PALESTINIAN SYRIAC LECTIONARY

OF THE GOSPELS

THE

PALESTINIAN SYRIAC LECTIONARY

OF THE GOSPELS

RE-EDITED FROM TWO SINAI MSS. AND FROM P. DE LAGARDE'S EDITION

OF THE

"EVANGELIARIUM HIEROSOLYMITANUM"

BY

AGNES SMITH LEWIS, M.R.A.S.

AUTHOR OF "TRANSLATION OF THE FOUR GOSPELS FROM THE SINAI PALIMPSEST"
"A PALESTINIAN SYRIAC LECTIONARY FROM THE PENTATEUCH, PROPHETS, ACTS AND EPISTLES," ETC.

AND

MARGARET DUNLOP GIBSON, M.R.A.S.

AUTHOR OF "A CATALOGUE OF THE ARABIC MSS. IN THE CONVENT OF ST. CATHERINE"
"A NINTH CENTURY ARABIC VERSION OF SOME OF ST. PAUL'S EPISTLES," ETC.

WIPF & STOCK · Eugene, Oregon

Wipf and Stock Publishers
199 W 8th Ave, Suite 3
Eugene, OR 97401

A Palestinian Syriac Lectionary of the Gospels
By Lewis, Agnes Smith and Gibson, Margaret Dunlop
ISBN 13: 978-1-60608-916-3
Publication date 3/29/2010
Previously published by Kegan Paul, Trench, Trubner & Co., 1899

JACOBO RENDEL HARRIS

VIRO DOCTISSIMO ET HVMANISSIMO

AMICO ET STVDIORVM SOCIO

QVI ET ORATIONEM ARISTIDIS APOLOGETICAM

VERO AVCTORI RESTITVIT

ET LECTIONARIVM EVANGELIORVM ALTERVM SINAITICVM

PALAESTINO-SYRIACA LINGVA SALVATORI VERNACVLA SCRIPTVM

SVMMA CVM SOLLERTIA REPERIT

Dant Dicant Dedicant

AGNES SMITH LEWIS ET MARGARETA DVNLOP GIBSON

PREFACE.

ALTHOUGH full justice has already been done to the text of the *Evangeliarium Hierosolymitanum*—the Palestinian Syriac Lectionary of the Gospels in the Library of the Vatican—by Count Miniscalchi Erizzo and by Dr. Paul de Lagarde, we think that the text of the two Sinai manuscripts also merits attention, both as supplementing that of the Vatican one, and as presenting some remarkable features of its own. These MSS., moreover, lie in a place so difficult of access, that it seemed almost a duty to give scholars the opportunity of comparing their several peculiarities, both of spelling and of diction, with those of their sister manuscript.

The printing of this work, with its numerous reference-letters, has been a tedious business, and has lasted over five years. During that period I have received such substantial assistance from my twin sister, Mrs. Margaret D. Gibson, that it is only fair to associate her name with mine on the title-page. In the spring of 1897 she revisited Sinai with me, and there revised the proofs of Codex B with the original, whilst I did the same to those of Codex C. I am also indebted to the Rev. Professor Nestle of Ulm (now of Maulbronn) for his careful reading of my proof-sheets, and for many valuable suggestions. He has been especially attentive to the collation from Codex A.

I have to thank Mr. J. F. Stenning, of Magdalen College, Oxford, for photographing a few pages of Codex B in 1894; and lastly, I have to thank the printers for their skill and patience in the execution of a very troublesome work.

A. S. LEWIS.

CASTLE-BRAE,
CAMBRIDGE.
Jan. 1899.

CONTENTS.

INTRODUCTION.

The "Evangeliarium Hierosolymitanum" of the Vatican.

It is now nearly 140 years since the Maronites Stephen Evodius and Joseph Simon Assemani, in their Catalogue of the Syriac manuscripts in the Vatican Library, devoted 33 folio pages to the description of an ancient vellum codex (No. xix.) of 196 leaves, written in the Palestinian Syriac character, in two columns, and forming a Lectionary of the Gospels arranged in portions to be read throughout the year. "It is a unique specimen of its kind," they said, "and its inestimable value is increased by the fact of its containing the story of the woman taken in adultery (for the Feast of St. Pelagia), John vii. 53—viii. 11."

An inscription in the MS. copied by Assemani, half of which is now lost, says that it was written by the Presbyter Elias of Abbud, in the Monastery of the Abbot Moses in the city of Antioch (of the Arabs),[1] in the year 1341 of Alexander = A.D. 1030. It was bequeathed by him, along with other MSS., to a monastery which he built, that of Mar Elias in Kaukab, on the condition that it should never be bought nor sold. There is no record of how it was brought to the Vatican Library.

It was examined by Adler, when he visited Rome in 1781, and was described by him in his book *Novi Testamenti versiones Syriacae Simplex, Philoxeniana et Hierosolymitana*, published in 1789.

Adler says (p. 157) "Superest, ut usum et in re critica in primis valorem huius versionis ostendam, qui sane, me judice, tantus est, ut naevi omnes laudem eius detractare vix queant, et nesciam, an ullus probatissimorum codicum graecorum palmam ei praeripiat."

He observed that some of its readings agree with quotations in the works of Origen, Chrysostom, and others of the Early Fathers; and that the text which comes nearest it is that of the Codex Vaticanus (p. 201).

[1] Perhaps near Jerusalem.

Seventy-five years later (1864) Cardinal Angelus Maius and the Maronite Sahwan encouraged Count Miniscalchi-Erizzo to publish a very sumptuous edition of the text, with a Latin translation, in which he followed, as far as possible, the Vulgate; a useful glossary of Palestinian Syriac words; and an introduction, in which he brought forward some cogent arguments to prove that the dialect of this codex was the vernacular of Palestine in the time of our Lord, and therefore the language spoken by Him. He considered that it represents the form of Aramaic which was brought from Chaldæa by the returning Hebrew exiles in the time of Nehemiah, and which became mingled to a great extent with Hebrew words. He noticed its striking similarity to the language of the Targums and to that of the Babylonian Talmud, the chief difference between it and them being that it is written in a character nearly approaching to Estrangelo Syriac, whilst they are in Hebrew letters. So highly did Miniscalchi exalt his subject, that he considered this version to be older than either the Peshiṭta or the Curetonian, and to approach very nearly to the original of St. Matthew's Gospel.[1] There is some force in his argument, that if it was written for the benefit of Christian Jews who still spoke the language of the Targums in their native land, its origin cannot be later than the second century. There would have been no need, he says, for the production of this version after the Peshiṭta had become the Authorized Version of the Syriac Church. Miniscalchi perhaps gives too little weight to the fact that the Peshiṭta was, in the early centuries, accepted by the Monophysite section of that Church, whilst this was the Lectionary of the Malkites. It agrees in its division of Lessons with the Arabic Lectionary now in use amongst the latter, there being only some slight variations. There can be no doubt, however, as to the value of this version as a perfectly independent witness to the text of the Gospels.

Dr. Nöldeke complains that Miniscalchi's translation does not meet the wants of students, because the Latin language is incapable of giving full expression to the meaning of the Syriac. It is a matter of regret that it has not yet been rendered into Greek.[2]

Other MSS. in Palestinian Syriac.

For upwards of a century the Palestinian dialect of Syriac was represented by this solitary Codex. But in 1875 Dr. Land of Leyden published some fragments of the Gospels and of the Psalms, with portions of hymns, from two of the Nitrian MSS. in the British Museum (Add. 14664 and Add. 14450), and a number of fragments, 129 in number, brought by Tischendorf to the Imperial Library of St. Petersburg after his second and third journeys to the East. These consist of portions of the Gospels and of the Acts; and from the Old

[1] *Prolegomena*, p. xlv.

[2] *Zeitschrift der Deutschen Morgenländischen Gesellschaft*, vol. xxii. (p. 443).

Testament, of Deuteronomy, Job, the Psalms, Proverbs, and Isaiah, also from the Acts of St. Philemon, the homilies of St. John Chrysostom, and some hymns. Many of the St. Petersburg fragments are palimpsest, and were deciphered with difficulty, the upper writing being in the Georgian or Iberian language.

In 1890 Dr. Rendel Harris published some verses from Galatians, found on a vellum leaf in the Convent Library on Mount Sinai. And in 1891 five palimpsest leaves were sent to the Bodleian Library, Oxford, from Egypt, by the late Rev. Greville J. Chester. They contain some verses from the Book of Numbers, from Colossians, 1 Thessalonians, 2 Timothy, and Titus, and were published by the Rev. G. H. Gwilliam in 1893, in *Anecdota Oxoniensia.*

The Vatican Lectionary was again very carefully edited by Dr. Paul de Lagarde, who paid three visits to Rome (1890—91) for the purpose of collating it. It was published in *Bibliotheca Syriaca* in 1892, after his death. We cannot but regret deeply that this great scholar should have passed away just before two other MSS. of the same Lectionary, and many fresh specimens of the same dialect were brought to light.

Discovery of the Two Sinai Codices.

In February 1892, whilst my sister, Mrs. James Y. Gibson, and I were examining and photographing some of the treasures in the Convent of St. Catherine, on Mount Sinai, the Librarian, Father Galakteon, called my attention to a beautiful Codex whose value he was very desirous of knowing. He kept it apart from the others, wrapped in a cotton handkerchief, although it had come out of the same box as the now famous Palimpsest of the Syriac Gospels, which was then occupying my exclusive attention. He asked me to photograph a few pages, and take them to Europe, so that I might be able to give him an account of what the manuscript really was. It was more than a week before I could accede to his request, being anxious to obtain a complete copy of the Palimpsest. I then photographed the first two and the last two pages. Having done so, the idea occurred to me that it would be pleasanter if I were able to read what I intended to submit to the judgment of Cambridge scholars. So, with the help of Dr. Euting's table of Semitic alphabets, I managed to decipher a good deal, and was delighted beyond measure when I found it was Syriac, although differing from the literary language both in spelling and in much of its vocabulary. Galakteon was equally delighted when I was able to tell him that it began with the first chapter of St. John's Gospel, and ended with the story of Herodias as told by St. Mark; also that its date was 6612 from the time of Adam.

After our return home we developed my four photographs, and I was told successively by Dr. Rendel Harris, Professor Bevan, and Professor Robertson Smith that I had made a discovery, and that the Vatican Codex described by Assemanus and by Adler could no longer be considered unique.[1] When I returned to Sinai in the following spring (1893) I resolved that while Professor Bensly, Dr. Rendel Harris, and Mr. Burkitt should be engaged in copying the text of the Syriac Gospels from the Palimpsest, I would devote myself to the much easier task of collating the Palestinian Lectionary on the recently published text of Paul de Lagarde. But on the very first day of our arrival I found that my work was to be doubled; for amongst the manuscripts which were produced by Father Galakteon from the same box as the Palimpsest, Dr. Rendel Harris discovered another Palestinian Syriac Lectionary, and taxed me with not having said that there were two copies. The second one is written in a very different hand, and I feel almost certain that it was not shown to me in 1892.

It was necessary to give to each a distinctive title, so I named them according to the order of the dates which they bear, and of the date of their discovery; the Vatican Codex (A.D. 1030) being Codex A, the Sinai one discovered in 1892 (A.D. 1104[2]) being Codex B, and that discovered in 1893 by Dr. Rendel Harris (A.D. 1118[2]) being Codex C; and as Codex A has been already twice edited, I decided to give the text of B, with the variants of A and C in parallel columns. Both the Sinai manuscripts are complete in themselves, so that none of the stray leaves of Palestinian Syriac scattered about the Convent library can be attributed to either of them. Both are vellum, the writing being in two columns, and both are in good bindings of wood covered with leather.

Description of the Codices.

Codex B has 156 leaves, measuring 24 cm. by 18, and having 24 lines in each column. The writing, which is on the line, is distinct, upright, and rather stiff. The first leaf is a fly-leaf, scribbled over with Syriac and Arabic rubrics; folium 152 is the same; ff. 153, 154, 155, and 156 are leaves from another Palestinian Syriac Lectionary, of which two more leaves can be seen in the cover at the beginning and the end of the book. The quires contain eight leaves each, and are numbered with Syriac letters, of which the last is ܟ. Vertical lines have been ruled for the columns. Folium 2 has a corner damaged. It has been

[1] The discovery of this manuscript, and also the photographs, are, through an unaccountable mistake, attributed by Dr. Schwally, in his *Idioticon des Christlich Palästinischen Aramäisch*, to the late Professor Bensly, whose visit to Sinai occurred a year after the events I have narrated, and who, so far as I know, never read any part of the two Sinai Lectionaries.

[2] I have to express my regret for not having given these dates quite accurately in my Catalogue of the Syriac MSS. on Mount Sinai (*Studia Sinaitica*, No. 1). The mistake probably arose from a dispute which I had with Father Galakteon about the date of the Creation, a point on which he averred that the Eastern Church disagrees with the Western.

repaired by a vellum patch, on either side of which the lost text has been restored. This begins on the recto with ܟܘܠܐ ܒܗ ܐܬܒܪܝ (John i. 3), and ends with ܡܫܠܝܚ ܡܢ in v. 6. On the verso it begins with ܠܟܘܠ ܒܪܢܫ ܕܐܬܐ ܠܥܠܡܐ (John i. 9), and ends with ܕܒܢܝܢ ܠܐܠܗܐ in v. 12. The omission of a clause in verse 3, *καὶ χωρὶς αὐτοῦ ἐγένετο οὐδὲ ἕν*, is thus easily accounted for.

Codex C has 156 leaves, measuring 22 cm. by 16, with 22 to 24 lines in each column. The writing is on the line, and though upright is flowing, and sometimes a little careless. The first two leaves are scribbled over with Arabic rubrics. The last two (or possibly three) are in Estrangelo Syriac of the seventh or eighth century, and are about the praise of our Lord, of the Virgin Mary, and of various saints. There are vertical lines ruled for the columns. Its rubrics, especially at the beginning, are short and meagre compared with those of Codex B. The leaves of the text are divided into 19 quires, each containing 8 leaves, with the exception of the first, which has 14, the fourth, which has 6, and the nineteenth, which has 3. The last leaf contains a lesson from Luke iii. 23—38, the colophon, containing the date, being on the leaf preceding it.

Both manuscripts possess a distinct advantage over the Vatican one, in that, so far as the Gospel text is concerned, they have not been tampered with by a later hand. There are a few insertions between the lines of earlier writing in the rubrics of Codex B, made evidently with a different kind of pen and of ink, and less carefully; but the "puncta diacritica et alias particulas, praepositiones, ac verba," which were added to Codex A "sine ullo discrimine" by a "barbara et inscia manus,"[1] are happily absent from B and C.

It will readily be perceived that both the spelling and the grammatical forms used in the two Sinai codices fully justify the description given by Miniscalchi-Erizzo of those which distinguish the Palestinian Syriac dialect: "Abundantia quiescentium, *scriptio plena* nuncupata, quae semper occurrit, et orthographia inconstans, et irregularis, maximae antiquitatis indubium argumentum praebent."[2] And again: "Textus autem attenta lectione et Glossarii studio palam fiet, nostri Codicis linguam esse asperam, incomptam, contractionum et pleonasmûm amicam, litteras distinctas confundentem, elegantiae nesciam; sed robustam, sensus tenacissimam, valde perspicuam, ab ambiguitate penitus alienum, rustica vero quadam, et antiqua simplicitate ac venustate praeditam."[3]

Both the Sinai Codices show a frequent use of the phonetic *yod* after a consonant, which was probably pronounced with *Rebaṣa* or *Ḥebaṣa*. This is especially noticeable in the expression ܠܓܠܝܠ and in the demonstrative pronouns ܕܝܢ, ܗܕܝܢ, where Codex A has ܠܓܠܠ, ܕܢ, ܗܕܢ; and in the third person singular masculine of the preterite, and the

[1] Miniscalchi-Erizzo, *Prolegomena*, p. viii. [2] *Prolegomena*, p. xxxiv. [3] Idem, p. xxxvii.

noun agent of verbs, *e.g.* ܐܟܝܠ, ܡܟܝܒܢ, where Codex A has ܐܟܠ, ܡܟܒܢ. But in this they are not consistent; for sometimes it is A that shows the *yod*, whilst B and C are without it.

The inverted letter ܦ̈ with two dots is invariably used in A and B to represent π in loan words from the Greek, especially in proper names, such as ܦ̈ܝܠܛܘܣ. C has occasionally this ܦ̈, but more frequently replaces it by *beth*, as ܒܝܠܛܘܣ, ܒܛܪܘܣ; and occasionally the mistake of using ܦ̈ instead of ܒ causes grotesque forms in both B and C; for instance, ܕܗܘܐ ܒܥܘܦ̈ܗ ܕܐܦ̈ܘܗܝ, John i. 18, in Codex B.

In the Carshuni of the rubrics Professor Robertson Smith, while studying one of my photographs, pointed out to me that the Arabic خ is represented by a Syriac ܚ with two dots. As the Syriac letter ܟ̰ appears to me to be the equivalent of the Arabic خ, I have adopted it instead of ܚ̈ for Carshuni words. An example of this will be found in the Preface to Codex A, page 1, line 9, in the word ܟ̰ܡܣܝܐܢ, which De Lagarde edited ܚ̈ܡܣܝܐܢ. I trust I have thereby made the meaning of these somewhat barbarous rubrics less obscure. This remark does not in the least apply to the Syriac text.

Codices B and C contain some portions of the Gospels which are not in Codex A. These are S. Matthew v. 33*b*—41; vi. 24*b*—34; viii. 14—20*a*; xxii. 1; and S. Luke ii. 22*a*; iii. 23—38; xviii. 8*b*, 9; xix. 29—48. One lesson, S. Matt. xvii. 14—23, is found in A and C, but not in B.

Many portions are absent from B and C which we have in A. These are S. Matt. viii. 23—27; xiii. 44—54*a*; xv. 21—28; xvii. 10—13; xxiii. 13—39; xxviii. 16—20; S. Mark xii. 28—37; S. Luke i. 50, 53—55; viii. 9—15, 26; x. 1—12; xi. 29—33; xxii. 39; S. John viii. 1—11.

The lessons in all three codices follow the same order till the end of Lesson CLII. After that the divergence is considerable.

The Sinai Codices contain two remarkable readings, the full significance of which was first observed by Dr. Nestle. Both have ܡܬܒܣܡܘܢ for ܡܬܒܣܪܘܢ in Matt. xi. 5. Here the difference of a single letter gives the sense of *οἱ πτωχοὶ εὐφραίνονται* instead of *οἱ πτωχοὶ εὐαγγελίζονται*, a very natural result of their acceptance of our Lord's teaching (p. 275).

C alone exhibits what may possibly have been the second limb of an antithetical *Logion*, or saying of Jesus. In Matt. xii. 36, instead of the usual *λέγω δὲ ὑμῖν ὅτι πᾶν ῥῆμα ἀργὸν ὃ λαλήσουσιν οἱ ἄνθρωποι, ἀποδώσουσιν περὶ αὐτοῦ λόγον ἐν ἡμέρᾳ κρίσεως*, C has *λέγω δὲ ὑμῖν ὅτι πᾶν ῥῆμα καλὸν ὃ οὐ λαλήσουσιν, κ.τ.λ.* (pp. 78, 79).

The view held by Dr. Rendel Harris, that this once constituted the limb of a Logion, receives support from the fact that there is an undoubted antithesis in the sequence: *ἐκ γὰρ τῶν λόγων σου δικαιωθήσῃ, καὶ ἐκ τῶν λόγων σου καταδικασθήσῃ.*

I have been somewhat puzzled to account for the presence of a colophon after John viii. 2. Dr. Rendel Harris has supplied me with the following ingenious hypothesis: that the section *de adultera*, John vii. 53—viii. 11, was at one time appended to St. John's Gospel after the final colophon, and that in the Greek or Syriac MS. from which the lessons of the Palestinian Lectionary were taken, the section was removed to the place (between chap. vii. and chap. viii.) which it now usually occupies; but that this being done by scribes who were not highly endowed with intelligence, the colophon was transported with it. The section must, in this instance, have comprised only John viii. 2—11, which is present in codex A, but wanting in B and C (see page 60).

The Dialect.

The fact of these Lectionaries having been written at so late a period points to the conclusion that about the beginning of the twelfth century a Malkite community existed in the vicinity of Mount Sinai—perhaps in the Convent of St. Catherine itself—and that they were in the habit of using the Palestinian Syriac language in their church services. At the same time it is evident that Arabic was the language of their everyday life; else why should the rubrics be in Karshuni? Religious communities, especially when they are in the midst of a people hostile to their faith, are apt to cling tenaciously to the use of the dead language of their fathers. We have an instance of this in the case of the Coptic Church of Egypt; and we know the supreme place which the Church of Rome still gives to Latin. These Lectionaries, therefore, throw but scant light on the question of when Palestinian Syriac ceased to be a spoken language; and we shall be agreeably surprised if they do anything to dissipate the darkness which enshrouds the origin of the version of the Gospels which they represent. I have already quoted the opinion of Miniscalchi-Erizzo with regard to the antiquity of that origin, an opinion which is not shared by Dr. Nöldeke, who does not consider it to be earlier than A.D. 300, possibly later. Even if it be proved that it represents the Galilean dialect of Syriac which was probably spoken by our Lord, and which provoked the retort of the maid-servant to St. Peter,[1] "Thy speech bewrayeth thee," this is not conclusive of its antiquity; for it has survived, in a very corrupt form, down to our own day in several

[1] Dr. Nöldeke does not concur in this view, because he considers that the texts which we possess in this dialect probably had their origin in Judaea, rather than in Galilee, and he detects a certain stiffness of locution which points to the translation having been made when the dialect was no longer in common use. "In this respect the text of the Curetonian and of the Sinai Palimpsest have a decided advantage over it, but of course the Palestinian must have been very nearly related to that spoken by Jesus." (*Letter to the Editor.*)

It is perhaps worth observing that the *lemà* of Matt. xxvii. 46 and the *lamà* of Mark xv. 34 is Palestinian; the Edessene, as represented in the Old Syriac and in the Peshiṭta being *lemana.*

villages of the Lebanon near to Damascus, such as Nebk, Ain et Tineh, and Ma'lula. Dr. Nöldeke has traced some of the most characteristic Palestinian forms—*e.g.* the use of *yod* instead of *nun* in forming the imperfect of verbs, and the *nun epentheticon*—in the speech of the inhabitants of these places,[1] from whom my sister and I received a very hearty welcome when we visited them in 1895. We are indebted to Dr. Dalman for the clear way in which he tells the story of how the dialect was carried northwards:

"After the war against Hadrian," he says, "Jewish scholarship, which was very poorly represented in 'Darom,' *i.e.* the ancient Philistia, wandered towards Lower Galilee, and occupied the districts of Uscha (now Chirbet Husche), Schephar Am (Schafa 'Amr), Sichnin (Suchnin), Zipporin (Ṣaffurije), Tiberias, and Cæsarea. The learning which was transferred from Judaea, in so far as it was Aramaic, clothed itself in the robe of the dialect spoken by the Jews of Galilee, which had been always distinguished from the Jewish both philologically and grammatically, although it has become known to us only by the product of a later period. This dialect is very nearly akin to the so-called Christian Palestinian dialect of the *Evangeliarium Hierosolymitanum*, whose exact origin is unknown to us."[2]

Most of the specimens of the Old or the New Testament in Palestinian Syriac which have yet been discovered appear to be portions of service-books. "But," as Mr. Gwilliam observes, "Lesson Books do not belong to the earliest periods of transcription. MSS. were marked for the Lessons long before separate copies were made for use in the Church. . . . Our oldest fragments appear to date from the eighth century at least. To that era belongs the commencement of the composition of Church Lesson Books. There is no proof that the Syro-Palestinian Lectionaries are translations from Greek Lectionaries; and it may be regarded as certain that they were preceded by complete copies of the Acts and the Pauline Epistles, and of parts, if not of the whole of the Old Testament."[3]

Dr. Nestle, however, considers that all the three codices which form the subject of the present volume are translations from Greek Lectionaries. "In one of the parallel passages of Codd. A and B, John xvii. 7," he says, "occurs the word ἔγνων, which in Greek allows of two meanings, and it is taken in Lesson XLII. (p. 53) in the meaning of ܝܕܥܬ 'I knew,' and in Lesson CL. (p. 190) in that of ܝܕܥܘ 'they knew.' This would not have been the case if the copyist had copied both passages from the same Syriac Gospel."

Dr. Nestle considers that Codex C cannot be a mere copy of B, for C has passages missing in B.

B cannot be a copy of C, its earlier date would preclude this; but there are too many variations betwixt them. B is sometimes more closely connected with A, sometimes with C.

[1] *Z. D. M. G.*, xxi., p. 183.
[2] *Grammatik des Jüdisch Palästinischen Aramäisch*, p. 31.
[3] G. H. Gwilliam, *Anecdota Oxoniensia*, Semitic Series, vol. i., part v., p. xix.

Nevertheless, B and C are more closely related to each other than to A, for there is a very slight difference in the arrangement of their lessons.

These conclusions will be easily verified by means of the list of variations and peculiarities in the three codices which we give on pp. xix.—lxiv.

Latest Discoveries.

The materials available for forming a judgment on these questions have been doubled, even since the words we have quoted were written, without the problems which they present to us being any nearer to a solution. Besides the three MSS. which form the subject of the present volume, and the fragments published by Dr. Land and Dr. Harris, which we have already mentioned, we have now a leaf from Exodus, published by Mr. Gwilliam, and a leaf from Wisdom, transcribed by Mr. J. F. Stenning of Magdalene College, Oxford, both brought to the Bodleian Library from Egypt by Professor Sayce; also a fragment of 3 Kings, transcribed by Mr. Stenning from a very curious double palimpsest in the Convent library on Mount Sinai; a leaf of Job, discovered in the same place by Mr. F. C. Burkitt; and some twenty leaves containing a homily of St. John Chrysostom, found in the cover of an Arabic book by Mrs. Bensly. These have all been published in *Anecdota Oxoniensia.* Dr. Rendel Harris also, when at Sinai in 1893, discovered another leaf of Galatians, and two verses of a hymn in honour of SS. Peter and Paul.

In 1895 another Lectionary came into my own possession, containing many readings from the Old Testament—chiefly the Messianic prophecies,—from the Acts, and the Pauline Epistles. It contains 226 vellum leaves, measuring 15 cm. by 10. It was published in 1897 as *Studia Sinaitica* No. vi. Unfortunately, the last eight leaves are lost, so that I can assign no date to it, but it appears to be older than the "Liturgy of the Nile," now in the British Museum, of which specimens were given by G. Margoliouth in the Royal Asiatic Society's Journal for October 1896.

A few palimpsest leaves of Palestinian Syriac written over in Hebrew have been discovered by Dr. Schechter amongst the collection of fragments which he brought from the Genizah of Cairo to Cambridge in 1897. The text of these, so far as they have been read, is: Deut. xxxi. 3—8*a*, 12—14; Jeremiah xxix. 32—xxx. 10; xxxi. 8—15*a*; xxxi. 39—xxxii. 2; xxxii. 35—39; Hosea xiv. 3—9; Joel i. 1—6; ii. 10—20; 2 Corinthians iii. 2—iv. 9; 1 Thess. iii. 1—13; iv. 1—14. There are also an early Creed and a fragment of the life of S. Antony. It is worthy of remark that on the same page where the text of Hosea ends that of Joel begins, a space of nine lines being left between them, and that there is no trace of a rubric.

These leaves are therefore portions of a continuous version, like those published by Mr. Gwilliam, and they are probably derived from the same locality, though they do not form part of the same MS.

On my visits to Sinai in 1893 and 1895 I paid no attention to the rubrics of Codex C. It was not, therefore, possible to include the whole of them in this work; these I have given in the form of collations (or entire where the variations were too many), being copied either from the MS. itself, in 1897, or from photographs. Separate lists are therefore given of those rubrics in A and C which it has not been possible to place along with the text.

A. S. L.

LIST OF VARIANTS IN THE THREE CODICES.

THE following notes are designed to show the chief variations betwixt the text of the three Palestinian Syriac Lectionaries of the Gospels and the text of Westcott and Hort. I have not included in it a few phrases which are merely introductory to some of the Lessons, nor any variations which do not affect the meaning, nor those that are due to the superfluity of pronouns in Syriac, as against their occasional suppression, when they might be present by implication, in Greek. Nor have I always noticed the presence or absence of ܕܝܢ or of *καὶ εἶπεν αὐτῷ* after *ἀπεκρίθη*, nor of *ὁ κύριος* before or instead of *'Ιησοῦς*, nor whether *ἀμὴν* occurs once or twice. To do so would have been to burden my pages without profit to anyone. In some instances I have considered that where forms like ܬܠܡܝܕܗܝ, ܥܒܕܗܝ, occur in B or C instead of ܬܠܡܝܕܘܗܝ, ܥܒܕܘܗܝ, as we find them in A, it is rather a case of contraction or of the ܘ being dropped, than a case of the possessive pronoun *αὐτοῦ* being omitted. Such instances will be found in Matt. xi. 1 on p. 77, Matt. xi. 2 on page 275, and Matt. xxi. 34 on page 152. In the numbering of verses I have kept strictly to that of De Lagarde's text, which is that of the Vulgate. I think this will lead to a greater facility of reference between his book and ours. In the rare cases where there is a discrepancy between his numbers and those of Westcott and Hort, I have given a second figure in brackets. When the number of a page is given in brackets it must be understood that the variant occurs on that page only.

For Codex A, I have kept strictly to the text of De Lagarde. This contains some instances where the prefix to the third person of the imperfect tense of the verb is the Edessene *nun* instead of the Palestinian *yod*. To take these words as if they were in the first person plural would be to do violence to the sense of the passages. Such instances will be found in Matt. i. 23, iii. 9; also in Matt. vi. 34, where Miniscalchi read a *yod*.

OMISSIONS DUE TO HOMŒOTELEUTON.

In all Three Codices.

		PAGE.
Matt. xiv. 23.	*καὶ ἀπολύσας τοὺς ὄχλους.*	81
Luke xxi. 35.	*πάντας τοὺς καθημένους ἐπὶ.*	133
John iii. 17.	*ἵνα κρίνῃ τὸν κόσμον.*	236
vii. 45.	*ἐκεῖνοι Διάτι οὐκ ἠγάγετε αὐτόν, ἀπεκρίθησαν οἱ ὑπερέται.*	59
viii. 14.	*ὑμεῖς δὲ οὐκ οἴδατε πόθεν ἔρχομαι ἢ ποῦ ὑπάγω.*	30

			PAGE
John	viii. 47.	τὰ ῥήματα τοῦ θεοῦ.	37
	xiv. 21.	με ἀγαπηθήσεται and μου.	51
	xiv. 29.	ἵνα ὅταν γένηται.	53
	xvi. 33.	ἐν τῷ κόσμῳ θλίψιν ἔχετε.	190
	xix. 28-30.	ἵνα τελειωθῇ ἡ γραφὴ λέγει Διψῶ. Σκεῦος ἔκειτο ὄξους μεστόν· σπόγγον οὖν μεστὸν τοῦ ὄξους ὑσσώπῳ περιθέντες προσήνεγκαν αὐτοῦ τῷ στόματι. ὅτε οὖν ἔλαβεν τὸ ὄξος [ὁ] Ἰησοῦς εἶπεν Τετέλεσται (p. 238 only).	238

In Codex A.

Matt.	v. 44.	καὶ προσεύχεσθε ὑπὲρ τῶν . . . . ὑμᾶς.	65
	x. 40.	καὶ ὁ ἐμὲ δεχόμενος δέχεται.	77
	xviii. 18.	δεδεμένα ἐν οὐρανῷ καὶ ὅσα ἐὰν λύσητε ἐπὶ τῆς γῆς ἔσται.	61
	xxii. 30.	οὔτε γαμοῦσιν.	157
	xxiii. 10.	ὅτι καθηγητὴς ὑμῶν ἐστὶν εἷς.	90
	xxiv. 33.	ὅταν ἴδητε πάντα ταῦτα.	162
	xxv. 38.	ἢ γυμνὸν καὶ περιεβάλομεν;	97, 129
Mark	vii. 34.	ὅ ἐστιν Διανοίχθητι·	142
Luke	viii. 38.	ὁ ἀνὴρ, ἀφ' οὗ ἐξεληλύθει.	109
	ix. 39.	ἀποχωρεῖ ἀπ' αὐτοῦ.	111
	xxii. 27.	ἢ ὁ διακονῶν; οὐχὶ ὁ ἀνακείμενος;	172
John	i. 9.	Ἦν τὸ φῶς.	2
	iii. 31.	ἐκ τῆς γῆς ἐστὶν καὶ ἐκ τῆς γῆς.	11
	v. 29.	οἱ τὰ ἀγαθὰ ποιήσαντες εἰς ἀνάστασιν ζωῆς.	15
	v. 45.	πρὸς τὸν πατέρα· ἔστιν ὁ κατηγορῶν ὑμῶν.	17
	xii. 24.	πεσὼν εἰς τὴν γῆν ἀποθάνῃ (168). 26. ἐμοί τις διακονῇ (168). 33. ἔλεγεν, σημαίνων ποίῳ θανάτῳ (48).	48, 168
	xii. 40.	τῇ καρδίᾳ καὶ τραφῶσιν.	169
	xvi. 17.	καὶ πάλιν μικρὸν καὶ ὄψεσθέ με;	188
	xvii. 3.	αὕτη δέ ἐστιν ἡ αἰώνιος ζωή. 8. ὅτι τὰ ῥήματα ἃ ⌜ἔδωκάς⌝ μοι δέδωκα αὐτοῖς.	190
	xvii. 9.	καὶ τὰ ἐμὰ πάντα σά ἐστιν.	52
	xix. 29.	μεστόν· σπόγγον οὖν μεστὸν τοῦ ὄξους.	206
	xx. 25.	τὸν δάκτυλόν μου εἰς τὸν τύπον τῶν ἥλων καὶ βάλω.	223

In Codex B.

			PAGE
Matt.	i. 19.	*ἐβουλήθη λάθρᾳ ἀπολῦσαι αὐτήν.*	253
	xii. 33.	*Ἢ ποιήσατε τὸ δένδρον καλὸν καὶ τὸν καρπὸν αὐτοῦ καλόν.*	78
	xiv. 26.	*ἐπὶ τὴν θάλασσαν· οἱ δὲ μαθηταὶ ἰδόντες αὐτὸν . . . . . . περιπατοῦντα.*	81
	xxiii. 10.	*ὅτι καθηγητὴς ὑμῶν ἐστὶν εἷς.*	90
	xxvii. 48.	*καλάμῳ ἐποτίζεν αὐτόν.*	204
Mark	ix. 19.	*καὶ ἤνεγκαν αὐτὸν πρὸς αὐτόν.*	143
	xvi. 15.	*κόσμον . . . . κηρύξατε τὸ εὐαγγέλιον πάσῃ.*	218
Luke	viii. 38.	*ὁ ἀνὴρ, ἀφ' οὗ ἐξεληλύθει.*	107
	ix. 34.	*ταῦτα δὲ αὐτοῦ λέγοντος.*	292
	xiv. 21.	*τότε ὀργισθεὶς ὁ οἰκοδεσπότης.*	115
	xviii. 25.	*εὐκοπώτερον γάρ ἐστιν κάμηλον διὰ τρήματος βελόνης εἰσελθεῖν ἢ πλούσιον εἰς τὴν βασιλείαν τοῦ θεοῦ εἰσελθεῖν.*	121
	xxi. 35.	*ἐπεισελεύσεται . . ἐπὶ πάντας τοὺς καθημένους.*	128
John	i. 3.	*καὶ χωρὶς αὐτοῦ ἐγένετο οὐδὲ ⸂ἕν.*	2
	iii. 31.	*ἐκ τῆς γῆς.*	11
	v. 23.	*ἵνα πάντες τιμῶσι τὸν υἱόν.*	15
	v. 45.	*πρὸς τὸν πατέρα· ἔστιν ὁ κατηγορῶν ὑμῶν.*	17
	vii. 22 [23].	*εἰ . . . [ὁ] ἄνθρωπος ἐν σαββάτῳ.*	29
	xii. 35.	*καὶ ὁ περιπατῶν ἐν τῇ σκοτίᾳ.*	168
	xiii. 31.	*καὶ ὁ θεὸς δοξάσει αὐτὸν ἐν αὐτῷ.*	182
	xiv. 3.	*καὶ ἐὰν πορευθῶ καὶ ἑτοιμάσω τόπον ὑμῖν.*	50
	xiv. 12.	*καὶ μείζονα τούτων ποιήσει.*	51
	xiv. 27.	*Εἰρήνην ἀφίημι ὑμῖν.*	184
	xvi. 19.	*καὶ πάλιν μικρὸν καὶ ὄψεσθέ με.*	56
	xvii. 11.	*ἐν τῷ κόσμῳ* after ⸂*αὐτοί*⸃	52

In Codex C.

Matt.	v. 35.	*ὑποπόδιόν ἐστιν τῶν ποδῶν αὐτοῦ· μήτε εἰς Ἱεροσόλυμα, ὅτι.*	64
	x. 37.	*καὶ ὁ φιλῶν υἱὸν ἢ θυγατέρα ὑπὲρ ἐμὲ, οὐκ ἔστιν μου ἄξιος,* Less. LV.	66
	xi. 7, 8.	*κάλαμον ὑπὸ ἀνέμου σαλευόμενον; ἀλλά τι ἐξήλθατε ἰδεῖν;*	275
	xi. 8.	*μαλακοῖς . . . . ἰδοὺ οἱ . . . . φοροῦντες*	276
	xii. 31.	*τοῖς ἀνθρώποις ἡ δὲ τοῦ πνεύματος βλασφημία οὐκ ἀφεθήσεται.*	78
	xviii. 31.	*ἐλυπήθησαν σφόδρα, καὶ ἐλθόντες διεσάφησαν τῷ κυρίῳ ἑαυτῶν πάντα τὰ γενόμενα.*	85

			PAGE
John	v. 29.	οἱ τὰ ἀγαθὰ ποιήσαντες εἰς ἀνάστασιν ζωῆς.	15
	v. 45.	πρὸς τὸν πατέρα· ἔστιν ὁ κατηγορῶν ὑμῶν. 46. Μωυσεῖ, ἐπιστεύετε ἂν ἐμοί.	17
	vii. 18.	ὁ ἀφ' ἑαυτοῦ λαλῶν.	29
	viii. 46.	περὶ ἁμαρτίας; εἰ ἀλήθειαν λέγω, διὰ τί ὑμεῖς οὐ πιστεύετέ μοι;	37
	ix. 22.	ἤδη γὰρ συνετέθειντο οἱ Ἰουδαῖοι.	45
	x. 18.	καὶ ἐξουσίαν ἔχω πάλιν λαβεῖν αὐτήν.	41
	xi. 44.	καὶ ἄφετε αὐτὸν.	149
	xii. 26.	ἐκεῖ . . . ἔσται.	48
	xii. 34.	τίς ἐστιν οὗτος ὁ υἱὸς τοῦ ἀνθρώπου;	168
	xiii. 32.	καὶ εὐθὺς δοξάσει αὐτόν.	182
	xiv. 27.	Εἰρήνην ἀφίημι ὑμῖν.	184
	xv. 2.	καὶ πᾶν τὸ καρπὸν φέρον καθαίρει αὐτὸ.	53
	xv. 10.	μενεῖτε ἐν τῇ ἀγάπῃ μου, καθὼς ἐγὼ τοῦ ⸢πατρὸς⸣ τὰς ἐντολὰς.	186
	xv. 19.	ἀλλ' ἐγὼ ἐξελεξάμην ὑμᾶς ἐκ τοῦ κόσμου.	24
	xv. 26.	τὸ πνεῦμα τῆς ἀληθείας ὃ παρὰ τοῦ πατρὸς.	187
	xvii. 11.	ἐν τῷ κόσμῳ after ⸢αὐτοὶ⸣.	52
	xvii. 20.	ἐρωτῶ μόνον, ἀλλὰ καὶ περὶ τῶν.	58
	xviii. 17.	λέγει οὖν τῷ Πέτρῳ ἡ παιδίσκη ἡ θυρωρός.	193
	xx. 25.	εἰς τὸν τύπον τῶν ἥλων καὶ βάλω.	223
	xxi. 17.	ἐλυπήθη ὁ Πέτρος ὅτι εἶπεν αὐτῷ τὸ τρίτον Φιλεῖς με;	226

Some Peculiarities of the Syriac Text.

Matt.	ii. 6.	B has a superfluous ܡܢܟܝ ἔκ σου after the first Ἰούδα. It is evidently in anticipation of a word two lines below it, and may be compared with the ܘܐܬܚܙܝ of the Sinai palimpsest in Luke xxiv. 33.	256
	iv. 24.	It is curious to find ܕܠܘܡܣܝܡ ܠܘܡܣܝܡ in B and C for the ܕܠܘܡܣܝܡ ܠܡܣܝܡ of A. It is certainly a better rendering of the Greek.	61
	vi. 34.	B translates αὔριον by ܡܚܪ ܠܡܚܪ.	71
	vii. 11.	In Less. LIII. we have the curious phrase ܟܡܐ ܚܕ ܟܡܠܐ as a translation of πόσῳ μᾶλλον. In Less. CXXVI. it is rendered ܚܕ ܟܡܐ ܟܡܠܐ	64, 135

PAGE

Matt. x. 5. A has ܗܘ̇ ܠܒܪ ܒܥܬܗܘܢ where B and C have ܠܗܠܝܢ ܫܠܚ ܝܬܗܘܢ τούτους ἀπέστειλεν. ܒܥ̇ܬ may possibly be the Arabic بعث ἀπέστειλε, but ܠܒܪ must be a mistake. 245, 246

x. 37. ܒܪ ܐܘ ܒܪܐ in A and in C, p. 76, is evidently meant for υἱὸν ἢ θυγατέρα. 66, 76

xvii. 25. ܐܒܪܗܡ in B and C is evidently a mistake for ܐܒܪ ܐܡ. 82

xxv. 4. ܗܢܝܢ in A and C is probably a mistake for ܗܠܝܢ. 95

xxviii. 8. It is interesting to find the name ܚܩܠ ܐܕܡܐ, Aceldama. 199, 209

Mark i. 9. Here B shows us the cause of a frequent mistake in Pal. Syr. MSS. The letter ܦ is usually formed by writing a ܒ, and then drawing a vertical stroke through it. When the scribe has forgotten this stroke we have words like ܒܗܠܝܢ in place of ܦܗܠܝܢ. Another instance is in Matt. xiv. 15 (p. 79): ܒܪܒܪ = ܦܪܒܪ. Cf. p. xxv., Luke ix. 32. 79, 265

vii. 35. B has ܐܘܪܘ (εὐθὺς) at the beginning of the verse, where A and C have ܘܗܘܐ (καὶ ἦν). 142

ix. 19. B has ܘܡܪܦܣܬ instead of the ܘܡܪܦܪܬ (ἀφρίζων) of A and C. 143

ix. 22. C has ܕܐܕܐܡ where A and B have ܕܐܢ (εἰ). 143

ix. 24. C has ܐܒܐ where A and B have ܟܐܪ (for ἐπετίμησεν). 143

xv. 46. B and C both have ܡܢ ἀπὸ instead of the ܙܒܢ ἀγοράσας of A. Probably, in an older manuscript, the upper part of a ܙ was rubbed away, and the remainder with ܒ appeared to be a ܦ. 19, 207

Luke ii. 22. In A we have the original form of the Afel ܐܣܠܩܘ, and in B and C the contracted form ܐܣܩܘ. 23. C translates μήτραν by ܒܝܬ ܒܬܘܠܝܗ. 272

ii. 36. The ܒܬܘܬܐ of B is evidently a scribe's blunder for ܒܬܘܠܘܬܐ. 273

vii. 14. B and C translate τῆς σοροῦ by ܠܐܪܢܐ. We have probably the same word in the Sinai palimpsest of the Syriac Gospels, though only the initial ܐ and the final are legible. I read the final ܐ in 1897. 100

vii. 25. All three codices translate εἰσίν by ܡܬܗܒܝܢ, ܡܬܗܒܝܢ or ܡܬܗܒܝܢ (διδόασι). We may surmise that the word ܡܬܒܝܢ (καθίστανται) has lost the upper stroke of its ܬ, and has thus become ܡܗܒܝܢ. In both the Sinai MSS. ܬ appears like ܗ with the central stroke heightened. Cf. *Studia Sinaitica* No. vi., p. xxix., and this Lectionary at John viii. 2. 274

viii. 6. ܡܦܠ in A seems to be a mistake for ܘܦܠ. 104

PAGE

Luke viii. 29. ܡܬܕܒܪ in B is evidently a mistake for ܡܬܕܒܪ. 108

ix. 32. B and C translate *βεβαρημένοι* by ܝܩܝܪܝܢ, A by ܝܩܪܝܢ. 291

x. 20. B and C have the Hebrew plural ܥܒܪܘܬܗܘܢ instead of ܥܒܪܬܗܘܢ. 233

John i. 16. ܒܘܠܗ in all three Codices is probably a mistake for ܒܘܠܝܗ. 3

iii. 8. B and C have ܢܫܒܐ where A has ܢܫܒܐ *πνεῖ*. 9

iii. 28. A translates *αὐτοὶ* by ܗܢܘܢ, B by ܗܢܝܢܘܢ, and C by ܗܢܝܢܘܢ. It is probably a corruption of ܗܡܘܢ, see John xii. 26, *infra*. 11

vi. 18. C has ܕܢܫܒܝܢ and B ܕܢܫܒܝܢ for ܕܢܫܒܐ (*πνέοντος*). 18

ix. 8. ܡܣܬܗܕܡ is a very curious word for *προσαίτης*, see Nöldeke, *Z.D.M.G.*, vol. xxii., p. 464, on the change of the ה into ו. See also Schwally, *Idioticon*, p. 66, sub ܣܗܕ, and Goldzieher, *Muhammedanische Studien*, vol. ii., pp. 387-393. 44

x. 38. ܘܡ in B is evidently *καὶ ἐν*. 43

xii. 26. The curious word ܦܫܝܢ becomes, in the parallel passage on p. 167, ܦܢܚܝܢ in A and ܦܦܫܝܢ in B and C. 48

xv. 20, xvi. 4. Possibly ܚܢܕܡ may be a contraction of ܚܗܕܡ on p. 54: B and C have ܚܝܕܡ, C also on p. 24. For the change of the second radical ܗ into yod in such words, see Nöldeke in the *Z.D.M.G.*, vol. xxii., p. 464. 24, 84, 186, 187

xx. 17. Either Hebrew or Arabic influence is shown in the plural suffixes to ܘܐܒܘܟܘܡ and ܘܐܠܗܟܘܡ *καὶ πατέρα ὑμῶν, καὶ Θεὸν ὑμῶν* in C. 223

xxi. 4. B and C translate ⌜*εἰς*⌝ *τὸν αἰγιαλόν* ܟܐܦܐ, whilst A has the more idiomatic ܥܠ ܐܝܕ ܝܡܐ (*ἐπὶ τὴν χεῖρα τῆς θαλάσσης*). 225

Variations in the Three Codices.

Matt. i. 3, 5. All om. *τῆς*. 6. All add *γυναικὸς* after *τῆς*. 11. All add *δὲ ἐγέννησε τὸν Ἰωακεὶμ*, Ἰωακεὶμ after *Ἰωσείας*, thus adding another generation. 252

i. 20. All agree with the Sinai palimpsest and Cureton in having *ἐξ αὐτῆς* instead of *ἐν αὐτῇ*: the Peshiṭta has *ἐν αὐτῇ*. 21. A has *καλέσεις*, or *καλέσει*, B has *καλεσόμενος*, and C *καλέσεται*. 22. All add *Ἡσαίου* after *διὰ*: C om. *λέγοντος*. 25. A and C om. [*οὗ*]:

		PAGE
	A adds *αὐτῆς τὸν πρωτότοκον* after *υἱόν*: B and C have ܘܩܪܐ "and he called," whilst A has ܘܩܪܬ "and she called," for *καὶ ἐκάλεσεν*.	253
Matt. ii. 4.	C has *συναγαγόντες* for *συναγαγὼν*.	255
ii. 6.	B om. *λεὲμ*, and has *ἐκ σοῦ* after the word *Ἰούδα*, occurring twice, the first time being evidently a *lapsus calami*: B om. *οὐδαμῶς* and *γὰρ*: B om. *μου* after *λαόν*: C has *αὐτοῦ* for *μου*. 7. A adds *αὐτοῖς* after *φαινομένου*. 8. All add *ἰδοὺ* after *εἶπεν*: all add *ἐλθόντες* after *εὕρητε*. 9. C om. *ἐστάθη*. 12. B adds *ἀλλὰ* before *δι' ἄλλης ὁδοῦ*.	256
ii. 13.	A and C have *τῶν μάγων* instead of *αὐτῶν*: all add *αὐτῷ* after *λέγων*: B om. *γὰρ*. 18. B om. *κλαίουσα*. 19. All om. *κατ' ὄναρ*: all add *αὐτῷ* after *λέγων*. 21. All have *ἦλθεν* for *εἰσῆλθεν*.	257
iii. 1.	B om. *Ἐν δὲ ταῖς ἡμέραις ἐκείναις* (261): all om. it on p. 260: C interpolates *καὶ εἶπεν. ἐγὼ* between *βαπτιστὴς* and *κηρύσσων*. 2. B om. *γὰρ*. 3. All om. *λέγοντος*. 4. All add *ζωσθεῖσαν* after *δερματίνην*.	261
iii. 5.	All add *χώρα* after *Ἰουδαία*.	260, 261
iii. 9.	All have *ἄρξητε* for *δόξητε*. 10. All om. *οὖν*. 11. A om. *μὲν*: all om. *ὀπίσω μου ἐρχόμενος* and *καὶ πυρί*.	260
iii. 13.	All add *τῆς χωρας* before *τῆς Γαλιλαίας*. 14. All add *Ἰωάννης* after *δὲ*. 16. B om. *ἀνέβη ἀπὸ τοῦ ὕδατος· καὶ*: all add *αὐτῷ* after *ἠνεῴχθησαν*: all have *καὶ μένον* for *ἐρχόμενον*. 17. All have *Σύ εἰ* for *Οὗτός ἐστιν* and *ἔν σοι* for *ἐν ᾧ*: C om. *ὁ υἱός*.	265
iv. 1.	All have *Σατανᾶ* instead of *διαβόλου*. 3. All add *αὐτῷ* after *προσελθὼν*: B and C add *ὁ* before *υἱὸς*. 3. B and C have *τοῖς λίθοις ἵνα* for *ἵνα οἱ λίθοι*. 4. A and B add *αὐτῷ* and C *αὐτοῖς* after *εἶπεν*: all om. *ἐκπορευομένῳ διὰ στόματος*. 5, 8, 11. All have *Σατανᾶς* for *διάβολος*. 6. All add *ἐντεῦθεν* before *κάτω*: B and C have *εἰς τὴν γῆν* for *κάτω*: A and B om. *πότε*. 7. All om. *Πάλιν*: B adds *γὰρ* after *γέγραπται*. 8. C om. *λίαν*: all add *πᾶσαν* before *τὴν δόξαν*. 11. C has *ὁ ἄγγελος αὐτοῦ* instead of *ἄγγελοι*. 12. All add *ὁ κύριος Ἰησοῦς* after *δὲ*: all have *χώραν τῆς Γαλιλαίας*. 13. C has *καταλιπόντες* for *καταλιπὼν*.	266, 267
iv. 15.	All om. *καὶ* after *Ζαβουλὼν*. 16. All have *σκότῳ* instead of *χώρᾳ* (cf. Tischendorf): C has *ὑμῖν* for *αὐτοῖς*. 17. B om. *γὰρ*.	268
iv. 18.	All add *αὐτῶν* after *ἀμφίβληστρον*, and *ἰχθύων* after *ἁλεεῖς*. 20. All add *αὐτῶν* after *δίκτυα*. 21. C om. *τὸν τοῦ Ζεβεδαίου*.	68, 69

PAGE

Matt. iv. 23. All add *ὁ κύριος Ἰησοῦς* after *περιῆγεν*. 24. A and B add *πάντας* after *αὐτούς*. 61, 62, 69

v. 5 [4]. A and B add *νῦν* after *πενθοῦντες·* 11. All add *οἱ ἄνθρωποι* after *ὀνειδίσωσιν ὑμᾶς*: C adds *ῥῆμα* after *πονηρὸν*. 12. B and C om. *γὰρ*. 61, 62

v. 18. B om. *γὰρ*: all add *ἢ ἀπὸ τῶν προφητῶν* after *νόμου*. 271, 272

v. 20. A om. *λέγω*: B om. *μὴ*: B has *τοῦ θεοῦ* for *τῶν οὐρανῶν*. 21. B has *πρῶτον* for *τοῖς ἀρχαίοις*. 22. All add *εἰκῆ* after the first *αὐτοῦ*: B has *τῇ κρίσει* for *τῷ συνεδρίῳ*: B has *εἰς τὸ πῦρ τῆς γεέννης*. 23. C has *καὶ πάλιν* for *κἀκεῖ*: all add *ἐν σεαυτῷ* after *μνησθῇς*. 26. C om. *κοδράντην*. 27. All add *τοῖς ἀρχαίοις* after *ἐρρέθη*. 62, 63

v. 32. All add *τοῦ ἀνδρὸς αὐτῆς* after *ἀπολελυμένην*. 33. B has *εἶπε* for *ἐρρέθη*. 37. B om. *περισσὸν*. 39. B and C om. *καὶ*. 40. B and C add *σου* after *ἱμάτιον*: A wanting. 63, 64

v. 43. A and C add *ὑμῖν* after *ἐρρέθη*. 44. All add after *ἐχθροὺς ὑμῶν καὶ εὐλογεῖτε τοὺς καταρωμένους ὑμᾶς· καὶ καλῶς ποιεῖτε τοὺς μισοῦντας ὑμᾶς*: A adds *καὶ διώκοντας*: B and C have *καὶ προσεύχεσθε ὑπὲρ τῶν κακῶς ποιούντων ὑμᾶς καὶ διωκόντων*. 46. B om. *καὶ*. 65, 66

vi. 1. B om. *οὐκ*. 2. A adds *σάλπιγγα* after *σαλπίσῃς*: all add *καὶ ἐν ταῖς στοαῖς* after *ῥύμαις*. 4. B adds *σε* after *βλέπων*: all add *ἐν τῷ φανερῷ* after *σοι*. 6. All om. *σου* after *θύραν*: A adds *βλέποντι* after *κρυπτῷ*: A and C add *ἐν τῷ φανερῷ* after *σοι*. 8. All om. *γὰρ* [*ὁ θεὸς*]. 130, 131

vi. 11. All have *περιουσίας* instead of *τὸν ἐπιούσιον*. 13. All add *ὅτι σού ἐστιν ἡ βασιλεία καὶ ἡ δύναμις καὶ ἡ δόξα εἰς τοὺς αἰῶνας ἀμήν*. 14. B om. *γὰρ*: all add *τὰ παραπτώματα ὑμῶν* after *οὐράνιος*. 15. C om. *μὴ* before *ἀφῆτε* and adds *ὁ ἐν τοῖς οὐρανοῖς* after *πατὴρ ὑμῶν*. 16. All om. *γὰρ*: C om. *τὰ πρόσωπα αὐτῶν ὅπως*. 18. B and C add *σε* after *βλέπων*: C adds *ἐν τῷ φανερῷ* after *σοι*. 21. C has *κεκρυμμένον* for *γὰρ*. 131, 132

vi. 23. C om. *τὸ σκότος* before *πόσον*. 24. B has *καταφρονήσει* for *ἀνθέξεται* and *ἀνθέξεται* for *καταφρονήσει*. 25. B and C om. [*ἢ τί πίητε*]: 26. C om. ܫܡܝܢܐ, an essential part of *ὁ οὐράνιος*. 28. B om. *τί*. 32. B om. *γὰρ*. 33. B and C add *τοῦ θεοῦ* after *βασιλείαν*: A wanting from v. 25 to v. 34 inclusive. 70, 71

vi. 34. B and C add *καὶ τῇ ὥρᾳ ἡ αἰσχύνη αὐτῆς*. This conflation is found in no other MS.: C om. *γὰρ*. 71

PAGE

Matt. vii. 4. C om. *ἰδού*. 6. All om. *ὑμῶν*. 9. All add *ἐκ χειρὸς αὐτοῦ* before *ἄρτον*. 67, 68

vii. 9. B adds *ἐκ χειρὸς αὐτοῦ* before *ἄρτον* in Less. LIII. 10. B has *ἰχθύας* for *ἰχθὺν* in Less. CXXVI. (135). 12. C om. *οὖν*: B om. *καὶ* after *οὕτως*. 13. All add *ἡ πύλη* after *πλατεῖα*: B om. *ὁδὸς*. 16. B om. *ἀπὸ* before *τριβόλων*. 18. C om. *ποιεῖν*. 64, 65, 135

vii. 24, 26. All om. [*τούτους*]. 25. All place *καὶ ἔπνευσαν οἱ ἄνεμοι* before *καὶ κατέβη ἡ βροχὴ*: C om. *γὰρ*. 27. B has *αἱ βροχαὶ* for *ἡ βροχή*, and adds *τεθεμελίωτο γὰρ ἐπὶ τὴν ἄμμον*: all add *σφόδρα* after *μεγάλη*. 28. All add *πάντες* before *οἱ ὄχλοι*. 69

viii. 1. B has *ἐγένετο* for *ἰδού*. 2. C om. *ἐὰν*. 3. All add *ὁ κύριος Ἰησοῦς* after *ἐκτείνας*. 4. All have *ἀπὸ τῆς λέπρας αὐτου* for *αὐτοῦ ἡ λέπρα*, and *τοῖς ἱερεῦσι* for *τῷ ἱερεῖ*: all add *σου* after *δῶρον*: C om. *εἰς μαρτύριον αὐτοῖς*. 69, 70, 71

viii. 7. All add *ὁ κύριος Ἰησοῦς* after *αὐτῷ*: C om. *ἐλθὼν* and *Κύριε*. 9. All om. *ὑπὸ ἐξουσίαν* [*τασσόμενος*]: all have *τῇ ἐξουσίᾳ μου* for *ἐμαυτὸν*. 10. B has *ἀμὴν* twice: all have *τοιαύτην* for *τοσαύτην*. 12. All have *ἐξέλθωσιν* for *ἐκβληθήσονται*. 13. All add *καὶ ὑποστρέψας ὁ ἑκατοντάρχος εἰς τὸν οἶκον αὐτοῦ ἐν αὐτῇ τῇ ὥρᾳ εὗρεν τὸν παῖδα ὑγιαίνοντα*. 72, 73

viii. 15. B adds *προσελθὼν* before *ἥψατο*: C om. *ἥψατο*. 18. B and C have *πολλοὺς ὄχλους* instead of ⌜*ὄχλον*⌝. 20. A om. *καὶ λέγει αὐτῷ ὁ Ἰησοῦς, Αἱ ἀλώπεκες φωλεοὺς ἔχουσιν καὶ τὰ πετεινὰ τοῦ οὐρανοῦ κατασκηνώσεις, ὁ δὲ υἱὸς τοῦ ἀνθρώπου*: C om. *ποῦ*. 71, 72

viii. 24. A adds *ἦν γὰρ ὁ ἄνεμος ἐναντίος αὐτοῖς*: B and C wanting to v. 27. 25. A adds *οἱ μαθηταὶ αὐτοῦ* before *ἤγειραν*; and *ἡμᾶς· ἰδού* after *σῶσον*. 245

viii. 28. All have *ἐλθόντων αὐτῶν* for *ἐλθόντος αὐτοῦ*: all have *Γαργασηνῶν* for *Γαδαρηνῶν*. 29. All om. *ἰδού*: all add *Ἰησοῦς* before *υἱέ*. 30. All have *ἐκεῖ* instead of *μακρὰν ἀπ᾽ αὐτῶν*. 31. C om. *λέγοντες*: all add *ὁ κύριος Ἰησοῦς* before *Ὑπάγετε*. 32. All have *εἰς τὴν ἀγέλην τῶν χοίρων* instead of *εἰς τοὺς χοίρους*: all omit *ἰδοὺ*: B has *τῇ θαλάσσῃ* for *τοῖς ὕδασιν*. 34. C has *ἐγένετο* for *ἰδού*: B has *πᾶσαι αἱ πόλεις ἐξῆλθον* for *πᾶσα ἡ πόλις ἐξῆλθεν*. 74, 75

ix. 2. All om. *ἰδού*: B om. *τὴν πίστιν αὐτῶν*: all add *μου* after *τέκνον*. 4. All add *αὐτοῖς* after *εἶπεν*. 6. All have *ἀνδρὸς* for *ἀνθρώπου*. 76

ix. 10. All have *αὐτῶν ἀνακειμένων* for *αὐτοῦ ἀνακειμένου*. 12. All have *καὶ ἀπεκρίθη ὁ κύριος Ἰησοῦς* instead of *ὁ δὲ ἀκούσας*: all add

PAGE

αὐτοῖς after *εἶπεν*. 13. All add *εἰς μετάνοιαν* after *ἁμαρτωλούς*. 14. All add *πολλὰ* after *νηστεύομεν*. 16. All have *ῥάκος* for *ἐπίβλημα ῥάκους* and *νέου* for *ἀγνάφου*: all add *παλαίου* after *ἱματίου*: all add *ἰδού* before *χεῖρον*: all have *τοῦ πρῶτου* for *γίνεται*. 17. B om. *εἰ δὲ*: all have *ῥήγνυται ὁ οἶνος τοὺς ἀσκοὺς* for *ῥήγνυνται οἱ ἀσκοί*. 73, 74

Matt. ix. 18. All om. *ταῦτα αὐτοῦ λαλοῦντος αὐτοῖς*: B adds *τῷ κυρίῳ*, A and C *τῷ κυρίῳ Ἰησοῦ* after *προσελθὼν*, and B adds *κύριε* before *Ἡ θυγάτηρ*. 25. All have *ἐξῆλθεν* for *ἐξεβλήθη*, and *ἤγειρε* for *ἠγέρθη*. 26. B and C om. *ἐκείνην*. 75

ix. 28. C om. *ἐλθόντι*: all add *δύο* before and *παρακαλοῦντες αὐτὸν* after *τυφλοὶ*, and *ὑμῖν* after *ποιῆσαι*. 29. All add *αὐτοῖς* after *λέγων*. 30. All add *εὐθέως* before *ἠνεῴχθησαν*. 31. C om. *ἐξελθόντες*. 32. All have *ἄνθρωπον κωφόν τινα* for *κωφὸν*. 33. All have *ἐξελθόντος* for *ἐκβληθέντος*. 35. All add *ἐν τῷ λαῷ* after *μαλακίαν*. 77, 78

ix. 36. All add *ὁ κύριος Ἰησοῦς* after *δὲ*. 287

x. 1. All have *ὁ κύριος Ἰησοῦς* after *προσκαλεσάμενος*, and C om. *αὐτοῦ* after *μαθητὰς* in Less. CLXIV. (245): B adds *ἐν τῷ λαῷ* (288). 2, 3. All add *υἱὸς* after *Ἰάκωβος ὁ bis*, and *Λεβαῖος ὁ καλούμενος* before *Θαδδαῖος*. 5. A om. *τούτους τοὺς δώδεκα ἀπέστειλεν* in Less. CLXIV.: B and C om. *δώδεκα* in Less. CLXIV. 245, 287, 288

x. 6. All om. *μᾶλλον*. 8. All om. *νεκροὺς ἐγείρετε*. 246, 288

x. 16. B and C have *γρηγοροῦντες* for *φρόνιμοι*. 18. All have *βασιλεῖς καὶ ἡγεμόνας*: B and C om. *ἐμοῦ*. 290

x. 19. B om. *πῶς ἢ*: All have *ἡμέρᾳ* for *ὥρᾳ*. 291

x. 32, 33. All om. *μου*. 33. A and B have *ἐγὼ* for *κἀγὼ*. 66

x. 42. B adds *ὕδατος* after *ποτήριον*. xi. 1. B adds *τοῦτο* before *διατάσσων*. 77

xi. 2. B adds *καὶ* before *τὰ ἔργα*: all have *δύο* for *διὰ*. 4. A and B have *βλέπετε καὶ ἀκούετε*: C has *ἐβλέψατε καὶ ἠκούσατε*. 5. B and C have *εὐφραίνονται* for *εὐαγγελίζονται*. 8. B and C have *ἢ* for *ἀλλὰ*. 9. All add *γὰρ* after *οὗτος*. 10. All om. *σου* after *ὁδόν*. 11. All add *γὰρ* after *ὑμῖν*: B adds *καὶ* before *μικρότερος*. 12. All om. *ἕως ἄρτι*. 15. All add *ἀκούειν* after *ὦτα*. 275, 276

xi. 27. All om. *μου* after *πατρός*: all add *αὐτὸς ἀπεκάλυψεν*. 29. C om. *καὶ εὑρήσετε ἀνάπαυσιν ταῖς ψυχαῖς ὑμῶν. ὁ . . . ζυγός μου*. 239

xii. 31. A adds *ὑμῖν*, and B *πᾶσι* before *τοῖς ἀνθρώποις*: C om. the clause: all add *ἁγίου* before *πνεύματος*. 33, 34. B om. *γὰρ*. 33. B om. *αὐτοῦ* after *καρπὸν*. 35. A and B add *τοῦ ἐν τῇ καρδίᾳ αὐτοῦ*

PAGE

after *θησαυροῦ bis*: C adds it the first time only. 36. C has a remarkable reading *Λέγω ὑμῖν ὅτι πᾶν ῥῆμα καλὸν ὁ οὐ λαλήσουσιν οἱ ἄνθρωποι, ἀποδώσουσιν περὶ αὐτοῦ λόγον ἐν ἡμέρᾳ κρίσεως·* 78, 79

Matt. xiii. 44. A adds *πάντα* before *ὅσα*. 45. A adds *ἀνθρώπῳ* before *ἐμπόρῳ*: B and C wanting to verse 54. 48. A has *εἰς τὰ ἄγγη αὐτων*. 51. A begins *καὶ εἶπεν αὐτοῖς ὁ κύριος Ἰησοῦς οἴδατε καὶ συνήκατε*. 54. A has *πόλιν* for *πατρίδα*. 241, 242

xiv. 14. All add *ὁ Ἰησοῦς* before *εἶδεν*: B adds *πάντας* before *τοὺς ἀῤῥώστους*. 15. All add *τὰς πλησίας* after *κώμας*. 19. B adds *ἔδωκαν* after *μαθηταὶ*. 79, 80

xiv. 22. A and C add *ὁ Ἰησοῦς* and B *ὁ κύριος Ἰησοῦς* after *ἠνάγκασεν*: 23. B and C om. *ἀνέβη εἰς τὸ ὄρος κατ' ἰδίαν προσεύξασθαι*: A om. *κατ' ἰδίαν*. All agree with א in omitting *καὶ ἀπολύσας τοὺς ὄχλους*. It is possible that there was a Greek text *ἕως οὗ ἀπολύσῃ τοὺς ὄχλους. ὀψίας δὲ γενομένης*. 24. All add *μέσον τῆς θαλάσσης* before *βασανιζόμενον*. 25. All add *ὁ κύριος Ἰησοῦς* after *αὐτοὺς*. 26. A and C have *τῶν ὑδάτων* for *τῆς θαλάσσης*. 28. All have *πάρεχε μοι ἐξουσίαν* for *κέλευσόν με*: All have *ἵνα ἔλθῃ* for *καὶ ἦλθεν*: A and C add *περιπατῶν* after *πρός σε*. 29. B has *τὴν θάλασσαν* instead of *τὰ ὕδατα*. 30. All add *ἰσχυρὸν* after *ἄνεμον*. 32. All have *ἀνάβαντος αὐτοῦ* for *ἀναβάντων αὐτῶν*: all add *ἤγγισαν καὶ* before *προσεκύνησαν*. 81

xv. 21. A has *Τότε ἦλθε* for *Καὶ ἐξελθὼν ἐκεῖθεν ἀνεχώρησεν*. 24. A adds *αὐτοῖς* after *εἶπεν*. 25. A adds *γυνὴ* after *δὲ*. 25, 26. *κύριε, βοήθει μοι. ὁ δὲ ἀποκριθεὶς εἶπεν, Οὐκ ἔστιν καλὸν λαβεῖν* has perished from A. 27. A om. [*γὰρ*]: A adds *καὶ ζῶσιν*. 28. A om. *ἀποκριθεὶς*: B and C wanting. 296, 297

xv. 32. All add *τοῦτον* after *ὄχλον*, *δώδεκα* before *μαθητὰς*, and *αὐτοῖς* after *εἶπεν*: C om. *μοι* (after *προσμένουσιν*). 33. B has *τοῦτον* for *τοσοῦτον*. 34. B adds *ἄρτους* after *Ἑπτὰ*. 38. All add *ὡσεὶ* before *τετρακισχίλιοι*. 80

xvi. 13. C om. *τῆς Καισαρίας*: all add *τότε* before *ἠρώτα*: all have *ἀνδρὸς* for *ἀνθρώπου*. 286

xvi. 14. All add *αὐτῷ* after *εἶπαν*, and *ἐξ αὐτῶν εἶπον* before *Ἰωάννην*: A adds *Ἰησοῦς* after *αὐτοῖς*. 17. All om. *μου* after *πατήρ*. 18. C om. *μου* before *τὴν ἐκκλησίαν*. 287

xvii. 1. All om. *μεθ' ἡμέρας ἓξ*. 2. All add *ὁ κύριος Ἰησοῦς* before *μετεμορφώθη*. 292

PAGE

Matt. xvii. 3. All om. *ἰδού*. 4. B and C om. *εἰ*: C om. *ὧδε*. 5. B and C om. *νεφέλη*: B has *τοῦ οὐρανοῦ* for *τῆς νεφέλης*. 6. All om. *καὶ ἀκούσαντες*. 7. All om. *Ἐγέρθητε καὶ*. 9. All have *ἀνδρὸς* for *ἀνθρώπου*. 292, 293

xvii. 11. A adds *κύριος Ἰησοῦς* after *δὲ*, and *αὐτοῖς* after *εἶπεν*. 12. A has *ἀνδρὸς* for *ἀνθρώπου*: B and C wanting. 289

xvii. 14. C has *καὶ ἐλθόντος τοῦ κυρίου Ἰησοῦ* and om. *πρὸς*. 15. A and C have *πάσχει* instead of ⸢*ἔχει*⸣. 17. A and C add *τότε* before *ἀποκριθεὶς*: B wanting. 18. C has *τὰ δαιμόνια* for *τὸ δαιμόνιον*. 82, 83

xvii. 20. All have *ἔσται δύσκολον* for *ἀδυνατήσει*. 22. A and C have *ἀνδρὸς* instead of *ἀνθρώπου* and om. *καὶ ἐλυπήθησαν σφόδρα*: B wanting. 83

xvii. 24. All om. *εἰς Καφαρναοὺμ*. 25. B and C have *λέγουσι* instead of *λέγει Ναί*, an obvious corruption, and om. *αὐτὸν* after *προέφθασεν*: all have *Πέτρος* for *Σίμων*; B. om. *ἢ κῆνσον*. 27. B. and C have *λαβὼν δὸς* where A has *δὸς* only. 82

xviii. 1. All have *ἡμέρᾳ* instead of *ὥρᾳ*. 2. All add *ὁ κύριος Ἰησοῦς* after *προσκαλεσάμενος*. 4. B om. *οὖν*. 82

xviii. 10. B and C have *ἀπολέσητε* and A has *πικρανῆτε* for *καταφρονήσητε*. 10, 14. All om. *μου* after *πατρός*. 14. All three codices omit *ἵνα ἀπόληται ἓν τῶν μικρῶν τούτων*. 15. All add *κατὰ σοῦ* after *ὁ ἀδελφός σου*. 16. C om. *ἐὰν δὲ μὴ ἀκούσῃ, παράλαβε* ⸢*μετὰ σου ἔτι*: all add *σου* after *ἀκούσῃ*, and *καὶ* before *αὐτῶν*. 17. All have *συναγωγῇ* and *συναγωγῆς* instead of *ἐκκλησίᾳ* and *ἐκκλησίας*: all have *οἱ ἐθνικοὶ* for *ὁ ἐθνικὸς*. 19. All om. *μου* after *πατρὸς*. 20. C om. *εἰς τὸ ἐμὸν ὄνομα*. 60, 61

xviii. 23. All om. *Διὰ τοῦτο*: B has *τοῦ δούλου* for *τῶν δούλων*. 24. B om. *ὀφειλέτης*. 26. All add *Κύριε* before *Μακροθύμησον*. 27. All om. [*ἐκείνου*]. 29. B adds *ἰδού* before *παρεκάλει*: all add *τὸ πᾶν* after *σοι*. 85

xviii. 31. A and B add *τότε* before *ἐλυπήθησαν*. 32. C om. *αὐτὸν*: B and C om. *ἐκείνην*. 34. All add *ἐπ' αὐτὸν* after *ὀργισθεὶς*. 35. A and C add *οὖν* after *οὕτως*: all om. *μου*: all add *τὰ παραπτώματα αὐτῶν* after *αὐτοῦ*: B adds *πάντων* before *καρδιῶν*. 86

xix. 3. All add *ἀνθρώπῳ* after *ἔξεστιν*. 5. All have *ἀνὴρ* for *ἄνθρωπος*. 8. All have *ἐναντίον* for *πρὸς*. 9. All have *μοιχεύει αὐτὴν* for *μοιχᾶται* and add *ὁ δὲ ἀπολελυμένην ἀπὸ τοῦ ἀνδρὸς αὐτῆς λαμβάνων γυναῖκα μοιχᾶται*. 83, 84

xix. 10. All have *ἀνδρὸς* for *ἀνθρώπου* and add *ἀνθρώπῳ* before *γαμῆσαι*: C om. *Εὐ*. 12. All add *εὐνοῦχοι* after *οὕτως*. 84

PAGE

Matt. xix. 16. All om. ἰδού: all have τῷ κυρίῳ Ἰησοῦ instead of αὐτῷ: B om. ἀγαθὸν after τί: all have ἀγαθὲ after Διδάσκαλε: all have κληρονομήσω for σχῶ. 17. B has ὁ Θεὸς before ὁ ἀγαθὸς. 18. B om. ἔφη: C has καὶ οὐ κλέψεις καὶ οὐ μοιχεύσεις. 19. A om. καὶ ἀγαπήσεις τὸν πλησίον σου ὡς σεαυτόν. 20. All add ἐκ νεότητός μου after ἐφύλαξα. 21. All add πάντα before τὰ ὑπάρχοντα, and αὐτὸ after δὸς. 22. All om. [τοῦτον]: B om. γάρ. 23. All om. Ἀμὴν. 25. All om. σφόδρα. 26. All have ἀποκριθεὶς instead of ἐμβλέψας: C om. ταῦτα. 86, 87

xix. 27. C om. τί ἄρα ἔσται ἡμῖν. 28. All translate πάλιν by ἀπ' ἀρχῆς: all have ἀνδρὸς for ἀνθρώπου. 29. All om. οἰκίας ἢ after ἀφῆκεν and add ἢ οἰκίας after ἀγροὺς. 66, 67

xx. 1. B om. γὰρ: all have ἀνδρὶ for ἀνθρώπῳ. 3. B om. ἐν τῇ ἀγορᾷ: C has ἐν ταῖς ἀγοραῖς. 4. C om. καὶ before ὑμεῖς. 276

xx. 6. All add ἀργοὺς after ἑστῶτας. 7. A adds καὶ ὃ ἐὰν ᾖ δίκαιον δώσω ὑμῖν. 8. All have διακόνῳ for ἐπιτρόπῳ. 11. A and B add καὶ αὐτοὶ ἀνὰ δηνάριον after λαβόντες δὲ. 12. B om. ἡμῖν. 13. A and B have Ἀγαπητέ μου and C Ἑταῖρε μου. 15. B and C add ἢ before οὐκ: A om. οὐκ ἔξεστιν . . . . μοι ποιῆσαι. 16. All add πολλοὶ γάρ εἰσι κλητοὶ ὀλίγοι δὲ ἐκλεκτοί, but B om. γὰρ. 277

xx. 30. B om. Κύριε, and all add Ἰησοῦς after ἡμᾶς. 31. A and C om. Κύριε. 34. A has an interpolation from Luke xviii. 43, δοξάζων τὸν Θεὸν, καὶ πᾶς ὁ λαὸς ἰδὼν ἔδωκεν αἶνον τῷ θεῷ. 86

xxi. 1. All add καὶ εἰς Βηθανίαν after Βηθφαγὴ: all have πλησίον before εἰς τὸ Ὄρος. 2. All add αὐτοὺς after ⌜ἀγάγετέ⌝. 3. B and C have an additional αὐτῶν dependent on κύριος. 4. All add πᾶν after δὲ. 5. B adds καὶ ταπεινὸς after πραῢς. 7. All have αὐτοῦ for αὐτῶν after ἐπάνω. 9. B and C om. αὐτὸν. 149

xxi. 15. All add ὁ κύριος Ἰησοῦς after ἐποίησεν. 16. All om. καὶ after νηπίων and add σοι after κατηρτίσω. 17. All om. καταλιπὼν αὐτοὺς. 150

xxi. 19. C om. αὐτῇ. 21. C om. εἶπεν αὐτοῖς: οὐ μόνον τὸ τῆς συκῆς ποιήσετε is incorrectly translated in all three codices by οὐ μόνον τὴν συκῆν ποιήσετε: all add οὕτως after γενήσεται. 23. All have τοῦ κυρίου Ἰησοῦ instead of αὐτοῦ: A adds αὐτῷ after λέγοντες. 152, 153

xxi. 25. All have ἐν ταῖς καρδίαις αὐτῶν instead of ⌜ἐν⌝ ἑαυτοῖς: all om. οὖν. 27. All add ὁ κύριος Ἰησοῦς after αὐτός. 28. All add τις after ἄνθρωπος: all add μου after τέκνον. 29. All add ὑπάγω after κύριε. 30. All add εἰς τὸν ἀμπελῶνα. 31. All add

PAGE

αὐτοῦ after *πατρός*; and *αὐτῷ* after *λέγουσιν*: all have *ἀμὴν* twice. 33. All add *τις* after *ἄνθρωπος*: all have *καὶ* for *ὅστις*: all add *ἐν αὐτῷ* after *ᾠκοδόμησεν*. 153, 154, 88

Matt. xxi. 34. C om. *αὐτοῦ* after *καρποὺς*. 35. All om. *οἱ γεωργοὶ* in Less. CXLI. (154): all om. *αὐτοῦ* after *δούλους* (154). 38. All add *αὐτοῦ* after *υἱὸν*: all om. *αὐτοῦ* after *κληρονομίαν* in Less. CXLI. 41. C om. *αὐτῷ* after *ἀποδώσουσιν* (89). 42. All have *διέτεμον* for *ἀπεδοκίμασαν*. 154, 88

xxii. 1. A om. *καὶ ἀποκριθεὶς ὁ Ἰησοῦς πάλιν εἶπεν*: all transfer *πάλιν εἶπεν* before *ὡμιώθη*. 2. All have *ἀνδρὶ* for *ἀνθρώπῳ*: B om. *καὶ* before *σιτιστοὶ*. 4. A and C have *ἕτοιμον* for *ἡτοίμακα*, and B has *ἡτοιμάκασιν*: B om. *μου* after *ταῦροι*. 14. B om. *γὰρ*. 90, 91

xxii. 7. All add *ἀκούσας* after *βασιλεὺς*: all om. *ἐκείνους*. 11. All have *τινα* after *ἄνθρωπον*. 13. All have *χεῖρας καὶ πόδας*. 91

xxii. 15. A and B add *κατὰ τοῦ Ἰησοῦ* (p. 87), and all add *κατ' αὐτοῦ* after *ἔλαβον* (p. 156). 87, 156

xxii. 16. C om. *γὰρ* (87): all om. *γὰρ* (156). 17. C om. *ἔξεστιν* (156). 18. B adds *αὐτοῖς* after *εἶπεν* (88). 20. All have *τότε* for *καὶ* (88): A has *τότε* after *καὶ* (156): all add *ὁ κύριος Ἰησοῦς* after *αὐτοῖς*. 21. All add *αὐτῷ* after *λέγουσιν*: all om. *τότε* (88): A also on p. 156: B and C add *τότε* before *Ἀπόδοτε* (156): B and C om. *οὖν* (156): B om. *οὖν* (88). 87, 156

xxii. 23. All have *οἵτινες λέγουσι* for *λέγοντες*: all add *νεκρῶν* after *ἀνάστασιν*. 25. B om. *παρ' ἡμῖν*. 27. All add *καὶ* before *ἡ γυνή*. 28. All add *τῶν νεκρῶν* after *ἀναστάσει*. 30. All add *τῶν νεκρῶν* after *ἀναστάσει*: A om. *οὔτε γαμοῦσιν*: B and C have *οὔτε γαμίζονται οὔτε γαμοῦσιν*: all add *τοῦ θεοῦ* after *ἄγγελοι*. 35. B om. *ἐξ αὐτῶν*. 157

xxii. 36. All add *λέγων* after *αὐτὸν*. 37. All have *ὁ κύριος Ἰησοῦς* instead of *ὁ*: all add *καὶ ἐν ὅλῃ τῇ δυνάμει σου* after *ψυχῇ σου* on p. 92, and after *καρδίᾳ σου* on p. 157. 42. All add *υἱὸς* before *Τοῦ Δαυείδ*. 43. All have *ὁ κύριος Ἰησοῦς* after *αὐτοῖς*: B has *με* instead of *αὐτὸν* after *καλεῖ* (92). 92, 157, 158

xxii. 44. All add *ὑποπόδιον* before *ὑποκάτω*. 45. All add *ἐν πνεύματι* after *Δαυεὶδ*: B has *με* instead of *αὐτὸν* (92). 46. B om. *αὐτῷ* (92). 93, 158

xxiii. 4. C om. *δεσμεύουσιν δὲ φορτία βαρέα* (89): all add *καὶ δυσβάστακτα*. 5. All add *τῶν ἱματίων αὐτῶν* after *κράσπεδα*. 7. All have *Ῥαββεί* twice. 8. All have *μὴ καλέσητε ἄνθρωπον* instead of *μὴ*

PAGE

κληθῆτε: B om. *γὰρ* after *εἷς*: after *εἷς γὰρ* A has the interpolation *ὑμῶν ὁ κύριος· ὑμεῖς δὲ μὴ κληθῆτε διδάσκαλοι· εἷς γάρ ἐστιν*. 9. C om. *γὰρ*. 158, 89

Matt. xxiii. 10. B and C om. *ὅτι καθηγητὴς ὑμῶν ἐστὶν εἷς*: B adds *εἰ μὴ* before *χριστός*. 12. All add *γὰρ* after *ὅστις*. 90

xxiii. 14. A adds *Οὐαὶ ὑμῖν γραμματεῖς καὶ φαρισαῖοι ὑποκριταὶ ὅτι κατεσθίετε τὰς οἰκίας τῶν χηρῶν καὶ προφάσει μακρὰ προσευχόμενοι· διὰ τοῦτο λήψεσθε περισσότερον κρίμα*. 18. A has *τοῦ θυσιαστηρίου* instead of *αὐτοῦ*. 19. A adds *μωροὶ καὶ* before *τυφλοὶ*. 24. A has *τῶν τυφλῶν* instead of *τυφλοί*. 26. A adds *οὖν* after *καθάρισον*. 28. A adds *πάσης* before *ἀνομίας*: B and C wanting from ver. 15 to ver. 28. 159

xxiii. 37. B and C add *ἐν σοί* after *τέκνα σου*, an interpolation from Luke xix. 44. 232

xxiii. 37. A and C add ܟܠ *πᾶν* between ܗܝܟ and ܢܐ *ὃν τρόπον*. 38. All add *ἔρημος* after *ὑμῶν*. 160, 232

xxiv. 3. All have *τοῦ κυρίου Ἰησοῦ* instead of *αὐτοῦ*: all add *αὐτοῦ* after *μαθηταὶ*: B om. *κατ' ἰδίαν* (160). 5. B om. *γὰρ* (160). 6. All add *ταῦτα* before *γενέσθαι*. 5. A adds after *πλανήσουσιν*, *καὶ ὁ καιρὸς ἤγγικεν· μὴ πορευθῆτε ὀπίσω αὐτῶν* from Luke xxi. 8 (160). 7. All add *λοιμοὶ καὶ* before *λιμοί*. 12. B has *τὰς ἀνομίας αὐτῶν* for *τὴν ἀνομίαν* (155). 13. B adds *ἢ* before *ὁ δὲ ὑπομείνας* (161). 15. A has *ἐγὼ* after *ἑστὸς*, evidently a mistake (155): C has *ὅς* for *ὁ ἀναγινώσκων*. 20. B adds *ἡμέρᾳ* before *χειμῶνος* (161). 21. All om. *τότε*. 155, 160, 161

xxiv. 23. All add *Ἰδού* before the second *ὧδε*: A and C om. the first *ὧδε* (161): A has *οὗτος* for the second *Ὧδε* (155). 26. A has *εἴπῃ* for *εἴπωσιν* (155). 26. A and C add *ἢ* before the second *Ἰδοὺ*, B also on p. 155. 27. All add *καὶ* after *ἔσται*: all have *ἀνδρὸς* for *ἀνθρώπου*. 29. A and C om. *Εὐθέως*, B also on p. 155: all have *τοῦ μέσου* before *τοῦ οὐρανοῦ*. 30. All have *ἀνδρὸς* for the first *ἀνθρώπου*, B has *ἀνδρὸς* for the second *ἀνθρώπου* (162). 31. A and C have *τότε* before *ἀποστελεῖ* (156), B also on p. 162: all add *φωνῆς* before *σάλπιγγος*, and *πάντας* before *τοὺς ἐκλεκτοὺς*. 32. All add *γὰρ* after *ὅταν*. 155, 156, 161, 162

xxiv. 33. C om. *καὶ*: B has *γενήσεται* for *ἴδητε*. 162

xxiv. 34. B om. *ἕως*. 36. All have *ἢ* for *καὶ*. 37. B and C om. *γὰρ* (93): B om. *γὰρ* (162): C adds *τῇ γενεᾷ* after *Ὥσπερ* (93): B has *ἐπὶ ταῖς ἡμέραις* and A and C *ἐν ταῖς ἡμέραις* for *αἱ ἡμέραι* (93): all have *ἐν ταῖς ἡμέραις* (162): A and C add *καὶ* after *ἔσται* (93): all add *καὶ* after *ἔσται* (162): all have *ἀνδρὸς* for *ἀνθρώπου* (93): C has *ἀνδρὸς* for *ἀνθρώπου* (162). 93, 162

PAGE

Matt. xxiv. 38. B has *γαμοῦντες* for *γαμίζοντες* (162). 39. All add *καὶ* after *ἔσται*: A and C om. *ἧς ἡμέρας* (163). 39, 44. All have *ἀνδρὸς* instead of *ἀνθρώπου* (93): B has *ἀνδρὸς* for *ἀνθρώπου* (163). 40. C has *τοῖς ἀγροῖς* for *τῷ ἀγρῷ* (163). 41. A adds *λέγει ὁ κύριος* after *ἀφίεται* in Less. CXCIV. (163). 43. All have *ὥρᾳ* for *φυλακῇ* on page 94, and A alone has it in Less. CXCIV., p. 163. 46. B adds *ἢ οὗτος* after *δοῦλος* (163). 93, 94, 163

xxiv. 48. All add *τοῦ ἔρχεσθαι* after *κύριος*. 50. A and C om. *ἐκείνου*. 163

xxv. 2. C om. *ἐξ αὐτῶν* (164). 4. All add *αὐτῶν* after *ἀγγείοις*. 5. All om. *πᾶσαι* in Less. LXXXIV.* and A in Less. CCCX. 6. A and B on p. 164, and all on p. 96, add *ἔρχεται* after *νύμφιος*: all add *ἐγέρθητε* before *ἐξέρχεσθε* (96): all have *ἐγέρθητε* for *ἐξέρχεσθε* on p. 164, except Less. CCCCX. which adds it: all add *αὐτοῦ* after *ἀπάντησιν*. 8. All add *τότε* before *αἱ δὲ μωραὶ* (96): A and C add *οὖν* after *αἱ δὲ* (164): all add *ἰδού* after *ὅτι*: C om. *σβέννυνται* (96). 9. All om. *μᾶλλον*. 95, 96, 164

xxv. 11. A om. *καὶ* after *ἔρχονται* in p. 164: all om. *καὶ* on p. 96. 13. A alone has *ἐν ᾗ ὁ υἱὸς τοῦ ἀνθρώπου ἔρχεται* added by a later hand in Less. CCCCX. 96, 164

xxv. 14. All om. *Ὥσπερ* (94): all have *ἀνὴρ* instead of *ἄνθρωπος*. 94, 164

xxv. 15. All have *εὐθέως* before *ἀπεδήμησεν* (165). 17. B adds *λαβὼν* after *τὰ δύο* (165): all add *καὶ* after *ὡσαύτως*. 94, 165

xxv. 17. In Less. LXXXIV., whilst A and C have *ὁ τὰ δύο ἐκέρδησεν ἄλλα δύο*, B has *ὁ λαβὼν δύο τάλαντα καὶ ἄλλα δύο ἐκέρδησεν ἐπ' αὐτοῖς* (94): in Less. CXLIV., B adds after *δὺο*, *τάλαντα ἠργάσατο ἐν αὐτοῖς καὶ* (165). 94, 165

xxv. 19. B om. *ἐκείνων*. 20. All om. *προσήνεγκεν ἄλλα πέντε τάλαντα*: C om. *πέντε ταλαντά μοι παρέδωκας*: A and B om. *Κύριε*: all add *ἐπ' αὐτοῖς* after *ἐκέρδησα*: B om. the last *τάλαντα* (94): C om. the last *τάλαντα* (165). 22. A om. *ἄλλα* (94): all add *λαβὼν* after the first *τάλαντα* in Less. LXXXIV. (94) and CXLIV. (165): all add *ἐπ' αὐτοῖς* after *ἐκέρδησα*. 24. All om. *σε* after *ἔγνων*: all have *ἀνὴρ* for *ἄνθρωπος*: all have *ὅ τι* for *ὅπου* (95). 94, 95, 165

xxv. 26. C adds *Ἰησοῦς sic* after *κύριος αὐτοῦ* (95): B and C have the curious reading *πόθεν ᾔδεις* (165), whilst A has the usual *ᾔδεις* before *ὅτι θερίζω ὅπου οὐκ ἔσπειρα*: C only has *πόθεν ᾔδεις* on p. 95. 27. All have *τῷ τόκῳ αὐτοῦ* for *τόκῳ*. 95, 165

xxv. 28. All om. *οὖν* (165). 28, 29. *ἔχει* and *ἔχοντι* are translated *more semitice ἐν τῇ χειρὶ αὐτοῦ* (166). 29. C adds *δέκα τάλαντα* after *ἔχοντι* (95). 95, 165, 166

PAGE

Matt. xxv. 31. B has ἀνδρὸς for ἀνθρώπου in Lessons LXXXIV.* (96), and CXLIV. (166): all have ἀνδρὸς for ἀνθρώπου in Less. CXX. (129): B om. ἐν τῇ δόξῃ αὐτοῦ in Less. LXXXIV.* (96): All have αὐτοῦ after ἄγγελοι. 96, 129, 166

xxv. 32. B adds τότε after καὶ before συναχθήσονται. 96, 166

xxv. 34. A om. αὐτοῦ after δεξιῶν (129): all om. αὐτοῦ after δεξιῶν (96). 96, 129

xxv. 34. C om. ἐρεῖ (129): all om. μου. 166, 129

xxv. 36. B om. ἤμην after φυλακῇ (97), but all add it after γυμνὸς, where the Greek idiom does not express it. 97, 129

xxv. 37. C om. αὐτῷ: C om. καὶ ἐθρέψαμεν (129). 129, 166

xxv. 39. B has καὶ for ἢ before ἐν φυλακῇ 97

xxv. 40. B om. ἀδελφῶν μου, and adds καὶ before ἐμοί. 97, 166

xxv. 40. C om. τῶν ἀδελφῶν μου in Less. CXX. 129

xxv. 41. A and B have Σατανᾷ instead of διαβόλῳ (97): all have Σατανᾷ in Less. CXLIV. (166) and CXX. (129). 97, 128, 166

xxv. 44. B om. καὶ αὐτοὶ (97): B om. αὐτοὶ (130). 97, 130

xxv. 44. C has ἢ γυμνὸν before ἢ ξένον. 130

xxv. 45. All add τῶν ἀδελφῶν μου after τούτων in Less. CXLIV. (167), but not in Less. CXX. (97): B adds it in Less. LXXXIV.* (97): A adds καὶ, and B καὶ ὁ βασιλεὺς after ἀποκριθήσεται (97). 97, 167

xxv. 45. All add καὶ after ἀποκριθήσεται. 130, 167

xxv. 46. B om. οὗτοι (97): B has εἰς πῦρ, whilst A has εἰς κόλασιν in Less. LXXXIV.* (97): B has κολάσεις for κόλασιν (130, 167). 97, 130, 167

xxvi. 1. B has ἰδοὺ for ἐγένετο: B om. πάντας. 2. B has ἀνδρὸς instead of ἀνθρώπου. 98

xxvi. 6. B adds μὴ before γενομένου (175). 7. All have ἐν τῇ χειρὶ αὐτῆς for ἔχουσα. 8. A and B add αὐτοῦ after μαθηταί. 175, 170

xxvi. 8. All add τοῦ μύρου after αὕτη, and τὸ μύρον after τοῦτο. 10. B om. γὰρ (170): all om. γὰρ (175). 11. All om. γὰρ. 12. All om. γὰρ (175). 13. C has ὅτι πᾶς ὃς κηρύξει for ὅπου ἐὰν κηρυχθεῖ (170): all om. καὶ: all om. αὐτῆς. 170, 175

xxvi. 14. All add αὐτοῖς after εἶπεν. 16. All add αὐτοῖς after παραδῷ (170). 17. A and B add αὐτοῦ after μαθηταί: B adds αὐτῷ after λέγοντες. 18. All add αὐτοῖς after εἶπεν: B om. μου. 170, 175, 176

xxvi. 21. All add αὐτοῖς after εἶπεν. 23. All add κύριος Ἰησοῦς after δὲ. 24. All have ἀνδρὸς instead of the first ἀνθρώπου. 25. B has οὗτος for ἐγώ. 27. B has ἐξ ἐμοῦ after πίετε instead of ἐξ

PAGE

αὐτοῦ. 28. All add νέας before διαθήκης: C om. μου, and has therefore the reading τὸ αἷμα τῆς νέας διαθήκης: C has ὑμῶν instead of πολλῶν. 177, 178

Matt. xxvi. 29. All om. μου after πατρός. 31. All add τοῖς μαθηταῖς αὐτοῦ after Ἰησοῦς: B adds γὰρ after ὑμεῖς: A om. τὰ πρόβατα τῆς, and has ἡ ποίμνη αὐτοῦ for ποίμνης: B and C add αὐτοῦ after ποίμνης. 32. All have ἰδοὺ before προάξω. 33. All have καὶ after Εἰ. 39. All om. μου after Πάτερ, and add θέλεις after σου. 44. C om. πάλιν: all om. the second πάλιν. 45. All add αὐτοῦ after μαθητὰς: all om. ἰδού. 49. All add αὐτῷ after εἶπεν: A om. καὶ κατεφίλησεν αὐτόν. ὁ δὲ. 50. All om. αὐτῷ. 52. All om. σου after μάχαιραν, and γὰρ after πάντες: C om. αὐτῷ. 178, 179

xxvi. 53. All add νῦν after δύναμαι, and om. μου after πατέρα. 55. All add μεθ' ὑμῶν after ἡμέραν. 57. B om. ὅπου (180): C has ἡμῖν for ὅπου (180). 59. All add καὶ οἱ πρεσβύτεροι after ἀρχιερεῖς. 62. All add καὶ before Οὐδὲν. 180, 195

xxvi. 57. All add οἱ δὲ στρατιῶται before οἱ κρατήσαντες (194): all add οἱ ἀρχιερεῖς καὶ after ὅπου. 180, 194, 195

xxvi. 59. All add καὶ οἱ πρεσβύτεροι after ἀρχιερεῖς. 180, 195

xxvi. 60. C om. μαρτύρων. 180

xxvi. 62. All add καὶ before Οὐδὲν. 180, 195

xxvi. 63. C adds τοῦ ζῶντος after Θεοῦ. 180, 195

xxvi. 64. B has ἀνδρὸς for ἀνθρώπου (181): all have ἀνδρὸς for ἀνθρώπου (195). 65. All add αὐτοῦ after βλασφημίαν. 181, 195

xxvi. 67. All add κολάφους after αὐτὸν, and ῥαπίσματα after ἐράπισαν. 69. B has τῆς αὐλῆς for ἐν τῇ αὐλῇ (181): B om. Καὶ (195): C has τὸν Ναζαρηνὸν for τοῦ Γαλιλαίου (196). 181, 195, 196

xxvi. 70. All add οὔτε ἐπίσταμαι. 71. All have καὶ for Οὗτος on p. 181, and καὶ before Οὗτος on p. 196. 72. All have τοῦτον τὸν ἄνδρα instead of τὸν ἄνθρωπον. 73. All om. καὶ σὺ ἐξ αὐτῶν εἶ (181): B om. καὶ γὰρ: A and C om. γὰρ on p. 181. 74. All add τοῦτον after ἄνθρωπον. 75. All add αὐτῷ after εἰρηκότος. 181, 196

xxvii. 1. B om. πάντες (181): B has κρατῆσαι instead of θανατῶσαι (181): 2. All add Ποντίῳ before Πειλάτῳ except C on p. 208. 181, 208

xxvii. 1. All om. πάντες and τοῦ λαοῦ and παρέδωκαν and τῷ ἡγεμόνει: all have ὑπερέται for πρεσβύτεροι: C adds Χριστοῦ after Ἰησοῦ. 237

xxvii. 3. B has καὶ before Ἰούδας (199). 4. C om. Ἥμαρτον (199). 5. All om. ἀνεχώρησεν except A and B on p. 208. 7. B has μετ' ἀλλήλων for ἐξ αὐτῶν, probably a mistake (199). 199, 208

PAGE

Matt. xxvii. 9. A and B have ἐτίμησαν for ἐτιμήσαντο in both Lessons, and C has προσήνεγκαν on p. 199. 10. C adds Ἰησοῦς after κύριος (199). 11. A om. ὁ ἡγεμὼν (209). 199, 209

xxvii. 14. All add μᾶλλον after ὥστε. 16. All add τίνα after δέσμιον: all have Ἰησοῦν before Βαραββᾶν. 17. All om. οὖν: all add τῶν δύο after τίνα, and Ἰησοῦν before [τὸν] Βαραββᾶν: B adds καὶ before Ἰησοῦν τὸν Βαραββᾶν on p. 209. 19. All have ἐν ὀνείρατί μου for κατ' ὄναρ. 200, 209

xxvii. 22. B has σταυρώση twice and C once for σταυρωθήτω on p. 200, and on p. 210 B has Σταυρώση. 23. B and C have σταυρώση for σταυρωθήτω on p. 201, and B has it on 210: C has σταύρωσον (210). 200, 210

xxvii. 24. All have αὐτοῦ after χεῖρας and C has τὴν χεῖρα for τὰς χεῖρας on p. 210: all add τοῦ δικαίου after τούτου. 26. All add αὐτοῖς after παρέδωκεν: all have σταυρῶσιν αὐτὸν for σταυρωθῇ. 29. C om. βασιλεῦ on p. 210. 30. B has τὸ πρόσωπον αὐτοῦ instead of αὐτὸν. 31. B has ἐξέδυσαν instead of ἐνέδυσαν: all add τότε before ἐνέδυσαν. 32. B has ἐξερχόμενος instead of ἐξερχόμενοι. 201, 210

xxvii. 33. All add οἱ στρατιῶται after ἐλθόντες. 203

xxvii. 33. B has τὸν τόπον τοῦτον for τόπον and has Κράνιος for Κρανίου τόπος. 35. C adds ἐπ' αὐτοῖς after ⌜βάλλοντες⌝. 210, 211

xxvii. 35. All add ἵνα πληρωθῇ τὸ λεγόμενον ὑπὸ τοῦ προφήτου τοῦ λέγοντος· διεμερίσαντο τὰ ἱμάτιά μου ἑαυτοῖς καὶ ἐπὶ τὸν ἱματισμόν μου ἔβαλον κλῆρον. 38. C has σταυροῦσι for σταυροῦνται. 44. C has συνσταυροῦντας for συνσταυρωθέντες (203). 39. All om. παραπορευόμενοι (211). 203, 211, 212

xxvii. 40. All add τοῦ Θεοῦ after ναὸν: all place εἰ υἱὸς εἶ τοῦ Θεοῦ after καὶ κατάβηθι ἀπὸ τοῦ σταυροῦ. 203, 211

xxvii. 42. B adds εἰ before Ἄλλους (212): all add εἰ before βασιλεὺς. 43. All add εἰ before πέποιθεν. 44. C om. καὶ after δ' αὐτὸ (212). 46. All om. τοῦτ' ἔστιν, Θεέ μου, Θεέ μου, ἱνατί με ἐγκατέλιπες; on p. 204. 48. B om. καλάμῳ ἐπότιζεν αὐτόν on p. 204. 49. C om. ἔρχεται (212): all om. [ἄλλος δὲ λαβὼν λόγχην ἔνυξεν αὐτοῦ τὴν πλευρὰν καὶ ἐξῆλθεν ὕδωρ καὶ αἷμα on p. 212]. 50. C om. κράξας (212). 51. All have εὐθέως instead of ἰδοὺ. 53. All om. μετὰ τὴν ἔγερσιν αὐτοῦ. 203, 204, 205, 212

xxvii. 54. C om. ἐφοβήθησαν. 55. All add καὶ before γυναῖκες. 213

		PAGE
Matt. xxvii. 57.	C om. ὃς καὶ αὐτὸς ⌜ἐμαθητεύθη⌝ τῷ Ἰησοῦ. 60. All om. αὐτοῦ. 62. All have γραμματεῖς for Φαρισαῖοι. 63. All add αὐτῷ after λέγοντες. 64. All add αὐτοῦ after μαθηταὶ. 65. All add Ἰδοὺ before Ἔχετε.	214
xxviii. 2.	B has ἦν instead of ἰδοὺ and om. γὰρ: all add ἀπὸ τῆς θύρας τοῦ μνημείου after λίθον. 3. C adds ὡς before λευκὸν. 6. All add ὁ κύριος after ἔκειτο. 7. C has ἦν instead of ἰδού. 8. C om. ἀπαγγεῖλαι. 9. A adds αὐταῖς after λέγων. 10. All have ἀλλὰ before ὑπάγετε. 12. All om. συμβούλιόν τε and ἔδωκαν.	215
xxviii. 16.	B om. εἰς τὴν Γαλιλαίαν before εἰς τὸ ὄρος in Less. CLI. 17. B om. αὐτὸν (CLI.); οἱ δὲ is translated literally but not correctly. 19. A and C add μοι after μαθητεύσατε.	216
Mark i. 1.	All have Εὐαγγέλιον for Ἀρχὴ τοῦ εὐαγγελίου. 6. All add δεδεμένην after δερματίνην: all have τοῦ ὄρους for ἄγριον.	262, 263
i. 9.	All add ποταμὸν after Ἰορδάνην. 10. All have ἠνεῳγμένους for σχιζομένους. 11. B om. [ἐγένετο]: all add λέγων after οὐρανῶν.	265
i. 37.	All have πᾶς ὁ λαὸς instead of πάντες: all om. ἀλλαχοῦ. 39. All add ἄνθρωπός τις before λεπρὸς. 40. All add Κύριε before Ἐὰν, and ὁ κύριος Ἰησοῦς before σπλαγχνισθεὶς. 41. All add λαλοῦντος αὐτοῦ before εὐθὺς. 42. All add αὐτοῦ after λέπρα. 44. All add τὸ κορβᾶν σου after προσένεγκε.	138, 139
ii. 1.	B and C add ὁ κύριος Ἰησοῦς, and A ὁ Ἰησοῦς after εἰσελθὼν, ὀλίγων after ἡμερῶν, and περὶ αὐτοῦ after ἠκούσθη. 4. All have αὐτὸν πρὸς τὸν κύριον Ἰησοῦν instead of αὐτῷ: B om. ὅπου ἦν: A and C add ὁ κύριος Ἰησοῦς after ὅπου ἦν. 5. All add μου after Τέκνον. 6. All have βλασφημίας; for βλασφημεῖ and C adds γάρ. 7. All add μόνος after Θεὸς: B om. ταῦτα. 9. All have ὅτι εἴπομεν instead of εἰπεῖν *bis*.	139
ii. 9.	C om. τῷ παραλυτικῷ. 12. All place εὐθὺς before ἠγέρθη instead of before ἄρας.	139, 140
ii. 14.	All add υἱὸν after τὸν: all add Ἀναστὰς before ἀκολούθει.	140
ii. 15.	All have τῇ δοχῇ instead of τῇ οἰκίᾳ αὐτοῦ. 15. All add ἐκεῖ after γάρ. 16. All have τῶν Ἰουδαίων instead of τῶν Φαρισαίων: all add αὐτὸν after ἰδόντες: all om. ἁμαρτωλῶν καὶ: all have ἐσθίετε καὶ πίετε for ἐσθίει. 17. All add εἰς μετάνοιαν.	140
ii. 24.	All add οἱ μαθηταί σου after ποιοῦσιν: B adds αὐτοῖς after ἔξεστιν. 25. B om. Οὐδὲ. 26. B has εἰσῆλθεν τῇ οἰκίᾳ for ἐπὶ Ἀβιάθαρ: all add αὐτῷ after ἔξεστιν and μόνοις after ἱερεῖς.	136

		PAGE
Mark iii. 5.	συνλυπούμενος is expressed by two Syriac words: all add τὴν χεῖρα αὐτοῦ after ἐξέτεινεν, they omit it after ἀπεκατεστάθη and add ὡς ἡ ἄλλη.	137
v. 24.	After πολὺς all add καὶ συνελθόντος αὐτοῦ ἰδοὺ ὄχλος πολύς: C om. ἰδού. 26. All add ἐκεῖθεν after χεῖρον. 29. B om. αὐτῆς. 30. All add ἔβλεψεν after ἐπιστραφεὶς. 32. All om. περὶ . . . 33. C om. ὃ γέγονεν.	248
v. 34.	All have ὁ κύριος Ἰησοῦς instead of ὁ δὲ: C om. ὕπαγε εἰς εἰρήνην.	249
vi. 1.	All have εἰς τὴν πόλιν for εἰς τὴν πατρίδα αὐτοῦ. 2. All add οὕτως after τοιαῦται. 3. All om. ὁ τέκτων: all om. οὐκ before εἰσὶν. 4. B adds ἰδοὺ before ἔλεγεν: all have πόλει for πατρίδι: C om. καὶ ἐν τῇ οἰκίᾳ αὐτοῦ.	258
vi. 14.	B has something unintelligible for φανερὸν: all have τοῦ κυρίου Ἰησοῦ for αὐτοῦ: A adds ὃν ἐγὼ ἀπεκεφάλισα after βαπτίζων. 15. All add ἢ before ὡς.	293
vi. 17.	B has ἔβαλεν for ἔδησεν. 20. All have ἐποίησε for ἠπόρει. 22. All om. αὐτοῦ. 23. All om. καὶ ὤμοσεν αὐτῇ ⌜Ὅτι⌝ ⌜ἐάν με⌝ αἰτήσῃς δώσω σοι. 26. All om. περὶ . .: all have συγκειμένους for ἀνακειμένους. 27. All om. ὁ βασιλεύς. 29. All have ἔδωσαν for ἔθηκαν. 30. C has κύριον for Ἰησοῦν.	294
vii. 24.	A adds ὁ Ἰησοῦς, B and C ὁ κύριος Ἰησοῦς after ἀπῆλθεν: all om. [καὶ Σιδῶνος]. 26. All translate Ἑλληνὶς by ἐθνική. 26, 29. C has δαιμόνια for δαιμόνιον. 27. All om. γάρ. 28. All om. αὐτῷ: A adds καὶ ζῶσιν. 29. All add ὁ κύριος Ἰησοῦς after αὐτῇ. 30. B and C have δαιμόνια for δαιμόνιον: A and B om. αὐτῆς. 31. All add ὁ κύριος Ἰησοῦς after ἐξελθὼν. 34. The explanation ὅ ἐστιν Διανοίχθητι, which is omitted in the earlier A, appears in the later B and C. It is quite unnecessary in a Syriac version, and one wonders if it is a replacement of what occurred in an earlier MS., or was added through the misplaced zeal for accuracy of a later reviser. 35. All add τότε before ἠνοίγησαν and εὐθὺς before ἐλύθη: B adds εὐθὺς before ἐλάλει.	141
vii. 37.	A has an interpolation καὶ ὅσα αὐτὸς πεποίηκεν after Καλῶς πάντα πεποίηκεν.	142
viii. 29.	All three codices add ὁ υἱὸς τοῦ Θεοῦ, and C further adds τοῦ ζῶντος. 31. B om. ἀναστῆναι.	143, 144
viii. 34.	τὸν σταυρὸν αὐτοῦ in A is added by a later hand. 35. All om. γὰρ: A om. ἐμοῦ after ἕνεκεν: all repeat ἕνεκεν before τοῦ	

PAGE

εὐαγγελίου: A om. δ' ἂν ἀπολέσῃ τὴν ψυχὴν αὐτοῦ probably by mistake. 37. All have εἰ τί instead of τί γὰρ: B om. ἄνθρωπος. 38. B has ἀνδρὸς instead of ἀνθρώπου: A and B add αὐτοῦ after ἀγγέλων. 140, 141

Mark ix. 16 (17). All add καὶ λέγει αὐτῷ after ὄχλου: C om. πνεῦμα. 17 (18). All add αὐτοῦ after ὀδόντας. 19 (20). All have ὁ κύριος 'Ιησοῦς for ὁ: A has ὅταν before ἤνεγκαν. 20 (21). A and B have ὁ κύριος 'Ιησοῦς, and C has ὁ κύριος after ἐπηρώτησεν: all add λέγων after αὐτοῦ. 21 (22). B and C have εἰς τὴν θάλασσαν, instead of εἰς τὰ ὕδατα: C has ἐμοὶ and ἐπ' αὐτὸν where A and B have ἡμῖν and ἐφ' ἡμᾶς: all add κύριε before σπλαγχνισθεὶς. 23 (24). All add μετὰ δακρύων after παιδίου: A and C add κύριε before βοήθει. 25 (26). All add ἐξ αὐτοῦ after ἐξῆλθεν. 27 (28). All have 'Ιησοῦς for αὐτοῦ after εἰσελθόντος. 28 (29). All add ἐν νηστείᾳ καὶ before προσευχῇ. 142, 143

ix. 32 (33). All add ὁ κύριος 'Ιησοῦς καὶ οἱ μαθηταὶ αὐτοῦ after ἦλθον, and λέγων after αὐτοὺς. 33 (34). All add μετ' ἀλλήλων after διελογίζεσθε. 249

ix. 37 (38). All have ἀπεκρίθη ..... λέγων instead of Ἔφη. 40 (41). All add μου after ὀνόματι: C adds μαθηταὶ before Χριστοῦ. 250

x. 32. All add ὁ κύριος 'Ιησοῦς after παραλαβὼν: all om. πάλιν. 34. All have τῷ προσώπῳ αὐτοῦ instead of αὐτῷ. 35. All om. [δύο]. 38. All add ἀπεκρίθη καὶ after 'Ιησοῦς. 39. All om. αὐτῷ. 144, 145

x. 40. C has ἐκ δεξιῶν and ἐξ εὐωνύμων where A and B have ἐκ δεξιῶν μου and ἐξ εὐωνύμων μου: all add εἷς before ἐκ, and καὶ εἷς before ἐξ: all om. δοῦναι. 41. All add ἄλλοι before δέκα: C om. πάντων. 145

xi. 23. C om. πιστεύῃ: all add ὅσα ἂν εἴπῃ. 25. C om. στήκετε: all om. εἴ: all add ἐν ταῖς ψυχαῖς ὑμῶν after ἔχετε. 134

xii. 29. B and C wanting from ver. 28 to 37: A adds ἐντολὴ αὕτη after Πρώτη: A has σου for ⌜ἡμῶν⌝. 30. A om. ἐξ ὅλης τῆς διανοίας σου: A adds αὕτη ἡ πρώτη ἐντολή. 31. A has καὶ δευτέρα ὁμοία ταύτῃ. 32. A adds Θεὸς after εἷς. 33. A adds ἡμῶν after καρδίας, and has ὅτι ἀγαπῶμεν instead of τὸ ἀγαπᾷν, and adds καὶ ἐξ ὅλης τῆς ψυχῆς after συνέσεως. 36. A adds γὰρ after αὐτὸς, and adds ὑποπόδιον before ὑποκάτω. 37. A has Εἰ οὖν for αὐτὸς. 232, 233

xii. 38. B and C have στοαῖς for στολαῖς: all add καὶ τῶν ὀρφανῶν after χηρῶν. 40. B om. κρίμα, evidently by a scribe's mistake. 41. All have ἑστὼς instead of καθίσας, and all add ὁ κύριος 'Ιησοῦς: C om. ἐθεώρει. 250

PAGE

Mark xv. 17. All add τότε before ἐνδιδύσκουσιν, and χλαμύδα κοκκίνην καὶ after αὐτὸν: B om. αὐτῷ, and adds further ἐπὶ τῆς κεφαλῆς αὐτοῦ: all add λέγοντες after αὐτόν. 201

xv. 20. All add χλαμύδα καὶ before πορφύραν. 21. All add ὀνόματι after τινα: B has θῇ for ἄρῃ. 23. All add τοῦ πιεῖν after αὐτῷ. 24. C has ἐπὶ τὰ ἱμάτια αὐτοῦ instead of ἐπ' αὐτὰ. 25. All add ὡς before ὥρα. 26. All add ἐπ' αὐτοῦ after ἐπιγεγραμμένη: C om. ἡ ἐπιγραφὴ τῆς αἰτίας αὐτοῦ. 27. A and B om. αὐτοῦ. 28. All add καὶ ἐπληρώθη ἡ γραφὴ ἡ λέγουσα καὶ μετ' ἀνόμων ἐλογίσθη. 29. B has καὶ instead of Οὐὰ: B adds αὐτοῦ after ναὸν. 32. All add ἐστιν after Ἰσραήλ. 202

xv. 43. All have πλούσιος instead of εὐσχήμων, and on p. 207 B and C have τῷ Πειλάτῳ instead of βουλευτής: all om. τολμήσας. 46. B adds καὶ Ἰωσὴφ before ἀγοράσας: all add τότε before ἔθηκεν: C om. λίθον ἐπὶ (207). 47. B has ἦν for τέθειται (207). 19, 207

xv. 47. B and C have Μαρία ἡ θυγάτηρ Ἰακώβου καὶ Ἰωσῆτος: A adds μήτηρ Ἰακώβου καὶ before Ἰωσῆτος (19): θυγάτηρ Ἰακώβου occurs in the Sinai palimpsest. 19, 207

xvi. 1. B and C have θυγάτηρ Ἰακώβου: all add ἐλθοῦσαι before ἠγόρασαν: A and B have τὸν κύριον, and C τὸν κύριον Ἰησοῦν for αὐτόν. 2. C om. μιᾷ (217). 3, 4. All three codices agree with the Sinai palimpsest in placing the statement ἦν γὰρ μέγας σφόδρα in what seems its natural place, at the end of verse 3: A om. ἡμῖν (217). 4. All three have καὶ ἐλθοῦσαι εὗρον instead of καὶ ἀναβλέψασαι θεωροῦσιν. 5. All om. ἐν τοῖς δεξιοῖς (217). 6. B om. ἠγέρθη (19). 7. All add ἰδοὺ after ὅτι: B has προάγω ἐγὼ for προάγει. 19, 217

xvi. 9. All have μιᾷ instead of πρώτῃ: A om. πρῶτον. 12. A om. πορευομένοις. 14. All om. [ἐκ νεκρῶν]. 15. B and C om. αὐτοῖς: A adds μου after εὐαγγέλιον. 16. B adds καὶ before ὁ πιστεύσας. 17. All add καιναῖς after γλωσσαῖς. 18. All om. [καὶ ἐν ταῖς χερσὶν]. 19. All add ταῦτα after αὐτοῖς. 20. All om. συν 218

Luke i. 3. All om. πᾶσιν: all add οὖν before κράτιστε. 8. B adds καὶ before ἐν τῇ τάξει. 9. All have θεοῦ for κυρίου. 11. B om. τοῦ θυμιάματος. 13. All add ἰδοὺ before ἡ γυνή: B and C have καλέσεται for καλέσεις. 15. All have ἐν κοιλίᾳ for ἐκ κοιλίας. 18. B om. γὰρ. 284, 285

i. 24. All have Ζαχαρίου for αὐτοῦ. 25. B om. μου. 28. All add ὁ ἄγγελος after εἰσελθὼν, and σοι after Χαῖρε. 29. All add αὐτοῦ after λόγῳ. 31. B and C have καλοῦνται for καλέσεις. 34. All add μοι after ἔσται. 278

		PAGE
Luke i. 35.	C adds *ἐκ σου* before *γεννώμενον*. 36. B and C om. *καὶ αὐτὴ*: A om. *αὐτὴ*. 37. All have *ἔσται δύσκολον* for *ἀδυνατῆσαι*. 38. All add *ἐγὼ* after *Ἰδοὺ*: C om. *μοι*.	279
i. 44.	All add *εὐθέως* after *γὰρ*: A has *διῆλθε* for *ἐγένετο*. 48. B has *σε* instead of *με*.	234
i. 55.	A adds *πάντα ἃ* before *ἐλάλησεν*: B and C wanting.	235
i. 58.	C has *οἱ περίοικοι αὐτῶν*. 60. B om. *Οὐχὶ*: A and C om. *ἀλλὰ*: all add *τὸ ὄνομα αὐτοῦ* before *Ἰωάννης*. 62. B has *καλέσαι* instead of *καλεῖσθαι*: all om. *αὐτό*. 66. C om. *παιδίον*. 76. B and C om. *γὰρ*: all add *προσώπου* after *ἐνώπιον*.	285, 286
ii. 2.	B om. *ἡγεμονεύοντος τῆς Συρίας*: A om. *ἡγεμονεύοντος*, and has *ἐν Συρίᾳ*. 7. A and C om. *αὐτοῖς*. 8. All add *ἐκεῖ* after *ἦσαν*. 9. B adds *ἰδοὺ* before *ὁ ἄγγελος*. 11. All have *κυρίου* instead of *κύριος*. 12. All add *ἰδού*, and B also *ἐλθόντες* before *εὑρήσετε*.	254
ii. 14.	A and B have *ἡ εὐδοκία*: C has *ἡ εὐδοκία σου*. 15. B has *ἰδοὺ* instead of *ἐγένετο*. 16. B has *ἐλθόντες εἶδον* instead of *ἀνεῦραν*. 18. All add *πάντων* before *τῶν λαληθέντων*.	255
ii. 20.	B has *εἶδον καὶ ἤκουσαν* (255): all add *ὑπὸ τῶν ἀγγέλων*.	255, 259
ii. 21.	All add *τῷ παιδὶ* after *ὀκτῷ*.	259
ii. 22.	A adds *οἱ συγγενεῖς τοῦ παῖδος τοῦ Ἰησοῦς* after *ἀνήγαγον*. 24. All have *καθὼς εἴρηκα* for *κατὰ τὸ εἰρημένον*: B has *νόμος* for *ἐν τῷ νόμῳ*. 25. C om. *ἰδοὺ*: B has *ἀπὸ* instead of *ἐν*: all om. the second *ἄνθρωπος*.	272
ii. 27.	All add *τοῦ κυρίου Ἰησοῦ* after *γονεῖς*: all have *αὐτὸν* for *τὸ παιδίον*. 28. All have *Συμεὼν* instead of *αὐτὸς*. 33. All have *ὁ Ἰωσὴφ* instead of *ὁ πατὴρ αὐτοῦ*: B has *ἑστῶς* for *καὶ ἡ μήτηρ*. 37. C has *κυρίου* after *ἱεροῦ*. 38. All have *κυρίῳ* for *θεῷ*: B has *περὶ πάντων* for *περὶ αὐτοῦ πᾶσιν*, evidently a mistake: all add *ἐν* before *Ἱερουσαλήμ*. 39. C adds *τὰ γεγραμμένα* after *πάντα*. 40. All add *τῇ ἡλικίᾳ* after *ἐκραταιοῦτο*: C adds *πνεύματι* (259).	259, 273
ii. 42.	C has *τρεῖς καὶ δέκα* for *δώδεκα*: all add *εἰς Ἱερουσαλὴμ* after *αὐτῶν*. 48. C om. *ἰδόντες αὐτὸν*: all add *μου* after *Τέκνον*: B om. *ἡμῖν*: all have *ἐγὼ καὶ ὁ πατήρ σου*. 49. B has *αὐτῷ* by mistake for *οὐκ*: A has *ἐν τῷ οἴκῳ*, B *ἐν τῇ χειρὶ*, and C *υἱὸς* for *ἐν τοῖς*.	259
ii. 52.	All have *τῇ ἡλικίᾳ καὶ τῇ σοφίᾳ καὶ τῇ συνέσει καὶ τῇ χάριτι*.	260

PAGE

Luke iii. 4. All have τοῦ λέγοντος after προφήτου: C has μου for αὐτοῦ: B om. αὐτοῦ. 5. All add πάντα before τὰ σκολιὰ, and πᾶσαι before αἱ τραχεῖαι: C om. πᾶν before ὄρος. 263

iii. 12. All add ὑπ' αὐτου after βαπτισθῆναι. 13. All add ποιῆτε μηδὲ before πράσσετε: B and C om. πᾶσιν. 16. All om. ἰσχυρότερός μου. 265

iii. 18. A and B have αὐτοὺς for τὸν λαόν. 265

iii. 19. B and C om. πάντων. 22. All add λέγων after γενέσθαι. 268

iii. 23. C has ἀρχόμενος, B πληρωσάμενος: A wanting up to ver. 38: B and C add υἱὸς 'Ιακώβου after 'Ιωσὴφ: C om. τοῦ 'Ηλεί. 24. C om. τοῦ Λευεὶ and τοῦ 'Ιανναί. 25. B om. τοῦ 'Αμώς: C om. τοῦ Ματταθίου, τοῦ Ναοὺμ and τοῦ Ναγγαί. 26. B has υἱὸς Μαλ, and C υἱὸς Βάλ for τοῦ Μαάθ: C om. τοῦ Σεμεεὶν and τοῦ 'Ιωδά. 27. C om. τοῦ 'Ρησά and τοῦ Σαλαθιήλ. 28. C om. τοῦ Μελχεί, τοῦ Κωσὰμ, and ῞Ηρ. 29. C om. τοῦ 'Ελιέζερ and τοῦ Μαθθάτ, and adds υἱὸς 'Ελία before τοῦ Λευεί. 261

iii. 30. C adds after τοῦ Λευεί, υἱὸς 'Ιανναὶ υἱὸς Ματταθίου υἱὸς Ναοὺμ υἱὸς Ναγὶρ υἱὸς Ματλὰτ υἱὸς Σχυὶ υἱὸς 'Ιουδὰ υἱὸς 'Ρησὰ υἱὸς Σαλαθιὴλ υἱὸς Μελχεὶ υἱὸς Κωσὰμ υἱὸς ῞Ηρ υἱὸς 'Ελιέζερ υἱὸς Μαθὰτ υἱὸς Λευεὶ. 32. B and C have 'Ιωβήδ for 'Ιωβήλ. 33. B and C add after τοῦ Ναασσών, υἱὸς 'Αρὰμ, υἱὸς 'Αμιναδάβ. 35. C has Γαὺ for 'Ραγαύ: τοῦ is translated by υἱὸς throughout the genealogy. 262

iv. 16. All add ὁ κύριος 'Ιησοῦς after ἦλθεν: all agree with the Sinai palimpsest in placing καὶ ἀνέστη ἀναγνῶναι after προφήτου 'Ησαίου. 17. B om. αὐτῷ, and has τοῦτο after βιβλίον. 18. B has ἔστειλε instead of ἔχρισεν: all add ἰάσασθαι τοὺς συντετριμμένους τὴν καρδίαν after ἀπέσταλκέν με. 229

iv. 22. All add πᾶσι after ἐπὶ (229 also), and κύριος 'Ιησοῦς *sic* after αὐτοῦ: all om. ἐμαρτύρουν αὐτῷ καὶ. 23. B has λόγον for παραβολὴν: all have ὅτι ἐποίησας for γενόμενα. 23, 24. All have πόλει for πατρίδι. 24. All add αὐτοῖς after δὲ. 25. All add προφήτου after 'Ηλείου: all have ἐκλείσθησαν for ἐκλείσθη, and probably οὐρανοὶ for οὐρανὸς: all om. πᾶσαν. 27. All add ταῖς ἡμέραις before 'Ελισαίου. 283

iv. 31. All add ὁ κύριος 'Ιησοῦς after κατῆλθεν. 33. B adds ἐκεῖ after ἦν: all add τις after ἄνθρωπος, and εἰπὼν after μεγάλῃ and om. ῎Εα. 34. B and C om. τίς. 36. All add μεγάλῃ after δυνάμει: B and C om. ἐπιτάσσει. 98

PAGE

Luke v. 1. A and B have ὁ κύριος Ἰησοῦς instead of αὐτὸς. 2. B and C om. ἔπλυνον: all add ἐσχίσθη γὰρ. 3. A adds ἐκάθισε after ἐμβὰς δὲ: A has αὐτῶν instead of τῶν πλοίων, and adds Πέτρου after Σίμωνος: A om. καθίσας. 4. A has Ἐπαναγάγετε for Ἐπανάγαγε. 5. A om. ἀποκριθεὶς. 6. A om. πλῆθος. 7. All add τότε: B om. ἐν τῷ ἑτέρῳ πλοίῳ. 8. All add τότε after Πέτρος. 99

v. 17. A and B add Ἰησοῦς and C ὁ κύριος Ἰησοῦς after ἐγένετο: all have διῆλθε for ἐγένετο, probably by mistake: all om. καὶ Ἰουδαίας: all have πάντας for αὐτὸν. 20. All add αὐτῷ after εἶπεν. 22. All add κακὰ after Τί. 23. All have ἵνα εἰπώμεθα for εἰπεῖν bis. 24. All have ἀνδρὸς for ἀνθρώπου: all add τότε before εἶπεν. 25. All add τὸ κλινίδιον after ἄρας. 26. B om. λέγοντες. 27. All om. μετὰ ταῦτα: B and C add ὁ κύριος Ἰησοῦς: A adds Ἰησοῦς only. 28. C has ἦλθε for ἀκολούθει αὐτῷ. 32. All have οὐ γὰρ for οὐκ. 100, 102

vi. 1. All om. ἐγένετο: A and B have Ἰησοῦν and C τὸν κύριον for αὐτὸν, and all add τὸν κύριον Ἰησοῦν περιπατοῦντα: B om. αὐτοῦ after μαθητὰς. 2. All add αὐτοῖς after εἶπαν. 3. A om. the οὐ of Οὐδὲ: all add ἵνα ποιῶμεν after ἔξεστιν. 4. All om. λαβὼν: A and B add καὶ before τοῖς. 5. All add γὰρ: all have ἀνδρὸς instead of ἀνθρώπου. 6 All add τις after ἄνθρωπος: B om. ἵνα. 8. All have Ἐλθὲ before Ἔγειρε: all om. ἀναστὰς. 9. B adds ἡμῖν after ἔξεστιν. 10. All add μετ' ὀργῆς after αὐτοὺς: B and C come nearer to the majority of Greek MSS. in having only καὶ εἶπεν αὐτῷ, while A has τῷ ἀνδρὶ τῷ ξηρὰν ἔχοντι τὴν χεῖρα: all add οὕτως before ἐποίησεν, and ὡς τὴν ἄλλην after αὐτοῦ. 103

vi. 17. In Less. CCIX., A om. vv. 18, 19, and the greater part of ver. 17: B and C add ὁ κύριος Ἰησοῦς after ἔστη: all add καὶ ἀπὸ after παραλίου: C has παρὰ τοῦ Ἰορδάνου for τῆς παραλίου. 19. All add αὐτοῦς before πάντας. 20. A and C add τῷ πνεύματι and B πνεύματος after πτωχοὶ: B has αὐτῶν for ὑμετέρα: all have τῶν οὐρανῶν for τοῦ Θεοῦ. 21. All transfer the second clause (οἱ κλαίοντες) to the first place. 22. All have ἀνδρὸς for ἀνθρώπου. 23. C om. πολὺς. 270

vi. 31. All add καὶ before αὐτοῖς. 32, 33, 34. B has μακαρισμὸς for χάρις. 33. All om. [γὰρ]. 33, 34. All add γὰρ after the second καὶ. 36. All add οὖν after Γίνεσθε and καὶ χρηστὸς after οἰκτίρμων. 101

vii. 1. All begin Ἦλθεν ὁ Ἰησοῦς εἰς τὰς ἀκοὰς τοῦ λαοῦ. 2. B om. τινος: all add γὰρ after ἤμελλεν. 6. All om. οὐ before μακρὰν:

		PAGE
	C om. *μή*. 8. B and C add *μου* after *ἐξουσίαν*: all have *ὑπὸ τὴν χεῖρά μου* for *ὑπ' ἐμαυτόν*. 9. All om. *ταῦτα*. 10. All have *τοιαύτην* for *τοσαύτην*: all add *τότε* after *καί*.	105
Luke vii. 11.	All add *ὁ κύριος 'Ιησοῦς* before *ἐπορεύθη*: B and C om. *ἰδού*. 12. All have *ἐξῆλθε* for *ἐξεκομίζετο*. 13. B om. *αὐτήν*: all add *Ιησοῦς* after *ὁ κύριος*: C om. *αὐτῇ*. 16. B adds *τὸν τῶν πιστευόντων τῷ λόγῳ αὐτοῦ*.	102
vii. 20.	All have *τὸν κύριον 'Ιησοῦν* for *αὐτόν*. 21. All add *ὁ κύριος 'Ιησοῦς* after *ἐθεράπευσεν*. 22. All add *ὁ κύριος 'Ιησοῦς* after *ἀποκριθείς*: B and C have *εὐφραίνονται* for *εὐαγγελίζονται*. 24. All add *ὁ κύριος 'Ιησοῦς* after *ἤρξατο*. 25. B has *ἢ* for *ἀλλά*: all have *ἠμφιεσμένοι* for *ὑπάρχοντες*: all om. *καὶ τρυφῇ*. 27. All add *γὰρ* after *οὗτος*: A om. *γέγραπται*: A and C om. *σου* after *ὁδόν*: B has *σοι*. 28. All add *ἀμὴν* before *λέγω*. 29. All have *ἐδόξασαν* for *ἐδικαίωσαν*: all have *ὑπὸ* for *τὸ βάπτισμα*.	274, 275
vii. 36.	B adds *καὶ εἶπε τῷ κυρίῳ 'Ιησοῦ* after *Φαρισαίων*, and has *εἰσέλθῃ* for *φάγῃ*. 39. All om. *ὁ καλέσας αὐτὸν* and *λέγων*.	279
vii. 41.	All add *εἶπεν αὐτῷ* after *φησίν*, and C adds further *ὁ κύριος 'Ιησοῦς*: all add *αὐτῷ* after *ὤφειλεν*, and *δηνάρια* after *πεντήκοντα*. 42. All add *εἰπέ μοι*. 44. B om. *μου*, also A in Less. CCCXXXI. 46. B and C have *τοὺς πόδας* for *τὴν κεφαλήν*. 47. C om. *ἠγάπησεν*.	280
viii. 1.	All have *ὁ κύριος 'Ιησοῦς* for *αὐτός*, and om. *ἐν τῷ καθεξῆς*.	289
viii. 2.	All om. *ἡ καλουμένη*.	290
viii. 5.	All add *'Ιδοὺ* before *ἐξῆλθεν*. 6. B adds *καὶ οὐκέτι* before *φυέν*. 8. B adds *πολὺν* after *καρπόν*. 10. A has *ὁ δὲ 'Ιησοῦς* for *ὁ*, and adds *αὐτοῖς* after *εἶπεν*: B and C wanting from ver. 9 to ver. 15. 11, 13. A has *τὸ δὲ πεσὸν* instead of *οἱ δέ*. 12. A has *τὸν λογὸν* after *ἀκούσαντες*, *καὶ* for *εἶτα*, and *ὁ σατανᾶς* instead of *ὁ διάβολος*. 13. A has *ὑγρότητα* for *ῥίζαν* and A *σκανδαλίζονται* for *ἀφίστανται*. 15. A adds *πεσὸν* after *τὸ δέ*, and *πολὺ* after *καρποφοροῦσιν*: it adds also *'Ο ἔχων ὦτα ἀκούειν ἀκουέτω*. 16. A om. the second *τίθησιν*. 18. All have *ἔχει* for *δοκεῖ ἔχειν*.	104, 107
viii. 26.	A has *καὶ ἐλθὼν ὁ κύριος 'Ιησοῦς* instead of *καὶ κατέπλευσαν*. 27. C adds *γὰρ* after *ἱκανῷ*. 29. B and C have *τῶν δαιμονίων* for *τοῦ δαιμονίου*. 30. All add *τὸ ὄνομά μου* after *λεγιών*. 32. All have *ἐπιστείλῃ* for *ἐπιτρέψῃ*: all add *χοίρους* after *ἐκείνους*.	108
viii. 33.	All add *πᾶσα* before *ἡ ἀγέλη*: B alone adds *καὶ ἀπέθανον* after *ἀπεπνίγη*. 37. All add *γὰρ* after *μεγάλῳ*.	108, 109

		PAGE
Luke viii. 41.	All om. καὶ ἰδού. 43. A alone adds ἥτις ἰατροῖς προσαναλώσασα ὅλον τὸν βίον. 45. A alone adds καὶ λέγεις· τίς μου ἥψατο; 46. All have αὐτοῖς after εἶπεν. 47. B has φοβηθεῖσα καὶ τρέμουσα where A has τρέμουσα only: C defective.	110
viii. 52.	B om. αὐτήν: all add ἡ παῖς after ἀπέθανεν. 54. All add ἐκβαλὼν ἔξω πάντα τὸν λαὸν τότε before κρατήσας.	111
ix. 1.	All have τότε before συνκαλεσάμενος and ὁ κύριος Ἰησοῦς after δὲ: all add ἀποστόλους after δώδεκα: A and C om. θεραπεύειν. 2. All add τὰς ἀσθενείας after ἰᾶσθαι.	109
ix. 5.	All add καὶ before τὸν κονιορτὸν.	109
ix. 28.	All add ὁ κύριος Ἰησοῦς after παραλαβὼν. 29. B adds καὶ before τὸ εἶδος. 30. B and C have ἐγένετο for ἰδού. 31. A adds περὶ after ἔλεγον. 32. B om. τὴν δόξαν αὐτοῦ καὶ τοὺς δύο.	291
ix. 33.	C om. καλόν. 35. All have ἀγαπητὸς for ἐκλελεγμένος. 36. C om. ὧν ἑώρακαν.	292
ix. 37.	All add μετὰ ταῦτα after ἡμέρᾳ: all have αὐτοῖς for αὐτῷ. 39. All have ῥίπτει for σπαράσσει. 42. All have ἔρρεψεν for ἔρρηξεν.	111
ix. 57.	C adds κύριε after αὐτόν: all add κύριε after ἀπέρχῃ. 58. A and B om. [ὁ] Ἰησοῦς. 58. All have ἀνδρὸς for ἀνθρώπου. 59. All add κύριε before Ἐπιτρέψον: B om. πρῶτον: all om. μου after πατέρα. 60. All add ὁ κύριος Ἰησους after αὐτῷ.	113
x. 1.	B and C wanting: A om. Μετὰ δὲ ταῦτα and [δύο]: A has καὶ for ἑτέρους and adds μαθητὰς after ἑβδομήκοντα, and πάντα before τόπον. 2. A om. οὖν. 6. A adds ἡ εἰρήνη ὑμῶν after ἀνακάμψει. 11. A adds ἐφ' ὑμᾶς after ἤγγικεν. 12. A adds γὰρ before τῇ πόλει.	230
x. 16.	All add καὶ ὁ ἀκούων ἐμοῦ ἀκούει τοῦ ἀποστείλαντός με at the end of the verse. 17. All om. [δύο]: B has σοι for ἡμῖν.	233
x. 19.	All add δύναμιν καὶ after ὑμῖν. 20. All add ἰδοὺ before τὰ ὀνόματα. 21. All add ὁ κύριος Ἰησοῦς after ἠγαλλιάσατο.	114, 233
x. 21.	B and C om. αὐτὰ νηπίοις and have ἡμῶν instead of σου: C om. τῷ αγίῳ.	234
x. 27.	B and C om. ἐξ ὅλης τῆς καρδίας σου: A has it after τῇ ψυχῇ σου. 29. B om. πρὸς. 31. All have καὶ ἐξῆλθον κατ' αὐτοῦ λῃσταὶ instead of καὶ λῃσταῖς περιέπεσεν.	112
x. 34.	All have δοὺς ἐπ' αὐτὰ for ἐπιχέων. 36. All add οὖν after τίς: all have τούτου καθ' οὗ ἔπεσον λῃσταὶ; instead of τοῦ ἐμπεσόντος εἰς τοὺς λῃστάς;	112, 113

		PAGE
Luke x. 38.	All have *αὐτὸν* for *αὐτούς*, and A adds *τὸν κύριον Ἰησοῦν*: all add *αὐτῆς* after *οἰκίαν*. 40. All add *Μάρθα* before *εἶπεν*. 41. All om. *ἢ ἑνός*.	235
xi. 27.	All have *τῷ κυρίῳ Ἰησοῦ* instead of *αὐτῷ*: all have *οἱ ἐθήλασάν σε* for *οὓς ἐθήλασας*. 28. All om. *Μενοῦν*.	235
xi. 29.	B and C wanting: A adds *ὁ κύριος Ἰησοῦς* before *ἤρξατο*. 30. A om. *καὶ* and has *ἀνδρὸς* instead of *ἀνθρώπου* and adds *σημεῖον*.	241
xii. 3.	All add *καὶ ἐν ταῖς ἀγοραῖς*. 7. A adds *πάντων* after *στρουθίων*. 8. B om. *πᾶς*. 8, 10. All have *ἀνδρὸς* for *ἀνθρώπου*. 9. All have *ἀπαρνήσω αὐτὸν καὶ ἐγὼ* for *ἀπαρνηθήσεται*.	244
xii. 16.	A adds *καὶ ἐποίησεν αὐτῷ καρποὺς πολλούς*. 18. C om. *καὶ εἶπεν Τοῦτο ποιήσω*: all add *αὐτοὺς* before *μείζονας*. 19. All add *μου ἰδοὺ* after *Ψυχή*. 21. All add *πᾶς* after *οὕτως*: A adds *ταῦτα λέγων ἐφώνει· ὁ ἔχων ὦτα ἀκούειν ἀκουέτω* from Luke viii. 8.	113, 114
xii. 34.	B om. *γάρ*. 36. All translate *ἀναλύσῃ* by *ἐπιστρέψῃ καὶ ἔλθῃ*. 38. All add *αὐτοὺς* after *εὕρῃ* and *δοῦλοι* after *ἐκεῖνοι*. 40. All have *ἀνδρὸς* for *ἀνθρώπου*.	116
xiii. 11.	B has *ἦν* for *ἰδού*: all add *τις* after *γυνή*. 12. All add *ἰδοὺ* before *ἀπολέλυσαι*. 15. All add *Ἰησοῦς* after *ὁ κύριος*.	115
xiii. 17.	A and B om. *ὑπ' αὐτοῦ*.	115
xiii. 20.	C has *ὁμιώσεται* for *ὁμιώσω*. 22. B adds *πάσας* before *κώμας*, and all add *πάσας* before *πόλεις*. 23. B has *θέλοι* for *ὀλίγοι*, evidently a mistake. 24. All om. *λέγω ὑμῖν*. 25. A om. *ἀφ' οὗ*: all om. *τὴν θύραν*: all have *Κύριε* twice: B has *τίνες* instead of *πόθεν*. 26. B om. *ἐνώπιόν σου* and *ἡμῶν*. 27. All have *ἀμὴν λέγω ὑμῖν* instead of *λέγων ὑμῖν*: all add *γὰρ* after *πάντες*. 28. All om. *καὶ πάντας τοὺς προφήτας*. 29. B and C om. *καὶ ἀπὸ βοῤῥᾶ*.	117, 118
xiv. 1.	All have *τὸν κύριον Ἰησοῦν* instead of *αὐτόν*: B has *ἐν ἡμέρᾳ σαββάτου* for *σαββάτῳ*. 2. A has *ἦν* for *ἰδού*: all add *ὃς* after *τις*. 3. All om. *λέγων*. 5. All have *ὄνος* for *υἱός*. 9. B has *ἔλθῃ* for *ᾖ*. 10. All add *μου* after *Φίλε*. 11. B om. *ὅτι*.	119, 120
xiv. 16.	All om. *μέγα*: C om. *τις*: A and C om. *καὶ ἐκάλεσεν πολλούς*. 17. C om. *καὶ ἀπέστειλεν τὸν δοῦλον αὐτοῦ τῇ ὥρᾳ τοῦ*: all have *ἰδοὺ* for *ἤδη*. 18. All add *ἰδοὺ* before *ἔχω*: B om. *ἰδεῖν*: 18, 19. All have *ὅτι οὐ δύναμαι ἐλθεῖν* for *με παρῃτημένον*. 21. B has *παραγενόμενοι οἱ δοῦλοι ἀπήγγειλαν*, and all have *τῷ οἰκοδεσπότῃ* for *τῷ κυρίῳ αὐτοῦ*: B and C om. *τότε ὀργισθεὶς ὁ οἰκοδεσπότης*: all add *οὖν* after *Ἔξελθε*: all om.	

PAGE

καὶ χωλούς. 22. All have *τῷ κυρίῳ αὐτοῦ* after *δοῦλος*: A has *κύριε, γέγονεν ὡς εἶπες*, while B and C have *ἐποίησα πᾶν ὅ τι ἐπέταξας.* 24. B om. *μου*: A adds *πολλοί εἰσιν κλητοὶ, ὀλίγοι ἐκλεκτοί* from Matt. xxii. 14. 116, 117

Luke xv. 11. B om. *Ἄνθρωπος*: C om. *τις.* 12. All om. *αὐτῶν*: all have *αὐτοῦ* after *πατρὶ*: all add *μου* after *μέρος* and *σου* after *οὐσίας*: A and C have *αὐτῷ* instead of *αὐτοῖς* and add *αὐτοῦ* after *βίον.* 13. All have *ὀλίγας* for *οὐ πολλὰς*: all have *πᾶσαν τὴν οὐσίαν* for *πάντα.* 15. All om. *αὐτοῦ* after *ἀγρούς.* 17. All add *ἐν τῷ οἴκῳ* before *τοῦ πατρός* and om. *μου.* 18. All om. *μου.* 20. All add *ἐπ' αὐτῷ.* 21. All add *αὐτοῦ* after *υἱὸς*: all om. [*ποίησόν με ὡς ἕνα τῶν μισθίων σου*]. 24. B adds *ἰδοὺ* before ⌜*ἀνέζησε*⌝. 126, 127

xv. 25. B has *ἤκουσαν* for *ἤκουσεν*: all have *ψαλμῳδίας* for *χωρῶν.* 26. All add *αὐτῷ λέγων* after *ἐπυνθάνετο.* 27. C has *καὶ ἔθυσεν αὐτῷ ὁ πατήρ σου*: B om. the clause, evidently by a mistake, whilst A has *καὶ ἀπέλαβεν αὐτὸν ὁ πατήρ σου καὶ ἔθυσεν αὐτῷ.* 31. All add *μου* after *Τέκνον.* 127

xvi. 10. B om. *καὶ* after *ἐλαχίστῳ.* 13. All om. *γὰρ.* 14. All om. *ταῦτα πάντα.* 121

xvi. 21. A adds *καὶ οὐδεὶς ἐδίδου αὐτῷ* after *πλουσίου* from chap. xv. 16. 22. A adds *καὶ κατέβη εἰς ᾅδου καὶ ὄντος.* 23. All om. *ὑπάρχων ἐν βασάνοις.* 24. All have *ἄψηται* for *καταψύξῃ*: all add *ἰδοὺ* before *ὀδυνῶμαι.* 25. All add *μου* after *Τέκνον.* 25, 27. All add *αὐτῷ* after *εἶπεν* or *εἶπεν δέ.* 27. All om. *οὖν* and add *Ἀβραὰμ* after *πάτερ*: B has *με* for *αὐτὸν*: all om. *μου* after *πατρός.* 29. All add *αὐτῷ* after *δὲ.* 30. All add *οὐ* before *μετανοήσουσιν.* 31. A adds *Ἀβραὰμ* after *αὐτῷ*: B adds *αὐτῷ* after *πεισθήσονται*: C om. ver. 31. 106, 107

xvii. 4. All add *ἄφες μοι*: B and C om. *ἀφήσεις αὐτῷ.* 6. All add *αὐτοῖς* after *δὲ.* 7. All om. *Εὐθέως*: B om. *αὐτῷ.* 8. B has *ἐν τῇ ἡμέρᾳ* instead of *τι.* 9. All have *αὐτῷ* instead of *τῷ δούλῳ.* 10. B has *ἠγαπήσαμεν* for *ὠφείλομεν*, probably a mistake. 122, 123

xvii. 11. A adds *τὸν κύριον Ἰησοῦν* after *πορεύεσθαι.* 14. All om. *ἰδὼν* and add *κύριος Ἰησοῦς* after *αὐτοῖς.* 118, 119

xviii. 2. C om. *μὴ* before *φοβούμενος.* 3. All add *αὐτῷ* after *λέγουσα.* 4. All add *πολὺν* after *χρόνον*: all om. *καὶ* after *Εἰ.* 8. All have *ναὶ* before *λέγω*: all om. *ὁ υἱὸς τοῦ ἀνθρώπου*: A om. from *πλὴν* to *λοιποὺς* in v. 9. 9. All add *εἶπεν ὁ κύριος* after *λοιπούς*: B and C add *λέγων* after *ταύτην.* 11. All have *λέγων* after *προσηύχετο.* 12. All add *γὰρ* after *νηστεύω.* 124, 125

PAGE

Luke xviii. 19. C om. εἷς, but adds μόνος after Θεός. 20. B adds καὶ before Μὴ three times, A and C once: A adds καὶ τὸν πλησιόν σου ὡς σεαυτόν in the space betwixt the two columns from Matt. xxii. 39. 21. All add αὐτῷ after εἶπεν, and μου after νεότητος. 24. All om. Πῶς. 25. A and C add γὰρ before πλούσιον: B wanting. 27. C om. δυνατὰ, and has οὐ for ἀδύνατα. 120, 121

xviii. 35. All have τὸν κύριον Ἰησοῦν instead of αὐτὸν: all have καὶ ἰδοὺ before τυφλός. 40. All add τότε before ἐπηρώτησεν, and λέγων after αὐτὸν. 41. B adds αὐτῷ after εἶπεν. 43. All om. ἠκολούθει αὐτῷ. 121, 122

xix. 1. B and C add ὁ κύριος Ἰησοῦς after εἰσελθὼν: A adds ὁ Ἰησοῦς. 2. All add τις after ἀνὴρ. 3. B has πόθεν instead of τίς. 5. All add ὁ κύριος Ἰησοῦς after ἦλθεν, and om. ὁ Ἰησοῦς after ἀναβλέψας. 8. All add Ἰησοῦν after κύριον. 10. All have ἀνδρὸς for ἀνθρώπου. 123, 124

xix. 29. B and C om. ἐγένετο and τὸ καλούμενον: both have ἦλθεν for ἤγγισεν: A wanting to ver. 48. 30. Both add αὐτοῖς after λέγων. 31. Both have καὶ λέγει ὑμῖν after ἐρωτᾷ, and τὸν πῶλον after λύετε. 32. B and C add πῶλον ἑστῶτα: C adds further δεδεμένον. 34. B adds αὐτοῖς after εἶπαν. 39. Both have γραμματέων for Φαρισαίων. 40. Both add αὐτοῖς after εἶπεν. 42. Both add σου after εἰρήνην. 48. B has ἀπολέσωσιν αὐτὸν instead of ποιήσωσιν. 227, 228

xx. 2. All om. λέγοντες: all add τινα after λόγον. 4. All add πόθεν after Ἰωάννου. 5. B adds ἐσίγησαν καὶ before συνελογίσαντο: all add ἡμῖν after ἐρεῖ. 269

xxi. 3. All add αὐτοῖς after εἶπεν. 4. B om. γὰρ: all add Ὁ ἔχων ὦτα ἀκούειν ἀκουέτω from Luke viii. 8. 126

xxi. 8. B om. γάρ. 9. B om. οὐκ by mistake: C om. εὐθέως. 128

xxi. 9. B om. εὐθέως (132). 10. A and C have ὑμῖν for αὐτοῖς. 11. All place λιμοὶ before λοιμοὶ. 12. All add ἐπὶ before ἡγεμόνας. 132, 240

xxi. 12. All three codices begin the verse with προσέχετε, and A adds further ἀπὸ τῶν ἀνθρώπων, evidently from Matt. x. 17 (240): B and C add οἱ ἄνθρωποι after αὐτῶν (240), C also on p. 133. 13. All add ταῦτα after ὑμῖν. 133, 240

xxi. 15. B om. γὰρ: all om. ⌜ἅπαντες⌝. 19. All add καὶ γὰρ before ἐν: B adds καὶ before τὰς ψυχὰς. 240

xxi. 27, 36. All have ἀνδρὸς for ἀνθρώπου (128). 27. All add τῶν οὐρανῶν after νεφέλῃ (133). 28. All om. Ἀρχομένων δὲ τούτων γίνεσθαι (133). 34. All om. πότε. 35. All om. γὰρ (133). 36. B om. πάντα (133): B has ἀνδρὸς for ἀνθρώπου (134). All have ἀνδρὸς for ἀνθρώπου (128). 128, 133, 134

PAGE

Luke xxii. 3. B om. *τὸν καλούμενον* (before *'Ισκαριώτην*). 6. C adds *ἰδοὺ* before *ἐζήτει*. 170

xxii. 10. B has *ὧδε* for *ἰδοὺ*: C om. *βαστάζων*. 11. All have *φάγωμεν* for *φάγω*. 13. All add *ὁ κύριος 'Ιησοῦς* after *αὐτοῖς*. 14. All add *δώδεκα* before *ἀπόστολοι*. 20. C om. *Τοῦτο τὸ ποτήριον*. 22. All have *ὅστις διὰ τῆς χειρὸς αὐτοῦ* for *δι' οὗ*. 171

xxii. 25. B adds *κύριοι* before *εὐεργέται*. 28. C om. *μου*. 29. All om. ⌜*μου*⌝. 30. All add *δώδεκα* before *θρόνων*. 31. All add *καὶ εἶπεν ὁ κύριος 'Ιησοῦς* before *Σίμων*. 34. All add *κύριος 'Ιησοῦς* after *δὲ*. 36. A adds *μάχαιραν* after *ἔχων*. 37. B and C add *ἔτι* after *ὅτι*, probably A also: all om. *δεῖ*: B and C om. *ἐν ἐμοί*. 39. B and C wanting: A adds *ὁ κύριος 'Ιησοῦς* after *ἐξελθὼν*, and *αὐτοῦ* after *μαθηταί*. 172, 173

xxii. 44. Whilst A and C have *ὡς ἐν ἀγωνίᾳ*, B has *ὡς ἐν τῇ ἡμέρᾳ ταύτῃ*: C om. *αἵματος*. 45. All om. *ἀπὸ τῆς λύπης*, and add *ἦσαν γὰρ αὐτῶν οἱ ὀφθαλμοὶ βεβαρημένοι* from Matt. xxvi. 43. 179

xxiii. 32. All add *σὺν τῷ κυρίῳ 'Ιησοῦ* after *"Ηγοντο δὲ*, and om. *σὺν αὐτῷ*: all have *σταυρωθῆναι* instead of *ἀναιρεθῆναι*. 33. C adds *αὐτοῦ* after *δεξιῶν* and *ἀριστερῶν*. 34. C om. *Πάτερ*: B and C have ܗܘܘ before *Διαμεριζόμενοι*. 35. All have *υἱοῦ* after *χριστὸς* and *αὐτοῦ* after *ἐκλεκτός*. 38. All om. *καὶ*: all add after *αὐτῷ*, *γράμμασιν ἑλληνιστὶ καὶ ῥωμαιστὶ καὶ ἑβραιστὶ οὗτός ἐστιν*. 204, 205

xxiii. 39. All have *σταυρωθέντων* for *κρεμασθέντων* and add *σὺν αὐτῷ*: all have *λέγων* after *αὐτὸν*, and *σῶσον* before *ἡμᾶς*: B has *Εἰ* for *Οὐχὶ*. 40. B om. *τῷ αὐτῷ* (211): all have *καὶ ἡμεῖς* instead of *εἶ*. 41. All have *ἀληθῶς* for *δικαίως*. 42. All have *τῷ κυρίῳ 'Ιησοῦ* for *'Ιησοῦ*, and C adds *κύριε* after *μνήσθητί μου*. 43. All add *'Απεκρίθη δὲ ὁ κύριος 'Ιησοῦς*: B om. *μετ' ἐμοῦ* (211 only). 44. All om. *ἤδη*. 205, 211

xxiii. 45. All om. *καὶ σκότος ἐγένετο ἐφ' ὅλην τὴν γῆν ἕως ὥρας ἐνάτης*: A has an interpolation from Matt. xxiv. 29 and xxvii. 52, 53, *καὶ ἡ σελήνη ἔκρυψε τὸ φέγγος αὐτῆς καὶ οἱ ἀστέρες ἔπεσαν καὶ αἱ πέτραι ἐσχίσθησαν, καὶ τὰ μνημεῖα ἀνεῴχθησαν καὶ πολλὰ σώματα τῶν ἁγίων ἠγέρθησαν καὶ ἐνεφανίσθησαν πολλοῖς·* 46, 47. C adds *υἱὸς τοῦ θεοῦ* after *οὗτος*. 48. All om. *συν . . . .*: all add *πάντα* before *τὰ γενόμενα*. 205

xxiv. 1. B and C add *καὶ τίνες σὺν αὐταῖς*. 2. All add *τῆς θύρας* after *ἀπὸ*. 5. All add *οἱ δὲ ἄνδρες* before *εἶπαν*. 7. All have *ἀνδρὸς* instead of *ἀνθρώπου*. 8, 9. All add *τότε* before *ἐμνήσθησαν*, and before *ἀπήγγειλαν*. 10. B and C have *θυγάτηρ*, and A *μήτηρ* before *'Ιακώβου*. 12. B adds *καὶ* before *ἐπὶ*. 219

		PAGE
Luke xxiv. 12.	A has *Σίμων* for *Πέτρος*, and *κείμενα* after *μόνα*: B and C wanting. 13. All add *ἑκατὸν καὶ* before *ἑξήκοντα*. 17. All add *ὁ κύριος Ἰησοῦς* after *αὐτούς*: A om. *καὶ ἐστάθησαν σκυθρωποί*. 18. All add *ἐξ αὐτῶν* after *εἷς*: all add *ἐκ πάντων τῶν παροίκων* after *παροικεῖς*: all add *πάντα* before *τὰ γενόμενα*. 19. All add *ἐναντίον* before *παντὸς*. 20. A has *τοῦ λαοῦ* for *ἡμῶν*. 21. All add *σήμερον* after *ἄγει*. 25. All have *ὁ κύριος Ἰησοῦς* for *αὐτὸς*. 34. All add *αὐτοῖς* after *λέγοντας*. 35. B has *τὰ λεγόμενα αὐτοῖς ὑπ' αὐτοῦ ἐν τῇ ὁδῷ* for *τὰ ἐν τῇ ὁδῷ*: all add *αὐτοῖς* after *ἐξηγοῦντο*.	4–6
xxiv. 36.	All have *ἦλθεν ὁ κύριος Ἰησοῦς καὶ* instead of *αὐτὸς*: all add *ἐγώ εἰμι· μὴ φοβεῖσθε* after *ὑμῖν* from Matt. xiv. 27. 38. B and C add *κακοὶ* after *διαλογισμοὶ*. 39. A and C add *καὶ νοεῖτε* after *πόδας μου*. 41. All have *τι ἵνα φάγωμεν* instead of *τι βρώσιμον*. 42. All add *καὶ ἀπὸ μελισσίου κηρίου* after *μέρος* and have *καὶ φαγὼν ἐνώπιον αὐτῶν καὶ λαβὼν τὰ ἐπίλοιπα ἔδωκεν αὐτοῖς* for *καὶ λαβὼν ἐνώπιον αὐτῶν ἔφαγεν*. 44. All add *μου* after *λόγοι*: all have *καὶ τοῖς ψαλμοῖς* before *καὶ τοῖς προφήταις*: C om. *πάντα*. 45. All have *τὴν καρδίαν* instead of *τὸν νοῦν*. 47. A and C om. *ὑμεῖς*.	220
xxiv. 49.	All om. *μου* after *πατρός*: all add *Ἱερουσαλὴμ* after *πόλει*. 51. A and B have *ἰδοὺ* for *ἐγένετο*.	221
John i. 3.	B om. *καὶ χωρὶς αὐτοῦ ἐγένετο οὐδὲ ἕν*, but this is due to an accident (vide Introduction, p. xiii.). 7. B adds *ὃς* after *οὗτος*. 12. B adds *πᾶσι* before *τοῖς πιστεύουσιν*. 15. All have *ὃν εἶπον* for *ὁ εἰπών*.	2
i. 18.	All om. *θεὸς*: all add *αὐτοῦ* after *πατρὸς* and *ἡμῖν* after *ἐξηγήσατο*. 21. B om. *Ὁ προφήτης εἶ σύ; καὶ ἀπεκρίθη Οὔ*. 22. B om. *οὖν*, and all add *αὐτοῖς* after *ἔφη*. 24. All have *γραμματέων* for *Φαρισαίων*. 26. All om. *αὐτοῖς*. 27. All add *ὅτι πρῶτος μου ἐγένετο*. 28. B has *Βηθαβαρᾷ* instead of *Βηθανίᾳ ..... πέραν*. 29. C om. *πρὸς αὐτόν*.	3, 4
i. 29.	All om. *Τῇ ἐπαύριον* (266): all add *ὁ Ἰωάννης* after *βλέπει*.	4, 266
i. 34.	C adds *ὁ μονογενὴς αὐτοῦ* after *Θεοῦ*: A and B add *ὁ ἐκλεκτὸς αὐτοῦ*.	4
i. 45.	All have *ἐν τοῖς προφήταις* for *οἱ προφῆται*. 48. All add *οὖν* after *αὐτῷ*: C om. *Φίλιππον*. 49. All om. *αὐτῷ* and add *καὶ λέγει* after *Ναθαναὴλ*. 50. All add *εἰ δὲ οὕτως* after *πιστεύεις;* 51. B has *σοι* for *ὑμῖν* and C *αὐτοῖς* for *αὐτῷ*: all add *ἀπ' ἄρτι* before *ὄψεσθε*.	137, 138
ii. 5.	All add *πᾶν* before *Ὅτι*. 7. B om. *καὶ ἐγέμισαν αὐτάς*. 8. All add *ὁ κύριος Ἰησοῦς* after *αὐτοῖς*. 11. A om. *ἐποίησεν*.	12, 13

PAGE

John ii. 12. All have ὁ κύριος Ἰησοῦς for αὐτὸς. 13. B adds ἰδοὺ before ἐγγὺς. 15. All add ὡς after ποιήσας. 16. B om. ταῦτα: all om. οἶκον τοῦ πατρός μου: A and C add μου after the second οἶκον. 17, 22. All add τότε before Ἐμνήσθησαν. 18, 20, 22. All om. οὖν. 9, 10

iii. 1. All add τις after ἄνθρωπος. 2. B adds ὃς after οὗτος: all have τὸν κύριον Ἰησοῦν for αὐτὸν: B om. γὰρ. 8. C om. οἶδας. 9. A om. Πῶς δύναται. 12. B om. ἐὰν. 8, 9

iii. 13, 14. All have ἀνδρὸς instead of ἀνθρώπου, and add ὁ ὢν ἐν τῷ οὐρανῷ to v. 13. 16. C om. μὴ (236). 17. All add αὐτοῦ after υἱὸν. 9, 236

iii. 25. All om. οὖν. 26. All have πᾶς ὁ λαὸς for πάντες. 27. All add ὑπ' ἑαυτοῦ after οὐδὲν. 31. B om. ἐπάνω. 33. B and C have ἑώρακα instead of ἐσφράγισεν. 11

iv. 5. A and B add ὁ κύριος Ἰησοῦς, and all om. οὖν after Ἔρχεται. 6. All om. οὖν and οὕτως: all have ἡμέρα for ὥρα, and add ὥρα after ἕκτη. 7. All add τις after γυνή: B and C add ὕδατα before πεῖν. 9. All om. οὖν and ἡ Σαμαρεῖτις. 11. All add ἡ γυνὴ after αὐτῷ, and om. οὖν. 16. All add ὁ κύριος Ἰησοῦς after αὐτῇ. 17. All have ἔχεις for the second ἔχω. 18. C om. γὰρ. 34, 34

iv. 20. B om. προσκυνεῖν. 22. A adds γὰρ after ὑμεῖς. 23. A adds ἰδοὺ after ἀλλὰ: C om. ἀληθινοί and προσκυνήσουσιν: all add τοὺς προσκυνοῦντας αὐτὸν ἐν πνεύματι at the end of ver. 23, but C om. ἐν πνεύματι. 25. All have μεθερμηνευόμενος for λέγομενος. 28. All om. ἡ γυνή: A and C om. οὖν. 29. A and B om. ὅς. 35

iv. 36. All om. ἤδη. 39. B om. πολλοὶ: all add καὶ λεγούσης after μαρτυρούσης. 40. All om. οὖν: all have παρ' αὐτοῖς for ἐκεῖ. 41. All add ἐπ' αὐτὸν after ἐπίστευσαν. 42. All add αὐτοῦ after ἀκηκόαμεν. 49. C om. κύριε. 35, 36

iv. 46. B adds ἰδοὺ before ἦν: A has δοῦλος τις βασιλέως for βασιλικὸς. 50. B adds ἰδοὺ before Πορεύου: A and C add it before ὁ υἱός. 51. All add ἰδοὺ before ὁ παῖς and have σου for αὐτοῦ. 48, 52, 53. All om. οὖν. 53. All add τοῦ παιδὸς after ὁ πατὴρ: all have ἰδοὺ before ὁ υἱός. 20

v. 1. A and B have αὐτῶν instead of τῶν Ἰουδαίων. 2. All have εἴσοδον for προβατική, and B has τῆς κολυμβήθρης for κολυμβήθρα. 3. B has ἦν for κατέκειτο. 3, 4. All add ἐκδεχομένων ὕδατος κίνησιν· ἄγγελος γὰρ κατὰ καιρὸν κατέβαινεν ἐν τῇ κολυμβήθρᾳ καὶ ἐτάρασσε τὸ ὕδωρ· ὁ οὖν πρῶτος ἐμβὰς τῶν ἀσθενούντων ὁ

PAGE

μετὰ τὴν ταραχὴν τοῦ ὕδατος, ὑγιὴς ἐγένετο, ᾧ δήποτε κατείχετο νοσήματι. 5. C om. ἐν τῇ ἀσθενείᾳ αὐτοῦ. 6. C adds ὁ κύριος Ἰησοῦς before θέλεις. 7. All add καὶ εἶπεν ναὶ before κύριε: all add καταβαίνειν after ἔρχομαι. 25

John v. 12. All add τὸν κράββατόν σου after Ἆρον. 13. All have ἐπορεύετο ἀπὸ τόπου εἰς τόπον for ἐξένευσεν: B has πολλοῦ after ὄχλου: all have ἐπ' αὐτῷ for ἐν τῷ τόπῳ. 14. All add τὸν τεθεραπευμένον after αὐτὸν: all om. γέγονας: all add τούτου after χεῖρον. 15. All have εἰσῆλθε for ἀπῆλθε: A om. αὐτὸν ὑγιῆ: C om. ὁ ποιήσας αὐτὸν ὑγιῆ: B has ἐμὲ for αὐτὸν. 26

v. 17. All add κύριος Ἰησοῦς after δὲ: all om. μου. 18, 19. All om. οὖν. 19. All add αὐτοῦ after πατέρα. 14

v. 25. All have τοῦ ἀνδρὸς instead of τοῦ Θεοῦ. 27. All have ἀνδρὸς instead of ἀνθρώπου. 29. In B the clause ending ἀνάστασιν κρίσεως precedes that ending ἀνάστασιν ζωῆς, which is wanting in A and C by *homœoteleuton.* 15

v. 32. All add αὐτοῦ after μαρτυρία. 35. All add ἰδοὺ before ἐκεῖνος. 38. B has μου for αὐτοῦ: A adds ἐμὲ between ὅτι and ὃν. 43. All om. μου: B and C add οὐ after ἐκεῖνον. 46. All have καὶ for ἂν: all om. γὰρ after περὶ. 16, 17

vi. 9. All have τι after παιδάριον: C om ὧδε. 10. All add ἐκεῖ after δὲ. 5, 10, 11, 13, 14. All om. οὖν. 12. B om. ἵνα. 14. All add ὁ κύριος Ἰησοῦς after σημεῖα. 39

vi. 18. All add κατ' αὐτῶν after διεγείρετο. 14, 19, 21, 28. All om. οὖν. 19. All add κόπῳ after ἐληλακότες. 21. All have εὑρέθη κείμενον for ἐγένετο. 22. All om. εἰ μὴ ἓν and add ἐν ᾧ ἀνέβησαν οἱ μαθηταὶ τοῦ κυρίου Ἰησοῦ. 23. All have καὶ for ἀλλὰ and add ἕτερα after πλοῖα. 26. B om. ἀλλ' (18). 27. All add τὴν παρελθοῦσαν καὶ after βρῶσιν: all have ἀνδρὸς for ἀνθρώπου. 18, 21

vi. 26. B and C interpolate τοῖς Ἰουδαίοις after ἀμὴν, ἀμὴν λέγω ὑμῖν. 30, 32, 41, 52. All om. οὖν. 32. All om. μου after πατρὸς: all om. τὸν ἀληθινὸν. 33. All add ὁ ἀληθινὸς after ἄρτος. 38. B om. ἵνα. 39. All add τοῦ πατρὸς after θέλημα *bis*, and B adds ὁ πατὴρ after μοι. 40. All add τοῦ πέμψαντός με after πατρὸς. 51. All add ἣν ἐγὼ δώσω after ἐστὶν: C om. τῆς . . . . ζωῆς·. 53. All have ἀνδρὸς for ἀνθρώπου. 54. All add ἰδοὺ before ἔχει. 21, 22, 23

vi. 55. B om. γὰρ. 59 (58). All add ὑμῶν τὸ μάννα after πατέρες, and A adds ἐν τῇ ἐρήμῳ. 61 (60). All add τοῦτον τὸν λόγον after

PAGE

ἀκούσαντες. 63 (62). All have ἀνδρὸς instead of ἀνθρώπου. 66 (65). All add ἄνωθεν before ἐκ τοῦ πατρός. 67 (66). All add οὖν after τούτου. 67 (68). All add γὰρ after ῥήματα. 26, 27

John vi. 69. All have ὁ Χριστὸς ὁ υἱος for ὁ ἅγιος, and add ζῶντος after Θεοῦ. 27

vii. 2. C om. τῶν Ἰουδαίων. 3. All om. οὐν. 4. B and C om. γὰρ. 7. B om. the second ὅτι. 8. All om. ὅτι. 11. B om. οὖν. 28

vii. 15, 16, 25. All om. οὖν. 16. All add πατρός after με. 17. All add μου after διδαχῆς. 29

vii. 26. All add ἀληθῶς before ὁ χριστός. 28. All om. οὖν: A has τίς for πόθεν. 30

vii. 39. All add ἅγιον δοθέν after πνεῦμα. 40. All add πολλοὶ before ἐκ τοῦ ὄχλου. 41. All om. ἄλλοι ἔλεγον Οὗτός ἐστιν ὁ χριστός. 43, 45. All om. οὖν. 45. All add καὶ γραμματεῖς after ἀρχιερεῖς and om. ἐκεῖνοι. 46. All add ὡς ὁ ἄνθρωπος οὗτος ἐλάλει. 50. All have τὸν κύριον Ἰησοῦν for αὐτὸν. 52. B om. καὶ before σὺ. 59

vii. 52. C om. ἐρεύνησον καὶ ἴδε ὅτι ἐκ τῆς Γαλιλαίας προφήτης. 59

viii. 2. After chap. viii. 2, all have a rubric Ἐτελειώθη τὸ εὐαγγέλιον Ἰωάννου ἑλληνιστὶ ἐν Ἐφέσῳ: C has βοηθείᾳ τοῦ χριστοῦ instead of ἑλληνιστῇ ἐν Ἐφέσῳ. 60

viii. 3. A adds καὶ τότε before Ἄγουσιν, and has πρὸς τὸν κύριον Ἰησοῦν after Φαρισαῖοι: B and C wanting from ver. 3 to ver. 11. 3, 4. A has ἁμαρτανομένη for ἐπὶ μοιχείᾳ and for μοιχευομένη: A has νῦν for ἐπ' αὐτοφώρῳ. 5. A om. [ἡμῖν]: A om. οὖν. 242

viii. 6. A adds τὸ πρόσωπον αὐτοῦ εἰς τὴν γῆν after κύψας. 7. A adds τότε before and τὸ πρόσωπον αὐτοῦ after ἀνέκυψεν. 8. A adds τὸ πρόσωπον αὐτοῦ after κατακύψας. 9. A has ἤρξαντο ἐξελθεῖν for ἀκούσαντες ἐξήρχοντο, om. ἀρξάμενοι, and adds ἕως τῶν παίδων after πρεσβυτέρων: A adds εἰς τὸν οἶκον αὐτοῦ after εἷς: A has εὑρέθη for καταλείθη: A has ἑστῶσα for οὖσα. 10. A has ἑαυτὸν after ἀνακύψας. 11. A adds αὐτῇ after the second εἶπεν. 243

viii. 13. All have Ἰουδαῖοι instead of Φαρισαῖοι. 14. All om. περὶ ἐμαυτοῦ. 19. All om. μου after πατέρα, *bis*. 20. B and C om. αὐτοῦ after ὥρα. 14, 24. All om. ὅτι. 22, 24. A and C om. οὖν. 25. A and C have ἀπεκρίθησαν for οὖν. 30, 31

viii. 27. All add αὐτοῦ after πατέρα. 28. All add αὐτοῖς πάλιν after οὖν: all have ἀνδρὸς for ἀνθρώπου: all add οὐκ ἦλθον καὶ after ἐμαυτοῦ. 31. A om. Ἰουδαίους. 33. All add οἱ Ἰουδαῖοι after ἀπεκρίθησαν, and ἡμῖν after λέγεις. 31, 38. All om. οὖν.

PAGE

38. All add ὑμῶν after πατρὸς. 40. A and B add ἰδοὺ before ζητεῖτε: B and C have ἐμὲ for ἄνθρωπον: all have πατρὸς for Θεοῦ: C om. ver. 42. 32, 33

John viii. 42. All add τοῖς Ἰουδαίοις after Ἰησοῦς. 43. C om. διὰ τί: A and C om. Ἰησοῦς. 44. B adds ἀκούετε after διαβόλου ἐστέ: all have Σατανᾶ for διαβόλου: all add γὰρ after ἐκεῖνος. 45. B om. ὅτι. 49. All om. μου after πατέρα. 37

viii. 52. B adds ἀπέθανον after προφῆται. 54. All om. μου after πατήρ. 55. All add καλῶς after λόγον αὐτοῦ: B and C om. τηρῶ. 57. All om. οὖν. 58. B om. αὐτοῖς. 59. All have οἱ Ἰουδαῖοι for οὖν, and add further αὐτὸς δὲ διελθὼν διὰ μέσου αὐτῶν ἐπορεύετο from Luke iv. 30. 38

ix. 1. All add ὁ κύριος Ἰησοῦς after παράγων: A adds further καὶ οἱ μαθηταὶ αὐτοῦ: all add τινα after ἄνθρωπον. 3. All have ἐν τούτοις for ἐν αὐτῷ. 4. All add γὰρ after ἔρχεται. 5. A and C om. εἰμὶ. 6. All add αὐτοῦ after πτύσματος: all have ἐπέχρισεν for ⸢ἐπέθηκεν⸣, and add τοῦ τυφλοῦ ἐκείνου after ὀφθαλμοὺς. 7, 8, 10, 11, 15, 16, 17, 18, 20, 24. All om. οὖν. 8. All add καὶ ὅτι οὐκ ἔβλεψε after προσαίτης ἦν: the word used for προσαίτης presents some difficulty, being apparently μάρτυρες, but see note on Syriac text p. xxv. 11. All add ὁ τυφλὸς after ἐκεῖνος, and τοὺς ὀφθαλμούς σου after νίψαι. 12. All add ὁ ἄνθρωπος after ἐκεῖνος. 15. All add λέγοντες after Φαρισαῖοι, and ἰδοὺ before βλέπω: all have ἀνέβλεψας for ἀνέβλεψεν. 17. All have τῷ ἀνθρώπῳ ὃς ἦν τυφλὸς for τῷ τυφλῷ. 43, 44

ix. 21. B adds ὅπως ἀποκρίνηται περὶ ἑαυτοῦ after ἡλικίαν ἔχει. 24. All have εἶπεν for Ἐφώνησαν and om. καὶ εἶπαν αὐτῷ: all add γὰρ after ἡμεῖς. 25, 26. All om. οὖν. 25. All add ὁ ἄνθρωπος after ἐκεῖνος: all add ἰδοὺ before ἄρτι. 27. B om. ὑμῖν. 30. B has a second οἴδατε after ἐστίν: C has τίνα for πόθεν. 45

ix. 35. All om. Ἤκουσεν Ἰησοῦς ὅτι ἐξέβαλον αὐτὸν ἔξω: B adds ὁ κύριος and C ὁ κύριος Ἰησοῦς before εἶπεν, and all add ἰδοὺ after it: all have τοῦ Θεοῦ instead of τοῦ ἀνθρώπου. 46

ix. 39. All add τοῖς Ἰουδαίοις after Ἰησοῦς. 40. All add τὰ ῥήματα after ταῦτα. 41. All add ἰδοὺ before λέγετε: all have αἱ ἁμαρτίαι ὑμῶν μένουσιν for ἡ ἁμαρτία ὑμῶν μένει. 40

x. 1. B om. εἰς τὴν αὐλήν. 3. B om. ἴδια. 4. All have ταῦτα for τὰ ἴδια πάντα. 7. All om. οὖν. 40

x. 8. All om. πρὸ ἐμοῦ. 15. All add μου after προβάτων. 40, 246, 247

PAGE

John x. 18. All om. μου. 21. C om. ἄλλοι. 22. All om. τότε. 24. All om. οὖν: C om. ἡμῖν. 25. All om. μου. 26. All add ὥσπερ πάντα ταῦτα ἃ ἐλάλουν ὑμῖν after τῶν ἐμῶν, but B has ἤμην for ἐλάλουν, and C om. ἐλάλουν. 29. All om. μου. 41, 42

x. 33. All have τῆς βλασφημίας σου. 35. All add ἡ λέγουσα after γραφή. 36. All add μοι before λέγετε. 37. All om. μου. 38. C om. εἰ: A om. τοῖς ἔργοις πιστεύετε, ἵνα: B has an unintelligible word, which may mean καὶ ἐν, before τοῖς ἔργοις. 42, 43

xi. 1. B adds ὀνόματι before Λάζαρος. 3. All have τὸν κύριον Ἰησοῦν instead of αὐτὸν. 146

xi. 4. C has πατρὸς instead of Θεοῦ. 6. All add ἐκεῖ after ἔμεινεν. 7, 8, 12. All have αὐτοῦ after μαθηταῖς and μαθηταί. 9. All add καὶ εἶπεν αὐτοῖς after Ἰησοῦς: C om. ὧραι. 13. B om. αὐτοῦ. 3, 14, 16, 19. All om. οὖν. 12. A and B om. οὖν. 16. B and C add αὐτοῖς after εἶπεν: A om. ὁ λεγόμενος. 17. A om. οὖν: all add εἰς Βηθανίαν after Ἰησοῦς, and B adds ἀποθανόντα before τέσσαρας: C om. ἤδη: B and C have ἔνδον τοῦ μνημείου where A has ἔχοντα ἐν τῷ μνημείῳ. 146, 147

xi. 20. A om. οὖν: all add τότε before ὑπήντησεν. 21. All om. οὖν. 22. All add ἀλλὰ before καί. 24, 25. B om. αὐτῷ and αὐτῇ. 25. C has ἡ ζωὴ καὶ ἡ ἀνάστασις, and adds οὐ before ἀποθάνῃ. 26. C om. κἂν. 27. C adds ζῶντος after Θεοῦ. 31. All have λέγοντες for δόξαντες. 147, 148

xi. 33, 38. All om. οὖν. 36. A and C om. οὖν. 37. B and C om. ἵνα καὶ before οὗτος. 39. All add αὐτοῖς after λέγει: C om. Μάρθα: all om. ἰδοὺ before τεταρταῖος: B om. γάρ. 40. B and C add τότε before ὄψῃ. 40. A om. οὖν: all add αὐτοῦ after ὀφθαλμοὺς. 43. B and C om. μεγάλῃ: all add ἔξελθε before ἔξω. 44. All add καὶ εὐθέως before καὶ ἐξῆλθεν: A om. περιεδέδατο. 45. All om. οὖν: A adds ὁ κύριος Ἰησοῦς after ἐποίησεν. 148, 149

xi. 47. All om. οὖν. 48. All add ἰδοὺ before οὗτος: all add ἡμῶν after τόπον and after ἔθνος. 49. All add ὀνόματι before Καιάφας: C om. ὢν τοῦ ἐνιαυτοῦ ἐκείνου. 50. All have ἡμῖν for ὑμῖν. 52. B om. καὶ after ἵνα. 53, 54. All om. οὖν. 46, 47

xii. 1, 2, 3. All om. οὖν. 2. All om. ἐκεῖ: all add αὐτοῖς after διηκόνει. 3. All add τῆς κεφαλῆς after θριξὶν: A and B have αὐτοὺς and C αὐτὸν instead of τοὺς πόδας αὐτοῦ: all have πᾶσα after οἰκία. 150, 151

xii. 6, 7, 17. All om. οὖν: all have ἣν ἐν τῇ χειρὶ αὐτοῦ for ἔχων. 7. A and B have ὁ κύριος for Ἰησοῦς. 8. All om. γάρ. 12. A and

PAGE

B add *συνήγαγεν* and C *συνήγαγον* after *πολὺς*. 13. B adds *λέγοντες* after *ἐκραύγαζον*. 16. A and C have *αὐτοῦ* after *μαθηταὶ*. 17. B om. *αὐτὸν*. 152

John xii. 17. B om. *ὅτε* (167). 18. C om. *αὐτῷ* (47): B om. *ὅτι* (47): all add *καὶ* before *ὁ ὄχλος* (167). 19. All add *πᾶς* before *ὁ κόσμος*. 17, 19, 21. All om. *οὖν*. 22. All add *ἔρχεται καὶ* before *λέγει* and *καὶ* before *'Ανδρέας* in Less. XXXVIII. (47): C om. *ὁ Φίλιππος* (167). 23. B has *ἀνδρὸς* for *ἀνθρώπου* (168): all have *ἀνδρὸς* for *ἀνθρώπου* (47). 24. All add *καὶ ἀπεκρίθη ὁ κύριος 'Ιησοῦς καὶ εἶπεν* before *ἀμὴν* (47). 47, 167, 168

xii. 24. C om. *πολὺν καρπὸν φέρει*. 48

xii. 27, 31. All add *ἰδοὺ* before *νῦν*. 28, 34. All om. *οὖν*: all add *λέγων* after *οὐρανοῦ* (48). 28. All om. *Καὶ*. 29. All om. [*οὖν*]. 30. All add *αὐτοῖς* after *εἶπεν*. 48, 168

xii. 31. All om. *νῦν κρίσις ἐστὶν τοῦ κόσμου τούτου* (48). 32. All om. *ἐκ τῆς γῆς* (48): C om. *ἑλκύσω* (168). 48, 168

xii. 33. All add *πάν* before *ἔλεγεν* (168). 34. All have *ἀνδρὸς* instead of *ἀνθρώπου bis* (48): B has *ἀνδρὸς* for *ἀνθρώπου bis* (168): A and B add *εἶπεν οὖν αὐτῷ* before *τίς ἐστιν* (48). 35. All om. *οὖν*: C om. *οὐκ οἶδεν* (169). 37. All have *Τοιαῦτα* for *τοσαῦτα* (169): A om. *σημεῖα* (169). 38. B has *αὐτοῦ* instead of *Κυρίου* (49). 40. All have *στραφῶσιν* for *νοήσωσιν* and *νοήσωσιν* for *στραφῶσιν* (49): all have *στραφῶσιν* for *νοήσωσιν* (169): A om. *τῇ καρδίᾳ καὶ στραφῶσιν* (169). 41. All have *τοῦ θεοῦ* instead of *αὐτοῦ* after *δόξαν*: and in Less. CXLV. all have *τοῦ κυρίου 'Ιησοῦ* instead of the second *αὐτοῦ* (169). 43. C om. *γὰρ* (169). 48, 49, 168, 169

xii. 44. B adds *πατέρα* after *τὸν πέμψαντά με*. 49

xii. 47. *μὴ* is placed before *ἀκούσῃ* instead of before *φυλάξῃ*: C om. *γὰρ* (169): B om. *γὰρ* (49). 49, 169

xii. 48. All three interpolate *ὁ ἐμὲ ἀθετῶν οὐκ ἐμὲ ἀθετεῖ ἀλλὰ τὸν ἀποστείλαντά με* from Luke x. 16, and add *ἰδοὺ* before *ἔχει τὸν κρίνοντα*: B and C om. *ἐμὲ* before the first interpolated *ἀθετῶν*. 169

xiii. 1. B om. *αὐτοῦ* before *ἡ ὥρα*: all add *αὐτοῦ* after *πατέρα*. 2. All have *τοῦ σατανᾶ* instead of *τοῦ διαβόλου*, add *τοῦ 'Ιούδα* after *καρδίαν*, and om. *Ιούδας Σίμωνος 'Ισκαριώτης*. 173

xiii. 3. All add *ὁ κύριος 'Ιησοῦς* after *εἰδὼς*. 4. All add *αὐτοῦ* after *ἱμάτια*. 5. A and B add *αὐτοῦ* after *μαθητῶν* (174): all add it on p. 176. 7. C om. *ποιῶ* and *γνώσῃ* (174). 8. All have *σου τοὺς πόδας* instead of *σε*. 10. All om. *ἀλλ'* before and add *γὰρ* after *ἐστιν*. 173, 174, 176

PAGE

John xiii. 13. All have ὁ κυριος καὶ ὁ διδάσκαλος. 14. B has ἀγαπᾶτε instead of ὀφείλετε. 16. All om. the second μείζων. 174, 177

xiii. 15. B and C om. γὰρ. 17. A om. οἴδατε. 177

xiii. 31. All have ἀνδρὸς for ἀνθρώπου. 32. A om. αὐτὸν at the end of the verse. 34. All add πλὴν before ἄρτι: B om. the second ἵνα. 35. All have πᾶς ὁ λαὸς for πάντες. 36. All have καὶ εἶπεν αὐτῷ after Ἰησοῦς. 37. There is a stop (: ·:) after ἀκόλουθεῖν: thus ἄρτι belongs to the second clause of the verse; we have a similar punctuation in the Sinai palimpsest. 38. All add καὶ εἶπεν αὐτῷ after Ἰησοῦς. 182

xiv. 2. All om. μου. 3. All add πρὸς ὑμᾶς after ἔρχομαι. B om. ἵνα (183). 4. All have καὶ after οἴδατε and ὑμεῖς οἴδατε after ὁδόν. 50, 51, 182, 183

xiv. 5. C om. αὐτῷ (50): All have δυνάμεθα εἰδέναι instead of οἴδαμεν. 7. All om. μου. 9. C has μοι for ἡμῖν (50). 10. All om. αὐτοῦ. 11. All om. ⸢αὐτὰ⸣. 13. B adds ὃ after τοῦτο: all add ἐμοὶ before τῷ υἱῷ except B on p. 51. 50, 51, 183

xiv. 14. All three codices om. ἐάν τι αἰτήσητέ [με] ἐν τῷ ὀνόματί μου ⸢τοῦτο⸣ ποιήσω. 51, 183

xiv. 15. C om. με (51). 16. All have ἵνα μένῃ instead of ἵνα ᾖ, except C on p. 184. 18. C om. πρὸς ὑμᾶς (184). 20. All om. μου. 21. All add πᾶς before ὁ ἔχων: all om. μου after πατρὸς. All om. με ἀγαπηθήσεται (p. 51 only). 22. A has perhaps τί ἐποίησας for τί γέγονεν, but see p. lxxii.: C om. οὐχ. 23. All om. μου after πατήρ. 24. All add μου after λόγος. 25. C om. ὑμῖν after λελάληκα. 27. All om. ἐγὼ δίδωμι: C adds γὰρ after οὐ. 28. All om. ὅτι before ὁ πατὴρ (53). 51, 53, 184, 185

xv. 1. All om. μου: A interpolates καὶ ὑμεῖς τὰ κλήματα (135); this is found also in a few other MSS. 2. All om. καθαίρει αὐτὸ ἵνα (185). 3. C om. διὰ τὸν λόγον ὃν λελάληκα ὑμῖν (54). 4. All add γὰρ after καθῶς (54), A and C also on p. 185. 5. All om. ὅτι (185). 6. The first word of this verse is rather πλὴν than ἐὰν μὴ, B alone retains μὴ in ἐὰν μή τις μείνῃ ἐν ἐμοί: B has γὰρ after ὡς (185). 7. B alone interpolates μὴ in ἐὰν μὴ ἐν μείνητε ἐμοί (p. 54 only): B has δοθήσεται instead of γενήσεται (54, 185). 53, 54, 135, 185

xv. 8. All om. μου. 10. All have καὶ after καθὼς. 136, 185

xv. 13. All om. τις. 15. All add μου after φίλους: all om. μου after πατρὸς. 16. All add εἰς τὸν αἰῶνα after μένῃ: all have πᾶν before ὅτι: all add ἵνα δοξασθῇ ὁ πατὴρ ἐν τῷ υἱῷ (C adds αὐτοῦ). 19. All add τούτου after the first and second κόσμου.

PAGE

20. B and C on p. 186 and C on p. 24 appear to have *γρηγορεῖτε* for *μνημονεύετε*, but see notes on p. xxv. for this verse: B has *ὑμῖν* for *τὸν ὑμέτερον* (187). 23, 24. All om. *μου* after *πατέρα*. 24, 186, 187

John xvi. 1. C om. *ἵνα* (54). 2. All have *δῶρον* for *λατρείαν*. 24, 54, 187

xvi. 3. All add *ὑμῖν* after *ποιήσουσιν*. 4. All om. *αὐτῶν* after *ὥρα*: B and C appear to have *γρηγορῆτε* for *μνημονεύητε*, but see notes on the Syriac text p. xxv.: all om. *ὑμῖν* before *ἐξ ἀρχῆς*: B om. *ἵνα* (187). 6. C om. *ἀλλ'* (187). 7. B and C add *γὰρ* after *συμφέρει* (55): all add *γὰρ* after *συμφέρει* (187): A om. the second *πρὸς ὑμᾶς* (188). 54, 55, 187, 188

xvi. 11. B om. *ὅτι* (188). 12. B om. *ἔχω* (188). 13. B om. *ἐκεῖνος* (188). 14. B has *αὐτὸν* for *ἐμὲ* (55). 15. All add *ὑμῖν* after *εἶπον*. 16. All add *καὶ ἐγὼ ὑπάγω πρὸς τὸν πατέρα*: B om. *καὶ* on p. 55. 17, 18. All om. *οὖν*. 17. All om. *Τί ἐστιν τοῦτο* (55): all have *οὐκέτι* for *οὐ*. 18. All om. *λέγει*: C om. *οὐκ* (188). 19. C om. *ἤθελον* (56). 22. All om. *οὖν*: B adds *πολὺ* after *χαρήσεται* (56). 23. All have *πᾶν ὅ τι* instead of *ἄν τι*. 24. All om. *ἐν τῷ ὀνόματί μου*. 55, 56, 188, 189

xvi. 27. C om. *ὅτι* before *ἐγὼ* (189): all have *Θεοῦ* instead of *πατρὸς*. 28. All add *γὰρ* after *ἐξῆλθον*. 29. All add *αὐτῷ* after *Λέγουσιν*. 30. C om. *σε*. 57, 189

xvi. 32. B and C om. *ἐλήλυθεν* (190), C also on p. 57: B om. *ἵνα* (190): all translate *εἰς τὰ ἴδια* by *εἰς τὸν τόπον αὐτοῦ*: B om. *ὅτι* before *ὁ πατὴρ* (190). 57, 190

xvii. 1. B has *τὸν ὀφθαλμὸν* for *τοὺς ὀφθαλμοὺς*: all add *σου* after *υἱός*. 2. B has *μοι* for *αὐτῷ bis* on p. 190: on p. 52 B and C have *μοι* for the first *αὐτῷ*, and C for the second *αὐτῷ*. 3. C adds *με* after *ἀπέστειλας*. 7. A and B have *ἔγνων* for *ἔγνωκαν* (52). 11. B and C add *ἓν ὦμεν* after *ἡμεῖς* (191): B adds *καὶ σὺ ἓν ὦμεν* and C *ἓν ὦμεν* (53). 12. All add *ἐν τῷ κόσμῳ* after *αὐτῶν*. 15. All add *σε* after *ἐρωτῶ*: B om. the second *ἵνα*. 52, 53, 190, 191

xvii. 18. C has *ἀπέστειλέ με ὁ πατὴρ* for *ἐμὲ ἀπέστειλας*, and om. *εἰς τὸν κόσμον*. 57

xvii. 20. B om. *εἰς ἐμέ* (191). 21. All add *ἓν* after *ἡμῖν*. 58, 191

xvii. 26. All om. *καὶ ἐγνώρισα αὐτοῖς τὸ ὄνομα σου καὶ γνωρίσω*. 58, 192

xviii. 1. All have *Κατρεσια* for *Κέδρων*. 2. C has *ὁ λεγόμενος* instead of *ὁ παραδιδοὺς*. 3, 4, 6. All om. *οὖν*: B om. *καὶ* before [*ἐκ*]. 4. C om. *'Ιησοῦς*. 5. A and B add *ὁ κύριος 'Ιησοῦς* after *αὐτοῖς*: all have *αὐτοῖς* instead of *μετ' αὐτῶν*. 192

xviii. 7. All add *καὶ εἶπεν αὐτοῖς* after *αὐτοὺς*: all add *πάλιν* before *εἶπαν*.

		PAGE
	8. All add καὶ εἶπεν αὐτοῖς after Ἰησοῦς. 7, 8, 10, 11, 12, 16, 17. All om. οὖν. 8. C om. Εἶπον: B om. τούτους. 10. All add αὐτοῦ after μάχαιραν, and have ἐν τῇ χειρὶ αὐτοῦ for ἔχων. 11. All have τὸν τόπον αὐτοῦ for τὴν θήκην: B has τοῦ πιεῖν instead of οὐ μὴ πίω. 13. All om. ἦν γὰρ πενθερὸς τοῦ Καιάφα: A agrees with the Sinai palimpsest in adding καὶ ὁ Ἄννας ἀπέστειλεν τὸν κύριον Ιησοῦν πρὸς Καιάφαν from verse 24. For the importance of this transposition see Dr. Blass's "Philology of the Gospels," p. 59. The clause appears again as ver. 24. 14. B has ὅτι οἱ Ἰουδαῖοι instead of τοῖς Ἰουδαίοις.	193
John xviii. 16.	In all εἰσήγαγε is feminine, its nominative being ἡ θυρωρὸς. 17. All have αὐτῇ for ἐκεῖνος. 19, 24, 25, 27, 28. All om. οὖν. 20. All add καὶ εἶπεν αὐτῷ after Ἰησοῦς. 25. All add εἶς after σύ.	193, 194
xviii. 29.	All add αὐτοῖς after φησὶν. 30. C has κακὸς for κακὸν ποιῶν. 28, 29, 31, 33, 40. All om. οὖν.	196, 197
xviii. 33.	B and C omit Σὺ εἶ ὁ βασιλεὺς τῶν Ἰουδαίων; ἀπεκρίθη Ἰησοῦς: A has εἶπεν αὐτῷ ὁ κύριος Ἰησοῦς for ἀπεκρίθη Ἰησοῦς. 35. All add καὶ εἶπεν αὐτῷ after Πειλᾶτος: B and C add ὁ βασιλεύς after τὸ σὸν, evidently by a mistake. 36. All add καὶ εἶπεν αὐτῷ after Ἰησοῦς: A has ὁ κύριος for Ἰησοῦς: B and C om. οὐκ ἔστιν: all add ὑπὲρ ἐμοῦ after ἂν: B has εἰς τὰς χεῖρας αὐτῶν instead of τοῖς Ἰουδαίοις. 37. All add καὶ εἶπεν αὐτῷ after Ἰησοῦς: all have ἀλήθεια instead of ἐκ τῆς ἀληθείας. 38. C om. ἐν αὐτῷ. 40. All have πάντες instead of πάλιν: all om. οὖν.	197
xix. 1.	All add μετὰ μαστίγων.	197
xix. 4.	All add οὖν before πάλιν. 6, 10. All om. οὖν. 6. All add τότε before ἐκραύγασαν: B has σταυρώσῃ for σταύρωσον (237): C has σταυρώσῃ (198): A and B add αὐτὸν after σταύρωσον (198): all add αὐτὸν (237).	198, 237
xix. 7.	All add καὶ εἶπαν before αὐτῷ. 10. All have σταυρῶσαι for ἀπολῦσαι and vice versa: C om. Ἐμοὶ (198). 11. A and C om. κατ' ἐμοῦ (198). 12. A and C add οὖν before Ἰουδαῖοι.	198, 237
xix. 7, 8.	All om. Ἡμεῖς νόμον ἔχομεν, καὶ κατὰ τὸν νόμον ὀφείλει ἀποθανεῖν, ὅτι υἱὸν θεοῦ ἑαυτὸν ἐποίησεν. Ὅτε οὖν ἤκουσεν ὁ Πειλᾶτος τοῦτον τὸν λόγον, μᾶλλον ἐφοβήθη, καὶ εἰσῆλθεν εἰς τὸ πραιτώριον (on p. 237 only). 9. B has εἶπαν for λέγει. 11. All om. διὰ τοῦτο ὁ παραδούς μέ σοι μείζονα ἁμαρτίαν ἔχει: ver. 12 is also omitted (p. 237 only).	237

			PAGE
John	xix. 15.	All have *ἔλεγον* instead of *ἐκραύγασαν*: all om. *οὖν*: all have *λέγοντες* after *ἀρχιερεῖς* (237): C has *σταυρώσωσι* for *σταυρώσω* (237): A repeats *ἀπεκρίθησαν* twice. 16. All om. *οὖν* (199). 17. A adds *εἰς τὸ πραιτώριον* after *Ἰησοῦν* (237).	199, 237
	xix. 17.	All have *ἐπεθήκαν ἐπ' αὐτὸν τὸν σταυρόν αὐτοῦ καὶ βαστάζων αὐτὸν* for *καὶ βαστάζων αὐτῷ τὸν σταυρὸν*: C om. *λέγεται*. 19. All add *ἐπ' αὐτῷ* after *γεγραμμένον*. 15, 20, 26. All om. *οὖν*. 26. B om. *ἴδε* before *ὁ υἱός* (281): B adds *ἤ* before *ὃν* (238).	237, 238, 281
	xix. 25.	B adds *καὶ* before the first *Μαρία* (238). 26. All om. *οὖν*. 27. All have *ἡμέρας* instead of *ὥρας*. 28. B om. *ἤδη* before *πάντα* (238). A and C have *ἴδε* for *ἤδη*: all have *ἴδε* for *ἤδη* (206).	206, 238
	xix. 28.	All add *καὶ ἔδωκαν εἰς τὸ δίψος μου ὄξος* after *γραφή*: A adding *μοι* and C *αὐτῷ* after *ἔδωκαν*: all add *ἰδοὺ* before *Διψῶ*. 29. All add *ἐκεῖ* after *ἔκειτο*: C om. *σκεῦος*.	206
	xix. 29.	All om. *οὖν* and *περιτιθέντες*: all add *καὶ ἔπλησαν* before *σπόγγον*, and om. *μεστὸν*: all have *χολῇ* for *ὑσσώπῳ*: all om. *περιθέντες*. 30. All add *μετὰ τῆς χολῆς* after *ὄξος*: all add *καὶ* after *εἶπεν* and *πάντα* after *Τετέλεσται*.	206
	xix. 30.	All have an interpolation *παραδόντος δὲ αὐτοῦ τὸ πνεῦμα*.	206, 238
	xix. 30.	B and C add further, on p. 206 only, *καὶ τὸ καταπέτασμα τοῦ ναοῦ ἐσχίσθη εἰς δύο ἀπὸ ἄνωθεν ἕως τῆς γῆς* from Mark xv. 38: C om. *ἕως τῆς γῆς* and B adds *μέσον* after *ναοῦ*. 31. B om. *οὖν*: C om. *γὰρ*: all add *ἡμέρα* before *μεγάλη*. 32. All om. *οὖν*.	206
	xix. 31.	B and C on p. 213, and all on p. 238, place *ἐκείνη γὰρ ἡ ἡμέρα τοῦ σαββάτου ἡμέρα μεγάλη* after *καὶ ἀρθῶσιν*, whilst A only on p. 213 has *ἦν γὰρ ἡ ἡμέρα ἐκείνου τοῦ σαββάτου ἡμέρα μεγάλη*, and places the clause after *ἐν τῷ σαββάτῳ* (213).	213, 238
	xix. 32.	All om. *οὖν*: C om. *οἱ στρατιῶται*.	213
	xix. 33.	A om. *ὡς εἶδον ἤδη αὐτὸν* (213): all om. *εἶδον αὐτὸν* (207): A also om. p. 213: B and C translate *ἤδη* by ܟܒܪ, whilst A has the unintelligible ܟܕܪ*: A has ܟܒܪ on p. 238: all have *εὐθέως* before *ὡς*.	207, 213, 238
	xix. 34.	B om. *στρατιωτῶν* (207). 36. All om. *ταῦτα*: B and C have *ἐκεῖ* for *πάλιν* (213): C also on p. 207.	207, 213
	xix. 38.	All have *αὐτὸ* instead of *τὸ σῶμα αὐτοῦ*. 39. All have *τὸν κύριον Ἰησοῦν* instead of *αὐτὸν*: all add *ἀρώματα* after *φέρων*. 40. All om. *οὖν*.	208
	xx. 1.	All add *ἡμέρᾳ* after *μιᾷ* and *στόματος τοῦ* before *μνημείου*. 2. B and C add *μου* after *κύριον*. 4. All om. *οἱ δύο*.	221

* Miniscalchi edits this ܟܒܪ.

		PAGE
xx. 5.	B has *ἐπὶ τῷ τόπῳ* instead of *εἰσῆλθεν*. 6. C om. *Σίμων*. 8. B and C have *καὶ εἶδον καὶ ἐπίστευσαν*. 13. All add *ἐκ τοῦ μνημείου* after *μου*. 16. All have *μεθερμηνεύεται* for *λέγεται*: all add *καὶ ἔδραμεν ἅψεσθει αὐτοῦ* like the Sinai palimpsest. 17. All add *ἰδοὺ* before *'Αναβαίνω*: all om. *μου* after *πατέρα*.	221–223
xx. 19.	All add *συνηγμένοι* after *μαθηταί*. 19, 21. All om. *αὐτοῖς*. 20. All om. *οὖν*. 24. B om. *εἷς*. 25. All have *τόπον* instead of *τύπον* before *τῶν ἥλων*, and B has *τόπον τῶν ποδῶν αὐτοῦ* instead of the second *τύπον τῶν ἥλων*.	223
xx. 26.	All have *ὁμοῦ* for *αὐτοῦ*. 30. All add *αὐτοῦ* after *μαθητῶν*.	224
xxi. 1.	All om. *πάλιν*. 3. A adds *ἰχθύας* after *ἁλιεύειν*: all add *εὐθέως* after *ἀνέβησαν*.	224
xxi. 5.	All om. *οὖν*: all have *ἐν ταῖς χερσὶν ὑμῶν* for *ἔχετε*: C adds *τότε*: all add *καὶ εἶπεν* before *αὐτῷ*: A and C om. *αὐτῷ*. 6. All om. *οὖν*. 7. C om. *οὖν* after *λέγει*, and B after *Σίμων*. 8. B om. *ἀλλὰ*. 9. All om. *οὖν*: A om. *κειμένην καὶ ὀψάριον*: C om. *καὶ ὀψάριον ἐπικείμενον*: A adds *καὶ ὀψάριον* after *ἄρτον*: C adds *καὶ ἰχθύας* before *ἄρτον*. 10. A and C add *οὖν* after *αὐτοῖς*. 11. C om. *τριῶν*. 13. All add *καὶ εὐλόγησεν* after *ἄρτον*. 14. All add *αὐτοῦ* after *μαθηταῖς*.	225
xxi. 17.	C om. *Σίμων 'Ιωάνου*: all om. *'Ιησοῦς*. 18. C om. *ἐζώννυες*: A and C om. *σε* (after *ζώσει*).	226
xxi. 21.	All om. *οὖν*. 23. All add *μαθητὰς* after *ἀδελφούς*, and om. *μαθητής*: B and C om. *τί πρὸς σέ;* 25. B and C om. *ἐάν*.	226, 227

A. S. L.

LIST OF PASSAGES IN THE GOSPELS WHICH ARE NOT EXTANT IN PALESTINIAN SYRIAC.

[*The numbers are all inclusive.*]

Matthew iii. 11 *καὶ πυρὶ*—12; vii. 19—23; x. 9—15, 23—31, 34—36; xi. 16—26; xii. 1—29, 38—50; xiii. 1—43, 54 *ὥστε*—58; xiv. 1—13, 35, 36; xv. 1—20, 29—31; xvi. 1—12, 20—28; xvii. 21, 23*b* *καὶ ἐλυπήθησαν σφόδρα*; xviii. 5—9, 21, 22; xix. 1, 2, 13—15; xx. 17—28; xxi. 44—46; xxvi. 40—43*a* *καθεύδοντας*.

Mark i. 12—34, 45; ii. 13, 18—22; iii. 6—35; iv. 1—41; v. 1—23, 34*b*—43; vi. 6—13; 31—56; vii. 1—23; viii. 1—26, 32, 34*a*—*αὐτοῖς*; ix. 1—15, 31, 41—50; x. 1—32*a* *ἐφοβοῦντο*, 46—52; xi. 1—21, 26—33; xii. 1—27; xiii. 1—37; xiv. 1—72; xv. 1—15, 32*b* *καὶ οἱ συνεσταυρωμένοι*—42.

Luke i. 51, 52, 68*b* *ὅτι ἐπεσκέψατο*—75, 77—79; iv. 1—15, 37—44; v. 1*a*—*τοῦ Θεοῦ*, 12—16, 33—39; vi. 11—16, 23*b* *κατὰ τὰ αὐτὰ*—30, 37—49; vii. 1*a*, 17—18*a* *τούτων*, 30—35; viii. 1*a*—*καθεξῆς*, 4, 22—25, 40; ix. 7—28*a* *ὀκτὼ*, 44—56; x. 13—15, 22—24; xi. 1—26, 34—54; xii. 1, 13—15, 22—31, 41—59; xiii. 1—10, 30—35; xiv. 12—15, 25—35; xv. 1—10; xvi. 1—9, 16—18; xvii. 1, 2, 20—37; xviii. 1, 15—17, 28—34; xix. 11—28; xx. 9—45; xxi. 5—7, 20—24, 37, 38; xxii. 40—42, 46—71; xxiii. 1—31, 50—56.

John ii. 23—25; iii. 34—36; iv. 1—4, 43—46*a* *οἶνον*; vi. 34, 45—47, 70, 71; vii. 30—36; xi. 46, 55—57; xiii. 18—31*a* *Ἰησοῦς*; xiv. 14; xix. 8, 21—24, 29.

INDEX TO THE LESSONS.

[*Numbers of Lessons below 152 coincide in the three Codices.*]

ERRATA.

Page 47, line 14 Transpose the figure **19** one line lower down.

,, 59, ,, 20. Transpose the figure **49** one line lower down.

,, 85, ,, 18. Transpose the figure **32** two lines lower down.

,, 106, ,, 30. For ܕܡܣܡܪ read perhaps ܕܡܣܡܕ

,, 164, ,, 25. In A column, for ܐܡܓܒ̈ܪܝܢ [θ n] read ܐܡܓܒ̈ܪܝܢ [n]

,, 184, ,, 17. In B column, for ܐܬ ܒܒܕ read probably ܐܬܒܒܕ

,, 198, ,, 28. In B column, for ܚܕܝܢ read ܚܕܝܢ [k]; and in A column, for [i] *add* ܚܢܝܢ read [k] *add* ܚܢܝܢ.

,, 201, ,, 9. In C column, for ܠܥܠܝܦܘܪܘܢ read ܠܩܠܝܦܘܪܘܢ

,, 206, ,, 23. In A column, for *omit* . . . ܕܒ ܕܢ read *omit* . . . ܐܬܦܠܓ

,, 210, ,, 8. In B column, for ܡܣܓܠܘܒ [w] read ܡܣܓܠܘܒ [w o]

,, 210, ,, 9. In C column, for ܡܣܓܠܘܒ [x] read ܡܣܓܠܘܒ [o]

,, 225, ,, 1. For ܘܡܣܡ [f] read ܘܡܘܡ [f]

,, 233, Luke x. 19. In C column, for ܕܬܕܥܘܢ [i] ܘܥܘܠܠܥܘܢ [h] read ܥܘܠܠܥܘܢ [h] ܘܕܬܕܥܘܢ [i]

,, 235, line 1. For **50** read **56**

,, 261, ,, 24. Delete ܒܪܗ in Codex C.

,, 276, ,, 5. In B column, add **10** before ܗܕܡ [l]

,, 278, ,, 9. In B column, for ܪܢܫܒܐ read ܕܢܫܒܐ

,, 296, ,, 12. For 96, 97 read 95, 96.

Lectionarivm

Sanctorvm Evangeliorvm

[illegible]

[illegible]

[illegible]

ܒܪ ܬܡ

ܫܒܚ ܡܪܐ ܐܠܗܢ ܐܠܗܘܪܘܗ

ܒܝܘܡܝ ܚܠܦܝܢ ܘܡܫܬܐ ܒ ܡܬܝܕܥ ܠܟܝ

ܗܘܝ ܡܬܦܫܩܝܢ ܡܠܟܘܬ ܒܪܝܬܝܢܐ

ܘܕܝܢ ܒ ܐܦܣܡ

ܐܡܝܢ

ܡܫܝܚܝܐ

PALESTINIAN SYRIAC LECTIONARY.

Preface to Codex A. (Vatican.)

بسم الاب والابن [والروح القدّس] كتب الاناجيل التى تقرا فى جميع ايام السنه الاربعه ܐܠܥܡܕ ܠܥܠܡ
ܐܠܕܝ ܝܓܒܪ ܥܠܝ ܐܠܩܘܐ ܦܝ ܥܠܘܡܗܡ : ܘܐܠܐܬܦܐܩ ܦܝ ܡܥܐܢܝܗܡ : ܘܐܠܬܒܝܢ ܦܝ
ܐܩܐܘܝܠܗܡ ܘܐܠܝܩܝܢ ܦܝ ܡܢܐܗܓܗܡ : ܐܕܐ ܐܩܐܡܘܐ ܦܝ ܡܥܐܠܡܗܡ ܘܩܕܪ
ܦܝ ܐܬܬܦܐܩܗܡ ܙܟܘܪ ⁘ ܘܠܗܡ ܦܝ ܩܪܒ ܐܠܟܐܒ ܘܡܫܒܗ ܦܝ ܫܟܗ ܐܠܚܘܐܠ ⁘
ܘܐܚܫܒܘ ܦܝ ܐܠܓܠܒ ܘܬܘܬܘ ܒܐܠܓܠܒܪ : ܥܡܒܪܐ ܡܚܝܢܐ ܥܠܐ ܡܢܐ ܓܡܝܥܗܡ
ܬܬܠܘܐܗ ⁘ ܘܫܬܪܒܘܐ ܦܝ ܓܝܡ ܡܢܐ ܐܓܬܪܐܝܐ ܥܠܝܗ ⁘ ܦܡܢܐ ܐܠܬܘܦܝܩ
ܐܠܐ ܒܗ ܒܪܐܝ ܐܠܥܠܡܝܢ :

[f. 1b] ܩܪܐܬ ܐܢܓܝܠ ܡܢ ܝܘܚܢܐ ܐܠܡܐܐܒܕܐܝܐ ܘܗܘܝ ܡܢ ܐܠܦܨܚ ܐܠܐ ܐܠܥܢܨܪ
ܗܝ ܡܬܘܒܗ ܥܠܝ ܘܪܩ ܥܠܝ ܘܒܕܕܗܐ ܫܡܥܘܢܐ ܐܓܝܠ ⁘ ܘܡܢܐ ܕܦܫܚܐ ܦܝ
ܐܠܡܘܕܗ ⁘

Preface to Codex B. (Sinai.)

[f. 2a] ✠ ܒܫܡܗ ܕܐܠܗܐ ܐܒܐ ܕܝܢ ܒܥܠܡܐ
ܢܫܪܝ ܒܟܬܒ ܐܠܗ ܢܫܬܘܒ ܐܠܐܢܓܝܠ
ܐܠܡܩܕܣ : ܘܗܘ ܐܪܒܥ ܒܪܐܝ ܐܠܐܘܠ
ܡܢܗܐ ܒܪܝܬ ܝܘܚܢܐ ܘܗܘܝ ܡܢ ܐܠܦܨܚ
ܐܠܐ ܐܠܥܢܨܪܗ ܬܘܡܪܐ ܘܒܕܕܗܐ ܫܡܥܘܢ
ܐܓܝܠ : ܘܗܘܝ ܡܬܘܒܗ ܥܠ ܘܪܩ ܥܠ
ܝܘܪܐ ܝܘܡ ܚܕ ܐܠܦܨܚ ܦܝ ܐܠܡܘܕܗ
ܡܢ ܝܘܚܢܐ : ܐ

Preface to Codex C. (Sinai.)

[f. 3a] ܒܫܡܗ ܕܐܒܐ ܘܒܪܐ ܘܪܘܚܐ ܕܩܘܕܫܐ
ܠܥܠܡ ܥܠܡܝܢ. ܐܡܝܢ ܢܫܪܝ ܒܟܬܒ
ܐܠܡܩܕܣ ܐܠܐܢܓܝܠ ܐܠܡܩܕܣܗ ܐܠܗ
ܡܚܒ (*sic*) ܥܠܐ ܐܬܡܡ ܒܫܦܬ ܐܦܫܪܗ
ܘܓܡܝܥ ܐܠܩܕܝܣܝܢ ܐܡܝܢ ܐܡܝܢ ܐܡܝܢ
ܐܠܥܠ ܡܢܗܐ ܚܢܢ ܗܘܝ ܫܡܥܘܢ ܐܓܝܠ
ܠܗܘܡ ܐܠܥܝܢ ܡܢ ܒܫܘܪܗ ܕܚܢܢܐ ✠

Codex A.	Codex B.	Codex C.

I.

John I. 1—17.

Codex B.

1 ܡܢ ܫܪܘ ܗܘܬ[a] ܡܠܬܐ ܘܡܠܬܐ ܗܘܬ ܠܘܬ
2 ܐܠܗܐ : ܘܐܠܗܐ[b] ܗܘ[c] ܡܠܬܐ : ܗܕܝܢ ܗܘܐ
3 ܡܢ ܫܪܘ ܠܘܬ ܐܠܗܐ ܟܘܠܐ ܒܗ ܐܬܒܪܝ :
4 [d]ܡܕܐ ܕܐܬܒܪܝ ܒܗ [o]ܚܝܝܢ ܗܘܘ ✠ ܘܚܝܝܐ
5 [fe]ܢܗܘܪܗܘܢ ܕܒܢܝܢܫܐ ⁘ ܘܢܗܘܪܐ ܒܚܒܠܐ
6 ܡܢܗܪ ⁘ ܘܚܒܠܐ ܠܐ ܕܒܩ ܠܗ ⁘ ܐܬܒܪܝ
ܓܒܪ [g]ܡܫܠܚ ܡܢ [h]ܐܠܗܐ ܕܫܡܗ [i]ܝܘܚܢܢ :
7 ܗܕܝܢ [k]ܕܐܬܐ [l]ܠܣܗܕܘ ⁘ [m]ܕܝܣܗܕ ܥܠ [n]ܢܗܘܪܗ
ܕܢܗܘܪܐ : [o]ܒܓܠܠ ܕܟܘܠܐ ܝܗܝܡܢܘܢ ܒܐܝܕܗ :
8 ܠܐ ܗܘܐ ܗܘ ܢܗܘܪܐ : ܐܠܐ [m]ܕܝܣܗܕ ܥܠ ܢܗܘܪܗ
[f. 2b]
9 ܕܢܗܘܪܐ : [p]ܗܘܐ ܢܗܘܪܐ ܩܘܫܛܐ ܗܕܝܢ
[r]ܕܡܢܗܪ ܠܟܘܠ ܒܪܢܫ ܕܐܬܐ [s]ܠܥܠܡܐ :
10 [t]ܒܥܠܡܐ ܗܘܐ [u]ܘܥܠܡܐ ܒܗ ܐܬܒܪܝ[u] :
11 ܘܥܠܡܐ ܠܐ [v]ܐܫܟܪ ܝܬܗ ⁘ [w]ܠܕܝܠܗ ܐܬܐ
12 ܘܕܝܠܗ ܠܐ ܩܒܠܘ ܝܬܗ ⁘ ܒܟܠ[†] ܗܠܝܢ ܕܝ
ܕܩܒܠܘ ܝܬܗ [x]ܝܗܒ ܠܗܘܢ ܫܘܠܛܢ ܕܒܢܝܢ
ܠܐܠܗܐ ܝܗܘܢ : [y]ܠܟܘܠ [z]ܗܠܝܢ ܕܡܗܝܡܢܝܢ
13 ܒܫܡܗ ⁘ ܗܠܝܢ ܕܠܐ ܡܢ ܐܕܡ [‡] ܘܠܐ ܡܢ
ܪܓܝܓ ܕܒܣܪ ܘܠܐ ܡܢ ܪܓܝܓ [a]ܕܓܒܪ ܐܠܐ
14 ܡܢ ܐܠܗܐ ܐܬܝܠܕܘ ⁘ ܘܡܠܬܐ [b]ܒܣܪ
ܐܬܥܒܕܬ : ܘܫܪܬ ܒܝܢܢ : ܘܚܡܝܢܗ
ܬܫܒܘܚܬܗ ܗܝܟ ܬܫܒܘܚܐ : [c]ܕܝܚܝܕܝ ܡܢ
15 ܠܘܬ [d]ܐܒܐ ܡܠܐ [e]ܚܣܕ [f]ܘܩܘܫܛ : [g]ܝܘܚܢܢ
[h]ܡܣܗܕ ܥܠ [i]ܕܓܒܪ ܘܐܓܥܝ ܘܐܡܪ : [k]ܗܕܝܢ
ܗܘ ܕܐܡܪܬ : ܗܕܝܢ ܕܐܬܐ ܡܢ ܒܬܪܝ [l]ܕܩܕܡܝ[m]

Codex A.

[f. 1b]
[a] ܗܘܬ
[b] ܘܐܠܗܐ [c] ܗܘܬ
[d] add ܘܠܒܪ ܡܢܗ ܟܠܘܡ ܠܐ ܐܬܒܪܝ:
[e] add ܗܘܘ
[f] ܢܗܘܪܗܘܢ
[g] ܡܫܠܚ
[h] add ܠܘܬ [k] ܕܐܬܐ
[m] ܕܝܣܗܕ [n] ܢܗܘܪܗ
[o] ܒܓܠܠ
[p] omit ܗܘܐ ܢܗܘܪܐ
[r] ܕܡܢܗܪ [s] ܠܥܠܡܐ
[t] ܒܥܠܡܐ [u] ܘܥܠܡܐ
[v] ܐܫܟܪ
[x] ܝܗܒ
[y] omit ܠܟܘܠ [z] ܗܠܝܢ
‡ f. 2a.
[a] ܕܓܒܪ
[b] ܒܣܪ
[c] ܕܝܚܝܕܝ
[d] ܐܒܘܗܝ [e] ܚܣܕ
[f] ܘܩܘܫܛܐ
[k] ܗܘ [l] ܕܐܡܪܬ
[m] add ܓܒܪ

Codex C.

[a] ܗܘܬ
[c] ܗܘܬ
[d] add ܘܠܒܪ ܡܢܗ ܟܠܘܡ ܠܐ ܐܬܒܪܝ:
[o] ܚܝܝܢ
[e] add ܗܘܐ
[f] ܢܗܘܪܗܘܢ
[g] ܡܫܠܚ [h] add ܠܘܬ
[i] ܘܝܘܚܢܢ [k] omit ܕ
[l] ܠܣܗܕܘܬܗ
[n] ܢܗܘܪܗ
[p] omit ܗܘܐ ܢܗܘܪܐ
[r] ܕܡܢܗܪ
[s] ܠܥܠܡܐ
† f. 3b.
[u] omit ܘܥܠܡܐ ܒܗ ܐܬܒܪܝ
[w] ܠܕܝܠܗ [x] ܝܗܒ
[y] omit ܠܟܘܠ
[b] ܒܣܪ
[e] ܚܣܕ [f] ܘܩܘܫܛ
[g] ܝܘܚܢܢ
[h] ܡܣܗܕ [i] omit ܕ
[m] add ܓܒܪ

Codex A.

¹ܐܬܒܪܝܬܢ ᵐܕܡܟܐܢ

ⁿܐܢܢ ᵒܟܘܠܗ

ᵖܢܣܒܢܢܗ

ᑫܘܚܣܕ ʳܚܠܦ

ˢܚܣܕ ᵗܚܣܕܐ

ᵘ*omit* ܒܐܝܕ ʷܫܠܡ

ᶻܠܝܬ

ᵃܐܠܗܐ ᵇܝܚܝܕܝܐ

ᶜ*omit* ܝܬܝܪܐ

ᵈ*add* ܥܒܕ

ᶻܠܝܬܗ ᵃܕ

ᵇܒܥܘܒܗ ᶜܕܐܒܘܗܝ

ᵈ*omit* ܕܝ ᶠܝܗܘܕܝܐ

ʰܘܠܒܘܢܝܐ ⁱ*add* ܐܬ

ʲܘܐܘܕܝ ᵏܠܒܪܢܐ

ˡܘܫܐܠܘ ᵐܐܠܒܘܗܝ

ⁿ*omit* ܗܘ ܕܝ

‡ f. 2*b*.

ᵒܘܐܡܪ

ᵖ*add* ܢܒܝܐ ܐܬ

ܘܐܥܢܐ ܘܐܡܪ ܠܐ

ᑫܡܢ ʳ*add* ܐܘ

ᵗܐܥܢܘ ᵘܕܡܕܒܪܐ

ᵛܐܫܥܝܐ

ʷܐܠܒܘܗܝ ˣܢܒܝ

ᵃܡܥܡܕ

ᵇܒܡܥܡܘܕܝܬܐ ᶜܕ

ᵈܗܘ ᵉܕܩܕܡܝ

ᶠܕ ᵍܫܘܐ

ʰܕܫܘܝܗ

ⁱܐܬܒܪܝܢ

ᵏ*add* ܒܥܝܢܐ ˡܒܥܒܪܗ

ᵐܕܝܪܕܢܐ

Codex B.

16 ¹ܐܬܒܪܝܬܢ ᵐܘܡܟܝܢ ܡܢܗ ܗܘܐ : ܕܡܢ ܡܠܝܘܬܗ

ⁿܐܢܚܢܗ ᵒܕܟܘܠܗ ᵖܢܣܒܢܢܗ : ᑫܘܚܣܕ ܕܝ

17 ʳܚܠܦ ˢܚܣܕ : ܕܢܡܘܣܐ ܒܐܝܕܗ ܕܡܘܫܐ

ܐܬܝܗܒ : ᵗܚܣܕܐ ܕܝ ܘܩܘܫܛܐ ᵘܒܐܝܕܗ

ܕܝܫܘܥ ܡܫܝܚܐ ܐܬܒܪܝܢ : : ʷܫܠܡ

II.

John I. 18—34.

18 ᶻܠܝܬ ᵃܐܠܗܐ ܡܢ ᵇܝܚܝܕܝܐ ᶜܝܬܝܪܐ ᵈܠܐܠܗܐ

ܐܢܫ ܡܢ ᶻܝܘܡܝܢ ܠܐ ܚܙܐ : ܚܙܐ ܒܪܐ

[f 3*a*]

ᵃܕܝ ܕܗܘܐ ᵇܒܥܘܒܗ ᶜܕܐܒܘܗܝ ܗܘ ܬܢܝ ܠܝ :

19 ܘܗܕܐ ܗܝ ܣܗܕܘܬܗ ᵈܕܝ ᵉܕܝܘܚܢܢ ܟܕ ܫܠܚܘ

ᶠ†ܝܗܘܕܝܐ ܡܢ ᵍܐܘܪܫܠܡ ܠܘܬܗ ܟܗܢܝܢ ʰܘܠܐܘܝܢ

20 ܕܢܫܐܠܘܢ ܝܬܗ ⁱܡܢ ܐܬ : ܘܐܘܕܝ ܘܠܐ

ܟܦܪ : ʲܘܐܘܕܝ ܕܐܢܐ ᵏܠܝܬ ܐܢܐ ᵏܡܫܝܚܐ ⁘

21 ¹ܘܫܐܠܘ ܝܬܗ ܡܐ ܐܘ ܐܬ ⁘ ᵐܐܠܝܐܘ ܐܬ :

22 ⁿܘܗܘ ܕܝ ᵒܐܡܪ ܠܝܬ ܐܢܐ : ‡ᵖܐܡܪܝܢ ܠܗ ᑫܡܐ

ʳܐܬ ˢܕܢܬܠ ᵗܐܥܢܘ ܠܗܠܝܢ ܕܫܠܚܘ ܝܬܢ : ܡܐ

23 ܐܬ ܐܡܪ ܥܠ ܢܦܫܟ ⁘ ܘܐܡܪ ܠܗܘܢ

ܐܢܐ ܩܠ ܡܩܪܐ ܒܡܕܒܪܐ ܐܫܘܘ ܐܘܪܚܗ

24 ᵘܕܡܪܝܐ . ܗܝܟ ܕܐܡܪ ᵛܐܫܥܝܐ ܢܒܝܐ : ܘܗܠܝܢ

25 ܕܐܫܬܠܚܘ ܗܘܘ ܡܢ ܦܪܝܫܐ : ܘܫܐܠܘ ܝܬܗ

ܘܐܡܪܘ ܠܗ ⁘ ܡܐ ܐܘ ܐܬ ܡܥܡܕ ܐ

ܠܝܬ ܐܬ ܡܫܝܚܐ : ܘܠܐ ʷܐܠܝܐ ܘܠܐ ˣܢܒܝܐ ⁘

26 ʸܘܐܥܢܐ ᶻܝܘܚܢܢ ܘܐܡܪ ⁘ ܐܢܐ ܡܢ ᵃܡܥܡܕ

ܒܡܝܢ : ᵇܒܡܥܡܘܕܝܬܐ ܕܝ ܩܐܝܡ ᶜܕܝܢ ܕܠܝܬ

27 ܐܬܘܢ ܚܟܡܝܢ : ᵈܗܘܝܢ ܕܐܬܐ ܡܢ ܒܬܪܝ

ᵉܕܡܟܝܢ ܡܢܝ ܐܬܒܪܝ : ᶠܕܝܢ ܕܠܝܬ ܐܢܐ ᵍܫܘܐ

28 ܕܐܫܪܐ ܒܪܘܬܐ ʰܕܫܘܝܗ : ܗܠܝܢ ⁱܐܬܒܪܝܢ

[f. 3*b*]

ᵏܒܒܝܬ ˡܥܒܪܐ ᵐܕܝܪܕܢܐ : ܗܢ ܕܗܘܐ ⁿܝܘܚܢܢ

Codex C.

¹ܐܬܒܪܝܢ ᵐܕܡܟܝܢ

ⁿܐܢܗ ᵒܟܘܠܗ

ᵖܢܣܒܢܗ ᑫܘܚܣܕ

ʳܚܠܦ ˢܚܣܕ

ᵘ*omit* ܒܐܝܕ

ʷ*omit* ܫܠܡ

ᵇܝܚܝܐ ܝܬܝܪܐ ᶜ*omit*

ᵈ*add* ܡܢ ܒܣܘܪܗ

ܘܒܝܬܗ ܡܢܪܘܣܐ

ᵇܒܥܘܒܗ ᶜܕܐܒܘܗܝ

† f. 4*a*.

ᵉܕܝܘܚܢܢ ᶠܝܗܘܕܝܢ

ᵍܐܘܪܫܠܡ ʰܘܠܘܝ

ⁱ*add* ܐܬ ʲܘܐܘܕܝ

ˡܘܫܐܠܘ ᵐܐܠܝܗ

ⁿ*omit* ܗܘ ܕܝ

ᵒܘܐܡܪ

ᵖ*add* ܡܐ ܐܬ ܢܒܝܐ

ܘܐܥܢܐ ܘܐܡܪ ܠܐ :

ᑫܡܢ ʳ*add* ܐܘ

ˢܕܢܬܠ ᵛܐܫܥܝܐ

ʷܐܠܝܗ ˣܢܒܝ

ʸܘܐܥܢܐ ᶻܝܘܚܢܐ

ᵃܡܥܡܕ ᵍܫܘܐ

ʰܕܫܘܝܗ

ⁱܐܬܒܪܝܢ

ᵏ*add* ܒܝܬܐ ˡܥܒܪܗ

ᵐܕܝܘܪܕܢܐ ⁿܝܘܚܢܢ

Codex A. | *Codex B.* | *Codex C.*

Codex B.

29 [o]ܡܟܒܢ : ܘܠܘܡܒܐ [p]ܐܘܫܝܐ ܣܓܝܐ [q]ܘܡܫܝܟ
ܠܡܒܪܐ ܫܘܐ ܐܬܐ [r]ܠܘܬܗ : ܘܐܡܪ ܗܐ
ܪܒܝܥܗ ܕܐܠܗܐ [s]ܗܕܝܢ ܕܡܪܝܡ [t]ܫܒܠܬܗ
30 [u]ܕܠܒܫܐ : [s]ܗܕܝܢ ܐܬܐ ܗܘ [w]ܕܝܢ ܕܐܡܪܬ
ܠܐ ܕܐܠܗܘ ܕܐܬܐ ܡܢ ܒܬܪܢ : ܒܟܪܐ ܕܝܢ
ܕܗܘ [x]ܡܘܕܟܢ ‡ܐܬܟܒܕ : [y]ܕܡܘܟܢ ܗܟܢ ܗܘܐ
31 ܘܐܢܐ ܠܐ [z]ܗܘܬ ܡܒܪ ܠܗ : ܐܠܐ [a]ܠܓܠܝܠ
ܕܐܬܕܢ [b]ܠܐܡܡܐܘܣ [a]ܠܓܠܝܠ [c]ܕܕܝܢ ܐܬܬܐ ܐܢܐ
32 [d]ܡܟܒܢ ܒܡܟܢܐ : [e]ܘܐܡܫܢ ܘܫܢܝܢ ܘܐܡܪ :
ܕܫܡܥܬ ܪܘܚܐ [g]ܫܢܬܐ ܗܘܝܢ ܘ ܡܢ ܠܗ ܠܘ
33 ܥܡܡܐ ܘܡܬܪܬ [h]ܒܠܒܗ : ܘܐܢܐ ܠܐ [i]ܕܝ
[k]ܗܘܬ [l]ܡܒܪ ܠܗ . ܐܠܐ [s]ܗܕܝܢ [m]ܕܫܠܝܢ ܬܪܝ
[n]ܐܟܒܢ ܒܡܟܢܐ ܗܘ ܐܡܪ ܠܝ : [s]ܗܕܝܢ ܕܐܬ
ܡܟܐ ܪܘܚܐ ܫܢܬܐ ܘܡܬܬܪܐ [o]ܒܠܒܗ : [s]ܗܕܝܢ
ܐܬܐ ܗܘ [p]ܕܝܢ ܕܡܟܒܢ ܒܪܘܚܐ ܕܩܘܕܫܐ :
34 ܘܐܢܐ ܫܡܥܬ [q]ܘܐܡܫܬ [r]ܕܗܕܝܢ ܗܘ [s]ܒܪܗ
ܕܐܠܗܐ [t]ܒܫܪܗ ⁘

Codex A.

[o]ܡܟܒܢ [p]ܫܘܐܐ
[s]ܗܕܝ [t]ܫܒܠܬܗ
[u]ܕܠܒܫܐ [w]ܕ
[x]ܡܘܕܟܢ
[y]ܕܡܘܟܢ
‡ f. 3*a*.
[a]ܠܓܠܝܠ
[b]ܠܐܡܡܐܘܣ
[c]ܒܕ [d]ܡܟܒܢ
[g]ܫܢܬܐ [h]ܒܠܒܗ
[i] *omit* ܕܝ
[l]ܡܒܪ [m]ܕܫܠܝܢ
[n]ܕܡܟܒܢ [o]ܒܠܒܗ
[p]ܕ [q]ܘܐܡܫܬ
[r]ܕܗܕ [s]ܒܪܗ
[t]ܒܫܪܗ

Codex C.

[o]ܡܟܒܢ [p]ܫܘܐܐ
[q]ܘܡܫܝܟ
[r] *omit* ܠܘܬܗ
[t]ܫܒܠܬܐ
[z]ܗܘܬ
[b]ܠܐܡܘܣ
[d]ܡܟܒܢ [e]ܘܐܡܫ
[g]ܫܢܬܐ
[i] *omit* ܕܝ
[k]ܗܘܬ [l]ܡܒܪ
[m]ܕܫܠܝܢ
[n]ܕܡܟܒܢ [o]ܒܠܒܗ
[q]ܘܐܡܫܬ [r]ܗܕܝܢ
[s]ܒܪܗ [t]ܕܫܪܗ

III.

Luke XXIV. 12—35.

Codex B.

[a]ܗܢܘܢ ܐܬܠܬܐ ܡܢ [b]ܠܘܩܕܐ [c] [e][d]ܘܗܘܐ [f]ܐܠܘܫܘܗܘܢ
ܡܢ [g]ܐܬܐܡܝܠ [h]ܐܠܘܫܘܗܝ [i]ܗܘܘ ܐܡܠܝܠ
13 [d][i]ܒܟܐܘܢ : [k] [z]ܗܘܐ ܬܪܝܢ ܡܢܗܘܢ : ܒܗ
ܒܝܘܡܐ : ܗܘܘ ܐܙܠܝܢ ܠܩܪܝܐ ܪܚܝܩܐ [f. 4*a*]
ܡܢ [a]ܐܘܪܫܠܡ [b]ܡܝܠܐ [c]ܫܬܝܢ [d]ܐܡܐܘܣ
14 ܕܫܡܗ [e]ܥܡܐܘܣ : ܘܗܘܘ [f]ܕܝ
ܡܡܠܠܝܢ ܚܕ ܥܡ ܚܕ ܥܠ [g]ܟܠ ܗܠܝܢ
15 [h]ܕܐܬܓܫ : ܘܗܘܐ ܟܕ ܗܘܘ ܡܡܠܠܝܢ
ܘܡܬܒܥܝܢ ⁘ [i]ܘܗܘܐ ܝܫܘܥ [k]ܩܪܒ ܘܗܘܐ

Codex A.

[b]ܠܘܩܕܐ [c] *add* ܪܒܐ
[e]ܘܗܘܐ [f] *omit* ܐܠܘܫܘܗܘܢ
[g]ܐܬܐܡܝܠ
[h] *add* ܡܢ ܩܪܝܐ
[i] *omit* ܗܘܘ . . .
. . . ܒܟܐܘܢ
[k] *add* الخامس
[z] *add* ܒܫܒܬܐ 12
ܡܢ ܩܪܝܐ ܡܢܗܘܢ
ܕܝ ܡܢ ܐܙܠܝܢ
ܠܩܪܝܐ . ܘܐܡܝܢ
ܫܬܝܢ ܡܝܠܐ ܕܡܢ
ܐܘܪܫܠܡ . ܘܐܡܪ ܠܗ
ܥܡܐܘܣ ܕܫܡܗ
ܥܠ ܟܠ ܕܗܘܐ
[a]ܐܘܪܫܠܡ [b]ܡܝܠܐ
[c]ܫܬܝܢ [d]ܐܡܐܘܣ
[e]ܥܡܐܘܣ
[f] *omit* ܕܝ [k]ܩܪܒ

Codex C.

[a]ܗܢܘܢ
[d]ܡܢ ܒܟܐܘܢ ܕܗܘܘ
[d]ܐܙܠܝܢ
[z] *add* ܒܫܒܬܐ
ܡܢ ܩܪܝܐ
[b]ܡܝܠܐ [d]ܐܡܐܘܣ
[f] *omit* ܕܝ [g]ܟܠ
[h]ܕܐܬܓܫ
[i]ܘܗܘܐ [k]ܩܪܒ

Codex A.

[h]ܐܙܠ [i]ܗܘ̈ܘ

‡ f. 3b.

[j]ܢܕ̈ܥܘܢ [k]ܗ̈ܘܝܢ

[l] omit ... ܘܡܟܐܒܝܢ

... ܒܝܫܝܢ

[o]ܩܠܝܘܦ̈ܐܣ

[q]ܒܠܚܘܕܝܟ

[s]ܒܡܕܝܢ̈ܬܗ

[t]ܕܐܘܪܫܠܡ

[v]ܕܐܬܥܒܕ [w]ܒܗ̇

[x] omit ܘܡܢܐ ܗܘ

[y]ܐܡܪ̈ܘ [a]ܢܨܪܝܐ

[b]ܗ̇ܕܝܢ [c]ܕܗܘܐ

[e]ܥܡܐ [f] omit ܠܗ̇

[g]ܪ̈ܒܝܐ [h]ܐܪ̈ܟܘܢܘܗܝ

[i] add ܕܒܡܘܬܐ

[j] omit ܐܢܚܢ [k]ܗ̇ܕܝܢ

[l] omit ܕܝ

[m]ܠܐܝܣܪܐܝܠ

[n]ܗܕ̇ܝܢ [o]ܬܠܝܬܝܐ

[p]ܝܘܡܢܐ

[q]ܕܐܬܥܒ̈ܕܝ

‡ f. 4a.

[r]ܢܫ̈ܝܢ [s]ܕܐܬ̈ܝ

[t]ܐܬ̈ܝ [u]ܐܡܪ̈ܢ

[v]ܕܐܘܦ [w]ܡܠܐܟ̈ܐ

[x]ܕܐܡܪ̈ܢ [y]ܚ̇ܝ

[z]ܢ̈ܫܝܐ [a]ܚܣܝܪ̈ܝ

[b]ܬܪ̈ܥܝܬܐ [c]ܘܝܩܝܪ̈ܐ

[d]ܢܒ̈ܝܐ [e]ܩ̈ܠܝܦܘܣ

[f] add ܐܘܦ

Codex B.

16 [h]ܐܙܠ ܒܥܡܗܘܢ : ܘܒܝܢܝܗܘܢ [i]ܗܘܘ [j]ܢܕܥܘܢ
17 ܕܠܐ ‡ ܢܚܙܘܢ ܠܗ : ܘܐܡܪ ܠܗܘܢ ܡܪܝܐ
ܦܫܘܫܘ : ܡܢܐ [k]ܗܘܝܢ ܗܠܝܢ ܡܠܝܐ ܕܐܬܘܢ
ܡܬܚܒܒܝܢ ܚܕ ܥܡ ܚܕ ܘܡܗܠܟܝܢ [l]ܘܡܟܐܒܝܢ
18 ܠܗܘܢ [m]ܐܩܝܡܘܢ ܒܝܫܝܢ[l] : [n]ܘܐܦܢܝ ܚܕ
ܡܢܗܘܢ ܕܫܡܗ [o]ܩܠܝܘ̈ܦܣ ܘܐܡܪ ܠܗ :
ܐܢܬ [q]ܒܠܚܘܕܝܟ ܬܘܬܒܐ ܡܢ [r]ܒܟܠ [s]ܒܡܕܝܢܬܗ
[t]ܕܐܘܪܫܠܡ : ܘܠܐ ܝܕܥܬ [u]ܒܟܠ ܗܠܝܢ [v]ܕܐܬܥܒܕܝ
19 [w]ܒܗ ܒܗܠܝܢ ܝܘܡܬܐ :· ܗܘ ܕܝܢ ܐܡܪ ܠܗܘܢ
[x]ܘܡܢܐ ܗܘ[x] ܗܠܝܢ : ܘܗܢܘܢ [y]ܐܡܪܝܢ ܠܗ : [†]ܥܠ
ܝܫܘܥ ܕܡܢ [a]ܢܨܪܬ : [b]ܗܕܝܢ [c]ܕܗܘܐ ܓܒܪܐ
ܘܢܒܝܐ ܚܝܠ ܒܥܒܕܐ ܘܒܡܠܬܐ : ܩܕܡ
20 ܐܠܗܐ ܘܩܕܡ ܟܠܗ [e]ܥܡܐ : ܐܝܟ ܕܫܠܡܘ
[f]ܠܗ [g]ܪܒܝ ܟܗܢܐ ܐܦ [h]ܐܪܟܘܢܗ [i]ܠܕܝܢܗ
21 ܕܡܘܬܐ ܘܨܠܒܘ ܠܗ : ܘܐܢܚܢ ܗܘܝܢ [j]ܐܢܚܢ
ܡܣܒܪܝܢ ܕܗܘ [k]ܗܕܝܢ [f. 4b] ܕܥܬܝܕ [l]ܕܝ ܕܢܦܪܘܩ
ܗܘܐ [m]ܠܐܝܣܪܝܠ : ܐܠܐ ܥܡ ܟܠ ܗܠܝܢ [n]ܗܕܝܢ
ܝܘܡ [o]ܬܠܬܝܐ : ܐܝܬ ܗܘ [p]ܝܘܡܢ ܕܗܘܝܢ ܡܢ
22 [q]ܕܐܬܥܒܕܝ ܗܠܝܢ ܐܠܐ ܐܦ [r]ܢܫܝܢ ܡܢ
ܕܝܠܢ ܐܬܕܡܪܢ ܠܢ : [s]ܕܐܬܝ ܡܢ ܠܘ
23 ܩܒܪܐ ܥܠ ܡܥܡܘܪܬܐ ܘܟܕ ܠܐ ܐܫܟܚܘ
ܦܓܪܗ [t]ܐܬܝܢ [u]ܐܡܪܢ : [v]ܐܦ ܚܙܘܢܐ
ܕܡܠܐܟܐ [w]ܚܙܝܢ ܗܠܝܢ [x]ܕܐܡܪܝܢ ‡ ܕܗܘ
24 ܚܝ : ܘܐܙܠܘ ܐܢܫܝܢ ܡܢ ܗܠܝܢ ܕܗܘܘ
ܥܡܢ ܠܡܥܡܘܪܬܐ : ܘܐܫܟܚܘ [y]ܟܢ
ܗܟܢ ܕܐܡܪܝ [z]ܢܫܐ : ܐܠܐ ܕܠܐ ܚܙܘ
25 ܠܗ :· ܘܐܡܪ ܠܗܘܢ ܡܪܝܐ ܦܫܘܫܘ :
ܐܘ [a]ܚܣܝܪܐ [b]ܬܪܥܐ [c]ܘܝܩܝܪܐ ܠܒܐ :
ܕܗܝܡܢܘܢ ܠܟܠ ܡܐ ܕܡܠܠܘ [d]ܢܒܝܐ :
26 ܠܐ ܗܠܝܢ ܗܘܐ ܠܗ [e]ܩ̈ܠܝܦܘܣ ܕܢܚܫ
27 ܡܫܝܚܐ ܘܢܥܘܠ [f]ܠܬܫܒܘܚܬܗ ܘܫܪܝ ܡܢ

Codex C.

[h]ܐܙܠ ܗܘܝ

[l]ܘܡܟܐܒ [m]ܐܩ̈ܝܡ

[n]ܘܐܦܢܝ

[o]ܩܠܝܘܦܐܣ [r]ܒܟܠܗ

[s]ܒܡܕܝܢܬܗ [u]ܒܟܠܗ

[v]ܕܐܬܥܒܕ [w]ܒܗ

[x] omit ܘܡܢܐ ܗܘ

† f. 5a.

[y]ܐܡܪܘ

[c]ܕܗܘܐ

[h]ܐܪܟܘܢܘܗܝ

[j] omit ܐܢܚܢ

[l] omit ܕܝ

[m]ܠܝܣܪܝܠ

[r]ܢܫܝܢ

[t]ܐܬܝ [v]ܕܐܘܦ

[z]ܢܫܝܐ

[a]ܚܣܝܪ

[e]ܩ̈ܠܝܦܘܣ

[f] add ܐܘܦ

Codex A.	Codex B.	Codex C.
ܢܒܝܐ [h]	ܡܫܒܚܐ ܗܘܝ ܒܠܚܘܕܝܗܘܢ ܢܒܝܐ[h] : ܡܬܝܠܕ	
	ܠܗܘܢ ܡܢ ܗܘܐ ܕܒܟܠ ܥܠܡܐ ܟܠ	
ܠܥܝܕܬܐ [i] ܐܬܠ [k]	28 ܕܠܟܘܢ ܘܐܡܪܗ ܠܥܝܕܬܐ[i] ܕܗܘܐ ܐܡܪ ܠܗ :	
ܠܢܗܪܐ [l]	ܗܘܐ ܒܟܠ ܥܒܪܗ ܐܬܠ[k] ܠܢܗܪܐ[l] ܕܝܘܪܕܢ :	ܠܢܗܪܐ [l] ܚܙܐ [m]
	29 ܘܐܬܚܙܝ ܝܘܚܢܢ ܐܡܪ ܚܙܐ[m] ܗܢܐ : ܕܝܠܗ[†] ܗܘ	† f. 5b.
ܘܐܡܪ [o] ܕܢܚܐ [n]	30 ܠܟܘܢ ܕܢܚܐ[n] ܘܐܡܪ[o] ܡܛܠ : ܒܬܪܝ ܐܬܐ	ܕܢܚܐ [n]
ܕܐܬܐ [p]	ܩܕܡܝ : ܘܗܘܐ ܡܢ ܩܕܡܝ ܕܐܬܐ[p] ܒܬܪܝ	ܕܐܬܐ [p]
ܘܐܢܐ [q]	[f. 5a] ܩܕܡܝ : ܒܬܪ ܝܘܡܐ ܘܐܢܐ[q] ܕܝܕܥܬܗ	ܘܗܘܐ [r]
ܘܗܘܐ [r]	31 ܘܗܘܐ[r] ܠܐ ܝܕܥܬܗ ܠܗܘܢ ܕܢܬܓܠܐ ܠܐܝܣܪܐܝܠ	
[s] add ܥܠܝܗ	ܘܐܡܪ ܝܘܚܢܢ[s] : ܗܘ ܕܝܢ ܐܬܐ ܕܐܥܡܕ ܒܡܝܐ :	
ܢܚܬ [t]	32 ܘܐܡܪ ܕܚܙܝܬ ܠܪܘܚܐ ܕܢܚܬ[t] ܡܢ ܫܡܝܐ	ܡܢ ܫܡܝܐ [u]
	ܐܝܟ : ܝܘܢܐ ܘܩܘܝܬ[u] ܥܠܘܗܝ[v] ܘܐܢܐ :	[v] omit . . . ܘܐܢܐ . . . ܠܐ
	33 ܕܠܐ ܝܕܥܬܗ ܗܘܐ ܕܠܘܬܗ ܠܗ[v] ܐܠܐ : ܗܘ[w] ܕܫܕܪܢܝ	ܕܫܕܪܢܝ [w]
[z] add ܠܗܘܢ	ܗܘ[x] ܕܥܡܕ ܒܡܝܐ[y] ܗܘ[z] ܐܡܪ ܠܝ[a] : ܕܥܠ ܡܢ	ܥܠܘܗܝ [x] ܕܚܙܝܬ [y]
‡ f. 4b.	‡ ܕܬܚܙܐ[b] ܪܘܚܐ ܕܢܚܬܐ : ܘܩܘܝܐ	[z] add ܠܗܘܢ
ܠܝܘܚܢܢ [a]	34 ܕܗܘܝܘ ܕܥܡܕ : ܘܐܢܐ ܚܙܝܬ ܘܐܣܗܕܬ	ܠܝܘܚܢܢ [b]
ܠܡܥܡܕ [b]	35 ܡܢ ܒܬܪ ܝܘܡܐ ܐܚܪܢܐ ܩܐܡ : ܗܘܐ	
[c] omit ܠܗܘܢ ܗܘܐ	ܗܘܐ ܩܐܡ ܝܘܚܢܢ ܠܘܬ ܗܘܐ ܕܩܐܡ ܗܘܐ[c] ܠܗܘܢ[c] :	[c] omit ܠܗܘܢ ܗܘܐ
	ܘܐܡܪܝܢ : ܗܐ ܐܡܪ ܠܗܘܢ ܒܡܫܝܚܐ	
[d] omit ܥܠܘܗܝ	ܕܐܬܐ : : [d] ܥܠܘܗܝ .	[d] omit ܥܠܘܗܝ

IV.

JOHN I. 35—51.

Codex A.	Codex B.	Codex C.
ܐܬܠܘܗܝ [a] ܝܫܘܥ [b] (sic)	ܒܗ ܐܬܪܐ ܕܗܘܐ ܐܬܚܙܝ[a] ܠܗ ܝܫܘܥ[b] : [c]	ܐܬܠܘܗܝ [a] ܝܫܘܥ [b]
[c] add ܘܥܒܕ ܡܫܒܚܘܬܗ	35 ܘܠܬܠܡܝܕܐ ܕܝܘܚܢܢ ܕܗܘܐ ܗܘܐ ܝܫܘܥ : ܘܐܡܪ[z]	[c] add ܡܢ ܒܡܫܒܚܘܬܗ ܕܥܒܕܐ ܘܒܬܠܡܝܕܘܗܝ ܢܗܘܐ
ܘܐܡܪ [z]	36 ܘܐܡܪ ܡܢ ܬܠܡܝܕܘܗܝ[a] ܘܐܬܚܙܝ[b] ܠܡܫܪܝܐ	ܬܠܡܝܕܘܗܝ [a] ܘܐܡܪ [z]
ܬܠܡܝܕܘܗܝ [a]	ܝܫܘܥ ܗܘ ܕܗܘܐ ܡܫܝܚܐ[c] ܘܐܡܪܝܢ : ܗܘ ܐܡܪ	[e] add ܥܠܘܗܝ [d] omit ܗܘ
ܘܐܬܚܙܝ [b] ܡܫܝܚܐ [c]	37 [d] ܗܘ ܕܫܡܥܘܢ ܕܐܠܗܐ : ܘܫܡܥܘ[e] ܬܪܝܢ ܡܢ	ܬܠܡܝܕܘܗܝ [f]
[e] add ܥܠܘܗܝ [d] omit ܗܘ	ܬܠܡܝܕܘܗܝ[f] ܡܡܠܠ[g] : ܘܐܙܠܘ ܒܬܪ ܝܫܘܥ :	[h] omit ܘܐܬܐ ܡܢ ܒܬܪ ܝܫܘܥ
ܡܡܠܠ [g] ܘܐܬܐ [h]	38 [h] ܘܐܬܐ ܡܢ ܒܬܪ ܝܫܘܥ[h] ܘܚܙܐ ܐܢܘܢ ܕܐܬܝܢ	

ܒܗ ܕ ܕܒܬܪ ܥܪܘܒܬܐ يوم الاربعا السابع

Codex A.

ܥܠܘܗܝ[h]

[l] *add* ܐܘ

ܘܠܓܒܗ[m] ܘܒܝܘܡܐ[o]

[p] *omit* ܗܘܝ

ܗܕ[q] ܘܡܬܐܡܪ[r]

‡ f. 5*a*.

ܐܫܟܚܢ[t] ܘܐܡܪܝܢ[u]

[v] *add* ܘܐܡܪ

ܗܘ[w] *add* ܒܪܗ[x]

ܕܢܘܢܐ[y] ܕܡܬܩܪܐ[z]

ܡܫܝܚܐ[a] ܠܦܝܠܛܘܣ[b]

ܦܝܠܛܘܣ[c]

ܡܢܗ[d]

ܕܝܢ *add*[e] ܘܐܢܕܪܐܘܣ[g]

ܘܐܫܟܚ[h]

ܦܝܠܝܦܘܣ[i]

ܠܢܬܢܐܝܠ[k]

ܗܕ[l] ܕܟܬܒ[m]

ܘܒܢܒܝܐ[o]

ܐܫܟܚܢ[p] ܠܗ[r]

ܢܬܢܐܝܠ[t] ܢܚܠ[u]

ܒܓܠܝܠ[v] ܦܝܠܝܦܘܣ[w]

[y]*omit* ܕܝܢ ܠܢܬܢܐܝܠ[x]

ܘܟܦܫ[z] ܐܝܣܪܝܠ[a]

[b] *add* ܗܕ

‡ f. 5*b*.

ܕܢܟܠ[c] ܢܬܢܐܝܠ[d]

ܡܟܝܪ[e] ܡܢ *add* [g]

ܦܝܠܝܦܘܣ[h]

Codex B.

[f. 5*b*]

39 ܐܬܝܢ ܠܘܬܗ[h] : ܘܐܡܪ ܠܗܘܢ ܡܢܐ ܐܢܬܘܢ

ܒܥܝܢ : ܗܢܘܢ ܕܝܢ ܐܡܪܘ ܠܗ ܪܒܢ[i] : ܡܢܐ

ܕܗܘ ܡܬܬܪܓܡ ܡܠܦܢܐ : ܗܢ ܐܝܬ ܥܡܪ :

ܘܐܡܪ ܠܗܘܢ[k] ܐܬܘ ܘܐܬܘܢ ܚܙܝܢ : †ܐܬܘ[l]

ܘܚܙܘ ܗܢ ܗܘ ܒܒܪ[m]ܘܠܓܝܒܗ ܒܬܪܗ

ܗܘܝ ܝܘܡܐ : ܘܗܘܐ ܝܘܡܐ ܗܘ ܒܟܫܪ

40 ܥܣܪ : ܘܗܘܐ ܐܢܕܪܐܘܣ[n] ܐܚܘܗܝ ܕܫܡܥܘܢ

‡ܟܐܦܐ ܣܦܘܢ : ܚܕ ܡܢ ܬܪܝܢ ܕܫܡܥܘ ܡܢ[o]ܝܘܚܢܢ

41 ܘܕܒܬܪܗ[p] ܗܘܝ ܠܡܪܢܐ ܘܐܫܟܚ[q] ܗܢܘܢ[r] ܡܫܬܥܐ

ܠܐܚܘܗܝ[s] ܕܝܠܗ ܠܫܡܥܘܢ ܘܐܡܪ ܠܗ :

ܐܫܟܚܢܢ[t] ܠܡܫܝܚܐ ܡܢ ܕܗܘ ܡܬܬܪܓܡ

42 ܡܫܝܚܐ : ܘܐܝܬܝܗ[u] ܗܘܝ ܠܘܬ ܡܪܢܐ

ܝܫܘܥ : ܘܐܚܙܝܗ ܒܗ ܡܪܢܐ ܝܫܘܥ[v] ܐܢܬ[w]

ܫܡܥܘܢ[x] ܒܪܗ ܕܝܘܢܐ[y] ܐܢܬ ܬܬܩܪܐ

ܟܐܦܐ ܡܢܐ ܕܗܘ ܡܬܬܪܓܡ ܟܐܦܐ ܦܛܪܘܣ :

43 ܘܠܝܘܡܐ ܕܡܚܪ ܨܒܐ ܕܢܦܘܩ[z] ܠܓܠܝܠܐ :

ܘܗܘ ܐܫܟܚܗ[a] ܠܦܝܠܝܦܘܣ[b] : ܘܐܡܪ ܠܗ

44 ܡܪܢܐ ܝܫܘܥ ܕܬܐܬܐ ܒܬܪܝ : ܗܘܐ ܕܝܢ

ܦܝܠܝܦܘܣ[c] ܡܢ ܒܝܬ ܨܝܕܐ ܡܢ ܡܕܝܢܬܗ[d][e]

45 ܕܐܢܕܪܐܘܣ[f] ܘܐܢܕܪܐܘܣ[g] : ܘܐܫܟܚܗ[h] ܦܝܠܝܦܘܣ[i]

ܠܢܬܢܐܝܠ[k] ܘܐܡܪ ܠܗ : ܗܘ[l] ܕܟܬܒ[m]

ܡܘܫܐ ܒܢܡܘܣܐ[n] ܘܒܢܒܝܐ[o] : ܐܫܟܚܢܢ[p]

ܠܗ ܠܝܫܘܥ ܒܪܗ[q] ܕܝܘܣܦ[r] ܗܘ ܕܡܢ[s] ܢܨܪܬ :

46 ܘܐܡܪ ܠܗ ܢܬܢܐܝܠ[t] ܡܢ ܢܨܪܬ ܡܫܟܚܐ[u]

ܡܕܡ[v] ܛܒ ܕܢܗܘܐ : ܐܡܪ ܠܗ ܦܝܠܝܦܘܣ[w]

[f. 6*a*]

47 ܐܬܐ ܘܚܙܝ : ܘܚܙܐ ܡܪܢܐ ܝܫܘܥ

ܠܢܬܢܐܝܠ[x] ܕܐܬܐ ܠܘܬܗ ܘܐܡܪ ܥܠ ܕܝܠܗ :

ܗܐ[y] ܕܝܢ ܡܢ ‡ ܫܪܝܪܐܝܬ[z] ܐܝܣܪܝܠܝܐ[a] [b] ܕܢܟܠ[c]

48 ܠܝܬ ܒܗ : † ܐܡܪ ܠܗ ܢܬܢܐܝܠ[d] ܡܢ ܗܝܟܐ

ܐܢܬ ܡܟܝܪ[e] ܠܝ : ܐܝܟܢܐ[f] ܡܪܢܐ ܝܫܘܥ

ܘܐܡܪ ܠܗ : ܕܥܕܠܐ[g] ܢܩܪܐ ܠܟ ܦܝܠܝܦܘܣ[h]

Codex C.

ܥܠܘܗܝ[h] ܪܒܢ[i]

ܠܗܘܢ [k] *omit*

ܐܘ [l] *add*

† f. 6*a*.

ܘܠܓܒܗ[m]

ܐܢܕܪܐܘܣ[n]

ܘܒܝܘܡܐ[o]

[p] *omit* ܗܘܝ

ܘܡܫܬܥܐ[r] ܠܐܚܘܗܝ[s]

ܘܐܡܪܝܢ[u]

[v] *add* ܘܐܡܪ.

ܒܪ[x] [w] *add* ܗܘ

ܕܝܘܢܐ[z] ܡܫܝܚܐ[a]

ܠܦܝܠܝܦܘܣ[b]

ܦܝܠܝܦܘܣ[c]

ܕܝܢ [e] *add* ܕܐܢܕܪܐܘܣ[f]

ܘܐܢܕܪܐܘܣ[g]

ܘܐܫܟܚ[h]

ܦܝܠܝܦܘܣ[i]

ܠܢܬܢܐܝܠ[k] ܕܟܬܒ[m].

ܒܢܡܘܣܐ[n]

ܕܝܘܣܦ[q] ܠܗܝ[r]

ܢܨܪܬ[s] ܢܬܢܐܝܠ[t]

ܒܓܠܝܠ[v] ܢܚܠ[u]

ܦܝܠܝܦܘܣ[w]

[y] *omit* ܕܝܢ ܠܢܬܢܐܝܠ[x]

ܐܝܣܪܝܠ[a]

ܗܘܝܢ [b]*add* ܕܢܟܠ[c]

† f. 6*b*.

ܢܬܢܐܝܠ[d] ܐܝܟܢ[f]

[g] *add* ܡܢ

Codex A.	Codex B.	Codex C.
ܬܬܐܢܬܐ[e]	ܘܐܢܬ ܬܚܘܬ ܬܬܐܢܬܐ[e] ܚܙܝܬ ܝܬܟ : ܐܥܢܐ 49	
	ܢܬܢܐܝܠ ܘܐܡܪ ܠܗ : ܪܒܝ ܐܢܬ ܗܘ ܒܪܗ	
ܕܐܝܣܪܐܝܠ[f]	ܕܐܠܗܐ : ܐܢܬ ܗܘ ܡܠܟܗ ܕܐܝܣܪܐܝܠ[f] :	ܕܐܣܪܐܝܠ[f]
	ܐܥܢܐ ܝܫܘܥ ܘܐܡܪ ܠܗ : ܕܐܡܪܬ ܠܟ 50	
ܬܬܐܢܬܐ[g]	ܕܚܙܝܬ ܝܬܟ ܬܚܘܬ ܬܬܐܢܬܐ[g] ܐܢܬ [h]ܡܗܝܡܢ :	ܡܗܝܡܢ[h]
[j] omit ܐܢܬ	[i]ܪܒܪܒܢ ܡܢ ܗܠܝܢ [j]ܐܢܬ ܚܙܐ : ܘܐܡܪ ܠܗ 51	ܪܒܪܒܢ[i]
ܐܡܪܢܐ[k]	ܐܡܝܢ ܐܡܝܢ [k]ܐܡܪ ܐܢܐ[k] ܠܟܘܢ : ܕܡܢ ܟܕܘ	[j] omit ܐܢܬ
ܡܬܦܬܚܝܢ[l]	ܬܚܙܘܢ ܫܡܝܐ [l]ܡܬܦܬܚܝܢ [m]ܘܡܠܐܟܝ	ܐܡܪܢܐ[k]
ܘܡܠܐܟܘܗܝ[m]	ܕܐܠܗܐ ܣܠܩܝܢ [n]ܘܢܚܬܝܢ ܥܠ ܒܪܗ ܕܓܒܪܐ :	ܬܦܬܚܝܢ[l] ܘܢܚܬܝܢ[n]
[o]ܥܠܝܟ	[o]ܥܠܝܟ	

V.

John III. 1—15.

ܩܪܝܢܐ ܕܝܘܡ ܚܡܫܐ يوم الخميس من بكرة الثامن

Codex A.	Codex B.	Codex C.
[a b] add ܐܠܡܣܝܚܐ	[b a]ܗܘܐ ܐܠܡܣܝܚܐ [dc]ܒܪܗ ܕܐܠܗܐ[bd] ܡܢ ܢܝܩܕܝܡܘܣ[ac] :	[a] add ܐܠܡܣܝܚܐ
[b]ܐܠܡܣܝܚܐ[b]	1 ܘܗܘܐ[b] ܚܕ[b] ܓܒܪܐ ܡܢ [c]ܦܪܝܫܝ [d]ܕܫܡܗ	ܡܢ ܦܪܝܫܝܐ[c]
[d] omit ܒܪܗ ܕܐܠܗܐ	2 [e]ܢܝܩܕܝܡܘܣ ܪܝܫܐ [f]ܕܝܗܘܕܝ : [g]ܗܢܐ [h]ܕܐܬܐ	[c]ܕܝܗܘܕܝܐ
[a] add ܘܒܚܢܬܗ ܡܝܪܘܣܐ	ܠܘܬ ܝܫܘܥ ܒܠܠܝܐ : ܘܐܡܪ ܠܗ ܪܒܝ	[a] add ܘܒܚܢܬܗ ܡܝܪܘܣܐ
	ܝܕܥܝܢ ܐܢܢ ܕܡܢ ܐܠܗܐ ܐܬܝܬ [i]ܡܠܦܢ :	
[b] omit ܗܘܐ	ܐܝܬ[k] ܠܐ[l] ܐܢܫ[m] [n]ܕܗܘܐ ܩܕܝܡ ܗܠܝܢ	[d] omit ܕ ... [b]ܘܗܘܐ ܚܕ[b]
‡ f. 6a.	ܐܬܝܢ[‡] [f. 6b] ܕܐܢܬ ܥܒܕ : ܐܠܐ [o]ܐܢ [p] ܐܠܗܐ	[h] omit ܕ ... [f]ܕܝܗܘܕܝ
[d] omit ܕ ... ܦܪܝܫܝܐ[c]	3 ܥܡܗ : ܐܥܢܐ ܝܫܘܥ ܘܐܡܪ	[l] add ܠܟ ... [k]ܐܝܬ
ܢܝܩܕܝܡܘܣ[e]	ܠܗ : ܐܡܝܢ ܐܡܝܢ ܐܡܪ ܐܢܐ ܠܟ :	[n] omit ܕ ... [m]ܠܐ
ܕܝܗܘܕܝܝ[f] ... ܗܢܐ[g]	[q]ܕܐܢ ܠܐ ܡܬܝܠܕ [r]ܐܢܫ ܡܢ [s]ܠܥܠ	[p] add ܗܘܐ ... [o]ܐܠܐ
[h] omit ܕ	ܠܐ [t]ܡܫܟܚ ܕܝܚܙܐ ܡܠܟܘܬܗ ܕܐܠܗܐ :	[q]ܕܐܢ ... [r]ܐܢܫ
[l] add ܠܟ ... ܡܠܦܢ[i]	4 ܐܡܪ ܠܗ [u]ܢܝܩܕܝܡܘܣ ܗܝܟ [w]ܡܫܟܚ [x]ܐܢܫ	[w]ܡܫܟܚ ... [x]ܐܢܫ
[p] add ܗܘܐ ... ܠܐ[m]	ܡܬܝܠܕ ܟܕ ܗܘ [y]ܣܒ : [z]ܕܠܡܐ [w]ܡܫܟܚ ܗܘ	[y]ܣܒ ... [z] add ܠܐ
ܠܥܠ[s] ... ܢܫܟܚ[t]	ܕܢܥܘܠ ܠܟܪܣܗ [a]ܕܐܡܗ ܡܢ ܬܢܝܢ : ܘܡܬܝܠܕ :	[a]ܕܐܡܗ
ܢܝܩܕܝܡܘܣ[u]	5 [b]ܐܥܢܐ ܝܫܘܥ ܘܐܡܪ : ܐܡܝܢ ܐܡܝܢ	[b]ܐܥܢܐ ... [c]ܕܐܢ
ܢܫܟܚ[w] ... ܣܒ[y]	[†]ܐܡܪ ܐܢܐ ܠܟ : [c]ܕܐܢ [d]ܕܝ ܠܐ ܡܬܝܠܕ	† f. 7a.
ܕܐܡܗ[a]	[e]ܐܢܫ ܡܢ ܡܝܐ ܘܡܢ ܪܘܚܐ ܠܐ [f]ܡܫܟܚ ܕܢܥܘܠ	[e]ܐܢܫ ... [d] omit ܕܝ
[d] omit ܕܝ ... ܢܫܟܚ[f]	6 ܠܡܠܟܘܬܗ ܕܐܠܗܐ : ܗܢܐ [g]ܕܝܠܝܕ ܡܢ ܒܣܪܐ	[f]ܡܫܟܚ ... [g]ܕܝܠܝܕ

Codex A.

ܒܣܪܐ[g] ܪܘܚܐ[i]
[k] *add* ܕ ܠܥܠ[l]
ܕܨܒܝܐ[m] ܢܫܒܐ[n]
ܫܡܥ[o] ܝܕܥ[p]
[q] *omit* ܗܘ ܐܙܠܐ[r]
ܗܟܢܢ[s] ܕܝܠܕ[t]
[u] *add* ܗܘ
ܢܝܩܕܝܡܘܣ[v]
[w] *omit* ܝܟܠ ܗܟܢ
‡ f. 6b.
ܕܗܘܝܢ[x] ܝܫܘܥ[y]
ܕܐܝܣܪܝܠ[z]
[a] ܠܝܬ ܐܢܬ ܝܕܥ[a]
[b] *add* ܐܡܝܢ
ܕܐܝܕܥܢܢ[c] ܕܚܡܝܢܢ[d]
ܐܢܬܘܢ[e] ܡܩܒܠܝܢ[f]
[g] *add* ܘ [h] *omit* ܠܟܘܢ
ܠܐ ܗܝܡܢܬܘܢ[i] [m] *add* ܐܢ
ܐܝܟܢܐ[n] [q] *add* ܕ
ܗܘ[r] ܒܫܡܝܐ[s]
ܒܫܡܝܐ[u]
ܒܪܗ[w] ܠܚܝܐ[x]
ܚܝܝܢ[y] ܕܠܥܠܡ[z]
[a] *add* ܥܠܡ

Codex B.

ܒܣܪܐ[g] ܗܘ : ܘܡܐܢ ܕܝܠܕ[h] ܡܢ ܪܘܚܐ ܪܘܚܐ[i]
7 ܗܘ : ܠܐ ܬܬܡܗܘܢ[j] ܠܡܠܬܐ ܕܐܡܪܬ ܠܟ
ܕܘܠܐ[k] ܠܟܘܢ ܕܬܬܝܠܕܘܢ ܡܢ ܠܥܠ[l] :
8 ܪܘܚܐ ܡܢ ܕܨܒܝܐ[m] ܢܫܒܐ[n] : ܘܩܠܗ ܐܢܬ
ܫܡܥ[o] : ܐܠܐ ܠܝܬ ܐܢܬ ܝܕܥ[p] ܡܢ ܗܢ ܗܢ
ܗܘ ܐܬܝܐ ܘܠܗܢ ܗܘ[q] ܐܙܠܐ[r] ܗܟܢܢ[s] ܗܘ
9 ܟܠ ܡܢ ܕܝܠܕ[t] ܡܢ ܪܘܚܐ : ܐܡܪ[u] ܢܝܩܕܝܡܘܣ[v]
10 ܘܐܡܪ ܠܗ : ܗܟܢ[w] ܝܟܠ ܗܠܝܢ ܕܗܘܝܢ[x] : ܐܡܪ
ܥܢܐ ܝܫܘܥ[y] ‡ ܘܐܡܪ ܠܗ ܐܢܬ ܗܘ ܡܠܦܢܐ
[f. 7a]
11 ܕܐܝܣܪܝܠ[z] ܘܗܠܝܢ ܠܝܬ ܐܢܬ ܝܕܥ[a] : ܐܡܝܢ[b]
ܐܡܪ ܐܢܐ ܠܟ ܕܡܢ ܕܐܝܕܥܢܢ[c] ܡܡܠܠܝܢ ܐܢܢ
ܘܡܢ ܕܚܡܝܢܢ[d] ܣܗܕܝܢ : ܘܣܗܕܘܬܢ ܠܐ ܐܢܬܘܢ[e] ܡܩܒܠܝܢ[f] :
12 ܐܢ[g] ܕܒܐܪܥܐ ܐܡܪܬ ܠܟܘܢ[h] ܠܐ ܗܝܡܢܬܘܢ[i] : ܐܢ[k]
ܕܐܡܪ ܐܢܐ ܠܟܘܢ ܕܒܫܡܝܐ ܐܝܟܢܐ ܬܗܝܡܢܘܢ[l]
ܬܗܝܡܢܘܢ : ܘܠܐ[m] ܐܢܫ ܣܠܩ[n] ܠܫܡܝܐ ܐܠܐ
13 ܗܘ : ܕܢܚܬ[o] ܡܢ ܫܡܝܐ ܒܪܗ[p] ܕܐܢܫܐ ܕܗܘ[r] ܒܫܡܝܐ
14 ܘܐܝܟ ܕܐܪܝܡ[s] ܡܘܫܐ ܚܘܝܐ ܒܡܕܒܪܐ : ܗܟܢܐ
ܥܬܝܕ ܠܡܬܪܡܡܘ[u] ܒܪܗ : ܕܐܢܫܐ[w] ܕܟܠ
15 ܡܢ ܕܡܗܝܡܢ ܒܗ ܠܐ ܢܐܒܕ ܐܠܐ : ܢܗܘܘܢ ܠܗ ܚܝܝܢ[x]
ܕܠܥܠܡ[y] ∴[a]

Codex C.

ܕܝܠܕ[h] ܪܘܚܐ[i]
[k] *add* ܕ ܬܬܡܗܘܢ[j]
ܕܨܒܝܐ[m]
ܫܡܥ[o]
[p] *omit* ܝܕܥ
[q] *omit* ܗܘ ܐܙܠܐ[r]
[a] ܠܝܬ ܐܢܬ ܝܕܥ[a]
ܕܐܝܕܥܢܢ[c] ܕܚܡܝܢܢ[d]
ܐܢܬܘܢ[e] ܡܩܒܠܝܢ[f]
[g] *add* ܘ
ܠܐ ܗܝܡܢܬܘܢ[i] ܐܢ[k]
[m] *add* ܐܢ ܘܠܐ[l]
ܐܝܟܢܐ[n]
ܕܢܚܬ[o]
[p] *omit* ܐܢ
[q] *add* ܕܗܘ
ܒܫܡܝܐ[s]
ܚܝܝܢ[y]
[a] *add* ܥܠܡ

VI.

John II. 12—22.

ܝܘܡ ܚܕ ܕܥܣܪܐ — يوم الجمعة العاشر

Codex A.

[b] *omit* ܒܬܪ
ܐܠܗܢ[c] ܢܚܬ[d]
[z] *add* ܥܡ ܗܘ[a]
ܘܐܚܘܗܝ[b] ܘܐܡܗ[c]
ܘܬܠܡܝܕܘܗܝ[d]
ܘܗܘܐ[f] ܕܝܗܘܕܝܐ[h]

Codex B.

ܒܬܪ[a b] ܗܠܝܢ ܢܚܬ ܐܠܗܢ[c] ܡܢ ܢܚܬ[d] ܐ
12 ܠܟܦܪܢܚܘܡ[z] : ܒܢ ܗܘ ܘܐܡܗ ܥܡ[a] ܗܘ[†]
ܘܐܝܬ ܬܠܡܝܕܘܗܝ : ܗܘ ܘܐܡܗ[b]
ܘܐܚܘܗܝ[c] ܘܬܠܡܝܕܘܗܝ[d] : ܘܬܡܢ ܠܐ ܩܘܝܘ ܝܘܡܝܢ[e]
13 ܣܓܝܐܝܢ : ܘܗܘܐ[f] ܩܪܝܒ ܦܨܚܐ[g] ܕܝܗܘܕܝܐ[h] : ܘܣܠܩ

Codex C.

ܐܚܘܗܝ ܘܐܡܗ[a]
ܐܠܗܢ ܡܢ ܢܚܬ[a]
† f. 7b.
ܘܐܚܘܗܝ[c] ܘܬܠܡܝܕܘܗܝ[d]
ܝܘܡܝܢ[e] ܘܗܘܐ[f]
ܦܨܚܐ[g] ܕܝܗܘܕܝܐ[h]

Codex A. | *Codex B.* | *Codex C.*

Codex B.

14 ܡܪܐ ܝܫܘܥ [h]ܠܢܝܩܕܝܡܘܣ [i]ܘܐܢܫܝܢ ܒܒܝܬ
ܢܫܝܐ : ܠܗܠܝܢ [j]ܕܡܗܝܡܢܝܢ ܬܘܪܬܐ ‡ ܘܐܡܪܝܢܐ
ܘܢܒܝܐ : ܘܠܗܠܝܢ [k]ܕܦܪܝܫܝܢ ܦܪܝܫܝܐ ܡܬܝܢ .
[f. 7b]
15 ܘܟܕܘ ܗܦܟ [l]ܠܪܓܠ ܡܢ [m]ܣܚܠ : [n]ܘܐܫ̈ܟܚ
ܒܠܒܗܘܢ ܡܢ ܢܘܗܪܐ : ܐܡܪܝܢܐ [o]ܘܬܘܪܬܐ :
ܘܟܬܒܝ ܦܪܝܫܝܗܘܢ [p]ܕܦܪܝܫܝܐ : ܘܐܘܦ
16 [q]ܦܪܘܫܝܗܘܢ ܟܦܝ : [r]ܘܗܠܝܢ [s]ܕܡܢܝܢ ܢܒܝܐ :
[t]ܘܐܡܪ [u]ܠܗܘܢ [v]ܐܪܝܡܘ ܡܢ ܟܐ : ܘܠܐ
17 ܬܟܒܕܘܢ [w]ܒܢܬ ܘܒܢܝܢ ܘܒܢܝܢ[w] : [x]ܘܒܟܝܢ
ܐܕܟܪܘ [y]ܬܬܠܡܝܕܘܬܗ ܕܟܬܒܝ ܗܘ ܕܢܘܬܗ ܕܟܝܬܝ
18 ܐܩܠܬ ܫܬܝ : [z]ܐܟܠܒܘ [a]ܢܕܘܝܢ [b]ܘܐܡܕܘ ܠܗ :
ܡܐ ܐܬ [c]ܡܘܕܝܢ[d] [j]ܠܝ [e]ܕܗܠܝܢ ܐܬ ܒܒܕ :
19 ܐܟܠܒܝ ܡܪܐ ܝܫܘܥ ܘܐܡܪ ܠܗܘܢ : ܫܪܘ
[f]ܗܕܝܢ ܢܘܗܪܐ ܘܬܬܠܬܬܐ [g]ܝܘܡܝܢ [h]ܡܩܝܡ
20 ܠܗ : ܘܐܡܪܘ ܠܗ [i] [k]ܝܘܕܝܢ : ܠܐܪܒܥܝܢ [l]ܘܫܬܝܢ
[m]ܫܢܝܢ ܐܬܒܢܝ [f]ܗܕܝܢ ܢܘܗܪܐ ܘܬܬܠܬܬܐ [n]ܝܘܡܝܢ
21 ܐܬ ܡܩܝܡ ܠܗ : ܗܘ ܕܝ ܗܘܐ ܐܡܪ ܥܠ
22 ܗܝܟܠ [o]ܢܘܗܪܐ ܕܦܓܪܗ : † ܟܕ ܕܝ ܩܡ [p]ܡܢ
ܒܝܬ [q]ܡܝܬܝܐ [r]ܒܟܝܢ [s]ܐܕܟܪܘ [t]ܬܬܠܡܝܕܘܗܝ [u]ܕܗܕܐ
ܗܘܐ ܐܡܪ : ܘܗܝܡܢܘ ܠܟܬܒܐ : [w]ܘܠܡܠܬܐ
ܗܕܐ ܕܐܡܪ ܡܪܐ ܝܫܘܥ :· [x]

Codex A.

[h]ܠܢܝܩܕܝܡܘܣ
‡ f. 7a.
[l]ܥܙܝܙ [m]ܣܚܠ
[n]ܘܐܫܟܚ [o]ܘܬܘܪ̈ܬܐ
[p]ܕܦܪܘܫܝܐ
[q]ܦܬܘܪ̈ܝܗܘܢ
[r]ܘܠܗ̈ܠܝܢ [t]omit ܘ
[u]omit ܠܗܘܢ
[v]add ܗ̈ܠܝܢ
[w]ܒܢܬܝ ܐܒܢ ܘܐܒܗܢ[w]
[x]ܘܟܒܢ [y]ܬ̇ܠܡܝܕܘܗܝ
[a]ܝܗܘܕ̈ܝܢ [b]ܘܐܡܪܘ
[c]add ܐܬ [d]ܡܘܕܝܢ
[f]ܗܕܢ [g]ܝܘ̈ܡܝܢ
[i]add ܕܝ [k]ܝܗܘܕ̈ܝܢ
[m]ܫ̈ܢܝܢ [n]ܝܘ̈ܡܝܢ
[o]ܢܘܐܗܐ
[q]ܡܝܬ̈ܝܐ [r]ܒܟܝܢ
[s]ܐܬܕܟܪܘ
[t]ܬ̇ܠܡܝܕܘܗܝ
[u]ܕܗ̈ܕܐ [w]ܘܡܠܬܐ

Codex C.

[h]ܠܢܝܩܕܝܡܘܣ
[i]ܘܐܢܫܝܢ
[j]ܕܡܗܝܡܢܝܢ
[k]ܕܦܪܝܫܝܐ
[l]ܥܙ̈ܝܠ [m]ܣܚܠ
[n]ܘܐܫܟܚ (sic)
[p]ܕܦܪܘ̈ܫܝܐ
[q]ܦܬܘ̈ܪܝܗܘܢ
[r]ܘܠܗܠܝܢ [s]ܕܡܗܝܡܢܝܢ
[u]omit ܠܗܘܢ [t]omit ܘ
[v]add ܗܠܝܢ
[w]ܒܢܬܝ ܐܒܢܝ ܘܐܒܢܝܗܘܢ[w]
[y]ܬܠܡܝܕܘܗܝ
[z]ܐܟܠܒܝ [a]ܝܗܘܕܝܢ
[j]add ܐܬ [d]ܡܘܕܝܢ
[g]ܝܘܡܝܢ [e]omit ܕ
[i]add ܕܝ [h]ܡܩܝܡ
[l]ܘܫ̈ܬܝܢ [k]ܝܗܘܕܝܢ
[n]ܝܘ̈ܡܝܢ
† f. 8a.
[p]omit ܡܢ [o]ܢܘܐܗܐ
[q]ܡܝ̈ܬܝܐ [t]ܬ̇ܠܡܝܕܘܗܝ
[x]add ܥܠܡ

يوم السبت الحادى عشر وهى جمعة القديمة

VII.

John III. 22—33.

Codex B.

[a]ܐܫܬܟܚ ܝܫܘܥ ܐܫܬܠܚ[b] ܒܬܪ [c]ܐܠܦܫܘܢ ܡܢ
22 [d]ܝܗܘܕܝܐ ܘܒܬܪܗ ܦܪܘܫܝܐ : [a]ܘܡܢ ܒܬܪ [b]ܒܬܪܝ
ܐܬܐ ܡܪܐ [c]ܝܫܘܥ [d]ܗܘ [e]ܘܬܠܡܝܕܘܗܝ

Codex A.

[a]omit ܐܫܬܟܚ
[b]add ܡܢ [d]ܝܗܘܕܝܐ
[a]omit ܘ [b]ܒܬܪ
[c]ܝܫܘܥ [d]omit ܗܘ
[e]ܘܬ̇ܠܡܝܕܘܗܝ

Codex C.

[b]add ܡܢ
[c]ܐܠܦܫ [d]ܝܗܘܕܝܐ
[d]omit ܗܘ
[e]ܘܬ̇ܠܡܝܕܘܗܝ

Codex A.

‡ f. 7b.

[f] ܕܝܗܘܕܐ [h] ܡܥܡܕ

[i] ܝܘܚܢܢ [j] omit ܕܝ

[l] ܕܗܘ [m] ܡܝܢ

[n] ܝܘܚܢܢ [o] ܒܦܠܝܩܐ

[p] omit ܡܢܐ

[r] ܕܝܘܚܢܢ

[s] ܝܗܘܕܝ

[t] ܕܕܘܟܝܐ [u] ܕܝܘܪܕܢܐ

[w] ܐܣܗܕܬ [x] ܥܠܘܗܝ

[y] ܡܥܡܕ [z] ܒܢܫܐ

[c] omit ܠܗ [d] ܝܟܠ

[e] ܕܝܣܒ [f] add ܗܘܐ

[g] ܝܗܒ [h] ܣܗܕܝܢ

[i] ܡܫܡܥܝܢ [k] ܥܠܐܝ

[l] ܕܐܡܪܬ ܐܢܐ [l]

[m] ܡܫܠܚ ܐܢܐ [m]

[n] ܩܕܡܘܗܝ [o] ܗܕܝܢ

[q] ܕܩܐܡ [r] ܚܕܘܐ

[s] ܠܓܠܠ [t] ܩܠܗ

‡ f. 8a.

[u] ܡܫܠܡܐ [v] ܪܒܝ

[w] ܕܝ [x] ܠܥܠ

[y] add ܠܥܠ [z] ܕܝ

[a] add ܡܢ ܐܪܥܐ

[b] ܡܡܠܠ [c] ܗܕܝ

[d] ܠܥܠ [f] ܗܕܝ

[g] ܚܬܡ.. [h] ܡܫܪܪ

[i] omit ܗܘ

Codex B.

‡ ܠܐܪܥܐ [f]ܕܝܗܘܕܐ : ܘܬܡܢ ܗܘܐ ܥܡܪ
23 ܥܡܗܘܢ [g]ܘܗܘܐ [h]ܡܥܡܕ : ܗܘܐ ܕܝ
ܐܘܦ [f. 8a] [i]ܝܘܚܢܢ [h]ܡܥܡܕ [j]ܕܝ ܒܥܝܢܘܢ ܩܪܝܒ
[k]ܠܫܠܝܡ : [l]ܕܗܘܘ ܬܡܢ [m]ܡܝܝܢ ܣܓܝܢ : ܘܗܘܘ
24 ܐܬܝܢ ܘܡܬܥܡܕܝܢ : ܥܕ ܟܕܘ ܓܪ ܠܐ ܗܘܐ
25 [n]ܝܘܚܢܢ ܪܡܐ [o]ܒܦܠܩܐ : ܐܬܥܒܕ ܕܝ ܒܥܝܘ
[p]ܡܢܐ ܒܝܢ [q]ܬܠܡܝܕܘܗܝ [r]ܕܝܘܚܢܢ ܠܒܝܢ [s]ܝܗܘܕܝ
26 ܥܠ ܕܟܝ [t]ܕܘܟܝܐ : ܘܐܬܘ ܠܘܬ [n]ܝܘܚܢܢ
ܘܐܡܪܘ ܠܗ : ܪܒܝ ܗܘ ܕܗܘܐ ܥܡܟ
ܒܥܒܪܗ [u]ܕܝܘܪܕܢܐ : ܗܕܝܢ ܕܐܬ [w]ܐܣܗܕܬ
[x]ܥܠܘܗ : ܗܐ ܗܘ [y]ܡܥܡܕ ܘܟܘܠ [z]ܒܢܝܢܫܐ
27 ܐܬܝܢ ܠܘܬܗ : [a]ܐܓܝܒ [n]ܝܘܚܢܢ ܘܐܡܪ [c]ܠܗ :
ܠܐ [d]ܡܟܠ ܒܪܢܫ [e]ܕܢܣܒ ܟܘܠܡ ܡܢ ܓܪܡܗ :
ܐܠܐ ܐܢ [f] [g]ܝܗܒ ܠܗ ܡܢ ܓܘ ܫܡܝܐ :
28 ܐܬܘܢ [h]ܣܗܕܝܢ [i]ܡܫܡܥܝܢ [k]ܥܠܝ : [l]ܕܐܢܐ
ܐܡܪܬ [l] ܠܝܬ ܐܢܐ ܡܫܝܚܐ : ܐܠܐ [m]ܡܫܠܚ
29 [n]ܩܕܡܘܗܝ : [o]ܗܕܝܢ † ܕܒܥܡܗ ܟܠܬܐ ܗܘ ܐܬܢ
ܗܘ ܚܬܢܐ : ܪܚܡܗ ܕܝ ܕܚܬܢܐ ܗܘ [p]ܕܡ
[q]ܕܩܝܡ ܘܫܡܥ ܡܢܗ : [r]ܚܕܐ ܗܘ ܚܕܐ
[s]ܠܓܠܠ [t]ܩܠܗ ܕܚܬܢܐ : ܗܕܐ ܐܘܢ
30 ܚܕܘܬܐ ‡ ܕܝܠܝ [u]ܒܡܫܠܡܐ ܗܝ : ܠܗܘ ܘܠܗ ܢܦܠ
ܕܗܘܐ [v]ܪܒܝ : ܠܝ ܕܝ ܕܗܘܐ ܐܢܐ ܙܥܘܪ :
[w]ܕܡ ܕܐܬܐ ܡܢ [x]ܠܥܠ [y] ܡܢ ܟܘܠܐ ܗܘ :
31 [z]ܕܡ ܕܗܘܐ ܡܢ ܐܪܥܐ [a] ܗܘ [b]ܡܡܠܠ : [c]ܗܕܝܢ
ܕܐܬܐ ܡܢ ܫܡܝܐ [d]ܠܥܠ ܡܢ ܟܘܠܐ ܗܘ :
32 ܡܐ ܕܚܡܐ ܘܫܡܥ ܗܕܐ ܗܘ ܡܣܗܕ :
33 ܘܣܗܕܘܬܗ [e]ܐܢܫ ܠܐ ܢܣܒ : [f]ܗܕܝܢ ܕܝ
ܕܢܣܒ ܣܗܕܘܬܗ [g]ܚܬܡܬ ܕܐܠܗܐ [h]ܡܫܪܪܐ
[i]ܗܘ ܀ [k]

Codex C.

[f] ܕܝܗܘܕܝ [g] ܘܗܘܐ

[h] ܡܥܡܕ [i] ܝܘܚܢܢ

[j] omit ܕܝ [k] ܠܫܠܝܡ

[l] ܕܗܘ [m] ܡܢ

[o] ܒܦܠܩܐ [p] omit ܡܢܐ

[q] ܬܠܡܝܕܘܗܝ

[r] ܕܝܘܚܢܢ [t] ܕܕܘܟܝܐ

[u] ܕܝܘܪܕܢܐ

[x] ܥܠܘܗܝ [y] ܡܥܡܕ

[z] ܒܢܫܐ

[a] ܐܓܝܒ [c] omit ܠܗ

[d] ܝܟܠ [e] ܕܢܣܒ

[f] add ܗܘܐ

[h] ܣܗܕܝܢ

† f. 8b.

[i] ܡܫܡܥܝܢ

[l] ܕܐܡܪܬ ܐܢܐ [l]

[m] ܡܫܠܚ ܐܢܐ [m]

[n] ܩܕܡܘܗܝ [p] ܕܝ

[q] ܕܩܐܡ [r] ܚܕܘܐ

[u] ܡܫܠܡܐ

[v] ܪܒܝ [y] add ܠܥܠ

[e] ܐܢܫ

[i] omit ܗܘ

[k] add ܥܠܡ

Codex A.	Codex B.	Codex C.

VIII.

John XX. 26.

Codex B.

[a]ܦܘܩ [b]ܚܕ ܐܘܢܓܠܝܘܢ ܡܢ ܝܘܚܢܢ : ܐܘܢܓܠܝܘܢ ܡܢ
26 [c]ܐܝܟܢܐ ܠܘܩܝܢܗ[a] ⁘ ܘܡܢ ܒܬܪ[a] [b]ܬܡܢܝܐ
[c]ܝܘܡܝܢ : [d]ܬܘܒܢ ܗܘܘ[d] [f]

[Lectio octava eadem est atque pars lectionis centesimae quinquagesimae secundae, itaque illam hoc loco tres codices omiserunt.]

Codex A. (margin: يوم الاحد الجديد الاول صبوحية)

[a] ܦܘܩ ܐܠܦܐ
ܐܘܢܓܠܝܘܢ ܡܢ
ܝܘܚܢܢ ܐܘܢܓܠܝܘܢ ܡܢ
ܐܝܟܢܐ ܠܘܩܝܢܗ[a]

[a] *add* ܕܝܢ

[f] *add* ܬܠܡܝܕܘܗܝ

Codex C.

[b]ܠܚܕ [c]ܐܝܟܢܐ
[b]ܬܡܢܝܐ [c]ܝܘܡܝܢ

[d] *omit* ܬܘܒܢ ܗܘܘ

IX.

John II. 1—11.

Codex B.

ܘܗܘܐ ܡܘܬܪܐ [a] ܕܝܘܡܗ [d]ܐܠܝܬܝܡ[d] : [e]ܐܟܠ ܦܢܝ
ܡܘܬܪܐ [f]ܗܘܐ ܠܢܦܫܗ [g]ܕܥܠܝܡܝ[h] [i]ܐܫܟܚܬ
[j]ܐܬܐܡܪܗ[k] [e]ܐܬܐܫܟܚܘ ܡܢ ܐܬܬܝܡ ܡܢ ܝܘܚܢܢ[l] [m]
1 [y]ܐܡܪ : ܘܒܝܘܡܐ ܬܠܝܬܝܐ : ܘܠܥܘܬܐ ܗܘܬ ܒܩܛܢܐ
ܕܓܠܝܠܐ ܘܗܘܬ [z]ܐܡܗ ܕܝܫܘܥ[a] ܬܡܢ ܗܘܬ
2 [b]ܐܦ ܝܫܘܥ ܐܬܩܪܝ ܗܘ ܘܬܠܡܝܕܘܗܝ ܠܡܫܬܘܬܐ
[c]ܘܐܦ ܗܘ [d]ܘܬܠܡܝܕܘܗܝ [e]ܐܬܩܪܝܘ ܠܡܫܬܘܬܐ :
3 ܘܟܕ ܐܬܚܣܪ [f]ܚܡܪܐ ܐܡܪܬ [g]ܐܡܗ [h]ܕܝܫܘܥ
4 ܠܗ [i]: ܚܡܪܐ ܠܝܬ ܠܗܘܢ : ܘܐܡܪ ܠܗ
* ܝܫܘܥ [i]: ܡܐ [j]ܠܝ [j]ܘܠܟܝ ܐܢܬܬܐ : ܠܐ ܐܬܬ
5 [†]ܥܕܢ ܫܥܬܝ[k] [l]: ܐܡܪܬ ܐܡܗ : ܘܐܡܪܬ
[g]ܐܡܗ ܠܡܫܡܫܢܐ : ܟܠ ܡܕܡ [‡]ܕܐܡܪ
6 ܠܟܘܢ ܥܒܕܘ : [m]ܘܗܘܝ ܬܡܢ ܓܪܒܐ ܕܟܐܦܐ
[n]ܫܬܐ ܕܡܝܐ : ܣܝܡܢ [o]ܠܬܕܟܝܬܐ [p]ܕܝܗܘܕܝܐ
[q]ܕܡܫܬܡܥܢ : [r]ܕܡܫܬܡܥܢ ܡܢ ܬܪܬܝܢ ܐܘ ܬܠܬ
7 [t]ܡܟܝܠܢ : ܘܐܡܪ ܠܗܘܢ ܝܫܘܥ : ܡܠܘ
8 [u]ܓܪܒܐ [v]ܡܝܐ [w]ܥܕܡܐ ܠܠܥܠ [w] : ܘܐܡܪ

[* Cod. B. ܠܟܪܝܢܐ (sic)]

Codex A.

[a] *add* ܡܢ [d]ܐܠܝܬܝܡ
[f]ܗܘܐ [g]ܕܥܠܝܡܝ
[h] *add* التاسع [i]ܐܫܟܚܬ
[j]ܐܬܐܡܪܗ
[k]ܐܬܐܡܪܗ [l]ܝܘܚܢܢ
[y] *omit* ܐܡܪ
[z]ܐܡܗ ܕܝܫܘܥ
[a]ܘܟܕ [b]ܐܦ ܝܫܘܥ
[c]ܘܐܦ ܗܘ
[d]ܘܬܠܡܝܕܘܗܝ
[e] *omit* ܐܬܩܪܝܘ
[f]ܚܡܪܐ [g]ܐܡܗ
[k]ܫܥܬܝ [l]ܐܡܪܬ
[m]ܘܗܘܝ [n]ܓܪܒܐ

‡ f. 8*b*.

[o]ܠܬܕܟܝܬܐ
[p]ܕܝܗܘܕܝܐ [q]ܕܡܫܬܡܥܢ
[r]ܕܡܫܬܡܥܢ
[t]ܡܟܝܠܢ [u]ܓܪܒܐ
[v] *add* ܡܠܘ ܐܢܘܢ
[w]ܥܕܡܐ ܠܠܥܠ[w]

Codex C.

[a] *add* ܡܢ
[d]ܘܗܘܐ ܐܠܝܬܝܡ[d]
[e]*omit* ܐܟܠ . . .
. . . ܐܫܟܚܬ
ܝܘܚܢܢ[l]
[m] *add* ܐܡܗ ܕܝܫܘܥ
[y] *omit* ܐܡܪ
[z]ܐܡܗ ܕܝܫܘܥ
[d]ܘܬܠܡܝܕܘܗܝ
[h]ܠܡܫܬܘܬܐ
[i] *omit* ܠܗ . . . ܝܫܘܥ
[j]ܘܠܟܝ [k]ܐܬܬ
[l]ܥܕܢ [m]ܗܘܝ

† f. 9*a*.

[n]ܓܪܒܐ
[o]ܠܬܕܟܝܬܐ
[p]ܕܝܗܘܕܝܐ
[q]ܕܡܫܬܡܥܢ
[r]ܕܡܫܬܡܥܢ [s]*omit* ܡܢ
[t]ܡܟܝܠܢ [u]ܓܪܒܐ
[v] *add* ܡܠܘ ܐܢܘܢ

Codex A.	Codex B.	Codex C.
ʷܐܬܝܠܕܘ ˣܘܐܬܐܡܪ	ܠܗܘܢ ܡܪܢ ܝܫܘܥ : ʷܐܠܗܐ ܕܒܪܘ ˣܘܐܬܐܡܪ ܠܟܝܢ	ˣܘܐܬܐܡܪ ᶻܐܬܡܠܟܘ
ᵃܦܪܫܝܢ	9 ܦܪܝܫܝܐ : ܥܢܘܢ ܕܝܢ ᶻܐܬܘ : ܘܟܕ ᵃܦܪܫܝܢ	ᵃܦܪܫܝܢ
ᵇܒܫܒܝܠ	ܐܝܟ ܦܪܝܫܝܐ ܒܫܒܐ ᵇܒܫܒܝܠ ܣܓܝ : ܘܠܐ	
	[f. 9a]	
	ܗܘܐ ܚܕ ܡܢ ܗܘܢ ܗܘ : ܡܫܡܫܢܐ ܕܝܢ ܗܘܐ	
ᶜadd ܗܠܝܢ ᵈܘܡܟܝܠ	ᶜܡܢܝܢ ܕܐܠܗܐ ܒܫܒܐ : ܘܐܡܪ ܐܝܟ ܕܒܥܒܪܐ	ᶜadd ܗܠܝܢ
ᵉܣܓܝܐܐ ᶠomit ܗܘ	10 ܠܫܬܐܠܐ ܘܐܡܪ ܠܗ : ܟܠ ܐܢܫ ᵈܘܡܟܝܠ	ᵈܘܡܟܝܠ
ᵍܢܘܪܐ ʰܠܗ	ᵉܣܓܝ ܦܪܫܐ ᶠܗܘ ܒܫܡܫܐ : ܘܟܕ ᵍܢܘܪܐ	ᶠomit ܗܘ
ⁱܣܓܝܐܐ ܦܪܫܐⁱ	ʰܠܗܘܢ ܕܫܡܫܐ ܗܘ ܒܫܠܘܡ : ܐܬܐ ܕܝܢ ܠܦܪܘܩ	ⁱܣܓܝܐܐ ܦܪܫܐⁱ
ʲomit ܕܒܥܒܪ	11 ⁱܣܓܝ ܦܪⁱ ܒܫܡܫܐ ܠܒܪܗ : ܗܘܐ ܒܫܡܐ ʲܕܒܥܒܪ	ᵏܐܬܐ ʲomit ܕ
ᵏܐܬܐܘܢ	ܡܪܢ ܝܫܘܥ ܐܝܟ ᵏܐܬܐ ܒܡܠܐ ܕܠܠܡܐ	ˡܬܠܡܝܕܘܗܝ
ᵐadd ܥܠܡ	ܘܟܠܗ ܬܫܒܘܚܬܗ ܘܫܡܗ ܒܗ ˡܬܠܡܝܕܘܗܝ ᵐ: ⁘	ᵐadd ܥܠܡ

X.

John III. 16—21.

Codex A.	Codex B.	Codex C.
ܡܢ ... ᵇomit ܐܬܬܠܝܗ	ܐܠܗܐ ܗܘ ܐܬܬܠܝܬܐ ᵃᵇܡܢ ᶜܐܫܬܡܥ ᵇܐܬܬܠܝܗ	ܡܢ ᵃomit ᶜܐܫܬܡܥ
ᵈܒܫܘܒܚܐ	ܡܢ ᵈܒܫܘܒܚܐ : ᶻܘܒܬܪܗ ܒܝܘܡܐᶻ : ܐܡܪ ܡܪܢ	ᵈܫܘܒܚܐ
ᶻomit ܘܒܬܪܗ	16 ᵃܬܠܡܝܕܘܗܝ : ᵇܗܟܢܐ ܓܝܪ ܐܚܒ ܐܠܗܐ	ᵃܬܠܡܝܕܘܗܝ
ܒܝܘܡܐ	ᶜܠܥܠܡܐ : ᵈ†ܕܠܒܪܗ ܝܚܝܕܝܐ ܝܗܒ ܕܟܠ ܡܢ	† f. 9b.
ᵃܬܠܡܝܕܘܗܝ	ᵉܕܡܗܝܡܢ ܒܗ ܠܐ ᶠܢܐܒܕ : ܐܠܐ ܢܗܘܐ ܠܗ	ᶜܠܥܠܡܐ
ᵇܗܟܢܐ ᶜܠܥܠܡܐ	17 ᵍܚܝܐ ʰܕܠܥܠܡ : ܠܐ ܓܝܪ ⁱܫܕܪ ܐܠܗܐ ʲܠܒܪܗ	ᵈܕܠܒܪܗ ᵉܕܡܗܝܡܢ
‡ f. 9a.	ᵏܠܥܠܡܐ ...... : ‡ ܐܠܐ ܕܢܚܐ ˡܥܠܡܐ	ᵍܚܝܐ ʰܠܥܠܡ
ᵈܕܠܒܪܗ ᵉܕܡܗܝܡܢ	18 ܒܐܝܕܗ : ܡܢ ᵉܕܡܗܝܡܢ ܒܗ ܠܐ ܡܬܕܝܢ	ⁱܫܕܪ ʲܠܒܪܗ
ᶠܢܐܒܕ ᵍܚܝܐ	ᵏܡܢ ܕܝܢ ܕܠܐ ܡܗܝܡܢ ᵐܟܒܪ ܗܘ ⁿܕܢ :	ᵏܠܥܠܡܐ ᵐܠܒܪ
ʰܕܠܥܠܡ ʲܠܒܪܗ	ܕܠܐ ᵒܗܝܡܢ ܒܫܡܗ ܕܝܚܝܕܝܐ ܒܪܗ	ⁿܕܐܝܢ ᵒܗܝܡܢ
ᵏܠܥܠܡܐ ˡܥܠܡܐ	19 ܕܐܠܗܐ : ᵖܗܢܘ ܕܝܢ ܗܘ ܕܝܢܐ ܕܢܘܗܪܐ	
ᵏܕܝܢ ᵒܗܝܡܢ	ܐܬܐ ᑫܠܥܠܡܐ : ʳܘܐܚܒܘ ܒܢܝܢܫܐ ܚܫܘܟܐ	ᑫܠܥܠܡܐ
ᵖܗܢܘ ᑫܠܥܠܡܐ	ܝܬܝܪ ܡܢ ܢܘܗܪܐ : ܗܘܘ ܓܝܪ	ʳadd ܘ
ʳadd ܘ	20 ܥܒܕܝܗܘܢ ˢܒܝܫܝܢ : ܟܠ ܡܢ ܓܝܪ ܕܥܒܕ	ˢܒܝܫܝܢ

D

Codex A.

ˢܒܫܥܬ
ᵗ *omit* ܗܘ
ᵘܬܬܚܘܒܘܢ
ˣܕ ᶻܒܘܒܕܝܗܘܢ
ᵃܥܒܝܕܝܢ

Codex B.

ˢܒܫܥܬ ܫܒܥܐ ᵗܗܘ ܫܒܩܬܗ ܠܚܡܘܪܐ : ܘܠܐ ܐܬܬܐ
ܠܘܬܗ ܢܗܘܪܐ ܕܠܐ ᵘܬܬܚܘܒܘܢ ʷܒܘܒܕܝ :
21 ˣܕܝܢ ܕܝ ܕܒܟܝܢ ʸܘܡܫܬܒܩܐ ܐܬܬܐ ܗܘ
ܠܘܬܗ ܢܗܘܪܐ : ܕܡܬܚܒܪܘܢ ᶻܒܘܒܕܝܗܘܢ
ܕܒܐܠܗܐ ܗܘܘܢ ᵃܥܒܝܕܝܢ ∴

XI.

John V. 16—24.

ᵃܗܐܕܝܢ ܒܬܪ ܗܦܟ ᵃ ܐܠܦܢܒܐ ᵇ ܥܡ ᶜܝܫܘܥ :
16 ʸܘܒܝܬܗ ܡܪܘܕܦܐʸ : ᶻܐܡܪ ܡܪܝܐᶻ ᵃ ᶻ [f. 9b] ᵇܠܬܠܡܝܕܝ
ᶜܕܝܢ ܗܘܘ ᵈܝܗܘܕܝܢ ᵉܪܕܦܝܢ ܠܡܪܢܐ ܝܫܘܥ ܕܗܘܠܝܢ
17 ܗܘܐ ܥܒܕ ܒܫܒܬܐ : ܗܘ ܕܝ ܡܪܢܐ ܝܫܘܥ
ܐܥܢܝ ܘܐܡܪ ܠܗܘܢ ܐܒܐ ܥܕ ܟܕܘ ᶠܥܡܠ
18 ܘܐܦܐ ᶠܥܡܠ : ᵍܠܬܠܝܠ ᵇܥܕܝܢ ܡܠܘܢ ܗܘܘ
ⁱܝܗܘܕܝܢ ܒܥܝܢ ʲܕܝܩܛܠܘܢ ܝܬܗ : ܕܠܐ ܒܠܚܘܕ
ܫܒܬܐ ܗܘܐ ܫܪܐ : ܐܠܐ ᵏܐܘܦ ܐܠܗܐ
ˡܗܘ ܐܡܪ ܕܗܘ ᵐܐܒܘܝ : ܘܥܒܕ ܢܦܫܗ
19 ⁿܫܘܝܐ ܠܐܠܗܐ : ܐܥܢܝ ܕܝ ܡܪܢܐ ܝܫܘܥ
ܘܐܡܪ ܠܗܘܢ : ‡ ܐܡܝܢ ܐܡܝܢ ᵒܐܡܪ ᵖܐܢܐᵒ
ܠܟܘܢ : ܕܠܐ ᵠܝܟܝܠ ܒܪܐ ܕܝܥܒܕ ᵗ ʳܟܘܠܡ
ܡܢ ܢܦܫܗ : ܐܠܐ ܡܐ ˢܕܝܚܡܐ ᵗܐܒܘܝܗ
ܥܒܕ : ᵘܡܐ ܕܝ ܕܗܘ ܥܒܕ ܗܠܝܢ ܐܘܦ ܒܪܐ
20 ᵛܥܡ ʷܘܥܒܘܕ ܥܒܕʷ : ܐܒܐ ܕܝ ܪܚܡ ˣܠܒܪܐ
ܘܟܘܠܐ ܗܘ ʸܡܚܘܝ ܠܗ : ᶻܡܐ ܕܗܘ ܥܒܕ
ᵃܘܪܒܝܢ ܡܢ ܗܠܝܢ ܥܒܕܝܐ ܗܘ ᵇܡܚܘܝ
ܠܗ ᶻ : ᵈܠܬܠܝܠ ܕܐܢܬܘܢ ᵉܬܗܘܘܢ ᶠܬܡܗܝܢ :
21 ܗܝܟ ܡܐ ܕܝ ܕܐܒܐ ܡܩܝܡ ᵍܠܡܝܬܝܐ
ʰܘܡܚܝܐ ܠܗܘܢ : ⁱܗܟܕܝܢ ܐܘܦ ܒܪܐ ᵏܠܡܢ

Codex C.

ˢܒܫܥܬ
ᵘܬܬܚܘܒܘܢ ʷܒܘܒܕܝ
ʸܘܡܫܬܒܩܐ
ᶻܒܘܒܕܝ

ᶜܝܫܘܥ
ᶻ *omit* ܐܡܪ ܡܪܝܐ
ᵇܘܬܠܝܠ
ᵉܪܕܦܝܢ
ᶠܥܡܠ

ᵏܕܐܘܦ ˡܗܘܐ
ᵐܐܒܘܝ ⁿܫܘܐ
ᵖ *omit* ܐܢܐ
ᵠܝܟܠ
ʳܟܘܠܡ (*sic*)
† f. 10a.
ᵗܐܒܘܝ
ᵘ *omit* ܡܐ . . . ܥܒܕ
ʷܘܥܒܘܕ ܥܒܕʷ
ˣܠܒܪܗ ʸܡܚܘܝ
ᶻ *omit* ܡܐ . . . ܠܗ
ᶠܬܡܗܝܢ
ᵍ *omit* ܠ ʰܘܡܚܝܐ
ᵏܠܡܢ

Codex A. (continued)

ᵃܡܪܐܗ ᵃ
ᵇ *add* ܐܠܗܟܘܢ
ܐܠܦܢܘܗܝ
ᶜܝܫܘܥ
ʸ *omit* ܘܒܝܬܗ
ܡܪܘܕܦܐ
ᵃ *add* ܠܬܠܡܝܕܘ
ᵇܘܬܠܝܠ ᶜܥܕ
ᵈܝܗܘܕܝܢ ᶠܥܡܠ
ᵍܠܬܠܝܠ ʰܥܕ
ⁱܝܗܘܕܝܢ
‡ f. 9b.
ʲܕܝܩܛܠܘܢ
ᵏܕܐܘܦ ˡܗܘܐ
ᵐܐܒܘܝ ⁿܫܘܐ
ᵒܐܡܪܢܐ ᵠܝܟܠ
ˢܕܝܚܡܐ ᵗܐܒܘܝ
ᵛܥܡ ʷܘܥܒܘܕ ܥܒܕʷ
ᵃܘܪܒܝܢ ᵇܡܚܘܝ
ᵈܠܬܠܝܠ ᵉܬܗܘܘܢ
ᵍ *omit* ܠ ⁱܗܟܕ

Codex A.

ܫܠܡ [f]

[g] *add* ܕܟܘܠܗܘܢ ܝܗܘܢ
ܡܝܩܪܝܢ ܠܒܪܐ

ܕܫܠܚ [j] ܐܡܪܢܐ [k]

ܒܕܝ [m]

ܕܫܠܚ [n] ܗܘܐ [o]

ܚܝܝܢ [p] ܕܠܥܠܡ [q]

ܥܒܪ [r]

Codex B.

22 ܕܝܢܐ ܗܘ [f] ܡܫܠܡ : ܐܒܐ ܓܪ ܠܐܢܫ ܠܐ
23 ܕܐܝܢ : ܐܠܐ ܟܘܠܗ ܕܝܢܐ ܝܗܒ ܠܒܪܐ : [g] ܗܟܢ
ܟܡܐ [h] ܕܡܝܩܪܝܢ ܠܐܒܐ : ܡܢ ܕܠܐ ܡܝܩܪ
ܠܒܪܐ ܠܐ ܡܝܩܪ ܠܐܒܐ [i] ܠܕܝܢ [j] ܕܫܠܚ
24 ܝܬܗ : ܐܡܝܢ ܐܡܝܢ [k] ܐܡܪ ܐܢܐ [k] ܠܟܘܢ :
[l] ܕܡܢ ܕܫܡܥ ܡܠܝ ܘܡܗܝܡܢ [m] ܒܕܝܢ
[n] ܕܫܠܚ ܝܬܝ [o] ܐܝܬ ܠܗ [p] ܚܝܝܢ [q] ܕܠܥܠܡ
ܘܠܕܝܢܐ ܠܐ ܐܬܐ : ܐܠܐ [r] ܥܒܪ ܡܢ
ܡܘܬܐ ܠܚܝܝܐ [s] ⁘

Codex C.

ܡܫܠܡ [f]

[g] *add* ܕܟܘܠܗܘܢ ܝܗܘܢ
ܡܝܩܪܝܢ ܠܒܪܐ

[h] ܕܡܝܩܪܝܢ (*sic*)

ܘܠܕܝܢ [i] ܕܫܠ [j]

[l] *omit* ܕ

ܕܫܠܚ [n] ܗܘܐ [o]

ܥܒܪ [r]

[s] *add* ܕܠܥܠܡ

XII.

John V. 25—30.

Codex A.

[b] *omit* ܐܬܒܫܪ

[c] *omit* ܡܢ

ܐܡܪܢܐ [z]

ܕܐܬܝܐ [a]

‡ f. 10*a*.

ܚܝܝܢ [b] ܚܝܝܢ [c]

ܗܒ [d] ܝܗܒ [e]

ܒܩܒܪܝܗܘܢ [f]

ܘܢܦܩܘܢ [h]

ܕܕܝܢ [i]

[k] *omit* ܘܗܠܝܢ . . .
. . . ܕܚܝܝܢ

ܢܟܠ [l] [m] *add* ܐܢܐ

ܕܗܕ [q]

ܕܫܠܚ [r]

Codex B.

[f. 10*a*]
[b a] ܐܬܒܫܪ ܒܗ ܐܠܝܫܥ [c] ܡܢ ܐܦܘܣܛܘܠܗ
25 ܡܢ ܝܘܚܢܢ [a] ܐܡܪ ܡܪܐ ܐܡܝܢ ܐܡܝܢ
[z] ܐܡܪ ܐܢܐ [z] ܠܟܘܢ : [a] ܕܐܬܝܐ ܫܥܬܐ ܘܟܒܪ
ܗܝ ܕܟܕ ܝܫܡܥܘܢ ܡܝܬܐ ܩܠܗ ܕܒܪܗ
26 ܕܐܠܗܐ : ܘܗܠܝܢ ‡ ܕܫܡܥܝܢ [b] ܚܝܝܢ : ܗܟܢ ܟܡܐ
ܓܪ ܕܐܒܐ ܒܗܘ [c] ܚܝܝܢ ܒܩܢܘܡܗ : [d] ܗܟܢ [e] ܝܗܒ
27 ܐܘܦ ܠܒܪܐ ܚܝܝܢ ܕܢܗܘܘܢ ܒܗ ܒܩܢܘܡܗ : ܘܫܘܠܛܢܐ
ܝܗܒ ܠܗ ܕܝܥܒܕ ܕܝܢܐ ܕܗܘ ܒܪܗ ܕܓܒܪܐ :
28 ܠܐ ܬܬܡܗܘܢ ܒܗܕܐ ܕܐܬܝܐ ܫܥܬܐ ܗܕܐ
ܕܒܗ ܟܘܠ ܗܠܝܢ ܕܒܩܒܘܪܬܐ [f] ܝܫܡܥܘܢ
29 [g] ܩܠܗ [h] ܘܢܦܩܘܢ : ܗܠܝܢ ܕܥܒܕܘ ܛܒܬܐ
ܠܩܝܡܬܐ [i] ܕܚܝܝܢ : [k] ܘܗܠܝܢ ܕܥܒܕܘ ܒܝܫܬܐ
30 ܠܩܝܡܬܐ ܕܕܝܢ : ܠܝܬ ܐܢܐ [l] ܝܟܠ [m] ܕܐܥܒܕ
ܟܘܠܡ ܡܢ [n] ܢܦܫܝ : ܗܟܢ ܟܡܐ ܕܐܫܡܥ
ܐܢܐ ܕܐܢ : ܘܕܝܢܝ ܕܝܠܝ [o] ܩܫܝܛ ܗܘ : ܕܠܝܬ
ܐܢܐ [p] ܒܥܐ ܨܒܝܢܝ ܕܝܠܝ : ܐܠܐ [q] ܕܗܕܝܢ
[r] ܕܫܠܚ ܝܬܝ ⁘

Codex C.

[a] ܬܐܒܫܪ ܒܗ
ܐܦܘܣܛܘܠܗ ܕܝܘ
ܐܠܝܫܥ ܡܢ ܣܘܢܐ
ܘܟܬܒܗ [a]

ܕܐܬܝܐ [a]

ܚܝܝܢ [b]

ܚܝܝܢ [c] ܝܗܒ [e]

ܡܠܟܗ [g] ܕܕܝܢ [i]

[k] *omit* ܘܗܠܝܢ . . .
. . . ܕܚܝܝܢ

ܡܢܠ [l] ܪܚܡܘ [n]

† f. 10*a*.

ܡܥܛ [o]

ܒܥܐ [p] ܗܕܝܢ [q]

ܕܫܠܚ [r]

XIII.

John V. 31—VI. 2.

Codex B.

[a]ܬܬܠܬ ܒܥܪ[b] ܗܘܐ ܐܠܗܐܘܬܗ [c]ܡܢ ܐܒܘܗ[c]
25 ܐܬܝܗܒܬܗ ܡܢ ܗܘܝܘܗܝ[a]:[z] ܐܡܪ ܡܪܢ ܐܡܝܢ
31 ܐܡܝܢ [a]ܐܡܪ ܐܢܐ[a] ܠܟܘܢ : ܐܢ ܐܢܐ
[b]ܡܣܗܕ ܥܠ [c]ܢܦܫܝ ܣܗܕܘܬܝ ܠܝܬ ܗܝ
32 [d]ܩܫܝܛܐ : [e]ܚܘܪܢ [f]ܕܝ ܗܘ [g]ܗܕܝܢ [h]ܕܡܣܗܕ
ܥܠ ܕܝܠܝ : ܘܝܕܥ ܐܢܐ [i]ܕܩܘܫܛܐ ܗܝ
ܣܗܕܘܬܗ : ܗܕܐ ܕܗܘ [k]ܡܣܗܕ ܥܠ ܕܝܠܝ :
33 ܐܢܬܘܢ ܫܠܚܬܘܢ ܠܘܬ [l]ܝܘܚܢܢ ܘܐܣܗܕ ܥܠ
34 ܩܘܫܛܐ : ܐܢܐ ܕܝ ܡܢ ܒܪܢܫ ܠܝܬ ܐܢܐ
ܢܣܒ ܣܗܕܘ : ܐܠܐ ܐܢܐ ܗܠܝܢ ܐܡܪ
35 ܕܐܢܬܘܢ [m]ܬܚܝܘܢ : [n]ܗܘܐ [o]ܗܘ ܒܘܨܝܢܐ
[f. 10b]
[p]ܕܕܠܩ [q]ܘܡܢܗܪ : ܐܢܬܘܢ [r]ܕܝ ܒܥܝܬܘܢ
36 ‡[s]ܕܬܬܚܕܘܢ [t]ܠܫܥܬܐ ܒܢܗܘܪܗ : ܐܢܐ ܕܝ
ܒܥܝ ܣܗܕܘ ܪܒܐ ܡܢ [u]ܝܘܚܢܢ : ܒܥܒܕܐ
ܕܝ ܗܠܝܢ ܕܝܗܒ ܠܝ ܐܒܐ ܕܐܫܠܡ ܝܬܗܘܢ :
[v]ܝܬܗ ܒܥܒܕܐ ܗܠܝܢ ܕܐܢܐ ܥܒܕ ܡܣܗܕܝܢ
37 ܥܠ ܕܝܠܝ ܕܐܒܐ [w]ܫܠܚܢܝ ܝܬܝ ܘܐܒܐ
[x]ܕܫܠܚܢܝ ܝܬܝ ܗܘ [y]ܡܣܗܕ ܥܠ ܕܝܠܝ : [z]ܗܕܝܢ
ܕܩܠܗ [a]ܡܢ ܝܘܡܟܘܢ ܠܐ ܫܡܥܬܘܢ[a] :
38 ܘܚܙܘܗ ܠܐ ܚܡܝܬܘܢ : [b]ܘܡܠܬܝ ܠܝܬ
ܗܝ [c]ܡܒܝܬܐ ܒܟܘܢ : [d]ܕܗܕܝܢ ܕܫܠܚ[e]
39 ܗܘ ܠܝܬ ܐܢܬܘܢ [f]ܡܗܝܡܢܝܢ : ܦܫܦܫܘ ܒܟܬܒܐ
ܕܐܢܬܘܢ ܣܒܪܝܢ ܕܒܗܘܢ ܠܟܘܢ [g]ܚܝܝ
[h]ܕܠܥܠܡ : ܘܗܢܘܢ ܡܣܗܕܝܢ ܥܠ ܕܝܠܝ :
40 ܘܠܝܬ ܐܢܬܘܢ ܨܒܝܢ ܕܬܝܬܘܢ ܠܘܬܝ : ܕܗܘܐ
41 ܠܟܘܢ [g]ܚܝܝ : ܫܘܒܚܐ ܡܢ ܒܢܝܢܫ ܠܝܬ
42 ܐܢܐ ܢܣܒ : [i]ܐܠܐ ܐܚܙܬ ܝܬܟܘܢ ܕܪܚܡܬܗ
43 ܕܐܠܗܐ ܠܝܬ ܗܝ [j]ܒܟܘܢ : ܐܢܐ ܐܬܝܬ

Codex A.

[b] *omit* ܒܥܪ
[c] *omit* ܡܢ ܐܒܘܗ
[z] *add* ܝܫܘܥ
[a]ܐܡܪܢܐ
[c] *omit* ܢܦܫܝ
[d]ܩܫܝܛܐ [f] *omit* ܕܝ
[g]ܗܕܝܢ [h]ܕܡܣܗܕ
[i]ܕܩܫܝܛܐ [k]ܡܣܗܕ
[n]ܗܘܐ [o]ܗܘܐ
[s]ܕܬܬܚܕܘܢ
‡ f. 10b.
[t]ܠܫܥܬܐ [u]ܕܝܘܚܢܢ
[v]ܝܬܗܘܢ
[w]ܫܠܚ [x]ܕܫܠܚ
[y]ܡܣܗܕ [z]ܗܕܝܢ
[b]ܘܡܠܬܗ
[c]ܡܒܝܬܐ
[d]ܕܗܕܝܢ [e] *add* ܝܬܝ
[g]ܚܝܝ
[h]ܕܠܥܠܡ
[j]ܒܟܘܢ

Codex C.

[a]ܐܬܝܗܒܬ ܒܥܪ
ܐܒܘܗ ܐܬܝܗܒܬܗ
ܗܘܐ ܐܠܗܐܘܬܗ ܡܢ
ܚܝܝܐ ܘܒܫܠܝܛܘܬܗ
ܦܪܘܫܘܬܐ[a]
[b]ܡܣܗܕ
[c] *omit* ܢܦܫܝ
[d]ܩܫܝܛܐ [e]ܚܘܪܢ
[f] *omit* ܕܝ
[i]ܕܩܫܝܛܐ [l]ܝܘܚܢܢ
[m]ܬܚܝܘܢ [o]ܗܘܐ
[p]ܕܕܠܩ [q]ܘܡܢܗܪ
[r] *omit* ܕܝ
[s]ܕܬܬܚܕܘܢ
[t]ܠܫܥܬܐ [u]ܕܝܘܚܢܢ
[v]ܝܬܗܘܢ
[w]ܫܠܚ [x]ܕܫܠܚ
[a]ܠܐ ܫܡܥܬܘܢ
ܡܢ ܝܘܡܟܘܢ[a]
[b]ܘܡܠܬܗ
[c]ܡܒܝܬܐ [d]ܕܗܕܝܢ
[f]ܡܗܝܡܢܝܢ
† f. 11a.
[g]ܚܝܝ
[i]ܘܠܐ
[j]ܒܟܘܢ

Codex A.	Codex B.	Codex C.
ᵏܐܬܐ	ܒܫܡܗ ܕܐܒܐ : ܘܠܝܬ ܐܢܬܘܢ ܡܩܒܠܝܢ	
ᵒܦܠܚ ᵐomit ܠܝܬ	ܠܝ : ܘܐܢ ᵏܐܬܐ ˡܐܚܪܢ ܒܫܡܗ ܕܓܪܡܗ	ᵏܐܬܐ ˡܐܚܪܢ
ᵖܘܬܫܒܘܚܬܐ	44 ᵐܠܝܬ ܐܢܬܘܢ ܡܩܒܠܝܢ : ܗܝܟ ܐܢܬܘܢ ⁿܝܟܠܝܢ	ⁿܝܟܠܝܢ
ᵠܗܕܝܢ ʳܒܠܚܘܕܘܗܝ	ܕܬܗܝܡܢܘܢ ܘܬܫܒܘܚܬܐ ܩܒܠܝܢ ܡܢ	
ˢܡܩܛܪܓ	ᵒܦܠܚ ܐܢܬܘܢ ܢܣܒܝܢ : ᵖܘܬܫܒܘܚܬܐ ܕܡܢ	
ᵗadd ܠܘܬ ܐܒܐ ܐܢܐ ܡܢ ܕܡܩܛܪܓ ܠܟܘܢ	ܗܕܐ ܕܡܢ ᵠܗܕܝܢ ܕܗܘ ʳܒܠܚܘܕܘܗܝ ܐܠܗܐ	ʳܒܠܚܘܕܘܗܝ
	45 ܠܝܬ ܐܢܬܘܢ ܒܥܝܢ : ܠܐ ܬܗܘܘܢ ܣܒܪܝܢ	
‡ f. 11a.	ܕܐܢܐ ˢܡܩܛܪܓ ‡ ܠܟܘܢ ᵗ: ܡܘܫܐ ܗܕܝܢ	ˢܡܩܛܪܓ ᵘܕܒܠܗ
ᵘܕܒܠܗ	46 ᵘܕܒܠܗ ᵛܣܒܪܬܘܢ : ܐܠܘ ܓܪ ܗܝܡܢܬܘܢ	ᵛܣܒܪܬܘܢ
ᵛܣܒܪܬܘܢ	ܡܗܝܡܢܝܢ ʷܠܡܘܫܐ : ܐܘܦ ܠܝ ˣܗܝܡܢܬܘܢ	ʷomit ܠܡܘܫܐ . . .
ˣܗܝܡܢܬܘܢ	47 ܡܗܝܡܢܝܢ ʷ ܗܘ ᶻܟܬܒܘܝ ܥܠ ܕܝܠܝ : ᵃܐܢ ܕܝܢ [f. 11a]	. . . ܡܗܝܡܢܝܢ
ᶻܟܬܒܝ ᵃܐܢ	ᵇܠܟܬܒܘܝ ܕܗܘ ܠܝܬ ܐܢܬܘܢ ܡܗܝܡܢܝܢ : ܗܝܟ	ᵃܐܢ
ᵇܠܟܬܒܘܗܝ ᶜܠܡ̈ܠܝ	VI. 1 ᶜܠܡܠܝܐ ܕܝܠܝ ܬܗܝܡܢܘܢ : ܘܡܢ ᵈܒܬܪ ܕܒܝܢ ᵈ	ᶜܠܡܠܝ
ᵈܒܬܪܟܢ ᵉܐܙܠ	ᵉܐܙܠ ܠܗ ܡܪܢ ܝܫܘܥ ܠܥܒܪܗ ܕܝܡܐ	ᵉܐܙܠ
ᶠܕܛܒܪܝܐ	2 ܕܓܠܝܠܐ ᶠܕܛܒܪܝܐ : ܘܗܘܐ ᵍܕܒܩ ܠܗ	
ᵍܕܒܩ ʰܐܘܟܠܘܣ	ʰܐܟܠܘܣ ܣܓܝ : ܕܗܘܘ ܚܙܝܢ ܐܬܐ ܕܗܘܐ	ʰܐܘܟܠܘܣ
ⁱܒܝܫ̈ܝܐ	ܥܒܕ ܥܠ ⁱܒܝܫܝܐ ∴	

XIV.

John VI. 14—27.

Codex A.	Codex B.	Codex C.
ܘܐܢܫܐ ܚܙܘ ᵇomit	ᵃ ᵇܘܐܢܫܐ ܚܙܘ ᵇ ܗܘ ܐܬܐ ᶜܕܥܒܕ ܡܢ ᵈܝܫܘܥ :	ᵃܐܢܫܐ ᵈܝܫܘܥ
ᶜadd ܡܢ ܐܠܗܗ ܐܠܗܘܬܗ	14 ᶻܘܒܥܘܬܗ ܡܪܘܫܐ : ᵃܗܝܟ ܒܚܝܫܐ ܕܝ †ܕܚܟܐ	† f. 11b.
ᵃܗ̈ܠܝܢ ᶻadd ܪܒ	ܕܚܡܘ ᵇܐܬܐ ܕܥܒܕ ܡܪܢ ܝܫܘܥ ܗܘܘ	
ᶜadd ܡܢ ᵇܐܬܐ	ܐܡܪܝܢ : ܕܗܕܝܢ ܗܘ ᶜ ܡܢ ᵈܩܘܫܛ ᵉܢܒܝܐ ᶠ	ᵈܩܘܫܛ ᵉܢܒܝܐ
ᵈܩܘܫܛ ᵉܢܒܝܐ		ᶠadd ܕܝܢ
ᶠadd ܕ ᵍܠܥܠܡܐ	15 ܕܐܬܐ ᵍܠܥܠܡܐ : ܘܡܪܢ ʰܝܫܘܥ ܟܕ ܝܕܥ	ᵍܠܥܠܡܐ
ʰܝܕܥ ⁱܕܐܬܘܢ	ܕܗܘܢ ܒܥܝܢ ⁱܕܝܬܘܢ ᵏܘܢܚܛܦܘܢ ܝܬܗ	ⁱܕܐܬܘܢ
ᵏܘܢܚܛܦܘܢ	ܘܡܥܒܕܘܢ ܝܬܗ ʲܡܠܟ : ᵏܐܙܠ ܠܗ ܡܢܗܘܢ	ʲܡܠܟ ᵏܐܙܠ
ᵏܐܙܠ ˡܒܠܚܘܕܘܗܝ	16 ܠܛܘܪܐ ܗܘ ˡܒܠܚܘܕܘܗܝ : ܟܕ ܕܝܢ ܗܘܐ	ˡܒܠܚܘܕܘܗܝ
ᵐܪܡܫܐ	ᵐܪܡܫܐ ܢܚܬܘ ⁿܬܠܡܝܕܘܗܝ :ᵒ ܥܠ ᵖܓܝܦ ܝܡܐ	ᵐܪܡܫܐ
ⁿܬܠܡܝܕܘܗܝ		ⁿܬܠܡܝܕܘܗܝ
ᵖܓܒ ᵠܘܣܠܩܘ	17 ᵠܘܣܠܩܘ ܠܐܠܦܐ : ܘܗܘܘ ܐܬܝܢ ܠܥܒܪܗ ܕܝܡܐ	ᵒadd ܘܗܘ ᵠܘܣܠܩܘ

Codex A.

^s ܕܢܒܥܘ ^u ܚܠܡܘܗܝ
‡ f. 11b.
^w ܒܡܘܒܝܢܐ
^x ܘܡܣܒܒܢܐ
^y ܐܣܦܠܕܝܢ ^z ܫܬܝܢ
^a ܗܘܘ
^b ܬܕܚܠܘܢ
^c ܡܢܗ
^d ܐܟܠܘܣܐ
^e ܐܝܟ ^f ܐܠܗ
^g ܗܢܝ
^h ܬܠܡܝܕܘܗܝ
^i ܬܠܡܝܕܘܗܝ
^l ܘܣܪܝܢܐ
^m ܐܬܝܢ
^o omit ܕܝ
^p ܐܟܠܘܣܐ
^r ܠܐܠܗܐ
^s ܘܐܡܪ
^t ܐܡܪܢܐ ^u ܒܚܝܢ
^v ܠܚܠܠ
‡ f. 12a.
^x add ܐܠܐ
^y ܒܟܠܗ
^z ܘܐܒܝܕܐ
^a ܡܬܩܠܬܐ
^b ܠܢܝܢ ^c ܕܠܝܒܠܡ
^d ܠܗܕܝܢ
^e add ܥܠܡ

Codex B.

ܠܦܘܪ ܢܝܫܗ : ^r ܘܗܘܐ ܡܫܠܝܐ ܚܒܪ ܘܠܐ
ܗܘܐ ܕܐܬܪܐ ܒܗ ܒܗܘ ܡܕܝܢܐ ܫܡܫܘ ܠܘܬܗܘܢ :
18 ܒܟܐ ܕܝ ^s ܕܢܒܥܒ ܙܘܥ ^t ܐܟܪ : ܐܬܬܚܝܠ ܡܠܟܐ
19 ܘܥܡ ܠܗ ^u ܚܠܡܘܗܝ : ܘܗܘܝܢ ^‡ ܕܒܪܘ ^w ܒܡܘܒܢܐ
ܒܦܪܝܢ ^x ܘܡܣܒܒܢܐ ^y ܐܣܦܠܕܝܢ : ܐܝܟ ܬܠܬܝܢ :
ܘܗܘܝܢ ^z ܣܒܘ ܠܡܪܐ ܫܡܫܐ ܡܫܡܠܝܢ ܟܠ
20 ܫܒܐ ܘܡܦܠܓܐ ܠܐܠܗܐ ܘܕܝܠܗ : ^a ܗܘܘ * ܕܝ
21 ܐܡܪ ܠܗܘܢ ܐܢܐ ܗܘ ܠܐ ^b ܬܕܚܠܘܢ : ܗܘܘ
ܕܝ ܒܚܝܢ ܕܫܡܥܘ ܡܢܗ ܠܐܠܗܐ : ܘܒܥܘܐ
ܐܬܒܣܬܪܘ ܐܠܗܐ ^c ܡܢܗ ܒܐܪܒܐ ܠܗܘܢ
22 ܕܗܘܘ ܐܝܠܝܢ : ܘܠܡܘܒܢܐ ܢܘܗܪܐ ܗܘ ^d ܐܟܠܘܣܐ
[f. 11b]
ܕܗܘܐ ^e ܥܡ ܒܒܪܗ ܕܫܒܐ : ܣܒܘ ܕܠܐ ܗܘܬ
ܬܦܢ ^f ܐܠܗܐ ܣܘܪܝ : ܐܠܐ ܐܢ ^g ܗܢܐ ܕܗܠܘ
ܠܗ ^h ܬܠܡܝܕܘܗ ܕܡܪܐ ܫܡܘܢ : ܘܕܠܐ ܟܠ
ܡܪܐ ܫܡܘܢ ܒܥ ^h ܬܠܡܝܕܘܗ ܠܐܠܗܐ : ^† ܐܠܐ
23 ^i ܬܠܡܝܕܘܗܝ ^k ܒܠܫܘܕܗܘܢ ܐܙܠܘ ^l ܘܣܪܝܢ ܐܠܦܝܢ
^m ܐܬܝܢ ܡܢ ^n ܦܠܚܘܐ : ܦܪܝܢ ܠܐܬܪܐ ܗܘ
24 ܕܐܬܠܘ ܠܣܒܐ : ܒܗ ^o ܕܝ ܐܬܒܘܕܝ ܡܪܐ :
ܒܗ ܕܝ ܫܒܐ ^p ܐܟܠܘܣܐ ܕܡܪܐ ܫܡܘܢ
ܠܬܪ ܗܘ ܬܦܢ : ܘܠܐ ^q ܬܠܡܝܕܘܗܝ ܦܠܚܘ ܗܘܝܢ
^r ܠܐܠܗܐ ܘܐܬܘ ܠܦܘܪ ܢܝܫܗ : ܒܚܝܢ ܠܡܪܐ
25 ܫܡܘܢ ܘܐܡܒܣܘ ܢܗܘ ܒܒܪܗ ܕܫܒܐ :
^s ܘܐܡܪܘ ܠܗ ܪܒܝ : ܐܡܪܢܝ ܐܬܬܐ ܠܒܐ :
26 ܐܚܝܒ ܡܪܐ ܫܡܘܢ ܘܐܡܪ ܠܗܘܢ : ܐܡܝܢ
ܐܡܝܢ ^t ܐܡܪ ܐܢܐ ^t ܠܟܘܢ ^u ܒܚܝܢ ^‡ ܐܬܘܢ
ܠܝ ܠܐ ^v ܠܚܠܠܠ ܕܬܚܙܘܢ ^w ܐܬܝܢ ^x :
27 ܕܐܬܠܘܬܘܢ ܡܢ ܠܣܒܐ ܘܫܒܚܬܘܢ : ^y ܒܟܠ
ܠܐ ܡܬܩܠܬܐ ܕܒܒܪܐ ^z ܘܐܒܝܕܐ : ܐܠܐ
^a ܡܬܩܠܬ ܗܕܐ ܕܡܒܬܪܐ ^b ܠܢܝܢ ^c ܕܠܝܒܠܡ :
ܗܕܐ ܕܒܪܗ ܕܠܒܪܐ ܫܒ ܠܒܘܢ ^d ܕܗܕܝܢ
ܠܪ ܣܢܬܦ ܐܒܐ ܐܠܗܐ ^e ∴

Codex C.

^r ܘܗܘܐ
ܕܢܒܥܘ ^t ܐܟܪ
^w ܒܡܘܩܒܢܐ (sic)
^x ܘܡܣܒܒܢܐ
^z ܣܒܝܢ ^a ܗܘ
[* *Sic* in Cod. B.]
^d ܐܟܠܘܣܐ
^e ܐܝܟ
^f ܐܠܗ ^g ܗܢܝ
^h ܬܠܡܝܕܘ
† f. 12a.
^i ܬܠܡܝܕܘ
^k add ܗܘܘ
^l ܘܣܪܝܢ ^n ܦܠܚܘܗ
^o omit ܕܝ
^p ܐܟܠܘܣܐ
^q ܬܠܡܝܕܘ
^w ܐܬܝܢ
^x add ܐܠܐ
^z ܘܐܒܝܕܐ
^a ܡܬܩܠܬܐ
^b ܠܢܝܢ
^d ܠܗܕܝܢ

Codex A. | Codex B. | Codex C.

XV.

Mark XV. 43—XVI. 8.

Codex B.

ܦܪܣܩܒܝ[y] ܗܘܐ ܐܢܫ[z] ܐܬܐ[a] ܡܢ[b c] ܒܬܪ
43 ܐܠܝܣܦ[d] ܡܢ[h] ܪܡܐܬܐܘܣ ܡܕܝܢܬܗ ܡܝܩܪܐ[e] : ܘܐܬܐ
ܒܘܠܘܛ[a] ܕܡܢ[b] ܪܒܢܬܗ : ܒܠܘܛܝܣ[c] ܚܒܪ
ܕܐܘܦ ܗܘ ܗܘܐ ܡܣܟܐ ܠܡܠܟܘܬܗ ܕܐܠܗܐ :
ܘܗܘ[d] ܥܠ ܠܘܬ ܦ̈ܝܠܛܘܣ : ܘܫܐܠ ܦܓܪܗ
44 ܕܝܫܘܥ ܦܝܠܛܘܣ ܕܝ ܬܡܗ[e] ܐܝܟ
[f. 12a]
ܟܒܪ ܡܝܬ : ܘܩܪܐ ܠܩܢܛܪܝܘܢܐ[f] ܘܫܐܠ ܝܬܗ
45 ܐܢ ܟܒܪ ܡܝܬ : ܘܟܕ ܝܕܥ ܡܢ ܩܢܛܪܝܘܢܐ :
46 ܝܗܒ[g] ܡܘܬܢܐ ܦܓܪܐ[h] ܠܝܘܣܦ[i] : ܘܙܒܢ[j]
ܕܝ ܡܢ[k] ܣܕܘܢ[l] † ܘܐܚܬܗ[m] ܝܬܗ ܘܟܪܟܗ
ܒܣܕܘܢܐ[n] : ܘܣܡܗ[o] ܐܫܟܒ[p] ܝܬܗ ܒܩܒܘܪܬܐ
ܕܗܘܬ ܚܨܝܒܐ ܒܟܐܦܐ[q] : ܘܓܠܓܠ[r] ܟܐܦ[s] ܥܠ
47 ܬܪܥܗ[t] ܕܩܒܘܪܬܐ : ܡܪܝܡ ܕܝ ܡܓܕܠܝܬܐ
ܘܡܪܝܡ ܒܪܬ[u] ܝܥܩܘܒ[u] ܘܝܘܣܦ[o] ܚܙܝܢ[v] ܗܘ
XVI. 1 ܗܘܐ ܡܬܬܣܡ[w] : ܘܒܬܪ ܕܝ[x] ܥܒܪ ܫܒܬܐ :
‡ ܡܪܝܡ[y] ܡܓܕܠܝܬܐ ܘܡܪܝܡ[z] ܒܪܬ[a] ܝܥܩܘܒ[b]
ܘܫܠܘܡܝ ܐܙܠܝ ܙܒܢ ܒܣܡܝܢ[c] ܕܐܬܝܢ[d]
2 ܘܡܫܚܢ[e] ܝܬܗ ܠܡܦܪܐ[f] ܘܒܨܦܪܐ ܠܚܕ[g] [h]
ܘܒܫܒܘܥܐ[i] ܗܘܢ[k] ܐܬܝܢ[l] ܥܠ ܩܒܘܪܬܐ
3 ܟܕ [m]ܕܢܚ [n]ܫܡܫܐ : [o]ܘܗܘܝ [p]ܐܡܪܢ[o] [q]ܠܡܩܒܠ
[r]ܡܢܗܘ ܡܢ [s]ܡܓܠܓܠ ܠܢ ܟܐܦܐ ܡܢ [u]ܬܪܥܐ
4 ܕܩܒܘܪܬܐ : [w]ܗܘܬ ܓܝܪ ܪܒܐ ܠܚܕܐ :
5 ܘܥܠܝ ܘܐܫܟܚܝ ܛܠܝܐ ܡܓܠܓܠܐ : ܘܟܕ
[s]ܐܬܝܢ [t]ܠܓܘ ܩܒܘܪܬܐ : [u]ܚܙܝ [v]ܥܠܝܡ
[w]ܝܬܒ ܡܢ ܝܡܝܢܐ ܠܒܝܫ ܐܣܛܠܐ ܚܘܪܐ
6 ܘܕܚܠܝ : ܗܘ ܕܝ ܐܡܪ [x]ܠܗܘܢ ܠܐ [y]ܬܕܚܠܝܢ :
ܠܝܫܘܥ [z]ܢܨܪܝܐ [a]ܐܬܝܢ [b]ܒܥܝܢ [c]ܗܘܝܢ
ܕܐܙܕܩܦ[d] ܠܝܬ ܗܘ ܗܟܐ : ܗܐ ܐܬܪܐ ܗܢ
7 ܕܐܣܒܘܗ ܬܡܢ : ܐܠܐ ܐܙܠܝܢ ܐܡܪܝܢ

Codex A.

[y] omit ܦܪܣܩܒܝ
[a] ܐܬܠܬܠܬ
[c] omit ܡܢ [d] ܐܠܝܣܦ
[a] ܒܘܠܘܛ [b] ܪܒܢܬܗ
[d] ܥܠ [f] ܘܐܬܐ
[g] ܝܗܒ [i] ܠܝܘܣܦ
[j] ܘܙܒܢ [k] ܡܢ
[l] ܣܕܘܢ [m] ܘܐܚܬܗ
[n] ܒܣܕܘܢܐ [o] ܘܣܡܗ
[q] ܒܟܐܦܐ [r] ܘܓܠܓܠ
[t] ܬܪܥܐ
[u] ܐܡܗ ܕܝܥܩܘܒ [u]
[o] ܘܕܝܘܣܦ [v] ܚܙܝܢ
[w] ܡܬܬܣܡ [x] ܥܒܪܬ
[z] ܘܡܪܝܡ
[a] omit ܒܪܬ
[b] ܕܝܥܩܘܒ
[c] ܒܣܡܝܢ
‡ f. 12b.
[d] ܕܐܬܝܢ
[e] ܘܡܫܚܢ [g] ܠܚܕ ܐ
[h] add ܒܚܕ [i] omit ܘ
[k] ܗܘܝܢ [l] ܐܬܝܢ
[m] ܕܢܚ [n] ܫܡܫܐ
[p] ܐܡܪܢ [q] ܠܡܩܒܠ
[s] ܡܓܠܓܠ
[u] ܬܪܥܐ [s] ܥܠܝ
[t] omit ܠܓܘ [u] ܚܙܝܢ
[v] ܥܠܝܡ [w] ܝܬܒ
[x] ܠܗܝܢ [y] ܬܕܚܠܝܢ
[z] ܢܨܪܝܐ [a] ܐܬܝܢ
[b] ܒܥܝܢ [c] ܗܘܝܢ
[d] add ܡܢ

Codex C.

[z] ܠܢܫ
43 ܡܢ . . . ܐܠܝܣܦ [b] omit
[e] add ܐܡܪܐ
[c] ܒܠܘܛܝܣ
[d] ܥܠ
44 [e] ܬܡܗ
46 [g] ܝܗܒ [h] ܦܓܪܗ
† f. 12b.
[i] ܠܝܘܣܦ [l] ܣܕܘܢ
[m] ܘܐܚܬܗ [n] ܒܣܕܘܢܐ
47 [p] ܐܫܟܒ
[s] ܟܐܦܐ [t] ܬܪܥܐ
XVI. 1 [o] ܘܕܝܘܣܦ [w] ܡܬܬܣܡ
[y] add ܕܝ
[c] ܒܣܡܝܢ
2 [d] ܕܐܬܝܢ
[g] ܠܚܕ ܐ [f] add ܒܨܦܪ
3 [i] omit ܘ
[m] ܕܢܚ [n] ܫܡܫܐ
4 [o] ܘܗܘܝ ܐܡܪܢ
5 [r] ܡܢܗܘ
[s] ܡܓܠܓܠ [w] ܗܘ
[s] ܥܠܝ [t] omit ܠܓܘ
6 [w] ܝܬܒ
[a] ܐܬܝܢ [b] ܒܥܝܢ
[d] add ܡܢ

(Left margin, Arabic, vertical:) حديوو الثلث من صبوحيه

Codex B.

ܠܬܠܡܝܕܘܝ[e] ܘܠܦܪ̈ܘܫܝܗ[f] : ܕܗܘܐ [g]ܐܝܟ [h]ܡܥܡܕ
ܠܗܘܢ ܠܓܠܝܠܐ ܬܘܒ † ܘܫܡܥܘܢ ܬܢܗ ܗܘܝ
8 ܗܢܐ ܕܐܡܪ ܠܗܘܢ : ܘܟܕ ܢܦܩ ܡܢ ܡܥܡܘܕܝܬܐ
ܚܙܝܢ ܗܘܐ ܠܗ ܐܬܬܐ ܚܕܐ [f. 12b] [i]ܠܗܘܢ ܘܫ̈ܠܡܐ :
ܘܠܐܝܫ [j]ܒܥܠܡ ܠܐ [k]ܐܡܪܝܢ [l]ܕܫܠܡ [m]ܗܘܘܢ
ܠܟ : [n]ܥܠܡ ∴

XVI.

John IV. 46—54.

[a]ܦܬܓܡܐ [b]ܘܐܬ [b]ܐܬܠܝܡ [c]ܒܗ ܐܣܒܗ [d]ܐܠܬܐܗ
46 ܡܢ [e]ܝܫܘܥ [f]ܘܒܢܝܬܗ ܡܢܝܪܘܬܐ : [z]ܘܗܘܐ
ܚܕ ܡܢ [a]ܕ[b]ܡܠܟܐ ܕܗܝܢ ܕܗܘܐ ܒܪܗ [c]ܟܐܝܒ
47 ܒܟܦܪ ܢܚܘܡ : ‡ [d]ܗܕܝܢ ܟܕ ܫܡܥ [e]ܡܪܝܐ
ܝܫܘܥ ܐܬܐ ܡܢ ܝܗܘܕܐ ܠܓܠܝܠܐ : [f]ܐܙܠ ܠܘܬܗ
[g]ܘܗܘܐ ܒܥܐ ܡܢܗ ܕܢܚܘܬ [h]ܘܝܐܣܐ ܬܢܗ
48 ܠܒܪܗ ܗܘܐ ܓܝܪ ܟܒܪ ܕܢܡܘܬ : ܘܐܡܪ
ܠܗ ܡܪܝܐ [o]ܝܫܘܥ ܐܢ ܠܐ ܐܬܝܢ [i]ܘܬܡܗܝܢ
49 ܬܚܙܘܢ ܠܐ ܬܗܝܡܢܘܢ : ܐܡܪ ܠܗ ܗܘ
[k]ܡܢ [l]ܕܡܠܟܐ : [m]ܡܪܝܐ ܚܘܬ ܥܕ ܠܐ ܡܐܬ
50 ܒܪܝ : ܐܡܪ ܠܗ ܡܪܝܐ ܝܫܘܥ : [n]ܗܐ [f]ܐܙܠ
[o]ܒܪܟ ܚܝ : [p]ܘܗܝܡܢ [q]ܓܒܪܐ ܠܡܠܬܐ
ܕܐܡܪ ܠܗ ܡܪܝܐ ܝܫܘܥ : ܘܗܘܐ [f]ܐܙܠ
51 ܘܟܕ ܗܘ ܢܚܬ ܐܪܥܘ ܝܬܗ [s]ܥܒܕܘܝ ܘܐܡܪܝܢ
52 ܠܗ ܗܐ ܒܪܟ ܚܝ : ܘܗܘܐ ܕܝ ܫܐܠ
ܠܗܘܢ ܠܗ ܚܠ ܠܦܝ ܫܥܬܐ ܕܐܬܢܫܡ ܒܗ :
ܘܐܡܪܘ ܠܗ [t]ܐܬܡܠܝ ܒܫܥܘܒ ܫܒܝܥ ܫܥܘܬ
53 ܬܢܗ [u]ܐܫܬܐ : ܘܝܕܥ [v]ܐܒܘܝ ܕܦܠܓܐ ܕܬܢܗ
[w]ܫܥܬܐ ܐܡܪ ܠܗ ܡܪܝܐ ܝܫܘܥ ܗܐ ܒܪܟ
54 ܚܝ : ܘܗܝܡܢ ܗܘ † ܘܒܝܬܗ ܟܠܗ : ܗܕܝܢ
[x]ܬܒܐ ܐܬܐ ܬܢܝܢܐ ܥܒܕ ܡܪܝܐ ܝܫܘܥ ܟܕ
ܐܬܐ ܡܢ ܝܗܘܕܐ ܠܓܠܝܠܐ : [y]ܥܠܡ ∴

Codex A.

[e]ܠܬܠܡܝܕܘܗܝ
[g] *omit* ܐܝܟ
[h]ܡܥܡܕ [i]ܠܗܘܢ
[j]ܒܥܠܡ
[k]ܐܡܪܝܢ [l]ܕܫܠܡ
[m]ܗܘܘܢ [n]*omit* ܥܠܡ

[a] *omit* ܦܬܓܡܐ
[c] *omit* ܒܗ
[d]ܐܠܬܐܗ
‡ f. 13*a*.
[e]ܝܫܘܥ
[f] *add* ܦܬܚ
[z]ܘܗܘܐ [a]*add* ܚܕ
[b] *omit* ܕ [d]ܗܕܝܢ
[e]ܕܡܪܝܐ [f]ܐܙܠ
[g]ܘܗܘܐ [h]ܘܝܐܣܐ
[i]ܘܬܡܗܝܢ
[k]ܕܡܢ [l]ܡܠܟܐ
[n] *omit* ܗܐ
[o] *add* ܗܐ
[q]*add* ܘܗܐ [s]ܥܒܕܘܗܝ
[t]ܐܬܡܠܝ
[u]ܐܫܬܐ [v]ܐܒܘܗܝ
[x]ܬܒܐ
[y]ܥܠܡ

Codex C.

[e]ܠܬܠܡܝܕܘܝ
† f. 13*a*.
[f]ܘܠܦܪܘܫܝܗ
[g] *omit* ܐܝܟ
[h]ܡܥܡܕ [k]ܐܡܪܝܢ
[n] *omit* ܥܠܡ

[b]ܡܢ ܝܫܘܥ ܘܐܬ
[b]ܐܬܠܝܡ
[e]ܝܫܘܥ
[z]ܘܗܘܐ [c]ܚܝܠ
[g]ܘܗܘܐ
[h]ܘܝܐܣܐ
[o]ܝܫܘܥ
[k]ܕܡܢ ܡܪܝܐ [m]*omit*
[n] *omit* ܗܐ
[o] *add* ܗܐ
[p]ܘܗܝܡܢ
[q] *add* ܘܗܐ
[s]ܥܒܕܘܗܝ
[u]ܐܫܬܐ
[v]ܐܒܘܗܝ *add* ܕܗܝ
† f. 13*b*.
[y]ܥܠܡ

Codex A.	Codex B.	Codex C.

XVII.

John VI. 26—33.

Codex B.

[a] [Syriac] [b] [Syriac] [c] [Syriac] [d] [Syriac]
26 [Syriac] [e] [Syriac] [z] [Syriac] [a] [Syriac]
27 [b] [Syriac] [b] [Syriac] : [c] [Syriac] ‡ [d] [Syriac] [e] [Syriac]
[f. 13a] [Syriac] [f] [Syriac]
[Syriac] [g] [Syriac] [h] [Syriac] [i] [Syriac] :
[Syriac] [j] [Syriac] [k] [Syriac]
28 [Syriac] [l] [Syriac] : [Syriac]
[Syriac] [m] [Syriac] [n] [Syriac] [o] [Syriac]
29 [Syriac] : [Syriac] :
[p] [Syriac] [q] [Syriac] [r] [Syriac] [s] [Syriac]
30 [Syriac] [t] [Syriac] [u] [Syriac] : [Syriac]
[Syriac] [w] [Syriac] : [Syriac] [x] [Syriac] [y] [Syriac]
31 [Syriac] : [Syriac] : [z] [Syriac]
[Syriac] [a] [Syriac] [b] [Syriac] :
[c] [Syriac]
32 [d] [Syriac] : [e] [Syriac] : [Syriac]
[Syriac] : [Syriac]
[Syriac] : [Syriac]
[Syriac] :
33 [f] [Syriac] [g] [Syriac] [h] [Syriac]
[Syriac] : [i] [Syriac]
[Syriac] [k] [Syriac] [l] [Syriac] [m] ⁘

Codex A.

[a] omit [Syriac]
[b] omit [Syriac]
‡ f. 13b.
[d] [Syriac]
[z] add [Syriac] [b] [Syriac]
[c] omit [Syriac]
[d] [Syriac]
[f] [Syriac]
[h] [Syriac] [i] [Syriac]
[j] [Syriac] [k] [Syriac]
[m] [Syriac] [o] [Syriac]
[p] [Syriac] [r] omit [Syriac]
[t] [Syriac] [u] [Syriac]
[w] add [Syriac]
[x] omit [Syriac]
[a] [Syriac] [c] [Syriac]
[d] [Syriac]
[e] add [Syriac]
[f] [Syriac] [g] [Syriac]
[h] [Syriac] [i] [Syriac]
[k] [Syriac] [l] [Syriac]
[m] add [Syriac]

Codex C.

[b] [Syriac] [c] add [Syriac]
[d] [Syriac] [e] [Syriac]
[a] omit [Syriac]
[c] omit [Syriac]
[e] add [Syriac]
[f] [Syriac]
[g] [Syriac] [j] [Syriac]
[k] [Syriac] [l] [Syriac]
[m] [Syriac] [n] [Syriac]
[q] [Syriac]
[r] omit [Syriac]
[s] [Syriac] [w] [Syriac]
[x] omit [Syriac]
[y] [Syriac]
[z] [Syriac]
[b] [Syriac] [c] [Syriac]
[e] add [Syriac]
[g] [Syriac] [h] [Syriac]
[k] [Syriac] [l] [Syriac]
[m] add [Syriac]

XVIII.

John VI. 35—39.

Codex B.

[a] [Syriac] [b c] [Syriac]
35 [d] [Syriac] [c] [Syriac] [e] [Syriac] : [z] [Syriac]
[Syriac] † [Syriac] : [a] [Syriac]

Codex A.

[a] omit [Syriac]
[b] omit [Syriac] [d] [Syriac]
[e] [Syriac]
[z] add [Syriac] [a] [Syriac]

Codex C.

[c] omit [Syriac] ... [Syriac]
[e] [Syriac]
[z] add [Syriac]
† f. 14a.

Codex A.	Codex B.	Codex C.
[b] ܟܦܢ	ܕܐܬܐ ܠܘܬܝ ܠܐ [b]ܟܦܢ [c]ܘܕܗܝܡ ܕܡܗܝܡܢ	
[c] ܘܕܝܢ	36 ܒܝ ܠܐ ܨܗܐ ܠܥܠܡ : ܐܠܐ ܐܡܪܬ ܠܟܘܢ	
‡ f. 14a.	ܘܚܙܝܬܘܢ ܝܬܝ ‡ܘܠܝܬ ܐܢܬܘܢ [d]ܡܗܝܡܢܝܢ :	[d] ܡܗܝܡܢܝܢ
[e] ܘܚܙܝܬܘܢ	37 ܟܘܠ ܡܐ ܕܝܗܒ ܠܝ ܐܒܐ ܠܘܬܝ ܐܬܐ :	
[f] ܡܦܩ	[e]ܘܗܕܝܢ ܕܐܬܐ ܠܘܬܝ ܠܝܬ ܐܢܐ [f]ܡܦܩܝܢ	[f] ܡܦܩܝܢ
[g] ܕܢܦܫܝ	38 ܠܗ ܠܒܪ ܕܢܚܬܬ ܡܢ ܓܘ ܫܡܝܐ : ܠܐ [f. 13b]	[g] ܕܢܦܫܐ
[h] ܨܒܝܢܐ	[g]ܗܘܐ ܐܢܐ ܥܒܕ [h]ܨܒܝܢܗ ܕܢܦܫܝ : ܐܠܐ	[h] ܨܒܝܢܐ
[i] ܕܗܕܝܢ [l] add ܕܝܢ	39 ܨܒܝܢܗ ܕܐܒܐ [i]ܗܕܝܢ ܕܫܠܚ ܝܬܝ : ܗܕܝܢ[l]	[l] add ܕ
[k] ܕܫܠܚܢܝ [m] omit ܐܒܐ	ܗܘ ܨܒܝܢܗ ܕܐܒܐ ܕܗܒ [k]ܕܫܠܚܢܝ ܝܬܝ	
[n] ܝܒܕ [p] ܒܥܒܪܬܐ	ܕܟܘܠ ܡܐ ܕܝܗܒ ܠܝ [m]ܐܒܐ ܠܐ [n]ܝܘܒܕ	[m] omit ܐܒܐ
[q] add ܥܠܡ	ܡܢܗ : ܐܠܐ [o]ܝܩܝܡ ܝܬܗ ܒܝܘܡܐ [p]ܒܚܪܬܐ[q] ܀	[n] ܝܒܕ [o] ܝܩܝܡ

XIX.

John VI. 40—44.

Codex A.	Codex B.	Codex C.
[a] omit ܬܫܡܫܬ ܨܦܪ	[a]ܬܫܡܫܬ ܨܦܪ ܝܘܡ ܐܠܚܡܝܣ [b][c]ܦܝ ܐܣܒܘܥܗ	[c] omit ܐܬܠܬܗ ... ܦܝ
[b] omit ܦܝ	[d]ܐܬܠܬܗ[c] ܡܢ [e]ܝܘܚܢܢ : ܘܟܬܒܗ ܡܪܩܘܣܐ[x]	[e] ܝܘܚܢܢ
[d] ܐܬܠܬܗ	40 [y]ܗܕܝܢ ܓܝܪ [z]ܐܝܬܘܗܝ ܨܒܝܢܗ [a]ܕܗܕܝܢ ܕܫܠܚ	[z] ܐܝܬܘܗܝ [b] ܠܐܒܐ
[e] ܝܘܚܢܢ	ܝܬܝ [b]ܐܒܐ : [c]ܕܟܘܠ ܡܢ ܕܚܡܐ ܠܒܪܐ [d]ܘܗܝܡܢ	[d] ܘܗܝܡܢ
[x] add ܐܡܪ ܡܪܢ ܝܫܘܥ	ܒܗ [e]ܝܗܘܐ ܠܗ [f]ܚܝܝ [g]ܕܠܥܠܡ : ܘܐܢܐ	[e] omit ܝܗܘܐ
[y] ܗܕܝܢ [a] ܕܗܕܝܢ	41 [h]ܡܩܝܡ ܠܗ ܒܝܘܡܐ [i]ܒܚܪܬܐ : ܘܗܘܘ	[f] ܚܝܝܢ [h] ܡܩܝܡ
[c] omit ܕ [d] ܘܗܝܡܢ	[k]ܝܘܕܝܐ [l][m]ܡܪܢܢܝܢ [n]ܥܠܘܝ : ܕܐܡܪ ܐܢܐ [o]ܗܘ	[l] add ܕܝܢ [m] ܡܪܢܢܝܢ
[f] ܚܝܝܢ [g] ܕܠܥܠܡ	42 ܠܚܡܐ [p]ܕܢܚܬܬ ܡܢ ܓܘ ܫܡܝܐ : ܘܗܘܘ	[n] ܥܠܘܗܝ [o] omit ܗܘ
[i] ܒܚܪܬܐ	ܐܡܪܝܢ [a]ܠܐ [q]ܗܕܝܢ ܗܘ ܝܫܘܥ ܒܪܗ [r]ܕܝܘܣܦ :	[p] ܕܢܚܬܬ
[k] ܝܘܕܝܐ [l] add ܕܝܢ	[q]ܗܕܝܢ ܕܐܢܢ ܡܟܝܪܝܢ [s]ܐܒܘܝ [t]ܘܐܡܗ ܗܝܟ	[a] ܠܗ [s] ܐܒܘܗܝ
[n] ܥܠܘ [p] ܕܢܚܬܬ	ܗܘ ܗܕܘ ܐܡܪ ܕܡܢ ܓܘ ܫܡܝܐ ܢܚܬܬ :	[t] ܘܐܡܗ
[q] ܗܕܝܢ [r] ܕܝܘܣܦ	43 [u]ܐܓܝܒ ܕܝܢ ܝܫܘܥ ܘܐܡܪ ܠܗܘܢ	[u] ܐܓܝܒ [w] ܐܢܫ
[s] ܐܒܘܝ [v] ܦܠܓ	44 ܠܐ ܬܪܛܢܘܢ ܦܠܓܘܢ ܥܡ [v]ܦܠܓ : [w]ܐܢܫ ܠܐ	[x] omit ܡܨܐ
[x] ܡܨܐ [y] ܕܝܬܐ	[x]ܡܨܐ [y]ܕܝܬܐ ܠܘܬܝ : ܐܠܐ ܐܢ ܐܒܐ	[y] ܕܝܬܐ [z] ܡܩܝܡ
[a] ܒܚܪܬܐ	ܕܫܠܚ ܝܬܝ ܝܓܪܕ ܝܬܗ : ܘܐܢܐ [z]ܡܩܝܡ ܠܗ	[a] ܒܚܪܬܐ
	ܒܝܘܡܐ [a]ܒܚܪܬܐ ܀ [b]ܥܠܡ	[b] omit ܥܠܡ

Codex A. | **Codex B.** | **Codex C.**

XX.

John VI. 48—54.

Codex B.

[a]ܒܙܒܢ ܗܘ [b]ܐܬܟܬܫܘܗܝ [d][c]ܥܡ ܐܘܚܕܗ
[e]ܐܬܠܬܗ [d] ܡܢ [f]ܝܗܘܕܝܐ[g]: [z]†‡ ܐܡܪ ܡܪܢ
47 [a]ܐܬܘ [b]ܡܗܝܡܢܐ ܐܡܝܢ ܐܡܝܢ ܐܡܪ ܐܢܐ ܠܟܘܢ
48 49 ܐܢܐ ܗܘ ܠܚܡܐ ܕܚܝܐ: ܐܒܗܬܟܘܢ ܐܟܠܘ
50 ܡܢܢܐ [e]ܒܡܕܒܪܐ ܘܡܝܬܘ: [f]ܗܕܝܢ ܗܘ
ܠܚܡܐ [g]ܗܕܝܢ ܕܡܢ [h]ܫܡܝܐ [i]ܢܚܬ:
51 [k]ܕܐܢܫ ܢܐܟܘܠ ܐܢܫ ܡܢܗ ܘܠܐ ܢܡܘܬ: ܐܢܐ
ܗܘ ܠܚܡܐ [l]ܕܚܝܐ [m]ܕܡܢ ܠܗ [n]ܘ ܫܡܝܐ
[f. 14a]
[o]ܢܚܬ ܡܢ [q]ܕܐܟܠ ܡܢ [f]ܗܕܝܢ ܠܚܡܐ [s]ܚܝܐ
[t]ܠܥܠܡ: ܘܠܚܡܐ [u]ܕܐܢܐ ܝܗܒ ܗܘ ܒܣܪܝ
ܗܕܝܢ [x]ܕܐܢܐ ܝܗܒ ܥܠ ܐܦܝ [w]ܚܝܘܗܝ
52 [y][x]ܕܥܠܡܐ: ܘܗܘܘ [z]ܝܗܘܕܝܐ ܢܚܝܢ ܦܠܓܘܗܝ
ܡܢ [a]ܦܠܓܗ ܘܐܡܪܝܢ: ܗܟܢ [b]ܗܕܝܢ [c]ܡܫܟܚ
[d]ܕܢܬܠ ܠܢ ܒܣܪܗ ܕܢܐܟܘܠ ܡܢܗ: ܘܐܡܪ
53 ܠܗܘܢ ܡܪܢ ܝܫܘܥ: [e]ܐܡܝܢ ܐܡܪ ܐܢܐ
ܠܟܘܢ [f]ܕܐܢ ܠܐ [g]ܬܐܟܠܘܢ ܒܣܪܗ ܕܒܪܗ
ܕܐܢܫܐ ܘܬܫܬܘܢ ܐܕܡܗ: ܠܝܬ ܚܝܐ ܒܟܘܢ
54 [h]ܚܝܝ ܒܟܘܢ: [i]ܘܡܢ [j]ܕܐܟܠ ܒܣܪܝ ܘܫܬܐ
ܐܕܡܝ ܗܘ ܒܗ [k]ܚܝܝ [l]ܕܠܥܠܡ: ܘܐܢܐ
[m]ܡܩܝܡ ܐܢܐ ܠܗ ܒܝܘܡܐ [n]ܚܪܝܐ [o]ܥܠܡ

Codex A.

[a] omit ܒܙܒܢ
‡ f. 14b.
[b] ܐܬܟܬܫܘܗܝ
[c] omit ܥܡ [e] ܐܬܠܬܗ
[g] add ܠܬܠܡܝܕܘܗܝ (sic)
[z] add ܝܫܘܥ
[a] omit ܐܬܘ [b] ܠܗܝܡܢܘܬܝ
[e] ܒܡܕܒܪܐ
[f] ܗܢܘ [g] omit ܗܕܝܢ
[h] add ܠܗ [i] ܢܚܬ
[l] ܚܝܐ [n] ܡܢ
[o] ܢܚܬ [q] ܕܐܟܠ
[s] ܚܝܐ [y] ܕܥܠܡܐ
[z] ܝܗܘܕܝܐ [a] ܦܠܓܗ
[b] ܗܢܐ [d] ܕܢܬܠ
[e] add ܐܡܝܢ
[g] ܬܐܟܠܘܢ
[h] ܚܝܝ [i] omit ܘ
[j] ܕܐܟܠ [k] ܚܝܝ
[l] ܕܠܥܠܡ [n] ܒܚܪܝܐ

Codex C.

[b] ܐܬܟܬܫܘܗܝ
† f. 14b.
ܥܡ ... ܐܬܠܬܗ [d] omit
[f] ܝܗܘܕܝܐ
[z] add ܘܡܪܢ
ܝܫܘܥ
[b] ܕܡܢܐ
[h] add ܠܗ [i] ܢܚܬ
[k] ܕܐܟܠ [l] ܚܝܐ
[q] ܕܐܟܠ
[s] ܚܝܐ [t] ܠܥܠܡ
[u] ܕܐܢܐ
[w] omit ܚܝܘ
[x] omit ܕ [z] ܝܗܘܕ
[b] omit ܗܕܝܢ
[c] ܡܫܟܚ [d] ܕܢܬܠ
[e] add ܐܡܝܢ [f] ܕܐܢ
[h] ܚܝܝ [i] omit ܘ
[j] ܕܐܟܠ [k] ܚܝܝ
[m] ܡܩܝܡ [o] omit ܥܠܡ

XXI.

John XV. 17—XVI. 2.

Codex B.

[a]ܦܩܕ ܘܒܙܒܢ ܗܘ ܐܬܠܬܗ[b] ܡܢ [c]ܝܫܘܥ:[a]
[z]ܘܡܪܢ ܝܫܘܥ[z] ܐܡܪ ܡܪܢ [a]ܠܬܠܡܝܕܘܗܝ

Codex A.

[a]ܒܙܒܢ ܗܘ ܐܬܟܬܫ
ܐܡܪ ܗܘܐ ܐܬܠܬܗ
ܡܢ ܝܫܘܥ[a]
[z] omit ܘܡܪܢ
ܝܫܘܥ
[a]ܠܬܠܡܝܕܘܗܝ

Codex C.

[b]add ܐܬܠܬܗ ܐܡܪ
[c]ܝܫܘܥ
[z] omit ܘܡܪܢ
ܝܫܘܥ
[a]ܠܬܠܡܝܕܘܗܝ

Codex A.	Codex B.	Codex C.
[b] ܒܡܫܝܚܐ	17 ܗܠܝܢ ܐܡܪ [b] ܡܫܝܚܐ ܠܗܘܢ ܕܢܬܗܘܢ ܡܗܝܡܢܝܢ	[b] ܡܫܝܚܐ
[c] ܠܥܠܡܐ [e] ܫܠܝܚܬܐ	18 ܘܠܟܠܗܘܢ [c] ܠܥܠܡܐ : [d] ܐܝܟ ܐܢܬ [e] ܫܠܝܚܬܐ	[d] ܐܝܟ [g] ܗܢܘ
[f] ܦܐܡܪܝܢ [h] ܕܝ	ܗܢܐ ܢܬܒܥܘܢ : ܢܣܒܝܢ ܐܢܬܘܢ ܕܠܝ [f] ܡܫܚܐ	
[i] ܗܘܐ	ܡܢܗܘܢ [g] ܗܢܐ : ܐܠܘ † ܗܘܝܬܘܢ ܡܢ [h] ܕܝܢ	† f. 15a.
‡ f. 15a.	19 [e] ܫܠܝܚܬܐ : ‡ [e] ܫܠܝܚܬܐ ܠܕܝܠܗ [i] ܗܘ ܪܚܝܩ	[i] ܗܘܐ
[l] ܕܠܝܬ [m] ܗܕܝܢ	[o] ܠܟܠܟ ܕܝ [l] ܠܝܬ ܐܢܬܘܢ ܡܢ [m] ܗܕܝܢ [e] ܫܠܝܚܬܐ :	[l] ܕܠܝܬ
	[n] ܐܠܐ ܐܢܐ ܒܨܒܘܬ ܢܬܒܥܘܢ ܡܢ [e] ܫܠܝܚܬܐ [n]	[n] ܐܠܐ ... *omit* ... ܫܠܝܚܬܐ
[o] ܠܟܠܟ [p] ܒܕܝ	20 [o] ܠܟܠܟ [p] ܒܕܝܢ [e] ܫܠܝܚܬܐ ܗܢܐ ܢܬܒܥܘܢ : ܗܘܘ	
	[q] ܒܕܝܢ ܡܠܬܐ ܗܕܐ ܕܡܠܠܬ ܠܗܘܢ : ܕܠܝܬ	[q] ܒܕܝܢ
	ܒܪܐ ܙܒ ܡܢ ܡܪܗ : [r] ܐܝܟ ܠܝ ܙܕܩܐ ܐܘܦ	[r] ܐܝܟ
	ܠܗܘܢ ܗܘܝܢ ܙܕܩܝܢ : ܐܠܘ ܢܛܪܘ ܡܠܬܝ	
	21 ܐܘܦ ܕܝܠܗܘܢ ܗܘܘ ܡܛܪܝܢ : ܐܠܐ ܒܗܠ	
[s] ܠܟܠܟ	ܗܠܝܢ ܡܒܕܝܢ ܠܗܘܢ [s] ܠܟܠܟ ܫܡܝ : ܕܠܐ	
[t] ܕܫܕܪܢ	22 ܡܒܪܝܢ ܠܕܝܢ [t] ܕܫܕܪܢ ܢܬܝ : ܐܠܘ ܠܐ ܐܬܝܬ [f. 14b]	[t] ܕܫܕܪܢ
	ܘܡܠܠܬ ܠܗܘܢ ܚܛܝܐ ܠܐ ܗܘܐ ܠܗܘܢ :	
	ܒܪܘ ܕܝ ܥܠܬܐ ܠܝܬ ܠܗܘܢ ܥܠ ܚܛܗܝ	
[u] ܫܒܩܬܗܘܢ	23 [u] ܫܒܩܬܗܘܢ : ܡܢ ܕܣܢܐ ܠܝ ܐܘܦ ܠܐܒܐ	
	24 ܗܘ ܣܢܐ : ܐܠܘ ܠܐ ܕܥܒܕܬ ܒܥܒܕܐ	
	ܒܗܘܢ ܡܢ ܕܐܢܫ [v] ܚܘܪܢ ܠܐ ܥܒܕ :	[v] ܚܘܪܢ [w] ܗܘܐ
	ܫܠܝܐ ܠܐ [w] ܗܘܬ ܠܗܘܢ : [x] ܒܪܘ ܕܝ ܚܙܘ	[x] ܒܪ [y] ܕܬܫܠܡ
[y] ܕܬܫܠܡ	25 ܘܣܢܘ ܐܘܦ ܠܝ ܘܠܐܒܐ : ܐܠܐ [y] ܕܬܫܠܡ	[z] ܕܟܬܝܒܐ
	ܡܠܬܐ ܗܕܐ [z] ܕܟܬܝܒܐ [a] ܒܢܡܘܣܗܘܢ	[a] ܒܢܡܘܣܗܘܢ
[c] ܒܐܬܐ	26 ܕܫܢܘ [b] ܢܬܝ ܠܡܟܢ : ܒܪ [c] ܢܬܐ ܡܒܣܝܡܢܐ	[b] *add* ܠܝ [c] ܢܬܐ
[d] ܕܝ [e] ܡܫܕܪ	[d] ܕܝܢ ܕܐܢܐ [e] ܡܫܕܪ * ܠܗܘܢ ܡܢ ܠܘܬ ܐܒܐ	[* *Sic* in Cod. B.]
	ܪܘܚܐ ܕܩܘܕܫܐ : [d] ܕܝܢ ܕܡܢ ܠܘܬ ܐܒܐ ܢܦܩ	[e] ܡܫܕܪ
	27 ܗܘ [g] ܡܣܗܕ ܥܠ ܕܝܠܝ : ܘܐܘܦ ܐܢܬܘܢ	[g] ܡܣܗܕ
	XVI. 1 ܡܣܗܕܝܢ ܕܡܢ ܪܝܫ ܐܢܬܘܢ ܥܡܝ : ܗܠܝܢ	[h] ܢܬܟܫܠܘܢ
[h] ܢܬܟܫܠܘܢ	2 ܡܠܠܬ ܠܗܘܢ ܠܒܪܢܠ ܕܠܐ [h] ܢܬܟܫܠܘܢ ܡܢ	[i] ܒܢܫܬܐ [j] ܢܫܘܢ
‡ f. 15b.	[i] ܒܢܫܬܐ [j] ܢܫܘܢ ‡ ܢܬܒܥܘܢ : ܐܠܐ ܐܬܝܐ	[k] ܕܩܛܠ [l] ܠܟܘܢ
[j] ܢܫܘܢ [m] ܫܒܪ	ܫܥܐ ܕܟܠ ܡܢ [k] ܕܢܩܛܠ [l] ܢܬܒܥܘܢ ܗܘܐ [m] ܫܒܪ	[m] ܫܒܪ
	ܕܢܘܪܡ ܗܘ ܡܩܪܒ ܠܐܠܗܐ ⁘	

Codex B.

XXII.

John V. 1—15.

ܐܬܐܡܝܢ ܘܒܪܟܝܢ[a] ܗܘܐ ܐܠܗܐ[b] ܐܡܪ[c] ܡܢ ܟܕ
ܐܠܗܟܘܢ ܡܢ[e] ܘܫܠܚܗ[f]: ܘܟܬܒܗ ܡܪܝܐ:
1 ܘܡܢ ܒܬܪ[a] ܗܠܝܢ ܗܘܐ[b] ܥܐܕܐ ܕܝܗܘܕܝܐ[c]:
2 ܘܗܘܐ ܒܐܘܪܫܠܡ[d]: ܐܝܬ ܗܘܐ[e]
ܒܐܘܪܫܠܡ[f] ܥܠ[g] ܕܡܥܡܘܕܝܬܐ[h][i] ܕܒܝܬ ܚܣܕܐ:
[j]ܗܘܐ[k] ܕܡܬܩܪܝܐ[l] ܒܥܒܪܝܐ[m] ܒܝܬ ܚܣܕܐ:
3 ܘܗܘܐ ܠܗ[n] ܚܡܫܐ ܐܣܛܘܢ[o]: ܘܒܗܘܢ
ܗܘܐ[p] ܪܡܝܢ ܟܪܝܗܐ: ܣܡܝܐ ܘܚܓܝܪܐ
ܘܝܒܝܫܐ[q]: ܕܗܘܘ ܡܣܟܝܢ ܠܙܘܥܗ[r] ܕܡܝܐ:
4 ܕܐܝܬ ܐܡܪ[s]: ܚܕ ܡܠܐܟܐ ܗܘܐ ܢܚܬ ܗܘܐ
ܠܡܥܡܘܕܝܬܐ ܘܡܙܝܥ ܗܘܐ ܠܗܘܢ ܠܡܝܐ[t]
[f. 15a]
ܠܡܝܐ: ܡܢ[u] ܕܗܘ ܩܕܡ ܢܚܬ ܗܘܐ[v] ܒܬܪ
ܙܘܥܐ: ܡܢ ܟܪܝܗܘܬܐ[w] ܕܐܝܬ ܗܘܐ[x] ܚܠܝܡ
ܗܘܐ ܡܢ ܟܠ ܟܐܒ[y]: ܡܢ ܟܠ[z] ܟܐܒ ܗܘܐ:
5 ܘܗܘܐ[a] ܬܡܢ[b]: ܓܒܪܐ ܚܕ ܕܬܠܬܝܢ ܘܬܡܢܐ ܫܢܝܢ
ܕܗܘܐ ܠܗ ܒܟܘܪܗܢܗ[c] ܫܢܝܢ[d] ܟܕ[e]:
6 ܠܗܢܐ[f] ܚܙܐ ܝܫܘܥ ܟܕ ܪܡܐ ܘܝܕܥ[g]
ܕܙܒܢܐ ܣܓܝܐ ܐܝܬ ܠܗ: ܘܐܡܪ ܠܗ ܨܒܐ ܐܢܬ[h]
7 ܐܢܐ[k] ܕܬܬܚܠܡ: ܥܢܐ ܗܘ ܟܪܝܗܐ ܘܐܡܪ ܠܗ:
ܐܝܢ ܡܪܝ ܠܝܬ[l] ܠܝ ܐܢܫ[m]: ܕܡܐ ܕܐܙܕܘܥܘܢ ܡܝܐ
ܠܡܥܡܘܕܝܬܐ: ܥܕ ܐܢܐ ܐܬܐ ܐܚܪܢܐ ܢܚܬ[o] ‡ ܩܕܡܝ.
8 ܐܡܪ[p] ܠܗ ܝܫܘܥ: ܩܘܡ ܫܩܘܠ ܥܪܣܟ ܘܗܠܟ †
9 ܘܡܚܕܐ ܚܠܡ ܓܒܪܐ ܗܘ: ܘܩܡ ܫܩܠ[r] ܥܪܣܗ
ܘܗܠܟ[q]: ܫܒܬܐ[t] ܕܝܢ[s] ܗܘܬ ܗܘ ܝܘܡܐ
ܕܗܘܐ[u]: ܘܗܘܬ ܗܝ ܫܒܬܐ ܒܗܘ ܝܘܡܐ:
10 ܘܐܡܪܘ[v] ܝܗܘܕܝܐ ܠܗܘ[w] ܕܐܬܐܣܝ:
ܫܒܬܐ ܗܝ ܘܠܐ ܫܠܝܛ[x] ܠܟ ܠܡܫܩܠ ܥܪܣܟ

Codex A.

[a] *omit* ܘܒܪܟܝܢ ܐܬܐܡܝܢ
[b] ܐܠܗܐ ܡܢ [c] *omit*
ܐܠܗܟܘܢ ܐܠܗܐ [f] *add*
ܐܠܗܟܘܢ ܐܠܗܐ
[a] ܗܠܝܢ
[b] ܥܐܕܐ
[e] *add* ܗܘ
[g] ܘܗܘܬ ܠܗ [h] *omit* ܕ
[k] ܕܡܬܩܪܝܐ
[l] ܒܥܒܪܝܐ
[m] ܕܚܣܕܐ [n] ܚܡܫܐ
[o] ܐܣܛܘܢ
[p] *add* ܕܗܘܘ
[q] ܘܝܒܝܫܐ
[r] ܠܙܘܥܗ
[s] ܚܕ [t] ܢܚܬ
[u] ܗܘ [w] ܟܪܝܗܘܬܐ
[x] ܚܠܝܡ [z] ܟܐܒ
[d] ܫܢܝܢ [f] ܠܗܢܐ
[h] *omit* ܕ [j] ܡܪܝ
[k] ܕܐܙܕܘܥܘܢ

‡ f. 16a.

[m] ܐܝܢ [n] ܐܢܫ
[o] ܩܕܡܝ [p] ܐܡܪ
[q] ܘܗܠܟ:
[s] ܕܝܢ [t] ܫܒܬܐ
[u] ܕܗܘܐ [v] ܝܗܘܕܝܐ
[w] ܕܐܬܐܣܝ

Codex C.

[f. 15b]

[c] *omit* ܡܢ
[d] ܐܠܗܟ [e] ܘܫܠܚܗ
[b] ܥܐܕܐ
[c] *add* ܕܝܗܘܕܝܐ
[d] ܒܐܘܪܫܠܡ
[e] *add* ܗܘ
[f] ܒܐܘܪܫܠܡ [h] *omit* ܕ
[i] ܚܣܕܐ
[j] ܗܘܐ [k] ܕܡܬܩܪܝܐ
[l] ܒܥܒܪܝܐ
[p] *add* ܕܗܘܘ
[r] ܠܙܘܥܗ
[s] ܚܕ [v] ܟܪܝܗܘܬܐ
[y] ܟܐܒ [z] ܟܐܒ
[a] *add* ܗܘ [b] ܬܡܢ
[c] ܒܟܘܪܗܢܗ
[e] *omit* ܟܕ
[g] ܘܝܕܥ
[i] *add* ܗܘܐ ܪܡܐ
[k] ܕܬܬܚܠܡ [l] ܠܝܬ
[m] ܐܢܫ [n] ܡܪܝ
[o] ܩܕܡܝ [p] ܐܡܪ

† f. 16a.

[r] ܫܩܠ (*sic*)
[s] ܗܘܬ

[x] ܫܠܝܛ

الخامس وهو الرابع من صبوحية (left margin, printed sideways)

Codex A.	Codex B.	Codex C.
	11 ܒܪܡܫܐ : ܗܘ ܕܝܢ [y]ܐܬܠܟܒ ܘܐܡܪ ܠܗܘܢ :	[y]ܐܬܠܟ
[z]ܕܝ [a]ܫܠܝܚܐ	[z]ܕܝܢ ܕܗܘܐ ܗܘܐ [a]ܒܪܐ ܗܘ ܐܡܪ ܠܗ ܗܘ	[b]ܗܘܠܟܝ [c]ܘܫܐܠܘ
[c]ܘܫܐܠܘ	12 ܒܪܡܫܐ [b]ܗܘܠܟܝ : [c]ܘܫܐܠܘ ܝܬܗ ܘܐܡܪܝܢ ܠܗ :	[d] *add* ܗܕܝܢ
[d] *add* ܗܕܝ	ܡܢ ܗܘ [d]ܒܪܢܫܐ [e]ܗܕܝܢ ܕܐܡܪ ܠܟ ܗܒ	[e] *omit* ܗܕܝܢ
[e] *omit* ܗܕܝܢ	13 ܒܪܡܫܐ [f]ܗܘܠܟܝ : ܗܘ ܕܝܢ [g]ܕܐܬܐܣܝ ܠܐ	
[f]ܘܗܠܟܝ	ܗܘܐ ܝܕܥ ܡܢ ܗܘ : ܗܘ ܓܝܪ ܝܫܘܥ	
[g]ܕܐܬܐܣܝ [h]ܐܙܠ	[h]ܐܙܠ ܠܗ ܡܢ ܐܬܪ ܠܐܬܪ : ܕܗܘܐ	
[k] *omit* ܒܬܪ	14 [i]ܘܐܫܟܚܗ [k]ܒܬܪ [l]ܟܠܗܝܢ : ܘܡܢ ܒܬܪ ܗܠܝܢ	[i]ܐܫܟܚܗ
[l]ܟܠܗܝܢ [m]ܐܫܟܚܗ	[m]ܐܫܟܚܗ ܝܬܗ ܝܫܘܥ ܠܗܘܢ ܕܐܬܐܣܝ	[l]ܟܠܗܝܢ [k] *omit* ܒܬܪ
[o]ܡܫܬܒܠ	[f. 15*b*] ܒܗܝܟܠܐ ܘܐܡܪ ܠܗ : ܗܐ ܐܢܬ ܚܠܝܡ ܡܢ	[m]ܐܫܟܚܗ
[p]ܒܪ [q]ܘܐܙܠ	ܒܪ ܠܐ ܬܘܒ ܬܚܛܐ ܕܠܐ [o]ܡܫܬܒܠ ܗܘܐ ܠܟ	[o]ܡܫܬܒܠ
[r]ܠܝܗܘܕܝܐ [s]ܕܝ	15 ܗܝܕܝܢ ܡܢ [p]ܒܬܪ [q]ܘܐܙܠ ܗܘ ܒܪܢܫܐ ܘܐܡܪ	[q]ܘܐܙܠ
[u] *omit* ܗܘ ܒܪܐ	[r]ܠܝܗܘܕܝܐ ܕܝܫܘܥ ܗܘ [s][t]ܕܝܢ ܕܗܘܐ	
[w] *add* ܥܠܡ	[u]ܗܘ ܒܪܐ [u][t] ܀ [w]	[t] *omit* ܒܪܐ . . . ܕܝܢ

XXIII.

JOHN VI. 55*b*—70.

Codex A.	Codex B.	Codex C.
[a]ܘܟܕ ܐܬܟܢܫܘ ܐܠܡܝܕܘܗܝ ܠܘܬܗ ܡܢ ܗܘܝܘ ܠܬܠܡܝܕܐ[a]	[a]ܘܟܕ ܐܬܟܢܫܘ ܗܢ ܐܠܡܝܕܘܗܝ ܠܘܬܗ ܬܠܡܝܕܘܗܝ ܘܒܬܪܝܗܘܢ ܡܢ ܗܘܝܘ[a] : [x]ܐܡܪ ܝܫܘܥ	[a]ܬܠܡܝܕܘܗܝ ܘܒܬܪܝܗܘܢ ܘܟܕ ܐܬܟܢܫܘ ܡܢ ܗܘܝܘ[a]
[x] *add* ܝܫܘܥ	56 ܠܗܘܢ[y] [z]ܕܡܫܬܘܬܦ [a]ܒܝ ܡܢ [b]ܦܓܪܝ : [c]ܒܗܕܐ ܡܢ	[x]*add* ܘܒܬܠܡܝܕܘܗܝ ܝܫܘܥ
[z]ܐܡܠܝ [a]ܒܝ	[d]ܘܫܬܝ ܡܢ ܕܡܝ ܗܘ : ܘܐܡܪ ܠܗܘܢ ܡܢ	[y] *add* ܐܝܬܘܗܝ (*sic*)
[b]ܦܓܪܝ [c] *add* ܗܢܐ	57 [d]ܘܫܬܝ ܡܢ ܕܡܐ ܐܝܬܘܗܝ ܗܘ : ܡܢ [e]ܕܐܟܠ	[z]ܕܡܫܬܘܬܦ [a]ܒܝ
‡ f. 16*b*.	[f]ܠܚܡܐ ‡ ܕܢܚܬ ܡܢ ܫܡܝܐ ܗܘ ܗܢܐ	[e] *add* ܗܢܐ
[d]ܘܫܬܝ [e]ܕܐܟܠ	58 ܘܐܟܠܐ ܚܝܐ [h]ܥܕܡܐ ܕܐܢܬ ܚܝ ܐܢܬ	[f]ܒܗܕܐ
[f]ܒܗܕܐ [k]ܠܚܡܐ	ܐܟܠܐ ܚܝܐ ܚܝܐ [i]ܫܡܝܐ [k]ܠܚܡܐ ܐܟܠ :	[h] *add* ܘ [i]ܚܝ
[l]ܘܗܘ [m]ܕܐܟܠ	[l]ܘܗܘ [m]ܕܐܟܠ ܠܗ ܢܚܝܐ ܗܘ [n]ܚܝܐ [o]ܠܚܡܐ :	[m]ܕܐܟܠ
[n]ܫܡܝܐ [o]ܠܚܡܐ	59 ܗܕܝܢ † ܗܘ ܡܠܠ ܒܟܢܘܫܬܐ ܡܢ [p]ܟܕ ܡܠܦ ܗܘܐ :	† f. 16*b*.
[p] *omit* ܟܕ	ܠܐ ܗܘܐ ܕܐܟܠܘ ܐܬܡܗܘ ܒܗܕܐ ܡܠܬܐ[q]	[s] *omit* ܡܢ [u]ܫܡܝܐ
[q] *add* ܒܟܢܘܫܬܐ	ܘܬܡܗܘ : ܡܢ [r]ܕܐܟܠ [s]ܡܢ [t]ܗܕܝܢ ܠܬܠܡܝܕܐ [u]ܚܝܐ	[w]ܠܬܠܡ [x]ܬܠܡܝܕܘܗܝ
[s] *omit* ܡܢ [r]ܕܐܟܠ	60 [w]ܠܬܠܡ : ܘܐܡܪ ܐܡܪ [x]ܬܠܡܝܕܘܗܝ [y]ܘܗܠܟܘ	[y]ܘܗܠܟܘ
[t]ܗܕܝ [y]ܘܗܠܟܘ		

Margin of Codex A (written vertically): ܘܟܕ ܕܝ ܐܡܝܕ ܕ

Codex A.

[o] add ܥܠܝ
[a] ܦܫܢܝܐ
[b] ܢܚܠ
[d] ܡܪܢܢܝܢ
[g] ܒܣܪܐ [h] ܒܠܘܡ
[i] ܪܘܚ [j] ܘܚܝܝܢ
[k] ܗܢܘܢ
ܕ [o] add [p] ܠܛܠܠ
[q] ܟܕܢ
[r] ܝܟܠ
[t] ܝܗܒ
‡ f. 17a.
[u] ܠܟܠ
[y] ܕܚܝܝܢ
[z] ܕܠܥܠܡ
[a] add ܥܠܝ

Codex B.

61 ܒܒܦܪ ܢܦܫܗ[o] ܝܫܘܥ ܐܘܢ ܡܢ [z]ܬܠܡܝܕܘܝ
ܕܝ ܫܡܥܘ ܗܕܐ ܡܠܬܐ : ܐܡܪܘ [a]ܕܝܢܬܐ*
ܗܝ ܗܕܐ ܡܠܬܐ ܡܢ [b]ܡܚܝܠ ܕܫܡܥܘܢ ܡܢܗ :
62 [c]ܘܝܕܥ ܡܪܢܐ ܝܫܘܥ ܒܢܦܫܗ ܕܪܛܢܝܢ
[d]ܡܪܢܢܝܢ ܥܠ ܟܢ ܗܕܐ [e]ܬܠܡܝܕܘܝ : ܘܐܡܪ
63 ܠܗܘܢ ܗܕܐ ܡܥܠܐ ܠܟܘܢ : [f]ܐܢ ܐܘܢ
ܬܚܡܘܢ ܠܒܪܗ ܕܓܒܪܐ ܣܠܩ ܠܗܢ ܠܗ ܕܗܘܐ
64 ܡܢ ܩܕܡ : ܪܘܚܐ ܗܝ ܗܕܐ ܕܡܚܝܝܐ :
[g]ܒܣܪܐ [h]ܒܠܘܡ ܠܐ ܡܗܢܝܐ : ܡܠܝܐ ܗܠܝܢ ܕܡܠܠܬ
65 ܠܟܘܢ [i]ܪܘܚܐ [k]ܗܢܘܢ [j]ܘܚܝܝܢ [k]ܗܢܘܢ : ܐܠܐ
ܐܝܬ ܐܢܫܝܢ ܡܢܟܘܢ ܕܠܝܬ ܗܢܘܢ ܡܗܝܡܢܝܢ
[f. 16a]
[l]ܝܕܥ ܗܘܐ ܓܪ ܡܪܢܐ ܝܫܘܥ ܡܢ ܪܫ [m]ܡܢ
ܗܢܘܢ ܗܠܝܢ[m] ܕܠܐ [n]ܡܗܝܡܢܝܢ : ܘܡܢ ܗܘ[o]
66 ܕܡܫܠܡ ܠܗ : ܘܗܘܐ ܐܡܪ [p]ܠܛܠܠ [q]ܟܕܝܢ
ܐܡܪܬ ܠܟܘܢ : ܕܐܢܫ ܠܐ [r]ܝܟܠ ܕܝܐܬܐ
ܠܘܬܝ : ܐܠܐ [s]ܐܢ ܗܘܐ [t]ܝܗܒ ܠܗ ܡܢ
67 [u]ܠܟܠ ܡܢ ܠܘܬ ܐܒܐ : ‡ ܡܢ [p]ܠܛܠܠ [v]ܗܕܐ
ܐܘܢ ܦܫܝ ܡܢ ܬܠܡܝܕܘܝ : ܐܙܠܘ [w]ܠܗܘܢ
ܠܒܣܬܪܐ : ܘܟܕܘ ܠܐ ܗܘܘ ܡܗܠܟܝܢ ܟܡܗ :
68 ܘܐܓܝܒ ܡܪܢܐ ܝܫܘܥ ܘܐܡܪ ܠܬܪܥܣܪܬܐ :
ܕܠܡܐ ܐܘܦ ܐܢܬܘܢ ܒܥܝܢ ܕܬܐܙܠܘܢ ܠܟܘܢ :
69 ܐܓܝܒ ܫܡܥܘܢ [x]ܦܛܪܘܣ ܘܐܡܪ ܠܗ : †ܡܪܢܐ
ܠܘܬ ܡܢ ܐܢܢ ܐܙܠܝܢ : ܡܠܝܢ ܓܪ [y]ܕܚܝܝܢ
[z]ܕܠܥܠܡ ܥܡܟ : ܘܐܢܢ ܗܝܡܢܢ ܘܐܟܪܢܢ
ܕܐܢܬ ܗܘ ܡܫܝܚܐ ܒܪܗ ܕܐܠܗܐ ܚܝܐ[a] ⁘

Codex C.

[z] ܬܠܡܝܕܘܝ
[* Sic in Cod. B.]
[a] ܡܫܢܝܐ
[c] ܘܝܕܥ
[e] ܬܠܡܝܕܘܝ
[f] ܐܝܢ
[g] ܒܣܪܐ
[i] ܪܘܚ [j] ܘܚܝܝܢ
[l] ܝܕܥ
[m] ܡܢ ܗܠܝܢ ܗܢܘܢ
[n] ܡܗܝܡܢܝܢ
ܕܡܢ [o] add [r] ܝܟܠ
[s] ܐܝܢ [t] ܝܗܒ
[v] ܗܕܐ
[w] omit ܠܗܘܢ
† f. 17a.
[x] ܦܛܪܘܣ
[y] ܕܚܝܝܢ
[a] add ܥܠܝ

XXIV.

John VII. 1—13.

Codex A: [a] ܐܬܗܠܟ ܐܪܟܗ[a] · [b] omit ܐܪܟܗ ܘܒܬܪܝܢ · [c] omit ܒܫܘܪܗ · [d] ܕܚܘܝܢܢ [z] add ܐܢܫ

ܒܗ ܫܥܬܐ ܗܘ [a]ܐܬܗܠܟ ܐܪܟܗ[a] : [b]ܐܪܟܗ
ܘܒܬܪܝܢ [b] ܡܢ [c]ܒܫܘܪܗ [d]ܕܚܘܝܢܢ : [z]ܘܒܬܘܗ

Codex C: [a] ܐܬܗܠܟ ܐܪܟܗ[a] · [b] omit ܐܪܟܗ ܘܒܬܪܝܢ · [c] omit ܒܫܘܪܗ · [d] ܚܘܝܐ

Codex B.

1 ܦܪܘܣܐ : ܘܡܢ ܒܬܪ [a]ܒܕܝܢ ܗܘܐ ܡܪܐ
ܝܣܘܣ [b]ܡܗܠܟ ܒܓܠܝܠܐ : ܠܐ ܓܝܪ ܗܘܐ
ܨܒܐ [c]ܕܡܗܠܟ ܒܝܗܘܕܐ ܕܗܘܘ [d]ܝܗܘܕܝܢ
2 ܒܥܝܢ [e]ܕܝܩܛܠܘܢ ܝܬܗ : ܗܘܐ ܕܝ ܩܪܝܒ
3 [f]ܡܛܠܛܘܠܗܘܢ [g]ܕܝܗܘܕܝܢ [h]ܕܡܛܠܠܬܐ : [i]ܘܐܡܪܝܢ
ܠܗ ܐܚܘܗܝ ܦܢܝ ܡܢ [j]ܗܟܐ [k]ܘܐܙܠ ܠܟ
ܠܝܗܘܕܐ : [l]ܠܓܠܝܠ [m]ܕܐܘܦ [n]ܬܠܡܝܕܝܟ ܢܚܡܘܢ
4 [o]ܥܒܕܝܟ ܗܠܝܢ ܕܐܢܬ [q]ܥܒܕܬ : ܠܝܬ ܐܢܫ[p]
ܥܒܕ ܒܛܘܫ [r]ܒܦܪܣܝܡ ܘܒܥܐ ܕܗܘ ܢܗܘܐ
ܒܦܪܣܝܐ : ܐܢ ܗܠܝܢ ܐܢܬ ܥܒܕ ܓܠܝ ܢܦܫܟ
5 [s]ܠܥܠܡܐ : ܐܘܦ [t]ܠܐܚܘܗܝ ܓܝܪ ܠܐ ܗܘܘ
6 ܡܗܝܡܢܝܢ ܒܗ : ܐܡܪ ܠܗܘܢ ܐܘܢ ܡܪܐ
[f. 16b]
ܝܣܘܣ ܥܕܢܝ ܕܝܠܝ ܥܕ ܟܥܢ ܠܝܬ ܗܘ :
‡ ܥܕܢܟܘܢ ܕܝ ܕܝܠܟܘܢ ܒܟܘܠ ܥܕܢ ܗܘ
7 [u]ܡܬܩܢ : ܠܐ [w]ܝܟܠ [x]ܥܠܡܐ ܕܝܗܘܐ ܣܢܐ
ܠܟܘܢ : ܠܝ ܗܘ ܣܢܐ ܕܐܢܐ ܡܣܗܕ [y]ܥܠܘܝ :
8 [z]ܒܥܒܕܘܗܝ ܒܝܫܝܢ ܗܢܘܢ : ܐܬܘܢ ܣܩܘ
[a]ܠܥܐܕܐ [b]ܡܛܠܬܐ : ܐܢܐ ܕܝ ܥܕܢ ܠܝܬ ܐܢܐ
ܣܠܩ [c]ܠܡܛܠܬܐ [d]ܗܕܝܢ : [e]ܥܕܢܝ ܕܝܠܝ ܥܕ
9 ܟܥܢ ܠܐ [f]ܫܠܡ : ܗܕܐ ܕܝ ܐܡܪ ܠܗܘܢ ܗܠܝܢ
10 [g]ܟܬܪ ܗܘ ܒܓܠܝܠܐ : ܘܟܕ ܣܠܩܘ [h]ܐܚܘܗܝ
[i]ܠܡܛܠܬܐ : [k]ܒܟܝܢ ܐܘܦ ܗܘ ܣܠܩ ܠܐ
[l]ܒܓܠܝܐ : ܐܠܐ ܗܝܟ [m]ܒܛܘܫܝܐ :
11 † [n][o]ܝܗܘܕܝܢ ܗܘܘ ܒܥܝܢ ܠܗ [p]ܒܡܛܠܬܐ :
12 ܘܗܘܘ ܐܡܪܝܢ ܗܢ ܗܘ [q]ܗܘܐ : ܘܪܛܢ
ܣܓܝ ܗܘܐ ܥܠ ܐܦܘܗ [r]ܕܐܘܟܠܘܣܐ :
ܡܢܗܘܢ ܗܘܘ ܐܡܪܝܢ ܕܗܘ ܛܒ : [s]ܘܐܚܪܢܝܢ
ܗܘܘ ܐܡܪܝܢ ܠܐ : ܐܠܐ ܡܛܥܐ ܗܘ
13 ܥܡܐ : [t]ܐܢܫ ܕܝ ܒܦܪܣܝܐ ܠܐ ܗܘܐ
ܡܡܠܠ ܥܠ ܐܦܘܗ : [u]ܠܓܠܝܠ [v]ܕܕܚܠܬܗܘܢ
[w]ܕܝܗܘܕܝܢ [x] ⁘

Codex A.

[a]ܒܬܪ [b]ܡܗܠܟ
[c]ܕܝܗܠܟ [d]ܝܗܘܕܝܐ
[e]ܕܝܩܛܠܘܢܗ
[f]ܡܛܠܛܘܠܗܘܢ
[g]ܕܝܗܘܕܝܐ
[h]ܕܡܛܠܠܬܐ
[k]ܘܐܙܠ [l]ܠܓܠܝܠ
[m] omit ܕ
[n]ܬܠܡܝܕܝܟ
[o]ܒܥܒܕܝܟ [p] add ܓܝܪ
[q]ܥܒܕ [r]ܒܦܪܗܣܝܐ
[s]ܠܥܠܡܐ
[t]ܠܐ ܐܚܘܗܝ
‡ f. 17b.
[w]ܝܟܠ [x]ܥܠܡܐ
[z] add ܕ
[a]ܠܥܐܕܐ [b]ܡܛܠܬܐ
[c]ܠܡܛܠܬܐ [d]ܗܕܐ
[e]ܥܕܢܝ [f]ܫܠܡ
[g]ܟܬܪ [h]ܐܚܘܗܝ
[i]ܠܡܛܠܬܐ [k]ܒܟܝܢ
[n]ܝܗܘܕܝܐ
[o] add ܐܘܦ
[p]ܒܡܛܠܬܐ
[q]ܗܘܐ
[r]ܕܐܘܟܠܘܣܐ
[s]ܘܐܚܪܢܝܢ [u]ܠܓܠܝܠ
[w]ܕܝܗܘܕܝܐ
[x] add ܥܠܡ

Codex C.

[b]ܡܗܠܟ
[c]ܕܡܗܠܟ
[f]ܡܛܠܛܠܗܘܢ
[g] omit ܕܝܗܘܕܝܢ
[i]ܘܐܡܪܘ
[j] omit ܗܟܐ
[n]ܬܠܡܝܕܝܟ
[q]ܥܒܕ
[s]ܠܥܠܡܐ
[t]ܠܐ ܐܚܘܗܝ
[u]ܡܬܩܢ
[y]ܥܠܘܝ
[z] add ܕ
[e]ܥܕܢܝ
[g]ܟܬܪ [h]ܐܚܘܗܝ
[l]ܒܓܠܝܐ
[m]ܒܛܘܫܝܐ
† f. 17b.
[o] add ܐܘܦ
[r]ܕܐܘܟܠܘܣܐ
[s]ܘܐܚܪܢܝܢ
[t]ܐܢܫ
[v]ܕܕܚܠܬܗܘܢ (sic)

Codex A.	Codex B.	Codex C.

XXV.

John VII. 14—29.

Codex B.

ܫܒܬܐ [a]ܘܪܒܥܝܢ ܝܘܡ [b]ܐܪܒܥܬܐ ܒܚܕ [c]ܐܠܝܫܒܥܝܢ
14 ܡܢ [d]ܡܘܥܕܗ: [y][z]ܟܕ ܕܝ ܗܘܐ [a]ܡܨܥܬܐ ܒܥܐܕܗ:
ܘܣܠܩ ܡܪܢ ܝܫܘܥ ܠܗܝܟܠܐ [b]ܗܘܐ [c]ܡܠܦ:
15 [d]ܘܗܘܘ [e]ܡܬܕܡܪܝܢ ܝܗܘܕܝ̈ܐ ܘܐܡܪܝܢ: ܗܟܢ
ܗܕܝܢ ܝܕܥ ܟܬܒܝܢ [f]ܘܗܘ ܠܐ [g]ܝܠܦ:
16 [h]ܘܐܬܝܒ ܡܪܢ ܝܫܘܥ ܘܐܡܪ ܠܗܘܢ:
ܐܘܠܦܢܝ ܕܝܠܝ ܠܝܬ ܗܘ ܕܝܠܝ: ܐܠܐ ܕܐܒܐ
17 [i]ܕܝܢ [j]ܕܫܠܚܢܝ ‡ ܐܝܢ: ܐܢ ܐܢܫ ܨܒܐ [k]ܕܢܥܒܕ
ܨܒܝܢܗ: [l]ܡܕܥ [m]ܗܘ ܥܠ [n]ܐܘܠܦܢܗ [o]ܕܐܘܠܦܢܝ:
[f. 17a]
ܐܢ ܡܢ ܐܠܗܐ [p]ܗܘܐ: ܐܘ ܐܢ ܐܢܐ ܡܢ
18 ܢܦܫܝ ܐܢܐ [q]ܡܡܠܠ: [s][r]ܗܕܝܢ ܕܡܢ ܢܦܫܗ
ܗܘ [t]ܡܡܠܠ[r]: ܬܫܒܘܚܬܗ ܕܢܦܫܗ ܗܘ
ܒܥܐ: [u]ܕܝܢ ܕܝ [v]ܕܒܥܐ ܬܫܒܘܚܬܗ [w]ܕܕܝܢ
ܕܫܠܚ ܐܝܬܗ [x]ܗܕܝܢ [y]ܩܘܫܛ ܗܘ: [z]ܘܫܩܪ ܠܝܬ
19 ܒܗ: ܠܐ ܡܘܫܐ [a]ܝܗܒ ܠܟܘܢ ܢܡܘܣܐ:
20 ܘܐܢܫ ܡܢܟܘܢ ܠܐ ܥܒܕ ܢܡܘܣܐ: ܠܡܐ
21 ܐܬܘܢ ܒܥܝܢ [b]ܕܬܩܛܠܘܢ ܝܬܝ: [c]ܐܬܝܒ
[d]ܐܘܟܠܘܣܐ ܘܐܡܪ ܠܗ: ܫܐܕ ܠܟ: ܡܢ ܒܥܐ
ܕܝܩܛܠ ܝܬܟ: [c]ܐܬܝܒ [e]ܕܝ ܡܪܢ † ܝܫܘܥ
ܘܐܡܪ ܠܗܘܢ: ܚܕ [j]ܥܒܕ ܥܒܕܬ ܘܟܘܠܟܘܢ
22 [v]ܬܡܗܝܢ: [f]ܠܒܓܠ [g]ܕܝܢ ܡܘܫܐ ܝܗܒ ܠܟܘܢ
[h]ܓܙܘܪܬܐ ܠܐ ܗܝܟ ܕܡܢ ܡܘܫܐ ܗܝ ܐܠܐ
ܡܢ ܐܒܗܬܐ: [i]ܘܒܫܒܬܐ ܐܬܘܢ ܓܙܪܝܢ
23 ܒܪܢܫ: [k]ܢܣܒ [h]ܓܙܘܪܬܐ ܕܠܐ [l]ܝܫܪܐ ܢܡܘܣܐ
ܕܡܘܫܐ: [m]ܥܠܝ ܗܟܢ ܐܬܘܢ ܡܬܚܡܬܝܢ:
24 ܕܟܘܠܗ ܒܪܢܫܐ ܥܒܕܬ [n]ܒܪܐ *ܒܫܒܬܐ: ܠܐ
[o]ܬܕܘܢܘܢ ܒܡܣܒ ܒܐܦܝܢ: [p]ܐܠܐ ܕܝܢܐ
25 ܕܟܝܢܐ ܕܘܢܘ: ܘܗܘܘ ܕܝ ܐܡܪܝܢ ܐܢܫܝܢ ܡܢ

Codex A.

[a]ܘܒܪܒܥܝܢ
[b]ܐܪܒܥܬܐ
[c]ܐܠܝܫܒܥܝܢ
[a]ܡܨܥܬܐ [y]*add* ܕܝܢ
[b]*add* ܘ [c]ܡܠܦ
[e]ܡܬܕܡܪܝܢ [g]ܝܠܦ
[i]*omit* ܕܝܢ [j]ܕܫܠܚܢܝ
‡ f. 18*a*.
[k]ܕܢܥܒܕ [l]ܡܕܥ
[n]ܐܘܠܦܢܗ [p]ܗܘ
[s]ܗܘ̈ܢ [t]ܡܡܠܠ
[u]ܕܝ [v]*omit* ܕ
[w]ܕܕܝ [x]ܗܘܢ
[y]ܩܘܫܛ
[z]ܘܫܩܪ [a]ܝܗܒ
[b]ܕܬܩܛܠܘܢ
[e]*omit* ܕܝ
[j]ܥܒܕ
[f]ܠܒܓܠ [g]ܕܝܢ
[h]ܓܙܘܪܬܐ
[k]*add* ܐܢ ܒܫܒܬܐ ܒܪܢܫ
[l]ܝܫܪܐ
[m]ܥܠܝ [n]ܣܠܝܩ
[o]ܬܕܘܢܘܢ
[p]ܐܦܝܢ

Codex C.

[b]ܐܪܒܥܬܐ [d]ܡܨܥܐ
[z]ܟܕ
[b]*add* ܘ [c]ܡܠܦ
[d]*omit* ܘܗܘܘ
[e]ܡܬܕܡܪܝܢ [f]ܘܗܘܐ
[g]ܝܠܦ [h]ܘܐܬܝܒ
[i]*omit* ܕܝܢ [j]ܕܫܠܚܢܝ
[k]ܕܢܥܒܕ [l]ܡܕܥ
[m]*omit* ܗܘ [n]ܐܘܠܦܢܗ
[o]ܘܐܘܠܦܢܝ [p]ܗܘ
[q]ܡܡܠܠ
[r]*omit* ܗܕܝܢ . . . ܡܡܠܠ . . .
[v]ܕܒܥܐ [y]ܩܘܫܛ
[z]ܘܫܩܪ [a]ܝܗܒ
[c]ܐܬܝܒ
[d]ܐܘܟܠܘܣܐ
[e]*omit* ܕܝ
† f. 18*a*.
[j]ܥܒܕ [v]ܬܡܗܝܢ
[f]ܠܒܓܠ
[i]ܘܒܫܒܬܐ
[k]*add* ܐܢ ܒܫܒܬܐ ܒܪܢܫ
[l]ܝܫܪܐ [m]ܥܠܝ
[* Cod. ܕܒܫܒܬܐ]
[o]ܬܕܘܢܘܢ

Codex A.

[r]ܗܘ̈ܝ [s]ܕ̈ܝ
[t]ܕܡܫܠܚܬܢܝ
‡ f. 18*b*.
[v]ܘܥܠܡܐ [w]ܕܐܠܗܐ
[x]ܡܫܠܚ [y]ܕܗܘ̈ܝ
[z] add ܕܝܢ [c]ܡ̈ܚܪ
[d] omit ܕܝܢ
[e]ܡܠܝܠ [f] add ܘ
[g] omit ܗܘܝ
[h]ܡܫܠܚ
[i]ܗܘ̈ܝ
[k] add ܥܠܡ

[a] omit ܗܘܐ ܘܥܢܝܢ
[c] omit ܕܝܢ [d]ܐܠܗܘܢ
[e]ܐܬ̈ܘܗܘܢ
[z] add ܝܫܘ
[a]ܕܥܠܡܐ [c]ܗܘ
[d] add ܕ [e]ܡܗܠܟ
[f]ܢܗܘܪܐ [h]ܢܗܘ̈ܘܕܢܢ
[i]ܡ̈ܫܡܥܝܢ [l]ܡܫܠܚܐ
[o]ܐܢܬܘܢ ܐܢ
[p]ܡܫܠܚܐ ܗܘܝ
[q]ܐܙܠ [r] add ܕ
[s]ܘܐܢ ܕܝ ܐ̈ܢܐ
[t]ܡܫܠܚ [u]ܘܕ̈ܝ
[v]ܕܥܠܝ
‡ f. 19*a*.

Codex B.

ܟܢ [q]ܢܘܪ̈ܝܫܠܡ : ܠܐ [r]ܗܕܝܢ ܗܘ [s]ܕܝܢ ܕܗܘܘ
26 ܣܓܝܢ [t]ܕܡܠܠܢ : ܘܗܐ ܕܦ̈ܪܫܢܐ ܗܘ [u]ܡܡܠܠ :
[v]ܘܒܠܡ ܠܐ ܐܡܪܝܢ ܠܗ : [w]ܕܡܒܐ ‡ ܡܢ [x]ܡܘܫܠܚ
ܐܒܘܝ ܐܪܚܡܢܐ [y]ܕܗܕܝܢ ܗܘ ܡܢ [x]ܡܘܫܠܚ
27 ܡܫܝܚܐ : ܐܠܐ ܠܕܝܢ ܐܝܬܗ ܡܡܪܝܢ ܡܢ ܗܘܝ
ܗܘ : ܡܫܝܚܐ [z]ܕܝ [a]ܐܬܬܐ [b]ܐܢܫ ܠܐ [c]ܡܡܪܝܢ
28 ܡܢ ܗܘܝ ܗܘ : ܘܐܬܝܚܝܕ [d]ܕܝܢ ܡܡܪܐ ܐܝܫܘܥ
[f. 17*b*]
[e]ܡܠܝܠ ܒܚܘܫܒܢܐ ܘܐܡܪ ܐܘܦ ܠܝ ܐܢܬܘܢ
ܡܡܪܝܢ [f]ܡ̈ܢ [g]ܗܘܝ ܐܢܐ ܐܢܬܘܢ ܝܕܥܝܢ :
ܘܡܢ ܚܝ̈ܡܒ ܠܐ ܐܬܬܝܬ : ܐܠܐ [h]ܘܡܫܠܚ ܗܘ
[i]ܗܕܝܢ ܕܥܠܝ ܡܬܝ : [i]ܗܕܝܢ ܕܐܬܘܢ ܠܐ ܡܡܪܝܢ
29 ܠܗ : ܐܢܐ ܕܝ ܡܡܪ ܠܗ ܕܡܢ ܠܘܬܗ ܐܢܐ
ܐܬܬܝܬ : ܘܗܘ ܥܠܝ ܡܬܝ [k] ⁘

XXVI.

John VIII. 12*a*—20.

[a]ܬܘܒ [b]ܘܥܢܝܢ ܗܘܐ ܐܠܗܘܢ [c]ܕܝ [d]ܐܝܫܘܥ
12 [e]ܐܬ̈ܘܗܘܢ ܡܢ [f]ܢܗܘܪܢ [z]: ܐܡܪ ܡܡܪܐ ܝܫܘܥ : ܐܢܐ
ܗܘ ܢܗܘܪܗ [a]ܕܥܠܡܐ . ܡܢ [b]ܗ̈ܘ [c]ܗܘܐ [d]ܕܝܢ ܠܝ
ܠܐ [e]ܡܗܠܟ ܒܚܫܘܟܐ : ܐܠܐ † ܗܘܐ ܚܝܗܘܢ
13 [f]ܢܗܘܪܗ ܕܚܝܝܐ : ܐܡܪܝܢ ܠܗ ܐܢܘܢ [h]ܦܪܝܫܝܐ
ܐܢܬ [i]ܡܫܡܥ ܥܠ [k]ܢܦܫܟ ܣܗܕܘܬܟ
14 ܠܝܬ ܗܝ [l]ܡܫܠܚܐ : [m]ܐܡܪ [n]ܠܗܘܢ ܝܫܘܥ
ܘܐܡܪ ܠܗܘܢ : [o]ܐܢ [o]ܐܢܬܘܢ ܐܢܐ [i]ܡܫܡܥ
ܣܗܕܘܬܝ [p]ܗܝ ܡܫܠܚܐ [p]: ܐܢܐ ܝܕܥ ܡܢ ܗܘܝ
15 ܐܬܝܬ ܘܠܗܢ ܐܢܐ [q]ܐܙܠ : ܐܢܬܘܢ ܠܗ ܝܕܥܝܢ
[r]ܡܢܐ ܐܢܬܘܢ ܕܐܙܠܝܢ : ܐܢܐ ܠܝܬ ܐܢܐ
16 ܕܐܝܢ ܠܐܢܫ : [s]ܘܐܢ ܕܝܢ ܐ̈ܢ [s]ܕܝܢ ܕܝܠܝ
[t]ܡܫܠܚ ܗܘ : ܕܠܝܬ ܐܢܐ ܠܚܘܕܝ ܐܠܐ
17 ܐܢܐ [u]ܘܕܝܢ [v]ܕܥܠܝ ‡ ܡܬܝ ܐܒܐ : ܘܒܢܡܘܣܐ

Codex C.

[q]ܢܘܪ̈ܫܠܡ
[u]ܡܡܠܠ
[z] add ܕܝ [a]ܐܬܬܐ
[b]ܐܢܫ [c]ܡ̈ܚܪ
[d] omit ܕܝܢ
[e]ܡܠܝܠ [f] add ܘ
[h]ܡܫܠܚ
[k] add ܥܠܡ

[b]ܘܥܢܝܢ
[c] omit ܕܝ ܐܝܫܘܥ
[e]ܐܬܘܢ [f]ܢܗܘܪ
[z] add ܘܒܢܘܗܪܗ ܕܥܠܡܗ
† f. 19*b*.
[b] add ܗܝ [c]ܗܘ
[d] add ܕ
[f]ܢܗܘܪܐ [h]ܦܪܝܫ̈ܝ
[k] omit ܥܠ [l]ܡܫܠܚܐ
[m]ܐܡܪ [n] add ܕܝ
[o]ܐܢܬܘܢ ܐܢ
[p]ܡܫܠܚܐ ܗܝ
[r] add ܕ
[s]ܘܐܢ ܕܐܝܢ
[t]ܡܫܠܚ [v]ܕܥܠܝ

Codex A.

ʷܓܒܪܝܢ ʸܒܢܝܢܐ
ᶻܡܣܗܕ
ᵇܘܡܣܗܕ ᶜܕܝ
ᵈܕܥܠܝܢ
ᵉܐܦܘܢ
ʰܘܦܪܢܣܐ
ⁱܡܠܠ ᵏܟܕ
ˡܕܐܬܬ ᵐܥܕܢܗ

Codex B.

ܕܝ ܕܬܠܬܗܘܢ ʷܓܒܪܝܢ ˣܕܣܗܕܘܬܗܘܢ ܕܫܪܝܪ
18 ʸܒܢܝܢܐ ᶻܘܡܣܗܕ ܗܘ : ܐܢܐ ᵃܡܣܗܕ ܥܠ ܢܦܫܝ
ܒܐܒܘܝ : ᵇܘܡܣܗܕ ܥܠ ܕܫܠܚܢܝ ܐܒܐ ᶜܕܝ
19 ᵈܕܥܠܝܢ ܠܗ : ܘܐܡܪܝܢ ܐܡܪܝܢ ܠܗ ܗܘ ܗܘ
ᵉܐܦܘܢ : ᶠܐܝܢܐ ܗܘܐ ܐܒܘܟ ܘܐܡܪ ܠܗܘܢ
ܠܐ ܠܝ ܚܟܡܝܢ ܐܢܬܘܢ ܘܠܐ ܠܐܒܘܝ : ܐܠܘ
ܗܟܢܐ ܠܝ ܚܟܡܝܢ ܐܢܬܘܢ ܐܦ ܠܐܒܘܝ ܗܘܝܬܘܢ
[f. 18a]
20 ܚܟܡܝܢ : ܗܠܝܢ ܡܠܝܐ ᵍܡܠܠ ܒܒܝܬ ʰܘܦܪܢܣܐ
ⁱܡܠܦ ʲܒܗܝܟܠܐ ܘܐܢܫ ܠܐ ᵏܟܕ ܬܗ : ܕܒܕ
ܕܠܐ ܗܘܐ ˡܕܐܬܬ ᵐܫܥܬܗ ⁿܥܠܡ ⁘

XXVII.

John VIII. 21—30.

ᵃᵇܗܟܢ ܘܒܬܪܝܢ ܝܘܡ ᶜܐܠܦܗܡ ᵈܦܢ ܐܫܘܥ
21 ܐܡܪܗܘܢ ܡܢ ᵉܝܫܘܥ ᵃ: ᶻܘܐܡܪ ܠܗܘܢ ܡܪܢܐ
ܝܫܘܥ ܐܢܐ ᵃܐܙܠ ܠܝ ᵇܘܐܬܘܢ ᶜܗܘܝܢ
ܒܥܝܢ ܠܝ : ᵈܘܒܚܛܝܬܟܘܢ ܐܢܬܘܢ ᵉܡܝܬܝܢ :
ܘܠܗܘܢ ܕܐܢܐ ⁱܐܙܠ ܐܢܬܘܢ ܠܝܬ ܐܢܬܘܢ ܝܟܠܝܢ
22 ܕܝܗܘܕܝܐ : ᶠܗܘܘ ᵍܐܘܢ ʰܝܗܘܕܝܐ ܐܡܪܝܢ ᵗܕܡܐ
ܡܛܠ ܗܘ ܢܦܫܗ : ܕܗܘ ܐܡܪ ᵛܠܗܘܢ ܕܐܢܐ
ⁱܐܙܠ ܐܢܬܘܢ ܠܝܬ ܐܢܬܘܢ ʲܝܟܠܝܢ ᵏܕܬܬܘܢ :
23 ˡܘܗܘܐ ܐܡܪ ܠܗܘܢ ܐܢܬܘܢ ܡܢ ܗܠܝܢ ܕܠܬܚܬ
ܐܢܬܘܢ : ܐܢܐ ᵐܡܢ ܗܠܝܢ ⁿܕܠܥܠ ܐܢܐ :
ܐܢܬܘܢ ܡܢ ᵒܗܕܝܢ ᵖܥܠܡܐ ܐܢܬܘܢ : ᵠܘܐܢܐ
24 ʳܠܝܬ ܐܢܐ ܡܢ ܗܕܝܢ ᵖܥܠܡܐ : ܐܡܪܬ
ܠܟܘܢ ˢܐܘܢ ܕܐܢܬܘܢ ᵗܡܝܬܝܢ ᵘܒܚܛܝܬܟܘܢ :
ܐܢ ܓܝܪ ܠܐ ܬܗܝܡܢܘܢ ܕܐܢܐ ܗܘ : ᵛܡܝܬܝܢ
25 ܐܢܬܘܢ ‡ ᵘܒܚܛܝܬܟܘܢ : ʷܗܘܘ ˣܐܘܢ
ʸܐܡܪܝܢ ܠܗ : ܐܢܬ ܡܢ ܐܢܬ : ʸܐܡܪ
ܠܗܘܢ ܡܪܢܐ ܝܫܘܥ : ܪܝܫܐ ܕܐܢܐ ᶻܡܡܠܠ

Codex C.

ʷܓܒܪܝܢ
ˣܕܣܗܕܘܬܗܘܢ
ʸܒܢܝܢܐ ᶻܡܣܗܕ
ᵃܡܣܗܕ ᵈܕܥܠܝܢ
ᵉܐܦܘܢ ᶠܐܝܢܐ
ᵍܡܠܠ ʰܘܦܪܢܣܐ
ʲܒܗܝܟܠܐ ᵏܟܕ
ˡܕܐܬܬ ܥܠܡ ⁿomit

Codex A.

ᵃܗܟܢ ܐܠܦܗܡ ܐܠܦܗܡ
ܐܡܪܗܘܢ ܐܠܒܪܗܘܢ
ܡܢ ܝܫܘܥ ᵃ
ᶻadd ܐܡܪ ᵃܐܙܠ
ᵇܘܐܬܘܢ ᶜܗܘܝܢ
ᵈܒܚܛܝܬܟܘܢ
ᵉܡܝܬܝܢ ᶠadd ܘ
ᵍomit ܐܘܢ ʰܝܗܘܕܝܐ
ᵛܠܗܘܢ ⁱܐܙܠ
ʲܝܟܠܝܢ ˡܗܘܘ
ᵐadd ܕܝ ⁿܕܠܥܠ
ᵖܥܠܡܐ ᵠomit ܘ
ʳadd ܕܝ ˢomit ܐܘܢ
ᵗܡܝܬܝܢ
ᵘܒܚܛܝܬܟܘܢ
ᵛܡܝܬܝܢ ʷܗܘܘܢ

‡ f. 19b.

ˣܐܡܪܝܢ ʸadd ܘ
ᶻܡܡܠܠ

Codex C.

ᵇܗܟܢ ᶜܐܠܦܗܡ
ᵈomit ܦܢ ᵉܝܫܘܥ
ᶻadd ܘܐܡܪ ܠܗܘܢ ܡܪܢܐ
ᵇܘܐܬܘܢ ᶠadd ܘ
ᵍomit ܐܘܢ ʰܝܗܘܕܝܐ

† f. 19a.

ᵛܠܗܘܢ
ʲܝܟܠܝܢ ᵏܕܬܬܘܢ
ˡܗܘܐ
ᵐadd ܕܝ
ᵒܗܕܝܢ ᵠomit ܘ
ʳadd ܕܝ
ˢomit ܐܘܢ
ᵗܡܝܬܝܢ
ʷܗܘܘܢ
ˣܐܡܪܝܢ ʸadd ܘ

Codex B.

26 ܐܢܐ ܣܓܝܐܢ : ܘܣܓܝܢ ܠܝ [a]ܕܐܡܠܠ [b]ܥܠ
[c]ܕܐܬܕܝܢܟܘܢ [d]ܘܕܝܢ : ܐܠܐ ܕܝܢ ܕܫܠܚ ܝܬܝ
[e]ܡܗܝܡܢ ܗܘ : ܘܐܢܐ ܡܐ ܕܫܡܥܬ ܡܢܗ ܗܠܝܢ
27 ܐܢܐ [f]ܡܡܠܠ [g]ܒܥܠܡܐ : ܘܠܐ ܚܟܡܘ ܕܥܠ
28 ܐܒ̈ܘܗܝ [h][i]ܗܘܐ ܐܡܪ ܠܗܘܢ : [j]ܐܡܪ ܠܗܘܢ
ܐܘܢ [k]ܬܪܝܡܘܢ ܒܪܗ ܕܐܢܫܐ[l] ܒܕ [m]ܕܝܢ [n]ܬܚܟܡܘܢ
[f. 18b]
[o]ܠܒܪܗ ܕܐܢܫܐ : [p]ܒܟܝܢ ܐܬܘܢ ܚܟܝܡܝܢ ܕܐܢܐ
ܗܘ ܘܡܢ ܓܪܡܝ ܠܐ ܐܬܝܬ ܘܠܐ ܥܒܕܬ
[q]ܟܠܘܡ : ܐܠܐ ܗܟܢ ܡܐ [r]ܕܐܠܦܢܝ ܐܒܝ
29 ܐܡܠܠ ܗܠܝܢ ܐܢܐ [s]ܡܡܠܠ : [t]ܘܕܝܢ ܕܫܠܚ
ܝܬܝ ܥܡܝ ܗܘ : ܘܠܐ ܫܒܩ ܝܬܝ ܠܚܘܕܝ :
ܕܐܢܐ ܡܐ ܕܫܦܪ ܠܗ ܐܢܐ ܥܒܕ ܟܘܠ
30 ܙܒܢ : ܟܕ ܕܝܢ ܕܗܘܐ [u]ܡܡܠܠ ܗܠܝܢ ܣܓܝܐܝܢ
ܗܝܡܢܘ ܒܗ[w] ⁘

Codex A.

[a] ܕܡܡܠܠ
[c] ܕܐܬܕܝܢܟܘܢ
[d] ܘܕܝܢ [e] ܡܗܝܡܢ
[f] ܡܡܠܠ [g] ܒܥܠܡܐ
[h] add ܕ [i] ܗܘܐ
[j] add ܘ [k] omit ܬܪܝܡܘܢ
[l] add ܬܪܝܡܘܢ
[m] omit ܕܝܢ
[n] ܬܚܟܡܘܢ
[o] ܠܒܪܗ [p] ܒܟܝܢ
[q] ܟܠܘܡ [r] ܕܐܠܦܢܝ
[t] ܘܕܝܢ
[w] add ܥܠܝܗ

Codex C.

[a] ܕܡܡܠܠ ܠܗ [b] add
[d] ܘܕܝܢ
[e] ܡܗܝܡܢ
[f] ܡܡܠܠ
[h] add ܕ [j] add ܘ
[k] omit ܬܪܝܡܘܢ
[l] add ܬܪܝܡܘܢ [m] omit ܕܝܢ
[n] ܬܚܟܡܘܢ
[o] ܠܒܪܗ [r] ܕܐܠܦܢܝ
[s] ܡܡܠܠ
[u] ܡܡܠܠ
[w] add ܥܠܝܗ

XXVIII.

JOHN VIII. 31—42.

Codex B.

[a]ܬܫܒܘܚܗ ܘܒܥ̈ܪܝܢ ܝܘܡ ܐܪܒܥܬ † [b]ܒܫ
31 ܐܠܗܘܡܗ [a]ܐܡܪ ܠܗܘܢ ܡܢ ܝܗܘܕܝܐ[b] :[y] [z]ܐܡܪ
[a]ܡܪܢܐ ܗܘ· ܕܝܢ[a] ܡܪܢܐ[z] ܝܫܘܥ [b]ܐܡܪ[d]
ܠܗܠܝܢ ܕܗܝܡܢܘ ܒܗ [e]ܡܢ ܝܗܘܕܝ[e] : [f]ܐܢ
ܐܬܘܢ ܬܬܩܘܡܘܢ ܒܡܠܬܝ ܕܝܠܝ : ܡܢ [g]ܡܗܝܡܢ
32 [h]ܬܠܡܝܕܝ ܐܬܘܢ : ܘܬܚܟܡܘܢ ܩܘܫܬܐ
33 ܘܩܘܫܬܐ [i]ܡܚܪܪ ܝܬܟܘܢ : ܐܡܪܘ [k]ܝܗܘܕܝ[l]
ܘܐܡܪܝܢ ܠܗ : ܙܪܥܗ ܕܐܒܪܗܡ ܐܢܚܢ ܘܠܐ
ܠܐ [m]ܐܫܬܥܒܕܢ ܡܢ [n]ܡܢܝܢ : ܗܝܟ
ܐܬ ܐܡܪ ܠܢ ܐܬ ‡ ܕܐܬܘܢ ܚܪ̈ܝܪܝܢ :
34 [o]ܐܓܝܒ ܡܪܢܐ ܝܫܘܥ ܘܐܡܪ ܠܗܘܢ : ܐܡܝܢ
ܐܡܝܢ ܐܡܪ ܐܢܐ ܠܟܘܢ : ܕܟܘܠ ܡܢ ܕܥܒܕ
35 [p]ܚܛܝܬܐ ܥܒܕܗ [a]ܕܚܛܝܬܐ ܗܘ : ܘܥܒܕܐ
ܠܐ [q]ܡܬܒܬܪ ܒܒܝܬܐ [r]ܠܥܠܡ : ܒܪܐ ܕܝܢ ܡܬܒܬܪ

Codex A.

[a] ܝܘܡ ܐܪܒܥܬ ܒܫ̈ܒܘܥܐ ܐܠܦܐܡܝ[a]
[y] add ܐܝܫ
[a] omit ܡܪܢܐ ܗܘ ܕܝܢ
[b] omit ܐܡܪ
[d] add ܠܝܗܘ̈ܕܝܐ
[e] omit ܡܢ ܝܗܘܕܝ
[g] ܡܗܝܡܢ
[h] ܬܠܡܝܕܝ ܐܝܬܝ
[i] ܡܚܪ̈ܪܐ [k] ܝܗܘ̈ܕܝܐ
[l] add ܕܝ
‡ f. 20a.
[m] ܐܫܬܥܒܕܢܢ
[n] ܒܢܝܢܫ
[p] ܚܛܝܬܐ
[a] ܕܚܛܝܬܐ [q] ܡܬܒܬܪ

Codex C.

[b] ܡܢ ܝܗܘܕܝ ܡܢ ܝܗܘܕܝ[b]
† f. 19b.
[y] add ܒܝܫܘܥ
[z] ܘܗܘܐ ܕܝܢ ܡܪܢܐ[z]
[b] omit ܐܡܪ
[f] ܐܢ
[h] ܬܠܡܝܕܝ
[n] ܒܢܝܢܫ
[o] ܐܓܝܒ
[q] ܡܬܒܬܪ [r] ܠܥܠܡ

Codex A.	Codex B.	Codex C.

Codex B.

36 [Syriac]
37 [Syriac]
[Syriac]
[Syriac]
38 [Syriac]
[f. 19a]
[Syriac]
[Syriac]
39 [Syriac]
[Syriac]
[Syriac]
40 [Syriac]
[Syriac] †
[Syriac]
41 [Syriac]
[Syriac]
[Syriac]
42 [Syriac]
[Syriac]
[Syriac] ⁘

XXIX.

John IV. 5—42.

[Syriac] ‡
[Syriac]
5 [Syriac]
[Syriac]
6 [Syriac]
[Syriac]
[Syriac]
[Syriac]

Codex A. (variants)

[u] [Syriac]
[w] [Syriac]
[x] [Syriac]
[y] [Syriac]
[z] [Syriac]
[b] [Syriac]
[c] [Syriac]
[d] [Syriac]
[f] [Syriac]
[h] [Syriac] [i] *omit* [Syriac]
[k] [Syriac]
[m] [Syriac]

[a] [Syriac] (*sic*) [Syriac] (*sic*) [Syriac] [a]

‡ f. 20b.

[y] *add* [Syriac]
[a] [Syriac] [b] *add* [Syriac]
[c] [Syriac]
[e] [Syriac]
[f] [Syriac] [g] [Syriac]
[h] [Syriac]
[i] *omit* [Syriac]

Codex C. (variants)

[r] [Syriac] [s] [Syriac]
[t] [Syriac] [v] [Syriac]
[x] [Syriac]
[y] [Syriac]
[z] [Syriac]
[a] *add* [Syriac]
[e] [Syriac]
† f. 20a.
[g] [Syriac]
[l] *omit* . . . [Syriac] . . .

[a] [Syriac] [a]
[y] *add* [Syriac]
[z] *omit* [Syriac]
[d] *omit* [Syriac]
[e] [Syriac]
[h] [Syriac]
[k] [Syriac] [i] [Syriac]

[Syriac]

Codex B.

7 [j]ܒܥܕܢܐܬܐܝܢ [k]ܘܐܬܬܐ ܚܕܐ [l]ܐܬܬ ܡܢ
[m]ܫܡܪܝܢ ܕܬܡܠܐ ܡܝܢ܆ ܘܐܡܪ ܠܗ ܡܪܐ
8 ܗܒܝ܆ ܗܒܝ ܠܝ [n]ܡܝܢ ܕܐܫܬܐ܆ [o]ܬܠܡܝܕܘܗܝ
ܓܝܪ ܗܘܘ[p] [q]ܐܙܠܝܢ [r]ܠܡܕܝܢܬܐ [s]ܕܝܙܒܢܘܢ
[f. 19b]
9 ܡܝܟܘܠ܆ ܘܐܡܪܐ ܠܗ [t]ܗܝ ܐܬܬܐ ܗܝܟ
[u]ܐܢܬ[v] [w]ܝܗܘܕܝ܆ ܡܒܥܐ ܐܢܬ ܡܢܝ ܠܡܫܬܝ ܡܢ
ܐܬܬܐ ܫܡܪܝܐ܆ ܠܐ ܓܝܪ ܡܬܚܠܛܝܢ [x]ܝܗܘܕܝ
10 ܥܡ [y]ܫܡܪܝܝ܆ [z]ܐܓܝܒ ܡܪܐ ܝܫܘܥ ܘܐܡܪ
ܠܗ܆ ܐܠܘ ܗܘܝܬܝ [a]ܝܕܥܐ [b]ܡܘܗܒܬܗ
ܕܐܠܗܐ܆ ܘܡܢ [c]ܗܘ [d]ܗܕܝܢ ܕܐܡܪ ܠܟܝ
ܗܒܝ ܠܝ ܕܐܫܬܐ ܐܬܝ ܗܘܝܬܝ [e]ܫܐܠܐ
11 ܡܢܗ ܘܗܘ ܝܗܒ ܠܟܝ ܡܝܢ [f]ܕܚܝܢ܆ [g]ܐܡܪܐ
ܠܗ ܐܬܬܐ ܡܪܝ ܠܐ [h]ܕܠܘ ܥܡܟ܆ ܘܒܝܪܐ
ܥܡܝܩܐ ܗܝ܆ ܡܢ ܗܢ ܠܟ ܡܝܢ [f]ܕܚܝܢ܆
12 †ܕܡܐ ܐܢܬ [i]ܪܒ. ܡܢ ܐܒܘܢ ܝܥܩܘܒ ܗܕܝܢ
ܕܝܗܒ ܠܢ ܡܒܘܥܐ܆ ܘܗܘ ܡܢܗ [j]ܗܘ ܫܬܐ܆
13 [k]ܘܒܢܘܗ ܘܒܥܝܪܗ܆ ‡[l]ܐܓܝܒ ܡܪܐ ܝܫܘܥ ܘܐܡܪ
ܠܗ܆ ܟܘܠ ܡܢ ܕܝܫܬܐ ܡܢ ܗܠܝܢ ܡܝܢܐ [m]ܝܗܡܐ
14 ܗܘ [n]ܬܘܗܡ܆ ܡܢ[o] ܕܝܫܬܐ ܡܢ [p]ܗܠܝܢ ܡܝܢܐ[q]
ܕܐܢܐ ܝܗܒ ܠܗ ܠܐ ܝܗܐ [a]ܠܥܠܡ܆ ܐܠܐ
ܡܝܢܐ ܕܐܢܐ ܝܗܒ ܠܗ ܡܬܥܒܕܝܢ ܒܓܘܗ܆
[b]ܡܒܘܥܐ [c]ܕܡܝܢ ܡܫܘܪܝܢ [r]ܠܚܝܝ [s]ܕܠܥܠܡ܆
15 [t]ܐܡܪܐ ܠܗ ܐܬܬܐ ܡܪܝ܆ ܗܒ ܠܝ ܗܠܝܢ
ܡܝܢܐ ܕܠܐ ܐܨܗܐ ܐܢܐ ܝܗܡܐ܆ ܘܠܐ ܐܬܐ
16 ܕܐܡܠܐ [u]ܟܐ܆ ܐܡܪ ܠܗ ܡܪܐ ܝܫܘܥ ܐܙܠܝ
17 [v]ܩܪܝ ܠܒܥܠܟܝ [w]ܘܐܬܝ [x]ܠܟܐ܆ [y]ܐܓܝܒܬ
ܐܬܬܐ [z]ܘܐܡܪܬ ܠܗ܆ ܠܝܬ ܠܝ ܒܥܠ܆ ܐܡܪ
ܠܗ ܡܪܐ ܝܫܘܥ [a]ܝܐܘܬ ܐܡܪܬܝ ܕܒܥܠ
18 ܠܝܬ ܠܝܟܝ܆ [b]ܚܡܫܐ [c]ܓܝܪ [d]ܒܥܠܝܢ [e]ܗܘܐ ܠܟܝ܆
ܘܕܘܒ [f]ܗܕܝܢ ܕܐܡܬܟܝ ܠܝܬ ܗܘ ܒܥܠܟܝ
[g]ܕܝܠܟܝ ܗܕܐ ܡܢ [h]ܩܘܫܛ ܐܡܪܬܝ܆

Codex A.

[j]ܕܒܥܕܢܐܬܐܝܢ
[n] *omit* ܡܝܢ
[o]ܬܠܡܝܕܘܗܝ
[p] *add* ܕܝ   [q]ܐܙܠܘ
[r]ܠܡܕܝܢܬܐ
[s]ܕܝܙܒܢܘܢ
[v] *add* ܕܐܢܬ
[w]ܝܗܘܕܝܐ
[x]ܝܗܘܕܝܐ
[y]ܫܡܪܝܐ   [a]ܝܕܥܐ
[b]ܡܘܗܒܬܗ
[d]ܗܕܝ   [e]ܫܐܠܐ
[f]ܚܝܝܢ   [g]ܐܡܪܐ
[h]ܕܠܘ
[i]ܪܒ
[j]ܗܘܐ   [k]ܘܒܢܘܗܝ
‡ f. 21a.
[m]ܝܗܡܐ   [n]ܬܘܗܡ
[o] *add* ܕܝ
[p] *omit* ܗܠܝܢ
[q] *add* ܗܠܝܢ
[b]ܡܒܘܥ
[c]ܕܡܝܢ   [r]ܠܚܝܝܢ
[s]ܕܠܥܠܡ   [t]ܐܡܪܐ
[u] *add* ܡܢ
[v]ܩܪܝ   [w]ܘܐܬܝ
[b]ܚܡܫܐ   [d]ܒܥܠܝܢ
[e]ܗܘܘ   [f]ܗܕܝ
[g]ܕܝܠܟܝ   [h]ܩܘܫܛ

Codex C.

[j]ܕܒܥܕܢܐܬܐܝܢ
[k]ܘܐܬܬܐ   [l]ܐܬܬܐ
[m]ܫܡܪܝ   [o]ܬܠܡܝܕܘܗܝ
[q]ܕܐܙܠܘ
[t] *omit* ܗܝ
[u]ܕܐܢܬ   [v] *add* ܐܢܬ
[x]ܝܗܘܕܝܐ
[z]ܐܓܝܒ   [a]ܝܕܥܐ
[b]ܡܘܗܒܬܗ
[c] *omit* ܗܘ
[e]ܫܐܠܐ
[f]ܕܚܝܝܢ   [g]ܐܡܪܐ
† f. 20b.
[i]ܪܒ   [j]ܗܘܐ
[l] *add* ܕܝ   [m]ܝܗܡܐ
[n]ܬܘܗܡ   [o] *add* ܕܝ
[p] *omit* ܗܠܝܢ
[q] *add* ܗܠܝܢ
[a]ܠܥܠܡ
[b]ܡܒܘܥ   [r]ܠܚܝܝܢ
[t]ܐܡܪܐ
[u] *add* ܡܢ   [v]ܩܪܝ
[x] *omit* ܠܟܐ
[y]ܐܓܝܒܬ
[z]ܘܐܡܪܬ
[a]ܝܐܘܬ
[c] *omit* ܓܝܪ   [d]ܒܥܠܝܢ
[e]ܗܘܘ
[g] *omit* ܕܝܠܟܝ

Codex A.

[i] ܐܡܪܐ [k] ܒܗܕܢ
[l] ܕܒܝܪܘܫܠܡ
[m] *add* ܕܝܣܓܘܕ
[p] ܒܗܕܢ
[s] ܬܣܓܕܘܢ
[t] *add* ܠܐ [u] ܣܓܕܝܢ
[w] ܐܢܚܢ [x] ܕܐܢܚܢ
[y] ܝܗܘܕܝܐ
[z] *add* ܗܐ [a] ܫܥܬܐ
‡ f. 21*b*.
[c] ܫܪܝܪܐ
[d] ܝܣܓܕܘܢ
[e] ܣܓܘܕܝܐ
[g] *omit* ܒܪܘܚܐ
[h] *add* ܝܬܗ
[i] ܗܕܝܢ [j] ܕܡܬܩܪܐ
[k] *add* ܗܘ
[l] ܕܡܡܠܠ
[m] ܘܒܟܝܢ [n] ܬܠܡܝܕܘܗܝ
[r] ܡܡܠܠ
[s] *add* ܘ [t] *omit* ܐܘܢ
[u] ܠܡܕܝܢܬܐ
[v] *omit* ܘ [y] ܗܕܝܢ
[n] ܡܕܝܢܬܐ [z] *omit* ܘ
[a] ܬܠܡܝܕܘܗܝ
[t] *add* ܘ [c] ܐܟܘܠ
[d] ܬܠܡܝܕܝܐ

Codex B.

19 [i]ܐܡܪܐ ܠܗ ܐܢܬܬܐ ܡܪܝ ܚܡܝܐ ܐܢܐ
20 ܕܐܢܬ ܢܒܝܐ : ܕܐܒܗܬܢ [k]ܒܗܕܝܢ ܛܘܪܐ ܣܓܕܘ
[f. 20*a*]
ܘܐܢܬܘܢ ܐܡܪܝܢ [l]ܕܒܝܪܘܫܠܡ ܗܘ ܐܬܪܐ
21 ܗܘ ܕܝܠܦܣܐ [m] ܐܡܪ ܠܗ ܡܪܢܐ ܝܫܘܥ
ܗܝܡܢܝ ܠܝ [o]ܐܢܬܬܐ ܕܐܬܝܐ ܫܥܬܐ : ܕܠܐ ܠܐ
[p]ܒܗܕܝܢ ܛܘܪܐ ܘܠܐ [q]ܒܝܪܘܫܠܡ [s]ܬܣܓܕܘܢ
22 ܠܐܠܗܐ : ܐܢܬܘܢ [t] [u]ܣܓܕܝܢ ܠܡܐ [r]ܕܠܝܬ ܐܢܬܘܢ
ܚܟܡܝܢ : † [w]ܐܢܚܢ ܕܝ ܣܓܕܝܢ ܠܡܐ [r] [x]ܕܐܢܚܢ
23 ܚܟܡܝܢ : ܕܚܝܝܐ ܡܢ [y]ܝܗܘܕܝܐ ܗܘܘ : ܐܠܐ
[z]ܐܬܝܐ [a]ܫܥܬܐ ‡ ܘܟܒܪ ܗܝ : ܟܕ ܣܓܘܕܝܐ
[c]ܫܪܝܪܐ [d]ܝܣܓܕܘܢ [c]ܠܐܒܐ ܒܪܘܚܐ ܘܒܩܘܫܛܐ :
ܡܛܠ ܐܒܐ ܕܒܥܝܗܘܢ ܕܗܠܝܢ [e]ܣܓܘܕܝܐ ܗܘ
24 ܒܥܐ : [f]ܗܠܝܢ ܕܣܓܕܝܢ ܠܗ [g]ܒܪܘܚܐ ܪܘܚ ܗܘ
ܐܠܗܐ : ܘܗܠܝܢ ܕܣܓܕܝܢ ܠܗ ܒܪܘܚܐ ܘܒܩܘܫܛܐ :
25 ܢܦܠ ܠܗܘܢ ܕܝܗܘܢ ܣܓܕܝܢ ܠܗ : ܐܡܪܐ
ܠܗ [h] ܐܢܬܬܐ : ܚܟܡܐ ܐܢܐ ܕܡܫܝܚܐ ܐܬܐ
[i]ܗܕܝܢ [j]ܕܡܬܩܪܐ ܡܫܝܚܐ : ܟܕ ܝܐܬܐ
26 ܗܘ [k] ܡܚܘܐ ܠܢ ܟܘܠܐ : ܐܡܪ ܠܗ ܡܪܢܐ
ܝܫܘܥ ܐܢܐ ܗܘ ܗܕܝܢ [l]ܕܡܡܠܠ ܥܡܝܟܝ :
27 [m]ܘܒܟܝܢ ܐܬܘ [n]ܬܠܡܝܕܘܗܝ ܘܗܘܘ [o]ܬܡܗܝܢ
ܕܥܡ [p]ܐܢܬܬܐ ܗܘܐ [r]ܡܡܠܠ : [q]ܐܢܫ ܕܝ
ܠܐ ܐܡܪ ܠܗ ܡܐ ܐܢܬ ܒܥܐ : ܐܘ ܡܐ
28 ܐܢܬ [r]ܡܡܠܠ ܥܡܗ : [s]ܫܒܩܬ [t]ܐܘܢ ܩܘܠܬܗ
29 ܘܐܙܠܬ [u]ܠܡܕܝܢܬܐ : ܘܐܡܪܬ ܠܒܢܝܢܫܐ ܐܬܘ
[v]ܘܚܡܘ ܓܒܪ [w]ܐܡܪ ܠܝ [x]ܟܘܠ ܡܐ ܕܥܒܕܬ
30 ܕܟܡܐ [y]ܗܕܝܢ ܗܘ ܡܫܝܚܐ : ܘܢܦܩܘ ܡܢ
31 [n]ܡܕܝܢܬܐ ܘܐܬܘ ܠܘܬܗ : [z]ܘܒܝܢܬܝܢ ܒܥܘ
ܡܢܗ [a]ܬܠܡܝܕܘܗܝ [t]ܐܡܪܝܢ ܠܗ [b]ܪܒܝ [c]ܟܘܠ :
[f. 20*b*]
32 ܗܘ ܕܝ ܐܡܪ ܠܗܘܢ : ܐܢܐ ܡܝܟܘܠܐ ܐܝܬ
ܠܝ ܕܐܟܘܠ : ܡܐ ܕܐܢܬܘܢ ܠܐ ܚܟܡܝܢ :
33 ܘܗܘܘ ܕܝ [d]ܬܠܡܝܕܘܗܝ ܐܡܪܝܢ ܦܠܓܗܘܢ

Codex C.

[i] ܐܡܪܐ
[l] ܕܒܝܪܘܫܠܡ
[m] *add* ܕܝܣܓܘܕ
[o] *add* ܐܬܝ
[q] ܒܝܪܘܫܠܡ
[r] *omit* ܕܠܝܬ . . .
. . . ܠܡܐ
† f. 21*a*.
[x] ܕܐܢܚܢ [y] ܝܗܘܕܝܐ
[c] *omit* ܫܪܝܪܐ ܝܣܓܕܘܢ
[e] ܣܓܘܕܝܐ [f] ܠܗܠܝܢ
[g] *omit* ܒܪܘܚܐ
[j] ܕܡܬܩܪܐ
[n] ܬܠܡܝܕܝ
[o] ܬܡܗܝܢ [p] ܐܬܬܐ
[q] ܐܢܫ
[s] *add* ܘ [t] *omit* ܐܘܢ
[v] *omit* ܘ [w] *add* ܕ
[x] ܟܘܠܐ
[z] *omit* ܘ
[a] ܬܠܡܝܕܝ [b] ܪܒܝ
[c] ܐܟܘܠ
[d] ܬܠܡܝܕܝܐ

Codex A.

ܠܥܠܡ[d] ܕܬܬܚܪܪܘܢ[f]
[g] *add* ܘ
ܕܥܠܡ[h]
‡ f. 22*a*.
ܗܝ[j] *add* ܕܐܒܪܗܡ[k]
ܝܗܘܕܝ[l] ܘܗܘ[m]
ܕܫܪܝ[n] ܐܪܥܬ[o]
ܘܡܫܡܫ[q] ܠܫܢܝ[r]
ܕܠܥܠܡ[s] ܠܥܠܡ[u]
ܕܗܘ[v] ܕܫܪܝ[w]
ܕܫܪܝܢ[x] ܬܗܘܢ[y]
ܘܫܪܝܢ[a] ܬܗܘܢ[b]
ܕܫܪܝ[c]
ܕܐܬܚܙܝܬܘܢ[d]
ܠܐܒܘ[e] ܥܠܒܝܢ[f]
ܥܠܒܬܗܘܢ[g]
ܡܬܚܫܒܝܢ[h] *add* ܦܟܝܢ[i]
ܥܒܕܝܢ[k] ܠܥܠܡ[l]
ܘܬܒܥܘܢ[p] ܦܟܝܢ[q]
ܠܥܠܡ[r] ܘܠܐܠܗܐ[s]
ܡܥܠܝܬܢ[t]
ܐܢܫ[u] ܥܒܕܝܢܗ[w]
ܘܐܢܫ[x] ܘܫܒܩ[y]
ܕܥܠܡܐ[z] ܥܠܡ[a]

Codex B.

ܠܥܠܡ[d] : ܕܗܟܐ ܐܢܬ [e]ܐܡܪ ܠܗ [f]ܕܬܬܚܪܪܘܢ :
34 [g]ܐܡܪ ܠܗܘܢ ܡܪܢ ܝܫܘܥ ܒܩܘܫܛܐ
† ܕܟܠ ܗܘ ܕܥܒܕ ܚܛܝܬܐ ܥܒܕܐ [h]ܕܚܛܝܬܐ
35 ܗܘ : [i]ܘܥܒܕܐ ܒܒܝܬܐ : ܠܐ ‡ ܩܐܡ ܠܥܠܡ
ܕܒܪܐ ܐܚܪܢܐ ܩܐܡ ܠܥܠܡ ܘܒܪܐ ܐܠܗܐ :
ܗܐ ܐܢܐ [j]ܐܡܪ ܠܟܘܢ : ܬܠܬ ܟܢܫܝܢ
ܘܫܪܘ [k]ܐܪܒܥܝܢ ܕܗܘܘ [l]ܫܪܝܢ ܠܚܕܐ :
36 [m]ܘܗܘ [n]ܕܫܪܝ [o]ܐܪܥܗ ܗܘ [p]ܢܦܩ : [q]ܘܡܫܡܫ
ܬܪܝܢ [r]ܠܫܢܝ [s]ܕܠܥܠܡ : [u]ܠܥܠܡ ܕܗܘܝܢ ܕܝܢ
37 [v]ܘܗܘܝܢ [w]ܕܫܪܝܢ ܗܘܝܢ ܫܒܝܐ ܫܒܝܘܢ : ܒܗܘܝܐ
ܐܪ ܗܘ ܡܠܬܐ ܕܗܘܡܢܬܐ : [x]ܕܐܘܫܪܝܢ ܗܘ
[y]ܗܘܝܢ [z]ܕܐܬܒ [a]ܘܐܘܫܪܝܢ ܗܘ [b]ܗܘܝܢ [c]ܕܫܪܝ :
38 ܐܢܐ ܥܒܕܬ ܡܬܒܥܘ [d]ܕܬܚܙܘܢ ܡܢܐ ܕܐܬܘܢ
ܠܐ ܐܠܗܬܘܢ : ܫܘܪܝܢ [e]ܠܐܠܘ ܘܐܬܘܢ
39 [f]ܥܠܬܘܢ [g]ܠܠܝܬܘܗܘܢ : ܡܢ ܗܘ ܕܝ [h]ܡܬܕܒܪ ܐܬܐ[i]
ܗܘܡܢܘ ܒܗ ܡܢ [k]ܥܒܕܝ [l]ܠܥܠܡ ܡܠܬܗ
ܕܐܬܬܐ : [m]ܕܐܫܬܕܪܬ ܘܐܡܪܬ ܕܐܡܪ ܠܝ ܒܟܠ
40 ܡܢܐ ܕܒܒܕܬ : ܘܒܕ ܐܬܘ ܠܗܬܗ [k]ܥܒܕܝ
ܒܟܘ ܡܢܘ ܕܡܬܪ [n]ܠܒܗܘܢ : ܘܡܬܪ ܠܒܗܘܢ
41 ܬܪܝܢ [o]ܢܩܡܝܢ : [p]ܘܦܩܠܝܢ [q]ܦܩܠܝܢ ܗܝܡܢܘ ܒܗ
42 [r]ܠܥܠܡ ܡܠܬܗ : [s]ܘܠܐܠܗܝ [s]ܐܬܬܐ ܘܗܘ
ܐܡܪܝܢ ܕܒܗܕ ܡܢ ܒܕܘ ܠܐ [r]ܠܥܠܡ [t]ܡܠܝܬܢܐ
ܐܢܘܢ ܡܗܝܡܢܝܢ : [u]ܐܝܢ ܐܪ [w]ܥܒܕܝܢ ܡܢܘܢ
[x]ܘܐܝܢ ܢܕܒܝܢ ܡܢ [y]ܘܫܒܩ ܕܗܘܝܢ ܗܘ ܡܢܝܢܘܢ
[z]ܕܥܠܡܐ : [a]ܥܠܡ ⁘

XXX.

John VIII. 42—51.

[f. 21*a*]
ܬܠܬܝܢ ܝܘܡ ܐܠܗܝܢ ܦܢ ܐܡܥܘ [b]ܐܠܫܥܝܘܢ
ܡܢ [c]ܢܫܝܢ[a] :[y] ܐܡܪ [z]ܠܗܘܢ ܡܪܢ[a] [b]ܫܡܥܘ :

Codex C.

ܐܢܬ[e] ܕܬܚܪܘܢ[f]
ܕܥܠܡ[h]
† f. 21*b*.
ܘܥܠܡ[i]
ܗܝ[j] *add* ܫܪܝܢ[l]
ܕ[n] *omit* ܐܪܥܗ[o]
ܕܢܦܩ[p] ܘܡܫܡܫ[q]
ܠܫܢܝ[r] ܕܠܥܠܡ[s]
ܘܗܘܝܢ[v] ܕܫܪܝܢ[x]
ܗܘܝܢ[y] *omit*
ܕܐܬܒ[z] ܘܫܪܝܢ[a]
ܕܫܪܝ[c]
ܕܬܚܙܘܢ[d] ܠܐܘ[e]
ܥܠܬܘܢ[f]
ܥܠܬܗܘܢ[g]
ܦܟܝܢ[i] *add*
ܐܬܕܘܪܬ[m]
ܠܒܗܘܢ[n]
ܢܩܡܝܢ[o] ܘܦܩܠܝܢ[p]
ܦܟܝܢ[q] ܘܠܐܠܗܝܬܐ[s]
ܡܠܝܬܢܐ[t]
ܐܝܢ[u] ܥܒܕܝܢ[w]
ܘܐܝܢ[x] ܕܥܠܡܐ[z]
ܥܠܡ[a] *omit*

ܐܠܫܥܝܘܢ[b] ܢܫܝܢ[c]
[y] *add* ܒܬܪܗ ܡܪܢ
[z] *omit* ܠܗܘܢ
[a] *add* ܠܬܠܡܝܕܘܗܝ
[b] *omit* ܫܡܥܘ

(Codex A, lower:)

ܝܘܡ ܐܠܗܝܢ[a]
ܦܢ ܐܠܫܥܝܘܢ
ܐܠܗܝܢܫܥܘ ܡܢ
ܢܫܝܢ[a]
[z] *omit* ܠܗܘܢ
[a] *add* ܠܬܠܡܝܕܘܗܝ
[b] *omit* ܫܡܥܘ

Codex A.	Codex B.	Codex C.
[b] omit ܘܐܡܪ	ܘܐܡܪ[b] ܠܗܘܢ ܐܠܘ ܗܘܐ ܐܠܗܐ ܐܒܘܟܘܢ[c] ܐܪܚܡܬ 42	ܐܒܘܟܘܢ[c]
‡ f. 22b.	ܗܘܝܬܘܢ[‡†] ܪܚܡܝܢ ܠܝ : ܐܢܐ ܓܝܪ ܡܢ ܐܠܗܐ	† f. 22a.
ܐܒܘܟܘܢ[c]	ܢܦܩܬ ܘܐܬܝܬ ܠܐ ܓܝܪ ܡܢ ܢܦܫܝ ܐܬܝܬ :	
	ܐܠܐ ܗܘ ܫܠܚ ܠܝ : [d]ܠܡܢܐ [e]ܠܡܠܠܝ ܕܝܠܝ 43	ܠܡܢܐ [d] omit [e]ܠܡܠܠܝ
ܐܢܬܘܢ[f] [g]ܡܠܝ	ܠܝܬ ܐܢܬܘܢ ܚܟܡܝܢ : ܕܠܝܬ [f]ܐܢܬܘܢ [g]ܡܠܝ	ܐܢܬܘܢ[f]
ܡܠܬܝ[h]	ܕܬܗܘܢ ܫܡܥܝܢ [h]ܡܠܬܐ ܕܝܠܝ : ܐܢܬܘܢ ܡܢ 44	ܡܠܬܝ[h]
ܥܒܕܝܢ ܐܢܬܘܢ [i] omit	ܐܒܘܟܘܢ ܣܛܢܐ ܐܢܬܘܢ [i]ܥܒܕܝܢ ܐܢܬܘܢ[i]	ܥܒܕܝܢ ܐܢܬܘܢ [i] omit
	[j]ܘܬܐܘܬܗ ܕܐܒܘܟܘܢ ܐܢܬܘܢ ܨܒܝܢ	[j]ܘܬܐܘܬܗ
ܩܛܘܠ[k]	ܕܬܥܒܕܘܢ ܥܒܕܝܢ : ܗܘ ܓܝܪ [k]ܩܛܘܠ [l]ܐܢܫܝܢ ܗܘܐ	ܩܛܘܠ[k] [l]ܐܢܫܝܢ
	ܡܢ ܫܪܝܐ : ܘܒܩܘܫܛܐ ܠܐ ܗܘܐ ܩܐܡ ܕܠܝܬ	
ܘܩܘܫܛ[m]	ܘܩܘܫܛ[m] ܒܓܘܗ : ܟܕ ܡܡܠܠ [n]ܡܡܠܠ ܕܓܕܠ	ܘܩܘܫܛ[m]
ܡܡܠܠ[n] [o]ܕܓܕܠ	ܡܢ ܕܝܠܗ ܗܘ [n]ܡܡܠܠ : ܕܟܕܒ [o]ܕܓܕܠ ܐܝܬ	
[q] add ܕ ܐܒܘܗܝ[p]	ܗܘ : ܘܐܒܘܗ [p]ܐܒܘܗܝ* : ܐܢܐ ܕܝ [q]ܐܢܐ ܐܡܪ 45	[* Sic in Cod. B.]
	ܩܘܫܛܐ ܠܝܬ ܐܢܬܘܢ ܡܗܝܡܢܝܢ ܠܝ : ܡܢ 46	[q] add ܕ ܐܒܘܗܝ[p]
	ܡܢܟܘܢ ܡܟܣ ܠܝ [r]ܥܠ ܚܛܐ ܚܕܐ : ܐܢ	[r] omit ܠܝ . . . ܥܠ
	ܩܘܫܛܐ ܐܢܐ ܐܡܪ ܠܡܢܐ ܠܝܬ ܐܢܬܘܢ	
ܠܡܠܠ[s]	ܡܗܝܡܢܝܢ ܠܝ[r] : ܡܢ ܕܗܘ ܡܢ ܐܠܗܐ ܗܘ 47	
[t] add ܐܢܬܘܢ	ܫܡܥ : [s]ܠܡܠܠ ܕܐܠܗܐ[t] ܠܝܬ ܐܢܬܘܢ ܫܡܥܝܢ	[t] add ܐܢܬܘܢ
ܝܗܘܕܝܐ[u]	ܕܠܝܬ ܐܢܬܘܢ ܡܢ ܐܠܗܐ : ܘܐܬܝܒܘ [u]ܝܗܘܕܝܐ 48	
[v] omit ܕ	ܘܐܡܪܘ ܠܗ ܠܐ ܫܦܝܪ ܐܡܪܝܢ[v] [j]ܕܫܡܪܝܐ	
ܕܫܡܪܝܐ[j]	ܐܢܬ ܘܫܐܕ ܠܟ : ܐܬܝܒ ܝܫܘܥ ܘܐܡܪ 49	
ܠܟܐ[k]	ܘܐܡܪ ܠܗܘܢ : ܐܢܐ ܫܐܕ ܠܝܬ [k]ܠܟܐ : ܐܠܐ	
ܡܝܩܪ[y] [z]ܡܩܠܢ	[a]ܡܝܩܪ[y] ܐܢܐ ܠܐܒܐ ܘܐܢܬܘܢ [z]ܡܩܠܢ ܠܝ : ܐܢܐ 50	ܡܝܩܪ[y] [z]ܡܩܠܢ
[a] add ܕܝ [c]ܕܒܥܐ	[b]ܠܝܬ ܒܥܐ ܫܘܒܚܝ : ܐܝܬ [c]ܕܒܥܐ ܘܕܐܢ :	[a] add ܕܝ [b]ܠܝܬ ܐܢܐ
ܢܛܪ[e]	ܐܡܝܢ [d]ܐܡܝܢ ܐܡܪ ܐܢܐ ܠܟܘܢ : ܐܢ [e]ܢܛܪ 51	ܐܡܝܢ [d] omit [e]ܢܛܪ
‡ f. 23a.	ܐܢܫ ܡܠܬܝ ܠܐ ܚܙܐ ܡܘܬܐ ܠܥܠܡ . [f]ܥܠܡ ‡ ⁘	[f] omit ܥܠܡ

XXXI.

John VIII. 51—59.

Codex A.	Codex B.	Codex C.
[a]ܝܘܡ ܐܬܠܬܝܬܐ	ܘܐܡܪ[c a] ܝܫܘܥ ܠܝܗܘܕܝܐ ܕܗܝܡܢܘ [b]ܒܗ ܐܡܝܢ	[b]ܡܢ ܝܫܘܥ[b]
ܐܠܝܡܡ ܐܡܝܢ		
ܐܠܝܫܘܥ ܡܢ	ܐܠܝܫܘܥ ܕܢ ܐܠܝܡܡ ܡܢ ܝܫܘܥ[a b] : ܐܡܝܢ 51	ܘܐܡܝܢ[c]
ܝܫܘܥ[a]		

Codex A.	Codex B.	Codex C
ܠܝܗܘܕܝܐ : [w] add	52 ܘܗܘܘ ܝܗܘܕܝܐ [w] ܐܡܪܝܢ ܠܗ [x] ܒܝܢܝܗܘܢ : ܕܐܝܟ	
ܐܡܝܢ ܐܡܝܢ ܐܡܪ	ܡܫܟܚ ܗܢܐ ܒܣܪܗ : ܐܡܪ ܠܗܘܢ [y] ܘܝܫܘܥ	
ܐܢܐ ܠܟܘܢ . ܕܐܢ	ܡܫܟܚ ܗܢܐ [z] : ܘܐܡܪ [b] ܐܡܝܢ ܐܡܝܢ ܐܡܪ ܐܢܐ	ܐܡܝܢ [b] [z] omit ܡܫܟܚ
ܠܐ ܬܐܟܠܘܢ ܒܣܪܗ	53 ܠܟܘܢ ܠܐ [c] ܐܟܠܝܢ [d] ܡܢ ܒܣܪܗ [e] ܠܐ [f] ܠܚܝܝܢ : [†] ܕܥܠܡܐ	† f. 22b.
ܕܒܪܗ ܕܐܢܫܐ	ܐܢܬ ܠܐ ܐܟܠܝܢ ܒܣܪܗ [g] ܕܒܪܗ ܕܐܢܫܐ : ܘܐܢܬ	ܐܟܠܝܢ [c] ܕܒܪܗ [d] ܕܐܢܫܐ
ܠܚܝܝܢ :	[h] ܠܐ ܫܬܝܢ ܕܡܗ : ܡܢ ܐܢܬ ܚܝܝܢ ܒܢܦܫܟܘܢ :	[g] ܕܝ ܗܘ
[x] ܘܝܗܘܕܝܐ [y] ܘܐܬܚܪܝܘ	54 [i] ܐܟܠ ܒܣܪܝ ܘܫܬܐ ܕܡܝ ܐܝܬ ܠܗ : ܚܝܝ	[i] ܐܟܠ
ܡܫܟܚ [z] omit ܐܡܝܢ [b]	ܐܢܐ ܡܩܝܡ ܐܢܐ [j] ܠܗ ܒܝܘܡܐ ܐܚܪܝܐ	
[e] omit ܠܐ ܒܣܪܗ [d]	[k] ܕܥܠܡܐ : ܐܢܬ ܗܘ ܐܟܠܐ ܕܡܬܚܘܐ ܠܢ : ܗܢܘܢ	
[f] ܠܚܝܝܢ [h] ܘܫܬܝܢ	55 ܕܒܫܪܐ ܐܬܐܟܠ ܕܚܝܝܢ [l] ܠܥܠܡܝܢ : ܘܐܠܐ	
[j] ܐܬܚܫܒܘܬܐ	ܐܟܪܬܐ ܗܘܐ : ܐܢܐ ܕܝ [m] ܡܬܒܣܪ ܠܗ : [n] ܘܐܢܐ	ܡܬܒܣܪ [m] [n] ܘܐܢܐ
[k] ܒܐܚܪܝܐ	[o] ܒܣܪܝ ܕܝܠܝ ܐܢܐ [p] ܡܫܬܪ ܠܗ : ܗܘ ܟܠܗ [q] ܐܢܐ	[q] omit ܐܢܐ
[l] ܐܠܗܐ ܠܥܠܡܐ	[r] ܕܐܟܠ ܕܝܠܝ ܠܥܠܡܐ : ܐܟܠ ܡܢܗ ܐܢܐ ܠܗ	
[o] ܢܦܫܗ [p] ܡܫܬܪ	56 ܘܡܢܬܗ ܐܢܐ ܠܗ [s] : ܐܡܪ ܠܗܘܢ ܘܐܡܪ	
[r] ܕܐܟܠ ܠܥܠܡ [s] add	ܐܬܚܫܒܘ ܕܗܘܐ ܗܢܐ ܕܝܠܝ : [t] ܘܡܚܫܒܐ	ܘܐܬܚܫܒܐ [t] ܘܐܡܪܘ [u]
[w] add ܕܝ [x] ܝܗܘܕܝܐ	57 [u] ܘܐܡܪܘ : ܐܡܪܝܢ ܠܗ [w] [x] ܝܗܘܕܝܐ ܡܢ ܗܢܐ	[w] add ܕܝ [x] ܝܗܘܕܝܐ
[y] ܫܡܥܝܢ	[y] ܫܡܥܝܢ ܡܠܝܢ ܠܗ ܠܝ [z] ܘܐܡܪܝܢ ܠܡܠܬܐ :	[y] ܫܡܥܝܢ
[z] ܘܐܡܪܝܢ	58 ܐܡܪ [a] ܡܢܐ ܝܗܘܕܝܐ ܐܡܪܝܢ ܐܡܪ ܐܢܐ ܐܢܐ	[z] ܘܐܡܪܝܢ
[a] add ܠܗܘܢ	ܠܗܘܢ : ܕܗܘ ܠܐ ܗܘܐ ܐܡܪܝܢ ܐܢܬ ܐܢܐ :	[a] add ܠܗܘܢ
[b] ܝܗܘܕܝܐ	59 ܘܡܫܟܚ [b] ܝܗܘܕܝܐ ܕܡܢ [c] ܕܐܬܚܫܒܘ ܡܢܗ :	[b] ܝܗܘܕܝܐ
[c] ܕܐܬܚܫܒܘ	ܡܢ ܝܗܘܕܝܐ [d] ܐܬܚܫܒܘ ܘܐܡܪܘ [e] ܠܗ ܡܢ	[e] omit ܠܗ [d] add ܕܝ
[d] add ܕܝ	ܗܘܐ : ܘܗܘܐ ܡܢܗ [f] ܘܐܡܪ ܠܗܘܢ	[g] ܐܬܚܫܒܘܢ
[f] ܘܐܡܪ	[g] ܐܬܚܫܒܘܢ [h] ܥܠܡܐ ⁘	[h] omit ܥܠܡܐ
[g] ܐܬܚܫܒܘܢ		

XXXII.

John VI. 3—14.

Codex A.	Codex B.	Codex C
ܐܬܐ ܝܫܘܥ ܘܬܠܡܝܕܘܗܝ [a]	ܐܬܐ [a] ܘܬܠܡܝܕܘܗܝ ܥܡܗ ܠܛܘܪܐ [b] ܥܠ ܐܚܪܢܐ	ܡܢ ܝܫܘܥ [b]
ܥܡܗ ܠܛܘܪܐ ܡܢ	ܠܥܠܡܐ ܡܢ ܝܫܘܥ [a] [b] ‡ [y] ܘܡܢܗ ܕܐܬܐ :	
[a] ܝܫܘܥ		
‡ f. 23b.		
[z] add ܠܗ [y] add ܕܝ	3 ܘܥܠܝܡ [z] . ܝܗܘܕܝܐ ܠܛܘܪܐ : ܘܬܡܢ ܗܘܐ	[z] add ܠܗ
[a] ܝܬܒ [b] ܬܠܡܝܕܘܗܝ	4 [a] ܝܬܒ ܥܡ [b] ܬܠܡܝܕܘܗܝ : ܗܘܐ ܕܝ ܦܨܚܐ	[b] ܬܠܡܝܕܘܗܝ

Codex A.	Codex B.	Codex C.
ᵈܟܡܐ ܕܒܥܠܡܐ	5 ᶜܟܡܐ ᵈܕܒܥܠܡܐ ᵉܐܢܐ : ܢܗܘܪܗ ܕܥܠܡܐ [f. 22a] ܐܢܐ	ᶜܟܡܐ
ᵉܕܐܢܐ ᶠܢܗܘܪܗ	ܗܘܝܬ ᶠ† ܗܘ ᵍܒܥܠܡܐ ʰܐܢܐ ܕܝܠܝ ܐܝܬܝ	† f. 23a.
ᵍܕܥܠܡܐ ʰܐܢܐ	ܠܗܘܢ ᶦܐܡܪ ܠܬܠܡܝܕܘܗܝ : ܟܕ ܗܘ ʲܐܝܬܝ	ᵈܕܒܥܠܡܐ
ʲܐܢܐ ᶦ add ܘ	6 ܘܟܕ ᵏܐܡܪ ˡܗܠܝܢ ܡܠܝܐ : ܪܩ ܥܠ ܐܪܥܐ	ᵉܕܐܢܐ ᶠܢܗܘܪܗ
ᵏܐܡܪ ˡܗܠܝܢ	ܘܓܒܠ ܛܝܢܐ ܡܢ ܪܘܩܗ : ܘܛܫ ܥܠ ܥܝܢܘܗܝ	ᵍܕܥܠܡܐ ʰܐܢܐ
ᵐܕܣܡܝܐ	7 ܕܗܘ ܣܡܝܐ : ܘܐܡܪ ܠܗ ᵐܙܠ ܐܫܝܓ	ᵏܐܡܪ ᶦ add ܘ
ⁿ omit ܠܗ ᵒܒܥܝܢܐ	ᵒܒܥܝܢܐ ܕܫܠܝܚܐ : ᵖܘܐܙܠ ܐܫܝܓ ⁿܠܗ ܘܐܡܪ	ˡܗܠܝܢ
ᵖܘܐܙܠ ᵠ omit ܘ	ܘܐܬܐ ᵠܟܕ ܚܙܐ ܕܐܬܐ ᵏܐܡܪ ܠܗܘܢ ܗܠܝܢ	ᵐܕܣܡܝܐ
ʳܕܡܢ ܩܕܡ	8 ܠܗܘܢ : ܐܡܪ ܠܗ ܡܢ ܥܠ ʳܕܡܢ ܩܕܡ ˢܐܬܚܙܝ	ⁿ omit ܠܗ ᵒܒܥܝܢܐ
ˢܐܬܚܙܝ	9 ܐܚܪܢܐ ᵗܕܡܐ ܠܗ : ܐܡܪ ᵘܗܘ ܗܘ ܗܘ	ᵖܘܐܙܠ ᵠ omit ܘ
ʷܐܢܐ	ʷܐܢܐ ܕܡܛܠ ᵏܐܡܪ ܠܗ ܕܐܢܐ ܗܘ	ʳܕܡܢ ܩܕܡ (sic)
ˣܕܐܬܦܬܚ	ܗܘ : ܐܡܪ ܠܗ ܐܝܟܢܐ ܗܠܝܢ ܐܬܦܬܚܘ :	ˢܐܬܚܙܝ
ᵃ add ܕܝܢ	10 ܐܡܪܘ ܠܗ ܐܝܟܢܐ ܐܬܦܬܚܘ ܥܝܢܝܟ	ᵗ omit ܕ ᵘ omit ܗܘ
ᵇܥܝܢܝܟ	ˣܕܐܬܦܬܚܘ : ܗܘ ܕܝܢ ܐܡܪ ʸܓܒܪܐ ܗܘ	ʷܐܢܐ
ᶜܥܝܢܝ ᵈܡܢ	ܕܡܬܩܪܐ : ᶻܐܡܪ ᵃܠܝ ܓܒܠ ܛܝܢܐ : ܘܛܫ	ʸ omit ܒ ᶻܐܡܪ
ᶠ omit ܕܝܢ ᵉ add ܕܝܢ	11 ᵇܥܝܢܝ ܘܐܡܪ ᶜܠܝ ܙܠ ܐܫܝܓ : ܘܐܙܠܬ	ᵃ add ܕܝܢ ᵇܥܝܢܝ
ᵍܘܐܬܦܬܚܘ	ܐܫܝܓܬ ܒܥܝܢܐ ܕܫܠܝܚܐ : ܘܚܙܝܬ ܠܗܘܢ	ᵉ add ܕܝܢ ᵛܘܐܡܪܘ
ᶦ add ܕ ʰܕܐܝܟܐ	ᵛܘܐܡܪܘ ܠܗ : ᵈܐܝܟܐ ᵉܗܘ : ܐܡܪ ܠܗܘܢ ܠܐ	ᵍܘܐܬܦܬܚܘ
ˡܐܒܘܗܝ ᵏܒܪܬ	12 ܝܕܥ ܐܢܐ : ܐܡܪ ᶠܕܝܢ ܐܒܘܗܝ ܕܗܘܐ ܐܡܪ	ᶦ add ܕ ʰܕܐܝܟܐ
ᵒܥܝܢܘܗܝ ⁿܕܦܬܚ	ᵍܘܐܬܦܬܚܘ ʰܥܝܢܝ ᶦܠܐ ᵏܕܝܢ ᵏܒܪܬ	ᵐܐܬܦܬܚ
‡ f. 24a.	13 ˡܠܦܪܝܫܐ : ‡ܕܝܢ ᵐܐܬܦܬܚ ⁿܕܦܬܚ	ⁿܕܦܬܚ ᵖܥܝܢܘܗܝ
ᵠ add ܕܝܢ	ᵒܡܢ ܥܝܢܘܗܝ ᵖܕܣܡܝܐ : ܗܘܐ ܕܐܬܦܬܚ	ᵠ add ܕܝܢ ˢ add ܗܘ
ˢ add ܗܘ ʳܕܥܒܕ	14 ܥܠ ܕܗܠܝܢ : ܡܠܝܐ ᵠܒܫܒܬܐ : ܗܘܐ ܕܝܢ	ᵘ omit ܗܘ ᵗܛܝܢܐ
ʷ add ܕ ᵘ omit ܗܘ	ʳܕܥܒܕ ܗܘܐ ܛܝܢܐ ˢܘܦܬܚ	ʷ add ܕܝܢ
ˣ omit ܗܘ ܫܡܥ	ᵗܛܝܢܐ ᵘܗܘ ܐܡܪ : ʷ ˣܗܘ ܕܝܢ ܐܬܦܬܚ	ˣ omit ܗܘ ܫܡܥ
ᶻ add ܥܠ ʸܠܦܪܝܫܐ	ʸܠܦܪܝܫܐ ᶻ : ⁘	ʸܠܦܪܝܫܐ

XXXIII.

John IX. 39—X. 9.

Codex A.	Codex B.	Codex C.
ᵃܘܐܡܪ ܐܝܫܘܥ	ᵃܐܡܪ ܝܫܘܥ ܠܬܠܡܝܕܘܗܝ ᵇܐܢܐ ܐܬܝܬ ᶜܠܥܠܡܐ ܗܢܐ	ᶜ omit . . . ܥܠ
ܠܥܠܡܐ	[f. 22b] ᶜܠܕܝܢܐ ܡܢ ܥܠܡܐ : ʸ ܘܐܡܪ ܗܘܐ ܗܢܐ ܕܝܢ	. . . ܠܥܠܡܐ
ܠܕܝܢܐ ܡܢ ᵃܥܠܡܐ		ʸ add ܘܐܡܪ
ʸ add ܐܡܪ		

Codex A.

[z] ܠܝܗܘܕܝܢ

[b] ܠܥܠܡܐ [c] ܗܕܝܢ

[d] ܦܪܝܫܝܐ

[e] ܘܐܡܪܝܢ

[f] ܐܢܚܢ

[g] ܘܚܛܝܬܟܘܢ

[h] ܩܐܡܝܢ [i] ܗܘܝܢ

[k] ܕܬܪܥܐ

[l] *add* ܠܕܪܬܐ

[n] ܘܠܝܣܛܝܣ

[p] ܕܥܠܠ [q] *add* ܕ

[r] ܐܡܪܬܐ [t] ܦܬܚ

[u] *omit* ܘ [v] ܫܡܥܝܢ

[x] *omit* ܕܝ [y] ܐܡܪܬܗ

[z] *omit* ܕܝ [a] ܚܕܐ

[e] ܩܕܡܝܗܘܢ

‡ f. 24*b*.

[d] ܘܡܗܠܟ [e] ܠܩܕܡܝܗܘܢ

[q] ܢܦܩ [r] ܒܬܪܗ

[f] ܡܬܕܒܪܝܢ

[g] ܐܙܠ [h] ܘܐܡܪܬܐ

[i] ܕܝܕܥܝܢ [j] ܕܗܘܝܢ

[k] ܡܚܪܝܢ [l] ܢܘܟܪܝ

[m] ܥܪܩܝܢ [n] ܠܩܠܗܘܢ

[o] ܕܢܘܟܪܝ [p] ܗܕܝܢ

[q] *omit* ܕ

[w] *omit* ܗܘ

[y] ܘܠܣܛܝܢ [z] ܫܡܥܘ

[a] ܐܡܪܬܐ

[h] *omit* ܫܠܡ

Codex B.

39 [z] ܠܝܗܘܕܝܢ : [a] ܠܕܝܢ ܐܬܝܬ [b] ܠܥܠܡܐ [c] ܗܕܝܢ :
ܕܗܠܝܢ ܕܠܐ ܚܙܝܢ ܢܚܙܘܢ : ܘܗܠܝܢ ܕܚܙܝܢ
40 ܢܣܡܘܢ ܡܢ ܬܠܡܝܕܘܗܝ : ܘܫܡܥܘ [d] ܦܪܝܫܝܐ ܕܗܘܘ
ܥܡܗ ܗܠܝܢ ܡܠܝܐ [e] ܘܐܡܪܘ ܠܗ : ܕܠܡܐ
41 ܐܘܦ [f] ܐܢܚܢ ܣܡܝܢ ܐܢܚܢ : ܐܡܪ ܠܗܘܢ
ܡܪܢ ܝܫܘܥ ܐܠܘ ܗܘܝܬܘܢ ܣܡܝܢ ܠܐ
ܗܘܬ ܠܟܘܢ ܚܛܝܐ : ܟܕܘ ܕܝ ܗܐ ܐܬܘܢ
ܐܡܪܝܢ ܕܐܢܚܢ ܚܙܝܢ [g] ܘܚܛܝܬܟܘܢ [h] ܩܝܡܝܢ
X. 1 [i] ܗܘܝܢ : ܐܡܝܢ ܐܡܝܢ ܐܡܪ ܐܢܐ ܠܟܘܢ :
ܕܡܢ ܕܠܐ [j] ܥܠܠ ܡܢ [k] ܬܪܥܐ [l] ܕܐܡܪܬܐ :
ܐܠܐ ܣܠܩ ܠܗ ܡܢ ܕܘܟܝ : ܗܘ ܗܘ [m] ܓܢܒ
2 ܐܝܬܘ ܗܘ [n] ܘܠܝܣܛܝܣ : ܕܝܢ [o] ܕܝ [p] ܥܠܠ ܡܢ
3 [q] ܬܪܥܐ ܗܘ ܪܥܝܐ [r] ܕܐܡܪܬܐ : ܠܗܕܝܢ
[s] ܬܪܥܐ [t] ܦܬܚ [s] : [u] ܘܐܡܪܬܐ ܠܩܠܗ [v] ܫܡܥܝܢ :
[w] ܘܗܘ [x] ܕܝ ܩܪܐ [y] ܠܐܡܪܬܐ ܒܫܡ [z] ܕܝ
4 [a] ܟܕ [b] [c] ܡܦܩܗܘܢ ܟܠܗܘܢ : [d] ܘܡܗܠܟ [e] ܠܗܘܢ
ܘܟܕ [q] ܢܩܦܝܢ [r] ܒܬܪܗ [f] ܡܬܕܒܪܝܢ ‡ ܗܘ
ܘܗܐ [g] ܐܙܠ : [h] ܘܐܡܪܬܐ [i] ܕܝܕܥܝܢ ܩܠܗ
5 [j] ܕܗܘܝܢ [k] ܡܚܪܝܢ ܩܠܗ : ܒܬܪ [l] ܢܘܟܪܝ ܕܝ
ܠܐ [i] ܕܝܕܥܝܢ : ܐܠܐ [m] ܥܪܩܝܢ ܡܢܗ ܕܠܐ
6 [k] ܝܕܥܝܢ [n] ܠܩܠܗ [o] ܕܢܘܟܪܝ [p] ܗܕܝܢ ܡܬܠܐ
ܐܡܪ ܠܗܘܢ ܡܪܢ ܝܫܘܥ : ܗܢܘܢ ܕܝ ܠܐ
7 ܝܕܥܘ ܡܢ [q] ܕܗܘܐ [s] ܡܡܠܠ ܠܗܘܢ : ܘܐܡܪ
ܠܗܘܢ ܬܘܒ ܡܪܢ ܝܫܘܥ : ܐܡܝܢ ܐܡܝܢ
8 ܐܡܪ ܐܢܐ ܠܟܘܢ : ܕܐܢܐ [w] ܗܘ ܬܪܥܐ
ܕܐܡܪܬܐ : ܟܘܠ ܗܠܝܢ ܕܐܬܘ [x] ܩܕܡܝ
ܗܘܘ [y] ܠܣܛܝܢ : ܐܠܐ ܠܐ [z] ܫܡܥܘܢ ܠܗܘܢ
9 [a] ܐܡܪܬܐ : † ܐܢܐ ܗܘ ܬܪܥܐ [b] ܡܢ [c] ܕܥܐܠ
ܒܝ [d] ܕܥܠܠ ܚܝܐ : [f] ܘܥܠܠ ܘܢܦܩ ܘܡܫܟܚ
ܡܪܥܝܐ : [h] ܫܠܡ ⁘

Codex C.

[z] ܠܝܗܘܕܝܢ

[a] *omit* ܠܕܝܢ

[b] ܠܥܠܡܐ

[e] ܘܐܡܪܝܢ

[f] ܐܢܗ

[h] ܘܩܐܡܝܢ [j] ܥܠܠ

[k] ܕܬܪܥܐ

[l] *add* ܠܕܪܬܐ

[m] ܓܢܒܐ [n] ܘܠܝܣܛܝܣ

[o] *omit* ܕܝ [p] ܕܥܠܠ

[q] *add* ܕ

[s] ܦܬܚ ܬܪܥܐ [s]

[w] ܘܗܘܘ

[y] *omit* ܠ [z] *omit* ܕܝ

[b] *add* ܘܚܕ [d] ܘܡܗܠܟ

[q] ܢܦܩ [f] ܡܬܕܒܪܝܢ

[i] ܕܝܕܥܝܢ

[j] *omit* ܕ

[n] ܠܩܠܗ

[o] ܕܢܘܟܪܝ

[q] *omit* ܕ [s] ܡܡܠܠ

[x] ܓܢܒܝܢ [y] ܘܠܝܣܛܝܢ

[c] ܕܥܠܠ [d] ܕܥܠܠ

† f. 24*a*.

[f] ܘܥܠܠ

[h] *omit* ܫܠܡ

Codex A. | Codex B. | Codex C.

XXXIV.

John X. 17—28.

Codex B.

ܐܪܒܥܗ^a ܘܬܠܬܝܢ ܝܘܡ ^bܐܠܟܣܢܕܪܘܣ ܒܝ ܐܘܫܥܢܗ
ܐܠܦܣܩܘܣ ܡܢ ܝܘܚܢܢ^{ba} : ^yܐܡܪ^z ^aܠܝܫܘܥ
17 ^bܗܠܝܢ ^cܕܐܒܘ ^dܠܟܠܠ ܕܢܝ^d ܐܒܐ ܪܚܡ ܠܝ
ܕܐܢܐ ^eܣܐܡ ܢܦܫܝ : ܕܬܘܒ ^gܐܣܒ ܝܬܗ
18 ^fܐܢܫ ܠܐ ^gܢܣܒ ܝܬܗ ܡܢܝ : ܐܠܐ ^hܐܢܐ
ܣܐܡ ܝܬܗ ܡܢ ܓܪܡܝ : ܫܠܝܛ ܐܢܐ ^iܕܐܣܝܡ
ܝܬܗ ^kܘܫܠܝܛ ܐܢܐ ܬܘܒ ܕܐܣܒ ܝܬܗ^k : ܗܕܝܢ
19 ܦܘܩܕܐ ܕܝ ܢܣܒܬ ܡܢ ܐܒܐ ^lܘܗܘܐ ܬܘܒ
ܐܬܒܙܥܘ ܒܝܢ ^mܝܗܘܕܝ ^nܠܟܠܠ ܗܠܝܢ ܡܠܝܐ :
20 ܘܗܘܘ ܕܝ ܣܓܝ ܡܢܗܘܢ ܐܡܪܝܢ ܫܐܕ ^oܥܠܝ*
ܘܗܘ ܡܫܬܦܐ ܠܡܐ ܐܬܘܢ ܫܡܥܝܢ ܠܗ :
21 ^pܘܚܘܪܢܝܢ ܗܘܘ ܐܡܪܝܢ ܗܠܝܢ ܡܠܝܐ ܠܝܬ
^qܗܢܘܢ ܕܐܢܫ ܕܥܠܘܝ ܫܐܕ : ܕܡܐ ܫܐܕ ^rܝܟܝܠ
22 ‡ܕܡܬܚܕ ܒܝܢܝܗܘܢ ܕܡܒܪܘܢ : ^sܘܐܬܚܕܒܕ
23 ܕܝ ^tܚܕܘܬܐ ^uܒܝܪܘܫܠܡ : ^vܘܣܬܘܐ ܗܘܐ :
ܘܗܘܐ ܡܪܢܐ ܝܫܘܥ ^wܡܗܠܟ ܒܢܘܣܐ
24 ܒܐܣܛܘܗ ^xܕܫܠܝܡܘܢ : ܘܚܕܪܘ ܝܬܗ ^yܝܗܘܕܝ
ܘܗܘܘ ܐܡܪܝܢ ܠܗ ܥܕ ^zܡܬܝ ܐܬ ܢܣܒ
^aܢܦܫܢ : ܐܢ ܐܬ ܗܘ ܡܫܝܚܐ ^bܐܡܪ ^cܠܢ
25 ܒܓ̈ܠܝܐ : ^dܐܓܝܒ ܡܪܢܐ ܝܫܘܥ ܘܐܡܪ
ܠܗܘܢ : ܐܡܪܬ ܠܟܘܢ ܘܠܝܬ ܐܬܘܢ
ܡܗܝܡܢܝܢ : ܥܘܒܕܐ ܗܠܝܢ ܕܐܢܐ ܥܒܕ ܒܫܡܗ
26 ܕܐܒܐ ܗܢܘܢ ܡܣܗܕܝܢ ܥܠ ܕܝܠܝ : ܐܠܐ
ܐܬܘܢ ܠܝܬ ܐܬܘܢ ܡܗܝܡܢܝܢ : ܕܠܝܬ ܐܬܘܢ ܡܢ
[f. 23b]
27 ^eܐܡܪܬܐ ܕܝܠܝ : ܗܝܟ ܒܠ ܡܒܐ ^{gf}ܕܗܘܬ ܠܟܘܢ^f
^hܕܐܡܪܬܐ ܕܝܠܝ ܠܩܠܝ ^iܫܡܥܢ ^jܫܡܥܝܢ :
28 ܘܐܢܐ ^kܡܟܪ ^mܠܗܘܢ : ܘܒܬܪܝ ^hܗܢܘܢ
^lܐܬܝܢ : ܘܐܢܐ ܝܗܒ ^mܠܗܘܢ ^nܚܝܝ ^oܕܠܥܠܡ^p ⁘

Codex A.

^a ܝܘܡ ܐܠܟܣܢܕܪܘܣ ܐܠܦܣܩܘܣ ܐܠܝܘܚܢܢܣ ܡܢ ܝܘܚܢܢ^a
^z add ܡܪܢܐ
^a ܠܝܫ̈ܘܥ
^b ܐܝܢ   ^c omit ܕ
^d ܠܟܠܠ ܕܢܝ
^e ܣܐܡ
^i ܕܐܣܝܡ   ^l ܘܗܘܐ
^m ܝܗܘܕ̈ܝܐ   ^n ܠܟܠܠ
^o ܥܠܘ
^q ܗ̈ܢܘܢ
^r ܕܝܟܝܠ   ^s ܘܐܬܚܕܒܕ
‡ f. 25a.
^t ܚܕܘܬܐ   ^v ܘܣܬܘܐ
^w ܡܗܠܟ
^x ܕܫܠܝܡܘܢ
^y ܝܗܘܕ̈ܝܐ
^z ܡܬܝ   ^a ܢܦܫ̈ܢ
^e ܐܡܪ̈ܬܐ
^g ܕܐܡܪܬ
^h ܕܐܡܪ̈ܬܐ
^i ܫܡܥܢ   ^j ܫ̈ܡܥܝܢ
^l ܐܬܝܢ
^m ܠܗܘܢ   ^n ܚ̈ܝܝܢ
^o ܕܠܥܠܡ ܥܠܡ ^p add

Codex C.

^b ܐܠܟܣܢܕܪܘܣ ܡܢ ܝܘܚܢܢ^b
^y add ܘܒܬܪܗ ܦܪܘܩܢܐ
^z add ܡܪܢܐ
^a ܠܝܫܘܥ   ^b ܐܝܢ
^c omit ܕ   ^e ܣܐܡ
^f ܐܢܫ   ^g ܢܣܒ
^h ܣܐܡ ܐܢܐ^h
^k omit ܘܫܠܝܛ . . . ܝܬܗ . . .
[* Sic in Cod. B.]
^l ܘܗܘܐ   ^o ܥܠܘܝ
^p omit ܘܚܘܪܢܝܢ
^s add ܚܕ
^t ܚܕܘܬܐ
^u ܒܝܪܘܫܠܡ
^v ܘܣܬܘܐ
^x ܕܫܠܝܡܘܢ
^z ܐܡܬܝ
^a ܢܦܫܢ   ^b ܐܡܪ
^c omit ܠܢ   ^d ܐܓܝܒ
^f omit ܗܘܬ ܠܟܘܢ
^h ܕܐܡܪܬܐ   ^k ܡܟܪ
^l ܐܬܝܢ
^n ܚܝܝܢ

Codex A. — *Codex B.* — *Codex C.*

XXXV.

John X. 25—38.

Codex B.

[a]ܫܒܥܣܪܗ ܘܬܠܬܝܢ †ܝܘܡ [b]ܐܫܒܘܥܬ ܡܢ [c]ܝܘܚܢܢ[a] : [z]
25 [a]ܐܓܝܒ ܡܪܢ ܝܫܘܥ ܘܐܡܪ ܠܗܘܢ : ܐܡܪܬ
ܠܟܘܢ ܘܠܝܬ ܐܢܬܘܢ ܡܗܝܡܢܝܢ : ܥܒܕܝܐ
ܗܠܝܢ ܕܐܢܐ ܥܒܕ ܒܫܡܗ ܕܐܒܐ ܗܢܘܢ
26 ܡܣܗܕܝܢ ܥܠ ܕܝܠܝ : ܐܠܐ ܐܢܬܘܢ ܠܝܬ
ܐܢܬܘܢ ܡܗܝܡܢܝܢ ܕܠܝܬ ܐܢܬܘܢ ܡܢ [b]ܐܡܪܬܐ
ܕܝܠܝ : ܗܝܟ ܟܘܠ ܡܐ ܕܐܡܪܬ ܠܟܘܢ :
27 [c]ܕܐܡܪܬܐ ܕܝܠܝ ܠܩܠܝ [d]ܗܢܘܢ [e]ܫܡܥܝܢ : ܘܐܢܐ
ܡܟܪ [f]ܠܗܘܢ ܘܒܬܪܝ ‡[d]ܗܢܘܢ [g]ܐܬܝܢ : ܘܐܢܐ
28 ܝܗܒ [f]ܠܗܘܢ [h]ܚܝܝܢ [i]ܕܠܥܠܡ ܘܠܐ [j]ܝܒܕܘܢ
[k]ܠܥܠܡ : ܘܠܐ ܚܛܦ [l]ܝܬܗܘܢ ܐܢܫ ܡܢ
29 [m]ܟܦܝ [n]ܐܒܘܝ : ܕܐܒܐ [o]ܕܝܢ ܕܝܗܒ ܠܝ ܪܒ
ܗܘ ܡܢ ܟܘܠܐ ܘܐܢܫ ܠܐ [p]ܝܟܠ ܕܝܗܘܐ
30 ܚܛܦ ܡܢ [q]ܐܝܕܗ ܕܐܒܐ : ܘܐܢܐ ܘܐܒܐ
31 [b]ܫܕܐ ܐܬ̈ܝܗ : ܘܦܟܒܘ ܛܘܦܝܢ [r]ܝܗܘܕܝ [s]ܟܐܦܝ
32 [t]ܕܢܪܓܡܘܢ ܝܬܗ : [a]ܐܓܝܒ [v]ܕܝܢ ܡܪܢ ܝܫܘܥ
ܘܐܡܪ ܠܗܘܢ : ܣܓܝ ܥܒܕܝܢ [u]ܛܒܝܢ [w]ܐܘܕܥܬ
ܠܟܘܢ ܡܢ ܠܘܬ ܐܒܐ : [x]ܠܐܝܠܝܢ [y]ܗܕܝܢ
33 ܥܘܒܕ ܡܢܗܘܢ ܐܢܬܘܢ ܪܓܡܝܢ ܝܬܝ : ܐܓܝܒܘ
[z]ܝܗܘܕܝ ܘܐܡܪܝܢ ܠܗ : ܥܠ ܛܒ ܥܘܒܕ ܛܒ
ܠܝܬ ܐܢܚܢ [b] ܪܓܡܝܢ ܝܬܟ : ܐܠܐ [c]ܥܠ [d]ܓܕܘܦ
34 [e]ܕܐܢܬ ܒܪܢܫ [f]ܘܥܒܕ ܓܪܡܟ ܐܠܗܐ : [a]ܐܓܝܒ
ܡܪܢ ܝܫܘܥ ܘܐܡܪ ܠܗܘܢ : ܠܐ [g]ܟܬܒ
[f. 24a]
[h]ܒܢܡܘܣܟܘܢ ܕܐܢܐ ܐܡܪܬ ܕܐܢܬܘܢ
35 [i]ܐܠܗܝܢ : ܐܢ [k]ܠܗܠܝܢ ܐܡܪ [l]ܐܠܗܝܢ ܗܠܝܢ
[m]ܕܠܘܬܗܘܢ ܗܘܬ ܡܠܬܗ ܕܐܠܗܐ : † ܘܠܐ
36 [n]ܝܟܠ ܟܬܒܐ ܗܕܝܢ ܕܐܡܪ ܕܝܫܬܪܝ : [o]ܗܕܝܢ
ܕܐܒܐ [p]ܩܕܫܗ [q]ܘܫܠܚܗ [r]ܠܥܠܡܐ : ܐܢܬܘܢ

Codex A.

ܟܕ ܐ

[a]ܝܘܡ ܐܠܫܒܬ
ܦܝ ܐܠܓܡܥܗ
ܐܠܣܐܕܣܗ ܡܢ
ܝܘܚܢܐ[a]

[b]ܐܡܪ̈ܬܝ
[c]ܕܐܡܝܪ̈ܬܝ
[d]ܗܢܝܢ [e]ܫܡ̈ܥܝܢ
‡ f. 25b.
[f]ܠܗ̈ܝܢ [g]ܐܬ̈ܝܢ
[h]ܚ̈ܝܝܢ [i]ܕܠܥܠܡ
[j]ܝܒ̈ܕܢ [l]ܝܬ̈ܗܝܢ
[m]*omit* ܟܦܝ [n]ܐܒܘܐ̈ܝ
[o]ܕܝܢ
[q]ܐܒܘܗ [b]ܫܕܘ
[r]ܝܗܘܕܝ̈ܝ [s]ܟܐܦ̈ܝܢ
[t]ܕܢܪ̈ܓܡܘܢ
[v]*omit* ܕܝܢ
[x]ܠܐܝܠܝܢ [y]ܗܕܝܢ
[z]ܝ̈ܗܘܕܝ [b]ܐܢ̈ܚܢ
[c]*add* ܛܒ
[d]ܓܕ̈ܘܦܝܢ [e]*add* ܘ
[g]ܟܬܝܒ
[i]ܐܠܗ̈ܝܢ
[m]ܕܠܘ̈ܬܗܘܢ
[n]ܝܟܠ [o]ܗ̇ܕܝܢ
[p]ܩܕܫܗ [r]ܠܥܠܡܐ

Codex C.

† f. 24b.
[b]*add* ܐܫܒܘܥܗ
ܐܠܣܐܕܣܗ
[c]ܝܘܚܢܐ
[z]*add* ܘܒܬܗ ܡܪܘܣܐ
[a]ܐܓܝܒ
[b]ܐܡܪܬܝ
[c]ܕܐܡܪܬܝ
[h]ܚܝܐܝܢ
[k]ܠܥܠܡ
[m]*omit* ܟܦܝ [o]ܕܝܢ
[p]ܝܟܠ
[b]ܫܕܘ [s]ܟܐܦܝܢ
[a]ܐܓܝܒ [v]*omit* ܕܝܢ
[u]ܛܒܐܝܢ [w]ܐܘܕܥܬ
[y]ܗܕܝܢ
[b]ܐܢܚܢ [c]*add* ܛܒ
[e]*add* ܘ [f]ܘܥܒܕܬ
[h]ܒܢܡܘܣܟܘܢ
[i]ܐܠܗܝܢ [k]ܠܗܠܝܢ
[l]ܠܗܝܢ
[m]ܕܠܘܬܗܘܢ
† f. 25a.
[q]ܘܫܠܚ ܝܬܗ[q]
[r]ܠܥܠܡܐ

Codex A.

^sܡܫܒܚ

^uܚܡܝܬܘܢ

^xomit ܠܒܪܢܫ ... ܡܢ

^yܕܬܬܒܪܟܘܢ

ܐܢ ^zadd ^aܕܐܒܐ

^badd ܥܠܡ

‡ f. 26a.

Codex B.

ܐܡܪܝܢ ܠܗ ܕܐܢܬ ^sܡܫܒܚ : ܕܐܡܪܬ ܕܐܢܐ
37 ܒܪܗ ܕܐܠܗܐ : ^tܐܢ ܠܝܬ ܐܢܐ ܥܒܕ ^uܚܡܝܬܘܢ
38 ܕܐܒܐ ܠܐ ^vܬܗܝܡܢܘܢ ܠܝ : ܐܢ ܕܝ ܥܒܕ
ܐܢܐ ܐܘܦ ^tܐܢ ܠܝ ܠܝܬ ܐܢܬܘܢ ܡܗܝܡܢܝܢ
^wxܡܢ ܠܥܒܕܝܐ ܗܝܡܢܘ ܠܒܪܢܫ ^x ^yܕܬܬܒܪܟܘܢ
ܘܬܬܒܪܟܘܢ ^zܕܐܒܐ ܒܝ ܘܐܢܐ ^aܒܐܒܐ ‡ ⁘ ^b

Codex C.

^sܡܫܒܚ

^tomit ܐܢ

ܚܡܝܬܘܢ ^u

^vܬܗܝܡܢܘܢ

^womit ܡܢ

^yܕܬܬܒܪܟܘܢ

ܒܐܒܐ ^a

XXXVI.

John IX. 1—38.

Codex A.

ܕܕܐ ܚܕܐ ܘ يوم حد الاعمى الثامن من صبوحية

^aܘܟܕ ܥܒܪ ܝܫܘܥ
ܐܫܟܚܗ ܗܘܐ ܝܒܗ
ܠܠܒܝܬܐ ܕܡܢ ܟܪܣܗ
ܕܐܡܗ ܗܘܐ ܣܡܝܐ. ܘܫ
^aܐܠܗܐ

^bomit ܕ ^aadd ܒܪܘܟ

^cadd ܬܠܡܝܕܘܗܝ
ܝܫܘܥ

ܘܐܡܪܘ ^d

^eܬܠܡܝܕܘܗܝ

^fܘܐܡܪܘ

^hadd ܘ ^gܬܠܡܝܕܘܗܝ

^iܐܬܩܛܠ ^jܗܢܐ

^kܕܝܠܕܘ ^lܡܢ ܣܡܐ

^nܕܗܘܐ ^oܐܬܩܛܠ

^pܚܡܝܬܘܢ

^tadd ܕܝ ^vܚܡܝܬܘܢ

^zadd ܗܘ ^xܕܫܠܚ

^aomit ܗܘ ^bܠܠܝܐ

^cܢܚܠ ^dܕܢܥܒܕܠ

^eܥܒܕ ^fܒܥܠܡܐ

^gadd ܐܢܐ

^hܕܥܠܡܐ

^iomit ܐܢܐ

^jܪܩ ^kܠܐܪܥ

^lܘܛܦܠ ^mܠܐܪܥܐ

^nܐܙܝܠ ^oܕܫܠܝܚܐ

Codex B.

^aܗܫܬܐ ܘܟܕ ܥܒܪ ܝܫܘܥ ^bܐܫܟܚܗ ^cܗܘܐ
ܝܒܗ ܠܠܒܝܬܐ ܗܘܐ ^cܡܢ ^dܡܘܠܕܗ ^a : ^eܘܚܙܝܗ
1 ܣܡܝܐ : ^aܘܗܘܐ ^bܕܗܘܐ ܒܪ ܟܪܣ ܐܡܗ ^c :
2 ^dܘܫܐܠܘ ܝܬܗ ܬܠܡܝܕܘܗܝ ^e ܡܢ ܬܠܡܝܕܘܗܝ : ^fܘܐܡܪ
ܠܗ ^gܬܠܡܝܕܘܗܝ ^hܐܡܪܝܢ ܠܗ : ܪܒܢ ܡܢ
^iܐܬܩܛܠ ^jܗܢܐ ܐܘ ܐܒܗܘܢ ^kܕܝܠܕܘܢ ^lܡܢ ܣܡܐ
3 ܐܬܝܠܕ : ^mܐܬܦܢܝ ܝܫܘܥ ܘܐܡܪ ܠܗܘܢ :
ܠܐ ^nܗܢܐ ^oܐܬܩܛܠ ܘܠܐ ܐܒܗܘܬܗ : ܐܠܐ
4 ܕܢܬܚܙܘܢ ^pܚܡܝܬܘܢ ܕܐܠܗܐ^q : ܒܗܠܝܢ *^{s t}
ܠܡܥܒܕ ܕܫܠܚܢܝ ^uܒܥܠܡܐ ^vܚܡܝܬܘܢ ^wܕܗܘܝܢ
^xܕܫܠܚܢܝ ܥܕ : ^yܚܒܪ ܝܘܡܐ ܐܢܬ ܗܘ : ^zܐܬܐ
ܠܝ ^aܗܘ ^bܠܠܝܐ ܕܒܗ ܠܐ ^cܡܫܟܚ ܐܢܫ ^dܕܢܥܒܕ
5 ܒܗ : ^eܒܥܕ ܐܢܐ ^fܒܥܠܡܐ ܢܗܘܪܗ ^g
6 ^hܕܥܠܡܐ ^iܐܢܐ : ܗܠܝܢ ܒܕ ܐܡܪ ^jܪܩ
ܒܐܪܥܐ ܘܥܒܕ ^kܛܝܢ ܡܢ ܪܘܩܗ ^lܘܛܦܠ
ܥܝܢܘܗܝ ܕܗܘ ܣܡܝܐ ܡܢ ܗܘ ^mܛܝܢܐ
[f. 24b]
7 ܘܐܡܪ ܠܗ : ^nܐܙܝܠ ܐܫܝܓ ܒܥܡܝܕܬܐ ^oܕܫܠܝܚܐ :

Codex C.

ܐܫܟܚܗ ^b

^comit ܗܘܐ ... ܗܘܐ

^eadd ܪܒܗ ^dܘܫܐܠ

^aadd ܒܪܘܟ

^eܬܠܡܝܕܘܗܝ

^hadd ܘ ^gܬܠܡܝܕܘܗܝ

^lܡܢ ܣܡܐ

^nܕܗܘܐ ^mܐܬܦܢܝ

^qadd ܗܘ ^oܐܬܩܛܠ

[* Cod. ܒܗܠܝܢ]

^sadd ܠܝ ܕܝ

^uܒܥܠܡܐ ^vܚܡܝܬܘܢ

^wܕܗܠܝܢ ^xܕܫܠܚ

^zadd ܗܘ ^yܒܥܕ

^aomit ܗܘ ^bܠܠܝܐ

^gadd ܐܢܐ ^eܒܥܕ

^iomit ܐܢܐ ^jܪܩ

^kܛܝܢ ^lܘܛܦܠ

^oܕܫܠܝܚܐ

Codex B.

ܡܢ ܕܗܘ ܡܬܘܪܟ ܡܫܠܡܢܐ: [n]ܐܙܠ[q] ܐܡܝܟ
8 ܘܐܬܐ ܫܡܥܐ: ܗܠܝܢ [r]ܕܝܢ [s]ܡܬܓܡܪܝܢ ܘܗܠܝܢ ܕܗܘܘ
ܫܡܝܢ ܢܬܗ ܡܢ [†] ܩܘܕܡ ܕܗܘܐ ܡܫܬܘܕܝܢ ܘܕܠܐ
ܫܡܥܐ ܗܘܘ [t]ܕܝܢ ܐܡܪܝܢ ܠܐ ܗܕܝܢ ܗܘ ܕܝܢ
ܕܗܘܐ [u]ܢܬܒ ܡܫܝܚܐ: ܫܘܪܝܢ[v] ܗܘܘ ܐܡܪܝܢ
9 ܗܘ ܗܕܝܢ: ܘܫܘܪܝܢ ܗܘܘ ܐܡܪܝܢ ܠܐ ܠܐ ܐܠܐ
ܕܡܢܐ ܗܘ ܠܗ: ܘܗܘ ܗܘܐ [‡] ܐܡܪ [w]ܕܐܢܐ
10 ܗܘ: ܗܘܘ[v] ܐܡܪܝܢ ܠܗ ܗܝܟ ܐܝܟ [x]ܐܬܦܬܚܬ
11 [y]ܥܝܢܝܟ: [z]ܐܢܫ ܗܘ ܡܬܩܪܐ ܘܐܡܪ ܠܗܘܢ:
[a]ܗܘ [b]ܒܪܢܫܐ [c]ܕܝܢ [d]ܕܡܬܩܪܐ ܝܫܘܥ: ܥܒܕ
[e]ܛܝܢ [f]ܘܛܫܠ ܥܝܢܝ ܘܐܡܪ ܠܝ [g]ܐܙܠ
[h]ܠܫܝܠܘܚܐ ܘܐܫܝܓ [y]ܥܝܢܝܟ: ܐܙܠܬ [z]ܕܝܢ ܘܥܒܕ
12 [i]ܐܫܝܓܬ ܘܚܙܝܬ: ܘܐܡܪܝܢ ܠܗ [j]ܗܢ [k]ܗܘ
ܒܪܢܫܐ: ܐܡܪ ܠܗܘܢ [l] [m]ܠܝܬ ܐܢܐ ܝܕܥ:
13 [n]ܘܐܝܬܘ ܠܗ ܠܘܬ [o]ܦܪܝܫܐ ܠܗܘ ܕܗܘܐ ܡܢ
14 ܩܕܡ ܥܘܝܪ: ܗܘܬ ܕܝܢ ܫܒܬܐ [p]ܝܘܡܐ
ܕܒܗ ܓܒܠ ܝܫܘܥ [q]ܛܝܢܐ ܘܦܬܚ [r]ܥܝܢܘܗܝ:
15 ܘܬܘܒ ܫܐܠܘ ܠܗ [o]ܦܪܝܫܐ ܘܐܡܪܝܢ ܗܝܟ
ܐܝܟ ܚܙܐ: ܗܘ ܕܝܢ ܐܡܪ ܠܗܘܢ [s]ܛܝܢ ܣܡ
16 ܥܠ [a]ܥܝܢܝ [b]ܘܐܫܝܓܬ ܘܗܐ ܚܙܐ ܐܢܐ: ܗܘܘ
ܕܝܢ ܐܡܪܝܢ ܐܢܫܝܢ ܡܢ [c]ܦܪܝܫܐ ܠܘܬ ܗܕܝܢ ܡܢ
ܐܠܗܐ ܒܪܢܫܐ [d]ܕܠܐ [t]ܢܛܪ ܫܒܬܐ: ܫܘܪܝܢ
ܕܝܢ ܗܘܘ ܐܡܪܝܢ ܗܝܟ [u]ܡܨܐ ܒܪܢܫܐ [w]ܚܛܝܐ
ܕܢܥܒܕ ܟܕܐ ܕܝܠܗ ܗܠܝܢ ܐܬܘܬܐ: ܘܗܘܐ
17 [x]ܦܠܓ ܒܝܢܬܗܘܢ: ܘܬܘܒ ܗܘܘ ܐܡܪܝܢ ܠܗܘ
ܥܘܝܪܐ ܕܗܘܐ ܡܢ ܩܕܡ: ܡܢܐ ܐܢܬ ܐܡܪ ܥܠ
[f. 25a]
[y]ܗܘ ܕܦܬܚ [z]ܥܝܢܝܟ: ܗܘ ܕܝܢ ܐܡܪ [a]ܠܗܘܢ
18 ܕܢܒܝܐ ܗܘ: ܘܠܐ ܗܝܡܢܘ [b] [c]ܝܗܘܕܝܐ ܥܠ
[y]ܗܘ ܕܗܘܐ ܥܘܝܪ ܘܚܙܐ: ܥܕܡܐ ܕܩܪܘ
19 ܠܐܒܘܗܝ [‡] [d]ܕܗܕܝܢ ܕܚܙܐ: ܘܫܐܠܘ ܐܢܘܢ
ܘܐܡܪܝܢ ܠܗܘܢ: ܗܕܝܢ ܗܘ ܒܪܟܘܢ [e]ܗܕܝܢ

Codex A.

[n] ܢܐܙܠ — [q] add ܕܝܢ
[s] ܬܬܓܡܪܘܢ
[t] omit ܕܝܢ
[u] ܬܬܒ — [v] add ܕܝܢ
[w] omit ܕ
‡ f. 26b.
[x] ܐܬܦܬܚ
[a] ܘܗܘ — [b] ܒܪܢܫܐ
[c] ܕܝܢ — [d] ܕܡܬܩܪܐ
[e] ܛܝܢ — [f] ܘܛܫܠ
[g] ܐܙܠ — [h] ܠܫܝܠܘܚܐ
[i] ܐܫܝܓܬ — [j] add ܘ
[k] add ܗܘ — [l] add ܕܝܢ
[n] ܘܐܝܬܝܘ — [o] ܦܪܝܫܐ
[p] ܝܘܡܐ — [q] ܛܝܢܐ
[r] ܥܝܢܘܗܝ
[s] ܛܝܢ
[a] ܥܝܢܝ
[b] ܘܐܫܝܓܬ
[c] ܦܪܝܫܐ
[d] omit ܕ — [t] ܢܛܪ
[u] ܡܨܐ — [w] ܚܛܝܐ
[y] add ܕ
[a] omit ܠܗܘܢ
[b] add ܕܝܢ — [c] ܝܗܘܕܝܐ
‡ f. 27a.
[d] ܕܗܢܘ — [e] ܗܢܘ

Codex C.

[q] add ܕܝܢ
[r] omit ܕܝܢ
† f. 25b.
[t] omit ܕܝܢ
[v] add ܕܝܢ
[x] ܐܬܦܬܚ
[y] ܥܝܢܝܟ — [z] ܐܟܠܒ
[b] ܒܪܢܫܐ
[f] ܘܛܫܠ
[h] ܠܫܝܠܘܚܐ
[j] add ܘ — [z] ܘܥܒܕ
[m] ܕܠܝܬ
[n] ܘܐܝܬܝܘ
[p] ܝܘܡܐ
[r] ܥܝܢܘܗܝ
[w] ܚܛܝܐ
[x] ܦܠܓ
[y] add ܕ — [z] ܥܝܢܝܟ
[a] omit ܠܗܘܢ
[b] add ܕܝܢ

Codex A.	*Codex* B.	*Codex* C.
[f] *add* ܕܝܢ	†ܕܐܬܘܢ ܐܡܪܝܢ ܕܣܡܝ ܐܬܝܠܕ ܗܝܟ[f] ܗܘ	† f. 26a.
ܘܐܡܪܘ[g]	20 ܚܡܐ ܟܕܘ: ܐܬܝܒܘ ܕܝܢ ܐܒܗܘܬܗ ܘܐܡܪܘ[g]	[f] *add* ܕܝܢ
ܕܗܕܝܢ[d]	ܠܗܘܢ: ܝܕܥܝܢ ܐܢܢ [d]ܕܗܕܝܢ ܗܘ [h]ܒܪܢ	
ܒܪܢ[h]	21 ܘܕܣܡܝ ܐܬܝܠܕ: ܗܝܟ ܕܝܢ ܗܘ ܚܡܐ ܟܕܘ	ܐܢܢ[i] ܥܝܢܘܗܝ[k]
ܥܝܢܘܗܝ[k]	ܠܝܬ [i]ܐܢܢ ܝܕܥܝܢ: ܐܘ ܡܢ ܦܬܚ ܠܗ [k]ܥܝܢܝܗ[l]	[l] *add* ܗܘ ܐܢܢ
[l] *add* ܗܟܢ	ܠܝܬ [i]ܐܢܢ ܝܕܥܝܢ: ܠܗ ܫܐܠܘ: ܠܡܠܐ [m]ܕܝܠܕ	[m] *omit* ܕܝܠܕ ܥܠ
[m] *omit* ܕܝܠܕ ܥܠ	ܥܠ[m] ܢܦܫܗ ܗܘ ܕܗܘ [a]ܡܡܠܠ ܥܠ ܦܓܪ ܢܦܫܗ:	ܡܡܠܠ[a]
ܐܡܪܝܢ[n] ܕܚܠܝܢ[o]	22 ܗܠܝܢ [n]ܐܡܪܝܢ ܐܒܗܘܬܗ ܕܗܘܘ [o]ܕܚܠܝܢ ܡܢ	ܐܡܪܝܢ[n] ܝܗܘܕܝܐ[p]
[q] *omit* ܒܕ ܝܗܘܕܝܐ[p]	[p]ܝܗܘܕܝܐ: [t]ܟܒܪ ܓܝܪ ܗܘܐ [q]ܒܕ [r]ܐܬܦܢܝܘ	[t] *omit* ܟܒܪ ... ܝܗܘܕܝܐ
ܝܗܘܕܝܐ[s] [r] *add* ܕ	[s]ܝܗܘܕܝܐ[t] ܒܝܢܬܗܘܢ [u]ܕܐܢ ܝܘܕܐ ܒܗ ܐܢܫ	ܕܐܢ[u]
ܢܦܩ[w] ܟܢܫܬܐ[x]	ܕܗܘ ܡܫܝܚܐ: ܝܗܐ [w]ܢܦܩ ܠܒܪ ܡܢ [x]ܟܢܫܬܐ:	
ܠܓܠܠ[y] ܟܕ[z]	23 [y]ܠܓܠܠ [z]ܟܕܝܢ [a]ܐܡܪܘ ܐܒܗܘܬܗ ܠܡܠܐ[f] ܢܦܫܗ	ܐܡܪܘ[a] ܠܟ[f]
ܐܡܪܘ[a]	24 ܗܘ ܘܠܗ ܫܐܠܘ: ܘܐܡܪܘ ܡܢ ܬܢܝܢܘ ܝܬܗ	
ܣܡܝ[b] ܗܒ[c]	ܓܒܪܐ ܕܗܘܐ [b]ܣܡܝ: [c]ܗܒ ܬܫܒܘܚܬܐ	ܣܡܝ[b] ܗܒ[c]
ܓܒܪܐ[d]	ܠܐܠܗܐ: ܐܢܢ ܓܝܪ ܝܕܥܝܢ ܕܗܕܝܢ [d]ܓܒܪܐ	ܓܒܪܐ[d]
ܚܛܝܐ[e]	25 [e]ܚܛܝܐ ܗܘ: ܐܬܝܒ ܗܘ ܓܒܪܐ ܘܐܡܪ	
	ܠܗܘܢ: [g]ܐܢ [e]ܚܛܝܐ ܗܘ ܠܝܬ ܐܢܐ ܝܕܥ:	ܐܢ[g]
ܗܘܝܬ[h]	ܚܕܐ ܕܝܢ ܐܢܐ ܝܕܥ ܕܣܡܝ [h]ܗܘܝܬ ܗܘܐ	
	26 ܟܕܘ ܐܢܐ ܚܡܐ: ܘܐܡܪܝܢ ܠܗ ܡܢܐ ܥܒܕ	
[y] *add* ܠܟܘܢ	27 ܠܟ ܗܝܟ ܦܬܚ [x]ܥܝܢܝܟ: ܘܐܬܝܒ ܘܐܡܪ	ܥܝܢܝܟ[x]
‡ f. 27b.	ܠܗܘܢ: ܐܡܪܬ [y]ܟܒܪ ܘܠܐ ܫܡܥܬܘܢ: ‡ܡܢܐ	[y] *add* ܠܟܘܢ
	ܬܘܒ ܐܬܘܢ ܨܒܝܢ ܕܬܫܡܥܘܢ ܕܠܡܐ ܐܘܦ	ܬܠܡܝܕܘܗܝ[z]
	28 ܐܬܘܢ ܨܒܝܢ ܕܬܗܘܘܢ [z]ܬܠܡܝܕܘܗܝ: ܘܐܠܘ [f. 25b]	[i] *add* ܕܝܬܗ
[i] *add* ܕܝܬܗ	ܝܬܗ ܘܐܡܪܘ ܠܗ: ܐܢܬ [i]ܬܠܡܝܕܗ ܐܢܬ: ܐܢܢ	ܬܠܡܝܕܘܗܝ[j]
ܕܡܘܫܐ[k]	29 ܕܝܢ [j]ܬܠܡܝܕܘܗܝ [k]ܕܡܘܫܐ ܐܢܢ: [l]ܐܢܢ ܝܕܥܝܢ	[l] *add* ܕ ܕܡܘܫܐ[k]
[l] *add* ܕ ܡܠܠ[m]	ܕܥܡ ܡܘܫܐ [m]ܡܠܠ ܐܠܗܐ: ܠܗܕܝܢ ܕܝܢ	
ܝܕܥܝܢ[n]	30 [n]ܠܝܬ ܐܢܢ[n] ܝܕܥܝܢ ܡܢ ܗܢ ܗܘ ܐܬܝܒ ܝܬܗ	ܝܕܥܝܢ[n]
	ܓܒܪܐ ܘܐܡܪ ܠܗܘܢ: ܒܗܕܐ ܓܝܪ ܗܘ ܬܡܗܐ	[o] *omit* ܗܢ
[p] *omit* ܝܕܥܝܢ	ܕܐܬܘܢ ܠܐ ܝܕܥܝܢ ܡܢ [o]ܗܢ ܗܘ [p]ܝܕܥܝܢ	[p] *omit* ܝܕܥܝܢ
ܥܝܢܝ[r] ܚܛܝܐ[s]	31 [q]ܘܦܬܚ [r]ܥܝܢܝ: ܝܕܥܝܢ ܐܢܢ ܕܝܢ ܕܥܡ [s]ܚܛܝܐ	ܥܝܢܝ[r] [q] *omit* ܘ
ܫܡܥ[t]	ܠܐ [t]ܫܡܥ ܐܠܗܐ: ܐܠܐ ܐܢ ܗܘܐ ܐܢܫ	ܫܡܥ[t]

Codex A.	*Codex* B.	*Codex* C.
[u] ܕܐܙܠ	[u]ܕܐܙܠ ܗܝ ܠܩܒܪܐ ܘܒܟܝܐ ܬܡܢ : † ܡܢ ܗܕܝܢ	† f. 26*b*.
[x] ܠܩܒܪܐ	32 ܗܘ ܥܡܟ : ܡܢ [w]ܝܫܘܥ [x]ܠܩܒܪܐ ܕܝ ܠܐ	[w] ܝܫܘܥ
[y] ܚܝܝ	ܐܬܡܝܬܬ ܕܦܬܚ ܐܚܝ ܕܐܚܝ [y]ܚܝܝ ܕܐܬܐܠ	
[a] ܢܚܠ [b] ܕܡܚܝܢ	33 [z]ܡܚܡܪ : ܐܠܘ ܠܐ ܕܗܘܐ ܗܕܝܢ ܡܢ ܐܠܗܐ :	[z] ܡܚܡܪ
[c] ܒܘܠܡ	34 ܠܐ ܗܘܐ [a]ܢܚܠ [b]ܕܡܚܝܢ [c]ܒܘܠܡ : ܘܐܟܝܒܗ	[b] ܕܡܚܝܢ
[d] *omit* ܐܬ [e] ܒܫܢܒܠܡ	ܘܐܡܪܝܢ ܠܗ [d]ܐܬ [e]ܒܫܢܒܠܡ ܐܬ ܒܘܠܢ	[d] *omit* ܐܬ
[f] ܡܠܒܘ [g] ܘܐܒܟܘ	ܐܬܠܕܬ : ܘܐܬ [f]ܡܠܒܘ ܢܬܢ : [g]ܘܐܒܟܘ ܢܬܗ	[f] ܡܠܒܘ
[h] ܐܫܟܚܝ	35 ܠܒܪ : ܘܟܕ [h]ܐܫܟܚܝ ܢܬܗ [i]ܡܪܝܐ [k]ܐܡܪ ܠܗ :	[k] *add* ܝܫܘܥ
[i] *omit* ܡܪܝܐ	36 ܗܐ ܐܬ ܡܣܝܒܡ ܒܒܪܗ ܕܐܠܗܐ : ܗܘ ܕܝ	
	ܐܟܝܒܗ ܘܐܡܪ ܠܗ : ܘܡܢ ܗܘ ܡܪܝ ܕܡܣܝܒܡ	
[l] ܗܕܝܢ	37 ܒܗ : ܐܡܪ ܠܗ ܡܪܝܐ ܫܡܥܘܢ ܫܡܝܬ ܢܬܗ ܘܗܘ	
[m] ܕܡܬܒܠܠ	38 [l]ܗܕܝܢ [m]ܕܡܬܒܠܠ ܒܡܝܢ : ܘܐܡܪ ܠܗ ܡܣܝܒܡ	
‡ f. 28*a*.	ܐܢܐ ܡܪܝ ܘܦܩܕ ܠܗ : [n]ܫܠܡ ⁘ ‡	[n] *omit* ܫܠܡ

XXXVII.

John XI. 47—54.

Codex A.	*Codex* B.	*Codex* C.
[a] ܗܘܐ ܐܠܬܝܢ / ܐܬܟܢܫܘ ܐܬܘܪܗܘܢ [a]	[a]ܗܟܢܫܘ ܘܬܠܬܝܢ ܗܘܐ ܐܠܬܝܢ[a][b] ܡܢ [c]ܝܫܘܥ :[a]	[b] *add* ܐܬܟܢܫܘ ܐܬܘܪܗܘܢ
[a] *add* ܬܠܬܝܗ ܘܒܢܝ ܦܪܝܫܝܐ	47 [b]ܘܐܡܪܝܢ [c]ܡܪܝܐ[b] ܘܒܢܝܗ [d]ܪܒܢܐ ܒܗܢܝܐ [e]ܘܦܪܝܫܝܐ	[c] ܝܫܘܥܐ
[b] *omit* ܘܐܡܪܝܢ ܡܪܝܐ	[f]ܒܝܬܐ : [g]ܘܗܘܘ ܐܡܪܝܢ ܡܢܐ ܐܢܫ [h]ܥܒܕܝܢ	[a] *add* ܘܬܠܬܝܗ ܦܪܝܫܝܐ
[d] ܪܒܢܐ [e] ܘܦܪܝܫܝܐ	48 ܕܗܘܐ [i]ܗܕܝܢ ܒܪܢܫܐ ܥܒܕ [k]ܐܬܝܢ ܣܓܝ : [l]ܘܐܢ	[c] *omit* ܡܪܝܐ [b] *omit* ܘ
[f] ܒܝܬܐ [h] ܥܒܕܝܢ	ܫܒܩܝܢ ܐܢܫܗ ܠܗ [n]ܟܕܝܢ ܒܘܠܐ ܡܗܝܡܢܝܢ	[g] ܘܗܘܘ [l] ܘܐܢ
[i] ܗܕܝܢ [k] ܐܬܝܢ	ܒܗ : ܘܐܬܝܢ [o]ܪܘܡܝܐ ܘܢܣܒܝܢ [p]ܐܬܪܢ [q]ܘܥܡܢ	[n] ܟܕܝܢ
[o] ܪܘܡܝܐ	[f. 26*a*] 49 [r]ܥܡܢ : ܚܕ [s]ܕܝ ܐܢܫ ܡܢܗܘܢ ܕܫܡܗ	[q] ܘܥܡܢ
[p] ܐܬܪܢ [q] ܘܥܡܢ	[t]ܩܝܦܐ ܪܒ ܟܗܢܐ [u]ܗܘܐ [v]ܗܘܐ [w]ܫܢܬܐ :[u]	*add* ܚܕ [r] ܥܡܢ
[t] ܩܝܦܐ	ܘܐܡܪ ܠܗܘܢ : ܐܬܘܢ ܠܐ ܝܕܥܝܢ [x]ܒܘܠܡ :	[t] ܩܝܦܐ
[v] *add* ܕ [w] ܫܢܬܐ	50 ܘܠܐ ܡܬܚܫܒܝܢ ܕܦܩܚ ܠܢ ܕܚܕ ܒܪܢܫ ܡܡܘܬ	[u] *omit* ܗܘܐ ... ܫܢܬܐ
[x] ܒܘܠܡ	[y]ܚܠܦ ܥܡܐ : ܘܠܐ [z]ܕܟܘܠܗ [a]ܥܡܐ [b]ܝܒܕ :	[z] *omit* ܕ [y] ܚܠܦ
[y] ܚܠܦ [a] ܥܡܐ	51 ܗܕܐ ܕܝ ܡܢ ܢܦܫܗ ܠܐ ܐܡܪ : ܐܠܐ ܕܗܘܐ	[b] ܝܒܕ
[b] ܝܒܕ	ܪܒ ܟܗܢܐ ܕܗܝ [c]ܫܢܬܐ [d]ܘܐܬܢܒܝ : ܕܗܘܐ	[c] ܫܢܬܐ [d] ܘܐܬܢܒܝ
[c] ܫܢܬܐ	[e]ܥܬܝܕ ܡܪܝܐ ܝܫܘܥ ܕܡܡܘܬ ܚܠܦ [f]ܥܡܐ :	[e] ܥܬܝܕ [f] ܥܡܐ

Codex A.	Codex B.	Codex C.
[g] add ܕܐܘܦ	52 ܘܠܐ ܚܘܠܦ [f]ܥܡܐ ܒܠܚܘܕ: ܐܠܐ[g] [h]ܚܘܠܦ	[f]ܥܡܡܝܐ
[h] omit ܚܘܠܦ	[i]ܒܢܝ ܕܐܠܗܐ ܗܠܝܢ[†] ܕܡܒܕܪܝܢ ܡܟܢܫ [j]ܠܚܕܐ:	† f. 27a.
[i]ܒܢܘܗܝ	53 ܘܡܢ ܗܘ ܝܘܡܐ ܕܝ ܐܬܡܠܟܘ [k]ܕܝܩܛܠܘܢ	[i]ܒܢܘܗܝ [g] add ܕܐܘܦ
[k]ܕܝܩܛܠܘܢ	54 ܝܬܗ: ܘܗ ܕܝ ܡܪܢܐ ܝܫܘܥ ܒܬܪ ܠܐ ܗܘܐ	[j] add ܝܬܗܘܢ
[m]ܝܗܘܕܝܐ	ܡܗܠܟ ܒܦܪܗܣܝܐ [l]ܒܝܢ [m]ܝܗܘܕܝ: ܐܠܐ	[l]ܒܐܝܢ
[n]ܐܙܠ [o]ܠܐܦܪܝܡ	[n]ܐܙܠ ܠܗ ܡܢ ܬܡܢ ܠܐܬܪ ܩܪܝܒܐ ܠܡܕܒܪܐ	[o]ܠܐܦܪܝܡ
[p]ܕܡܬܐܡܪܐ	[o]ܠܐܦܪܝܡ: ܗܕܐ [p]ܕܡܬܐܡܪܐ ܡܕܝܢܬܐ ܘܬܡܢ	[q]ܬܠܡܝܕܘܗܝ
[q]ܬܠܡܝܕܘܗܝ	ܗܘܐ ܥܒܪ ܥܡ [q]ܬܠܡܝܕܘܗܝ: [r]ܥܠܡ ⁘	[r] omit ܥܠܡ

XXXVIII.

John XII. 18—36a.

Codex A.	Codex B.	Codex C.
[a]ܝܘܡ ܐܬܠܬܐ ܡܢ	[a]ܬܡܢܝܗ ܘܬܠܬܝܢ ܝܘܡ ܐܬܠܬܐ [b]ܒܬܪ ܐܠܦܣܚ	[b] omit ܒܬܪ . . .
[a]ܝܘܚܢܢ	ܦܝ ܐܘܟܡ ܐܘܣܕܘܣܗ[b] ܡܢ [c]ܝܘܚܢܢ[a] [d]ܘܒܬܪܗ	. . . ܐܘܣܕܘܣܗ
[d] add ܪܫܐ	18 ܡܝܢܝܘܡܐ: ‡ [a]ܠܓܠܓܠ [b]ܒܝܘܡ [c]ܦܕܝܡ [d]ܝܬܗ	[c]ܝܘܚܢܢ
‡ f. 28b.	19 [e]ܐܘܟܠܘܣܝܐ: [f]ܡܥܟܒܘ [g]ܕܝܒܒܪ ܗܕܝܢ [h]ܐܬܬܐ:	[d] omit ܝܬܗ [c]ܦܕܝܡ
[a]ܠܓܠܓܠ [b]ܒܝܘܡ	[i]ܦܪܝܫܝ ܕܝ ܐܡܪܘ ܒܝܢܝܗܘܢ [k]ܠܚܒܪܝܗܘܢ: ܚܙܝܢ	[e]ܐܘܟܠܘܣܝܐ
[c]ܦܕܝܡ [e]ܐܘܟܠܘܣܝܐ	ܐܬܘܢ ܕܠܝܬ ܐܬܘܢ [l]ܡܗܢܝܢ [m]ܟܠܘܡ: [n]ܗܐ	[f]ܡܥܟܒܘ [g]ܕܝܒܒܪ
[f]ܡܥܟܒܘ [g]ܕܝܒܒܪ	20 ܟܠܗ [o]ܥܠܡܐ [p]ܐܙܠ [q]ܠܗ ܒܬܪܗ: ܘܗܘܘ ܕܝ	[l]ܡܗܢܝܢܝܢ
[h]ܐܬܬܐ [i]ܦܪܝܫܝܝܢ	ܐܢܫܝܢ [r]ܐܪܡܝܢ ܡܢ ܗܠܝܢ ܕܣܠܩܘ [s]ܕܝܣܓܕܘܢ	[n] omit ܗܐ
[k]ܠܚܒܪܝܗܘܢ [m]ܟܠܘܡ	21 [t]ܒܥܐܕܐ: ܗܠܝܢ ܕܝ ܩܪܒܘ [u]ܠܦܝܠܝܦܘܣ ܕܡܢ	[q] omit ܠܗ [p]ܐܙܠ
[o]ܥܠܡܐ	ܒܝܬ ܨܝܕܐ ܕܓܠܝܠܐ: ܘܗܘܘ [v]ܒܥܝܢ ܡܢܗ	[r]ܐܪܡܝܢ
[s]ܕܝܣܓܕܘܢ	[w]ܘܐܡܪܝܢ ܡܪܝ ܨܒܝܢ [x]ܐܢܢ [y]ܕܢܚܙܝ ܠܡܪܢܐ	[u]ܠܦܝܠܝܦܘܣ
[t]ܒܥܐܕܐ	22 ܝܫܘܥ: ܘܐܬܐ [z]ܦܝܠܝܦܘܣ ܘܗܘ ܐܬܐ ܘܐܡܪ	[x]ܐܢܢ [y]ܕܢܚܙܝܐ
[u]ܠܦܝܠܝܦܘܣ	[a]ܠܐܢܕܪܐܘܣ: ܘܐܬܐ ܐܘܦ [b]ܐܢܕܪܐܘܣ [c]ܘܦܝܠܝܦܘܣ [f. 26b]	[z]ܦܝܠܝܦܘܣ
[v]ܒܥܝܢ [w]ܘܐܡܪܝܢ	23 ܘܐܡܪܘ ܠܡܪܢܐ ܝܫܘܥ: ܗܘ ܕܝ ܡܪܢܐ	[c]ܘܦܝܠܝܦܘܣ
[x]ܐܢܢ [y]ܕܢܚܙܝܐ	ܝܫܘܥ [d]ܐܓܝܒ ܘܐܡܪ ܠܗܘܢ: ܐܬܬ	
[a]ܠܐܢܕܪܐܘܣ	24 ܫܥܬܐ ܕܝܫܬܒܚ ܒܪܗ ܕܓܒܪܐ: ܘܐܓܝܒ	[d]ܐܓܝܒ
[b]ܐܢܕܪܐܘܣ	ܡܪܢܐ ܝܫܘܥ ܘܐܡܪ ܐܡܝܢ ܐܡܝܢ ܐܡܪ ܐܢܐ	
[c]ܘܦܝܠܝܦܘܣ	ܠܟܘܢ: [e]ܕܐܢ ܠܝܬ [f]ܦܪܕܐ ܕܚܛܬܐ ܢܦܠܐ	[e]ܕܐܢ [f]ܦܪܕܬܐ
[f]ܦܪܕܬܐ	ܒܐܪܥܐ [g]ܘܡܝܬܐ ܗܝ ܠܒܠܚܘܕܗ ܡܬܩܝܡܐ:	[g]ܘܡܝܬܐ
[g]ܘܡܝܬܐ		

Codex A.

[c]ܡܝܬܝܬܐ
[e]ܡܝܬܝܬܐ [f]ܕܪܚܡ
[g]ܥܠܡܐ [h]ܠܚܝܝ
‡ f. 29*a*.
[i]ܕܠܥܠܡ [j]ܢܛܪ
[m]ܡܫܡܫ
[p]ܡܫܡܫ
[r]ܡܝܡܪ [s]ܗܕܐ
[t]ܠܓܠܠ [u]ܗܕܐ
[w] *omit* ܐܢܐ
[CLXXVI.]
[[β]ܠܫܡܟ]
[x]ܐܟܠܘܣܐ
[z]ܩܐܝܡ
[c] *add* ܗܕܐ
[d]ܠܓܠܠܝ
[e]ܠܓܠܠܟܘܢ
[f]ܕܗܕܐ [g]ܥܠܡܐ
[h]ܐܬܪܘܡܡܬ
[i]ܐܡܪ ... ܗܘܐ *omit*
[k]ܥܢܘ [m]ܐܟܠܘܣܐ
[p] *add* ܐܢܬ
[s]ܗܕܐ
[t]ܙܥܝܪ
[u]ܕܡܗܠܟ
[v]ܐܙܠ [w]ܕܒܢܝܗ
[x] *add* ܕ [z] *add* ܥܠܡ
‡ f. 29*b*.

Codex B.

[b]ܐܢ ܕܝ [c]ܡܝܬ [d]ܣܓܝ ܦܐܪܝܢ ܗܘܝ [e]ܡܝܬܝܐ [d]:
25 ܡܢ [f]ܕܪܚܡ ܢܦܫܗ ܡܘܒܕ ܗܘ ܠܗ : ܘܡܢ ܕܣܢܐ
ܢܦܫܗ ܒܗܕܝܢ [g]ܥܠܡܐ [h]ܠܚܝܝ [i]ܕܠܥܠܡ ܗܘ
26 [j]ܡܛܪ ܠܗ : ‡ [k]ܐܢ ܠܝ ܗܘܐ [l]ܐܢܫ [m]ܡܫܡܫ
ܠܝ ܝܗܐ ܕܒܗ [n]: ܘܗܢ ܕܐܢܐ ܬܡܢ ܗܘܐ
[o]ܬܡܢ ܗܘܐ [o]ܐܘܦ ܡܫܡܫܢ : ܐܢ ܗܘܐ ܐܢܫ
27 [p]ܡܫܡܫ ܠܝ † [q]ܡܝܩܪ ܗܘ ܠܗ ܐܒܐ : ܗܐ ܟܕܘ
ܢܦܫܝ ܡܬܪܒܟܐ ܘܡܐ [r]ܐܡܪ : ܐܒܐ ܐܚܝ
ܝܬܝ ܡܢ [s]ܗܕܐ ܫܥܬܐ : ܐܠܐ [t]ܠܓܠܠ [u]ܗܕܐ
28 [w]ܐܢܐ ܐܬܝܬ ܠܗܕܐ ܫܥܬܐ : ܐܒܐ ܫܒܚ ܝܬܗ
[β]ܠܫܡܟ : ܘܐܬܐ ܩܠܐ ܡܢ ܫܡܝܐ ܘܐܡܪ
29 ܫܒܚܬ ܘܬܘܒ ܐܢܐ ܡܫܒܚ : [x]ܐܟܠܘܣܐ
ܕܝ [y]ܕܗܘܐ [z]ܩܝܡ ܘܫܡܥ ܗܘܐ ܐܡܪ :
ܕܪܥܡ ܐܬܥܒܕ : ܚܘܪܢܝܢ ܕܝ ܗܘܘ ܐܡܪܝܢ
30 ܡܠܐܟ [a]ܡܠܠ ܥܡܗ : [b]ܐܬܝܒ ܡܪܐ ܝܫܘܥ
ܘܐܡܪ ܠܗܘܢ ܠܐ ܐܬܚܒܕ ܩܠܐ [c] [d]ܠܓܠܠܝ
31 ܐܠܐ [e]ܠܓܠܠܟܘܢ : ܗܐ ܟܕܘ ܐܪܟܘܢܗ
32 [f]ܕܗܕܝܢ [g]ܥܠܡܐ ܡܬܪܕܝ ܠܒܪ : ܘܐܢܐ ܟܕ
33 [h]ܐܬܪܘܡܡܬ ܟܘܠܐ ܐܢܐ ܓܪܕ ܠܘܬܝ : ܗܕܐ
ܕܝ ܗܘܐ [i]ܐܡܪ [j]ܡܘܕܥ ܒܗܕܝܢ ܡܘܬ ܡܝܬ [i]ܗܘܐ
[f. 27*a*]
34 [k]ܡܥܢܝ ܕܝܠܗ : [l]ܐܬܝܒ [m]ܐܟܠܘܣܐ ܘܐܡܪܝܢ
ܠܗ : [n]ܐܢܚܢ ܫܡܥܢܢ ܡܢ ܢܡܘܣܐ [o]ܕܡܫܝܚܐ
ܡܩܘܝ ܠܥܠܡ : ܘܐܝܟ ܐܢܬ [p]ܐܡܪ [q]ܕܡܬܬܠܝܘ
ܠܗ ܕܝܬܪܘܡܡ ܒܪܗ ܕܓܒܪܐ : [r]ܐܡܪܝܢ ܠܗ
35 ܐܘܢ [r] ܡܢ ܗܘ [s]ܗܕܝܢ ܒܪܗ ܕܓܒܪܐ : ܐܡܪ
ܠܗܘܢ ܡܪܐ ܝܫܘܥ ܥܘܕ [t]ܙܥܝܪ ܐܬܘܢ
ܢܗܘܪܐ ܒܡܨܥܟܘܢ ܐܝܬ ܗܘ : ܗܠܟܘ ܥܕ
ܕܒܟܘܢ ܢܗܘܪܐ : ܕܠܐ ܚܫܘܟ ܝܕܪܟܟܘܢ ܡܠܟܐ :
ܘܡܢ [u]ܕܡܗܠܟ ܒܚܫܘܟܐ ܠܐ ܝܕܥ ܠܗܢ ܗܘ
36 [v]ܐܙܠ : ܥܕ ܕܒܟܘܢ ܢܗܘܪܐ ܗܘܘ ܡܗܝܡܢܝܢ
‡ ܒܢܗܘܪܐ [w]ܕܒܢܝ [x]ܢܗܘܪܐ [y]ܬܗܘܢ ⁘ [s]

Codex C.

[b]ܐܢ [c]ܡܝܬܝܬܐ
ܣܓܝ ... [d] *omit*
... ܡܝܬܝܐ
[f]ܕܪܚܡ [h]ܠܚܝܝ
[j]ܢܛܪ [k]ܐܢ
[l]ܐܢܫ [m]ܡܫܡܫ
† f. 27*b*.
[n] *add* ܠܝ
[o] *omit* ܬܡܢ ܗܘܐ
[p]ܡܫܡܫ [q]ܡܝܩܪ
[w] *omit* ܐܢܐ
[x]ܐܟܠܘܣܐ
[y] *omit* ܕ [z]ܩܡ
[a]ܡܠܠ [b]ܐܬܝܒ
[c] *add* ܗܕܝܢ
[e]ܠܓܠܠܟܘܢ
[h]ܐܬܪܘܡܡܬ
[j]ܡܘܕܥ
[k]ܥܢܘ [l]ܐܬܝܒ
[m]ܐܟܠܘܣܐ
[n] *omit* ܐܢܚܢ [o]ܕܡܫܝܚܐ
[p] *add* ܐܢܬ
[q]ܕܡܬܬܠܝܘ
[r] *omit* ... ܐܡܪܝܢ
... ܐܘܢ
[v]ܐܙܠ
[y]ܬܗܘܢ

Codex A.

ᵃ ܗܘܐ ܐܠܦܢܐ
ܐܠܦܘܢܗܘܢ
ᵃܐܠܗܘܕܝܗ

ᶻ *add* ܝܫܘܥ

ᵃܠܝܗܘܕܝܐ

ᵉܘܐܙܠ

ᵍܠܡܫܠܡ

ⁱܠܡܫܡܥܬܢ

ʲ *add* ܡܪܢܐ

ᵏܠܡܫܠܡ ˡܒܕܝܢ

ᶻܒܠܒܗܘܢ

ʳܘܐܣܐ

ˢܐܫܥܝܐ

ᵇܒܪܡ

ᶜܠܡܫܠܡ ᵈܦܪܝܫܝ

ᵉܢܦܩܘܢ

ˣܫܒܘܚܬܗܘܢ

ʸܫܒܘܚܬܗ

ᶠ*add* ܕܝ ᵍܕܡܗܝܡܢ

ʰܡܗܝܡܢ ⁱܒܕܝܢ

ᵏܕܫܠܚ ܐܒܐ ˡ *omit*

ᵒܠܥܠܡܐ ܡܢ ᵖ *omit*

ᵠܡܬܚܪ ʳܡܐܡܪܝ

‡ f. 30 r.

ˢܘܡܛܪ ᵗܠܗܘܢ

ᵘ *add* ܓܪ ᵛܒܥܠܡܐ

ʷ *add* ܟܠܗ

Codex B.

XXXIX.

John XII. 36*b*—47.

ᵃܬܫܒܚܬܗ ᵇܐܬܬܠܘܢ ܗܘܐ ᶜܐܠܦܢܐ ܦܝ ܐܫܒܚܗ
ᵃܐܫܒܚܐܘܗ ܡܢ ܗܘܫܝܢܘᶜ : ᶻܐܡܪ ܡܪܢܐ
36 ᵃܠܝܗܘܕܝܐ ܗܠܝܢ ᵇܡܠܠ ܡܪܢܐ ܝܫܘܥ † ᵉܘܐܙܠ
37 ܐܬܛܡܪ ܡܢܗܘܢ : ܘܟܘܠ ܗܠܝܢ ܐܬܘܬܐ
ܗܘܐ ܥܒܕ ܩܕܡܝܗܘܢ : ܘܠܐ ܗܘܘ
38 ܡܗܝܡܢܝܢ ܒܗ : ᵍܠܡܫܠܡ ܡܠܬܗ ʰܕܐܫܥܝܐ
ܢܒܝܐ ܬܬܡܠܐ : ܗܕܐ ܕܐܡܪ ܡܪܢܐ ܡܢ
39 ܗܝܡܢ ⁱܠܡܫܡܥܬܢ : ܘܐܕܪܥܗ ʲ ܠܡܢ
ܐܬܓܠܝ : ᵏܠܡܫܠܡ ˡܒܕܝܢ ܠܐ ܗܘܘ ܝܟܠܝܢ
40 ᵐܡܗܝܡܢܝܢ : ܕܬܘܒ ܐܡܪ ⁿܐܫܥܝܐ : ܣܡܝ
ܥܝܢܝܗܘܢ ܘܥܒܕ ᵒܠܠܒܗܘܢ : ܕܠܐ ܢܚܙܘܢ
ܒܥܝܢܝܗܘܢ ᵖܘܢܬܒܘܢ * ᶻܒܠܒܗܘܢ
41 ܘܢܬܦܢܘܢ ʳܘܐܣܐ ܝܬܗܘܢ : ܗܠܝܢ ܐܡܪ
ˢܐܫܥܝܐ ܕܚܙܐ ܫܒܘܚܬܗ ܕܐܠܗܐ
42 ᵘܘܡܫܠܡ ܒܠ ܕܐܦܠܗ : ᵇܒܪܡ ܕܝ ܐܘܦ ܡܢ
ܐܪܟܘܢܐ ܣܓܝ ܗܝܡܢܘ ܒܗ : ܐܠܐ ᶜܠܡܫܠܡ
ᵈܦܪܝܫܝ ܠܐ ܗܘܘ ܡܘܕܝܢ ܒܗ : ܕܠܐ
[f. 27b]
43 ᵉܢܦܩܘܢ ܡܢ ʷܟܢܫܬܐ : ܐܚܒܘ ܓܪ
ˣܫܒܘܚܬܗܘܢ ܕܒܢܝܢܫܐ ܣܓܝ ܡܢ
44 ʸܫܒܘܚܬܗ ܕܐܠܗܐ : ܘܡܪܢܐ ܝܫܘܥ ᶠܐܓܥܝ
ܘܐܡܪ : ܡܢ ᵍܕܡܗܝܡܢ ܒܝ ܠܐ ʰܡܗܝܡܢ
45 ܒܝ : ܐܠܐ ⁱܒܕܝܢ ᵏܕܫܠܚ ܝܬܝ ˡܐܒܐ : ܘܡܢ
46 ܕܚܙܐ ܠܝ ܚܙܐ ᵐܠܕܝܢ ܕܫܠܚ ܝܬܝ : ܐܢܐ
ܢܗܘܪܐ ܐܬܝܬ ᵒܠܥܠܡܐ : ܕܟܘܠ ᵖܡܢ ܕܡܗܝܡܢ
47 ‡ ܒܝ ܠܐ ᵠܡܬܚܪ ܒܚܫܘܟܐ : ܘܡܢ ܕܠܐ ܫܡܥ
ʳܡܐܡܪܝ ˢܘܡܛܪ ᵗܠܗܘܢ : ܐܢܐ ܠܐ ܐܕܝܢ
ܝܬܗ : ܠܐ ᵘܐܬܝܬ ܕܐܕܘܢ ʸܒܥܠܡܐ : ܐܠܐ
ܕܐܚܐ ᵛܒܥܠܡܐ ʷ ⁖

Codex C.

ᵇܐܬܬܠܘܢ

ᶜܐܠܦܢܐ ܡܢ ܚܝܠܐ ᶜ

† f. 28*a*.

ᶻ*add* ܘܒܬܪ ܡܪܝܡܬܗ

ᵃܠܝܗܘܕܝܐ ᵇܡܠܠ

ʰܕܐܫܥܝܐ

ⁱܠܡܫܡܥܬܢ

ʲ *add* ܡܪܢܐ

ᵐܡܗܝܡܢܝܢ

ⁿܐܫܥܝܐ ᵒܠܠܒܗܘܢ

ᵖܘܢܬܒܘܢ

[* Cod. ܘܢܬܦܢܘܢ]

ᶻܒܠܒܗܘܢ

ʳܘܐܣܐ ˢܐܫܥܝܐ

ᵘܘܡܫܠܡ

ᵉܢܦܩܘܢ ʷܟܢܫܬܐ

ᶠ *add* ܕܝ

ᵍܕܡܗܝܡܢ

ʰܡܗܝܡܢ ⁱܒܕܝܢ

ᵏܕܫܠܚ ܐܒܐ ˡ*omit*

ᵐܠܕܝܢ

ᵒܠܥܠܡܐ ᵠܡܬܚܪ

ܡܠܝ ˢܘܡܛܪ

ᵘ *add* ܓܪ ܠܗܘܢ

Codex A.

ᵃ ܐܠܝܫܒܥܗ
ܐܠܝܫܒܥܗ ܡܢ
ܝܘܚܢܢ ᵃ

ᶜ ܡܢ
ᵍ ܐܙܠ
ʰ *add* ܘܐܢ ܐܙܠ
ܘܐܬܩܢ ܠܟܘܢ ܐܬܪ
ⁱ ܕܗܝܟ
ᵏ ܐܙܠ

‡ f. 30*b*.

ⁿ ܕܒܐܠܝ

ᵠ ܦܝܠܝܦܘܣ
ʳ ܘܡܣܦܩ
ˢ ܗܕܝܢ
ᵗ ܦܝܠܝܦܐ
ᵘ ܐܘܕܝ ʷ ܡܗܝܡܢ
ˣ *add* ܐܢܬ ܗܘ ܥܠܡ .

Codex B.

XL.

John XIV. 1*b*—10*a*.

ᵃ ܐܪܒܥܝܢ ܝܘܡ ܐܠܝܫܒܥ ᵇ ܠܥܠܘܡܗ ܕܕܝܫܢܐ
ܘܗܘ ܡܢ ܐܢܓܠ ܐܠܝܫܒܥ ܐܡܗ ܕܝܘܚܢܢ ܘܗܘܝܢ
ܕܗܘܝ ܡܩܛܠܝܢ ܐܬܐ ܡܪܢܐ ܫܡܥܘ ܘܗܕܝܢ
ܠܡܦܪܐ ܫܦܐܪ ܐܬܠܒܫ ܡܢ ܐܠܝܫܒܥܗ
ܘܗܘ ܐܬܬܐ ܥܡ ܕܝ ܒܡܦܪܐ ܘܫܪ ܘܐܪܟܒܝܢ
ܝܘܡ ܐܠܝܫܒܥܗ ܒܬܪ ܐܫܠܘܡ ܡܢ ܝܘܚܢܢ ᵃᵇ :
1 ܐܡܪ ܡܪܢܐ ᵃ ܠܬܠܡܝܕܘܗܝ ܗܘܘ ܡܗܝܡܢܝܢ
2 ܒܐܠܗܐ ܘܒܝ ܗܘܘ ܡܗܝܡܢܝܢ : ܒܒܝܬܗ
ܕܐܒܐ ܐܝܬ ܡܢܝܚ ܣܓܝ : ܐܠܘ ܕܝ ᶜ ܠܝܢ
ܐܝܬ ܐܢܐ ܐܡܪܬ ܠܟܘܢ ܕܐܢܐ ᵍ ܐܙܠ
3 ܕܐܬܩܢ ܠܟܘܢ ܐܬܪ : ʰ ܘܬܩܢ ܐܢܐ † ܐܬܐ
ܠܘܬܟܘܢ ܘܕܒܪ ܠܟܘܢ ܠܘܬܝ : ⁱ ܕܗܝܟ ܕܐܢܐ
4 ܗܘܐ ܐܦ ܐܢܬܘܢ ܬܗܘܘܢ : ܘܠܗܝܟ ܕܐܢܐ
ᵏ ܐܙܠ ܝܕܥܝܢ ܐܢܬܘܢ : ܐܦ ܐܘܪܚܐ ܐܢܬܘܢ
5 ܡܕܥܝܢ : ܐܡܪ ˡ ܠܗ ܬܐܘܡܐ ܡܪܢܐ ܠܝܬ ܐܢܗ
ܝܕܥܝܢ ܠܗܢ ܐܢܬ ᵏ ܐܙܠ : ܘܗܝܟ ܐܢܗ ܝܟܠܝܢ
6 ܕܢܕܥ ܐܘܪܚܐ : ܐܡܪ ᵐ ܠܗ ܡܪܢܐ
ܐܢܐ ܗܘ ܐܘܪܚܐ ܘܩܘܫܛܐ ‡ ܘܚܝܝܐ :
[f. 28*a*]
ܐܢܫ ܠܐ ܐܬܐ ܠܘܬ ܐܒܐ ܐܠܐ ܐܢ ܒܝ
7 ⁿ ܕܒܝ : ᵒ ܐܢ ܐܚܟܡܬܘܢ ܝܬܝ ܐܦ ܠܐܒܐ
ܐܢܬܘܢ ܗܘܝܢ ܡܚܟܡܝܢ : ܘܡܢ ܟܕܘ ܐܢܬܘܢ
8 ܡܚܟܡܝܢ ܠܗ ܘܚܡܝܬܘܢ ܝܬܗ : ܐܡܪ ܠܗ
ᵠ ܦܝܠܝܦܘܣ : ܡܪܢܐ ܐܚܘܝ ܠܝ ܐܒܐ ʳ ܘܡܣܦܩ ܠܢ :
9 ܐܡܪ ᵐ ܠܗ ܡܪܢܐ ܝܫܘܥ ܟܘܠ ˢ ܗܕܝܢ ܐܙܒܢܐ
ܐܢܐ ܥܡܟܘܢ ܘܠܐ ܐܚܟܡܬ ܝܬܝ ᵗ ܦܝܠܝܦܐ :
ܡܢ ܕܚܡܐ ܝܬܝ ܚܡܐ ܠܐܒܐ : ܘܗܝܟ ܐܬ
10 ܐܡܪ ᵘ ܐܘܕܝ ᵛ ܠܝ ܐܒܐ : ܠܝܬ ܐܬ ʷ ܡܗܝܡܢ
ܕܐܢܐ ܒܐܒܐ ܘܐܒܐ ܒܝ : ˣ ∴

Codex C.

ᵇ ܠܥܠܘܡܗ ܐܠܝܫܒܥ
ܐܡܗ ܡܢ ܐܠܝܫܒܥܗ
ܘܫܪ ܘܐܪܟܒܝܢ ܝܘܡ
ܐܠܝܫܒܥܗ ܡܢ ܝܘܚܢܢ
ܘܒܬܪܗ ܫܪ ᵇ

ᵃ ܠܬܠܡܝܕܘܗܝ

† f. 28*b*.
ʰ *add* ܘܐܢ ܐܙܠ
ܘܐܬܩܢ ܠܟܘܢ ܐܬܪ

ˡ *omit* ܠܗ

ᵐ *omit* ܠܗ

ⁿ ܕܒܐܠܝ
ᵒ ܐܢ

ᵠ ܦܝܠܝܦܘܣ
ʳ ܘܡܣܦܩܝܢ
ܘܠܝܢ ᵗ ܦܝܠܝܦܐ
ᵘ ܐܘܕܝ ᵛ ܠܝ
ʷ ܡܗܝܡܢ
ˣ *add* ܐܢܬ ܗܘ

Codex A.	Codex B.	Codex C.

XLI.

John XIV. 10b—21.

Codex B.

ᵇᵃ ܐܢܬܘܢ ܘܐܡܪܬܘܢ ܗܘܐ ܐܡܪܬ ܠܟܘܢ ᶜܒܪܐ ܕܐܠܗܐ ᵇᶜ
ܡܢ ᵈܢܦܫܝ : ܘܒܟܘܬܗ ᶻ ܡܪܘܡܬܐ : ܐܡܪ ܒܪܐ
10 ᵃܠܬܠܡܝܕܘܗܝ ܡܠܠ ܗܠܝܢ ܕܐܢܐ ᵇܡܡܠܠ ܠܟܘܢ
ܡܢ ܢܦܫܝ ܠܐ ܐܢܐ ᶜܡܡܠܠ : ܐܒܐ ᵈܗܘ ܕܫܪܐ
11 ܕܒܝ ܗܘ ܥܒܕ ᵉܥܒܕܘܗܝ : ܗܝܡܢܘ ܠܝ
ܠܝ ܕܐܢܐ ܒܐܒܐ ܘܐܒܐ ܒܝ : ᶠܘܐܢ ܠܐ
12 ᵍܡܢ ܡܠܠ ܥܒܕܐ ܗܘܘ ܡܗܝܡܢܝܢ : ܐܡܝܢ
ܐܡܝܢ ܐܡܪ ܐܢܐ ܠܟܘܢ ܕܡܢ ᵸܕܡܗܝܡܢ ܒܝ
ܥܒܕܐ ܗܠܝܢ ܕܐܢܐ ܥܒܕ ܐܦ ܗܘ ܢܥܒܕ ⁱ:
13 ܕܐܢܐ ܠܘܬ ܐܒܐ ܐܙܠ ʲ : ܘܡܕܡ
ᵏܕܬܫܐܠܘܢ ܒܫܡܝ ܗܘ ܐܢܐ ˡܕܐܢܐ ܥܒܕ :
15 ᵐܠܡܠܠ ܕܬܫܒܘܚ ܐܒܐ ⁿܒܒܪܐ : ᵒ† ܐܢ ܪܚܡܝܢ
16 ܐܢܬܘܢ ᵖܠܝ ᵍܦܘܩܕܢܝ ‡ ʳܛܪܘ : ܘܐܢܐ ܐܒܥܐ ܡܢ
ܐܒܐ : ܘܗܘ ܝܗܒ ܠܟܘܢ ˢܦܪܩܠܛܐ ܐܚܪܢ
17 ܕܝܗܘܐ ܥܡܟܘܢ ܠܥܠܡ ᵗ : ܪܘܚܐ
ܕܩܘܫܬܐ : ܗܘ ܕܥܠܡܐ ᵘ ܠܐ ᵛܝܟܠ ܕܢܩܒܠ
ܕܠܐ ܚܙܐ ܠܗ ܘܠܐ ܝܕܥ ܠܗ : ܐܢܬܘܢ ܕܝ
ܝܕܥܝܢ ܠܗ ܕܠܘܬܟܘܢ ܗܘ ܫܪܐ : ܘܒܟܘܢ
18 ܗܘ ܗܘܐ : ܠܐ ܐܫܒܘܩ ܐܢܐ ܠܟܘܢ ʷܝܬܡܐ :
[f. 28b]
19 ܐܬܐ ܐܢܐ ܠܘܬܟܘܢ : ܘܥܘܕ ˣܩܠܝܠ
ʸܘܥܠܡܐ ܡܢ ܗܕܐ ܠܐ ᶻܚܙܐ ܠܝ ܐܢܬܘܢ
ܕܝ ܚܙܝܢ ܠܝ ܕܐܢܐ ܚܝ ܘܐܢܬܘܢ ᵃܚܝܝܢ
20 ܐܢܬܘܢ ܗܘܘ ܝܕܥܝܢ ᵇܕܬܕܥܘܢ ܕܐܢܐ
21 ܒܐܒܐ ܘܐܢܬܘܢ ܒܝ : ܘܐܢܐ ܒܟܘܢ : ܟܠ
ܡܢ ܕܐܝܬ ᶜܦܘܩܕܢܝ ܘܢܛܪ ܠܗܘܢ ܗܘ ܗܘ
ᵈܗܘ ܕܪܚܡ ܠܝ : ܘܡܢ ܕܪܚܡ ܠܝ ܢܬܪܚܡ ܡܢ ܐܒܐ :
ᵉܘܐܢܐ ܐܪܚܡܝܘܗܝ : ܘܐܢܐ ᶠܐܚܘܝܘܗܝ ܠܗ
ܢܦܫܝ ᵍܥܠܡ ܀

Codex A.

ᵇ ܗܘܐ ܐܠܗܘܬܐ
ᵇ ܐܬܓܠܝܬ ܕܒܪܗ ܗܘ
ᶻ omit ܘܒܟܘܬܗ
ܡܪܘܡܬܐ
ᵃ ܠܬܠܡܝܕܘܗܝ
ᵇ ܡܡܠܠ ᵈ ܗܘܐ
ᵉ ܒܥܒܕܐ
ᵍ ܡܢ
ʰ ܕܡܗܝܡܢ
ⁱ add ܡܢ ܘܥܒܕܝܢ
ܗܠܝܢ ܥܒܕ
ˡ omit ܕ ʲ ܐܙܠ
ⁿ add ܒܪ ᵐ ܠܡܠܠ
‡ f. 31a.
ᵍ ܦܘܩܕܢܝ
ᵗ ܠܥܠܡ
ᵘ ܕܥܠܡܐ
ʷ ܝܬܡܝܢ
ˣ ܩܠܝܠ
ʸ ܘܥܠܡܐ
ᶻ ܚܙܝܢ
ᵃ ܚܝܝܢ
ᶜ ܦܘܩܕܢܝ
ᵈ ܗܘܐ
ᶠ ܐܚܘܝܘܗܝ
ᵍ omit ܥܠܡ

Codex C.

ᵃ ܐܢܬܘܢ
ᶜ omit ܒܪܐ ܕܐܠܗܐ
ᵈ ܢܦܫܝ
ᵃ ܠܬܠܡܝܕܘܗܝ
ᵇ ܡܠܠ ᶜ ܡܡܠܠ
ᶠ ܘܐܢ
ʰ ܕܡܗܝܡܢ
ⁱ add ܡܢ ܘܥܒܕܝܢ
ܗܠܝܢ ܥܒܕ
ˡ omit ܕ ᵏ ܕܬܫܐܠܘܢ
† f. 29a.
ᵒ ܐܢ ⁿ add ܒܪ
ʳ add ܕܝ ᵖ omit ܠܝ
ᵗ ܠܥܠܡ ˢ ܦܪܩܠܛܐ
ᵛ ܝܟܠ
ʷ ܝܬܡܝܢ
ˣ ܩܠܝܠ
ᵇ ܬܕܥܘܢ
ᶠ ܐܚܘܝܘܗܝ ᵉ omit ܘ
ᵍ omit ܥܠܡ

Codex A.	*Codex* B.	*Codex* C.
ܣܘܦ ܐܠܝܫ. ܐܠܗܐ ܠܠܐܫܠܝܚܘܬ ܗܘܐ ܐܘܢܓܠܝܘܢ ܕܡܢ ܐܠܝܫ ܡܢ ܣܘܦܗ. Sequitur rubrica quae legi non potest praeter بكره et ننت	**XLII.** JOHN XVII. 1—13. ܬܫܒܚܬܐ ܘܐܘܪܝܬܐ ܡܢ ܐܠܝܫ [b]ܐܡܪ ܕܒܪܝ. ܐܠܗܝܐ ܗܘܐ ܠܠܐܫܠܝܚܐ ܡܢ ܣܘܦܗ[b] :[y]	[b]ܝܘܡ ܐܠܝܫܘܥܬܗ ܗܘܐ ܐܘܢܓ ܕܒܪ ܐܡܪ ܡܢ ܝܘܚܢܢ[b]
[y]*add* ܘܒܬܘܠܬܐ ܘܐܪܒܥܐ	1 ܗܠܝܢ [s]ܡܠܠ ܝܫܘܥ : ܘܐܪܝܡ [a]ܥܝܢܘܝ ܠܫܡܝܐ ܘܐܡܪ : ܐܒܐ [b]ܐܬܬ ܫܥܬܐ ܫܒܚ ܠܒܪܟ ܕܒܪܟ [c]ܢܫܒܚܟ : [d]ܐܝܟ ܕܝܗܒܬ ܠܗ :	[y] *add* ܘܒܬܘܠܬܐ [a]ܥܝܢܘܝ [b]ܐܬܬ [c]ܫܒܚ [d]ܐܝܟ
[z]ܥܠ [a]ܥܝܢܘܗܝ [b]ܐܬܬ [c]ܫܒܚ [d]ܐܝܟ [e]ܠܗ [g]ܫܘܠܛܢܐ ܥܠ ܒܣܪ[g]	2 ܫܘܠܛܢܐ ܥܠ ܟܠ [e]ܒܣܪ [f]ܕܟܠ ܡܐ [g]ܕܝܗܒܬ ܠܗ [h]ܢܬܠ ܠܗܘܢ	[f]ܕܟܠ [g]ܫܘܠܛܢܐ ܥܠ ܒܣܪ[g]
[i]ܚܝܐ [j]ܕܠܥܠܡ [l]ܢܕܥܘܢ [m]ܠܟ ܒܠܚܘܕܝܟ [n]ܘܡܢ [p]ܕܫܕܪܬ [q]ܡܫܝܚܐ [h]ܥܒܕܬ [i]ܫܘܠܡܐ [r]ܠܥܠܡܐ	[k]ܗܠܝܢ ܕܝܢ [i]ܚܝܐ [j]ܕܠܥܠܡ : ܗܠܝܢ ܐܢܘܢ 3 [j]ܕܠܥܠܡ : [l]ܕܢܕܥܘܢ ܠܟ ܐܢܬ ܗܘ ܐܠܗܐ ܫܪܝܪܐ [m]ܒܠܚܘܕܝܟ : [n]ܘܠܡܢ [o]ܕܫܕܪܬ 4 ܝܫܘܥ ܡܫܝܚܐ : ܐܢܐ ܫܒܚܬܟ ܥܠ ܐܪܥܐ : [p]ܫܘܠܡܐ ܕܥܒܕܐ [q]ܕܝܗܒܬ ܠܝ 5 ܠܡ ܕܐܥܒܕ : [†]ܘܗܫܐ [h]ܫܒܚܢܝ ܐܢܬ ܐܒܐ ܠܘܬܟ [i]ܒܬܫܒܘܚܬܐ ܗܝ ܕܗܘܬ ܠܝ 6 ܡܢ ܩܕܡ ܕܢܗܘܐ [r]ܥܠܡܐ : ܐܘܕܥܬ ܫܡܟ ܠܒܢܝܢܫܐ : ܗܠܝܢ ܕܝܗܒܬ ܠܝ ܡܢ [r]ܥܠܡܐ : ܕܝܠܟ ܗܘܘ ܘܠܝ ܝܗܒܬ ܐܢܘܢ : ܘܡܠܬܟ ܢܛܪܘ	[h]ܠܟ [k]*omit* ܐܢܘܢ [o] *add* ܗܘ [q]ܡܕܡ † f. 29*b*.
[u]*add* ܡܢ [t]*omit* ܕ [w]ܘܒܬܪ	7 ܗܫܐ [s]ܝܕܥܘ [t]ܕܟܠ ܡܐ ܕܝܗܒܬ ܠܝ [u]ܡܢ ܠܘܬܟ 8 ܗܘ : ܡܛܠ ܕܡܠܐ ܕܝܗܒܬ ܠܝ ܝܗܒܬ ܠܗܘܢ : [f. 29*a*] ܘܗܢܘܢ ܩܒܠܘ ܘܝܕܥܘ ܫܪܝܪܐܝܬ [w]ܕܡܢ ܠܘܬܟ ܢܦܩܬ : ܘܗܝܡܢܘ ܕܐܢܬ ܫܕܪܬܢܝ : 9 ܐܢܐ ܥܠ ܕܝܠܗܘܢ ܒܥܐ : ܠܐ ܥܠ [x]ܕܥܠܡܐ ܐܢܐ ܒܥܐ : ܐܠܐ [y]ܥܠ ܗܠܝܢ ܕܝܗܒܬ ܠܝ : [z]ܕܕܝܠܟ ܐܢܘܢ : [a]ܘܟܠ 10 ܡܐ ܕܝܠܝ ܕܝܠܟ ܐܢܘܢ : [a]ܘܕܝܠܟ ܕܝܠܝ ܘܐܢܐ 11 ܡܫܬܒܚ ܒܗܘܢ : ܘܠܐ [b]ܠܘܬ [c]ܐܢܐ [b]ܒܥܠܡܐ[d] : ܘܗܢܘܢ [e]ܐܢܘܢ ܘܐܢܐ ܠܘܬܟ : ܐܢܐ ܐܬܐ [f]ܐܒܐ ܩܕܝܫܐ ܛܪ ܐܢܘܢ [g]ܒܫܡܟ ܕܝܗܒܬ ܠܝ :	[s]ܝܕܥܘ [w]ܘܒܬܪ [y] *omit* ܥܠ [c] *omit* ܐܢܐ [f]ܐܒܐ
[x]ܕܥܠܡܐ [z]ܕܕܝܠܟ [a]*omit* ܘܟܠ...ܐܢܘܢ [b]ܠܘܬܟ [d]ܒܥܠܡܐ [e]*add* ܕܒܥܠܡܐ [f]ܐܒܐ [g]ܒܫܡܟ		

بلا لانها روهو لسا . . . . . . من

Codex B.

ܕܗܘܢ ܚܙܐ ܗܟܢ[h] ܕܐܒܘܗܝ[i] ܘܐܦ ܚܙܐ[i]
12 ܒܪ[h] ܗܘܬ ܚܡܝܗܘܢ [j]ܒܥܠܡܐ : ܐܢܐ [k]ܗܘܝܬ
ܡܛܪ ܠܗܘܢ ܒܫܡܟ [g]ܗܒܬ ܕܝܗܒܬ
ܠܝ : [l]ܘܢܛܪܬ ܘܐܢܫ ܡܢܗܘܢ ܠܐ
[m]ܐܘܒܕ ܐܠܐ[‡] ܐܢ ܒܪܗ ܕܐܒܕܢܐ : [n]ܠܡܫܠܡ
13 ܕܬܬܡܠܐ [o]ܟܬܒܐ : ܒܪܘ ܕܝܢ ܠܘܬܟ ܐܢܐ
ܐܬܐ : ܘܗܠܝܢ ܐܢܐ [p]ܡܡܠܠ [q]ܒܥܠܡܐ :
ܕܬܗܘܐ ܚܡܝܗܘܢ [r]ܚܕܘܬܐ ܕܝܠܝ : ܡܫܠܡܐ
ܒܓܘܗܘܢ ⁘

XLIII.

John XIV. 27—XV. 7.

ܐܡܪܗ ܘܐܡܪܢ ܝܗܒ ܐܠܗܢ[b] ܗܝ ܐܫܒܩ[a]
ܐܫܒܩܗ ܡܢ [c]ܢܝܫܝ :[z] ܐܡܪ ܡܪܐ
27 [a]ܠܬܠܡܝܕܘܗܝ ܠܐ ܢܬܒܪܒ ܠܒܟܘܢ ܘܠܐ ܢܕܚܠ :
28 ܫܡܥܬܘܢ ܕܐܢܐ ܐܡܪܬ ܠܟܘܢ : ܕܐܢܐ [b]ܐܙܠ
[†]ܘܐܬܐ ܠܘܬܟܘܢ : ܐܠܘ ܗܘܝܬܘܢ ܡܚܒܝܢ
ܠܝ : ܐܢܬ [c]ܚܕܝܬܘܢ ܕܐܢܐ [b]ܐܙܠ ܠܘܬ ܐܒܐ :
29 ܐܒܐ ܪܒ ܗܘ ܡܢܝ : ܐܘܦ ܟܕܘ ܐܡܪܬ
ܠܟܘܢ ܡܢ ܩܕܡ ܠܐ [d]ܬܬܥܒܕ ܬܗܝܡܢܘܢ :
30 ܒܬܪ ܠܘܬ ܐܢܐ [e]ܡܡܠܠ ܒܥܡܟܘܢ ܣܓܝ :
ܐܬܐ ܗܘ [f]ܓܝܪ[f] ܐܪܟܘܢܗ [g]ܕܗܕܝܢ [h]ܥܠܡܐ :
31 [i]ܘܒܝ ܠܝܬ [j]ܠܗ [k]ܟܠܘܡ : ܐܠܐ [l]ܕܝܕܥ
[f. 29b]
[h]ܥܠܡܐ ܕܐܢܐ ܪܚܡ ܠܐܒܐ : ܘܗܟܢ ܡܐ
ܕܦܩܕ ܠܝ ܐܒܐ ܗܟܢ[m] ܐܢܐ ܥܒܕ ܩܘܡܘ
XV. 1 [n]ܐܙܠ ܡܢ ܗܟܐ :[o] ܐܢܐ ܗܘ ܓܘܦܢܐ [p]ܕܩܘܫܛܐ
2 ܘܐܒܐ ܗܘ ܦܠܚܐ : ܟܠ [q]ܫܒܫܒܬܐ ܕܒܝ
ܕܠܐ [r]ܡܝܬܝܐ ܦܐܪܝܢ ܡܣܝܒ ܗܘ ܠܗ : [s]ܘܟܠ
[t]ܗܝܐ [u]ܕܡܝܬܝܐ ܦܐܪܝܢ ܡܕܟܐ ܗܘ ܠܗ :[s]
3 [x]ܠܡܠܠ ܕܦܢܝܬ ܥܡܟܘܢ ܬܗܘܐ : ܒܬܪ ܐܬܘܢ

Codex A.

[h] add ܗܟܐ
[i] omit ܘܐܦ ܚܙܐ
[j] ܒܥܠܡܐ [k] ܗܘܝܬ
[g] ܗܒܬ
‡ f. 32a.
[l] ܘܢܛܪܬ [m] ܐܘܒܕ
[p] ܡܡܠܠ [q] ܒܥܠܡܐ
[r] ܚܕܘܬܐ
[a] ܗܝ ܐܫܒܩ ܐܠܗܝܢ
[a] ܐܫܒܩܗ
[c] ܢܝܫܝ
[a] ܠܬܠܡܝܕܘܗܝ
[b] ܐܙܠ
[c] ܚܕܝܬܘܢ
[d] ܬܬܥܒܕ
[e] ܡܡܠܠ
[g] ܕܗܕܝܢ [h] ܥܠܡܐ
[k] ܟܠܘܡ [l] ܕܝܕܥ
[m] ܗܟܢ [n] ܐܙܠ
[o] add ܩܘܡܘ
[p] ܕܩܘܫܛܐ
[q] ܫܒܫܒܬܐ [r] ܡܝܬܝܐ
[t] ܗܝܐ [u] ܕܡܝܬܝܐ
[x] ܠܡܠܠ

Codex C.

[h] add ܗܟܐ
[i] omit ܘܐܦ
[m] ܐܘܒܕ [n] ܠܡܫܠܡ
[o] add ܕ
[p] ܡܡܠܠ
[r] ܚܕܘܬܐ
[b] omit ܗܝ [c] ܘܢܝܫܐ
[z] add ܘܐܡܪ ܡܪܢ ܝܫܘܥ
[a] ܠܬܠܡܝܕܘܗܝ
† f. 30a.
[c] ܚܕܝܬܘܢ
[d] ܬܬܥܒܕ
[f] ܓܝܪ ܗܘ[f]
[i] ܘܒܝ [j] ܗܘ
[k] ܟܠܘܡ [l] ܕܝܕܥ
[n] ܘܐܙܠ
[s] omit ܘܟܠ . . . ܠܗ

Codex A.	Codex B.	Codex C.
[w] ܕܐܡܪ [x] ܠܥܠܠ	[w] ܕܐܡܪܬ [x] [y] ܠܥܠܠ ܡܠܬܐ ܕܐܡܠܠܬ ܠܟܘܢ [y] :	[y] ܠܥܠܠ ... ܠܟܘܢ omit
‡ f. 32b.	4 ܩܘܡܘ ܒܝ ܘܐܢܐ ܒܟܘܢ : ܗܝܟ ‡ [z] ܡܐ ܕ	[z] ܡܐ omit
[a] ܕܡܬܩܪܝܬܐ [b] ܢܥܠܐ	[a] ܕܡܬܩܪܝܬܐ ܠܐ [b] ܢܥܠܐ [c] ܡܥܒܕܐ ܦܐܪܝܢ ܡܢ	[a] ܕܡܬܩܪܝܬܐ
[c] ܡܥܒܕܐ	ܓܪܡܗ : ܐܠܐ ܐܢ ܬܩܘܡ ܒܓܘܦܢܐ :	
[d] ܗܟܕܢ	[d] ܗܟܕܢ ܐܦ ܐܢܬܘܢ ܠܐ ܬܥܒܕܘܢ	
[e] ܡܬܩܪܝܬܐ	5 ܒܝ : ܐܢܐ ܗܘ ܓܘܦܢܐ ܘܐܢܬܘܢ [e] ܡܬܩܪܝܬܐ :	[e] ܡܬܩܪܝܬܐ
	ܡܢ ܕܩܐܝܡ ܒܝ ܘܐܢܐ ܒܗ ܗܢܐ ܝܥܒܕ ܦܐܪܝܢ	
[f] ܡܕܡ [g] ܠܐ omit	ܣܓܝܐܝܢ : ܕܡܢ ܒܠܥܕܝ ܠܐ ܬܫܟܚܘܢ ܠܡܥܒܕ	
[h] ܕܡܬܩܪܝܬܐ	6 ܟܠܡܕܡ [f] : ܐܠܐ ܗܘܐ ܐܢܫ	[f] ܡܕܡ [g] ܠܐ omit
[i] ܘܝܒܫ	[g] ܠܐ ܩܐܝܡ ܒܝ ܢܬܪܡܐ ܠܒܪ ܗܝܟ ܡܐ	[h] ܕܡܬܩܪܝܬܐ
[k] ܘܦܚܡܝܢ [l] ܘܢܦܩܝܢ	[h] ܕܡܬܩܪܝܬܐ [i] ܘܝܒܫ : ܘܠܩܛܝܢ ܡܟܢܫܝܢ	[k] ܘܦܚܡܝܢ
[m] ܠܐ omit	ܠܗ [k] ܘܦܚܡܝܢ* ܒܢܘܪܐ [l] ܘܝܩܕܝܢ :	[* Sic in Cod. B.]
[o] ܬܫܐܠܘܢ	7 ܐܢ ܕܝܢ [m] ܠܐ ܬܩܘܡܘܢ ܒܝ [n] ܘܡܠܝ	[m] ܠܐ omit [l] ܘܝܩܕܝܢ
[p] ܘܡܬܥܒܕ	ܒܟܘܢ [o] ܬܫܐܠܘܢ : ܡܐ ܕܐܢܬܘܢ ܨܒܝܢ	[n] ܘܡܠܝ [o] ܬܫܐܠܘܢ
[q] ܥܠܡ add	ܫܐܠܘ [p] ܘܡܬܥܒܕ ܠܟܘܢ [q] ⁘	[p] ܘܡܬܥܒܕ

XLIV.

John XVI. 1—13.

Codex A.	Codex B.	Codex C.
ܦܓܢܐ ܩܪܝ [a] ܡܢ ܐܘܢܓܠܝܘܢ ܕܝܘܚܢܢ ܒܗ ܕܐܬܠܟܣܢܕܪܘܣ [a]	[a] ܡܢ ܐܘܢܓܠܝܘܢ ܕܝܘܚܢܢ [b] ܒܗ	[b] ܡܢ ܝܘܚܢܢ [b]
	1 ܐܡܪ [y] [ab] ܡܪܢ ܝܫܘܥ [z] ܠܬܠܡܝܕܘܗܝ † ܗܠܝܢ	† f. 30b.
	2 ܡܠܠܬ ܠܟܘܢ : [a] ܠܡܕܠ ܕܠܐ ܬܬܟܫܠܘܢ ܡܢ	[y] ܘܡܠܘ ܡܪܢ ܝܫܘܥ add
[c] ܢܦܩܘܢ	[b] ܟܢܘܫܬܐ [c] ܢܦܩܘܢ ܠܟܘܢ : ܐܠܐ ܐܬܝܐ ܫܥܬܐ	[z] ܠܬܠܡܝܕܘܗܝ
[d] ܩܪܒ	ܕܟܠ ܡܢ ܕܝܩܛܠ ܝܬܟܘܢ ܢܗܘܐ [d] ܩܪܒ [e] ܩܘܪܒܢܐ	[a] ܠܡܕܠ omit
[f] ܡܣܒܪ	3 ܗܘ [f] ܡܣܒܪ ܠܐܠܗܐ : ܘܗܠܝܢ ܥܒܕܝܢ [g] ܠܟܘܢ	[b] ܟܢܘܫܬܐ
[g] ܠܟܘܢ	4 ܠܟܘܢ ܕܠܐ ܚܟܡܘ ܠܐܒܐ ܘܠܐ ܠܝ : ܐܠܐ	[e] ܩܘܪܒܢܐ
[h] ܫܥܬܐ	ܗܠܝܢ ܡܠܠܬ ܠܟܘܢ [f. 30a] ܕܟܕ ܬܐܬܐ [h] ܫܥܬܐ	[f] ܡܣܒܪ [h] ܫܥܬܐ
[i] ܬܥܗܕܘܢ [j] ܠܗܝܢ	ܬܗܘܘܢ [i] ܥܗܕܝܢ [j] ܠܗܝܢ ܕܐܢܐ ܐܡܪܬ ܠܟܘܢ :	[j] ܠܗܝܢ
[k] ܕܝܢ omit	ܘܗܠܝܢ ܕܝܢ ܡܢ ܪܫ [k] ܠܐ ܕܝܢ ܐܡܪܬ ܠܟܘܢ	[k] ܕܝܢ omit
[l] ܗܘܝܬ [n] ܐܙܠ	5 [l] ܗܘܝܬ : ܟܕ ܕܝܢ ܐܢܐ [n] ܐܙܠ ܠܘܬ ܡܢ ܕܫܠܚ	
‡ f. 33a.	ܠܝ : ܘܐܢܫ ‡ ܡܢܟܘܢ ܠܐ ܫܐܠ ܠܝ ܠܗ	

Codex A.

ᵐܐܙܠ ⁿ *add* ܕ
°ܥܩܬܐ
ᵖ *omit* ܓܝܪ
ᑫܐܙܠ ˢܡܢܚܡܢܐ
ᵗܐܙܠ
ʷܠܥܠܡܐ ˣܩܫܝܛܘܬܐ
ᶻ *omit* ܘ
ⁿܐܙܠ ᵇ *add* ܕܝ
ʷܠܥܠܡܐ ᶜܕܐܡܪ
ᵈܕܬܛܥܢܘܢ
ᵉܐܬܐ ʰܠܟܘܢ
ⁱܒܟܘܠ ܩܘܫܛܐ
ᵏ *add* ܥܠܡ

Codex B.

6 ܐܬ ᵐܐܙܠ : ܐܠܐ ܕܗܠܝܢ ⁿܡܠܠܬ ܠܟܘܢ
7 °ܥܩܬܐ ܡܠܬ ܠܒܟܘܢ : ܐܠܐ ܐܢܐ ܩܘܫܛܐ
ܐܢܐ ܐܡܪ ܠܟܘܢ : ܛܒ ܠܟܘܢ ᵖܓܝܪ ܕܐܢܐ
ᑫܐܙܠ : ʳܐܢ ܠܝܬ ܐܢܐ ܓܝܪ ᵐܐܙܠ ˢܡܢܚܡܢܐ
ܠܐ ܐܬܐ ܠܘܬܟܘܢ . ʳܐܢ ܕܝ ᵗܐܙܠ ܐܢܐ
8 ܡܫܠܚ ܢܬܗ ܠܘܬܟܘܢ : ܘܟܕ ᵘܐܬܐ ܗܘ
ᵛܡܟܣܐ ʷܠܥܠܡܐ ܥܠ ܚܛܝ ˣܩܫܝܛܘܬܐ ܘܥܠ
9 ܚܛܝ ܕܝܢܐ ܘܥܠ ʸܚܛܝ ܕܠܝܐ : ᶻܘܥܠ ܚܛܝ
10 ˣܩܫܝܛܘܬܐ ܕܠܐ ᵃܡܗܝܡܢܝܢ *ܒܝ : ܥܠ ܚܛܝ
ᵇܕܝܢܐ ܕܐܢܐ ܠܘܬ ܐܒܐ ⁿܐܙܠ ܘܠܒܪ :
11 ܠܝܬ ܐܢܬܘܢ ܚܙܝܢ ܠܝ : ܥܠ ܚܛܝ ܕܝܢܐ ܕܝ
12 ܕܐܪܟܘܢܗ ܕܗܕܝܢ ʷܠܥܠܡܐ ܐܬܕܝܢ : ܥܘܕ
ܣܓܝ ܠܝ ᶜܕܐܡܪ ܠܟܘܢ : ܐܠܐ ܠܝܬ ܐܢܬܘܢ
13 ܡܫܟܚܝܢ ᵈܕܬܛܥܢܘܢ ܟܕܘ ܕܝ ᵉܐܬܐ ᶠܗ̈ܘ
ܪܘܚܐ ܕܩܘܫܛܐ ܗܘ ܡܕܒܪ ʰܠܟܘܢ ⁱܒܟܘܠ ܩܘܫܛ
ʲܒܟܠܗ . ᵏ ⁘

Codex C.

°ܥܩܬܐ
ʳܐܢ ˢܡܢܚܡܢܐ
ᵗܐܙܠ
ᵘܐܬܐ
ᵛܡܟܣܐ
ʸܚܛܝ
[* Cod. ܕܝ]
ᵃܡܗܝܡܢܝܢ
ᶜܕܐܡܪ
ᵉܐܬܐ ᶠܗܘ
ʰܠܟܘܢ
ⁱܕܩܘܫܛܐ ʲܒܟܠܗ

XLV.

John XVI. 14—23.

Codex A.

ᵃܗܘܬܗ ܘܐܪܒܥܝܢ ᵃ*omit*
ᵃ *add* ܒܥܠܐ ܕܐܒܐ
ᵇܠܝ ᶜܘܡܚܘܐ
ᵈܡܛܠ
ᵉܘܐܢܐ
‡ f. 33*b*.
ᶠܐܙܠ ʰܠܦܠܓܗܘܢ
ⁱܙܥܘܪ
ᵏܐܙܠ

Codex B.

ᵃܗܘܬܗ ܘܐܪܒܥܝܢ ᵃܝܘܡ ܐܪܒܥܐ ܡܢ ᵇܘܫܒܥܐ :ʸ
14 ܐܡܪ ܡܪܢܐ ᶻܬܠܡܝܕܘܗܝ ᵃ ܗܘ ܡܫܒܚ ᵇܠܝ :
15 ܕܡܢ ܕܝܠܝ ܗܘ ܢܣܒ ᶜܘܡܚܘܐ ܠܟܘܢ : ܟܠ
ܡܐ ܕܐܠܐܒܐ ܕܝܠܝ ܗܘܝ : † ᵈܡܛܠ ܗܕܝܢ
ܐܡܪܬ ܠܟܘܢ ܕܡܢ ܕܝܠܝ ܗܘ ܢܣܒ ܘܡܚܘܐ
16 ܠܟܘܢ : ܙܥܘܪ ܘܠܒܪ ܠܝܬ ܐܢܬܘܢ ܚܙܝܢ ܠܝ :
ܘܬܘܒ ܙܥܘܪ ܘܐܢܬܘܢ ܚܙܝܢ ܠܝ ᵉܐܢܐ
17 ᶠܐܙܠ ܠܘܬ ܐܒܐ : ܐܡܪܘ ܕܝ ܐܢܫܝܢ ‡ ܡܢ
ᵍܬܠܡܝܕܘܗܝ ܦܠܓܗܘܢ ʰܠܦܠܓܗܘܢ ܕܗܘ ܐܡܪ ܠܢ
[f. 30*b*]
ⁱܙܥܘܪ ܘܠܒܪ ܠܝܬ ܐܢܬܘܢ ܚܙܝܢ ܠܝ : ܘܬܘܒ
ⁱܙܥܘܪ ܘܐܢܬܘܢ ܚܙܝܢ ܠܝ : ܘܐܢܐ ᵏܐܙܠ

Codex C.

ᵇܘܫܒܥܐ
ʸ *add* ܒܥܘܬܗ
ᶻܬܠܡܝܕܘܗܝ ᵇܠܝ
† f. 31*a*.
ᶜܘܡܚܘܝܢ ᵈܡܛܠ
ᵉܘܐܢܐ
ᵍܬܠܡܝܕܘܗܝ (*sic*)

Codex A.	Codex B.	Codex C.
[l] *add* ܕܝܢ [m]ܗܕܝܢ	18 ܠܡܬܐ ܐܡܪܐ : ܗܘܘ [l]ܐܡܪܝܢ ܡܐ ܗܘ [m]ܗܕܝܢ	[l] *add* ܕܝܢ
[i]ܝܕܥܝܢ [n]ܡܡܠܠ	[i]ܝܕܥܝܢ ܠܢܢ ܐܝܟ ܕܐܡܪ ܡܐ ܗܘ [n]ܡܡܠܠ :	[q] *omit* ܕ [p] *omit* ܕܝܢ
[o] *add* ܘ [s]ܫܐܠܝܢ	19 ܘܝܕܥ ܝܫܘܥ ܕܗܘܘ ܒܥܝܢ [p]ܕܝܢ [q]ܕܢܫܐܠܘܢܗ	[o] *add* ܘ
[w] *add* ܝܫܘܥ ܘܐܡܪ	ܠܗ : [o]ܐܡܪ ܠܗܘܢ ܥܠ ܗܕܐ ܒܥܝܢ ܐܢܬܘܢ[t]	[t] *add* : ܗܕܐ ܐܢܬܘܢ
ܘܐܢܬܘܢ ܬܚܕܘܢ	ܡܬܚܫܒܝܢ ܥܡܟܘܢ [r]ܥܡ [s]ܫܐܠܝܢ : [q]ܕܐܡܪܬ	ܥܡ [r] *omit* [s]ܫܐܠܝܢ
ܬܗܘܢ :	20 [i]ܝܕܥܝܢ ܘܟܘܬ ܐܢܬܘܢ ܒܟܝܢ ܘܬܗܘܢ :[w] ܐܡܝܢ ܐܡܝܢ	[w] *add* ܝܫܘܥ ܘܐܡܪ
[x]ܘܬܬܒܥܘܢ	ܐܡܪ ܐܢܐ ܠܟܘܢ ܕܐܢܬܘܢ ܬܒܟܘܢ [x]ܘܬܬܐܠܠ :	ܘܐܢܬܘܢ ܬܚܕܘܢ
[y]ܥܠܡܐ [z]ܬܬܥܨܒܘܢ	[y]ܥܠܡܐ ܕܝܢ ܢܚܕܐ : ܐܢܬܘܢ [z]ܬܬܥܨܒܘܢ ܐܠܐ	ܬܗܘܢ
	21 ܥܨܒܘܬܟܘܢ ܠܚܕܘܐ ܬܗܘܐ ܡܬܗܦܟܐ : ܐܢܬܬܐ	[x]ܘܬܬܒܥܘܢ
[a]ܕܝܠܕܐ [b]ܥܨܒܐ	ܟܕ ܗܝ [a]ܕܝܠܕܐ [b]ܥܨܒܐ ܗܘܐ ܠܗ ܕܐܬܬ	[c]ܬܫܠܡ [b]ܥܨܒܐ
[d]ܡܬܕܟܪܐ [e]ܠܐܘܠܨܢܐ	ܫܥܬܗ : ܟܕ ܕܝܢ [c]ܬܫܠܡ ܝܠܕܐ ܟܕܘ ܠܐ	[d]ܡܬܕܟܪܐ [e]ܠܐܘܠܨܢܐ
[f]ܠܓܠܠ [g]ܕܐܬܝܠܕ	[d]ܡܬܕܟܪܐ [e]ܠܐܘܠܨܢܐ [f]ܠܓܠܠ ܚܕܘܬܐ	[g]ܕܐܬܝܠܕ
[h]ܠܥܠܡܐ [k]ܥܨܒܐ	22 [g]ܕܐܬܝܠܕ ܒܪܢܫ [h]ܠܥܠܡܐ : [i]ܘܐܦ ܐܢܬܘܢ	[i] *omit* ܘܐܦ
[l]ܚܕܬܐ [m]ܚܙܐ	ܗܫܐ ܕܝܢ [k]ܥܨܒܐ ܐܝܬ ܠܟܘܢ : ܬܘܒ ܕܝܢ	
[n] *omit* ܡܢܟܘܢ	ܐܚܙܐ [l]ܚܕܬܐ ܠܟܘܢ ܘܠܒܟܘܢ [m]ܚܙܐ [n]ܡܢܟܘܢ :	[l]ܚܕܬܐ [m]ܚܙܐ
[o]ܘܚܕܘܬܟܘܢ	[o]ܘܚܕܘܬܟܘܢ ܐܢܫ ܠܐ ܢܣܒ ܡܢܟܘܢ :	[n] *omit* ܡܢܟܘܢ
[p]ܬܫܐܠܘܢ	23 ܘܒܝܘܡܗ ܗܘܐ ܠܐ ܠܝ ܬܫܐܠܘܢ ܐܢܬܘܢ [p]ܬܫܐܠܘܢ	
[q]ܟܠܡܕܡ [r]ܐܡܪܐ	[q]ܟܠܡܕܡ : ܐܡܝܢ ܐܡܝܢ [r]ܐܡܪ ܐܢܐ [r] ܠܟܘܢ :	[q]ܟܠܡܕܡ
	ܕܟܠ ܡܐ [s]ܕܬܫܐܠܘܢ ܡܢ ܐܒܐ ܒܫܡܝ	[s]ܕܬܫܐܠܘܢ [t]ܝܗܒ ܗܘ
[u] *add* ܠܟܘܢ [t]ܝܗܒ	ܗܘ [t]ܝܗܒ ܠܟܘܢ [u] :	[u] *add* ܠܟܘܢ

XLVI.

John XVI. 23—33.

Codex A.	Codex B.	Codex C.
[a]ܫܡܥܘܢ	[a]ܫܡܥܘܢ [b]ܘܐܡܪܝܢ ܗܘܐ ܐܠܝܫܘܥ [c]ܟܕ ܐܫܡܥ	[b]ܘܐܡܪܝܢ
[b]ܘܐܡܪܝܢ	ܐܫܡܥܢܐ ܡܢ ܝܫܘܥ [c z]ܐܡܪ ܡܪܢ [a]ܠܬܠܡܝܕܘܗܝ	[c]ܡܢ ܝܫܘܥ [c]
[c]ܡܢ ܝܫܘܥ [c]	23 ܐܡܝܢ ܐܡܝܢ [b]ܐܡܪ ܐܢܐ [b] ܠܟܘܢ : ܕܟܠ ܡܐ	[z] *add* ܡܪܢ ܘܐܡܪ
‡ f. 34a. [z] *add* ܡܪܢ ‡	ܕܬܫܐܠܘܢ ܡܢ ܐܒܐ ܒܫܡܝ ܗܘ ܝܗܒ	[a]ܠܬܠܡܝܕܘܗܝ
[a]ܠܬܠܡܝܕܘܗܝ	24 ܠܟܘܢ : ܥܕ ܟܕܘ ܠܐ [d]ܫܐܠܬܘܢ [e]ܟܠܡܕܡ :	[d]ܫܐܠܬܘܢ
[b]ܐܡܪܐ	ܫܐܠܘ ܘܬܣܒܘܢ [f]ܕܬܗܘܐ [g]ܠܓܠܠ [h]ܚܕܘܬܟܘܢ	[f]ܕܬܗܘܐ [e]ܟܠܡܕܡ
[e]ܟܠܡܕܡ [g]ܠܓܠܠ	25 ܗܕܐ ܒܡܬܠܐ : ܡܠܝܬ ܥܡܟܘܢ ܡܠܠܬ ܠܟܘܢ :	
[h]ܕܚܕܘܬܟܘܢ		

Codex A.	Codex B.	Codex C.
	[f. 31a] ܐܬܝܐ[i] ܫܥܐ ܕܗܘܐ ܒܡܬܠܝܢ ܠܐ[k] ܡܡܠܠ	ܐܬܝܐ[i] ܡܡܠܠ[k]
	ܠܟܘܢ : ܐܠܐ ܒܦܪܣܝܐ ܥܠ ܐܒܘܝ ܕܐܒܐ	[l] add ܕܝܢ
[l] add ܕܝܢ [m] omit ܕܝܢ	26 ܐܢܐ ܡܚܘܐ ܠܟܘܢ : ܒܗܘ[l] ܝܘܡܐ [m] ܕܝܢ	[m] omit ܕܝܢ
ܬܫܐܠܘܢ[n]	ܐܬܘܢ [n] ܬܫܐܠܘܢ ܒܫܡܝ ܘܠܝܬ ܐܢܐ[o] ܐܢܐ ܐܡܪ	[o] omit ܐܢܐ
	ܠܟܘܢ : ܕܐܢܐ ܒܥܐ ܡܢ ܐܒܐ ܥܠ ܕܝܠܟܘܢ :	
	27 ܗܘ ܓܝܪ ܐܒܐ ܪܚܡ ܠܟܘܢ ܕܐܬܘܢ ܪܚܡܬܘܢ	
	ܠܝ : ܘܗܝܡܢܬܘܢ ܕܐܢܐ ܡܢ ܠܘܬ ܐܠܗܐ	
[p] omit ܕܝܢ	28 ܢܦܩܬ ܕܝܢ[p] ܢܦܩܬ ܓܝܪ ܡܢ ܠܘܬ ܐܒܐ ܘܐܬܝܬ	[p] omit ܕܝܢ
ܠܥܠܡܐ[q] ܥܠܡܐ[r]	ܠܥܠܡܐ[q] : ܘܬܘܒ ܐܢܐ ܫܒܩ ܥܠܡܐ[r] ܘܐܙܠ[s][t]	ܠܥܠܡܐ[q]
ܘܐܙܠ[s] [t] add ܠܝ	29 ܠܘܬ ܐܒܐ ܐܡܪܝܢ ܠܗ ܬܠܡܝܕܘܗܝ[u] ܗܐ ܗܫܐ	ܬܠܡܝܕܘܗܝ[u]
	ܒܦܪܣܝܐ ܐܢܬ ܡܡܠܠ[v] : ܘܡܬܠ ܚܕ ܠܐ	ܡܡܠܠ[v]
ܐܡܪܬ[x]	30 ܗܫ [w] ܝܕܥܝܢ ܐܢܬ ܡܡܠܠ[x] : ܒܗܘ ܐܢܬ ܝܕܥ ܕܐܢܬ	ܐܡܪܬ[x] [w] omit ܝܕܥܝܢ
	ܝܕܥ ܟܘܠܐ : ܘܠܝܬ ܐܢܬ ܨܪܝܟ ܕܝܫܐܠ ܠܟ[y]	[y] omit ܠܟ
	ܐܢܫ : ܒܗܕܐ ܐܢܢ ܡܗܝܡܢܝܢ ܕܡܢ ܐܠܗܐ	
[z] omit ܐܢܬ	31 ܐܢܬ[z] ܢܦܩܬ : ܐܡܪ[a] ܠܗܘܢ ܝܫܘܥ ܘܐܡܪ	ܐܡܪ[a] [z] omit ܐܢܬ
ܐܡܪ[a]	32 ܠܗܘܢ : ܗܐ ܐܬܘܢ ܡܗܝܡܢܝܢ : ܗܐ ܐܬܝܐ	ܘܐܬܬ[b]
	ܫܥܐ ܘܐܬܬ[b] ܕܬܬܒܕܪܘܢ[c] ܟܠ ܚܕ ܠܘܬ ܕܝܠܗ	(sic) ܕܬܬܒܕܪܘܢ[c]
‡ f. 34b.	ܒܝܬܗ ܠܒܝܬܗ : ‡ ܘܠܝ ܠܚܘܕܝ ܐܢܬܘܢ	
	ܫܒܩܝܢ[d] : ܘܠܝܬ ܐܢܐ ܠܚܘܕܝ ܕܐܒܐ ܥܡܝ	ܫܒܩܝܢ[d]
ܡܠܠܬ[e]	33 ܐܢܝܢ : ܗܠܝܢ ܡܠܠܬ ܠܟܘܢ ܡܠܠܬ[e] ܕܒܝ	
[f] add ܫܠܡ	ܫܠܡ ܝܗܘܐ ܠܟܘܢ :[f] :·	

XLVII.

John XVII. 18—26.

Codex A.	Codex B.	Codex C.
		ܫܠܚܬܢܝ[b]
		ܘܐܦ ܫܠܚܬܗܘܢ ܡܢ[c]
		ܠܥܠܡܐ[c]
ܘܟܡܐ[a] ܕܫܠܚܬܢܝ	ܘܟܡܐ[a] ܕܐܫܠܚܬܢܝ ܐܘܦ ܫܠܚܬܢܝ[b] ܡܢ[c]	ܘܟܡܐ[a] ܕܫܠܚ[b]
ܫܠܚܬܗܘܢ ܡܢ	18 ܠܥܠܡܐ[ca] : ܘܐܦ ܐܢܐ ܫܠܚܬܗܘܢ ܐܢܐ[a] ܡܢ	[c] add ܐܢܐ
ܠܥܠܡܐ[a]	ܕܝܫܠܚ[b] ܠܗܘܢ[c] ܠܥܠܡܐ[d] : ܐܢܐ ܫܠܚܬ[c] ܐܢܘܢ	[d] omit ܠܥܠܡܐ
ܠܥܠܡܐ[d] ܫܠܚܬ[e]	19 ܠܥܠܡܐ[f] : † ܘܥܠ ܕܝܠܗܘܢ ܐܢܐ ܡܩܕܫ[g]	† f. 32a. ܠܥܠܡܐ[f] ܫܠܚ[e]
ܠܥܠܡܐ[f] ܡܩܕܫ[g]	ܢܦܫܝ : ܕܝܗܘܢ ܐܦ ܗܢܘܢ ܡܩܕܫܝܢ[h]	[i] omit ܕ ܡܩܕܫ[g]
ܡܩܕܫܝܢ[h]	20 ܒܩܘܫܛܐ : ܠܐ ܥܠ ܕܝܠܗܘܢ[i] ܕܗܠܝܢ[j] ܐܢܐ	[j] omit ܐܢܐ . . . ܕܗܠܝܢ

Codex A.	*Codex* B.	*Codex* C.
	ܒܥܐ ܠܩܛܠܝ : ܐܝܠܐ ܐܘܦ ܚܠ ܕܬܠܒܘܢ	
	ܕܗܠܝܢ [f. 31b] [j] [k]ܕܡܗܡܢܝܢ ܒܗ ܒܬܪܗ ܕܡܠܬܗܘܢ :	[k]ܕܡܗܡܢܝܢ
[l] omit ܡܐ	21 ܕܒܠܗܘܢ ܚܕܐ ܗܘܘ : ܗܟܢ [l]ܡܐ ܕܐܬ	
	ܐܒܐ ܒܟܘܢ : ܘܐܢܐ ܐܘܦ ܐܢܐ ܒܟܘܢ :	[m]ܕܗܘܡܢ
	ܕܐܘܦ ܗܘܐ ܒܟܘܢ ܚܕܐ ܗܘܘ : [m]ܕܗܘܡܢ*	[* Cod. ܕܗܘܡܢ]
ܒܠܝܡܐ[n]	22 [n]ܒܠܝܡܐ ܕܐܬ ܥܒܕܬ ܠܟܘ : ܘܐܢܐ [o]ܬܬܒܥܘܢܐ	ܬܬܒܥܘܢܐ[o]
	ܗܕܐ ܕܗܘܝܬ ܠܝ ܗܘܝܬ ܠܗܘܢ : ܕܗܘܘ ܚܕܐ	
	23 ܗܟܢ ܡܐ ܕܐܢܐ ܚܕܐ : ܐܢܐ ܒܟܘܢ	
ܠܓܠܠ[p]	ܘܐܬ ܒܟܘܢ : [p]ܠܓܠܠ ܕܗܘܘܢ ܡܫܠܡܝܢ	
	ܠܚܕܐ : ܘܕܗܘܐ [n]ܒܠܝܡܐ ܗܕܐ ܕܐܬ	
ܘܐܬܒܥܬ[q]	ܥܒܝܕܬ ܠܝ : [q]ܘܐܬܒܥܬ ܠܗܘܢ ܗܟܢ ܡܐ	
	24 ܕܐܬܒܥܬ ܠܝ : ܐܢܐ ܡܐ ܕܗܘܝܬ ܠܝ ܠܟܐ	
[r]ܕܗ ܘ [s]ܬܬܒܥܘܢ	ܐܢܐ [r]ܕܗܘܘ ܕܐܢܐ ܗܘܐ ܐܘܦ ܗܘܢ	[r]ܕܗ
[t]ܢܡܘܣܗ [u]ܕܒܠܝܡܐ	ܗܘܘ ܒܫܒܐ : ܕܗܘܘ ܫܠܡܝܢ [s]ܬܬܒܥܘܢ	
‡ f. 35a.	ܗܕܐ ܕܗܘܝܬ ܠܝ [‡] ܕܐܬܒܥܬ ܠܝ ܡܢ ܩܘܕܡ	
[w]ܘܒܠܝܡܐ	25 [t]ܢܡܘܣܗ [u]ܕܒܠܝܡܐ : ܐܢܐ ܓܕܘܦܐ [w]ܘܒܠܝܡܐ	[t]ܢܡܘܣܗ
[x]ܐܡܪ	ܠܐ [x]ܐܡܪܬ ܠܝ : ܐܢܐ ܕܝ ܐܡܪܬ ܠܝ :	
[y] omit ܐܬ	26 ܘܐܘܦ ܗܠܝܢ ܐܡܪܘ ܕܐܬ ܥܒܝܕܬ ܠܝ :	[y] omit ܐܬ
	ܕܫܒܬܐ [y]ܕܐܬ ܐܬܒܥܬ ܠܝ ܒܟܘܢ ܗܕܐ :	
	ܘܐܢܐ ܒܟܘܢ ∴	

XLVIII.

JOHN VII. 37—VIII. 2.

Codex A.	*Codex* B.	*Codex* C.
[a]ܐܬܝܚܝܠ	ܠܝܘܡ ܗܒܬ ܐܠܥܝܕܐ : [f]ܘܗܘܐ ܡܢ [a]ܐܬܝܚܝܠ	[f]ܐܠܦܝܘܗܝ [a]ܐܬܝܚܝܠ
[b]ܐܠܝܘܕܢܝܐ ܒܥܐܪܐ	ܐܠܦܝܘܗܝ [b]ܐܠܝܘܕܢܝܐ [g]ܘܒܥܘ [d]ܝܚܘܫ ܐܡܪ	[g] omit ܩܠܝܪܘܗܝ ... ܘܒܥܘ
[b] الحادى عشر	ܡܕܐ ܗܘܐ ܠܡܝܩܪ [e]ܩܠܝܪܘܗܝ [g] [i h]ܕܗܘܐ	[h]ܠܝܘܡ ܐܠܝܘܕ
[d]ܝܚܘܫ [e]ܩܠܝܪܘܗܝ	37 ܠܝܘܡ [i] ܚܕ ܐܠܥܝܕܐ [y h]: [z]ܘܡܘܩܡܐ ܕܝ ܒܥܡܐ	[h]ܐܠܥܝܕܐ ܡܢ ܚܕܐ
[i] omit ܠܝܘܡ ܕܗܘܐ	[a]ܕܡܒܫܢܝܐ ܪܒܐ ܗܘܐ ܡܕܐ ܝܫܘܥ [b]ܘܩܐܡ	[y] add ܘܒܥܡܗ
[y] add ܘܒܥܡܗ ܡܢ ܥܝܕܐ	ܘܐܬܝܚ ܘܐܡܪ : ܡܢ ܕܨܗܐ ܝܐܬܐ ܠܘܬܝ	[z] omit ܘ
[a]ܕܡܒܫܢܝܐ [z] omit ܘ	38 ܘܫܬܐ ܡܢ ܕܡܗܝܡܢ ܒܝ ܗܝܟ [c]ܡܐ ܕܐܡܪ	[b]ܘܩܐܡ
[c] omit ܡܐ		

Codex B.

ܟܬܒܐ : ܢܗܪܝܢ ܕܡܝܢ [d]ܚܝܝܢ ܝܓܕܘܢ ܡܢ ܟܪܣܗ :
39 ܗܕܐ ܕܝ ܐܡܪ ܥܠ [e]ܪܘܚܐ [f]ܕܩܘܕܫܐ : ܕܗܘܐ
ܕܗܘܘ ܥܬܝܕܝܢ ܕܢܣܒܘܢ ܗܠܝܢ ܕܡܗܝܡܢܝܢ
ܒܗ : ܥܕ ܟܕܘ ܓܝܪ ܠܐ [g]ܗܘܐ ܪܘܚܐ
ܕܩܘܕܫܐ [h]ܡܬܝܗܒܐ : [i]† ܡܛܠ ܕܡܪܐ ܝܫܘܥ
40 ܠܐ ܗܘܐ [k]ܡܫܬܒܚ ܥܕ ܟܕܘ ܫܡܥܘ ܐܘ
ܡܢ [l]ܐܟܠܘܣܐ ܥܕ [m]ܫܡܥܘ ܗܠܝܢ ܡܠܝܐ ܗܘܘ
ܐܡܪܝܢ : ܗܕܝܢ ܗܘ [n]ܡܢ [o]ܩܘܫܛ [p]ܢܒܝܐ :
41 [q]ܘܐܚܪܢܝܢ ܗܘܘ ܐܡܪܝܢ ܕܗܢܐ ܓܝܪ ܡܢ ܓܠܝܠܐ
42 [r]ܡܫܝܚܐ [r]ܐܬܐ : ܠܐ [s]ܟܬܒܐ ܐܡܪ [t]ܡܢ [u]ܙܪܥܗ
‡ [v]ܕܕܘܝܕ ܘܡܢ ܒܝܬ [w]ܠܚܡ ܩܪܝܬܐ ܗܝ ܕܗܘܐ
43 [x]ܕܘܝܕ [y]ܐܬܐ ܡܫܝܚܐ[y] : ܘܦܠܓ ܐܬܥܒܕ [z]ܒܝܢ
44 [a]ܐܟܠܘܣܐ [b]ܡܛܠܬܗ : ܐܢܫܝܢ ܕܝ ܡܢܗܘܢ ܗܘܘ
ܨܒܝܢ [c]ܕܢܬܦܣܘܢ ܝܬܗ : ܐܠܐ ܐܢܫ ܠܐ ܐܪܡܐ
45 [d]ܥܠܘܗܝ [e]ܐܝܕܐ : [f]ܘܐܬܘ [g]ܗܡܪܓܠܝܐ ܠܘܬ [h]ܪܒܝ
ܟܗܢܝܐ ܘܦܪܝܫܐ [i]ܘܦܪܝܫܝܢ ܘܐܡܪܘ ܠܗܘܢ :
46 ܡܢ [v]ܡܬܚܝܢ ܠܐ [k]ܡܠܠ ܒܪܢܫ [l]ܟܕܝܢ ܗܟܢ
47 [m]ܕܗܕܝܢ ܒܪܢܫܐ [n]ܡܡܠܠ : ܘܐܓܝܒܘ [o]ܦܪܝܫܝ
48 [p]ܘܐܡܪܘ ܠܗܘܢ : ܕܠܡܐ ܐܘܦ ܐܢܬܘܢ ܛܥܝܬܘܢ :
49 ܕܠܡܐ ܐܢܫ ܡܢ ܐܪܟܘܢܐ [h]ܗܝܡܢ ܒܗ : ܐܘ ܡܢ
[q]ܦܪܝܫܝ : ܐܠܐ ܗܕܝܢ [r]ܐܟܠܘܣܐ ܕܠܐ [s]ܡܕܪܝܢ
50 ܢܝܩܕܡܘܣ ܠܓܒܝܗܘܢ : ܘܐܡܪ [t]ܠܗܘܢ
[u]ܢܝܩܕܡܘܣ [w]ܠܡܦܠܚܘܢ : ܗܕܝܢ ܕܐܬܐ
ܠܘܬܗ ܡܪܐ ܝܫܘܥ ܡܢ ܩܕܡ : [x]ܗܕܝܢ ܕܗܘܐ
51 ܚܕ ܡܢܗܘܢ : ܕܗܢܐ [y]ܢܡܘܣܢ [z]ܕܝܢ [a]ܠܒܪܢܫܐ
ܐܠܐ ܐܢ ܫܡܥ ܡܢܗ [b]ܩܕܡܝܢ ܘܝܕܥ
52 ܡܐ ܗܘ [c]ܥܒܕ : ܐܓܝܒܘ ܕܝ ܘܐܡܪܝܢ
ܠܗ ܕܗܢܐ [d]ܐܦ ܐܢܬ ܡܢ ܓܠܝܠܐ ܐܢܬ [e]ܦܫܦܫ
53 ܘܚܙܝ : ܕܡܢ ܓܠܝܠܐ ܢܒܝܐ [e]ܠܐ ܩܐܡ : [f]ܘܐܙܠܘ
[f. 33b]
VIII. 1 ܠܗܘܢ ܟܠ ܐܢܫ ܠܒܝܬܗ : ܡܪܐ ܝܫܘܥ[g]
2 [h]ܐܙܠ ܠܗ ܠܛܘܪܐ [i]ܕܙܝܬܐ : ܘܬܘܒ ܡܢ

Codex A.

[d] ܚܝܝܢ
[e] ܪܘܚܗ [f] ܕܩܘܕܫܐ
[g] ܗܘܬ
[h] ܡܬܝܗܒܐ [i] ܡܛܠ
[k] ܕܐܫܬܒܚ
[l] ܐܘܟܠܘܣܐ
[m] ܫܡܥܘ
[t] ܕܡܢ [u] ܙܪܥܐ
[v] ܕܕܘܕ [x] ܕܘܕ
[z] omit ܒܝܢ
‡ f. 35b.
[a] ܒܐܘܟܠܘܣܐ
[b] ܡܛܠܬܗ [c] ܕܢܬܦܣܘܢ
[d] ܥܠܘܗܝ [e] ܐܝܕܐ
[f] add ܕܝ
[g] ܗܡܪܓܠܝܐ
[h] ܪܒܝܐ [i] ܘܦܪܝܫܝܢ
[k] ܡܡܠܠ [l] ܟܕ
[o] ܦܪܝܫܝܢ
[p] ܘܐܡܪܝܢ
[q] ܦܪܝܫܝܢ
[r] ܐܘܟܠܘܣܐ
[s] ܡܕܪܝ ܠܗܘܢ [t] omit
[u] ܢܝܩܕܡܘܣ
[w] ܠܡܦܠܚܘܢ
[x] ܗܕܝܢ [z] ܕܐܝܢ
[a] ܠܒܪܢܫܐ [b] ܡܩܕܡܝܢ
[d] add ܐܘܦ
[g] add ܕܝ
[h] ܐܙܠ [i] ܕܙܝܬܐ

Codex C.

[d] ܚܝܝܢ
[e] ܪܘܚܗ [f] ܕܩܘܕܫܐ
[g] ܗܘܬ
[k] ܕܐܫܬܒܚ
† f. 32b.
[l] ܐܘܟܠܘܣܐ
[m] ܫܡܥܘ ܡܢ [n] omit
[o] ܩܘܫܛ [p] ܢܒܝܐ
[q] ܘܐܚܪܢܝܢ
[r] ܡܫܝܚܐ ܐܬܐ [r]
[s] ܟܬܒܐ [t] ܕܡܢ
[u] ܙܪܥܐ [w] ܠܚܡ
[y] ܡܫܝܚܐ ܐܬܐ [y]
[z] omit ܒܝܢ
[a] ܒܐܘܟܠܘܣܐ [d] ܥܠ
[e] ܐܝܕܗ [f] add ܕܝ
[g] ܗܡܪܓܠܝܐ [h] ܪܒܝܐ
[i] ܘܦܪܝܫܝܢ
[v] ܡܛܠ [k] ܡܠܠ
[m] omit ܕ [n] ܡܡܠܠ
[p] ܘܐܡܪܝܢ [h] ܗܝܡܢܘ
[r] ܐܘܟܠܘܣܐ [s] ܡܕܪܝ
[t] omit ܠܗܘܢ
[y] ܢܡܘܣܢ [z] ܕܐܝܢ
[a] ܠܒܪܢܫ [b] ܡܩܕܡܝܢ
[c] omit ܗܘ
[d] add ܐܘܦ
[e] omit ܦܫܦܫ . . . ܢܒܝܐ
[f] ܘܐܙܠ [g] add ܕܝ

Codex A.	Codex B.	Codex C.
ܦܪܝܫܝܐ [k]	ܦܪܝܫܝܐ [k] ܐܬܬ ܠܢܘܗܪܐ : ܒܥܠܡܐ ܘܟܠܗ † ܗܘܐ ܗܘܐ	† f. 33a.
‡ f. 36a.	ܐܬܬ ܠܒܝܬܗ : [l] ܘܩܡܬ ‡ [m] ܠܗ [n] ܘܗܘܐ ܘܟܠܗ °	ܦܪܝܫܝܐ [k] ܘܩܡܬ [l]
ܘܗ[ܘ]ܐ [n] ܘܟܠܗ °	ܠܗܘܢ ÷ [q p] ܥܠ ܟܢܘܫܗ ܕܝܘܚܢܢ [r] ܡܠܝܫܘܥ	ܠܗܘܢ [m] ܘܟܠܗ °
ܥܠܝܗ [q] ܡܠܝܫܘܥ [r]	ܒܐܘܢܓܠܝܘܢ [s] [p]	ܥܠܝܟܬ ܕܝܘܚܢܢ [p]
ܒܐܘܢܓܠܝܘܢ [s]		ܫܠܝܚܐ ܕܟܠܗܘܢ
		ܐܠܗܝܢ ܘܗܘܐ
		ܗܝ ܕܝܘܚܢܢ ܕܐܬܬ
		ܐܠܗܝܢ [p]

XLIX.

Matt. XVIII. 10—20.

Codex A.

ܚܘܐ [a] ܡܢ ܡܫܬܐܠܘܬܐ
ܗܘܐ ܐܬܬܐܡܪܐ
ܒܗ ܐܠܗܝܢܗ [a]
ܗܘܫܘ [z] *omit*
ܬܬܒܥܘܢ [b]
ܐܡܪ *omit* [c]
ܕܡܬܐܡܪܝܢ [d]
[e] ܟܠܗ ܥܡܡܐ [e]
ܗܘܐ [g] [f] *add* ܕ
ܐܡܬܟܝܢ [j] ܡܢܐ [i]
ܡܚܝܢ [k] ܠܒܪܐ [m]
ܘܐܝܬ [n]
ܗܘܐ [b] ܘܐܡܪܝܢ [c]
ܕܗܘܐ [d] ܢܬܬܪ [o]
ܫܡܥ [s] ܐܝܬ [t]
ܟܢܫܐ [u] ܟܠܘܢܝ [w]
ܬܫܡܥ [x]
ܚܒܪ [z]
ܐܐ [d]
ܐܡܪܬ [e]
ܕܬܫܪܘܢ [h]

Codex B.

ܚܙܘ [a] ܐܬܘܢ ܐܠܗܝܢܗ ܡܢ ܡܫܬܐܠܘܬܐ ܗܘܘ
ܒܗ ܘܒܝܬܗ ܡܫܬܐܠܘܬܗܘܢ ܕܝܢ ܡܢ ܐܒܝ ܐܠܗܝܢ [a y]
10 ܐܡܪ ܡܢܐ [z] ܗܘܫܘ [z] ܫܡܥ ܕܠܐ [b] ܬܬܒܥܘܢ
ܫܡ ܡܢ ܗܝܟܢ ܠܒܝܫܐ : [c] ܐܡܪ ܐܢܐ ܠܗܘܢ
ܗܝ [d] ܕܡܬܐܡܪܝܢ [e] ܒܥܡܘܢܐ ܟܢܫܠ ܗܝ ܫܡܝܢ
12 ܐܡܪܝܢ ܕܐܡܐ [f] ܟܠܗ ܥܡܡܐ : ܡܢܐ [g] ܗܘܐ
ܠܗܘܢ [h] ܐܝܬ ܗܘܐ [i] ܡܢܐ ܠܚܒܪܝ [j] ܐܡܬܟܝܢ
ܬܬܚܙܐ ܫܪܝܐ [k] ܡܚܝܢ : ܠܐ ܐܝܬ ܬܬܚܙܝܢ
[l] ܘܬܫܡܥ ܥܠ [m] ܠܒܪܐ : [n] ܘܐܝܬ ܟܢܫܐ ܗܝ
13 ܕܬܚܙܐ : [a] ܘܐܢ [b] ܗܘܐ [c] ܐܫܟܚܝܢ ܠܗ : ܐܡܝܢ
ܐܡܪ ܐܢܐ ܠܗܘܢ : [d] ܗܘܐ ܫܪܐ ܒܠܚܘܕ [o] ܢܬܬܪ
ܡܢ ܕܟܠ ܬܬܚܙܝܢ [p] ܘܬܫܡܥ ܕܠܐ [q] ܬܚܙܝܢ :
14 ܘܗܟܢ ܠܝܬ ܨܒܝܢ ܘܗܘܐ ܐܡܪ ܟܠܗ ܥܡܡܐ :
15 [r] ܐܢ ܕܝܢ [s] ܢܫܡܥ ܥܠܝܟ ܐܚܘܟ [t] ܐܝܬ
[u] ܠܚܘܕܘܗܝ ܒܝܢܟ ܠܒܝܢܗ [w] ܟܠܘܢܝ : [r] ܐܢ
16 [x] ܕܬܫܡܥ ܠܟ ܐܬܪܒܚܬ ܐܚܘܟ : [y] ܐܢ ܕܝܢ ܠܐ
ܢܫܡܥ ܠܟ ܕܒܪ ܥܡܟ [z] ܚܕ [a y] [b] ܚܕ ܐܘ ܐܐ
ܬܪܝܢ : ܕܟܠ [c] ܦܘܡ ܬܪܝܢ [d] ܐܘ ܬܠܬܐ ܣܗܕܝܢ
ܬܩܘܡ ܟܠ ܡܠܐ : [r] ܐܢ ܕܝܢ ܐܦ ܠܐ
17 ܠܗܘܢ ܠܐ ܢܫܡܥ [e] ܐܡܪ [f] ܠܥܕܬܐ : [r] ܐܢ
ܕܝܢ ܐܦ [g] ܠܐ [f] ܠܥܕܬܐ ܠܐ ܢܫܡܥ ܢܗܘܐ
18 ܠܟ ܐܝܟ ܡܟܣܐ ܘܚܢܦܐ : ܐܡܝܢ ܐܡܪ
ܐܢܐ ܠܗܘܢ : ܕܟܠ ܡܐ [h] ܕܬܫܪܘܢ ܥܠ

Codex C.

ܠܚܘܕ [a] ܐܬܘܢ
ܐܠܗܝܢܗ ܡܢ
ܡܫܬܐܠܘܬܐ [a]
[y] *add* ܘܒܝܬܗ
[z] *omit* ܗܘܫܘ
[a] *add* ܠܬܠܡܝܕܘܗܝ
ܕܡܬܐܡܪܝܢ [d]
[e] ܟܠܗ ܥܡܡܐ [e]
[f] *add* ܕ
ܐܝܬ [h] ܗܘܐ [g]
ܐܡܬܟܝܢ [j] ܡܢܐ [i]
ܘܐܝܬ [n] ܘܬܫܡܥ [l]
ܗܘܐ [b] ܕܗܘܐ [d]
ܘܬܫܡܥ [p] ܬܚܙܝܢ [q]
ܐܝܬ [r]
ܟܢܫܐ [u]
ܕܬܫܡܥ [x]
[y] *omit* ܐܢ . . . ܚܕ
[a] *add* ܐܘܦ [b] ܚܕ
ܐܐ [d] ܦܘܡ [e]
ܠܥܕܬܐ [f]
[g] *omit* ܠܐ
ܕܬܫܪܘܢ [h]

Codex A.

‡ f. 36b.

[i] omit ܐܡܪ . . . ܗܘܐ . . .

[m] ܫܡܥܘܢ

[p] add ܥܠܡ

ܐܬܠܬܐ [b]

[y] ܝܫܘܥ [a] ܘܡܟܪܙ

[b] ܒܣܒܪܬܐ [d] ܘܟܠ

[f] add ܗܘܘܢ [g] ܒܝܫܝܢ

[h] ܒܟܐܒܝܢ

[j] ܕܬܘܢܟܝܢ [j] ܬܘܢܟܝܢ

[l] ܠܟܘܠܗܘܢ

[m] omit ܟܢܫܝܢ

[o] add ܟܢܫܝܢ

[CCLXXXII.]

[f. 176a]

[a] add ܘܟܢܬܗ ܡܢܝܪܘܣܐ

[β] ܐܘܟܠܘܣܝܢ ܟܢܫܝܢ [β]

[γ p] ܕܩܦܘܠܝܣ

[δ q] ܝܗܘܕܐ [ε r] ܕܝܘܪܕܢܢ

[[ζ] ܐܘܟܠܘܣܝܢ]

[η v] ܡܠܦ

‡ f. 37a.

[θ y] ܕܡܬܐܒܠܝܢ

[ι a] ܕܗܘܢ

[[κ] ܡܬܒܝܐܝܢ]

Codex B.

[f. 33a]

‡ ܐܪܒܥܐ ܗܘܐ [i] ܐܡܪ ܟܠܗ ܫܡܥܘܢ : ܘܒܥܠ
ܡܢ ܕܬܫܪܘܢ ܠܐ ܐܪܒܥܐ ܗܘܐ [i] ܫܪܐ ܟܠܗ
19 ܫܡܥܘܢ : ܬܘܒܢ [k] ܐܡܟܢ ܐܡܪ ܐܢܐ ܠܟܘܢ :
[l] ܕܐܢ [m] ܫܡܥܘܢ ܬܘܪܝܢ ܡܢܟܘܢ ܠܐ ܐܪܒܥܐ : ܠܐ
ܟܘܠ ܡܫܡܥܐ ܕܫܡܥܘܢ ܬܒܥܕ ܠܗܘܢ : ܡܢ
20 ܠܘܬ ܐܒܐ ܕܟܠܗ ܫܡܥܘܢ : ܗܘ ܠܐ ܕܬܘܪܝܢ
[n] ܐܐ † ܬܠܬܐ ܚܝܢܝܢ [o] ܕܝܢܝܢ ܕܝܠܗ ܬܘܒܢ
ܐܢܐ ܒܡܢܒܬܘܢ [p] ⁘

L.

MATT. IV. 23—V. 13.

[a] ܢܦܩ [b] ܐܬܠܬܐ ܒܝܕ ܐܠܝܫܪܗ ܡܢ ܡܬܐܘܣ
23 [x] ܘܟܢܬܗ ܡܢܝܪܘܣܐ [x] : ܘܗܘܐ [y] ܝܫܘܥ [z] ܡܕܪܐ
ܫܘܘܣ ܒܟܘܠܗ ܓܠܝܠܐ : ܘܡܠܦ ܒܟܢܫܬܗܘܢ
[a] ܘܡܟܪܙ [b] ܒܣܒܪܬܐ ܕܡܠܟܘܬܐ : [c] ܘܡܐܣܐ
24 ܟܘܠ ܒܘܫܝܢ [d] ܘܟܘܠ [e] ܡܪܥܘ ܒܥܡܐ : ܘܢܦܩ
ܡܫܡܥܗ ܒܟܘܠܗ ܣܘܪܝܐ : ܘܩܪܒܘ ܠܗ ܟܘܠ
[f] ܕܠܝܢ [g] ܕܒܝܫܝܢ [h] ܒܟܐܒܝܢ ܒܟܘܫܝܢ [i j] ܕܬܘܢܟܝܢ
[j] ܬܘܢܟܝܢ : ܘܡܬܚܠܝܢ ܡܢ ܫܐܕܝܢ :
ܘܡܬܢܟܝܢ ܡܢ ܚܝܕܝܢ ܘܟܠܝܘܢ [k] ܒܢܬܗܝܪܝܢ
ܘܡܫܪܝܢ : ܘܐܣܝ ܐܢܘܢ [l] ܠܟܘܠܗܘܢ
25 [α] ܘܐܬܘ ܒܬܪܗ [β m] ܟܢܫܝܢ [n] ܐܘܟܠܘܣܝܢ [o β] : ܡܢ
ܓܠܝܠܐ ܘܕܩܦܘܠܝܣ [γ p] ܕܩܦܘܠܝܣ ܘܡܢ ܐܘܪܫܠܡ :
ܘܡܢ [δ q] ܝܗܘܕܐ ܘܡܢ ܥܒܪ [ε r] ܕܝܘܪܕܢܢ :
V. 1 ܘܟܕ ܚܡܐ [ζ s] ܐܘܟܠܘܣܝܢ ܣܠܩ ܠܛܘܪܐ :
2 ܘܟܕ ܝܬܒ [t] ܠܗ ܩܪܒܘ ܠܗ [u] ܬܠܡܝܕܘܗܝ : ܘܦܬܚ
ܦܘܡܗ ܘܗܘܐ [η v] ܡܠܦ ‡ ܠܗܘܢ ܘܐܡܪ :
3 ܛܘܒܝܗܘܢ ܠܡܣܟܢܐ ܒܪܘܚܐ [w] ܕܕܝܠܗܘܢ ܗܝ
4 ܡܠܟܘܬܐ ܕܫܡܝܐ : ܛܘܒܝܗܘܢ [x] ܗܠܝܢ [θ y] ܕܡܬܐܒܠܝܢ
[f. 33b]
5 [z] ܕܗܘ [a] ܗܘܢ [κ] ܡܬܒܝܐܝܢ : ܛܘܒܝܗܘܢ ܠܡܟܝܟܐ

Codex C.

[i] ܐܡܪܐ

[k] omit ܐܡܟܢ

[l] ܕܐܢ [m] ܫܡܥܘܢ

[n] ܐܘ

† f. 33b.

[o] omit ܕܝܢܝܢ

[a] ܢܦܩ

[x] omit ܘܟܢܬܗ ܡܢܝܪܘܣܐ

[y] ܝܫܘܥ [z] ܡܕܪ

[b] ܒܣܒܪܬܐ [c] ܘܡܐܣܐ

[e] ܡܪܥܘܬ

[f] add ܗܘܘܢ

[g] ܕܒܝܫܝܢ [h] ܒܟܐܒܝܢ

[i] ܕܬܘܢܟܝܢ

[k] ܒܢܬܗܝܪܝܢ

[l] omit ܠܟܘܠܗܘܢ

[m] omit ܟܢܫܝܢ

[n] ܐܘܟܠܘܣܝܢ

[p] ܕܩܦܘܠܝܣ [o] add ܟܢܫܝܢ

[s] ܐܘܟܠܘܣܝܢ

[t] omit ܠܗ

[u] ܬܠܡܝܕܘܗܝ [v] ܡܠܦ

[x] omit ܗܠܝܢ [w] omit ܕ

[y] ܐܬܐܒܠܝܢ

[z] omit ܕܗܘ [a] ܕܗܘܢ

Codex B.

6 ܕܟܦܢܝܢ [bλ]ܘܨܗܝܢ ܠܗ ܠܟܐܢܘܬܗ : ܛܘܒܝܗܘܢ
ܗܠܝܢ ܕܟܦܢܝܢ ܘܨܗܝܢ [e]ܠܙܕܩܐ ܕܗܢܘܢ [μe]ܣܒܥܝܢ :
7 ܛܘܒܝܗܘܢ ܪܚܡܢܝܐ : ܕܥܠܝܗܘܢ [νf]ܗܘܢ
8 ܪܚܡܢܝܐ : ܛܘܒܝܗܘܢ ܗܠܝܢ ܕܕܟܝܢ ܒܠܒܗܘܢ
9 ܕܗܢܘܢ ܚܡܝܢ ܝܬܗ ܠܐܠܗܐ : ܛܘܒܝܗܘܢ
ܗܠܝܢ ܕܥܒܕܝܢ [ξ]ܫܠܡܐ ܕܗܢܘܢ [ωg]ܒܢܘ ܕܐܠܗܐ
10 ܝܬܩܪܘܢ : ܛܘܒܝܗܘܢ ܗܠܝܢ [πh]ܕܪܕܦܝܢ ܠܒܕܠ
ܙܕܩܐ ܕܕܝܠܗܘܢ [†] ܗܝ ܡܠܟܘܬܐ [i]ܕܫܡܝܐ :
11 [a]ܛܘܒܝܗܘܢ ܟܕ ܚܣܕܘ ܝܬܟܘܢ ܒܢܝܢܫܐ
[ρk]ܘܪܕܦܘܢ [σl]ܝܬܟܘܢ [m]ܘܐܡܪܘܢ ܥܠܝܟܘܢ
12 ܟܠ [n]ܒܝܫ ܡܕܓܠܝܢ [o]ܠܒܕܠܝ : ܐܬܘܢ [τp]ܚܕܘ
[q]ܘܐܬܦܨܚܘ [υr]ܕܐܓܪܟܘܢ ܣܓܝ ܒܓܘ ܫܡܝܐ :
[s]ܗܟܕܝܢ [t]ܪܕܦܘ ܠܢܒܝܐ [u]ܕܡܢ ܩܕܡܝܟܘܢ :
13 ܐܢܬܘܢ ܗܘܝܢ ܡܠܚܗ ܕܐܪܥܐ : [w]ܐܢ ܕܝ
ܡܠܚܐ ܦܟܗ ܒܡܐ ܗܝ ܡܬܡܠܚܐ : [x]ܠܡܠܡ
ܒܕܘ ܠܐ ܚܫܚܐ : ܐܠܐ [w]ܐܢ ܕܡܬܪܡܝܐ ܠܒܪ
ܘܡܬܕܝܫ ܡܢ ܒܢܝܢܫܐ : [y] ⁘

Codex A.

[λb]ܘܨܗܘܢ
[μe]ܣܒܥܘܢ
[f]ܗܘܢ [ν][ܗܘܝܢ]
[ξ][ܫܠܡܐ] [ωg]ܒܢܝܗ
[πh]ܕܪܕܦܝܢ
[[a]ܛܘܒܝܗܘܢ]
[ρk]ܘܪܕܦܘܢ
[lσ] *omit* ܝܬܟܘܢ
[o]ܠܒܕܠ [τp]ܚܕܘ
[υr]ܕܐܓܪܟܘܢ
[s]ܗܟܕܝܢ [t] *add* ܠܟܢ
[u]ܕܡܢ
[x]ܠܡܠܡ
[y] *add* ܥܠܡ

Codex C.

[e] *add* ܠܒܕܠ ܙܕܩܐ
[i]ܕܫܡܝܐ :
† f. 34*a*.
[k]ܘܪܕܦܘܢ
[m]ܘܐܡܪܘܢ
[n] *add* ܡܠܐ
[q]ܘܐܬܦܨܚܘ
[u]ܕܡܢ
[w]ܐܢ

LI.

Matt. V. 20—30.

Codex B.

[a]ܝܘܡ ܐܠܐܪܒܥܐ ܡܢ [b]ܡܬܐܘܣ[a] : [y]ܐܡܪ ܡܪܐ
20 [z]ܠܬܠܡܝܕܘܗܝ [a]ܐܡܪ ܐܢܐ ܠܟܘܢ ܕܝܢ ܕܐ[b]
ܬܬܝܬܪ [c]ܙܕܩܬܟܘܢ : [‡]ܣܓܝ ܡܢ ܣܦܪܝܐ
[d]ܘܦܪܝܫܝܐ ܠܐ [e]ܬܥܠܘܢ [f]ܠܡܠܟܘܬܗ [g]ܕܐܠܗܐ :
21 ܫܡܥܬܘܢ ܕܐܬܐܡܪ [h]ܠܩܕܡܝܐ ܕܠܐ ܬܩܛܘܠ ܕܡܢ
22 [i]ܘܩܛܠ ܚܝܒ [j]ܗܘܐ ܒܕܝܢܐ : ܐܢܐ ܕܝ ܐܡܪ
ܠܟܘܢ ܕܟܠ ܡܢ ܕܪܓܙ ܥܠ ܐܚܘܝ [k]ܠܡܓܢ
ܚܝܒ ܗܘܐ ܒܕܝܢܐ : ܘܡܢ [l]ܕܐܡܪ ܠܐܚܘܝ
ܪܩܐ ܚܝܒ ܗܘܐ [m]ܒܟܢܫܐ : ܘܡܢ [n]ܕܝܐܡܪ
[f. 34*a*]
[o]ܫܛܝܐ ܚܝܒ ܗܘܐ [p]ܒܢܘܪܐ ܕܓܗܢܐ[p] :

Codex A.

[b]ܡܬܐܘܣ [y]*add* ܫܢܝ
[z]ܠܬܠܡܝܕܘܗܝ
‡ f. 37*b*.
[b]*add* ܠܐ [a]*omit* ܐܡܪ
[e]ܬܥܠܘܢ
[f]ܠܡܠܟܘܬܐ
[g]ܕܫܡܝܐ [h]ܠܩܕܡܝܢ
[i]ܕܩܛܠ [nl]ܕܝܐܡܪ
[m]ܒܟܢܫܬܐ [o]ܫܛܝܐ
[p]ܒܓܗܢܐ ܕܢܘܪܐ[p]

Codex C.

[a]ܠܝܘܡ ܐܠܐܪܒܥܐ
ܐܠܟܒܝܪܗ ܡܢ
[a]ܡܬܐܘܣ
[y] *add* ܘܟܬܒܗ
[b]*add* ܠܐ [z]ܠܬܠܡܝܕܘܗܝ
[c]ܙܕܩܬܟܘܢ
[d]ܘܦܪܝܫܝܐ
[f]ܠܡܠܟܘܬܐ
[g]ܕܫܡܝܐ [h]ܠܩܕܡܝܢ
[j]*omit* ܗܘܐ [k]ܠܡܓܢ
[nl]ܕܝܐܡܪ
[m]ܒܟܢܫܬܐ [o]ܫܛܝܐ
[p]ܒܓܗܢܐ ܕܢܘܪܐ[p]

Codex A.

[t]ܩܘܒܠ [u]ܕܚܘܒܢ
[w]ܘܐܙܠ [x]ܩܕܡܝ
[y]ܐܬܪܥܝ
[a]ܘܩܘܪܒܢܟ [b]ܪܥܝ
[c]ܠܐܢܛܝܕܝܩܘܣܟ
[d]ܒܥܓܠ
[e]ܐܢܛܝܕܝܩܘܣܐ
[f]ܠܕܝܢܐ
[h]ܠܦܪܟܛܘܪܐ
[j]ܬܦܘܩ [l]ܠܩܕܡܝܢ
[n]ܐܢܬܬܐ
[q]ܘܛܪܝ
[r]ܐܒܪܝܟ [s]ܠܓܗܢܐ
‡ f. 38*a*.
[v]ܘܦܣܩܝܗ [w]ܐܒܪܝܟ
[x]ܝܐܙܠ [y]ܠܓܗܢܐ
[z] *add* ܟܠܗ

Codex B.

23 ܐܢ ܐܘܢ ܬܩܪܒ ܩܘܪܒܢܟ ܥܠ ܡܕܒܚܐ
[r]ܘܬܡܢ [s]ܬܕܟܪ ܒܠܒܒܗ ܕܐܚܘܟ ܥܠܝܟ
24 [t]ܩܘܒܠܟ : [u]ܫܒܘܩ ܬܡܢ ܩܘܪܒܢܟ [v]ܩܘܕܡ
ܡܕܒܚܐ : [w]ܘܐܙܠ [x]ܩܕܡܝ [y]ܐܬܪܥܝ ܠܐܚܘܟ :
25 ܘܒܬܪܟܢ ܐܬܐ [z]ܩܪܒ [a]ܩܘܪܒܢܟ : ܗܘܝ [b]ܪܥܝ
[c]ܠܐܢܛܝܕܝܩܘܣܟ [d]ܒܥܓܠ : ܥܕ ܐܢܬ ܥܡܗ
ܒܐܘܪܚܐ : ܕܠܐ ܐܡܣܪܟ ܡܫܠܡܢܘܬ ܠܟ
[e]ܐܢܛܝܕܝܩܘܣܟ [f]ܠܕܝܢܐ : [g]ܘܕܝܢܐ [h]ܠܦܪܟܛܘܪܐ
26 [i]† ܘܠܫܘܒܐ ܬܬܪܡܐ : ܘܐܡܝܢ ܐܡܪ ܐܢܐ
ܠܟ ܕܠܐ [j]ܬܦܘܩ ܡܢ ܬܡܢ ܒܕܡܐ ܕܬܦܪܥ
27 [k]ܘܗܘܐ ܐܫܡܥܐ : ܫܡܥܬܘܢ ܕܐܬܐܡܪ [l]ܠܩܕܡܝ
28 ܕܠܐ [m]ܬܓܘܪ : ܐܢܐ ܕܝ ܐܡܪ ܠܟܘܢ ܕܟܠ
ܡܢ ܕܚܙܐ [n]ܐܢܬܬܐ ܗܘܝܢ ܕܝܬܪܓܝܓ ܠܗ
29 ܟܒܪ ܓܪܗ ܠܒܗ : [o]ܐܢ ܕܝ ܥܝܢܟ ܕܝܡܝܢܐ
ܡܟܫܠܐ ܠܟ [p]ܗܦܟܝܗ [q]ܘܛܪܝ ܝܬܗ ܡܢܟ : ܦܩܕ
ܠܟ ܓܪ ܕܝܐܒܕ ܚܕ ܡܢ [r]ܐܒܪܝܟ : ܘܠܐ ܟܠܗ
30 ‡ ܦܓܪܟ ܝܬܪܡܐ [s]ܠܓܗܢܐ : [t]ܘܐܢ [u]ܐܝܕܟ
ܕܝܡܝܢܐ ܡܟܫܠܐ ܠܟ [v]ܦܣܩܝܗ ܘܛܪܝ ܝܬܗ
ܡܢܟ : ܦܩܕ ܠܟ ܓܪ ܕܝܐܒܕ ܚܕ ܡܢ [w]ܐܒܪܝܟ :
ܘܠܐ ܟܠܗ ܦܓܪܟ [x]ܝܐܙܠ [y]ܠܓܗܢܐ [z] ⁘

Codex C.

[r]ܘܬܡܢ [s]ܬܕܟܪ
[v]ܩܕܡ (*sic*) [x]ܩܕܡܝ
[y]ܐܬܪܥܝ [z]ܩܪܒ
[b]ܪܥܝ [c]ܠܐܢܛܝܕܝܩܘܣܟ
[d]ܒܥܓܠ
[e]ܐܢܛܝܕܝܩܘܣܐ
[g]ܘܕܝܢܐ
† f. 34*b*.
[h]ܠܦܪܟܛܘܪܐ
[i]ܘܠܫܘܒܐ
[j]ܬܦܘܩ ܘܗܘܐ [k]*omit*
[m]ܬܓܘܪ
[o]ܐܢ
[p]ܗܦܟܝܗ [q]ܘܛܪܝ
[s]ܠܓܗܢܐ [t]ܘܐܢ
[u]ܐܝܕܟ
[v]ܦܣܩܝܗ
[x]ܝܐܙܠ
[z] *add* ܟܠܗ

LII.

Matt. V. 31—41.

Codex A.

[a]ܘܐܡܪ ܐܠܫܘܥ ܡܢ
ܬܠܡܝܕܘܗܝ[a]
[a] *omit* ܠܬܠܡܝܕܘܗܝ
[c]ܫܘܒܩܢ
[d]ܕܝܫܪܐ [e]ܕܙܢܘ
[f]ܕܬܓܘܪ [g]ܕܫܒܝܩܐ
[h]ܓܘܪ
[j]ܫܡܥܬܘܢ [k]ܕܐܬܐܡܪ

Codex B.

[a]ܘܐܡܪ ܐܠܫܘܥ ܡܢ ܬܠܡܝܕܘܗܝ[a] : ܐܡܪ ܡܪܢ
31 [a]ܠܬܠܡܝܕܘܗܝ : ܐܬܐܡܪ ܕܝ ܕܡܢ ܕܝܫܪܐ ܐܢܬܬܗ :
32 ܝܬܠ ܠܗ [b]ܐܓܪܬ [c]ܫܘܒܩܢ : ܐܢܐ ܕܝ ܐܡܪ
ܠܟܘܢ : ܕܟܠ ܡܢ [d]ܕܝܫܪܐ ܐܢܬܬܗ ܒܪ ܡܢ
ܡܠܬ [e]ܕܙܢܘ ܥܒܕ ܗܘ ܠܗ [f]ܕܬܓܘܪ : ܘܡܢ
ܕܝܫܬܒܩܐ ܠܡܣܒܐ [g]ܕܫܒܝܩܐ ܡܢ ܒܥܠܗ [h]ܓܘܪ
33 ܬܘܒ ܗܘ : [j]ܫܡܥܬܘܢ ܡܫܬܥܝܬܘܢ [k]ܕܐܬܐܡܪ

Codex C.

[a]ܠܡܐ ܐܠܫܘܥ
ܟܕ ܐܠܝܙܗ ܡܢ
ܬܠܡܝܕܘܗܝ[a]
[a] *omit* ܠܬܠܡܝܕܘܗܝ
[b]ܐܓܪܬ [c]ܫܘܒܩܢ
[d]ܕܝܫܪܐ [f]ܕܬܓܘܪ
[g]ܕܫܒܝܩܐ
[k]ܕܐܬܐܡܪ

Codex A.	Codex B.	Codex C.
¹ *desunt ab* ܠܡܩܒܠܗ݀ (*v.* 33) *ad* ܥܠܡ (*finem*).	ܠܡܩܒܠܗ݀ ¹ : ܕܠܐ ܬܬܒܗܬ ܘܐܡܪܐ ܩܕܡܘܗܝ ܟܠ ܫܪܪܐ ܕܐܬܥܒܕܬ	ᵐ ܗܝܡܢܘܬܟܝ
	[f. 34b] 34 ܠܒܪܬܐ ᵐܗܝܡܢܘܬܟܝ : ܐܚܝ ܕܝܢ ⁿܐܡܪ ܠܗܘܢ	ⁿ ܐܡܪܐ (*sic*)
	ᵒܕܠܐ ܬܬܒܗܬܘܢ ᵖܗܘܠܦܘܗܝ : ܠܐ ܒܥܝܪܬܐ ܗܘܐ	ᵖ ܗܘܠܦܘܗܝ ᵒ *omit* ܕ
	35 ܕܝܢ ܡܬܚܒܠܝܢ ܕܐܠܗܐ : ܘܠܐ ᵍܒܪܢܫܐ	ᵍ ܒܪܢܫܐ
	ܕܗܘܝܢ ʳ ܢܦܫܐ ܕܝܠܗܘܢ : ܘܠܐ ܒܢܘܗܪܐ	ʳ *omit* . . . ܢܦܫܐ
	36 ܕܗܘܝܢ ʳ ܡܬܚܒܠܝܢ ܕܗܠܟܝܢ ܢܦܫܐ : ܘܐܡܪ ܠܗ ܠܐ	. . . ܕܗܘܝܢ
	ܬܕܚܠܝܢ : † ܠܒܪܬܐ ܕܠܐ ܬܬܒܗܬ ܐܝܟ ܡܐ ܕܐܬܥܒܕ	† f. 35*a*.
	37 ܫܒܩ ܕܝܢ ܠܐ ˢܐܢܫ ܐܚܪܢܐ : ܕܢܐܬܐ ܕܝܢ	ˢ ܐܢܫ
	ᵗܥܠܘܗܝ ᵘܐܠܐ ܐܢ ܠܐ ܠܗ : ܡܢ ܕܝܢ ᵛ	ᵗ ܥܠܘܗܝ
	38 ܡܢ ܗܠܝܢ ܡܢ ܕܒܝܬܐ ܗܘ ܥܒܕܝܢ ܕܝܢ	ᵛ *add* ܕܝܠܗ ᵘ ܐܝܟ ܡܢ
	ᵂܐܬܡܐܝܢ ܡܢ ܫܠܡ ܡܢ : ܘܡܢ ܫܠܡ ܡܢ :	ˣ *omit* ܕܝܢ ᵂ ܕܐܬܡܐܝܢ
	39 ܐܡܪ ܕܝܢ ܐܡܪ ܠܗܘܢ ܕܠܐ ˣ ܕܝܢ ʸ ܬܬܒܗܬܘܢ	ʸ ܬܬܒܗܬܘܢ
	ܠܡܩܒܠ ܒܢܝܢܐ ܐܠܐ ܡܢ ܕܡܫܒܚ ܠܟ ܠܐ ܒܟ	
	40 ܕܗܘܝܢܐ ܗܘܝܬ ܠܗ ᶻܐܡܪܐ : ܘܡܢ ܕܐܬܐ	ᵃ ܕܐܬܐܡܪ ᶻ ܐܡܪܐ
	ᵃ ܕܐܬܐܡܪ ܒܢܝܢ ܘܡܢܘ ᵇܫܠܡܟ ܥܒܕܘ ܠܗ	ᵇ ܫܠܡܟ
	41 ܐܡܪ ᶜ ܡܐܡܢܟ : ܘܡܢ ᵈܕܐܬܐܡܪ ܠܟ ܐܢܐ ܐܡܪܐ	ᵈ ܕܐܬܐܡܪ ᶜ ܡܐܡܢܟ
	ܡܢܠ ᵉܫܒܩ ܐܢܐ ܠܟܘܢ ܕܬܬܒܪ : ᶠܥܠܡ ⁘	ᶠ *omit* ܥܠܡ ᵉ ܫܒܩ

LIII.

MATT. VII. 9—18.

Codex A.	Codex B.	Codex C.
[Vide Lagarde, p. 263, subscriptum 39. 1.]	9 ᵃ ܡܢܘ ܐܠܦܘܢܟܘܢ ܡܢ ܕܡܬܐܡܪ ᵃ : ᶻ ᵃܐܡܪ	ᵃ ܡܢܘ ܐܠܦܘܢܟܘܢ
ᵃ ܒܪܢܫ ܡܢܘ ܕܡܬܐܡܪܝܢ (*sic*) ܒܢܘܗܝ ܐܠܦܘܢܟܘܢ ܒܪܢܫܐ ܐܠܦܘܢܟܘܢ ᵃ ܕܡܬܐܡܪ	ܒܪܗ ܡܢ ܗܘ ܡܢܘܢ ܒܢܝܐ ᵇ ܕܗܒܐ ᶜ ܐܡܪܐ ᵈ	ܒܪܗ ܐܠܦܘܢܟܘܢ ܡܢ ܕܡܬܐܡܪ ᵃ
ᵃ *desunt ab* ܐܡܪ (*ver.* 9) *ad* ܫܒ (*ver.* 11).	10 ܒܪܗ ᶠ ܒܐܝܕܗ ᵍ ܠܚܡܐ : ܕܗܒܐ ܒܢܝܐ ܗܘ	ᶻ *add* ܘܡܬܐܡܪܝܢܘܗܝ ܒܪܗ
	ʰ ܡܬܒܥܐ ܠܗ : ܐܦ ܐܡܪ ܐܢ ܐܢܐ ܒܢܝܐ ܠܟ	ᵇ *add* ܕܗܒܐ ᶜ ܕܗܒܐ
	11 ܕܗܒܐ ⁱ ܢܦܫܐ ܗܘ ʰ ܡܬܒܥܐ ܠܗ : ܐܢ ܐܢ	ᵈ *add* ܒܢܝܗ
	ܐܢܬܘܢ ܕܐܢܬܘܢ ܒܝܫܝܢ : ܐܢܬܘܢ ܝܕܥܝܢ	ᶠ *omit* ܒܐܝܕܗ
	ܕܬܬܠܘܢ ܛܒܬܐ ᵏ ܡܘܗܒܬܐ ܠܒܢܝܟܘܢ :	ᵍ ܠܚܡܐ ʰ ܡܬܒܥܐ
	ܒܟܡܐ ܝܬܝܪ ᵃ ܐܒܘܟܘܢ ܕܒܫܡܝܐ	ᵏ ܡܘܗܒܬܐ ⁱ ܢܦܫܐ
ᵒ ܛܒܬܐ ⁿ ܢܬܠ	ܢܬܠ ⁿ : ܛܒܬܐ ᵒ ܠܗܢܘܢ ᵖ ܕܫܐܠܝܢ ܠܗ :	ᵖ ܕܫܐܠܝܢ ⁿ ܢܬܠ
ᵖ ܕܫܐܠܝܢ ᵍ [ܠ]ܗ	12 ᵍ ܟܠ ܕܐܢܬܘܢ ʳ ܐܡܪܐ ˢ ܐܢ ܕܬܬܒܥܘܢ	ˢ *omit* ܐܢ
ʳ ܐܡܪܐ		

Codex A.	Codex B.	Codex C.
[a] ܗܟܕܢ	ܠܟܘܢ ܒܫܡܝܐ : [a] ܗܟܕܢ [b] ܐܪܕܦܘܢ ܗܘܘ ܩܕܡܝܢ	[b] add ܐܦܘܢ
[b] add ܐܦܘܢ	[f. 35a] ܠܗܘܢ [c] ܗܘܝܢ ܒܪ ܗܘ ܡܫܝܚܐ [d] ܘܢܒܝܐ	[d] ܘܢܒܝܐ [e] ܠܚܡܝܐ
[c] ܗܘܝܢ [d] ܘܢܒܝܐ	13 ܒܟܠ ܕܪܕܐ [e] ܠܚܡܝܐ : ܕܡܬܡܪ ܗܘ ܪܕܐ	[f] ܐܪܥܝܐ
[f] ܐܪܥܝܐ [g] omit ܕ	[f] ܐܪܥܝܐ ܗܘܐ [g] ܗܘܢ [h] † ܕܡܬܟܠܐ ܠܥܠܡܐ :	† f. 35b.
[h] add ܗܘܐ ܐܪܥܝܐ	14 ܘܠܐ ܗܘܐ ܟܠ [i] ܕܒܟܠ ܒܗ : ܗܟܢ [k] ܥܠܝܗ	[h] add ܗܘܐ ܐܪܥܝܐ
[i] ܕܟܠܡ [l] omit ܗܝ	ܪܕܐ ܘܡܬܡܠܝܐ ܗܝ ܐܪܥܝܐ ܗܘܐ [l] ܕܗܘܢ	[k] ܥܠܝܗܝ
[n] ܡܬܚܡܫ [o] ܢܒܝܐ	ܡܟܠܡ ܠܥܠܡܐ : [n] ܡܬܚܡܫ ܗܘܐ ܟܠܡ	[n] ܡܬܚܡܫ
[p] ܕܐܬܝܢ	15 ܕܡܬܚܡܫ ܗܘܬ : ܗܟܢ ܠܟܘܢ ܡܢ [o] ܢܒܝܐ	[o] ܢܒܝܐ
‡ f. 39a.	ܕܐܬܠܐ ܟܠܡ [p] ܕܐܬܝܢ ܠܡܬܩܢ ‡ ܠܟܘܢ ܘܟܠܡ	[p] ܕܐܬܝܢ
[q] ܕܐܡܬܝܢ	[q] ܕܐܡܬܝܢ [r] ܘܗܢ ܠܟܘ ܕܝ ܗܘܐ [s] ܕܗܒܢ	[r] omit ܘ [s] ܕܗܒܢ
[r] omit ܘ [s] ܕܗܒܢ	16 ܫܠܡܘܢ : ܡܢ ܦܘܡܗ ܗܘܘ ܡܢܝܢ ܢܘܗܪܐ :	[t] ܠܡܠܟܝܢ [u] ܒܫܡܝܢ
[t] ܠܡܠܟܝܢ [u] ܒܫܡܝܢ	ܕܗܟܢ [t] ܠܐܡܠܟܝܢ ܡܢ ܒܫܡܝܐ [u] ܒܫܡܝܢ : [v] ܐܢܐ	[v] add ܡܢ [w] ܐܡܠܟ
[v] add ܡܢ [x] ܠܟܘ	17 ܕܐܢܬܘܢ ܢܗܝܪܝܢ : ܗܟܢܐ ܒܟܠ [w] ܐܡܠܟ [x] ܠܟܘܢ	[x] ܠܟܘ [y] omit ܗܝ
[y] omit ܗܝ [z] ܒܟܪ	ܦܘܡܝ ܠܟܘܢ [y] ܗܝ [z] ܒܟܪ ܘܐܡܠܟܐ ܒܟܠܐ	[z] ܒܟܪ [c] ܐܬܝܬ
[a] ܒܟܠ [c] ܐܬܝܬ	18 ܦܘܡܝ ܒܟܠܝܢ ܒܟܪ : ܠܐ [a] ܒܟܠ ܐܡܠܟܐ ܠܟܘܢ	[d] omit ܕܝ [e] ܠܟܘܢ
[d] omit ܕܝ [e] ܠܟܘܢ	ܕܦܘܡܝ ܒܟܠܝܢ [c] ܐܬܝܬ : ܘܠܐ [d] ܕܝ ܐܡܠܟܐ	[f] omit ܒܟܪ
[g] omit ܥܠܡ	ܒܟܠܐ ܕܦܘܡܝ [e] ܠܟܘܢ ܗܝ ܐܢܐ : [f] ܒܟܪ : [g] ܥܠܡ ⁘	[g] omit ܥܠܡ

LIV.

Matt. V. 42—48.

Codex A.	Codex B.	Codex C.
[a] ܡܢ ܐܢܫ ܐܢܬܘܢ ܐܠܠܐ ܡܢ ܒܟܪ ܐܠܗܝܢܘܗܝ ܡܢ ܫܡܝܐ [a] ܕܒܫܡܝܐ	[a] ܡܢ ܐܢܫ ܡܢ ܡܪܐܢܘ ܗܘܐ ܐܠܠܐ ܗܒܬ	[a] ܠܡܢ ܐܢܫ ܐܢܬ ܐܠܠܐ ܡܢ ܡܪܐܬܘܢ [a]
[a] add ܐܡܪ ܡܪܝܐ	42 ܒܟܪ ܐܠܗܝܢܘܗܝ [a][za] ܠܡܢ [b] ܕܫܐܠ ܡܢܟ [c] ܗܒ ܠܗ :	[z] add ܘܡܢܗܘܢ
[c] ܗܒ [d] ܕܢܙܦ	ܘܡܢ ܕܨܒܐ [d] ܕܢܙܦ ܡܢܟ ܠܐ ܬܟܠܐ ܠܗ :	[a] add ܐܡܪ ܡܪܝܐ
[e] add ܠܟܘܢ	43 ܫܡܥܬܘܢ [e] ܕܐܬܐܡܪ [e] ܕܬܪܚܡ ܠܩܪܝܒܟ ܘܬܣܢܐ	[b] ܕܫܐܠ [c] ܗܒ
[f] ܠܒܥܠܕܒܒܝܟܘܢ	44 ܠܒܥܠܕܒܒܟ : ܐܢܐ ܕܝ ܐܡܪ ܐܢܐ ܠܟܘܢ ܐܚܒܘ	[d] ܕܢܙܦ
[g] ܕܠܐܠܝܢ [h] ܕܡܐܫܝܢ	[f] ܠܒܥܠܕܒܒܝܟܘܢ ܘܒܪܟܘ ܠܐܝܠܝܢ [g] ܕܠܛܝܢ	[e] add ܠܟܘܢ
[i] omit ܘܨܠܘ...ܥܠܝܟܘܢ	ܠܟܘܢ : ܘܥܒܕܘ ܛܒܬܐ ܠܐܝܠܝܢ [h] ܕܣܢܝܢ	[f] ܠܒܥܠܕܒܒܝܟܘܢ
[k] ܠܟܠܠ [l] omit ܕܝ	ܠܟܘܢ [i] ܘܨܠܘ ܥܠ ܗܠܝܢ ܕܪܕܦܝܢ ܠܟܘܢ [i]	[l] omit ܕܝ
[m] ܒܢܘܗܝ [o] ܕܒܫܡܝܐ	45 ܘܐܪܡܝܢ : [k] ܠܟܠܠ [l] ܕܝ ܕܬܗܘܘܢ [m] ܒܢܝ [f. 88b]	[n] add ܕ
	[n] ܐܒܘܟܘܢ ܕܒܫܡܝܐ : [o] ܕܫܡܫܗ ܗܘ	

Codex A.

[p]ܡܬܒܝܫ [r]ܛܠܝܢ
[s]ܥܡܗܘܢ [t]ܐܡܪ
[u]add ܐܢܘܢ
‡ f. 39b.
[w]ܒܬܠܡܝܕܘܗܝ
[x]ܕܐܡܝܢܢ
[y]ܡܢ ܚܪ ܕܝܢ [z]ܗܕܐ
[a]ܥܠܡܝܢ [b]add ܕ
[d]add ܥܠܡ

Codex B.

[p]ܡܬܒܝܫ ܥܠ ܚܒܝܫܝܢ ܘܥܠ [q]ܛܠܝܢ : ܘܡܚܦܛܪ
46 ܥܠ ܕܢܡܠܠ ܥܡ [r]ܟܢܫܝܢ : ܐܢ ܐܡܗ ܘܐܚܘܗܝ
ܩܝܡܝܢ ܕܡܒܥܝܢ [s]ܠܡܠܠܐ ܥܡܗ : ܐܡܪ [t]ܠܗ ܚܕ ܐܢܫ
47 ܠܗܘܢ : ܠܐ [u]‡ ܗܐ ܐܡܟ ܘܐܚܝܟ : [v]ܘܐܡܪ
ܐܬܢܘܢ [w]ܠܬܠܡܝܕܘܗܝ [x]ܕܐܡܝܢܢ ܥܠܝܗ ܕܝܢ
ܡܢ [y]ܗܕܐ ܕܝܢ † ܐܡܪ ܠܗܘܢ : ܠܐ ܐܢܘܢ ܒܢܝܐ
48 ܚܢܢܐ [z]ܚܕܡ ܠܗܘܢ : ܗܘܘ ܐܡܪ ܐܢܘܢ ܐܡܪ
[a]ܥܠܡܝܢ ܗܢܝܢ [b]ܐܡܘܢ ܕܥܒܕ ܥܡܘܢܐ
[c]ܥܠܡ ܐܢܬ ܗܘ [d] ∴

Codex C.

[q]ܛܠܝܢ
[r]ܛܠܝܢ
[s]ܥܡܗܘܢ [t]ܐܡܪ
[u]add ܐܢܘܢ [v]ܘܐܡܪ
[w]ܒܬܠܡܝܕܘܗܝ
† f. 36a.
[z]ܗܕܐ
[a]ܥܠܡܝܢ
[b]add ܕ [c]ܥܠܡ

LV.

Matt. X. 32, 33, 37—40.

Codex A.

[b]ܡܢ ܩܕܡܘܗܝ[b]
[y]add ܕܝܢ
[z]ܠܡܠܐܟܘܗܝ
[c]ܕܢܟܦܘܪ [e]ܐܟܦܘܪ
[h]ܐܡܪ [i]ܒܪ
[k]ܒܪ ܐܒ ܒܪܐ[k]
[l]ܕܠܝ
[m]ܕܡܩܒܠ
[p]ܡܩܒܠ
[q]ܕܡܩܒܠ [r]ܡܩܒܠ
[t]ܕܫܠܚ

Codex B.

[a]ܗܘܐ ܐܡܪ ܐܠܗܐ [b]ܡܢ ܩܕܡ ܐܠܗܢܐ ܡܢ
32 ܩܕܡܘܗܝ[a b] : [y]ܐܡܪ ܡܪܢܐ [z]ܠܡܠܐܟܘܗܝ : ܟܠ
ܡܢ ܐܢܘܢ [a]ܕܝܘܕܐ ܒܝ ܩܕܡ ܒܢܝܢܫܐ : ܐܘܕܐ
ܐܢܐ ܒܗ ܒܗ [b]ܩܕܡ ܐܒܐ ܕܒܫܡܝܐ ܥܡܘܢܐ
33 ܘܡܢ [c]ܕܢܟܦܘܪ ܒܝ ܩܕܡ ܒܢܝܢܫܐ [d]ܐ[e]ܟܦܘܪ
37 [f]ܐܢܐ ܒܗ[f] ܩܕܡ ܐܒܐ ܕܒܫܡܝܐ : ܘܡܢ
ܕܪܚܡ ܐܒ [g]ܐܘ [h]ܐܡ ܝܬܝܪ ܡܢ ܕܠܝ ܠܝܬ
ܗܘ ܫܘܐ [i]ܠܝ : [j]ܘܡܢ ܕܪܚܡ [k]ܒܪܐ ܐܘ
38 ܒܪܬܐ[k] ܝܬܝܪ ܡܢ [l]ܕܠܝ ܠܝܬ ܗܘ ܫܘܐ ܠܝ[j]:
ܘܡܢ ܕܠܐ ܢܣܒ ܨܠܝܒܗ ܘܐܬܐ ܒܬܪܝ ܠܝܬ ܗܘ
39 ܫܘܐ ܠܝ : ܡܢ [m]ܕܡܫܟܚ ܢܦܫܗ [n]ܡܘܒܕ ܗܘ
ܠܗ : ܘܡܢ [o]ܕܡܘܒܕ ܢܦܫܗ ܠܡܛܠܬܝ [p]ܡܫܟܚ
40 ܠܗ : ܡܢ [q]ܕܡܩܒܠ ܠܟܘܢ ܠܝ ܗܘ [r]ܡܩܒܠ :
ܘܡܢ [q]ܕܡܩܒܠ ܠܝ [r]ܡܩܒܠ ܠܡܢ [t]ܕܫܠܚ
ܠܝ ∴

Codex C.

[a]ܐܡܪ ܐܠܗܐ ܐܠܗ
[a]ܡܢ ܡܠܐܟܘܗܝ
[y]add ܘܟܠ ܡܢ ܕܝܘܕܐ ܒܝ
[z]ܠܡܠܐܟܘܗܝ
[a]ܕܝܘܕܐ
[b]omit ܩܕܡ
[d]add ܐܢܐ ܐܢܘܢ
[e]ܐܟܦܘܪ
[f]ܒܗ ܐܢܐ[f] [g]ܐܘ
[h]ܐܡ [i]ܒܪ
[j]omit ܒܪ . . . ܘܡܢ
[m]ܕܡܫܟܚ [n]ܡܘܒܕ
[o]ܕܡܘܒܕ [p]ܡܫܟܚ
[q]ܕܡܩܒܠ [r]ܡܩܒܠ
[t]ܕܫܠܚ

Matt. XIX. 27—30.

Codex A.

[w]ܟܦܐ
[z]add ܠܟ [a]ܒܬܪܟ

Codex B.

27 [w]ܗܝܕܝܢ ܐܡܪ [x]ܟܐܦܐ ܘܐܡܪ ܠܗ : ܗܐ ܐܢܚܢܢ
ܫܒܩܢ ܟܠܡܕܡ [y]ܘܐܬܝܢ[z] [a]ܒܬܪܟ : [c]ܡܢܐ

Codex C.

[x]ܟܐܦܐ
[y]ܘܐܬܝܢ [a]ܠܟ :
[c]omit ܡܢܐ ܐܢܐ
ܗܘܐ ܠܢ

In margin: ܡܬ ܕܝ ܠ

Codex B.

28 ܐܪܐ ܗܘܐ ܠܟ[c]: ܐܝܟܢܐ ܕܐ ܨܒܝܐ ܘܐܣܬܣܝܬ
[f. 36a] ‡ ܘܐܡܪ ܠܗܘܢ ܐܡܝܢ[d] ܐܡܪ ܐܢܐ ܠܟܘܢ
ܕܐܬܘܢ [e]ܕܐܬܬܒܥܘܢ ܠܟܘܢ ܒܬܪܝ [f]ܒܬܠܡܝܕܘܬܐ
ܕܡܢ [g]ܙܒܢ: ܟܕ [h]ܝܬܒ ܒܪܗ ܕܓܒܪܐ ܥܠ
[i]ܟܘܪܣܝܐ ܕܫܘܒܚܗ: [j]ܬܬܝܒܘܢ ܐܦ
ܐܢܬܘܢ ܥܠ [k]ܬܪܬܥܣܪܐ [l]ܟܘܪܣܝܢ [m]ܕܐܢܝܢ
29 ܬܪܬܥܣܪܬܐ [n]ܫܒܛܝܐ [o]ܕܐܝܣܪܐܝܠ: ܘܟܠ ܡܢ
ܕܫܒܩ ܐܚܝܢ ܐܘ [p]ܐܚܘܬܐ ܐܘ ܐܒ ܐܘ
† [q]ܐܡܐ ܐܘ ܒܢܝܢ: ܐܘ ܚܩܠܝܢ ܐܘ [r]ܒܬܝܢ
30 ܡܢ ܠܓܠܠ ܫܡܝ: [s]ܡܐܐ [t]ܒܥܠܡܐ ܗܕܝܢ:
[u]ܘܚܝܝܢ [w]ܕܠܥܠܡ ܢܣܒ: ܣܓܝ ܕܝܢ [x]ܩܕܡܝܢ
ܝܗܘܘܢ ܒܬܪܝܝܢ ܘܒܬܪܝܝܢ [y]ܝܗܘܘܢ [x]ܩܕܡܝܢ:
[z]ܥܠܡ ⁘

Codex A.

‡ f. 40a.
[f] ܒܬܠܡܝܕܘܬܐ
[g] ܙܒܢ [h] ܝܬܒ
[j] ܬܬܝܒܘܢ [k] ܬܪܬܥܣܪ
[l] ܟܘܪܣܘܢ
[m] ܕܐܢܝܢ
[o] ܕܐܝܣܪܐܝܠ
[q] ܐܡܐ [r] ܒܬܝܢ
[s] *add* ܕ [t] ܒܥܠܡ
[w] ܕܠܥܠܡ [x] ܩܕܡܝܢ
[y] *omit* ܝܗܘܘܢ

Codex C.

[d] *add* ܐܡܝܢ
[e] ܕܐܬܬܒܥܘܢ
[h] ܝܬܒ
[i] ܟܘܪܣܘܗ
[j] ܬܬܝܒܘܢ [l] ܟܘܪܣܘܢ
[m] ܕܐܢܝܢ [n] ܫܒܛܝܢ
[p] ܐܚܘܢ [q] ܐܡܐ
† f. 36b.
[s] *add* ܕ [t] ܒܥܠܡ
[u] ܘܚܝܝܢ [x] ܩܕܡܝܢ
[y] *omit* ܝܗܘܘܢ
[z] *omit* ܥܠܡ

LVI.

MATT. VII. 1—11.

Codex B.

[a]ܒܝܘܡ ܐܪܒܥܬ ܐܬܝܐ [b]ܡܢ ܒܬܪ ܐܠܝܦܪܗ ܡܢ
1 ܡܬܝܐܘܣ[a b]: [y] [z]ܐܡܪ ܡܪܢ ܠܐ [a]ܬܕܘܢܘܢ ܕܠܐ
2 ܬܬܕܘܢܘܢ: ܒܕܝܢܐ ܓܝܪ ܕܐܬܘܢ ܕܐܢܝܢ ܒܗ
ܬܬܕܝܢܘܢ [b]ܘܒܡܟܝܠܬܐ ܕܐܬܘܢ ܟܝܠܝܢ
3 [c]ܚܘܠܦܗ ܡܬܟܝܠ ܠܟܘܢ: ܡܢܐ ܕܝ ܐܬ
ܚܙܐ: [d]ܩܝܣܐ ܕܒܥܝܢܗ ܕܐܚܘܟ ܘܩܪܝܬܐ
4 [e]ܕܒܥܝܢܐ ܕܝܠܟ ܠܝܬ ܐܬ ܚܙܐ: ܐܝܟ ܗܟܢ
[f]ܐܬ ܐܡܪ ܠܐܚܘܟ ܫܒܘܩ [g]ܕܐܦܩ [d]ܩܝܣܐ
ܡܢ ܥܝܢܟ: [h]ܘܗܐ ܩܪܝܬܐ ܒܥܝܢܟ ܕܝܠܟ:
5 ܫܩܪܢܐ [i]ܐܦܩ [j]ܩܕܡܝ ܩܪܝܬܐ ܡܢ ܥܝܢܟ
[k]ܘܒܬܪ ܐܬ ܚܙܐ [l]ܕܬܦܩ [d]ܩܝܣܐ ܡܢ ܥܝܢܗ
6 ܕܐܚܘܟ: ܠܐ ܬܬܠܘܢ [m]ܘܩܕܫܐ ܠܟܠܒܝܐ:
ܘܠܐ ܬܪܡܘܢ ‡ ܡܪܓܠܝܬܐ ܩܘܕܡ [n]ܚܙܝܪܝܐ
ܕܠܐ ܐܬܗܘܢ [o]ܕܘܫܝܢ [p]ܬܗܘܢ [q]ܒܪܓܠܝܗܘܢ

Codex A.

ܡܢ ... ܡܬܐܘܣ [b]*omit*
[y] *add* ܐܡܪ
[a] ܬܬܕܝܢܘܢ
[b] ܘܒܡܟܝܠܬܐ
[c] ܚܘܠܦܗܘܢ
[d] ܩܝܣܐ
[e] ܕܒܥܝܢܟ
[f] ܐܬ ܐܡܪ [f]
[g] ܕܐܦܩ [i] ܐܦܩ
[k] ܘܒܬܪ [l] ܕܬܦܩ
[n] ܚܙܝܪܝܐ
[o] ܕܘܫܝܢ
‡ f. 40b.
[q] ܒܪܓܠܝܗܘܢ

Codex C.

[a] ܠܝܘܡ ܐܪܒܥܬ
ܐܬܝܐ ܡܢ ܡܬܝܐ [a]
[y] *add* ܡܬܝܐܘܣ ܡܦܪܫܝܢܐ
[z] *omit* ܐܡܪ ܡܪܢ
[b] ܘܒܡܟܝܠܬܐ
[d] ܩܝܣܐ
[e] ܕܒܥܝܢܟ
[f] ܐܬ ܐܡܪ [f]
[g] ܕܐܦܩ [h] ܘܗܐ
[i] ܐܦܩ [j] ܩܕܡܝ
[l] ܕܬܦܩ
[m] ܘܩܕܫܐ
[o] ܕܘܫܝܢ [p] ܬܗܘܢ

Codex B.

7 ܘܦܪܝܫܝܢ[r] ܘܨܕܘܩܝܢ ܣܓܝܐܝܢ : ܥܠܘ

[f. 36b]

ܘܡܬܥܡܕܝܢ ܠܗܘܢ ܒܗ ܘܐܡܪ ܠܗܘܢ ܡܡܚܝܢ :

8 ܐܪܬܘ ܘܡܬܦܬܘ ܠܟܘܢ : ܒܥܠ ܡܢ ܚܪ

ܕܥܠ[s] ܢܦܩ : ܘܕܢܒܚܐ[t] ܡܥܒܕܝܢ ܘܠܗܕܝܢ

9 ܕܡܬܪܬܝܢ[u] ܡܬܦܬܘ ܠܗ : ܐܐ ܡܢ[w] ܗܘ ܡܢܟܘܢ[w]

ܒܪܢܫܐ[x] ܕܝܒܚܐ[z] ܒܐܝܕܗ ܒܪܗ[a] ܠܚܝܠ ܕܡܚܐ

10 ܒܢܦ ܗܘ[b] ܡܥܢܝܦ ܠܗ : ܐܐ ܦܘܐ ܐ

ܝܒܚܐ ܢܘ ܕܡܚܐ[c] ܚܝܘܐ ܗܘ[b] ܡܥܢܝܦ ܠܗ :

11 ܐ[d] ܐܘ ܐܬܘ ܕܐܬܘ ܒܝܫܝܢ : ܐܬܘ

ܡܕܒܝܢ[†] ܕܬܗܘܢ[e] ܡܗܡܢ[f] ܡܬܘܠܝܢ[g] ܛܒܝܢ

ܠܒܢܝܟܘܢ : ܚܕ ܒܡܐ ܡܠܘ ܐܒܘܟܘܢ

ܕܒܫܘ ܥܘܡܪܐ[h] ܡܬܠ[i] ܛܒܝܢ ܠܗܠܝܢ[k] ܕܫܐܠܝܢ

ܠܡܢܗ :[l]

Codex A.

[r] ܘܦܪܝܫܝܢ

[s] ܕܥܠ [t] ܘܕܢܒܚܐ

[u] ܕܡܬܪܬܝܢ

[x] *add* ܗܕܝܢ

[a] ܠܚܝܠ [b] ܡܥܢܝܦ

[c] ܚܝܘܐ

[e] ܡܗܡܢ

[f] ܡܬܘܠܝܢ [g] ܛܒܝܢ

[i] ܛܒܝܢ

[k] ܕܫܐܠܝܢ [l] *add* ܥܠܡ ܥܠܡ

Codex C.

[r] ܘܦܪܝܫܝܢ

[s] ܕܥܠ [u] ܕܡܬܪܬܝܢ

[w] ܡܢܟܘܢ ܗܘ[w]

[x] *add* ܗܕܝܢ

[z] ܒܐܝܕܗ

[b] ܡܥܢܝܦ

[c] ܚܝܘܐ [d] ܐܝܢ

† f. 37a.

[e] ܡܗܡܢ

[h] ܡܬܠ [i] ܛܒܐܝܢ

LVII.

Matt. IV. 17—23.

Codex B.

[a] ܒܝܘܡ ܐܠܗܐ ܐܬܐܡܪ[b] ܡܢ ܒܬܪ ܐܠܗܢܝܢ[b]

17 ܡܢ[c] ܗܝܕܝܢ[a] :[x] ܘܫܪܝܬܗ[y] ܡܫܪܝܢܐ : ܒܬܪ[z] ܡܢ

ܠܡܟܪܙ[a] ܝܫܘܥ ܘܐܡܪ ܬܘܒܘ[b] ܡܢܗܝܢ : ܘܗܘܬ[c] ܡܢܒܐ ܒܪ ܡܠܟܘܬܐ[d]

ܕܫܡܝܐ : ܘܗܘܐ[e] ܡܗܠܟ ܥܠ ܝܡܐ ܕܓܠܝܠܐ

18 ܕܓܠܝܠܐ : ܚܙܐ ܬܪܝܢ[f] ܐܚܝܢ ܫܡܥܘܢ

ܗܘ ܕܡܬܩܪܐ ܟܐܦܐ[g] : ܘܐܢܕܪܐܘܣ[h] ܐܚܘܗ[i] :

ܪܡܝܢ[j] ܡܨܝܕܬܗܘܢ ܠܝܡܐ ܗܘܘ ܓܝܪ ܨܝܕܝܢ

19 ܕܢܘܢܝܢ[k] : ܘܐܡܪ ܠܗܘܢ ܐܬܘ[l] ܒܬܪܝ

20 ܘܐܢܐ ܐܥܒܕ‡ ܠܟܘܢ ܨܝܕܝܢ ܕܒܢܝܢܫܐ : ܘܫܒܩܘ

21 ܡܨܝܕܬܗܘܢ ܘܐܬܘ ܒܬܪܗ : ܘܥܒܪ ܡܢ

ܬܡܢ ܘܚܙܐ ܬܪܝܢ ܐܚܝܢ ܐܚܪܢܝܢ[n] ܝܥܩܘܒ[o]

ܒܪܗ[p] ܕܙܒܕܝ[q] ܘܝܘܚܢܢ[r] ܐܚܘܗ[s] ܒܐܠܦܐ ܥܡ

ܙܒܕܝ[t] ܐܒܘܗܘܢ ܡܬܩܢܝܢ ܡܨܝܕܬܗܘܢ :

22 ܘܩܪܐ ܠܗܘܢ : ܘܗܢܘܢ ܫܒܩܘ ܥܘܕ ܐܠܦܐ

Codex A.

ܓ ܕ ܕ

[b] *omit* ܡܢ . . . ܐܠܗܢܝܢܗ . . .

[c] ܫܪܝܬܗ

[x] *add* ܝܫܘܥ [z] ܒܬܪ

[b] ܡܢܒܝܢ [c] ܘܗܘܬ

[e] ܥܠ

[h] ܘܐܢܕܪܐܘܣ

[i] ܐܚܘܗ [j] ܪܡܝܢ

‡ f. 41a.

[o] ܝܥܩܘܒ

[q] ܕܙܒܕܝ

[r] ܘܝܘܚܢܢ

[t] ܙܒܕܝ

Codex C.

[a] ܠܒܝܘܡ ܐܠܗܐ ܐܬܐܡܪ ܡܢ ܗܝܕܝܢ[a]

[y] *omit* ܡܫܪܝܢܐ

[a] *omit* ܠܗܘܢ

[d] ܡܠܟܘܬܗ

[f] ܐܚܝܢ

[g] ܟܐܦܐ

[j] ܪܡܝܢ [k] ܢܘܢܝܢ

[l] ܐܬܘ

[n] ܐܚܪܢܝܢ

[p] *omit* ܒܪܗ ܕܙܒܕܝ

[r] ܘܝܘܚܢܢ [s] ܐܚܘܗ

Codex A.	Codex B.	Codex C.
	23 ܠܐܟܣܢܝܘܬܗܘܢ ܘܐܬܬ ܒܬܪܗ : ܘܗܘܐ ᵘܫܠܝܐ	ᵘܫܠܝܐ
ᵛܒܪܐ	[f. 37a] ᵛܒܪܐ ܝܫܘܥ ܒܟܘܠܗ ܓܠܝܠܐ : ܘܡܠܦ	ᵛܒܪܐ
ᵂܘܡܟܪܙ	ܒܟܢܫܬܗܘܢ ᵂܘܡܟܪܙ ᵡܒܣܒܪܬܐ ܕܡܠܟܘܬܐ :	ᵡܒܣܒܪܬܐ
	ᵞܘܡܐܣܐ ܟܠ ܟܐܒ ܘܟܠ ܟܘܪܗܢ ᶻܡܪܥܐ	ᵞܘܡܐܣܐ ᶻܡܪܥܐ
ᵃ*add* ܥܠܡ	ܒܥܡܐ : ᵃ ⁘	

LVIII.

Matt. VII. 24—29.

Codex A.	Codex B.	Codex C.
		ᵃܗܟܘܬ ܐܡܝܢ
ᵃܗܟܘܬ ܐܡܝܢ ܐܬܐܬ	ᵃܐܡܝܢ ܐܬܐܬ ܡܢ ܒܬܪ ܐܠܦܝܢ ܡܢ	ᵃܐܬܐܬ ܡܢ ܬܠܡܝܕܘܗܝ
ᵃܡܢ ܬܠܡܝܕܘܗܝ	24 ܬܠܡܝܕܘܗܝ :ᵃ ᵂܐܡܪ ܝܫܘܥ : ܟܘܠ ܡܢ ܕܝܫܡܥ	ᵂ*add* ܒܬܠܡܝܕܘܗܝ ܘܐܡܪ
ᵂ*add* ܐܡܪ	ᵡܡܠܝ ܗܠܝܢ ᵞܘܥܒܕ ᶻܕܡܐ ܠܓܒܪ ܚܟܝܡ	ᵡܡܠܝ ᶻܕܡܐ
ᵞܢܛܪ ᶻܕܡܐ	25 ᵃܕܒܢܐ ܒܝܬܗ ܥܠ ᵇܫܘܥܐ : ܘܢܚܬ	ᵃܕܒܢܐ ᶜܘܐܬܘ
ᵃܕܒܢܐ ᵇܫܘܥܐ	ܡܛܪܐ ܘܐܬܘ ܢܗܪܘܬܐ ܘܢܫܒܘ ܪܘܚܐ : ᶜܘܐܬܘ	ᵈ*omit* ܒܝܬܐ
ᵈ*omit* ܒܝܬܐ	ܒܗ ܒܝܬܐ ܘܠܐ ܢܦܠ ᵈܒܝܬܐ ᵉܕܫܬܐܣܘܗܝ	ᵉ*omit* ܕ
ᵉܫܬܐܣܘܗܝ ʰܫܘܥܐ	26 ᶠܗܘܐ ᵍܓܝܪ ܥܠ ʰܫܘܥܐ : ܘܟܠ ܡܢ ܕܫܡܥ	ᵍ*omit* ܓܝܪ ᶠܗܘ
ʲܢܛܪ ᵏܕܡܐ	ⁱܡܠܝ ܠܐ ܥܒܕ ʲܢܛܪ : ᵏܕܡܐ ܠܓܒܪ	ⁱܡܠܝ
ˡܣܟܠ ᵐܕܒܢܐ	27 † ˡܣܟܠܐ ᵐܕܒܢܐ ܒܝܬܗ ܥܠ ܚܠܐ : ⁿܘܢܚܬ	† f. 37b.
ⁿܘܢܚܬ ᵒܡܛܪܐ	ᵒܡܛܪܐ ܘܐܬܘ ܢܗܪܘܬܐ ܘܢܫܒܘ ܪܘܚܐ ᵖܘܐܬܘ	ᵏܕܡܐ ˡܣܟܠ
ᵠܘܡܦܘܠܬܗ ʳܪܒܬܐ	ܒܗ ܒܝܬܐ ܘܢܦܠ : ܘܗܘܬ ᵠܡܦܘܠܬܗ ʳܪܒܐ	ᵐܕܒܢܐ ⁿܘܢܚܬ
ˢ*omit* ܠܚܕܐ ... ܠܐ	ܠܚܕܐ : ˢܠܚܕܐ ܕܗܘ ܡܣܬܒܪ ܥܠ ܚܠܐ :ˢ	ᵒܡܛܪܐ ᵖܘܐܬܘ
‡ f. 41b.	28 ‡ ܘܗܘܐ ܟܕ ܫܠܡ ܝܫܘܥ ܡܠܘܗܝ ܗܠܝܢ :	ᵠܘܡܦܘܠܬܗ
ᵗܐܟܠܘܣܐ	ܗܘܘ ܡܬܗܡܝܢ ܟܠ ᵗܐܟܠܘܣܐ ܥܠ ܡܠܦܢܘܬܗ :	ˢ*omit* ܠܚܕܐ ... ܠܐ
ᵘܫܠܝܛ	29 ܗܘܐ ܓܝܪ ܡܠܦ ܠܗܘܢ ܐܝܟ ᵘܫܠܝܛ ܘܠܐ	ᵗܐܟܠܘܣܐ
	ܐܝܟ ܣܦܪܝܗܘܢ : ⁘	ᵘܫܠܝܛ

Matt. VIII. 1—4.

Codex A.	Codex B.	Codex C.
ᵃܐܟܠܘܣܝܢ	1 ܘܟܕ ܢܚܬ ܡܢ ܛܘܪܐ ܐܙܠܘ ܒܬܪܗ ᵃܐܟܠܘܣܝܢ	ᵃܐܟܠܘܣܐ
ᵇܘܗܐ ᶜܡܢܪܐ	2 ܣܓܝܐܝܢ : ᵇܘܗܐ ܚܕ ܓܒܪ ᶜܡܢܪܐ ᵈܘܗܘܐ ܣܓܕ	ᵇܘܗܐ ᵈܘܗܘ
ᵍ*add* ܐܢܬ ᶠܨܒܐ	ܠܗ ܘܐܡܪ : ܡܪܝ ᵉܐܢ ܨܒܐ ܐܢܬ ᶠܨܒܐ ᵍ	ᵉ*omit* ܐܢ
ʰܐܝܕܗ	3 ܡܕܟܐ ܠܝ : ܘܦܫܛ ʰܐܝܕܗ ܝܫܘܥ ܘܩܪܒ	ᵍ*add* ܐܢܬ

Codex A.	Codex B.	Codex C.
	[Syriac text]	
[i] [Syriac text]	4 [i] [Syriac text]	[i] [Syriac text]
[k] [Syriac text] [l] [Syriac text]	[Syriac text] [k] [Syriac text] [l] [Syriac text]	
[m] [Syriac text] [n] [Syriac text]	[Syriac text] [m] [Syriac text] [f. 37b]	[o] omit [Syriac text]
[o] [Syriac text]	[n] [Syriac text] [o] [Syriac text] [p] [Syriac text]	[p] omit [Syriac text]

LIX.

Matt. VI. 22—34.

Codex A.	Codex B.	Codex C.
		[a] [Syriac text]
[b] [Syriac text]	[a] [Syriac text] [b] [Syriac text]	[a] [Syriac text]
[b] [Syriac text]	22 [Syriac text] [a b] [v] [Syriac text] [w] [Syriac text]	[v] add [Syriac text]
[v] add [Syriac text]	[Syriac text] [x] [Syriac text]	[x] [Syriac text] [w] [Syriac text]
[y] [Syriac text]	23 [Syriac text] [y] [Syriac text] [z] [Syriac text]	[z] omit [Syriac text] [y] [Syriac text]
	[Syriac text] [a] [Syriac text]	[a] add [Syriac text]
	[Syriac text] [b] [Syriac text] [b] [c] [Syriac text]	[b] [Syriac text] [b]
[d] [Syriac text] [e] [Syriac text]	24 [Syriac text] [d] [Syriac text] [e] [Syriac text]	[c] omit [Syriac text]
[f] [Syriac text]	[Syriac text] [f] [Syriac text]	[f] [Syriac text] [e] [Syriac text]
[g] [Syriac text] [h] [Syriac text]	[Syriac text] [g] [Syriac text] [h] [Syriac text] [i] [Syriac text]	[g] [Syriac text] [h] [Syriac text]
[i] [Syriac text] [k] [Syriac text]	† [Syriac text] [k] [Syriac text] [l m] [Syriac text]	† f. 38a.
[l] desunt ab [Syriac text] ad finem.	25 [n] [Syriac text]	[i] [Syriac text] [k] [Syriac text]
	[Syriac text]	[m] [Syriac text]
	[o] [Syriac text]	[n] [Syriac text]
	[Syriac text]	[o] [Syriac text]
	26 [Syriac text]	
	[Syriac text] [q] [Syriac text]	[q] [Syriac text]
	[Syriac text] [r] [Syriac text]	[r] omit [Syriac text]
	27 [Syriac text]	
	[Syriac text] [s] [Syriac text]	[s] [Syriac text]
	28 [Syriac text] [t] [Syriac text]	[t] add [Syriac text]
	[Syriac text] [u] [Syriac text]	[u] [Syriac text]

Codex A.

(*desunt ad finem.*)

Codex B.

29 ܕܠܐ [w]ܠܐܝܠܝܢ ܘܠܐ [x]ܥܒܪܝܢ : ܘܐܡܪܝ ܐܢܐ
ܠܗܘܢ ܕܐܘܦ ܠܐ [y]ܫܠܛܘܢ ܒܥܠܡܗ
ܬܫܒܘܚܬܗ ܠܐ ܠܒܢܝ ܗܘܝ ܚܙܐ ܡܢ ܗܠܝܢ :
30 [z]ܐܘ [a]ܕܝ ܠܚܘܒܗ ܕܦܠܓܪܐ ܕܚܙܝܪܝܢ [b]ܗܘܘ :
[f. 38a]
[c]ܡܣܓܝ ܠܬܘܪܐ ܗܘ ܡܬܪܥܝܐ ܐܠܗܐ ܒܝܢܝ
[d]ܡܠܟܝܢ : ܠܐ ܒܠ ܕܡܥܠܬܪ ܕܝ ܫܐܕܘܢ
31 [e]ܐܒܘܪܝ [f]ܗܝܡܢܘܬܐ : ܠܐ ܐܘܢ ܗܘܬܘܢ
ܚܝܝܢ ܘܐܡܪܝܢ ܡܢܐ [g]ܢܦܩܘܬ ܐܢܐ ܡܢܐ ܢܫܒܬܐ
32 ܐܢܐ ܡܢܐ ܢܠܒܫ : [h]ܒܠܗܘܢ ܗܠܝܢ [i]ܡܢܝܢܐ
ܒܝܢ : ܘܒܗ ܗܘ ܟܪ ܐܒܘܒܘܢ ܕܩܛܠܘ ܫܘܡܝܐ
33 ܕܐܬܘܢ ܦܪܚܝܢ ܠܗܠܝܢ ܒܠܗܘܢ : ܒܒܗ ܕܝ
ܡܒܝ ܡܠܟܘܬܗ ܕܐܠܗܐ ܦܪܘܩܗ ܘܗܠܝܢ
34 ܒܠܗܘܢ ܡܬܘܒܩܝܢ ܠܗܘܢ : ܠܐ ܐܘܢ
ܬܦܩܘܢ [k]ܡܣܓܝ ܠܡܣܓܝ : ܡܣܓܝ [l]ܟܪ ܦܢܩ
ܟܪܝܡܗ : [m]†ܡܫܡܫܬܗ ܘܡܢܐ ܒܢܬܗ [n]ܘܢܫܬܐ
ܦܪܝܗ ∴

Codex C.

[w]ܠܐܝܠܝܢ [x]ܥ̈ܒܪܝܢ
[y]ܫܘܠܛܢܝܢ
[z]ܐܝܡ [a]ܕܐܝ
[b]ܗܘ :
[c]ܘܡܣܓܝ
[d]ܡܠܟܝܢ [e]ܐܒܘܪܐ
[f]ܕܗܝܡܢܘܬܐ
[g]ܢܦ̈ܩܘܬ [h]ܒܠܗܘܢ
[i] *add* ܟܪ
[k] *omit* ܡܣܓܝ
[l] *omit* ܟܪ
† f. 38b.
[m]ܡܫܡܫܬܗ [n]ܘܫܒܬ

LIX.*

Matt. VIII. 14—23.

Codex A.

desunt ab ver. 14 *ad ver.* 20.

Codex B.

[a]ܘܩܒ ܐܫܟܚܬ ܐܪܟܒ ܡܢ ܡܬܐܘܦ [a]ܘܒܢܬܗ
14 ܡܫܪܘܦܐ : ܘܟܕ ܐܬܐ ܡܪܢ ܝܫܘܥ ܠܒܝܬܗ
ܕܟܐܦܐ ܚܙܐ ܠܚܡܬܗ ܪܡܝܐ ܒܐܫܬܐ
15 [a]ܘܩܪܒ [b]ܓܝܪ [c]ܒܐܝܕܗ ܘܫܒܩܬ ܠܗ [d]ܐܫܬܐ
16 ܘܩܡܬ ܘܫܡܫܬ ܡܫܡܫܐ ܠܗ : ܘܟܕ ܗܘܐ
[f]ܪܡܫܐ ܩܪܒܘ ܠܗ ܗܠܝܢ ܕܒܝܫܝܢ ܣܓܝܐܝܢ
ܫܐܕܝܢ : [g]ܘܐܦܩ ܪܘܚܬܐ [h]ܒܡܠܬܐ : ܘܟܠ
17 ܗܠܝܢ ܕܗܘܘ ܒܝܫܝܢ [i]ܒܟܐܒܝܢ ܐܣܝ : ܠܡܠܠ
ܕܐܬܡܠܠܬ ܡܢ ܕܐܬܡܪ [j]ܒܝܕ ܢܒܝܐ ܕܐܡܪ :[k]
ܒܟܐܒܝܗ ܗܘ [l] ܢܣܒ [m]ܘܡܟܐܘܒܝܗ ܛܥܝܢ :
18 ܘܟܕ ܚܙܐ ܡܪܢ ܝܫܘܥ ܣܓܝ [n]ܐܘܟܠܘܣܝܢ

Codex C.

[a]ܠܘܩܒܠ ܐܫܟܚܬ
[a]ܐܪܟܒ ܡܢ ܡܬܐ
[a]ܘܩܪܒ [b]*omit* ܓܝܪ
[c]ܠܐܝܕܗ [d]ܐܫܬܐ
[f]ܪܡܫܐ
[g]ܘܐܦܩ [h]ܒܡܠܬܐ
[i]ܒܟܝܫܬ
[j]ܒܐܝܕܐ
[k] *add* ܗܘ [l] *omit* ܗܘ
[m]ܘܡܟܐܘܒܝܗ
[n]ܐܘܟܠܘܣܝܢ

Codex A.

ܘܐܓܪܐ . . . [q] omit
ܕܓܢܒܐ . . .
[u] ܕܝܢܫܩ
[v] ܫܘܪ ܠܟ [w] omit ܕܝ
‡ f. 42a.
[x] ܬܠܡܝܕܘܗܝ [y] ܥܠܝܟ
[a] ܕܐܙܠ [c] ܠܒܐܒܝ
[d] ܡܢܟ [e] add ܕܝ
[f] ܘܡܒܥܒܝܢ
[g] ܒܐܬܪܗ [i] add ܥܠܡ

Codex B.

19 ܒܠܒܝ [o] ܥܡܝܩ ܕܐܝܬܝܠܗܘܢ ܠܟܢܫܐ : ܘܡܛܘ
ܣܩ ܫܦܪ [z] ܐܓܪܐ ܠܗ : ܒܡܛܠܠܬܐ [p] ܐܬܐ
20 [a] ܒܐܬܪܟ ܠܗܘܢ ܕܐܬܐ ܐܙܠ : [q] ܘܐܓܪܐ ܠܗ
ܡܢܐ ܫܡܥ ܬܠܡܝܕܐ [r] ܫܘܪܝܢ ܐܢܬ ܠܗܘܢ :
ܘܠܦܪܫܬܐ ܕܒܡܘܥܐ ܡܢܝܢ : ܒܢܗ ܕܓܢܒܐ [q]
[f. 38b]
21 ‡ ܠܝܬ ܠܗ [t] ܗܘܢ [u] ܕܝܢܫܡ ܪܒܥܗ : [v] ܫܘܪܝܢ [w] ܕܝ
ܡܢ [x] ܬܠܡܝܕܘܗܝ ܐܡܪ ܠܗ : ܡܪܝ [y] ܥܠܝܟ ܬܝܒ
22 [z] ܘܐܡܪܝ [a] ܕܐܙܠ [b] ܘܡܩܒܪ [c] ܠܐܒܘܝ : [d] ܡܢܐ
ܫܡܥ [e] ܐܡܪ ܠܗ : ܐܬܐ ܠܟ ܒܬܪܝ [f] ܘܫܒܘܩ
23 ܡܝܬܝܐ ܡܩܒܪܝܢ ܡܝܬܝܗܘܢ : ܘܟܕ ܣܠܩ
ܠܐܠܦܐ ܐܬܘ [g] ܒܐܬܪܗ † [h] ܬܠܡܝܕܘܗܝ : [i] ⁘

Codex C.

[o] ܥܡܝܩ [z] ܘܐܓܪܐ
[p] ܐܬܐ [a] ܒܐܬܪܟ
[r] ܫܘܪܝܢ
[t] omit ܗܘܢ [w] omit ܕܝ
[x] ܬܠܡܝܕܘܗܝ [y] ܥܠܝܟ
[z] ܡܐܡܪ [a] ܕܐܙܠ
[b] ܘܡܩܒܪ [c] ܠܐܒܐ
[d] ܡܢܐ
[g] ܒܐܬܪܗ [h] ܬܠܡܝܕܘܗܝ
† f. 39a.

LX.

Matt. VIII. 5—13.

Codex A.

[b] ܡܢ ܡܕܝܢܬܗܘܢ [b]
[z] add ܪܒܝ
[a] ܡܦܠܓܝܢ
[b] ܛܠܝܐ [c] ܡܫܪܝ
[d] ܒܝܫܐܝܬ
[g] ܘܐܓܒܐ
[h] ܗܐܘ [k] ܕܡܦܠܓܝ
[l] ܠܬܚܘܬ
[n] ܐܡܪܬ
[q] ܪܘܡܝܢ
[r] ܠܗܕܝܢ [s] ܐܙܠ
[u] ܐܬܬܡܗ [x] ܒܐܬܪܗ
[y] omit ܐܡܝܢ

Codex B.

[a] ܘܟܕ ܐܠܝܫ ܐܬܒܝ [b] ܡܢ ܒܬܪ ܐܠܦܝܢܗ ܡܢ
5 ܒܬܐܘܣ [b] [a] : [z] ܘܒܝܬܗ ܡܢܝܘܣܐ : ܘܒܕ ܒܠ
ܠܒܦܪ ܫܘܩ ܡܢܝ ܠܗ ܣܪ [a] ܡܦܠܓܝܢ ܒܒܐ
6 ܡܢܗ ܘܐܡܪ ܡܪܝ : [b] ܛܠܝܐ ܪܒܐ ܒܒܗ ܒܝܬܐ
7 [c] ܡܫܪܝ [d] ܒܝܫܐܝܬ ܡܬܢܦܪ : ܘܐܡܪ ܠܗ
ܡܢܐ ܫܡܥ ܐܢܐ [e] ܐܬܐ [f] ܡܐܣܝ ܠܗ :
8 [g] ܐܓܒܐ [h] ܗܘ ܡܦܠܓܝܢܐ ܘܐܡܪ : [i] ܡܪܝ
ܠܝܬ ܐܢܐ [k] ܕܡܘܐܠ ܕܬܥܘܠ [l] ܠܬܚܘܬ [m] ܪܒܝܫ
ܐܠܐ ܒܠܚܘܕ [n] ܐܡܪ [o] ܒܡܠܐ [p] ܘܡܬܐܣܐ
9 [b] ܛܠܝܐ : ܡܛܠ ܐܘܦ ܐܢܐ ܒܪܢܫ ܐܢܐ : ܘܐܝܬ
ܬܚܘܬ ܫܘܠܛܢܝ [q] ܪܘܡܝܢ : ܘܐܡܪ ܐܢܐ
[r] ܠܗܕܝܢ [s] ܐܙܠ ܘܗܘ [s] ܐܙܠ : [t] ܘܠܫܢܪ ܐܬܐ
ܘܗܘ ܐܬܐ : ܘܠܥܒܕܝ ܥܒܕ ܗܕܐ ܘܗܘ ܥܒܕ :
10 ܘܟܕ ܫܡܥ ܡܢܐ ܫܡܥ [u] ܐܬܬܡܗ : ܘܐܡܪ
ܠܗܠܝܢ [w] ܕܐܬܝܢ [x] ܒܐܬܪܗ : ܐܡܝܢ [y] ܐܡܝܢ

Codex C.

[a] ܠܒܬܪ ܐܠܝܫ
[a] ܐܬܐܒܝ ܡܢ ܒܬܐܘ
[b] ܛܠܝܐ [d] ܒܝܫܐܝܬ
[e] omit ܐܬܐ
[f] ܡܐܣܝ [g] ܘܐܓܒܐ
[h] omit ܗܘ
[i] omit ܡܪܝ
[k] ܕܡܘܐܠ [m] ܪܒܝܫ
[o] ܒܡܠܐ [p] ܘܡܬܐܣܐ
[r] ܠܗܕܝܢ [t] ܘܠܫܢܪ
[u] ܬܗܘܐ
[w] ܕܐܬܝܢ [x] ܒܐܬܪܗ
[y] omit ܐܡܝܢ

Codex A.	Codex B.	Codex C.
	ܐܡܝܪ ܐܢܐ ܠܟܘܢ : [z]ܕܠܘܬ ܐܢܫ ܗܟܢ ܗܕܐ	[z] *omit* ܕ
[b]ܒܐܝܣܪܐܝܠ	11 ܗܝܡܢܘܬܐ ܠܐ [a]ܐܫܟܚܬ [b]ܒܐܝܣܪܐܝܠ : ܐܡܪ	[a]ܐܫܟܚܬ
‡ f. 42b.	‡ ܐܢܐ ܠܟܘܢ ܕܝܢ ܕܣܓܝܐܝܢ ܡܢ ܡܕܢܚܐ ܘܡܢ	
[c]ܘܝܪܬܘܢ	ܡܥܪܒܐ ܝܐܬܘܢ [c]ܘܝܪܬܘܢ ܥܡ ܐܒܪܗܡ [f. 39a]	
[d]ܘܐܝܣܚܩ	[d]ܘܐܝܣܚܩ ܘܝܥܩܘܒ ܒܡܠܟܘܬܐ ܕܫܡܝܐ :	
[f]ܢܦܩܘܢ	12 [e]ܘܒܢܝܗ ܕܡܠܟܘܬܐ [f]ܢܦܩܘܢ ܠܒܪܐ ܚܫܘܟܐ :	[e]ܘܒܢܝܗ
[g]ܕܫܢܝܐ [h]ܠܗܘܢ ܘܐܡܪ	ܬܡܢ ܗܘܐ ܒܟܝܐ ܘܚܘܪܩܘܩܝܢ [g]ܕܫܢܝܐ	[g]ܕܫܢܝܐ
[i]ܩܢܛܪܘܢܐ	ܘܐܡܪ ܡܪܢ ܝܫܘܥ [h]ܠܗܘܢ [i]ܠܩܢܛܪܘܢܐ	[i]ܩܢܛܪܘܢܐ
[k]ܐܙܠ [l] *omit* ܕ	[k]ܐܙܠ ܗܝܟ [l]ܕܗܝܡܢܬܐ ܬܬܥܒܕ ܠܟ :	[l] *omit* ܕ
[m]ܘܐܬܐܣܝ	13 [m]ܘܐܬܐܣܝ † ܛܠܝܐ ܡܢ ܗܝ ܫܥܬܐ : ܘܗܦܟ	† f. 39b.
[n]ܩܢܛܪܘܢܐ	ܗܘ [n]ܩܢܛܪܘܢܐ ܠܒܝܬܗ ܒܗ ܒܫܥܬܗ [o]ܘܐܫܟܚ	[o]ܘܐܫܟܚ
[o]ܘܐܫܟܚ [p]ܛܠܝܐ	[p]ܠܛܠܝܐ ܚܠܝܡ ⁘	[p]ܛܠܝܐ

LXI.

Matt. IX. 9—17.

Codex A.	Codex B.	Codex C.
[b]ܐܠܝܣܛܣ	[a]ܒܗ ܐܫܥܬܐ [b]ܐܠܝܣܛܣ [c]ܒܪ ܐܠܦܝܘܣ ܡܢ	[a]ܒܗ ܐܫܥܬܐ
[c]ܡܢ ܡܬܠܘܗܝ[c]	9 ܡܬܐܡܪ[a c] : [z] ܘܒܬ ܒܬܪ ܡܪܢ ܝܫܘܥ ܡܢ	[a]ܐܠܝܣܛܣ ܡܢ ܡܬܠܬܐ
[z] *add* ܘܒܬܗ ܡܪܢ ܝܫܘܥ	ܬܡܢ : ܚܙܐ ܓܒܪ [a]ܝܬܒ ܥܠ ܡܟܣܐ	[z] *add* ܘܒܬܗ
[a]ܝܬܒ [o]ܡܬܩܪܐ	[o]ܡܬܐܡܪ [b]ܡܬܝ : ܘܐܡܪ ܠܗ : ܐܬܐ ܒܬܪܝ	[b]ܡܬܝ [o]ܡܬܩܪܐ
[c]ܘܩܡ [d] *omit* ܘ	10 [c]ܘܩܡ [d]ܘܐܬܐ ܒܬܪܗ : ܘܗܘܐ ܗܝܟ ܕܗܘܐ	[d] *omit* ܘ
[e]ܡܟܣܐܝܢ	ܣܡܝܟ ܒܒܝܬܐ ܘܗܐ ܣܓܝ [e]ܡܟܣܐܝܢ	[e]ܡܟܣܝܢ
[f]ܬܠܡܝܕܘܗܝ	ܘܚܛܝܝܢ ܐܬܘ ܘܗܘܘ ܣܡܝܟܝܢ ܥܡ ܡܪܢ ܝܫܘܥ	
[g]ܦܪܝܫܝܐ [i]ܡܟܣܐܝܢ	11 ܘܥܡ [f]ܬܠܡܝܕܘܗܝ : ܘܟܕ ܚܙܘ [g]ܦܪܝܫܝܐ ܗܘܘ	[f]ܬܠܡܝܕܘܗܝ
[j]ܘܚܛܝܝܢ	ܐܡܪܝܢ [h]ܠܬܠܡܝܕܘܗܝ : ܠܡܢܐ ܥܡ [i]ܡܟܣܐܝܢ	[h]ܠܬܠܡܝܕܘܗܝ
[k]ܡܬܠܘܥܣܝܢ	12 [j]ܘܚܛܝܝܢ [k]ܡܬܠܘܥܣ [l]ܐܟܠ [m]ܘܐܫܬܐ	[i]ܡܟܣܐܝܢ [j]ܘܚܛܝܝܢ
[l]ܐܟܠ [m]ܘܫܬܐ	ܡܪܢ ܝܫܘܥ ܘܐܡܪ ܠܗܘܢ : ܠܐ ܨܪܝܟܝܢ	[m]ܘܐܫܬܐ
[n]ܕܒܝܫܝܢ [p]ܝܠܦܘ	ܚܠܝܡܝܢ ܕܒܪܝܢ ܠܐܣܝܐ : ܐܠܐ ܚܠܝܡܝܢ [n]ܕܒܝܫܝܢ	
‡ f. 43a.	13 [o]ܒܫܐܠܬܐ : ‡ ܐܙܠܘ ܕܝܢ [p]ܝܠܦܘ ܡܢܐ ܗܘ [q]ܕܪܚܡܝܢ	[o]ܒܫܐܠܬܐ [q]ܕܪܚܡܝܢ
[r]ܕܒܚܬܐ	ܐܢܐ ܨܒܐ ܘܠܐ [r]ܕܒܚܝܢ : ܠܐ ܓܝܪ ܐܬܝܬ ܕܐܩܪܐ	
[s] *add* ܥܠ [t]ܒܟܝܢ	14 ܙܕܝܩܝܢ ܐܠܐ ܚܛܝܝܢ ܠܬܝܒܘ[s] : [t]ܒܟܝܢ ܩܪܒܘ	

Codex A.

ܬܠܡܝܕܘܗܝ
[u] ܕܝܘܚܢܢ
[g] ܘܦܪܝ̈ܫܝܐ [v] ܨܝܡܝܢ
[w] ܘܬܠܡܝ̈ܕܝܟ
[x] ܝܟܠܝܢ [y] ܒܢܝ
[z] ܕܡܬܐܒܠܘܢ
[b] add ܕ [c] add ܕܝ
[d] ܕܡܬܢܣܒ [e] ܘܒܗܝܢ
[g] ܡܪܘܩܥܬܐ [i] ܡܐܢܐ
[j] ܘܗܘܝܐ [l] ܚܡܪ
[m] ܚܕܬ [n] add ܐܠܐ ܕܝ
[o] ܟܝ [q] ܚܡܪܐ
[r] ܡܬܐܫܕ [s] ܐܒܕܝܢ
[t] ܚܡܪ [u] ܚܕܬ

Codex B.

ܠܗ [f] ܬܠܡܝܕܘܗܝ [u] ܕܝܘܚܢܢ ܐܡܪܝܢ ܠܡܢܐ ܐܢܢ
[g] ܘܦܪܝܫܝܐ· [v] ܨܝܡܝܢ ܣܓܝ [w] ܘܬܠܡܝܕܝܟ ܠܐ
15 [v] ܨܝܡܝܢ: ܘܐܡܪ ܠܗܘܢ ܡܪܢ ܝܫܘܥ: ܕܠܡܐ
[f. 39b]
[x] ܝܟܠܘܢ [y] ܒܢܝ ܓܢܘܢܐ [z] ܠܡܬܐܒܠܘܢ: ܟܕ [a] ܥܡܗܘܢ
ܐܡܬܝ [b] ܚܬܢܐ ܒܝܢܬܗܘܢ: ܐܬܝܢ [c] ܝܘܡܝܢ
ܟܕ [d] ܝܬܢܣܒ ܚܬܢܐ ܡܢܗܘܢ: [e] ܘܒܗܝܢ ܝܨܘܡܘܢ:
16 ܠܝܬ [f] ܐܢܫ ܪܡܐ [g] ܡܪܘܩܥܐ ܚܕܬܐ ܥܠ ܡܐܢܐ
ܒܠܝܐ: [h] ܢܣܒܐ ܗܝ ܓܝܪ ܡܠܘܝܗ ܡܢ [i] ܡܐܢܐ
17 ܒܠܝܐ: [j] ܘܗܘܐ [k] ܒܙܥܐ ܒܝܫ ܡܢ ܩܕܡܐ: ܘܠܐ
ܪܡܝܢ [l] ܚܡܪܐ [m] ܚܕܬܐ ܒܙܩܝܢ ܒܠܝܢ: [n] ܠܐ
[o] ܕܝܢ [p] ܡܬܒܙܥ ܗܘ † [q] ܚܡܪܐ ܠܙܩܝܐ:
[q] ܘܚܡܪܐ [r] ܡܬܐܫܕ ܘܙܩܝܐ [s] ܐܒܕܝܢ: ܐܠܐ
ܪܡܝܢ [t] ܚܡܪܐ [u] ܚܕܬܐ ܒܙܩܝܢ ܚܕܬܝܢ ܘܬܪܝܗܘܢ
ܡܬܢܛܪܝܢ: [w] ܥܠܡ ⁘

Codex C.

[u] ܕܝܘܚܢܐ
[x] ܝܟܠܝܢ [y] ܒܢܝܐ
[z] ܕܡܬܐܒܠܘܢ [a] ܟܕܘ
[b] add ܕ [c] add ܕܝ
[f] ܐܢܫ [g] ܡܪܘܩܥܬܐ
[h] ܢܣܒܐ [i] ܡܐܢܐ
[j] ܘܗܘܝܐ [k] ܒܙܥ
[l] ܚܡܪ [m] ܚܕܬ
[n] add ܐܢ
† f. 40a.
[p] ܡܬܒܙܥ [q] ܚܡܪܐ
[t] ܚܡܪ [u] ܚܕܬ
[w] omit ܥܠܡ

LXII.

Matt. VIII. 28—IX. 1.

Codex A.

[b] ܐܠܝܫܥܗܘܢ (sic)
[c] ܡܢ ܡܬܐܬܘܢ
[z] ܕܓܪܓܣܝܐ
[b] ܗܟܢ [c] ܢܓܠ
[e] add ܥܠ [f] ܕܒܝܬܗ
‡ f. 43b.
[g] ܓܥܘ [h] ܘܐܡܪܝܢ
[i] ܕܬܫܢܩܝܢ
[j] ܕܚܙܝ̈ܪܝܢ
[m] ܡܦܩܬ [n] ܫܠܚ
[o] ܕܚܙܝܪܝܐ
[p] omit ܕܝ

Codex B.

[a] ܒܗܘ ܙܒܢܐ [b] ܐܠܝܫܥܗܘܢ [c] ܟܕ ܐܬܥܒܪ ܡܢ
28 [a c] ܡܬܐܬܘܢ ܘܒܚܝܬܗ ܡܢܘܗܒܐ ܘܒܚܕ ܐܬܪܐ
ܠܐܬܪܐ [z] ܕܓܪܓܣܝܐ ܠܟܦܪܐ: ܐܪܥܘ ܝܬܗ
ܬܪܝܢ ܕܒܠܝܗܘܢ ܫܐܕܝܢ ܢܦܩܝܢ ܡܢ ܒܝܬ ܩܒܘܪܬܐ
ܒܝܫܝܢ ܠܚܕܐ: [a b] ܗܟܢܢ ܕܐܢܫ ܠܐ ܗܘܐ [a c] ܡܫܟܚ
29 [d] ܕܢܥܒܪ ‡ [e f] ܒܝܬܗ ܐܘܪܚܐ: ܘܗܐ ܓܥܘ [g]
[h] ܘܐܡܪܘ ܡܐ ܠܢ ܘܠܟ ܝܫܘܥ ܒܪܗ ܕܐܠܗܐ:
ܐܬܝܬ ܠܟܐ ܡܢ ܩܕܡ ܙܡܢܗ [i] ܕܬܫܢܩ ܝܬܢ:
30 ܗܘܬ ܕܝ ܪܚܝܩ ܡܢܗܘܢ [j] ܕܚܙܝܪܝܢ ܣܓܝ ܪܥܝܐ:
31 ܒܥܘܢ ܕܝ ܫܐܕܐ ܗܘܘ ܒܝܢ ܡܢܗ [k] ܘܐܡܪܝܢ:
[l] ܐܢ ܐܢܬ [m] ܡܦܩ ܠܢ [n] ܫܠܚ ܝܬܢ ܠܡܪܥܝܬܐ
32 [o] ܕܚܙܝܪܐ: ܘܐܡܪ ܠܗܘܢ ܡܪܢ ܙܠܘ ܐܝܠܘ:
ܗܢܘܢ ܕܝ ܢܦܩܘ ܘܐܙܠܘ [p] ܕܝ ܠܡܪܥܝܬܐ

Codex C.

[a] ܒܗܘ ܙܒܢܐ ܐܠܝܫ
ܐܠܝܫܥܗܘܢ ܡܢ
ܡܬܐܬ [a]
[z] ܕܓܪܓܣܝܐ
[a] ܗܟܢܢ ܕܐܢܫ ܠܐ
ܗܘܐ [a]
[d] ܕܢܥܒܪ [e] add ܥܠ
[g] ܓܥܘ
[i] ܕܬܫܢܩ
[j] ܕܚܙܝܪܐ
[k] omit ܘܐܡܪܝܢ
[l] ܐܢ [m] ܡܦܩ
[n] ܫܠܚ
[p] omit ܕܝ

Codex B.

[q] ܕܚܙܝܪܐ : ܘܐܪܗܛܬ ܒܟܠܗ ܡܪܥܝܬܐ [r]
[s] ܠܡܚܕܘܪܬܐ ܠܝܡܐ : [t] ܘܡܝܬܘ [u] ܒܡܝܐ :
[f. 40a]
33 ܗܠܝܢ [v] ܕܗܘܘ ܪܥܝܢ ܥܪܩܘ ܘܐܙܠܘ [w] ܠܡܕܝܢܬܐ
34 ܘܐܡܪܘ ܟܘܠܐ : [x] ܘܗܠܝܢ ܕܕܝܘܢܝܢ : [y] ܘܗܐ
[z] ܟܘܠܗܘܢ [a] ܡܕܝܢܬܐ [b] ܢܦܩܘ ܠܐܘܪܥܘܬܗ
ܕܡܪܢܐ ܝܫܘܥ : ܘܟܕ ܚܡܘ ܝܬܗ ܒܥܘ ܡܢܗ :
IX. 1 ܕܢܥܒܪ ܡܢ [c] ܬܚܘܡܗܘܢ : ܘܣܠܩ ܠܐܠܦܐ
ܘܥܒܪ ܘܐܬܐ [d] ܠܡܕܝܢܬܐ ܕܝܠܗ ∴

Codex A.

[q] ܕܚܙ̈ܝܪܝܐ
[r] *add* ܟܠ
[s] ܕܡܚܕܘܪܬܐ
[u] ܒܡ̈ܝܐ [v] ܕܝ ܗܘܘ
[w] ܠܡܕܝܢܬܐ
[x] ܘܗ̇ܠܝܢ
[z] ܟܘܠܗ [a] ܡܕܝܢܬܐ
[b] ܢܦܩܬ [d] ܠܐܘܪܥܘܬܗ

Codex C.

[r] *add* ܟܠ
[s] ܠܡܚܕܘܪܬܐ
[t] ܘܡܝܬܘ [u] ܒܡܝܐ
[v] ܕܝ ܗܘܘ [v]
[x] ܘܗܠܝܢ [y] ܘܗܐ
[z] ܟܘܠܗ [b] ܢܦܩܬ
[c] ܬܚܘܡܗܘܢ

LXIII.

Matt. IX. 18—26.

Codex B.

[a] ܒܗܝ ܫܥܬܐ [b] ܐܬܐ ܚܕ [c] ܐܪܟܘܢ ܡܢ
18 ܡܬܐܘܗ [z c] ܘܗܐ [a] ܚܕ ܐܪܟܘܢ ܩܪܒ [b] ܠܡܪܢܐ [c]
ܣܓܕ ܠܗ ܘܐܡܪ [d] ܡܪܝ ܒܪܬܝ ܟܕܘ [†] ܡܝܬܬ
ܐܠܐ ܐܬܐ [e] ܐܘܫܛ [f] ܐܝܕܟ ܥܠܝܗ ܘܗܝ
19 ܚܝܐ : ܘܩܡ ܡܪܢܐ ܝܫܘܥ [‡] ܘܐܙܠ [g] ܗܘ
20 [h] ܘܬܠܡܝܕܘܗܝ : ܘܗܐ ܚܕܐ [i] ܐܢܬܬܐ ܕܗܘܬ
ܐܝܬ ܒܐܕܡܐ [j] ܬܪܬܥܣܪܐ [k] ܫܢܝܢ [l] : ܩܪܒܬ ܡܢ
21 [m] ܠܒܣܬܪܗ ܘܐܬܩܪܒܬ ܠܟܢܦܬܐ [n] ܕܟܬܘܢܗ : ܗܘܬ ܒܪ
ܐܡܪܐ ܒܪܥܝܗ : ܐܢ ܒܠܒܘܫܗ ܐܩܪܒ [o] ܠܡܚܝܐ
22 ܚܝܐ ܐܢܐ : ܘܐܬܦܢܝ ܝܫܘܥ [p] ܬܡܢ ܘܚܙܐ ܝܬܗ
ܘܐܡܪ ܠܗ : ܐܬܚܝܠܝ ܒܪܬܐ ܗܝܡܢܘܬܟܝ
[q] ܐܚܝܬܟܝ ܘܚܝܬ : ܘܚܝܬ [r] ܐܢܬܬܐ ܡܢ ܗܝ
23 ܫܥܬܐ : ܘܟܕ ܐܬܐ ܡܪܢܐ ܝܫܘܥ ܠܒܝܬܗ
ܕܐܪܟܘܢܐ ܚܙܐ ܙܡܪܐ [s] ܘܐܘܟܠܘܣܐ
24 ܡܬܒܥܒܥܝܢ : ܘܗܘܐ ܐܡܪ [t] ܦܘܩܘ ܠܐ ܓܝܪ
[u] ܡܝܬܬ ܛܠܝܬܐ : ܐܠܐ [v] ܕܡܟܒܐ ܗܝ ܘܗܘܘ
25 ܓܚܟܝܢ ܥܠܘܝ : ܟܕ ܕܝ ܢܦܩ [w] ܐܘܟܠܘܣܐ ܟܠ
[x] ܘܥܠ [y] ܒܐܝܕܗ [z] ܘܐܩܝܡ ܝܬܗ ܠܛܠܝܬܐ :
27 ܘܢܦܩ ܛܒܗ [a] ܒܟܘܠܗ [b] ܐܪܥܐ ∴

Codex A.

[b] ܐܫܬܐܘܗ
[c] ܡܢ ܟܢܫܬܗ [c]
[z] *add* ܘܟܢܫܬܗ ܕܝܘܕܝܐ
[b] ܐܬܐ [a] *omit* ܘ
[c] *add* ܝܫܘܥ
[d] *omit* ܡܪܝ
‡ f. 44*a*.
[e] ܐܘܫܛ [f] ܐܝܕܟ
[g] *add* ܥܡܗ [i] ܐܢܬܐ
[j] ܬܪܬܥܣܪܐ
[k] ܫܢ̈ܝܢ [m] ܠܒܣܬܪܐ
[n] ܕܡܢܐ [o] ܠܒܘܫܗ
[s] ܘܐܘܟ̈ܠܘܣܐ
[t] ܦܘܩܘ
[v] ܕܡܟܒܐ
[w] ܐܘܟ̈ܠܘܣܐ
[y] *add* ܝܬܗ
[a] ܒܟܘܠ [b] *add* ܗܝ

Codex C.

[a] ܒܝܘܡ
[z] *add* ܘܟܢܫܬܗ ܕܝܘܕܝܐ
[a] *omit* ܘ
† f. 40*b*.
[c] *add* ܝܫܘܥ
[d] *omit* ܡܪܝ
[g] *add* ܥܡܗ
[h] ܘܬܠܡܝܕܘܗܝ
[j] ܬܪܬܥܣܪܐ
[l] *add* ܘܗܝ
[m] ܠܒܣܬܪܐ [n] ܕܡܢܐ
[o] ܠܒܘܫܗ [p] ܬܡܢ
[q] ܐܚܝܬܟܝ [r] ܐܢܬܐ
[s] ܘܐܘܟܠܘܣܐ
[t] ܦܘܩܘ
[u] ܡܝܬܬ [v] ܕܡܟܒܐ
[w] ܐܘܟܠܘܣܐ
[x] ܘܥܠ [y] *add* ܝܬܗ
[z] ܘܐܩܝܡ [a] ܒܟܘܠ

Codex A.	Codex B.	Codex C.

LXIV.

Matt. IX. 1—8.

Codex B.

ᵃܒܗܘ ܐܠܝܢ ᵇܐܘܢܓܠܝܘܢ ᶜܒܕ ܐܠܥܒܪܗ ܡܢ
1 ܡܬܐܘܣ ᵃᶜ: ܘܟܢܫܗ ܡܢܫܘܬܐ : ܘܥܠ ܠܐܠܦܐ
[f. 40b]
2 ܘܥܒܪ ܘܐܬܐ ᶻܠܡܕܝܢܬܗ ܕܝܠܗ : ܘܗܐ ܩܪܒܘ
ܩܪܒܘ ܠܗ ܚܕ ᵃܡܫܪܝ ܪܡܐ ܒܥܪܣܐ : ܘܚܙܐ
ܝܫܘܥ ᵇܗܝܡܢܘܬܗܘܢ ܘܐܡܪ ܠܡܫܪܝܐ ܬܘܪܘܬ ܒܪܝ
3 ᶜܫܒܝܩܝܢ ܠܟ ᵈܚܛܗܝܟ : ܘܗܐ ܐܢܫ ‡ܡܢ ܣܦܪܐ
4 ܐܡܪܘ ܒܠܒܗܘܢ : ᵘܗܕܝܢ ܡܓܕܦ : ܘܚܙܐ ᵉ
ܝܫܘܥ ܡܚܫܒܬܗܘܢ ܘܐܡܪ ܠܗܘܢ ܠܡܢܐ
5 ܐܢܬܘܢ † ܡܬܚܫܒܝܢ ᶠܒܝܫ ᵍܒܠܒܒܝܟܘܢ : ܡܢܐ
ܗܘ ܦܫܝܛ ʰܕܐܡܪ ⁱܫܒܝܩܝܢ ܠܟ ᵈܚܛܗܝܟ :
6 ܐܘ ʰܕܐܡܪ ܩܘܡ ʲܗܠܟ : ᵏܠܟܠܠ ܕܝ
ˡܕܬܕܥܘܢ ܕܫܠܝܛ ܗܘ ܒܪܗ ܕܐܢܫܐ ܥܠ
ܐܪܥܐ ܕܝܫܒܘܩ ᵐܚܛܗܝܢ : ܟܕܝܢ ܐܡܪ
ܠܡܫܪܝܐ ܩܘܡ ܫܩܘܠ ܥܪܣܟ ⁿܘܐܙܠ ܠܒܝܬܟ :
7 ܘܩܡ ᵒܐܙܠ ܠܒܝܬܗ : ܟܕ ܕܝ ܚܙܘ ᵖܐܟܠܘܣܐ
8 ܕܚܠܘ ܘܫܒܚܘ ܠܐܠܗܐ : ᵠܠܗܕܝܢ ܕܝܗܒ ܫܘܠܛܢܐ ʳ
ˢܫܘܠܛܢܘܬܐ ᵗܠܒܢܝ ܐܢܫܐ : ʷܫܠܡ ⁘

Codex A.

ᵇܐܘܢܓܠܝܘܢ
ᶜܡܢ ܡܬܐܘܣ ᶜ
ᶻܠܡܕܝܢܬܗ
ᵇ *add* ܝܫܘܥ
ܠܗܝܡܢܘܬܗܘܢ

‡ f. 44b.

ᶜܫܒܝܩܝܢ ᵈܚܛܗܝܟ
ᵉ *add* ܕܝ ᵘܗܕܝܢ
ᵍܒܠܒܒܝܟܘܢ
ʰܕܢܐܡܪ ⁱܫܒܝܩܝܢ
ʲܗܠܟ
ᵏܠܟܠܠ ˡܕܬܕܥܘܢ
ᵐܚܛܗܝܢ ⁿܘܐܙܠ
ᵒܐܙܠ ᵖܐܟܠܘܣܐ
ʳ *add* ܗܕܐ ᵠܠܗܕܝܢ
ˢܫܘܠܛܢܘܬܐ
ʷ *omit* ܫܠܡ

Codex C.

ᵃܒܗܘ ܐܠܝܢ
ᵃܐܘܢܓܠܝܘܢ ܡܢ ܡܬܐܘܣ
ᵃܡܫܪܝ
ᵇ *add* ܝܫܘܥ
ܠܗܝܡܢܘܬܗܘܢ
ᵉ *add* ܕܝ ᶜܫܒܩ

† f. 41a.

ᶠܒܝܫ
ʲܗܠܟ (*sic*)
ᵖܐܟܠܘܣܐ
ʳ *add* ܗܕܐ
ᵗܕܒܢܝܐ
ʷ *omit* ܫܠܡ

LXV.

Matt. X. 37—XI. 1.

Codex B.

ᵃܒܗܘ ܐܠܝܢ ܐܘܢܓܠܝܘܢ ܒܕ ܐܠܥܒܪܗ ܡܢ
37 ܡܬܐܘܣ ᵃʸ ܐܡܪ ܡܪܢ ܡܢ ܕܪܚܡ ܐܒ ܐܘ ܐܡ
ܝܬܝܪ ܡܢ ᶻܕܝܠܝ : ܠܝܬ ܗܘ ܫܘܐ ܠܝ : ܘܡܢ ܕܪܚܡ
ᵃܒܪ ܐܘ ᵇܒܪܬܐ ܝܬܝܪ ܡܢ ᶻܕܝܠܝ ܠܝܬ ܗܘ ܫܘܐ
38 ܠܝ : ܘܡܢ ܕܠܐ ܢܣܒ ܨܠܝܒܗ ܘܐܬܐ ܒܬܪܝ ܠܝܬ
39 ܗܘ ܫܘܐ ܠܝ : ܡܢ ᶜܕܡܫܟܚ ܢܦܫܗ ᵈܡܘܒܕ ܗܘ
ܠܗ : ܘܡܢ ᵉܕܡܘܒܕ ܢܦܫܗ ᶠܒܕܝܠܝ ᵍܡܫܟܚ ܠܗ :

Codex A.

ᵃܒܗܘܢ ܐܪܒܥܬ
ܐܘܢܓܠܝܘܢ ܡܢ
ᵃܡܬܐܘܣ
ᶻܕܝܠܝ ᵃܒܪ
ᵇܒܪܬܐ
ᶜܕܡܫܟܚ
ᶠܒܕܝܠܝ ᵍܡܫܟܚ

Codex C.

ᵃܒܗܘ ܐܪܒܥܬ
ᵃܐܘܢܓܠܝܘܢ ܡܢ ܡܬܐܘܣ
ʸ *add* (*sic*) ܘܡܬܐܘܣ
ܡܢܫܘܬܐ
ᵃܒܪ ᵇܒܪܬܐ
ᵈܡܘܒܕ ᵉܕܡܘܒܕ
ᶠܒܕܝܠܝ ᵍܡܫܟܚ

Codex A.

[i] *omit* ܘܡܢ . . . ܡܫܡܫܠ

ܘܡܢ [j] ܕܚܠܝܫ [k]

ܕܡܦܩܠ [g]

ܢܦܫܐ [l] ܕܢܦܫܐ [o]

‡ f. 45*a*.

ܕܝܕܝܥ [q]

[s] *omit* ܕܚܝܝܢ

[v] *omit* ܗܕܝܢ [t] *add* ܕ

ܦܬ [z]

[c] *add* ܨܠܡ

Codex B.

40 ܡܢ ܕܡܫܡܫܠ ܠܟܘܢ ܠܝ. ܗܘ ܡܫܡܫܠ : [i]ܘܡܢ
[f]ܕܡܫܡܫܠ ܠܝ [h]ܡܫܡܫܠ[i] [j]ܠܗܕܝܢ [k]ܕܚܠܝܫ ܬܗܝ :
41 ܡܢ [g]ܕܡܫܡܫܠ [l]ܢܦܫܝ [m]ܒܟܝܢܐ ܢܦܫܐ : [n]ܐܚܪܢ
[f. 41*a*]
[o]ܢܦܫܐ ܗܘ ܢܫܒܩ : ܘܡܢ [g]ܕܡܫܡܫܠ ܝܕܝܥ :
[m]ܒܟܝܢܐ [p]ܝܕܝܥ [n]ܐܚܪܢ [q]ܝܕܝܥ ܗܘ ܢܫܒܩ :
42 ܘܡܢ ܕܢܦܫܐ ‡ ܠܝܬ ܡܢ ܗܠܝܢ ܕܗܘܐ [r]ܒܗ
[s]ܕܚܝܝܢ [t]ܡܬܬܝܗܒ ܠܟܘܢ ܒܟܝܢܐ [u]ܬܠܡܝܕܐ :
ܐܡܝܢ ܐܡܪ ܐܢܐ ܠܟܘܢ ܕܠܐ ܢܦܩ ܐܚܪܢܗ :
XI. 1 ܘܗܘܐ ܟܕ ܨܠܐ ܡܪܢܐ ܝܫܘܥ [v]ܗܕܝܢ [w]ܡܫܒܚ
[x]ܬܗܘܢ ܠܬܪܥܣܪܬܐ [y]ܬܠܡܝܕܘܗܝ [z]ܦܬܚ ܡܢ
ܬܡܢ † ܠܟܠܒ ܕܝܠܗ [a]ܘܡܪܢ [b]ܒܡܕܝܢܬܗܘܢ [c] ⁘

Codex C.

ܕܡܫܡܫܠ [f][g] ܡܫܡܫܠ [h]

ܢܦܫܐ [l] ܒܟܝܢܐ [m]

ܐܚܪܢ [n]

[p] *omit* ܝܕܝܥ

[s] *omit* ܕܚܝܝܢ ܒܗ [r]

ܬܠܡܝܕܐ [u] [t] *add* ܕ

[v] *omit* ܗܕܝܢ

ܡܫܒܚܝܢ [w]

ܠܗܘܢ [x] ܬܠܡܝܕܘܗܝ [y]

ܘܡܪܢ [a] ܒܡܕܝܢܬܐ [b]

† f. 41*b*.

LXVI.

Matt. IX. 27—35.

Codex A.

[a]ܐܠܝܫܥ ܐܫܒܥܝ.

[a]ܡܢ ܡܬܐܘܢ

[x] *add* ܕܝܢ

[y]ܒܠܝܫܢ

[z]ܕܕܘܕ

[b]ܡܪܢܐ ܗܝܡܢܝܢ[c]

[d]ܢܓܠ ܐܝܢ[e]

[f]ܡܪܢܐ ܕܟܡ[g] ܡܬܚ[h]

[i]ܡܬܦܬܚܢܗܘܢ

[j]ܬܬܚܒܕ

[l]ܢܦܩܘ ܘܐܫܬܥܘ[m]

[n]ܒܟܠܗ ܥܢܝ

[o] *omit* ܕܝ [p]ܢܦܩܘ

[q]ܕܟܠܗܝ

Codex B.

[a]ܢܦܩ ܐܠܝܫܥ ܐܫܒܥܝ. ܟܕ ܐܠܝܫܥܢܗ ܡܢ
27 ܡܬܐܘܢ[a] : [x] ܘܟܕܬܗ ܡܬܪܘܢܐ ܘܗܘܝܢ ܕܗܘ
ܒܬܪ ܡܢ ܬܡܢ ܡܪܢܐ ܝܫܘܥ : ܕܟܦܘ ܬܗܘ
ܬܪܝܢ ܥܘܝܪܝܢ ܡܩܥܝܢ ܘܐܡܪܝܢ ܐܬܪܚܡ [y]ܒܠܝܫܢ
28 ܒܪܗ [z]ܕܕܘܕ : ܘܟܕ [a]ܐܬܐ ܠܒܝܬܐ ܩܪܒܘ ܠܗ
ܬܪܝܢ ܥܘܝܪܐ ܒܟܝܢ ܡܕܘܗ : ܘܐܡܪ ܠܗܘܢ
[b]ܡܪܢܐ ܝܫܘܥ [c]ܗܝܡܢܝܢܬܘܢ ܐܢܬܘܢ ܕܐܝܟܐ
[d]ܡܨܠ ܕܥܒܕ ܠܟܘܢ ܗܕܐ : ܐܡܪܝܢ ܠܗ [e]ܐܝܢ
29 [f]ܡܪܝ : [g]ܒܟܝܢ [h]ܩܪܒ ܠܥܝܢܝܗܘܢ ܘܐܡܪ
ܠܗܘܢ ܗܝܟ [i]ܗܝܡܢܘܬܟܘܢ [j]ܬܬܥܒܕ ܠܟܘܢ :
30 [k]ܘܐܬܦܬܚܘ ܐܬܦܬܚ ܥܝܢܝܗܘܢ : ܘܐܟܐܐ
ܒܗܘܢ ܡܪܢܐ ܝܫܘܥ ܘܐܡܪ ܚܙܘ ܕܐܢܫ
31 ܠܐ [l]ܢܕܥ : ܗܢܘܢ ܕܝܢ ܢܦܩܘ [m]ܘܐܫܬܥܘ ܥܠܘܗܝ
32 [n]ܒܟܠܗ ܐܪܥܐ : ܘܟܕ [o]ܕܝܢ ܢܦܩܘ ܗܐ ܩܪܒܘ
33 ܠܗ ܚܕ ܓܒܪܐ [p]ܚܪܫܐ [q]ܕܟܠܝ ܫܐܕ : ܘܟܕ ܢܦܩ

Codex C.

[a]ܐܠܝܫܥ ܐܫܒܥܝ.

[a]ܡܢ ܡܬܐܘܢ

[a] *omit* ܐܬܐ

[c]ܗܝܡܢܝܢ

[e]ܐܝܢ

[j]ܬܬܥܒܕ

[k]ܘܐܬܦܬܚܘ

[l]ܢܕܥ

[m] *omit* ܘܐܫܬܥܘ

[n]ܒܟܠܗ ܥܢܝ[n]

[o] *omit* ܕܝ

Codex B.

ܥܒܕܐ[r] ܡܡܠܠ[s] ܚܪܫܐ : ܘܐܬܡܗܘ ܐܘܟܠܘ̈ܣܐ[t]
ܐܡܪܝܢ ܕܡܢ[i] ܥܠܡܝܢ[u] ܠܐ ܐܬܚܡܝܬ ܟܕܝܢ
34 ‡ ܒܐܪܟܘܢ[w] : ܦܪܝܫܝܐ[k] ܕܝܢ[x] ܗܘܘ ܐܡܪܝܢ
[f. 41b]
ܒܐܪܟܘܢܗܘܢ[y] ܕܫܐܕܐ ܗܘ ܡܦܩ[z] ܫܐܕܐ
35 ܘܗܘܐ ܡܚܕܪ ܝܫܘܥ ܥܠ ܡܕܝܢܬܐ[a] ܘܩܘܪܝܗܘܢ[b] :
ܘܗܘܐ[c] ܘܡܠܦ[d] ܒܟܢܘܫܬܗܘܢ ܘܡܟܪܙ[e] ܒܣܒܪܬܐ
ܕܡܠܟܘܬܐ : ܘܡܐܣܐ[f] ܟܠ ܟܐܒ ܘܟܠ
ܡܪܥܘ[g] ܒܥܡܐ : ܫܠܡ[h] ⁘

Codex A.

ܡܡܠܠ[s] ܐܘܟܠܘ̈ܣܐ[t]
ܕܡܢ[i] ܥܠܡܝܢ[u]
‡ f. 45b.
ܒܐܪܟܘܢܬܐ[w]
ܦܪܝܫܝܐ[k]
ܒܐܪܟܘܢܗܘܢ[y]
ܡܦܩ[z] ܡܕܝܢܬܐ[a]
ܒܩܘܪܝܗ[b] ܡܠܦ[d]
ܘܡܐܣܐ[f]
[h] *omit* ܫܠܡ

Codex C.

ܥܒܕܐ[r] ܡܡܠܠ[s]
ܐܘܟܠܘ̈ܣܐ[t]
ܕܡܢ[i] ܥܠܡܝܢ[u]
ܕܝܢ[x] ܡܦܩ[z]
ܘܗܘܐ[c] ܡܠܦ[d]
ܘܡܟܪܙ[e] ܘܡܐܣܐ[f]
ܡܪܥܝܢ[g]
[h] *omit* ܫܠܡ

LXVII.

Matt. XII. 30—37.

Codex B.

ܝܘܡ[a] ܐܚܕܒܫܒܐ ܐܘܢܓܠܝܘܢ ܕܡܬܝ ܡܢ
30 ܡܬܝܐܘܣ[a] :[y] ܐܡܪ ܡܪܢ : ܡܢ ܕܠܝܬ ܗܘ ܥܡܝ
ܠܩܘܒܠܝ[z] ܗܘ : ܘܡܢ ܕܠܐ ܡܟܢܫ[a] ܥܡܝ
31 ܡܒܕܪ[b] ܐܝܬ ܗܘ[c] : ܠܒܕܠ ܟܕܝܢ ܐܢܐ ܐܡܪ
ܠܟܘܢ : ܕܟܠ ܚܛܐ ܘܓܕܘܦ ܡܫܬܒܩ[d] ܠܗܘܢ
ܠܟܠ ܠܒܢܝܢܫܐ[e] : ܓܕܘܦܐ ܕܝܢ ܕܥܠ ܪܘܚܐ
32 ܕܩܘܕܫܐ ܠܐ ܡܫܬܒܩܐ[e] : ܘܡܢ ܕܐܡܪ[f]
ܡܠܐ ܥܠ ܒܪܗ ܕܓܒܪܐ ܡܫܬܒܩ ܠܗ : ܘܡܢ
ܕܐܡܪ[f] ܥܠ ܪܘܚܐ ܕܩܘܕܫܐ ܠܐ[g] ܡܫܬܒܩ
ܠܗ : ܠܐ[h] ܒܗܕܝܢ[i] ܥܠܡܐ ܘܠܐ[k] ܒܗܘ ܕܐܬܐ :[l]
33 ܐܘ ܥܒܕܘ ܐܝܠܢܐ ܛܒܐ ܘܦܐܪܝ[m] ܛܒܝܢ :
ܡܢ ܦܐܪܘܗܝ[p] ܐܝܠܢܐ[q] ܗܘ[r] ܡܬܝܕܥ :
34 ܝܠܕܘܗܝ[s] ܕܐܟܕܢܐ[t] ܗܝܟ ܐܬܘܢ ܡܠܘ[u]
ܕܬܡܠܠܘܢ ܛܒܢ[w] : ܘܐܬܘܢ ܒܝܫܝܢ : ܡܢ
35 ܡܘܬܪܐ[x] [y] ܕܠܒܐ[z] ܦܘܡܐ[a] ܡܡܠܠ : ܒܪܢܫܐ
ܛܒܐ ܡܢ ܣܝܡܬܐ[b] ܛܒܬܐ[c] ܕܠܒܗ[d][d] ܡܦܩ[e]
ܛܒܬܐ ܘܒܪܢܫܐ ܒܝܫܐ[f] ܡܢ ‡ ܣܝܡܬܐ[b] ܒܝܫܬܐ[g]
36 ܕܠܒܗ[h] ܡܦܩ[e] ܒܝܫܬܐ[i] : ܐܡܪ ܐܢܐ ܠܟܘܢ[k]

Codex A.

ܘܦܢܐ[a] ܐܡܪ ܐܡܬ
ܐܬܐܡܪ ܡܢ ܡܬܝܐܘܣ[a]
ܠܩܘܒܠܝ[z] ܡܒܕܪ[b]
ܐܝܬܘܗܝ[c]
ܡܫܬܒܩܘܢ[d]
ܠܟܘܢ[e] ܕܝܐܡܪ[f]
ܕܝܢ[h] ܒܥܠܡܐ[i]
ܘܒܗܘ[k]
[l] *add* ܐܠܐ ܒܕܝܢܐ ܐܝܠܢܐ ܛܒ ܘܦܐܪܘܗܝ ܛܒܝܢ
ܘܦܐܪܘܗܝ[m]
[r] *omit* ܗܘ [p] *add* ܓܝܪ
ܘܠܝܠܕܘܗܝ[s]
ܕܐܟܕܢܐ[t] ܡܠܝܢ[u]
ܛܒܢ[w] ܡܘܬܪܐ[x]
[z] *omit* ܕ [y] *add* ܓܝܪ
ܡܡܠܠ[a] ܣܝܡܬܐ[b]
ܛܒܬܐ[c] ܡܦܩ[e]
‡ f. 46a.
ܕܠܒܗ[h] [k] *add* ܕܝܢ

Codex C.

ܠܝܘܡ[a] ܐܚܕܬ
ܐܬܐܡܪ ܡܢ ܡܬܝ[a]
[y] *add* ܘܐܬܝ ܝܫܘܥ ܡܪܢ
ܡܟܢܫ[a] ܡܒܕܪ[b]
ܡܫܬܒܩܘܢ[d]
† f. 42a.
ܠܟܠ . . . [e] *omit*
. . . ܡܫܬܒܩܘܢ
ܒܗܕܝܢ[h] [g] *add* ܕ
ܒܐܝܢܘܢ[k]
[l] *add* ܐܠܐ ܒܕܝܢܐ ܐܝܠܢܐ ܛܒ ܘܦܐܪܘܗܝ ܛܒܝܢ
ܘܦܐܪܘܗܝ[m] [p] *add* ܓܝܪ
ܐܝܠܢܐ[q] [r] *omit* ܗܘ
ܕܐܟܕܢܐ[t] ܛܒܢ[w]
ܛܒܬܐ[c] [y] *add* ܓܝܪ
[d] ܗܘ ܕܠܒܗ[d]
ܡܦܩ[e] ܒܝܫܬܐ[f]
ܒܝܫܐ[g] [h] *omit* ܕܠܒܗ
ܒܝܫܐ[i] [k] *add* ܕܝܢ

Codex A.

ܕܝ ᵐ*omit* ᵒܣܓܝܐܢ
ᵖܒܝܘܡܗ ᵠܡܠܝܟ

ᵃܐܠܝܫ ܐܬܗܡܬܝܢ
ܡܢ ܡܬܝܬܘܣ ᵃ
ᶻ*add* ܦܫܘ
ᵃܢܦܩ ܚܡܐ ᵃ
ᵇܐܬܪܚܡܐ
ᶜ*omit* ܟܘܠ
ᵈܟܐܢܫܗܘܢ
ܕܝ ᵉ*add* ᶠܪܡܫܐ
ܠܗ ʰ*omit* ⁱܐܬܪܐ
ᵏܚܪܒ ˡܐܘܟܠܘܣܐ
ᵐܠܩܘܪܝܐ ⁿܕܩܪܝܒܝܢ
ᵒܕܝܙܒܢܘܢ
ᵛܡܙܘܢܝܢ
ᵖܕܝܐܙܠܘܢ
ᵠܕܝܐܟܠܘܢ
ʳܚܡܫܐ
ܠܗܘܢ ᵗ*omit* ᵘܠܟܐ
ʷܘܦܩܕ ܝܬܗ ˣ*omit*
ʸܠܐܘܟܠܘܣܐ
ᶻܕܝܣܬܡܟܘܢ
ᵃܚܡܫܬܐ ᵇܢܘܢܝܐ
ᶜܘܐܕܝܩ
ᵉ*omit* ܝܗܒܘ
ᶠܠܐܘܟܠܘܣܐ
‡ f. 46b.
ⁱܚܡܫܬܐ ʲܢܫܝܢ

Codex B.

ܕܟܘܠ ܡܠܟܐ ˡܠܩܠܠܐ ᵐܕܝ ⁿܕܡܡܠܠܝܢ ܒܢܝܢܫܐ :
ܡܛܠܗ ܒܠܝܗ ᵒܣܓܝܢ ᵖܒܝܘܡܐ ܕܕܝܢܐ :
37 ܡܢ ᵠܡܠܝܟ ܓܝܪ ܬܙܕܕܩ ܘܡܢ ᵠܡܠܝܟ ܬܬܚܝܒ :
ʳܥܠܡ ⁘

LXVIII.

Matt. XIV. 14—22.

ᵃܢܦܩ ܐܠܝܫ ܐܬܗܡ ܒܬܪ ܐܠܒܫܝܪܗ ܡܢ
[f. 42a]
14 ܡܬܐܘܣ ᵃ ᶻ ܘܒܫܥܬܗ ܦܪܘܫܐ ܘܟܕ ܢܦܩ ᵃܚܡܐ ܟܢܫܐ
ܣܓܝ ᵃ ᵇܐܬܪܚܡ ܥܠܘܗܝ : ܐܬܐܣܝ ܟܪܝܗܘܢ :
15 ܘܐܡܫ ᶜܟܘܠ ᵈܟܘܢܫܗܘܢ : ܘܟܕ ᵉܗܘܐ ᶠܪܡܫܐ
ܩܪܒܘ ܠܗ ᵍܬܠܡܝܕܘܗܝ ܘܐܡܪܝܢ ʰܠܗ ⁱܐܬܪ
ᵏܚܪܒ ܘܫܥܬܐ ܥܒܪ ܥܒܪܬ : ܦܢܝ ˡܐܘܟܠܘܣܐ
ܕܐܙܠܘܢ ᵐܠܩܘܪܝܐ ⁿܕܩܪܝܒܝܢ ᵒܕܝܙܒܢܘܢ ܠܗܘܢ
16 ᵛܡܙܘܢ : ܡܪܐ ܝܫܘܥ ܕܝ ܐܡܪ ܠܗܘܢ ܠܐ
ܨܪܝܟܝܢ ᵖܕܝܐܙܠܘܢ. ܗܒܘ ܠܗܘܢ ܐܢܬܘܢ
17 ᵠܕܝܐܟܠܘܢ : ܗܢܘܢ ܕܝ ܐܡܪܘ ܠܗ : ܠܝܬ ܠܢ
18 ܗܟܐ ܐܠܐ ʳܚܡܫ ˢܠܚܡ †ܘܬܪܝܢ ܢܘܢܝܢ : ܗܘ ܕܝ
ܐܡܪ ᵗܠܗܘܢ : ܐܝܬܘ ܝܬܗܘܢ ܠܝ ᵘܠܗܟܐ :
19 ʷܘܦܩܕ ˣܝܬܗ ʸܠܐܘܟܠܘܣܐ ᶻܕܝܣܬܡܟܘܢ ܥܠ
ܥܣܒܐ : ܘܢܣܒ ᵃܚܡܫܬܐ ܠܚܡܝܢ ܘܬܪܝܢ
ᵇܢܘܢܝܢ ᶜܘܐܕܝܩ ܠܫܡܝܐ : ᵈܘܒܪܟ ܘܩܨܐ
ܘܝܗܒ ܠܚܡܐ ܠܬܠܡܝܕܘܗܝ ܘܬܠܡܝܕܝܐ ᵉܝܗܒܘ
20 ᶠܠܐܘܟܠܘܣܐ : ܘܐܟܠܘ ܟܠܗܘܢ ܘܣܒܥܘ
ܘܐܪܝܡܘ ܡܘܬܪܢܐ ᵍܕܩܨܝܐ ʰܬܪܬܥܣܪ ܩܠܝܢ
21 ܡܠܝܢ : ܗܠܝܢ ܕܝ ܕܐܟܠܘ ‡ܗܘܘ ܗܟܢ ⁱܚܡܫܐ
22 ܐܠܦܝܢ ܕܓܒܪܝܢ ܠܒܪ ܡܢ ʲܢܫܝܢ ܘܛܠܝܢ : ܘܡܚܐ

Codex C.

ˡܠܩܠܐ ܕܝ ᵐ*omit*
ⁿܠܐ ܡܡܠܠܝܢ ⁿ
ᵒܣܓܝܢ ᵖܒܝܘܡܗ
ʳ*omit* ܥܠܡ

ᵃܠܝܘܡ ܐܠܝܫ
ܐܬܐܡܪ ܡܢ ܡܬܐ ᵃ
ᵃܚܙܐ ܝܫܘܥ ܚܡܐ ᵃ
ᵇܐܬܪܚܡ
ᶜ*omit* ܟܘܠ
ᶜܒܐܢܫܗܘܢ
ܕܝ ᵉ*add* ᵍܬܠܡܝܕܘܗܝ
ܠܗ ʰ*omit* ⁱܐܬܪܐ
ᵏܚܪܒ ˡܐܟܠܘܣܐ
ᵐܠܩܘܪܝܐ ⁿܕܩܪܝܒܝܢ
ᵛܠܡܙܘܢܝܢ
ᵖܕܝܐܙܠܘܢ
ᵠܕܝܐܟܠܘܢ
† f. 42b.
ʳܚܡܫܐ ˢܠܚܡ
ܠܗܘܢ ᵗ*omit* ᵘܠܟܐ
ʷܘܦܩܕ ܝܬܗ ˣ*omit*
ʸܠܐܟܠܘܣܐ
ᶻܕܝܣܬܡܟܘܢ
ᵇܢܘܢܐ ᵈܘܒܪܟ
ᵉ*omit* ܝܗܒܘ
ᶠܠܐܘܟܠܘܣܐ
ᵍܕܩܨܝܐ ʰܬܪܬܥܣܪ
ⁱܚܡܫܐ ʲܢܫܝܢ

Codex A.	Codex B.	Codex C.
ˡܠܬܠܡܝܕܝܐ ᵐܕܝܫܘܥ ⁿܠܐܟܠܘܣܝܐ ᵒadd ܥܠܡ	ᵏܐܝܬܗ ˡܠܬܠܡܝܕܘܝ ᵐܕܝܫܘܥ ܠܐܠܗܐ : ܘܡܫܒܚܝܢ ܝܬܗ ܠܐܒܘܢܐ ܕܒܫܡܝܐ ܕܝܗܒܐ ⁿܠܐܟ̈ܠܘܣܝܐ ᵒ ⁘	ᵏܐܝܬܗ ⁿܠܐܟ̈ܠܘܣܝܐ

LXIX.

Matt. XV. 32—39.

Codex A.	Codex B.	Codex C.
ᵃܝܘܡ ܐܪܒܥܬ ܐܬܐܡܫ ܡܢ ܡܬܝܘܣ ᵃ ˣ add ܝܫܘܥ ᵃܬܠܡܝܕܘܗܝ ᶜomit ܕܝܢ ᵇܐܬܪܚܡ ᵈܐܘܟ̈ܠܘܣܐ ᵉܠܝ ᶠܕܝܐܟܠܘܢ ᵍܐܝܟܢ ʰܢܫܒܘܩ ᵏܠܚܡ ⁱadd ܡܢ ˡadd ܗܟܝܢ ᵐܐܘܟܠܘܣ ⁿܕܗܘܝܢ ᵇܫܒܥܐ ᵃadd ܕܝܢ ᶜomit ܠܚܡ ᵈܘܢܘܢܝܢ ᵉܠܐܘܟ̈ܠܘܣܐ ᵖܕܢܬܒܥܘܢ ᵠܘܗܘܐ ʳܠܐܟ̈ܠܘܣܝܐ ˢܟܠܗܘܢ ᵛܢܬܥܘܢ ‡ f. 47a. ʷܠܐܘܟ̈ܠܘܣܝܐ ˣܠܬܚܘܡܝܐ	ᵃܝܘܡ ܐܪܒܥܬ ܐܬܐܡܫ ܒܒܪ ܐܘܢܓܠܝܘܢ ܡܢ 32 ܡܬܐܝ ᵃ: ˣ ܘܒܬܪܗ ʸܡܪܘܫܐ : ܗܘ ܕܝܢ ܩܪܐ ܝܫܘܥ ᶻܩܪܐ ܠܬܠܡܝܕܘܬܐ ᵃܬܠܡܝܕܘܝ : ܘܐܡܪ ܠܗܘܢ ᵇܐܬܪܚܡ ܐܢܐ ᶜܕܝܢ ܥܠ ܗܕܝܢ ᵈܐܘܟ̈ܠܘܣܝܐ ܕܗܐ ܟܒܪ ܬܠܬܐ ܝܘܡܝܢ ܗܢܘܢ ܡܬܥܪܝܢ ᵉܥܡܝ ܘܠܝܬ ܠܗܘܢ ܡܗ ܐܝܟܘܠ ᶠܕܝܐܟܠܘܢ : [f. 42b] ܘܕܫܒܩ ܝܬܗܘܢ ᵍܐܝܟܢ ܠܝܬ ܐܢܐ ܒܥܐ 33 ܕܠܐ ܐܡܬܢܝ ʰܢܦܠܘܢ ܒܐܘܪܚܐ : ܘܐܡܪܝܢ ܠܗ ܬܠܡܝܕܝܐ ⁱܡܢ ܐܢ ܠܢ ܒܡܕܒܪܐ ᵏܠܚܡ 34 ܟܘܠ ܟܕܝܢ ˡܕܢܣܒܥ ᵐܐܟ̈ܠܘܣ ⁿܗܕܝܢ : ܘܐܡܪ ܠܗܘܢ ܡܢܐ ܐܝܬ ܠܟܘܢ ᵒܠܚܡ ܒܟܝܢ : ܗܢܘܢ ᵃܐܡܪܘ ᵇܫܒܥܐ ᶜܠܚܡ ᵈܘܢܘܢܝܢ 35 ܩܠܝܠ : ܘܦܩܕ ᵉܠܐܟ̈ܠܘܣܝܐ ᵖܕܝܬܒܘܢ ܥܠ 36 ܐܪܥܐ : ܘܢܣܒ ܫܒܥܬܐ ܠܚܡܐ ܘܢܘܢܝܐ : ܘܐܘܕܝ ܘܩܨܐ † ᵠܘܗܘ ܝܗܒ ܠܬܠܡܝܕܝܐ 37 ܘܬܠܡܝܕܝܐ ʳܠܐܟ̈ܠܘܣܝܐ : ܘܐܟ̈ܠܘ ܟܘܠܗܘܢ ܘܣܒܥܘ : ܘܡܘܬܪܢܐ ܕܝܢ ܕܦܨܝܐ ܐܪܝܡܘ 38 ᵇܫܒܥܐ ܩܘܦܝܢ ˢܡܠܝܢ : ܗܠܝܢ ܕܝܢ ᵗܐܟ̈ܠܘ ‡ ܗܘܘ ܗܟܝܢ ܐܪܒܥܐ ܐܠܦܝܢ ᵘܕܓܒܪܝܢ ܠܒܪ 39 ܡܢ ᵛܢܫܝܢ ܘܛܠܝܢ : ܘܟܕ ܫܪܐ ʷܠܐܟ̈ܠܘܣܝܐ : ܣܠܩ ܠܐܠܦܐ ܘܐܬܐ ˣܠܬܚܘܡܐ ܕܡܓܕܢ ⁘	ᵃܠܝܘܡ ܐܪܒܥܬ ᵃܐܬܐܡܫ ܡܢ ܡܬܐܝ ʸomit ܡܪܘܫܐ ᶻܩܪܐ ᵃܬܠܡܝܕܘܝ ᶜomit ܕܝܢ ᵇܐܬܪܚܡ ᵈܐܘܟܠܘܣܐ ᵉomit ܥܡܝ ᶠܕܝܐܟܠܘܢ ⁱadd ܡܢ ʰܢܫܠܘܢ ˡadd ܗܟܝܢ ᵐܐܟ̈ܠܘܣ ᵒܠܚܡ ᵘܕܗܘܝܢ ᵇܫܒܥܐ ᵃadd ܕܝܢ ᶜomit ܠܚܡ † f. 43a. ᵈܘܢܘܢܝܢ ᵉܠܐܘܟ̈ܠܘܣܐ ᵠܘܗܘܐ ʳܠܐܟܠܘܣܐ ᵗadd ܕܝܢ ˢܡܠܝܢ ᵘܕܓܒܪ ˣܠܬܚܘܡܝܐ

Codex A.	Codex B.	Codex C.
	LXX.	
	MATT. XIV. 22—34.	
[a]ܣܘܥܪܐ ܐܠܨ̇ ܐܬܐܘܣܒ ܡܢ ܒܬܐܘܣ[a]	[a]ܐܠܨ̇ ܐܬܐܘܣܒ ܡܢ ܒܬܪ ܐܠܒܝܢܗ ܡܢ	[a]ܠܝܘܡ ܐܠܨ̇
[a] add ܡܬܥܪܘܒ ܝܬܡ ܘܒܝܘܬܐ	22 ܒܬܐܘܣ[a a] ܘܩܕܡܐ[b] ܐܢܘܢ[c] ܡܪܐ ܝܫܘܥ	[a]ܐܬܐܘܣܒ ܡܢ ܒܬܐ
[c] omit ܡܪܐ	[d]ܠܬܠܡܝܕܝܐ [o]ܕܝܫܘܥ ܠܐܠܦܐ : ܘܡܕܒܪܘܢ	[a]add ܘܒܝܬܡ ܡܬܥܪܒܘܢܐ
[o]ܕܝܒܩܘܢ	ܠܗܘܢ ܠܥܒܪܐ ܕܝܡܐ ܕܝܢܐ [e]ܠܘܬܗ	[c]omit ܡܪܐ [b]ܝܫܘܥ
[e] omit ܠܘܬܗ	23 [f]ܠܐܘ̈ܟܠܘܣܝܐ [g]ܘܒܬܪ ܗܘܐ [h]ܪܡܫܐ ܗܘ	[d]ܠܬܠܡܝܕܘܗܝ
[f]ܠܐܘܟ̈ܠܘܣܝܐ	24 [i]ܠܒܘܕܗ ܗܘܐ ܬܡܢ : ܐܠܦܐ ܕܝܢ ܒܒܪ ܗܘܬ	[e] omit ܠܘܬܗ
[g] add ܘܣܠܩ ܠܛܘܪܐ ܠܡܨܠܝܘ	[j]ܪܚܝܩܐ ܡܢ ܐܪܥܐ ܐܣܛܕܝܢ ܣܓܝ : [k]ܡܬܢܚܬܐ	[i]ܠܒܘܕܝ [k]ܡܬܢܚܬܐ
[h]ܪܡܫܐ [i]ܠܒܘܕܝ	ܕܝܡܐ ܡܢ ܓܠܠܝܐ : ܗܘܐ ܓܝܪ	[m]ܡܩܒܠܬܐ
[j]ܪܚܝܩܐ [k]ܡܬܢܚܬܐ	25 ܪܘܚܐ ܘܐܝܟ [l]ܠܡܛܠܝܢܘܢ : [m]ܡܩܒܠܬܐ	[n]ܕܝܢ [o]ܪܒܝܥܝܬܐ
[l]ܠܡܛܠܝܢܘܢ	[n]ܕܝܢ [o]ܪܒܝܥܝܬܐ ܕܠܝܠܝܐ : ܐܬܐ ܠܘܬܗܘܢ	[q] add ܥܠ ܝܡܐ
[m]ܡܩܒܠܬܐ	26 ܡܪܐ ܝܫܘܥ [p]ܡܗܠܟ [q]ܥܠ ܝܡܐ : ܐܬܚܙܝܘ	ܘܬܠܡܝܕܘܗܝ ܟܕ ܚܙܘ ܠܘܬܗ ܡܗܠܟ
[o]ܕܝܒܥܝܬܐ [p]ܡܗܠܟ	[f. 43a]	[r]ܐܬܡܪܘ [s]ܕܚܙܘܢܐ
[q] add ܥܠ ܝܡܐ	[r]ܐܬܡܪܘ [s]ܕܚܙܘܢܐ ܗܘ : ܘܡܢ ܕܚܠܬܐ [t]ܐܬܝܥܘ :	[t]ܐܬܝܥܘ [v]ܘܐܡܪ
ܘܬܠܡܝܕܘܗܝ ܟܕ ܚܙܘ ܠܘܬܗ ܡܗܠܟ	27 ܘܥܠܘ [u]ܡܠܠ ܠܗܘܢ ܡܪܐ ܝܫܘܥ [v]ܐܡܪ :	[y]ܬܩܪܘܣ [x] add ܕܝܢ
[u]ܡܠܠ [w]ܬܕܚܠܘܢ	28 ܐܬܒܝܠܘ ܐܢܐ ܗܘ ܠܐ [w]ܬܕܚܠܘܢ : ܐܠܝܒ[x]	[a]ܕܐܬܝ
[z]ܓܢܝ [a]ܕܐܬܝ	[y]ܬܩܪܘܣ ܘܐܡܪ ܠܗ : ܡܪܐ ܐܢ ܐܢܬ ܗܘ	[b] add ܡܗܠܟ
[b] add ܡܗܠܟ	29 [z]ܦܩܘܕ ܠܝ [a]ܕܐܬܝ ܠܘܬܟ [b]ܥܠ ܡܝܐ : ܗܘ	† f. 43b.
[c] add ܠܗ [d]ܐܬܝ	ܕܝܢ [c]ܐܡܪ [d]ܐܬܝ : †ܘܢܚܬ [y]ܬܩܪܘܣ ܡܢ ܐܠܦܐ	[c] add ܠܗ [d]ܐܬܝ
‡ f. 47b.	[o]ܘܗܠܟ ܥܠ [p]ܡܝܐ : ܕܢܐܬܐ ܠܘܬ ܡܪܐ	[e] add ܕܝܢ [p]ܡܝܐ
[o]ܘܗܠܟ [p]ܡܝܐ	30 ܝܫܘܥ : [e]ܚܙܐ ܪܘܚܐ ܚܝܠܐ [f]ܘܕܚܠ ‡ ܘܫܪܝ	[h] omit ܕܝܢ
[e] add ܕܝܢ [f]ܘܕܚܠ	[g]ܕܢܛܒܥ : ܘܐܓܥܐ [h]ܕܝܢ ܘܐܡܪ ܡܪܝ ܐܚܝܢܝ	[j]ܡܪܐ ܝܫܘܥ ܐܝܕܗ[j]
[h] omit ܕܝܢ [g]ܕܢܛܒܥ	31 ܠܘܬܝ : ܘܥܠܘ [i]ܕܝܢ ܦܫܛ[i] ܐܝܕܗ[j] ܡܪܐ ܝܫܘܥ[j]	[k]ܙܥܘܪܝ
[i]ܕܦܫܛ	ܘܐܚܕܗ ܘܐܡܪ ܠܗ [k]ܙܥܘܪܝ ܗܝܡܢܘܬܐ ܠܡܢܐ	[l] omit ܒܕ
[j]ܡܪܐ ܝܫܘܥ ܐܝܕܗ[j]	32 [h]ܕܝܢ ܐܬܦܠܓܬ : ܘ[l]ܒܕ ܣܠܩܘ ܠܐܠܦܐ ܫܠܐ	[n] add ܘ [m] omit ܘ
[k]ܙܥܘܪܝ	33 ܪܘܚܐ : ܗܠܝܢ ܐܝܟ ܕܗܘܘ [h]ܕܝܢ ܒܐܠܦܐ	[o]ܡܫܬܓܕܝܢ
[n] add ܘ [m] omit ܘ	ܩܪܒܘ [h]ܕܝܢ [m]ܘܣܓܕܘ ܠܗ [n]ܐܡܪܝܢ [o]ܡܫܬܓܕܝܢ	
[p]ܕܓܢܣܪ	34 ܐܢܬ ܗܘ ܒܪܗ ܕܐܠܗܐ : ܘܒܕ ܥܒܪܘ ܐܬܘ ܥܠ	
[q] add ܝܡܐ	ܐܪܥܐ [p]ܕܓܢܣܪ[q] ∴	

Codex A. | *Codex* B. | *Codex* C.

LXXI.

Matt. XVII. 24—XVIII. 4.

Codex B.

24 [c][a] ܘܟܕ ܥܠ ܐܝܫܘܥ ܠܟܦܪܢܚܘܡ ܡܢ [b] ܬܠܡܝܕܘܗܝ [c]: [y] [z] ܘܒܬܪ
ܕܝ ܐܬܘ ܦܛܪܘܤ [a] ܠܗܘܢ ܕܢܤܒܝܢ ܕܝܢܪܐ ܘܐܡܪܘ
[b] ܠܦܛܪܘܤ [c] ܡܠܦܢܟܘܢ ܠܐ ܝܗܒ ܐܝܢܐ [d] ܕܝܢܪܐ
25 [e] ܐܡܪ ܐܝܢ: ܟܕ [f] ܕܝ [g] ܥܠ ܠܒܝܬܐ [h] ܩܕܡܝܗ [i] ܝܫܘܥ
ܘܐܡܪ ܫܡܥܘܢ ܘܐܡܪ: ܡܐ ܗܘܐ ܠܟ [j] ܦܛܪܘܤ:
ܡܠܟܝܐ ܕܐܪܥܐ ܡܢ ܡܢ ܢܤܒܝܢ ܡܟܤܐ [k] ܡܢ
26 ܒܢܝܗܘܢ ܐܘ ܡܢ [l] ܢܘܟܪܝܐ: ܗܘ ܕܝ ܐܡܪ
ܡܢ ܢܘܟܪܝܐ: ܟܕ ܕܝ ܐܡܪ ܠܗ ܡܪܢ ܫܡܥܘܢ
ܗܟܐ ܐܘܢ [m] ܒܢܝܐ ܚܪܝܢ ܐܢܘܢ ܒܢܝܐ:
27 [n] ܠܡܠܠ ܕܝ ܕܠܐ ܢܟܫܠ ܐܢܘܢ [o] ܐܙܠ
[f. 43b]
ܠܝܡܐ ܘܪܡܝ [p] ܚܟܬܐ [q] ܘܢܘܢܐ ܩܕܡܝܐ
ܕܤܠܩ ܤܒ [r] ܘܦܬܚ ܦܘܡܗ ܘܐܬ [s] ܡܫܟܚ
[t] ܐܤܛܛܪ ܬܡܢ [u] ܤܒ ܘܗܒ ܠܗܘܢ [v] ܚܠܦܝ
XVIII. 1 [w] ܘܚܠܦܟ: ܒܗ [x] ܒܫܥܬܐ [y] ܩܪܒܘ ܬܠܡܝܕܐ
ܬܠܡܝܕܝܐ [‡] ܠܘܬ ܝܫܘܥ ܐܡܪܝܢ: ܡܢ ܐܪܐ
2 ܪܒ ܒܡܠܟܘܬܐ [†] ܕܫܡܝܐ: ܘܩܪܐ ܡܪܐ
ܝܫܘܥ ܠܛܠܝܐ [z] ܘܐܩܝܡ ܝܬܗ [a] ܒܡܨܥܬܗܘܢ:
3 ܘܐܡܪ ܐܡܝܢ ܐܡܪ ܐܢܐ ܠܟܘܢ: [b] ܕܐܢ
ܠܐ ܬܬܘܒܘܢ ܘܬܗܘܘܢ ܗܝܟ [c] ܕܛܠܝܐ ܠܐ
4 [d] ܬܥܠܘܢ [e] ܠܡܠܟܘܬܐ ܕܫܡܝܐ: ܟܠ [f] ܡܢ
ܕܡܟܝܟ ܢܦܫܗ ܗܝܟ ܗܕܝܢ [g] ܛܠܝܐ [h] ܗܕܝܢ
[i] ܐܝܬܘܗܝ [k] ܪܒ [l] ܒܡܠܟܘܬܐ ܕܫܡܝܐ ܀

Codex A.

[c] ܘܩܪܝܐ ܐܘܢܓܠܝܘܢ ܐܠܟܣܢܕܪܝܢ ܡܢ ܡܬܝܐ (sic)
[y] *add* ܪܒܢ ܘܒܢܝܬܗ ܡܢܪܘܤܐ
[z] *omit* ܘ [b] ܠܩܤܛܪܝܢ
[c] ܡܠܦܢܟܘܢ [d] ܕܙܘܙܐ
[e] ܐܡܪ ܐܝܢ [e]
[f] *omit* ܕܝ
[g] ܥܠ [i] ܩܕܡܝܗ
[k] *add* ܐܘ ܡܢܤܒܢ
[l] ܢܘܟܪܝܐ [m] ܒܢܝܐ
[n] ܠܡܠܠ [o] ܐܙܠ
[p] ܚܟܬܐ
[q] ܘܢܘܢܐ [r] ܘܦܬܚ
[s] ܡܫܟܚ [t] ܐܤܛܛܪ
[u] *omit* ܤܒ
‡ f. 48*a*.
[v] ܚܠܦܝ
[w] ܘܚܠܦܟ
[x] ܒܗܘ [c] *omit* ܕ
[d] ܬܥܠܘܢ
[f] ܡܢ ܐܘ [f]
[h] ܗܕܝܢ [i] ܐܝܬ ܗܘ [i]
[k] ܪܒ

Codex C.

[a] ܠܟܦܪ [b] ܡܬܐ
[y] *add* ܘܒܢܝܬܗ ܡܢܪܘܤܐ
ܠܗ *add* [a] [b] ܠܦܛܪܘܤ
ܕܝ *omit* [f] [g] ܥܠ
[h] ܒܝܬܗ [i] ܩܕܡܝܗ
[j] ܦܛܪܘܤ
[k] *add* ܐܘ ܡܢܤܒܢ
[l] ܢܘܟܪܝܐ
[r] ܘܦܬܚ [s] ܡܫܟܚ
[t] ܐܤܛܛܪ
[v] ܚܠܦܝ
[y] ܩܪܒܘ
[z] ܘܐܡܪܝܢ (sic)
† f. 44*a*.
[a] ܠܡܨܥܬܗܘܢ
[b] ܕܐܢ [c] *omit* ܕ
[e] ܠܡܠܟܘܬܗ
[f] *add* ܐܘ
[g] ܛܠܝܐ [i] ܐܝܬ
[l] *add* ܕܝ

Codex A. | *Codex* C. | *Codex* B.

LXXII.

Matt. XVII. 14—23.

Codex C.

[a] ܠܟܦܪ ܐܠܝܫܥ ܐܠܟܤܢܕܪܝܢ ܡܢ ܡܬܐ [a] ܘܒܢܝܬܗ
14 ܡܢܪܘܤܐ: ܘܟܕ [a] ܐܬܐ [β a] ܡܪܢ ܝܫܘܥ [b γ]

Codex A.

[CCCLXVIII.]

[a] ܘܩܪܝܐ ܐܠܝܫܥ ܐܠܟܤܢܕܪܝܢ ܡܢ
[a] ܡܬܝܘܤ [ܘܐܬܐ[a]]
[a β] *omit* ܡܪܢ ܝܫܘܥ
[b γ] *add* ܠܘܬ

Codex B.

(*deest*)

Codex A.	Codex C.	Codex B.
[c]ܐܦ̈ܩܠܘܣܝܐ	[cρ]ܐܦ̈ܩܠܘܣܝܐ : ܡܢܟܘܢ ܠܗ ܚܕ ܒܪܢܫ ܡܕܡ ܚܠ	(deest)
[ܐܦ̈ܩܠܘܣܝܐ[ρ]]	15 ܐܪܡܠܬܗ : ܘܐܡܪ ܡܪܝ : ܐܬܚܙܝ [dδ]ܚܠܘܢ	
[dδ]ܚܠ [eζ]ܚܒܪܬ	ܚܙܘ ܕܡܗ ܡܬܚܙܝܐ ܡܢ [eζ]ܚܒܪܬ [fη]ܘܐܬܚܝܪ	
[fη]ܘܐܬܚܝܪ [gθ]ܘܡܥܒܕܝܐܬ	[gθ]ܘܡܥܒܕܝܐܬ ܗܘ [iλ]ܢܣܒܝ : [k]ܘܗܟܢ ܐܚܝܡ ܠܟ	
[iλ]ܢܣܒܝ [k]add ܘ	16 ܗܘ ܢܗܠ ܠܚܡܪܐ : ܘܗܟܢ ܐܚܝܡ ܠܡܥܒܕ :	
[iμ]ܠܬܠܡܝܕܘܗܝ	ܘܩܪܒܬ ܬܘܗ ܠܬܠܡܝܕܘܗܝ[iμ] ܘܠܐ [m]ܡܩܠܐ ܕܐܡܗܘܢ	
[f. 191a]		
[m]ܡܩܠ [ܡܩܠܐ]	17 ܢܘܗ : ܚܡܢ [nν]ܐܝܟ ܡܪܐ ܫܡܥܘ ܐܚܪܢ : ܐܘ	
[nν]ܐܝܟܢ [[ξ]ܗܕܡܐ]	ܕܪܐ [ξ]ܗܕܡܐ ܕܠܐ ܡܗܝܡܢܐ [oς]ܘܡܗܦܟܝܢ : ܥܕ [pπ]ܡܬܝ ܐܝܬܝ	
[oς]ܘܡܗܦܟܢ [ܗܘܐ[ρ]]	ܐܝܟ [ρ]ܗܘܐ ܥܡܟܘܢ ܥܕ [pπ]ܡܬܝ [q]ܥܕ ܕܐܣܝܒܪ[σ]	
[pπ]ܡܬܝ [p]ܐܝܬܝ	18 ܥܡܟܘܢ : ܐܝܬܘ ܢܘܗ ܠܝ ܠܗܟܐ : ܘܟܐܒ ܗܘ	
[q]omit ܥܕ [ܕܐܣܝܒܪ[σ]]	ܡܪܐ ܫܡܥܘ ܘܢܦܩ ܡܢܗ [rτ]ܫܐܕܐ : ܘܐܬܐܣܝ	
[rτ]ܫܐܕܐ [[φ]ܡܢ]	19 ܛܠܝܐ ܡܢ ܗܝ ܫܥܬܐ : [φ]ܚܡܢ ܡܢܗ [‡] [sχ]ܬܠܡܝܕܘܗܝ	
‡ f. 48b.		
[sχ]ܬܠܡܝܕܘܗܝ	ܠܡܪܐ ܫܡܥܘ ܚܒܝܫܝܢ ܠܚܘܕܝܗܘܢ : [tψ]ܘܐܡܪܝܢ ܠܗ ܠܡܢܐ	
[tψ]ܘܐܡܪܝܢ [uω]ܢܟܠܝܗ	20 ܠܐ ܐܬܟܠܢ [uω]ܢܟܠܝܗ [va]ܕܢܦܩ ܢܘܗ : ܗܘ [wβ]ܕܐܡܪ ܐܡܪ	
[va]ܕܢܦܩ [wβ]ܕܐܡܪ	ܠܗܘܢ [xγ]ܠܓܠܠ [yδ]ܕܠܐ ܗܝܡܢܘܬܟܘܢ : ܐܡܝܢ	
[xγ]ܠܓܠܠ [yδ]ܕܠܐ ܗܝܡܢܘܬ	ܐܢܐ ܐܡܪ ܐܢܐ ܠܟܘܢ [zε]ܕܐܝܢ ܐܝܬ ܒܟܘܢ	
[zε]ܕܐܝܢ [aη]ܕܚܪܕܠ	ܗܝܡܢܘ ܗܟܢ ܟܦܪܐ [aη]ܕܚܪܕܠ [bθ]ܬܐܡܪܘܢ [cι]ܠܛܘܪܐ	
[f. 44b]		
[b]ܬܐܡܪܘܢ	ܦܫܘܛ ܡܢ ܗܪܟܐ ܠܬܡܢ : ܘܢܦܫܛ	
[ܬܐܡܪܘܢ[θ]]	22 ܠܐ ܢܫܬܐܠ ܡܢܟܘܢ : ܡܗܠܟܝܢ ܕܝܢ ܒܓܠܝܠܐ	
[cι]ܠܛܘܪܐ	[η]ܒܓܠܝܠܐ ܐܡܪ ܠܗܘܢ ܡܪܐ ܫܡܥܘ ܥܬܝܕ ܗܘ	
[[η]ܕܓܠܝܠܐ]	ܒܪܗ ܕܐܢܫܐ [dζ]ܕܢܫܬܠܡ [eθ]ܠܐܝܕܝ [fκ]ܕܒܢܝܢܫܐ	
[[dζ]ܕܢܫܬܠܡ]	23 [gλ]ܘܢܩܛܠܘܢܗ ܘܠܬܠܬܐ ܝܘܡܝܢ ܢܩܘܡ ܘܐܬܟܪܝܘ ܛܒ ܐ	
[eθ]ܠܐܝܕܝ [fκ]ܕܒܢܝܢܫܐ		
[gλ]ܘܢܩܛܠܘܢܗ		

Codex A.	Codex B.	Codex C.
	LXXIII.	
	MATT. XIX. 3—12.	
[a]ܘܩܪܒܘ ܠܘܬܗ ܦܪܝܫܐ	[a]ܘܩܪܒܘ ܠܘܬܗ ܦܪܝܫܐ ܕܢܢܣܘܢܗ ܘܐܡܪܝܢ ܠܗ	[a]ܘܩܪܒܘ ܠܘܬܗ ܦܪܝܫܐ
[a]ܘܐܡܪܝܢ ܠܗ ܐܢ ܫܠܝܛ	3 ܕܢܣܝܘܢܗ : [a]ܘܐܡܪܝܢ : ܕܐܢ ܫܠܝܛ : [a]ܐܡܪ ܘܐܡܪܘ	[a]ܘܐܡܪܝܢ ܠܗ
[a]omit ܐܡܪܝܢ	ܠܗ [b]ܦܪܝܫܐ ܡܢܗܘܢ ܢܘܗ [c]ܐܡܪܝܢ : [d]ܐܢ	[a]omit ܐܡܪܝܢ
[c]add ܘ [b]ܦܪܝܫܐ		[c]add ܘ [d]ܐܢ

Codex A.

[g]ܕܗܘܐܘ [h]add ܕ
[k]ܒܪܐ
[l]ܠܐܒܘܗܝ
[m]ܘܠܐܡܗ
[n]ܡܦܪܫ
[o]ܐܓܪܬ [p]ܫܘܒܩܝܢ
‡ f. 49a.
[r]ܠܡܫܒܩ [s]ܫܒܩ
[t]ܢܫܝܟܘܢ
[u]ܒܝ [w]add ܕܝ
[y]ܕܙܢܘ [z]ܕܡܓܘܪ
[a]ܕܡܫܬܒܩܐ
[b]ܕܢܣܒܐ
[c]ܐܡܪܘ ܗܘ[c]
[e]ܬܠܡܝܕܘܝ
[g]ܒܝ [h]ܐܝܬ ܗܘܝ[h]
[i]ܕܡܢ [l]omit ܐܢ
[m]add ܕ
[p]ܕܐܡܗܬܗܘܢ
[r]omit ܕܝ
[s]ܒܢܝܢܫܐ [t]ܒܠܠ
[u]ܕܝܟܠ
[v]ܕܡܣܒܠ [w]ܡܣܒܠ

[a]ܘܡܬܠܐ ܐܡܪ ܡܪܢ
[a]ܐܡܪ ܒܪܐ ܡܢ ܡܬܠܐ
[x]ܐܬܕܡܬ

Codex B.

[e]ܥܐܠܝܢ ܠܡܠܟܘ [f]ܕܫܡܝܐ ܐܬܬܗ ܒܠ ܟܘܠ ܟܠܐ :
4 ܗܘ ܕܝ ܐܡܟܝܟ ܘܐܡܪ ܠܗܘܢ : ܠܐ ܬܕܚܠܘܢ
[g]ܕܗܘ [h]ܒܪܐ ܡܢ ܙܥܪ ܕܒܪ ܘܢܣܒܐ ܒܒܪ
5 ܬܗܘܘܢ ܘܐܡܪ : [i]ܒܠܠ ܗܕܐ ܡܣܒܬ [k]ܒܪ
[l]ܠܐܒܘܗ [m]ܘܠܐܡܗ ܘܝܕܒܩ ܠܐܬܬܗ ܘܝܗܘܢ
6 ܬܪܝܗܘܢ ܠܚܕ ܒܣܪ : ܗܘܐ ܐܘܢ ܡܢ ܒܬܪ
ܠܝܬ ܗܘܢ ܬܪܝܢ ܐܠܐ ܚܕ ܒܣܪ : ܡܐ ܐܘܢ
ܕܐܠܗܐ ܙܘܓ ܒܪܢܫ ܠܐ ܝܗܐ [n]ܡܦܪܫ.
7 ܐܡܪܝܢ ܠܗ : ܘܡܢܐ ܐܘܢ ܡܘܫܐ ܦܩܕ ܕܝܬܠ
8 [o]ܐܓܪܬ ‡ [p]ܫܘܒܩܝܢ [q]ܘܠܡܫܪܐ : ܐܡܪ ܠܗܘܢ
ܕܡܘܫܐ [r]ܠܩܒܠ ܩܫܝܘܬ ܠܒܟܘܢ [s]ܫܒܩ
ܠܟܘܢ ܠܡܫܪܐ [t]ܢܫܝܟܘܢ : ܡܢ ܫܪܝ ܕܝ
9 [u]ܒܝܢ ܠܐ ܗܘܐ : ܐܡܪ ܐܢܐ ܠܟܘܢ [w] ܕܟܠ
ܡܢ [x]ܕܡܫܪܐ ܐܬܬܗ ܠܒܪ ܡܢ ܡܠܐ [y]ܕܙܢܘ [f. 44a]
ܘܢܣܒ ܐܚܪܢ ܚܒܪ ܗܘ ܠܗ [z]ܕܡܓܘܪ : ܘܗܘ
[a]ܕܡܫܬܒܩܐ ܠܗ [b]ܕܢܣܒܐ ܡܢ ܒܪ ܓܒܪܗ ܓܒܪ
10 [c]ܐܡܪܘܢ : ܐܡܪܝܢ ܠܗ [d]ܕܝ [e]ܬܠܡܝܕܘܝ : [f]ܐܢ
[g]ܒܝܢ [h]ܐܝܬܘܝ ܥܠܬܐ [i]ܕܡܢ ܒܪܐ ܠܐܬܬܐ
11 † [j]ܠܐ [k]ܛܒ [l]ܐܢ [m]ܡܫܬܒܩ ܐܚܕ : ܗܘ ܕܝ
ܐܡܪ ܠܗܘܢ : ܠܐ ܟܘܠܐ ܡܣܬܝܒܪܝܢ ܡܠܬܐ
ܐܠܐ ܗܠܝܢ ܕܝܗܒ ܠܗܘܢ : ܐܝܬ ܓܝܪ ܡܗܝܡܢܝܢ
12 ܗܠܝܢ [o]ܕܡܢ ܟܪܣܗ [p]ܕܐܡܗܘܢ ܐܬܝܠܕܘ [g]ܒܕܡ
ܡܗܝܡܢܝܢ : [q]ܘܐܝܬ ܡܗܝܡܢܝܢ ܕܐܬܡܗܝܡܢܘ [r]ܕܝ ܡܢ
[s]ܒܢܝܢܫܐ : ܘܐܝܬ ܡܗܝܡܢܝܢ ܗܠܝܢ ܕܡܗܝܡܢܘ
ܓܪܡܗܘܢ [t]ܒܠܠ ܡܠܟܘܬܐ ܕܫܡܝܐ : ܡܢ
[u]ܝܟܠ [v]ܕܡܣܒܠ [w]ܡܣܒܠ ⁘

LXXIV.

Matt. XVIII. 23—35.

[a]ܢܘܡ ܐܠܝܐ ܐܠܝܐܒܒܪ ܒܒܪ ܐܠܒܝܪܗ ܡܢ
23 ܡܬܐܝ[a]: [w]ܐܡܪ ܡܪܐ ܗܕܐ ܡܬܠܐ : [x]ܐܬܕܡܬ

Codex C.

[e]ܥܐܠܝܢ [f]ܕܫܡܝܐ
[h]add ܕ [i]ܒܠܠ
[k]ܒܪܐ [l]ܠܐܒܘܗܝ
[o]ܐܓܪܬ [p]ܫܘܒܩܝܢ
[q]ܘܠܡܫܪܐ [s]ܫܒܩ
[u]ܒܝܢ [t]ܢܫܝܟܘܢ
[w]add ܕܝ
[x]ܕܡܫܪܐ [z]ܕܡܓܘܪ
[a]ܕܡܫܬܒܩܐ
[b]ܕܢܣܒܐ
[d]omit ܕܝ [f]omit ܐܢ
[g]ܒܝܢ [i]ܕܡܢ
[j]omit ܠܐ [k]ܛܒ
† f. 45a.
[l]omit ܐܢ [m]add ܕ
[o]omit ܕ
[p]ܕܐܡܗܬܗܘܢ
[q]ܘܐܝܬ [r]omit ܕܝ
[u]ܕܝܟܠ

[a]ܗܘ ܡܬܠܐ ܐܡܪ ܡܪܢ
ܒܪܐ ܡܢ ܡܬܠܐ[a]
[w]add ܗܕܐ
[x]ܐܬܕܡܬ

Codex A.

ᵞܡܠܟܘܬܐ ᶻܡܠܟ
ᵃܫܘܪܝܗ ᶜܚܫܒܢܘܢ
‡ f. 49b.
ᵈܚܝܒܝ ᵉadd ܫܢܝܢ
ᶠadd ܐܦܪܫܢ
ᵍomit ܘܠܡ ʰܦܩܕ
ʲܘܒܢܘܗܝ ᵏܥܒܕܐ
ˡadd ܗܘܐ ᵐܐܘܪܟ
ⁿܥܠܐܝ ᵒadd ܕܝܢ
ᵖܥܠܘܝ ᑫܘܐܘܦ
ʳܐܫܟܚ ˢܡܐܐ
ᵘܟܢܘܬܗ ʷܘܗܘܐ
ˣܐܘܪܟ ʸܥܠܐܝ
ᶻomit ܕܝܢ
ᵇܐܙܠ ᶜܒܦܠܩܘܬܐ
ᵒܕܢܫܠܡ ᵖomit ܠܗ
ᵈadd ܕ ᶠܐܬܟܪܝܘ
ᵍܠܡܪܗܘܢ ʰܟܕܢ
ᵏadd ܐܘܦ
ˡadd ܗܐ
ᵐܡܛܠ ⁿܬܬܪܚܡ
ᵒܟܢܘܬܟ ʳܥܠܘܝ
ˢܝܬܗ ᵗܠܡܫܢܩܢܝܐ * *
ᵘܗܟܕܢ ᵛadd ܐܘܦ
‡ f. 50a.
ʷܬܫܒܩܘܢ
ˣomit ܐܢܫ
ᶻadd ܡܢ ܠܒܒܟܘܢ
ᵃܣܟܠܘܬܗܘܢ
ᵇomit ܡܢ...ܠܒܒܟܘܢ

Codex B.

ᵞܡܠܟܘܬܗ ܕܫܡܝܐ : ܠܓܒܪ ᶻܡܠܟܢ ܕܗܡ ܕܝܬܒܐ
24 ܘܟܕ ᵃܫܪܝܢ ᵇܠܡ ᶜܚܫܒܢܗ : ܥܠ ܕܝܢ ᵈܚܝܒܐ
25 ܘܟܕ ܐܬܦܢܝ ܠܗ ܫܕ ᵉ ‡ ܪܒܗ ᶠܠܡܙܒܢܗ ᵍܘܠܡ
ܕܠܐ ܗܘܐ ܠܗ ܕܝܦܪܥ : ʰܦܩܕ ܡܪܗ ⁱܕܝܙܕܒܢ
ܗܘ ܘܐܢܬܬܗ ʲܘܒܢܘܗ : ܘܟܠ ܡܐ ܕܗܘܐ ܠܗ
26 ܘܐܬܦܢܝ : ܘܢܦܠ ܐܘܦ ܗܘ ᵏܥܒܕܐ ˡܘܣܓܕ
ܠܗ ܘܐܡܪ : ܡܪܝ ᵐܐܘܪܟ ܪܘܚܐ ⁿܥܠܝ
27 ܘܟܘܠܐ ܐܢܐ ܦܪܥ ܠܟ : ܐܬܪܚܡ ᵒܡܪܗ
ܕܥܒܕܐ ᵖܥܠܘܗ ܘܫܪܝܗ ܠܗ : ᑫܘܐܦ ܚܘܒܬܐ
28 ܢܦܩ ܠܗ : ܟܕ ܕܝܢ ܢܦܩ ܗܘ ܥܒܕܐ ʳܐܫܟܚ
[f. 44b]
ܚܕ ܡܢ ܟܢܘܬܗ ܕܗܘܐ ܚܝܒ ܠܗ ˢܡܐܐ ܕܝܢܪܝܢ :
ᵗܘܐܚܕ ܝܬܗ ܘܗܘܐ ܚܢܩ ܠܗ ܘܐܡܪ : ܦܪܥ ܠܝ ܡܐ
29 ܕܐܬ ܚܝܒ : ܢܦܠ ܐܘܦ ᵘܟܢܘܬܗ ʷܗܘܐ ܒܥܐ
ܡܢܗ ܘܐܡܪ ˣܐܘܪܟ ܪܘܚܐ ʸܥܠܝ ܘܟܘܠܐ
30 ܐܢܐ ܦܪܥ ܠܟ : ܗܘ ܕܝܢ † ܠܐ ܗܘܐ ܨܒܐ
ܐܠܐ ᶻܕܝܢ ᵃ ᵇܐܙܠ ܐܪܡܐ ܝܬܗ ᶜܒܦܠܩܐ ܕܐܣܝܪܐ
31 ܕܝܚܙܐ ܡܐ ᵒܫܠܡ : ܥܕ ܕܝ ܚܙܘ ᵖܠܗ
32 ܟܢܘܬܗ ܡܐ ᵈܕܐܬܥܒܕ : ᵉܟܪܝܢ ᶠܐܘܕܥܘ
ܠܡܪܐ ܘܐܬܘ ܘܐܡܪܘ ᵍܠܡܪܗܘܢ ܟܠ ܡܐ
ܕܐܬܥܒܕ ᵉ : ʰܟܕܝܢ ܩܪܐ ⁱܝܬܗ ܡܪܗ ʲܘܐܡܪ
ܠܗ : ᵏܥܒܕܐ ܒܝܫܐ ܟܠ ˡܚܘܒܬܐ ܫܒܩܬ
33 ܠܟ ᵐܡܛܠ ܕܒܥܝܬ ܡܢܝ : ܠܐ ܗܘܐ ܐܘܦ
ܐܘܦ ܐܢܬ ⁿܐܬܪܚܡܬ ܥܠ ᵒܟܢܘܬܟ ܗܝܟ
34 ᵖܡܐ ܕܐܘܦ ܐܢܐ ᑫܐܬܪܚܡܬ ܥܠܝܟ : ܘܪܓܙ
ʳܥܠܘܗ ܡܪܗ ܘܐܫܠܡܗ ˢܠܗ ᵗܠܡܫܢܩܢܝܐ ‡ ܥܕܡܐ
ܕܝܦܪܥ ܟܠ ܡܐ ܕܗܘܐ ܚܝܒ ܠܗ :
35 ᵘܗܟܕܝܢ ᵛܐܘܦ ܐܒܐ ܕܒܫܡܝܐ ܥܒܕ
ܠܟܘܢ : ܐܢ . ܠܐ ʷܬܫܒܩܘܢ ܟܠ ܐܢܫ
ˣܐܢܫ ʸܠܐܚܘܗ ᶻ ᵃܚܘܒܬܗܘܢ ᵇܡܢ ܟܠ
ܠܒܒܟܘܢ ᵇ ⁘

Codex C.

ᵃܫܘܪܝܢ ᵇܠܡܡ (sic)
ᶜܚܫܒܢܝ ᵈܚܝܒܝ
ᵉadd ܫܢܝܢ ʰܦܩܕ
ⁱܕܝܙܕܒܢ ʲܘܒܢܝ
ˡadd ܗܘܐ
ⁿܥܠܘܝ
ᵒadd ܕܝܢ
ᵖܥܠܘܝ ᑫܘܐܘܦ
ᵗܘܐܚܕ
ʷܕܗܘܐ
ˣܐܘܪܟ
† f. 45b.
ᶻomit ܕܝܢ ᵃadd ܗܘܐ
ᵒܕܫܠܡ
ᵖomit ܠܗ ᵈadd ܕ
ᵉomit ܟܪܝܢ . . .
. . . ܕܐܬܥܒܕ
ⁱomit ܝܬܗ ʲomit ܘ
ˡadd ܗܐ ⁿܬܬܪܚܡ
ᵖomit ܡܐ ᑫܐܬܪܚܡ
ʳܥܠܘܝ ˢܝܬܗ
ᵛadd ܐܘܦ
ʷܬܫܒܩܘܢ
ˣomit ܐܢܫ
ʸܠܐ ܐܚܘܗܝ ʸ
ᶻadd ܡܢ ܠܒܒܟܘܢ
ᵇomit ܡܢ...ܠܒܒܟܘܢ

LXXV.

Matt. XX. 29—34.

Codex A.

ᵃ ܠܗܘܢ ܐܡܪ ܥܒܕ
ᵃ ܐܬܠܚܒܪ ܡܢ ܬܠܡܝܕܘܗܝ

ᵃ *add* ܗܘ ܡܢ ܡܕܐ ܒܥܘܒܕ

ᵇ ܐܟܠܘܣ ᶜ ܝܬܒܝܢ

ᵈ ܠܟܒ ᵉ *add* ܡܪܢ

ᵍ ܕܕܘܕ ʰ ܐܟܠܘܣܐ

ⁱ ܗܘܐ ʲ ܝܟܐܡ

ᵏ ܕܢܫܬܩܘܢ

ˡ *omit* ܕܝ ᵐ *omit* ܡܪܢ

ⁿ ܥܠܝܢ ᵒ ܠܗ

ᵖ ܡܪܢ ʳ ܡܪܢ

ˢ ܕܢܬܦܬܚܢ ᵗ ܥܝܢܝܢ

ᵘ *add* [ܕܝ ܡܫܒܚܝܢ
ܠܐܠܗܐ ܘܟܠܗܘܢ
ܥܡܐ ܕܚܙܐ ܫܒܚ
ܗܘܐ ܠܐܠܗܐ]

Codex B.

ᵃ ܝܘܡ ܥܒܪ ܐܬܠܚܒܪ ܡܢ ܬܠܡܝܕܘܗܝᵃ: ܘܒܬܪܗ
29 ᶻ ܡܢ ܝܪܝܚܘᵃ: ܘܗܘܐ ܕܗܢܘܢ ܢܦܩܝܢ ܡܢ ܝܪܝܚܘ
30 ܐܬܐ ܒܬܪܗ ᵇ ܐܟܠܘܣ ܣܓܝ: ܘܗܐ ܬܪܝܢ
ܣܡܝܢ ܗܘܘ ᶜ ܝܬܒܝܢ ܥܠ ᵈ ܝܕ ܐܘܪܚܐ:
ܘܟܕ ܫܡܥܘ ܕܝܫܘܥ ܥܒܪ: ܗܘܘ ܡܙܥܩܝܢ
ܘܐܡܪܝܢ ᵉ: ܐܬܪܚܡ ᶠ ܥܠܝܢܢ ܝܫܘܥ ܒܪܗ
31 ᵍ ܕܕܘܕ: ʰ ܐܟܠܘܣܐ ܕܝ ⁱ ܗܘܘ ʲ ܝܟܐܡ ܒܗܘܢ
[f. 45a]
ᵏ ܕܢܫܬܩܘܢ: ܗܢܘܢ ܕܝ ܥܠ ܕܡܩܕܡܬܪ ܗܘܘ ˡ ܕܝ
ܡܙܥܩܝܢ ܐܡܪܝܢ: ᵐ ܡܪܢ ܐܬܪܚܡ ⁿ ܥܠܝܢ ܒܪܗ
32 ᵍ ܕܕܘܕ: ܘܩܡ ᵒ ܕܝ ᵖ ܡܪܢ ܫܡܥܘܢ: ܘܩܪܐ
33 ܠܗܘܢ ܘܐܡܪ: ܡܐ ܐܢܬܘܢ ܨܒܝܢ ᑫ ܕܐܥܒܕ
ܠܟܘܢ: ܐܡܪܝܢ ܠܗ ʳ ܡܪܢ ˢ ܕܢܬܦܬܚܢ ᵗ ܥܝܢܝܢ:
34 ܗܘ ܕܝ ᵖ ܡܪܢ ܫܡܥܘܢ ܐܬܪܚܡ ܥܠܝܗܘܢ ܘܩܪܒ
ܠܥܝܢܝܗܘܢ ܘܡܚܐ ܚܙܘ ܘܐܬܘ ܒܬܪܗ ᵘ ⁘

Codex C.

ᵃ ܠܗܘܢ ܐܡܪ ܥܒܕ
ᵃ ܐܬܠܚܒܪ ܡܢ ܬܠܡܝܕܘܗܝ

ᶻ *omit* ܡܢ ܝܪܝܚܘ

ᶜ ܝܬܒܝܢ

ᵉ *add* ܡܪܢ ᶠ ܥܠܝܢ

ʰ ܘܐܟܠܘܣܐ ⁱ ܗܘܐ

ʲ ܝܟܐ ᵏ ܕܢܫܬܩܘܢ

ˡ *omit* ܕܝ

ᵐ *omit* ܡܪܢ

ⁿ ܥܠܝܢ ᵒ ܠܗܘܢ

ᵖ ܡܪܢ ᑫ ܕܐܥܒܕ

ʳ ܡܪܢ ˢ ܕܢܬܦܬܚܢ

ᵗ ܥܝܢܝܢ

LXXVI.

Matt. XIX. 16—26.

Codex A.

ᵃ ܠܗܘܢ ܐܡܪ ܝܫܘܥ
ܐܬܠܡܝܕܘܗܝ ܡܢ
ᵃ ܟܢܫܗ ܕܬܠܡܝܕܘܗܝ

ʸ *add* ܛܒ ʷ *add* ܚܕ

ᶻ ܕܐܚܝ ᵃ ܕܠܥܠܡ

ᵇ ܫܐܠ ᶜ ܐܝܬ ܗܘ ᶜ

‡ f. 50b.

ᵈ *omit* ܐܠܗܐ

ᶠ *add* ܐܬ ʰ ܛܪ

ⁱ *add* ܐܡܪ

ʲ ܬܩܛܠܘܢ ˡ ܬܓܘܪ

ᵐ ܬܣܗܕ ᵒ ܐܒܘܟ

ᵖ ܘܐܡܟ

ᑫ *omit* . . . ܘܬܪܚܡ

. . . ܠܩܪܝܒܟ

Codex B.

ᵃ ܝܘܡ ܚܕ ܬܠܡܝܕܝ ܡܢ ܟܕ ܐܠܗܝܢܐ ܡܢ
16 ܡܬܐܘܬܐ ʷᵃ ܘܟܢܫܗ ˣ ܡܢ ܝܪܝܚܘ ᵗ ܘܩܪܒ ܚܕ ܠܘܬ
ܡܪܢ ܫܡܥܘܢ ܘܐܡܪ ܠܗ: ‡ ܡܠܦܢܐ ܛܒܐ ܡܐ ʸ
17 ܐܥܒܕ ᶻ ܕܐܚܝ ᵃ ܕܠܥܠܡ ܚܝܝܢ: ܗܘ ܕܝ ܐܡܪ
ܠܗ: ܡܐ ܐܬ ᵇ ܫܐܠ ܠܝ ܥܠ ܛܒ ܛܒܐ:
ܚܕ ᶜ ܐܝܬܘܗܝ ᵈ ܐܠܗܐ ܛܒܐ: ᵉ ܐܢ ܕܝ ܨܒܐ ᶠ
18 ᵍ ܕܬܥܒܠ ܠܚܝܝܐ ʰ ܛܪ ܦܩܘܕܝܐ: ܐܡܪ ܠܗ
ܗܠܝܢ ܗܘ ܕܝ ܡܪܢ ܫܡܥܘܢ ⁱ ܕܠܐ ܬܩܛܠ
ᵏ ܘܠܐ ˡ ܬܓܘܪ ܘܠܐ ᵏ ܬܓܢܘܒ ܘܠܐ ᵐ ܬܣܗܕ
19 ⁿ ܕܓܠܝܢ: ܐܘܩܪ ᵒ ܐܒܘܟ ᵖ ܘܐܡܟ ᑫ ܘܬܪܚܡ

Codex C.

ᵃ ܠܗܘܢ ܐܡܪ ܝܫܘܥ ܐܬܠܡ
ᵃ ܟܢܫ ܡܢ ܡܬܠܡܝܕ

ˣ *omit* ܡܢ ܝܪܝܚܘ

† f. 46a.

ʸ *add* ܛܒ

ᶻ ܕܐܚܝ ᵇ ܫܐܠ

ᵈ *omit* ܐܠܗܐ

ᶠ *add* ܐܬ ᵉ ܐܢ

ᵍ ܕܬܥܒܠܘܢ ʰ ܛܪ

ⁱ *add* ܐܡܪ

ᵏ ܘܠܐ ܬܓܢܘܒ ܘܠܐ
ᵏ ܬܓܘܪ

ⁿ *add* ܣܗܕܘܬܐ

ᵒ ܐܒܘܟ

Codex A.	Codex B.	Codex C.
	20 ܠܡܪܢܒܝܢ ܗܘܢ ܕܠܟܪܥܝܢ[q]: ܐܡܪ ܠܗ ܗܘ	
[r]ܒܠܡܗܝܡܢܘܬܐ	[r]ܒܠܡܗܝܡܢܘܬܐ ܟܘܠ ܡܠܝܢ ܢܦܩܬ ܡܢ ܓܠܝܠܘܬܟܘܢ:	[r]ܒܠܡܗܝܡܢܘܬܐ
[s]ܢܨܝܒ	21 ܡܢܐ ܒܘܕ ܐܢܐ [s]ܫܡܥܝܢ: ܐܡܪ ܠܗ ܡܪܢܐ	[s]ܫܡܥܝܢ
[t]*add* ܐܢܬ [w]ܐܙܠ	ܫܡܥܘܢ: ܐܢܐ [t]ܐܢܬ ܒܢܐ ܕܬܗܘܐ [u]ܡܫܠܡ	[t]*add* ܐܢܬ
[x]ܙܒܢ ܝܬܗ [y]*omit*	[w]ܐܙܠ [x]ܙܒܢ ܒܗܘܢ ܡܢܝܢ ܘܗܒ [y]ܝܬܗ	[u]ܡܫܠܡ ܝܬܗ [y]*omit*
[z]ܘܗܘܐ	ܠܡܣܟܢܝܐ: [z]ܘܗܘܐ ܠܟ [a]ܫܝܡܐ ܒܫܡܝܐ	[z]ܘܗܘܐ [a]ܫܝܡܐ
	22 ܫܡܥܝܢ: ܘܐܬܐ ܕܗܘܐ ܝܬܒ: ܘܒܕ ܫܡܥ	
[b]ܒܠܡܬܐ	ܗܘ [b]ܒܠܡܬܐ ܡܠܬܐ [w]ܐܙܠ ܠܗ [c]ܡܟܝܪ:	[b]ܒܠܡܬܐ
[c]ܟܪܝܗ [d]*add* ܠܗ	23 ܗܘܐ ܠܗ [d] [e]ܡܢܝܢ ܣܓܝܢ: ܘܡܪܢܐ ܝܫܘܥ ܕܝܢ	[e]ܡܢܝܢ [d]*add* ܠܗ
[e]ܡܢܝܢ	ܐܡܪ [f]ܠܬܠܡܝܕܘܗܝ: ܐܡܪ ܐܢܐ ܠܟܘܢ [g]ܕܥܬܝܪ	[f]ܠܬܠܡܝܕܘܗܝ
[v]ܒܡܣܟܢܐ	[f. 45*b*] 24 [v]ܡܣܟܢܐ ܥܘܠ [h]ܠܡܠܟܘܬܐ ܕܫܡܝܐ: ܬܘܒ ܕܝܢ	[g]ܕܥܬܝܪ [v]ܡܣܟܢܐ
ܕܝܢ [i]*omit* [j]ܒܚܘܡܪܐ	ܐܢܐ ܐܡܪ ܠܟܘܢ: ܕܢܝܚ [i]ܕܝܢ ܗܘ ܠܓܡܠܐ	[h]ܠܡܠܟܘܬܗ
[k]ܠܡܠܟܘܬܐ	ܕܝܥܘܠ [j]ܒܚܘܡܪܐ ܕܡܚܛܐ: ܐܘ ܥܬܝܪ [k]ܠܡܠܟܘܬܗ	ܕܝܢ [i]*omit*
	25 ܕܐܠܗܐ ܟܕ ܕܝܢ ܫܡܥܘ ܬܠܡܝܕܘܗܝ ܗܘܘ	
[l]ܡܬܒܗܠܝܢ [m]ܢܟܠ	[l]ܡܬܒܗܠܝܢ ܘܐܡܪܝܢ: ܐܝܢ ܡܢ [m]ܝܟܠ ܕܝܚܐ:	[l]ܡܬܒܗܠܝܢ [n]ܐܬܒܝܢ
[q]ܢܚܝܐ	26 [n]ܐܬܒܝܢ [o]ܕܝܢ ܡܪܢܐ ܫܡܥܘ ܘܐܡܪ ܠܗܘܢ:	ܕܝܢ [o]*omit*
‡ f. 51*a*.	ܠܘܬ ܒܢܝܢܫܐ [p]ܗܕܐ ‡ ܠܐ † [q]ܐܬܚܝܐ: ܠܘܬ	† f. 46*b*.
[s]*add* ܥܠܡ	ܐܠܗܐ ܕܝܢ ܒܘܠܐ [m]ܝܟܠ [s]ܚ	[q]ܡܚܠܐ [p]*omit* ܗܕܐ

LXXVII.

Matt. XXII. 15—22.

Codex A.	Codex B.	Codex C.
[a]ܒܗܘܢܪܐ ܐܣܬܒܪ ܡܢ ܡܠܒܟܝܪܬܐ [a]ܗܘܢܬܐ	[a]ܒܚܕ ܡܢ ܬܠܬܝܪ ܒܬܪ ܐܠܒܠܝܘܢ ܡܢ ܡܠܦܘܬܗ[a a]	[a]ܠܝܘܡ ܐܣܬܒܪ ܐܬܠܬܐ ܒܬܪ ܡܢ [a]ܡܬܐ
[a]*add* ܒܚܘܬܐ ܘܡܬܚܘܪܗܘܢ	15 [b]ܒܟܝܡ ܐܙܠܘ [c]ܦܪܝܫܝ ܢܣܒܘ [d]ܡܠܟܐ ܥܠ ܫܡܥܘܢ[e]	[a]*add* ܘܚܘܬܗ
[b]ܒܟܝܡ [c]ܦܪܝܫܝܢ	16 [f]ܕܝܨܕܘܢ ܝܬܗ ܒܡܠܬܐ: ܘܫܕܪܘ ܡܫܠܡܝܢ	[e]*omit* ܫܡܥܘܢ
[d]ܡܠܟܝܢ [f]ܕܝܨܕܘܢ	[g]ܠܗ [h]ܬܠܡܝܕܝܗܘܢ ܥܡ [i]ܗܪܘܕܝܢܘܣ ܐܡܪܝܢ:	[g]ܠܗ [i]ܗܪܘܕܝܢܘܣ
[g]ܠܗ [h]ܬܠܡܝܕܝܗܘܢ	ܡܠܦܢܐ ܝܕܥܝܢ ܐܢܢ ܕܩܫܝܛ ܐܢܬ [k]ܘܐܘܪܚܗ	[k]ܘܐܘܪܚܗ
[i]ܗܪܘܕܝܢܘܣ	ܕܐܠܗܐ [l]ܒܩܘܫܛ ܐܢܬ [m]ܡܠܦ: ܘܠܐ [n]ܒܛܝܠ	[l]ܒܩܘܫܛ [m]ܡܠܦ
[l]ܒܩܘܫܛ [m]ܡܠܦ	ܠܟ ܒܐܢܫ: ܠܘܬ ܐܢܬ [o]ܚܙܐ ܒܐܦܐ [p]ܕܒܢܝܢܫܐ	[o]*omit* ܚܙܐ [n]ܒܛܝܠ
[n]ܒܛܝܠ [p]ܕܒܢܝܢܫ	17 ܐܡܪ ܠܢ [q]ܟܡܐ: ܐܡܪ ܠܝ ܐܢܬ ܡܢܐ ܗܘܐ ܠܢ:	[q]ܐܡܪ [r]ܥܠܝܛ
	[r]ܥܠܝܛ [s]ܕܢܬܠ ܡܢܝܢ ܠܩܣܪ ܐܘ ܠܐ:	[s]ܕܢܬܠ

Codex A.	*Codex B.*	*Codex C.*
[t] [illegible]	18 [t] [illegible] [u] [illegible]	[t] [illegible]
[u] [illegible]	[v] [illegible] [w] [illegible]	[v] *omit* [illegible]
[v] *omit* [illegible]	19 [illegible]	[w] *omit* [illegible]
[x] [illegible]	20 [illegible] [x] [illegible]	
[y] [illegible]	[illegible] [y] [illegible]	[y] [illegible]
[z] *add* [illegible]	21 [illegible] [z]	[z] *add* [illegible]
[a] [illegible]	22 [illegible]	
[b] *omit* [illegible]	[a] [illegible] [b] [illegible] ⁘	[b] *omit* [illegible]

LXXVIII.

Matt. XXI. 33—42.

Codex A.	*Codex B.*	*Codex C.*
[a] [illegible] [a]	[a] [illegible] [a] [y] [illegible] [z] [illegible]	[a] [illegible] [a]
[z] [illegible] [a] [illegible]	33 [illegible] [a] [illegible] [b] [illegible]	[y] *add* [illegible]
‡ f. 51*b*.	[f. 46*a*]	[a] [illegible] [b] [illegible]
[c] [illegible] [d] [illegible]	[c] [illegible] ‡ [d] [illegible]	[e] [illegible]
[e] [illegible] [f] [illegible]	[illegible] [e] [illegible]	
[g] [illegible] [a] [illegible]	34 [f] [illegible] [g] [illegible]	[a] [illegible] [b] [illegible]
[b] [illegible] [c] [illegible]	[a] [illegible] [b] [illegible] [c] [illegible]	† f. 47*a*.
[i] *omit* [illegible] [j] [illegible]	35 [i] [illegible] [j] [illegible] † [illegible] [c] [illegible] [k] [illegible]	[i] *omit* [illegible] [j] [illegible]
[k] [illegible]	[illegible] [l] [illegible] [m] [illegible] [n] [illegible]	[k] [illegible] [l] [illegible]
[m] [illegible] [m]	36 [illegible] [o] [illegible] [p] [illegible] [e] [illegible] [q] [illegible]	[m] [illegible] [m]
[n] *omit* [illegible]	[r] [illegible] [s] [illegible]	[p] [illegible] [e] [illegible]
[o] [illegible] [p] [illegible]	37 [t] [illegible] [u] [illegible]	[q] [illegible] [r] [illegible]
[e] [illegible] [q] [illegible]	38 [illegible] [c] [illegible]	[t] [illegible] [w] [illegible]
[r] [illegible] [s] [illegible]	[illegible] [w] [illegible] [x] [illegible]	[z] *omit* [illegible]
[t] [illegible] [u] [illegible]	39 [illegible] [z] [illegible] [a] [illegible]	[a] [illegible]
[x] [illegible] [z] *omit* [illegible]	40 [illegible] [b] [illegible]	[b] [illegible]
[a] [illegible] [c] [illegible]	[c] [illegible] [d] [illegible]	[c] [illegible]
[d] [illegible] [f] [illegible]	41 [illegible] [e] [illegible] [f] [illegible]	[e] [illegible] [f] [illegible]

Codex A. | **Codex B.** | **Codex C.**

Codex B.

ܠܗܘܢ : ܘܒܪܝܫܐ ܗܘ ܗܟܢ ܠܐܪܝܫܝܢ
[g]ܐܘܣܪܢܝܢ : ܘܠܝܬ [h]ܕܝܗܒ [i]ܠܗ ܦܬܓܡܐ
42 [j]ܒܦܘܪܫܢܗܘܢ : ܐܡܪ ܠܗܘܢ ܒܪܐ ܝܫܘܥ :
ܡܢ [k]ܝܘܡܢܐ [l]ܕܝܢ ܠܐ ܐܬܡܪܚܘ ܒܥܬܝܒܘܬܐ
[m]ܕܢܫܐܠܘܢ ܗܘܐ ܕܢܫܐܠ [n]ܒܢܝܢ ܐܬܡܪܚܘ ܕܝܢ
ܠܢܫܐܠܘܬܐ : ܡܢ ܠܗܢ [o]ܒܪܐ ܐܬܡܪܚܘ ܗܘܐ
ܗܘܝܢ ܒܬܘܩܠܐ [p]ܒܢܝܢ : [q]ܫܠܡ ⁘

Codex A.

[g]ܘܣܪܢܝܢ [h]ܕܝܗܒ
[j]ܒܦܘܪܫܢܗܘܢ
[i] *omit* ܕܝܢ
[m]ܕܢܫܐܠܐ [n]ܒܢܝܢ
[o]ܒܪܐ
[p]ܒܢܝܢ

Codex C.

[g]ܘܣܪܢܝܢ [h]ܕܝܗܒ
[i] *omit* ܠܗ
[j]ܒܦܘܪܫܢܗܘܢ
[k]ܝܘܡܢܐ
[l] *omit* ܕܝܢ
[n]ܒܢܝܢ
[q] *omit* ܫܠܡ

LXXIX.

Matt. XXIII. 1—12.

Codex B.

[a]ܝܘܡ ܥܪܘܒܬܐ ܕܫܒܘܥܐ ܪܒܐ ܐܘܢܓܠܝܘܢ ܡܢ
1 ܡܬܝ[a] : [a] [b]ܘܒܗܝܢ [c]ܡܠܠ ܝܫܘܥ ܒܪܐ ܥܡܐ
2 [d]ܠܐܘܟܠܘܣܝܐ [e]ܘܠܬܠܡܝܕܘܗܝ : [f]ܐܡܪ ܥܠ
[f. 46b]
ܡܘܬܒܗ ܕܡܘܫܐ ܝܬܒܘ ܣܦܪܐ [g]ܘܦܪܝܫܐ :
3 ܒܟܠ ܡܐ ܕܝܢ [h]ܕܢܐܡܪܘܢ ܠܟܘܢ ܥܒܕܘ
ܘܛܪܘ : [i]ܗܟܢ † [k]ܒܥܒܕܝܗܘܢ ܕܝܢ ܕܠܡܐ
ܠܐ ܬܥܒܕܘܢ ܐܡܪܝܢ : ܗܢܘܢ ܓܝܪ
4 ܘܠܐ ܥܒܕܝܢ : [a][b]ܘܐܣܪܝܢ ܡܘܒܠܝܢ [c]ܝܩܝܪܝܢ[a]
[d]ܘܣܡܝܢ [l]ܠܐ [l]ܫܩܝܠܝܢ [m]ܘܡܬܩܦܩܦܝܢ : [n]ܥܠ ܟܬܦܝܗܘܢ
ܥܠ ܟܬܦܬܗܘܢ ܕܒܢܝܢܫܐ : ܗܢܘܢ ܕܝܢ
[o]ܒܐܨܒܥܬܗܘܢ ܠܐ ܨܒܝܢ ܕܢܙܝܥܘܢ [p]ܠܗܘܢ :
5 ܒܟܠ ܕܝܢ [q]ܥܒܕܝܗܘܢ ܥܒܕܝܢ ܕܢܬܚܙܘܢ : ܗܟܢ
ܕܡܦܬܝܢ ܠܒܢܝܢܫܐ [r]ܬܦܠܝܢ ܗܢܘܢ [s]ܕܝܢ ܓܝܪ
ܡܪܚܒܝܢ ܬܦܠܝܗܘܢ [t]ܘܡܘܪܟܝܢ ܬܟܠܬܗܘܢ [u]ܕܠܒܘܫܝܗܘܢ :
6 ܘܪܚܡܝܢ [v]ܪܫ ܡܫܟܒܐ ܒܚܫܡܝܬܐ : ܘܪܫܐ
7 ܡܘܬܒܐ [w]ܒܟܢܘܫܬܐ : [x]ܘܫܠܡܐ ܒܫܘܩܐ
ܒܫܘܩܐ : ܘܕܢܬܩܪܘܢ [y]ܪܒܝ ܪܒܝ ܡܢ
8 ܒܢܝܢܫܐ [z]ܪܒܝ ܪܒܝ[z] : ܐܢܬܘܢ [a]ܕܝܢ ܠܐ ܬܬܩܪܘܢ
ܪܒܝ ܪܒܝ : ܚܕ ܗܘ [b]ܓܝܪ [d]ܪܒܟܘܢ ܕܝܠܟܘܢ
9 ܕܝܢ ܐܚܝܢ ܐܢܬܘܢ : ܘܐܒܐ ܠܐ ܬܬܩܪܘܢ ܠܟܘܢ

Codex A.

[a]ܝܘܡ ܥܪܘܒܬܐ ܕܫܒܘܥܐ ܪܒܐ ܐܘܢܓܠܝܘܢ ܡܢ ܡܬܝ[a]
[a] *add* ܐܝܟ ܕܟܬܝܒ ܡܬܝ ܡܠܐܟܐ :
[b]ܘܒܗܝܢ [c]ܡܠܠ
[d]ܠܐܘܟܠܘܣܝܐ
[e]ܘܠܬܠܡܝܕܘܗܝ
[g]ܘܦܪܝܫܐ
[h]ܕܢܐܡܪܘܢ
[k]ܒܥܒܕܝܗܘܢ
[b]ܘܐܣܪܝܢ [c]ܝܩܝܪܝܢ
[l]ܠܐ [m]ܘܡܬܩܦܩܦܝܢ
[n]ܥܠ
[o]ܒܐܨܒܥܬܗܘܢ
[p]ܠܗܘܢ
[q]ܥܒܕܝܗܘܢ
[s] *omit* ܕܝܢ
[u]ܕܠܒܘܫܝܗܘܢ
[w]ܒܟܢܘܫܬܐ [x]ܘܫܠܡܐ
[b] *add* ܓܝܪ ܕܝܢ
ܐܢܬܘܢ ܠܐ ܬܬܩܪܘܢ
ܠܟܘܢ ܡܠܦܢܐ : ܚܕ
ܗܘ ܓܝܪ
[d]ܡܠܦܢܟܘܢ

Codex C.

[a]ܝܘܡ ܥܪܘܒܬܐ ܕܫܒܘܥܐ ܪܒܐ ܡܢ ܡܬܝ[a]
[a] *add* ܘܒܗܝܢ
[e]ܘܠܬܠܡܝܕܘܗܝ
[f] *add* ܘ
† f. 47b.
[h]ܕܢܐܡܪܘܢ
[i]ܗܟܢ
[a] *omit* ܘܐܣܪܝܢ . . . ܝܩܝܪܝܢ . . .
[d]ܘܣܡܝܢ [l]ܠܐ
[m]ܘܡܬܩܦܩܦܝܢ
[o]ܒܐܨܒܥܬܗܘܢ
[p]ܠܗܘܢ
[r]ܬܦܠܝܢ [r] *omit* ܕܝܢ
[t]ܘܡܘܪܟܝܢ (*sic*) [v]ܪܫ
[y]ܪܒܝ
[z]ܪܒܝ [a] *omit* ܕܝܢ
[b] *add* ܓܝܪ

Codex A.	Codex B.	Codex C.
ᵉܗܘ ܓܝܪᵉ	ܠܐ ܐܪܒܐ: ܚܕ [f e]ܓܝܪ ܗܘ[e] ܐܒܘܟܘܢ ܕܒܫܡܝܐ	[f] omit ܓܝܪ
[g] add ܚܕ ܗܘ ܓܝܪ ܡܕܒܪܢܟܘܢ	10 ܫܡܥܝܢܐ: ܘܠܐ ܬܬܩܪܘܢ ܡܕܒܪܢܝܢ:[g] [h]ܐܠܐ	[h] omit ܐܠܐ
‡ f. 52b.	‡ 11 ܡܕܒܪܢܐ: ܕܝܢ ܕܝ ܕܒܟܘܢ ܪܒ ܝܗܐ	
[h] omit ܐܠܐ	[i] 12 ܫܡܫܟܘܢ: ܟܘܠ ܡܢ ܓܝܪ ܕܢܪܘܡ ܓܪܡܗ	
[i] ܫܡܫܟܘܢ	ܡܬܡܟܝܟ: [k]ܘܟܘܠ ܡܢ ܕܡܡܟܟ ܓܪܡܗ	
[k] ܟܘܠ		
[m] omit ܥܠܡ	ܡܬܪܘܡ: [m]ܥܠܡ ⁘	[m] omit ܥܠܡ

LXXX.

Matt. XXII. 1—14.

Codex A.	Codex B.	Codex C.
[a] ܘܡܢܝܐ ܝܘܡ ܐܪܟܝܦܛܪܝ (sic) ܡܢ ܡܬܠܘܗܝ[a]	[a]ܘܐܡ ܝܫ ܐܪܟܝܦܛܪܝ ܒܒܪ ܐܠܟܣܢܕܪܘܣ ܡܢ	[a]ܠܝܘܡ ܐܠܟܣ ܐܪܟܝ ܒܒܪ ܡܢ ܡܬܠܐ[a]
[a] add ܐܡܪ ܡܪܢ ܗܕܐ ܡܬܠܐ:	1 ܡܬܠܘܗܝ[a] :[a] [b]ܘܐܡܠܝܟ ܡܪܢ ܝܫܘܥ ܘܐܡܪ	[a] add ܘܒܢܝܗܘܢ
[b] omit ܘܐܡܠܝܟ . . . ܐܡܪ . . .	2 ܠܗܘܢ ܒܡܬܠܝܢ: ܕܡܘܝܐ ܐܡܪ[b] [c]ܐܬܕܡܝܬ	ܡܠܟܐ[d]
[c]ܐܬܕܡܝܬ	ܡܠܟܘܬܐ ܕܫܡܝܐ: ܠܓܒܪ [d]ܡܠܟܐ [e]ܗܕܝܢ	
[d]ܡܠܟܐ [e]ܗܕܝ	[f. 47a]	
[f]ܘܫܠܚ [g]ܠܥܒܕܘܗܝ	3 ܕܥܒܕ ܡܫܬܘ ܠܒܪܗ: [f]ܘܫܠܚ [g]ܠܥܒܕܘܗܝ ܕܢܩܪܘܢ	[f]ܘܫܠܚ [g]ܠܥܒܕܘܗܝ
[h]ܠܡܫܬܘܬܐ	ܠܗܠܝܢ ܕܩܪܝܢ [h]ܠܡܫܬܘ † ܘܠܐ ܗܘܘ ܨܒܝܢ	† f. 48a.
[i]ܕܝܐܬܘܢ [j]ܥܒܕܝܢ	4 [i]ܕܝܬܘܢ: ܘܬܘܒ ܫܠܚ [j]ܥܒܕܝܢ ܐܚܪܢܝܢ ܐܡܪ:	[h]ܠܡܫܬܘܬܐ
[l]omit ܕܝ [k]ܐܡܪܘ	[k]ܐܡܪܘ ܠܗܠܝܢ ܕܩܪܝܢ ܗܐ [l]ܕܝ ܡܫܬܘܝ	[i]ܕܝܬܘܢ
[m]ܬܘܪܝ [n]ܬܘܪܝ	[m]ܬܘܪܝ [n]ܬܘܪܝ [o]ܦܛܡܐ [p]ܢܟܝܣܝܢ ܘܟܘܠܐ	[l] omit ܕܝ
[o]ܘܦܛܝܡܐ	5 [q]ܬܘܪܝܢ: ܐܬܘ ܠܡܫܬܘܬܐ: ܗܢܘܢ ܕܝ ܒܣܘ	[m]ܬܘܪܝ [n]ܬܘܪܝ
[p]ܢܟܝܣܝܢ [q]ܬܘܪܝ	ܘܐܙܠܘ ܠܗܘܢ: ܚܕ [r]ܠܚܩܠܗ ܠܚܘܠܩܗ ܘܚܕ	[o]ܘܦܛܡܐ [p]ܢܟܝܣܝܢ
[r]ܡܢ [s]ܠܬܓܪܘܬܗ:	6 [s]ܠܬܓܪܘܬܗ: [t]ܫܪܟܐ ܕܝ [u]ܐܚܕܘ [v]ܠܥܒܕܘܗܝ	[q]ܬܘܪܝ [r]ܡܢ
[t]ܫܪܟܐ [u]ܐܚܕܘ	7 ܘܐܨܥܪܘ ܘܩܛܠܘ: ܡܠܟܐ ܕܝ ܟܕ ܫܡܥ [w]ܪܓܙ	[u]ܐܚܕܘ [v]ܠܥܒܕܘܗܝ
[v]ܠܥܒܕܘܗܝ [w]ܪܓܙ	[x]ܘܫܠܚ [y]ܚܝܠܘܗܝ [z]ܘܐܘܒܕ ܠܩܛܘܠܐ ܘܠܡܕܝܢܬܗܘܢ	[w]ܪܓܙ [y]ܚܝܠܘܗܝ
[x]ܘܫܠܚ [y]ܚܝܠܘܗܝ	8 ܐܘܩܕ: [a]ܒܟܢ ܐܡܪ [b]ܠܥܒܕܘܗܝ ܡܫܬܘܬܐ ܡܢ	[z]ܘܐܘܒܕܘ [b]ܠܥܒܕܘܗܝ
[a]ܒܟܢ [b]ܠܥܒܕܘܗܝ	ܬܘܩܢܐ ܐܝܬ ܗܝ: ܘܗܠܝܢ ܕܗܘܘ ܩܪܝܢ ܠܐ	
[d]ܦܪܫܘܬܗܘܢ	9 ܗܘܘ [c]ܫܘܝܢ: ܐܙܠܘ ܐܘ ܥܠ [d]ܦܪܫܘܬܗܘܢ	[c]ܫܘܝܐܢ
‡ f. 53a.	ܕܐܘܪܚܬܐ ܘܟܘܠ ܗܠܝܢ ܕܐܫܟܚܘܢ ܩܪܘܢ ܠܗܘܢ	[d]ܦܪܫܘܬܗܘܢ
[e]ܥܒܕܝܐ [f]ܒܝܫܝܢ	10 ܠܡܫܬܘܬܐ: ܘܢܦܩܘ [e]ܥܒܕܝܐ ‡ ܗܠܝܢ ܠܐܘܪܚܬܐ	
	ܘܟܢܫܘ ܟܘܠ ܗܠܝܢ ܕܐܫܟܚܘ [f]ܒܝܫܝܢ ܘܛܒܝܢ:	[f]ܒܝܫܝܢ
[g] add ܕܝ	11 ܘܐܬܡܠܝ ܒܝܬ ܡܫܬܘܬܐ ܡܢ ܪܒܘܥܝܐ: ܟܕ[g]	[g] add ܕܝ

Codex B.

ܥܠ ܟܠܗܘܢ ܕܫܡܥܐ ܪܒܘܬܐ ܫܡܥܐ ܗܘܝܢ ܗܘ
ܟܢܫܝ ܕܠܐ ܗܘܐ[h] ܠܒܢܝ[i] ܠܒܝܬ ܕܡܫܝܚܐ :
12 ܘܐܡܪ ܠܗ ܫܒܪܐ ܗܝܟ ܥܠܬ ܠܗܢܐ ܕܠܐ ܕܠܒܫܬ[j] ܠܟ
ܠܒܝܬ ܕܡܫܝܚܐ : ܗܘ[k] ܐܫܬܬܩ[l] ܕܫܬܩܬ :
13 ܗܝܕܝܢ[m] ܐܡܪ ܡܠܟܐ ܠܡܫܡܫܢܐ ܦܟܪܘ[n] ܐܝܕܘܗܝ ܘܪܓܠܘܗܝ
ܘܐܦܩܘܗܝ[o] ܠܚܫܘܟܐ[p] ܒܪܝܐ[q] ܬܡܢ ܢܗܘܐ
ܒܟܝܐ : ܘܚܘܪܩ ܫܢܝܐ[r]
14 ܣܓܝܐܝܢ[s] : ܓܝܪ ܩܪܝܐ[t] ܢܐ ܕܝܢ ܒܚܝܪܐ[u] ܕܝܢ ܐܢܘܢ[w]
ܗܘܘ ܒܚܝܪܐ ❖

LXXXI.

Matt. XXIV. 1—13.

[a] ܩܪܝܢܐ ܕܡܫܝܚܐ ܕܝܘܡ ܬܠܬܐ ܕܒܫܒܬܐ ܕܚܫܐ
[f. 47b]
1 ܕܡܬܐ[a] : ܢ[w] ܘܢܦܩ ܝܫܘܥ ܡܢ ܗܝܟܠܐ ܘܐܙܠ
ܗܘܐ[x] ܐܙܠ[y] : ܘܩܪܒܘ ܬܠܡܝܕܘܗܝ[z] ܕܢܚܘܘܢܝܗ[a]
ܠܗ ܒܢܝܢܐ ܕܗܝܟܠܐ ܗܘ ܕܝܢ[b] ܐܡܪ ܘܐܡܪ
2 ܠܗܘܢ : ܚܙܝܢ ܐܢܬܘܢ ܗܠܝܢ ܟܠܗܘܢ[c] :
ܐܡܝܢ ܐܡܪ ܐܢܐ ܠܟܘܢ ܕܠܐ ܬܫܬܒܩ[d] ܟܐ
3 ܟܐܦ ܥܠ ܟܐܦ ܕܠܐ ܬܫܬܪܐ : ܘܟܕ ܝܬܒ ܗܘܐ
ܥܠ ܛܘܪܐ ܕܙܝܬܐ[e] : ܩܪܒܘ ܠܗ
ܬܠܡܝܕܘܗܝ[f] ܒܝܢܝܗܘܢ ܠܒܠܚܘܕ ܘܐܡܪܝܢ[g] :
ܐܡܪ[h] ܠܢ ܐܡܬܝ[i] ܗܠܝܢ ܢܗܘܝܢ : ܘܡܢܐ
ܗܝ[j] ܐܬܐ[k] ܕܡܐܬܝܬܟ[l] ܘܕܫܘܠܡܗ[m]
4 ‡ [n] ܕܥܠܡܐ : ܗܘ[o] ܕܝܢ ܝܫܘܥ ܥܢܐ ܘܐܡܪ
ܠܗܘܢ : ܚܙܘ ܕܠܐ ܐܢܫ ܢܛܥܝܟܘܢ :
5 ܣܓܝܐܐ ܓܝܪ[p] ܢܐܬܘܢ ܒܫܡܝ ܘܢܐܡܪܘܢ ܕܐܢܐ[q]
6 ܡܫܝܚܐ[r] ܘܣܓܝܐܐ ܢܛܥܘܢ : ܥܬܝܕܝܢ ܐܢܬܘܢ
[s] ܕܝ[t] ܕܝܢ[u] ܬܫܡܥܘܢ ܩܪܒܐ ܘܫܡܥܐ ܕܩܪܒܐ
ܚܙܘ : ܠܐ ܬܬܕܠܚܘܢ : ܘܠܐ ܕܝܢ ܗܘܐ
ܓܝܪ ܠܡܗܘܐ ܕܢܗܘܝܢ[v] : ܐܠܐ ܕܝܢ ܠܐ[w] ܥܕܟܝܠ

Codex A.

[j] ܕܠܒܫܬ [k] add ܕܝܢ
[l] ܐܫܬܬܩ ܗܘ [m] ܗܝܕܝܢ
[n] ܦܟܪܘ ܐܝܕܘܗܝ [o] ܘܐܦܩܘܗܝ
[p] ܠܚܫܘܟܐ
[q] ܒܪܝܐ
[r] ܘܚܘܪܩ ܫܢܝܐ
[s] ܣܓܝܐܝܢ [t] add ܓܝܪ
[w] ܐܢܘܢ

[a] ܩܪܝܢܐ ܐܘܢܓܠܝܘܢ ܕܡܫܝܚܐ ܡܢ ܕܡܬܐ[a]
[w] add ܘܢܦܩ ܝܫܘܥ ܡܢ ܗܝܟܠܐ
[x] ܗܘܐ [y] ܐܙܠ
[a] ܕܢܚܘܘܢܝܗ
[b] ܐܡܪ

[e] ܕܙܝܬܐ [g] ܘܐܡܪܝܢ
[i] ܐܡܬܝ [k] ܐܬܐ
[l] ܕܡܐܬܝܬܟ
[m] ܘܕܫܘܠܡܗ
‡ f. 53b.
[n] ܕܥܠܡܐ [o] ܘܐܡܪ
[p] ܢܐܬܘܢ
[q] add ܗܘ [r] ܡܫܝܚܐ
[s] omit ܕܝ
[u] ܕܬܫܡܥܘܢ
[v] ܕܢܗܘܝܢ [w] ܡܢ

Codex C.

[h] ܗܘ [i] ܠܒܝܬ

[k] add ܕܝܢ

[o] ܕܐܦܩܘ [q] ܘܐܦܩܘ

[w] omit ܘ [u] add ܓܝܪ

[a] ܠܝܘܡ ܐܬܠܬ ܐܘܢܓܠܝܘܢ ܡܢ ܕܡܬܐ[a]
[w] add ܘܢܦܩ ܝܫܘܥ ܡܢ ܗܝܟܠܐ
[x] ܗܘܐ [z] ܬܠܡܝܕܘܗܝ
[a] ܕܢܚܘܘܢܝܗ [b] ܐܡܪ
[c] ܟܠܗܘܢ [d] ܠܐ

[f] ܬܠܡܝܕܘܗܝ
[g] ܘܐܡܪܝܢ [h] ܐܡܪ
[j] omit ܗܘ
[l] ܕܡܐܬܝܬܟ
[o] ܘܐܡܪ [p] ܢܛܥܝܟܘܢ
[q] add ܗܘ

[s] omit ܕܝ [t] ܕܝܢ
[u] ܕܬܫܡܥܘܢ
[v] ܕܢܗܘܝܢ

Codex A.	Codex B.	Codex C.

7 ܗܘܐ ܥܝܪܘܬܐ : ܢܦܩܘ ܠܗ ܡܢ ܟܠ ܡܢ
ܕܡܛܝܘܢ ܟܠ ܕܡܛܘ : ܘܗܘܘ ܡܛܘܬܢ ܘܡܡܟܝܢ
8 ܘܡܘܕܝܢ ܒܐܬܪܝܢ ܐܬܪܝܢ : ܒܟܠ ܙܒܢ ܕܝ
9 ܦܪܥ ܚܠܦܝܢ : ܡܢ ܒܨܒܝܢ ܒܢܗܪܐ ܫܘܒܚܐ
ܠܠܝܫܘܥ ܘܡܫܬܡܥܝܢ ܫܘܒܚܐ : ܘܐܬܝܢ
ܗܘܝܢ ܡܛܘܬܢ ܡܢ ܟܠܗܘܢ ܥܡܡܐ ܠܟܠ
10 ܥܠܡܐ : ܘܡܢ ܫܡܝܐ ܕܟܠ ܡܠܟܘܬܐ
ܠܡܠܟܐ ܡܫܝܚܐ : ܘܡܫܝܚܐ ܘܠܟܘܢ
11 ܠܡܠܟܐ : ܘܡܠܟ ܥܡܗ ܕܐܝܬܝ ܡܫܝܚܐ
12 ܘܠܥܠܡ ܥܠܡܝܢ : ܘܠܥܠܡ ܕܥܠܡ ܚܕܐ
13 ܫܡܝܐ ܫܒܝܚ ܒܗܘܢ ܡܠܟܐ ∴ † ܘ ܕܡܢ
[f. 48a]
ܕܫܡܝܐ ܠܝܫܘܥ ܗܘ ܡܪܐ : ܐܡܝܢ ∴

† f. 49a.

r omit ܐܡܝܢ

LXXXII.

Matt. XXII. 35—46.

ܗܘܐ ܚܕ ܡܢ ܢܡܘܣܝܐ ܚܕ ܐܬܩܪܒ ܡܢ
35 ܬܠܡܝܕܘܗܝ : ܘܢܣܝ ܠܗ ܘܐܡܪ ܠܗ ܚܕ
36 ܡܠܦܢܐ : ܐܝܕܐ ܦܘܩܕܢܐ ܪܒ ܒܢܡܘܣܐ
37 ܘܐܡܪ ܠܗ ܝܫܘܥ : ܬܪܚܡ ܠܡܪܝܐ ܐܠܗܟ
ܒܟܠܗ ܠܒܟ : ‡ ܘܒܟܠܗ ܢܦܫܟ ܘܒܟܠܗ
ܚܝܠܟ : ܘܒܟܠܗ ܪܥܝܢܟ ܘܒܟܠ
38 ܗܢܘ ܦܘܩܕܢܐ ܪܒܐ ܘܩܕܡܝܐ : ܗܢܘ ܕܝܢ
39 ܬܢܝܢܐ ܕܕܡܐ ܠܗ : ܬܪܚܡ ܠܩܪܝܒܟ
40 ܐܝܟ ܢܦܫܟ : ܒܗܠܝܢ ܬܪܝܢ ܦܘܩܕܢܝܢ
41 ܢܡܘܣܐ ܟܠܗ ܘܢܒܝܐ ܬܠܝܢ : ܟܕ
ܕܝܢ ܟܢܝܫܝܢ ܦܪܝܫܐ : ܫܐܠ ܐܢܘܢ
42 ܝܫܘܥ ܘܐܡܪ : ܡܢܐ ܐܡܪܝܢ ܐܢܬܘܢ
ܥܠ ܡܫܝܚܐ ܒܪ ܡܢ ܗܘ : ܐܡܪܝܢ ܠܗ
43 ܕܕܘܝܕ : ܐܡܪ ܠܗܘܢ ܘܐܝܟܢܐ ܕܘܝܕ
ܒܪܘܚ ܩܪܐ ܠܗ ܡܪܝܐ

b add ܕ

‡ f. 54a.

o omit ܘ

p add ܕܝ

p add ܕܝ

r omit ܐܡܝܢ

Codex A.	Codex B.	Codex C.
ܬܐܒ[p]	44 ܕܐܡܪ : ܐܡܪ ܡܪܢܐ ܠܡܚܪܝ [p]ܬܐܒ ܡܢ ܡܚܝܢ	ܕܐܬܝܢ[q]
[r]ܒܡܠܒܫܝܗܝܢ	ܒܪܡܐ [q]ܕܐܬܝܢ [r]ܒܡܠܒܫܝܗܝܢ [s]ܒܒܬܝܢ ܬܚܘܬ	[r]ܒܡܠܒܫܝܗܝܢ
[s]ܒܒܬܝܢ [t]ܐܝܠܝܢ	45 [t]ܐܝܠܝܢ : ܐܢ ܐܘܢ [n]ܕܚܙܘ ܒܪܘܚܐ ܡܪܐ [o]ܠܗ	[s]ܒܒܬܝܢ [t]ܐܝܠܝܢ :
[n]ܕܚܙܘ [o]ܠܗ	46 ܡܪܝ : ܗܘܝܢ ܗܘ ܒܪܗ : ܘܐܢܫ ܠܐ ܗܘܐ	[o]ܠܗ [u]ܡܠܠ
[w]ܕܝܬܒ	[u]ܡܠܠ [w]ܕܝܬܒ [x]ܡܠܟܐ : ܘܠܐ ܕܝ [z]ܐܚܝܢܘܢ	[w]ܕܝܬܒ ܬܐܬܗ [x]*add*
[x]*add* ܬܐܬܗ [z]ܐܚܝܢܘܢ	ܐܢܫ ܡܢ ܗܘ ܝܘܡܐ ܕܝܫܐܠ ܬܐܬܗ ܒܘܕ ⁘	[z]ܐܚܝܢܘܢ

LXXXIII.

Matt. XXIV. 34—44.

Codex A.	Codex B.	Codex C.
[a]ܘܡܥܪܒܐ ܐܘܕܥܬ ܐܘܠܥܙܪ ܡܢ [a]ܡܝܬܝܢ	[a]ܝܘܡ ܚܡܫܬ ܦܨܚܐ ܒܬܪ ܐܠܥܙܪ ܡܢ	[a]ܠܝܘܡ ܐܘܕܥܬ ܐܘܡܪܐ ܒܬܪ ܡܢ [a]ܡܝܬܐ
[x]*add* ܐܢܫ	34 ܡܬܐܝ [a] :[w] [x]ܐܡܪ ܡܪܢܐ [y]ܐܡܝܢ ܐܡܝܢ ܐܡܪ	[w]*add* ܘܒܬܪܗ ܡܝܬܪܘܬܐ
[y] *omit* ܐܡܝܢ	ܐܢܐ ܠܟܘܢ : ܕܠܐ ܝܥܒܘܪ ܗܕܝܢ ܕܪܐ [z]†	† f. 49b.
[z] *add* ܒܪܡܐ	35 ܕܗܠܝܢ ܟܘܠܗܘܢ [a]ܝܬܥܒܕܘܢ : ܫܡܝܐ [b]ܕܝ	[y] *omit* ܐܡܝܢ
[a]ܝܬܥܒܕܘܢ	[c]ܘܐܪܥܐ [d]ܝܥܒܪܘܢ [e]ܘܡܠܝ ܕܝܠܝ ܠܐ	[z] *add* ܒܪܡܐ
‡ f. 54b.	36 [d]ܝܥܒܪܘܢ : ‡ ܥܠ [f]ܝܘܡܐ ܗܘ [g]ܗܘ ܐܐ	[c] *add* ܕܝ [e]ܘܡܠܝ
[b] *omit* ܕܝ	[f. 48b] ܫܥܬܐ ܐܢܫ ܠܐ ܝܕܥ ܐܘܦ ܠܐ ܡܠܐܟܝܐ	
[d]ܝܥܒܪܘܢ	ܕܫܡܝܐ ܐܘܦ ܠܐ ܒܪܐ : ܐܠܐ ܐܢ ܐܒܐ	
[f] *add* ܕܝ [e]ܘܡܠܝܗ	37 [h]ܒܠܚܘܕܝ : ܗܝܟ ܡܐ [i]ܕܗܘܘ [k]ܥܠ [l]ܝܘܡܝ	[k] *omit* ܥܠ [i] *add* ܠܒܪ
[g]ܗܘܐ [h]ܒܠܚܘܕܘܗܝ	ܕܢܘܚ : ܗܟܕܝܢ [m]ܬܗܘܐ [n]ܡܝܬܝܬܗ ܕܒܪ	[l]ܒܝܘܡܝ
[k] *omit* ܥܠ [i] *add* ܠܒܪ	38 ܕܐܢܫܐ : ܗܝܟ ܡܐ ܠܒܪ ܕܗܘܐ [o]ܒܝܘܡܝܐ	[m] *add* ܐܘܦ
[l]ܒܝܘܡܝ	ܗܠܝܢ : ܗܠܝܢ ܕܡܢ ܩܕܡ ܛܘܦܢܐ ܕܗܘܘ	
[m] *add* ܐܘܦ	ܐܟܠܝܢ ܘܫܬܝܢ : [p]ܡܫܬܬܦܝܢ ܘܡܫܬܬܦܝܢ : ܒܪܡܐ	[p]ܡܫܬܬܦܝܢ
[n]ܡܝܬܝܬܗ	39 ܠܝܘܡܐ ܕܥܠ ܢܘܚ ܠܩܒܘܬܐ : ܘܠܐ ܝܕܥܘ	
[o]ܒܝܘܡܝܐ	ܒܪܡܐ ܕܐܬܐ ܛܘܦܢܐ ܘܢܣܒ ܟܘܠܗܘܢ :	
[q]ܗܟܕܝܢ	[q]ܗܟܕܝܢ ܬܗܘܐ ܐܘܦ [r]ܡܝܬܝܬܗ ܕܒܪܗ	
[r]ܡܝܬܝܬܗ	40 ܕܐܢܫܐ : ܒܗܝܢ ܬܪܝܢ ܝܗܘܘܢ ܒܚܩܠܐ ܚܕ	
[u]ܝܗܘܘܢ [s] *omit* ܕܝ	41 [s]ܕܝ ܡܬܕܒܪ ܘܚܕ ܡܫܬܒܩ : ܬܪܬܝܢ [u]ܝܗܘܘܢ	[s] *omit* ܕܝ
[v]ܛܚܢܢ [t]ܬܬܕܒܪ	[v]ܛܚܢܢ ܒܪܚܝܐ ܚܕܐ [t]ܬܬܕܒܪ ܘܚܕܐ ܬܫܬܒܩ :	[u]ܝܗܘܘܢ [v]ܬܬܕܒܪ
[w]ܗܘ [x]ܗܢܕܝܢ	42 [w]ܗܘܐ ܐܘܢ ܥܝܪܝܢ ܕܠܝܬ ܐܢܬܘܢ ܝܕܥܝܢ	[w]ܗܘܘ
[y]ܡܪܟܘܢ	43 [x]ܕܗܕܝܢ ܝܘܡ [y]ܡܪܝܟܘܢ ܐܬܐ : ܗܕܐ ܕܝ	[x]ܗܕܝܢ

Codex A.	*Codex* B.	*Codex* C.

[illegible]
[illegible]
44 [illegible]
[illegible]
[illegible] ⁘

LXXXIV.

Matt. XXV. 14—30.

[a] [illegible]
14 [illegible] ‡ [illegible]
[illegible]
15 [illegible] † [illegible]
[illegible]
16 [illegible]
[f. 49a]
[illegible]
17 [illegible]
[illegible]
[illegible]
18 [illegible]
19 [illegible]
[illegible]
20 [illegible]
[illegible]
21 [illegible]
[illegible]
[illegible]
22 [illegible]
[illegible]
[illegible]
23 [illegible]

Codex A notes: [a] [illegible] ‡ f. 55a. [a] [illegible] [b] [illegible] [c] *omit* [illegible] [d] *omit* [illegible] [e] *omit* [illegible] [g] *add* [illegible] ...

Codex C notes: [z] *add* [illegible] [a] [illegible] [c] [illegible] † f. 50a. [f] [illegible] [l] [illegible] [n] [illegible] [o] [illegible] [q] [illegible] [r] *omit* [illegible] [s] *omit* [illegible] [t] [illegible] [u] *omit* [illegible] [q] [illegible] [w] *add* [illegible] [s] *add* [illegible] [w] *omit* [illegible] [v] *add* [illegible] [x] [illegible] [y] [illegible] [b] [illegible] [d] *add* [illegible] [e] *omit* [illegible] . . . [illegible]

Codex A.	Codex B.	Codex C.

Codex B.

ܐܦ ʰܒܙܥܘܪܐ ܗܘܝܬ ܡܗܝܡܢܐ ܥܠ ⁱܣܓܝܐܝܢ
ᵏܐܩܝܡܝܢܟ ܡܗܝܡܢ: ܥܠ ܚܕܘܬܐ ܕܡܪܟ ˡܐܥܘܠ ܠܟ:
24 ܩܪܒ ܠܗ ܐܦ ܗܘ ܕܢܣܒ ܟܟܪܐ ܚܕ: ᵐܡܪܝ ܝܕܥ ⁿܗܘܝܬ
ᵒܕܐܢܬ ᵖܓܒܪܐ ܩܫܝܐ ܐܢܬ: ܚܨܕ ᵠܐܝܟܐ ܕܠܐ ܙܪܥܬ
ܘܟܢܫ ܐܝܟܐ ˢ‡ ܕܠܐ ܒܕܪܬ:
25 ᵗܘܕܚܠܬ: ܘܐܙܠܬ ܛܡܪܬ ܟܟܪܟ ܒܐܪܥܐ: ܗܐ ܕܝܠܟ ܗܘ
ᵘܘܥܢܐ ܡܪܗ ᵛܘܐܡܪ ܠܗ ʷܥܒܕܐ ܒܝܫܐ ܘܚܒܢܐ:
26 ܝܕܥ ܗܘܝܬ ᶻܕܚܨܕ ܐܢܐ ʸܐܝܟܐ ܕܠܐ ܙܪܥܬ ܘܟܢܫ ܐܢܐ
ܐܝܟܐ ܕܠܐ ᵇܒܕܪܬ: ᶜܘܠܐ ܡܢ ܕܝܠܟ ܕܝܢ
ᵈܘ ܡܢ ܗܘ ܕܠܐ †ܙܪܥܬ: ᵉܘܡܟܝܠ ܡܢ [f.49b]
27 ᶠܐܠܐ ܗܘܐ ܠܟ ܕܬܫܕܐ ܟܣܦܝ: ܠᵍܬܪܘܬܐ ʰܥܠ ܬܚܘܝܐ: ܘܐܢܐ
ⁱܗܘܝܬ ܐܬܐ ʲܘܬܒܥ ܗܘܝܬ ܕܝܠܝ ܥܡ ܪܒܝܬܗ:
28 ᵏܣܒܘ ܗܟܝܠ ܡܢܗ ܟܟܪܐ ܘܗܒܘܗܝ ܠܗܘ
29 ܕܐܝܬ ܠܗ ܥܣܪܐ ܟܟܪܝܢ: ܟܠ ܓܝܪ ܕܐܝܬ ܠܗ
ᵐܢܬܝܗܒ ܠܗ ⁿܘܢܬܝܬܪ ܠܗ: ܡܢ ܕܝܢ ᵒܕܠܝܬ
ܠܗ ܐܦ ܗܘ ܕܐܝܬ ܠܗ ᵖܢܫܬܩܠ ܡܢܗ:
30 ܘܠܥܒܕܐ ᵠܒܛܝܠܐ ʳܐܦܩܘ ܠܒܪ ܠܚܫܘܟܐ
ܬܡܢ ܢܗܘܐ ܒܟܝܐ ˢܘܚܘܪܩ ܫܢܐ ᵗ:·

LXXXIV.*

Matt. XXV. 1—13.

ᵃܗܝܕܝܢ ܬܬܕܡܐ ܡܠܟܘܬܐ ܕܫܡܝܐ ܠܥܣܪ ܒܬܘܠܢ ᵃ ܓܕܐ ˣ:
1 ܐܝܠܝܢ ܕܢܣܒ ʸܠܡܦܐܕܝܗܝܢ ᶻܘܢܦܩ ܠܐܘܪܥ ܚܬܢܐ ܘܟܠܬܐ:
ܚܡܫ ᵃܡܢܗܝܢ ᵇܚܟܝܡܢ ܘܚܡܫ ܣܟܠܢ: ᶜܘܗܢܝܢ ᵈܣܟܠܬܐ ᵉܢܣܒ ᶠܠܡܦܐܕܝܗܝܢ
2 ᵍܘܠܐ ʰܢܣܒ ⁱܥܡܗܝܢ ᵏ ˡܡܫܚܐ ᵐ:
3 ⁿܘܚܟܝܡܬܐ ᵒܢܣܒ ᵖܡܫܚܐ ܒܡܐܢܐ ᵠܥܡ ʳܠܡܦܐܕܝܗܝܢ ˢ
4 ᵗܟܕ ܕܝܢ ᵘܐܘܚܪ ܚܬܢܐ ᵛܢܡ ᵗܟܠܗܝܢ ᵗܘܕܡܟ

Codex A.

ʷܒܡܐ̈ܢܝܗܘܢ
ʸܘܗ̈ܘܝ ᶻܕܡܟ̈ܢ
ᵃܒܦܠܓܘܬܗ
ᵇܐܬܥܒܕܬ ᵈܒܟܢ
ᶠܠܡܦ̈ܕܝܗܘܢ
ᵍܐܡܪ̈ܝ ⁱܗ̈ܒܢ
ʲܡܫܚܟܘܢ
ᵏܠܡܦ̈ܕܝܢ
ᵐܐܓܝܒܘ ⁿܘܐܡܪ̈ܝ
ᵖ *add* ܕܠܐ
ʰܐܙܠܢ ⁱܘܙܒ̈ܢܢ
ᵏܠܟܢ ᵐܕܝܙܒܢܢ
ⁿܕܗ̈ܘܝ ᵒܡܛܝܒ̈ܢ
ᵖܥ̈ܠܝ ʳܒܢ
ˢܐܬ̈ܝܐܢ ᵗܫܪܝܬ

‡ f. 195*b*.

ᵘܐܡܪ̈ܢ ᵛܡܪ̈ܢ
ˣ *add* ܐܡܝܢ ᶻܡܚܪ
ᵃ *add* ܕܐܬܐ ܒܗ
ܒܪܗ ܕܐܢܫܐ

Codex B.

5 ʷܒܡܐܢܝܗܘܢ ܥܡ ܠܡܦ̈ܕܝܗܘܢ : ܟܕ ܕܝ ܐܘܚܪ
6 ܚܬܢܐ ˣܢܐܡܘ ʸܘܗܘܘ ᶻܕܡܟ̈ܢܝܢ ∴ ᵃܒܦܠܓܗ
ⁿܕܝ ܕܠܠܝܐ ܩܥܘܐ ᵇܐܬܥܒܕܬ : ܗܐ ܚܬܢܐ
7 ܐܬܐ ܩܘܡܘ ܦܘܩܘ ᶜܠܐܘܪܥܘܬܗ : ᵈܒܟܝܢ
ܩܡܘ ܟܘܠ ܒܬܘܠܬܐ ᵉܗܠܝܢ ܘܬܩܢܝܢ
8 ᶠܠܡܦ̈ܕܝܗܘܢ : ᵈܒܟܝܢ ᵍܐܡܪܝܢ ᵉܗܠܝܢ ܛܦܫܬܐ
ʰܠܦܩܝܚܬܐ : ⁱܗܒܘ ܠܢ ܡܢ ʲܡܫܚܟܘܢ ܕܗܐ
9 ᵏܠܡܦ̈ܕܝܢ ˡܛܦܝܢ : ᵐܐܓܝܒܘ ܕܝ ܦܩܝܚܬܐ
ⁿܘܐܡܪܝܢ ᵒ † ܠܐ ᵖ ܐܡܬܝ ܠܐ ܢܣܦܩ ܠܢ
[f. 50*a*]
ᵠܘܠܟܝܢ : ʰܐܙܠܝܢ ܕܝ ܠܘܬ ܗܠܝܢ ܕܡܙܒܢܝܢ
10 ⁱܘܙܒܢܝܢ ᵏܠܟܘܢ ∴ ܟܕ ܕܝ ˡܐܙܠܝ ᵐܕܝܙܒܢܝܢ
ܐܬܐ ܚܬܢܐ : ܘܗܠܝܢ ⁿܕܗܘܘ ᵒܡܛܝܒܝܢ ᵖܥܠܘ
11 ܥܡܗ ܠܒܝܬ ܚܘܠܢܐ ᵠܘܐܬܚܕ ܬܪܥܐ ∴ ܒܬܪ
ʳܕܝܢ ˢܐܬܝ ᵗܫܪܟ ܒܬܘܠܬܐ ⁿܐܡܪܝܢ ᵛܡܪܢ
12 ᵛܡܪܢ ܦܬܚ ܠܢ : ܗܘ ܕܝ ܐܓܝܒ ‡ ܘܐܡܪ :
ʷܐܡܝܢ ˣܐܡܪ ܐܢܐ ᵏܠܟܘܢ ܕܠܝܬ ܐܢܐ
13 ᶻܡܚܟܢ ܠܟܘܢ ܗܘܘ ܐܘܢ ܚܟܡܝܢ ܕܠܝܬ ܐܢܬܘܢ
ܝܕܥܝܢ ܝܘܡܐ ܘܠܐ ܫܥܬܐ .ᵃ

Codex C.

ʷܒܡܐܢܝܗܘܢ
ˣܢܗܡܘ ᵃܒܦܠܓܘܬܗ
ᶜܠܐܘܪܥܘܬܗ
ᵉ *omit* ܗܠܝܢ . . .
. . . ܐܡܪܝܢ
ʰܠܦܩܝܚܬܐ
ʲܡܫܚܟܘܢ
ⁿ *omit* ܘ ˡ *omit* ܛܦܝܢ

† f. 51*a*.

ᵒ *add* ܠܗܘܢ
ᵖ *add* ܕܠܐ
ᵠܘܠܟܘܢ ʰܐܙܠܝ
ˡܐܙܠܘ ᵐܕܝܙܒܢܘܢ
ᵒܡܛܝܒܢ ᵖܥܠܝ
ᵠܘܐܚܕ ˢܐܬܐ
ᵗܫܪܝܬ ᵘܐܡܪܢ
ʷ *add* ܠܗܘܢ
ˣ *add* ܐܡܝܢ

Codex A.

[CXX.]

ᵃܟܕ ᵇܕܝ ᵇܐܬܐ
ᵈ *add* ܒܫܒܘܚܬܗ
ᵉܡܠܐܟ̈ܘܗܝ

‡ f. 75*b*.

ᶠ *omit* ܒܟܝܢ
ᵍܠܩܕܡܘܗܝ
ʰܡܦܪܫ ⁱܘܡܩܝܡ
ʲܣܡܐܠܗ ∴ ᵏܒܟܢ
ˡܐܡܪ ᵐܡܒܪ̈ܟܘܝ
ⁿܝܪܬܘ ᵒܕܡܬܒܕܐ
ᵖܫܘܪܝܗ ᵠܕܥܠܡܐ

Codex B.

Matt. XXV. 31—XXVI. 2.

31 ᵃܘܟܕ ᵇܐܬܐ ܒܪܗ ܕܓܒܪܐ ᵈܘܟܘܠ ᵉܡܠܐܟܘܗ
ܥܡܗ : ܒܟܝܢ ܗܘ ܝܬܒ ܥܠ ܡܬܒܘܬܒܝܬܐ
32 ܕܫܒܘܚܬܗ : ᶠܘܒܟܝܢ ‡ ܡܬܟܢܫܝܢ ᵍܠܘܩܕܡܘܗ
ܟܘܠܗܘܢ ܥܡܡܝܐ : ܘܗܘ ʰܡܦܪܫ ܠܗܘܢ
ܗܠܝܢ ܡܢ ܗܠܝܢ : ܗܝܟ ܡܢ ܕܪܥܝܐ ʰܡܦܪܫ
33 ܐܡܪܝܐ ܡܢ ܓܕܝܐ : ⁱܘܡܩܝܡ ܐܡܪܝܐ ܡܢ
34 ܝܡܝܢܗ ܘܓܕܝܐ ܡܢ ʲܣܡܐܠܗ : ᵏܒܟܝܢ ˡܝܐܡܪ
ܡܠܟܐ ܠܗܠܝܢ ܕܡܢ ܝܡܝܢܗ : ܐܬܘ ᵐܡܒܪܟܝ
ܕܐܒܐ ⁿܝܪܬܘ ܡܠܟܘܬܐ ܗܕܐ ᵒܕܡܬܒܕܬܐ
35 ܠܟܘܢ ܡܢ ᵖܫܘܪܝܗ ᵠܕܥܠܡܐ : ܟܦܢܬ ܓܪ

Codex C.

(*deest in hoc loco*)

Codex A.

[s] ܕܐܟܘܠ   [t] *omit* ܘ
[v] ܐܟܣܢܝܐ
[x] ܒܪܬܠܠܐ
[y] ܐܬܟܪܗܬ
[z] *add* ܗܘܝܬ
[a] ܘܐܬܝܬܘܢ
[b] ܠܘܬܝ   [c] ܒܟܡ
[o] ܘܐܡܪܝܢ   [d] ܚܙܝܢܟ
[e] ܟܦܢ   [f] ܘܬܪܣܝܢܟ
[g] ܨܗܐ   [h] ܘܐܫܩܝܢܟ
[i] ܐܟܣܢܝܐ   [k] ܘܟܢܫܢܟ
[l] *omit* ܐܘ̈ ... ܗܘܝܢ :
[m] ܒܐܝܫ   [n] *add* ܐܘ̈
[o] ܒܒܝܬܐܣܝܪܐ   [p] ܘܐܬܝܢ
[q] *omit* ܐܡܝܢ   ‡ f. 76*a*.
[r] ܐܡܪ ܐܢܐ   [s] *add* ܐܫܝܢ
[t] *omit* ܐܘܦ   [u] ܒܟܡ
[w] ܐܡܪ   [z] ܕܠܥܠܡ
[a] ܕܡܛܝܒܐ   [b] ܠܣܛܢܐ
[c] ܘܠܡܠܐܟܘܗܝ :
[d] ܕܐܟܘܠ   [e] ܐܟܣܢܝܐ
[f] ܘܒܪܬܠܠܐ
[h] ܘܒܒܝܬܐܣܝܪܐ   [i] ܒܟܡ
[k] *add* ܐܦ ܗܢܘܢ
[m] ܘܢܐܡܪܘܢ
[n] ܚܙܝܢܟ   [o] ܟܦܢ
[p] ܨܗܐ   [r] ܒܪܬܠܠܐ
[s] ܒܒܝܬܐܣܝܪܐ
[t] ܫܡܫܢܟ   [k] ܢܥܢܐ
[l] ܠܗܘܢ   [m] ܘܢܐܡܪ
[n] *omit* ܠܗܘܢ
[o] ܠܚܕ ܡܢ   [p] *omit* ܐܚܕ
[q] *add* ܠܐ   [r] ܘܢܐܙܠܘܢ
[s] *omit* ܠܢܘܪܐ
[t] *add* ܗܠܝܢ ܠܓܗܢܐ
[u] ܕܠܥܠܡ

Codex B.

ܘܝܗܒܬܘܢ ܠܝ [s]ܕܐܟܘܠ [t]ܘܨܗܝܬ ܘܐܫܩܝܬܘܢ
ܗܘܝ : [v]ܐܟܣܢܝܐ ܗܘܝܬ ܘܟܢܫܬܘܢ ܗܘܝ :
36 [x]ܒܪܬܠܠ ܗܘܝܬ ܘܐܠܒܫܬܘܢ ܗܘܝ : [y]ܐܬܟܪܗܬ
37 ܘܣܥܪܬܘܢ ܗܘܝ : ܒܒܝܬܐܣܝܪܐ [z] [a]ܘܐܬܝܬܘܢ
[b]ܠܘܬܝ : [c]ܒܟܡ ܢܥܢܘܢ ܠܗ ܙܕܝܩܐ [o]ܘܢܐܡܪܘܢ :
ܡܪܢ : ܐܡܬܝ [d]ܚܙܝܢܢ ܗܘܝܢ [e]ܟܦܢ [f]ܘܬܪܣܝܢ
38 ܗܘܝܢ : ܐܘ [g]ܨܗܐ [h]ܘܐܫܩܝܢ ܗܘܝܢ : ܐܡܬܝ
[d]ܚܙܝܢܢ ܗܘܝܢ [i]ܐܟܣܢܝܐ [k]ܘܟܢܫܢ ܗܘܝܢ : [l]ܐܘ̈
39 ܒܪܬܠܠ ܘܐܠܒܫܢ ܗܘܝܢ :[l] ܐܡܬܝ [d]ܚܙܝܢܢ [f. 50*b*]
ܗܘܝܢ [m]ܟܪܝܗ [n] [o]ܘܒܟܠܘܐ [p]ܘܐܬܝܢ ܠܘܬܟ :
40 ܘܢܥܢܐ ܡܠܟܐ ܘܐܡܪ ܠܗܘܢ : [q]ܐܡܝܢ
ܐܡܝܢ [r]ܐܡܪ ܐܢܐ[r] ‡ ܠܟܘܢ ܕܟܕ ܟܠ ܐܡܬܝ
41 ܕܥܒܕܬܘܢ ܠܚܕ ܡܢ ܗܠܝܢ[s] ܙܥܘܪܐ [t]ܐܘܦ
ܠܝ ܥܒܕܬܘܢ : [u]ܒܟܡ ܗܘ [w]ܢܐܡܪ ܐܘܦ
ܠܗܠܝܢ ܕܡܢ ܣܡܠܐ : ܐܙܠܘ ܠܟܘܢ ܡܢܝ
ܠܝܛܐ ܠܢܘܪܐ [z]ܕܠܥܠܡ : [a]ܕܡܛܝܒܐ [b]ܠܐܟܠܩܪܨܐ
42 [c]ܘܠܡܠܐܟܘܗܝ : ܟܦܢܬ ܓܝܪ ܘܠܐ ܝܗܒܬܘܢ ܠܝ
[d]ܕܐܟܘܠ : ܘܨܗܝܬ ܘܠܐ ܐܫܩܝܬܘܢ ܗܘܝ :
43 [e]ܐܟܣܢܝܐ ܗܘܝܬ ܘܠܐ ܟܢܫܬܘܢ ܗܘܝ : [f]ܒܪܬܠܠ
ܘܠܐ ܐܠܒܫܬܘܢ ܒܝ : ܟܪܝܗ [h]ܘܒܟܠܘܐ
44 ܘܠܐ ܣܥܪܬܘܢ ܗܘܝ : [i]ܒܟܡ ܢܥܢܘܢ[k]
[m]ܘܢܐܡܪܘܢ : ܡܪܢ : ܐܡܬܝ [n]ܚܙܝܢܢ ܗܘܝܢ :
[o]ܟܦܢ ܐܘ̈ [p]ܨܗܐ ܐܘ̈ [e]ܐܟܣܢܝܐ ܐܘ [r]ܒܪܬܠܠ
ܐܘ ܟܪܝܗ ܐܘ [s]ܒܟܠܘܐ ܘܠܐ [t]ܫܡܫܢܝܢ
45 ܗܘܝܢ : [i]ܒܟܡ [k]ܢܥܢܐ ܐܘܦ [l]ܡܠܟܐ [m]ܘܢܐܡܪ
[n]ܠܗܘܢ : ܐܡܝܢ ܐܡܝܢ ܐܡܪ ܐܢܐ ܠܟܘܢ :
ܕܟܕ ܟܠ ܐܡܬܝ ܕܠܐ ܥܒܕܬܘܢ [o]ܥܡ [p]ܐܚܕ
ܗܠܝܢ ܙܥܘܪܐ ܐܘܦ [q] ܠܝ ܠܐ ܥܒܕܬܘܢ :
46 [r]ܘܢܐܙܠܘܢ [s]ܠܢܘܪܐ[t] [u]ܕܠܥܠܡ : ܘܙܕܝܩܐ ܠܚܝܐ

Codex C.

(*deest*)

Codex A.	Codex B.	Codex C.
[CXLIV.]	XXVI. 1 ᵘܕܠܥܠܡ: ᵛܘܗܘܐ ܟܕ ᵂܫܠܡ ܡܪܢ ܝܫܘܥˣ	(deest)
ᵘܕܠܥܠܡ ᵛܘܗܘܐ	ܟܠܗܘܢ ܡܠܝܐ ܗܠܝܢ ʸܠܬܠܡܝܕܘܗܝ ܐܡܪ ܠܗܘܢ	
ᵂܫܠܡ ˣadd ܟܠ	2 ܕܡܢ ܒܬܪ ܬܪܝܢ ܝܘܡܝܢ ᶻܦܨܚܐ ܡܬܥܒܕ:	
ʸܠܬܠܡܝܕܘܗܝ	ܘܒܪܗ ᵃܕܓܒܪܐ ᵇܡܫܬܠܡ ᶜܕܢܨܛܠܒ:	
ᶻܦܨܚܐ ᵃܕܓܒܪܐ	ܫܠܡܬ ᵃܩܪܝܢܬ ܐܠܒܘܪ ܡܬܐ: ܗܘܐ ܕܝܢ ܡܠܦܪ	
ᵇܡܬܡܫܠܡ	ܬܘܪܝܐ ܐܠܝܫܘܥ ܘܐܠܥܡܘܢܬ ܡܢ ܒܪܝܬܐ ܟܕ	
ᶜܕܢܨܛܠܒ	ܟܕ ܐܬܝܠܕܐ: ᵃ	
ᵃܩܪܝܢܬ ܐܠܒܘܪ (sic)	* ܫܪ ܡܢܓܝܠܐ ܕܝܫܘܥ ܡܫܝܚܐ ܡܢ ܒܬܪ ܕܐܬܝܠܕ	
ܡܫܝܚܘܬܗ ܗܘܐ	ܐܝܟܢ ܕܝܠܕܬܗ ܗܘܐ ܐܡܪ ܐܠܗܐ	
ܫܝܬܢܐ ܬܘܪܝܐ	* Manu recentiore scriptum.	
ܐܠܝܫܘܥܕܘ (sic)		
ᵃܘܐܠܥܡܘܢܬ		

LXXXV.

Luke IV. 31—36.

Codex A.	Codex B.	Codex C.
ܩܪܝܢܬ ܐܠܝܫܘܥ	[f. 51a] ᵃܒܝܘܡ ܚܕ ܩܪܝܢܬ ܐܠܒܘܪ ܠܥܡܐ ܬܘܪܝܐ	
ܐܠܒܪܝܬ ܐܠܥܡܘܢ	ܐܠܥܡܘܢܬ ܘܐܠܝܫܘܥ ܡܩܠܬ ܐܠܠܗ ܟܕ ܐܬܝܠܕ.ᵃᵃ	
ܠܘܩܐ قرات انجيل	31 ‡ܘܢܚܬ ܡܪܢ ܝܫܘܥ ܠܟܦܪ ܢܚܘܡ ᵇܡܕܝܢܬܐ	
البشر (sic) اطاهر لوقا	ܕܓܠܝܠܐ: ܘܗܘܐ ᶜܡܠܦ ܠܗܘܢ ܒܫܒܬܐ	ᶜܡܠܦ
ᵃܘܩܪܝܢܐ ܐܫܒܬ	32 ܘܗܘܘ ܡܬܕܡܪܝܢ ܥܠ ܝܘܠܦܢܗ: ᵈܕܒܫܘܠܛܢܐ	ᵈܕܒܫܘܠܛܢܐ
ᵃܐܠܐܠܗ ܡܢ ܠܘܩܐ	33 ܘܗܘܐ ܡܠܬܗ: ܘܗܘܐ ᵉܬܡܢ ᶠܒܟܢܘܫܬܐ ܚܕ ܓܒܪ	ᵉomit ܬܡܢ
‡ f. 56a.	ܕܗܘܐ ܒܗ ᵍܪܘܚ ʰܕܫܐܕ ⁱܛܢܦܐ: ʲܘܐܙܥܩ	ᶠܒܟܢܘܫܬܐ ᵍܪܘܚܐ
ᵃadd: ܘܡܠܦ ܡܢܗܘܢ ܘܗܘܘ	34 ᵏܒܩܠܐ ᵏܪܒܐ ܘܐܡܪ: ܡܐ ܠܢ ܘܠܟ ܝܫܘܥ	ʰܕܫܐܕ ʲܘܐܙܥܩ
ᵇܒܟܢܘܫܬܐ ᶜܡܠܦ	ˡܢܨܪܝܐ: ܐܬܝܬ ܠܡܘܒܕܘ ܠܢ ܝܕܥ ܐܢܐ ܠܟᵐ	ᵏܒܩܠܐ ܪܒᵏ
ᵉomit ܬܡܢ ᵍܪܘܚܐ	35 ⁿܡܢܘ ܩܕܝܫܗ ܕܐܠܗܐ: ܘܟܐܐ ܒܗ ܡܪܢ	ⁿomit ܕ
ʰܕܫܐܕ ⁱܛܢܦܐ	ܝܫܘܥ ܘܐܡܪ ܣܟܘܪ ܦܘܡܟ ܘܦܘܩ ܡܢܗ	ᵒܫܐܕܐ ᵖܠܡܨܥܬܗ
ᵏܒܩܠ ܪܒᵏ	ᵒܫܐܕܐ ᵖܠܡܨܥܬܐ † ܘܢܦܩ ܡܢܗ ᑫܕܠܐ ܢܟܝܬ ܠܗ	† f. 51b.
ˡܢܨܪܝܐ ᵐadd ܡܢ	36 ܐܦܠܐ ܡܕܡ: ܘܗܘܬ ܬܗܪܐ ܥܠ ܟܠܗܘܢ:	ᑫܕܠܐ ܢܟܝܬ
ⁿomit ܕ	ܘܗܘܘ ܡܡܠܠܝܢ ʳܥܡ ܚܕܕܐ ܘܐܡܪܝܢ ˢ	ʳܥܡ ܚܕܕܐ
ᑫܕܠܐ ܢܟܝܬ	ܘܐܡܪܝܢ: ܡܢܐ ܗܝ ᵗܡܠܬܐ ᵗܗܕܐ ܕܒܫܘܠܛܢܐ	ˢܘܐܡܪܝܢ
ʳܥܡ ܚܕܕܐ	ܘܒܚܝܠ ᵘܦܩܕ ܠܪܘܚܐ ᵂܛܢܦܬܐ ˣܘܢܦܩܝܢ	ᵗܗܕܐ ܡܠܬܐᵗ
ᵗܗܕܐ ܡܠܬܐᵗ	ʸܢܦܩܝܢ: ᶻܫܠܡ ⁘	ᵘܦܩܕ
ʷadd ܡܢܗ		ᶻomit ܫܠܡ
ˣܘܢܦܩܝܢ ʸܢܦܩܝܢ		

Codex A. | *Codex* B. | *Codex* C.

LXXXVI.

Luke V. 1, 2*a*, 7—11.

ܘܗܘܐ[a] ܗܘ ܝܫܘܥ ܐܙܠ ܒܚܕ ܐܝܠܝܢ ܡܢ

1 ܝܘܡܝܐ[a][w] ܘܗܘܐ ܩܐܡ ܥܠ[x][y] ܓܝܦ ܝܡܐ[y] ܥܠ

2 ܝܡܐ[b] ܕܓܢܣܪ: ܘܚܙܐ ܬܪܬܝܢ[z] ܐܠܦܝܢ

ܩܝܡܢ ܥܠ ܝܡܐ[b]: ܘܨܝܕܐ ܕܢܚܬܘ

ܡܢܗܘܢ[c] [d]: [g] ܘܡܫܝܓܝܢ[e] ܗܘܘ ܡܨܕܬܗܘܢ. ܘܪܡܙ

7 ܠܫܘܬܦܝܗܘܢ[i] ‡ [h] ܕܢܐܬܘܢ ܘܢܥܕܪܘܢ

ܕܢܐܬܘܢ[j] ܘܢܫܩܠܘܢ ܐܬܘ ܘܡܠܘ

ܬܪܬܝܢ ܐܠܦܐ[k]: ܥܕܡܐ ܕܩܪܒܘ[l] ܠܡܛܒܥ:

[f. 51*b*]

8 ܟܕ ܚܙܐ ܫܡܥܘܢ[m] ܟܐܦܐ[n] ܢܦܠ

ܥܠ ܪܓܠܘܗܝ[o] ܕܝܫܘܥ ܘܐܡܪ[p] ܒܥܘ

ܐܙܠ[q] ܠܝ ܡܪܝ[r] ܕܓܒܪܐ ܚܛܝܐ ܐܢܐ:

9 ܬܗܪܐ ܓܝܪ[s] ܐܚܕܗ[t] ܘܠܟܠܗܘܢ ܕܥܡܗ

10 ܥܠ ܨܝܕܐ ܕܨܝܕܘ: ܗܟܢܐ[u] ܐܦ

ܠܝܥܩܘܒ[w] ܘܠܝܘܚܢܢ[x] ܒܢܝ[y] ܙܒܕܝ[z]: ܕܗܘܘ

ܫܘܬܦܐ[a] ܕܫܡܥܘܢ: ܘܐܡܪ ܝܫܘܥ ܠܫܡܥܘܢ

ܠܐ ܬܕܚܠ: ܡܢ ܗܫܐ ܬܗܘܐ ܨܐܕ

11 ܠܒܢܝ ܐܢܫܐ: ܘܩܪܒܘ ܐܠܦܐ[c] ܠܝܒܫܐ:

ܘܫܒܩܘ ܟܠܡܕܡ[d] ܘܐܙܠܘ ܒܬܪܗ:

ܘܠܘܗܝ[e] ܟܠ :·

LXXXVII.

Luke V. 17—26.

ܘܗܘܐ[b] ܒܚܕ[a] ܡܢ ܝܘܡܝܐ ܗܘܐ ܝܫܘܥ[a] ܡܠܦ[b]:

Codex A.—cont.]

ܘܠܝܘܚܢܢ[x] ... [w] ... [u] ... ܘܠܟܠܗܘܢ[t]

... [d] ... [a] ... [z] ... [y]

... [a]

Codex C.: ܠܝܫܘܥ[a] ܡܢ ܝܘܡܐ[a] ... [w] add ... [y] omit ... [z] ... [h] omit ܘ ... [i] add ... [j] add (sic) ... [k] ... [m] ... [o] ... [t] ... [x] ... [y] ... [b] ... [c] ... [e] omit ܟܠ ... [b] ... [b]

Codex A.

ܐܪܓ ^x *add* ^a ܫܘܟܐ

^b ܟܠܝܠ ^d ܟܘܒܝܢ

^e ܘܟܠܝܠܗ

^f ܘܩܪܝܐ ^h ܫܪܐܡܐ

^j ܓܡܝܠ ^l ܕܝܠܗ

^n ܡܘܕܝܢ

‡ f. 57*a*.

^o ܟܘܕܐ ^a ܫܠܡ

^c ܐܘܩܠܘܣܐ

^d *omit* ܘ

^q ܕܡܢܝܢܝܢ

^t *omit* ܬܗ

^u ܡܢܝܢܝܢܗ

^x ܟܘܪܝܐ

^y ܥܒܝܩ ^z ܗܚܠܬܟ

^a ܘܥܡܝܗ ^b ܘܦܪܢܘܢ

^d ܕܡܚܠܠ ^e ܢܚܠ

^f ܗܦܠܡ ^g ܕܒܪ

^h ܠܡܒܠܘܢ

^i ܟܕܘܢ ^k ܕܟܒܪܬ

^l ܥܒܝܩ ^m ܗܚܠܬܟ

^n ܕܟܒܪܬ

^o ܗܠܝܟ ^p *add* ܕܝ

^q ܕܙܒܝܢܗ

^r ܥܠܠܝܗ ^s ܦܨܠܡ

^t ܒܚܡ ^u ܐܦܪܬ

^w ܗܒ ^x ܘܐܘܠ

^y ܡܢ ^z ܢܫܒ

^a ܒܠܝܗ ^b ܘܐܬܦܠܓ

‡ f. 57*b*.

^c *add* ܐܡܪܝܢ

^e ܡܩܒܣܝܢ

Codex B.

17 ^x ܘܐܠܒܫܘܗ ^y ܐܪܓܘܢܐ : ܘܐܬܟܪܟܘ ^z ܟܘܒܝܢ ^† ܟܠܝܠ
ܡܢ ^a ܫܘܟܐ ܘܗܘܐ ܫܐܠܝܢ ^b ܒܫܠܡܗ : ܘܗܘܘ
ܕܝ ^c ܫܪܝܢ ^d ܟܘܪܝܢ ^e ܘܡܠܟܝܢ ܕܝܗܘܕܝܐ :
ܗܠܝܢ ܕܐܬܐܘ ܡܢ ܟܠ ^f ܘܩܪܝܐ ܕܓܠܝܠܐ ܘܡܢ
^g ܐܘܪܫܠܡ : ܘܣܝܡܘ ܕܐܠܗܐ ܗܘܐ ^h ܡܫܝܚܐ
18 ܒܠܝܠܘܢ : ^i ܘܗܐ ܐܢܫܝܢ ܕܝ ܗܘܘ ܡܢܬܗܘܢ
ܒܠ ܒܪܫܐ ܟܘܪܝ ܕܗܘܐ ^‡ ^j ܡܟܪܝܙ : ܘܗܘܘ
^k ܒܟܝܢ ^l ܕܡܒܠܝܢ ܬܗ ^m ܘܡܣܦܕܝܢ ܬܗ
19 ^n ܡܘܕܝܢ : ܘܡܢ ܕܠܐ ܐܫܟܚܘ ^o ܟܘܕܐ
^a ܡܒܠܝܢ ܬܗ ^b ܠܟܕܠ ^c ܐܘܩܠܘܣܐ : ^d ܘܫܠܚܘ
ܠܐ ^p ܐܬܪܐ ܒܠ ^q ܕܡܢܝܢܝܢܗ ܘܐܬܚܘܐ ܬܗ
^r ܒܡ ܒܪܫܗ ܠܡܟܪܙܬܐ ^s ܠܡܘܕܢ ܡܢ ܪܫܐ ܘܫܘܐ :
20 ܘܗܘܐ ܫܡܥܐ ^t ܬܗ ^u ܡܢܝܢܝܢܗܘܢ ܘܐܡܪ
21 ^w ܠܗ ^x ܟܘܪܝܐ ^y ܥܒܝܩ ܠܟ ^z ܗܚܠܬܟ : ^a ܘܥܡܪ
ܡܬܚܡܝܢ ܗܦܪܐ ^b ܘܦܪܢܘܢ ܐܡܪܝܢ ^c ܡܢ ܗܘ
[f. 52*a*]
ܗܕܝܢ ^d ܕܡܚܠܠ ܒܕܝܢ : ܡܢ ^e ܐܚܒܠ ܕܥܡܝܗ
22 ^f ܗܚܠܡ ܐܠܐ ܒܠܡܕ ܐܠܗܐ : ܘܡܢ ^g ܕܒܪ
ܡܪܐ ܫܡܘܗ ܢܒܝܗܘܢ : ܐܒܝܕ ܘܐܡܪܬ
^h ܠܡܒܠܘܢ : ܡܢ ܐܬܘܢ ܡܬܚܡܝܢ ^i ܟܕܘܢ
23 ܒܠܒܒܟܘܢ ܡܢ ܚܝܕ ^k ܕܟܒܪܬ ^l ܥܒܝܩ ܠܟ
^m ܗܚܠܬܟ : ܐܐ ^n ܕܟܒܪܬ ܡܘܡ ^o ܗܠܝܟ :
24 ^p ܠܟܕܠ ^q ܕܙܒܝܢܗ ܕܐܬܐ ^r ܥܠܠܝܗ ܠܒܪܗ
ܕܒܪܐ ܒܠ ܐܪܒܐ ܕܡܥܡܘܢ ^s ܦܨܠܡ : ^t ܒܚܡ
ܐܡܪ ܠܡܪܥܠܐ ܠܟ ܐܢܐ ^u ܐܡܪ ܡܘܡ ^w ܗܒ
25 ܒܪܫܟ ^x ܘܐܘܠ ܠܒܝܬܟ : ܘܡܪ ܥܒܬܗ ܕܝ
^y ܡܐܡ ܠܒܝܬܗܘܢ : ^† ^z ܢܫܒ ܒܪܫܐ ܕܗܘܐ
ܪܡܐ ^a ܒܗ ^x ܘܐܘܠ ܠܒܝܬܗ ܡܫܒܚ ܠܐܠܗܐ :
26 ܘܬܡܗܐ ^‡ ܢܫܒ ܠܟܠܗܘܢ ܘܗܘܘ ܡܫܒܚܝܢ
ܠܐܠܗܐ : ^b ܘܐܬܦܠܓܘ ^c ܕܝܠܗ ^d ܕܚܙܝܢ ^e ܡܫܒܚܝܢ
ܘܡܕܝܢ ܀

Codex C.

† f. 52*a*.

^y *omit* ܡܘܪܝܐ

^z *add* ܒܪܐ ^a ܫܘܟܐ

^c ܫܪܝܢ ^f ܘܩܪܝܐ

^g ܐܘܪܫܠܡ ^h ܡܫܝܚܐ

^i *omit* ܘ

^k ܒܟܝܢ ^m ܘܡܣܦܕܝܢ

^n ܡܘܕܝܢܗ

^b ܠܟܕ ^c ܠܐܘܩܠܘܣܐ

^d *omit* ܘ ^p ܐܬܪܐ

^q ܕܡܢܝܢܝܢܗ

^r ܒܠ ^s ܡܘܕܢ

^t *omit* ܬܗ

^w ܠܗܘܢ ^x ܟܘܪܝܐ

^b ܘܦܪܢܘܢ

^d ܕܡܚܠܠ ^e *omit* ܡܢ

^g ܕܒܪ

^h ܠܡܒܠܘܢ

^l ܥܒܝܩ

^p *add* ܕܝ

^q ܕܙܒܝܢܗ

^w ܗܒ

^y ܡܢ

† f. 52*b*.

^z ܢܫܒ ^a ܒܠܝܗ

^b ܘܐܬܦܠܓ

^c *add* ܐܡܪܝܢ

^d ܕܚܙܝܢ

LXXXVIII.

Luke VI. 31—36.

Codex A.

ᵇܐܬܐܢܝܢ
ᶜ*omit* ܒܥܝܢ ܐܝܠܝܢ
ᶻ*add* ܘ ᵃܒܢܝ
ᶜ*omit* ܘܟܕܘܬ ᵇܗܝ
ᵈܪܚܡܝܢ
ᵍܡܚܒܝܢ ܐܢܬܘܢᵍ
ⁱ*omit* ܓܝܪ ʰܛܒܘ
ʲܕܡܚܒܝܢ
ᵏܛܒܝܢ
ᵐܗܕܐ
ⁿܛܒܘ ᵖܡܝܦܝܢ
ᑫܗܢ
ʳܛܒܘ
ˢܒܪܡ
ᵗܠܒܥܠܕܒܒܝܟܘܢ
ᵘܛܒܝܢ
ʷܐܓܪܟܘܢ
ʸܒܣܝܡ
ᶻܐܝܬ ܗܘᶻ
ᵇ*add* ܥܠܡ
‡ f. 58*a*.

Codex B.

ᵃܘܗܝܟܢܐ ܐܠܝܢ ᵇܐܬܐܢܝܢ ᶜܒܥܝܢ ܐܝܠܝܢᶜ ܕܝ
31 ʸᵃܠܗܘܢ ᶻܐܥܒܕ ᵃܒܢܝ ܐܢܫܐ : ܘܗܟܢ ܥܒܕܐ
ܕܐܬܘܢ ܨܒܝܢ ܕܢܥܒܕܘܢ ܠܟܘܢ ܒܢܝܢܫܐ : ᵇܗܝܢ
32 ᶜܘܟܕܘܬ ܐܘܦ ܐܢܬܘܢ ᵈܪܚܡܝܢ ᵉܠܗܘܢ : ᶠܘܐܢ
ᵍܐܢܬܘܢ ܡܚܒܝܢᵍ ܠܗܠܝܢ ܕܡܚܒܝܢ ܝܬܟܘܢ
ܡܐ ʰܛܝܒܘ ܠܟܘܢ : ܐܘܦ ⁱܓܝܪ ܚܛܝܐ ܗܠ
ܠܗܠܝܢ ʲܕܡܚܒܝܢ ܝܬܗܘܢ ܗܢܘܢ ܡܚܒܝܢ :
33 ᶠܘܐܢ ܐܢܬܘܢ ܥܒܕܝܢ ᵏܛܒܝܢ : ܠܗܠܝܢ ܕܥܒܕܝܢ
ܠܟܘܢ ᵏܛܒܝܢ : ᵐܗܕܐ ⁿܛܝܒܘܬܐ ᵒܐܝܬ ܠܟܘܢ :
34 ᵖܡܝܦܝܢ ܐܘܦ ܚܛܝܐ ᑫܗܢ ܥܒܕܝܢ : ܘܐܢ
ܡܘܙܦܝܢ ܐܢܬܘܢ ܠܗܠܝܢ ܕܐܬܘܢ ܡܣܒܝܢ
[f. 52*b*]
ܕܬܬܦܪܥܘܢ ܡܢܗܘܢ ܡܐ ʳܛܝܒܘܬܐ ܠܟܘܢ :
ᵖܡܝܦܝܢ ܐܘܦ ܚܛܝܐ ܠܚܛܝܐ ܡܘܙܦܝܢ
35 ܕܝܬܦܪܥܘܢ ܡܢܗܘܢ ᑫܗܢ ܘܟܘܬ : ˢܒܪܡ ܕܝ
ܐܚܒܘ ᵗܠܒܥܠܕܒܒܝܟܘܢ : ܘܥܒܕܘ ᵘܛܒܝܢ
ܘܐܘܙܦܘ ܘܠܐ ܬܣܒܪܘܢ ܡܕܝܪܐ : ᵛܘܗܘܐ
ʷܐܓܪܟܘܢ ܣܓܝ : ܘܬܗܘܘܢ ܒܢܘܗܝ
ˣܕܡܪܘܡܡܐ : ܕܗܘ ʸܒܣܝܡ ᶻܐܝܬܘܗ ܥܠ
36 ܗܠܝܢ ܕܠܝܬ ܗܢܘܢ ܡܫܬܒܚܝܢ ܘܒܝܫܝܢ : ܗܘܘ
ܐܘܢ ܚܢܢܝܢ ܗܝܟ ܕܐܒܘܟܘܢ ܚܢܝܢ ܘܪܚܝܡ
ᵃܐܝܬ ܗܘᵃ ᵇ ⁘ ‡

Codex C.

ᵃܠܗܘܢ ܐܠܝܢ ܐܬܐܢܝܢ
ܗܝ ܠܗܘܢᵃ
ʸ*add* ܘܒܝܬܗܘܢ
ᶜ*omit* ܘܟܕܘܬ
ᵈܥܒܕܘ ᵉܠܗܘܢ
ᶠܘܐܢ
ᵍܡܚܒܝܢ ܐܢܬܘܢᵍ
ⁱ*omit* ܓܝܪ ʰܛܒܘ
ʲܕܡܚܒܝܢ ᵏܛܒܝܢ
ᵒ*omit* ܐܝܬ ⁿܛܒܘ
ʳܛܒܘ
ᵗܠܒܥܠܕܒܒܝܟܘܢ
ᵘܛܒܝܢ ᵛܘܗܘܐ
ˣܕܡܪܘܡܡܐ
ᵃ*omit* ܐܝܬ ܗܘ

LXXXIX.

Luke V. 27—32.

Codex A.

ᵃܘܡܪܢܐ
ᵇ*omit* ܡܪܢܐ ᵃ*omit* ܘ
ᶜܡܟܣ
ᵈܠܝܘܝ ᵉܝܬܒ

Codex B.

ᵃܠܗܘܢ ܐܫܒܚ ܐܬܐܬ ܡܢ ᵇܠܗܘܢ : ܘܚܙܝܗ
27 ܡܪܢܐ ᵃ† ܘܚܙܐ ᵇܡܪܢܐ ܝܫܘܥ ܡܟܣܐ
ᶜܡܟܣܐ ܕܫܡܗ ᵈܠܘܝ : ᵉܝܬܒ ܥܠ ܒܝܬ

Codex C.

ᵃܠܗܘܢ ᵇܠܗܘܢܐ
† f. 53*a*.
ᶜܡܟܣ

Codex B.

ܡܟܣܐ ܘܐܡܪ ܠܗ ܐܬܐ ܒܬܪܝ ܘܫܒܩ
28 29 ܟܘܠܐ ܘܩܡ [f]ܕܝ [g]ܘܐܬܐ [h]ܒܬܪܗ : ܘܥܒܕ
ܠܗ [d]ܠܘܝ ܡܫܬܘ ܪܒ ܒܒܝܬܗ ܘܗܘܐ
[i]ܐܟܠܘܣ ܣܓܝ [k]ܕܡܟܣܝܢ : ܘܐܘܦ ܕܣܘܪܝܢ
30 ܗܠܝܢ ܕܗܘܘ ܪܒܝܥܝܢ ܥܡܗܘܢ : ܘܗܘܘ ܡܪܛܢܝܢ
[a]ܦܪܝܫܝ ܘܣܦܪܝܗܘܢ [b]ܠܩܒܠ [l]ܬܠܡܝܕܘܝ
ܐܡܪܝܢ : ܠܡܢܐ ܥܡ ܡܟܣܝܐ ܘܥܡ ܚܛܝܝܐ
31 ܐܬܘܢ ܐܟܠܝܢ ܘܫܬܝܢ : [m]ܘܐܓܝܒ ܡܪܢ ܝܫܘܥ
ܘܐܡܪ ܠܗܘܢ : ܠܐ ܨܪܝܟܝܢ ܗܠܝܢ ܕܒܪܝܢ
ܠܐܣܝܐ ܐܠܐ ܗܠܝܢ [n]ܕܒܝܫܝܢ [o]ܒܝܫܐܝܬ :
32 ܠܐ ܓܪ ܐܬܝܬ ܕܐܩܪܐ ܨܕܝܩܝܢ : ܐܠܐ ܚܛܝܝܢ
ܠܬܝܒܘ : [p] ⁘

XC.

Luke VII. 11—16.

11 [b a]ܝܘܡ ܐܠܝܫ ܐܬܠܬ ܡܢ ܠܘܩܣ : [c]ܙܥܪ : [b] [z] : [a]ܟܬܪ
[b]ܒܕܝܡ [c]ܗܘܐ ܡܪܢ ܝܫܘܥ ܐܙܠ [d]ܠܡܕܝܢܬܐ
[f. 53a]
[e]ܕܡܬܩܪܝܐ ܢܐܝܢ : ܘܗܘܘ ܐܙܠܝܢ ܥܡܗ [f]
12 [g]ܬܠܡܝܕܘܗܝ [h]ܘܐܟܠܘܣܝܢ ܣܓܝ : ܘܟܕ [i]ܩܪܒ
ܠܬܪܥܐ [k]ܕܡܕܝܢܬܐ : [l]ܘܗܘܐ ܚܕ [m]ܡܝܬ ܗܘܐ
ܢܦܩ ܒܪ [n]ܝܚܝܕܝ [o]ܠܐܡܗ : ܘܗܝ ܗܘܬ [‡]ܐܪܡܠܐ :
[p]ܘܐܟܠܘܣܝܢ ܣܓܝ ܡܢ [q]ܡܕܝܢܬܐ ܗܘܐ ܥܡܗ :
13 ܘܟܕ ܚܡܐ [r]ܡܪܢ ܝܫܘܥ [s]ܐܬܪܚܡ ܥܠܝܗ :
14 ܘܐܡܪ [t]ܠܗ ܠܐ [u]ܬܒܟܝܢ : [v]ܘܩܪܒ [w]ܐܬܠܚܡ
[x]ܠܐܪܢܐ ܘܗܠܝܢ ܕܗܘܘ [y]ܛܥܢܝܢ [z]ܩܐܡܘ :
ܘܐܡܪ [a]ܒܥܠܝܡܐ ܠܟ ܐܢܐ ܐܡܪ ܩܘܡ :
15 [†]ܘܝܬܒ ܗܘ ܡܝܬܐ ܘܫܪܝ [b]ܗܘ [c]ܡܡܠܠ :
16 ܘܝܗܒ ܝܬܗ [d]ܠܐܡܗ : ܘܢܦܠܬ ܕܚܠܬܐ
ܠܟܘܠܗܘܢ ܘܗܘܘ ܡܫܒܚܝܢ ܠܐܠܗܐ [e]ܘܐܡܪܝܢ :
ܕܢܒܝܐ [f]ܪܒ [g]ܩܡ ܒܝܢܬܢ : ܘܟܕ [h]ܦܩܕ
ܐܠܗܐ ܠܥܡܗ [i]ܕܝܗܘܒܢ ܒܫܠܘܬܗ [i] ⁘

Codex A.

[f] omit ܕܝ [g] omit ܘ
[d] ܠܝܘܝ [i] ܐܟܠܘܣܝܢ
[k] ܕܡܟܣܝܢ
[a] ܦܪܝܫܝܝ
[b] ܠܩܘܒܠ
[m] ܘܐܓܝܒ
[p] add ܥܠܡ

[a] ܘܒܬܪܐ ܙܥܪ [c] omit
[z] add ܘܒܬܪܗ ܡܝܠܐ
[b] ܒܬܪ [c] ܗܘ
[d] ܠܡܕܝܢܬܐ
[e] ܕܡܬܩܪܝܐ
[f] add ܥܡܗ
[g] ܬܠܡܝܕܘܝ
[h] ܘܐܟܠܘܣܗ [i] ܩܪܒ
[k] ܕܡܕܝܢܬܐ [l] ܘܗܐ
‡ f. 58b.
[m] ܡܝܬܐ [n] ܝܚܝܕܝ
[p] ܘܐܟܠܘܣܗ
[q] ܡܕܝܢܬܐ
[r] add ܡܪܢ [v] ܘܩܪܒ
[w] ܐܬܠܚܡ [x] ܠܐܪܢܐ
[y] ܛܥܢܝܢ [z] ܩܡܘ
[a] ܒܥܠܝܡܐ
[b] omit ܗܘ
[c] ܡܡܠܠ [e] omit ܘ
[g] ܩܡ [h] ܦܩܕ
[i] omit ܕܝܗܘܒܢ ܒܫܠܘܬܗ

Codex C.

[f] omit ܕܝ [g] omit ܘ
[h] omit ܒܬܪܗ
[i] ܐܟܠܘܣ
[l] ܬܠܡܝܕܘܝ
[m] ܘܐܓܝܒ
[n] ܕܒܝܫܝܢ [o] ܒܝܫܐܝܬ

[b] ܝܘܡ ܐܠܝܫ
[b] ܐܬܠܬ ܡܢ ܠܘܩܣ
[z] add ܘܒܬܪܗ
[a] add ܘܒܢ
[c] ܗܘ [d] ܠܡܕܝܢܬܐ
[g] ܬܠܡܝܕܘܝ
[h] ܘܐܟܠܘܣ [i] ܩܪܒ
[k] ܕܡܕܝܢܬܐ [o] ܠܐܡܗ
[p] ܘܐܟܠܘܣܗ
[r] add ܡܪܢ
[s] ܐܬܪܚܡ [t] omit ܠܗ
[u] ܬܒܟܝܢ [v] ܘܩܪܒ
[w] ܐܬܠܚܡ [x] ܠܐܪܢܐ
[z] ܘܩܡܘ [a] ܒܥܠܝܡܐ
[b] omit ܗܘ
† f. 53b.
[d] ܠܐܡܗ [e] omit ܘ
[f] ܐܡܪܝܢ [g] ܩܡ
[h] ܦܩܕ
[i] omit ܕܝܗܘܒܢ ܒܫܠܘܬܗ

Codex B.

XCI.

Luke VI. 1—10.

ᵃܘܩܪܝܐ ܐܘܢܓܠܝܘܢ ᵇܐܡܪܒܒ ܒܚܕ ܚܕ ܐܝܟܢܐ
1 ܡܢ ܠܗܘܢ ᵇᵃ: ˣ ʸܘܐܬܚܒܒܪ ᶻ ᵃܝܫܘܥ ܐܙܠ ᵇ
ܒܫܒܬܐ : ܗܘܐ ܡܪܢܐ ܝܫܘܥ ܡܗܠܟ ܒܝܢ
ܙܪܥܐ : ܘܗܘܘ ᶜܬܠܡܝܕܘܗܝ ܡܦܠܟܝܢ ᵈܫܘܒܠܝܢ
2 ܘܡܦܪܟܝܢ ᵉܒܐܝܕܝܗܘܢ ܘܐܟ̈ܠܝܢ : ܘܐܢܫܝܢ ܡܢ
ᶠܦܪ̈ܝܫܝ ܐܡܪܘ ܠܗܘܢ : ܡܢܐ ܐܬܘܢ ܥܒܕܝܢ
3 ܡܢܐ ܕܠܐ ܫܠܝܛ ܕܝܥܒܕ ܒܫܒܬܐ : ᵍܘܐܓܝܒ
ܡܪܢܐ ܝܫܘܥ ʰܘܐܡܪ ܠܗܘܢ : ܐܘܦ ⁱܠܗܕܐ
ᵏܠܐ ܩܪܝܬܘܢ ܡܢܐ ܥܒܕ ˡܕܘܕ ܟܕ ᵐܟܦܢ ܗܘ
4 ܘܗܠܝܢ ᵒܕܥܡܗ : ܗܝܟ ᵖܕܥܠ ܠܒܝܬܗ ܕܐܠܗܐ
ᵍܘܠܣܒ ʳܐܣܒܘܬܬܐ ˢܐܟ̈ܠ ܘܝܗܒ ᵗܐܘܦ
ᵘܠܗܠܝܢ ‡ ܕܗܘܘ ܥܡܗ : ܠܗܠܝܢ ܕܠܐ [f. 53b] ᵛ ܫܠܝܛ
ܠܗܘܢ ʷܕܝܐܟ̈ܠܘܢ : ܐܠܐ ˣ ܠܟܗܢܝܐ ܒܠܚܘܕ :
5 ʸܘܗܘ ܐܡܪ ܠܗܘܢ ᶻܡܪܗ ܕܫܒܬܐ ܒܪ
6 ܗܘ ܒܪܗ ܕܐܢܫܐ : ᵃܘܐܬܚܒܕ ᵇܕܝ ܒܫܒܬܐ
ܚܘܪܢܬܐ ܕܝܥܘܠ ᶜܠܟܢܝܫܬܐ ᵈܘܝܠܦ : ܘܐܝܬ
ᵉܕܗܘܐ ܬܡܢ ܓܒܪ ܚܕ ᶠܘܐܝܕܗ ܕܝܡܝܢܐ
7 ܗܘܬ ܝܒܝܫܐ ܘܗܘܘ ܣܦܪܝܐ ᵍܘܦܪ̈ܝܫܝ ܡܢܛܪܝܢ
ܠܗ ʰܐܢ ⁱܗܘ ᵏܡܐܣܐ ܒܫܒܬܐ ˡܡܫܟܚܘܢ
8 ᵐܕܝܦܪܓܢܘܢ ܥܠܘܗܝ : ܗܘ ܕܝ ܗܘܐ ܝܕܥ
ܚܫܒܘܬܗܘܢ : †ܘܐܡܪ ⁿܠܓܒܪܐ ܕܐܝܕܗ ܝܒܝܫܐ :
9 ᵒܐܬܝ ܩܘܡ ܒܡܨܥܬܐ ܘܗܘ ᵖܩܐܡ : ܘܐܡܪ
ܠܗܘܢ ܡܪܢܐ ܝܫܘܥ : ܫܐܠ ܐܢܐ ܠܟܘܢ
ܡܢܐ ᵍܫܠܝܛ ʳܠܡ ܒܫܒܬܐ ܕܢܥܒܕ ܛܒ ܐܘ
ܕܢܒܒܫ ܒܝܫ : ˢܢܚܝܝ ᵗܢܦܫ ܐܘ ᵘܕܢܘܒܕ :
10 ܘܐܕܡܟܝ ʷܒܟܠܗܘܢ ܒܪܓܙ : ܘܐܡܪ ˣܠܗܘ ʸ
ܦܫܘܛ ᶻܐܝܕܟ : ܘܗܘ ܥܒܕ ᵃܒܝܢ ܘܐܬܬܩܢܬ
ᵇܐܝܕܗ ܗܝܟ ᶜܐܚܪܬܐ ⁘

Codex A.

ᵇܐܡܪܒܒ ܡܢ ܠܗܘܢ ᵇ

ˣ*add*: ܘܒܢܬܗ ܩܕܝܫܬܐ

ʸܘܐܬܚܒܪ

ᶜܬܠܡܝܕܘܗܝ

ᵈܫ̈ܘܒܠܝܢ

ᵉܒܐܝ̈ܕܝܗܘܢ

ᶠܦܪ̈ܝܫܝ ⁱܠܗܕܐ ⁱ

ᵏ *omit* ܠܐ

ˡܕܘܝܕ ᵐܟܦܢ

ᵖ *omit* ܕ ᵍܘܠܣܒ

ʳܐܣܒܘܬܬܐ

ˢܐܟ݂ܠ ᵘܠܐܠܝܢ

‡ f. 59*a*.

ᵛ *add* ܗܘܐ

ʷܕܝܐܟ̈ܠܘܢ

ˣ *add* ܐܠܐ ʸܘܗܘܐ

ᶻܡܪܝ ᵇ *omit* ܕܝ

ᶜܠܟܢܝܫܬܐ ᵈܘܐܠܦ

ᵉ *omit* ܕ ᵍܘܦܪ̈ܝܫܝܢ

ⁱ*omit* ܗܘ ᵏܡܐܣܐ

ˡ *add* ܕ

ᵐܘܢܦܪ̈ܓܢܘܢ

ᵒܐܬܐ ᵖܩܡ

ʳ *omit* ܠܡ

ˢܕܢܚܝܐ ᵗܢܦܫ

ʸ*add* ܠܓܒܪܐ ܕܐܝܕܗ ܝܒܝܫܐ

ᶻܐܝܕܟ ᵃܟܢ

ᵇܐܝܕܗ ᶜܚܠܝܡܬܐ

Codex C.

ᵃܠܘܩܐ ܐܘܢܓܠܝܘܢ

ᵃܐܡܪܒܒ ܡܢ ܠܗܘܢ ᵃ

ˣ *add* ܘܒܢܬܗ

ʸܘܐܬܚܒܪ

ᶻ *add* ܕܝ

ᵃ *omit* ܝܫܘܥ

ᵇ *add* ܡܪܢܐ

ᶜܬܠܡܝܕܘܗܝ ᵈܫܘܒܠܝܢ

ᵉܒܐܝܕܝܗܘܢ

ᵍܘܐܓܝܒ

ʰ*omit* ܘܐܡܪ ᵐܟܦܢ

ᵒܕܗܘܘ ܥܡܗ ᵒ

ᵖ *omit* ܕ ᵍܘܠܣܒ

ʳܐܣܒܘܬܬܐ

ˢܐܟܠ ᵗ*omit* ܐܘܦ

ᵛ *add* ܗܘܐ

ˣ *add* ܐܠܐ ʸܘܗܘܐ

ᶻܡܪܝ ᵃܘܐܬܚܒܕ

ᵇ *omit* ܕܝ ᵈܘܝܠܦ

ᵉ *omit* ܕ ᶠܘܐܝܕܗ

ʰܐܝܢ ⁱ *omit* ܗܘ

ᵏܡܐܣܐ ˡ *add* ܕ

† f. 54*a*.

ⁿܠܓܒܪܐ

ᵒܐܬܐ ᵖܩܡ

ᵍܫܠܝܛ ʳ *omit* ܠܡ

ˢܕܢܚܝܐ ᵘܕܢܘܒܕ

ʷܒܟܠܗܘܢ ˣܠܗ

ᶻܐܝܕܟ

ᶜܚܠܝܡܬܐ

Codex A.	Codex B.	Codex C.
ᵃ ܘܡܬܠ ܐܠܝܫ ᵃ ܠܙܒܢܐ ܡܢ ܠܗܘܢ ᵃ ܕܢܙܪܥ ᶜ ܠܓܒ ᵈ ܐܚܪܢܬܐ ᵉ ܘܐܘܚܪܢ ᶠ omit ܕ ᵍ ܫܘܥܐ ʰ omit ܟܕ ܠܐ ⁱ add ܘܡܢ ʲ ܕܨܡܚ ᵏ ܝܒܫ ‡ f. 59b. ˡ ܠܓܠܠ ᵐ ܠܝܬ ⁿ ܠܚܝܐ ᵒ ܘܐܘܚܪܢ ᵠ add ܟܘܒܝܢ ʳ omit ܟܘܒܝܐ ᵗ ܘܐܘܚܪܢ ᵘ omit ܡܐܐ ᵛ ܡܐܐ ܐܦ ʸ omit ܫܡܥ	# XCII. Luke VIII. 5—15. ᵃ ᵇ ܒܗܘ ܐܠܝܫ ܐܘܟܡܐ ܡܢ ᶜ ܠܗܘܢ ᵃ: ʸ ܐܡܪ 5 ܡܪܐ ܗܘܐ ܡܬܠܐ : ܗܘܐ ܢܦܩ ᶻ ܙܪܘܥܐ ᵃ ܕܢܙܪܥ ܙܪܥܗ : ܘܟܕ ܗܘܐ ܙܪܥ ᵇ ܐܝܬ ܕܢܦܠ ܥܠ ᶜ ܓܒ ܐܘܪܚܐ ܘܐܬܕܝܫ : ܘܦܪܚܬܐ 6 ܕܫܡܝܐ ᵈ ܐܟܠܘ ܝܬܗ : ᵉ ܘܐܘܚܪܢ ᶠ ܕܢܦܠ ܥܠ ᵍ ܫܘܥܐ ʰ ܟܕ ܠܐ ʰ ⁱ ‡ ʲ ܡܨܡܚ ᵏ ܝܒܫ : ˡ ܠܓܠܠ ܕܠܐ 7 ܗܘܐ ᵐ ܠܗ ⁿ ܠܚܝܐ : ᵒ ܘܐܘܚܪܢ ᵖ ܢܦܠ ܒܝܢ ܟܘܒܝܐ 8 ܘܨܡܚܘ ᵠ ܥܡܗ ʳ ܟܘܒܝܐ ˢ ܘܚܢܩܘ ܝܬܗ : ᵗ ܘܐܘܚܪܢ ܢܦܠ ܒܐܪܥܐ ܛܒܬܐ : ܘܨܡܚ ܘܥܒܕ ܦܐܪܝܢ ᵘ ܡܐܐ ᵛ ܡܢܝܐ ʷ ܟܦܠܝܢ : ܗܠܝܢ ܟܕ ܗܘܐ ܐܡܪ : [f. 54a] ܗܘܐ ܡܨܘܚ : ܡܢ ܕܠܗ ܐܕܢܝܢ ܕܡܫܡܥ ˣ ܢܫܡܥ ʸ ܫܡܥ ˣ	ᵇ ܠܗܘܢ ᶜ ܠܗܘܢ ʸ add ܡܬܠܗ ᶻ ܙܪܘܥܐ ᵇ ܐܝܬ ᵈ ܐܚܪܢܬܐ ᵉ ܘܐܘܚܪܢ ᶠ omit ܕ ʰ omit ܟܕ ܠܐ ⁱ add ܘܡܢ ʲ ܕܨܡܚ ᵏ ܝܒܫ ⁿ ܠܚܝܐ ᵖ add ܕܝܢ ᵠ add ܟܘܒܝܐ ʳ omit ܟܘܒܝܐ ˢ ܘܚܢܩ ᵗ ܘܐܘܚܪܢ ᵘ omit ܡܐܐ ᵛ ܡܢܐ ʷ ܟܦܠܝܢ ˣ omit ܫܡܥ ܢܫܡܥ

Codex A.

[Exhibet hic in margine manu correctoris antiqui.]

9 10 ܘܫܐܠܘ ܝܬܗ ܬܠܡܝܕܘܗܝ ܘܐܡܪܝܢ ܠܗ. ܡܐ ܗܘ ܡܬܠܐ ܗܢܐ. ܐܡܪ ܠܗܘܢ ܝܫܘܥ.
ܠܟܘܢ ܐܬܝܗܝܒ ܕܬܕܥܘܢ ܪܐܙܐ ܕܡܠܟܘܬܐ ܕܐܠܗܐ. ܠܫܪܟܐ ܕܝܢ ܒܡܬܠܐ. ܕܟܕ ܚܙܝܢ
11 ܠܐ ܚܙܝܢ. ܘܟܕ ܫܡܥܝܢ ܠܐ ܢܣܬܟܠܘܢ. ܗܢܐ ܗܘ ܡܬܠܐ. ܙܪܥܐ ܐܝܬܘܗ ܡܠܬܐ
12 ܕܐܠܗܐ. ܗܘ ܕܝܢ ܕܢܦܠ ܥܠ ܓܒ ܐܘܪܚܐ. ܗܠܝܢ ܐܢܘܢ ܕܫܡܥܝܢ ܠܡܠܬܐ ܘܐܬܐ.
13 ܣܛܢܐ ܫܩܠ ܠܗ ܠܡܠܬܐ ܡܢ ܠܒܗܘܢ ܕܠܐ ܢܗܝܡܢܘܢ ܘܢܚܘܢ. ܗܘ ܕܝܢ ܕܢܦܠ ܥܠ
ܫܘܥܐ. ܗܠܝܢ ܕܫܡܥܝܢ ܠܡܠܬܐ ܘܡܩܒܠܝܢ ܠܗ ܒܚܕܘܬܐ. ܘܥܩܪ ܠܝܬ ܠܗܘܢ ܬܠܝܬܘܬܐ. ܐܝܠܝܢ
14 ܠܙܒܢܐ ܗܘ ܡܗܝܡܢܝܢ. ܘܒܙܒܢܐ ܕܢܣܝܘܢܐ ܡܫܬܢܝܢ. ܗܘ ܕܝܢ ܕܢܦܠ ܒܝܢ ܟܘܒܝܐ.
ܗܠܝܢ ܕܫܡܥܝܢ ܘܐܙܠܝܢ ܡܬܚܢܩܝܢ ܒܪܢܝܐ ܘܒܥܘܬܪܐ ܘܒܪܓܝܓܬܐ ܕܥܠܡܐ. ܘܦܐܪܐ
15 ܠܐ ܝܗܒܝܢ. ܗܘ ܕܝܢ ܕܢܦܠ ܒܐܪܥܐ ܛܒܬܐ. ܗܠܝܢ ܕܫܡܥܝܢ ܠܡܠܬܐ ܒܠܒܐ ܕܟܝܐ
ܘܛܒܐ ܘܐܚܝܕܝܢ ܠܗ ܘܡܝܬܝܢ ܦܐܪܐ ܒܡܣܝܒܪܢܘܬܗܘܢ. ܡܢ ܕܐܝܬ ܠܗ ܐܕܢܝܢ
ܕܢܫܡܥ ܢܫܡܥ ܀

Codex A.	Codex B.	Codex C.

XCIII.

Luke VII. 1—10.

Codex A.

ܡܢ ܠܗܘܢܐ[c]
[a] add ܡܪܢ ܘܥܠܬܗ ܝܫܘܥ
ܟܦܪܢܚܘܡ

[d] omit ܠܘܬ [b] omit ܘ
ܠܟܦܪܢܚܘܡ[e]
[g] add ܕܝܠܗ ܥܠ[f]
[h]ܩܢܛܪܘܢܐ [i]ܥܒܕܗ
ܕܝ ܕܩܪܝܒ[l] [k] add ܕܝ
[n]ܘܐܬܘ [o]ܠܝܫܘܥ

‡ f. 60a.

[q]ܗܢܐ [s]ܫܐܠܝܢ
[t]ܘܒܥܝܢ ܗܘܬ [u]ܐܙܠ
[v]ܘܟܕ ܕܝ [w] omit ܕܝ
[j] add ܡܢ [x] add ܕܝ
[y]ܩܢܛܪܘܢܐ
[b]ܬܬܥܡܠ [c]ܕܬܥܘܠ
[d]ܠܡܠܠ [e]ܟܪ
[f]ܕܝܠܟ [g]ܛܠܝܐ
[h]ܡܬܚܝܒ [i] omit ܘ
[k]ܫܠܝܛܘ [l]ܡܬܟܢܫ
[m]ܐܙܠ [n]ܘܐܙܠ
[o]ܐܬܐ [p]ܠܗ
[q]ܐܙܠ [r]ܐܙܠ
[s]ܘܠܥܒܕܝ [t]ܘܬܡܗ
[u]ܠܐܘܟܠܘܣܐ [w]ܕܝ
[x]ܟܗܕܐ ܐܦ
ܘܗܘ
[a] omit ܫܠܝܡ

Codex B.

ܘܗܘܐ ܐܫܠܡܬ[b] ܐܠܗܐ[c] ܟܕ ܐܬܠܝܛ ܡܢ
1 ܠܥܡܐ[b] :[a] ܘܐܬܐ[b] [c]ܝܫܘܥ ܠܘܬ[d] ܟܦܪܢܚܘܡ[e]
2 ܕܥܡܠܐ : [f]ܒܥܠ ܠܚܡܪ ܢܣܘܩ : ܘܥܒܕܗ[g]
[h]ܕܩܢܛܪܘܢܐ ܕܗܘܐ [i]ܥܒܕ [j]ܒܝܫܐܝܬ : ܗܘܐ
ܟܪ [i]ܥܒܕ ܕܝܩܝܪܬ ܘܗܕܡ ܗܘܐ ܩܪܝܒ ܠܗ :
3 ܟܕ[k] ܫܡܥ ܥܠ ܡܪܢ ܝܫܘܥ : ܫܠܚ[†] ܠܘܬܗ ܡܢ
ܘܫܝܫܐ[l] ܕܝܗܘܕܝܐ ܟܒܐ ܡܢܗ[m] ܕܝܐܬܐ
4 ܘܝܚܝܐ ܥܒܕܗ : [n]ܗܢܘܢ ܐܬܘ ܠܘܬ [o]ܡܪܐ
ܝܫܘܥ : ܘܒܥܘ ܡܢܗ [p]ܚܦܝܛܐܝܬ ܐܡܪܝܢ : ܕܗܘ
5 ܫܘܐ [q]ܗܘܝܢ ܕܬܥܒܕ ܠܗ ܗܕܐ [r]ܡܚܝܒ ܗܘ
6 ‡ ܟܪ [s]ܚܒܝܒ [t]ܘܒܝܬ ܥܒܕܐ ܗܘ ܒܢܐ ܠܢ : ܘܡܪܐ
ܝܫܘܥ ܗܘܐ [u]ܐܙܠ ܥܡܗܘܢ : [v]ܘܟܕ [w]ܕܝ
ܗܘ[x] ܪܚܝܩ[j] ܒܝܬܐ ܫܠܚ ܠܘܬܗ ܪܚܡܘܗܝ ܗܘ
[y]ܩܢܛܪܘܢܐ : [z]ܐܡܪ ܠܗ ܡܪܝ [a]ܠܐ [b]ܬܬܥܡܠ :
ܠܝܬ ܐܢܐ ܟܪ [c]ܫܘܐ ܕܬܥܘܠ ܠܬܚܘܬ
7 ܛܠܠܝ : [d]ܠܡܠܠ [e]ܕܗܝܢ ܐܦ ܠܐ ܟܪܝܬ ܠܐ
[f]ܕܝܢܬ ܫܘܐ ܕܐܬܐ ܠܘܬܟ : ܐܠܐ ܐܡܪ
8 ܒܡܠܐ ܘܢܬܐܣܐ [g]ܛܠܝ : [h]ܡܛܠ ܐܢܐ ܒܪܢܫ
ܐܢܐ [i]ܘܬܚܘܬ [k]ܫܘܠܛܢܝܬܝ ܐܢܐ [l]ܡܬܟܢܫ :
ܘܐܝܬ ܬܚܘܬ [m]ܐܘܕܝ [n]ܦܪܫܝܢ : ܘܐܡܪ [o]ܐܡܪ
[p]ܠܗܕܝܢ [q]ܐܙܠ ܘܗܘ [r]ܐܙܠ [s]ܘܠܗܕܝܢ ܐܬܐ
ܘܗܘ ܐܬܐ : ܘܠܥܒܕܝ ܥܒܕ ܗܕܐ ܘܗܘ ܥܒܕ :
9 ܟܕ ܕܝ ܫܡܥ ܡܪܐ ܝܫܘܥ ܐܬܡܗ ܥܠܘܝ
[t]ܘܬܡܗ ܐܡܪ [u]ܠܐܘܟܠܘܣܐ [w]ܕܝܢ ܕܐܬܐ
[f. 54b]
ܒܬܪܗ : ܐܡܪ ܐܢܐ ܠܟܘܢ ܕܐܦ ܠܐ
[x]ܒܐܝܣܪܝܠ ܗܟܢ ܗܕܐ ܗܝܡܢܘܬܐ ܠܐ
10 [y]ܐܫܟܚܬ : [z]ܘܗܦܟܘ ܗܢܘܢ ܠܒܝܬܗ ܘܠܩܘ
ܕܐܫܬܠܚܘ ܘܐܫܟܚܘ ܒܥܒܕܐ ܚܠܝܡ : [a]ܫܠܝܡ ∴

Codex C.

[a]ܠܗܘܢ [b]ܐܠܝܢܗܘܢ
[c]ܡܢ ܠܗܘܢܐ[c]
[a] add ܡܪܢ ܘܥܠܬܗ
[c] add ܡܪܐ [b] omit ܘ
[d] omit ܠܘܬ
ܠܟܦܪܢܚܘܡ[e]

† f. 54b.

[g] add ܕܝܠܗ ܥܠ[f]
[h]ܩܢܛܪܘܢܐ [j]ܒܝܫܐܝܬ
ܕܝܗܘܕܝܐ[l] [k] add ܕܝ-
ܗܢܘܢ[n] [m]ܕܝܐܬܐ
[p]ܚܦܝܛܐܝܬ [r]ܡܚܝܒ
[w] omit ܕܝ [v]ܘܟܕ
[j] add ܡܢ [x] add ܕܝ
[a] omit ܠܐ [z]ܘܐܡܪ
[b]ܬܬܥܡܠ
[c]ܕܬܥܘܠ
[f]ܕܝܢܬ
[g]ܛܠܝܐ
[l]ܡܬܟܢܫ
[m]ܐܘܕܝ
[p]ܠܗܕܝܢ [r]ܐܙܠ
[s]ܘܠܥܒܕܝ

[t]ܘܬܡܗ

[y]ܐܫܟܚܬ

Codex A. | Codex B. | Codex C.

XCIV.

Luke XVI. 19—31.

Codex B.

[a]ܘܦܢܐ ܗܘܐ ܐܠܝܫܥ. ܐܠܝܫܥܘܗܝ ܡܢ ܠܗܘܢ ܘܗܘܐ
ܠܠܫܢܐ ܡܟܝܟ ܡܢ ܐܝܟܢ [x][a] ܘܒܝܬܗ [y]ܦܘܪܦܘܪܐ
19 ܓܒܪ ܕܝ ܚܕ ܗܘܐ ܥܬܝܪ : ܘܗܘܐ ܠܒܝܫ
[z]ܒܐܪܓܘܢܐ [a]ܘܒܘܨܐ : ܘܗܘܐ ܝܘܡ ܒܟܠ
20 ܡܦܢܩ [b]ܢܗܝܪܐܝܬ : ܘܚܕ ܡܣܟܝܢ ܗܘܐ ܫܡܗ
ܐܠܥܙܪܘܣ : ܘܗܘܐ ܪܡܐ ܩܕܡ ܬܪܥܗ ܡܚܐ.
21 [c]ܘܗܘ ܒܥܝܢܐ : ܘܗܘܐ ܡܬܚܡܕ ܕܢܣܒܥ
ܡܢ ܡܐ ܕܢܦܠ ܥܠ ܦܬܘܪܗ ܕܝܠܗ ܕܥܬܝܪܐ :[d]
ܐܠܐ ‡ ܕܐܘܦ ܟܠܒܝܐ ܗܘܘ ܐܬܝܢ ܡܠܚܟܝܢ
22 [e]ܡܫܚܘܬܗ : [f]ܘܐܬܥܒܕ ܕܡܝܬ ܗܘ
ܡܣܟܢܐ : ܘܐܘܒܠܘ ܝܬܗ ܡܠܐܟܝܐ ܠܥܘܒܗ
ܕܐܒܪܗܡ : [g]ܡܝܬ ܕܝ ܐܘܦ ܝܬܗ ܥܬܝܪܐ :
23 ܘܐܬܩܒܪ : [h] [i]ܘܒܓܗܢܐ ܙܩܦ ܬܠܐ [j]ܥܝܢܘܗܝ
ܘܚܙܐ [k]ܠܐܒܪܗܡ ܡܢ ܪܚܘܩܐ [l]ܘܠܠܥܙܪܘܣ
24 ܒܥܘܒܗ : ܘܗܘ ܩܪܐ ܘܐܡܪ : ܐܒܐ ܐܒܪܗܡ
ܐܬܪܚܡ [m]ܥܠܝ : [n]ܘܫܠܚ [o]ܠܠܥܙܪܘܣ ܕܝܛܒܠ
ܪܝܫ ܐܨܒܥܗ ܒܡܝܐ : ܘܝܩܪܪ [q]ܠܠܫܢܝ : ܕܗܐ
25 ܐܢܐ [r]ܡܫܬܢܩ ܒܗܕܐ ܫܠܗܒܝܬܐ : [s]ܐܡܪ ܠܗ
ܕܝ ܐܒܪܗܡ : ܒܪܝ [t]ܐܕܟܪ ܕܩܒܠܬ [u]ܛܒܬܟ
[w]ܒܚܝܝܟ [x]ܘܐܠܥܙܪܘܣ [y]ܚܡ ܘܩܒܠܬ [z]ܒܝܫܬܗ :

[f. 55a]

ܘܒܕܘ ܟܐ ܗܘ [a]ܡܬܢܚܡ ܘܐܢܬ ܡܬܫܢܩ :
26 ܘܒܟܠ ܗܠܝܢ ܕܝ [b]ܦܚܬ [c]ܪܒ ܐܝܬ ܒܝܢܢ
ܠܒܝܢܝܟܘܢ [d]ܡܬܩܢ : ܠܡܠܐ ܕܗܠܝܢ ܕܨܒܝܢ
[e]ܕܢܥܒܪܘܢ ܡܢ ܟܐ ܠܘܬܟܘܢ ܠܐ [f]ܝܟܠܝܢ :
27 ܘܠܐ ܡܢ ܬܡܢ ܠܘܬܢ : ܠܐ [g]ܡܥܒܪܝܢ : † ܘܗܘ
ܐܡܪ ܠܗ : ܐܢܐ ܒܥܐ ܡܢܟ ܐܒܐ ܐܒܪܗܡ :
28 [h]ܕܬܫܠܚ [i]ܝܬܗ ܠܒܝܬܗ ܕܐܒܐ : ܐܝܬ [k]ܠܝ
ܚܡܫ [l]ܐܚܝܢ ܕܝ [m]ܕܝܣܗܕ ܠܗܘܢ : ܕܠܐ ܐܘܦ

Codex A.

[a]ܘܦܢܐ ܐܠܝܫܥ
ܐܠܝܫܥܘܗܝ ܡܢ ܠܗܘܢ[a]
[x] *add* ܥܬܝܪ
[z]ܒܐܪܓܘܢܐ
[a]ܘܒܘܨܐ
[c] *omit* ܗܘ
[d] *add* ܘܠܐ ܐܢܫ
ܝܗܒ ܗܘܐ ܠܗ
‡ f. 60b.
[f]ܡܫܚܘܬܗ [g]ܡܣܟܢܐ
[h] *add* ܘܢܦܩ ܒܫܘܠܛܢ
ܘܒܕ ܗܘ
[i]ܘܒܓܗ [j]ܥܝܢܘܗܝ
[k] *add* ܝܬܗ
[m]ܥܠܝ [n]ܘܫܠܚ
[q]ܠܠܫܢܝ
[r]ܡܫܬܢܩ [s]ܘܐܡܪ
[t]ܐܬܕܟܪ [u]ܛܒܬܟ
[x]ܘܠܥܙܪܘܣ
[y]ܚܡ [z]ܒܝܫܬܗ
[c]ܪܒܐ [d]ܡܬܩܢ
[e]ܕܢܥܒܪܘܢ
[f]ܝܟܠܝܢ [g]ܕܢܥܒܪܘܢ
[h]ܕܬܫܠܚ [i]ܝܬܗ
[l]ܐܚܝܢ [m]ܢܗܕ

Codex C.

[a]ܠܗܘܢ ܐܠܝܫܥ
ܐܠܝܫܥܘܗܝ ܡܢ ܠܗܘܢ[a]
[y] *omit* ܦܘܪܦܘܪܐ
† f. 55a.
[z]ܒܐܪܓܘܢܐ
[b]ܢܗܝܪܐܝܬ
[c] *omit* ܗܘ
[e]ܡܫܚܘܬܗ [f]ܘܐܬܥܒܕ
[g]ܡܝܬ [j]ܟܕ ܗܘܐ
[k] *add* ܝܬܗ
[l]ܘܠܠܥܙܪܘܣ
[m]ܥܠܝ [n]ܘܫܠܚ
[o]ܐܠܥܙܪܘܣ
[q]ܠܠܫܢܝ
[s]ܘܐܡܪ [u]ܛܒܬܟ
[w]ܒܚܝܝܟ
[x]ܘܠܠܥܙܪܘܣ
[z]ܒܝܫܬܗ [a]ܡܬܢܚܡ
[b]ܦܚܬ
[f]ܝܟܠܘܢ
† f. 55b.
[h]ܕܬܫܠܚ [i]ܝܬܗ
[k]ܠܗ

Codex B.

ܗܢܘܢ ܒܥܐܬܘܢ ܠܡܕܝܢܬ ܐܘܬܪܐ ‡ ܕܓܝܪܣܝܢܝܐ :
29 ܘܐܡܪ ܠܗ ܐܒܘܢܗܘܢ : ܐܝܬ ܠܗܘܢ ܟܐܒܐ
30 [n]ܘܠܓܝܘܢܐ [o]ܕܝܢ ܡܫܬܟܚܝܢ ܠܗܘܢ [p]ܗܘ ܕܝܢ
ܐܡܪ ܠܐ ܐܒܐ ܐܒܘܢܗܘܢ ܐܠܐ ܐܢ [q]ܐܢܫ
ܡܢ ܒܢܝ ܡܕܝܢܬܐ [r]ܣܐܝܒ ܠܬܘܬܗܘܢ ܠܐ
31 ܢܬܗܘܢ : [s]ܐܡܪ ܠܗ [t][u]ܕܝܢ ܐܢ ܠܡܗܡܢܐ
[w]ܘܠܓܝܘܢܐ ܠܐ [x]ܫܟܚܝܢ : [y]ܐܘܦ ܠܐ ܐܢ
ܐܢܫ [z]ܡܢ ܒܢܝ [a]ܡܕܝܢܬܐ [b]ܢܦܩ [c]ܠܐ
[d]ܡܗܡܢܝܢ [e]ܠܗ : [f][s] ⁘

XCV.

Luke VIII. 16—21.

[a]ܩܪܝܢܐ [b]ܢܦܩ ܐܘܢܓܠܝܘܢ ܕܐܘܢܓܠܣܛܐ ܡܢ ܠܘܩܐ[a] : [y]
16 ܐܡܪ [z]ܠܗ ܡܪܢ [a]ܠܬܠܡܝܕܘܗܝ : ܠܝܬ ܐܢܫ ܕܝܢ
[b]ܕܕܠܩ ܒܨܝܪ : ܘܡܟܣܐ [c]ܒܡܐܢܝܢ [d] : ܐܘ̈
ܡܣܝܡ ܠܗ ܬܚܘܬ ܥܪܣܐ : ܐܠܐ [e]ܡܣܝܡ ܠܗ[e]
ܥܠ ܡܢܪܬܐ ܕܗܠܝܢ [f]ܕܥܐܠܝܢ ܚܙܝܢ [g]ܢܘܗܪܐ :
17 ܠܝܬ ܓܝܪ ܦܣܝܪ ܕܠܐ ܢܬܓܠܐ ܘܠܐ ܟܣܝ
18 ܕܠܐ [h]ܢܬܝܕܥ : [i]ܘܐܬܐ [j]ܠܓܠܝܐ ܚܙܘ ܐܘ
ܗܟܢ ܐܬܘܢ [k]ܫܡܥܝܢ : ܡܢ ܓܝܪ ܕܐܝܬ ܠܗ
ܢܬܝܗܒ ܠܗ : ܘܡܢ ܕܠܝܬ ܠܗ ܐܦ ܗܘ
19 ܐܘܦ ܡܐ ܕܣܒܪ ܢܬܢܣܒ ܡܢܗ : ܘܐܬܘ
[l]ܐܡܗ ܘܐܚܘܗܝ ܠܘܬܗ : ܘܠܐ ܕܝܢ ܗܘܘ [m]ܡܫܟܚܝܢ
[n]ܕܢܬܩܪܒܘܢ ܠܘܬܗ : [o]ܠܓܠܠ [f. 55b] [p]ܐܘܟܠܘܣܐ :
20 ܘܐܬܐܡܪ ܠܗ [q]ܕܐܡܟ ܘܐܚܝܟ [r]ܩܝܡܝܢ
21 ܠܒܪ ܨܒܝܢ ܕܢܚܙܘܢ ܠܟ : ܗܘ ܕܝܢ ܐܦܢܝ
ܘܐܡܪ ܠܗܘܢ : [s]ܐܡܝ [t]ܘܐܚܝ ܗܢܘܢ
ܗܠܝܢ ܕܫܡܥܝܢ ܡܠܬܗ ܕܐܠܗܐ ܘܥܒܕܝܢ :
[u]ܫܠܡ ⁘

Codex A.

‡ f. 61a.
[n]ܘܠܓܝܘ̈ܢܐ [o]omit ܕܝܢ
[p]ܗܘܘ [r]ܣܐܝܒ
[t]add ܐܒܘܢܗܘܢ
[u]omit ܕܝܢ
[w]ܘܠܓܝܘ̈ܢܐ
[x]ܫܟܚܝܢ [y]ܘܐܘܦ
[z]add ܢܦܩ [a]ܡܕܝܢܬܐ
[b]omit ܢܦܩ
[c]omit ܠܐ [d]ܡܗܡܢܝܢ
[e]omit ܠܗ [f]add ܫܠܡ

[b]omit ܢܦܩ
[z]omit ܠܗ [y]add ܝܫܘܥ
[a]omit ܬܠܡܝܕܘܗܝ
[b]ܕܕܠܩ [c]add ܠܗ
[d]ܡܐܢܐ
[e]omit ܡܣܝܡ ܠܗ
[f]ܕܥܐܠܝܢ [g]ܢܘܗܪܐ
[h]ܢܬܝܕܥ [i]ܘܐܬܐ
[j]ܠܓܠܝܐ [k]ܫܡܥܝܢ
[l]ܐܡܗ [m]ܡܫܟܚܝܢ
[n]ܕܢܬܩܪܒܘܢ [o]ܠܓܠܠ
[p]ܐܘܟܠܘܣܐ
[q]ܕܐܡܟ
[r]ܩܝܡܝܢ [s]ܐܡܝ
[t]ܘܐܚܝ
[u]omit ܫܠܡ

Codex C.

[o]omit ܕܝܢ
[q]ܐܢܫ
[s]omit ܐܡܪ . . . ܠܗ . . .

[a]ܠܘܩܐ ܐܘܢܓܠܣܛܐ
[a]ܐܘܢܓܠܝܘܢ ܡܢ ܠܘܩܐ
[y]add ܬܠܡܝܕܘܗܝ
[z]omit ܠܗ
[a]omit ܬܠܡܝܕܘܗܝ
[b]ܕܕܠܩ [c]add ܠܗ
[d]ܡܐܢܐ [f]ܕܥܐܠܝܢ
[k]ܫܡܥܝܢ
[m]ܡܫܟܚܝܢ
[q]ܕܐܡܟ [r]ܘܐܚܝܟ
[s]ܐܡܝ [t]ܘܐܚܝ
[u]omit ܫܠܡ

Codex A. | *Codex B.* | *Codex C.*

XCVI.

Luke VIII. 26—39.

Codex B.

[a] † ܘܡܦܪܐ ܐܠܝܫ ܐܘܣܪܘܗ [b] ܕܚܕ ܐܓܠܝܠ ܡܢ
27 ܠܩܘܒܠ [a] [b] : [u] ‡ ܘܟܕ [w] ܢܦܩ ܥܠ ܐܪܥܐ ܐܘܪܥܗ
ܓܒܪ ܚܕ ܡܢ [x] ܡܕܝܢܬܐ ܕܗܘܘ [y] ܒܠܝܘܗ ܫܐܕܝܢ :
[z] ܘܐܫܢܝܢ ܣܓܝܢ [a] ܠܐ ܐܬܟܣܝ [b] ܒܡܐܢܝܢ [e] ܘܒܒܝܬ
28 ܠܐ ܒܒܝܬ ܐܠܐ [f] ܗܘܐ [g] ܒܡܩܒܪܬܐ : ܘܟܕ
ܚܙܐ ܠܝܫܘܥ ܡܩܥܐ ܘܢܦܠ [h] ܩܕܡܘܗܝ :
ܘܒܩܠܐ ܪܒܐ ܐܡܪ ܡܐ ܠܝ ܘܠܟ ܝܫܘܥ
ܒܪܗ ܕܐܠܗܐ ܡܪܝܡܐ : ܒܥܐ ܐܢܐ ܡܢܟ
29 ܠܐ [i] ܬܫܢܩܢܝ : ܗܘܐ ܓܝܪ [j] ܡܦܩܕ [k] ܠܪܘܚܐ
ܠܛܡܐܬܐ [l] ܕܬܦܘܩ ܡܢ ܒܪܢܫܐ : ܣܓܝ ܓܝܪ
ܐܫܢܝܢ ܗܘܬ [m] ܚܛܦܐ ܠܗ : ܘܗܘܐ [n] ܡܬܐܣܪ
ܒܫܫܠܬܐ ܘܒܟܒܠܐ [o] ܡܬܢܛܪ : ܘܗܘܐ [p] ܡܦܣܩ
[q] ܐܣܘܪܝܐ [r] ܘܡܬܕܒܪ ܡܢ [s] ܫܐܕܐ [t] ܠܡܕܒܪܐ :
30 [u] ܘܫܐܠܗ ܡܪܢ ܝܫܘܥ [v] ܘܐܡܪ ܡܐ ܗܘ
ܫܡܟ : ܘܗܘ ܐܡܪ [w] ܠܓܝܘܢ [x] ܗܘ ܫܡܝ :
31 ܕܥܠܝܢ ܫܐܕܝܢ ܣܓܝ ܠܓܘܗ : ܘܗܘܘ ܒܥܝܢ ܡܢܗ
ܕܠܐ [y] ܢܦܩܕ ܐܢܘܢ [z] ܕܝܐܙܠܘܢ [a] ܠܬܗܘܡܐ :
32 ܘܗܘܬ ܬܡܢ ܡܪܥܝܬ [b] ܕܚܙܝܪܝܢ ܣܓܝܐܢ ܪܥܝܐ
ܒܛܘܪܐ : ܘܒܥܘ ܡܢܗ [c] ܕܝܫܒܘܩ ܢܬܗܘܢ
33 [z] ܕܝܐܠܘܢ ܠܗܠܝܢ [d] ܚܙܝܪܝܐ : [e] ܘܫܒܩ ܐܢܘܢ
ܘܢܦܩܘ [f] ܫܐܕܐ ܡܢ ܗܘ ܒܪܢܫܐ [g] ܘܥܠ [h] ܒܚܙܝܪܝܐ :
[f. 56a]
[i] ܘܐܫܬܕܝܬ ܟܠܗ ܡܪܥܝܬܐ ܥܠ [v] ܕܡܩܘܪܬܐ
34 ܠܝܡܐ ܘܐܬܚܢܩܘ [j] ܘܡܝܬܘ : ‡ ܟܕ ܕܝ † ܚܙܘ
ܗܠܝܢ ܕܗܘܘ ܪܥܝܢ ܡܐ [k] ܕܐܬܥܒܕ ܥܪܩܘ ܘܬܢܘ
35 [l] ܒܡܕܝܢܬܐ ܘܒܩܘܪܝܐ : ܘܢܦܩܘ [m] ܕܝܚܙܘܢ ܡܐ
ܐܬܥܒܕ : ܘܐܬܘ ܠܘܬ ܡܪܢ ܝܫܘܥ : ܘܐܫܟܚܘ
[n] ܠܗܘ ܒܪܢܫܐ ܕܢܦܩܘ ܡܢܗ ܫܐܕܐ [o] ܝܬܝܒ
ܘܡܠܒܫ [p] ܘܡܢܟܦ ܗܘ [q] ܕܪܓܠܘܗܝ ܕܡܪܢ ܝܫܘܥ

Codex A.

[b] ܡܢ ܠܩܘܒܠܐ [b]

‡ f. 61*b*.

[w] *add* ܘܒܝܬܗ

ܡܢܗܘܢ : 26 ܘܟܕ
ܐܬܐ ܡܪܢ ܝܫܘܥ
ܠܐܪܥܐ ܕܓܪܓܫܝܐ
ܗܕܐ ܕܗܝ ܠܩܘܒܠ
ܓܠܝܠܐ ܕܓܠܝܠܐ :

[x] ܡܕܝܢܬܐ [y] ܒܠܝܘܗ

[z] ܘܐܫܢܝܢ

[b] ܒܡܐܢܝܢ

[e] ܘܒܒܝܬ

[f] *omit* ܗܘܐ

[g] ܒܡܩܒܪܬܐ

[i] ܬܫܢܩܢܝ [j] ܡܦܩܕ

[m] ܚܛܦܐ [n] ܡܬܐܣܪ

[o] ܡܬܢܛܪ [p] ܡܦܣܩ

[q] ܐܣܘܪܝܐ

[r] ܘܡܬܕܒܪ [s] ܫܐܕܐ

[t] ܠܡܕܒܪܐ

[u] ܘܫܐܠ ܠܗ [u] [v] *omit* ܘ

[w] ܠܓܝܘܢ [x] *omit* ܗܘ

[y] ܢܦܩܕ [z] ܕܝܐܙܠܘܢ

[a] ܠܬܗܘܡܐ

[b] ܕܚܙܝܪܝܢ

[c] ܕܝܫܒܘܩ [d] ܚܙܝܪܝܐ

[e] ܘܫܒܩ [f] ܫܐܕܐ

‡ f. 62*a*.

[g] ܘܥܠܘ [h] ܒܚܙܝܪܝܐ

[v] *omit* ܕ

[j] *omit* ܘܡܝܬܘ

[k] ܕܐܬܥܒܕ

[l] ܒܡܕܝܢܬܐ

[p] ܘܡܢܟܦ [q] ܕܪܓܠܘܗܝ

Codex C.

[a] ܠܩܘܒܠ ܐܠܝܫ
ܐܘܣܪܘܗ ܡܢ ܠܩܘܒܠܐ [a]

† f. 56*a*.

[u] *add* ܘܒܝܬܗ

[w] ܢܦܩ [y] ܒܠܝ

[z] ܘܐܫܢܝܢ

[a] *add* ܓܝܪ [b] ܒܡܐܢܝܢ

[e] ܘܒܒܝܬ

[f] *omit* ܗܘܐ

[h] ܩܕܡܘܗܝ [i] ܬܫܢܩܢܝ

[j] ܡܦܩܕ [k] ܠܪܘܚܬܐ

[l] ܕܬܦܘܩ [m] ܚܛܦܐ

[n] ܡܬܐܣܪ [p] ܡܦܣܩ

[q] ܐܣܘܪܝܐ

[r] ܘܡܬܕܒܪ

[u] ܘܫܐܠ ܠܗ [u]

[v] *omit* ܘ

[w] ܠܓܝܘܢ [x] *omit* ܗܘ

[y] ܢܦܩܕ [z] ܕܝܐܙܠܘܢ

[b] *omit* ܕ

[c] ܕܝܫܒܘܩ

[e] ܘܫܒܩ [f] ܫܐܕܐ

[g] ܘܥܠܘ [i] *add* ܟܠ

[v] *omit* ܕ

† f. 56*b*.

[j] *omit* ܘܡܝܬܘ

[k] ܕܐܬܥܒܕ

[m] ܕܢܚܙܘܢ

[n] ܠܗܘ [o] ܝܬܝܒ

[p] ܘܡܢܟܦ [q] ܕܪܓܠܘܗܝ

Codex A.	Codex B.	Codex C.
	36 ܘܕܚܙܘ : ܘܬܢܘ ܠܗܘܢ [r]ܗܝܟܢ ܕܚܣܘ ܗܘܝ	[r]ܗܝܟܢ [s]ܡܢ
[u]ܕܐܪܥܗܘܢ	37 ܐܬܟܢܫܘ [s]ܗܘ [t]ܕܓܕܝܣܗ : ܘܒܥܘ ܡܢܗ ܟܘܠ	[t]ܕܓܕܝܣܐ
[v]ܕܓܪܓܫܢܝ	ܣܓܝܐܐ [u]ܕܐܪܥܗܘܢ [v]ܕܓܪܓܫܝܐ [w]ܕܐܙܠ	
[w]ܕܐܙܠ [x]ܐܚܝܕܝܢ	ܠܗ ܡܢܗܘܢ ܒܕܚܠܬܐ ܪܒܬܐ ܓܪ ܗܘܘ	
[y]ܐܙܠ	[x]ܐܚܝܕܝܢ : ܘܗܘ ܣܠܩ ܠܐܠܦܐ ܘܬܒ [y]ܐܙܠ	[x]ܐܚܝܕܝܢ
	38 ܠܗ : ܘܗܘܐ ܕܝ ܒܥܐ ܡܢܗ [z]ܓܒܪܐ ܕܢܦܩܘ ܕܗܘܐ	[z] *add* ܗܘܝܢ ܕܕܒܝܩ ܡܢܗ
	39 ܥܡܗ : ܘܫܪܐ ܝܬܗ ܘܐܡܪ ܠܗ : ܬܘܒ ܠܟ	
	ܠܒܝܬܟ : ܘܬܢܝ ܟܠ ܡܐ ܕܥܒܕ ܠܟ ܐܠܗܐ :	
[a]ܘܐܙܠ [c]ܡܟܪܙ	[a]ܘܐܙܠ ܒܟܠ [b]ܡܕܝܢܬܐ [c]ܡܟܪܙ ܟܠ ܡܐ	[b]ܡܕܝܢܬܐ
	ܕܥܒܕ ܠܗ ܝܫܘܥ : [d]ܫܠܡ ⁘	[d] *omit* ܫܠܡ

XCVII.

Luke IX. 1—6.

ܩܢ ܐ

Codex A.	Codex B.	Codex C.
[a]ܐܫܒܘܥܬ ܐܠܝܫܒܥ	[a]ܘܩܪܝܐ ܝܘܡ ܐܪܒܥܬ ܐܫܒܘܥ ܒܬܪ ܐܨܠܝܒܐ	[a]ܠܝܘܡ ܐܫܒܘܥ
ܡܢ ܠܘܩܐ[a]	1 ܡܢ ܠܘܩܣ[a] : ܘܩܪܐ ܗܘ [y]ܠܬܪܥܣܪܐ : [z]ܘܝܗܒ ܗܘ	ܐܫܒܥ ܡܢ ܠܘܩܐ[a]
[z]ܘܩܪܐ	ܡܪܢ ܝܫܘܥ ܡܪܐ ܠܬܪܥܣܪܬܐ [a]ܫܠܝܚܐ :	[y] *omit* ܩܘܪܣܐ
[c]ܕܝܐܚܘܢ	ܘܝܗܒ ܠܗܘܢ [b]ܫܘܠܛܢܐ ܘܚܝܠ ܥܠ ܟܠ ܫܐܕܐ	[z]ܘܩܪܐ [a]ܫܠܝܚܐ
[d] *omit* ܡܟܐܒ	2 ܘܠܡܐܣܝܐ [c]ܕܝܚܘܢ [d]ܡܟܐܒ : [e]ܘܫܕܪ ܐܢܘܢ	[b]ܫܘܠܛܢܐ [c]ܕܝܚܘܢ
[e]ܘܫܕܪ [g]ܟܠܘܡ	ܕܢܟܪܙܘܢ ܡܠܟܘܬܗ ܕܐܠܗܐ : ܘܢܐܣܘܢ ܟܪܝܗܐ	[d] *omit* ܡܟܐܒ [e]ܘܫܕܪ
‡ f. 62*b*.	3 ܘܐܡܪ ܠܗܘܢ [g]ܟܠܘܡ [†]ܠܐ [‡]ܬܫܩܠܘܢ ܠܐܘܪܚܐ	† f. 57*a*.
[j]ܠܚܡ [k]ܟܣܦ	ܠܐ [h]ܚܘܛܪܐ ܘܠܐ [i]ܬܪܡܠ ܘܠܐ [j]ܠܚܡ ܘܠܐ	[h]ܚܘܛܪ [i]ܬܪܡܠ
[l]ܬܠܬܝܢ [m]ܘܒܝܬܐ	[k]ܟܣܦ ܘܠܐ ܬܪܬܝܢ [l]ܟܘܬܝܢ ܝܗܘܐ ܠܟܘܢ : [f. 56*b*]	[l]ܬܠܬܝܢ [m]ܘܠܒܝܬܐ
[v]ܕܬܥܠܘܢ	4 [m]ܘܒܝܬܐ [v]ܕܬܥܠܘܢ ܠܗ ܬܡܢ ܩܘܘ : ܘܡܢ	[v]ܕܬܥܠܘܢ
	5 ܬܡܢ ܗܘܘ ܢܦܩܝܢ : ܘܟܠ ܡܢ ܕܠܐ ܡܩܒܠ ܠܟܘܢ	[n]ܢܦܩܝܢ [o] *add* ܗܘܘ
	ܢܦܩܘ ܡܢ ܬܡܢ [n]ܢܦܩܝܢ [o] [q]ܡܢ ܗܟܐ[q]	[q] *omit* ܡܢ ܗܟܐ
[r]ܡܕܝܢܬܐ	[r]ܡܕܝܢܬܐ ܐܘܦ ܥܦܪܐ ܡܢ [s]ܪܓܠܝܟܘܢ ܢܦܛܘ	
[s]ܪܓܠܝܟܘܢ	6 ܥܠܝܗܘܢ ܠܣܗܕܘ : ܟܕ ܕܝ ܢܦܩܘ ܗܘܘ ܚܕܪܝܢ	
[t]ܩܘܪܝܐ	ܒܟܠ [t]ܩܘܪܝܐ ܡܣܒܪܝܢ ܘܡܐܣܝܢ ܒܟܠ	
	ܐܬܪ ⁘	

Codex A. | Codex B. | Codex C.

XCVIII.

Luke VIII. 41—56.

Codex B.

ܩܪܝܢܐ[a] ܗܘܟ[b] ܐܘܢܓܠܝܘܢ ܐܠܘܫ[c] ܟܕ ܐܬܝܠܕ.
41 ܡܢ ܠܘܩܣ[a c] : ܘܒܫܥܬܗ[x] ܡܢܪܘܫܐ ܐܬܐ ܚܕ
ܓܒܪ ܕܫܡܗ[y] ܝܐܝܪܘܣ : ܘܗܘ[z] ܗܘܐ ܪܝܫ
ܟܢܫܬܐ[a] : ܘܢܦܠ ܩܕܡ[b] ܪܓܠܘܗܝ ܕܡܪܢ ܝܫܘܥ :
42 ܘܗܘܐ ܒܥܐ ܡܢܗ ܕܝܥܘܠ ܠܒܝܬܗ : [c]ܠܛܠܝܠ
ܕܝܚܝܕܐ ܒܪܐ[d] ܝܚܝܕܗ ܗܘܬ ܠܗ : ܗܘܝܢ[e] ܒܪܬ
[f]ܬܪܬܥܣܪܐ[g] ܫܢܝܢ : ܘܗܝ ܗܘܬ[h] ܡܝܬܐ :
ܘܒܡܐ[i] ܕܗܘܐ[j] ܐܙܠ[k] ܐܟܠܘܣܝܐ ܗܘܘ
43 ܡܕܚܩܝܢ ܠܗ : [l]ܘܐܢܬܬܐ ܕܗܘܬ ܒܕܘܒܗ[m] ܕܕܡܐ
[n]ܬܪܬܥܣܪ[g] ܫܢܝܢ : ܗܕܐ[o] [p]ܕܠܐ ܝܟܠܬ[q] ܡܬܐܣܝܐ
44 ܡܢ ܐܢܫ : ܩܪܒܬ[r] ܠܐܘܚܪܝܐ[s] ܘܐܬܩܪܒܬ
ܠܟܢܦܐ ܕܠܒܘܫܗ ܘܒܪ ܫܥܬܗ[‡] [t]ܩܡ ܠܗ ܡܥܝܢܗ
45 [m]ܕܕܡܐ : ܘܐܡܪ ܡܪܢܐ ܝܫܘܥ ܡܢ ܗܘ[u]
[v]ܕܩܪܒ ܠܝ : ܟܕ ܕܝ ܗܘܘ[w] ܡܟܦܪܝܢ ܟܘܠܗܘܢ :
ܐܡܪ ܠܗ ܦ̈ܛܪܘܣ ܪܒܝ[x] ܐ̈ܟܠܘܣܝܐ[y] ܗܘܘ
46 ܡܕܚܩܝܢ ܠܟ ܘܡܠܚܨܝܢ[z] : ܘܡܪܢܐ ܝܫܘܥ ܐܡܪ
ܠܗܘܢ[a] ܐܢܫ[b] ܩܪܒ ܠܝ : ܐܢܐ ܓܝܪ ܝܕܥܬ
47 ܒܚܝܠܐ ܕܢܦܩ ܡܢܝ : ܘܟܕ ܚܙܬ ܐܢܬܬܐ[†] ܕܠܐ
[c]ܛܫܝܐ[d] ܘܐܬܬܐ[e] ܕܚܝܠܐ ܘܡܪܬܬܐ[f] ܘܐܬܬ[e]
ܘܢܦܠܬ[g] ܩܕܡܘܗܝ : ܘܗܝ ܗܘܬ ܡܬܢܝܐ[h] ܠܛܠܝܠ
[f. 57a]
[i]ܗܝܕܐ ܥܠܐ ܩܪܒܬ ܠܗ ܠܥܝܢ[k] ܟܘܠܗ ܥܡܐ :
48 ܘܗܝܟ[l] ܐܬܐܣܝܬ ܒܪ ܫܥܬܗ : ܘܗܘ ܐܡܪ
ܠܗ ܒܪܬܐ ܗܝܡܢܘܬܟܝ[a] ܐܚܝܬ ܝܬܟܝ ܐܙܠܝ
49 [b]ܒܫܠܡܐ : [m]ܟܕ ܗܘ[n] ܡܡܠܠ ܐܬܐ ܚܕ ܡܢ
ܕܒܝܬ[o] ܪܝܫ ܟܢܫܬܐ : ܐܡܪ ܡܝܬܬ ܒܪܬܟ ܡܢ ܟܕܘ
50 ܠܐ[p] ܕܝ ܬܛܪܚܝ ܠܡܠܦܢܐ : ܡܪܢܐ[q] ܝܫܘܥ[r] ܕܝ
ܟܕ ܫܡܥ : ܐܬܦܢܝ ܘܐܡܪ[s] ܠܗ ܠܐ ܬܕܚܠ :
51 ܐܠܐ ܒܠܚܘܕ ܗܝܡܢ ܘܗܝ ܚܝܐ : ܟܕ ܕܝ ܐܬܐ

Codex A.

[b] *omit* ܗܘܟ
[c] ܡܢ ܠܘܩܐ [c]
[y] ܝܐܝܪܘܣ [z] ܗܘ ܕܝ [z]
[a] ܟܢܫܬܐ [b] ܪܓܠܘܗܝ
[c] ܠܛܠܝܠ [d] ܝܚܝܕܐ
[f] ܬܪܬܥܣܪܐ [g] ܫܢܝܢ
[h] ܡܝܬܐ ܠܡܡܬ [h]
[j] ܐܙܠ [k] ܐ̈ܟܠܘܣܝܐ
[l] ܘܐܢܬܬܐ [m] ܕܕܘܒܐ
[n] ܬܪܬܥܣܪܐ
[o] *add* ܐܢܬܬܐ ܩܛܝܥܐ ܕܟܘܠ
ܟܠ ܡܢܝܢܗ ܐܘܒܕܬ
[p] ܠܐ [q] ܡܬܐܣܝܐ
‡ f. 63*a*.
[r] ܠܐܘܚܪܗ [s] ܘܐܬܩܪܒܬ
[t] ܩܡ [m] ܕܕܘܒܐ
[u] *add* ܕܝ [v] ܕܩܪܒ
[w] ܡܟܦܪܝܢ
[x] ܐ̈ܟܠܘܣܝܐ
[y] *omit* ܗܘܘ
[z] *add* ܘܐܬܐ ܐܡܪ
ܡܢ ܗܘ ܕܝ ܕܩܪܒ ܠܝ
[b] ܩܪܒ [c] ܛܫܝܐ
[d] ܐܬܬܐ
[e] *omit* ܘ ܕܚܝܠܐ
[f] *omit* ܘܐܬܬ
[g] ܩܕܡܘܗܝ [h] ܠܛܠܝܠ
[m] *add* ܘ [a] ܐܚܝܬ
[p] *omit* ܕܝ [o] ܟܢܫܬܐ

Codex C.

[a] ܠܘܩܐ ܐܠܘܫ
[a] ܐܘܢܓܠܝܘܢ ܡܢ ܠܘܩܐ
[x] *omit* ܡܢܪܘܫܐ
[y] ܝܐܝܪܘܣ
[d] ܝܚܝܕܐ [e] ܒܪܬ
[f] ܬܪܬܥܣܪܬܐ
[h] ܡܝܬܐ [i] ܕܗܘܐ
[m] ܕܕܘܒܐ
[r] ܠܐܘܚܪܗ [s] ܘܐܬܩܪܒܬ
[u] *add* ܕܝ
[w] ܡܟܦܪܝܢ
[y] *omit* ܗܘܘ
[a] ܐܢܫ [b] ܩܪܒ
[c] ܛܫܝܐ [d] ܘܐܬܬܐ
† f. 57*b*.
[e] *omit* . . . ܕܚܝܠܐ
ܘܐܬܬ . . .
[g] ܩܕܡܘܗܝ [i] ܗܝܕܐ
[k] ܟܘܠܗ [l] ܐܬܐܣܝܬ
[a] ܐܚܝܬ [b] ܒܫܠܡܐ
[m] *add* ܘ [n] ܡܡܠܠ
[p] *omit* ܕܝ [q] *add* ܕܝ
[r] *omit* ܕܝ
[s] *omit* ܠܗ

Codex A.	Codex B.	Codex C.
ᵘܘܠܐܘܪܫܠܡ	ܠܟܘ ܟܢܘܬܐ ܠܗ ܥܒܘ ܠܐܬܪ ܕܢܐܠܠ ܚܡܣ :	ᵗܠܦܪܨܘܦܗ
ᵛܘܠܡܒܥܘܬܗ	ܐܠܐ ܐ ܠ ᵗܠܦܪܨܘܦܗ ᵘܠܐܘܪܫܠܡ ᵛܠܡܒܥܘܬܗ :	ᵘܠܐܘܪܫܠܡ
ʷܘܐܙܠܘ	52 ʷܘܐܙܠܘ ܕܫܡܪܝܐ ˣܠܩܪܝܬܐ ܕܫܡܪܝܐ : ܘܗܘܘ ܚܡܣ	ʷܘܐܙܠܘ
ˣܘܐܝܬܝܗ	ܟܕܠܡܘܢ ܘܒܥܘܬܗ ʸ: ܘܗܘ ܐܡܪ ܠܗ ᶻܬܠܡܝܕܘܗܝ ܠܐ ܢܬܒܥܘ :	ʸ add ܠܗ ᶻܬܠܡܝܕܘܗܝ
‡ f. 63b.	ܠܐ ܓܪ ܐܬܝܬ ܠܡܘܒܕܐ ܢܦܫܬܐ : ‡ܐܠܐ ᵃܕܢܚܝܐ ܗܘ :	
ʸ add ܠܗ	53 ܘܗܘܘ ܚܡܣ ܟܠܗܘܢ ܕܗܘܘ ܥܡܗ ܕܢܬܒܥܘܢ :	ᵇܗܢܘ ᶜܐܚܪ
ᶻܬܠܡܝܕܘܗܝ ᵃܕܢܚܝܐ	54 ܗܘ ܕܝܢ ᵇܗܢܘ ᶜܚܙܐ ᵈܟܠܗܘܢ ܚܡܣ ܠܒܪ : ܚܡܣ	ᵈܟܠܗ ᵉܟܝܢ
ᶜܐܚܪ ᵈܟܠܗ	ᵉܐܝܟ ܐܢܫܐ ܚܕ ܐܡܪ ܘܐܬܐ ᶠܠܗ ܠܩܪܝܬܐ	ᵍܡܣܬܟܠ
ᶠomit ܠܗ ᵉܟܝܢ	55 ᵍܡܣܬܟܠ : ܘܐܬܐ ᶠܠܗ ܢܦܫܗ ܘܡܢܟܐ ʰܗܘ ܐܬܢ	ᵍܡܣܬܟܠ ʰܘܡܢܟܐ ⁱܚܡܣ
	56 ܥܢܝܗ : ܘܚܡܣ ܕܠܐܬܪܟܘܢ ܠܗ ܕܬܬܟܠܠ : ܘܗܘܘ	ᵏܘܡܢܟܐܘܬ
ⁱܚܡܣ ᵏܐܬܪܟܘܢ	ܐܚܪܢܝܬܐ ܡܬܬܟܠܠܝܢ : ܘܗܘ ⁱܚܡܣ ܢܦܫܗܘܢ	ˡܕܐܬܝܬ
ᵐomit ܥܠܡ	ܕܐܠܐ ܠܗ ᵏܡܬܚܪܝܢ ܡܢܐ ˡܕܐܬܝܬ : ᵐܥܠܡ ⁘	ᵐomit ܥܠܡ

XCIX.

Luke IX. 37—43.

Codex A.	Codex B.	Codex C.
ᵃܘܗܘܐ ܐܚܪܢܐ ܐܢܫܐ	ᵃܘܗܘܐ ܗܘܐ ܐܢܫ ܐܬܐ ܟܕ ܐܝܠܝܢ	ᵃܠܗܘܢ ܐܢܫܐ
ᵃܐܬܐ ܡܢ ܠܗܘܢ	37 ܡܢ ܠܗܘܢ ᵃ: ᶻܘܗܘܐ ᵃܠܗܘܢ ᵇܐܚܪܢܐ	ᵃܐܬܐ ܡܢ ܠܗܘܢ
ᶻadd ܘܒܥܘܬܗ ܐܚܪܢܐ	ᶜܕܟܠܬܗܘܢ ܟܕ ᵈܢܚܬܘ ܡܢ ܛܘܪܐ : ᵉܐܬܐ	ᶻadd ܘܒܥܘܬܗ ܐܚܪܢܐ
ᵇܐܚܪܢܐ ᶜܕܟܠܬܗܘܢ	38 ܟܢܫܐ ᶠܣܓܝܐܐ ܥܡܗ : ܘܗܐ ܓܒܪܐ ܚܕ	ᵃܟܢܫܐ
ᵉܐܬܐ	ᵍܡܢ ܟܢ ʰܣܓܝܐܐ ܩܥܐ ܘܐܡܪ : ܡܠܦܢܐ	ᵇܐܚܪܢܐ ᵈܢܚܬ
ᶠܣܓܝܐܐ	ܐܬܐ ܒܥܐ ܡܢܟ ⁱܐܬܚܢܢ ⁱܥܠ ܒܪܝ ܕܗܘ	ᵉܐܬܐ
ⁱܐܬܚܢܢ ܥܠ ܒܪܝ ⁱ	[f. 57b]	† f. 58a.
	39 ܝܚܝܕ ܠܝ : ܘܗܐ ܪܘܚܐ ܢܣܒܐ ܠܗ ܡܢ ܥܠܡ	ᵍܡܢ ʰܣܓܝܐܐ
ˡܘܡܫܬܢܩܐ	ܗܘ ܩܥܐ : ܘܡܫܬܢܩ ܠܗ ܘܗܘ ᵏܡܬܚܒܠ :	ᵏܡܬܚܒܠ ˡܘܡܫܬܢܩ
ᵐomit ܪܘܚܐ ... ܕܗܘܐ	ˡܘܡܫܬܢܩ ܗܘ ᵐܪܘܚܐ ܡܢܗ ܡܢ ܕܗܘܐ ᵐܚܠܡܐ	ⁿܬܠܡܝܕܝܟ
ᵒܕܢܦܩܘܢ	40 ܠܗ : ܘܒܥܝܬ ܡܢ ⁿܬܠܡܝܕܝܟ ᵒܕܢܦܩܘܢ ܠܗ	ᵒܕܢܦܩܘܢ ᵖܐܬܟܠܘ
ᵖܒܟܠܗ ᵠܘܐܬܒܝܬ	41 ܘܠܐ ᵖܫܟܚܘ : ᵠܘܐܬܒܝܬ ܠܗ ܝܫܘܥ ܘܐܡܪ	ʳܘܗܝܡܢܘܬܐ
ʳܗܝܡܢܘܬܐ	ܐܘ ܕܪܐ ܕܠܐ ʳܗܝܡܢܘܬܐ ˢܘܡܥܩܡܢܘܬܐ ܥܕ ܐܡܬܝ	ˢܘܡܥܩܡܢܘܬܐ
ᵘܐܣܝܒܪ	ܐܗܘܐ ܥܡܟܘܢ ܘܡܣܝܒܪ ܐܢܐ ܠܟܘܢ : ܩܪܒܘ	ᵗܠܗ ܗܪܐ ᵗ
‡ f. 64a.	42 ᵗܠܗ ܗܪܟܐ ܥܕ ܗܘ ‡ ܕܝܢ ᵘܐܣܝܒܪ ܠܗ ܪܘܚܐ	ᵘܐܣܝܒܪ ᵛܝܚܝܕܐ
ˣܠܗ	ܗܘ ᵛܝܚܝܕܐ ܘܗܘܐ ʷܚܝܪ ˣܠܗ : ܘܟܐܒ ܪܘܚܐ	ʷܚܝܪ ˣܠܗ
ʸܪܘܚܐ	ܗܘܝܐ ʸܪܘܚܬܐ ܠܩܕܝܫܬܐ : ܘܐܣܝ ܠܛܠܝܐ	ʸܪܘܚܐ

Codex A.	*Codex* B.	*Codex* C.
[z] [Syriac]	43 [Syriac] [z] [Syriac]	[z] [Syriac]
	[Syriac] ⁘	

C.

Luke X. 25—37.

Codex A.	*Codex* B.	*Codex* C.
[a] [Syriac]	[a] [Syriac] [b] [Syriac]	[a] [Syriac]
[b] *omit* [Syriac] ... [Syriac]	25 [Syriac] [b] [y] [Syriac]	[b] *omit* [Syriac] ... [Syriac]
[y] *add* [Syriac]	[z] [Syriac] [a] [Syriac]	[y] *add* [Syriac]
[z] [Syriac] [a] [Syriac]	26 [b] [Syriac] [c] [Syriac] [d] [Syriac]	[a] [Syriac]
[b] [Syriac] [c] [Syriac]	[Syriac] [e] [Syriac] [e] [Syriac]	[b] [Syriac] [d] [Syriac]
[g] [Syriac] [h] [Syriac]	27 [f] [Syriac] [g] [Syriac] [h] [Syriac]	[e] [Syriac] [e]
[i] *add* [Syriac]	[Syriac] [i] [Syriac]	[f] *omit* [Syriac] [g] [Syriac]
	[Syriac]	
	28 [Syriac] [j] [Syriac] [k] [Syriac]	[j] [Syriac] [k] [Syriac]
	29 [Syriac]	
[l] [Syriac]	30 [Syriac] [l] [Syriac]	[l] [Syriac]
[m] [Syriac]	[Syriac] [m] [Syriac]	
[n] [Syriac] [o] [Syriac]	[Syriac] [n] [Syriac] [o] [Syriac]	[o] [Syriac]
	[Syriac] † [Syriac] [f. 58*a*]	† f. 58*b*.
[p] [Syriac] [r] *omit* [Syriac]	[Syriac]	
[u] [Syriac]	31 [p] [Syriac] [q] [Syriac] [r] [Syriac] [s] [Syriac]	[p] [Syriac] [q] [Syriac]
[w] *add* [Syriac] [x] [Syriac]	32 [Syriac] [t] [Syriac]	[r] *omit* [Syriac] [s] [Syriac]
‡ f. 64*b*.	‡ [u] [w] [Syriac] [x] [Syriac]	[t] [Syriac] [w] *add* [Syriac]
[z] [Syriac] [a] [Syriac]	33 [Syriac] [y] [Syriac] [z] [Syriac]	[y] [Syriac] [a] [Syriac]
[c] [Syriac] [d] [Syriac]	[Syriac] [a] [Syriac]	[b] [Syriac] [c] [Syriac]
[e] [Syriac] [f] [Syriac]	34 [Syriac] [b] [Syriac] [c] [Syriac]	[d] [Syriac] [e] [Syriac]
[g] [Syriac] [h] [Syriac]	[d] [Syriac] [e] [Syriac] [f] [Syriac]	[g] [Syriac] [h] [Syriac]
[i] [Syriac]	[Syriac] [g] [Syriac] [h] [Syriac]	[i] [Syriac]
[k] [Syriac] [l] *omit* [Syriac]	35 [Syriac] [i] [Syriac]	[k] [Syriac] [l] *omit* [Syriac]
[m] [Syriac]	[Syriac] [k] [Syriac] [l] [Syriac]	[m] [Syriac]
[n] [Syriac]	[m] [Syriac] [n] [Syriac]	[n] [Syriac]

Codex A.	Codex B.	Codex C.
^j^ ܡܬ̈ܩܝܡ ^k^ omit ܘ	ܬܐܡܪ ܐܬܬܐ ^i^ ܒܗܠ ܡܢܐ ܕܐܬܬ ^j^ ܡܬ̈ܩܝܡ ܒܠܗܝ :	^i^ ܘܐܬܬܐ ^j^ ܡܬ̈ܩܝܡ
^l^ ܬܠܬܝܬܐ ^n^ add ܕܝ	36 ^k^ ܘܒܬܘܪ ܐܢܐ ܒܥܐ ܠܟ : ܡܢ ܐܢܘܢ ܡܢ ܗܠܝܢ	^l^ ܬܠܬܝܬܐ ^k^ omit ܘ
^o^ ܒܠܒܗ ^q^ ܐܙܠ	^l^ ܬܠܬܝܬܐ ܗܢܐ ܠܟ ܕܗܘܐ ^m^ ܡܪܚܡܗ ^n^ ܕܢܦܠ	^m^ ܡܪܚܡܝܢ ^n^ add ܕܝܢ
^r^ ܐܘܦ̮ ܐܬ ^r^	37 ^o^ ܒܠܒܗ ^p^ ܠܡܦ̮ܠܛܐ : ܗܘ ܕܝ ܐܡܪ ܕܡ ܕܒܒܕ	^o^ ܒܠܒܗ ^p^ ܠܡܦ̮ܠܛܐ
^s^ add ܗܘܝ	^o^ ܒܠܒܗ ܪܚܡܝܢ : ܘܐܡܪ ܠܗ ܡܪܝܐ ܝܫܘܥ ^q^ ܐܙܠ	^r^ ܐܘܦ̮ ܐܬ ^r^
^t^ ܚܡ ^u^ omit ܥܒܕ	^r^ ܐܬ ܐܘܦ̮ ^r^ ^s^ ܒܒܕ ^t^ ܚܡ : ^u^ ܥܒܕ ܀	^u^ omit ܥܒܕ

CI.

Luke IX. 57—62.

Codex A.	Codex B.	Codex C.
^b^ ܡܢ ܠܘܩܒܠܐ ^b^	^a^ ܘܗܘܪܐ ܐܬܗܦ̮ܟ ܐܬܐܘܣܒ ^b^ ܟܕ ܐܬܩܒܠ ܡܢ	^a^ ܠܘܩܒܠ ^b^ ܡܢ ܠܘܩܒܠܐ ^b^
	57 ^b^ ܠܘܩܒܠ : ܘܒܡܬܗ ^z^ ܡܢܪܘܫܐ ܘܗܘܐ ܗܘܝܢ	^z^ omit ܡܢܪܘܫܐ
	ܕܗܠܟܘܢ ܐܙܠܝܢ ܒܐܘܪܚܐ : ܐܡܪ ܠܗ ܚܕ ^a^	^a^ add ܡܢܝܗ
^b^ ܐܙܠ	58 ܥܬܗ ܒܬܪܟ ܠܗܘܢ ܕܐܬ ^b^ ܐܙܠ ܡܪܢܐ : ^c^ ܗܘ	^c^ omit ܗܘ ܕܝ
	^c^ ܕܝ ܐܡܪ ܠܗ ^d^ ܠܬܥܠܒܐ ܒܝܬ : ܘܠܦ̮ܪܚܬܐ	^d^ add ܡܪܢܐ ܝܫܘܥ
^e^ ܩܢܝܢ ^f^ ܕܒܢܝܗ	ܕܫܡܝܐ ^e^ ܩܢܝܢ : ܒܪܗ ܕܓ̰ܒܪܐ ܕܝ ܠܝܬ ܠܗ	^e^ ܩܢܝܢ ^g^ ܠܡܣܡܟ
^i^ ܥܠܝܟ ^j^ add ܡܚܕܐ	59 ܗܘ ^f^ ܕܢܝܚܡ ܪܫܗ : ܘܐܡܪ ^g^ ܠܡܣܡܟ ܐܬܐ	^h^ ܡܪܝ ^i^ ܥܠܝܟ
‡ f. 65a.	ܒܬܪܝ : ܗܘ ܕܝ ‡ ܐܡܪ ^h^ ܡܪܢܐ ^i^ ܥܠܝܟ ܬܘܝ ^j^	^j^ add ܡܚܕܐ
^l^ omit ܕ ^m^ omit ܕܝ	60 ^k^ ܕܐܙܠ ^l^ † ܕܐܩܒܘܪ ^m^ ܕܝ ܠܐܒܐ : ܘܐܡܪ ^n^ ܠܗ	† f. 59a.
^p^ ܐܙܠ ^q^ ܟܡܣܝܪ	[f. 58b] ܡܪܢܐ ܫܒܘܩ ܥܒܕܘ ܡܝܬܬܐ ܡܩܒܪܝܢ ^o^ ܡܝܬܝܗܘܢ :	^k^ ܕܐܙܠ ^l^ omit ܕ
^r^ ܡܠܟܘܬܐ ^s^ ܚܘܪܝ	ܐܬ ܕܝ ^p^ ܐܙܠ ^q^ ܟܡܣܝܪ ^r^ ܕܡܠܟܘܬܗ ܕܐܠܗܐ :	^m^ omit ܕܝ ^n^ omit ܠܗ
^u^ ܦ̮ܚܐܝ ^v^ ܥܠܝܟ	61 ܘܐܡܪ ܠܗ ^s^ ܚܘܪܝܢ ^t^ ܡܬܐܬܐ ܒܬܪܟ ܡܪܢܐ :	^o^ ܡܝܬܝܗܘܢ
^w^ ܕܒܐܙܠ ^x^ ܒܛܥܢܬܝ	^u^ ܡܚܕܐ ܕܝ ^v^ ܥܠܝܟ ܬܘܝ ^w^ ܕܐܙܠ ^x^ ܬܛܥܢܬ ܡܢ	^r^ ܡܠܟܘܬܗ ^t^ ܬܘܝ
	62 ܗܠܝܢ ܕܒܒܝܬܝ : ܐܡܪ ܠܗ ܕܝ ܡܪܢܐ ܝܫܘܥ	^w^ ܕܐܙܠ
^y^ ܙܡܕܝ ^z^ ܐܒܪܗܡ	ܠܝܬ ܐܢܫ ^y^ ܙܡܕܐ ^z^ ܐܕܗ ܒܠ ܦ̮ܕܢܐ ܘܡܣܬܟܠ	^y^ ܙܡܕܝ ^a^ ܠܚܘܪܐ
^a^ ܠܚܘܪܐ ^b^ omit ܕܝ	^a^ ܠܚܘܪܐ ܘܡܥܒܝ ^b^ ܕܝ ܠܡܠܟܘܬܗ ܕܐܠܗܐ ܀	^b^ omit ܕܝ

CII.

Luke XII. 16—21.

Codex A.	Codex B.	Codex C.
^b^ ܘܗܘܪܐ ^c^ omit . . . ܟܕ . . . ܐܬܩܒܠ		
^a^ ܥܬܝܪ ܚܕ ^a^ ^b^ ܚܠܝܬܐ ^c^ add ܘܐܚܠܬ ܠܗ ܚ̈ܠܬܐ ܡ̈ܬܐܝܬܐ (in intercolumnio manus non recens).	^a^ ^b^ ܘܐܡܪ ܐܠܝܫܥ ܐܬܗܦ̮ܟ ^c^ ܟܕ ܚܕ ܐܬܩܒܠ ^c^ ܡܢ	^a^ ܠܘܩܒܠ ܐܠܝܫܥ ^a^ ܐܬܦ̮ܟ[ܒ]ܡܢ ܠܘܩܒܠܐ
	16 ^z^ ^a^ ܠܘܩܒܠܐ ܐܡܪ ܡܪܢܐ ܗܕܐ ܡܬܠܬܐ : ^a^ ܚܕ	^z^ add ܘܒܡܬܗ
	^a^ ܥܬܝܪ ܗܘܐ ^b^ ܚܠܝܬ ܘܐܬܠܝܫܬ ܠܗ ܐܪܥܗ : ^c^	^a^ ܥܬܝܪ ܚܕ ^b^ ܚܠܝܬ

Codex A.	Codex B.	Codex C.
ᵈܕܠܝܬ ᵉomit ܕܝ ᶠܕܡܚܝܒ ᵍܦܪܝܢ ⁱܘܐܪܘܢܐ ᵏܝܚܝܒ ˡܫܠܝܐ ᵐܘܦܠܚܬܝ ⁿܠܚܝ ᵖܡܣܬܡܟ ᵠܥܠܝ ᵗܘܐܫܬܝ ᵘܘܚܡܕܝ ʷܒܗܕܐ ˣܠܠܝܐ ʸܒܥܝܢ ᶻܐܬܩܢܬ ᵃܝܗܘܘܢ ᵇܕܐܩܝܪ ᶜܥܬܪ ‡ f. 65b. ᵈadd ܘܟܕ ܐܡܪ ܗܠܝܢ . ܡܢܐ ܘܐܡܪ ܡܢ ܕܐܝܬ ܠܗ ܐܕܢܐ ܕܡܫܡܥ ܢܫܡܥ ⁘ (in intercolumnio manus non recens). ᵉomit ܥܠܡ	17 ܘܗܘܘܐ ܡܬܘܣܦܝܢ ܒܠܒܗܘܢ ܐܡܪܝܢ ܡܢܐ ܡܟܕܢ : ᵈܠܝܬ ܠܝ ᵉܕܝ ܗܘ ᶠܕܡܚܝܒ ᵍܦܪܝܢ : ʰܘܐܡܪ 18 ܗܕܐ ܐܢܐ ܟܒܕܐ ʰ: ܦܬܪ ܐܢܐ ⁱܐܘܪܢܝ ܘܟܠܢܐ ܬܗܘܘܢ ܙܟܪܝܢ : ʲܘܠܬܠܬܗܘܢ ᵏܡܚܝܒ 19 ܟܘܠ ˡܫܠܝ ᵐܘܦܠܚܬܝ : ܘܐܢܐ ܐܡܪ ܠܢܦܫܝ ܢܦܫܝ ܗܐ ⁿܠܝܬ ܠܝ ᵒܦܠܚ ᵖܡܣܬܡܟ ܠܡܦܠܚ ᵠܥܠܝ : ʳܐܬܢܝܚܝ ˢܘܐܟܘܠܝ ᵗܘܐܫܬܝ ᵘܘܚܡܕܝ : 20 ܘܐܡܪ ܠܗ ܐܠܗܐ : ܦܟܗܐ : ʷܒܗܕܐ ˣܠܠܝܐ ʸܒܥܝܢ 21 ܢܦܫܟ ܡܢܟ : ܘܗܠܝܢ ܕܝ ᶻܕܐܬܩܢܬ ܠܡܢ ᵃܝܗܘܘܢ : ܗܟܕܝܢ ܗܘ ܟܘܠ ܡܢ ‡ ᵇܕܐܩܝܪ ܠܗ ܘܠܐ ᶜܥܬܪ ܒܐܠܗܐ :ᵈ ᵉܥܠܡ ⁘	ᵈܕܠܝܬ ᵉomit ܕܝ ᶠܕܡܚܝܒ ʰomit ܘܐܡܪ ... ܟܒܕܐ ⁱܐܘܪܢܝ ʲܘܠܝܬ ܡܢ ᵏܡܚܝܒ ˡܫܠܝ ᵒܦܠܚܝܢ ʳܐܬܢܝܚܝ ˢܘܐܟܘܠܝ ᵘܘܚܡܕܝ ˣܠܠܝܐ ᶻܐܬܩܢܬ ᵇܕܐܩܝܪ ᶜܥܬܪ ᵉomit ܥܠܡ

CIII.

Luke X. 19—21.

ܟܒ ܐ		
ᵇܡܢ ܠܘܩܣ ᵇ ᵃܠܬܠܡܝܕܘܗܝ ᵈܘܫܠܛܢܘ ᵉܕܬܕܘܫܘܢ ᶠܠܟܠ ᵍܚܘܝܬܐ ʰܕܒܥܠܕܒܒܐ ⁱܒܪܡ ᵏadd ܕܝ ˡܡܫܬܥܒܕܝܢ ᵐܫܡܗܬܟܘܢ ⁿܟܬܝܒܝܢ ᵒܠܛܠܝܢ ᵖܐܝ ᵠܕܗܟܕܝܢ ʳomit ܕܝ ˢܨܒܝܢܐ	ᵃܩܪܝܢܐ ܐܘܟܬ ܐܠܟܣܢܕܪ ᵇܒܬܪ ܒܬܪ ܐܦܝܦܢ 19 ܡܢ ܠܘܩܣ ᵇᵃ: ᶻ ܐܡܪ ܡܪܢ ᵃܠܬܠܡܝܕܘܗܝ : ܗܐ ܝܗܒܬ ᶜܠܟܘܢ ܫܠ ᵈܘܫܠܛܢ ᵉܕܬܕܘܫܘܢ ᶠܠܟܠ ܡܢ ᵍܚܘܝܬܐ ܘܥܩܪܒܝܐ : † ܘܥܠ ܟܘܠ ܚܝܠܗ ʰܕܒܥܠܕܒܒܐ : ܘܡܕܡ ܠܐ ܠܐ ܡܟܐ ܢܬܟܘܢ : 20 ⁱܒܪܡ ᵏܒܗܕܐ ܠܐ ܬܚܕܘܢ ܕܪܘܚܬܐ ˡܡܫܬܥܒܕܝܢ [f. 59a] ܠܟܘܢ : ܚܕܘ ܕܝ ܕܗܘܐ ᵐܫܡܗܬܟܘܢ ⁿܟܬܝܒܝܢ 21 ܒܫܡܝܐ : ܘܒܗ ܒܫܥܬܐ ܐܬܦܨܚ ܡܪܢ ܒܪܘܚܐ ܕܩܘܕܫܐ ܘܐܡܪ : ܡܫܬܘܕܐ ܐܢܐ ܠܟ ܐܒܐ ܡܪܐ ܕܫܡܝܐ ܘܕܐܪܥܐ : ܕܛܡܪܬ ܗܠܝܢ ܡܢ ܚܟܝܡܝܢ ܘܡܢ ܡܣܟܘܬܢܝܢ : ܘܓܠܝܬ ܐܢܘܢ ᵒܠܛܠܝܢ ᵖܐܝ ܐܒܐ ᵠܕܗܟܕܝܢ ܐܬܟܒܕ ʳܕܝ ˢܨܒܝܢܐ ܩܕܡܝܟ ⁘	ᵃܠܝܘܡ ܐܘܟܬ ᵃܐܠܟܣܢܕܪ ܡܢ ܠܘܩܣ ᶻadd ܘܒܬܪܗ ܦܢܝܐ ܘܐܡܪ ᶜomit ܠܟܘܢ † f. 59b. ᵈܘܫܠܛܢܘ ʰܕܒܥܠܕܒܒܐ ᵏadd ܕܝ ⁿܟܬܝܒܝܢ ᵒܠܛܠܝܢ ᵖܐܝ ᵠܕܗܟܢ ʳomit ܕܝ

CIV.

Luke XIII. 11—17.

ܟܓ ܐ		
ᵇܦܢܝܐ ᶜܡܢ ܠܘܩܐ ᵃadd ܘܒܬܪܗ ܦܢܝܐ ܘܐܡܪ ᵇܗܘܬ ܐܬܬܐ ᵇ	ᵃᵇܦܩܘ ܐܠܝܫܥ ܐܠܟܣܢܕܪ ᶜܒܬܪ ܒܬܪ ܐܦܝܦܢ ܡܢ 11 ܠܘܩܣ ᵃᶜ: ᵃ ᵇܘܗܘܐ ܐܬܬܐ ᵇ ܚܕܐ ᶜ ܕܗܘܐ ܠܗ	ᵃܠܝܘܡ ܐܠܝܫܥ ᵃܐܠܟܣܢܕܪ ܡܢ ܠܘܩܐ ᵃadd ܘܒܬܪܗ ᵇܗܘܬ ܐܬܬܐ ᵇ ᶜomit ܕ

Codex A.	Codex B.	Codex C.
ܬܬܡܠܟܘܢ [d]	ܕܢܚܬ ܥܠܝܟ [c] ܕܬܬܡܠܟܘܢ [d] ܥܠܝ [e] : ܘܗܘܬ ܠܒܘܫܐ	[c] *omit* ܕ ܕܬܬܡܠܟܘܢ [d]
[e] ܥܠܝ [f] ܟܠܝܠܐ	12 ܘܠܐ ܗܘܬ [f] ܟܠܝܠܐ ܕܐܬܬܐ [g] ܠܒܫ ܗܘܝܬ : ܗܐ [h]	[f] ܟܠܝܠܐ [h] *add* ܕܝ
[g] ܠܒܫ [h] *add* ܕܝ	ܢܚܬܐ ܠܗ ܡܢ ܫܡܝܐ ܘܐܬܐ [i] ܘܝܬܒ ܥܠ [i]	[k] ܩܝܡܝܢ
‡ f. 66a.	ܠܗ: ܐܬܐ ܗܘ ܐܢܬ [j] ܘܐܡܪ [k] ܩܝܡܝܢ ‡ ܡܢ ܩܕܡܝܟܘܢ :	[l] ܘܐܫܘܬ [m] ܥܠܝ
[i] ܐܢܬ [j] ܐܡܪ	13 [l] ܘܐܫܘܬ [m] ܥܠܝ [n] ܐܝܕܗ ܘܟܬܒܗ ܕܡܬܬܕܒܪܐ	[n] ܐܝܕܗ [o] ܡܫܒܚܐ
[k] ܩܝܡܝܢ [m] ܥܠܝ	14 ܘܗܘܬ [o] ܡܫܒܚܐ ܠܐܠܗܐ : ܘܐܬܒܪܟ ܘܐܡܪ	[q] *omit* ܕܝ
[n] ܐܝܕܗ [o] ܡܫܒܚܐ	[p] ܟܬܒܬܐ ܗܘܬ [q] ܕܝ [r] ܒܬܘܠܬܐ ܐܝܟ ܡܢ ܫܡܝܐ	[r] ܕܒܬܘܠܬܐ
[p] ܟܬܒܬܐ [q] *omit* ܕܝ	ܗܘܝܢ [t] ܘܐܬܐ [u] ܠܐܠܒܫܐ : [w] ܐܝܟܐ [x] ܡܢ	[t] *omit* ܘ
[r] ܕܒܬܘܠܬܐ	ܗܘܝܢ ܕܗܘܘ ܠܘܩܒܠ [y] ܕܢܘܗܪܐ [z] ܕܟܘܠܗܘܢ	[u] ܠܐܠܒܫܐ
[u] ܠܐܠܒܫܐ	ܟܕ ܐܝܟ ܗܘܘ ܐܬܪ [a] ܡܬܚܙܐ : ܘܠܐ	[x] ܡܢ [y] ܕܢܘܗܪܐ
[w] ܐܝܟܐ [x] ܡܢ	15 ܒܐܝܕܐ ܕܒܬܘܠܬܐ : ܐܡܪܬ [v] ܡܢ ܫܡܝܐ	[a] ܡܬܚܙܐ [v] *add* ܕܝ
[y] ܕܢܘܗܪܐ [z] ܕܟܘܠܗܘܢ	ܘܐܡܪ ܠܗ : ܥܡܐ ܟܠ ܐܢܫ ܡܢܗܘܢ ܠܐ [b]	[b] *add* ܗܘ
[d] ܘܐܬܬ [v] *add* ܕܝ	ܥܠܡܐ ܬܬܒܪܟ [c] ܐܢܐ : ܡܢ ܫܡܝܐ ܘܐܬܐ	[c] ܗܘ
[g] ܕܐܬܐ	16 ܒܬܘܠܬܐ [d] ܘܐܬܬ † ܡܪܝܐ ܠܗ : ܘܗܘܐ ܕܝ	† f. 60a.
[h] ܬܬܡܠܟܘܢ [i] ܥܠܝ	[e] ܕܗܘܝ ܒܐܬܪܗ [f] ܕܡܪܝܐ [g] ܕܐܬܐ ܗܘܐ ܡܢ	[e] ܗܘܝ [f] ܕܡܪܝܐ
[k] ܐܡܪ [l] *add* ܕܗܘܘ	[h] ܬܬܡܠܟܘܢ [i] ܥܠܝ : ܠܐ ܗܘܐ ܠܘܩܒܠ ܕܬܬܒܪܟ	[h] ܬܬܡܠܟܘܢ [h]
[m] ܩܕܡܝ [n] ܠܡܫܠܡ	17 ܡܢ ܗܘܝ [k] ܐܡܪ ܠܐܠܗܐ ܕܒܬܘܠܬܐ : ܘܫܠܡ [f. 59b]	[k] ܐܡܪ
[o] ܘܟܠ [p] ܐܠܒܫܐ	ܗܘܐ ܐܡܪ : ܘܗܘܘ ܒܫܡܝܐ ܡܢ ܟܠ ܫܠܡ [l]	[l] *add* ܕܗܘܘ
[q] ܬܫܒܚܬܐ	[m] ܕܩܕܡ [n] ܠܡܫܠܡ : [o] ܘܟܠܗܘܢ [p] ܐܠܒܫܐ	[m] ܩܕܡܝ [o] ܘܟܠ
[r] ܡܬܒܪܟܝܢ	ܗܘܐ ܐܢܫ ܥܠ ܟܠ [q] ܬܫܒܘܚܬܗ ܕܗܘܘ	[q] ܬܫܒܚܬܐ
[t] *omit* ܥܠܡ	[r] ܡܬܒܪܟܝܢ : [s] [t] ܥܠܡ ⁘	[t] *omit* ܥܠܡ [s] *add* ܡܢܗ

CV.

Luke XII. 32—40.

Codex A.	Codex B.	Codex C.
[a] ܫܒܬܐ ܕܩܕܡ ܥܐܕܐ	[a] ܫܒܬܐ ܕܩܕܡ ܥܐܕܐ ܕܝܠܕܗ ܕܡܪܢ ܡܢ	[a] ܫܒܬܐ ܕܩܕܡ ܥܐܕܐ
[a] ܕܝܠܕܗ ܡܢ ܠܘܩܐ	32 ܠܘܩܐ [z a] ܐܡܪ ܡܪܢ ܠܐ [a] ܬܕܚܠܘܢ [b] ܡܪܥܝܬܐ	[a] ܡܢ ܠܘܩܐ
[a] ܬܕܚܠܘܢ	ܙܥܘܪܬܐ : [c] ܕܨܒܐ ‡ ܐܒܘܟܘܢ ܕܢܬܠ ܠܟܘܢ	[z] *add* ܡܪܥܝܬܐ ܙܥܘܪܬܐ
‡ f. 66b.	33 ܡܠܟܘܬܐ : ܙܒܢܘ ܩܢܝܢܝܟܘܢ ܘܗܒܘ [d] ܕܝ	[d] *omit* ܕܝ [c] *omit* ܕ
[b] ܡܪܥܝܬܐ	[e] ܨܕܩܬܐ : ܥܒܕܘ ܠܟܘܢ [f] ܟܝܣܝܢ ܕܠܐ ܒܠܝܢ	[e] ܠܨܕܩܬܐ [f] ܟܝܣܝܢ
[d] *omit* ܕܝ [f] ܟܝܣܝܢ	[g] ܘܣܝܡܬܐ ܕܠܐ [h] ܚܣܪܐ ܒܫܡܝܐ : ܗܘ	[g] ܘܣܝܡܬܐ [h] ܚܣܪܐ
[h] ܚܣܪܐ		

عد. ٣ قبل عيد الميلاد بسبتين

Codex B.

34 ⁱܕܟܕ ܠܐ ʲܦܪ̈ܝܫܝ ܘܫܡܥܐ ܠܐ ᵏܫܪܝܘ : ܗܘܢ ˡ
ᵐܕܗܘܐ ⁿܦܣܬܩܘܬܗܘܢ ܬܡܢ °ܗܘܐ ܐܘܦ
35 ᵖܠܒܝܒܗܘܢ : ܡܢܗܘܢ ܣܪܝܒܗܘܢ ᵠܐܫܪܝܢ
36 ʳܘܡܢܣܝܒܗܘܢ ܕܠܡܢ : ܘܐܬܘܢ ܗܘܢ ܗܘܢ
ˢܐܢܫ ܕܡܫܡܥ ᵗܠܡܪ̈ܗܘܢ ܐܡܬܝ ܡܬܒ
ᵘܘܐܬܐ ܡܢ ᵛܡܫܒܬܐ : ܕܒܗ ʷܐܬܐ ܘܪܬܘ
37 ˣܫܐܠܐ ʸܡܬܦܬܚܝܢ ܠܗ : ܠܦܪܘܩܗܘܢ ᶻܒܒܝܬܐ
ܗܠܝܢ ܒܟܐ ᵃܕܐܬܐ ᵇܡܪ̈ܗܘܢ ᶜܡܫܒܚܝܢ
ܡܬܗܘܢ ܒܝܪܝܢ : ᵈܐܡܪܝܢ ܐܡܪ ܐܢܐ ܠܟܘܢ
ܕܗܘ ᵉܐܫܟܚ ܣܪܝܩܝܢ ܘܡܪܒܒܢ ܡܬܗܘܢ
38 ᶠᵍܘܢܦܠ ܘܫܒܫܒ ܡܬܗܘܢ ᵍ: ܐܘܦ ʰܐܢ
ⁱܐܬܐܬܐ ᵏܡܦܘܪܬܐ ˡܬܫܝܢܝܬܐ ᵐܘܡܬܠܬܠܬܐ
ⁿܫܒܚ ܡܬܗܘܢ °ܗܕܒܝܢ : † ܠܦܪܘܩܗܘܢ ܠܗܠܝܢ
39 ܒܒܝܬܐ : ܗܕܐ ܕܝ ܗܘܘ ܝܕܥܝܢ ܕܐܠܘ ᵖܝܕܥ
ܡܪܗ ܕܒܝܬܐ ʳܒܗܕܐ ܫܥܬܐ ˢܓܢܒܐ ܐܬܐ
ᵗܗܘ ܐܬܝ ܗܘܐ ܫܗܪ ܘܠܐ ܗܘܐ ܫܒܩ ܒܝܬܗ
40 ܕܡܬܚܬܪ : ‡ ܐܘܦ ܐܬܘܢ ܗܘܘ ܡܬܝܕܥܝܢ
[f. 60*a*]
ܕܒܫܥܬܐ ܕܠܝܬ ܐܬܘܢ ܡܣܒܪܝܢ ܒܪܗ ܕܓܒܪܐ
ܐܬܐ ⁘

CVI.

Luke XIV. 16—24.

ᵃܢܘܡ ܐܠܝܗ ܕܝܫܒܪ ܒܒܗ ܐܪܠܝܒ ܡܢ ܠܗܘܡ ᵃ: ᶻ
16 ܐܡܪ ܡܪܢ ܡܬܠܐ ܗܢܐ : ܒܪܢܫ ᵃܚܕ ܚܕ
17 ᵇܥܒܕ ܚܫܡܝܘ ᶜܘܫܕܪ ܠܥܒܕܗ ᶜ: ᵈᵉܘܫܕܪ ᶠܒܫܝܘܬܗ
ܒܫܥܬܗ ܕᵉܚܫܡܝܬܐ ᵍܠܡܐܡܪ ܠܡܙܡܢܐ ܐܬܘ
18 ܕܗܐ ܟܘܠܐ ʰܡܬܩܢ : ⁱܘܫܪܝܘ ܒܟܘܠܗܘܢ ܡܢ
ܚܕ ܕܠܐ ܥܣܩܝ : ܩܕܡܝܐ ܐܡܪ ܠܗ : ᵏܚܩܠ
ܙܒܢܬ ܘܐܝܬ ܠܝ ˡܢܦܩܘ ᵐܠܡܩܘܡ ⁿܚܬܗ :
ܐܒܥܐ ܒܟܐ ܡܢܟ ܗܘܝ ܫܒܩ ܠܝ ܕܠܝܬ ܐܢܐ
19 °ܡܛܠ ܕܐܬܝܐ : ᵖܐܘܚܪܢܐ ܐܡܪ ᵠܙܘܓܐ ܕܬܘܪܝܢ

Codex A.

ⁱܕܒܪܫܐ
ʲܦܪ̈ܝܫܝ ᵏܡܫܬܩܝܢ
ˡ*add* ܓܝܪ ᵐܕܗܘܐ
ⁿܫܒܩܘܬܗܘܢ
°ܗܘܐ ᵖܠܒܝܬܗܘܢ
ᵠܐܫܪܝܢ
ᵗܠܡܪ̈ܗܘܢ
ᵘ*omit* ܘ ˣܫܐܠ
ʸܡܬܦܬܚܝܢ
ᵃܕܐܬܐ ᵇܡܪ̈ܗܘܢ
ᶜܡܫܒܚܝܢ ᵉܐܫܟܚ
ᶠܘܢܦܘܠ ᵏܡܦܘܪܬܐ
ˡܬܫܝܢܝܬܐ
ᵐܘܡܬܠܬܠܬܐ
ⁿ*add* ܘ °ܗܕܒܝܢ
ᵖ*add* ܗܘܐ

‡ f. 67*a*.

ʳܒܗܕܐ ˢܓܢܒܐ
ᵗܗܘܐ

ᵃܢܘܡܪܐ ܐܠܝܗ ܕܝܫ
ᵃܒܒܪܐ ܡܢ ܠܗܘܡܐ
ᵇܡܥܡܝܬܐ ܙܒܝܬܐ ᵇ
ᶜ*omit* ܠܥܒܕܗ ܘܡܪܐ
ᵈܘܫܕܪ ᶠܒܫܝܘܬܗ
ʰܡܬܩܢ ⁱܘܫܪܝܘ
ˡܢܦܩܘ ᵐܕܝܩܘܡ
ⁿ*add* ܒܥܒܕ °ܢܚܬ
ᵖܘܫܪܝܐ
ᵠܙܘܓܢܝܐ

قبل الميلاد في حدين

Codex C.

ˡ*add* ܓܝܪ
°ܗܘܐ ᵖܠܒܝܬܗܘܢ
ʳܘܡܢܣܝܒܗܘܢ
ˢܐܢܫ ᵘ*omit* ܘ
ᵛܡܫܒܬܐ ʷܐܬܐ
ˣܫܐܠ ʸܡܬܦܬܚܝܢ
ᶻܒܒܝܬܐ ᵃܕܐܬܐ
ᶜܡܫܒܚ ᵈ*add* ܐܡܪܝܢ
ᵉܐܫܟܚ
ᵍ*omit* . . . ܘܢܦܠ
. . . ܡܬܗܘܢ
ʰܐܢ ⁱܐܬܐ

† f. 60*b*.

ᵏܡܦܘܪܬܐ
ˡܬܫܝܢܝܬܐ ⁿ*add* ܘ
ᵖ*add* ܗܘܐ

ᵃܠܗܘܡ ܐܠܝܗ ܕ
ܐܠܝܗܝ ܒܒܪ ܡܢ
ᵃܠܗܘܡܐ
ᶻ*add* ܘܒܬܪܗ ܕܐܝܟܢܐ
ᵇܚܫܡܝܬܐ ᵃ*omit* ܚܕ
ᶜ*omit* ܠܥܒܕܗ ܘܡܪܐ
ᵉ*omit* . . . ܘܫܕܪ
. . . ܒܫܥܬܗ ܕ
ᵍܕܐܡܪ ʰܡܬܩܢ
ᵏܚܩܠ ᵐܕܝܩܘܡ
ⁿ*add* ܒܥܒܕ
ᵖܘܫܪܝܐ

Codex A. | *Codex B.* | *Codex C.*

Codex B.

ܕܬܦܩܝܢ ܠܒܪ : ܘܐܡܪ ^r ܝܫܘܥ ܕܡܛܠ ܙܥܘܪܘܬ ܗܝܡܢܘܬܟܘܢ :
ܐܡܢ ܒܟܐ ܡܫܝܚ ܗܘܘ ^s ܫܢܝܒ ܠܝ ܕܠܝܬ ܐܡܢ
20 ^o ܐܟܘܬ ^t ܕܐܡܪܬ : ^u ܘܐܘܪܚܐ ܐܡܪ ܐܬܬܐ
ܢܦܩܬ ^v ܘܠܓܠܝܠ ܒܪܡ ^w ܠܝܬ ܐܡܢ ^w ^o ܐܟܘܬ
21 ܕܐܡܪܬ : ^x ܘܐܡܪܬ ܠܗ ^y ܒܒܪܢܐ ^z ܘܬܒܥ ܗܘܠܝܢ
ܠܡܪܗ ܕܒܝܬܐ ^a : ܘܐܡܪ ^b ܠܒܢܝܗ ^c ܦܘܩܘ
ܐܘܦ ^d ܒܐܘܦܪܝܢ ^e ܠܥܘܒܕܢܐ ܘܠܐܒܘܢܝܐ
^f ܕܡܕܝܢܬܐ : ^g ܘܐܟܠܘ ܠܒܐ ܠܡܣܟܢܐ ܘܠܚܓܝܪܐ
22 ܘܠܣܡܝܐ : ܘܐܡܪ ܒܒܪܐ ܠܡܪܗ ^{h†} : ^i ܒܒܪܬ
ܟܘܠ ܡܐ ܕܦܩܕܬ ^i ܘܒܒ ^‡ ܒܪܘ ܐܝܬ ܐܬܪ :
23 ܘܐܡܪ ܡܪܗ ܕܒܒܪܐ ܠܗ ܦܘܩ ܠܐܘܪܚܬܐ :
^j ܘܠܣܝܓܐ : ^k ܘܐܠܘܨ ܢܬܘܢ ܕܒܥܠܘܢ ^l ܕܢܬܡܠܐ
24 ܒܝܬܝ ^m ܐܡܪ ܐܢܐ ^m ܠܟܘܢ ܕܝ ^n ܚܕ ܡܢ
ܗܢܘܢ ܓܒܪܐ ^o ܕܐܬܩܪܘ ܠܐ ^p ܢܛܥܡܘܢ
^q ܡܢܚܡܫܝܐ ^r ^s ܥܠܡ ܀

Codex A.

^r ܝܫܘܥ ^o ܐܟܘܬ
^u ܘܐܘܪܚܐ ^v ܘܠܓܠܝܠ
^w ܠܝܬ ܐܡܢ ^x ܘܐܡܪܬ
^y ܒܒܪܢܐ ^z ܘܬܒܥ
^a *add* ܡܢܗܘܢ ܐܝܟ ܡܪܗ ܕܒܝܬܐ
^b ܠܒܢܝܗ ^c ܦܘܩܘ
^d ܒܦܪܘܒ ^e ܠܥܘܒܕܢܐ
^f ܕܡܕܝܢܬܐ ^g ܘܐܟܠܘ.
^h *add* ܡܢ ܗܘܘ ܐܝܬ ܕܐܡܪܬ.
^i *omit* ܒܒܪܬ . . . ܕܦܩܕܬ . . .
‡ f. 67*b*.
^j ܘܠܣܝܓܐ
^k ܘܐܠܘܨܘܗܝ ^l ܕܢܬܡܠܐ
^m ܐܡܪܢܐ ^n ܕܚܕ
^o ܕܐܬܩܪܝܘ
^p ܢܛܥܡܘܢ
^q ܡܢܚܡܫܝܐ
^r *add* ܩܠܝܠܝܢ ܐܢܘܢ ܩܪܝܐ ܘܒܚܝܪܝܢ ܙܥܘܪܐ :
(manus satis vetusta in intercolumnio addidit).
^s *omit* ܥܠܡ

Codex C.

^s ܫܢܝܒ ^o ܐܟܘܬ
^t ܕܐܡܪܬ ^u ܘܐܘܪܚܐ
^x ܘܐܡܪܬ ^y ܒܒܪܢܐ
^z ܘܬܒܥ
^d ܒܦܪܘܒ
^g ܘܐܟܠ
† f. 61*a*.
^j ܘܠܣܝܓܐ
^l ܕܢܬܡܠܐ
^n ܕܚܕ
^q ܡܢܚܡܫܝܐ
^s *omit* ܥܠܡ

CVII.

Luke XIII. 18—29.

Codex B.

^a ܘܩܪܝܐ ܐܘܢܓܠܝܘܢ ܐܬܐܡܪ ܒܬܪ ܐܢܓܠܝܘܢ ܡܢ
ܠܘܩܐ ^a : ^x ^{zy} ܘܗܘܐ ܡܪܢ ܝܫܘܥ ܐܡܪ ܠܗܘܢ :^y [f. 60*b*]
18 ܠܡܢ ܗܝ ܕܡܬܝܐ ^a ܡܠܟܘܬܗ ^b ܕܐܠܗܐ : ^c ܘܠܡܢ
19 ܗܝ ^c ܕܡܝܐ ܠܗ : ܕܡܬܝܐ ܗܝ ܠܦܪܕܐ ܕܚܪܕܠ
^d ܢܣܒ ܓܒܪܐ ܙܪܥܗ ܠܗ ܒܓܢܬܗ ^e ܘܪܒܬ
ܘܐܬܚܒܪܬ ^f ܐܝܠܢ : ܘܦܪܚܬܐ ܕܫܡܝܐ ^g ܐܫܟܠܠܬ
20 ^h ܒܣܘܟܝܗ ܘܬܘܒ ^i ܗܘ ܐܡܪ : ܠܡܢ ^j ܕܡܝܐ
21 ^k ܡܠܟܘܬܗ ܕܐܠܗܐ : ܕܡܝܐ ܗܝ ^l ܠܚܡܝܪ ^m ܕܡܢ
ܕܢܣܒܬ ^n ܐܢܬܬܐ ܘܛܡܪܬܗ ܠܗ ^o ܒܬܠܬ ^p ܐܣܐܝܢ
22 ^q ܕܩܡܚ : ܒܕܡܝܐ ^r ^s ܕܚܡܝܪ ܟܘܠܗ ܘܗܘܐ

Codex A.

^a ܘܩܪܝܐ ܡܢ ܠܘܩܐ
^a ܐܘܢܓܠܝܘܢ ܕܡܢ ܠܘܩܐ
^y *omit* ܘܗܘܐ . . . ܠܗܘܢ . . .
^z *add* ܐܡܪ ܡܪܢ ܗܘܐ ܠܬܠܡܝܕܘܗܝ :
^c ܘܠܡܢ ܕܡܝܐ ^c
^e ܘܐܬܥܒܪܬ ^f ܐܝܠܢ
^g ܐܫܟܠܠܬ ^h ܒܣܘܟܝܗ
^i ܗܘܐ ^l ܠܚܡܝܪ
^m ܕ ^p ܣܐܝܢ
^r *add* ܕܗܘܐ.

Codex C.

^a ܠܘܩܐ ܐܘܢܓܠܝܘܢ
ܐܘܢܓܠܝܘܢ ܕܡܢ ^a ܠܘܩܐ
^x *add* ܘܬܘܒ
^a ܡܠܟܘܬܐ
^b ܕܐܠܗܐ
^c ^c ܘܠܡܢ ܕܡܝܐ
^d *add* ܕ ^g ܐܫܟܠܠܬ
^h ܒܣܘܟܬܐ
^i ܗܘܐ ^j ܕܡܝܐ
^k ܡܠܟܘܬܗ
^l ܠܚܡܝܪ
^n *add* ܗܝ ^o ܒܬܠܬ
^p ܣܐܝܢ ^q ܕܩܡܚܐ
^s ܕܚܡܝܪ

(ܥܕܐ ܕܝ ܦـ ܣبت قبل الميلاد)

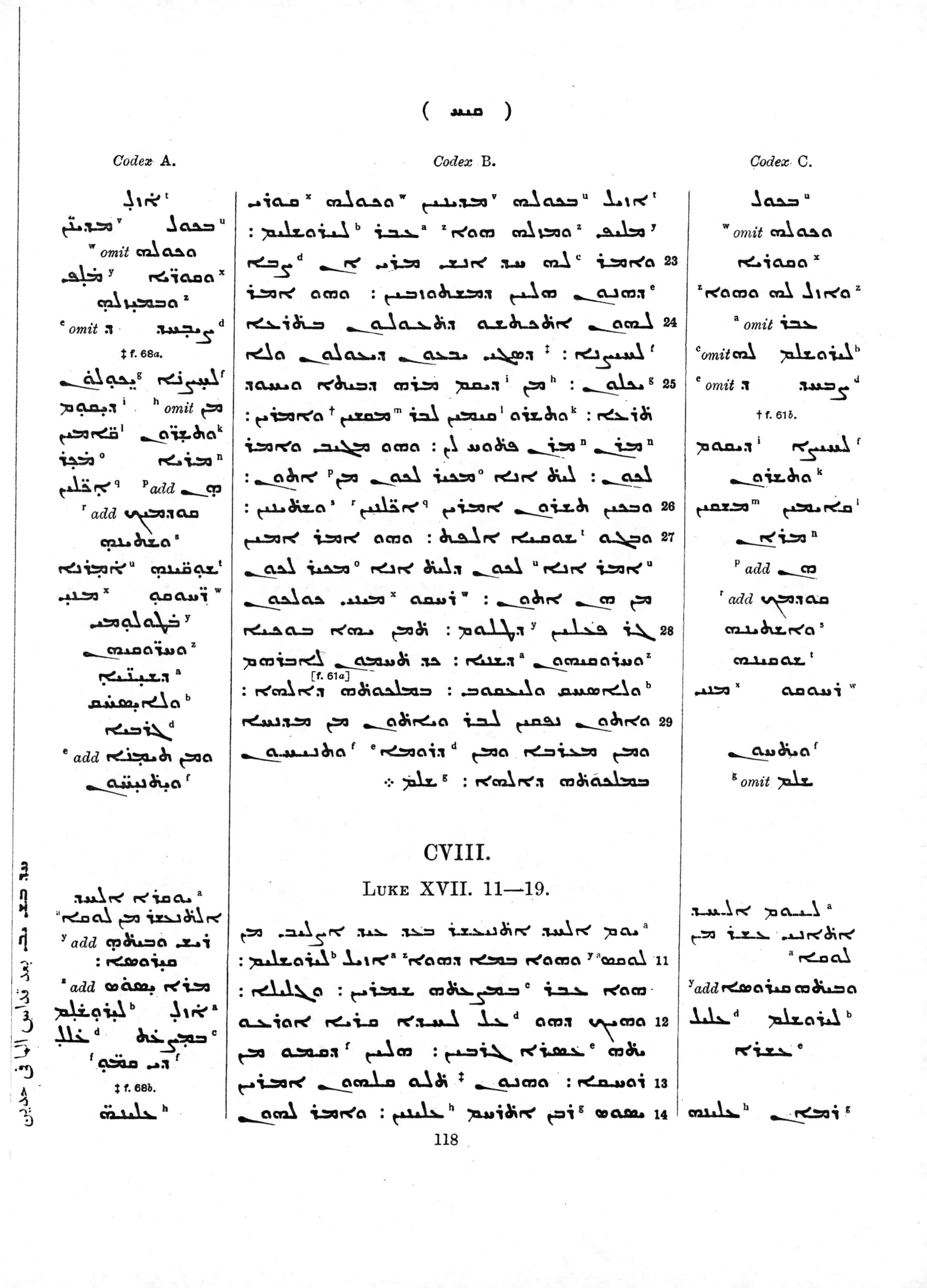

Codex A.	Codex B.	Codex C.
[t] [u] [v] [w] omit [x] [y] [z] [d] [e] omit ܕ	[t] [u] [v] [w] [x] [illegible]	[u] [w] omit [x] [z]
‡ f. 68a.	[y] [z] [a] [b] [illegible] :	[a] omit
[f] [g] [h] omit [i] [k] [l] [n] [o] [p] add [q] [r] add [s] [t] [u] [w] [x] [y] [z] [a] [b] [d] [e] add [f]	23 [c] [d] [illegible]	[b] [c] omit [d] [e] omit ܕ
	[e] [illegible]	† f. 61b.
	24 [illegible]	[f] [i] [k] [l] [m] [n] [p] add [r] add [s] [t] [w] [x] [f] [g] omit
	[f] ‡ [illegible]	
	25 [g] [h] [i] [illegible]	
	[k] [l] [m] † [illegible] :	
	[n] [n] [illegible]	
	[o] [p] [illegible] :	
	26 [q] [r] [s] [illegible] :	
	27 [t] [illegible]	
	[u] [u] [o] [illegible]	
	[w] [x] [illegible]	
	28 [y] [illegible]	
	[z] [a] [illegible]	
	[f. 61a] [b] [illegible] :	
	29 [illegible]	
	[d] [e] [f] [illegible]	
	[g] [illegible] :·	

CVIII.

Luke XVII. 11—19.

Codex A.	Codex B.	Codex C.
[a] [a] [y] add [z] add [a] [b] [c] [d] [f] [f]	[a] [illegible]	[a] [a] [y] add [b] [d] [e] [g] [h]
‡ f. 68b.	11 [y] [a] [z] [a] [b] [illegible] :	
[h]	[c] [illegible] :	
	12 [d] [illegible]	
	[e] [f] [illegible]	
	13 ‡ [illegible]	
	14 [g] [h] [illegible]	

Codex B.

ܡܢܗ ܝܘܡܝܢ : ܐܬܘ ܐܬܐܣܘ ܒܗܘܢ
ܠܫܒܬܐ : ܘܗܘܐ ܗܟܢ ܕܗܘܢ ܐܬܝܢ
15 ܐܬܒܪܘ[i] : ܘܥܢܐ ܡܪܢ ܕܝ ܒܪ ܫܡܥܐ
ܕܐܬܚܢܝ [j]ܬܐܒ ܒܡܠܐ ܕܒܐ ܡܫܒܚ ܠܐܠܗܐ :
16 ܘܢܦܠ ܥܠ [k]ܐܦܝܗ ܩܕܡ [†] [l]ܪܓܠܝ ܡܪܢܐ
17 ܠܗ : ܘܗܘ ܗܘܐ [m]ܫܡܪܝ : ܐܡܪ ܕܝ ܡܪܢܐ
ܠܗܘܢ ܐܡܪ ܠܐ ܥܣܪܐ ܐܬܕܟܝܘ : [n]ܬܫܥܝܢܐ
18 ܕܝ ܗܢ ܗܘܢ [o]ܠܐ [p]ܐܫܬܟܚܘ [q]ܕܝܬܘܢ
ܬܘܕܝܬ [r]ܕܝ [s]ܬܫܒܘܚܬܐ ܠܐܠܗܐ : [t]ܐܠܐ
19 ܕܗܢ ܫܡܘܪܐ ܢܘܟܪܝ ܗܘ : ܘܗܘ ܐܡܪ ܠܗ
ܩܘܡ [u]ܐܙܠ ܗܝܡܢܘܬܟ ܐܚܝܬ ܝܬܟ : [w]ܫܠܡ ܀

Codex A. (notes)

[j] ܬܐܒ [k] ܐܦܝܗ
[l] ܪܓܠܝܗ [m] ܫܡܪܝܢ
[n] ܬܫܥܝܢܐ [o] ܕܠܐ
[p] ܐܫܬܟܚܬܘܢ
[q] ܕܝܬܘܢ
[r] *omit* ܕܝ
[s] ܬܫܒܘܚܬܐ
[t] *add* ܕ [u] ܐܙܠ

Codex C. (notes)

[i] ܐܬܕܟܘ
[j] ܬܐܒ [k] ܐܦܝܗ
† f. 62*a*.
[m] ܫܡܪܝܢ
[n] ܬܫܥܝܢܐ
[o] ܕܠܐ
[r] *omit* ܕܝ [t] *add* ܕܝ
[w] *omit* ܫܠܡ

CIX.

Luke XIV. 1—11.

Codex B.

[a]ܘܦܪܐ ܥܪܘܒ ܬܠܬܫܒܬ ܒܒܬܪ ܚܒܪ ܐܠܝܒ
1 ܡܢ ܠܘܩܐ[a] : [z] ܘܗܘܐ ܒܥܠܐ ܕܐܬܐ ܡܪܢܐ
ܝܫܘܥ : ܠܒܝܬܗ ܕܚܕ [a]ܐܪܟܘܢܗܘܢ [b]ܕܦܪܝܫܝ
2 ܕܢܐܟܘܠ [c]ܠܚܡܐ [d]ܒܝܘܡ [e]ܫܒܬܐ : ܘܗܢܘܢ
ܗܘܘ ܡܛܪܝܢ ܠܗ : [f]ܘܗܐ ܚܕ ܒܪܢܫ ܗܕܝܡ
3 ܕܗܘܐ [g]ܗܕܪܘܩܝܢܘܣ : [h]ܘܥܢܐ : [i]ܘܐܡܪ
ܡܪܢܐ ܝܫܘܥ ܘܐܡܪ [j]ܠܡܠܦܢܐ ܢܡܘܣܝܐ [k]ܘܦܪܝܫܝ :
[f. 61*a*]
4 ܫܠܝܛ [‡] [l]ܕܢܐܣܐ ܒܫܒܬܐ ܐܘ ܠܐ : ܘܗܢܘܢ
ܗܘܘ [m]ܫܬܝܩܝܢ : ܘܐܚܕܗ ܘܐܣܝܗ ܘܫܪܝܗ
5 ܘܥܢܐ : ܘܐܡܪ ܘܐܡܪ ܠܗܘܢ ܡܢ [n]ܗܘ
ܡܢܟܘܢ ܕܚܡܪܗ ܐܘ [o]ܬܘܪܗ ܢܦܠ ܠܒܝܪܐ :
ܘܠܐ ܡܚܕܐ ܢܓܕ [p]ܘܡܣܩ ܠܗ ܒܝܘܡܐ
6 ܕܫܒܬܐ : ܘܠܐ [q]ܡܨܘ ܕܢܦܢܘܢ ܦܬܓܡ
7 [j]ܠܡܠܦܢܐ : [r]ܘܗܘ ܐܡܪ ܡܬܠܐ [j]ܠܡܠܦܢܐ
ܗܠܝܢ ܕܩܪܝܢ : ܚܙܐ ܗܝܟ ܗܘܘ [s]ܓܒܝܢ
8 [t]ܪܫܝ [u]ܡܫܟܒܝܬܐ ܘܐܡܪ ܠܗܘܢ : ܟܕ [v]ܕܝ

Codex A. (notes)

[a] ܥܪܘܒ ܬܠܬܫܒܬ ܐܠܝܒ
ܡܢ ܠܘܩܐ[a]
[‡] *add* ܡܬܡܠ ܡܢ ܬܫܥܝܬܗ ܕܠܘܩܐ :
[a] *add* ܡܢ
[b] ܕܦܪܝܫܝ
[c] ܠܡܐܟܠ [d] *omit* ܒܝܘܡ
[e] ܫܒܬܐ [f] ܘܗܐ
[g] ܗܕܪܘܩܝܢܘܣ
[j] ܠܡܠܦܐ [k] ܘܦܪܝܫܝ
‡ f. 69*a*.
[l] ܕܢܐܣܐ
[n] *omit* ܗܘ
[p] ܘܡܣܩ
[q] ܡܨܘ [r] ܘܗܘܐ
[s] ܓܒܝܢ
[u] ܡܫܟܒܝܬܐ
[v] *omit* ܕܝ

Codex C. (notes)

[a] ܠܘܩܐ ܐܘܢܓܠܝܘܢ
ܬܠܬܫܒܬ ܡܢ
ܠܘܩܐ[a]
[z] *add* ܘܐܬܐ
[a] *add* ܡܢ
[c] ܠܡܐܟܠ [d] *omit* ܒܝܘܡ
[e] ܫܒܬܐ
[g] ܗܕܪܘܩܝܢܘܣ
[h] ܘܥܢܐ [i] ܘܐܡܪ
[l] ܕܢܐܣܐ [m] ܫܬܝܩܝܢ
[n] *omit* ܗܘ
[o] ܬܘܪܗ
[p] ܘܡܣܩ
[r] ܘܗܘܐ
[t] ܪܫܝ [v] *omit* ܕܝ

Codex A.	*Codex* B.	*Codex* C.
ʷܐܢܫ ʸܡܬܩܘܡܝܢܐ	ܬܬܦܪܐ ܡܢ ʷܐܢܫ ˣܠܡܫܡܥܘܢ ܠܐ ܬܪܗܛܘܢ	ˣܠܡܫܡܥܘܢ
ᶻܗܘܐ ᵃܡܫܡܥܘܢ	ܒܬܪܝܗ ʸܡܬܩܘܡܝܢܐ : ܕܠܐ ܐܡܬܝ ᶻܡܛܬܐ	ʸܡܬܩܘܡܝܢܐ ᶻܗܘܐ
ᵇܘܐܬܬܐ ᵉܗܘܝܢ	9 ܐܢܫ ᵃܡܫܡܥܘܢ ܡܥܢ ܩܪܒܐ ܡܢܗ : ᵇܘܐܬܬܐ † ܕܝܢ	† f. 62*b*.
ᶠܠܗܕܝܢ ᵍܘܒܟܝܢ	ᶜܕܩܪܝܐ ܠܟܘܢ ܘܠܗܘܢ : ᵈܘܐܡܪܘܢ ܠܟܘܢ ᵉܗܘܝܢ	ᵇܘܐܬܐ ᶜܕܩܪܝܢ
ʰܒܒܗܬܬܐ	ܐܬܪܐ ᶠܠܗܕܝܢ : ᵍܘܒܟܝܢ ܬܥܪܬܐ ʰܒܒܗܬܬܐ	ᵈܘܐܡܪ ᵉܗܘܝܢ
	10 ⁱܐܟܕ ܐܬܪܐ ܐܚܪܢܐ : ܐܠܐ ܒܕ ܬܦܪܬܐ	ⁱܐܟܕ
ˡܐܡܪ	ˡܐܡܪ ܪܒܘܢ ܠܟܘܢ ܕܐܬܪܐ ܐܚܪܢܐ ܕܒܕ	
ᵐܕܝܢ	ܒܐܬܪܐ ᵐܕܝܢ ܕܩܪܐ ܢܬܟܘܢ ܐܡܪ ܗܘ ܠܟܘܢ	ⁿܪܚܡܘܢ
ⁿܪܚܡܘܢ ᵒܠܟܠ	ⁿܪܚܡܘܢ ܗܘܘ ܠܟܐ ᵒܠܟܠ : ᵍܘܒܟܝܢ ܗܘܝܐ	ᵖܬܫܒܚܬܐ
ᵠ*add* ܘܠܗܘܢ	ܠܟܘܢ ᵖܬܫܒܚܬܐ ܘܡܕܡ ܟܘܠ ᵠ ʳܕܒܝܢ ܒܟܘܢ :	ᵠ *add* ܘܠܗܘܢ
ʳܕܒܝܢ ˢܕܟܘܠ	11 ˢܟܘܠ ܡܢ ܕܡܬܘܡܡ ܚܘܒܝܗ ܬܬܡܚܡܝܢ : ܘܡܢ	ˢܕܟܘܠ ᵗܕܡܡܚܡܝܢ
‡ f. 69*b*.	ᵗܕܡܡܚܡܝܢ ܚܘܒܝܗ ܬܬܪܘܡܡ : ᵘܥܠܡ ‡ ⁘	ᵘ *omit* ܥܠܡ

CX.

Luke XVIII. 18—27.

Codex A.	*Codex* B.	*Codex* C.
ᶜܬܠܬܝܕܥܪ ܡܢ ܠܗܘܢ ᶜ	ᵃܘܩܪܐ ܐܢܫ ᵇܬܠܬܝܕܥܪ ᶜܟܕ ܚܕ ܐܪܟܘܢ	ᵃܠܗܘܢ ᶜܡܢ ܠܗܘܢ ᶜ
ᵃܚܕ ᵇܕܫܐܠܗ	18 ܡܢ ܠܗܘܢ ᵇᶜ : ܘܫܐܠܗ ܡܬܪܢܐ ᶻܘܫܐܠ ܠܗ	ᶻܘܫܐܠ
ᶜܕܠܗܠܝܢ ᵉܠܒܐ	ᵃܚܕ ܐܪܟܘܢ ܘܐܡܪ ܡܠܦܢܐ ܛܒܐ ܡܐ	ᵃܚܕ ᵇܕܫܐܠܗ
ᵍܚܕ ⁱ*add* ܕܝܢ	19 ܡܢܕܝ ᵇܕܫܐܠܗ ᶜܕܠܗܠܝܢ ܝܪܬ : ᵈܘܐܡܪ ܠܗ	ᵈ *omit* ܘ
ʲܬܦܠܚܘܪ ˡܠܐ	ܡܪܐ ܝܫܘܥ ܡܐ ܐܢܬ ܐܡܪ ܠܝ ᵉܛܒܐ :	ᵉܛܒܐ
ᵐܕܝܠܝܢ ⁿܠܐܒܘܟ	20 ܠܝܬ ᶠܛܒ ܐܠܐ ᵍܚܕ ܐܠܗܐ ʰ: ܦܘܩܕܢܐ ⁱ	ᶠܛܒ ܚܕ ᵍ *omit* ʰ *add* ܒܠܚܘܕܝ
ᵒܘܠܐܡܟ	ܐܢܬ ܝܕܥ : ܠܐ ʲܬܦܠܚܘܪ ᵈܘܠܐ ܬܓܢܘܒ : ˡܘܠܐ	ⁱ *add* ܕܝܢ
ᵖ *add* ܘܠܩܪܝܒܝܟ	ܬܓܘܢܒ ˡܘܠܐ ܬܣܗܕ ᵐܕܝܠܝܢ : ܐܘܩܪ	ⁿܠܐܒܘܟ
ܐܝܟ ܢܦܫܟ : (in intercolumnio manus non recens).	21 ⁿܠܐܒܘܟ ᵒܘܠܐܡܟ ᵖ: ܗܘ ܕܝ ܐܡܪ ܠܗ ܗܠܝܢ	ᵠܘܗܠܝܢ
ʳܢܦܫܝܐ ˢܘܐܡ	22 ᵠܟܘܠܗܝܢ ܢܛܪܬ ܡܢ ܛܠܝܘܬܝ : ܘܟܕ ܫܡܥ	ᵗ*omit* ܗܕܐ ʳܢܦܫܝܐ
ᵗ*omit* ܗܕܐ ᵘܘܦܠܓ	ܡܪܢ ܝܫܘܥ ܐܡܪ ܠܗ : ܚܕܐ ܚܣܝܪܐ ʳܢܦܫܝ	ᵘܘܦܠܓ ᵛܘܗܘܐ
ˣ *omit* ܒܕ ᵛܘܗܘܐ	ܠܟ : ܟܘܠ ܡܐ ܕܠܟ ˢܙܒܢ ᵗܗܕܐ ᵘܘܦܠܓܗ	† f. 63*a*.
ᶻܗܘܐ ʸܚܪܝܡ	ܠܡܣܟܝܢܐ : ᵛܘܗܘܐ ܠܟ † ܣܝܡܐ ܒܫܡܝܐ	ʷܒܐܬܪܝ ʸܚܪܝܡ
ᵃ*omit* ܕܝܢ	23 ܘܢܩܦܐ ܒܬܪܝ : ܘܐܬܐ ܠܟ ʷܒܬܪܝ : ܘܗܘܐ ˣܒܕ	ᵃ *omit* ܕܝܢ ᶻܗܘܐ
	ܫܡܥ ܗܠܝܢ ܗܘܐ ʸܚܫܝܫ ᶻܗܘ ᵃܕܝܢ ܥܬܝܪ	

In the left margin beside Codex A: ܣܒ ܕܡ ܒܝ ✗

Codex A.

ᵇܢܩܦܝܢ ᶜܠܬܠܡܝܕܘܬܗ
ᵈ*add* ܗܘ ܓܒܪ 25 ܢܟܠ
ܠܡܛܠܐ ܕܝܟܘܠ
ܒܢܘܡܘܣ ܕܡܫܝܚܐ:
ܐܠܐ ܓܒܪ ܚܕ
ܕܝܟܘܠ ܠܬܠܡܝܕܘܬܗ
ܕܐܠܗܐ:
ᵉܢܟܠ ‡ f. 70*a*.
ᶠܝܟܠܝܢ ᵍܗܢܘܢ

ᵃܒܙܒܢܐ ܗܘܝܘ ܗܟܢ
ܐܡܪ ܡܪܢ (*sic*) ܝܫܘܥ
ᵃܠܗܘܢ
ʸܡܗܝܡܢ
ᶻ*add* ܐܦ
ᶜܕܡܗܝܡܢ
ᵈ*omit* ܗܘ
ᵉܦܠܝܓ ᵍܒܡܡܘܢܐ
ʰ*omit* ܐܢܬܘܢ
ⁱܕܩܘܫܛܐ
ʲܕܝ ᵏܡܗܝܡܢ
ᵇܢܟܠ ᵐܠܡܪܐ
ⁿܘܠܡܡܘܢܐ
ˢܡܡܘܢܐ ᵗܢܟܠܝܢ
ᵘܘܠܡܡܘܢܐ
ˣܦܪܝܫܝܢ

ᵃܕܡܢ

ᵇ*omit* ܗܘܝܘ
ᶜ*omit* ܢܦܩ
‡ f. 70*b*.
ᶻ*add* ܘܒܪܬܗ
ܡܦܪܢܣܐ:

Codex B.

24 ܒܬܪ ܠܚܕܐ: ܘܣܓܝܐܐ ܡܬܗ ܕܢܐ ܡܫܘܢ
ܘܐܡܪ ܥܡܐ ܠܗܠܝܢ ܕܠܗܘܢ ᵇܢܩܦܝܢ ܕܝܚܒܘܢ
26 ᶜܠܬܠܡܝܕܘܬܗ ܕܐܠܗܐ: ᵈܘܐܡܪܘ ܗܠܝܢ ܕܫܡܥܘ
27 ܘܡܢ ᵉܡܚܝܠ ܕܝܚܝܐ: ‡ܗܘ ܕܝ ܐܡܪ ܗܠܝܢ ܕܝ
ܠܐ ᶠܝܟܠܝܢ ܠܡܬܐ ܒܡܠܟܘܬܐ: ܠܡܬܐ ܐܠܗܐ ᵍܗܢܘܢ
ʰܝܟܠܝܢ ⁘

CXI.

Luke XVI. 10—15.

ᵃܒܙܒܢܐ ܗܘܝܘ ܗܟܢ ܐܡܪ ܡܪܢ ܝܫܘܥ ܠܬܠܡܝܕܘܗܝ
10 ܡܢ ᵃˣܠܗܘܢ ܐܡܪ ܡܪܢ ܗܕܝܢ ܕܡܗܝܡܢ
ʸܡܗܝܡܢ ᶻ ᵃܒܩܠܝܠ ܗܘ ᵇܡܗܝܡܢ : ܘܕܝܢ
ᶜܕܡܗܝܡܢ ᵈܗܘ ᵉܦܠܝܓ ܐܦ ܒܩܠܝܠ ܗܘ
11 ܦܠܝܓ : ᶠܐܢ ܐܘܢ ᵍܒܡܡܘܢܐ ܕܦܠܝܓܘܬܐ
ܠܐ ʰܐܢܬܘܢ ܐܬܒܚܪܬܘܢ ܡܗܝܡܢܝܢ ⁱܒܩܘܫܛܐ
12 ʲܕܝ ܡܢ ᵏܡܗܝܡܢ ܠܟܘܢ : ˡܘܐܢ ܒܢܘܟܪܝܐ
ܡܗܝܡܢܝܢ ܠܐ ܐܬܒܚܪܬܘܢ : *ܕܝܠܟܘܢ ܕܝ
13 ܡܢ ᵃܝܬܠ ܠܟܘܢ : ܠܝܬ ܥܒܕ ܚܕ ᵇܡܨܐ ܕܢܦܠܚ
ܠܬܪܝܢ ܡܪܝܢ : ܐܠܐ ᵐܠܚܕ ܢܣܢܐ ⁿܘܠܚܕܐ
ᵒܢܚܒ : ܐܠܐ ᵖܡܢ ᵠܚܕ ʳܢܩܒܠ ܘܟܠ ˢܐܘܚܪܢܐ
[f. 62*b*]
ܢܣܒܪ : ܠܝܬ ܐܢܬܘܢ ᵗܝܟܠܝܢ ܕܬܦܠܚܘܢ
14 ܠܐܠܗܐ ᵘܘܠܡܡܘܢܐ : ʷܘܗܘܘ ܫܡܥܝܢ ˣܦܪܝܫܝܢ
ܕܗܘܘ ܪܚܡܝܢ ʸܟܣܦܐ ܘܗܘܘ ܡܡܝܩܝܢ ܒܗ
15 ܘܐܡܪ ܠܗܘܢ : ܐܢܬܘܢ ܗܘܝܢ ܕܡܙܕܩܝܢ
†ܓܪܡܟܘܢ ܩܕܡ ܒܢܝܢܫܐ : ܘܐܠܗܐ ᶻܝܕܥ
ܠܒܒܟܘܢ ܕܡܐ ᵃܕܪܡ ᵇ ᶜܒܒܢܝܢܫܐ ܛܢܦ ܗܘ
ܩܕܡ ܐܠܗܐ ⁘

CXII.

Luke XVIII. 35—43.

ᵃܒܙܒܢܐ ᵇܗܘܝܘ ܐܬܐ ܝܫܘܥ ‡ܠܐܪܝܚܘ ܡܢ ܠܗܘܢ :
35 ᶜܢܦܩ ᵃ: ᶻܘܗܘܐ ܟܕ ܩܪܒ ܡܢܐ ܚܕ ܝܬܒ ܗܘܐ ܠܝܪܝܚܘ :

Codex C.

ᶜܠܬܠܡܝܕܘܬܗ
ᵈ*add* ܗܘ ܓܒܪ 25 ܡܢ
ܠܡܛܠܐ ܕܝܟܘܠ
ܒܢܘܡܘܣ ܕܡܫܝܚܐ
ܐܠܐ ܓܒܪ ܚܕ
ܕܝܟܘܠ ܠܬܠܡܝܕܘܬܗ
ܕܐܠܗܐ:
ʰ*omit* ܝܟܠܝܢ ᵉ*omit* ܢܟܠ

ᵃܠܗܘܢ ܐܡܪ ܡܪܢ
ܝܫܘܥ ܡܢ ܐܡܪ
ᵃܠܗܘܢ
ˣ*add* ܠܬܠܡܝܕܘܗܝ ܘܐܡܪ
ᶻ*add* ܐܦ ᵃܒܩܠܝܠ
ᵇܡܗܝܡܢ ᵉܦܠܝܓ
ᶠ*omit* ܐܢ
ᵍܒܡܡܘܢܐ
ʰ*omit* ܐܢܬܘܢ
ⁱܕܩܘܫܛܐ ʲܕܝ
ᵏܡܗܝܡܢ ˡܘܐܢ
ᵃܝܬܠ ᵐܠܡܪܐ
ⁿܘܠܡܡܘܢܐ
ᵒܢܚܒ ᵖ*omit* ܡܢ
ᵠܠܚܕ ʳܢܩܒܠ
ᵗܝܟܠܝܢ ᵘܘܠܡܡܘܢܐ
ʷ*omit* ܘ ʸܟܣܦܐ
† f. 63*b*.
ᶻܝܕܥ
ᵇ*add* ܡܢ ᶜܒܢܝܢܫܐ

[* Cod. B ܕܝܠܟܘܢ]

ᵃܠܗܘܢ ܐܡܪ ܝܫܘܥ
ܐܡܪ ܡܪܢ ܐܬܐ
ᵃܠܗܘܢ
ᶻ*add* ܘܒܪܬܗ

Codex A.	Codex B.	Codex C.
[b] ܡܩܪܒܐ [d] ܥܠ	ܘܗܘܐ ܟܕ [b] ܡܩܪܒܐ ܗܘܐ [c] ܠܝܪܝܚܘ ܥܠ [d] ܚܕ	[c] ܠܝܪܝܚܘ ܕܝܢ [e] add
[e] add ܕܝܢ	36 ܐܘܪܚܐ ܡܚܙܪ : ܟܕ [e] ܫܡܥ [f] ܐܘܟܠܘܣܐ ܥܒܪ	[f] ܐܘܟܠܘܣܐ
[f] ܐܘܟܠܘܣܐ [g] ܗܘ	37 [g] ܗܘܐ [h] ܫܐܠ ܡܢܐ ܗܘ [i] ܗܕܝܢ : ܬܢܝܘ ܠܗ	[h] ܫܐܠ
[i] ܗܕܐ [j] add ܕ	38 [j] ܕܝܫܘܥ [k] ܢܨܪܝܐ ܥܒܪ : [l] ܘܗܘ ܐܟܝܚ ܘܐܡܪ	[l] ܘܗܘܐ
[k] ܢܨܪܝܐ [m] ܕܕܘܝܕ	39 ܝܫܘܥ ܒܪܗ [m] ܕܕܘܝܕ ܐܬܪܚܡ [n] ܥܠܝ : ܘܗܠܝܢ	
[n] ܥܠܝ [o] ܡܩܕܡܗ	ܕܗܘܘ ܐܙܠܝܢ [o] ܡܩܕܡܗ ܗܘܘ ܡܟܐܝܢ ܒܗ	[o] ܡܩܕܡܗ
[p] omit ܘ [q] ܕܝܬܝܪ	ܕܝܫܬܘܩ : [p] ܘܗܘ [e] ܥܠ [q] ܕܝܬܝܪ ܗܘܐ ܡܙܥܩ ܒܪܗ	[p] omit ܘ
	40 [m] ܕܕܘܝܕ ܐܬܪܚܡ [n] ܥܠܝ : ܩܡ ܕܝܢ ܡܪܢ ܝܫܘܥ	
[r] ܩܪܒ	ܘܦܩܕ ܕܝܬܝܬܘܢ ܝܬܗ ܠܘܬܗ : ܟܕ ܕܝܢ [r] ܩܪܒ	
[s] ܫܐܠ	41 [s] ܫܐܠܗ ܫܐܠ ܝܬܗ ܘܐܡܪ : ܡܢܐ ܐܢܬ ܒܥܐ	
[t] omit ܠܗ	ܕܐܥܒܕ ܠܟ : ܘܗܘ ܐܡܪ [t] ܠܗ ܡܪܝ ܕܝܚܙܐ :	[t] omit ܠܗ
	42 ܘܡܪܐ ܝܫܘܥ ܐܡܪ ܠܗ ܚܙܝ : ܗܝܡܢܘܬܟ	
	43 ܐܚܝܬ ܝܬܟ : ܘܒܪܫܥܬܗ ܚܙܐ : ܘܗܘܐ ܡܫܒܚ	
[v] omit ܕܝܢ	ܠܐܠܗܐ : ܘܟܠ [u] ܥܡܐ [v] ܕܝܢ [w] ܕܚܙܐ ܝܗܒܘ	[u] ܥܡܐ [v] omit ܕܝܢ
[x] ܬܫܒܘܚܬܐ	[x] ܬܫܒܘܚܬܐ ܠܐܠܗܐ ⁘	[w] ܕܚܙܐ

CXIII.

Luke XVII. 3—10.

Codex A.	Codex B.	Codex C.
ܐܡܪ [b] ܡܪܢ	[a] ܐܡܪ [b] ܡܪܢ ܝܫܘܥ ܠܬܠܡܝܕܘܗܝ [c] ܟܕ ܐܬܝܢ ܗܘܐ	[a] ܐܡܪ ܡܪܢ ܝܫܘܥ ܠܬܠܡܝܕܘܗܝ ܕܝܠܗ [a]
[c] ܡܢ ܠܗܘܢ	3 ܠܗܘܢ [c a] : [z] ܐܢ ܚܛܐ ܐܚܘܟ [a] ܠܐܝܩܒܘܠܟ :	[z] add ܠܘܬܗ
[z] add ܕܝܢ	ܐܢ [b] ܫܒܩ ܐܚܘܟ [‡] ܐܟܣܗ ܒܗ : [c] ܘܐܢ	[a] ܠܐܝܩܒܘܠܟ
[a] ܠܐܝܩܒܘܠܟ	4 ܬܘܒ ܫܒܩ ܠܗ [d] ܐܦ [c] ܐܢ [d] ܫܒܥܐ ⁽[f. 63a]⁾	[b] ܫܒܩ [c] ܘܐܢ
[b] ܫܒܩ	ܙܒܢܝܢ ܒܝܘܡܐ [e] ܫܒܩ ܠܟ : [f] ܘܫܒܥܐ	[e] ܐܫܒܩ
‡ f. 71a.	ܙܒܢܝܢ ܠܘܬܟ [g] ܘܝܐܡܪ ܬܝܒ ܐܢܐ [h] ܫܒܘܩ	[f] ܘܫܒܥܬܐ
[d] ܐܦ ܐܢ [d]	5 ܠܗ [†] : [i] [k] ܘܐܡܪܘ ܕܝܢ ܫܠܝܚܐ ܠܡܪܢ ܐܘܣܦ	† f. 64a.
[f] ܘܫܒܥܬܐ	6 ܠܢ ܗܝܡܢܘ : ܘܐܡܪ ܠܗܘܢ ܡܪܐ ܝܫܘܥ [l] ܐܢ	[k] ܘܐܡܪ [l] ܐܝܢ
[g] ܘܐܡܪܝܢ [h] ܫܒܘܩ	[m] ܐܝܬ ܒܟܘܢ ܗܝܡܢܘ ܗܝܟ ܦܪܕܐ ܕܚܪܕܠ	[m] add ܒܟܘܢ
[i] add : ܫܒܘܩ ܠܗ ܐܢ	ܐܡܪܝܢ ܗܘܝܬܘܢ ܠܬܘܬܐ ܗܕܐ ܐܬܥܩܪ	
	ܘܐܬܢܨܒ ܒܝܡܐ ܘܗܘܐ ܫܡܥ [n] ܠܟܘܢ :	[n] ܠܟܘܢ
[o] ܕܝܢ	7 ܡܢ [o] ܕܝܢ ܡܢܟܘܢ ܕܠܗ ܥܒܕ ܕܕܒܪ ܐܘ ܪܥܐ :	[o] ܕܐܝܢ

Codex A.	Codex B.	Codex C.
[r] add ܠܗ	ܕܟܕ [q] ܚܠܠ ܡܢ ܠܒܪܐ ܕܟܐ ܐܡܪ ܗܘ [r]	[q] ܚܠܠ ܠܗ [r] add
[s] ܒܒܪܐ	8 [s] ܒܒܪܐ ܕܒܕ ܠܟ: ܐܠܐ ܠܢܬ ܗܘ ܐܡܪ	[s] ܒܒܪܐ
[t] ܚܠܘܢ [u] ܒܢܘܟܐ	ܠܗ [t] ܚܠܘܢ [u] ܒܢܘܟܐ [w] ܕܝܠܟܘܢ: [x] ܘܐܡܪ	[t] ܚܠܘܢ [u] ܒܢܘܟܐ
[w] ܕܝܠܟܘܢ [x] ܘܐܡܪܘܢ	[y] ܢܝܫܐ ܘܡܚܕܐ ܢܠܝܢ: ܒܒܕܟܐ [z] ܕܢܩܒܠ	[w] ܕܝܠܟܘܢ [x] ܘܐܡܪܘܢ
[z] ܕܢܩܒܠ	9 ܘܠܬܒܐ: [a] ܘܡܠܐܒܝܢ ܠܡܠܟܘܬܐ: ܕܟܐ	[y] ܢܝܫܐ [z] ܕܢܩܒܠ
[a] ܘܡܠܐܒܝܢ	10 ܐܡܪ ܠܗ [b] ܠܒܪܐ ܕܒܕܐ ܕܟܐ ܕܐܬܒܢܝ: [c] ܗܕܝܢ	[b] ܠܒܪܐ
[b] ܠܒܪܐ [c] ܗܕܝܢ	ܐܦ ܐܢܬܘܢ ܟܕ ܬܥܒܕܘܢ: ܟܠ ܡܕܐ	
[e] ܢܝܫܐ [f] ܚܝܝܢ	[d] ܕܐܬܦܩܕܬܘܢ ܗܘܘ ܐܡܪܝܢ ܕܥܒܕܝܢ ܕܠܝܬ	[d] ܕܐܬܦܩܕܬܘܢ (sic)
	ܠܗܘܢ [e] ܢܝܫܐ ܐܢܘ: ܕܟܐ ܕܗܘܘ [f] ܚܝܝܢ	[f] ܚܝܝܢ
	ܕܢܥܒܕ ܥܒܕܢܗ ܀	

CXIV.

Luke XIX. 1—10.

Codex A.	Codex B.	Codex C.
[a] ܠܒܘܪܐ ܚܕ ܕ	[a] ܠܒܘܪܐ ܚܕ ܕܟܬܝܒ ܒܗ ܕܐܢܫ ܡܢ	[a] ܠܒܘܪܐ ܐܠܝܫ ܕ
‡ ܡܬܠܡܕܢܐ ܡܢ	ܠܐܒܐ [a] ܘܐܬܠܗ [z] ܡܪܘܬܐ: [a] ܘܒܒܪܐ [b] ܡܪܐ	ܐܠܝܫܥ ܒܪܐ ܡܢ
‡ f. 71b. [a] ܠܐܒܐ	1 ...	[a] ܠܐܒܐ
[b] omit ܡܪܐ [a] omit ܘ	2 ܒܝܘܡ [c] ܚܠ [d] ܚܠܝܐ ܒܢܝܫܐ: ܗܘܐ ܚܕ ܐܢܫ	[z] omit ܡܪܘܬܐ
[c] omit ܚܠ [d] ܚܠܝܐ	ܕܫܡܗ ܙܟܝ [e] ܘܐܟܪ: ܘܗܘ ܗܘܐ ܪܒ	[d] omit ܚܠܝܐ [a] omit ܘ
[e] ܘܐܟܪ	3 ܡܟܣܐ ܘܗܘܐ ܥܬܝܪ: ܘܗܘܐ ܒܥܐ ܕܢܚܙܐ	[e] ܘܐܟܪ
[f] omit ܡܢ [g] ܢܚܠ	ܠܝܫܘܥ ܡܢ [f] ܡܢ ܗܘ: ܘܠܐ ܗܘܐ	[f] omit ܡܢ
[h] ܐܟܠܘܣܐ	[f. 63b] [g] ܢܚܠ ܡܢ [h] ܐܟܠܘܣܐ: ܕܗܘܐ [i] ܕܗܘܐ [k] ܙܥܘܪ ܒܩܘܡܬܗ:	[h] ܐܟܠܘܣܐ
[i] ܕܗܘܐ [k] ܙܥܘܪ	4 ܘܪܗܛ [l] ܩܕܡ [m] ܠܩܘܕܡܐ ܘܣܠܩ [n] ܠܬܘܬܐ [o] ܠܬܐܢܬܐ:	[i] ܕܗܘܐ [k] ܙܥܘܪ
[m] ܠܩܘܕܡܝܢ	ܕܢܚܙܝܗ ܠܗ ܕܥܠ ܗܘ ܗܘܐ [p] ܚܠܘܢ	[l] ܩܕܡ
[n] add ܠܗ [p] ܚܠܘܢ	5 ܕܒܒܪܐ: ܘܟܕ ܐܬܐ ܡܪܐ [q] ܫܘܐ ܠܝܫܘܥ	[m] ܠܐܟܠܘܣܐ
[q] ܒܥܘܢ	ܐܬܪܐ ܐܬܟܠܬ ܘܚܙܝܗ † ܘܐܡܪ ܠܗ:	[n] add ܠܗ
	[e] ܘܐܟܪ ܐܬܒܥܝ ܢܚܘܬ [r] ܕܝܘܡܢܐ ܠܝ ܒܒܝܬܟ:	† f. 64b.
[r] ܕܝܘܡܢܐ	6 ܘܐܬܦܢܝ [s] ܢܚܬ ܘܐܬܒܥܝ: ܘܩܒܠܗ ܒܚܕܘܬܐ	[o] ܠܐܬܘܬܐ
	7 [t] ܘܟܠܗܘܢ ܚܙܘ: ܘܪܛܢܘ ܟܠܗܘܢ ܗܘܘ ܐܡܪܝܢ	[r] ܕܝ ܡܪܐ [r]
[u] ܗܟܠ [v] ܡܪ	8 ܕܠܘܬ ܓܒܪܐ ܚܛܝܐ ܥܠ [u] ܠܡܒܛܠ: [v] ܘܐܡܪ	[s] add ܘ
	ܕܝ [e] ܘܐܟܪ ܠܝܫܘܥ ܒܗܝ: ܗܐ [w] ܦܠܓܘܬ	[t] ܗܟܠ ܠܗ [v] ܡܪ
[x] ܡܢܟܣܝ	[x] ܡܢܟܣܝ ܠܡܣܟܢܐ ܝܗܒ ܐܢܐ: [y] ܘܐܢ	[w] ܦܠܓܘܬ
	ܕܝ [z] ܠܐܢܫ ܥܘܠ ܥܒܕܬ ܐܢܐ ܐܦܢܐ ܐܪܒܥܐ	[x] ܡܢܟܣܝ [y] ܘܐܢ
		[z] ܠܐܢܫ

Marginal note (Codex A): ܩܪܝܢܐ ܕ...

Codex A.	Codex B.	Codex C.
	9 ܒܚܠܝܢ : ܘܐܡܪ [a]ܠܗ ܡܪܐ ܝܫܘܥ ܝܘܡܢܕܝܢ	[a] *omit* ܠܗ
‡ f. 72*a*.	‡ ܚܝܝܢܐ [b]ܠܗܕܝܢ ܒܝܬܐ ܐܬܥܒܕܘ : ܗܝܢ ܡܢܐ	
[b]ܠܗܕܝܢ	10 ܕܐܘܦ ܗܕܝܢ ܒܪܗ ܕܐܒܪܗܡ ܐܝܬ ܗܘ ܐܬܐ	
[d]ܕܐܒܕ	ܓܝܪ ܒܪܗ ܕܓܒܪܐ ܕܢܒܥܐ ܘܢܚܝܐ ܡܐ [d]ܕܐܒܕ ⁘	

CXV.

Luke XVIII. 2—8*a*.

Codex A.	Codex B.	Codex C.
[a]ܦܬܚ ܦܬܓܡܢ ܐܬܪ [a]ܡܢ ܠܗܘܢ	[a]ܘܡܪܐ ܦܬܚ ܦܬܓܡܢ ܡܢ ܒܬܪ ܐܠܝܢ ܡܢ ܠܗܘܢ [z a]ܐܡܪ ܡܪܐ ܗܕܐ ܡܬܠܐ : ܘܐܡܪ	[a]ܠܝܢܘܢ ܐܦܬܓܡ ܐܘܪܐ ܒܒܪ ܡܢ [a]ܠܗܘܢ
[a]ܕܐܝܢ [b]ܡܕܝܢܬܐ	2 [a]ܕܐܝܢ ܚܕ ܗܘܐ ܒܚܕܐ [b]ܡܕܝܢܬܐ : [c]ܡܢ ܐܠܗܐ	[z] *add* ≡ ܘܒܝܬܗ
[c]ܕܡܢ [e]ܕܚܝܠ	[d]ܠܐ ܗܘܐ [e]ܕܚܝܠ : ܘܡܢ ܒܢܝܫ ܠܐ ܗܘܐ	[b]ܡܕܝܢܬܐ [c]ܕܡܢ
	3 ܡܬܒܝܢ : ܘܚܕܐ ܐܪܡܠܐ ܗܘܬ ܒܝܬܗ	[d] *omit* ܠܐ [e]ܕܚܠ
[f]ܡܕܝܢܬܐ	[f]ܡܕܝܢܬܐ : ܘܗܘܬ ܐܬܝܐ ܠܘܬܗ ܘܐܡܪܐ	
[g]ܚܒܝܪ [h]ܐܢܛܕܝܩܝ	4 ܠܗ [g]ܚܒܝܪ ܢܩܡܢܝ ܡܢ [h]ܐܢܛܕܝܩܝ : ܘܠܐ ܗܘܐ	[g]ܚܒܝܪ [h]ܐܢܛܕܝܩܝ
	ܨܒܐ ܒܙܒܢܐ ܠܣܓܝ ܐܝܟܢ : ܘܡܢ ܒܬܪ	
[i] *omit* ܕܝ	ܗܠܝܢ ܐܡܪ [i]ܕܝ ܒܠܒܗ [k]ܐܢ ܡܢ ܐܠܗܐ [f. 64*a*]	[k]ܐܢ [i] *omit* ܕܝ
[l]ܠܝܬܢܐ	[l]ܠܝܬ [l]ܐܢܐ [l]ܕܚܝܠ : ܘܡܢ ܒܢܝܫ [l]ܠܝܬ [l]ܐܢܐ	
[m]ܒܓܠܠ [n]ܕܗܕܐ	5 ܡܬܒܝܢ : [m]ܒܓܠܠ ܕܝ [n]ܗܕܐ ܐܪܡܠܬܐ	
[o]ܡܫܠܝܬܐ [p]ܚܠܝܐ	[o]ܡܫܠܝܬܐ [p]ܚܠܝܐ ܠܝܬ ܢܣܒ ܢܩܡܗ : ܕܠܐ	[o]ܡܫܠܝܬܐ
[q]ܠܥܠܡܝܢ	6 [q]ܠܥܠܡ ܬܗܘܐ ܐܬܝܐ ܡܫܢܩܐ ܠܝ : ܘܐܡܪ	
[r]ܫܡܥܘܢ	ܡܪܐ [r]ܫܡܥܘ ܡܐ [s]ܕܐܡܪ ܕܝܢܐ ܕܥܘܠܐ :	[r]ܫܡܥܘܢ [s]ܕܐܡܪ
[u]ܢܩܡܬܗܘܢ	7 †ܐܠܗܐ ܕܝ ܠܐ [t]ܥܒܕ [u]ܢܩܡܬܗܘܢ [v]ܕܓܒܝܘܗܝ :	† f. 65*a*.
‡ f. 72*b*.	ܗܠܝܢ ܕܩܥܝܢ ܠܘܬܗ ܐܝܡܡܐ ܘܠܠܝܐ : ‡ ܘܗܘ	[t]ܥܒܕ
[v]ܕܓܒܝܘܗܝ [w]ܡܓܪܓܝܢ	8 [w]ܡܓܪܓ ܪܘܚܗ ܥܠܝܗܘܢ : [x]ܐܢ ܐܡܪ ܐܢܐ	[x]ܐܢܐ
[y]ܒܥܓܠ	ܠܟܘܢ ܕܥܒܕ [u]ܢܩܡܬܗܘܢ [y]ܒܥܓܠ ⁘	[y]ܒܥܓܠ

CXVI.

Luke XVIII. 8*b*—14.

Codex A.	Codex B.	Codex C.
[a]ܐܡܪ ܕܝ ܦܬܓܡܐ ܐܬܪ ܡܢ ܠܗܘܢ ܐܠܦܪܢܘܣ [a]ܘܠܒܥܐܪ	[a]ܒܪܡ ܐܠܝܢ ܦܬܓܡܐ ܡܢ ܠܗܘܢ ܗܘܐ ܠܠܝܢ	[a]ܠܝܢܘܢ ܐܠܝܢܕ ܐܡܪ ܒܒܪ ܡܢ [a]ܠܗܘܢ
[b] *omit* ܪܫܝ [z] *omit* . . . ܒܪܡ ܠܪܫܝܬܐ . . .	ܐܠܝܢܗܘ ܡܢ ܐܒܐܦ : [b]ܪܫܝ :[a] :[y] [z]ܒܪܡ ܕܝ ܐܢܐ	[y] *add* ܘܒܝܬܗ

Codex B.

ܒܗ [a]ܕܗ [b]ܐܬܪܐ [c]ܢܚܡܝܢ [d]ܗܘܘ ܥܠ ܐܪܥܐ :
9 ܘܗܘܘܐ ܐܡܪܝܢ ܠܗܘܢ ܗܠܝܢ ܕܐܣܝܢ ܥܠ
ܒܪܝܗܘܢ [e]ܕܗܘܢ ܩܪܝܒ [f]ܘܡܠܟܘܬܗ [g]ܕܐܠܗܐ[z]
10 ܐܡܪ ܡܪܢ ܗܕܐ ܡܬܠܬܐ [h]ܘܐܡܪ[i] : ܬܘܒ
ܒܣܒܪ ܗܠܘ ܠܗܘܢ ܕܣܡܠܗ : ܣܗ [k]ܦܪܫܝܢ
11 [l]ܘܣܬܪܝܢ [m]ܡܟܐܢܐ : ܘܬܘܒ ܦܪܫܝܢ [n]ܐܟܘ
ܘܗܠܝܢ [o]ܠܡܥܠ ܒܪܝܗܘܢ : [p]ܘܗܘܘܐ ܡܬܠܐ ܘܐܡܪ
ܐܠܗܐ ܡܫܬܘܕܝ ܐܢܐ ܠܟ : ܕܠܝܬ ܐܢܐ
ܗܟܢ [q]ܕܫܪܝܬ ܒܣܝܢܐ ܣܦܘܩܐ ܘܦܠܛܘܢܐ
[r]ܘܠܒܘܪܐ : [s]ܐܦ ܐܘܦ ܒܗܬ [t]ܗܕܝܢ [u]ܡܟܐܢܐ :
12 [w]ܟܐܝܢ [x]ܠܟ ܐܢܐ[x] ܬܘܒ ܘܒܠܝܢ ܒܥܘܒܬܐ :
13 ܘܡܒܩܪ ܐܢܐ ܒܗܠ ܡܢ ܕܐܢܐ ܦܢܐ ܘܬܘܒ
ܡܟܐܢܐ ܡܢ ܪܘܫܢܐ ܗܘܐ [y]ܘܐܟܢ : ܘܠܐ
ܗܘܐ ܟܢ ܐܘܦ[z] [a]ܕܫܠܛܐ [b]ܒܣܝܗ [c]ܠܡܘܒܠܐ
[f. 64b]
ܐܠܐ ܗܘܐ ܡܣܟܢܐ ܥܠ ܣܕܝܗ ܘܐܡܪ ܐܠܗܐ
14 ܥܒܘܕ ܠܝ [d]ܠܚܛܝܐ : ܘܐܡܪ ܐܢܐ ܠܟܘܢ
ܕܢܚܬ ܗܕܝܢ [e]ܡܙܕܕܩ ܠܒܝܬܗ ܗܟܢ ܡܢ [f]ܗܘ :
ܕܟܠ ܡܢ [g]ܕܡܪܘܡܡ ܢܦܫܗ ܡܬܡܟܟ : ܘܡܢ
[h]ܕܡܡܟܟ ܢܦܫܗ [i]ܡܬܪܘܡܡ : [‡k] ⁘

CXVII.

Luke XX. 46—XXI. 4.

[‡][a]ܘܐܡܪ ܐܘܦ ܡܫܝܚܐ ܕܗ ܒܕܗ ܠܬܠܡܝܕܘܗܝ ܡܢ
46 [a]ܠܗܘܢ: [y]ܐܡܪ ܡܪܢ [z]ܠܗܘܢ [a]ܠܬܠܡܝܕܘܗܝ :
[†]ܐܙܕܗܪܘ ܡܢ ܣܦܪܐ ܗܠܝܢ ܕܨܒܝܢ ܕܢܗܠܟܘܢ
ܒܐܣܛܠܐ ܘܪܚܡܝܢ [b]ܫܐܠܐ [c]ܫܠܡܐ
ܒܫܘܩܝܐ : ܘܪܫܝ [d]ܡܬܟܬܒܐ [e]ܒܟܢܫܬܐ :
47 ܘܪܫܝ ܡܫܟܒܝܐ [f]ܒܚܫܡܝܬܐ : ܗܠܝܢ ܕܐܟܠܝܢ
[g]ܒܬܝܗܘܢ ܕܐܪܡܠܬܐ : ܘܒܥܠܬܐ ܡܨܠܝܢ
[h]ܐܪܝܟܝܢ : ܗܠܝܢ ܢܣܒܘܢ ܕܝܢܐ ܝܬܝܪܐ :

Codex A.

ܘܐܡܪ [h] *omit*
ܐܢܬ [i] *add*
[k]ܦܪܫܝܢ
[l]ܘܣܬܪܝܢ [m]ܡܟܐܢܐ
[n]ܐܟܘ [o]ܠܡܥܠ
[p] *omit* ܘ [q]ܕܫܪܝܬ
[r]ܘܠܒܘܪܐ
[t]ܗܕܝܢ [u]ܡܟܐܢܐ
[w]ܟܐܝܢ [x]ܐܢܐ ܠܟ[x]
[y]ܘܐܟܢ [z] *add* ܠܐ
[a]ܕܫܠܛܐ [b]ܒܣܝܗ
[c]ܠܡܘܒܠܐ [d]ܠܚܛܝܐ
[e]ܡܙܕܕܩ [f]ܘܐܦ
[g]ܕܡܪܘܡܡ
[h]ܕܡܡܟܟ
[k] *add* ܥܠܡ

[‡][a]ܘܐܡܪ ܐܘܦ ܡܫܝܚܐ ܠܬܠܡܝܕܘܗܝ
‡ f. 73*a*. [a]ܡܢ ܠܗܘܢ
[z] *omit* ܠܗܘܢ
[b]ܫܐܠ
[f]ܒܚܫܡܝܬܐ
[g]ܒܬܝܗܘܢ
[h]ܐܪܝܟܝܢ
8

ܡܚ
ܠ

Codex C.

ܒܗ [a] *omit* [b]ܐܬܪܐ
[c]ܢܚܡܝܢ [d]ܗܘܘܬܐ
[e] *omit* ܕ
[f]ܘܡܠܟܘܬ [g]ܠܐܠܗܐ
[l]ܘܣܬܪܝܢ [m]ܡܟܐܢܐ
[o]ܠܡܥܠ [p] *omit* ܘ
[q]ܕܫܪܝܬ [s]ܐܢܐ
[u]ܡܟܐܢܐ
[x]ܐܢܐ ܠܟ[x]
[b]ܒܣܝܗ
[d]ܥܠ ܚܛܝܬܝ[d]
[e]ܡܙܕܕܩ
[f]ܘܐܦ [g]ܕܡܪܘܡܡ
[h]ܕܡܡܟܟ
[i]ܡܬܪܘܡܡ (*sic*)

[a]ܠܗܘܢ ܐܡܪ ܡܫܝܚܐ
ܐܡܪ ܡܪܢ ܡܢ
[a]ܠܗܘܢ
[y] *add* ☰ ܘܬܠܡܝܕܘܗܝ
† f. 65*b*.
[z] *omit* ܠܗܘܢ
[a]ܠܬܠܡܝܕܘܗܝ [c]ܫܠܡܐ
[d]ܡܬܟܬܒܐ
[e]ܒܟܢܫܬܐ
[f]ܒܚܫܡܝܬܐ
[h]ܐܪܝܟܝܢ

Codex B.

XXI.

1 ܘܚܡܐ ܘܚܡܐ ܠܥܬܝܪܝܢ [i]ܕܪܡܝܢ ܒܩܘܪܒܢ [j]ܩܘܪܒܢܝܗܘܢ :
2 ܩܘܪܒܢܝܗܘܢ [k]ܒܓܙܐ : ܘܚܡܐ [l]ܚܕܐ ܐܪܡܠܐ
3 [m]ܡܣܟܢܬܐ [n]ܪܡܬ ܬܪܬܝܢ ܡܢ ܙܘܙ : ܘܐܡܪ
ܐܡܪ ܠܗܘܢ ܐܡܪ ܐܢܐ ܠܟܘܢ [o]ܕܗܕܐ ܐܪܡܠܬܐ
ܗܕܐ ܐܪܡܠܬܐ [p]ܡܣܟܢܬܐ ܝܬܝܪ ܡܢ
4 ܟܠܗܘܢ [q]ܪܡܬ : ܟܠ ܗܠܝܢ [r]ܡܢ ܡܝܬܪܬܐ
ܕܝܠܗܘܢ ܪܡܘ [s]ܒܩܘܪܒܢܐ : ܗܕܐ ܕܝܢ ܡܢ
ܚܣܝܪܘܬܗ : ܟܠ [t]ܚܝܝܗ ܕܗܘܐ ܠܗ [q]ܪܡܬ
ܡܢ ܕܝܠܗ ܐܢܫ [u]ܕܡܫܬܒܚ ܡܫܬܒܚ : [w]ܫܠܡ ⁘

CXVIII.

Luke XV. 11—32.

[a]ܐܡܪ ܡܪܢ ܡܬܠܐ ܗܢܐ : ܓܒܪ ܚܕ ܐܝܬ ܗܘܐ ܠܗ
ܬܪܝܢ ܒܢܝܢ : [f. 65a] [v] [a]ܐܡܪ ܒܪܐ ܙܥܘܪܐ ܐܒܘܗܝ
11 12 ܠܐܒܘܗܝ : [w] [x]ܐܒܐ ܗܒ ܠܝ ܡܢܬܐ ܕܡܛܝܐ ܠܝ : [‡] [y]ܘܐܡܪ
[z]ܙܥܘܪܐ [a]ܠܐܒܘܗܝ : ܐܒܐ ܗܒ ܠܝ ܡܢܬܐ [b]
ܡܢ [c]ܕܡܛܝܐ ܠܝ ܡܢ [d]ܩܢܝܢܐ ܕܝܠܟ : [e]ܘܦܠܓ
13 ܠܗܘܢ [f] [g]ܩܢܝܢܗ : ܘܡܢ ܒܬܪ [h]ܝܘܡܬܐ [i]ܩܠܝܠܝܢ
[k]ܟܢܫ ܒܪܗ ܙܥܘܪܐ ܟܠ ܡܕܡ [l]ܕܝܠܗ : [m]ܘܐܙܠ
ܠܗ [n]ܠܐܬܪܐ ܪܚܝܩܐ : [o]ܘܬܡܢ ܒܕܪ ܟܠ
14 ܩܢܝܢܗ ܕܚܝܐ ܒܐܣܘܛܘܬܐ [p] : ܘܡܢ [q]ܒܬܪ
[r]ܕܐܘܒܕ ܟܠܡܐ ܕܗܘܐ ܠܗ [s]ܗܘܐ ܟܦܢܐ ܒܐܬܪܐ
15 ܐܪܥܐ : ܘܫܪܝ ܕܢܚܣܪ [m]ܘܐܙܠ [t]ܐܬܕܒܩ ܠܚܕ
ܡܢ ܒܢܝ [†] [u]ܡܕܝܢܬܐ ܗܝ : ܘܫܕܪܗ
16 ܠܚܩܠܐ ܠܡܪܥܐ [w]ܚܙܝܪܐ : ܘܪܓܐ ܗܘܐ ܠܡܡܠܐ
ܟܪܣܗ ܡܢ ܚܪܘܒܐ ܕܐܟܠܝܢ [y]ܚܙܝܪܐ :
17 ܘܐܢܫ ܠܐ ܝܗܒ ܗܘܐ ܠܗ : [z]ܟܕ ܕܝܢ ܐܬܐ
ܠܢܦܫܗ ܐܡܪ : [a]ܟܡܐ ܐܓܝܪܝܢ ܐܝܬ ܒܒܝܬܗ ܕܐܒܝ
[b]ܕܝܬܝܪ ܠܗܘܢ ܠܚܡܐ : ܘܐܢܐ [c]ܗܪܟܐ [d]ܐܒܕ
18 [e]ܒܟܦܢܐ : ܐܩܘܡ ܐܙܠ ܠܘܬ ܐܒܝ ܘܐܡܪ :

Codex A.

[i] ܕܪܡܝܢ [j] ܩܘܪܒܢܝܗܘܢ

[k] ܒܓܙܐ

[n] ܪܡܬ

[o] ܕܡܣܟܢܬܐ

[p] ܡܣܟܢܬܐ

[q] ܪܡܬ [r] *add* ܗܢܘܢ

[a] ܚܕ ܡܢ ܬܠܡܝܕܘܗܝ ܡܢ ܠܘܬܗ [a]

[v] *add* ܝܫܘܥ

‡ f. 73b.

[w] *add* ܒܪܗ

[a] ܠܐܒܘܗܝ [e] ܘܦܠܓ

[f] ܠܗܘܢ [h] ܝܘܡܬܐ

[i] ܩܠܝܠܝܢ [k] ܟܢܫ

[m] ܘܐܙܠ

[r] ܕܐܘܒܕ [s] ܟܦܢܐ

[t] ܐܬܕܒܩ

[u] ܡܕܝܢܬܐ

[w] ܚܙܝܪܐ

[y] ܚܙܝܪܐ

[z] ܟܕ

[b] *omit* ܕܝܢ

[c] ܗܪܟܐ [d] ܐܒܕ

[f] ܐܙܠ

Codex C.

[i] ܕܪܡܝܢ [j] ܩܘܪܒܢܝܗܘܢ

[k] ܒܓܙܐ [l] ܚܕ

[m] ܡܣܟܢܬܐ [n] ܪܡܬ

[r] *add* ܗܢܘܢ

[s] ܒܩܘܪܒܢܐ

[t] ܚܝܝܗ

[w] *omit* ܫܠܡ [u] *omit* ܕ

[a] ܠܗܘܢ ܐܡܪ ܡܬܠܐ ܗܢܐ ܡܢ ܠܘܬܗ [a]

[v] *add* ܝܫܘܥ

[x] *omit* ܚܕ [w] *add* ܒܪܗ

[z] ܙܥܘܪܐ [y] *add* ܠܗ

[c] ܕܡܛܝܐ [b] *add* ܡܢ

[e] ܘܦܠܓ [d] ܩܢܝܢܐ

[g] ܩܢܝܢܗ [f] ܠܗܘܢ

[l] ܕܝܠܗ [h] ܝܘܡܬܐ

[o] *omit* ܘ [n] ܠܐܬܪܐ

[q] ܒܬܪ [p] ܒܐܣܘܛܘܬܐ

[t] ܐܬܕܒܩ [r] ܕܐܘܒܕ

† f. 66a.

[w] ܚܙܝܪܐ

[z] ܟܕ

[b] *omit* ܕܝܢ [a] ܟܡܐ

[d] ܐܒܕ [c] ܗܪܟܐ

[e] *omit* ܒ

Codex A.	*Codex* B.	*Codex* C.
	ܘܐܢܐ ܐܡܪ ܠܗ : ܐܒܐ ܐܣܟܠܬ ܒܫܡܝܐ	
[g]ܘܩܘܕܡܝܟ	19 [g]ܘܩܘܕܡܝܟ : ܟܥܢ ܠܝܬ ܐܢܐ ܫܘܐ ܕܢܬܩܪܐ	
[h]ܐܓܝ̈ܪܝܟ :	ܒܪܟ : ܥܒܕ ܝܬܝ ܗܝܟ ܚܕ ܡܢ [h]ܐܓܝ̈ܪܝܟ :	
[k] *omit* ܕܝ	20 ܘܩܡ ܐܬܐ ܠܘܬ [l]ܐܒ̈ܘܝ : ܘܥܕ ܗܘ ܪܚܝܩ	
‡ f. 74*a*.	ܚܡܐ ܝܬܗ [k]ܕܝ [l]ܐܒ̈ܘܝ ܘܐܬܪܚܡ ‡ [m]ܥܠܘܝ :	[k] *omit* ܕܝ
[l]ܐܒܘܗܝ [m]ܥܠܘܗܝ	21 ܘܪܗܛ ܢܦܠ ܥܠ ܨܘܪܗ ܘܢܫܩ ܝܬܗ : ܘܐܡܪ ܠܗ	[l]ܐܒܘܝ [m]ܥܠܝ
[n]ܒܫܡܝܐ	ܒܪܗ ܐܒܐ : ܐܣܟܠܬ [n]ܒܫܡܝܐ [g]ܘܩܘܕܡܝܟ :	
	22 ܟܥܢ ܠܝܬ ܐܢܐ ܫܘܐ ܕܢܬܩܪܐ ܒܪܟ ܘܐܡܪ	
[o]ܠܥܒ̈ܕܘܗܝ [p]ܐܦ̈ܩܘ	[f. 65*b*] [l]ܐܒ̈ܘܝ [o]ܠܥܒ̈ܕܘܝ ܒܥܪܒ [p]ܐܦ̈ܩܘ ܐܣܛܠܝܬܐ	[o]ܠܥܒܕܘܝ [p]ܐܦ̈ܩܘ
[s]ܒܪ̈ܓܠܘܗܝ [t]ܘܐܝܬܘ	[q]ܗܐܝ ܡܫܒܚܬܐ ܘܐܠܒܫܘ ܝܬܗ : ܘܗܒܘ ܥܙܩܬܐ	[q]ܕܗܝ [r]ܘܡܣܢܝܢ
[u]ܬܘܪܐ	23 ܒܐܝܕܗ : [r]ܘܡܣܢܝܢ [s]ܒܪ̈ܓܠܘܝ : [t]ܘܐܝܬܘ [u]ܬܘܪܐ	[s]ܒܪ̈ܓܠܘܗ [u]ܬܘܪܐ
[y]ܕܗܢܐ	ܦܛܡܐ [w]ܘܟܘܣܘ ܝܬܗ [x]ܢܝܟܘܠ ܘܢܒܣܡ :	[w]ܘܢܟܣܘ [x]ܕܢܝܟܘܠ
[z] *omit* ܗܐ	24 [y]ܕܗܕܝܢ ܒܪܝ ܗܘܐ ܡܝܬ [z]ܘܗܐ ܚܝܐ :	[z] *omit* ܗܐ [c]ܒܚܩܠܝܢ
[a]ܘܐܒܝܕ [b]ܘܒܪ̈ܗ	25 [a]ܘܐܒܕ ܘܐܫܬܟܚ : [b]ܘܒܪܗ [c]ܒܚܩܠܝܢ ܗܘܐ	[d]ܡܛܐ [e]ܘܫܡܥ
[c]ܒܚܩ̈ܠܝܢ [d]ܡܛܐ	ܕܝ ܟܕ ܗܘ ܩܪܐ ܒܦܪܘܐ : ܘܟܕ ܐܬܐ [d]ܡܛܐ	[f]ܐܫܡܘܥܬܐ
[e]ܘܫܡܥ [g]ܕܡܢ̈ܠܐ	ܠܗ ܕܒܝܬܐ [e]ܘܫܡܥ [f]ܐܫܡܘܥܬܐ [g]ܒܡܠܐ	[g]ܕܡܗܠܐ
	26 ܘܪܩܕܝܢ : [h]ܘܩܪܐ ܠܚܕ ܡܢ ܛܠܝܐ ܘܫܐܠ ܠܗ	[h]ܩܪܐ
[i] *omit* ܕܝ	27 [i]ܕܝ ܘܐܡܪ ܡܢ ܗܘܢ ܗܠܝܢ : ܗܘ ܕܝ	[i] *omit* ܕܝ
[k] *add* ܘܡܚܠܗ ܐܒܘܟ ܘܢܟܣ ܠܗ	ܐܡܪ ܠܗ ܕܐܬܐ ܐܚܘܟ :[k] [l]ܘܬܘܪܐ ܦܛܡܐ	[k] *add* ܘܐܒܘܟ ܢܟܣ ܠܗ
[l] *omit* ܘ [o]ܐܒܘܗܝ	28 [m]ܕܩܒܠܗ ܚܠܝܡ ܘܪܓܙ ܘܠܐ ܗܘܐ ܒܥܐ	† f. 66*b*.
[q]ܠܐܒܘܗܝ [r]ܫܢ̈ܝܢ	ܕܝܥܘܠ : [n]ܘܢܦܩ † [o]ܐܒ̈ܘܝ ܘܗܘܐ ܒܥܐ ܡܢܗ	[l] *omit* ܘ [m]ܘܡܚܠ ܠܗ
[s]ܦ̈ܠܚܐܢܐ [t]ܐܥܒܪܬ	29 ܗܘ ܕܝ [p]ܐܬܝܒ ܘܐܡܪ [q]ܠܐܒ̈ܘܝ : ܗܐ	[n]ܘܢܦܩ (*sic*) [o]ܐܒܘܝ
‡ f. 74*b*.	ܟܡܐ [r]ܫܢܝܢ ܐܢܐ ܡܫܡܫ ܠܟ : ܘܡܢ	[p]ܐܬܝܒ
[u]ܡܘܡ̈ܢ	[s]ܡܢܗܘܢ ܦܘܩܕܢܟ ܠܐ ‡ [t]ܥܒܪܬ : ܘܠܝ ܡܢ	[q]ܠܐܒܘܝ (*sic*)
[w]ܪ̈ܚܡܝ	[u]ܡܘܡܢ ܠܐ ܝܗܒܬ ܚܕ ܓܕܝ ܕܐܬܒܣܡ ܥܡ	[t]ܐܥܒܪܬ
[x]ܕܐܟܘܠ [y]ܡܢ̈ܟܣܝܟ	30 [w]ܪܚܡܝ : ܘܟܕ ܐܬܐ ܗܕܝܢ ܒܪܟ [x]ܕܐܟ̈ܠ	[w]ܪܚܡܝ [y]ܠܢܟܣܝܟ
[z] *add* ܐܢܬ [a]ܕܝܠܝ	[y]ܡܢܟܣܝܟ ܥܡ ܙܢܝ̈ܬܐ : ܢܟܣܬ ܠܗ ܬܘܪܐ	[z] *add* ܐܢܬ
[b] *omit* ܐܢܬܝ	31 ܦܛܡܐ : ܗܘ ܕܝ ܐܡܪ ܠܗ ܒܪܝ ܐܢܬ ܒܟܠ [z]	[b] *omit* ܐܢܬܝ
[d]ܘܢܬܚܕܐ	ܥܕܢ ܥܡܝ : ܘܟܠ ܡܐ [a]ܕܝܠܝ ܕܝܠܟ ܐܝܬ	[c] *omit* ܕܝ
[e]ܕܗܢܐ	32 ܗܘ : [b]ܐܢܬܝ ܕܢܒܣܡ [c]ܕܝ [d]ܘܢܬܚܕܐ ܗܘܐ	[d]ܘܢܬܚܕܐ
	ܠܡܣܟܐ : [e]ܕܗܕܝܢ ܐܚܘܟ ܗܘܐ ܡܝܬ ܘܚܝܐ :	

Codex A.	Codex B.	Codex C.
[f]ܘܐܬܢܟܣ	[f]ܘܐܒܕ [g]ܗܘܐ [h]ܘܐܬܢܟܣܘܢ : [i]ܫܠܒܬ ܡܪܝܐܬ	[g]omit ܗܘܐ
[k]ܐܠܟܣܢܕܪ ܠܗܘܐ	[k]ܐܠܟܣܢܕܪ ܠܗܘܐ ܗܘܝ ܫܟܦܣܪ[k] ܬܘܪܐ	[h]ܘܐܬܢܟܣܘܢ
ܗܘܝ ܫܟܦܣܪ[k]	ܐܠܝܣܘܕ [l]ܘܠܗܫܒܘܬ[i] ⁘	[i]ܫܠܒܬ ܡܪܝܐܬ
[l]ܘܐܠܗܫܒܘܬ		ܐܠܟܣܢܕܪ ܠܗܘܐ ܗܘܝ
		ܫܟܦܣܪ ܬܘܪܐ
		ܠܝܣܘܕ ܘܠܗܫܒܘܬ
		ܗܘܐ ܐܬܚܠܦ
		ܐܝܟ ܐܠܟܣܢܕܪܘܣ
		ܐܠܗܐ ܒܚܝܐ
		ܡܪܢܐ ܐܠܝܣ[i]

CXIX.

Luke XXI. 8, 9, 25—27, 33—36.

Codex B.

[f. 66a]

[a]ܘܩܪܝܐ ܝܘܡ ܫܒܬ ܡܢܘܚ. ܐܠܝܣܐ ܡܢ ܠܘܩܣ:[a] [z]

8 ܐܡܪ ܡܪܢܐ [a]ܠܬܠܡܝܕܘܗܝ ܚܙܘ [b c]ܠܐ ܬܛܥܘܢ:[c]

ܣܓܝ [d]ܐܝܬܘܢ ܥܠ ܫܡܝ ܐܡܪܝܢ ܐܢܐ ܗܘ :

ܘܙܒܢܐ [e]ܩܪܒ ܠܐ ܬܐܙܠܘܢ ܒܬܪܗܘܢ

9 ܟܕ ܕܝ [f]ܬܫܡܥܘܢ [g]ܩܪܒܝܢ [h]ܘܒܪܘܒܝܢ ܠܐ

[i]ܕܝ ܬܬܪܗܒܘܢ : ܩ̈ܠܝܦܘ ܓܝܪ ܠܗܠܝܢ [k]ܕܝܗܘܢ

[l]ܡܬܒܝ : [m]ܐܠܐ [n]ܥܕ̈ܡܐ ܗܘܐ [o]ܫܘܦܝܐ :

25 ܘܝܗܘܢ ܐܬܝܢ [p]ܒܫܡܫܐ ܘܒܣܗܪܐ ܘܒܟܘܟܒܝܐ

ܘܥܠ ܐܪܥܐ ܠܚܘܨܝܢ ܕܥܡܡܝܢ : [r]ܒܬܗܘܒܬܐ

26 ‡ [s]ܕܩܠܗ ܕܝܡܐ : [t]ܘܕܘܠܒܐ [u]ܕܢܦܫܝܢ ܢܦܩܬܐ

ܕܒܚܝܠܐ ܡܢ ܕܚܠܬܐ : ܘܡܢ [w]ܣܘܒܪܐ ܕܗܠܝܢ

[x]ܕܐܬܝܢ ܥܠ [y]ܥܡܘܪܬܐ : [z]ܚܝܠܝܐ [a]ܓܝܪ

27 [b]ܕܫܡܝܐ [c]ܡܙܕܥܙܥܝܢ : [d]ܘܒܟܝܢ ܚܙܝܢ ܠܗ

† ܠܒܪܗ ܕܓܒܪܐ ܐܬܐ [e]ܥܠ [f]ܥܢܢܐ ܥܡ ܚܝܠ

33 [g]ܘܬܫܒܘܚܬܐ ܣܓܝ ܫܡܝܐ ܘܐܪܥܐ [h]ܥܒܪܘܢ

34 [i]ܘܡܠܝ ܕܝܠܝ ܠܐ [k]ܥܒܪܢ : ܐܣܬܟܠܘ ܕܝ

ܠܓܪܡܟܘܢ ܕܠܐ [l]ܝܩܪܘܢ ܠܒܒܟܘܢ : [m]ܒܫܬܝ

ܕܚܡܪ ܘܒܪܘܝܘ : ܘܒܝܦܘܐ [n]ܕܥܠܡ ܘܢܩܘܡ

35 ܥܠܝܟܘܢ ܬܗܘ ܡܘܡܐ ܡܢ ܥܠܡܐ : ܗܝܟ ܦܚ

36 [o]ܒܪ ܥܠ ܟܘܠ [p]ܐܦܝܗ ܕܐܪܥܐ : ܗܘܘ ܕܝ

ܫܗܪܝܢ ܒܟܘܠ ܥܕܢ ܘܒܥܝܢ [r]ܕܬܫܟܚܘܢ

[s]ܠܡܥܪܩ ܡܢ ܟܘܠ ܗܠܝܢ [t]ܕܥܬܝܕܝܢ [u]ܕܝܗܘܢ :

[w]ܘܬܩܘܡܘܢ ܩܕܡ ܒܪܗ ܕܓܒܪܐ ⁘

Codex A.

[a]ܠܬܠܡܝܕܘܗܝ [b]ܕܠܐ

[d]add ܓܝܪ [e]ܩܪܒ

[f]ܬܛܥܘܢ

[g]ܩܪܒܝܢ [h]ܘܒܪܘܒܝܢ

ܕܝ [i]omit [k]ܕܝܗܘܢ

[l]ܡܬܒܝ [m]add ܠܐ

[o]ܫܘܦܝܐ [p]ܒܫܡܫܐ

[r]ܒܬܗܘܒܬܐ

[s]ܕܩܠܗ [t]ܘܕܘܠܒܐ

[u]ܕܢܦܫܝܢ [w]ܣܘܒܪܐ

[x]ܕܐܬܝܢ

‡ f. 75a.

[y]ܥܡܘܪܬܐ

[a]omit ܓܝܪ [b]add ܓܝܪ

[d]ܘܒܟܝܢ [e]omit ܥܠ

[f]ܥܢܢܐ

[g]ܘܬܫܒܘܚܬܐ

[h]ܥܒܪܘܢ

[i]ܘܡܠܝ

[l]ܝܩܪܘܢ

[m]ܒܫܬܝ

[o]add ܗܘ ܐܦܝ ܥܠ

ܟܘܠ ܗܠܝܢ ܕܥܬܝܕܝܢ

[t]ܕܥܬܝܕܝܢ [u]ܕܝܗܘܢ

Codex C.

[a]ܠܝܘܡ ܐܚܒܬ

ܡܢܘܚ ܐܠܝܣ ܡܢ

ܠܘܩܐ[a]

[z]add ܘܟܢ ܡܪܢܐ ܗܘܐ

[c]ܕܬܛܥܘܢ (sic)

[d]add ܓܝܪ [g]ܩܪܒܝܢ

ܕܝ [i]omit [k]ܕܝܗܘܢ

[l]ܡܬܒܝ [m]add ܠܐ

[n]omit ܥܕ̈ܡܐ

[o]ܫܘܦܝܐ

[r]ܒܬܗܘܒܬܐ

[t]ܘܕܘܠܒܐ [u]ܕܢܦܫܝܢ

[y]ܥܠܡܐ [z]ܚܝܠܝܐ

[a]omit ܓܝܪ [b]add ܓܝܪ

† f. 67a.

[c]ܡܙܕܥܙܥܝܢ

[g]ܘܬܫܒܘܚܬܐ

[i]ܘܡܠܝ [k]ܥܒܪܢ

[l]ܝܩܪܘܢ [m]ܒܫܬܝܐ

[n]ܕܥܠܡ

[o]add ܗܘ ܐܦܝ ܥܠ

ܟܘܠ ܗܠܝܢ ܕܥܬܝܕܝܢ

[p]ܐܦܝܗ [r]ܕܬܫܟܚܘܢ

[s]ܠܡܥܪܩ

[w]ܘܬܩܘܡܘܢ

Codex A. | Codex B. | Codex C.

CXX.

Matt. XXV. 31—46.

Codex B.

[a]ܡܘܕܥܐ ܗܘ ܚܕ ܡܢ ܐܠܝܫ ܡܢ ܡܠܐܟܘܗ[a]: [z]

31 ܐܡܪ ܡܪܢܐ [a]ܠܬܠܡܝܕܘܗ ܟܕ ܕܝ ܝܬܐ [b]ܒܪܗ

ܕܓܒܪܐ [d]ܒܫܒܚܘܬܗ ܘܟܠ [e]ܡܠܐܟܘܝ ܥܡܗ :

ܒܟܝܢ ܗܘ [f]ܝܬܒ ܥܠ [g]ܟܘܪܣܝܐ ܕܫܒܚܘܬܗ : [f. 66b]

32 ‡ ܘܡܬܟܢܫܝܢ [i]ܠܩܕܡܘܗ ܟܠܗܘܢ ܥܡܡܝܐ :

ܘܗܘ [j]ܡܦܪܫ ܠܗܘܢ ܗܠܝܢ ܡܢ ܗܠܝܢ : ܗܝܟ

ܡܐ ܕܪܥܝܐ ܡܦܪܫ ܐܡܪܝܐ ܡܢ ܓܕܝܐ :

33 [l]ܘܡܩܝܡ ܐܡܪܝܐ ܡܢ ܝܡܝܢܗ ܘܓܕܝܐ ܡܢ

34 ܣܡܠܗ : [n]ܒܟܝܢ [o]ܝܐܡܪ ܡܠܟܐ ܠܗܠܝܢ ܕܡܢ

[p]ܝܡܝܢܗ ܐܬܘ [q]ܡܒܪܟܝܢ ܕܐܒܐ [r]ܝܪܬܘ ܡܠܟܘܬܐ

ܗܕܐ [s]ܕܡܬܩܢܐ ܠܟܘܢ ܡܢ [t]ܫܪܘܝܗ [u]ܕܥܠܡܐ :

35 [w]ܒܦܢܬ ܓܝܪ ܘܝܗܒܬܘܢ ܠܝ [x]ܕܐܝܟܘܠ : [y]ܘܨܗܝܬ

ܘܐܫܩܝܬܘܢ ܠܝ : [z]ܐܟܣܢܝܐ [a]ܗܘܝܬ

36 ܘܟܢܫܬܘܢ ܠܝ : [b]ܥܪܛܠܝ ܗܘܝܬ ܘܐܠܒܫܬܘܢ

ܠܝ : [c]ܐܬܟܪܗܬ ܘܣܥܪܬܘܢ [d]ܠܝ : †ܒܐܣܘܪܐ

37 ܗܘܝܬ [e]ܘܐܬܝܬܘܢ [f]ܠܘܬܝ : [g]ܒܟܝܢ ܡܓܝܒܝܢ

[h]ܠܗ ܨܕܝܩܝܐ [i]ܘܐܡܪܝܢ : [j]ܡܪܢ ܐܡܬܝ

[k]ܚܡܝܢܢ ܝܬܟ [l]ܟܦܢ [m]ܘܝܗܒܢ ܝܬܟ : ܐܘ

38 [n]ܨܗܐ [o]ܘܐܫܩܝܢ ܝܬܟ : ܐܡܬܝ [k]ܚܡܝܢܢ

ܝܬܟ [p]ܐܟܣܢܝ [q]ܘܟܢܫܢ ܝܬܟ : [r]ܐܘ ܥܪܛܠܝ

39 [t]ܘܐܠܒܫܢ ܝܬܟ :[r] ܐܡܬܝ [c]ܚܡܝܢܢ ܝܬܟ : [u]ܟܪܝܗ

40 ܐܘ [v]ܒܡܛܪܐ [w]ܘܐܬܝܢ ܠܘܬܟ : [x]ܘܡܓܝܒ ܡܠܟܐ

ܘܐܡܪ ܠܗܘܢ : [y]ܐܡܝܢ [z]ܐܡܪ ܐܢܐ[z] ‡ ܠܟܘܢ

ܕܟܕ ܟܘܠ ܐܡܬܝ ܕܥܒܕܬܘܢ ܠܚܕ ܡܢ ܗܠܝܢ

41 [a]ܐܚܘܝ ܙܥܘܪܝܐ ܠܝ ܥܒܕܬܘܢ : [b]ܒܟܝܢ ܗܘ

ܐܡܪ ܐܦܘ ܠܗܠܝܢ ܕܡܢ [c]ܣܡܠܗ ܐܙܠܘ ܠܟܘܢ

ܡܢܝ [d]ܠܝܛܝܐ ܠܢܘܪܐ [e]ܕܠܥܠܡ ܕܡܬܩܢܐ [i]ܠܣܛܢܐ

42 [k]ܘܠܡܠܐܟܘܗܝ : ܒܦܢܬ ܓܝܪ ܘܠܐ ܝܗܒܬܘܢ ܠܝ

Codex A.

[a]ܘܐܡܪܐ ܠܝܫܘܥ
ܐܠܝܫ ܐܠܗܐ ܐܠܝܫ
ܡܢ ܡܠܐܟܐ[a]

[a]ܠܬܠܡܝܕܘܗܝ [b]ܒܪܗ

[e]ܡܠܐܟܘܗܝ [f]ܝܬܒ

[g]ܡܠܟܘܬܗ

‡ f. 75b.

[i]ܠܩܕܡܘܗܝ

[j]ܡܦܪܫ

[n]ܒܟܝܢ [p]ܝܡܝܢܗ

[q]ܡܒܪܟܝܢ

[r]ܝܪܬܘܢ [t]ܫܪܘܝܗ

[u]ܕܥܠܡܐ

[x]ܕܐܝܟܘܠ [y] omit ܘ

[z]ܐܟܣܢܝܐ

[b]ܥܪܛܠܝ

[c]ܐܬܟܪܗܬ

[e]ܘܐܬܝܬܘܢ [f]ܠܘܬܝ

[g]ܒܟܝܢ [k]ܚܡܝܢܢ

[l]ܟܦܢ [m]ܘܝܗܒܢ

[n]ܨܗܐ [o]ܘܐܫܩܝܢܢ

[p]ܐܟܣܢܝܐ

[q]ܘܟܢܫܢܢ

[r] omit ܐܘ . . . ܝܬܟ

‡ f. 76a.

[u]ܟܪܝܗ [v]ܒܡܛܪܬܐ

[w]ܘܐܬܝܢ [z]ܐܡܪܢܐ

[a]ܐܚܝ [b]ܒܟܝܢ

[e]ܕܠܥܠܡ [i]ܠܣܛܢܐ

Codex C.

[a]ܠܗܘܢ ܐܠܝܫ ܚܕ
ܐܠܝܫ ܡܢ ܡܠܐܟܐ[a]

[z]add ܘܒܬܫܡܫܬܗܘܢ

[a]ܠܬܠܡܝܕܘܗܝ [b]ܒܪܗ

[d]ܒܫܒܚܘܬܗ

[e]ܡܠܐܟܘܗܝ [f]ܝܬܒ

[g]ܡܠܟܘܬܐ

[i]ܠܩܕܡܘܗܝ [k]ܡܦܪܫ

[l]ܘܡܩܝܡ

[o] omit ܝܐܡܪ

[s]ܕܡܬܩܢܐ [w]ܒܦܢܬ

[y] omit ܘ [a]ܗܘܝܬ

[b]ܥܪܛܠܝ

[c]ܐܬܟܪܗܬ

[d] omit ܠܝ

† f. 67b.

[e]ܘܐܬܝܬܘܢ

[h] omit ܠܗ [j]ܡܪܢ

[k]ܚܡܝܢܢ

[m] omit ܘܝܗܒܢ ܝܬܟ

[n]ܨܗܐ [o]ܘܐܫܩܝܢ

[q]ܘܟܢܫܢ [t]ܘܐܠܒܫܢ

[c]ܚܡܝܢܢ [x]ܡܓܝܒ

[y]add ܐܡܝܢ

[a] omit ܐܚܘܝ

[c]ܣܡܠܗ

[d]ܠܝܛܝܐ

[k]ܘܠܡܠܐܟܘܗܝ

Codex B.

[l]ܕܡܝܟܘܠ : ܘܨܗܝܬ ܘܠܐ ܐܫܩܝܬܘܢ ܝܬܝ :
43 [m]ܐܟܣܢܝ ܗܘܝܬ ܘܠܐ ܟܢܫܬܘܢ ܝܬܝ :
[n][o]ܥܪܛܠܝ ܘܠܐ ܐܠܒܫܬܘܢ ܝܬܝ[o] : ܒܐܝܫ
44 [p]ܘܒܒܝܬ ܐܣܘܪܐ ܘܠܐ ܣܥܪܬܘܢ ܝܬܝ : [q]ܒܟܝܢ
ܝܥܢܘܢ [r] ܐܘܦ [s]ܘܐܡܪܝܢ [t]ܡܪܢ ܐܡܬܝ
[u]ܚܡܝܢܢ ܝܬܟ : [v]ܟܦܢ ܐܘ [w]ܨܗܝ ܐܘ [x]
[y]ܐܟܣܢܝ : [z]ܐܘ [a]ܥܪܛܠܝ[z] ܐܘ ܒܐܝܫ ܐܘ̈
45 [b]ܒܒܝܬܐ : ܘܠܐ [c]ܫܡܫܢܝܢ ܝܬܟ : [q]ܒܟܝܢ [d]ܝܥܢܐ
ܐܘܦ ܠܗܘܢ [f]ܘܐܡܪ : [h]ܐܡܝܢ ܐܡܪ ܐܢܐ
ܠܟܘܢ : [i]ܕܟܕ ܐܡܬܝ ܕܠܐ ܥܒܕܬܘܢ ܠܚܕ
ܡܢ ܗܠܝܢ ܙܥܘܪܝܐ ܐܘܦ [k]ܠܝ ܠܐ ܥܒܕܬܘܢ :
46 [l]ܘܐܙܠܘܢ [n]ܠܝܩܕܐ ܗܠܝܢ[n] [o]ܕܠܥܠܡ ܘܨܕܝܩܝܐ
ܠܚܝܝܐ [o]ܕܠܥܠܡ ⁘

Codex A.

[l]ܕܡܝܟܘܠ
[m]ܐܟܣܢܝܐ
[n]ܘܥܪܛܠܝܐ
[p]ܘܒܒܝܬ ܐܣܘܪܐ [q]ܒܟܝܢ
[r] add ܗܢܘܢ
[s]ܘܡܐܡܪܝܢ
[u]ܚܡܝܢܢ [v]ܒܟܝܢ
[w]ܨܗܝܐ [y]ܐܟܣܢܝܐ
[a]ܥܪܛܠܝܐ
[b]ܒܒܝܬܐ [c]ܫܡܫܢܝܢܟ
[h] add ܐܡܝܢ
[k] add ܠܐ [i] add ܟܠ
[l]ܘܐܙܠܘܢ
[n]ܗܠܝܢ ܠܝܩܕܐ[n]
[o]ܕܠܥܠܡ

Codex C.

[o] omit ܥܪܛܠܝ ... ܝܬܝ
[r] add ܗܢܘܢ
[t]ܡܪܢ
[x] add ܐܘ ܥܪܛܠܝ
[z] omit ܐܘ ܥܪܛܠܝ
[d]ܝܥܢܐ [f]ܘܐܡܪ
[h] add ܐܡܝܢ
[i] add ܟܠ
[k] add ܠܐ
[l]ܘܐܙܠܘ

CXXI.

Matt. VI. 1—13.

Codex B.

[a]ܘܦܪܐ ܝܘܡ ܥܪܘܒܬ ܡܪܥܒ [b]ܐܠܝܗܘܢ ܡܢ
1 ܡܬܐܘܣ[a][b]: [w]† ܐܡܪ [x]ܡܪܢܐ [y]ܝܫܘܥ [z]ܐܣܬܟܠܘ
[a]ܠܝܕܡܫܒܚܘܢ ܕܠܐ [b]ܬܗܘܘܢ [b]ܥܒܕܝܢ ܩܘܕܡ
ܒܢܝܢܫܐ : ܗܝܟ [c]ܕܬܬܚܡܘܢ ܠܗܘܢ : [d]ܐܘ ܕܝ
[e]ܠܝܬ [f]ܐܓܪ [g]ܐܝܬ ܠܟܘܢ [h]ܡܢ ܠܘܬ ܐܒܘܟܘܢ
2 ܕܒܫܡܝܐ : ܟܕ ܐܘܢ [i]ܗܘܝܬܐ ܥܒܕ ܨܕܩܐ
ܠܐ [j]ܬܩܪܝܢ[k] [l]ܩܕܡܝܟ ܗܝܟ ܡܐ ܕܥܒܪܝܢܐ
ܥܒܕܝܢ ܟܢ [m]ܒܟܢܫܬܐ ܘܒܫܘܩܐ ܘܒܫܘܩܝܐ
ܫܘܩܝܐ : ܠܡܒܥܠ ܕܝܫܬܒܚܘܢ ܡܢ ܒܢܝܢܫܐ :
[n]ܐܡܝܢ [o]ܐܡܪ ܐܢܐ[o] ܠܟܘܢ ܕܩܒܠܘ [p]ܐܓܪܗܘܢ :
[f. 67b]
3 ܐܢܬ ܕܝ ܟܕ ܗܘܝܬ ܥܒܕ ܨܕܩܐ ܠܐ [q]ܬܘܕܥ
4 [r]ܣܡܐܠܟ ܡܐ ܥܒܕܐ [s]ܝܡܝܢܟ : [t]ܠܡܠܠ
ܕܬܗܘܐ ܨܕܩܬܟ [u]ܒܛܡܝܪܘ [v]ܘܐܒܘܟ ܕܚܙܐ
[w]ܝܬܟ [x]ܒܛܡܝܪܘ ܗܘ ܝܦܪܥ ܠܟ [y]ܒܓܠܝ :
5 ܘܟܕ ܬܗܘܘܢ ܡܨܠܝܢ ܠܐ ܬܗܘܘܢ ܗܝܟ ܡܐ

Codex A.

[b]ܐܠܝܗܘܢ ܡܢ
‡ f. 76b. [b]ܡܬܐܘܣ‡
[y] omit ܝܫܘܥ
[a]ܠܝܕܡܫܒܚܘܢ
[f]ܐܓܪܐ [g]ܠܝܬ
[h] omit ܡܢ [j]ܬܩܪܐ
[k] add ܩܪܢܐ
[l]ܩܘܕܡܝܟ
[o]ܐܡܝܢܐ
[p]ܐܓܪܗܘܢ
[q]ܬܕܥ [r]ܣܡܠܟ
[s]ܝܡܝܢܟ [t]ܠܡܠܠ
[u]ܒܛܡܝܪܘ
[v]ܐܒܘܟ
[w] omit ܝܬܟ
[x]ܒܛܡܝܪܘ
[y]ܒܓܠܝܐ

Codex C.

[a]ܠܝܘܡ ܥܪܘܒܬ ܡܪܥܒ ܐܠܝܗܘܢ ܡܢ ܡܬܝ[a]
† f. 68a.
[w] add ܘܐܡܪ ܠܬܠܡܝܕܘܗܝ
[z] add ܡܫܝܚܐ [x]ܡܪܢ
[a]ܠܝܕܡܫܒܚܘܢ
[b]ܥܒܕܝܢ [b]ܬܗܘܘܢ
[c]ܕܬܬܚܡܘܢ
[e]ܠܝ [d]ܐܡܢ
[g]ܠܝܬ [f]ܐܓܪ
[h] omit ܡܢ [i]ܬܗܐ (sic)
[j]ܬܩܪܐ [m]ܒܟܢܫܬܐ
[n] add ܐܡܝܢ
[q]ܬܘܕܥ [r]ܣܡܠܟ
[s]ܝܡܝܢܟ [u]ܒܛܡܝܪܘ
[v]ܐܒܘܟ
[w] omit ܝܬܟ

Codex A.	*Codex* B.	*Codex* C.
[a] ܒܟܢܫܬܐ [b] ܩܝܡܝܢ	ܕܫܘܩܝܐ : [z] ܕܗܘܘܢ ܪܚܡܝܢ ܕܗܘܘܢ ܩܝܡܘ	[z] *omit* ܕܗܘܘܢ
[p] ܐܓܪܗܘܢ	[a] ܒܟܢܫܬܐ ܘܒܙܘܝܬܐ ܕܫܘܩܝܐ [b] ܩܐܡܝܢ ܡܨܠܝܢ :	[b] ܩܝܡܝܢ
[d] ܕܝܢ [e] ܘܐܚܕ	ܠܒܕܠ [c] ܕܢܬܚܘܘܢ ܠܒܢܝܢܫܐ : ܐܡܝܢ ܐܡܪ	[c] ܕܢܬܚܙܘܢ
[f] ܠܐܒܘܟ [g] ܠܗ	6 ܐܢܐ ܠܟܘܢ ܕܢܣܒܘ [p] ܐܓܪܗܘܢ :* ܐܢܬ [d] ܕܝ	[* Cod. B ܐܓܪܗܘܢ *sic.*]
‡ f. 77*a*.	ܟܕ ܬܗܘܐ ܡܨܠܐ : ‡ ܥܘܠ ܠܝ ܠܬܘܢܟ : [e] ܘܐܚܕ	
[h] *add* ܫܡܥܐ	ܬܪܥܐ : ܘܨܠܝ [f] ܠܐܒܘܟ [g] ܠܕܝ ܕܒܛܘܫܝܐ [h]	[e] ܘܐܚܕ [f] ܠܐܒܘܟ
[i] ܘܐܒܘܟ [j] ܝܦܪܥ	[i] ܘܐܒܘܟ ܕܚܙܐ ܒܛܘܫܝܐ [j] ܝܦܪܥ ܠܟ :[k]	[g] *omit* ܠܕܝ
[k] *add* ܒܓܠܝܐ	7 ܘܟܕ ܬܗܘܘܢ ܡܨܠܝܢ ܠܐ [l] ܐܡܪܝܢ ܡܠܝܢ ܒܛܠܢ	[i] ܘܐܒܘܟ
[l] ܐܡܪܝܢ	ܗܝܟ ܡܐ ܕܥܒܕܝܢ ܥܡܡܝܐ ܣܒܪܝܢ ܗܘܝܢ	[k] *add* ܒܓܠܝܐ
	8 ܕܝ ܕܒܣܓܝܐܘܬ ܡܠܝܗܘܢ ܡܬܫܡܥܝܢ : ܠܐ	
[m] ܐܒܘܟܘܢ	ܐܘܢ ܬܕܡܘܢ ܠܗܘܢ : ܝܕܥ ܗܘ [m] ܐܒܘܟܘܢ	[m] ܐܒܘܟܘܢ
	ܡܐ ܐܢܬܘܢ ܨܪܝܟܝܢ ܥܕ ܠܐ [n] ܬܫܐܠܘܢ	[n] ܬܫܐܠܘܢ
[p] ܫܡܝܐ	9 † ܗܟܢ : ܗܟܕܝܢ ܐܘܢ [o] ܐܢܬܘܢ ܗܘܘ ܡܨܠܝܢ :	† f. 68*b*.
[q] ܘܬܝܬܐ [r] ܝܬܥܒܕ	ܐܒܘܢ ܕܒܫܡܝܐ [p] ܫܡܝܐ ܝܬܩܕܫ ܫܡܟ	[o] *omit* ܐܢܬܘܢ
[s] ܕܬܕܝܪܐ	10 [q] ܬܝܬܐ ܡܠܟܘܬܟ [r] ܝܬܥܒܕ ܨܒܝܢܟ : ܗܝܟ	[q] ܘܬܝܬܐ
[t] ܝܘܡܕܝܢ	11 ܡܐ ܕܒܫܡܝܐ ܐܘܦ ܥܠ ܐܪܥܐ : ܠܚܡܢ	[s] ܕܬܕܝܪܐ
[u] ܠܚܝܒܝܢ	12 [s] ܕܬܕܝܪ ܗܒ ܠܢ [t] ܝܘܡܕܝܢ : ܘܫܒܘܩ ܠܢ	[u] ܠܚܝܒܝܢ
[v] ܬܥܠ [w] ܠܢܣܝܘܢ	ܚܘܒܝܢ ܗܝܟ ܕܐܘܦ ܐܢܢ ܫܒܩܝܢ [u] ܠܚܝܒܝܢ :	[v] ܬܥܠ
[x] ܦܨܝ [y] *add* ܟܠ	13 ܘܠܐ [v] ܬܥܠ ܝܬܢ [w] ܠܢܣܝܘܢ : ܐܠܐ [x] ܦܨܝ	[w] ܠܢܣܝܘܢ [z] ܕܕܝܠܟ
[a] ܘܬܫܒܘܚܬܐ	ܝܬܢ ܡܢ ܒܝܫܐ [y] [z] ܕܕܝܠܟ ܗܝ ܡܠܟܘܬܐ	[a] ܘܬܫܒܘܚܬܐ
[b] *omit* ܥܠܡ	ܘܚܝܠܐ [a] ܘܬܫܒܘܚܬܐ ܠܥܠܡܝܐ ܐܡܝܢ : [b] ܥܠܡ ∴	[b] *omit* ܥܠܡ

CXXII.

MATT. VI. 14—21.

Codex A.	*Codex* B.	*Codex* C.
[a] ܗܘܟ ܚܕ ܐܠܝܦܘܢ ܡܢ ܡܬܐܘܣ [a]	[a] ܩܪܝܢܐ ܗܘܟ ܚܕ ܡܦܪܫ ܐܠܝܦܘܢ ܡܢ ܡܬܐܘܣ :[a]	[a] ܠܝܘܡ ܐܠܝܦܘܢ ܡܪܦܘܣ ܐܠܝܦܘܢ ܡܢ ܡܬܐܘܣ [a]
[x] *add* ܓܝܪ	[f. 68*a*]	[w] *add* ܘܬܘܒ ܡܪܢ ܝܫܘܥ
‡ f. 77*b*.	14 [w] ܐܡܪ ܡܪܢ ܝܫܘܥ [x] ܐܢ ܬܫܒܩܘܢ ܠܒܢܝܢܫܐ	[x] *add* ܓܝܪ
[y] ܐܒܘܟܘܢ	ܣܪܘܚܢܘܬܗܘܢ ܐܘܦ ‡ [y] ܐܒܘܟܘܢ ܕܒܫܡܝܐ	[y] ܐܒܘܟܘܢ
[b] ܣܪܘܚܢܘܬܟܘܢ	15 ܫܡܝܐ ܝܫܒܘܩ ܠܟܘܢ ܣܪܘܚܢܘܬܟܘܢ : ܐܢ	[z] *add* ܗܟܢ
	ܕܝ [z] [a] ܠܐ ܬܫܒܩܘܢ ܠܒܢܝܢܫܐ [b] ܣܪܘܚܢܘܬܗܘܢ :	[a] *omit* ܠܐ
	ܐܘܦ ܠܐ [y] ܐܒܘܟܘܢ [c] ܠܐ ܝܫܒܘܩ ܠܟܘܢ	[b] ܣܪܘܚܢܘܬܗܘܢ
		[c] *add* ܕܒܫܡܝܐ

Codex A.

ᵍܘܫܡܝ
ˡܐܦܛܪܘܦܐ
ᵐܐܟܘܡܪܝܟܘܢ
ⁿܐܩܫܝܢ ᵒܠܥܠܡ
ᑫ*omit* ܕܝ ʳܠܐܩܘܡܢ
ˢܘܐܚܝܢ
ᵗ*omit* ܠܢ
ʷܐܘܣܦܝܢ
ˣܡܣܝܒܐܘܢ
ᶻܐܡܪܘ
ᵃܡܣܝܒܢ
ᵉܡܣܝܒܘܬܟܘܢ
ᶠܠܒܢܝܟܘܢ ᵍܗܘܝܐ

‡ f. 78*a*.

Codex B.

16 ܡܫܠܡܘܢܬܟܘܢ : ᵈܘܟܕ ܬܗܘܘܢ ܣܢܐܝܢ ܠܐ
ܬܗܘܘܢ ܣܢܝܢ ܡܢ ܟܠ ܕܒܫܡܝ: ܒܓܝܢ ᵉܐܫܡܝ :
ᶠܣܘܓܝ ᵍܗܘܢ ʰܐܩܝܡܘܢ ʰܠܒܝܬ ⁱܕܝܢܘܬܟܘܢ
ܠܡܠܟܐ ܘܫܠܝܛܝܢ: ᵏܐܡܝܢ ˡܐܡܪ ܐܢܐ ˡܠܟܘܢ
17 ܕܝܡܟܠܘ ᵐܐܟܘܡܪܝܟܘܢ : ܐܦ ܕܝ ܟܕ ܬܗܘܐ
ܐܝܟ ܡܢܟܘܢ ܣܘܦ ܠܪܫܟܘܢ ܘܐܫܝܬ ⁿܐܩܫܝܢ
18 ᵒܠܥܠܡ ܕܠܐ ᵖܬܬܚܙܝܐ ᑫܕܝ ܠܡܠܟܐ ܐܝܟ :
ܐܠܐ ʳܠܐܩܘܡܢ ܕܒܚܘܒܪܐ : ˢܘܐܚܝܢ
19 ܕܣܢܐ ᵗܠܢ ܟܦܘܪܢܐ † ܒܐܪܐ ܠܢ ᵘ: ܠܐ
ܬܗܘܢ ʷܐܘܣܦܝܢ ܠܟܘܢ ˣܡܣܝܒܐܘܢ ܒܠ
ܐܪܒܐ : ܗܢ ܕܡܣܒܐ ܘܐܩܠܝܐ ܡܪܢ : ܘܗܢ
20 ʸܕܒܒܝܐ ܚܝܪܝܢ ܘܒܒܝܢ : ᶻܐܡܪܘ ܠܟܘܢ ܕܝ
ᵃܡܣܝܒܢ ܒܗ ܥܡܡܐ : ܗܢ ܕܠܐ ᵇܡܡܢܐ
ܘܠܐ ܐܩܠܝܐ ܡܪܢ : ܘܗܢ ܕܠܝܬ ܒܒܝܢ ܚܝܪܝܢ
21 ܘܒܒܝܢ : ܗܢ ᶜܒܪ ᵈܗܘܝܐ ᵉܡܣܝܒܘܬܟܘܢ
ܬܡܢ ‡ܐܘܦ ᶠܠܒܢܝܟܘܢ ᵍܗܘܝܐ ∴

Codex C.

ᵈܗܘܝܢ ᵉܐܫܡܝ
ᶠܣܘܓܝܢ
ʰܐܩܝܡܘܢ ʰ*omit*
ܠܒܝܬ
ⁱܕܝܢܘܬܟܘܢ
ᵏ*add* ܐܡܝܢ ⁿܐܩܫܝܢ
ᵖܬܬܚܙܝܐ ܕܝ ᑫ*omit*
ʳܠܐܩܘܡܢ ˢܘܐܚܝܢ
ᵘ*add* ܒܟܠܗ

† f. 69*a*.

ʷܐܘܣܦܝܢ
ˣܡܣܝܒܐܘܢ
ʸܕܒܒܝܐ ᶻܐܡܪܘ
ᵃܡܣܝܒܢ
ᵇܡܡܢܐ ᶜܒܪ
ᵈܗܘܝܐ ᵈܗܘܝܐ
ᵉܡܣܝܒܘܬܟܘܢ
ᶠܠܒܢܝܟܘܢ ᵍܗܘܝܐ

CXXIII.

LUKE XXI. 8—15*a*, 25—36.

Codex A.

ᵇ*omit* ܗܕܗ
ᶜܐܝܟܘܢ
ᵈܐܠܦܐܕܫܒܐ
ᵈ: ܢܘܡܐ
ᵉ*add* ܒܫ ܐܡܪ ܗܘ
ܐܠܗܐ
ᵉܩܪܒ ᶠܬܐܠܘܢ
ᵍ*omit* ܕܝ
ʰܩܪܒܝܢ ⁱܘܫܓܘܫܝܢ
ᵐ*add* ܗܘܐ ܥܒܕܐ ᵏܕܝܗܘܢ
ⁿܫܘܠܡܐ
ᵒܢܩܘܡܘܢ ᵖܥܡܡ
ᑫܘܙܘܥܝܢ ʳܪܘܪܒܝܢ
ˢܘܡܘܬܢܝܢ

Codex B.

ᵃᵇܗܕܗ ܐܘܢܓܠܝܘܢ ܕܬܪܝܢ ܒܫ ᶜܐܝܟܘܢ ܐܠܦܐܕܫ
ܒܫ ᵈܐܡܪ ᵈܐܠܗܐ ܢܘܡ ܐܠܬܝܢ ܒܝܢܘ ᵉܡܢ
8 ܠܬܠܡܝܕܝ ᵃ: ܐܡܪ ܡܪܢ ᵃܢܫܝܘ ܚܙܘ ᶜܕܠܐ
ܬܛܥܘܢ : ܣܓܝ ܓܝܪ ܢܐܬܘܢ ܒܫܡܝ ܐܡܪܝܢ
ܐܢܐ ܗܘ : ᵉܘܙܒܢܐ ᵉܩܪܒ ܠܐ ᶠܬܐܠܘܢ
[f. 68*b*]
9 ܒܬܪܗܘܢ ܟܕ ᵍܕܝ ܬܫܡܥܘܢ ʰܩܪܒܝܢ ⁱܘܫܓܘܫܝܢ
ܠܐ ܬܬܪܗܒܘܢ : ܢܦܠܘܢ ܒܪ ܠܥܠܡ ᵏܕܝܗܘܢ
10 ˡܗܕܝܢ ܐܠܐ ܠܐ ᵐܗܘܐ ⁿܫܘܠܡܐ : ܟܕܝܢ ܐܡܪ
*ܠܗܘܢ ᵒܢܩܘܡܘܢ ᵖܥܡܡܝܢ ܥܠ ᵖܥܡܡܝܢ ܘܡܠܟܘ
11 ܥܠ ܡܠܟܘ : ᑫܘܙܘܥܝܢ ʳܪܘܪܒܝܢ ܒܐܬܪܝܢ ܐܬܪܝܢ
ܘܟܦܢܝܢ ˢܘܡܘܬܢܝܢ ܢܗܘܘܢ : ᵗܘܕܚܠܝܢ ܘܐܬܝܢ

Codex C.

ᵃܗܕܗ ܐܘܢܓܠܝܘܢ ܕ
ܬܪܝܢ ܒܫ ܐܠܦܐܕܫܒܐ
ܐܬܩܪܝܬ ܐܠܬܝܢ
ܒܫܡܐ ܢܘܡܐ ܐܠܬܝܢ
ᵃܡܢ ܠܬܠܡܝܕܝ
ᵃ*add* ܘܐܡܪ ܡܪܢ ܠܬܠܡܝܕܘܗܝ
ᶠܬܐܠܘܢ ʰܩܪܒܝܢ
ᵏܕܝܗܘܢ ᵐ*add* ܗܘܐ ܥܒܕܐ
ⁿܫܘܠܡܐ ᵒܢܩܘܡܘܢ
ᵖܥܡܡ ᑫܘܙܘܥܝܢ
[* Cod. B ܠܗܘܢ]
ʳܪܘܪܒܝܢ
ˢܡܘܬܢܝܢ ᵗܘܕܚܠܝܢ

Codex A.

[u] ܙ̈ܒܢܝܢ
[w] ܐܢܕܪܝܗܘܢ
[y] ܘܒܫܘܦܪܗܘܢ
[z] *omit* ܢܬܒܘܢ
[b] ܗܡܝܡܢܝܢ [c] ܠܟܠܟܠ
[e] ܒܠܒܒܗܘܢ
‡ f. 78b.
[f] ܡܬܠܚܡܝܢ
[g] ܕܬܬܠܘܢ
[i] ܒܥܡܠܐ
[k] ܠܡܣܝܒ
[n] ܘܕܘܒܪܐ
[o] ܕܢܦܩܝܢ [p] ܢܦܫܬܐ
[r] ܫܘܒܚܐ [s] ܕܐܬܝܬܐ
[w] ܠܒܪܗ [a] ܕܫܘܒܚܐ
[b] ܘܬܫܒܘܚܬܐ
[c] ܐܕܘܢ [e] ܕܦܘܪܩܢ
[s] ܦܘܪܩܢܗܘܢ
[t] ܬܘܬܬܐ [u] ܐܠܗܐ
[w] ܒܟܢܝܪ [x] ܕܢܒܘܢ
[y] ܫܪܕܐ
[z] ܡܬܒܒܕܝܢ
[a] ܕܒܗ [b] *omit* ܗܝ
[e] *omit* ܐܢܐ
[g] ܢܒܒܪܘܢ
‡ f. 79a.
[i] ܐܫܬܟܚܘ [k] ܢܦܪܘܢ
[m] ܘܡܣܟܢܘܢ
[o] ܐܬܩܢܗ
[r] *omit* ܐܬܘܢ

T

Codex B.

12 [u] ܙ̈ܒܢܝܢ ܡܢ ܫܘܡܠܝܐ ܚܝܠܗܘܢ : ܘܡܢ ܦܘܩܕܢ
ܗܠܝܢ ܒܗܠܝܢ ܢܩܡܘܢ ܒܠܒܗܘܢ [w] ܐܢܕܪܝܗܘܢ [x]
ܘܢܙܕܗܘܢ ܢܬܒܘܢ [y] ܘܢܫܬܪܘܢ [z] ܢܬܒܘܢ
ܒܚܫܝܫܘܬܐ ܘܒܫܘܒܩܢܐ [a] ܘܬܬܝܒܘܢ ܠܦܘܩܕܢ
ܡܠܟܝܢ ܘܠܦܘܩܕܢ [b] ܗܡܝܡܢܝܢ [c] ܠܟܠܟܠ ܫܢܝܢ :
13 14 [d] ܡܠܟܐ ܗ̇ܢ ܠܗܘܢ ܗܠܝܢ ܠܦܘܩܕܢ :: † ܐܫܬܡܥܘ
ܐܘ [e] ܒܠܒܗܘܢ ‡ ܕܠܐ ܡܢ ܦܘܩܕܢ ܬܗܘܘܢ
[f] ܡܬܠܚܡܝܢ [g] ܕܬܬܠܘܢ [h] ܐܬܩܠܦܢܐ : ܐܝܟ ܓܪ
25 ܢܬܠ ܠܗܘܢ ܟܡ ܘܫܘܒܚܐ : ܘܢܗܘܘܢ ܐܬܝܢ
[i] ܒܥܡܠܐ ܘܒܨܘܪܐ ܘܒܟܘܒܝܐ : ܘܒܠ ܐܘܪܚܐ
[k] ܠܫܘܝܢ ܕܡܫܝܚ [l] ܟܬܡܫܝܚܘܬܗ ܕܟܠܗ ܕܥܡܐ
26 [n] ܘܕܘܒܪܝܐ : [o] ܕܢܦܩܝܢ [p] ܢܦܫܬܐ ܕܒܫܝܢܐ ܡܢ
[q] ܕܫܠܡܬܐ : ܘܡܢ [r] ܫܘܒܚܐ ܕܗܠܝܢ [s] ܕܐܬܝܢ ܒܠ
[t] ܒܡܬܪܬܐ : [u] ܫܠܝܐ ܓܪ ܕܫܘܒܚܐ [v] ܢܕܒܪܘܢ :
27 ܘܒܟܝܢ ܢܫܒܚܘܢ [w] ܠܒܪܗ ܕܒܪܝܐ ܐܬܐ ܒܠ
ܒܢܫܘܗܘܢ [a] ܕܫܘܒܚܐ ܒܡ ܫܠ [b] ܘܬܫܒܘܚܬܐ
28 ܗܟܢ : [c] ܐܕܘܢ ܘܬܠܘܢ [d] ܙܢܝܚܘܢ [e] ܕܦܘܪܩܢ
29 [s] ܦܘܪܩܢܗܘܢ : ܘܐܡܪ ܠܗܘܢ ܡܬܠ : ܫܡܥܬܘܢ
30 [t] ܬܘܬܐ ܘܟܘܠ [u] ܐܠܗܐ : ܒܕ ܢܦܩܘܢ [w] ܒܟܢܝܪ
[f. 69a] ܡܦܪܟܝܢ : ܫܡܥ ܡܢܗܘܢ [x] ܢܕܒܘܢ ܕܦܘܪܩܢ ܗܘ
31 [w] ܒܟܢܝܪ [y] ܫܪܕܐ : ܗܟܕܝܢ ܐܘܦ ܐܬܘܢ ܒܕ
ܬܫܒܚܘܢ ܗܠܝܢ [z] ܡܬܒܒܕܝܢ [a] ܕܒܗ ܕܦܘܪܩܢܬ
32 [b] ܗܝ [c] ܡܠܟܘܬܗ ܕܐܠܗܐ : ܐܡܝܢ [d] ܐܡܪ [e] ܐܢܐ
ܠܗܘܢ ܕܠܐ ܢܒܒܘܪ ܗܕܝܢ ܕܐܪܐ ܒܕܡܐ
33 ܕܒܘܠܐ [f] ܡܬܒܒܢܝ ܫܘܒܚܐ ܘܐܪܒܐ [g] ܢܒܒܪܘܢ
34 ܘܟܠܗ ܕܠܗ ܠܐ ‡ [h] ܢܒܒܪܘܢ : [i] ܐܫܬܟܚܘ ܕܝ
ܠܓܪܡܗܘܢ ܕܠܐ [k] ܢܦܪܘܢ ܠܒܒܗܘܢ ܒܬܐܝܢ
ܕܫܡܝܐ ܘܒܪܘܚܐ [m] ܘܡܣܟܢܝܢ [n] ܕܒܠܝܛ : ܘܦܩܕ
35 ܒܠܒܗܘܢ ܢܬܗ ܢܡܘܣܐ ܡܢ ܥܠܝܐ ܗܢܝܢ ܒܢ
36 ܗܘ ܐܬܐ ܒܠ ܒܘܠ [o] ܐܬܩܢܗ ܕܐܪܒܐ : ܘܗܘ [p]
[q] ܥܡܪܝܢ ܒܟܠ ܢܝܪܗ : ܒܟܝܢ [r] ܐܬܘܢ

Codex C.

[x] *add* ܒܫܝܢܐ
[z] ܠܗܘܢ
[a] ܘܬܬܝܗܒܘܢ
[d] ܡܠܟܐ
† f. 69b.
[e] ܒܠܒܗܘܢ [g] ܕܬܬܠܘܢ
[h] ܐܬܩܠܦܢܐ
[k] ܠܡܣܝܒ
[l] ܟܬܒܘܬܗ
[n] ܘܕܘܒܪܝܐ [o] ܢܦܩܝܢ
[q] ܕܫܠܡܬܗܘܢ
[u] ܫܠܝܐ [v] ܕܢܕܒܪܘܢ
[w] ܠܒܪܗ
[d] ܙܢܝܚܘܢ
[s] ܦܘܪܩܢܗܘܢ
[w] ܒܟܢܝܪ
[x] ܕܢܒܘܢ
[b] *omit* ܗܝ
[c] ܡܠܟܘܬܐ
[d] *add* ܐܡܝܢ
[f] ܡܬܒܒܢܝ ܘܟܠܗ [f]
[h] ܢܒܒܪܘܢ
[k] ܢܦܪܘܢ
[m] ܘܡܣܟܢܘܢ
[n] ܕܒܠܝܛ [o] ܐܬܩܢܗ
[p] *add* ܗܝ [q] ܥܡܪܝܢ

Codex A.	Codex B.	Codex C.
[s]ܕܬܬܩܠܘܢ	[s]ܕܬܬܩܠܘܢ ܒܪܘܚ ܡܢ [u]ܗܠܝܢ ܕܥܬܝܕܝܢ ܕܝܗܘܢ :	[s]ܕܬܬܩܠܘܢ
[u]*add* ܟܘܠ [x]ܕܒܢܝܢܫܐ	† [w]ܘܬܬܩܝܡܘܢ ܩܕܡ ܒܪܗ [x]ܕܓܒܪܐ	[u]*add* ܟܘܠ
[y]*omit* ܫܠܡ	[y]ܫܠܡ ∴	† f. 70*a*.
		[w]ܘܬܬܩܘܡܘܢ
		[x]ܕܒܢܝܢܫܐ [y]*omit* ܫܠܡ

CXXIV.

Matt. VI. 1.

Codex A.	Codex B.	Codex C.
[b]ܐܙܕܗܪܘܢ	[a]ܐܡܪ ܐܠܗܐ ܒܒܣܪܗ [b]ܐܙܕܗܪܘ [c]ܘܡܐ ܗܒܬ	[a]ܠܡܐܡ [c]ܗܘܐ
[d]ܐܠܗܟܘܢ ܗܘܐ ܒܝ	ܡܘܗܒ [e d]ܐܠܗܟܘܢ [f]ܡܢ ܒܬܪܐ [d f] [a]ܐܡܪ	[e]ܐܠܗܟܘܢ
[d]ܡܬܝܗܒ	1 ܒܪܐ ܗܘܝܘܢ : [a]ܐܬܚܙܝܘ [b]ܠܒܢܝ ܢܫܐ : [c]ܕܝ	ܡܢ ܒܬܪܐ [f]*omit*
[a]*omit* ܐܡܪ ܒܪܐ	ܠܐ [d]ܬܗܘܘܢ [d]ܒܒܬܝܢ ܩܕܡ ܒܢܝܢܫܐ ∴	[c]*omit* ܕܝ
ܗܘܝܘܢ :		[d]ܬܗܘܘܢ ܒܒܬܝܢ [d]
[b]ܠܒܢܝ ܢܫܐ		
[c]*omit* ܕܝ		

CXXV.

Mark XI. 22—25.

Codex A.	Codex B.	Codex C.
[a]ܐܡܪ	[a]ܐܡܪ ܐܠܗܢܐ ܒܒܣܪܗ [a]ܡܢ ܡܪܢܘܗܝ : [a]ܘܐܡܪ	[a]ܗܘܐ ܠܡܐܡ
ܐܢ [b]*add* [c]ܬܗܘܐ	22 ܒܪܐ ܗܘܝܘܢ ܘܐܡܪ ܠܗܘܢ : [b] [c]ܬܗܘܐ ܒܟܘܢ	[a]ܐܠܗܢܐ ܒܒܣܪܗ
[g]*omit* ܘܗܘܐ	23 ܗܝܡܢܘܬܗ ܕܐܠܗܐ : ܐܡܝܢ ܐܡܪ ܐܢܐ ܠܟܘܢ	[a]ܐܡܪ [f]ܕܝܐܡܪ
[h]ܘܐܬܥܩܪܝ	ܕܡܢ [f]ܝܐܡܪ ܠܛܘܪܐ ܗܢܐ ܐܬܥܩܪ [g]ܘܗܘܐ	[g]*omit* ܘܗܘܐ
[i]ܘܬܬܪܡܝ [k]ܕܡܦܠܠ	[h]ܐܬܥܩܪ ܠܝܡܐ ܘܠܐ [i]ܬܬܦܠܓ ܒܠܒܗ : ܐܠܐ	[h]ܘܐܬܥܩܪܝ [i]ܘܬܬܦܠܓ
[l]ܬܬܥܒܕ [m]ܕܝܐܡܪ	[j]ܝܗܝܡܢ ܕܗܘ [k]ܕܡܡܠܠ [l]ܬܬܥܒܕ : ܝܗܘܐ ܠܗ	[j]*omit* ܝܗܝܡܢ
[p]ܡܗܝܡܢܝܢ	24 ܟܘܠ ܡܐ [m]ܕܝܐܡܪ : ܠܗܕܐ [f. 69*b*] ܟܕܝܢ ܐܢܐ [n]ܐܡܪ	[k]ܡܡܠܠ [l]ܬܬܥܒܕ
‡ f 79*b*.	ܠܟܘܢ ܕܟܘܠ ܡܐ [o]ܕܬܫܐܠܘܢ [‡] ܟܕ ܬܗܘܘܢ	[n]ܐܡܪ
[q]ܘܬܬܥܒܕ	ܡܨܠܝܢ ܗܘܘ [p]ܡܗܝܡܢܝܢ ܕܐܬܝܬܘܢ ܢܣܒܝܢ [q]ܘܡܬܥܒܕ	[o]ܕܬܫܐܠܘܢ
	25 ܠܟܘܢ : ܘܟܕ ܐܬܝܢ [r]ܡܩܝܡܝܢ ܡܨܠܝܢ ܗܘܘ	[p]ܡܗܝܡܢܝܢ
[s]*omit* ܕܐܝܬ	ܫܒܩܝܢ ܡܐ [s]ܕܐܝܬ [t]ܒܠܒܒܟܘܢ ܥܠ [u]ܐܢܫ	[q]ܘܡܬܥܒܕ
[t]ܒܠܒܒܟܘܢ	ܕܐܦ ܐܒܘܟܘܢ ܕܒܫܡܝܐ ܫܒܩ ܫܒܘܩ	[r]*omit* ܡܩܝܡܝܢ
[w]*omit* ܫܠܡ	ܠܟܘܢ ܣܟܠܘܬܟܘܢ : [w]ܫܠܡ ∴	[u]ܐܢܫ
		[w]*omit* ܫܠܡ

CXXVI.

Matt. VII. 7—11.

Codex A.	Codex B.	Codex C.
[b]ܬܠܡܝܕܘܗܝ	7 [a]ܐܡܪ ܝܫܘܥ ܡܫܝܚܐ ܒܒܣܪܗ ܠ[b]ܬܠܡܝܕܘܗܝ[a] : [y] ܐܡܝܢ	[a]ܐܡܪ ܝܫܘܥ ܡܫܝܚܐ
	ܒܪܐ ܗܘܝܘܢ ܫܐܠܘ ܘܡܬܝܗܒ ܠܟܘܢ : ܒܥܘ	[a]ܒܒܣܪܗ ܡܢ ܬܠܡܝܕܘܗܝ
		[y]*add* ܘܢܣܝܒܐ ܢܬܝܗܒ ܗܘܐ

Codex A.	Codex B.	Codex C.
	ܘܐܢܬܘܢ ܡܫܡܫܝܢ : ܐܝܬܝܘ ܘܡܬܦܬܚ ܠܗܘܢ :	
[a]ܘܕܒܥܐ [b]ܡܫܟܚ	8 ܟܘܠ ܡܢ ܕܢ [z]ܕܫܐܠ ܢܣܒ [a]ܘܕܒܥܐ [b]ܡܫܟܚ :	[z]ܕܫܐܠ [a]ܘܕܒܥܐ
[c]ܕܡܬܢܩܫ	9 ܘܗܕܝܢ [c]ܕܡܬܢܩܫ ܡܬܦܬܚ ܠܗ : ܐܘ ܡܢ ܗܘ	
[d]ܗܕܢ	ܡܢܟܘܢ ܓܒܪ [d]ܗܕܝܢ ܕܫܐܠ ܡܢܗ [e]ܒܪܗ	[e]ܒܪܗ
[f]ܠܚܡ [g]ܡܘܫܛ	10 [f]ܠܚܡ : ܕܟܐܦܐ ܝܗܒ ܗܘ [g]ܡܘܫܛ ܠܗ : ܐܘ	
[h]ܢܘܢ [i]ܚܘܝܐ	ܐܘܦ ܐܢ ܡܒܥܐ [h]ܢܘܢ : ܕܚܘܝܐ [i]ܚܘܝܐ ܗܘ	[h]ܢܘܢ
	11 ܡܘܫܛ ܠܗ : ܐܢ ܐܘܢ ܐܢܬܘܢ ܕܐܢܬܘܢ	
[l]ܛܒܝܢ [m]ܠܒܢܝ	ܒܝܫܝܢ ܐܢܬܘܢ ܝܕܥܝܢ ܕܬܗܒܘܢ ܡܘܗܒܢ [l]ܛܒܝܢ	
[n]ܡܠܝܘܢ	[m]ܠܒܢܝܢ ܠܒܢܝܟܘܢ : † ܟܕ ܟܡܐ [n]ܡܠܝܘܢ	† f. 70b.
[o]ܛܒܢ	ܐܒܘܟܘܢ ܕܒܫܡܝܐ ܝܬܠ [o]ܛܒܬܐ ܠܗܠܝܢ	[o]ܛܒܬܐ
[p]ܕܫ̈ܐܠܝܢ	[p]ܕܫܐܠܝܢ ܠܗ ⁘	[p]ܕܫܐܠܝܢ

CXXVII.

John XV. 1—12a.

Codex A.	Codex B.	Codex C.
[b]ܐܠܝܫܘܥ [d]ܢܘܚܐ ‡ f. 80a.	‡ [a]ܐܡܪ [b]ܐܠܝܫܘܥ ܠܬܠܡܝܕܘܗܝ [c]ܒܝܘܡܗ ܡܢ [d]ܢܘܚܐ [y]ܘܒܬܪܗ	[a]ܐܡܪ [c]ܒܝܘܡ
[y]omit ܘܒܬܪܗܘܢ	1 [z]ܦܪܘܩܢܐ[y] : ܐܡܪ ܡܪܢ ܐܢܐ ܗܘ ܓܘܦܢܐ	[z]omit ܦܪܘܩܢܐ
[c]add ܘܐܢܬܘܢ	2 [a]ܫܪܝܪܬܐ ܘܐܒܐ ܗܘ [b]ܐܪܡܢܐ[c] : ܟܘܠ [d]ܫܒܫܐ	[a]ܫܪܝܪܬܐ [b]ܐܪܡܢܐ
ܫܒܫܬܐ	ܕܒܝ [e]ܠܐ [f]ܡܝܬܝܐ ܦܐܪܝܢ ܡܦܣܩ [g]ܗܘ ܠܗ[g] :	[d]ܫܒܫܬܐ [e]ܕܠܐ
[d]ܫܒܫܬܐ [f]ܡܝܬܝܬܐ	ܘܟܘܠ ܗܕܐ [h]ܕܡܝܬܝܐ ܦܐܪܝܢ [i]ܡܢܩܐ ܗܘ ܠܗ	[f]ܡܝܬܝܐ [g]ܠܗ ܗܘ[g]
[h]ܕܡܝܬܝܬܐ [j]ܝܬܝܪܐ	3 ܠܡܬܠ ܕܦܐܪܝܢ ܡܘܬܪ [j]ܝܬܝܪܐ : ܟܕܘ ܐܢܬܘܢ	[h]ܕܡܝܬܝܐ [i]ܡܢܩܐ
[l]ܕܟܢܝܢ [m]ܗܟܢܐ	4 [l]ܕܟܢ ܠܡܬܠ ܡܠܬܐ ܕܐܡܪܬ ܠܟܘܢ ܒܗܝ ܘܡܬܪ [f. 70a]	[j]ܝܬܝܪܐ
[n]ܕܫܒܫܬܐ	ܟܢ ܘܐܢܐ ܒܟܘܢ : [m]ܗܟܢ ܡܐ[m] [n]ܕܫܒܫܬܐ	[n]ܕܫܒܫܬܐ
[o]ܝܟܠܐ [p]ܡܝܬܝܬܐ	ܠܐ [o]ܡܫܟܚܐ [p]ܡܝܬܝܐ ܦܐܪܝܢ ܡܢ ܢܦܫܗ	[o]ܝܟܠܐ [p]ܡܝܬܝܐ
[r]ܐܢ ܠܐ[r]	[r]ܐܠܐ ܡܫܬܪܝܐ ܒܓܘܦܢܐ ܗܟܢ ܐܘܦ ܐܢܬܘܢ	[r]ܐܢ ܠܐ[r]
	5 ܐܢ ܠܐ ܬܬܡܘܢ ܒܝ : ܐܢܐ ܗܘ ܓܘܦܢܐ	
[u]ܫܒܫܬܐ	ܘܐܢܬܘܢ [t]ܗܘܝܢ [u]ܫܒܫܬܐ : ܡܢ [v]ܕܝ	[t]omit ܗܘܝܢ
ܕܝ [v]omit [w]ܡܝܬܝ	ܕܡܫܬܪ ܒܝ ܘܐܢܐ ܒܗ : ܗܕܝܢ [w]ܕܡܝܬܝ	[u]ܫܒܫܬܐ
	ܦܐܪܝܢ ܣܓܝܐܢ : ܕܠܒܪ ܡܢܝ ܠܝܬ ܐܢܬܘܢ ܝܟܠܝܢ	[v]omit ܕܝ
[z]ܟܘܠܡܐ	6 [y]ܕܬܥܒܕܘܢ [z]ܟܘܠܡܐ : ܐܠܐ ܐܢ ܗܘܐ	[y]ܕܬܥܒܕܘܢ [z]ܟܘܠܡܐ
[a]omit ܠܐ	ܐܢܫ [a]ܠܐ ܡܬܡܪ ܒܝ ܫܪܝܐ ܠܒܪ ܗܝܟ	[a]omit ܠܐ
[b]ܕܫܒܫܬܐ	ܐܝܟ [b]ܕܫܒܫܬܐ ܘܝܒܫ ܘܟܢܫܝܢ ܠܗ ܡܚܡܝܢ	[b]ܕܫܒܫܬܐ

Codex A.	Codex B.	Codex C.
ܬܗܘܘܢ[c]	7 ܬܗܘܘܢ[c] ܘܪܥܝܢ[d] ܠܒܗܘܢ ܠܣܘܪܐ[e] ܘܐܡܪܝܢ[f] : ܐܝܟ[g]	ܘܪܥܝܢ[d] ܬܗܘܢ[c]
‡ f. 80b.	ܬܬܚܫܒܘܢ ܒܗ ܘܡܠܠ[h] ܒܠܒܒܟܘܢ ‡ ܡܬܚܫܒܘܢ[i] :	ܒܠܘܪܐ[e] ܘܐܡܪܝܢ[f]
ܘܡܠܐܟܝ[h] ܕܬܚܫܒܝܢ[i]	ܡܢܐ ܕܐܬܘܢ ܝܕܥܝܢ : ܫܒܘܩ ܘܡܬܒܥܒܥ[k] ܠܗܘܢ :	ܐܝܟ[g] ܘܡܠܠ[h]
ܘܡܬܒܥܒܥ[k]	8 ܒܗܕܐ ܫܥܬܐ ܝܕܥ ܐܢܐ ܕܪܘܚܝ ܝܡܝܢ ܬܚܫܒܘܢ[l] :	ܘܡܥܒܥܒ[k]
ܬܚܫܒܘܢ[l]	9 ܘܬܗܘܢ ܠܝ ܬܠܡܝܕܝ : ܗܟܢ ܡܢܐ ܕܐܝܬܝ	
ܐܝܬܝܬ[m]	ܬܗܝ ܐܢܐ ܐܘܦ ܐܢܐ ܐܝܬܝܬ[m] ܬܗܘܢ :	
ܬܚܫܒܘܢ[n]	10 ܒܬܪܘ † ܒܝܬܗܝ ܕܝܠܝ : ܐܝܟ[g] ܬܚܫܒܘܢ[n]	† f. 71a.
	ܦܘܩܕܝ ܡܬܢܛܪܝܢ ܐܬܘܢ ܒܝܬܗܝ ܕܝܠܝ :	
ܗܟܢܐ[o] ܦܘܩܕܝ[p]	ܗܟܢ ܡܢܐ[o] ܕܐܘܦ ܐܢܐ ܦܘܩܕܝ[p] ܕܐܒܐ	
ܡܠܠܬ[r]	11 ܢܛܪܬ : ܘܐܢܐ ܡܬܢܛܪ ܒܝܬܗ : ܗܠܝܢ[r] ܡܠܠܬ	
ܕܚܕܘܬܝ[s] ܬܗܘܢ	ܠܟܘܢ ܕܚܕܘܬܝ[s] ܕܝܠܝ ܬܗܘܐ ܒܟܘܢ :	
ܦܘܩܕܝ[t]	12 ܘܚܕܘܬܟܘܢ ܬܫܬܡܠܐ : ܗܕܝܢ ܗܘ[t] ܦܘܩܕܝ	
	ܕܝܠܝ ܕܬܗܘܢ ܡܚܒܝܢ ܚܕ ܠܚܕ ⁘	

CXXVIII.

Mark II. 23—III. 5.

Codex A.	Codex B.	Codex C.
ܩܪܝܢܬ[a] (sic) ܐܠܡܥܢܝܪ ܡܢܘܦܐ ܐܟܬܒܗ (sic) ܡܢ ܬܠܡܝܕܐ ܕܦܛܪܘܣ ܥܒܕ ܕ ܐܚܕܬܐ[a]	ܩܪܝܢܬ[a] ܐܠܡܥܢܝܪ ܡܢܘܦܐ ܐܟܬܒܗܐ ܡܢ	ܩܪܝܢܬ[a] ܐܠܡܥܢܝܪ ܡܢܘܦܐ ܐܟܬܒܗ ܡܢ ܬܠܡܝܕܐ ܕܦܛܪܘܣ[a]
ܘܬܠܡܝܕܘܗܝ[b]	23 ܬܠܡܝܕ ܕܦܛܪܘܣ[a] : ܘܒܙܒܢܗ ܦܪܘܫܐ[y] ܘܗܘܢ	ܦܪܘܫܐ[y] omit
ܘܐܙܠ[c] ܘܦܪܫܝܢ[c]	ܕܗܘܐ[z] ܥܒܪ[a] ܒܫܒܬܐ ܒܝܢ ܙܪܥܐ : ܘܬܠܡܝܕܘܗܝ[b]	ܕܗܘܘ[z] ܥܒܪ[a]
ܕܝ[f] omit	ܫܪܘ ܥܒܪܝܢ ܘܐܙܠ[c] ܡܩܛܦܝܢ ܫܒܠܝܢ[d] :	ܘܬܠܡܝܕܘܗܝ[b]
ܬܠܡܝܕܝܟ[g]	24 ܘܦܪܝܫܝܢ[e] ܗܘܘ ܕܝ[f] ܐܡܪܝܢ ܠܗ : ܚܙܝ ܕܝ[f]	ܫܒܠܝܢ[d] ܒ[c] omit
ܠܗܘܢ[h] omit	ܡܢܐ ܥܒܕܝܢ ܬܠܡܝܕܝܟ[g] ܒܫܒܬܐ ܡܢܐ ܕܠܐ	ܘܦܪܝܫܝ[e] ܕܝ[f] omit
‡ f. 81a.	25 ܫܠܝܛ[h] ܠܗܘܢ : ܘܗܘ ܐܡܪ ܠܗܘܢ ܡܢ	ܠܗܘܢ[h] omit
ܕܘܝܕ[j] ܠܐ[i] add	ܩܕܡܝܬܟܘܢ ‡ [i] ܩܪܝܬܘܢ ܡܢܐ ܥܒܕ ܕܘܝܕ[j] : ܟܕ	ܠܐ[i] add
ܒܝܬ[k] ܠܚܠ[l]	26 ܟܦܢ ܘܥܒܕ ܗܘ ܕܝ[f] ܘܥܠܝܢ ܕܥܒܕܗ : ܗܟܢ	ܕܐܒܝܬܪ[m] ܠܚܠ[l]
ܐܒܝܬܪ[m] ܐܦܐ[n]	ܒܝܬ[k] ܠܒܝܬܗ ܕܐܠܗܐ : ܠܚܠ[l] ܕܝ[f] ܠܒܝܬܪ[m]	ܐܦܐ[n] ܐܟܠ[o]
ܐܟܠ[o]	ܪܒܝ ܟܗܢܐ ܘܠܚܡ ܐܦ̈ܝܐ[n] ܐܟܠ[o] : ܡܢܐ	
	ܕܠܐ ܫܠܝܛ ܠܗ ܕܢܐܟܘܠ : ܐܠܐ ܐܢ ܠܟܗܢܐ	
ܒܠܚܘܕ[p]	27 ܒܠܚܘܕ[p] : ܘܗܒ ܐܘܦ ܠܗܠܝܢ ܕܥܡܗ : ܘܗܘ	
	ܐܡܪ ܠܗܘܢ ܫܒܬܐ ܠܒܪ ܐܢܫܐ ܐܬܒܪܝܬ :	

Codex B.

28 ܠܐ ܒܥܒܪܐ ܠܝܪܕܢܐ ܥܡܘܕܝܬܐ : ܗܘܐ ܐܘܢ ܡܥܡܕ
III. 1 [q]ܕܥܡܘܕܝܬܐ ܗܘ ܒܪܗ [q]ܕܒܢܝܐ : [r]ܘܡܟܠ ܐܬܐ
[s]ܠܡܕܒܪܬܐ ܘܗܘܐ ܐܬܐ ܒܪܝܫ ܕܐܪܥܗ ܕܝܗܘܕܐ
2 ܘܗܘܐ ܡܟܪܙ ܠܗ ܐܢ ܐܝܬ ܗܘ [t]ܡܐܡܪ
3 ܠܗ [†] ܒܥܡܘܕܝܬܐ [f]ܕܝ [u]ܕܬܝܒܘܬܐ ܠܡܫܒܩ ܚܛܗܐ : ܘܐܡܪ
ܠܒܝܫܐ ܕܐܝܢܗ ܡܢܝܫܐ ܡܢܟ [v]ܒܡܠܟܘܬܐ :
4 ܘܐܡܪ ܠܗܘܢ [w]ܫܠܝܛ [x]ܕܝܗܒ ܒܥܡܘܕܝܬܐ
[y]ܠܐܒܝ ܐܢܐ [z]ܕܝܗܒ ܠܟ : ܢܦܫܐ [a]ܕܝܢܐ ܐܢܐ
5 [b]ܕܝܘܒܠ : [c]ܗܘܢ ܗܘܘ [d]ܫܡܥܝܢ : [e]ܘܫܡܥܐ
ܠܗܘܢ [f]ܒܝܫܐ ܪܘܚܐ [g]ܡܠܝܐ ܥܠ [h]ܒܪܘܬܗ
[i]ܕܠܗܘܢ ܘܐܡܪ [j]ܠܗܘܢ ܒܝܫܐ ܒܝܫܐ [k]ܐܝܟܢ [f. 71a]
ܘܒܫܝܐ [l]ܐܝܟܢ [‡] [m]ܘܐܬܘܬܐ ܗܢܘܢ [n]ܕܐܬܪܝܐ [o] ⁘

CXXIX.

John I. 43—51.

[‡] [a]ܝܘܡ ܐܠܝܫܥ [b]ܐܠܘܠ ܡܢ ܐܝܓܘܢ[b] ܟܕܐ ܚܕ
[c]ܐܘܢܓܠܝܘܢ ܡܢ [d]ܝܘܚܢܢ : ܘܒܬܪܗ [x]ܦܪܘܟܣܐ :
43 ܘܠܝܘܡܐ ܕܒܬܪܗ ܨܒܐ [y]ܕܢܦܘܩ ܠܓܠܝܠܐ ܘܗܘܐ
ܡܫܟܚ [z]ܕܝ [a]ܠܦܝܠܝܦܘܣ ܘܐܡܪ ܠܗ ܗܒܪܐ
44 ܗܘܐ ܕܒܘܢ ܠܝܬ : ܗܘܐ ܕܝ [b]ܦܝܠܝܦܘܣ ܡܢ
ܒܝܬ ܨܝܕܐ : ܡܢ [c]ܡܕܝܢܬܗ [d]ܕܐܢܕܪܐܘܣ
45 [e]ܘܕܦܛܪܘܣ [f]ܘܐܫܟܚ [g]ܦܝܠܝܦܘܣ [h]ܠܢܬܢܐܝܠ :
ܘܐܡܪ ܠܗ : [i]ܐܫܟܚܢܢ ܗܘܝ [j]ܕܟܬܒ ܡܘܫܐ
ܒܢܡܘܣܐ ܘܒܢܒܝܐ ܠܝܫܘܥ ܒܪܗ [k]ܕܝܘܣܦ
46 [l]ܗܘܝ ܕܡܢ [m]ܢܨܪܬ : ܘܐܡܪ ܠܗ [n]ܢܬܢܐܝܠ : ܡܢ
[o]ܢܨܪܬ [p]ܡܨܝ [q]ܚܠܝܡ [r]ܛܒܐ ܕܗܘܐ : ܐܡܪ
47 ܠܗ [s]ܦܝܠܝܦܘܣ ܐܬܐ ܘܚܡܝ : ܘܚܡܐ ܡܪܢܐ
ܝܫܘܥ ܠܢܬܢܐܝܠ ܐܬܐ ܠܘܬܗ : ܘܐܡܪ ܥܠ
ܕܝܠܗ ܗܐ ܡܢ [t]ܘܩܫܛ [u]ܐܝܣܪܐܝܠ ܗܘܝ
48 ܕܢܟܝܠ ܠܝܬ ܒܗ : ܐܡܪ ܠܗ ܐܘܢ ܢܬܢܐܝܠ

Codex A.

[r]ܘܟܠ [s]ܠܡܕܒܪܬܐ
[f]*omit* ܕܝ
[v]ܒܡܠܟܘܬܐ [x]ܕܝܗܒ
[y]ܠܐܒܝ [b]ܕܝܘܒܠ
[c]ܗܘܢ [e]ܘܫܡܥܐ
[f]ܒܝܫܐ [h]ܒܪܘܬܗ
[j]ܠܗܘܢ [k]ܐܝܟܢ
[l]ܐܝܟܢ [m]ܘܐܬܘܬܐ
[n]ܕܐܬܪܝܐ
[o] *add* ܥܠܡ
‡ f. 81b.

[b]ܐܠܘܠ ܐܝܓܘܢ[b]
‡ f. 82a.
[c]ܐܘܢܓܠܝܘܢ [d]ܝܘܚܢܢ
[y]ܕܢܦܘܩ [z]*omit* ܕܝ
[b]ܦܝܠܝܦܘܣ
[c]ܡܕܝܢܬܗ
[d]ܕܐܢܕܪܐܘܣ
[f]ܘܐܫܟܚ
[g]ܦܝܠܝܦܘܣ
[h]ܠܢܬܢܐܝܠ
[i]ܐܫܟܚܢܢ
[k]ܕܝܘܣܦ [l]ܗܘܝ
[m]ܢܨܪܬ [n]ܢܬܢܐܝܠ
[o]ܢܨܪܬ [p]ܡܨܝ
[q]ܚܠܝܡ [r]ܛܒܐ
[s]ܦܝܠܝܦܘܣ [t]ܘܩܫܛ

Codex C.

[q] *omit* ܕܥܡܘܕܝܬܐ ܗܘ ܒܪܗ
[r]ܘܟܠ
[t]ܡܐܡܪ [u]ܕܬܝܒܘܬܐ
[v]ܒܡܠܟܘܬܐ [w]ܫܠܝܛ
† f. 71b.
[y]ܠܐܒܝ [z]ܕܝܗܒ
[a]ܕܝܢܐ [d]ܕܝܘܒܠ
[c]ܗܘܢ [d]ܫܡܥܝܢ
[g]ܡܠܝܐ
[i]ܕܠܗܘܢ
[k]ܐܝܟܢ [m]ܘܐܬܘܬܐ
[n]ܕܐܬܪܝܐ

[a]ܝܘܡ
[c]ܐܘܢܓܠܝܘܢ [d]ܝܘܚܢܢ
[x]*omit* ܦܪܘܟܣܐ
[y]ܕܢܦܩ [z]*omit* ܕܝ
[a]ܠܦܝܠܝܦܘܣ [b]ܦܝܠܝܦܘܣ
[e]ܘܕܦܛܪܘܣ
[f]ܘܐܫܟܚ [g]ܦܝܠܝܦܘܣ
[h]ܠܢܬܢܐܝܠ [j]ܕܟܬܒ
[o]ܢܨܪܬ [q]ܚܠܝܡ
[s]ܦܝܠܝܦܘܣ
[t]ܘܩܫܛ [u]ܐܝܣܪܐܝܠ

Codex A. | *Codex B.* | *Codex C.*

Codex B.

ܡܢ ܗܘ ܐܢܬ ܡܚܟܡ ܠܝ : ܐܓܝܒ ܡܪܢܐ ܝܫܘܥ
ܘܐܡܪ ܠܗ : ܡܢ ܩܕ ܠܐ ܢܩܪܐ ܠܟ ܦܝܠܝܦܘܣ[v]
49 ܘܐܢܬ ܬܚܘܬ † ܬܐܢܬܐ[w] ‡ ܚܡܝܬ ܠܟ : ܐܓܝܒ
ܢܬܢܐܝܠ ܘܐܡܪ ܪܒܝ ܐܢܬ ܗܘ ܒܪܗ ܕܐܠܗܐ
50 ܐܢܬ ܗܘ ܡܠܟܐ ܕܐܝܣܪܐܝܠ[x] : ܐܓܝܒ ܕܝܢ[y] ܡܪܢܐ
ܝܫܘܥ ܘܐܡܪ ܠܗ :[z] ܕܐܡܪܬ ܠܟ ܕܚܡܝܬ
[f. 71b]
ܬܚܘܬ ܬܐܢܬܐ[w] ܐܢܬ ܡܗܝܡܢ[a] : ܐܦ[b]
51 ܕܝܢ ܪܒܝܢ ܡܢ ܗܠܝܢ ܬܚܙܐ : ܘܐܡܪ
ܠܗ[c] ܐܡܝܢ ܐܡܝܢ ܐܡܪ ܐܢܐ ܠܟ[d] : ܕܡܢ
ܟܕܘ ܬܚܡܘܢ ܫܡܝܐ ܡܦܬܚܝܢ[e] ܘܡܠܐܟܘܗܝ[f]
ܕܐܠܗܐ ܣܠܩܝܢ ܘܢܚܬܝܢ ܥܠ ܒܪܗ[g] ܕܒܪܢܫܐ :
ܥܠܡ[h] ⁖

Codex A: ‡ f. 82b. — [w] ܬܐܢܬܐ — [x] ܕܐܝܣܪܐܝܠ — [y] omit ܕܝܢ — [z] add ܟܠ — [d] ܠܟܘܢ — [e] ܦܬܝܚܝܢ — [f] ܘܡܠܐܟܘܗܝ — [g] ܒܪܗ — [h] omit ܥܠܡ

Codex C: [v] omit ܦܝܠܝܦܘܣ — † f. 72a. — [a] ܡܗܝܡܢ — [b] ܐܢܬ — [c] ܠܟܘܢ — [d] ܠܟܘܢ — [e] ܦܬܝܚܝܢ — [g] ܒܪܗ — [h] omit ܥܠܡ

CXXX.

Mark I. 35—44.

[a][b]ܘܩܪܝܐ ܝܘܡ ܐܚܫܒܬ ܐܬܢܝܢ[b] ܡܢ ܐܘܢܓܠܝܘܢ
ܡܢ ܡܪܩܘܣ ܪܫܐ[c] [a] ܘܒܬܪܗ[y] ܩܝܪܝܐܠܐܝܣܐ[y] :
35 ܘܒܨܦܪܐ ܡܢ ܩܕܝܡܐ[z] ܠܚܕܐ ܩܡ ܢܦܩ ܘܐܙܠ
36 ܠܐܬܪ ܡܕܒܪ : ܘܬܡܢ ܗܘܐ ܡܨܠܐ ܘܪܗܛ
ܒܬܪܗ ܫܡܥܘܢ ܘܗܠܝܢ[a] ܕܥܡܗ[b] : ܘܟܕ
37 ܐܫܟܚܘܢ ܝܬܗ ܐܡܪܝܢ ܠܗ : ܟܘܠ ܥܡܐ ܗܘܘ
ܒܥܝܢ ܠܟ : ܘܐܡܪ ܠܗܘܢ ܢܝܙܠ[c] ܠܡܕܝܢܬܐ[d]
38 ܕܩܪܝܒܢ[e] ܕܐܘܦ ܬܡܢ ܢܟܪܙ : ܠܗܕܐ ܓܪ
ܢܦܩܬ : ܘܐܬܐ ܡܟܪܙ ܕܝܢ[f] ܒܟܢܫܬܗܘܢ
39 ܒܟܘܠܗ ܓܠܝܠܐ : ܘܫܐܕܝܐ[g] ܗܘܐ ܡܦܩ[h] :
40 ܘܐܬܐ ܠܘܬܗ ܚܕ ܓܒܪ ܓܪܒ[i] ܒܥܐ ܡܢܗ :
‡ ܘܢܦܠ ܥܠ ܐܪܟܘܒܬܗ ܘܡܬܟܫܦ[j] ܘܐܡܪ ܠܗ :
ܡܪܝܐ[k] ܐܢ ܨܒܐ ܐܢܬ ܡܫܟܚ[l] ܕܬܕܟܝܐ ܝܬܝ :
ܡܪܢܐ ܝܫܘܥ ܕܝܢ ܐܬܪܚܡ ܥܠܘܗܝ[m] ܘܦܫܛ
41 ܐܝܕܗ[n] ܘܩܪܒ ܠܗ : ܘܐܡܪ ܠܗ ܨܒܐ ܐܢܐ
ܐܬܕܟܝ[o] : ܘܟܕ ܐܡܪ ܗܟܢ ܐܙܠ[p] ܠܗ ܡܢܗ

Codex A: [a] ܝܘܡ ܚܫܒܬ ܬܐܢܝܢ ܡܢ ܐܘܢܓܠܝܘܢ ܡܢ ܡܪܩܘܣ[a] — [y] omit ܘܒܬܪܗ ܩܝܪܝܐܠܐܝܣܐ — [z] ܩܕܝܡܐ — [d] ܠܡܕܝܢܬܐ — [e] ܕܩܪܝܒܢ — [f] omit ܕܝܢ — [g] ܘܫܐܕܝܐ — [h] ܡܦܩ — ‡ f. 83a. — [j] ܘܡܬܟܫܦ — [l] ܡܫܟܚ — [m] ܥܠܘܗܝ — [o] ܐܬܕܟܝ — [p] ܐܙܠ

Codex C: [b] ܠܝܘܡ ܐܚܫܒܬ — [b] ܐܬܢܝܢ — [c] omit ܪܫܐ — [z] add ܟܘ — [a] ܘܗܠܝܢ — [b] add ܗܘܘ — [c] ܢܝܙܠ — [f] omit ܕܝܢ — [h] ܡܦܩܝܢ — [i] ܓܪܒ — [k] ܡܪܝܐ — [m] ܥܠܘܗܝ — [n] ܐܝܕܗ — [o] ܐܬܕܟܝ

Codex A.	Codex B.	Codex C.
[q]ܘܐܬܕܟܝ	42 ܓܪܒܗ [q]ܘܐܬܕܟܝ : ܘܐܟܐ [†]ܒܗ ܘܫܕܪܗ [r]ܐܦܩܗ	† f. 72b.
[s]ܟܠܘܡ [p]ܐܙܝܠ	43 ܬܡܢ ܘܐܡܪ ܠܗ ܚܙܝ ܕܠܐܢܫ ܠܐ ܬܐܡܪ	[q]ܘܐܬܕܟܝ [r]ܐܦܩܗ
[t]ܐܘܕܥ [v]ܘܩܪܒ	44 [s]ܟܠܡ : ܐܠܐ [p]ܐܙܠ [t]ܐܘܕܥ ܓܪܡܟ	[t]ܐܘܕܥ [u]ܠܟܗܢܐ
[w]ܕܕܟܝܘܬܟ [y]ܕܦܩܕ	[u]ܠܟܗܢܐ : [v]ܘܩܪܒ ܩܘܪܒܢܟ [f. 72a] ܥܠ [w]ܕܕܟܝܘܬܟ [x]	[v]ܘܩܪܒ ܗܘ [x]add
[z]add ܥܠܡ	ܡܐ [y]ܕܦܩܕ ܡܘܫܐ ܠܣܗܕܘ ܠܗܘܢ [z] ⁘	

CXXXI.

Mark II. 1—12.

Codex A.	Codex B.	Codex C.
[b]ܐܬܐ	[a]ܗܘܐ ܐܠܗܐ [b]ܐܬܐ ܡܢ ܐܢܫ ܡܢ ܩܕܡܘܗܝ :	[a]ܠܝܘܡ
[b]omit ܡܪܢܐ [a]omit ܘ	1 ܘܒܬܪ ܝܘܡܝܢ ܐܘܪܫܠܡ [a]ܘܐܬܐ [b]ܡܪܢܐ ܝܫܘܥ :	[a]omit ܘ
[d]ܠܗܘܢ [c]omit ܘ	[c]ܘܥܠ ܠܟܦܪ ܢܚܘܡ [d]ܠܗܘܢ ܓܒܪܐ ܕܝܢ	[d]ܠܗܘܢ
	2 ܘܐܬܟܢܫܘ ܣܓܝܐܐ ܕܗܘܐ ܒܒܝܬܐ : ܘܐܬܟܢܫܘ	
[e]ܡܫܡܫܝܢ	ܣܓܝܐܐ ܡܕܡ ܕܠܐ ܗܘܐ [e]ܡܫܡܫܝܢ : ܐܘܦ	[e]ܡܫܡܫܝܢ
[g]ܡܬܢܝܢ [i]ܡܬܠܟܠܟܝܢ	ܠܐ ܡܢܐ ܕܬܪܥܐ : ܘܗܘܐ [f]ܡܡܠܠ	[f]ܡܠܠ
[j]ܡܬܠܐ ܕܝ [k]omit	3 ܠܗܘܢ ܡܠܬܐ : ܘܐܬܘ ܠܘܬܗ [g]ܡܬܢܝܢ [h]ܡܫܪܝܐ	[h]ܡܫܪܝܐ
[l]ܐܟܠܘܣܐ	4 [i]ܡܬܠܟܠܟܝܢ ܡܢ ܐܪܒܥܐ : ܘܟܕ ܕܠܐ [j]ܡܬܠܐ	[k]omit ܕܝ
	[k]ܕܝ ܕܢܩܪܒܘܢ ܠܗ ܠܘܬܗ ܡܢ ܡܢ ܣܓܝܐܘܬ	[m]add ܗܘ ܕܗܘܐ ܡܫܪܝܐ ܝܫܘܥ
† f. 83b.	ܠܟܘܠ [l]ܐܟܠܘܣܐ : ܐܪܝܡܘ [‡]ܬܛܠܝܠܐ [m]ܘܚܦܪܘ	
[m]add ܗܘ ܕܗܘܐ ܡܫܪܝܐ ܝܫܘܥ	[k]ܕܝ ܘܫܒܩܘ [n]ܥܪܣܐ ܕܗܘܐ ܪܡܐ ܡܫܪܝܐ	[n]ܥܪܣܐ
[n]ܥܪܣܐ	5 ܥܠܝܗ : ܘܚܙܐ ܝܫܘܥ ܗܝܡܢܘܬܗܘܢ ܡܪܢܐ ܝܫܘܥ	
[o]ܠܡܫܪܝܐ [p]ܠܡܫܪܝܐ [q]ܫܒܝܩܝܢ	[o]ܠܗܝܡܢܘܬܗܘܢ : ܐܡܪ [p]ܠܡܫܪܝܐ ܒܪܝ [q]ܫܒܝܩܝܢ	
[o]ܠܗܝܡܢܘܬܗܘܢ	6 ܠܟ ܚܛܗܝܟ : ܘܗܘܘ ܐܢܫܝܢ ܡܢ ܣܦܪܐ	
[p]ܠܡܫܪܝܐ [q]ܫܒܝܩܝܢ	7 ܬܡܢ ܝܬܒܝܢ [r]ܘܡܬܚܫܒܝܢ ܒܠܒܗܘܢ ܡܢܐ	[s]ܡܡܠܠ
[r]ܘܡܬܚܫܒܝܢ	ܗܢܐ ܗܟܢܐ [s]ܡܡܠܠ [t]ܓܘܕܦܝܢ : ܡܢ [u]ܝܟܠ [v]ܕܫܒܩ	[t]add ܓܝܪ [u]ܝܟܠ
[s]ܡܡܠܠ [u]ܝܟܠ	ܚܛܗܝܢ ܐܠܐ ܐܢ ܚܕ [w]ܐܠܗܐ [x]ܒܠܚܘܕܘܗܝ :	[w]add ܗܘ [x]ܒܠܚܘܕܘܗܝ
[v]ܢܫܒܘܩ [x]ܒܠܚܘܕܘܗܝ	8 ܘܝܕܥ [y]ܡܚܕܐ ܡܪܢܐ ܝܫܘܥ [z]ܒܪܘܚܗ ܕܗܢܘܢ	[y]ܡܚܕܐ [z]ܒܪܘܚܐ
[y]ܡܚܕܐ	ܗܢܘܢ [†]ܡܬܚܫܒܝܢ ܒܠܒܗܘܢ : ܐܡܪ ܠܗܘܢ	† f. 73a.
[a]add ܩܠܝܠ	9 ܡܢܐ ܐܢܬܘܢ ܡܬܚܫܒܝܢ [a]ܒܠܒܒܟܘܢ : ܡܢܐ	[a]add ܩܠܝܠ
[b]ܦܫܝܩ [c]ܕܢܐܡܪ	[b]ܦܫܝܩ [c]ܕܢܐܡܪ [d]ܠܡܫܪܝܐ [q]ܫܒܝܩܝܢ ܠܟ ܚܛܗܝܟ :	[d]omit ܠܡܫܪܝܐ
[q]ܫܒܝܩܝܢ [e]ܩܘܡ	ܐܘ [c]ܕܢܐܡܪ ܩܘܡ [e]ܫܩܘܠ ܥܪܣܟ ܘܗܠܟ :	[e]ܘܫܩܘܠ

Codex A.	Codex B.	Codex C.
ᵍ ܐܝܬ ʰ ܫܘܠܛܢܐ	[f. 72b] 10 ᶠ ܕܬܕܥܘܢ ܕܝ ᵍ ܕܐܝܬ ʰ ܫܘܠܛܢܐ ܠܒܪܗ ܕܓܒܪܐ :	ᶠ ܕܬܕܥܘܢ
	ܥܠ ܐܪܥܐ ܠܡܫܒܩ ܚܛܗܝܢ : ܐܡܪ ܠܗܘ	ᵍ ܫܘܠܛܢܐ
ⁱ ܐܡܪ	11 ܡܫܪܝܐ ܠܟ ܐܢܐ ⁱ ܐܡܪ ܩܘܡ ܛܥܘܢ ܥܪܣܟ	ⁱ ܐܡܪ
ʲ ܘܐܙܠ ᵏ ܘܩܡ	12 ʲ ܘܐܙܠ ܠܒܝܬܟ : ᵏ ܘܩܡ ܗܘ ܘܛܥܢ ܥܪܣܗ	ˡ ܠܟܠܗ
‡ f. 84a.	ܘܢܦܩ ܩܕܡ * ܟܠܗܘܢ ˡ ܠܟܠܗ ‡ ܕܗܘܘ	[* Cod. B ܟܠܗܘܢ sic]
ᵐ ܡܬܡܗܝܢ	ᵐ ܡܬܡܗܝܢ ܟܠܗܘܢ : ܘܗܘܘ ܡܫܒܚܝܢ ܠܐܠܗܐ	ᵐ ܡܬܡܗܝܢ
ⁿ ܕܗܟܕܝܢ	ܘܐܡܪܝܢ : ⁿ ܕܗܟܕܝܢ ܡܢ ܥܠܡ ܠܐ ܚܙܝܢ :	ⁿ ܕܗܟܕܝܢ
ᵒ omit ܥܠܡ	ᵒ ܥܠܡ ⁘	ᵒ omit ܥܠܡ

CXXXII.

Mark II. 14—17.

	Codex A.	Codex B.	Codex C.
	ᵇ ܡܫܪܝ ܐܘܢܓܠܝܘܢ ᵇ	ᵃ ܒܗܘܢ ᵇ ܐܬܡܫܪܝ ܐܘܢܓܠܝܘܢ ᵇ ܡܢ ܐܘܢܓܠܝܘܢ ܕܡܪܩܘܣ :	ᵃ ܒܗܘܢ
ܢܛ / 1	ᶻ ܠܠܘܝ	14 ܘܒܥܒܪܗ ܡܢ ܬܡܢ ܚܙܐ ܠܘܝ ܒܪ ܚܠܦܝ	ᶻ ܠܠܘܝ
	ᵃ ܝܬܒ ᵇ ܥܠ ܒܝܬ	ᶻ ܠܠܘܝ ܒܪ ᵃ ܝܬܒ ᵇ ܥܠ ܒܝܬ ܡܟܣܐ :	ᶜ ܒܬܪܝ
	ᶜ ܒܬܪܝ ᵉ ܘܐܙܠ	ܘܐܡܪ ܠܗ ܐܬܐ ᶜ ܒܬܪܝ : ᵈ ܘܩܡ ᵉ ܘܐܙܠ	ᵈ omit ܩܡ ... ܒܬܪܗ ᵉ ܘܐܙܠ
	ᶠ ܒܬܪܗ ᵍ ܘܗܘܐ	15 ᶠ ܒܬܪܗ :ᵈ ᵍ ܘܗܘܐ ܟܕ ᵍ ܗܘ ʰ ܣܡܝܟ ܒܒܝܬܗ :	ᵍ ܘܗܘܐ
	ʰ ܣܡܝܟ	ܘܣܓܝܐܝܢ ܡܟܣܐ ܘܚܛܝܐ ܗܘܘ ܣܡܝܟܝܢ ܥܡ ܝܫܘܥ	ⁱ ܬܠܡܝܕܘܗܝ
	ⁱ ܬܠܡܝܕܘܗܝ	ܘܥܡ ⁱ ܬܠܡܝܕܘܗܝ : ܗܘܘ ܓܝܪ ܣܓܝܐܝܢ ܘܐܬܘ	ᵏ ܘܣܦܪܐ
	ˡ ܕܦܪܝܫܐ	16 ܘܟܕ ܚܙܘ ᵏ ܘܣܦܪܐ ˡ ܕܦܪܝܫܐ : ܟܕ ܚܙܘ	ˡ ܕܦܪܝܫܐ
	ⁿ omit ܗܘ	ܠܗ ᵐ ܕܗܘܐ ܐܟܠ ܥܡ ܡܟܣܐ ܘܚܛܝܐ	ⁿ omit ܗܘ ᵐ ܕܗܘܐ
	ᵖ ܘܫܬܐ	ⁿ ܗܘ ܐܡܪܝܢ ° ܠܬܠܡܝܕܘܗܝ : ܠܡܢܐ ܥܡ ܡܟܣܐ	° ܠܬܠܡܝܕܘܗܝ
	ᵠ add ܩܠܝܠ	17 ᵖ ܘܫܬܐ ܐܟܠ ܘܫܬܐ : ܘܟܕ ܫܡܥ	
	ʳ ܕܟܪܝܗܝܢ	ܝܫܘܥ ܐܡܪ ܠܗܘܢ † : ܠܐ ܣܢܝܩܝܢ ᵠ	† f. 73b.
	ˢ ܒܟܪܝܗܘܬܐ	ܚܠܝܡܐ ܠܐܣܝܐ : ܐܠܐ ʳ ܕܒܝܫ ܠܗܘܢ ˢ ܒܟܪܝܗܘܬܐ :	ᵠ add ܩܠܝܠ
	ᵘ add ܥܠܡ ᵗ ܚܛܝܐ	ܠܐ ܐܬܝܬ ܕܐܩܪܐ ܠܙܕܝܩܐ ܐܠܐ ᵗ ܚܛܝܐ ܠܬܝܒܘܬܐ ᵘ ⁘	ˢ ܒܟܪܝܗܘܬܐ

CXXXIII.

Mark VIII. 34—39.

	Codex A.	Codex B.	Codex C.
ܢܛ ܒܥܢܝ / 1	ᵇ ܐܠܚܕ ܐܬܦܠܬ ᵇ	ᵇᵃ ܒܗܘܢ ܐܠܚܕ ܐܬܦܠܬ ᵇ ܡܢ ܐܘܢܓܠܝܘܢ ܕܡܪܩܘܣ ˣ	ᵃ ܒܗܘܢ
	ʸ ܕܝܬܒܝܢ ᶻ ܒܬܪܝ	34 ܐܡܪ ܡܪܢ ܝܫܘܥ ܠܡܢ ܕܨܒܐ ʸ ܕܝܬܐ	ˣ add ܘܩܪܐ ܠܬܠܡܝܕܘܗܝ
	‡ f. 84b.	[f. 73a] ᶻ ܒܬܪܝ ܢܟܦܘܪ ‡ ܒܢܦܫܗ ܘܢܛܥܢ ܨܠܝܒܗ	ᶻ ܒܬܪܝ

Codex A.	Codex B.	Codex C.
[a]ܕܨܒܐ [b]ܢܦܫܗ	35 ܘܐܬܐ ܒܬܪܝ : ܡܢ [a]ܕܨܒܐ ܕܝܚܝܐ [b]ܢܦܫܗ	
[c]ܡܘܒܕ [d]ܢܦܫܗ	[c]ܡܘܒܕ [d]ܠܗ : [e]ܘܡܢ [f]ܕܝܘܒܕ ܢܦܫܗ[f] [g]ܠܒܓܠܠ	
[e]omit ܘ	36 ܘܠܒܓܠܠ ܒܣܒܪܬܐ ܝܚܝ ܠܗ : ܡܗ ܓܪ [h]ܡܘܬܪܐ	[h]ܡܘܬܪܐ [i]ܐܢ
[f]omit ܕܝܘܒܕ ܢܦܫܗ	ܒܪܢܫ : [i]ܐܢ [k]ܝܬܐܓܪ ܒܟܠܗ [l]ܥܠܡܐ	[k]ܝܬܐܓܪ [n]ܝܚܣܪ
[g]ܠܒܓܠܠ [h]ܡܬܘܬܪ	37 [m]ܘܢܦܫܗ [n]ܝܚܣܪ : ܐܘ ܡܗ ܝܬܠ [o]ܚܘܠܦ	[o]add ܒܪܢܫ
[k]ܝܬܐܓܪ [l]ܥܠܡܐ	38 [b]ܢܦܫܗ : ܡܢ ܓܪ ܕܝܒܗܬ ܒܝ ܘܒܡܠܝ [q]ܒܗܕܐ	[q]ܒܗܕܐ
[m]ܘܢܦܫܗ [n]ܝܚܣܪ	ܕܪܐ ܚܛܝܐ [r]ܘܓܝܪܬܐ : ܐܘܦ ܒܪܗ [s]ܕܓܒܪܐ	[s]ܕܓܒܪܐ
[o]add ܒܪܢܫ	ܝܒܗܬ ܒܗ : ܟܕ [t]ܗܘ [u]ܐܬܐ [v]ܒܬܫܒܘܚܬܗ	[t]omit ܗܘ [u]ܐܬܐ
[r]ܘܡܓܝܪܬܐ [s]ܕܓܒܪܐ	[w]ܕܝ [x]ܕܐܒܘܗܝ ܥܡ [y]ܡܠܐܟܘܗܝ [z]ܩܕܝܫܐ :	[w]omit ܕܝ [x]ܕܐܒܘܗܝ
[t]omit ܗܘ [u]ܝܬܐ	39 ܘܗܘܐ ܐܡܪ ܠܗܘܢ ܐܡܝܢ ܐܡܝܢ ܐܡܪ ܐܢܐ	[y]ܡܠܐܟܘܗܝ
[v]ܒܬܫܒܘܚܬܗ	ܠܟܘܢ : ܐܝܬ ܐܢܫܝܢ ܡܢ ܗܠܝܢ [a]ܕܗܟܐ	[a]ܕܗܟܐ
[w]omit ܕܝ [x]ܕܐܒܘܗܝ	[b]ܩܝܡܝܢ : [c]ܗܠܝܢ [d]ܕܠܐ [e]ܝܛܥܡܘܢ ܡܘܬܐ	[b]ܩܝܡܝܢ [c]omit ܗܠܝܢ
[z]ܩܕܝܫܐ [a]ܕܗܟܐ	ܥܕ ܕܝܚܡܘܢ ܡܠܟܘܬܗ ܕܐܠܗܐ ܐܬܝܐ	[d]omit ܕ
[b]ܩܝܡܝܢ	ܒܚܝܠܐ : [f]ܥܠܡ ⁘	[f]omit ܥܠܡ
[e]ܝܛܥܡܘܢ		
[f]omit ܥܠܡ		

CXXXIV.

Mark VII. 24—37.

Codex A.	Codex B.	Codex C.
[a]ܒܥܕܢ [b]ܐܪܐܟܒ	[a]ܒܥܕܢܐ ܐܗܟܬ [b]ܐܪܐܟܒ ܡܢ ܐܝܟܢ ܡܢ	[a]ܒܥܕܢ [b]ܐܪܐܟܒ
[a]add ܘܡܚܘܙܝܗ ܕܨܝܕܢ	24 ܡܪܢ [a]ܝܫܘܥ ܘܡܢ ܬܡܢ [b]ܩܡ ܘܐܬܐ [c]ܡܚܘܙܐ ܨܘܪ	[a]add ܘܡܚܘܙܝܗ ܕܨܝܕܢ
[c]omit ܡܚܘܙܐ [b]ܘܩܡ	ܠܬܚܘܡܝܗ ܕܨܘܪ : ܘܥܠ [d]ܠܒܝܬ ܠܓܘ ܒܥܐ ܠܐ	[b]ܘܩܡ [d]ܥܠ
[d]ܥܠ [f]ܝܕܥ	ܗܘܐ ܒܥܐ [e]ܕܐܢܫ [f]ܝܕܥ : ܘܠܐ ܝܟܠ ܕܝܬܛܫܐ :	[e]ܕܐܢܫ [f]ܝܕܥ
‡ f. 85a.	25 ܐܠܐ ܡܚܕܐ ܕܫܡܥܬ ܥܠ ܕܝܫܘܥ‡ [g]ܐܬܬܐ ܕܗܘܬ	[g]ܐܬܬܐ
[g]ܐܬܬܐ	ܠܒܪܬܗ ܪܘܚܐ ܦܟܝܬܐ ܘܐܬܬ ܘܢܦܠܬ ܩܕܡ	
	26 ܪܓܠܘܝ ܘܐܬܬܐ ܗܘܬ †ܐܪܡܝܬܐ ܡܢ ܣܘܪܝܐ	† f. 74a.
	ܕܦܘܢܝܩܐ : ܒܥܝܐ ܕܝܠܗ ܘܗܘܬ [h]ܕܝܦܩ ܫܐܕܐ ܡܢܗ :	[h]ܒܥܐ [i]ܕܒܩܘ
[i]ܕܒܩܘ	27 [i]ܕܒܩܘ [j]ܣܒܥܐ ܡܢ ܒܢܝܗ : [k]ܘܗܘܐ ܐܡܪ ܠܗ	[j]ܣܒܥܐ [k]ܘܗܘ
[l]omit ܕܝ	[l]ܕܝ ܫܒܘܩܝ ܩܕܡ ܕܝܣܒܥܘܢ ܒܢܝܐ : ܠܐ ܫܦܝܪ	[l]omit ܕܝ [m]ܕܢܣܒ(sic)
	[f. 73b] [m]ܕܢܣܒ [n]ܠܚܡܗܘܢ ܕܒܢܝܐ [o]ܘܢܪܡܝ ܠܟܠܒܝܐ :	[n]ܠܚܡܗܘܢ
[q]ܐܝ	28 ܘܗܝ ܐܬܝܒܬ [p]ܐܡܪܐ [q]ܐܝ ܡܪܝ ܐܘܦ	[o]ܘܢܪܡ (sic) [p]ܐܡܪܐ
[r]add ܘܡܪܢ	ܟܠܒܝܐ ܬܚܘܬ ܦܬܘܪܐ ܐܟܠܝܢ ܡܢ ܦܪܘܕܝܐ	[q]ܐܝ
[s]omit ܡܢ	29 ܕܛܠܝܐ : [r]ܘܐܡܪ ܠܗ ܡܪܢ ܝܫܘܥ [s]ܡܢ ܒܓܠܠ	[s]omit ܡܢ

U

Codex A.

[t]ܕܗܘܐ [u]ܡܫܝܠܬܐ
[l]*omit* ܕܝ
[x]ܘܫܒܚܐ [z]ܘܡܬܠܝܢ
[a]ܣܓܝܐ [b]ܡܡܠܠ
[c]ܕܢܫܩ [d]ܐܕܢܘܗܝ
[e]ܐܬܩܠܫܬܐ
[g]ܠܠܫܢܗ
‡ f. 85b.
[k]*omit* ܡܢ ܕܗܘܐ
ܐܬܦܬܚܝ
[l]ܐܬܦܬܚܘ
[m]ܡܫܡܥܘܗܝ
[n]ܕܠܫܢܗ [o]ܘܗܘܐ
[p]ܡܡܠܠ [r]ܘܦܩܕ
[s]ܢܐܡܪܘܢ
[u]ܡܬܩܠܒܝܢ
[w]*add* ܐܦܠ ܒܟܠܐ ܗܘ ܥܒܕ
[y]ܘܠܡܐܠܝܢ [z]*add* ܕ

Codex B.

[t]ܕܐܢ [u]ܡܫܝܚܐ : ܐܙܠܝ ܢܦܩ [v]ܥܒܕܐ ܡܢ ܒܪܬܗܘܢ :
30 ܘܟܕ [l]ܕܝ ܐܙܠܬ ܠܟܘ [w]ܒܬܘܗ ܐܫܟܚܬ ܠܬܠܡܝܕܬܐ
ܕܝܩܢܐ ܥܠ ܒܪܢܫܐ [x]ܘܫܒܝܚܐ ܕܢܦܩ ܡܢܗ :
31 ܘܫܪܝ ܒܗ ܢܦܩ ܡܢܐ ܫܡܥܘ ܡܢ [y]ܬܘܫܡܫܬܐ
ܕܚܙܘ : ܐܬܬ ܥܠ ܕܝܕܥܝܢ ܠܫܡܥܐ ܕܓܠܝܠܐ :
32 ܒܝܢ ܬܘܫܡܫܬܐ ܕܒܫܪܬܐ ܡܕܝܢܬܐ : [z]ܘܡܛܠܝܢ
ܠܗ [a]ܣܓܝ ܘܒܥܝܐ [b]ܡܡܠܠ ܘܟܒܘ ܡܢܗ
33 [c]ܕܢܫܩ [d]ܐܕܗ ܒܠܒܝ : ܘܢܫܩܗ ‡ ܒܝܢܗ ܘܠܗ
ܡܢ ܒܗ [e]ܐܬܩܠܫܬܐ ܘܢܡܘܣܐ ܐܝܟܢܬܗ [f]ܠܐܬܪܢܝ
34 ܘܝܬ ܘܡܢܝܒ [g]ܠܠܝܫܗ : ܘܫܡܥ ܠܫܡܥܐ [h]ܘܐܬܚܙܝ
ܘܐܬܡܪ ܠܗ [i]ܐܬܦܬܚܝ [k]ܡܢ ܕܗܘܐ ܐܬܦܬܚܝ[k] :
35 ܘܒܝܢ [l]ܐܬܦܬܚܝ [m]ܡܫܡܥܘܗܝ : ܘܫܪܐ ܐܣܪܐ
ܐܦܪܐ [n]ܕܠܫܢܗ : [o]ܘܫܪܐ [p]ܡܡܠܠ [q]ܫܦܝܐܝܬ :
36 [r]ܘܦܩܕ ܢܬܗܘܢ ܕܠܐܢܫ ܠܐ [s]ܢܐܡܪܘܢ : ܘܟܡܠ
ܡܐ ܕܗܘܐ ܡܦܩܕ ܠܗܘܢ : ܗܢܘܢ ܡܠܘܢ
37 ܒܠ [t]ܕܢܬܪ ܗܘܘ ܡܬܡܗܝܢ : ܘܟܠ ܕܡܫܬܪ ܗܘܘ
[u]ܡܬܩܠܒܝܢ ܘܐܡܪܝܢ : ܫܦܝܪ ܒܟܠܐ ܗܘ ܥܒܕ[w]
[x]ܐܦ ܠܚܪܫܝܢ ܗܘ ܥܒܕ[x] ܕܫܡܥܘܢ : [y]ܘܠܡܐܠܝܢ
ܕܠܐ ܡܡܠܠܝܢ [z]ܡܡܠܠܝܢ ⁘

Codex C.

[t]ܕܗܘܐ [v]ܥܒܕܐ
[w]ܒܬܘܗ
[y]ܬܘܫܡܫܬܐ
[e]ܐܬܩܠܫܬܐ
[f]ܠܐܬܪܢܝ
[g]ܠܫܢܗ [h]ܘܐܬܚܙܝ
[i]ܐܬܦܬܚܬ
[l]ܐܬܦܬܚܘ
[n]ܕܠܫܢܗ [o]ܘܗܘܐ
[p]ܡܡܠܠ [q]ܦܫܝܛܬ
[t]ܕܢܬܪ
[x]*omit* ܐܦ . . . ܥܒܕ
[y]ܘܠܡܐܠܝܢ [z]*add* ܕ

CXXXV.

Mark IX. 16—30.

Codex A.

ܥܪ. ܒܫܒ. ܕ

[a]*add* ܘܥܢܐ
[c]ܐܠܝܒܒ
[z]ܐܘܩܠܫܝܢܐ
[a]ܐܝܬܝܬ
[d]ܡܒܪܚܬ [e]ܫܢܘܗܝ
‡ f. 86a.
[f]ܠܬܠܡܝܕܝܟ
[g]ܕܢܦܩܘܢ [h]ܫܟܚܘ

Codex B.

[a] [b]ܫܐܠ ܐܠܝܫܥ † [c]ܐܬܐܡܪ ܡܢ ܐܝܟܘ [d] ܡܢ
[f. 74a]
16 ܒܪܢܫܐ : ܘܒܝܬܗ [y]ܡܚܘܡܐ : ܐܠܝܒܐ ܚܕ ܡܢ
[z]ܐܘܩܠܫܝܢܐ ܘܐܡܪ ܠܗ ܡܠܦܢܐ : [a]ܐܝܬܝܬ ܒܪܝ
17 ܠܘܬܟ ܕܠܗ [b]ܪܘܚ ܕܠܐ ܡܡܠܠܐ : ܘܗܝ [c]ܕܗܘܝ
ܕܒܥܐ ܠܗ ܗܝ ܢܒܥܐ ܠܗ : ܘܗܘܐ [d]ܡܒܪܚܬ
ܘܡܪܚܩ [e]ܫܢܘܗܝ ‡ ܘܒܥܫ ܘܐܡܪܬ [f]ܠܬܠܡܝܕܝܟ
18 [g]ܕܢܦܩܘܢ ܝܬܗ ܘܠܐ [h]ܫܟܚܘ : [i]ܘܐܡܪ
ܡܢܐ ܫܡܥܘ ܘܐܡܪ ܠܗܘܢ : ܐܘ ܕܪܐ ܕܠܐ

Codex C.

[b]ܠܝܫܥ
[d]*add* ܡܢ ܐܡܪܐ ܡܢ ܐܝܟܘ
† f. 74b.
[y]*omit* ܡܚܘܡܐ
[z]ܐܘܩܠܫܝܢܐ
[b]*omit* ܪܘܚ
[d]ܡܒܪܚܬ [c]*omit* ܕ
[e]ܫܢܘܗܝ
[g]ܕܢܦܩܘܢ
[h]ܫܟܚܘ [i]ܘܐܡܪ

Codex A.

^jܡܗܝܡܢܝܢ.

^kܐܡܬܝ ^lܐܬܪ̈ܘ

^m *add* ܘܟܕ ܐܬܝܬܘܢ ܠܘܬܗ:

^nܘܡܫܪܝܬ ^pܠܐܒܘܝ

^q *omit* ܘ

^sܘܠܡܠܟܐ ^vܢܟܠ

^yܕܐܦ ܐܢ^y ^zܢܟܠ

^a *add* ܡܗܝܡܢܝܢ

^bܠܟܘܢ ^cܕܡܗܝܡܢܝܢ

^dܢܘܚ ^eܐܒܘܝ

^fܒܕܡܟܬܝܢ ^gܡܗܝܡܢܝܢ.

^h *add* ܡܪܝ

^iܠܫܦܝܪܘܬ

^aܕܪܚܡ

‡ f. 86*b*.

^bܘܐܘܠܨܢܐ

^e *add* ܘܐ ^d *omit* ܠܗ

^jܘܚܪܝܬܐ

^kܡܟܝܢܐ ^lܬܬܟܠܝܢ

^m *omit* ܘ ^nܕܡܟܝܢܬ

^rܥܠ ^wܒܢ̈ܝܗܘܢ

^xܘܐܡ̈ܪܝܢ ^yܠܗ

^aܒܟܠܝܢ ^bܕܢܟܣ

^dܒܟܠܝܘܣ

^eܢܟܠܝܢ ^fܕܢܟ̈ܣܘ

^gܕܟܠܒܐ ^kܓܪ

^lܡܠܝܓ

^mܠܬܠܡܝܕܘܗܝ

^oܘܩܛܠܝܢ

^pܡܒܬܘܩܠ ^qܢܩ̈ܡܝܢ

Codex B.

^jܡܗܝܡܢܝܢ ܒܗ. ^kܡܐܬܝܬܝ ܐܢܐ ܗܘܐ ܠܘܬܟܘܢ:
ܒܗ. ^kܡܐܬܝܬܝ ܫܡܥܬ ܡܢܟܘܢ: ^lܐܝܟܢܐ ܗܘܬ
19 ܠܘܬܝ: ^mܘܫܡܥܬ ܗܘܬ ܪܘܚܐ ܘܚܘܐ ܒܓܘܬ
ܗܘܬ ܘܢܦܠ ܥܠ ܐܪܥܐ: ܘܗܘܐ ܡܬܬܟܠܝܢ
20 ^nܘܡܫܪܝܬ: ܘܐܢܟܠ ܡܪܐ ^oܫܘܐܠ ^pܠܐܒ̈ܘܝ
^qܘܐܡܪ: ܒܡܠܐ ܐܚܘܟ ܠܗ ܡܢ ܕܗܘܬ ܠܗ
21 ܗܕܐ ܘܐܡܪ ^rܡܢ ܩܠܝܠܘܬܗ: ܘܫܦܝܪ ܐܝܟܢ
ܠܟܘܪܐ ܗܘܬ ܪܘܚܐ ܠܗ ^sܘܠܡܠܟܐ ^tܕܬܘܒܢܝ
ܗܘܬ: ܐܠܐ ܡܢܐ ^uܕܐܝܬ ^vܢܟܠ ܫܒܩ ^wܠܝ
22 ܡܪܐ ܘܐܬܪܘܚܝ ^xܒܠܒܝܢ: ܘܡܪܐ ܫܡܥܘܢ
ܐܡܪ ܠܗ: ^yܕܐ ^zܐܬܟܠ ܐܬ ^aܒܡܠܐ ܢܟܠ
23 ^bܠܕܝܢ ^cܕܡܗܝܡܢܝܢ: ܘܫܘܚܐ ^dܐܢܘܚ ^eܐܒ̈ܘܝ
ܕܩܠܠܐ ^fܒܕܡܟܝܢ ܘܗܘܐ ܐܡܪ ^gܡܗܝܡܢܝܢ ܐܢܐ^h
24 ܫܒܩ ^iܠܫܦܝܪܘܬ ܡܗܝܡܢܘܬܝ: ܘܟܕ ܫܡܥ ܡܪܐ
ܫܘܒ ^aܪܚܡ ܟܠܗܝ ^bܐܘܠܨܢܐ: ^cܓܪ ܒܪܘܚܐ
ܠܚܝܘܬܐ ܘܐܡܪ ^dܠܗ ^eܪܘܚܐ ‡ ܕܠܐ ܡܬܟܠܠܐ
^jܘܚܪܝܬܐ ^kܡܟܝܢܐ ܐܢܐ ܠܟܝ: ܦܘܩܝ ܡܢܗ
25 ܘܡܢ ܒܪܗ ܠܐ ^lܬܬܟܠܝܢ ܠܗ ܘܢܘܚܬ ^mܘܫܒܩ
[f. 74*b*]
ܚܙܬ ܗܘܬ: † ܘܢܦܩܬ ܡܢܗ: ܘܐܬܒܪܟܬ ܗܝܢ
ܡܢܟܬ: ܗܟܝܠ ܕܫܒܩ ܗܘܘ ܐܡܪܝܢ ^nܕܡܪܬ:
26 ܘܡܪܐ ܫܘܐܠ ^oܚܙܐ ^pܒܐܢܫܗ ^qܘܐܘܡܝ ܗܘܬ
27 ܘܩܡ: ܘܟܕ ^rܥܠܐ ^sܫܘܐܠ ܠܒܝܬܐ: ^tܫܐܠܘ
ܗܘܬ ^uܬܠܡܝܕܘܗܝ ^wܒܢܝܗܘܢ ܘܠܗ ^xܐܡܪܝܢ
^yܠܡܪܐ: ܕܐܝܟ ܠܐ ^aܡܟܠܝܢ ^bܕܢܟ̈ܣܘ ܗܘܬ:
28 ܘܐܡܪ ܠܗܘܢ ܗܢܝܢ ^cܓܢܣܐ ^dܒܟܠܘܡ ܠܐ
^eܢܟܠ ^fܕܢܩܡ ܐܠܐ ܐܢ ܒܨܠܘܬܐ ܘܒܨܘܡܐ:
29 ܘܟܕ ܢܦܩܘ ܡܢ ܬܡܢ ܗܘܘ ܥܒܪܝܢ ܥܠ ^gܓܠܝܠܐ:
30 ܘܠܐ ܗܘܐ ܨܒܐ ^hܕܐܢܫ ^iܢܕܥ: ܗܘܐ
^kܓܝܪ ^lܡܠܦ ^mܠܬܠܡܝܕܘܗܝ ܘܐܡܪ ܠܗܘܢ ܕܒܪܗ
ܕܐܢܫܐ ܡܫܬܠܡ ܠܐܝܕܝ ^nܒܢܝܢܫܐ ^oܘܩܛܠܝܢ
ܠܗ: ܘܡܢ ܕܡܝܬ ^pܡܬܩܛܠ ܬܠܬܐ ^qܝܘܡܝܢ ܩܐܡ܀

Codex C.

^jܡܗܝܡܢܝܢ ^kܡܬܝ

^m *add* ܗܘܬ ܘܐܬܦܠܘ ܠܘܬܗ

^nܘܡܫܪܝܬ

^o *omit* ܫܘܐܠ

^pܠܐܒܘܝ

^r *add* ܠܗ ^q *omit* ܘ

^u *omit* ܕܐܝܬ ^tܕܬܘܒܢܝ

^wܬܘܒ ^xܟܠܘܝ

^yܕܐܦ ܐܢ^y

^zܢܟܠ ^cܕܡܗܝܡܢܝܢ

^dܢܘܚ ^eܐܒܘܝ

^fܒܕܡܟܝܢ ^gܡܗܝܡܢܝܢ

^h *add* ܡܪܝ

^iܠܫܦܝܪܘܬ

^aܕܪܚܡ ^cܘܟܕ

^jܘܚܪܝܬܐ

^lܬܬܟܠܝܢ

† f. 75*a*.

^nܕܡܟܝܢܬ ^oܚܙܐ

^pܒܐܢܫܗ (*sic*) ^qܘܐܘܡܝ

^rܥܠ ^s *add* ܡܪܐ

^tܫܐܠܘ ^uܬܠܡܝܕܘܗܝ

^yܠܗ: ܕܡܪܐ^y

^aܡܟܠܝܢ ^bܕܢܟܣ

^cܓܢܣܐ ^fܕܢܟ̈ܣܘ

^gܕܓܠܝܠܐ

^hܕܐܢܫ ^iܢܕܥ

^kܓܝܪ ^lܡܠܦ

^nܕܒܢܝܢܫܐ

^oܘܩܛܠܝܢ ^qܢܩܘܡ

Codex A.	Codex B.	Codex C.
	CXXXVI.	
	MARK VIII. 27—31.	
ܫܡܥܬ [b]	ܗܘܐ [a] ܫܡܥܬ [b] ܐܠܝܫܘܥ [c] ܡܢ ܐܬܪܐ ܡܢ	ܠܒܬܪ [a] ܐܠܝܫܘܥ [c]
ܐܠܝܫܘܥ [c] (sic)	27 ܬܠܡܝܕܘܗܝ: [a] ܘܢܦܩ ܡܢ ܬܡܢ ‡ ܗܘ [b] ܘܬܠܡܝܕܘܗܝ	[a] add ܘܬܠܡܝܕܘܗܝ ܥܡܗ
‡ f. 87a.	ܠܩܘܪܝܐ ܕܩܣܪܝܐ [c] ܕܦܝܠܝܦܘܣ: [d] ܘܒܐܘܪܚܐ [e] ܗܘܐ	ܕܦܝܠܝܦܘܣ [c]
[a] add ܘܬܠܡܝܕܘܗܝ ܥܡܗ	[f] ܫܐܠ [g] ܠܬܠܡܝܕܘܗܝ ܘܐܡܪ ܠܗܘܢ: ܡܢ ܐܡܪܝܢ	ܘܒܐܘܪܚܐ [d]
ܘܬܠܡܝܕܘܗܝ [b]	28 [h] ܥܠܝ ܒܢܝ ܐܢܫܐ: ܗܢܘܢ ܕܝ ܐܡܪܘ	[f] ܫܐܠ [g] ܠܬܠܡܝܕܘܗܝ
ܕܦܝܠܝܦܘܣ [c]	ܐܡܪܝܢ [i] ܝܘܚܢܢ [j] ܡܥܡܕܢܐ: [k] ܘܐܚܪܢܝܢ ܐܠܝܐ	[h] ܥܠܝ [i] ܝܘܚܢܢ
[d] ܘܒܐܘܪܚܐ [e] ܗܘܐ	29 [l] ܘܐܚܪܢܝܢ ܚܕ ܡܢ [m] ܢܒܝܐ: ܘܫܐܠ ܐܢܘܢ ܗܘ	ܡܥܡܕܢܐ [j]
[f] ܫܐܠ	[n] ܘܐܡܪ ܠܗܘܢ: ܐܢܬܘܢ ܕܝ ܡܢ ܐܢܬܘܢ	[k] ܘܐܚܪܢܝܢ [l] ܘܐܚܪܢܝܢ
[g] ܠܬܠܡܝܕܘܗܝ [h] ܥܠܝ	ܐܡܪܝܢ ܥܠܝ ܕܐܢܐ: [o] ܐܡܪ [p] ܕܝ [q] ܟܐܦܐ ܗܘ	[n] omit ܘ [o] ܐܡܪ
[k] ܘܐܚܪܢܝܢ	ܘܐܡܪ ܠܗ: ܐܢܬ ܗܘ ܡܫܝܚܐ ܒܪܗ ܕܐܠܗܐ: [r]	[p] omit ܕܝ [q] ܟܐܦܐ
[l] ܘܐܚܪܢܝܢ [m] ܢܒܝܐ	30 ܘܐܟܐ ܒܗܘܢ ܕܠܐ [s] ܢܐܡܪܘܢ [t] ܠܐܢܫ ܥܠܘܗܝ:	[r] add ܚܕ [t] ܠܐܢܫ
[p] omit ܕܝ	31 ܘܫܪܝ [u] ܡܠܦ ܠܗܘܢ [w] ܕܙܕܩ ‡ ܠܒܪܗ [f. 75a]	† f. 75b.
ܢܐܡܪܘܢ [s]	ܕܐܢܫܐ ܕܣܓܝ ܢܚܫ ܘܢܣܬܠܐ ܡܢ [x] ܩܫܝܫܐ	[u] ܡܠܦ [w] ܕܙܕܩ
[y] ܪܒܢܝ [z] ܘܩܡ	ܘܡܢ [y] ܪܒܝ ܟܗܢܐ: ܘܡܢ ܣܦܪܐ ܘܢܬܩܛܠ	[x] ܩܫܝܫܐ [z] ܘܩܡ
[a] add ܒܝܘܡ	ܘܒܬܪ ܬܠܬܐ [z] ܝܘܡܝܢ [a] ܢܩܘܡ ⁘	[a] add ܢܩܘܡ
	CXXXVII.	
	MARK X. 32—45.	
[a] ܗܘܐ [b] ܐܠܝ	ܗܘܐ [a] ܐܠܝ [b] ܐܠܝܫܘܥ [c] ܡܢ ܐܬܪܐ ܡܢ	[a] ܠܒܬܪ [c] ܐܠܝܫܘܥ
ܐܠܝܫܘܥ [c]	32 ܬܠܡܝܕܘܗܝ [a] ܘܐܡܪ ܠܬܪܥܣܪ [b] ܬܠܡܝܕܘܗܝ:	[a] add ܘܬܠܡܝܕܘܗܝ ܥܡܗ
[a] add ܘܬܠܡܝܕܘܗܝ ܥܡܗ	ܘܫܪܝ ܐܡܪ ܠܗܘܢ: ܗܠܝܢ ܕܥܬܝܕܢ [c] ܕܢܓܕܢ	
[b] ܠܬܪܥܣܪܬܐ	33 ܠܗ: ܕܗܐ ܣܠܩܝܢ [d] ܚܢܢ [e] ܠܐܘܪܫܠܡ ܘܒܪܗ	[d] ܣܠܩܝܢ
[c] ܕܢܓܕܢ	ܕܐܢܫܐ [f] ܡܫܬܠܡ [g] ܠܪܒܝ ‡ ܟܗܢܐ ܘܣܦܪܐ:	
‡ f. 87b.	[h] ܘܢܚܝܒܘܢܗ ܠܡܘܬܐ ܘܢܫܠܡܘܢܗ ܠܗ	
[d] ܣܠܩܝܢ [e] ܠܐܘܪܫܠܡ	34 ܠܥܡܡܐ: ܘܢܒܙܚܘܢ ܒܗ [i] ܘܢܪܩܘܢ [k] ܒܐܦܘܗܝ:	[i] ܘܢܪܩܘܢ
[f] ܡܫܬܠܡ	ܘܢܢܓܕܘܢܗ ܘܢܩܛܠܘܢܗ ܘܠܝܘܡܐ ܕܬܠܬܐ	[k] ܒܐܦܘܗܝ
[g] ܠܪܒܝ [h] ܘܢܚܝܒܘܢܗ	35 ܢܩܘܡ: [l] ܘܩܪܒܘ [m] ܠܗ [n] ܝܥܩܘܒ [o] ܘܝܘܚܢܢ	[l] ܘܩܪܒ [m] add ܕܝ
[k] ܒܐܦܘܗܝ [l] ܘܩܪܒܘ	[p] ܒܢܝ [q] ܙܒܕܝ: ܘܐܡܪܝܢ ܠܗ: ܡܠܦܢܐ ܨܒܝܢ	[o] ܘܝܘܚܢܢ [q] ܙܒܕܝ
[m] add ܕܝ [n] ܝܥܩܘܒ		
[p] ܒܢܝ [q] ܙܒܕܝ		

Left margin: ܝܕ ܒ (beside CXXXVI); ܝܚ ܟܐ ܒ (beside CXXXVII)

Codex A.	*Codex* B.	*Codex* C.
[r] ܕܢܫܡܠ	36 ܐܝܟ ܕܡܢܐ [r] ܕܢܫܡܠ ܡܢܝ ܐܬܟܬܒ ܠܝ: ܘܗܘܐ	[r] ܕܢܫܡܠ
	ܐܡܪ ܠܗܘܢ ܡܢܐ ܐܢܬܘܢ ܡܬܚܫܒܝܢ ܕܒܟܬܒܐ	
[m] *add* ܕܝ	37 ܠܗܘܢ: ܗܘܢ [m] [s] ܐܡܪܬ ܠܗ: ܡܢ ܠܝ ܕܢܬܒܥ	[s] ܐܡܪ
[t] ܡܬܒܠܝܟ	ܣܪ ܡܢ ܡܬܚܫܒ ܗܘܐ ܡܢ [t] ܡܬܒܠܝܟ [u] ܒܬܫܒܘܚܬܟ:	[t] ܡܬܐܠܝܟ
[u] ܒܬܫܒܘܚܬܟ	38 ܘܡܪܐ ܗܘܐ ܐܝܟܢܐ ܘܐܡܪ ܠܗܘܢ: ܠܝܬ	
	ܐܢܬܘܢ ܡܬܚܫܒܝܢ ܡܢܐ ܐܢܬܘܢ ܫܐܠܝܢ: [v] ܡܬܠܝܢ	[v] ܡܬܐܠܝܢ
	ܐܢܬܘܢ ܕܬܫܬܘܢ ܟܣܐ ܕܐܢܐ ܫܬܐ	
	ܘܬܬܛܒܠܘܢ ܡܢ ܡܥܡܘܕܝܬܐ ܕܐܢܐ [w] ܡܬܛܒܠ:	[w] ܡܬܛܒܠ
[x] ܐܡܪܘ	39 ܗܢܘܢ [x] ܐܡܪܝܢ [v] ܡܬܠܝܢ ܐܢܚܢ: ܘܐܡܪ ܝܫܘܥ	[v] ܡܬܐܠܝܢ
	ܐܡܪ ܠܗܘܢ: ܟܣܐ ܡܢ ܕܐܢܐ ܫܬܐ ܐܢܬܘܢ	
[y] ܡܬܛܒܠ	ܫܬܝܢ: ܘܡܥܡܘܕܝܬܐ ܕܐܢܐ [y] ܡܬܛܒܠ	[y] ܡܬܛܒܠ
	[f. 75*b*]	
	40 ܐܢܬܘܢ ܡܬܛܒܠܝܢ: [o] ܕܬܬܒܘܢ ܕܝ ܣܪ ܡܢ	[o] ܕܬܬܒܘܢ
‡ f. 88*a*.	[z] ܡܬܚܫܒ ‡ ܗܘܐ ܡܢ [a] ܡܬܒܠܝܟ: ܠܝܬ ܗܘ ܕܝܠܝ	[z] ܡܬܚܫܒ [a] ܡܬܐܠܝܟ
[c] ܕܗܘ	41 ܐܠܐ [b] ܕܗܠܝܢ [c] ܕܝ ܡܬܟܬܒܐ: ܘܒܪ ܫܡܥܘܢ	[b] ܠܗܠܝܢ [c] ܕܗܘ
[e] ܫܪܝܘ	[d] ܫܪܝܘܬ † ܒܡܫܪܝܬܐ [e] ܫܪܘ [f] ܡܬܪܓܙܝܢ ܥܠ	† f. 76*a*.
[g] ܒܥܘܠܡܗܘܢ	42 [g] ܒܥܘܠܡܗܘܢ ܘܥܠ [h] ܐܚܘܗܝ: ܘܩܪܐ ܐܢܘܢ ܝܫܘܥ	[f] ܐܚܝܢ [d] ܫܪܝܬ
[i] ܫܬܝܢ	ܫܡܗܘܢ ܘܐܡܪ ܠܗܘܢ [i] ܫܬܝܢ ܐܢܬܘܢ	[h] ܐܚܘܗܝ
[j] *add* ܕ	ܕܗܠܝܢ [j] ܡܫܬܒܚܝܢ ܕܗܘܝܢ ܪܫܐ ܥܠ ܥܡܡܐ	[j] *add* ܕ
	ܗܘܝܢ [k] ܡܬܐܡܪܝܢ ܥܠܝܗܘܢ ܘܪܘܪܒܢܝܗܘܢ	[k] ܡܬܐܡܪܝܢ
[m] ܒܟܘܢ [n] ܕܢܗܘܐ	43 [l] ܫܠܝܛܝܢ ܒܗܘܢ: [m] ܒܟܘܢ ܠܐ ܗܘܐ ܗܟܢܐ ܒܝܢܬܟܘܢ:	[l] ܫܠܝܛܝܢ ܒܗܘܢ [n] ܕܢܗܘܐ
[o] ܡܫܡܫܢܐ	ܐܠܐ ܡܢ ܕܨܒܐ [n] ܕܢܗܘܐ ܒܟܘܢ ܪܒ ܢܗܘܐ	[o] ܡܫܡܫܢܐ ܠܟܘܢ [o]
[q] ܡܫܡܫܢܟܘܢ	44 [o] ܡܫܡܫܢܟܘܢ: ܘܡܢ ܕܨܒܐ [p] ܕܢܗܘܐ [q] ܡܫܡܫܢܟܘܢ	[p] ܢܗܘܐ [q] ܡܫܡܫܢܟܘܢ
[r] ܠܟܠܟܘܢ	45 ܢܗܘܐ [r] ܠܟܠܟܘܢ [s] ܟܠܟܘܢ: ܡܛܠ ܒܪܗ	[r] ܠܟܘܢ ܟܠ [r]
[s] ܕܟܠܟܘܢ	ܕܐܢܫܐ ܠܐ ܐܬܐ ܕܢܫܬܡܫ ܐܠܐ [t] ܕܢܫܡܫ:	[s] *omit* ܟܠܟܘܢ
[u] ܢܦܫܗ [w] ܦܘܪܩܢ	ܘܢܬܠ [u] ܢܦܫܗ [w] ܦܘܪܩܢ ܚܠܦ ܣܓܝܐܐ ⁘	[t] ܕܢܫܡܫ

CXXXVIII.

John XI. 1—45.

Codex A.	*Codex* B.	*Codex* C.
[b] ܗܘܐ ܐܠܥܙܪ [b]	[a] ܗܘܐ [b] ܐܢܫ ܐܠܥܙܪ [b] ܠܠܥܙܪ ܡܢ ܒܝܬ ܥܢܝܐ[a]	[a] ܐܢܫ ܗܘܐ ܐܠܥܙܪ ܡܢ ܒܝܬ ܥܢܝܐ [a]
[c] *omit* . . . ܘܡܢ	[c] ܘܡܢ ܗܘܐ ܐܚܬܗ ܕܐܠܥܙܪ ܡܪܝܡ ܘܡܪܬܐ	[c] *omit* . . . ܘܡܢ
. . . ܐܠܥܙܪ	ܘܐܚܘܗ ܕܝ ܥܠ ܕܗܘܐ ܐܚܘܗ ܐܠܥܙܪ[c]:	. . . ܐܠܥܙܪ

ܥܠ ܕܐܠܥܙܪ (*sic*)

Codex A.

[a] *omit* ܕܥܢܕܗ

[b]ܠܒܝܪܘܣ [c]ܡܪܘܬܗ

[d]ܚܬܗ [e]ܡܪܝܢܫ

[g]ܒܒܝܫܘܬ [h]ܢ̈ܚܠܘܢ

[k]ܐܚܘܗ [l]ܠܒܝܪܘܣ

‡ f. 88b.

[a]ܘܐܡܪ̈ܝܢ [b]ܗܕܝܢ

[c] *add* ܕܝ

[d]ܠܡܒܥ

[m]ܬܒܥܘܬܗ

[q]ܒܐܬܪܐ [r]ܗܕܝܢ

[t] *omit* ܕܝ [u]ܢܝܚܠ

[w]ܠܡܘܕܝܐ

[y]ܐܡܪ̈ܝܢ [z]ܪܒܝ

[b]ܟܒܝܢ ܡܘܕܝܐ[b]

[c]ܕܢܬܟܢܫܘܢ [d]ܐܙܠ

[e]ܬܬܒܥܣܪ̈ܐ

[g]ܗܘ̈ܝܢ [h]ܒܟܘܒܐ

[m]ܕܢܘܗܪܗ [n]ܗܕܝܢ

[o]ܒܠܠܝܐ [p]ܗܘ

[t] *omit* ܗܘ

[u]ܡܬܬܠܝܠ

[v]ܗܘ ܕܢܘܗܪ[v]

‡ f. 89a.

[w]ܗܕܝܢ [x]ܠܒܝܪܘܣ

[y]ܕܡܫܝܚ [z]ܐܙܠ

[a]ܕܐܒܪ [c]ܬܠܡܝܕܘܗܝ

[e]ܠܒܗ [f]ܡܘܬܗ

[g]ܕܥܢܝܢܬܐ [i]ܒܟܝܢ

[k] *omit* ܡܪܝܐ ܫܡܥܘܢ

[l] *add* ܡܪܝܐ ܒܫܡܥܘܢ

Codex B.

1 ܘܒܬܪܗ ܡܢܝܪܘܣܐ : ܘܗܘܐ ܕܝ ܚܕ ܟܐܒ
[a]ܕܥܢܕܗ [b]ܐܠܒܝܪܘܣ ܡܢ ܒܝܬ ܒܢܝܐ ܡܢ [c]ܡܪܘܬܗ
2 ܕܡܪܝܢܫ ܘܕܡܪܝܢܬܐ [d]ܐܚܬܗ : ܗܘܬ ܕܝ [e]ܡܪܝܢܫ
[f]ܗܕܐ ܕܡܫܡܫܬ ܠܡܪܝܐ [g]ܒܒܝܫܘܬ : ܘܥܒܕܬ
[h]ܢ̈ܚܠܘܢ ܒܡܢܝܢܗ : ܗܕܐ [i]ܕܗܘܐ [k]ܐܚܘܗ
3 [l]ܐܠܒܝܪܘܣ ‡ ܒܐܟܝܢ : ܘܥܠܝܢ ܐܚܘܬܗ ܠܘܬ
ܡܪܝܐ ܫܡܥܘܢ [a]ܐܡܪܝܢ ܠܗ : ܡܪܝܐ ܗܐ [b]ܗܕܝܢ
4 ܕܐܬܐ ܙܢܘܢ ܒܐܟܝܢ : ܟܕ[c] ܥܒܕ ܡܪܝܐ ܫܡܥܘܢ
[f. 76a]
ܐܡܪ ܗܕܝܢ ܒܟܐܒܐ ܠܝܬ ܗܘ ܠܡܚܝܘܬ : ܐܠܐ
[d]ܠܡܒܥ [m]ܠܡܬܒܥܘܬܗ [n]ܕܐܠܗܐ : ܠܒܝܬ ܕܥܬܝܕ
5 ܒܪܗ ܕܐܠܗܐ ܒܬܪܒܗ : [o]ܗܘܐ ܕܝ ܡܪܝܐ
ܫܡܥܘܢ ܡܫܒܚ ܠܡܪܝܐ ܘܠܫܡܗ ܘܠܠܒܝܪܘܣ :
6 ܟܕ ܐܘ ܥܒܕ ܕܗܘ ܒܐܟܝܢ : ܒܟܝܢ [p]ܒܬܪ
ܬܘܡ [q]ܒܐܬܪܗ ܗܘ ܕܗܘܐ ܬܪܝܢ ܡܘܡܝܢ :
7 ܘܡܢ ܒܬܪ [r]ܗܕܝܢ ܐܡܪ [s]ܠܬܠܡܝܕܘܗܝ : ܐܬܘ
8 [u]ܕܢܝܚܠ [w]ܠܡܘܕܝܐ † [x]ܬܘܒܢ : [y]ܐܡܪܝܢ ܠܗ
[z]ܬܠܡܝܕܘܗܝ [a]ܪܒܝ : ܒܕ ܗܘܘ [t]ܕܝ [b]ܡܕܝܢ ܒܟܝܢ[b]
[c]ܕܢܬܟܢܫܘܢ ܠܘܬܟ : ܘܬܘܒܢ ܐܬ [d]ܐܙܠ ܠܬܡܢ :
9 ܐܬܒܟܝ ܡܪܝܐ ܫܡܥܘܢ ܘܐܡܪ ܠܗܘܢ : ܠܐ
[e]ܬܬܒܥܣܪ [f]ܥܒܕܝܢ [g]ܗܘܢ [h]ܘܒܟܝܐ : [i]ܐܢ ܗܘܐ
ܐܢܫ ܡܗܠܟ [k]ܒܟܘܒܐ ܠܐ [l]ܡܬܬܠܝܠ : [m]ܕܢܘܗܪܐ
10 [n]ܗܕܝܢ [o]ܒܠܝܠܝܐ [p]ܗܘܐ ܚܫܟܐ : [q]ܐܢ [r]ܕܝ
ܗܘܐ ܐܢܫ [s]ܡܗܠܟ ܒܠܠܝܐ [t]ܗܘ [u]ܡܬܬܠܝܠ
11 ‡ [v]ܕܢܘܗܪܐ[v] ܠܝܬ ܒܗܘܢ : ܗܠܝܢ ܐܡܪ ܘܡܢ
ܒܬܪ [w]ܗܕܝܢ ܐܡܪ ܠܗܘܢ [x]ܐܠܒܝܪܘܣ ܢܣܒ
[y]ܕܡܫܝܚ : ܐܠܐ [z]ܐܙܠ ܐܢܐ [a]ܕܐܒܪ ܢܦܫܗ :
12 ܐܡܪܝܢ[b] ܠܗ [c]ܬܠܡܝܕܘܗܝ ܡܪܝܐ ܐܢ [d]ܕܡܫܝܚ
13 ܚܝܐ ܗܘ : ܡܪܝܐ ܫܡܥܘܢ ܕܝ ܗܘܐ ܐܡܪ ܒܠ
[e]ܠܒܗ [f]ܕܡܘܬܐ : ܘܗܘܢ ܗܘܘ ܡܫܡܥܝܢ ܕܒܠ
14 ܠܒܗ ܕܡܟ̈ܐ [g]ܕܥܢܝܢܬܐ [h]ܗܘ ܐܡܪ : [i]ܒܟܝܢ
ܐܡܪ ܠܗܘܢ [k]ܡܪܝܐ ܫܡܥܘܢ[k] ܒܟ̈ܪܝܗܘܬܐ[l]

Codex C.

[a] *omit* ܕܥܢܕܗ

[f]ܗܕܝܢ [g]ܒܒܝܫܘܬܗ

[h]ܢܚܠܘܢ [i]ܕܗܘܬ

[a]ܘܐܡܪܝܢ

[c] *add* ܕܝ

[n]ܕܐܒܐ

[o] *omit* ܗܘܐ

[p]ܒܬܪ

[q]ܒܐܬܪܐ

[s]ܠܬܠܡܝܕܘܗܝ [u]ܢܝܚܠ

† f. 76b.

[x]ܬܘܒܢ [z]ܬܠܡܝܕܘܗܝ

[e]ܐܬܒܟܝܪܐ

[f] *omit* ܥܒܕܝܢ

[h]ܒܟܘܒܐ [i]ܐܢ

[k]ܒܟܘܒܟܐ [l]ܡܬܬܠܝܠ

[m]ܕܢܘܗܪܗ [n]ܕܝܢ

[o]ܒܠܠܝܐ [p]ܗܘ

[q]ܐܢ [s]ܡܗܠܟ

[x]ܠܠܒܝܪܘܣ

[b] *add* ܐܘ

[c]ܬܠܡܝܕܘܗܝ

[d]ܕܡܫܝܚ [e]ܠܒܗ

[f]ܡܘܬܗ [h] *omit* ܗܘ

Codex A.

ᵈܠܥܙܪܘܣ ᵉadd ܐܢܐ
ᶠܠܒܓܠܠܟܘܢ
ᵍܕܬܗܝܡܢܘܢ
ʰܢܐܙܠ ⁱܕܝ
ᵏܬܐܘܡܣ
ᵐomit ܕܡܬܩܪ
ⁿܠܚܒܪܘܗܝ ᵖܐܢܚܢ
ʳܕܝ ˢܡܪܢ
ᵗܘܐܫܟܚ
‡ f. 89b.
ᵘomit ܡܬܗ ʷܒܩܒܪ
ˣܒܡܩܒܪܬܐ
ʸܠܐܘܪܫܠܡ
ᶻܢܚܡܬܗܘܢ
ᵃܐܣܛܕܝܢ ᶜܝܗܘܕܝܐ
ᵈadd ܗܘܘ ᵍܕܝ
ʰܠܐܚܘܗܝܢ
ⁱܡܪܬܐ ʲadd ܕܝ
ˡܗܘܬ ᵐܡܐܝܬ
ⁿܕܬܫܐܠ
ᵒܩܐܡ ᵠadd ܠܗ
ˢܒܩܝܡܬܐ
ᵗܒܝܘܡܐ ᵘadd ܠܗ
ˣܩܝܡܬܐ
ᵈܕܚܝ ᵉadd ܕܝ
ᶠܒܥܠܡ ᵍܒܕ
ʰܐܝܢ ʲܠܥܠܡܐ
‡ f. 90a.
ˡܐܙܠܬ ᵐܠܡܪܝܡ
ⁿܐܚܬܗ ᵒܘܐܡܪܬ
ᵖܠܗ ᵒomit ܘ
ˢܒܥܓܠ ᵗܘܐܙܠܬ

Codex B.

15 ᵈܐܠܥܙܪ ܡܝܬ : ܘܐܢܐ ܚܕܐ ᵉ ᶠܠܒܓܠܠܟܘܢ
ᵍܕܬܗܝܡܢܘܢ ܕܠܐ ܗܘܝܬ ܬܡܢ : ܐܠܐ ܐܬܘ ʰܢܐܙܠ
16 ܠܘܬܗ : ܐܡܪ ⁱ ܠܗܘܢ ᵏ ܬܐܘܡܣ ˡ ᵐ ܕܡܬܩܪ
[f. 76b]
ܬܐܘܡܐ ⁿܠܚܒܪܘܗܝ ܬܠܡܝܕܝܐ ܐܬܘ ᵒܢܐܙܠ ܐܘܦ
17 ᵖܐܢܚܢ ᵠܕܢܡܘܬ ܥܡܗ : ܐܬܐ ʳܐܘܢ ˢܡܪܐ
ܘܫܟܚܗ ܠܒܝܬ ܟܠܝܐ ᵗܘܐܪܒܥܐ ܝܘܡܝܢ ܗܘܘ ܠܗ
ᵘܒܬܪ ܡܬܗ ᵘ ܐܪܒܥܐ ܝܘܡܝܢ ʷܒܩܒܪ ˣܡܩܒܪܬܐ :
18 ܗܘܬ ܕܝܢ ܒܝܬ ܥܢܝܐ ܩܪܝܒܐ ʸܠܐܘܪܫܠܡ :
19 ܗܝܟ ܚܡܫܬܥܣܪ ᵃܐܣܛܕܝܢ : ܣܓܝܐܝܢ ᵇܕܝܢ ܡܢ
ᶜܝܗܘܕܝܐ ᵈܐܬܘ ᵉܠܘܬ † ܡܪܬܐ ‡ ܘܡܪܝܡ
20 ܕܝܢܚܡܘܢ ܝܬܗܝܢ ܥܠ ᶠܐܚܘܗܝܢ : ܟܕ
ᵍܐܘܢ ܫܡܥܬ ܡܪܬܐ ܕܡܪܝܐ ܝܫܘܥ ܐܬܐ
ܢܦܩܬ ʰܠܩܘܕܡܘܗܝ : ⁱܡܪܝܡ ܕܝܢ ܗܘܬ
21 ܝܬܒܐ ܒܒܝܬܐ : ܐܡܪܬ ʲܡܪܬܐ ܠܡܪܐ
ܝܫܘܥ : ᵏܡܪܝ ˡܐܠܘ ܗܘܬ ܗܟܐ ܠܐ ܗܘܐ
22 ܐܚܝ ᵐܡܐܝܬ : ܐܠܐ ܐܘܦ ܒܗܘ ܝܕܥܐ
ܐܢܐ ܕܟܠܘܕܐ ⁿܕܬܫܐܠ ܡܢ ܐܠܗܐ ܝܗܒ
23 ܗܘ ܠܟ ܐܠܗܐ : ܐܡܪ ܠܗ ܡܪܐ ܝܫܘܥ
24 ᵒܩܐܝܡ ܗܘ ᵖܐܚܘܟܝ : ܐܡܪܐ ᵠ ܡܪܬܐ
ʳܝܕܥܐ ܐܢܐ ܕܗܘ ᵒܩܐܝܡ ˢܒܩܝܡܬܐ ܒܝܘܡܐ
25 ᵗܐܚܪܝܐ : ᵘܐܡܪ ܡܪܐ ܝܫܘܥ ܐܢܐ ܗܘ ʷ
ˣܩܝܡܬܐ ʸܘܚܝܝܐ : ܡܢ ܕܗܝܡܢ ܒܝ ᶻܐܘܦ
26 ᵃᶻ ܐܢ ᵇܝܡܘܬ ܚܝܐ ܗܘ : ܘܟܘܠ ܡܢ ᶜ ᵈܕܚܝ
ܘܡܗܝܡܢ ܒܝ ܠܐ ᵉܝܡܘܬ ᶠܠܥܠܡ : ܡܗܝܡܢܐ
27 ܐܢܬܝ ᵍܒܕܐ : ܐܡܪܐ ܠܗ ʰܐܝܢ ܡܪܝ ܐܢܐ
ܗܝܡܢܬ ܕܐܢܬ ܗܘ ܡܫܝܚܐ ܒܪܗ ܕܐܠܗܐ ⁱ:
28 ‡ ܗܕܝܢ ܕܐܬܝܐ ʲܠܥܠܡܐ : ܘܟܕ ᵏܐܡܪܬ ܗܠܝܢ
[f. 77a]
ܐܙܠܬ ˡܘܩܪܬ ᵐܠܡܪܝܡ ⁿܐܚܬܗ ᵒܘܐܡܪܐ ܠܗ
29 ܒܛܫܗ ᵖܘܠܗ ܡܠܦܢܐ ܐܬܐ ܘܗܘ ܩܪܐ ܠܝܟܝ :
ᵠܗܝ ܕܝܢ ܟܕ ܫܡܥܬ ʳܩܡܬ ˢܒܥܓܠ
30 ᵗܘܐܙܠܬ ܠܘܬܗ : ܥܕ ܟܕܘ ܕܝܢ ܠܐ ܗܘܐ

Codex C.

ᵈܠܠܥܙܪܘܣ
ᵍܕܬܗܝܡܢܘܢ
ʰܕܢܐܙܠ
ˡadd ܗܕܝܢ
ⁿܠܚܒܪܘܗܝ ᵒܢܐܙܠ
ᵠܕܢܡܘܬ
ᵘomit ܒܬܪ ܡܬܗ
ᵃܐܣܛܕܝܢ ᵇomit ܕܝ
† f. 77a.
ᵉܠܘܬܗ ᶠܐܚܘܗܝܢ
ʲadd ܕܝ
ᵏܡܪܝ
ⁿܕܬܫܐܠ
ᵖܐܚܘܟܝ ᵠadd ܠܗ
ʳܝܕܥܐ ᵘadd ܠܗ
ʷadd ܘ ܐܢܐ
ʸomit ܘܚܝܝܐ
ᶻomit ܐܘܦ ܐܢ
ᵇܝܡܘܬ ᵃadd ܠܐ
ᶠܠܥܠܡ ʰܐܝܢ
ⁱadd ܐܢܐ
ʲܠܥܠܡܐ ᵏܐܡܪܬ
ⁿܐܚܬܗ
ʳܘܩܡܬ
ˢܒܥܓܠ

Codex B.

ܕܐܬܐ ܡܪܢܐ ܝܫܘܥ [u]ܠܩܪܝܬܐ: ܐܠܐ [w]ܥܕ
ܥܕܘ [x]ܗܘܐ ܒܐܬܪܐ ܗܘ [y]ܕܥܪܥܬ ܠܗ
31 ܡܪܬܐ: [z]ܗܠܝܢ ܐܘܢ [a]ܝܗܘܕܝܢ [b]ܗܠܝܢ ܕܗܘܘ
†ܥܡܗ ܒܒܝܬܐ ܡܢܚܡܝܢ ܠܗ: ܟܕ ܚܙܘ
[m]ܠܡܪܝܡ [n]ܕܐܬܦܢܝܬ [o]ܘܐܙܠܬ ܘܢܦܩܬ [p]ܕܝ
ܕܢܦܩܐ ܗܘܬ ܐܡܪܝܢ: ܕܗܝ ܐܙܠܐ [q]ܠܡܩܒܘܪܬܐ
32 ܕܐܬܐܬܐ ܬܡܢ: [r]ܟܕ ܐܘܢ ܐܬܬ ܡܪܝܐܡ[r] ܠܗܘܢ
ܕܗܘܐ ܡܪܢܐ ܝܫܘܥ: [s]ܘܚܙܬܗ ܘܢܦܠܬ
ܗܘܢ [t]ܠܪܓܠܘܝ [u]ܘܐܡܪܐ ܠܗ ܡܪܝ ܐܠܘ
33 [v]ܗܘܬ ܟܐ ܠܐ ܗܘܐ ܐܚܝ [j]ܡܐܝܬ: ܡܪܢܐ
ܝܫܘܥ ܕܝ ܟܕ ܚܙܐ ܠܗ ܒܟܝܐ: [w]ܘܠܝܗܘܕܝܢ
[x]ܗܠܝܢ [y]ܕܐܬܘ ܥܡܗ ܒܟܝܢ: ܐܬܙܥܦ [z]ܒܪܘܚܐ
34 ܘܐܬܒܠܒܠ ܒܢܦܫܗ ܘܐܡܪ ‡ ܗܢ [a]ܐܣܡܬܘܢ
ܝܬܗ: ܐܡܪܝܢ ܠܗ ܡܪܢܐ ܐܬܐ [b]ܘܚܡܝ:
35 36 ܘܕܡܥ ܡܪܢܐ ܝܫܘܥ ܘܗܘ [c]ܐܘܢ [d]ܝܗܘܕܝܢ
37 ܐܡܪܝܢ ܚܡܘ ܐܝܟ [e]ܗܘ [f]ܪܚܡ ܠܗ: ܐܢܫܝܢ
ܕܝ ܡܢܗܘܢ ܐܡܪܘ ܠܐ ܗܘܐ [g]ܝܟܠ [h]ܗܢܕܝܢ
ܕܦܬܚ [i]ܥܝܢܘܝ [k]ܕܣܡܝܐ ܕܝܥܒܕ [l]ܗܢܕܝܢ ܠܐ
38 ܝܡܘܬ: ܡܪܢܐ ܝܫܘܥ [m]ܬܘܒ ܐܬܙܥܦ ܒܪܘܚܗ
ܘܐܬܐ [n]ܠܡܩܒܘܪܬܐ: ܗܘܬ ܕܝ ܡܥܪܐ
[f. 77*b*]
39 ܘܟܐܦ [o]ܗܘܐ [p]ܡܣܝܡ ܥܠܝܗ: [r]ܐܡܪ ܠܗܘܢ
ܡܪܢܐ ܝܫܘܥ ܐܪܝܡܘ ܟܐܦܐ: ܐܡܪܐ ܠܗ:
[t]ܐܚܬܗ [u]ܕܕܝܡ [v]ܕܓܐܙ [w]ܡܪܬܐ ܡܪܝ ܟܒܪ
[x]ܗܘܐ ܡܣܪܝ [y]ܗܐ ܠܗ[y] [z]ܐܪܒܥܐ ܝܘܡܝܢ:[a]
40 ܐܡܪ ܠܗ ܡܪܢܐ ܝܫܘܥ: ܠܐ ܐܡܪܬ ܠܟܝ
[b]ܕܐܢ [c]ܬܗܝܡܢܝܢ [d]ܚܡܝܢ [e]ܬܚܡܝܢ [f]ܕܝ
41 ܬܫܒܘܚܬܗ ܕܐܠܗܐ: [g]ܟܕ [h]ܐܘܢ ܐܪܝܡܘ
ܟܐܦܐ: [i]ܡܪܢܐ ܝܫܘܥ [j]ܬܠܐ [k]ܥܝܢܘܝ [l]ܠܥܠ
ܘܐܡܪ ܐܒܐ ܡܘܕܝܢܐ ܐܢܐ ܠܟ † ܕܫܡܥܬ
42 ܡܢܝ: ܐܢܐ ܕܝ [m]ܝܕܥ ܕܒܟܠ ܥܕܢ ܐܬ
[n]ܫܡܥ ܡܢܝ: ܐܠܐ [p]ܠܥܡܐ [r]ܐܘܟܠܘܣܐ

Codex A.

[u]ܠܩܪܝܬܐ
[w]*add* ܗܘܐ
[x]*omit* ܗܘܐ
[y]ܕܐܬܪܥܬ [a]ܝܗܘܕܝܢ
[b]*omit* ܗܠܝܢ
[m]ܡܪܝܡ [n]ܕܐܬܦܢܝܬ
[o]ܘܐܙܠܬ [p]*omit* ܕܝ
[q]ܠܡܩܒܘܪܬܐ
[r]ܡܪܝܐܡ ܕܝ ܟܕ
[r]ܐܬܬ
[s]ܘܚܙܬ [t]ܠܪܓܠܘܝ
[u]ܘܐܡܪܐ
[j]ܡܐܝܬ [w]ܘܠܝܗܘܕܝܢ
[x]*omit* ܗܠܝܢ [y]ܕܐܬܘ
[z]ܒܪܘܚܗ
‡ f. 90*b*.
[a]ܐܣܡܬܘܢ
[b]ܘܚܡܝ [c]ܕܝ
[d]ܝܗܘܕܝܢ [e]ܗܘܐ
[f]ܪܚܡ [g]ܝܟܠ
[h]ܕܝܢ [i]ܥܝܢܘܝ
[k]ܕܣܡܝܐ
[l]*add* ܕܐܦ
[m]*add* ܕܝ [n]ܠܡܩܒܘܪܬܐ
[o]*omit* ܗܘܐ
[p]ܡܣܝܡ [r]ܘܐܡܪ
[t]ܐܚܬܗ [u]ܕܡܝܬ
[v]ܕܐܙܠ [x]ܗܘ
[y]*omit* ܗܐ ܠܗ
[z]ܐܪܒܥܐ ܟܒܪ[z]
[a]*add* ܠܗ
omit ܕܝ [d]*omit* ܚܡܝܢ
[g]ܘܟܕ [h]*omit* ܐܘܢ
omit ܬܠܐ [i]*add* ܬܠܐ
[m]*add* ܬܘܒ [l]ܠܥܠ
[n]ܫܡܥ [p]ܠܟܠ
[r]ܐܘܟܠܘܣܐ

Codex C.

[u]ܠܩܪܝܬܐ
[z]ܗܠܝܢ
† f. 77*b*.
[n]ܕܐܬܦܢܝܬ [o]ܘܐܙܠܬ
[p]*omit* ܕܝ
[q]ܠܡܩܒܘܪܬܐ
[r]ܟܕ ܐܘܢ ܕܝ
ܐܬܬ ܡܪܝܐܡ[r]
[u]ܘܐܡܪܐ
[v]ܗܘܬ
[y]ܕܐܬܘ
[e]ܗܘܐ [f]ܪܚܡ
[k]ܕܣܡܝܐ
[m]*add* ܕܝ
[o]*omit* ܗܘܐ
[p]ܡܣܝܡ
[t]ܐܚܬܗ [v]ܕܐܙܠ
[w]*omit* ܡܪܬܐ [x]ܗܘ
[z]ܐܪܒܥܐ ܟܒܪ[z]
[b]ܕܐܢ
[c]ܬܗܝܡܢܝܢ
[e]ܬܚܡܝܢ
[f]*omit* ܕܝ [k]ܥܝܢܘܝ
† f. 78*a*.
[n]ܫܡܥ
[r]ܐܘܟܠܘܣܐ

Codex A.

[‡ f. 91a.] ܦܐܡܪ ᵗܐܢܫܐ ᵘadd ܐܢܐ
ʷܐܡܪ ܠܗ ʸadd ܗܘ
ᶻܠܒܝܬܐ ᵃܘܡܛܘ
ᵇܬܠܡܝܕܘ
ᵉܒܥܡܡܐ
ᶠܘܐܬܩܛܘ
ᵍadd ܢܒܝܐ
ʰܒܥܡܡܐ
ⁱomit ܗܘܘ ܚܙܝܢ
ʲܘܐܡܪ ᵏܘܒܥܘܘܢ
ˡܕܢܐܚܕ ᵐadd ܕܝ
ⁿܡܢܗܘܢ
ᵖܡܬܚܙܝܐ ʳܘܫܡܥܘ
ˢadd ܡܢܗ ܒܥܡܐ
ᵘadd ܥܠܡ

ܫܒܐ ܕܒܬܪ ܦܢܛܩܘܣܛܐ

ᵇܐܠܘܡ ܫܒ
ᵇܐܥܒܕܥܒ
ᶜܒܬܘܢܗ
ᵃaddܘܒܝܘܡܐ ܕܥܘܪܒܐ
ᵇܦܘܠ ᵉܕܝܢܝܒ
ⁱܠܡܕܝܢܬܐ
ˡܕܠܡܠܟܘܬܗ
ᵐܐܬܚܙܝ ⁿܘܡܠܟ
ᵒomit ܗܘܐ
ᵖܘܐܬܘܒ ˢܒܠܡܫ
ᵗܐܡܪܘ ᵘܕܐܡܪ
[‡ f. 91b.]
ˣܡܫܝܚ ᵛadd ܗܘ
ʸܐܬܒܥܒܕܬ ᶻܠܟܠܠ
ᵈomit ܡܫܝܚ
ᵉܘܐܬܒܥ ᶠܥܠܠ
ʰܐܬܐ
ⁱܐܬܐܡܘ ʲܘܐܬܘ
ᵏܡܫܝܚܐ ᵐomit ܕܝ
ⁿܒܐܬܢܐ
ᵒܘܩܒܠ ᵖܥܠ

Codex B.

‡ ˢܕܒܥܐ ᵗܘܐܬܩܛ ᵘܘܐܡܪ ʷܐܡܪܬ ܕܡܫܝܚܘܬܗ ܕܒܝܬ
43 ܥܠ ܗܕܐ ܐܡܪ: ܒܗܠܝܢ ܐܡܪ ܐܢܐ ܠܟܘܢ ʸܕܬܠܬ
44 ܘܐܡܪ: ᶻܠܒܝܬܗ ܐܬܐ ܗܘܐ ܠܒܪ: ᵃܘܡܛܘ
ܢܗܘ ܗܘܐ ܡܢܗ ᵇܬܠܡܝܕܘ ᶜܘܐܬܩܛܘ ᵈܐܡܪܝܢ
ᵉܒܥܡܡܐ: ᶠܘܐܬܩܛܘ ᵍʰܒܥܡܡܐ ⁱܗܘܘ ܚܙܝܢ:
ʲܐܡܪ ܠܗܘܢ ܡܢ ܐܢܫ ܫܡܥ ܒܪ ܗܘܐ
45 ᵏܘܒܥܘ ܗܘܐ ᵏܕܝ ˡܕܢܐܚܕ: ᵐܡܢ ܕܝ ⁿܘܢܚܕ
ܡܠܝ ܕܐܬܐ ܠܗܘܢ ᵖܡܚܙܝܢ: ʳܫܡܥ ܡܢ ܕܟܕ:
ᵗܡܫܝܚ ܒܗ ᵘ:·

CXXXIX.

Matt. XXI. 1—17.

ᵃܡܦܪܫܐ ܕܥܠ ᵇܫܒ ᵇܐܥܒܕܥܒܗ ܦܢܝ ܡܢ
1 ᶜܒܬܘܢܗ: ᵃ ᵃ: ܘܟܕ ᵇܩܪܒ ᶜܠܝܪܘܫܠܡ: ᵈܘܐܬܐ
ܠܒܝܬ ᵉܦܓܐ ܠܛܘܪܐ ܕܙܝܬܐ ᶠܠܛܘܪܐ
ܕܙܝܬܐ: ܗܝܕܝܢ ܐܝܫܘܥ ᵍܫܕܪ ܬܪܝܢ
2 ܡܢ ʰܬܠܡܝܕܘܗܝ: ܘܐܡܪ ܠܗܘܢ ܙܠܘ ⁱܠܩܪܝܬܐ
ᵏܕܠܘܩܒܠܟܘܢ ˡܕܠܩܘܒܠܟܘܢ: ܘܡܚܕܐ ܬܫܟܚܘܢ ܡܫܒܚܝܢ
ᵐܐܬܢܐ ⁿܘܥܠܐ ܒܪܗ: ܫܪܘ ᵒܐܝܬܝܘ
[f. 78a]
3 ᵖܘܐܢ ܐܢܫ ܢܐܡܪ ܠܟܘܢ ᵠܡܕܡ ܐܡܪܘ ܠܗ
ʳܡܪܢ ˢܨܒܐ: ᵗܐܡܪܘ ᵘܕܫܕܪ ܐܢܘܢ ᵛ ʷܡܚܕܐ
4 ܠܗܘܢ: ‡ ᵗܘܗܕܐ ܗܘܐ ˣܕܢܫܠܡ ܡܕܡ: ܗܕܐ
ܕܝ ܗܘܬ ʸܕܐܬܐܡܪ ᶻܠܟܠܠ ܕܢܒܝܐ ܕܐܡܪ
5 ܕܐܡܪܘ ܠܒܪܬ ܨܗܝܘܢ: ᵃܗܐ ܡܠܟܟܝ ܐܬܐ ܠܟܝ
ܢܝܚ ܗܘ ᵇܘܪܟܝܒ ܥܠ ᶜܥܠܐ ܒܪ ܐܬܢܐ
ᵈܡܫܝܚ ᵉܘܐܙܠܘ ᶠܥܠ ܐܒܐ ܘܥܒܕܘ ᵍܐܝܟ
6 ʰܐܬܐ: ܘܥܒܕ ܐܝܟ ܕܦܩܕ ܠܗܘܢ ܡܪܢ ܝܫܘܥ
7 ⁱܘܐܝܬܝܘ ܠܗܘܢ ܐܬܢܐ ܘܥܠܐ: ʲܘܣܡܘ
ᵏܥܠܝܗܘܢ ܡܐܢܝܗܘܢ: ˡܘܪܟܒ ᵐܗܘ ܥܠܝܗܘܢ
8 ⁿܘܣܓܝܐܐ: ᵒܘܦܪܣܘ ᵖܥܠ ܐܘܪܚܐ ܡܐܢܝܗܘܢ

Codex C.

ܕܒܥܐ ᵗܘܐܬܩܛ
ᶻܐܠܒܝܬ ᵃܘܡܛܘ
ᶜܘܐܡܪܝܢ ᵈܐܡܪܝܢ
ᶠܘܐܬܩܛܘ ʰܒܥܡܡܐ
ᵏomit ܗܘܐ ܘܒܥܘ
ˡܕܢܐܚܕ ᵐadd ܕܝ
ᵗܘܡܫܝܚ
ᵘadd ܥܠܡ

ᵃܠܝܘܡ ܐܠܘܡ ܫܒ
ܐܥܒܕܥܒ ܦܢܝ ܡܢ
ᵃܒܬܘܢܗ
ᵃaddܘܒܝܘܡܐ ܕܥܘܪܒܐ
ᵇܦܘܠ ᶜܠܝܪܘܫܠܡ
ᵈܘܐܬܐ ᶠܠܒܝܬ
ᵍܥܠܝܗ ʰܬܠܡܝܕܘܗܝ
ᵏomit ܗܘܐ
ˡܕܠܡܠܟܘܬܗ
ⁿܘܡܠܟ ᵒomitܗܘܐ
ᵖܘܐܢ ᵠܘܐܡܪ
ʳܐܡܪܘ ᵗܘܐܡܪܘ
ʷܡܚܕܐ
ʸܐܬܒܥܒܕ ᵃܐܡܪ
ᵇܡܠܟܟܝ ᶜܥܠܐ
ᵈomit ܡܫܝܚ
ᵉܘܐܙܠܘ ᶠܥܠܠ
ᵍܟܐܝܟ ʰܐܬܐ
ᵏܡܫܝܚܐ ˡܘܪܟܒ
ᵐomit ܕܝ ᵒܘܦܪܣܘ

Codex B.

ܕܝ [r]ܕܐܘܟܠܘܣܐ ܗܘܘ [s]ܡܚܣܝܢ † ܠܡܚܣܝܘܢ
ܒܐܘܪܫܠܡ : ܫܐܪܝܢ ܕܝ ܗܘܘ ܡܒܥܝܢ [t]ܠܝܫܘܥ
ܡܢ ܐܚܕܝܐ : ܘܗܘܘ [u]ܡܚܫܒܝܢ ܒܐܘܪܫܠܡ :
9 ܐܘܟܠܘܣܐ ܕܝ ܣܓܝ ܕܝܗܘܕܝ ܐܝܬܝܢ [w]ܘܝܕܥܝܢ :
ܘܗܠܝܢ [x]ܕܐܬܝܢ ܒܬܪܗ ܗܘܘ ܡܙܥܩܝܢ ܘܐܡܪܝܢ
[y]ܐܘܫܥܢܐ ܠܒܪܗ [z]ܕܕܘܕ : ܡܒܪܟ ܗܘ ܗܕܝܢ
ܕܐܬܐ ܒܫܡܗ [v]ܕܝ [a]ܕܡܪܝܐ [y]ܐܘܫܥܢܐ
10 ܒܡܪܘܡܝܐ : ܘܟܕ ܥܠ [b]ܠܐܘܪܫܠܡ ܙܥܬ ܟܘܠܗ
11 [c]ܡܕܝܢܬܐ ܘܐܡܪܐ ܡܢ ܗܘ [d]ܗܕܝܢ : [e]ܐܘܟܠܘܣܐ
ܕܝ ܗܘܘ ܐܡܪܝܢ : ܗܕܝܢ ܗܘ ‡ [f]ܢܒܝܐ ܝܫܘܥ
12 ܕܡܢ ܢܨܪܬ ܕܓܠܝܠܐ : ܘܟܕ ܡܪܢܐ ܝܫܘܥ
[v]ܠܢܘܣܐ : [o]ܘܐܦܩ ܟܠ ܗܠܝܢ ܕܡܙܒܢܝܢ [g]ܘܡܙܒܢܝܢ
ܒܢܘܣܐ : ܘܦܬܘܪܝܗܘܢ [h]ܕܨܪܦܝܐ ܟܦܟ :
[f. 78b]
ܘܡܘܬܒܝܗܘܢ ܕܗܠܝܢ [i]ܕܡܙܒܢܝܢ ܝܘܢܐ :
13 ܘܐܡܪ ܠܗܘܢ : ܟܬܝܒ ܕܒܝܬܝ ܒܝܬ ܨܠܘ
ܬܬܩܪܐ : ܐܢܬܘܢ ܕܝ ܥܒܕܬܘܢ ܝܬܗ ܡܥܪܐ
14 [j]ܕܠܝܣܛܝܢ : [k]ܘܐܬܩܪܒܘ [m]ܠܗ ܣܡܝܢ ܘܚܓܝܪܝܢ
15 ܘܡܣܝܐܝܢ [n]ܒܢܘܣܐ ܘܐܣܐ ܝܬܗܘܢ : ܘܟܕ
ܚܙܘ [o] [p]ܪܒܝ ܟܗܢܝܐ ܘܣܦܪܝܐ [q]ܬܕܡܘܪܬܐ ܕܥܒܕ
ܡܪܢܐ ܝܫܘܥ : ܘܛܠܝܐ ܡܙܥܩܝܢ [n]ܒܢܘܣܐ ܘܐܡܪܝܢ :
16 [r]ܐܘܫܥܢܐ ܠܒܪܗ [s]ܕܕܘܕ ܐܬܟܥܣܘ [t]ܘܐܡܪܘ
ܠܗ : ܫܡܥ ܐܢܬ [u]ܡܐ ܗܠܝܢ ܐܡܪܝܢ : ܗܘ ܕܝ
ܡܪܢܐ ܝܫܘܥ ܐܡܪ ܠܗܘܢ : [v]ܐܝܢ ܡܢ ܘܡܟܒܗܘܢ
ܠܐ ܩܪܝܬܘܢ ܕܡܢ [w]ܦܘܡܗܘܢ ܕܛܠܝܢ [x]ܝܢܩܝܢ
17 [y]ܐܫܟܠܠܬ ܠܟ [z]ܬܫܒܘܚܐ : † ܘܫܒܩ ܠܗܘܢ ܠܒܪ ܡܢ
[a]ܡܕܝܢܬܐ ܠܒܝܬ ܥܢܝܐ ܘܐܒܝܬ ܬܡܢ ⁘

Codex A.

[s]ܡܚܣܝܢ
[t]ܠܝܫܘܥ
[u]ܡܚܫܒܝܢ
[w]ܘܝܕܥܝܢ
[y]ܐܘܫܥܢܐ [z]ܕܕܘܕ
ܕܝ [v] *omit* [a]ܕܡܪܝܐ
[c]ܡܕܝܢܬܐ [d]ܗܕܝܢ
[e]ܐܘܟܠܘܣܐ [f]ܢܒܝܐ
‡ f. 92*a*.
[v]ܠܢܘܣܐ
[o]ܘܐܦܩ [g]ܘܙܒܢܝܢ
[h]ܕܨܪܦܝܐ
[j]ܕܠܝܣܛܝܢ
[k]ܘܐܬܩܪܒܘ ܠܘܬܗ[k]
[n]ܒܢܘܣܐ
[p]ܪܒܝ [q]ܬܕܡܘܪܬܐ
[r]ܐܘܫܥܢܐ [s]ܕܕܘܕ
[t]ܘܐܡܪܘ [u]ܡܐ
[v]ܐܝܢ [w]ܦܘܡܗܘܢ
[y]ܐܫܟܠܠܬ
[z]ܬܫܒܘܚܬܐ
[a]ܡܕܝܢܬܐ

Codex C.

† f. 78*b*.
[r]ܐܘܟܠܘܣܐ
[s]ܡܚܣܝܢ
[t]ܠܝܫܘܥ [u]ܡܚܫܒܝܢ
[x]ܕܐܬܝܢ
[y]ܐܘܫܥܢܐ
[b]ܠܐܘܪܫܠܡ
[e]ܘܐܘܟܠܘܣܐ
[o]ܘܐܦܩ [g]ܘܙܒܢܝܢ
[h]ܕܨܪܦܝܐ
[i]ܕܡܙܒܢܝܢ
[j]ܕܠܝܣܛܝܢ
[k]ܘܐܬܩܪܒܘ ܠܘܬܗ[k]
[m] *omit* ܠܗ
[o] *add* ܝܬܗܘܢ
[q]ܬܕܡܘܪܬܐ
[r]ܐܘܫܥܢܐ
[v]ܐܝܢ
[x]ܝܢܩܝܢ
† f. 79*a*.

CXL.

John XII. 1—18.

Codex B.

[a]ܩܕܡ ‡ ܡܢ [b]ܐܫܒܘܥܗ[b] ܕܝ ܐܠܦܣܚܐ
1 [a]ܦܣܚܐ : [x] ܗܘ ܕܝ ܡܪܢܐ ܝܫܘܥ ܡܢ ܦܘܩܕ

Codex A.

ܫܒ ܚܫ ܕܦܣܚܐ
[b]ܫܒ ܐܫܒܘܥܐ[b]
‡ f. 92*b*.
[x]*add* ܘܡܘܬܒܝܗܘܢ ܕܟܢܘܫܬܐ

Codex C.

[a]ܠܝܘܡ ܐܠܝܫܒ ܕܝ ܐܠܥܙܪ ܩܕܡ
ܐܫܒܘܥܗ ܕܦܣܚܐ[a]
[x] *add* ܘܡܘܬܒܝܗ

Codex B.

[y]ܫܬܬܐ ܝܘܡܝܢ [z]ܕܦܣܚܐ ܐܬܐ ܠܒܝܬ ܥܢܝܐ
ܗܢ ܕܗܘܐ [a]ܠܠܥܙܪܘܣ [b]ܗܕܝܢ [c]ܕܐܩܡ [d]
2 ܡܢ ܒܝܬ ܡܝܬܝܐ: ܡܪܢ ܝܫܘܥ ܥܒܕܘ ܠܗ[e]
ܡܟܠܘܣ: ܡܪܬܐ [f]ܕܝܢ ܗܘܬ ܡܫܡܫܢܝܬܐ ܠܗܘܢ:
[g]ܐܠܥܙܪܘܣ ܕܝܢ ܗܘܐ ܚܕ ܡܢ ܗܠܝܢ [h]ܕܪܒܥܝܢ
3 ܥܡܗ: [i]ܡܪܝܡ ܕܝܢ ܢܣܒܬ [j]ܠܝܛܪܐ ܕܒܣܡ
ܢܪܕܝܢ [k]ܦ̈ܝܣܛܝܩܘܣ ܕܣܓܝ ܕܡܝܗ: ܘܡܫܚܬ
[l]ܪ̈ܓܠܘܗܝ ܕܡܪܢ ܝܫܘܥ ܘܫܘܝܬ [m]ܬܗܘܢ
[n]ܒܣܥܪܗ ܕܪܝܫܗ: ܒܝܬܐ ܕܝܢ ܟܠܗ ܐܬܡܠܝ
[f. 79a]
4 ܡܢ ܪܝܚܗ [o]ܕܒܣܡܐ: ܐܡܪ ܕܝܢ ܝܗܘܕܣ
ܐܣܟܪܝܘܛܐ ܚܕ ܡܢ [p]ܬܠܡܝܕܘܗܝ: ܗܕܝܢ ܕܗܘܐ
5 ܒܬܪ ܕܡܫܠܡ ܠܗ [q]ܠܡܐ [r]ܗܕܝܢ [s]ܒܡܫܚܐ
ܠܐ ܐܙܕܒܢ ܒܬܠܬ [t]ܡܐܐ [u]ܕܝܢܪܝܢ ܘܐܬܝܗܒ
6 ܠܡܣܟܢܝܐ: ܗܕܐ ܕܝܢ ܐܡܪ ܠܐ [v]ܗܘܐ
ܚܝܣ ܠܡܣܟܢܝܐ: ܐܠܐ [w]ܗܘ [x]ܓܢܒ:
[y]ܘܓܠܘܣܩܡܐ ܗܘܐ [z]ܒܝܕܗ: ܘܡܕܡ ܕܗܘܐ
7 [‡]ܡܬܪܡܐ ܒܗ ܗܘ ܗܘܐ ܫܩܠ: ܐܡܪ ܕܝܢ
ܡܪܢ[a] [b]ܫܒܘܩܘ ܠܗ ܕܠܝܘܡܐ [c]ܕܩܒܘܪܝ
8 ܬܛܪܝܗ [d]ܠܗ: ܡܣܟܢܝܐ ܒܟܠ ܙܒܢ ܥܡܟܘܢ:
9 ܐܢܐ ܕܝܢ ܠܐ ܒܟܠ ܙܒܢ ܥܡܟܘܢ: [e]ܘܝܕܥ
ܐܘܟ̈ܠܘܣ ܣܓܝ [†]ܡܢ [f]ܝܗܘܕܝܐ [o]ܕܗܘ ܬܡܢ
ܘܐܬܘ ܠܐ ܠܒܠܚܘܕ ܡܛܠ [g]ܝܫܘܥ ܒܠܚܘܕ:
ܐܠܐ ܕܐܦ ܠܠܥܙܪܘܣ ܢܚܙܘܢ ܠܗܕܝܢ
10 [h]ܕܐܩܡ ܡܢ ܒܝܬ ܡܝܬܝܐ ܐܬܡܠܟܘ [i]ܕܝܢ
[j]ܪ̈ܒܝ ܟܗܢܐ [k]ܕܐܦ ܠܠܥܙܪܘܣ [l]ܢܩܛܠܘܢ:
11 ܕܣܓܝ ܡܢ [f]ܝܗܘܕܝܐ ܗܘܘ ܐܙܠܝܢ ܡܢ ܒܓܠܠܗ:
12 ܘܗܘܘ ܡܗܝܡܢܝܢ ܒܡܪܢ ܝܫܘܥ: ܘܠܝܘܡܐ
ܕܝܢ ܕܡܚܪ ܐܟ̈ܠܘܣ ܣܓܝ [m]ܐܬܟܢܫ: [n]ܗܕܝܢ
ܕܐܬܐ [o]ܠܡܥܕܥܕܐ: ܘܟܕ ܫܡܥܘ ܕܡܪܢ
13 ܝܫܘܥ ܐܬܐ ܠܐܘܪܫܠܡ: ܢܣܒܘ [p]ܫܒ̈ܫܒܝܢ
[q]ܕܕܩܠܝܢ ܘܢܦܩܘ ܠܐܘܪܥܘܬܗ: ܘܗܘܘ [r]ܡܙܥܩܝܢ

Codex A.

[a]ܠܥܙܪܘܣ [b]ܗܕܝܢ
[c]ܕܐܩܝܡ
[e]add ܕܝܢ
[g]ܠܥܙܪܘܣ
[i]ܡܪܝܡ [j]ܠܝܛܪܐ
[k]ܦ̈ܝܣܛܝܩܘܣ
[l]ܪ̈ܓܠܘܗܝ
[m]ܬܗܘܢ [n]ܒܣܥܪܐ
[o]ܕܒܣܡܐ
[r]ܗܕܝܢ
[s]ܒܡܫܚܐ [t]ܡܐܐ
[v]ܕܗܘܐ [w]ܕܗܘܐ
[x]ܓܢܒܐ
[y]ܘܓܠܘܣܩܡܐ
‡ f. 93a.
[f]ܝܗܘܕܝܐ
[h]ܕܐܩܝܡ
[j]ܪ̈ܒܝ [k]ܕܐܦ
[l]ܢܩܛܠܘܢ
[n]ܗܕܝܢ
[o]ܠܡܥܕܥܕܐ
[p]ܫܒ̈ܫܒܝܢ
[q]ܕܕܩܠܝܢ

Codex C.

[y]ܫܬܐ [z]ܕܦܨܚܐ
[a]ܐܠܥܙܪ ܝܬܗ [d]add
[e]add ܕܝܢ
[f]ܕܐܝܢ
[h]ܕܪܒܥܝܢ
[k]ܦ̈ܣܛܝܩܘܣ
[l]ܪ̈ܓܠܝ
[m]ܬܗܘ [n]ܒܣܥܪܗ
[p]ܬܠܡܝܕܝ
[q]ܠܡܐ
[t]ܡܐܐ [u]ܕܝܢܪܝܢ
[v]ܕܗܘܐ [x]ܓܢܒ
[y]ܘܓܠܘܣܩܡܐ
[z]ܒܐܝܕܗ
[a]add ܫܒܘܩܘ
[b]ܫܒܘܩ [c]ܕܠܩܒܘܪܝ
[d]ܠܗ
[e]ܘܝܕܥܘ
† f. 79b.
[o]ܕܗܘܘ
[g]omit ܝܫܘܥ
[h]ܕܐܩܡ [i]omit ܕܝܢ
[k]ܕܐܦ
[m]ܐܬܟܢܫܘ
[q]ܕܕܩܠܝܢ [r]ܡܙܥܩܝܢ

Codex A.

[r]ܘܐܡܪܝܢ *omit*
[s]ܗܘܫܥܢܐ [u]ܗܕܝܢ
‡ f. 93b.
[v]ܒܫܡܗ [w]ܕܡܪܝܐ
[x]ܕܝܢ *omit*
[y]ܕܐܝܣܪܐܝܠ
[a]ܕܐܙܠ ܗܘܐ[a]
[b] *add* ܐܫܟܚ
[c]ܥܝܪܐ [e]ܗܟܡܐ
[f]ܕܟܬܝܒ [g]ܬܕܚܠܝܢ
[h]ܥܠ [i]ܐܬܢ
[k]ܬܠܡܝܕܘܗܝ
[l]ܐܬܕܟܪܘ
[m]ܗܘܝ [n]ܟܬܝܒܢ
[r]ܘܐܩܝܡܗ [t]ܟܕ
[u]ܗܕܝܢ [w]ܐܬܬܐ

Codex B.

[r]ܘܐܡܪܝܢ : [s]ܐܘܫܥܢܐ ܡܒܪܟ [t]ܗܘ [u]ܗܕܝܢ ܕܐܬܐ
14 [v]ܒܫܡܗ [w]ܕܡܪܝܐ ܡܠܟܐ [x]ܕܝܢ [y]ܕܐܝܣܪܐܝܠ : ܘܟܡܐ
[z]ܕܝܢ [a]ܐܫܟܚ ܡܪܢܐ ܝܫܘܥ [b] ‡ [c]ܥܝܪ [d]ܘܪܟܒ
[f. 79b]
15 ܥܠܘܗܝ : [e]ܗܝܟ ܡܐ[e] [f]ܕܟܬܝܒ ܠܐ [g]ܬܕܚܠܝܢ
ܒܪܬܗ ܕܨܝܘܢ : ܗܐ ܡܠܟܝܟ ܐܬܐ ܪ̈ܟܝܒ ܥܠ
16 [h]ܥܠ ܒܪ [i]ܐܬܢ : ܗܠܝܢ ܠܐ ܝܕܥܘ [k]ܬܠܡܝܕܘܗܝ
ܡܢ ܩܕܡ : ܐܠܐ ܟܕ ܐܫܬܒܚ ܡܪܢܐ ܝܫܘܥ :
ܟܕܝܢ [l]ܐܕܟܪܘ ܕܗܠܝܢ [m]ܕܗܘܝ [n]ܟܬܝܒܝܢ [o]ܥܠܘܗܝ :
17 ܘܗܠܝܢ ܥܒܕܘ ܠܗ : ܗܘܐ ܕܝܢ ܡܣܗܕ [p]ܐܘܟܠܘܣܐ
ܗܕܝܢ ܕܗܘܐ ܥܡܗ [q]ܟܕ ܩܪܐ ܠܠܥܙܪ ܡܢ
ܩܒܘܪܬܐ [r]ܘܐܩܝܡ [s]ܗܝ ܡܢ ܒܝܢ ܡܝܬܝܐ :
18 ܠܟܢ [t]ܕܝܢ ܐܘܦ [p]ܐܘܟܠܘܣܐ ܢܦܩ ܠܘܬܗ :
ܕܫܡܥܘ ܕܥܒܕ [u]ܗܕܝܢ [w]ܐܬܐ ⁘

Codex C.

[r]ܘܐܡܪܝܢ *omit*
14 [s]ܐܘܫܥܢܐ
[t]ܘܗ *omit* [u]ܗܕܝܢ
15 ܕܐܝܣܪܐܝܠ [z]ܕܝܢ
[a]ܕܐܫܟܚܘ ܗܘܐ[a]
16 ܒܪܬ [f]ܕܟܬܝܒ
ܐܬܢ [k]ܬܠܡܝܕܘܗܝ
[o]ܥܠܘܗܝ
17 [p]ܐܘܟܠܘܣܐ
[q]ܟܕܝ
ܘܐܩܝܡ [s]*add* ܗܝ̈ܬ
18

CXLI.

Matt. XXI. 18—43.

Codex B.

[b][a]ܝܘܡ ܐܬܠܝܬܝ ܦܢܐ ܐܫܟܚܗ ܐܠܟܒܪܗ ܫܘܪ [c]ܡܢ
18 [d]ܟܬܐܝܢ : ܘܒܬܪܗ ܡܢܗܪܐ ܒܩܪܝܬܐ [z]ܕܝܢ ܗܦܟ
19 ܕܗܘ ܗܦܟ [a]ܠܡܕܝܢܬܐ [b]ܟܦܢ : ܘܚܡܐ [c]ܬܬܐ
ܚܕܐ ܥܠ ܐܘܪܚܐ : ܘܐܬܐ [d]ܥܠܝܗ [e]ܘܒܠܩܡ
ܠܐ [f]ܐܫܟܚ ܒܗ ܐܠܐ ܛܪܦܝܢ ܒܠܚܘܕ : ܘܐܡܪ
[g]ܠܗ ܡܢ ܟܕܘ ܡܢܟܝ ܦܐܪܝܢ ܠܐ ܢܗܘܘܢ
20 [h]ܠܥܠܡ [i]ܘܝܒܫܬ ܒܪ [i]ܫܥܬܗ [j]ܗܝ [k]ܬܐܢܬܐ : ܘܟܕ
ܚܙܘ ‡ [l]ܬܠܡܝܕܝܐ [l]ܬܡܗܘ [m]ܘܐܡܪܝܢ : ܗܝܟ
21 ܟܪ ܫܥܬܗ ܝܒܫܬ [k]ܬܐܢܬܐ : ܐܓܝܒ ܕܝܢ ܡܪܢܐ
ܝܫܘܥ [n]ܐܡܪ ܠܗܘܢ[n] : ܐܡܝܢ ܐܡܪ ܐܢܐ
ܠܟܘܢ : [o]ܕܐܢ ܬܗܘܐ ܒܟܘܢ [p]ܗܝܡܢܘ ܘܠܐ
[q]ܬܬܦܠܓܘܢ : ܠܐ ܒܠܚܘܕ ܗܕܐ [k]ܬܐܢܬܐ
ܬܥܒܕܘܢ : ܐܠܐ ܐܘܦ ܠܗܕܝܢ ܛܘܪܐ [r]ܐܢ
[s]ܬܐܡܪܘܢ ܐܬܥܩܪ ܘܐܬܪܡܝ ܠܝܡܐ [t]ܬܗܘܐ [u]ܟܢ :

Codex A.

ܝܘܡ ܒ ܒܫܒܐ ܕܚܫܐ

[a] *add* ܘܡܦܪܐ
[c] *add* ܒܝ̈ܦܪܐ
[d]ܟܬܝܒܘܗܝ
[z]ܕܝܢ *omit* [a]ܠܡܕܝܢܬܐ
[b]ܟܦܢ [c]ܬܐܢܬܐ
[d]ܥܠܝܗ̇ [e]ܘܒܠܩܡ
[k]ܬܐܢܬܐ [l]ܬܡܗܘ
‡ f. 94a.
[q]ܬܬܦܠܓܘܢ
[s]ܬܐܡܪܘܢ
[t]ܬܗܘܐ [u]ܟܢ

Codex C.

[b]ܠܝܘܡ
18 [d]ܟܬܐܘܗ
19
[f]ܐܫܟܚ
[g]ܠܗ *omit* [h]ܠܥܠܡ
20 ܘܒܪ ܫܥܬܗ ܝܒܫܬ[i]
[j]ܗܝ *omit*
21 ܬܡܗܘ [m]ܘ *omit*
ܐܡܪ ܠܗܘܢ [n]*omit*
ܕܐܢ [p]ܗܝܡܢܘܬܐ
ܐܢ [t]ܬܗܘܐ
[u]ܟܕܝܢ

Codex B.

22 ܘܒܥܠܡܐ[v] ܕܬܫܬܠܡܘܢ[w] ܒܝܠܘܬܐ ܘܡܬܒܣܡܝܢ [f. 80a]
23 ܬܫܒܚܘܢ : ܘܒܬܪ ܐܬܐ ܡܪܢ ܝܫܘܥ ܠܢܘܗܪܐ[x] :
ܡܛܘ ܠܗ ܗܢܘܢ ܕܗܘ ܡܠܟܐ [y]ܝܪܬ ܒܗܝܡܢܐ[y]
ܘܡܫܒܚܝܢ[z] ܕܗܘܠܐ ܐܡܪܝܢ[a] ܒܗܕܐ[b] ܫܠܝܚܘ[c]
ܐܬ ܒܬܪ ܗܠܝܢ : ܘܡܢ ܝܗܒ ܠܟ ܗܕܐ
24 ܫܠܝܚܘܬܐ[d] : ܐܝܟܢܐ ܕܝܢ ܡܪܢ ܫܡܥܘܢ ܘܐܡܪ
ܠܗܘܢ : ܢܫܐܠ ܐܬܒܥܘܢ ܐܘܦ ܐܢܐ ܚܕܐ
ܡܠܬܐ ܗܕܐ ܕܐܢ[e] ܬܐܡܪܘܢ[f] ܠܝ ܐܘܦ
ܐܢܐ ܐܡܪ[g] ܠܟܘܢ ܒܗܕܐ[h] ܫܠܝܚܘ ܐܢܐ
25 ܒܬܪ ܗܠܝܢ : ܡܥܡܘܕܝܬܐ[i] ܕܝܘܚܢܢ[j] ܡܢ ܗ
ܗܘܬ ܡܢ ܫܡܝܐ ܐܘ̈ ܡܢ ܒܢܝܢܫܐ : ܗܢܘܢ
ܕܝܢ ܗܘܘ ܡܬܚܫܒܝܢ[v]† ܒܠܒܒܗܘܢ[‡] ܘܐܡܪܝܢ :
[k]ܐܢ ܢܐܡܪ ܡܢ ܫܡܝܐ ܐܡܪ ܗܘ ܠܢ ܠܡܢܐ
26 ܠܐ ܗܝܡܢܬܘܢ ܠܗ : [l]ܘܐܢ [m]ܢܐܡܪ ܡܢ
ܒܢܝܢܫܐ [n]ܕܚܠܝܢ ܐܢܚܢ ܡܢ [o]ܐܟ̈ܠܘܣܐ : ܟܘܠܐ
27 ܓܝܪ ܝܕܥܝܢ [p]ܠܝܘܚܢܢ ܕܗܘ ܢܒܝܐ : ܘܐܦܢܝܘ
ܘܐܡܪܘ ܠܡܪܢ ܝܫܘܥ ܠܝܬ ܐܢܚܢ ܝܕܥܝܢ :
ܐܡܪ ܠܗܘܢ ܐܘܦ ܗܘ ܡܪܢ ܝܫܘܥ : ܐܘܦ[q]
ܐܢܐ ܠܝܬ ܐܢܐ [r]ܐܡܪ ܠܟܘܢ [s]ܒܗܕܐ
28 [t]ܫܠܝܚܘ ܐܢܐ ܒܬܪ ܗܠܝܢ : [u]ܡܢܐ[v] ܗܢܐ ܠܟܘܢ :
ܓܒܪܐ ܚܕ ܗܘܐ ܠܗ ܬܪܝܢ ܒܢܝܢ [w]ܘܩܪܒ
ܐܡܪ ܠܩܕܡܝܐ ܒܪܝ : ܐܙܠ ܝܘܡܢܐ ܦܠܘܚ
29 ܒܟܪܡܐ : ܗܘ ܕܝܢ ܐܥܢܐ ܘܐܡܪ ܐܢܐ ܡܪܝ
30 ܐܙܠ ܘܠܐ [x]ܐܙܠ : [y]ܗܘ ܕܝܢ[y] [z]ܩܪܒ[v] ܘܐܡܪ
ܠܬܪܝܢܐ [a]ܠܡ ܘܠܘܬܗ ܗܘ ܕܝܢ ܐܥܢܐ [b]ܐܡܪ
ܠܝܬ ܐܢܐ [c]ܨܒܐ : ܒܚܪܬܐ ܕܝܢ ܬܘܐ [d]ܘܐܙܠ
31 ܠܟܪܡܐ : ܡܢ ܡܢ ܗܠܝܢ ܬܪܝܢ ܥܒܕ ܨܒܝܢܗ
[e]ܕܐܒܘܗܝ : ܐܡܪܘ ܠܗ ܕܝܢ [f]ܒܚܪܝܐ : ܐܡܪ [f. 80b]
ܠܗܘܢ ܡܪܢ ܝܫܘܥ : ܐܡܝܢ ܐܡܝܢ [g]ܐܡܪ
ܐܢܐ[g] ܠܟܘܢ ܕܡܟܣܐ ܘܙܢܝܬܐ [h]ܡܩܕܡܝܢ
32 ܠܟܘܢ ܠܡܠܟܘܬܗ [i]ܕܝܢ ܕܐܠܗܐ : ܐܬܐ ܓܝܪ

Codex A.

[v] ܘܒܥܠܡܐ
[x] ܠܢܘܗܪܐ
[y] ܕ̈ܫܡܫܝܢܐ
[z] ܘܩܥܝܢ [a] add ܠܗ
[b] ܒܗܕܐ
[d] ܫܠܝܚܘܬܐ
[e] ܕܐܢ [f] ܬܐܡܪܘܢ
[g] ܐܡܪ [h] ܒܗܕܐ
[i] ܡܥܡܘܕܝܬܗ
[j] ܕܝܘܚܢܢ
‡ f. 94b.
[v] ܒܠܒܗܘܢ
[m] ܢܐܡܪ [n] ܕܚܠܝܢ
[o] ܐܟ̈ܠܘܣܐ
[p] ܠܝܘܚܢܢ
[q] add ܠܐ
[r] ܐܡܪ [s] ܒܗܕܐ
[t] ܫܠܝܚܘ [v] add ܕܝܢ
[w] ܘܩܪܒ
[x] ܐܙܠ
[y] omit ܗܘ ܕܝܢ
[z] ܩܪܒ [a] ܠܡ
[d] ܘܐܙܠ
[e] ܕܐܒܘܗܝ [f] ܒܚܪܝܐ
[g] ܐܡܪܝܢܐ
[i] omit ܕܝܢ

Codex C.

[w] ܕܬܫܬܠܡܘܢ
[c] ܫܠܝܚܘ
[e] ܕܐܢ
[i] ܡܥܡܘܕܝܬܗ
† f. 80b.
[k] ܐܢ
[l] ܘܐܢ
[n] ܕܚܠܝܢ
[q] add ܠܐ
[r] ܐܡܪ
[u] ܕܡܢܐ [v] add ܕܝܢ
[w] ܒܢܝܢ ܘܩܪܒ[w]
[y] omit ܗܘ ܕܝܢ
[b] omit ܐܡܪ
[c] ܨܒܐ
[h] ܡܩܕܡܝܢ
[i] omit ܕܝܢ

Codex B.

[j]ܢܡܘܣܗ ‡ ܠܘܬܟܘܢ [k]ܟܐܪܘܙ ܕܢܝܫܗ ܘܠܐ
ܡܫܬܡܥܝܢܘܢ ܠܗ : ܡܟܝܠܢܐ ܕܝܢ ܘܠܝܬܐ ܗܫܡܥܢܘ
ܠܗ : ܐܬܘܢ [l]ܫܡܥܬܘܢ ܘܠܐ ܬܫܡܥܬܘܢ
33 ܒܫܪܝܬܐ [m]ܕܝܢ [n]ܗܫܡܥܬܘܢ ܠܗ : [o]ܫܘܪܝܢ
ܡܛܠ [p]ܥܡܟܘܢ [q]ܒܪܢܫܐ ܚܕ[q] ܗ̇ܘܐ [r]ܡܪܝܐ
ܒܢ[r] : ܘܬܘܒ ܒܪܟ [t]ܘܫܠܡ ܗܘ [u]ܗܟܢ :
ܘܫܦܐ ܠܒܗܘܢ ܡܫܪܝܐ ܘܒܟܐ ܠܒܗܘܢ ܡܬܬܠ :
34 ܘܢܗܒ ܗܘܐ ܠܐܪܡܝܐ [v]ܘܐܘܠ [w]ܠܗ : † ܒܕ
[y]ܡܪܒ [z]ܡܪܘܫܘܗܝ [a]ܕܦܪܥܐ [b]ܚܠܝܡ [c]ܒܒܢܘܗܝ
35 ܠܘܬ [d]ܐܪܡܝܐ [e]ܕܫܡܥܢ ܡܢ [f]ܦܬܪ : [g]ܘܫܡܥܘܢ
[h]ܠܒܒܟܐ ܠܝܬ ܡܢ ܡܫܘ : [i]ܘܠܝܬ [j]ܡܢܠܐ
36 ܘܠܝܬ ܪܚܡܘ : ܘܬܘܒܢ [m]ܚܠܝܡ [n]ܒܒܢܝܢ [o]ܫܘܪܝܢ
ܗܟܢ ܡܢ [p]ܡܘܬܐ ܘܒܒܢܘ ܠܗܘܢ [q]ܒܢ ܘܒܡܘܬ :
37 ܒܫܪܝܬܐ ܕܝܢ ܚܠܝܡ ܠܘܬܗܘܢ ܒܪܗ ܐܡܪ
38 ܒܗܬܢ ܗܢܘܢ ܡܢ ܦܬܪ : [r]ܐܪܡܝܐ ܕܝܢ ܒܕ
ܫܡܥ ܠܒܪܗ ܐܡܪܘ ܒܠܒܗܘܢ : ܗܕܝܢ ܗܘ
ܢܘܪܐ ܘܐܬ ܢܦܠܬ ܗܘܬ ܘܗܘܬ [s]ܢܘܪܬܐ
39 ܕܠܟ : ܘܫܡܥܘ [t]ܗܘܬ [u]ܘܐܬܥܩܘ ܗܘܬ ܠܒܪ ܡܢ
40 ܒܪܡܝܐ ܘܡܠܠܘ ܗܘܬ : ܒܕ ܐܘܢ ܐܬܬܐ ‡ ܡܪܗ
ܕܒܪܡܝܐ ܡܟܐ ܗܘ [w]ܒܒܕ [x]ܠܗܠܝܢ ܐܪܡܝܐ[x] :
41 ܐܡܪܝܢ ܠܗ ܒܥܕ ܒܥܐܬ ܗܘ [z]ܡܟܒܕ [a]ܗܘܬܘܢ :
[f. 81a]
ܘܒܪܡܝܐ ܗܘ [b]ܢܗܒ ܠܐܪܡܝܐ [c]ܫܘܪܝܢ [d]ܗܠܝܢ
42 ܕܗܟܢܝܢ ܠܗ [e]ܦܬܪܗܘܢ [f]ܒܦܬܪܘܫܗ : ܐܡܪ
ܠܗܘܢ ܡܪܐ ܢܫܘܫ ܡܢ ܢܡܘܣܘܢ ܠܐ :
ܡܪܝܬܘܢ ܒܬܘܒܢܐ [g]ܐܒܢܐ ܗܕܐ ܕܫܦܠܘ
[h]ܒܢܐܝܢ ܗܝ ܐܬܒܒܕܬ ܪܚܡ ܠܢܫܬܐ : ܡܢ
ܠܘܬ [i]ܡܪܐ ܐܬܒܒܕܬ ܗܕܐ ܘܗܝ ܡܬܒܗܬܐ
43 [k]ܒܚܝܝܢ : [m]ܠܟܠܠ ܒܕܝܢ ܐܒܐ ܐܡܪ ܠܟܘܢ
[n]ܕܡܬܪܢܚܐ ܡܢܚܘܢ ܡܠܟܘܬܗ ܕܐܠܗܐ :
ܘܡܬܒܗܒܐ ܠܗܝ ܕܒܒܕ [o]ܦܬܪܗ ܀

Codex A.

‡ f. 95*a*.
[j]ܢܡܘܣܗ
[k]ܟܐܪܘܙܐ
[l] *add* ܕܝܢ
[n]ܗܫܬܡܥܬܘܢ
[o]ܫܘܪܝ [p]ܥܡܡܢ
[r]ܡܪܝܐ ܒܟܝ[r]
[v]ܘܐܘܠ
[y]ܡܪܒ [a]ܕܦܪܥܐ
[c]ܒܒܢܘܗܝ [e]ܕܫܡܥܢ
[f]ܦܬܪܝ [g]ܘܫܡܥܘܢ
[h]ܠܒܒܟܐ [i]ܠܝܬ
[j] *add* ܕܝܢ [m]ܚܠܝܡ
[n]ܒܒܢܝܢ [p]ܡܘܬܢ
[q]ܒܢ
[s]ܢܘܪܬܐ
[t] *omit* ܘ ܗܘܬ
‡ f. 95*b*.
[u]ܐܬܥܩܘ
[x]ܠܐܪܡܝܐ ܗܠܝܢ[x] [z]ܡܟܒܕ [b]ܢܗܒ
[e]ܦܬܪܐ
[f]ܒܦܬܪܘܫܗܘܢ
[g]ܕܫܦܠܐ
[h]ܒܢܐܝܢ
[i]ܡܪܐ
[m]ܠܟܠܠ

Codex C.

[k]ܟܐܪܘܙ
[l] *add* ܕܝܢ [m] *omit* ܕܝܢ
[n]ܗܫܬܡܥܬܘܢ
[q] *omit* ܒܪܢܫܐ ܚܕ
[r]ܡܪܐ ܒܢ[r]
[t]ܘܫܠܡ [u]ܗܟܢ
† f. 81*a*.
[w] *omit* ܠܗ
[z]ܡܪܘܫܘܗܝ
[a]ܕܦܪܥܐ [b]ܚܠܝܡ
[c]ܒܒܢܘܗܝ [d]ܐܪܡܝܐ
[e]ܕܫܡܥܢ
[f]ܦܬܪܝ [g]ܘܫܡܥܘܢ
[m]ܚܠܝܡ [o]ܫܘܪܝܢ
[p]ܡܘܬܢ
[r]ܐܪܡܝܐ
ܗܘܬ [t]*omit* ܘܐܬܥܩܘ[u]
[w]ܒܒܕ
[x]ܠܐܪܡܝܐ ܗܠܝܢ[x]
[z]ܡܟܒܕ [a]ܗܘܬܘܢ
[b]ܢܗܒ [c]ܫܘܪܝܢ
[d]ܗܕܝܢ [e]ܦܬܪܐ
[f]ܒܦܬܪܘܫܗܘܢ
[h]ܒܢܐܝܢ
[n]ܕܡܬܪܢܚܐ
[o]ܦܬܪܗ

[*Codex* A, vide p. 160.] *Codex* B. [*Codex* C, vide p. 160.]

CXLII.

Matt. XXIV. 3—35.

3 ܘܟܕ ܐܬܝܬܒ ܐܠܦܢܢ ܒܛܘܪ ܡܢ ܡܬܐܘܗܝ ܘܩܪܒܘ ܠܘܬܗ ܬܠܡܝܕܘܗܝ ܒܥܕ ܗܘܐ ܩܪܝܒܐ ܫܐܠܘܗܝ
ܘܐܡܪܝܢ ܠܗ ܐܡܪ ܠܢ ܐܡܬܝ ܬܗܘܝܢ ܗܠܝܢ ܘܡܢܐ ܗܝ ܐܬܐ ܕܡܐܬܝܬܟ ܘܕܫܘܠܡܗ ܕܥܠܡܐ ܐܡܪ ܠܗ
4 ܐܡܪ ܠܗܘܢ ܗܘܐ ܡܠܝܢ ܗܘ ܐܬܝܐ ܕܡܫܬܡܥܝܢ ܘܡܬܚܙܝܢ ܕܠܥܠܡܐ : ܘܐܡܪ ܠܗܘܢ
5 ܚܙܘ ܕܠܐ ܐܢܫ ܢܛܥܝܟܘܢ : ܣܓܝܐܝܢ ܓܝܪ ܢܐܬܘܢ ܒܫܡܝ ܘܢܐܡܪܘܢ ܕܐܢܐ ܗܘ ܡܫܝܚܐ
6 ܘܣܓܝܐܐ ܢܛܥܘܢ : ܥܬܝܕܝܢ ܐܢܬܘܢ ܕܬܫܡܥܘܢ ܩܪܒܐ ܘܫܡܥܐ ܕܩܪܒܐ : ܚܙܘ ܠܐ ܬܬܕܠܚܘܢ
ܕܘܠܐ ܗܘ ܕܢܗܘܝܢ ܗܠܝܢ : ܐܠܐ ܠܐ ܥܕܟܝܠ ܫܘܠܡܐ
7 ܢܩܘܡ ܓܝܪ ܥܡܐ ܥܠ ܥܡܐ ܘܡܠܟܘ ܥܠ ܡܠܟܘ : ܘܢܗܘܘܢ ܟܦܢܐ ܘܡܘܬܢܐ ܘܙܘܥܐ ܒܐܬܪ ܐܬܪ
8 ܗܠܝܢ ܕܝܢ ܟܠܗܝܢ ܪܫܐ ܐܢܘܢ ܕܚܒܠܐ : (*sic*)
[f. 81*b*]
9 ܗܝܕܝܢ ܢܫܠܡܘܢܟܘܢ ܠܐܘܠܨܢܐ ܘܢܩܛܠܘܢܟܘܢ ܘܬܗܘܘܢ ܣܢܝܐܝܢ ܠܟܠ ܥܡܡܐ ܡܛܠ ܫܡܝ
10 ܗܝܕܝܢ ܢܬܟܫܠܘܢ ܣܓܝܐܐ : ܘܢܫܠܡܘܢ ܚܕ ܠܚܕ ܘܢܣܢܘܢ ܚܕ ܠܚܕ
11 ܘܣܓܝܐܐ ܢܒܝܐ ܕܕܓܠܘܬܐ ܢܩܘܡܘܢ : ܘܢܛܥܘܢ ܠܣܓܝܐܐ
12 ܘܡܛܠ ܕܬܣܓܐ ܥܘܠܐ ܬܦܘܓ ܚܘܒܐ ܕܣܓܝܐܐ :
13 ܗܘ ܕܝܢ ܕܢܣܝܒܪ ܥܕܡܐ ܠܚܪܬܐ ܗܘ ܢܚܐ :
14 ܘܬܬܟܪܙ ܗܕܐ ܣܒܪܬܐ ܕܡܠܟܘܬܐ ܒܟܠ ܥܠܡܐ : ܠܣܗܕܘ
15 ܠܟܠܗܘܢ ܥܡܡܐ : ܘܗܝܕܝܢ ܬܐܬܐ ܫܘܠܡܐ : ܡܐ ܕܝܢ ܕܚܙܝܬܘܢ ܐܬܐ ܕܛܢܦܘܬܐ ܕܚܪܒܐ
ܕܐܬܐܡܪܬ ܒܝܕ ܕܢܝܐܝܠ ܢܒܝܐ ܕܩܝܡܐ ܒܐܬܪܐ ܩܕܝܫܐ : ܡܢ ܕܩܪܐ ܢܣܬܟܠ :
16 ܗܝܕܝܢ ܗܠܝܢ ܕܒܝܗܘܕ ܢܥܪܩܘܢ ܠܛܘܪܐ : ܘܡܢ ܕܒܐܓܪܐ ܠܐ ܢܚܘܬ ܠܡܣܒ ܡܕܡ
17 ܡܢ ܒܝܬܗ : ܘܡܢ ܕܒܚܩܠܐ ܠܐ ܢܗܦܘܟ ܠܒܣܬܪܗ ܠܡܣܒ ܠܒܘܫܗ : ܘܝ ܠܗܝܢ ܕܝܢ
18
19
20 ܕܒܛܢܢ ܘܠܗܠܝܢ ܕܡܝܢܩܢ ܒܗܢܘܢ ܝܘܡܬܐ : ܨܠܘ ܕܝܢ ܕܠܐ ܬܗܘܐ ܥܪܘܩܬܟܘܢ
21 ܒܣܬܘܐ ܘܠܐ ܒܫܒܬܐ : ܬܗܘܐ ܓܝܪ ܗܝܕܝܢ ܐܘܠܨܢܐ ܪܒܐ ܕܠܐ ܐܬܗܘܝ ܡܢ ܪܫ
22 ܥܠܡܐ ܘܥܕܡܐ ܠܗܫܐ ܘܠܐ ܢܗܘܐ : ܘܐܠܘ ܠܐ ܐܬܟܪܝܘ ܝܘܡܬܐ ܗܢܘܢ ܠܐ ܚܝܐ ܗܘܐ ܟܠ ܒܣܪ :
ܐܠܐ ܕܝܢ ܡܛܠ ܓܒܝܐ ܢܬܟܪܘܢ ܝܘܡܬܐ ܗܢܘܢ :
[f. 82*a*]
23 ܗܝܕܝܢ ܐܢ ܐܢܫ ܢܐܡܪ ܠܟܘܢ ܗܐ ܗܪܟܐ ܗܘ ܡܫܝܚܐ : ܐܘ ܗܐ ܬܡܢ ܠܐ ܬܗܝܡܢܘܢ :
24 ܢܩܘܡܘܢ ܓܝܪ ܡܫܝܚܐ ܕܕܓܠܘܬܐ ܘܢܒܝܐ ܕܕܓܠܘܬܐ : ܘܢܬܠܘܢ ܐܬܘܬܐ ܪܘܪܒܬܐ ܠܡܛܥܝܘ
25 ܐܦ ܠܓܒܝܐ : ܗܐ ܩܕܡܬ ܐܡܪܬ ܠܟܘܢ : ܐܢ
26 ܢܐܡܪܘܢ ܠܟܘܢ ܗܐ ܕܝܢ ܒܡܕܒܪܐ ܗܘ ܠܐ ܬܦܩܘܢ : ܐܘ ܗܐ ܒܬܘܢܐ ܗܘ ܠܐ
27 ܬܗܝܡܢܘܢ : ܐܝܟ ܓܝܪ ܕܒܪܩܐ ܢܦܩ ܡܢ ܡܕܢܚܐ ܘܡܬܚܙܐ ܥܕ ܡܥܪܒܐ ܗܟܢܐ ܬܗܘܐ :
28 ܡܐܬܝܬܗ ܕܒܪܗ ܕܐܢܫܐ : ܐܝܟܐ ܕܐܝܬ ܦܓܪܐ ܬܡܢ ܢܬܟܢܫܘܢ ܢܫܪܐ
29 ܒܥܓܠ ܕܝܢ ܒܬܪ ܐܘܠܨܢܐ ܕܝܘܡܬܐ ܗܢܘܢ ܫܡܫܐ ܢܚܫܟ : ܘܣܗܪܐ

Codex B.

ܠܐ ܝܬܠ ܢܗܘܪܗ ܘܟܘܟܒܝܐ ܢܦ̈ܠܘܢ ܡܢ ܓܘ ܫܡܝܐ : ܘܚܝܠܝ ܕܫܡܝܐ ܝܬܙܥܙܥܘܢ :
30 ܘܟܕܝܢ ܬܬܚܙܝܐ ܐܬܗ ܕܒܪܗ ܕܓܒܪܐ ܒܫܡܝܐ : ܘܟܕܝܢ ܝܚܒܛܘܢ ܟܠܗܘܢ ܫܒܛܝܐ
ܕܐܪܥܐ : ܘܝܚܡܘܢ ܠܒܪܗ ܕܝ ܕܓܒܪܐ ܐܬܐ ܥܠ ܥܢܢܝܗܘܢ ܕܫܡܝܐ ܥܡ ܚܝܠ
31 ܘܬܫܒܘܚܬܐ ܣܓܝ : ܘܟܕܝܢ ܗܘ ܡܫܠܚ ܡܠܐܟܘܗܝ ܥܡ ܩܠܗ ܩܪܢܐ ܪܒܐ ܘܡܟܢܫܝܢ ܠܒܚܝܪܘܗܝ ܡܢ ܟܠ
32 ܒܣܘܢܝ ܡܢ ܐܪܒܥܬܐ ܪܘܚܝܐ : ܡܢ ܪܝܫܗܘܢ ܕܫܡܝܐ ܥܕ ܣܦܝܐ ܪܝܫܗܘܢ : ܡܢ
ܬܬܢܐ ܝܠܦܘ ܡܬܠܐ ܗܝܟ ܡܐ ܕܠ ܕܢ ܕܟܕ ܣܘܟܗ ܐܬܥܒܕ ܪܟܝܟ : ܘܡܦܩܝܢ ܛܪ̈ܦܝܐ
[f. 82b]
33 ܚܟܡܝܢ ܕܩܪܝܒ ܗܘ ܩܝܛܐ : ܗܟܕܝܢ ܐܘܦ ܐܢܬܘܢ ܟܕ ܬܚܡܘܢ ܗܠܝܢ ܟܠܗܘܢ :
34 ܐܬܘܢ ܚܟܡܝܢ ܕܩܪܝܒ ܗܘ ܥܠ ܬܪܥܐ : ܐܡܝܢ ܐܡܪ ܐܢܐ ܠܟܘܢ ܕܠܐ ܡܥܒܪ
35 ܗܕܝܢ ܕܪܐ ܥܕ ܡܐ ܕܟܘܠ ܗܠܝܢ ܝܬܥܒܕܘܢ : ܫܡܝܐ ܘܐܪܥܐ ܝܥܒܪܘܢ ܘܡܠܝ̈
ܕܝ ܠܐ ܝܥܒܪܘܢ :

CXLIII.

Matt. XXII. 15—46.

Codex A.

[a] *omit* ܩܪܝܢܐ
ܡܬܝܐܘܣ [c]
[a] *add* ܘܒܬܪܗ ܦܪ̈ܘܣܐ
[b] ܦܪ̈ܝܫܝܢ
[d] ܕܝܨ̈ܕܘܢ [e] *omit* ܕܝ
[g] ܗܪ̈ܘܕܘܣܝ
[p] ܒܟܠ
[r] ܠܐܦ̈ܝܢ
[u] ܩܢܣܘܢ [w] ܝܕܥ
[x] ܒܝܫܘܬܗܘܢ
[z] ܕܩܢܣܘܢ
[a] *add* ܒܟܝܢ [b] ܐܡܪ
‡ f. 98a.
[c] ܕܡܢ [d] *omit* ܗܕܐ
[f] *omit* ܒܟܝܢ [g] ܗܒܘ
[h] *add* ܐܘܢ

Codex B.

[a]ܩܪܝܢܐ [b]ܝܘܡ ܬܠܝܬܝܐ ܗܫܢܝ ܡܢ [c]ܡܬܝܐܘܣ :[a]
15 ܒܟܝܢ ܐܙܠܘ [b]ܦܪܝܫܝܐ ܢܣܒܘ [c]ܡܠܟܝܢ ܒܠܘܝ.
16 [d]ܕܝܨܕܘܢ ܝܬܗ [e]ܕܝ ܒܡܠܬܐ : ܘܫܕܪܘܢ ܥܠܘܗܝ
ܠܗ ܬܠܡܝܕܝܗܘܢ ܥܡ [g]ܗܪܘܕܝܢܝ ܐܡܪܝܢ
ܡܠܦܢܐ ܝܕܥܝܢ ܐܢܢ ܕܐܬ ܡܫܪܪ ܘܐܘܪܚܗ
ܕܐܠܗܐ ܒܩܘܫܛ ܐܬ ܡܠܦ : ܘܠܐ [p]ܒܟܠ
ܠܟ [q]ܒܐܢܫ : ܠܐܦܝ ܐܬ ܚܙܝ [r]ܠܐܦ̈ܝܢ
17 ܕܒܢܝܢܫ : ܐܡܘܪ ܠܢ ܐܘܢ ܡܐ ܗܢܐ ܠܟ :
[s]ܫܠܝܛ [t]ܕܢܬܠ [u]ܩܢܣܘܢ ܠܩܣܪ ܐܘ ܠܐ :
18 [w]ܝܕܥ ܕܝ ܡܪܢܐ ܝܫܘܥ [x]ܒܝܫܘܬܗܘܢ ܘܐܡܪ
19 ܡܐ ܐܬܘܢ ܡܢܣܝܢ ܠܝ ܢܣܒܐܦܐ : ܐܘܕܒܘ
20 ܠܝ ܕܝܢܪܐ [z]ܕܩܢܣܘܢ : ܗܘܢ ܕܝ ܩܪܒܘ
‡ ܠܗ ܙܘܙ [a] [b]ܘܐܡܪ ܠܗܘܢ ܡܪܢܐ ܝܫܘܥ :
[c]ܠܡܢ ܗܝ ܗܕܐ ܨܘܪܬܐ [d]ܗܕܐ [e]ܘܐܟܬܒܬܐ :
21 ܐܡܪܝܢ ܠܗ ܕܩܣܪ : ܐܡܪ ܠܗܘܢ [f]ܒܟܝܢ
[g]ܗܐܒܘ † [h]ܕܩܣܪ ܠܩܣܪ : ܘܕܐܠܗܐ ܠܐܠܗܐ :

Codex C.

[a] *omit* ܩܪܝܢܐ [b]ܠܝܘܡ
[a] *add* ܘܒܬܪܗ ܦܪܘܣܐ
[c] ܡܠܟܝܢ [e] *omit* ܕܝ
[g] ܗܪܘܕܝܢܝ
[p] ܒܟܠ
[q] ܕܐܢܫ [r] ܠܐܦ̈ܝܢ
[s] *omit* ܫܠܝܛ
[t] ܕܢܬܠ [u] ܩܢܣܘܢ
[w] ܝܕܥ
[z] ܕܩܢܣܘܢ
[c] ܕܡܢ [d] ܘܗܕܐ
[e] *omit* ܘ [f] ܗܒܘ
† f. 83a.

Codex A.

[i]ܘܐܛܡܪܬܗ [k] *omit* ܘ
[m]ܘܚܟܡܬܐ [n]ܝܕܥܬܢܝ
[o]ܡܛܠܒܬܐ
[p]ܕܡܠܟܘܬܐ
[s]ܫܒܩ [t]ܐܪܝܘܟ
[u]ܘܦܩܕܗ
[y] *add* ܠܘܬܗ
[z]ܟܠܝܢ [a]ܡܢ [d]ܟܠܕܝܐ
[e]ܠܡܬܒܥܘܬܗ
[f] *omit* ܘ
[i]ܐܝܟ [k]ܕܡܢ
[l]ܥܩܪܬܗ
[m]ܗܘܝܐ [n] *add* ܕܝ
‡ f. 98b.
[o]ܕܠܝܬ [p]ܐܬܥܠܝܐ
[j] *omit* ܕܝ [q]ܡܥܬܩܝܢ
[r] *omit* ܘܠܐ ܥܡܬܩܝܢ
[t] *add* ܕܝ [u]ܡܬܚܙܝܢܐ
[w]ܐܠܗܝܢ [x]ܘܐܠܗܝܢ
[y]ܕܐܬܚܘܫܢ
[z]ܘܐܠܗܝܢ
[b]ܕܫܝܢ [c]ܐܬܚܠܦܐ
[f]ܘܟܕ ܥܩܒܘ ܦܬܟܪܐ
[h]ܠܕܘܩܝܢ
[i]ܘܥܩܠ ܗܘܬ
[k] *add* ܒܥܘܕܢ
[m]ܗܝܢ [n]ܠܚܙܘܐ
[o]ܐܠܗܘܢ [p]ܒܟܠܗ
[q]ܢܟܣܝܢ [r]ܣܢܝܢ
[s]ܕܗܝܢ [t]ܘܦܩܕܗ

Codex B.

22 ܘܗܘ ܥܡܝܩܢ [i]ܐܬܛܡܪܬܗܘܢ : ܘܝܕܥ ܡܐ ܗܘ ܘܢܗܘܪܐ
23 ܠܟܘܢ : [k]ܘܒܗ [l]ܒܘܢ [m]ܘܚܟܡܬܐ ܘܓܒܪܘ ܠܗ
[f. 83a]
[n]ܝܕܥܬܢܝ ܗܠܝܢ ܕܐܬܚܢܢ ܕܠܝܬ [o]ܡܛܠܒܬܐ
24 [p]ܠܡܠܟܘܬܐ : [q]ܘܐܙܠ ܠܘܬܗ : ܐܡܪܝܢ ܡܠܟܐ
ܡܠܟܐ ܐܡܪ : [r]ܕܐܝܟ ܡܢܗܘܢ [r]ܐܡܪ ܕܠܐ ܟܠܝܢ :
[s]ܫܒܩ [t]ܐܪܝܘܟ ܐܬܬܗ [u]ܘܦܩܕ [w]ܙܪܝܙ ܠܐܪܝܘܟ :
25 [x]ܘܗܘ ܕܝ [y]ܥܩܒܬܐ ܐܚܝܢ : ܘܦܩܕܝܢܐ ܐܬܥܬܩܘ
ܘܡܠܟܘܬܐ : ܘܡܢ ܕܠܐ ܗܘܐ ܠܗ [z]ܙܪܝܙ ܥܒܕ
26 ܐܬܬܗ ܠܐܪܝܘܟ ܀ [a]ܟܕ ܕܝ [b]ܘܒܥܬ ܐܘܦ[b] ܬܢܝܢܐ
27 ܘܬܠܝܬܝܐ [d]ܕܝ ܡܠܟܐ[d] [e]ܠܡܬܒܥܘܬܗܘܢ : [f]ܘܡܢ ܒܬܪ
28 ܕܝ ܒܥܠܘܗܝ [g]ܡܠܟܘܬ [h]ܐܘܦ ܐܬܬܐ : ܒܡܠܟܘܬܐ
[i]ܐܝܟ ܕܡܠܟܘܬܐ [k]ܕܗܕܝܢ ܡܢ [l]ܥܩܪܬܐ [m]ܗܘܐ
29 ܐܬܬܐ : ܒܥܠܘܗܝ ܒܪ ܢܫܡܗ ܗܘ : [n]ܐܟܠܝܒ
ܡܢ ܐܢܫܐ ܘܐܡܪ ܠܗܘܢ : ܝܠܕܝܢ ܐܬܘܢ [‡] :
[o]ܘܠܝܬ ܐܬܘܢ ܝܕܥܝܢ [p]ܒܬܠܬܐ ܘܠܐ ܚܝܠܗ
30 ܕܐܠܗܐ : ܒܡܚܟܡܬܐ ܒܪ ܕܡܢ ܠܟ ܠܐ [j]ܕܝ
[q]ܡܥܬܩܝܢ [r]ܘܠܐ [s]ܥܡܬܩܝܢ[r]. ܐܠܐ ܗܝܢ
31 ܡܠܟܘܬܝ ܕܐܠܗܐ ܗܘܝܢ ܟܠܗ ܥܡܝܩܬܐ : ܟܠ
[t]ܟܠ[u] ܡܬܚܙܝܢܐ ܕܡܠܟܘܬܐ ܠܐ ܦܪܫܘܢ ܡܢܐ
32 [v]ܕܐܬܡܪ ܠܟܘܢ ܡܢ ܐܠܗܐ ܕܐܡܪ : ܐܢܐ
ܗܘ [w]ܐܠܗܘܢ ܕܐܒܪܗܡ [x]ܘܐܠܗܘܢ [y]ܕܐܬܚܘܫܢ
[z]ܘܐܠܗܘܢ ܕܝܥܩܘܒ ܀ ܘܠܝܬ ܐܠܗܐ [a]ܕܡܠܟܘܬܝ
33 ܐܠܐ [b]ܕܫܝܢ : ܘܟܕ ܕܝ ܥܡܩܒ [c]ܐܬܚܠܦܐ
34 ܘܗܘ ܡܬܓܠܡܝܢ ܟܠ [†]ܐܘܠܦܢܗ [d] ܀ [f]ܦܪܫܢ
[g]ܟܕ ܥܩܒܘ [f]ܕܥܬܩ [h]ܠܕܘܩܝܢ ܐܬܟܒܫܘ ܗܝܢ
35 ܚܕܐ : [i]ܘܥܩܠܗ ܚܕ ܦܩܪ[k] ܡܒܫܠܐ ܠܗ
36 [l]ܘܐܡܪ ܀ ܡܠܟܐ [m]ܗܕܝܢ ܚܠܡܐ ܘܦܫܪܗ ܢܐܡܪ :
37 ܘܗܘ ܕܝ ܡܢܐ ܫܡܗ ܐܡܪ ܠܗ : ܕܬܚܒ
[f. 83b]
[n]ܠܡܢܐ [o]ܐܠܗܘܢ ܡܢ [p]ܒܟܠ ܠܒܟ : ܘܡܢ
ܒܟܠܗ [q]ܣܢܝܢ ܘܡܢ ܒܟܠܗ [r]ܢܟܣܝܢ ܘܡܢ ܒܟܠܗ
38 ܫܒܩܬܟ : [s]ܗܕܝܢ ܗܘ ܒܥܘܕ ܪܒܐ [t]ܘܦܩܕܐ :

Codex C.

[i]ܘܐܛܡܪܬܗ [l]ܒܢܘܗܝ
[n]ܝܕܥܬܢܝ
[o]ܡܛܠܒܬܐ [q]ܘܐܙܠ
[r]ܕܐܝܟ ܡܢܗܘܢ[r]
[s]ܫܒܩ [t]ܐܪܝܘܟ
[w]ܙܪܝܙ [x]ܗܘܐ
[y] *add* ܠܘܬܗ [z]ܙܪܝܙ
[b]ܐܘܦ ܘܒܥܬ[b]
[d]ܘܡܠܟܐ
[e]ܠܡܬܒܥܘܬܗܘܢ
[f] *omit* ܘ
[g]ܡܠܟܘܬ [h]ܐܘܦ
[j] *omit* ܕܝ [p]ܒܬܠܬܐ
[q]ܡܥܬܩܝܢ
[s]ܥܡܬܩܝܢ
[v]ܕܐܬܡܪ
[w]ܐܠܗܘܢ [x]ܘܐܠܗܘܢ
[y]ܕܐܬܚܘܫܢ
[z]ܘܐܠܗ [a]ܕܡܠܟܘܬܝ
† f. 83b.
[b]ܫܝܢ [d]ܐܘܠܦܢܗ
[g] *add* ܕܝ [h]ܠܕܘܩܝܢ
[i]ܘܥܩܠ ܠܗ
[k] *add* ܒܥܘܕܢ
[l] *omit* ܘ [p]ܒܟܠܗ

Codex A.	*Codex* B.	*Codex* C.
°ܕܕܡܝܐ ʳܘܢܒܝܝܐ	39 ܘܬܢܝܢܐ °ܕܕܡܝܐ ܠܗ: ܕܬܪܚܡ ܠܩܪܝܒܟ ܗܝܟ	°ܕܕܡܝܐ
‡ f. 99a.	40 ˢܠܢܦܫܟ: ᑫܒܗܠܝܢ ܬܪܝܢ ܦܘܩܕܝܐ ‡ ܟܘܠܗ	ᑫܒܗܠܝܢ
ˢ*add* ܕ ᵘ*add* ܕܝ	41 ܢܡܘܣܐ ʳܘܢܒܝܐ ܬܠܝܢ: ᵗܟܕ ᵘܗܘܘ ᵛܦܪܝܫܝܢ	ᵗܟܕܘ ᵛܦܪܝܫܝܢ
ᵛܦܪܝܫܝܝܐ	42 ܡܟܢܫܝܢ: ܫܐܠ ܝܬܗܘܢ ܡܪܢ ܝܫܘܥ ܘܐܡܪ:	
	ܡܐ ܗܝܐ ܠܟܘܢ ܠܡܣܒܪ ܕܡܫܝܚܐ ܒܪܗ ܕܡܢ	
ᵛܕܕܘܝܕ	43 ܗܘ: ܐܡܪܝܢ ܠܗ ܒܪܗ ᵛܕܕܘܕ: ܐܡܪ ܠܗܘܢ	
ʷܕܘܝܕ	ܡܪܢ ܝܫܘܥ: ܗܝܟ ܐܘܢ ʷܕܘܕ ܒܪܘܚܐ ܩܪܐ	
ˣܬܒ ʸܕܐܫܘܝ	44 ܠܗ ܡܪܝ: ܕܐܡܪ ܐܡܪ ܡܪܝܐ ܠܡܪܝ ˣܬܒ	ˣܬܒ
ᶻܒܥܠܕܒܒܝܟ	ܡܢ ܝܡܝܢܝ ܥܕܡܐ ʸܕܐܫܘܝ ᶻܒܥܠܕܒ̈ܒܝܟ ᵃܟܒܫ	ᶻܒܥܠܕܒܒܝܟ
ᵃܟܒܫ ᵇܪ̈ܓܠܝܟ	45 ܬܚܘܬ ᵇܪ̈ܓܠܝܟ: ᶜܐܢ ܐܘܢ ʷܕܘܕ ܒܪܘܚܐ	ᵇܪ̈ܓܠܝܟ ᶜܐܝܢ
	46 ܩܪܐ ܠܗ ܡܪܝ: ܗܝܟ ܗܘ ܒܪܗ: ܘܐܢܫ ܠܐ	
ᵈܡܫܟܚ ᶠ*add* ܕܝ	ܗܘܐ ᵈܡܫܟܚ ᵉܕܢܬܝܒ ܝܬܗ ܡܠܐ: ܘܠܐ ᶠ	ᵉܕܢܬܒ ᶠ*add* ܕܝ
ᵍܐܢܫ	ᵍܐܢܫ ܐܚܪ ܡܢ ܗܘ ܝܘܡܐ ܕܫܐܠ ܝܬܗ	ᵍܐܢܫ
	ܟܘܕ:	

[*Codex* B *deest.*] *Codex* A. [*Codex* C *deest.*]

Matt. XXIII. 1—XXIV. 2.

1 2 ܘܒܟܝܢ ܡܠܠ ܡܪܢ ܝܫܘܥ ܠܐܘܟܠܘܣܝܐ ܘܠܬܠܡܝܕܘܝ ܐܡܪ: ܥܠ ܡܬܘܬܒܗ ܕܡܘܫܐ
3 ܝܬܒܘ ܣܦܪܝܐ ܘܦܪܝܫܝܢ ܟܘܠ ܡܐ ܐܘܢ ܕܝܐܡܪܘܢ ܠܟܘܢ ܥܒܕܘ ܘܛܪܘ: ܗܝܟ
4 ܒܥܒܕܝܗܘܢ ܠܐ ܬܥܒܕܘܢ: ܐܡܪܝܢ ܐܢܘܢ ܓܪ ܘܠܐ ܥܒܕܝܢ: ܘܐܣܪܝܢ ܡܘܒܠܝܢ
ܝܩܝܪܢ ܘܩܫܝܢ ܠܡܛܥܢ [f.99b] ܘܡܣܝܡܝܢ ܝܬܗܘܢ ܥܠ ܟܬܦܬܗܘܢ ܕܒܢܝܢܫܐ: ܐܢܘܢ ܕܝ
5 ܒܐܨܒܥܬܗܘܢ ܠܐ ܨܒܝܢ ܕܝܙܝܥܘܢ ܝܬܗܘܢ: ܟܘܠ ܕܝ ܥܒܕܝܗܘܢ ܕܐܢܘܢ ܥܒܕܝܢ
ܗܝܟ ܕܝܬܚܡܘܢ ܠܒܢܝܢܫܐ: ܡܦܬܝܢ ܐܢܘܢ ܓܪ ܐܦܝܠܩܛܝܗܘܢ ܘܡܪܒܝܢ ܟܪܨܦܬܗܘܢ
6 ܕܡܐܢܝܗܘܢ: ܘܪܚܡܝܢ ܪܝܫ ܡܫܟܒܐ ܒܫܪܘܬܐ: ܘܪܝܫܝܐ ܡܬܘܬܒܬܐ ܒܟܢܫܬܐ:
7 8 ܘܫܐܠ ܫܠܡܐ ܒܫܘܩܝܐ: ܘܕܝܬܩܪܘܢ ܐܦܘ ܡܬܩܪܝܢ ܡܢ ܒܢܝܢܫܐ ܪܒܝ ܪܒܝ: ܐܢܬܘܢ ܕܝ
ܠܐ ܬܬܩܪܘܢ ܠܟܘܢ ܡܠܦܢܐ: ܚܕ ܗܘ ܓܪ ܪܒܟܘܢ. ܘܠܐ ܬܬܩܪܘܢ ܠܐܢܫ ܪܒܝ: ܚܕ ܗܘ
9 ܓܪ ܡܠܦܢܟܘܢ: ܟܘܠܟܘܢ ܕܝ ܐܚܝܢ ܐܢܬܘܢ: ܘܐܒܐ ܠܐ ܬܩܪܘܢ ܠܟܘܢ ܥܠ ܐܪܥܐ:
10 ܚܕ ܗܘ ܓܪ ܐܒܘܟܘܢ: ܕܒܫܡܝܐ: ܘܠܐ ܬܬܩܪܘܢ ܡܕܒܪܢܝܢ: ܚܕ ܗܘ ܓܪ ܡܕܒܪܢܟܘܢ
11 12 ܡܫܝܚܐ: ܪܒ ܕܝ ܕܒܟܘܢ ܝܗܝ ܫܡܫܟܘܢ: ܟܘܠ ܡܢ ܓܪ ܕܝܪܝܡ ܢܦܫܗ
13 ܡܬܡܟܟ: ܘܟܘܠ ܡܢ ܕܡܡܟܟ ܢܦܫܗ ܝܬܪܘܡܡ: ܘܝ ܠܟܘܢ ܣܦܪܝܐ ܘܦܪܝܫܝܢ ܢܣܒܝ ܒܐܦܐ:

Codex A.

[f. 100a]
ܕܐܢܬܘܢ ܐܚܕܝܢ ܡܠܟܘܬܐ ܕܫܡܝܐ ܩܕܡ ܒܢܝ̈ܢܫܐ: ܐܢܬܘܢ ܓܝܪ ܠܐ ܥܐܠܝܢ ܘܠܐܝܠܝܢ ܕܥܐܠܝܢ
14 ܠܝܬ ܐܢܬܘܢ ܫܒܩܝܢ ܕܢܥܘܠܘܢ: ܘܝ ܠܟܘܢ ܣܦܪ̈ܐ ܘܦܪ̈ܝܫܐ ܢܣܒܝ ܒܐܦܐ: ܕܐܢܬܘܢ ܐܟܠܝܢ
15 ܒ̈ܬܝܗܝܢ ܕܐܪ̈ܡܠܬܐ: ܘܒܥܠܬܐ ܡܨܠܝܢ ܐܪܝܟܬܐ: ܡܛܠ ܗܢܐ ܬܩܒܠܘܢ ܕܝܢܐ ܝܬܝܪܐ: ܘܝ
ܠܟܘܢ ܣܦܪ̈ܐ ܘܦܪ̈ܝܫܐ ܢܣܒܝ ܒܐܦܐ: ܕܐܢܬܘܢ ܟܪܟܝܢ ܝܡܐ ܘܝܒܫܐ ܕܬܥܒܕܘܢ ܚܕ ܓܝܘܪܐ ܀
16 ܘܡܐ ܕܡܬܥܒܕ ܐܢܬܘܢ ܥܒܕܝܢ ܠܗ ܒܪܗ ܕܓܗܢܐ: ܥܦܝܦ ܡܢܟܘܢ: ܘܝ ܠܟܘܢ ܥܘܝ̈ܪܐ
ܡܕܒܪ̈ܢܐ: ܗܠܝܢ ܕܐܡܪܝܢ ܡܢ ܕܝܡܐ ܒܗܝܟܠܐ ܠܝܬ ܗܘ ܡܕܡ: ܘܡܢ ܕܝܡܐ ܒܕܗܒܗ
17 ܕܗܝܟܠܐ ܚܝܒ ܗܘ: ܣܟ̈ܠܐ ܘܥܘܝ̈ܪܐ: ܡܢ ܓܝܪ ܪܒ ܕܗܒܐ ܐܘ ܗܝܟܠܐ ܗܘ ܕܡܩܕܫ ܠܗ
18 ܠܕܗܒܐ: ܘܡܢ ܕܝܡܐ ܒܡܕܒܚܐ ܠܝܬ ܗܘ ܡܕܡ: ܘܡܢ ܕܝܡܐ ܒܩܘܪܒܢܐ ܕܠܥܠ ܡܢ
19 ܡܕܒܚܐ ܚܝܒ ܗܘ: ܣܟ̈ܠܐ ܘܥܘܝ̈ܪܐ ܡܢܐ ܓܝܪ ܪܒ ܩܘܪܒܢܐ ܐܘ ܡܕܒܚܐ ܕܡܩܕܫ ܠܗ
20
21 ܠܩܘܪܒܢܐ: ܡܢ ܐܘ ܕܝܡܐ ܒܡܕܒܚܐ: ܝܡܐ ܒܗ ܘܒܟܠܡܕܡ ܕܠܥܠ ܡܢܗ: ܘܡܢ
[f. 100b]
22 ܕܝܡܐ ܒܗܝܟܠܐ ܝܡܐ ܒܗ ܘܒܡܢ ܕܥܡܪ ܒܗ: ܘܡܢ ܕܝܡܐ ܒܫܡܝܐ ܝܡܐ
23 ܒܗ ܒܟܘܪܣܝܗ ܕܐܠܗܐ ܘܒܡܢ ܕܝܬܒ ܠܥܠ ܡܢܗ: ܘܝ ܠܟܘܢ ܣܦܪ̈ܐ ܘܦܪ̈ܝܫܐ ܢܣܒܝ ܒܐܦܐ:
ܕܐܢܬܘܢ ܡܥܣܪܝܢ ܢܢܥܐ ܘܫܒܬܐ ܘܟܡܘܢܐ: ܘܫܒܩܬܘܢ ܝܩܝܪܬܗ ܕܢܡܘܣܐ: ܕܝܢܐ
24 ܘܪܚܡܐ ܘܗܝܡܢܘܬܐ: ܗܠܝܢ ܗܘܐ ܘܠܐ ܕܬܥܒܕܘܢ: ܘܗܠܝܢ ܠܐ ܬܫܒܩܘܢ: ܡܕܒܪ̈ܢܐ
25 ܕܥܘܝ̈ܪܐ: ܗܠܝܢ ܕܡܨܠܝܢ ܩܘܩܐ ܘܒܠܥܝܢ ܓܡܠܐ: ܘܝ ܠܟܘܢ ܣܦܪ̈ܐ ܘܦܪ̈ܝܫܐ ܢܣܒܝ ܒܐܦܐ:
ܕܐܢܬܘܢ ܡܕܟܝܢ ܒܪܝܬܗ ܕܟܣܐ ܘܕܦܝܢܟܐ: ܘܡܢ ܠܓܘ ܡܠܝܢ ܡܢ ܚܛܘܦܝܐ
26 ܘܥܘܠܐ: ܦܪܝܫܐ ܥܘܝܪܐ ܕܟܝ ܐܘܠ ܠܓܘܗ ܕܟܣܐ ܘܕܦܝܢܟܐ ܕܢܗܘܐ ܐܦ
27 ܒܪܝܬܗܘܢ ܕܟܝܐ: ܘܝ ܠܟܘܢ ܣܦܪ̈ܐ ܘܦܪ̈ܝܫܐ ܢܣܒܝ ܒܐܦܐ ܕܐܢܬܘܢ ܕܡܝܢ.. ܠܩܒܪ̈ܐ ܡܚܘܪ̈ܐ:
[f. 101a]
ܗܠܝܢ ܕܡܢ ܠܒܪ ܡܢ ܡܬܚܙܝܢ ܢܐܝ̈ܢ: ܘܡܢ ܠܓܘ ܡܠܝܢ ܓܪ̈ܡܐ ܕܡܝ̈ܬܐ ܘܟܠ
28 ܛܢܦܘ: ܗܟܢܐ ܐܦ ܐܢܬܘܢ ܡܢ ܠܒܪ. ܐܢܬܘܢ ܡܬܚܙܝܢ ܠܒܢܝ̈ܢܫܐ ܟܐܢܝܢ: ܘܡܢ ܠܓܘ
29 ܐܢܬܘܢ ܡܠܝܢ ܥܘܠܐ ܘܡܢ ܟܘܠ ܒܝܫ ܢܣܒܘ ܒܐܦܐ ⁜ ܘܝ ܠܟܘܢ ܣܦܪ̈ܐ ܘܦܪ̈ܝܫܐ ܢܣܒܝ ܒܐܦܐ:
30 ܕܐܢܬܘܢ ܒܢܝܢ ܩܒܪ̈ܬܗܘܢ ܕܢܒܝ̈ܐ: ܘܡܨܒܬܝܢ ܩܒܪ̈ܝܗܘܢ ܕܙܕܝܩ̈ܐ: ܘܐܢܬܘܢ ܐܡܪܝܢ
ܕܐܠܘ ܗܘܝܢ ܒܝܘܡ̈ܝ ܐܒܗ̈ܬܢ: ܠܐ ܗܘܝܢ ܫܘܬܦܝܢ ܠܗܘܢ ܒܕܡܐ ܕܢܒܝ̈ܐ:
31 ܗܘܐ ܗܟܝ ܐܦ ܐܢܬܘܢ ܡܣܗܕܝܢ ܥܠ ܢܦܫܟܘܢ ܕܐܢܬܘܢ ܒܢܝܗܘܢ ܕܗܠܝܢ ܕܩܛܠܘ ܠܢܒܝ̈ܐ:
32
33 ܐܦ ܐܢܬܘܢ ܡܠܘ ܡܟܝܠܬܗܘܢ ܕܐܒܗ̈ܬܟܘܢ: ܚܘܘܬܐ ܘܝܠܕܝܗܘܢ ܕܐܟܕ̈ܢܐ ܗܝܟ
34 ܬܥܪܩܘܢ ܡܢ ܕܝܢܐ ܕܓܗܢܐ: ܡܛܠ ܗܢܐ ܗܐ ܐܢܐ ܡܫܕܪ ܠܘܬܟܘܢ ܢܒܝ̈ܐ ܘܚܟܝ̈ܡܐ
ܘܣܦܪ̈ܐ: ܘܡܢܗܘܢ ܬܩܛܠܘܢ ܘܬܙܩܦܘܢ: ܘܡܢܗܘܢ ܬܢܓܕܘܢ ܒܟܢܘܫܬܟܘܢ:
35 ܘܬܪܕܦܘܢ ܡܢ ܡܕܝܢܐ ܠܡܕܝܢܐ: ܠܡܛܠ ܕܢܐܬܐ ܥܠܝܟܘܢ ܟܘܠ ܐܕܡ ܙܕܝܩ ܕܐܫܬܦܟ
[f. 101b]
ܥܠ ܐܪܥܐ: ܡܢ ܐܕܡܗ ܕܗܒܝܠ ܙܕܝܩܐ ܥܕܡܐ ܠܐܕܡܗ ܕܙܟܪܝܐ ܒܪ ܒܪܟܝܐ ܗܘ
36 ܕܩܛܠܬܘܢ ܒܝܢ ܢܘܣܐ ܠܡܕܒܚܐ: ܐܡܝܢ ܐܡܪ ܐܢܐ ܠܟܘܢ ܕܢܐܬܝܢ ܗܠܝܢ ܟܠܗܝܢ
37 ܥܠ ܫܪܒܬܐ ܗܕܐ.. ܐܘܪܫܠܡ ܐܘܪܫܠܡ ܗܝ ܕܩܛܠܐ ܢܒܝ̈ܐ ܘܪܓܡܐ ܠܗܠܝܢ ܕܫܠܝܚܝܢ

Codex A.

ܠܘܬܗ: ܟܡܐ ܙܒܢܝܢ ܨܒܝܬ ܕܐܟܢܫ ܒܢܝܟܝ ܗܝܟ ܟܘܠܬܐ ܕܬܪܢܓܠܬܐ ܡܟܢܫܐ ܦܪܘܓܝܗ
38 39 ܬܚܘܬ ܓܦܝܗ ܘܠܐ ܨܒܝܬܘܢ: ܗܐ ܫܒܝܩ ܠܟܘܢ ܒܝܬܟܘܢ ܚܪܒ: ܐܡܪ ܐܢܐ
ܠܟܘܢ ܓܝܪ ܕܠܐ ܬܚܙܘܢܝ ܡܢ ܟܕܘ ܥܕܡܐ ܕܬܐܡܪܘܢ ܡܒܪܟ ܗܘ ܕܐܬܐ
XXIV. 1 ܒܫܡܗ ܕܡܪܝܐ: ܘܢܦܩ ܝܫܘܥ ܡܢ ܗܝܟܠܐ ܘܗܘܐ ܐܙܠ: ܘܩܪܒܘ ܬܠܡܝܕܘܗܝ
2 ܕܢܚܘܘܢ ܠܗ ܒܢܝܢܗ ܕܗܝܟܠܐ: ܗܘ ܕܝܢ ܐܬܝܒ ܘܐܡܪ ܠܗܘܢ: ܠܝܬ ܐܢܬܘܢ ܚܡܝܢ
ܟܘܠܗܝܢ ܗܠܝܢ: ܐܡܝܢ ܐܡܪ ܐܢܐ ܠܟܘܢ ܕܠܐ ܬܫܬܒܩ ܗܟܐ ܟܐܦ ܥܠ ܟܐܦ
ܕܠܐ ܬܬܣܬܪ ܀

Codex A.

[CXLII.]

[b]ܐܬܐܬܝܢ ܒܛܘܪܗ ܡܢ
[b]ܡܢܬܘܬܗ
ܘܒܝܬܗ ܡܪܢܐ ܝܫܘܥ [w]*add*
[a]ܬܠܡܝܕܘܗܝ
ܒܝܚܘܕܝܗܘܢ *add* [b]
[d]ܘܐܡܪܝܢ
[f]ܘܕܫܘܠܡܗ
[g]ܕܥܠܡܐ [h]ܘܐܬܝܒ
ܓܝܪ *add* [i]

‡ f. 96*a*.

ܘܩܝܪܘܣܐ *add* [k]
ܩܪܒ ܠܐ ܬܬܕܠܚܘܢ
ܒܬܪܗܘܢ
[n]ܩܪ̈ܒܐ [o]ܘܫܡ̈ܥܝܢ
[p]ܕܝܗ̈ܘܢ [q]ܫܝܢܐ
[r]ܝܩܘܡܘܢ [s]ܥ̈ܡܝܢ
[t]ܡܘ̈ܬܢܝܢ [u]ܘܟ̈ܦܢܝܢ
[w]ܘܙ̈ܘܥܝܢ ܕܝܢ *omit*[x]
[y]ܝܫܠܡܘܢ
[z]ܠܐܘܠܨܢ
[a]ܟܘܠܗܘܢ [b]ܒܓܠܠ
[c]ܢܒ̈ܝܐ [d]ܕܓܠ̈ܝܢ
[e]ܘܒܓܠܠ

Codex B.

Matt. XXIV. 3—35.

[a]ܘܟܕ [b]ܐܬܐܬ ܒܛܘܪܗ ܐܝܠܢܝܗ ܡܢ
3 ܡܬܐܬܐ[ba]: [w]ܘܟܕ [x]ܗܘܐ ܡܪܢܐ ܝܫܘܥ [y]ܝܬܝܒ
ܥܠ ܛܘܪܐ [z]ܕܙܝܬܐ: ܩܪܒܘ ܠܗ [a]ܬܠܡܝܕܘܗܝ[b]
[c]ܘܐܡܪܘ [d]ܐܡܪܝܢ: [†]ܐܡܪ ܠܢ [e]ܐܡܬܝ ܗܘܝܢ
ܗܠܝܢ: ܘܡܢܐ ܗܝ ܐܬܐ ܕܡܬܒܘܬܟ [f]ܘܕܫܘܠܡܗ
4 [g]ܕܥܠܡܐ [h]ܘܐܬܝܒ ܡܪܢܐ ܝܫܘܥ ܘܐܡܪ ܠܗܘܢ
5 ܚܙܘ ܕܠܐ ܐܢܫ ܝܛܥܝ ܝܬܟܘܢ: ܣܓܝܐܝܢ [i]ܐܬܝܢ
ܥܠ ܫܡܝ ܐܡܪܝܢ ܐܢܐ ܗܘ ܡܫܝܚܐ ܘܣܓܝܐܝܢ
6 ܝܛܥܘܢ: [k][‡]ܥܬܝܕܝܢ ܐܢܬܘܢ [l]ܕܝܢ [m]ܕܬܫܡܥܘܢ
[f. 84*a*]
[n]ܩܪܒܝܢ [o]ܘܫܡܥܝܢ ܕܩܪܒܝܢ ܚܙܘ ܕܠܐ
ܬܬܪܗܒܘܢ: ܩ̈ܢܝܢ ܓܝܪ ܠܗܠܝܢ [p]ܕܝܗܘܢ:
7 ܐܠܐ ܠܐ ܟܕܘ ܗܘܐ [q]ܫܘܠܡܐ: [r]ܝܩܘܡ ܓܝܪ
[s]ܥܡ ܥܠ [s]ܥܡ ܘܡܠܟܘ ܥܠ ܡܠܟܘ: ܘܗܘܘܢ
[t]ܡܘܬܢܝܢ [u]ܘܟܦܢܝܢ [w]ܘܙܘܥܝܢ ܒܐܬܪܝܢ ܐܬܪܝܢ:
8 9 ܟܘܠ ܗܠܝܢ [x]ܕܝܢ ܪܝܫ ܚܒܠܝܢ: ܟܕܝܢ [y]ܝܫܠܡܘܢ
ܝܬܟܘܢ [z]ܠܐܘܠܨܢ ܘܝܩܛܠܘܢ ܝܬܟܘܢ:
ܘܬܗܘܘܢ ܣܢܐܝܢ ܡܢ [a]ܟܘܠ ܥܡܡܝܐ
10 [b]ܒܓܠܠ ܫܡܝ: ܘܟܕܝܢ ܝܬܟܫܠܘܢ ܣܓܝܐܝܢ:
ܘܝܫܠܡܘܢ ܠܚܕܕܝܢ ܘܝܣܢܘܢ
11 ܠܚܕܕܝܢ: ܘܣܓܝܐܝܢ [c]ܢܒܝܝܢ [d]ܕܓܠܝܢ
12 ܝܩܘܡܘܢ ܘܝܛܥܘܢ ܣܓܝܐܝܢ: [e]ܘܒܓܠܠ ܕܣܓܝ

Codex C.

[CXLII.]

[a]ܠܝܘܡ ܐܬܠܬܝܢ ܒܥܢܐ
[a]ܡܢ ܡܬܐܬܐ
ܘܟܕ ܝܬܒܗ ܡܪܢܐ ܝܫܘܥ [w]*add*
[x]ܐܬܐ [y]ܝܬܒ

† f. 81*b*.

[z]ܕܙܝܬܐ [a]ܬܠܡܝܕܘܗܝ
ܒܝܚܘܕܝܗܘܢ *add* [b]
[c]ܠܝܫܘܥ [e]ܐܡܬܝ
[h]ܘܐܬܝܒ ܓܝܪ *add*[i]
ܕܒܐܕ *add* [l]
ܕ *omit*[m] [o]ܘܫܡܥܝܢ
[r]ܝܩܘܡܘܢ
[s]ܥܡ
[t]ܡܘܬܢܝܢ [u]ܘܟܦܢܝܢ
ܕܝܢ *omit* [x]
[a]ܟܘܠ
[d]ܕܓܠܝܢ

Codex A.

[x]ܗܘ ܕܝ ܕܡܣܝܒܪ[x]

[y]ܘܬܬܟܪܙ [z]ܒܥܠܡܐ

[a]ܥܡܡܝܐ

[b]ܗܘܣܘܒܝܬܐ

[d]ܒܕܢܝܐܝܠ

[g]ܬܐܬܪ [h]ܘܗ

[i]ܕܒܠ [k]ܐܓܪܐ

‡ f. 96b.

[l]ܒܥܠܡ [m]ܘܗܘ

[o]ܕܝܣܒܢ [p]ܡܐܢܗ

[q]ܘܝ [t]ܕܡܝܢܩܝܢ

[u]ܒܝܘܡ

[w]ܒܪܘܡܝܗܘܢ

ܒܝܘܡ [x]*omit* [y]ܒܫܒܬܐ

[z]ܠܢܝܘܢ

[b]ܪܫܗ [c]ܕܥܠܡܐ

[d]ܬܬܒܒܕ [e]ܠܟܠܠ

[f]ܒܡܝܪܘܢ

ܕܝ [g]*omit* [l]ܗܟܐ

ܒܐ [m]*omit* [n]ܠܗܠ

[o]ܬܗܝܡܢܘܢ

[q]ܘܢܒܝܝܢ [r]ܐܬܘܢ

[t]ܘܓܒܘܪܘܢ

[v]ܒܟܠܗ [w]ܒܓܒܪܘܢ

[y]ܬܦܩܘܢ

[z]ܐܐ ܗܐ[z]

‡ f. 97a.

[a]ܘܡܬܚܙܝܐ

[b]ܡܥܪܒܐ

[c]ܡܐܬܝܬܗ

[d]ܕܗܘܐ

Codex B.

ܒܒܪ ܣܓܝܐܘܬ ܥܘܠܐ ܬܦܫܓ ܕܪܚܡܬܗ :
13 ܐܐ[x] ܗܘ ܕܡܣܝܒܪ[x] ܠܣܘܦܐ ܗܘ ܚܝܐ :
14 [y]ܘܬܬܟܪܙ ܗܕܝܢ ܒܣܒܪܬܐ ܕܡܠܟܘܬܐ ܒܒܠܗ
[z]ܒܥܠܡܐ ܠܣܗܕܘ ܠܟܠ ܥܡܡܝܐ : ܘܒܒܝܢ
15 ܐܬܝܐ [a]ܥܝܢܐ : ܟܕ ܐܘܢ ܬܚܙܘܢ [b]ܗܘܣܘܒܐܝܬܗ
ܕܚܘܪܒܐ [c]ܕܐܬܐܡܪ [d]ܒܕܢܝܐܝܠ ܢܒܝܐ [e]ܘܩܝܡ
ܒܐܬܪܐ ܩܕܝܫܐ ܗܘ [f]ܕܩܪܐ ܝܕܥ [g]ܬܐܬܪ :
16 ܒܒܝܢ ‡ ܗܠܝܢ ܕܒܝܗܘܕܐ ܥܪܩܘܢ ܠܛܘܪܝܐ : [h]ܘܐܗ
17 [i]ܕܠ [k]ܐܓܪܐ ܠܐ ܢܚܘܬ ܕܢܣܒ [l]ܒܥܠܡ ܡܢ
18 ܒܝ ܒܝܬܗ : [m]ܘܐܘܗ ܕܒܚܩܠܐ ܠܐ ܝܬܘܒ
19 [n]ܠܒܣܬܪܐ [o]ܕܝܣܒ [p]ܡܐܢܗ : †[q]ܘܐܝ [r]ܠܗܝܢ ܕܝ
[s]ܠܗܠܝܢ ܕܒܛܢܢ[s] ܘܠܗܠܝܢ [t]ܕܡܝܢܩܢ ܒܗܠܝܢ ܝܘܡܝܐ :
20 ܘܗܘ ܕܝ ܡܨܠܝܢ ܕܠܐ [u]ܝܗܘܝ [w]ܥܪܘܩܝܟܘܢ
[f. 84b]
ܠܐ [x]ܒܝܘܡ [y]ܫܒܬܐ : ܘܠܐ ܒܣܬܘܐ ܗܘܐ
21 ܒܪ [z]ܠܢܝܘܢ ܪܒ ܕܠܐ ܐܬܒܒܕ ܒܗܬܗ ܡܢ
[b]ܪܫܗ [c]ܕܥܠܡܐ ܥܕ ܟܕܘ ܘܐܘܦ ܠܐ
22 ܠܐ [d]ܬܬܒܒܕ : ܘܐܠܘ ܠܐ ܕܡܝܪܘ ܗܠܝܢ
ܝܘܡܝܐ : ܐܠܐ ܕܝ ܒܢ ܠܐ ܚܝܐ ܟܠ ܒܣܪ :
[e]ܠܟܠܠ ܕܝ ܒܚܝܪܝܐ [f]ܡܝܪܘ [g]ܕܝ ܝܘܡܝܐ [h]ܗܠܝܢ :
23 ܒܒܝܢ [i]ܐܝ [j]ܐܡܪܘ ܠܒܘܢ [k]ܐܝܟ [l]ܐܗ ܗܘ [m]ܒܐ
ܡܫܝܚܐ : ܐܐ ܗܐ [n]ܒܐ ܗܘ ܠܐ ܬܗܝܡܢܘܢ :
24 [o]ܝܩܘܡܘܢ ܓܪ ܡܫܝܚܝܢ [p]ܕܓܠܝܢ [q]ܘܢܒܝܝܢ [p]ܕܓܠܝܢ :
ܘܬܠܘܢ [r]ܐܬܘܢ [s]ܪܒܪܒܝܢ [t]ܘܓܒܘܪܝܢ ܠܡܛܥܝܐ
25 ܕܝܛܥܘܢ [u]ܐܝ [v]ܐܠܘ ܐܘܦ ܠܓܒܝܪܝܐ : ܗܐ
26 ܩܕܡܬ ܐܡܪܬ ܠܒܘܢ [u]ܐܝ ܐܘܢ [w]ܐܡܪܘ
ܠܒܘܢ ܗܐ [x]ܒܡܕܒܪܐ ܐܝܬ ܗܘ ܠܐ [y]ܬܦܩܘܢ :
[z]ܗܐ ܗܘ[z] ܒܬܘܢܝܐ ܗܘ ܠܐ ‡ ܬܗܝܡܢܘܢ :
27 ܗܟܢ ܗܐ ܓܪ ܕܒܪܩܐ ܢܦܩ ܡܢ ܡܕܢܚܐ
[a]ܘܡܬܚܙܝܐ ܥܕ ܡܥܪܒܐ [b]ܒܡܥܪܒܐ : ܗܟܕܝܢ
28 ܗܘܝܐ ܐܘܦ [c]ܡܐܬܝܬܗ ܕܒܪܗ ܕܓܒܪܐ : ܗ
[d]ܕܗܘܝܐ ܦܓܪܐ [e]ܠܬܡܢ ܡܬܟܢܫܝܢ ܢܫܪܝܐ :

Codex C.

[x]ܗܘ ܕܝ ܡܣܝܒܪ[x]

[z]ܒܥܠܡܐ [a]ܥܡܘܝܐ

[b]ܗܘܣܐܒܘܬܐ

[c]ܕܐܬܐܡܪ

[d]ܒܕܢܝܠ [e]ܩܡ

ܕܩܪܐ [f]*omit* [g]ܬܬܪ

[h]ܘܗ [i]ܕܒܠ

[j]ܠܛܘܪܐ [k]ܐܓܪܐ

[m]ܘܗܘ [n]ܠܒܣܬܪܐ

[q]ܘܝ [r]ܠܗܠܝܢ

† f. 82a.

[s]ܕܗܠܝܢ ܕܒܛܢܝܢ[s]

ܒܝܘܡ [x]*omit*

[y]ܫܒܬܐ.

[z]ܠܢܝܘܢ [b]ܪܫܗ

[c]ܒܥܠܡܐ [f]ܡܝܪܘܢ

ܕܝ [g]*omit* [h]ܗܠܝܢ

[i]ܐܝܢ [j]ܡܡܪܘܢ

[k]ܐܝܟ [l]ܗܟܐ

ܒܐ [m]*omit*

[n]ܠܗܠ [o]ܬܗܝܡܢܘܢ

[p]ܕܓܐܠܝܢ [q]ܘܢܒܝܢ

[s]ܪܒܪܒܝܢ [t]ܘܓܒܘܪܝܢ

[u]ܐܝܢ [v]ܡܠܠܘ

[w]ܡܡܪܘܢ [x]ܒܡܕܒܪܐ

[y]ܬܦܩܘܢ

[z]ܐܐ ܗܐ[z]

[a]ܘܡܬܚܙܝܐ

[b]ܡܥܪܒܐ

[c]ܡܐܬܝܬܗ

[d]ܕܗܘܐ [e]ܬܡܢ

Codex A.	*Codex* B.	*Codex* C.
[f]ܥܩܬܗ ܕܝܢ [g] *omit*	29 [f]ܒܬܪ ܕܝܢ ܡܢ ܥܩܬܗ [g]ܕܝܢ [h]ܠܝܘܡܝܗܘܢ ܗܠܝܢ	[f]ܥܩܬܐ ܕܝܢ [g] *omit*
[h]ܠܝܘܡܝܗܘܢ	ܘܫܡܫܐ : [i]ܫܡܫܐ [k]ܢܚܫܟܢ ܘܣܗܪܐ ܠܐ [l]ܝܬܠ	[k]ܢܚܫܟܢ [l]ܝܬܠ
[i]ܫܡܫܐ [k]ܢܚܫܟܢ	ܢܘܗܪܗ ܘܟܘܟܒܝܐ [m]ܢܦܠܘܢ ܡܢ ܫܡܝܐ :	
[l]ܝܬܠ [m]ܢܦܠܘܢ	30 [n]ܘܚܝܠܝܐ ܕܫܡܝܐ [o]ܡܙܕܥܙܥܝܢ : ܘܒܟܝܢ ܡܬܚܙܝܐ	[n]ܘܚܝܠܝܐ [o]ܡܙܕܥܙܥܝܢ
[p]ܓܒܪܐ [q]ܢܪܩܕܘܢ	ܐܬܗ ܕܒܪܗ [p]ܕܓܒܪܐ ܒܫܡܝܐ : ܘܒܟܝܢ	[q]ܢܪܩܕܘܢ
[r]ܫܪܒܬܗ	[q]ܡܪܩܕܘܢ * ܟܠܗܘܢ [r]ܫܪܒܬܐ ܕܐܪܥܐ :	[* *Sic* in Cod. B.]
[s]ܕܐܪܥܐ [t]ܕܫܡܝܐ	[f. 85*a*] ܘܚܙܝܢ ܠܒܪܗ [s]ܕܓܒܪܐ ܐܬܝ ܥܠ	[s]ܕܐܪܥܐ
[v]ܘܒܚܝܠ ܣܓܝ[v]	ܥܢܢܝܗܘܢ [t]ܕܫܡܝܐ : ܥܡ ܚܝܠ [u]ܘܬܫܒܘܚܐ	[u]ܘܬܫܒܘܚܐ
[m]ܪܒܬܐ [x]ܒܚܝܪܘܗܝ	31 ܣܓܝ : [v] † ܘܗܘ [w]ܡܫܠܚ ܡܠܐܟܘܗܝ ܥܡ ܩܠܗ	† f. 82*b*.
[y]ܐܪܒܥܬܗܘܢ	ܕܩܪܢܐ [m]ܪܒܐ ܘܡܟܢܫܘܢ ܟܘܠ [x]ܒܚܝܪܝ ܡܢ	[v]ܘܒܚܝܠ ܣܓܝ[v]
[z]ܪܫܝܗܘܢ [a]ܕܫܡܝܐ	[y]ܐܪܒܥܬܐ ܪܘܚܐ ܡܢ [z]ܪܝܫܝܗܘܢ [a]ܕܫܡܝܐ	[w]ܡܫܠܚ [m]ܪܒܬܐ
[b]ܬܐܢܬܐ [c] *add* ܕܝܢ	32 ܒܕ ܡܬܠܐ [z]ܪܝܫܗܘܢ : ܡܢ [b]ܬܐܢܬܐ [c] [d]ܝܠܦܘܢ	[c] *add* ܕܝܢ
‡ f. 97*b*.	ܡܬܠܐ : ܗܝܟ ܡܐ ܕܐ [e]ܕܒ ‡ ܥܒܪ [f]ܫܘܪܘܚܗ	[e]ܕܒܕ
[d]ܝܠܦܘܢ [e]ܕܒܕ	ܬܟܒܕ [g]ܪܒܝܢ [h]ܘܢܦܩܝܢ ܛܪܦܝܐ ܡܬܒܕܒ [i]ܕܝܢ	[g]ܪܒܝܢ [h]ܘܢܦܩܝܢ
[f]ܫܘܪܘܚܗ [h]ܘܢܦܩܝܢ	33 ܕܩܪܝܒ ܗܘ ܩܝܛܐ : ܗܟܕܝܢ [j]ܐܘܦ ܐܢܬܘܢ :	[i] *omit* ܕܝܢ
[i] *omit* ܕܝܢ	ܟܕ [n][o]ܬܚܙܘܢ ܗܠܝܢ ܟܠܗܘܢ [n]ܐܢܬܘܢ ܬܕܥܝܢ	[j] *omit* ܐܘܦ
[n] *omit* ܬܚܙܘܢ . . .	34 ܕܩܪܝܒ ܗܘ ܥܠ [p]ܬܪܥܐ : ܐܡܝܢ ܐܡܪ ܐܢܐ	[o]ܬܚܙܘܢ
. . . ܟܠܗܘܢ	ܠܟܘܢ ܕܠܐ [q]ܬܥܒܪ ܗܕܐ ܕܪܐ ܥܕܡܐ ܕܟܘܠ	[q]ܬܥܒܪ
[p]ܬܪܥܐ [s]ܢܬܥܒܕܘܢ	35 [r]ܗܠܝܢ [s]ܝܬܥܒܕܘܢ : ܫܡܝܐ ܘܐܪܥܐ [u]ܥܒܪܝܢ	[r]ܗܠܝܢ
[t]ܘܡܠܝ [u]ܥܒܪܝܢ	[t]ܘܡܠܝܐ ܕܝܠܝ ܠܐ [u]ܥܒܪܝܢ ⁘	[t]ܘܡܠܝ

CXLIV.

Matt. XXIV. 36—XXVI. 2.

Codex A.	*Codex* B.	*Codex* C.
ܣܗܕ ܐܬܬܠܬܐ	36 [y]ܥܠ ܝܘܡ [z]ܗܘ ܘܫܥܬܐ [a]ܗܝ [b]ܫܥܬܐ [c]ܐܢܫ ܠܐ	ܠܣܗܕ ܐܬܬܠܬܐ
ܒܡܝܬܗ ܐܬܓܠܠ	37 [d]ܝܕܥ : ܐܘܦ ܠܐ [e]ܡܠܐܟܝܐ ܕܫܡܝܐ : ܐܘܦ	ܒܫܒܐ ܗܘܐ ܐܬܓܠܠ
ܐܠܓܝܢܘܢ ܡܢ ܡܬܝ	† ܠܐ ܒܪܐ ܐܠܐ [o]ܐܒܐ [f]ܒܠܚܘܕܘܗܝ : [g]ܗܝܟ	ܐܠܓܝܢܘܢ ܡܢ ܡܬܝ
[y] *add* ܐܡܪ ܡܪܢ	ܡܐ [g][h]ܕܗܘܘ [i]ܒܝܘܡܝ [j]ܢܘܚ : [k]ܗܟܕܝܢ ܬܗܐ	[y] *add* ܐܡܪ ܡܪܢ ܝܫܘܥ
‡ f. 102*a*. [‡]ܝܫܘܥ	38 ܐܘܦ ܡܝܬܝܬܗ ܕܒܪܗ [l]ܕܓܒܪܐ : ܗܝܟ ܡܐ	† f. 84*a*.
[z] *add* ܕܝܢ [a]ܗܘ	ܕܗܘܘ [m]ܒܝܘܡܝܐ ܗܠܝܢ ܗܠܝܢ ܕܩܕܡ ܡܘܕܒ	[b] *add* ܠܐ [z] *add* ܕܝܢ
[b] *add* ܠܐ [d]ܝܕܥ	39 ܛܘܦܢܐ : ܕܗܘܘ ܐܟܠܝܢ ܘܫܬܝܢ [n]ܘܡܫܬܬܦܝܢ	[c]ܐܢܫ [d]ܝܕܥ
[f]ܒܠܚܘܕܘܗܝ		[o] *add* ܠܐ [f]ܒܠܚܘܕܘܗܝ
[h] *add* ܗܟ [g]ܗܝܟܢܐ		[h] *add* ܗܟ [i]ܕܗܘܘ
[j]ܒܝܘܡܝ		[l]ܕܓܒܪܐ
[k]ܗܟܢܐ [m]ܒܝܘܡܝܐ		
[n]ܘܡܫܬܬܦܝܢ		

Codex A.

ܘܡܫܬ̈ܬܦܝܢ[h]

[i] *omit* ܠܡܘܬܐ

ܗܟ̇ܢܢ[k] [l] *omit* ܕܝܢ

ܬܗܘܐ̣[m] ܕܒܪܢܫܐ[n]

ܚܕ[p]

CXLIV. [CXCIV.]

ܒ̈ܗܘܢ[r] ܦܢ̈ܝܢ[s]

ܬܬܕܒ̇ܪ[t]

[ξ] *add* ܐܚܪ̇ܢ ܐܚܪ̇ܢܐ

ܕܠܢܬܘܢ[u] ܒܗܢ̇ܕܝܢ[w]

ܗܢܘܢ[a] ܡܪ̈ܕܘܢ[βx]

ܢ̇ܕܒ[sy] [zη] *omit* ܢܕܒ

ܒܗܢܕܐ[δg] ܦ̇ܠܚܪܐ[h]

ܒ̇ܥܒܕܐ[e] [a] *add* ܗ̣ܘ

‡ f. 102b.

ܒܝܬܗ̣[ζb] ܠܚܠܠ̇[c]

ܒܕ[θ] ܕܒܪܢܫܐ[d]

[λ] *add* ܗ̣ܘ

[μ] *omit* ܐܝܬܘܗܝ

ܗ̇ܕ[e] [gξ] *add* ܢܬ̇ܗ̣

ܒܥ̈ܒܕܬܗ[πh]

ܡܪ̇ܘܚ̈ܢܘܢ[ρi]

[§ f. 158a.]

ܒܡܪ̇ܘܣܐ[j]

ܦ̇ܠܚܒ̇ܗ[τk] [φ] *add* ܗ̇ܘ

[l] *omit* ܐܐ

[χ] *omit* ܐܐ ܗܘ

ܕ[m] ܗ̇ܕܝܢ[ψ]

ܕܢܬ̇ܐ[n] [oα] *omit* ܕܝܢ

ܘܒ̇ܥܒܝܕ[p] ܒ̇ܥܒ̈ܝܕ[β]

[qγ] *add* ܢܬ̇ܗ̣

ܒܒܕ ܟ̇ܕܝܢ[δr] ܒܗܠ[σs]

ܐ̇ܡܘܪ[ζ] [wη] *omit* ܐܐ

ܘܐ̇ܗ[θ] ܠܒ̇ܢ̈ܝܬܗ̣[y]

ܘܐܟ̇ܠ[λz] ܘܐܥܬ̇ܝ[a]

Codex B.

ܘܡܫܬܬܦܝܢ[h]: ܒܕܡܘܬܐ ܠܡܘܬܐ[i] ܕܟܠ ܢܦܫ

ܠܚܕܘܬܐ: ܘܠܐ ܢܚܒ ܒܕܡܘܬܐ ܕܐܬܐ ܠܦܘܢܐ

ܘܢܣܒ ܒܥܠܘܡܗܘܢ: ܗܟܢܢ[k] ܕܝܢ[l] ܬܗܘܐ[m] ܐܘܦ

40 ܒܢܬܘܬܗ ܕܒܪܗ ܕܒܪܢܫܐ[n]: ܒܒܝܢ ܬܪܝܢ ܗܘܘܢ

41 ܒܦܠܚܐ[o]: ܐܚܕ[p] ܢܬܕܒܪ ܘܚܕ[q] ܡܬܬܒܗ: ܬܬܪܬܝܢ

[f. 85b]

ܗܘܘܢ[r] ܦܢܝܢ[s] ܒܪܝܚܐ ܚܕܐ ܬܬܕܒܪ[t] ܘܚܕܐ

42 ܬܬܥܒܕܒ:[ξ] ܗܘܘ ܐܘܢ ܒܪܢܫ ܕܠܢܬܘܢ[u] ܐܬܘܢ[u]

43 ܢܕܒܝܢ[w] ܗܕܝܢ[α] ܢܘܦ[x] ܡܪܕܘܢ[β] ܐܬܐ: ܗܕܐ

ܕܝܢ ܗܘܘ ܢܕܒܝܢ ܕܐܠܗܐ ܗܘܐ[y] ܕܝܢ[s] ܡܪܗ

ܕܒܢܬܐ[η] ܢܕܒ[z] ܒܗܕܐ[δ] ܦܠܚܪܐܬܐ[h] ܠܒܢܝܐ

ܐܬܐ ܐܬܐ ܗܘܐ[a] ܒܢܝܢ ܘܠܐ ܥܒܕ ܒܝܬܗ[ζb]

44 ܕܢܬܚܬܪ[c] ܠܚܠܠ[θ] ܒܕܝܢ ܐܘܦ ܐܬܘܢ ܗܘܘܢ

‡ ܒܬܕܝܢ ܕܒܥܒܬܐ ܕܠܢܬ ܐܬܘܢ ܡܥܒܕܝܢ ܒܪܗ

45 ܕܒܪܢܫܐ[d] ܐܬܐ: ܡܢ[λ] ܐܪܐ ܐܝܬܘܗܝ[μ] ܒܒܕܐ

ܡܗܡܢܐ ܘܦܩܝܕܐ ܗܕܝܢ[e] ܕܢܣܒ[f] [ξg] ܡܪܗ ܒܠ

ܒܥܒܕܘܬܗ[πh] ܕܢܬܠ ܠܗܘܢ ܡܪܘܚܢܘܢ[ρi]

46 ܒܡܪܘܣܗ[j]: ܦܠܚܒܢ[τk] ܒܒܕܐ[φ] ܐܐ[χl] ܗܘ ܕܝܢ[ψm]

ܕܐܬܐ[n] ܡܪܗ ܕܝܢ[αo] ܡܥܒܝܕܗ[βp] [q] ܕܒܕܝܢ[δr] ܒܒܕ[r]:

47 ܐܡܪ ܐܡܪ ܐܢܐ ܠܗܘܢ: ܕܒܠ[σs] ܒܗܠܘܢ

48 ܘܢܣܒܢܝܢ[t] ܢܣܒ[u] ܢܬܗ[§]: ܐܢ[v] ܕܝܢ ܡܥܒܪ[ζ]

ܐܐ[ηw] ܗܘ[θ] ܒܒܕܐ ܒܝܫܐ ܒܠܒܗ ܡܘܚܪ ܗܘ

49 ܡܪܝ ܕܢܬܐܬܐ: ܘܢܫܪܐ[x] ܡܚܝܐ[†] ܠܒܢܝܬܗ[y]:

50 ܘܐܟܠܝܢ[λz] ܘܐܫܬܐ[a] ܥܡ ܪܘܝܐ[b]: ܐܬܐ ܗܘ

ܡܪܗ ܕܗܘ[νc] ܒܒܕܐ ܒܝܘܡܐ[sd] ܕܠܐ ܡܣܟܐ

51 ܘܒܥܒܕܬܐ[e] ܕܠܐ ܡܒܝܢ[πf]: ܘܡܦܠܓ ܢܬܗ

ܘܢܣܝܡܗ ܕܝܢ[ρg] ܥܡ ܕܢܣܒܪܐ[h] [σ] ܢܣܒ[τi]: ܬܡܢ

ܗܘܐ[k] ܒܟܝܐ ܘܚܘܪܩܢܘܢ[υl] ܕܫܢܐ[φm]:

Codex A.—cont.]

ܪ̈ܘܢܝܢ[b] | [cν] *omit* ܗܘ | ܒܝܘܡ[sd] | ܘܒܥܒܕܐ[e]
ܢ̇ܕܒ[πf] | [gρ] *omit* ܕܝܢ | [σ] *add* ܗܘ | ܡܥܒ̇ܝܕ[τ]
ܒܟ̇ܝܐ[k] | ܘܚܘܪ̈ܩܢܘܢ[υl] | ܕܫ̈ܢܝܐ[φm]

Codex C.

ܘܡܫܬܦܝܢ[h]

[i] *omit* ܠܡܘܬܐ

[l] *omit* ܕܝܢ ܬܗܘܝ[m]

ܕܒܪܢܫܐ[n] ܒܦܠܚܐ[o]

ܚܕܐ[p] ܘܚܕܐ[q]

ܗܘ[r] ܦܢܝܢ[s]

ܕܗܕܝܢ[w]

ܢܕܒ[y]

[z] *omit* ܢܕܒ

ܒܦܠܚܪܐ[h] [a] *add* ܗܘ

ܒܝܬܗ[b] ܠܚܠܠ[c]

ܕܒܪܢܫܐ[d] ܕܢܣܒ[f]

[g] *add* ܢܬܗ ܒܥܒܕܬܗ[h]

ܒܡܪܘܣܐ[j]

[l] *omit* ܐܐ ܕܢܬܐ[n]

[o] *omit* ܕܝܢ

[p] ܘܡܥܒܝܕ ܢܬܗ [p]

[r] ܒܒܕ ܒܝܢ [r]

ܒܗܠ[s] ܘܢܣܒܢ[t]

ܢܣܒ[u] ܐܢ[v]

† f. 84b.

ܘܢܫܪܐ[x] ܘܐܫܬܝ[a]

ܪܘܝ[b] [c] *omit* ܗܘ

ܒܝܘܡ[d] ܘܒܥܒܕܐ[e]

ܢܕܒ[f] [g] *omit* ܕܝܢ

ܕܢܣܒܪܐ[h] ܢܣܒ[i]

Codex A.

CXLIV. [CCCCX.]

^β *add* ܐܡܪ ܡܪܢ ܗܕܐ ܡܬܠܐ

^γ ܒܟܢ ^δ ܬܬܕܡܐ

^g ܐܬܕܡܬ

^ζh ܡܠܟܘܬܐ

^ηm ܠܐܘܪܥܘܬܗ

‡ f. 103*a*.

^θ *omit* ܕܝ ^κp ܡܢܗܘܢ

^λ *add* ܕܝ ^μq ܣܟܠܢ

^u ^ξ *add* ܕܝ ^νs ܦܩܝܚܢ

^π ܡܫܚ ^sw ܥܡܗܘܢ

^σa ܒܡܐܢܝܗܘܢ

^τ *omit* ܟܘܠܗܘܢ

^φ ܘܗܘܝ ^b *omit* ܘܘܗܘ

^d ܘܕܡܟܝܢ ^χ ܕܡܟܝܢ

^ψe ܒܦܠܓܗ

^ωf ܐܬܥܒܕܬ

^β *add* ܦܘܩܘ ^γ ܒܟܢ

^δh ܟܘܠܗܘܢ ^δ ܟܘܠ

^k ܠܡܫܟܢܝܗ

^ζ *add* ܒܟܢ ܐܡܪܝܢ ܗܠܝܢ

^l *add* ܐܘ

^ηm ܣܟܠܬܐ ^θn ܐܡܪܢ

^θ *omit* ܐܡܪܝܢ

^κ ܗܒܝ ^p ܡܢ ܡܫܚܟܝܢ

^λ ܡܫܚܟܘܢ ^qς *omit* ܕܝ

^v ܠܡܫܟܢܝܢ [§ f. 195*b*.]

^μ ܠܡܫܟܢܝܗ

^νr ܐܬܥܢܝ ^s ܐܡܪܝ

^ξ ܘܐܡܪܝ ^tπ *add* ܕܠܐ

^ρw ܐܙܠܝܢ ^σx ܘܙܒܢܝܢ

‡ f. 103*b*.

^τy ܠܟܝܢ ^φa ܕܝܙܒܢܝܢ

^ψr ܡܬܛܝܒܢ ^b ܥܐܠܝ

^ω ܥܠܝ ^αc ܠܒܝܬ

^d ܘܐܬܚܕ ^e ܬܪܥܝܢ

^β ܬܪܥܐ ^γ ܐܬܝܐ

^δ *omit* ܐܘܦ ^f ܫܪܟܬ

Codex B.

XXV.

1 ^γβ ܘܒܗܝܢ ^δg ܬܬܕܡܝ ^ζh ܡܠܟܘܬܗ ܕܫܡܝܐ ܠܥܣܪ
^i ܒܬܘܠܢ ܗܠܝܢ ܕܢܣܒܘ ^k ܠܡܫܟܢܝܗܘܢ : ܘܢܦܩܘ
2 ^ηm ܠܐܘܪܥܘܬܗ ܕܚܬܢܐ : ܚܡܫ ^θo ܕܝ ^κp ܡܢܗܘܢ ^λ
[f. 86*a*]
3 ܗܘܝ ^μq ܣܟܠܢ ^r ܘܚܡܫ ^νs ܦܩܝܚܢ : ܣܟܠܬܐ ^ξu
ܕܢܣܒܘ ܫܦܝܬܐ ܠܡܫܟܢܝܗܘܢ ܠܐ ܢܣܒܘ
4 ^sw ܥܡܗܘܢ ^π ܡܫܚ : ‡ ܗܠܝܢ ܕܝ ^y ܦܩܝܚܬܐ
ܢܣܒܘ ^π ܡܫܚ ^σa ܒܡܐܢܝܗܘܢ ܥܡ ^k ܠܡܫܟܢܝܗܘܢ :
5 ܟܕ ܕܝ ܐܘܚܪ ܚܬܢܐ ܢܐܡܘ ^τ ܟܘܠܗܘܢ
6 ^φb ܘܘܗܘ ^χd ܕܡܟܝܢ : ^ψe ܒܦܠܓܗ ܕܝ ܕܠܠܝܐ
ܩܥܘ ^ωf ܐܬܥܒܕܬ ܗܐ ܚܬܢܐ ܐܬܐ ^g ܦܘܩܘ ^β
7 ܠܐܘܪܥܘܬܗ : ^γ ܗܝܕܝܢ ܩܡܝܢ ^δh ܟܘܠܗܘܢ
^i ܒܬܘܠܬܐ ܗܠܝܢ ܘܬܩܢܝܢ ^k ܠܡܫܟܢܝܗܘܢ :
8 ^ζj ܗܠܝܢ ^l ^ηm ܕܣܟܠܬܐ ^θn ܐܡܪܝܢ ܠܦܩܝܚܬܐ ^κ ܗܒܘ
ܠܢ ܡܢ ^λp ܡܫܚܟܘܢ ܕܗܐ ^sq ܕܝ ^μv ܠܡܫܟܢܝܢ
9 ܥܦܝܢ : ^νr ܐܬܥܢܝܢ ܕܝ ܦܩܝܚܬܐ ^ξs ܐܡܪܢ
ܠܐ ^πt ܐܡܬܝ ^u ܠܐ ܡܣܦܩ ܠܢ ^v ܘܠܟܝܢ : ^ρw ܐܙܠܝܢ
10 ܕܝ ܠܘܬ ܗܠܝܢ ܕܡܙܒܢܝܢ ^σx ܘܙܒܢܝܢ ^τy ܠܟܘܢ : ܟܕ
ܕܝ ^z ܐܙܠܝ ^φa ܕܝܙܒܢܝܢ ܐܬܐ ^q ܕܝ ܚܬܢܐ : ܘܗܠܝܢ
ܕܗܘܝ ^ψr ܡܬܛܝܒܢ ^ωb ܥܠ ܥܡܗ ^αc ܠܒܝܬ ܚܠܘܠܐ
11 ^d ܘܐܬܚܕ ܬܪܥܐ : ^βe ܒܬܪ ܕܝ ܗܟܝܢ ^γ ܐܬܝܢ ^δ ܐܘܦ
^f † ܫܪܟܬ ^ηg ܒܬܘܠܬܐ ^θh ܐܡܪܢ ^i ܡܪܢ ^i ܡܪܢ
12 ^κk ܦܬܚ ܠܢ : ܘܗܘ ^l ܕܝ ܐܬܥܢܝ ^§ ܘܐܡܪ ^m ܐܡܝܢ
^n ܐܡܝܢ ܐܡܪ ܐܢܐ ^μ ܠܟܘܢ ܕܠܝܬ ܐܢܐ ^o ܝܕܥ
13 ^p ܠܟܘܢ : ܗܘܘ ܐܘܢ ܥܝܪܝܢ ܕܠܝܬ ܐܢܬܘܢ ܝܕܥܝܢ
14 ܝܘܡܐ ܘܠܐ ܫܥܬܐ : ^ξ :* ܗܟܢ ܡܟܐ ܓܒܪ ܕܓܒܪ
ܚܒܪ ^q ܕܢܦܩ ܠܗ : ‡ ܩܪܐ ^r ܠܥܒܕܘܗܝ ܘܡܣܪ
15 ^s ܠܗܘܢ ܩܢܝܢܗ : ܠܚܕ ܡܢ ܝܗܒ ܚܡܫܐ

Codex C.

XXV.

1 ^g ܐܬܕܡܝܬ ^h ܡܠܟܘܬܐ

^i ܒܬܘܠܢ

2 ^k ܠܡܫܟܢܝܗܘܢ

3 ^o ܕܐܝ

^p *omit* ܡܢܗܘܢ

4 ^q ܣܟܠܬܐ ^r ܘܚܡܫܐ

^u *add* ܕܝ ^y ܦܩܝܚܢ

5 ^b *omit* ܘܘܗܘ

6 ^d ܘܕܡܟܝܢ

^e ܒܦܠܓܗ

7 ^g *omit* ܐܬܐ

^i ܒܬܘܠܬܐ ^j ܗܠܝܢ

8 ^k ܠܡܫܟܢܝܗܘܢ

^l *add* ܐܘ ܕܝ

9 ^m ܣܟܠܬܐ ^n ܐܡܪܝܢ

^q *omit* ܕܝ ^v ܠܡܫܟܢܝܢ

10 ^r ܐܬܥܢܝ ^t *add* ܕܠܐ

^u *omit* ܠܐ ^v ܘܠܟܘܢ

^z ܐܙܠܝܢ ^a ܕܝܙܒܢܘܢ

11 ^b ܥܐܠܝ ^c ܠܒܝܬ

† f. 85*a*.

12 ^e ܒܬܪܟܝܢ ^f ܫܪܟܬ

^g ܒܬܘܠܬܐ ^i ܡܪܢ

13 ^k ܦܬܚܘ ^l ܕܐܝ

14 ^m *add* ܠܗܘܢ ^o ܡܕܝܢ

^q ܕܢܦܩ ^r ܠܥܒܕܘܗܝ

15 ^s ܩܢܝܢܗ

Codex A.—cont.] ^g ܒܬܘܠܬܐ ^η ܒܬܘܠܬܐ
^θh ܡܪܢ ^κk ܦܬܚܘ ^n *omit* ܐܡܝܢ ^μ ܠܟܝܢ
^o ܡܕܝܢ ^p ܠܟܝܢ ^ξ *add* ܕܐܬܐ ܒܗ ܒܪܗ ܕܐܢܫܐ
^q ܕܢܦܩ ^r ܠܥܒܕܘܗܝ * Explicit CCCCX.

Codex B.

ܐܠܠܝܡ: ܘܠܒܫ ܐܬܪܝ: ܘܠܒܫ[b] ܚܕ: ܠܟܠ ܐܢܫ
16 ܠܡܟܠ ܚܝܠܗ: ܘܡܪܝܐ [e]ܐܡܪ ܠܗ: [f][g]ܘܡܪܝܐ
[e]ܐܡܪ[g] ܗܘ ܕܢܫܡܥ ܫܡܥܐ ܐܠܠܝܡ: [i]ܒܡܟܠ
[f. 86b]
17 ܒܡܘܢ[j] ܘܐܬܚܙܝ[k] ܫܘܪܝܐ[l] ܫܡܥܐ[k]: ܡܢ ܕܝܢ
ܘܒܘܬܐ ܐܘܦ ܗܘ [n]ܕܢܫܡܥ [o]ܬܪܝܢ [p]ܐܠܠܝܡ ܒܡܟܠ
18 ܒܡܘܢ[p] [q]ܘܐܬܚܙܝ ܫܘܪܝܐ[q] ܬܪܝܢ: ܗܘ [r]ܗܘ ܕܢܫܡܥ
[s]ܚܕܐ [e]ܐܡܪ [t]ܫܡܥ ܒܐܪܒܐ: [u]ܘܐܬܚܙܝ [v]ܕܝܢ
19 ܒܫܡܥ ܕܡܪܘܗ: ܡܢ ܒܬܪ ܕܝܢ ܗܠܝܢ [w]ܐܡܘܢ
ܐܬܐ [x]ܡܪܘܗ [y]ܕܒܒܪܐ ܗܠܝܢ ܘܒܒܪ ܒܡܘܢ
20 [a]ܫܡܥܝܢ: [b]ܘܦܪܘܩ ܗܘ ܕܢܫܡܥ ܫܡܥܐ ܐܠܠܝܡ
[c]ܘܐܬܚܙܝ [d]ܫܘܪܝܐ ܫܡܥܐ ܐܠܠܝܡ ܐܡܪ ܡܪܝ
ܫܡܥܐ ܐܠܠܝܡ ܡܫܪܬ ܠܝ: ܗܐ [e][f]ܫܘܪܝ
21 [g]ܫܡܥܐ[e] [h]ܐܠܠܝܡ [i]ܐܬܚܙܬ ܒܠܒܘܢ: ܐܡܪ
ܠܗ [j]ܕܝܢ ܡܪܘܗ ܐܘ ܒܒܪܐ [k]ܠܒܐ ܘܡܗܝܡܢܘܬܐ
ܒܠ ܝܫܘܥ [l]ܗܘܬ ܡܗܝܡܢ ܒܠ ܗܠܝܢ ܐܢܐ
22 [m]ܡܫܝܚ ܠܝ: ܒܟܠ ܠܫܪܘܬܗ ܕܡܪܝ [n]ܦܪܘܩ ܕܝܢ
ܐܘܦ ܗܘ ܕܢܫܡܥ ܬܪܝܢ ܐܠܠܝܡ: ܐܡܪ ܡܪܝ ܬܪܝܢ
ܐܠܠܝܡ[‡] ܡܫܪܬ ܠܝ: ܗܐ ܫܘܪܝܢ ܬܪܝܢ[†] ܐܠܠܝܡ
23 ܐܬܚܙܬ ܒܠܒܘܢ ܐܡܪ ܠܗ ܡܪܘܗ ܐܘ ܒܒܪܐ
ܠܒܐ ܘܡܗܝܡܢܘܬܐ: ܒܠ ܝܫܘܥ [l]ܗܘܬ ܡܗܝܡܢ
ܒܠ ܗܠܝܢ ܐܢܐ [m]ܡܫܝܚ ܠܝ ܒܟܠ ܠܫܪܘܬܗ
24 ܕܡܪܝ: [n]ܦܪܘܩ ܐܘܦ ܗܘ ܕܢܫܡܥ ܚܕ
[q]ܐܠܠܝܡ ܐܡܪ ܡܪܝ ܡܢܝܢ ܕܐܬܐ ܒܪܐ [r]ܘܐܡܪ:
25 [s]ܚܙܐ ܡܢ ܗܘ ܕܠܐ ܙܒܢܬ: [t]ܘܡܒܣܪ ܡܢ ܗܘ
ܕܠܐ ܒܙܘܢ: ܘܕܚܠܬ ܘܐܬܠܬ ܘܐܬܚܙܝܬ ܐܠܠܝܡ
[f. 87a]
26 ܒܐܪܒܐ ܗܐ ܠܝ ܕܠܝ: ܐܬܚܙܝ ܕܝܢ [u]ܡܪܘܗ
ܘܐܡܪ ܠܗ: ܒܒܪܐ ܒܫܡܐ [w]ܘܦܘܫܠܐ: [x]ܡܢ ܗܘ
ܙܒܢܬ[x] ܕܐܢܐ [s]ܚܙܐ ܡܢ ܗܘ ܕܠܐ ܙܒܢܬ:
27 [t]ܘܡܒܣܪ ܡܢ ܗܘ ܕܠܐ ܒܙܘܢ: ܗܘܐ ܐܘ
ܢܦܠ ܠܝ [y]ܕܬܪܥܝܬܐ ܒܫܡܐ [z]ܐܠܠܝܡܢܐ ܘܐܢܐ
[a]ܗܘܬ ܐܬܐ ܢܫܡܥ ܕܠܝ ܡܢ [b]ܪܒܘܬܗ:
28 ܫܒܩ ܒܫܡ ܐܠܠܝܡܐ ܘܫܡܥ [c]ܠܗܘ ܕܒܢܘܗ

Codex A.

[b]add ܕܝܢ [e]ܘܐܡܪ
[f]ܘܡܪܝܐ ܕܝܢ[f]
[i]ܒܡܟܠ [l]ܫܘܪܝܢܐ
ܕܢܫܡܥ [n]omit [o]ܬܪܝܢ
[p]omit ܐܠܠܝܡ ܒܡܟܠ
ܒܡܘܢ
[q]ܐܬܚܙܝܬ ܫܘܪܝܢ[q]
[r]add ܕܝܢ [s]ܚܕ
[t]ܫܡܥ [u]ܘܐܬܚܙܝ
[v]omit ܕܝܢ [w]ܐܡܘܢ
[x]ܡܪܘܗ
[a]ܫܡܥܝܢ [b]ܘܦܪܘܩ
[c]ܘܐܬܚܙܝ [f]ܫܘܪܝܢ
[g]ܫܘܪܝܢܐ
[n]ܦܪܘܩ
‡ f. 104a.
[q]ܐܠܠܝܡܐ [r]ܘܐܡܪ
[w]ܘܦܘܫܠܐ
[x]ܢܫܡܥ ܗܘܬ[x]
[t]ܘܡܒܣܪ
[y]ܕܬܪܥܝܬܐ
[z]ܐܠܠܝܡܢܐ

Codex C.

[b]add ܕܝܢ
[g]omit ܘܡܪܝܐ ܐܡܪ
[i]ܒܡܟܠ [j]ܘܐܬܚܙܝ
[k]ܫܡܥܐ ܫܘܪܝܢ[k]
[n]omit ܢܫܡܥ
[p]omit ܐܠܠܝܡ ܒܡܟܠ
ܒܡܘܢ
[q]ܐܬܚܙܝܬ ܫܘܪܝܢ[q]
[r]add ܕܝܢ [s]ܚܕ [t]ܫܡܥ
[v]omit ܕܝܢ [x]ܡܪܘܗܝ
[y]ܕܒܒܪܐ
[b]ܘܦܪܘܩ [d]ܫܘܪܝܢ
[e]ܫܡܥܐ ܫܘܪܝܢ[e]
[h]omit ܐܠܠܝܡ
[i]ܐܬܚܙܝܬ ܕܝܢ [i]omit
[k]ܠܒܐ [l]ܗܘܬ
[m]ܡܫܝܚ
† f. 85b.
[r]ܘܐܡܪ
[s]ܚܙܐ [t]ܘܡܒܣܪ
[u]ܡܪܘܗ
[w]ܘܦܘܫܠܐ
[t]ܘܡܒܣܪ
[y]ܕܬܪܥܝܬܐ
[z]ܐܠܠܝܡܢܘܬܐ
[a]ܗܘܬ [b]ܪܒܘܬܗ
[c]ܠܗܘܢ

z

Codex A.

[o]ܦܫܝܛܐ [p]ܐܦ̈ܩܘ
[q] *omit* ܝܬܗ [s]ܠܒܪ
[t]ܘܚܘܪܩܘܩܝܗܘܢ
‡ f. 104*b*.
[u]ܕܒܪܢܫܐ
[w]ܒܬܫܒܘܚܬܗ
[z]ܡܠܐܟܘܗܝ [a]ܢܬܒ
[b]ܡܘܬܒܘܬܐ
[c]ܕܬܫܒܘܚܬܗ
[d] *omit* ܒܟܝܢ
[e]ܘܢܬܟܢܫܘܢ
[g]ܡܦܪܫ [h]ܐܝܟܢܐ
[i]ܘܢܩܝܡ [j]ܢܐܡܪ
[k]ܡܒܪ̈ܟܘܗܝ
[l]ܐܪܬܘ [m] *omit* ܕܝ
[v]ܫܘܪܝܗ [o]ܕܥܠܡܐ
[q]ܕܐܟܘܠ [r]ܘܨܗܝܬ
[s]ܘܐܫܩܝܬܘܢܢܝ
[t]ܐܟܣܢܝܐ
[v]ܥܪܛܠܝܐ
[x]ܐܬܟܪܗܬ
[y]ܘܐܬܝܬܘܢ
[b]ܡܪܢ
[c]ܒܟܝܢ [d]ܘܐܝܟ
‡ f. 105*a*.
[e]ܨܗܝܐ [f] *add* ܕܝ
[g]ܐܟܣܢܝܐ
[i]ܥܪܛܠܝܐ
[a]ܐܚܝ̈
[n]ܐܡܪ ܐܘܦ[n]
[q]ܣܡܠܗ [s]ܕܠܥܠܡ
[t] *omit* ܗܕܐ
[u]ܘܠܡܠܐܟܘܗܝ
[v]ܟܦܢܬ [w]ܐܟܣܢܝܐ

Codex B.

29 ܒܫܪܐ ܛܠܠܝܢ: ܟܠ ܡܢ ܕܒܝܕܗ ܢܬܝܗܒ ܠܗ
[k]ܘܢܬܬܘܣܦ ܠܗ: ܗܘ ܕܝܢ ܕܠܝܬ ܒܝܕܗ [l]ܐܘܦ
30 ܡܢܐ ܕܒܝܕܗ[l] [n]ܡܫܬܩܠ ܡܢܗ: ܘܠܥܒܕܐ [o]ܦܫܝܛܐ
[p]ܐܦ̈ܩܘ [q]ܝܬܗ [s]ܠܒܪܐ ܠܚܫܘܟܐ ܒܪܝܐ :‡ ܬܡܢ
31 ܗܘܐ ܒܟܝܐ [t]ܘܚܘܪܩܘܩܝ ܕܫܢ̈ܐ: ܟܕ ܕܝ
ܐܬܐ ܒܪܗ [u]ܕܒܪܢܫܐ [w]ܒܫܘܒܚܘܬܗ ܘܟܠ
[z]ܡܠܐܟܘܗܝ ܥܡܗ: ܒܟܝܢ ܗܘ [a]ܢܬܒ ܥܠ [b]ܡܘܬܒܘܬܗ
32 [c]ܕܬܫܒܘܚܬܗ: [d]ܒܟܝܢ [e]ܢܬܟܢܫܘܢ [f]ܠܩܘܕܡܘܗܝ
ܟܠܗܘܢ ܥܡܡܐ ܘܗܘ [g]ܡܦܪܫ ܠܗܘܢ ܗܠܝܢ
ܡܢ ܗܠܝܢ [h]ܐܝܟ ܡܐ[h] ܕܪܥܝܐ [g]ܡܦܪܫ ܐܡܪܐ
33 ܡܢ ܓܕܝܐ: [i]ܘܢܩܝܡ ܐܡܪܐ ܡܢ [†]ܝܡܝܢܗ ܘܓܕܝܐ
ܡܢ ܣܡܠܗ: ܒܟܝܢ [j]ܢܐܡܪ ܡܠܟܐ ܠܗܠܝܢ ܕܡܢ
34 ܝܡܝܢܗ: ܐܬܘ [k]ܡܒܪܟܘܗܝ ܕܐܒܐ [l]ܝܪܬܘ [m]ܕܝ
ܡܠܟܘܬܐ ܕܡܛܝܒܐ ܠܟܘܢ ܡܢ [n]ܫܘܪܝܗ
[o]ܕܥܠܡܐ: ܟܦܢܬ ܓܝܪ ܘܝܗܒܬܘܢ ܠܝ [q]ܕܐܟܘܠ:·
35 [r]ܨܗܝܬ [s]ܘܐܫܩܝܬܘܢ ܢܝ: [t]ܐܟܣܢܝܐ ܗܘܝܬ
36 ܘܟܢܫܬܘܢ ܢܝ: [v]ܥܪܛܠܝ ܘܐܠܒܫܬܘܢ ܢܝ:
[f. 87*b*]
[x]ܐܬܟܪܗܬ ܘܣܥܪܬܘܢ ܢܝ: ܒܚܒܘܫܝܐ ܗܘܝܬ
37 [y]ܘܐܬܝܬ ܠܘܬܝ: ܒܟܝܢ [z]ܢܐܡܪܘܢ [a]ܠܗ ܙܕܝ̈ܩܐ
ܐܡܪܝܢ: [b]ܡܪܢ ܐܡܬܝ ܚܙܝܢܟ ܟܦܢ [c]ܒܟܝܢ
[d]ܘܐܘܟܠܢܟ: ܐܘ [e]ܨܗܐ ܘܐܫܩܝܢܟ:
38 ܐܡܬܝ[f] ܚܙܝܢܟ [g]ܐܟܣܢܝܐ [h]ܘܟܢܫܢܟ:
39 ‡ ܐܘ [i]ܥܪܛܠܝܐ [j]ܘܐܠܒܫܢܟ: ܐܡܬܝ ܕܝ
[k]ܚܙܝܢܟ ܟܪܝܗ ܐܘ ܒܚܒܘܫܝܐ [l]ܘܐܬܝܢ
40 ܠܘܬܟ: ܘܢܥܢܐ ܡܠܟܐ ܘܢܐܡܪ ܠܗܘܢ[m]
ܐܡܝܢ ܐܡܪ ܐܢܐ ܠܟܘܢ: ܕܟܕ ܒܟܠ ܐܡܬܝ
ܕܥܒܕܬܘܢ ܠܚܕ ܡܢ ܗܠܝܢ [a]ܐܚܝ̈ ܙܥܘܪ̈ܐ[a] ܠܝ
ܥܒܕܬܘܢ:· ܒܟܝܢ ܗܘ [n]ܐܘܦ ܐܡܪ[n] [p]ܠܗܠܝܢ ܕܡܢ
41 [q]ܣܡܠܐ: ܐܙܠܘ ܠܟܘܢ ܡܢܝ [r]ܠܝܛܐ ܠܢܘܪܐ
[s]ܕܠܥܠܡ [t]ܗܕܐ ܕܡܛܝܒܐ ܠܣܛܢܐ [u]ܘܠܡܠܐܟܘܗܝ:
42 [v]ܟܦܢܬ ܓܝܪ ܘܠܐ ܝܗܒܬܘܢ ܠܝ ܕܐܟܘܠ:· ܘܨܗܝܬ
43 ܘܠܐ ܐܫܩܝܬܘܢ ܢܝ: [w]ܐܟܣܢܝܐ ܗܘܝܬ ܘܠܐ

Codex C.

[k]ܘܢܬܬܘܣܦ
[l] *omit* ܐܘܦ ܡܢܐ
ܕܒܝܕܗ
[n]ܡܫܬܩܠ [o]ܦܫܝܛܐ
[p]ܐܦܩܘܗܝ [q] *omit* ܝܬܗ
[s]ܠܒܪ [u]ܕܒܪܢܫܐ
[z]ܡܠܐܟܘܗܝ
[d] *omit* ܒܟܝܢ
[e]ܘܢܬܟܢܫܘܢ
[f]ܠܩܘܕܡܘܗܝ [g]ܡܦܪܫ
† f. 86*a*.
[k]ܡܒܪ̈ܟܘܗܝ
ܕܝ [m] *omit* [v]ܫܘܪܝܗ
[q]ܕܐܟܘܠ
[r]ܘܨܗܝܬ
[y]ܘܐܬܝܬܘܢ
[z]ܒܟܝܢ
[a] *omit* ܠܗ
[b] *add* ܡܪܢ
[d]ܘܐܘܟܠܢܟ
ܕܝ [f] *add* [h]ܘܟܢܫܢܟ
[i]ܥܪܛܠܝܐ [j]ܘܐܠܒܫܢܟ
[k]ܚܙܝܢܟ [l]ܘܐܬܝܢ
[m] *add* ܐܡܝܢ
[a]ܐܚܝ̈ [a]ܙܥܘܪܐ
[n]ܐܡܪ ܕܐܘܦ[n]
[p]ܠܗ [q]ܣܡܠܗ
[r]ܠܝܛܐ [s]ܕܠܥܠܡ
[t] *omit* ܗܕܐ
[u]ܘܠܡܠܐܟܘܗܝ

Codex A.

ˣܡܬܪܓܠܝܢ
ᶻܘܒܣܘܕܪܐ
ᵃܡܪܢ ᵇܢܐܙܠ
ᶜܐܬܚܙܝ
ᵈܡܬܪܓܠܝܢ
ᶠܥܡܝܩܝܢ ⁱܥܒܕ
ᵏܠܡܪܝܐ ܘܒܣܘܕܪܐ ᵏ
‡ f. 105*b*.
ⁿܐܢܫܐ ᵖ*add* ܠܗ
ˢܠܥܙܪܐ ᵗܕܐܬܒܠܛ
ʷܩܒܝܡܢܐ ˣܡܬܐܟܠܝܢ
ʸܡܫܬܥܒܕܝܢ
ᶻܕܡܫܬܠܡ

Codex B.

ܒܥܡܬܗܘܢ ܗܘܐ :· ˣܡܬܪܓܠܝܢ ʸܘܠܐ ܐܬܟܫܦܘܢ
ܗܘܐ : ܒܐܝܕܐ ܘܒܟܠܝܠܐ ܘܠܐ ܦܪܨܘܦܗܘܢ ܗܘܐ :·
44 ܒܣܘܕܪܐ ܟܪܝܟܝܢ ܗܘܘ ܐܦܝܗܘܢ ᶻܘܡܣܘܕܪܐ
ᵃܡܪܢ ܐܡܪ ܠܗܘܢ ܫܪܘ ܐܢܘܢ ܘܫܒܩܘ ᵇܢܐܙܠܘܢ
ܐܠܐ ᶜܐܬܚܙܝܘ ܐܠܐ ᵈܡܬܪܓܠܝܢ † ܐܠܐ ܟܐܢܫܐ ܐܠܐ
ܒܟܠܝܠܐ ܘܠܐ ᶠܥܡܝܩܝܢ ܗܘܘ : ܒܣܘܡ ⁱܥܒܕ
45 ܐܦܠܐ ᵏܘܒܣܘܕܪܐ ܠܡܪܝܐ ᵏ : ˡܐܡܪܝܢ ܐܡܪܝܢ ܐܢܐ
ܠܟܘܢ ܕܒܬܪ ܟܠܗ ܐܡܪܘ ܕܠܐ ܡܬܚܙܝܢ
‡ ܠܗܢ ܡܢ ܗܠܝܢ ⁿܐܢܫܐ ܕܡܬܐܟܠܝܢ ᵖܐܦܠܐ ܠܐ
46 ܠܐ ܡܬܚܙܝܢ ܘܡܬܠܝܢ ܗܠܝܢ ˢܠܥܙܪܐ
ᵗܕܐܬܒܠܛ ܘܡܨܝܢܘܬܐ ܠܝܫܢܐ ᵗܕܐܬܒܠܛ ܗܘܐ ܒܗ [f. 88*a*]
XXVI. 1 ᵘܥܠܝܢ ܡܢܐ ܗܘܐ ܒܟܠ ܗܠܝܢ ܡܠܝܢ ܐܡܪܝܢ
2 ᵛܠܬܠܡܝܕܘܗܝ : ܘܒܣܘܡ ܐܬܘܢ ܕܡܢ ܒܬܪ ܬܠܬ
ܘܡܢ ʷܩܒܝܡܢܐ ˣܡܬܐܟܠܝܢ ܘܒܪܗ ܕܐܢܫܐ
ʸܡܫܬܥܒܕܝܢ ᶻܕܡܫܬܠܡ :·

Codex C.

ˣܡܬܪܓܠܝܢ
ʸ*add* ܗܘܬ
ᵇܢܐܙܠ
† f. 86*b*.
ᶠܥܡܝܩܝܢ ⁱܐܥܒܕ
ᵏܠܡܪܝܐ ܘܡܣܘܕܪܐ ᵏ
ˡ*add* ܐܡܝܢ
ⁿܐܢܫܐ
ˢܠܥܙܪܐ
ᵘܥܠܝܢ
ᵛܠܬܠܡܝܕܘܗܝ
ʷܦܘܣܚܐ ˣܡܬܐܟܠܝܢ
ᶻܕܡܫܬܠܡ

CXLV.

John XII. 17—50.

Codex A.

ᶜ*omit* ܐܡܪ
ᵃܐܟܠܘܣܐ ᵇܕܗܘܐ
ᶜ*add* ܒܗ
ʰܐܬܐ ⁱܦܪܝܫܝܢ
ᵏܕܝܢ ܐܡܪܘ ᵏ
ᵐܒܥܠܡܐ ⁿܒܬܪܗ
ᵒܐܙܠ ᵍܐܡܪܝܢ
ʳܟܡܐ ܕܡܘܢ
ˢܠܡܣܓܕ ܗܘܘ
ᵛܐܬܝܢ ˣܠܝܫܘܥ
‡ f. 106*a*.
ʸܦܠܝܓܘܗܝ

Codex B.

ᵃܗܘܝܬ ܐܘܟܠܘܣܐ ܗܘܐ ܥܡܗ ʰܘܡܣܗܕ :· ᶜܐܡܪ :
17 ܘܒܥܠܡܗ ܡܪܩܢܘܬܐ : ܗܘܐ ܕܝܢ ܒܗܕܐ ᵃܐܟܠܘܣܐ :
ᵇܗܘܝܢ ܕܗܘܐ ܥܡܗ ᶜܒܕܡܐ ܡܢ : ܠܠܥܙܪܐ ܗܘܐ ܡܢ
ܡܢ ܩܒܘܪܬܐ :· ᵈܘܐܩܝܡ ܐܢܘܢ ܡܢ ܒܝܬ ܡܝܬܐ :
18 ܠܗܠܝܢ ܒܗܝܢ ܐܬܐ ᵉᵃܐܟܠܘܣܐ ᶠܘܣܗܕܘ ܗܘܐ
19 ܕܥܒܕ ܗܕܐ ܐܬܐ ʰܐܡܪܝܢ :· ⁱܦܪܝܫܝܢ ᵏܐܡܪܘ
ᵏܕܝܢ ܚܕ ܠܚܕ : ܚܙܝܢ ܐܢܬܘܢ ܕܠܡܢ
ˡܐܢܬܘܢ ܡܢ ܒܥܠܡܐ ᵐܒܥܠܡܐ : ܗܐ ܒܬܪܗ ⁿܒܬܪܗ ܡܛܠܗ
20 ᵒܐܙܠ ܠܗ ܟܠܗ : ܗܘܘ ܕܝܢ ᵍܐܢܫܝܢ ܐܪܡܝܐ
ܡܢ ܗܠܝܢ ܕܣܠܩܘ ܠܡܣܓܕ ʳܒܥܐܕܐ :
21 ܗܠܝܢ ܕܝܢ ܩܪܒܘ ˢܠܦܝܠܝܦܘܣ ܕܡܢ ܒܝܬ ܨܝܕܐ
ܕܓܠܝܠܐ :· ܘܒܥܘ ‡ ܡܢܗ ܘܐܡܪܝܢ ᵗܡܪܢ
22 ܨܒܝܢ ᵛܐܢܚܢ ʷܕܢܚܙܐ ˣܠܝܫܘܥ :· ܘܐܬܐ ʸܦܝܠܝܦܘܣ

Codex C.

ᵃܠܗܘܢ ᵇܗܘܝܢܐ
ᶜ*omit* ܐܡܪ
ᶜ*add* ܒܗ
ᵈܘܐܩܝܡ
ᵉܐܘܟܠܘܣܐ ᶠܘܣܗܕ
ᵏܕܝܢ ܐܡܪܘ ᵏ
ˡ*omit* ܐܢܬܘܢ
ˢܠܦܝܠܝܦܘܣ
ᵗ*omit* ܡܪܢ
ʷܕܢܚܙܐ ˣܠܝܫܘܥ
ʸ*omit* ܦܝܠܝܦܘܣ

z 2

Codex A.	Codex B.	Codex C.
[z]ܠܐܢܕܪܐܘܣ	ܘܐܡܪ [z]ܠܐܢܕܪܐܘܣ :· ܘܐܬܐ [a]ܐܢܕܪܐܘܣ [b]ܘܦܝܠܝܦܘܣ	[b]ܘܦܝܠܝܦܘܣ
[a]ܐܢܕܪܐܘܣ	23 [†]ܘܐܡܪܘ ܠܡܪܢܐ ܝܫܘܥ : ܗܘ ܕܝܢ ܡܪܢܐ ܝܫܘܥ	† f. 87a.
[b]ܘܦܝܠܝܦܘܣ	[c]ܐܚܝܒ ܘܐܡܪ ܠܗܘܢ : ܐܬܬ ܫܥܬܐ ܕܝܫܬܒܚ	[c]ܐܚܝܒ [d]ܕܒܪܢܫܐ
[c]ܐܚܝܒ [d]ܕܒܪܢܫܐ	24 ܒܪܗ [d]ܕܓܒܪܐ : [e]ܐܡܝܢ ܐܡܝܢ [f]ܐܡܪ ܐܢܐ[f]	ܐܡܝܢ [e]omit
[f]ܐܡܝܢܐ [i]ܕܚܛܬܐ	ܠܟܘܢ :· [g]ܕܐܢ ܠܐ [h]ܦܪܕܬܐ [i]ܕܚܛܬܐ [j]ܢܦܠܐ	[g]ܕܐܢ [h]ܦܪܕܬܐ
ܢܦܠܐ . . . [j]omit	[k]ܕܝܢ ܒܐܪܥܐ [l]ܘܡܝܬܐ[j] ܠܓܪܡܗ ܗܝ ܡܬܟܬܪܐ [f. 88b]	[j]ܢܦܠܐ ܕܝܢ [k]omit
. . . ܘܡܝܬܬܐ	[m]ܐܢ ܕܝܢ ܡܝܬܬ ܣܓܝ ܦܐܪܝܢ ܗܝ [n]ܡܝܬܝܐ :	[l]ܘܡܝܬܐ
[n]ܡܝܬܐ [o]ܢܦܫܗ	25 ܡܢ ܕܪܚܡ [o]ܢܦܫܗ ܡܘܒܕ ܗܘ ܠܗ : ܘܡܢ [p]ܕܣܢܐ	[m]ܐܢ [n]ܡܝܬܐ
[p]ܕܣܢܐ [r]ܒܥܠܡܐ	ܢܦܫܗ ܒܗܕܝܢ [r]ܥܠܡܐ [s]ܠܚܝܝܢ [t]ܕܠܥܠܡ ܗܘ [u]ܢܛܪ	[s]ܠܚܝܝܢ
[s]ܠܚܝܝܢ [t]ܕܠܥܠܡ	26 ܠܗ : [m]ܐܢ ܠܝ ܢܗܘܐ [x]ܐܢܫ ܡܫܡܫ ܠܝ ܢܗܘܐ[x]	
[u]ܢܛܪ	[y]ܕܒܬܪܝ :· ܗܘ[y] ܕܐܢܐ [a]ܩܐܝܡ ܬܡܢ ܗܘܐ	[y]ܕܒܬܪܝ
ܐܢܫ ܡܫܡܫ [x]omit ܠܝ ܗܘܐ	ܐܘܦ ܡܫܡܫܝ :· [m]ܐܢ ܗܘܐ [c]ܐܢܫ ܡܫܡܫ ܠܝ	[c]ܒܪܢܫ
	27 [d]ܡܝܩܪ ܗܘ ܠܗ ܐܒܐ :· ܗܐ ܒܕܘ ܢܦܫܝ	
[a]ܡܫܡܫ [d]ܡܝܩܪ	ܡܬܬܪܒܒܐ ܘܡܐ ܐܡܪ : ܐܒܐ ܦܨܝ ܝܬܝ	
[f]ܗܕܐ [h]ܒܕܝܢ	ܡܢ [f]ܗܕܝܢ ܫܥܬܐ : ܐܠܐ ܠܒܕܠ [h]ܟܕܝܢ ܐܬܝܬ	[f]ܗܕܐ
[i]ܠܗܕܐ [k]ܫܒܚ	28 [i]ܠܗܕܝܢ ܫܥܬܐ : ܐܒܐ [k]ܫܒܚ ܝܬܗ [l]ܠܫܡܟ :	[i]ܠܗܕܐ
[l]ܠܫܡܟ [n]ܩܠܐ	ܐܬܐ ܩܠ [n]ܡܢ ܫܡܝܐ : ܫܒܚܬ	
‡ f. 106b.	29 ܘܬܘܒ ܐܢܐ [o]ܡܫܒܚ : [‡] [p]ܐܘܟܠܘܣܐ : ܕܗܘܐ	
[o]ܡܫܒܚ [p]ܐܘܟܠܘܣܐ	ܩܐܝܡ [q]ܘܫܡܥ ܐܡܪ : ܕܪܥܡ [s]ܐܬܥܒܕ :	[q]ܘܫܡܥ
[q]ܘܫܡܥ [s]ܐܬܥܒܕ	ܐܚܪܢܝܢ ܕܝܢ ܗܘܘ ܐܡܪܝܢ [t]ܡܠܐܟ [u]ܡܠܠ ܥܡܗ :	[t]ܡܠܐܟ
[u]ܡܠܠ	30 ܐܚܝܒ ܡܪܢܐ ܝܫܘܥ ܘܐܡܪ ܠܗܘܢ :· ܠܐ	
[w]ܠܒܕܠ [x]ܗܕܐ	[w]ܠܒܕܠܝ [x]ܗܕܝܢ ܩܠܐ ܐܬܥܒܕ : ܐܠܐ ܠܒܕܠܟܘܢ :·	
[z]ܥܠܡܐ	31 ܗܐ ܒܕܘ ܐܪܟܘܢܗ ܕܗܕܝܢ [z]ܥܠܡܐ ܡܬܪܡܝ	
[a]ܐܬܪܘܡܡ	32 ܠܒܪ : ܘܐܢܐ ܟܕ [a]ܐܬܪܘܡܡ ܡܢ ܐܪܥܐ ܟܘܠܐ	
	33 ܐܢܐ [b]ܢܓܕ ܠܘܬܝ : [†] ܗܕܐ ܕܝܢ ܒܡܠܗ ܗܘܐ	† f. 87b.
[c]omit ܕܝܢ [e]ܕܗܕܐ	ܐܡܪ [c]ܕܝܢ [d]ܡܚܘܕܥ [e]ܕܗܕܝܢ ܡܘܬܗ ܗܘܐ ܥܬܝܕ	ܢܓܕ [b]omit ܕܝܢ [c]omit
[g]ܐܘܟܠܘܣܐ	34 ܕܡܡܬ :· ܐܚܝܒ ܐܘܢ [g]ܐܘܟܠܘܣܐ ܘܐܡܪ	[d]ܡܚܘܕܥ
[i]ܕܡܫܝܚ	ܠܗ : ܐܢܚܢ ܫܡܥܢ ܡܢ ܢܡܘܣܐ [i]ܕܡܫܝܚܐ	[g]ܐܘܟܠܘܣܐ
[k]ܐܡܪ ܐܬ[k]	ܡܬܟܬܪ [j]ܠܥܠܡ :· ܘܗܝܟ ܐܬ [k]ܐܡܪ ܐܬ[k] [l]ܕܝܬܪܘܡܡ	[j]ܠܥܠܡ [l]ܕܝܬܪܘܡܡ
[m]ܕܒܪܢܫܐ	ܠܗ ܕܝܬܪܘܡܡ ܒܪܗ [m]ܕܓܒܪܐ [n]ܡܢ ܗܘ ܗܕܝܢ	[m]ܕܒܪܢܫܐ
[p]add ܕܝܢ	35 ܒܪܗ [m]ܕܓܒܪܐ[n] :· ܐܡܪ [o]ܠܗܘܢ [p]ܡܪܢܐ ܝܫܘܥ : [f. 89a]	ܡܢ . . . ܕܓܒܪܐ [n]omit
[q]ܙܥܝܪ	ܟܘܕ [q]ܙܥܝܪ ܐܘܫܢ ܢܗܘܪܐ ܒܓܘܟܘܢ ܐܬܘܢ :	[o]ܕܝܢ

Fol. 88*b*.

Page 168.

CODEX B.

(JOHN XII. 24—34.)

Codex B.

ܗܠܟܘ ܥܕ ܥܡܟܘܢ ܢܘܗܪܐ ܕܠܐ [o]ܝܕܪܟܘܢ
ܚܫܘܟܐ[o] ܡܗܠܟܐ ܀[p] [q]ܠܐ ܝܕܥ[q] [r]ܠܐܢ ܗܘ [s]ܐܙܠ ܀
36 ܥܕ ܥܡܟܘܢ ܢܘܗܪܐ ܗܘܘ [t]ܡܗܝܡܢܝܢ ܒܢܘܗܪܐ ܀
[u]ܕܒܢܘܝ [‡][v]ܕܢܘܗܪܐ ܬܗܘܘܢ ܀ ܗܠܝܢ ܡܠܠ ܡܪܢܐ
37 ܝܫܘܥ ܀ [w]ܘܐܙܠ [y]ܕܝ ܐܬܛܡܪ ܡܢܗܘܢ [z]ܘܕܟܡܐ
[a]ܥܒܕ [b]ܐܬܘܢ ܗܘܐ ܩܕܡ ܥܝܢܝܗܘܢ ܀ ܘܠܐ
38 ܗܘܘ ܡܗܝܡܢܝܢ ܒܗ ܀ ܠܡܫܠܡ ܕܡܠܬܗ [c]ܕܐܫܥܝܐ
ܢܒܝܐ [d]ܕܝ ܬܬܡܠܐ ܀ ܗܕܐ ܕܐܡܪ ܡܪܝܐ ܡܢ
[e]ܗܝܡܢ [f]ܠܡܫܡܥܢ ܀ ܘܐܕܪܥܗ [g]ܕܡܪܝܐ ܠܡܢ
39 ܐܬܓܠܝ ܀ ܠܡܫܠܡ [h]ܥܕܝܢ ܠܐ ܗܘܘ ܝܟܠܝܢ ܡܗܝܡܢܝܢ
40 ܕܬܘܒ ܐܡܪ [i]ܐܫܥܝܐ ܀ ܥܘܪ ܥܝܢܝܗܘܢ
ܘܩܫܝ [j]ܠܒܗܘܢ ܕܠܐ ܚܙܘܢ ܒܥܝܢܝܗܘܢ
41 [k]ܘܝܬܘܒܘܢ [l]ܒܠܒܗܘܢ ܀ [m]ܘܝܬܘܒܘܢ ܘܐܣܐ
ܝܬܗܘܢ ܀ ܗܠܝܢ ܡܠܠ [n]ܐܫܥܝܐ [o]ܕܚܙܐ [p]ܝܬܗ
42 [q]ܬܫܒܘܚܬܗ ܕܐܠܗܐ ܀ ܘܡܠܠ ܥܠ ܕܝܠܗ
ܕܡܪܝܐ ܒܫܘܦ ܀ ܒܪܡ ܕܝ ܐܘܦ ܡܢ [s]ܐܪܟܘܢܝܐ
ܣܓܝ ܗܝܡܢܘ ܒܗ ܀ ܐܠܐ [t]ܠܓܠܠ [u]ܦܪܝܫܝ ܠܐ
ܗܘܘ ܡܘܕܝܢ ܠܡܫܠܡ ܕܠܐ [v]ܢܦܩܘܢ ܡܢ [w]ܟܢܫܬܐ ܀
43 44 ܐܚܒܘ [x]ܓܝܪ [y]ܬܫܒܘܚܬܗܘܢ ܕܒܢܝܢܫܐ ܀ ܝܬܝܪ
ܡܢ [†] [z]ܬܫܒܘܚܬܗ ܕܐܠܗܐ ܀ ܘܩܥܐ [a]ܝܫܘܥ
[b]ܐܡܪ ܘܐܡܪ ܡܢ [c]ܕܡܗܝܡܢ ܒܝ ܠܐ [c]ܡܗܝܡܢ
[f. 89b]
45 ܒܝ ܐܠܐ ܒܡܢ [d]ܕܫܠܚ ܝܬܝ ܀ [‡]ܘܡܢ [f]ܕܚܙܐ
46 ܠܝ ܚܙܐ [g]ܠܡܢ [d]ܕܫܠܚ ܝܬܝ ܀ ܐܢܐ ܗܘ
[k]ܢܘܗܪ ܐܬܝܬ [l]ܠܥܠܡܐ ܀ ܕܟܠ ܡܢ ܕܡܗܝܡܢ
47 ܒܝ ܠܐ [m]ܡܗܠܟ ܒܚܫܘܟܐ ܀ ܘܡܢ ܕܠܐ ܫܡܥ
ܡܠܝ ܘܡܛܪ [p]ܠܗܝܢ ܀ ܐܢܐ ܠܐ ܕܐܝܢ ܝܬܗ ܀
ܠܐ [q]ܓܝܪ ܐܬܝܬ [r]ܕܐܕܘܢ [s]ܠܥܠܡܐ ܐܠܐ ܕܐܚܝܐ
48 [s]ܠܥܠܡܐ ܀ ܡܢ [t]ܕܡܣܠܐ [u]ܠܝ ܠܐ ܗܘ ܕܐܝܢ
ܐܠܐ [v]ܠܡܢ [d]ܕܫܠܚ ܝܬܝ ܀ ܘܡܢ ܕܡܣܠܐ ܠܝ
ܘܠܐ ܢܩܒܠ ܡܠܝ ܀ ܗܐ ܠܗ ܡܢ [w]ܕܐܕܝܢ
ܠܗ ܀ ܡܠܬܐ ܗܕܐ [x]ܕܡܠܠܬ ܗܝ [y]ܕܕܝܢܐ ܠܗ
49 ܒܝܘܡܐ ܐܚܪܝܐ ܀ ܕܐܢܐ ܡܢ ܪܥܝܢܝ ܠܐ

Codex A.

[p] *add* ܘܡܢ ܕܡܗܠܟ ܒܚܫܘܟܐ
[s] ܐܙܠ
‡ f. 107*a*.
[w] ܘܐܙܠ [y] *omit* ܕܝ
[z] ܘܕܟܡܐ [a] ܥܒܕ
[b] *omit* ܐܬܘܢ
[c] ܕܐܫܥܝܐ
[d] *omit* ܕܝ
[f] ܠܡܫܡܥܢ
[g] ܕܡܪܝܐ [h] ܥܕܝܢ
[i] ܐܫܥܝܐ [k] *omit* ܘ
[l] *omit* ܒܠܒܗܘܢ
[m] *omit* ܘܝܬܘܒܘܢ
[q] ܠܬܫܒܘܚܬܗ
[t] ܠܓܠܠ [u] ܦܪܝܫܝ
[v] ܢܦܩܘܢ
[y] ܬܫܒܘܚܬܗܘܢ
[z] ܬܫܒܘܚܬܗ
[a] *add* ܕܝ
[c] ܕܡܗܝܡܢ
‡ f. 107*b*.
[g] ܠܡܢ
[l] ܠܥܠܡܐ
[m] ܡܗܠܟ
[s] ܠܥܠܡܐ
[u] *add* ܠܝ
[v] ܠܡܢ
[w] ܕܐܕܝܢ
[x] ܕܡܠܠܬ [y] ܕܕܝܢܐ

Codex C.

[o] ܝܕܪܟܘܢ
[p] *add* ܘܡܢ ܕܡܗܠܟ ܒܚܫܘܟܐ
[q] *omit* ܠܐ ܝܕܥ
[r] ܠܗܢ (*sic*) [t] ܡܗܝܡܢܝܢ
[u] ܕܒܢܝ [v] ܢܘܗܪܐ
[y] *omit* ܕܝ [b] ܐܬܘܢ
[c] ܕܐܫܥܝܐ [d] *omit* ܕܝ
[e] ܗܝܡܢ [f] ܠܡܫܡܥܢ
[i] ܐܫܥܝܐ
[j] ܠܒܗܘܢ
[l] ܒܠܒܗܘܢ [m] ܘܝܬܘܒܘܢ
[n] ܐܫܥܝܐ
[o] *add* ܢܒܝܐ
[p] *omit* ܝܬܗ
[q] ܬܫܒܘܚܬܗ
[s] ܐܪܟܘܢܝܐ [u] ܦܪܝܫܝܢ
[w] ܟܢܫܬܐ [x] *omit* ܓܝܪ
† f. 88*a*.
[z] ܬܫܒܘܚܬܗ
[a] *add* ܕܝ
[b] ܐܡܪ [c] ܕܡܗܝܡܢ
[d] ܕܫܠܚ [f] ܕܚܙܐ
[g] ܠܡܢ [k] ܢܘܗܪܐ
[m] ܡܗܠܟ [p] ܠܗܝܢ
[q] *omit* ܓܝܪ [r] ܕܐܕܘܢ
[t] ܕܡܣܠܐ
[v] ܠܡܢ

Codex A.	Codex B.	Codex C.
ܡܛܠܠܬ[y] [z] *omit* ܕ	ܡܛܠܠܬ[y] ܐܠܐ ܕܐܬܐ[z] ܕܢܚܠܝܫ[a] ܢܚܬ ܗܘ	ܕܚܠܝܫ[a]
	ܗܘܐ ܠܝ ܦܘܡܝ : ܡܐ ܚܙܘ ܘܡܐ ܡܬܠܝܠ :	
ܬܐܡܝܢ[b] ܕܠܝܠܚܢ[c]	50 ܘܡܥܡܘܕܝܐ ܐܢܐ ܕܐܬܥܡܕ[b] ܬܐܡܝܢ[c] ܕܠܝܠܚܢ : [d]ܗܘ	ܗܘܐ[d]
ܡܫܬܐ[e]	ܡܐ ܐܢܐ ܕܐܢܐ ܡܬܠܝܠ : [e]ܗܟܢ ܡܐ[e]	
	ܕܐܬܐ ܠܝ ܐܠܐ : ܡܬܐ ܐܢܐ ܡܬܠܝܠ ⁖	

CXLVI.

Matt. XXVI. 6—16.

Codex A.	Codex B.	Codex C.
ܐܝܡܢܐ[b] ܡܬܡܬܠܘ[d]	ܒܬܪ[a] ܐܝܡܢܐ[b] ܥܒܝܕ ܕܝ[c] ܡܬܡܬܠܘ[d] : ܘܒܬܠܘ	ܠܒܬܪ[a] ܥܒܝܕ[c]
	6 ܒܝܬܐ : ܘܟܕ ܗܘܐ ܝܫܘܥ ܒܒܝܬܝܐ ܒܒܝܬ	ܡܬܡܬܠܘ[d]
ܕܒܝ[b] *omit* ܕܫܡܥܘܢ[d]	7 ܫܡܥܘܢ ܓܪܒܐ : ܐܬܬ[b] ܕܝ ܠܘܬܗ	ܕܝ[b] *omit*
‡ f. 108a.	ܠܗ ܐܢܬܬܐ[c] ܚܕܐ ‡ ܘܐܝܬ ܥܡܗ ܕܫܡܥܘܢ[d] ܡܫܚܐ	ܐܢܬܬܐ[c] ܕܫܡܥܘܢ[d]
ܪܫܗ[e]	ܕܒܣܡ : ܘܐܫܕܬ ܥܠܘܗܝ ܥܠ ܪܫܗ ܗܘ ܪܫܗ[e] :	ܬܠܡܝܕܘܗܝ[f]
ܗܘܢ ܘ[h] *add* [g] *omit* ܗܘܢ	8 ܚܙܘ ܕܝ ܬܠܡܝܕܘܗܝ[f] ܘܗܢܘܢ[g] ܐܬܪܥܡܘ[h]	ܗܘܢ[g] *omit*
ܕܒܣܡܐ[i] ܒܠܚܘܕ[j]	9 ܘܐܡܪܝܢ : ܠܡܢܐ ܗܘܐ ܐܒܕܢܐ ܕܒܣܡܐ[i] : ܡܛܠ[j]	ܗܘܐ[k] ܘ[h] *add*
ܗܘܐ[k]	ܗܘܐ[k] ܠܝ ܗܘܐ ܕܒܣܡܐ ܗܢܐ ܕܙܒܢ ܒܣܓܝ † ܘܢܬܝܗܒ	† f. 88b.
ܝܕܥ[n]	10 ܕܝ[b] ܠܡܣܟܢܐ : ܝܕܥ[n] ܕܝ[o] ܕܝܢ ܝܫܘܥ ܘܐܡܪ	ܠܡܣܟܢܐ[l]
ܡܥܠܝܢ[p]	ܘܐܡܪ ܠܗܘܢ : ܡܢܐ ܐܢܬܘܢ ܡܥܠܝܢ[p] ܠܐܢܬܬܐ ܗܕܐ	ܝܕܥ[n] ܕܝ[o] *omit*
[q] *add* ܠܝ	[f. 90a] 11 ܐܢܬܬܐ ܥܒܕܬ ܓܒܝ[q] ܒܥܒܕܐ ܠܝ : ܒܟܠ ܥܕܢ	[q] *add* ܠܝ
ܕܐܫܕܬ[r] ܒܣܡܐ[s]	ܡܣܟܢܐ ܥܡܟܘܢ : ܐܢܐ ܕܝ ܠܐ ܒܟܠ ܥܕܢ	
ܐܡܝܢ[u] ܕܬܬܟܪܙ[w]	12 ܥܡܟܘܢ : ܗܕܐ ܓܝܪ ܕܐܫܕܬ[r] ܗܢܐ ܒܣܡܐ[s] ܥܠ	
ܒܟܠܗ[x] ܥܠܡܐ[y]	13 ܦܓܪܝ ܗܟܢ ܠܩܒܘܪܬܝ ܥܒܕܬ ܗܕܐ : ܐܡܝܢ[t]	ܐܡܝܢ[t] *add*
[z] *add* ܠܗ	ܐܡܝܢ[u] ܐܡܪ ܐܢܐ[u] ܠܟܘܢ : ܕܟܠ[v] ܗܢ[w] ܕܬܬܟܪܙ	ܗܢ[v] ܕܬܟܪܙ[w]
ܠܕܘܟܪܢܗ[a]	ܗܕܐ ܣܒܪܬܐ ܒܟܠ[x] ܥܠܡܐ[y] ܬܬܡܠܠ ܗܕܐ	ܒܟܠܗ[x]
ܐܣܟܪܝܘܛܐ[b]	14 ܕܥܒܕܬ ܗܕܐ[z] ܠܕܘܟܪܢܗ[a] : ܒܗܝ ܫܥܬܐ ܐܙܠ ܚܕ ܡܢ	[z] *add* ܠܗ
ܝܗܘܕܐ[d]	ܬܪܥܣܪ ܐܣܟܪܝܘܛܐ[b] ܕܡܬܩܪܐ ܝܗܘܕܐ[d] ܠܘܬ	ܝܗܘܕܐ[d]
ܪܒܢܐ[e]	15 ܪܒܢܐ[e] ܕܟܗܢܐ : ܘܐܡܪ ܠܗܘܢ : ܡܢܐ ܨܒܝܢ	
ܕܬܬܠܠܘܢ[f]	ܐܢܬܘܢ ܕܬܬܠܠܘܢ[f] ܠܝ ܘܐܢܐ ܡܫܠܡ[g] ܠܗ ܠܟܘܢ :	ܝܗܒܝܢ[f] ܠܗ[g]
‡ f. 108b.	ܗܢܘܢ ܕܝ[h] ܐܬܩܝܡܘ ܠܗ ܬܠܬܝܢ ‡ ܕܟܣܦܐ :	ܕܝ[h] ܐܬܐ
ܗܘܐ[i] ܟܡ[t]	16 ܘܡܢ[t] ܗܝܕܝܢ ܗܘܐ[i] ܒܥܐ[k] ܠܗ ܦܘܪܣܐ[m] ܕܢܫܠܡܝܘܗܝ	ܒܥܐ[k] ܗܘܐ[i]
ܕܢܫܠܡܝܘܗܝ[m]	ܠܗ ܠܗܘܢ ⁖	ܕܢܫܠܡܝܘܗܝ[m]

Codex B.

CXLVII.

Luke XXII. 1—38.

[a]ܝܘܡ [b]ܐܠܚܡܝܣ ܐܠܟܒܝܪ ܣܚܪ ܡܢ [c]ܠܝܠܗ [a]:
1 [b]ܘܩܪܝܒ ܕܝܢ [c]ܥܐܕܥܕܐ ܕܦܛܝܪܐ [d]ܕܡܬܐܡܪ
2 [e]ܦܨܚܐ : ܘܗܘܘ ܒܥܝܢ [f]ܪܒܢܝ ܟܗܢܝܐ ܘܣܦܪܝܐ
ܗܝܟ [g]ܢܩܛܠܘܢ ܝܬܗ : ܗܘܘ ܕܝܢ [h]ܕܚܠܝܢ ܡܢ
3 [i]ܥܡܐ : ܘܥܠ ܣܛܢܐ [j]ܒܝܗܘܕܐ [k]ܕܡܬܩܪܐ ܐܣܟܪܝܘܛܐ :
4 ܕܗܘܐ ܡܢ [l]ܡܢܝܢܐ ܕܬܪܥܣܪܬܐ : [m]ܘܐܙܠ
ܡܠܠ ܥܡ [n]ܪܒܢܝ ܟܗܢܝܐ [o]ܘܐܣܛܪܛܓܝܐ :
5 ܕܗܝܟ [p]ܕܢܫܠܡܝܘܢ ܝܬܗ ܠܗܘܢ : ܘܚܕܘ ܘܩܝܡܘ
6 ܕܝܬܠܘܢ ܠܗ ܟܣܦ : † [q]ܘܐܫܬܘܕܝ [r]ܘܗܘܐ
ܒܥܐ ܦܪܨܘܦ ܕܛܒܐ ܕܢܫܠܡܝܘܢ ܝܬܗ ܠܗܘܢ :
7 ܕܠܐ [s]ܐܟܠܘܣܐ : ܘܐܬܐ ܝܘܡܐ ܕܦܛܝܪܐ
8 ܕܒܗ ܗܘܐ ܠܡܟܣܐ ܕܝܬܢܟܣ [t]ܦܨܚܐ : [u]ܘܫܠܚ
[w]ܕܝܢ [x]ܠܦܛܪܘܣ [y]ܘܠܝܘܚܢܢ [z]ܘܐܡܪ : ܐܙܠܘ ܥܒܕܘ
[f. 90b]
9 ܠܢ ܕܢܟܘܠ [t]ܦܨܚܐ : ܘܗܢܘܢ ܕܝܢ ܐܡܪܘ ܠܗ :
10 ܗܢ ܐܬ ܨܒܐ [a]ܕܢܥܒܕ : ܘܗܘ ܐܡܪ ܠܗܘܢ
[b]ܗܐ [c]ܟܕ ܬܥܠܘܢ [d]ܠܡܕܝܢܬܐ ܝܦܪܥ ܝܬܟܘܢ
ܓܒܪ ‡[e]ܛܥܝܢ ܓܪܒ ܕܡܝܢ : ܐܙܠܘ ܒܬܪܗ [f]ܠܒܝܬܐ
11 ܕܗܘ [g]ܥܐܠ : ܘܐܡܪܘܢ ܐܡܪܝܢ ܠܡܪܗ ܕܒܝܬܐ :
ܐܡܪ ܠܟ ܡܠܦܢܐ : ܗܢ ܗܘ ܒܝܬ ܡܫܪܝܐ ܗܢ
12 ܕܐܟܘܠ [h]ܦܨܚܐ ܥܡ [i]ܬܠܡܝܕܝ : ܘܗܘ [j]ܡܚܘܐ
ܠܟܘܢ [k]ܥܠܝܐ ܪܒܐ [l]ܕܝܢ ܡܫܘܐ : ܘܬܡܢ ܥܒܕܘ :
13 ܘܐܙܠܘ [l]ܕܝܢ ܘܐܫܟܚܘ [m]ܗܝܟ [n]ܕܐܡܪ ܠܗܘܢ
14 ܡܛܐ ܫܥܬܐ : ܘܥܒܕܘ [o]ܦܨܚܐ : ܘܟܕ ܗܘܬ
ܫܪܬܐ ܪܒܐ ܘܬܪܥܣܪܬܐ ܫܠܝܚܝܐ ܥܡܗ :
15 ܘܐܡܪ ܠܗܘܢ [p]ܒܬܝܒܘܬܐ ܐܬܝܒܬ ܕܢܟܘܠ
16 [q]ܗܕܝܢ [r]ܦܨܚܐ ܥܡܟܘܢ : ܥܕ ܠܐ ܚܫ : ܐܡܪ
ܐܢܐ ܠܟܘܢ ܕܝܢ ܕܡܢ ܟܕܘ ܠܐ ܐܟܘܠ ܡܢܗ [s]ܥܕܡܐ
17 ܕܬܬܡܠܐ [t]ܒܡܠܟܘܬܗ ܕܐܠܗܐ : [u]ܘܢܣܒ ܟܣܐ
ܘܐܫܬܘܕܝ ܘܐܡܪ ܣܒܘ ܗܕܝܢ ܦܠܓܘ [w]ܒܝܢܬܟܘܢ :

Codex A.

[b]ܐܠܚܡܝܣ
[a]add ܘܒܢܘܗܝ ܡܦܪܩܢܐ
[b]ܘܩܪܒ [c]ܡܥܕܥܐ
[d]ܕܡܬܐܡܪ
[e]ܦܨܚܐ [f]ܪܒܢܝ
[g]ܢܩܛܠܘܢܗ [h]ܕܚܠܝܢ
[i]ܣܛܢܐ [j]ܒܝܗܘܕܐ
[k]add ܕܡܬܩܪܐ
[m]ܘܐܙܠ
[o]ܘܐܣܛܪܛܓܝܐ
[p]omit ܕ [s]ܐܟܠܘܣ
[t]ܦܨܚܐ
[w]omit ܕܝܢ
[y]ܘܠܝܘܚܢܢ [z]omit ܘ
[a]ܕܢܥܒܕ [b]ܗܐ
[d]ܠܡܕܝܢܬܐ
‡ f. 109a.
[f]ܠܒܝܬܗ [g]ܥܐܠ
[i]ܬܠܡܝܕܝ
[k]ܥܠܝܐ [l]omit ܕܝܢ
[n]ܐܡܪ
[o]ܦܨܚܐ
[p]ܒܬܝܒܘܬܐ
[q]ܗܕܝܢ
[t]ܒܡܠܟܘܬܗ
[u]ܘܢܣܒ
[w]ܒܝܢܬܟܘܢ

Codex C.

[a]ܝܘܡ [b]ܐܠܚܡܝܣ
[c]ܠܝܠܗ
[a]add ܘܒܢܘܗܝ ܡܦܪܩܢܐ
[e]ܦܨܚܐ
[j]ܒܝܗܘܕܐ
[k]add ܕܡܬܩܪܐ
[l]ܡܢܝܢܐ (sic) [n]ܪܒܢܝ
[o]ܘܐܣܛܪܛܓܝܐ
[p]omit ܕ
† f. 89a.
[q]ܘܐܫܬܘܕܝ
[r]ܘܗܘܐ [s]ܐܟܠܘܣ
[t]ܦܨܚܐ [u]ܘܫܠܚ
[w]omit ܕܝܢ [x]ܠܦܛܪܘܣ
[y]ܘܠܝܘܚܢܢ [z]omit ܘ
[a]ܕܢܥܒܕ
[b]ܗܐ [c]ܟܕ
[e]omit ܛܥܝܢ
[g]ܥܐܠ
[h]ܦܨܚܐ [i]ܬܠܡܝܕܝ
[j]ܡܚܘܐ
[l]omit ܕܝܢ
[m]ܗܝܟ
[o]ܦܨܚܐ
[p]ܒܬܝܒܘܬܐ
[r]ܦܨܚܐ
[s]add ܕܡܢ (sic)
[u]ܘܢܣܒ
[w]ܒܝܢܬܟܘܢ

Codex A.

[o]ܕܝ [q]ܕܐܬܝܗܒܘܢ
[r]ܗܘܘ [s]ܠܕܘܟܪܢܝ
‡ f. 109b.
[t]ܟܢ [v]ܕܕܝܬܩܐ
[x]ܕܚܠܦܝܟܘܢ
[y]ܒܪܡ [z]ܕܕܝ
[b]ܐܙܝܠ [c]ܒܪܡ
[e] *omit* ܕܝܢ
[g]ܕܝ [h]ܕܥܬܝܕ
[i]ܒܝܢܬܗܘܢ
[k]ܓܒܪܗ
[m] *add* ܕܝܢ
[o]ܒܠܗܘܢ [p]ܕܫܠܝܛܝܢ
[q] *omit* ܡܪܝܢ
[r]ܡܬܩܪܝܢ
[t]ܟܕܝ [u]ܕܝ
[v]ܕܡܫܡܫ [w]ܕܪܒܥ
[x] *omit* ܐܐ . . . ܕܪܒܥ
[z]ܕܡܫܡܫ
[c]ܡܬܩܢ
‡ f. 110a.
[d]ܘܬܬܒܘܢ
[e]ܬܪܬܥܣܪܬܐ
[f]ܡܬܒܘܪܣܝܐ
[i]ܗܟܒܐ [j] *add* ܕܝܢ

Codex B.

18 ܐܡܪ ܐܢܐ ܠܟܘܢ ܓܪ ܕܠܐ ܐܫܬܐ ܡܢ ܟܕܘ ܡܢ
ܦܐܪܐ † ܕܓܘܦܢܐ : ܥܕܡܐ ܕܬܐܬܐ ܡܠܟܘܬܗ
19 ܕܐܠܗܐ : ܘܢܣܒ ܠܚܡܐ ܘܐܫܬܘܕܝ ܘܩܨܐ
ܘܝܗܒ ܠܗܘܢ ܘܐܡܪ [o]ܗܕܝܢ ܗܘ [p]ܦܓܪܝ
ܕܥܠ [q]ܕܝܠܟܘܢ ܡܬܝܗܒ : ܗܕܝܢ [r]ܗܘ ܥܒܕܝܢ
20 [s]ܠܕܘܟܪܢܝ ܕܝܠܝ : ‡ ܘܟܣܐ [t]ܟܢ ܘܟܘܬ ܡܢ ܒܬܪ
ܕܐܟܠܘ ܐܡܪ : [u]ܗܕܝܢ ܟܣܐ ܗܘ[u] [v]ܕܕܝܬܩܐ
ܚܕܬܐ [w]ܒܐܕܡܝ ܕܝܠܝ [x]ܕܚܠܦܝܟܘܢ ܡܫܬܦܟ :
[f. 91a]
21 [y]ܒܪܡ ܕܝܢ ܗܐ ܐܝܕܗ [z]ܕܕܝܢ ܕܡܫܠܡ [a]ܠܝ ܥܡܝ
22 ܥܠ ܦܬܘܪܐ : ܘܒܪܗ ܕܒܪܢܫܐ ܗܟܢ ܕܡܬܩܢܝܢ
ܠܗ [b]ܐܙܠ : [c]ܒܪܡ ܕܝܢ ܘܝ ܠܗ ܠܓܒܪܗ ܒܪܢܫܐ
23 [d]ܕܒܐܝܕܗ ܗܘ [e]ܕܝܢ ܡܬܡܣܪ : ܘܗܢܘܢ ܫܪܘ
ܡܬܒܥܝܢ [e]ܕܝܢ [f]ܠܡܒܥܐ ܠܓܒܝܗܘܢ ܕܡܢ ܡܢܗܘܢ
24 ܐܪܐ ܗܘ [g]ܕܝܢ [h]ܕܥܬܝܕ ܕܝܥܒܕ ܗܕܐ : ܘܗܘܐ
[i]ܒܝܢܝܗܘܢ ܐܘܦ [k]ܡܪܘܢ ܕܡܢ ܡܢܗܘܢ [l]ܣܒܪ
25 ܢܗܐ ܪܒ : ܗܘ [m]ܐܡܪ ܠܗܘܢ [n]ܡܠܟܝܗܘܢ
ܕܥܡܡܝܐ ܡܪܝܢ [o]ܒܗܘܢ : ܘܫܠܝܛܝܢ [p]ܕܥܠܝܗܘܢ
26 ܒܗܘܢ [q]ܡܪܝܢ ܡܛܒܢܝܢ [r]ܡܬܩܪܝܢ : ܐܬܘܢ
[s]ܕܝܢ ܠܐ [t]ܟܕܝܢ : ܐܠܐ ܪܒܐ ܕܒܟܘܢ ܢܗܐ
ܗܟܢ ܟܙܥܘܪܐ : ܘܪܒܐ ܗܟܢ [u]ܕܝܢ [v]ܕܡܫܡܫ :
27 ܡܢ ܓܪ ܪܒ ܕܝܢ [w]ܪܒܥ [x]ܐܘ [y]ܗܕܝܢ [z]ܕܡܫܡܫ
[a]ܠܐ ܗܕܝܢ ܕܪܒܥ[x] : ܐܢܐ ܕܝܢ ܒܝܢܬܟܘܢ ܗܟܢ
28 [u]ܕܝܢ [z]ܕܡܫܡܫ[a] : ܘܐܬܘܢ ܗܘܝܢ ܗܠܝܢ
29 ܕܟܬܪܬܘܢ ܥܡܝ [b]ܒܢܣܝܘܢܝ : ܘܐܘܦ ܐܢܐ
[c]ܡܬܩܢ ܠܟܘܢ ܗܟܢ ܕܐܬܩܢ ܠܝ ܐܒܐ :
30 ܡܠܟܘ : ܕܬܗܘܢ ܐܟܠܝܢ ‡ ܘܫܬܝܢ ܥܠ ܦܬܘܪܝ
ܒܡܠܟܘܬܝ : [d]ܘܬܬܒܘܢ ܥܠ [e]ܬܪܬܥܣܪܐ
[f]ܟܘܪܣܘܢ ܕܕܝܢܝܢ ܬܪܬܥܣܪܬܐ ܫܒܛܝܐ
31 †[g]ܕܐܝܣܪܐܝܠ : ܐܡܪ ܕܝܢ ܡܪܝܐ ܫܡܥܘܢ ܫܡܥܘܢ
ܫܡܥܘܢ : ܗܐ ܣܛܢܐ ܫܐܠ ܠܟܘܢ [h]ܕܢܪܒܠ
32 ܝܬܟܘܢ[h] [i]ܗܝܟ ܟܚܛܐ[i] ܕܣܠܬܐ : ܐܢܐ [j]ܒܥܝܬ
ܠܓܒܟ ܕܠܐ [k]ܬܚܣܪ ܗܝܡܢܘܬܟ : ܘܐܘܦ

Codex C.

† f. 89b.
[o]ܕܝܢ
[p]ܦܓܪܐ
[r]ܗܘܘ [s]ܠܕܘܟܪܢܐ
[u] *omit* ܗܕܝܢ ܟܣܐ ܗܘ
[w]ܒܐܕܡܐ
[x]ܕܚܠܦܝܟܘܢ [a]ܠܗ
[d]ܕܒܐܝܕܗ [e] *omit* ܕܝܢ
[f]ܠܡܒܥܝ [h]ܕܥܬܝܕ
[i]ܒܝܢܬܗܘܢ
[k]ܡܪܘܢ [l]ܫܒܪ
[m] *add* ܕܐܢ
[n]ܡܠܟܝܗܘܢ
[p]ܕܫܠܝܛܝܢ
[q] *omit* ܡܪܝܢ
[r]ܡܬܩܪܝܢ
[s] *omit* ܕܝܢ [v]ܕܡܫܡܫ
[w]ܕܪܒܥ [y]ܕܝܢ
[z]ܕܡܫܡܫ
[a] *omit* ܠܐ . . .
. . . ܕܡܫܡܫ
[b]ܕܢܣܝܘܢܝܐ
[d]ܘܬܬܒܘܢ
[e]ܬܪܬܥܣܪܬܐ
[f]ܡܬܒܘܪܣܝܢ
[g]ܕܐܝܣܪܐܝܠ
† f. 90r.
[h] *omit* ܕܢܪܒܠ
ܝܬܟܘܢ
[j] *add* ܕܝܢ [k]ܬܚܣܪ

Codex A.

[n]ܕܐܘܦ [o]ܠܥܠܡܐ
[p]ܥܬܝܕ [q]ܠܗܝ
[s]ܢܡܘܣܐ [t]ܡܡܪ
[v]ܩܝܘܡ · [w]ܕܡܬܐ
[x]ܚܝܠܬܟ
[y]ܐܬܡܫܠܡܘܬܢ
[z]ܢܗܝܪܐ ܢܗܝܪ [a]*add*
[c]*omit* ܕܝ
[d]ܘܐܝܬܘܢ
[e]ܕܒܢܐ [f]ܕܗܢܐ
[g]ܕܝ ܟܬܒܐ [g]
‡ f. 110*b*.
[h]ܕܐܬܢܟܠܬ [i]ܒܝ
[l]ܡܠܬܐ
[m]ܚܛܝܘܢ [o]ܫܡܥܢ
ܘܢܦܩ ܐܙܠ ܡܢ[p]*add*
[ܝ]ܫܘܥ ܘܢܣܝ
[ܗܘ]ܘ . ܐܠܘܦ
[ܠܗܘ]ܢ ܕܢܫܬܡܥܘܢ
[ܘܐܙ]ܠ ܠܒܝܬܗ
[ܐܘܦ]ܬܠܡܝܕܘܗܝ :·

[a]ܝܘܡ ܐܠܝܣܘܢ
(*sic*)ܠܛܘܒܐܠܝܘܚܢܢ
[a]ܡܢ ܦܘܚܡܐ
[a]*add*:ܘܒܘܬܗ ܕܐܘܡܐ
[b]ܡܩܕܡ [c]ܕܦܨܚܐ
[d]ܥܕܢܗ [z]ܕܢܦܩܐ
[f]ܠܥܠܡܐ [i]ܕܐܝܬܘ
[j]ܕܒܥܠܡܐ
[l]ܕܐܬܓܒܪ
[m]ܕܢܗܘܐ
[n]ܕܝܡܣܪܝܘܗܝ [q]ܐܙܠ
[s]*omit* ܕܝ [t]ܫܩܠ

Codex B.

[f. 91*b*]
ܐܢܬ ܒܝܬܝ ܬܘܒ [l]ܘܓܪܪ ܟܠܗܘܢ ܠܐܢܫܝܢ :
33 ܘܗܘ ܐܡܪ ܠܗ ܡܚܘܝ ܒܐܝܢ ܐܝܢܐ [m]ܒܡܘܬܐ
[n]ܐܘܦ [o]ܒܥܠܡܐ ܘܐܘܦ ܠܡܡܬܐ [p]ܥܬܝܕ :
34 ܗܘ ܕܝ ܡܢܝܐ ܫܡܥܘ ܐܡܪ [q]ܠܗ : ܐܡܪ ܐܢܐ
ܠܢ [r]ܒܢܡܘܣܐ ܕܠܐ [s]ܡܫܝܚܐ ܡܬܩܝܡ ܠܥܠܡ ܘܐܝܟܢ
ܒܐܡܪܐ ܕܬܬܪܡܐ ܐܝܢ ܒܪܗ ܕܓܒܪܐ ܒܝ : ܕܡܢܘ ܐܬ
35 [t]ܡܡܪܝ ܠܝ : ܘܐܡܪ ܠܗܘܢ ܒܪ ܥܠܝܡܬ ܢܘܗܪܗܘܢ
ܕܠܐ ܒܟܘܢ : ܘܕܠܐ [u]ܩܕܡ ܘܕܠܐ [v]ܬܫܘܟܝܢ : [w]ܕܠܐ
36 [x]ܒܥܠܡܐ [y]ܡܫܬܪܝܢ : ܗܝܟܢ ܕܝ ܐܡܪܘ ܘܠܐ
[x]ܒܥܠܡܐ :· ܗܘ ܕܝ ܐܡܪ ܠܗܘܢ ܐܠܗܐ ܒܕܘ ܡܢ
ܕܠܗ ܒܟܘܢ [z]ܢܗܝܪ ܘܒܢܝܢ ܘܒܝܬܐ ܐܘܦ ܩܕܡ
ܘܡܢ ܕܠܝܬ ܠܗ [a] [b]ܝܘܡ ܡܐܢܫܗ [c]ܕܝ ‡ [d]ܘܝܘܡ
37 ܠܗ ܫܡܥ : ܐܡܪ ܐܢܐ ܠܒܗܘܢ ܒܪ [e]ܕܒܢܐ
[f]ܗܕܐ [g]ܕܟܬܒܐ ܠܗ [h]ܕܐܬܢܟܠܬ [i]ܕܝ : [k]ܕܐܘܦ
ܒܢ [l]ܡܠܝܠܐ ܢܬܚܫܒ : ܡܢܐ ܒܪ ܕܒܠ ܕܢܦܠܝ
38 [m]ܚܛܝܘܢ ܠܗ : ܘܗܝܟܢ ܐܡܪܘ ܡܢܝܐ ܗܐ ܒܐ
ܬܘܪܝܢ ܫܦܝܢ : [n]ܘܗܘ ܕܝ ܐܡܪ ܠܗܘܢ [o]ܫܦܝܢ
ܗܘ :· [p]

CXLVIII.

John XIII. 1—11*a*.

[a][b]ܝܘܡ ܐܠܝܣܘܢ ܠܛܘܒܐ ܝܘܚܢܢ[b] ܡܢ ܦܘܚܡܐ[a] :[a]
1 ܡܢ ܩܕܡ ܕܝ [b]ܡܥܒܕܢܐ [c]ܕܦܨܚܐ : ܝܕܥ
ܡܪܢܐ ܝܫܘܥ ܕܐܬܬ [d]ܥܕܢܗ [z]ܕܢܦܩܐ ܡܢ [e]ܗܕܝܢ
[f]ܥܠܡܐ : ܠܘܬ [g]ܐܒܘܝ :· [h]ܒܡܐ [i]ܕܐܚܒ ܕܝܠܗ
ܗܠܝܢ [j]ܕܒܥܠܡܐ [k]ܠܚܝܘܝ ܐܚܒ ܢܘܗܪܘܢ :
2 ܘܒܡܐ [l]ܕܐܬܥܒܕ ܡܫܡܫܐ [†] ܘܣܛܢܐ ܒܒܪ
ܕܢܐܡܐ ܒܠܒܗ [m]ܕܝܗܒܗ [n]ܕܝ ܡܫܠܡ[n] ܢܘܗܝ :
3 ܘܒܡܐ ܕܝܕܥ ܡܪܢܐ ܫܡܥܘ ܕܟܘܠܐ ܝܗܒ ܠܗ
[f. 92*a*]
ܐܒܐ ܒܐܝܕܘܝ : [o]ܘܕܡܢ ܐܠܗܐ ܢܦܩ ܘܠܘܬ
4 ܐܠܗܐ [p]ܗܘ [q]ܐܙܠ : ܩܡ [r]ܕܝ ܡܢ ܡܫܡܫܐ
ܘܐܫܠܚ ܡܐܢܘܗܝ : ܘܢܣܒ [s]ܕܝ [t]ܫܘܫܦܐ

Codex C.

[l]ܘܓܪܪ
[m]ܒܡܘܬܐ [n]ܕܐܘܦ
[o]ܠܥܠܡܐ [p]ܥܬܝܕ
[r]ܒܢܡܘܣܐ [s]ܡܡܪ
[t]ܡܡܪ
[u]ܒܪ [v]ܬܫܘܟܝܢ
[w]ܕܡܬܐ [x]ܒܥܠܡܐ
[y]ܐܬܡܫܠܡܘܬܢ
[z]ܢܗܝܪ [b]ܝܘܡ
[c]*omit* ܕܝ [d]ܘܝܘܡܢ
[g]ܕܟܬܒܐ
[h]ܕܐܬܢܟܠܬ [k]*omit* ܕ
[m]ܚܛܝܘܢ
[n]*omit* ܘ [o]ܫܦܝܢ

[b]ܝܘܡ ܐܠܝܣܘܢ
[b]ܠܛܘܒܐ ܝܘܚܢܢ
[a]*add* ܘܒܘܬܗ
[c]ܕܦܨܚܐ [d]ܥܕܢܗ
[z]ܕܢܦܩܐ [e]ܗܕܝܢ
[h]ܕܒܡܐ [g]ܐܒܘܝ
[i]ܕܐܚܒ [k]ܠܚܝܘܝ
† f. 90*b*.
[l]ܕܐܬܥܒܕ
[m]ܕܝܗܒܗ
[n]ܕܝܡܫܠܡ
(*sic*) [o]ܘܕܡܢ
[r]ܕܝ [p]*omit* ܗܘ
[t]ܫܘܫܦ [s]*omit* ܕܝ

Codex A.	*Codex* B.	*Codex* C.
‡ f. 111a.	5 [u]ܘܐܫܪܝ [v]ܒܡܫܓܘܢ : ‡ ܘܫܪܝ ܕܝܫܐ ܡܝܢ [w]ܒܡܫܚܠܐ	[v]ܒܚܨܝܘܢ
[u]ܘܫܪܝ [w]ܒܡܫܚܠܬܐ	ܘܫܪܝ ܡܫܝܓ [x]ܪܓܠܝܗܘܢ [y]ܕܬܠܡܝܕܘܝ : ܘܡܫܝܦ	[x]ܪܓܠܝܗܘܢ
[x]ܪܓܠܝܗܘܢ	[z]ܒܡܫܚܠܬܐ ܗܕܐ ܕܗܘܐ [a]ܐܣܝܪ [b]ܒܚܨܝܘܢ :	[y]ܕܬܠܡܝܕܘܝ
[y]ܕܬܠܡܝܕܘܝ	6 ܐܬܐ ܐܘܢ ܠܘܬ ܫܡܥܘܢ [c]ܦܛܪܘܣ : ܐܡܪ	[a]ܐܣܝܪ [c]ܦܛܪܘܣ
[z]ܒܡܫܚܠܬܐ	7 ܠܗ ܡܪܝ [d]ܪܓܠܝ ܐܢܬ ܡܫܝܓ : ܘܐܓܝܒ ܡܪܢܐ	[d]ܪܓܠܝ
[b]ܒܚܨܝܘܢ [d]ܪܓܠܝ	ܝܫܘܥ ܘܐܡܪ ܠܗ : ܡܐ ܕܐܢܐ [e]ܥܒܕ ܠܝܬ	[e]*omit* ܥܒܕ
	ܐܢܬ ܝܕܥ ܟܕܘ : [f]ܝܕܥ ܐܢܬ ܕܝ ܡܢ ܒܬܪ [g]ܟܕܘܢ	ܝܕܥ [f]*omit* [g]ܟܕܘܢ
[h]*add* ܠܝ [i]ܪܓܠܝ	8 ܐܡܪ ܠܗ [c]ܦܛܪܘܣ : ܠܝܬ ܐܢܬ ܡܫܝܓ [h] [i]ܪܓܠܝ	[h]*add* ܠܝ
[j]ܠܥܠܡ	[j]ܠܥܠܡ : [k]ܐܓܝܒ ܡܪܢܐ ܝܫܘܥ ܘܐܡܪ ܠܗ :	[j]ܠܥܠܡ [k]ܐܓܝܒ
[m]ܪܓܠܝܟ	[l]ܐܢ ܠܝܬ ܐܢܐ ܡܫܝܓ ܠܟ [m]ܪܓܠܟ ܠܝܬ ܠܟ	[l]ܐܢ
	9 ܚܘܠܩ ܥܡܝ : ܐܡܪ ܠܗ ܫܡܥܘܢ ܦܛܪܘܣ	
[n]ܪܓܠܝ ܒܠܚܘܕ[n]	ܡܪܝ ܠܐ [n]ܪܓܠܝ [o]ܒܠܚܘܕ[n] : ܐܠܐ ܐܘܦ	[n]ܒܠܚܘܕ ܪܓܠܝ[n]
[p]ܐܝܕܝ	10 [p]ܐܝܕܝ ܘܪܝܫܝ : ܐܡܪ ܠܗ ܡܪܢܐ ܝܫܘܥ :	[p]ܐܝܕܝ
[q]ܗܘ ܕܝ [r]*omit*	[q]ܗܘܝܢ ܕܣܚܐ ܠܐ [r]ܕܝ ܨܪܝܟ ܐܠܐ [s]ܕܝܫܝܓ	ܕܝ [r]*omit* [s]ܕܝܫܝܓ
[t]ܪܓܠܘܝ	[t]ܪܓܠܘܝ : ܟܘܠܗ ܓܝܪ ܕܟܝ ܐܝܬ ܗܘ ܐܘܦ	[t]ܪܓܠܘܝ
[u]ܡܫܠܡܢܗ	ܐܢܬܘܢ ܕܟܝܢ ܐܢܬܘܢ ܐܠܐ ܠܐ ܟܘܠܟܘܢ :	[u]ܡܫܠܡܢܗ
ܥܠܡ [w]*omit*	11 ܝܕܥ ܗܘܐ ܓܝܪ ܡܢ ܗܘ [u]ܡܫܠܡܢܗ : [w]ܥܠܡ :	ܥܠܡ [w]*omit*

JOHN XIII. 12—17.

Codex A.	*Codex* B.	*Codex* C.
[a]*omit* ܒܫܘܪܗ	ܡܢ ܒܬܪ ܐܬܚܫܠ ܡܢ [a]ܒܫܘܪܗ [b]ܕܡܘܫܐ [y] [z]ܒܪ	[a]*omit* ܒܫܘܪܗ
[b]ܡܐܢܘܗܝ	12 ܐܘܢ ܐܫܝܓ [a]ܪܓܠܝܗܘܢ : ܘܢܣܒ [b]ܡܐܢܗ	[b]ܘܫܩܠ
[a]ܪܓܠܝܗܘܢ [b]ܡܐܢܘܗܝ	ܘܪܒܥ : ܘܬܘܒ ܐܡܪ ܠܗܘܢ ܝܕܥܝܢ ܐܢܬܘܢ ܡܐ	ܘܒܬܪ ܗܕܐ [y]*add* [z]ܘܒܪ
	13 [c]ܥܒܕܬ ܠܟܘܢ : ܐܢܬܘܢ ܩܪܝܢ ܠܝ ܡܪܢܐ ܘܡܠܦܢܐ	[a]ܪܓܠܝܗܘܢ
‡ f. 111b.	†ܘܝܐܝܬ ܐܢܬܘܢ ܐܡܪܝܢ : [d]ܟܝܢ ‡ ܓܝܪ ܐܢܐ [o]ܐܢ [f. 92b]	[b]ܡܐܢܘܗܝ [c]ܥܒܕ
[d]ܟܢ [e]ܐܫܝܓܬ	14 ܐܢ ܐܢܐ [e]ܐܫܝܓܬ [f]ܪܓܠܝܟܘܢ ܡܪܢܐ ܘܡܠܦܢܐ :	† f. 91a.
[f]ܪܓܠܝܟܘܢ	ܐܘܦ ܐܢܬܘܢ [g]ܚܝܒܝܢ ܐܢܬܘܢ ܕܬܗܘܢ ܡܫܝܓܝܢ	[o]ܐܢ
[g]ܚܝܒܝܢ [h]ܪܓܠܝ	15 [h]ܪܓܠܝ ܚܒܪܝܟܘܢ [i]ܠܥܠܡܟ : ܕܡܘ ܓܝܪ ܝܗܒܬ	[g]ܚܝܒܝܢ
[i]ܕܥܠܡܟ [j]ܕܗܝܟ	ܠܟܘܢ : [j]ܗܝܟ ܡܐ ܕܐܢܐ ܥܒܕܬ ܠܟܘܢ ܐܘܦ	[j]ܕܗܝܟ
	16 ܐܢܬܘܢ ܬܗܘܢ ܥܒܕܝܢ : [k]ܐܡܝܢ ܐܡܝܢ ܐܡܪ ܐܢܐ	[k]ܐܡܪ
[l]ܕܠܝܬ	ܠܟܘܢ : [l]ܠܝܬ ܥܒܕ ܪܒ ܡܢ ܡܪܗ : ܘܠܐ ܫܠܝܚ	[l]ܕܠܝܬ
	17 ܡܢ ܗܕܝܢ [m]ܕܫܠܚ ܝܬܗ : ܐܢ ܝܕܥܝܢ ܐܢܬܘܢ ܗܠܝܢ	[m]ܕܫܠܚ
	ܛܘܒܝܟܘܢ : ܐܢ ܗܘܝܬܘܢ ܐܢܬܘܢ ܥܒܕܝܢ [n]ܠܗܘܢ :	[n]ܠܗܘܢ

Codex A.	Codex B.	Codex C.

CXLIX.

Matt. XXVI. 1—20.

[a] ܗܘܐ ܐܘܢܓܠܝܘܢ [a] ܐܠܦܢܝܐ ܠܡܬܝܐܘܣ ܡܢ ܦܨܚܐ :·
1 ܐܡܪ ܡܪܢ ܝܫܘܥ [a] ܠܬܠܡܝܕܘܝ : ܝܕܥܝܢ ܐܢܬܘܢ
2 ܕܡܢ ܒܬܪ ܬܪܝܢ ܝܘܡܝܢ [b] ܦܨܚܐ [c] ܡܬܥܒܕ : ܘܒܪܗ
3 ܕܐܢܫܐ ܡܫܬܠܡ [e] ܠܡܙܕܩܦܐ : [f] ܘܟܢܫܘ ܐܬܟܢܫܘ
[g] ܪܒܝ ܟܗܢܝܐ [h] ܘܣܦܪܝ ܕܥܡܐ : ܠܕܪܬܗ ܕܪܒ
4 ܟܗܢܝܐ ܗܘ [i] ܕܡܬܩܪܐ [j] ܩܝܦܐ : ܘܐܬܡܠܟܘ
[k] ܕܝܫܘܥ [‡] ܝܬܗ ܠܡܐܚܕ ܒܢܟܠ ܘܠܡܩܛܠܗ
5 ܝܬܗ : ܗܘܘ ܕܝܢ ܐܡܪܝܢ ܠܐ [l] ܒܥܐܕܐ ܕܠܐ
6 [m] ܬܬܗܘܐ [n] ܫܓܘܫܝܐ [o] ܒܥܡܐ : [p] ܠܐ [p] ܕܝܢ
[q] ܟܕ ܗܘܐ ܝܫܘܥ ܒܒܝܬ ܥܢܝܐ ܒܒܝܬܗ
7 [r] ܕܫܡܥܘܢ ܓܪܒܐ : ܩܪܒܬ ܠܗ [s] ܐܢܬܬܐ [t] ܕܐܝܬ ܗܘܐ
[u] ܥܡܗ ܫܛܦܐ ܕܒܣܡܐ ܕܢܪܕܝܢ : ܘܐܫܦܝܬܗ ܥܠ
8 ܪܝܫܗ ܟܕ ܣܡܝܟ ܗܘܐ [v] ܚܙܘ : [w] ܗܘܘ [x] ܬܠܡܝܕܘܗܝ
[y] ܘܐܬܚܡܬܘ ܐܡܪܝܢ ܠܡܢܐ [z] [†] ܗܕܐ ܐܒܕܢܐ
9 [a] ܕܡܫܚܐ : [b] ܡܫܟܚ ܗܘܐ ܓܝܪ ܗܢܐ [c] ܡܫܚܐ
10 [d] ܕܢܙܕܒܢ ܒܣܓܝ ܘܢܬܝܗܒ [e] ܠܡܣܟܢܐ : [f] ܝܕܥ
[g] ܡܪܢ ܝܫܘܥ ܘܐܡܪ ܠܗܘܢ : ܡܢܐ ܐܢܬܘܢ
[h] ܡܫܪܚܝܢ ܠܐܢܬܬܐ ܥܠ ܥܒܕܐ ܛܒܐ ܥܒܕܬ
11 ܠܝ : ܟܠܙܒܢ ܓܝܪ ܡܣܟܢܐ ܐܝܬ ܠܟܘܢ : ܐܢܐ [i] ܠܐ
12 ܟܠܙܒܢ ܓܝܪ [j] ܕܝܢ ܐܝܬܝ ܥܡܟܘܢ : ܗܕܐ ܕܐܪܡܝܬ
[c] ܡܫܚܐ ܗܢܐ ܥܠ ܦܓܪܝ ܠܩܘܒܪܝ ܥܒܕܬ
13 ܗܕܐ : ܐܡܝܢ ܐܡܪ ܐܢܐ ܠܟܘܢ ܕܟܠ ܟܪ
[n] ܕܬܬܟܪܙ ܗܕܐ ܣܒܪܬܐ [o] ܒܟܠܗ [p] ܥܠܡܐ :
14 ܢܬܡܠܠ ܐܦ ܗܕܐ ܕܥܒܕܬ ܠܗ [r] ܠܕܘܟܪܢܗ : ܗܝܕܝܢ
[s] ܐܙܠ ܚܕ ܡܢ [t] ܬܪܥܣܪ ܕܡܬܩܪܐ ܝܗܘܕܐ
[‡] ܐܣܟܪܝܘܛܐ [u] ܠܘܬ ܪܒܝ [w] ܟܗܢܝܐ ܘܐܡܪ ܠܗܘܢ :
15 ܡܢܐ ܐܢܬܘܢ ܨܒܝܢ [x] ܠܡܬܠ ܠܝ ܘܐܢܐ ܡܫܠܡ
ܠܗ ܠܟܘܢ : ܗܢܘܢ [z] ܘܐܩܝܡܘ ܠܗ ܬܠܬܝܢ
16 [a] ܕܟܣܦ : ܘܡܢ [b] ܗܝܕܝܢ ܗܘܐ ܒܥܐ ܠܗ [d] ܦܘܪܣܐ

[f. 93a]

Codex A. [a] ܠܬܠܡܝܕܘܗܝ (sic) — ܐܠܦܢܝܐ — (sic) ܡܢ ܦܨܚܐ — [a] ܕܡܬܝܐܘܣ — [b] ܦܨܚܐ [c] ܡܬܥܒܕ — [f] ܘܟܢܫ [g] ܪܒܝ — [h] ܘܣܦܪܝ — [i] ܕܡܬܩܪܐ — [j] ܩܝܦܐ — ‡ f. 112a. — [k] ܕܝܫܘܥ — [l] ܒܥܐܕܐ — [n] ܫܓܘܫܝܐ — [o] ܒܥܡܐ — [p] omit ܕܝܢ ܠܐ — [q] ܟܕ ܗܘܐ — [r] ܕܫܡܥܘܢ — [t] ܥܡܗ [u] ܕܒܣܡܐ — [v] ܚܙܘ [w] add ܕܝܢ — [z] ܗܕܐ [a] ܕܡܫܚܐ — [b] ܡܫܟܚ [c] ܡܫܚܐ — [d] ܕܢܙܕܒܢ [e] ܠܡܣܟܢܐ — [f] ܝܕܥ [g] add ܕܝܢ — [h] ܡܫܪܚܝܢ [i] add ܕܝܢ — [j] omit ܕܝܢ — [n] ܕܬܬܟܪܙ [o] ܒܟܠܗ — [p] ܥܠܡܐ — [r] ܠܕܘܟܪܢܗ — [s] ܐܙܠ [t] ܬܪܥܣܪ — ‡ f. 112b. — [w] ܪܒܝ [x] ܠܡܬܠ — [z] add ܕܝܢ [a] ܕܟܣܦ — [b] ܡܢ [d] ܦܘܪܣܐ

Codex C. [a] ܠܬܠܡܝܕܘܗܝ ܡܢ ܦܨܚܐ [a] ܕܡܬܝܐܘܣ — [z] add ܘܟܢܫܘ ܐܬܟܢܫܘ — [a] ܠܬܠܡܝܕܘܗܝ [b] ܦܨܚܐ — [e] ܠܡܙܕܩܦܐ — [j] ܩܝܦܐ — [l] ܒܥܐܕܐ — [m] ܬܬܗܘܐ — [n] ܫܓܘܫܝܐ [p] ܠܐ — [r] ܕܫܡܥܘܢ — [s] ܐܢܬܬܐ [t] ܕܐܝܬ — [w] add ܕܝܢ — [x] ܬܠܡܝܕܘܗܝ — † f. 91b. — [y] ܘܐܬܚܡܬܘ — [g] add ܕܝܢ — [h] ܡܫܪܚܝܢ — [i] add ܕܝܢ — [j] omit ܕܝܢ — [n] ܕܬܬܟܪܙ [o] ܒܟܠܗ — [u] ܗܘܐ (sic) — [x] ܠܡܬܠ — [z] add ܕܝܢ — [b] ܡܢ

Codex A.	Codex B.	Codex C.
g omit ܕܝܢ	17 ܕܐܣܗܕܘܪ ܝܬܗ :f ܘܡܣܗܕܐ ܣܗܕܐ ܕܥܡܗ ܕܩܛܝܪܐ	g omit ܕܝܢ f add ܪܒܐ
i omit ܠܗ	ܡܢܘܗ g ܕܝܢ h ܬܠܡܝܕܘܗܝ ܠܡܪܐ ܚܫܘ ܗܘܘ ܘܐܡܪܝܢ	h ܬܠܡܝܕܝܐ
j ܕܟܬܝܒܐ m ܟ̈ܢܫܝܐ	i ܠܗ ܗܝ ܐܬܐ ܨܒܐ j ܕܟܬܝܒܢ k ܠܗ l ܕܥܒܕܘܠ	i omit ܠܗ
n ܠܡܕܝܢܬܐ p ܦܠܡ	18 m ܦܫܝܐ: ܗܘ ܕܝܢ ܐܡܪ ܠܗܘܢ ܐܝܠܘ n ܠܡܕܝܢܬܐ	j ܕܟܬܝܒܐ k ܠܗ
q ܡܢ̈ܘܗܘܢ	ܠܘܬ o ܐܢܫ p ܦܠܡ ܘܐܡܪܘ ܠܗ: ܡܠܦܢܐ ܐܡܪ:	l omit ܕܥܒܕܘܠ
r ܦ̈ܫܝܐ	q ܡܢܘܗܘܢ ܡܪܝܒ ܐܢܬ ܗܘ ܠܘܬܟ ܐܝܟܐ ܒܒܕ	m ܦܫܝܐ o ܐܢܫ
s ܬܠܡ̈ܝܕܘܗܝ	19 r ܦܫܝܐ ܟܡ s ܬܠܡܝܕܘܗܝ: ܘܟܬܒܘ ܬܠܡܝܕܝܐ	p ܦܠܡ q ܡܢܘܗܘܢ
t ܗܟܕܐ u ܕܐܬܘܢ	t ܗܝܟ ܟܐ t u ܕܐܬܘܡ ܠܗܘܢ ܡܪܐ ܝܫܘܥ	r ܦܫܝܐ w ܘܟܬܒܘ
w ܘܟܬܒܘ x omit ܕܝܢ	20 w ܘܟܬܒܘ x ܕܝܢ r ܦܫܝܐ: ܘܟܕ ܕܝܢ ܗܘܐ y ܪܓܫܐ	x omit ܕܝܢ z ܪܒܒ
y ܪܓܫܐ	ܗܘܐ z ܪܒܒ ܟܡ ܬܪܥܣܪܬܐ † ܬܠܡܝܕܝܐ:	† f. 92a.

John XIII. 3—17.

[f. 93b]

Codex A.	Codex B.	Codex C.
وهدا لا كلام (sic) من يحنا (sic) مضاف فيه	3 ܘܟܕܡܐ ܕܝܕܥ ܡܪܐ ܝܫܘܥ ܕܟܘܠܐ ܝܗܒ ܠܗ	
	ܐܒܐ w ܒܐܝܕܘܗܝ x ܘܕܡܢ ܐܠܗܐ ܢܦܩ: ܘܠܘܬ	w ܒܐܝܕܘܗܝ x ܘܐܘܕܗ
y ܐܙܠ a ܡܫܟܘܒܐ	4 ܐܠܗܐ ܗܘ y ܐܙܠ z ܩܡ ܕܝܢ ܡܢ a ܡܫܟܒܐ:	z ܩܐܡ
b ܡܐܢܘܗܝ	ܘܐܫܩ b ܡܐܢܝ ܘܢܣܒ ܫܒܫܢ c ܘܐܣܪ d ܚܨܘܗܝ:	d ܚܨܘܗܝ
‡ f. 113a.	5 ‡ ܘܟܕܝܢ ܪܡܐ e ܡܝ f ܒܡܫܠܐ ܘܫܪܝ ܡܫܝܓ	e ܡܝܢ
c ܘܐܫܪ d ܚܨܘܗܝ	g ܪ̈ܓܠܝܗܘܢ h ܕܬܠܡܝܕܘܗܝ ܘܡܫܘܦܪ ܒܫܘܫܦܬܐ	h ܬܠܡܝܕܘܗܝ
e ܡܝܢ f ܒܡܫܠܐ	6 ܗܕܐ ܕܗܘܐ i ܐܫܪ j ܒܫܪܝܢ: ܐܬܐ ܐܘܢ ܠܘܬ	
g ܪ̈ܓܠܝܗܘܢ	ܫܡܥܘܢ k ܦ̈ܛܪܘܣ ܘܐܡܪ ܠܗ ܡܪܝ l ܪ̈ܓܠܝ	k ܦܛܪܘܣ
i ܐܫܪ j ܚܨܘܗܝ	7 ܐܬ ܡܫܝܓ: m ܘܐܓܝܒ ܡܪܐ ܝܫܘܥ ܘܐܡܪ	m ܘܐܓܝܒ
l ܪ̈ܓܠܝ	ܠܗ: ܡܐ ܕܐܢܐ ܥܒܕ ܠܝܬ ܐܬ ܝܕܥ ܟܕܘ:	
n omit ܐܬ	ܝܕܥ ܐܬ ܕܝܢ ܡܢ ܒܬܪܟܢ: ܐܡܪ ܠܗ ܦ̈ܛܪܘܣ:	
o ܪ̈ܓܠܝ q ܐܓܝܒ	8 ܠܝܬ n ܐܬ ܡܫܝܓ ܠܝ o ܪ̈ܓܠܝ p ܠܥܠܡ: q ܐܓܝܒ	p ܠܥܠܡ q ܐܓܝܒ
	ܡܪܐ ܝܫܘܥ ܘܐܡܪ ܠܗ: r ܐܢ ܠܝܬ ܐܢܐ	r ܐܢ
s ܪ̈ܓܠܝܟ	ܡܫܝܓ ܠܟ s ܪ̈ܓܠܝܟ ܠܝܬ ܠܟ ܚܘܠܩ ܥܡܝ:	s ܪ̈ܓܠܝܟ
t ܪ̈ܓܠܝ	9 ܐܡܪ ܠܗ ܫܡܥܘܢ k ܦ̈ܛܪܘܣ: ܡܪܝ ܠܐ t ܪ̈ܓܠܝ	
u ܐܝܕܝ	10 ܒܠܚܘܕ: ܐܠܐ ܐܘܦ u ܐܝܕܝ ܘܪܫܝ: ܐܡܪ ܠܗ	
v ܗܝܢ w ܪ̈ܓܠܘܗܝ	ܡܪܐ ܝܫܘܥ: v ܗܕܝܢ ܕܣܚܐ ܠܐ ܨܪܝܟ ܐܠܐ	w ܪ̈ܓܠܝ x ܘܒܠܚܘܕܗ
y ܐܝܟ ܗܘ	ܕܡܫܝܓ w ܪ̈ܓܠܘܗܝ: x ܒܠܚܘܕܗ ܠܐ ܕܟܐ y ܐܝܬܘܗܝ	z ܕܐܢܬܘܢ
	ܐܘܦ ܐܢܬܘܢ z ܕܟܝܢ ܐܢܬܘܢ ܐܠܐ ܠܐ	

Codex B.

11 ܒܥܠܡܐ : ܢܫܒ ܓܝܪ ܗܘܐ ܡܢ ܗܘ ܕܡܣܟܢ
ܠܗ : ܠܓܒܝܠ [a]ܕܓܫܡ ܐܡܪ ܕܠܐ ܒܥܠܡܐ
12 [z]ܕܓܫܡ : ܗܕ ܐܝܬ ܐܚܝܕ [b]ܕܬܠܡܝܕܘܗܝ [c]ܘܢܫܒ
[d]ܡܐܢܐ ܘܢܦܩ : ܗܘܐ ܐܡܪ ܠܗܘܢ [‡]ܡܕܓܫܡ
13 ܐܢܬܘܢ ܡܢܐ ܒܥܕܢܐ ܠܗܘܢ : [†]ܐܢܬܘܢ ܗܘܝܢ ܠܗ
14 ܡܢܐ ܐܢܐ ܡܫܠܡܢܐ [e]ܘܡܐܬܐ ܐܢܬܘܢ ܐܡܪܝܢ : [f]ܗܘܝܢ
ܐܢܐ ܠܐ ܐܢܐ ܐܢܐ [g]ܐܚܝܕ [h]ܕܬܠܡܝܕܘܗܝ
ܡܢܐ ܡܫܠܡܢܐ : ܐܢܐ ܐܢܬܘܢ [i]ܝܗܒܝܢ ܐܢܬܘܢ
[j]ܬܘܗܘܢ ܡܥܒܕܝܢ [k]ܕܬܠܡܝܕܘ [f. 94a] ܦܠܓܘܬܐ [l]ܠܥܠܝܡ :
15 ܕܗܘ [m]ܡܣܬܒܪ ܠܗܘܢ : [n]ܕܗܘܝܢ ܡܢܐ [n] [o]ܕܐܢܐ
[p]ܒܓܒܝܠ [q]ܕܝ ܠܗܘܢ ܐܡܪ [q]ܕܝ ܐܢܬܘܢ ܬܗܘܘܢ
16 ܒܓܒܝܠ : ܐܡܝܢ ܐܡܪ ܐܢܐ ܠܗܘܢ ܕܠܐ
ܚܕ ܙܕ ܡܢ [r]ܡܢܗ : ܘܠܐ ܫܠܝܚ ܡܢ [s]ܗܕܝܢ
17 [t]ܕܫܠܝܚ ܐܢܬܘܢ : [u]ܐܢܐ [v]ܡܕܓܫܡ ܐܢܬܘܢ ܘܠܝܬ
ܠܡܠܟܘܬܗ [u]ܐܢܐ ܗܘܝܢ ܐܢܬܘܢ ܒܓܒܝܠ [w]ܠܗܘܢ :

Matt. XXVI. 21—39.

21 ܘܗܘܝܢ ܕܗܘܝܢ ܐܡܪܝܢ ܠܗܘܢ : [s]ܐܡܝܢ
ܐܡܪ ܐܢܐ ܠܗܘܢ : ܕܚܕ ܡܢܟܘܢ ܡܫܠܡ
22 ܘܟܪܝܐ : ܘܫܪܝܘ [t]ܡܬܥܣܩܝܢ ܠܚܕܐ ܚܕ ܐܡܪܝܢ
ܠܗ : ܕܠܡܐ ܚܕ ܡܢܢ ܡܫܠܡ : ܕܠܡܐ ܐܢܐ ܐܢܐ
23 ܗܘ ܕܝܢ : ܗܘ ܕܝ ܡܢܐ ܫܠܡ ܐܝܕܗ
ܘܐܡܪ : [u]ܗܘ [w]ܕܝܚܒܐ [x]ܐܝܕܗ ܒܡܐ [y]ܥܡܝ
24 [z]ܒܪܢܫܐ [a]ܗܘ ܡܫܠܡ ܐܝܕܗ : ܘܡܢܗ ܕܒܪܢܫܐ
[b]ܐܙܠ [c]ܘܗܘܝܢ ܕܟܬܝܒ [‡] ܥܠ ܕܒܓܠܗ : ܘܝ ܠܗ
ܕܝ ܠܗܘ ܓܒܪܐ ܗܘܝܢ ܕܡܫܬܠܡ ܒܪܗ ܕܓܒܪܐ
ܡܫܠܡܢܐ : ܛܒ ܗܘܐ ܠܗ [d]ܕܠܐ ܐܬܝܠܕ ܗܘ
25 ܓܒܪܐ : ܐܚܝܕ ܕܝ [e]ܝܗܘܕܐ ܗܘ [f]ܕܡܫܠܡ
ܠܗ [g]ܐܡܪ : [h]ܕܠܡܐ [i]ܐܢܐ ܗܘ ܪܒܝ ܘܐܡܪ ܠܗ
26 ܐܢܬ ܐܡܪܬ : ܗܕ ܕܝ ܗܘܘ ܐܟܠܝܢ : ܢܣܒ
ܡܢܐ ܝܫܘܥ ܠܚܡܐ [j]ܘܒܪܟ [†] ܘܩܨܐ
[k]ܠܬܠܡܝܕܘܗܝ ܘܐܡܪ ܣܒܘ [l]ܘܐܟܘܠܘ [u]ܗܢܐ ܐܢܘܢ

Codex A.

[a] ܚܕ
[b] ܕܬܠܡܝܕܘܗܝ
‡ f. 113b.
[d] ܡܐܢܘܢ
[f] ܗܘ [g] ܐܚܝܕܬ
[h] ܕܬܠܡܝܕܘܗܝ
[i] ܝܗܒܝܢ
[j] ܕܬܗܘܘܢ [k] ܕܬܠܡܝܕܘ
[l] ܕܥܠܝܡ ܚܕ [m] *add*
[n] ܕܗܘܝܢܗܘܢ
[q] ܕܝ *omit*
[s] ܗܢ [t] ܕܫܠܝܚ
[v] ܡܕܓܫܡ *omit*
[u] ܗܘ [w] ܕܝܚܒܐ
[x] ܐܝܕܗ ܥܡܝ *omit* [y]
‡ f. 114a.
[z] ܒܪܢܫܐ [a] ܗܘ ܕܝ
[b] ܐܙܠ [c] ܗܘܝܢܗܘܢ
[d] ܐܠܐ ܠܐ [d] [e] ܝܗܘܕܐ
[f] ܡܫܠܡ [i] ܐܢܐ
[j] ܘܒܪܟ
[k] ܠܬܠܡܝܕܘܗܝ
[l] ܘܐܟܘܠܘ [u] ܗܢܐ

ܡܐܬܘܢ ورجعنا الى متى

Codex C.

[z] ܕܐܓܫܡ ܘ [c] *omit*
[d] ܡܐܢܘܢ
† f. 92b.
[e] ܘܡܐܬܐ
[i] ܝܗܒܝܢ
[j] ܬܗܘܘܢ [k] ܕܬܠܡܝܕ
[o] *omit* ܕܐܢܐ
[p] ܕܒܓܒܝܠ ܕܝ [q] *omit*
[r] ܡܢܗ
[t] ܕܫܠܝܚ [u] ܐܢܐ
[w] ܠܗ
[s] *add* ܐܡܝܢ
[t] ܡܬܥܣܩܝܢ
[w] ܕܝܚܒܐ [x] ܐܝܕܗ
[y] *omit* ܥܡܝ
[z] ܒܪܢܫܐ [a] ܗܘ ܕܝ
[c] ܗܘܝܢ ܡܢܐ [c]
[e] ܝܗܘܕܐ [g] ܐܡܪ
[h] *omit* ܐܢܐ [i] ܐܢܐ
† f. 93a.

Codex B.

27 ܗܘ ܦܓܪ̈ܝ܆ ܘܢܣܒ ܟܣܐ ܘܐܫܬܘܕܝ ܘܝܗܒ
28 ܠܗܘܢ ܘܐܡܪ ܐܫܬܘ [l]ܡܢܗ ܒܟܠܟܘܢ܆ [m]ܗܢܘ
ܓܝܪ[n] *ܗܘ [o]ܐܕܡܝ [p]ܕܕܝܬܩܐ ܚܕܬܐ [q]ܕܚܠܦ
29 [r]ܣܓܝܢ [s]ܡܫܬܦܟ ܠܫܘܒܩܢ [t]ܕܚܘܒܝܢ: [u]ܐܡܪ [f. 94b]
ܐܢܐ[u] ܠܟܘܢ ܕܝ ܕܠܐ ܐܫܬܐ ܡܢ ܟܕܘ ܡܢ
ܗܠܝܢ ܦܐܪܐ ܕܓܘܦܢܐ ܥܕܡܟܐ ܠܝܘܡܐ ܗܘ [v]ܕܒܗ
[w]ܕܝ ܐܫܬܝܗ [x]ܚܕܬ ܥܡܟܘܢ ܒܡܠܟܘܬܗ ܕܐܒܐ:
30 31 ܘܐܫܒܚܘ ܕܝ [y]ܘܢܦܩܘ ܠܛܘܪܐ ܕܙܝܬܝܐ: ܘܟܕܝܢ
ܐܡܪ ܠܗܘܢ ܡܪܢ ܝܫܘܥ [z]ܠܬܠܡܝܕܘܗܝ: ܐܢܬܘܢ
ܟܠܟܘܢ [n]ܓܝܪ ܬܬܟܫܠܘܢ ܒܝ: [a]ܒܗܕܝܢ ‡ [b]ܠܠܝܐ
ܟܬܝܒ ܓܝܪ ܕܐܡܚܐ ܠܪܥܝܐ [c]ܘܢܬܒܕܪܘܢ
32 [d]ܐܡܪܝܢܐ [e]ܕܡܪܥܝܬܗ: ܘܡܢ ܒܬܪ ܕܐܢܐ [f]ܩܐܡ
33 ܗܐ ܐܢܐ [g]ܕܝ [h]ܡܩܕܡ ܠܟܘܢ ܠܓܠܝܠܐ: ܐܓܝܒ
ܕܝ [i]ܦ̈ܛܪܘܣ ܘܐܡܪ ܠܗ: ܐܢ ܐܘܦ ܟܠܗܘܢ
ܢܬܟܫܠܘܢ ܒܟ: ܐܢܐ ܠܥܠܡ ܠܝܬ ܐܢܐ ܡܬܟܫܠ:
34 ܐܡܪ ܠܗ ܡܪܢ ܝܫܘܥ: [j]ܐܡܝܢ ܐܡܝܢ ܐܡܪ
ܐܢܐ ܠܟ [k]ܕܒܗܕܝܢ ܠܠܝܐ [l]ܥܕ ܠܐ [m]ܢܩܪܐ
35 [n]ܬܪܢܓܘܠܐ [o]ܬܠܬܐ ܙܒܢܝܢ ܬܟܦܘܪ ܒܝ: ܐܡܪ
ܠܗ [i]ܦ̈ܛܪܘܣ ܐܘܦ [p]ܠܘܬ ܐܢܐ[p] ܕܝ [q]ܡܡܬ[q]
ܥܡܟ: [r]ܠܝܬ ܐܢܐ[r] ܟܦܪ ܒܟ: ܟܢ [s]ܘܟܘܬ
36 ܐܘܦ ܟܠܗܘܢ ܬܠܡܝܕܝܐ ܐܡܪܘ: ܒܟܢ ܐܬܐ
ܥܡܗܘܢ † ܡܪܢ ܝܫܘܥ ܠܩܪܝܐ ܕܡܬܩܪܝܐ
ܓܣܡܢܝܢ: ܘܐܡܪ [t]ܠܬܠܡܝܕܝܐ: ܬܒܘ ܗܟܐ
37 ܥܕܡܟܐ [u]ܐܙܠ [w]ܠܗܠ ܘܐܨܠܝ: ܘܕܒܪ [x]ܠܦ̈ܛܪܘܣ
ܘܬܪܝܢ [y]ܒܢܘܗܝ [z]ܕܙܒܕܝ: ܘܫܪܝ [a]ܡܬܥܝܩ ܘܡܬܟܪܝ:
38 ܒܟܢ ܐܡܪ ܠܗܘܢ ܡܬܥܝܩܐ ܗܝ [b]ܢܦܫܝ ܥܕ
ܡܛܐ [c]ܕܡܘܬܐ: ܩܘܝܘ [d]ܗܟܐ ܘܗܘܘ ܫܗܪܝܢ [f. 95a]
39 ܥܡܝ: [e]ܘܩܪܒ ܙܥܘܪ ܘܢܦܠ ܥܠ [f]ܐܦ̈ܘܗܝ ‡[g]ܡܨܠܐ
ܘܐܡܪ: ܐܒܐ ܐܢ ܡܫܟܚ ܡܥܒܪ ܡܢܝ ܗܕܝܢ
ܟܣܐ: ܒܪܡ ܕܝ ܠܐ ܗܝܟ ܕܐܢܐ ܨܒܐ ܐܠܐ
ܗܝܟ [h]ܕܝ ܕܐܢܬ ܨܒܐ ܀

Codex A.

[l] ܡܢܗ [m] ܗܢܘ
[n] add ܐܢܬ
[p] ܕܕܝܬܝܩܐ
[q] ܕܚܠܦ [s] ܡܫܬܦܟܝܢ
[t] ܕܚܘܒܝܢ [u] ܐܡܪܢܐ
[v] ܕܒܗ
[w] ܕܝ omit [x] ܚܕܬܐ
[y] ܘܢܦܩ
[z] ܠܬܠܡܝܕܘܝ
‡ f. 114b.
[n] ܓܝܪ omit [a] ܒܗܢ
[c] ܘܬܬܒܕܪ
[d] ܐܡܪܝܢܐ ܕ omit
[g] ܕܝ omit [h] ܡܩܕܡ
[k] ܕܒܗܕܝܢ
[n] ܬܪܢܓܘܠܐ
[o] ܬܠܬ [p] ܐܠܝܦܬ
[q] ܕܝܡܡܬ [r] ܠܝܬܢܐ
[s] add ܕܝ
[u] ܐܙܠ
[b] ܢܦܫܝ
[c] ܕܡܘܬܐ
‡ f. 115a.
[e] ܘܩܪܒ [f] ܐܦܘܝ
[h] ܕܝ omit

Codex C.

[l] ܡܢܗ [n] add ܐܢܬ
[o] ܐܕܡܗ
[* Cod. B, ܗܘ]
[p] ܕܕܝܬܩܐ
[q] ܕܥܠ ܕܝܠܟܘܢ [q]
[r] ܣܓܝܢ omit
[w] ܕܝ omit [x] ܚܕܬ
[y] ܘܢܦܩ
[z] ܠܬܠܡܝܕܘܝ
[n] ܓܝܪ omit [b] ܠܠܝܐ
[e] ܕܡܪܥܝܬܐ
[f] ܘܩܐܡ [g] ܕܝ omit
[h] ܡܩܕܡ [i] ܒܦܛܪܘܣ
[j] ܐܡܝܢ omit
[k] ܕܒܗܕܝܢ
[l] ܥܕܡܟܐ [m] ܕܢܩܪܐ
[p] ܐܢܐ ܠܘܬ [p]
[q] ܕܝܡܡܬ
[s] add ܕܝ
† f. 93b.
[t] ܠܬܠܡܝܕܝ
[u] ܐܙܠ [w] ܠܗ
[x] ܠܦܛܪܘܣ
[y] ܡܢ ܒܢܝ [y]
[z] ܕܙܒܕܝ [a] ܡܬܥܩܐ
[d] ܗܟܐ [e] ܘܩܪܒ
[f] ܐܦ̈ܝ [g] ܡܨܠܐ
[h] ܕܝ omit

Codex A.	Codex B.	Codex C.
	Luke XXII. 43—45.	
ܥܪܘܒܐ وهدا الفصل من لوقا	43 ܘܐܬܚܙܝ[w] ܠܗ ܕܝ ܡܠܐܟ[x] ܡܢ ܫܡܝܐ ܡܥܫܢ[y]	ܘܐܬܚܙܝ[w] ܡܠܐܟ[x]
ܡܥܫܢ[y]	44 ܘܗܘܐ ܒܐܓܘܢ: ܘܡܨܠܐ ܗܘܐ ܒܬܘܩܦܐ[z] ܘܗܘܐ	ܒܬܘܩܦܐ[z]
ܒܬܘܩܦܐ[z]	ܕܝܥܗ[z] ܐܝܟ ܢܛܦܐ ܕܕܡܐ ܕܢܚܬܐ	ܕܐܬܪܡܝܐ[a]
ܕܐܬܪܡܐ[b]	ܥܠ[a] ܐܪܥܐ[b] ܕܢܚܬܝܢ[c] ܥܠ	ܕܐܬܪܡܐ[b] omit
ܢܚܬܝܢ[c] ܘܩܡ[d]	45 ܘܩܡ[d]: ܡܢ ܨܠܘܬܗ ܘܐܬܐ ܠܘܬ	ܢܚܬܝܢ[c]
	ܬܠܡܝܕܘܗܝ ܘܐܫܟܚ ܐܢܘܢ ܕܕܡܟܝܢ[e] ܗܘܘ	ܕܕܡܟܝܢ[e]
	ܡܢ ܥܩܬܐ ܕܐܢܘܢ ܀	
ܡܬܝ ܡܬܝ ورجعنا الى متاى		
43 ܗܘܐ ܕܝ ܐ[a] add	**Matt. XXVI. 44—XXVII. 2.**	
ܒܥܝܢܝܗܘܢ ܝܩܝܪܢ	44 ܘܫܒܩ[a e] ܐܢܘܢ ܗܘܐ[f] ܘܐܙܠ[g] ܨܠܝ[h] ܬܘܒ	ܘܫܒܩ[e] ܐܢܘܢ omit[f]
ܘܫܒܩ[e] ܘܐܙܠ[g]	45 ܬܠܝܬܝܬ ܗܘܐ[i] ܡܠܬܐ ܐܡܪ ܒܬܪܟܢ ܐܬܐ	ܗܘܐ add[i]
ܬܘܒ[h] ܗܘܐ add[i]	ܠܘܬ ܬܠܡܝܕܘܗܝ[j] ܘܐܡܪ ܠܗܘܢ ܕܡܟܝܢ[k] ܗܘܘ	ܬܠܡܝܕܘܗܝ[j]
ܕܡܟܝܢ[k]	ܘܐܬܬܢܝܚܘ[l] ܗܐ ܡܛܬ ܫܥܬܐ ܘܒܪܗ ܕܐܢܫܐ	ܕܡܟܝܢ[k] ܘܐܬܬܢܝܚܘ[l]
ܡܫܬܠܡ[m]	46 ܡܫܬܠܡ[m] ܠܐܝܕܝܗܘܢ[n] ܕܚܛܝܐ[o] ܀ ܩܘܡܘ	ܠܐܝܕܝܗܘܢ[n]
ܕܚܛܝܐ[o]	47 ܢܐܙܠ[p] ܠܢ[q] ܗܐ ܡܛܐ[r] ܗܘ ܕܡܫܠܡ ܠܝ: ܘܥܕ	ܢܐܙܠ[p] ܡܢ ܠܢ[q]
ܢܐܙܠ[p] ܡܛܐ[r]	ܗܘ ܡܡܠܠ[s] ܗܐ ܝܗܘܕܐ ܚܕ ܡܢ ܬܪܥܣܪܬܐ	
ܡܡܠܠ[s] ܕܐܚܪܝܢ[t]	ܐܬܐ ܘܥܡܗ ܟܢܫܐ ܣܓܝ ܥܡ ܣܝܦܐ	
‡ f. 115b.	ܘܚܘܛܪܐ ܡܢ ܠܘܬ[t] ‡ ܪܒܝ ܟܗܢܐ[u] ܕܝ[w] ܘܩܫܝܫܐ	ܕܐܚܪܝܢ[t] ܕܝ omit[u]
ܘܩܫܝܫܐ[w] ܕܝ omit[u]	48 ܕܥܡܐ: ܘܗܘ[x] ܕܝ ܕܡܫܠܡ ܗܘܐ ܝܗܒ ܠܗܘܢ	ܕܝ[x] ܘܐܡܪ[y]
ܘܐܡܪ[y] ܡܛܐ[a]	ܐܬܐ[y] ܐܡܪ † ܗܘ ܕܐܢܫܩ ܐܢܐ ܠܗ ܗܘ ܐܚܘܕ	† f. 94a.
ܠܡܚܕܐ[b] ܫܠܡ[c]	49 ܘܗܘ ܩܪܒ[z] ܠܗ: ܘܡܛܐ[a] ܠܡܚܕܐ[b] ܝܫܘܥ	ܩܪܒ[z] ܡܛܐ[a]
ܘܢܫܩ . . . ܕܝ omit[d]	ܘܐܡܪ ܠܗ: ܫܠܡ[c] ܠܟ ܪܒܝ[d] ܘܢܫܩ	ܫܠܡ[c]
	50 ܠܗ[e]: ܗܘ ܕܝ[d] ܝܫܘܥ ܐܡܪ ܠܗ ܚܒܪܐ	ܠܗ[e]
ܐܬܝܬ[g]	[f. 95b] ܥܠ ܡܢܐ ܕܐܬܝܬ: ܗܝܕܝܢ ܩܪܒܘ[f] ܐܘܫܛܘ[g]	ܩܪܒܘ[f] ܐܘܫܛܘ[g]
	51 ܥܠ ܝܫܘܥ: ܘܐܚܕܘ ܗܘ: ܘܗܐ ܚܕ	
ܐܝܕܗ[h]	ܡܢ ܗܠܝܢ ܕܥܡ ܝܫܘܥ: ܦܫܛ ܐܝܕܗ[h]	
ܣܦܣܪܐ[i]	ܘܫܡܛ ܣܦܣܪܗ[i] ܘܡܚܝܗ ܠܥܒܕܗ[j] ܕܪܒ[k] ܟܗܢܐ	ܣܦܣܪܐ[i] ܠܥܒܕܗ[j]
ܘܐܦܝܩ[n]	52 ܘܐܡܪ[l] ܠܗ[u] ܕܝ ܝܫܘܥ: ܗܦܘܟ ܠܗ[m] ܣܦܣܪܐ	ܪܒ[k] ܘܐܡܪ[l]
	ܠܕܘܟܬܗ: ܟܠ ܓܝܪ ܕܢܣܒܘܢ[n] ܣܦܣܪܐ	ܠܗ omit[m] ܒܣܦܣܪܐ[p]
ܐܒܕܝܢ[q] ܕܢܣܒܘܢ[o]	53 ܕܢܣܒܘܢ[o] ܒܣܦܣܪܐ[p] ܐܒܕܝܢ[q]: ܐܘ[r] ܠܐ	ܐܒܕܝܢ[q] ܐܘ ܠܐ[r]

Codex B.

ܣܒܪ ܐܢܬ [p]ܕܠܝܬ ܐܢܐ ܡܫܟܚ ܒܗ ܕܐܒܥܐ
ܡܢ ܐܒܐ [q]ܘܢܩܝܡ ܠܝ ܗܫܐ [r]ܝܬܝܪ ܡܢ [s]ܬܪܥܣܪ
54 ܠܓܝܘܢܐ[s] [t]ܠܚܘܝܢ ܕܡܠܐܟܐ: ܗܝܟ [u]ܐܘܟܝ
ܢܬܡܠܘܢ [v]ܟܬܒܐ [w]ܕܗܟܢܐ ܗܘܐ [x]ܕܝܢ [y]ܙܕܩܘܗ̇
55 [z]ܕܡܬܟܬܒ: ܒܗ ܕܝܢ ܒܗܝ ܫܥܬܐ ܐܡܪ ܡܪܢܐ
ܝܫܘܥ ܠܘܬ ܐܟ̈ܠܘܣܐ ܗܝܟ ܕܥܠ [a]ܠܓܝܣܐ
ܢܦܩܬܘܢ ܥܡ ܣܝܦܝܢ ‡ ܘܚܘܛܪܝܢ [b]ܕܬܐܚܕܘܢܢܝ
ܠܝ: ܟܠܝܘܡ ܥܡ [c]ܐܢܐ ܠܘܬܟܘܢ ܒܗܝܟܠܐ
[d]ܗܘܝܬ [e]ܝܬܒ ܡܠܦ ܘܠܐ [o]ܐܚܕܬܘܢܢܝ ܠܝ:
56 ܗܕܐ [f] [g]ܕܟܠܗ [h*]ܐܬܥܒܕܬ ܕܢܬܡܠܘܢ
[i]ܟܬܒܝܗܘܢ. [j]ܕܢܒܝܐ ܗܝܕܝܢ ܟܠܗܘܢ [k]ܬܠܡܝܕܐ
57 ܫܒܩܘܗܝ ܘܥܪܩܘ: ܗܢܘܢ [l]ܕܐܚܕܘ ܠܡܪܢܐ
ܝܫܘܥ [m]ܐܘܒ̈ܠܘ* ܗܘ ܠܘܬ ܩܝܦܐ ܪܒ ܟܗܢܐ[n]
ܕܐܬܟܢܫܘ [o]ܪܒ̈ܝ ܟܗܢܐ ܘܣܦܪ̈ܐ ܘܩܫܝ̈ܫܐ:
58 [p]ܫܡܥܘܢ ܕܝܢ [q]ܗܘܐ ܐܬܐ [r]ܒܬܪܗ †ܡܢ ܪܘܚܩܐ
ܥܕܡܐ ܠܕܪܬܗ ܕܪܒ ܟܗܢܐ: ܘܥܠ [s]ܥܠ
ܠܓܘ ܗܘܐ [t]ܝܬܒ ܥܡ [u]ܗܘܦܪ̈ܛܝܐ ܕܢܚܙܐ
[f. 96a]
59 [v]ܫܘܠܡܐ: ܪܒ̈ܝ ܟܗܢܐ [w]ܘܩܫܝ̈ܫܐ [x]ܘܟܢܘܫܬܐ
ܟܠܗ ܗܘܘ ܒܥܝܢ ܣܗܕܘ ܕܓܠܐ ܥܠ ܡܪܢܐ
60 ܝܫܘܥ: ܗܝܟ ܕܢܡܝܬܘܢܝܗܝ: ܘܠܐ ܗܘܘ
ܡܫܟܚܝܢ: ܘܐܦ ܕܩܪܒܘ [y]ܣܗܕܐ ܕܓܠܐ ܣܓܝܐܐ
61 ܒܚܪܬܐ ܕܝܢ ܩܪܒܘ ܬܪܝܢ [z]ܘܐܡܪܘ: ܗܢܐ
ܐܡܪ ܡܫܟܚ [a]ܕܝܢ ܐܢܐ ܕܐܫܪܐ [b]ܢܘܣܗ ܕܐܠܗܐ
62 ܘܠܬܠܬܐ ܝܘܡܝܢ [c]ܡܒܢܐ ܐܢܐ ܠܗ: ܘܩܡ ܪܒ
ܟܗܢܐ ܘܐܡܪ ܠܗ ܐܘܦ ܠܐ ‡ ܚܕܐ [d]ܠܝܬ
ܐܬ ܡܦܢܐ ܡܢ ܡܕܡ [e]ܕܗܠܝܢ ܡܣܗܕܝܢ ܥܠܝܟ:
63 ܗܘ [f]ܕܝܢ ܡܪܢܐ ܝܫܘܥ ܗܘܐ [g]ܫܬܩ: ܘܪܒ
ܟܗܢܐ ܐܡܪ ܠܗ: ܡܘܡܐ ܐܢܐ ܠܟ
ܒܐܠܗܐ ܚܝܐ: [h]ܕܬܐܡܪ ܠܢ ܐܢ ܐܢܬ ܗܘ
64 ܡܫܝܚܐ ܒܪܗ ܕܐܠܗܐ: [i]ܐܡܪ ܠܗ ܡܪܢܐ
ܝܫܘܥ: ܐܢܬ ܐܡܪܬ: ܒܪܡ ܕܝܢ ܐܡܪ [k]ܐܢܐ

Codex A.

[q] ܘܢܩܝܡ
[r] ܝܬܝܪ̈ [s] ܬܪܬܥܣܪ
[v] ܟܬ̈ܒܐ
[w] ܕܗܟܢܐ [x] *omit* ܕܝܢ
[z] ܕܡܬܟܬܒ
[a] ܠܓܝܣܐ
‡ f. 116*a*.
[b] ܕܬܐܚܕܘܢܢܝ
[c] *omit* ܐܢܐ
[e] ܝܬܒ [f] *add* ܕܝܢ
[g] ܟܠܗ̇ [h] ܐܬܥܒܕܬ
[j] ܕܢܒ̈ܝܐ [k] ܬܠܡ̈ܝܕܘܗܝ
[* *Sic* in Cod. B.]
[l] *add* ܕܝܢ [m] ܐܘܒܠܘܗ̇
[n] *add* ܠܗ [o] ܪ̈ܒܝ
[u] ܗܘܦܪ̈ܛܝܐ
[v] ܫܘܠܡܗ̇ [w] *add* ܕܝܢ
[x] ܘܟܢܘܫܬܐ
[a] *omit* ܕܝܢ [b] ܢܐܘܣܗ
‡ f. 116*b*.
[f] *omit* ܕܝܢ
[h] ܕܬܐܡܪ
[k] *omit* ܐܢܐ

Codex C.

[p] ܠܝܬ
[r] ܘܝܬܝܪ [s] ܬܪܬܥܣܪ
[t] ܠܚܘܝܢ [u] ܐܘܐ
[v] ܟܬܒܐ [w] ܕܗܟܢܐ
[x] *omit* ܕܝܢ [y] ܒܙܕܩܘܗ̇
[a] ܠܓܝܣܐ
[b] ܕܬܐܚܕܘܢܢܝ
[c] *omit* ܐܢܐ
[d] ܗܘܬ [e] ܝܬܒ
[o] ܐܚܕܬܘܢܢܝ
[f] *add* ܕܝܢ [g] ܟܠܗ̇
[h] ܐܬܥܒܕܬ
[i] ܟܬܒܝܗܘܢ
[m] ܐܘܒܠܘܗ̇ [n] *add* ܠܗ
† f. 94*b*.
[p] ܟܐܦܐ
[q] *omit* ܗܘܐ
[r] ܒܬܪܗ [s] ܥܠ
[t] ܝܬܒ [u] ܗܘܦܪ̈ܛܝܐ
[x] ܘܟܢܘܫܬܐ [w] *add* ܕܝܢ
[y] *omit* ܣܗܕܐ
[z] ܘܐܡܪܘ
[b] ܢܘܣܗ [a] *omit* ܕܝܢ
[c] ܒܢܐ
[d] *omit* ܠܝܬ
[e] ܕܗܠܝܢ
[g] ܫܬܩ
[h] ܕܬܐܡܪ
[i] *add* ܝܫܘܥ

Codex B.

ܠܟܘܢ ܕܡܢ ܟܕܘ ܬܚܡܘܢ ܠܒܪܗ [i]ܕܒܪܢܫܐ
[j]ܝܬܒ ܡܢ [k]ܝܡܝܢܗ ܕܚܝܠܐ ܘܐܬܐ ܥܠ
65 ܥܢܢܝܗܘܢ ܕܫܡܝܐ : ܒܟܝܢ ܨܪܝ ܟܗܢܐ ܪܒܐ
[l]ܡܐܢܘܗܝ ܘܐܡܪ ܓܕܦ : ܡܐ ܥܘܕ [m]ܐܢܢ
[n]ܨܪܝܟܝܢ [o]ܠܣܗܕܝܢ ܗܐ ܟܕܘ [p]ܫܡܥܬܘܢ [q]ܓܕܘܦܗ
66 ܡܐ ܗܢܐ ܠܟܘܢ ܗܘܢ :[r] ܐܓܒܘ ܘܐܡܪܝܢ
67 ܚܝܒ ܗܘ ܒܡܘܬܐ : ܒܟܝܢ ܪܩܘ [s]ܒܐ̈ܦܘܗܝ
ܘܡܚܘ ܝܬܗ [t]ܘܡܠܟܡܝܢ : ܘܐܚܪ̈ܢܝܢ ܡܚܘ ܝܬܗ
68 ܡܣܦܩܝܢ : ܘܐܡܪܝܢ † ܐܬܢܒܝ ܠܢ ܡܫܝܚܐ ܡܢ
69 [u]ܗܘ [v]ܗܘܐ ܕܡܚܝ [j]ܠܟ : [w]ܦ̈ܛܪܘܣ ܕܝܢ ܗܘܐ
[x]ܝܬܒ ܠܒܪ [y]ܕܪܬܐ : ܘܩܪܒܬ ܚܕܐ [z]ܛܠܝܬܐ
[f. 96b]
ܐܡܪܐ ܠܗ ܐܦ ܐܢܬ [a]ܗܘ [b]ܥܡ ܝܫܘܥ
70 [c]ܓܠܝܠܐ : ܗܘ ܕܝܢ ܟܦܪ ܩܕܡ ‡ ܟܠܗܘܢ :
[d]ܐܡܪ ܠܝܬ ܐܢܐ ܝܕܥ ܡܐ ܐܬܝ ܐܡܪܐ
71 ܘܠܐ ܡܒܝܢ : ܘܟܕ ܕܝܢ ܢܦܩ [e]ܠܬ̈ܪܥܐ ܚܡܬ
ܝܬܗ ܐܚܪܝ ܘܐܡܪܐ [f]ܠܗܠܝܢ [g]ܕܝܢ ܕܗܘܘ
ܬܡܢ ܐܘܦ [g]ܕܝܢ ܗܘܐ ܥܡ ܝܫܘܥ ܢܨܪܝܐ :
72 [h]ܘܬܘܒ ܟܦܪ ܒܡܘܡܬܐ ܕܠܝܬ ܐܢܐ [i]ܡܒܝܢ
73 [j]ܠܗܕܡ [k]ܓܒܪܐ : ܘܒܬܪ [l]ܙܥܘܪ ܩܪܒܘ ܗܠܝܢ
ܕܩܝܡܝܢ ܘܐܡܪܘ [m]ܠܦ̈ܛܪܘܣ : [n]ܡܫܪܪܐܝܬ :[o]
74 ܡܡܠܠܟ ܒܒܕ ܠܟ [p]ܡܕܥ : ܒܟܝܢ ܫܪܝ
ܡܚܪܡ ܘܝܡܐ ܕܠܝܬ ܐܢܐ ܡܒܝܢ ܠܓܒܪܐ
75 [q]ܗܕܡ : ܘܫܥܐ ܩܪܐ [r]ܬܪܢܓܘܠܐ : [s]ܘܐܕܟܪ
[w]ܦ̈ܛܪܘܣ ܡܠܬܗ ܕܡܪܐ ܝܫܘܥ ܕܐܡܪ ܠܗ :
ܕܥܕ ܠܐ ܩܪܐ [r]ܬܪܢܓܘܠܬܐ ܬܠܬܐ ܙܒܢܝܢ
ܬܟܦܘܪ ܒܝ : ܘܢܦܩ ܠܒܪ ܘܒܟܐ [t]ܡܪܝܪܐܝܬ :
XXVII.
1 ܘܟܕ ܕܝܢ ܗܘܐ ܨܦܪܐ ܢܣܒܘ [u]ܡܠܟܝܢ [v]
[w]ܪܒ̈ܝ ܟܗܢܐ [x]ܘܣܒܝ̈ܝܗ ܕܥܡܐ ܥܠ ܡܪܢܐ
2 ܝܫܘܥ [y]ܕܢܩܛܠܘܢ ܝܬܗ ܘܟܦܬܘ ܝܬܗ ܘܐܘܒܠܘ
ܝܬܗ ܘܡܣܪܘ ܝܬܗ [z]ܠܦ̈ܢܛܝܘܣ ܦܝܠܛܘܣ
[a]ܗܓܡܘܢܐ [b] ⁘

Codex A.

[i] ܕܒܪܢܫܐ
[j] ܝܬܒ   [k] ܝܡܝܢܐ
[o] ܣܗ̈ܕܝܢ
[p] ܫ̈ܡܥܬܘܢ
[r] add ܕܝܢ   [s] ܒܐ̈ܦܘܗܝ
[t] ܡܠܟܡܝܢ
[v] ܗܘܝܢ
[y] ܒܕܪܬܐ   [z] ܛܠܝܬܐ
[a] ܗܘܝܬ   [c] ܓܠܝܠܝܐ
‡ f. 117a.
[g] omit ܕܝܢ
[h] ܘܬܘܒ   [j] ܠܗܝ
[k] ܠܓܒܪܐ   [l] ܙܥܘܪ
[o] add ܐܘܦ
[p] ܝܕܥ   [q] ܗܘܝܢ
[r] ܬܪܢܓܘܠܐ
[s] ܘܐܬܕܟܪ
[v] add ܟܘܠ   [w] ܪ̈ܒܢܝ
[x] ܘܣܒ̈ܝܝܗܘܢ
[y] ܕܢܩܛܠܘܢ
[z] ܠ̈ܦܢܛܝܘܣ
[a] ܗܓܡܘܢܐ
[b] add ܥܠܡ

Codex C.

[i] ܕܒܪܢܫܐ
[l] ܡܐܢܘ   [m] ܐܢܢ
[n] ܨܪܝܟܝܢ   [o] ܣܗܕܝܢ
[p] ܫܡܥܬܘܢ
[q] ܓܕܘܦܗ   [r] add ܕܝܢ
[s] ܒܐ̈ܦܘܗܝ
† f. 95a.
[u] omit ܗܘ   [j] ܝܬܟ
[w] ܦܛܪܘܣ   [x] ܝܬܒ
[y] ܒܕܪܬܐ   [a] ܗܘܝܬ
[b] add ܐܡܪܐ
[c] ܓܠܝܠܝܐ   [d] ܘܐܡܪ
[e] ܠܬܪܥܐ
[f] ܠܗܠܝܢ   [g] omit ܕܝܢ
[h] ܘܬܘܒ   [i] ܡܒܝܢ
[j] ܕܝܢ   [m] ܠܦܛܪܘܣ
[n] ܡܫܪܪܬ
[o] add ܐܘܦ
[t] ܡܪܝܪ
[u] ܡܠܟܝܢ   [v] add ܟܘܠ
[w] ܪܒܢܐ
[y] ܕܢܩܛܠܘܢ
[z] ܠܦܢܛܝܘܣ

Codex A.	Codex B.	Codex C.
	CL.	
	JOHN XIII. 31—XVIII. 1.	

Codex B.

ܨܦܪܐ[a] ܠܠܝܠܝܬ[b] ܐܘܢܓܠܝܘܢ † ܐܠܚܡܝܣ[c] ܕܡܢ
ܝܘܚܢܢ ܗܘܐ ܡܩܪܝܬ ܝܘܚܢܢ[a c]: [y] ܐܡܪ
31 ܡܪܢ[z] ܠܬܠܡܝܕܘܝ: ܗܐ ܐܫܬܒܚ ܒܪܗ ܕܐܢܫܐ
32 ܘܐܠܗܐ ܐܫܬܒܚ ܒܗ: [a] ܘܡܢ[b] ܚܝܐ ܗܘ
33 [c]ܡܫܬܒܚ[d] ܒܗ[b] ܒܢܝ ܙܥܘܪܝ[e] ܥܘܕ ܐܢܐ
ܥܡܟܘܢ: ܘܬܒܥܘܢܢܝ[f] ܘܗܝܟ ܕܐܡܪܬ ܠܗ: ܗܘܢ
ܠܝܗܘܕܝܐ[g] ܕܠܡܐ[h] ܕܠܗܢ ܕܐܢܐ ܐܙܠ
ܐܢܐ[i] ܐܢܬܘܢ[k] ܠܝܬ ܐܢܬܘܢ[l] ܝܟܠܝܢ ܠܡܐܬܐ:
34 ܘܟܕܘ ܠܟܘܢ ܐܢܐ ܐܡܪ: [m]ܦܘܩܕܢܐ ܚܕܬܐ
[n]ܕܬܚܒܘܢ ܚܕ ܠܚܕ ܐܝܟܢܐ ܕܐܚܒܬ ܠܟܘܢ: ܐܦ
ܐܢܬܘܢ ܬܚܒܘܢ ܠܚܕܕܐ[o]: ܒܗܕܐ
ܢܕܥܘܢ ܟܠ ܕܬܠܡܝܕܝ[p] ܐܢܬܘܢ: ܐܢ ܚܘܒܐ
35 [q]ܬܗܘܘܢ ܡܚܒܝܢ ܠܚܕܕܐ[o]: ܒܗܕܐ
[r]ܢܕܥܘܢ[s] ܟܠܗܘܢ ܕܐܢܬܘܢ ܬܠܡܝܕܝ[t]
[u]ܐܢ ܬܗܘܐ ܒܟܘܢ ܚܘܒܐ ܠܚܕܕܐ[o]:
36 ܐܡܪ ܠܗ ܫܡܥܘܢ ܟܐܦܐ[v] ܡܪܢ ܠܐܝܟܐ
ܐܙܠ[w] ܐܢܬ: ܐܡܪ ܠܗ ܝܫܘܥ ܠܐܝܟܐ ܕܐܢܐ
ܐܙܠ[x] ܠܝܬ ܐܢܬ[w] ‡[y] ܝܟܠ ܐܢܬ ܠܡܐܬܐ ܒܬܪܝ
ܗܫܐ[z]: ܒܚܪܬܐ[a] ܕܝܢ ܬܐܬܐ[b] ܒܬܪܝ
37 ܗܫܐ: ܐܡܪ ܠܗ ܫܡܥܘܢ[v] ܡܪܢ ܠܡܢܐ ܠܝܬ
ܐܢܐ[y] ܝܟܠ ܠܡܐܬܐ ܒܬܪܟ: ܢܦܫܝ[c] ܚܠܦܝܟ
38 [d]ܕܝܢ ܐܢܐ[e] ܐܣܝܡ: [f]ܐܡܪ ܠܗ ܝܫܘܥ ܢܦܫܟ
ܚܠܦܝ ܬܣܝܡ[e]: ܐܡܝܢ ܐܡܝܢ[g] ܐܡܪ ܐܢܐ ܠܟ[h]:
ܕܠܐ ܩܪܐ ܬܪܢܓܘܠܐ[i] ܥܕܡܐ ܕܬܟܦܘܪ ܒܝ ܬܠܬ
XIV. 1 ܙܒܢܝܢ[j]: ܠܐ ܢܬܕܠܚ ܠܒܟܘܢ ܗܝܡܢܘ ܒܐܠܗܐ
ܘܒܝ ܗܝܡܢܘ: ܒܒܝܬܗ ܕܐܒܝ ܡܘܬܒܐ ܣܓܝܐܝܢ
2 ܐܝܬ[k] ܘܐܠܘ ܠܐ: ܐܡܪ ܗܘܝܬ[l] † ܠܟܘܢ ܕܐܙܠ
ܐܢܐ[l] ܡܛܝܒ[m] * ܐܬܪܐ: ܘܐܢ ܕܝܢ[n] ܐܙܠ ܐܢܐ

Codex A.

[b] ܠܠܝܠܝܬ
[c] ܐܘܢܓܠܝܘܢ ܕܚܡܝܣ ܕܦܨܚܐ ܕܐܠܡܫܝܚ ܘܐܟܠܬ ܡܢ ܝܘܚܢܢ[c]
[z] ܠܬܠܡܝܕܘܝ
[a] *add* ܐܡܪ ܐܠܗܐ ܡܫܬܒܚ ܠܗ ܒܗ:
[c] ܡܫܬܒܚ [d] *omit* ܒܗ
[e] ܙܥܘܪܝ [f] ܗܘܢ
[g] ܠܝܗܘܕܝܐ [i] ܐܢܐ
[l] ܝܟܠܝܢ [m] ܚܕ
[n] ܕܬܚܒܘܢ
[o] ܠܚܕܕܐ
[p] ܕܐܢܬܘܢ
[r] ܢܕܥܘܢ [s] ܟܠ
[t] ܬܠܡܝܕܝ ܐܢܬܘܢ
[w] ܐܙܠ [x] ܕܐܢܐ
‡ f. 118*a*.
[y] ܝܟܠ [a] ܒܚܪܬܐ
[b] ܬܐܬܐ
[c] ܢܦܫܝ
[d] *omit* ܕܝܢ
[g] ܢܦܫܟ
[h] *add* ܐܡܝܢ [i] ܬܪܢܓܘܠܐ
[j] ܬܠܬ ܙܒܢܝܢ
[k] *omit* ܐܝܬ
[m] ܡܛܝܒ [n] ܐܢ

Codex C.

ܨܦܪܐ[a] ܠܠܝܠܝܬ ܐܘܢܓܠܝܘܢ : ܐܠܚܡܝܣ ܐܠܚܕܢܝܬ ܐܠܬ ܕܡܢ ܝܘܚܢܢ[a]
† f. 95*b*.
[y] *add* ܘܟܬܒܐ ܡܩܪܝܬܐ
[a] *add* ܐܡܪ ܐܠܗܐ ܡܫܬܒܚ ܠܗ ܒܗ
[b] *omit* ܘܡܢ . . . ܒܗ
[g] ܠܝܗܘܕܝܐ[g]
[h] ܠܗܘܢ
[k] *omit* ܐܢܬܘܢ
[l] ܝܟܠܝܢ
[n] ܕܬܚܒܘܢ
[p] ܕܐܢܬܘܢ
[q] *omit* ܬܗܘܘܢ
[u] ܐܢ
[v] ܟܐܦܐ
[x] ܕܐܢܐ
[z] ܗܫܐ [b] ܬܐܬܐ
[d] *omit* ܕܝܢ [e] ܐܣܝܡ
[f] ܐܡܪ [i] ܩܪܐ
[j] ܬܠܬ ܙܒܢܝܢ
[l] ܐܡܪ ܗܘܝܬ[l]
[m] ܡܛܝܒ
† f. 96*a*.

[* *Sic* in Cod. B.]

Codex A.	Codex B.	Codex C.
ⁿܐܙܝܠ ᵒܕܐܬܩܢ	ܐܢܐ ܐܡܪܬ ܠܟܘܢ : ܕܐܢܐ ⁿܐܙܠ ᵒܠܡܬܩܢ	ᵒܕܐܬܩܢ
	3 ܠܟܘܢ ܐܬܪ : ᵖܘܐܢ ᑫܐܙܠ ܘܐܬܩܢ ܠܟܘܢ	ᵖܘܐܝܢ ᑫܗܐܙܠ
ʳomit ܕܝ	ܐܬܪ : ܬܘܒܢ ܐܢܐ ܐܬܐ ʳܕܝ ܠܘܬܟܘܢ	ʳomit ܕܝ ⁿܕܡܬܩܢ
ˢܘܡܕܒܪ ᵗܕܗܝܟ	ˢܘܡܕܒܪ ܠܟܘܢ ܠܘܬܝ : ᵗܗܝܟ ܕܐܢܐ ܗܘܐ [f. 97b]	ˢܘܡܕܒܪ ᵗܕܗܝܟ
	4 ܐܘܦ ܐܢܬܘܢ ᵘܬܗܘܘܢ : ᵛܘܠܗܝܟ ܕܐܢܐ ⁿܐܙܠ	ᵘܬܗܘܢ ᵛܘܠܗܠܝܢ
	ܝܕܥܝܢ ܐܢܬܘܢ ܐܘܦ ܐܘܪܚܐ ܐܢܬܘܢ ܡܟܝܪܝܢ :	
ʷܡܪܢܐ ˣܠܝܬ ܐܢܢ	5 ܐܡܪ ܠܗ ܬܐܘܡܣ ʷܡܪܝ ˣܠܝܬܢ ܝܕܥܝܢ ܠܗܝܟ	ʷܡܪܢܐ ˣܠܝܬ ܐܢܢ
ʸܐܢܗ	ܐܬ ⁿܐܙܠ : ܘܗܝܟ ʸܐܢܢ ܝܕܥܝܢ ܕܢܚܙܐ	ʸܐܢܗ
‡ f. 118b.	6 ܡܟܝܪܝܢ ܐܘܪܚܐ : ܐܡܪ ܠܗ ܡܪܢܐ ‡ܝܫܘܥ	
	ܐܢܐ ܗܘ ܐܘܪܚܐ ᶻܘܩܘܫܛܐ ܘܚܝܝܐ : ᵃܐܢܫ	ᶻܘܩܘܫܛܐ ᵃܐܢܫ
	ܠܐ ܐܬܐ ܠܘܬ ܐܒܐ ܐܠܐ ܐܢ ܒܝ	
	7 ܕܒܝܠܝ : ᵇܐܢ ܐܚܪܬܘܢ ܠܝ : ܐܘܦ ܠܐܒܐ	ᵇܐܝܢ
	ܐܢܬܘܢ ᶜܗܘܝܢ ܡܟܝܪܝܢ : ܘܡܢ ܟܕܘ ܐܢܬܘܢ	ᶜomit ܗܘܝܢ
	8 ܡܟܝܪܝܢ ܠܗ ܘܚܡܝܬܘܢ ܝܬܗ : ܐܡܪ ܠܗ ʳܕܝ	
ᵈܦܝܠܝܦܘܣ	ᵈܦܝܠܝܦܘܣ ܡܪܢܐ ܐܘܕܥ ܠܢ ܐܒܐ ᵉܘܡܣܦܩܬܢ :	ᵈܦܠܝܦܘܣ ᵉܘܡܣܬܦܩܝܢ
ᵉܘܡܣܦܩܬܢ ᵍܗܕܝܢ	9 ܐܡܪ ܠܗ ܡܪܢܐ ܝܫܘܥ ܟܡܠ ᵍܗܕܝܢ ܐܙܒܢܐ	ᵍܗܕܐ
	ܐܢܐ ܥܡܟܘܢ ܘܠܐ ܐܚܟܡܬ ܝܬܝ ʰܦܝܠܝܦܐ :	ʰܦܠܝܦܐ
	ܡܢ ܕܚܡܐ ܝܬܝ ܚܡܐ ܠܐܒܐ : ܘܗܝܟ	
	10 ܐܬ ܐܡܪ ܐܘܕܥ ܠܢ ܐܒܐ ܠܝܬ ܐܬ	
	ܡܗܝܡܢ ܕܐܢܐ ܒܐܒܐ ܘܐܒܐ ܒܝ ܐܝܬ	
	ܗܘ : ܡܠܝܐ ܗܠܝܢ ܕܐܢܐ ⁱܡܠܠ ܠܟܘܢ ܡܢ	ⁱܡܡܠܠ
ʲⁱܡܡܠܠ ᵏܗܕܝܢ	ܢܦܫܝ ܠܝܬ ܐܢܐ ʲܡܡܠܠ : ܐܒܐ ᵏܗܕܝܢ	ʲܡܡܠܠ
	11 ܕܡܕܝܪ ܒܝ ܗܘ ܥܒܕ ܥܘܒܕܝܐ : ܗܘܘ	
ˡܠܝ	ܡܗܝܡܢܝܢ ˡܒܝ ܕܐܢܐ ܒܐܒܐ ܘܐܒܐ ܒܝ :	ᵐܘܐܝܢ ˡܠܝ
ⁿܦܝ ᵒܠܚܠܠ	ᵐܘܐܢ ܠܐ ⁿܒܝ ᵒܠܚܠܠ †ܥܘܒܕܝܐ ܗܘܘ	† f. 96b.
	12 ܡܗܝܡܢܝܢ : ܐܡܝܢ ܐܡܝܢ ܐܡܪ ܐܢܐ ܠܟܘܢ :	
	ܕܡܢ ܕܡܗܝܡܢ ܒܝ ܥܘܒܕܝܐ ܗܠܝܢ ܕܐܢܐ ܥܒܕ	ᵖܘܪܒܪܒܝܢ ᑫadd ܗܘ
‡ f. 119a.	ܐܘܦ ܗܘ ܥܒܕ : ᵖܘܪܒܝܢ ‡ܡܢ ܗܠܝܢ ᑫܥܒܕ :	ʳomit ܐܢܐ
ˢܐܙܝܠ	13 ܕܐܢܐ ܠܘܬ ܐܒܐ ʳܐܢܐ ˢܐܙܠ : ܘܡܐ	ᵗܕܬܫܐܠܘܢ
ᵘܐܢܐ	[f. 98a] * ᵗܕܬܫܐܠܘܢ ܒܫܡܝ ܗܕܐ ᵘܕܐܢܐ ܥܒܕ :	[* Ver. 14 is omitted.]
	15 ᵒܠܚܠܠ ܕܬܪܚܡܘܢ ܐܒܐ ܒܝ ܒܒܪܐ : ʷܐܢ	ᵘܐܢܐ ʷܐܝܢ

Codex A.	Codex B.	Codex C.
[g]ܦܘܩܕܐܢܝ	16 ܡܚܒܝܢ ܐܢܬܘܢ ܠܝ [g]ܦܘܩܕܝ ܛܪܘ: ܘܐܢܐ	
[i]ܚܪܢ	ܒܥܐ ܡܢ ܐܒܐ: ܘܗܘ ܝܗܒ ܠܟܘܢ [i]ܐܘܚܪܢ	[i]ܚܘܪܢ
	17 [j]ܡܢܚܡܢ ܕܝܗܐ [k]ܥܡܪ ܥܡܟܘܢ ܠܥܠܡ ܪܘܚܐ	[j]ܡܢܚܡܢ
[l]ܕܥܠܡܐ	ܕܩܘܫܛܐ ܗܢܐ [l]ܕܥܠܡܐ ܠܐ [m]ܝܟܠ ܕܝܩܒܠ	[k] omit ܥܡܪ [m]ܚܝܠ
[n]ܡܚܟܡ	ܕܠܐ ܚܡܐ ܠܗ ܘܠܐ [n]ܡܚܟܡ ܠܗ: ܐܢܬܘܢ	[n]ܡܚܟܡ
	ܕܝ ܡܚܟܡܝܢ ܝܬܗ ܕܒܝܢܬܟܘܢ ܗܘ ܥܡܪ	
	18 ܘܒܟܘܢ ܗܘ ܗܘܐ: ܠܝܬ ܐܢܐ ܫܒܩ ܝܬܟܘܢ	
[p]ܩܠܝܠ	19 ܝܬܡܝܢ: ܐܬܐ ܐܢܐ [o]ܠܘܬܟܘܢ: ܘܥܘܕ [p]ܩܠܝܠ	[o] omit ܠܘܬܟܘܢ
[s]ܘܥܠܡܐ	[s]ܘܥܠܡܐ ܡܢ ܟܕܘ ܠܐ ܚܡܐ ܠܝ: ܐܢܬܘܢ	
	ܕܝ ܚܡܝܢ ܠܝ: ܕܐܢܐ ܚܝ ܘܐܢܬܘܢ [t]ܚܝܝܢ	[t]ܚܝܐܢ
[v]ܬܕܥܘܢ	20 ܐܢܬܘܢ: [u]ܒܗܘ ܝܘܡܐ [v]ܬܕܥܘܢ ܕܐܢܐ	[u]ܒܐܗܘ
	21 ܒܐܒܐ ܘܐܢܬܘܢ ܒܝ ܘܐܢܐ ܒܟܘܢ: ܟܘܠ	
[x]ܦܘܩܕܐܢܝ	[w]ܡܢ ܕܒܝܕܗ [x]ܦܘܩܕܝ [y]ܘܢܛܪ ܠܗܘܢ ܝܬܗ ܗܘ	[w]ܕܡܢ [y]ܘܢܛܪ
	ܗܕܝܢ ܕܡܚܒ ܠܝ: ܘܡܢ ܕܡܚܒ ܠܝ ܡܬܪܚܡ	
	ܡܢ ܐܒܐ: ܘܐܢܐ ܡܚܒ ܠܗ ܘܐܢܐ	
‡ f. 119b.	22 [z]ܡܘܕܥ ܠܗ ܢܦܫܝ: ܐܡܪ ܠܗ ‡ ܝܗܘܕܐ [a]ܠܐ	[z]ܡܘܕܥ
	ܐܣܟܪܝܘܛܐ: ܡܪܝ ܘܡܢܐ ܐܬ [b]ܥܬܝܕ ܕܐܬ	[a] omit ܠܐ [b]ܥܬܝܕ
[d]ܠܥܠܡܐ	ܥܬܝܕ [c]ܕܬܘܕܥ ܠܢ ܢܦܫܟ ܘܠܐ [d]ܠܥܠܡܐ:	[c]ܕܬܘܕܥ
	23 ܐܓܝܒ ܡܪܢ ܝܫܘܥ † ܘܐܡܪ ܠܗ: ܐܢ ܐܝܬ	† f. 97a.
	ܐܢܫ ܡܚܒ ܠܝ ܡܠܬܝ ܝܗܘܐ [e]ܡܛܪ: ܘܐܒܐ	[e]ܡܛܪ
	ܡܚܒ ܠܗ ܘܠܘܬܗ ܐܬܝܢ ܐܢܚ: [f]ܘܡܫܪܝܬܐ	[f]ܘܡܫܪܝܬܐ
[g]ܐܢܚ	24 ܠܘܬܗ [g]ܐܢܚ ܥܒܕܝܢ: ܡܢ ܕܠܐ [h]ܡܚܒ ܠܝ	[h]ܡܚܒܒ (sic)
[i]ܢܛܪ	ܡܠܬܝ ܠܐ [i]ܡܛܪ: ܘܡܠܬܐ ܕܫܡܥܝܢ ܗܕܐ	[i]ܡܛܪ
	ܕܐܢܬܘܢ ܫܡܥܝܢ ܠܝܬ ܗܝ ܕܝܠܝ ܐܠܐ ܕܐܒܐ	[k]ܕܫܠܚܢ
[k]ܕܫܠܚܢ	25 [k]ܕܫܠܚܢ ܝܬܝ: ܗܠܝܢ ܡܠܠܬ [f. 98b] [l]ܠܟܘܢ ܟܕ ܐܢܐ	[l] omit ܠܟܘܢ
	26 ܥܡܪ ܠܘܬܟܘܢ: ܘܡܢܚܡܢܐ ܕܝ [m]ܪܘܚܐ	[m]ܕܪܘܚܐ
	ܕܩܘܕܫܐ ܕܝ ܕܡܫܠܚ ܐܒܐ ܒܫܡܝ: ܗܘ	
[n]ܘܡܕܟܪ	ܡܠܦ ܠܟܘܢ ܟܘܠܐ [n]ܘܡܕܟܪ ܠܟܘܢ ܟܘܠ	[o] add ܫܠܡܐ ܐܢܐ
[o] add ܫܠܡܐ ܐܢܐ	27 ܡܐ ܕܡܠܠܬ ܠܟܘܢ: [o] [p]ܫܠܡܐ ܕܝܠܝ ܐܢܐ	ܫܒܩ ܠܟܘܢ :
ܫܒܩ ܠܟܘܢ :	ܝܗܒ ܠܟܘܢ: ܠܐ [q] ܗܟܢ ܡܐ [r]ܕܥܠܡܐ	[q] add ܟܕ [p]ܫܠܡܝ
[p]ܫܠܡܝ [r]ܕܥܠܡܐ	ܝܗܒ ܠܟܘܢ ܠܐ ܢܬܒܗܠ ܠܒܒܟܘܢ ܘܠܐ	[r]ܕܥܠܡܐ

Codex A. | *Codex B.* | *Codex C.*

Codex B.

28 ܕܢܩܘܡ : ܡܩܕܡܬܘܢ ܕܐܢܐ ܐܩܕܡܬ ܠܟܘܢ
ܕܐܢܐ [n]ܐܙܠ ܘܐܬܐ ܠܓܠܝܠܘܢ : ܐܡܪ
ܗܘܐ ܟܐܦܐ [f]ܡܣܒܪ ܠܝ ܐܢܬ ܫܡܥܘܢ ܕܐܢܐ
[n]ܐܙܠ [g]ܠܘܬܟ ܐܒܐ[g] : ܕܐܒܐ ܪܒ ܗܘ ܡܢܝ :
29 ܐܡܪ ܒܗ ܐܡܪܬ ܠܟܘܢ ܡܢ ܟܕ ܠܐ
30 ܬܬܕܟܪ ܕܟܕ [‡] ܬܬܚܙܐ ܒܫܡܫܐ ܟܕ ܠܝܬ
ܐܢܐ [h]ܡܛܠܠ ܟܕܘܢ ܫܡܥ : [i]ܐܬܐ ܗܘ[i] ܐܢ
ܐܪܟܘܫ ܕܗܕܝܢ [j]ܟܠܗܘܢ : ܘܟܦܪܝ ܠܝܬ ܠܗ
31 [k]ܟܘܠܗ : ܐܠܐ [l]ܕܝܕܥܝ [j]ܟܠܗܘܢ ܕܐܢܐ
[m]ܡܫܝܚ ܠܟܐܦܐ : ܘܗܘܝܢ ܡܢܐ ܕܩܘܡ ܢܬܝ
ܐܟܢܐ [n]ܗܕܝܢ ܐܢܐ ܟܕ ܘܩܘܡ [o]ܫܘܠ [p] ܡܢ
XV. 1 ܟܕ : ܐܢܐ ܗܘ ܒܨܦܪܐ [†] [q]ܡܫܬܠܛܐ ܘܐܟܐ
2 ܗܘ ܐܪܫܘܐ : ܟܘܠ [r]ܒܡܟܪܐ ܕܟܕ ܕܠܐ
ܡܬܬܐ ܦܢܝܢ ܡܢܝܢ ܗܘ ܠܗ : ܘܟܘܠ [s]ܗܕܐ
3 [t]ܕܡܬܢܝܬܐ ܦܢܝܢ ܥܡܗ ܬܬܬܐ : ܟܕܪ [u]ܕܝ
ܐܬܘܢ ܕܡܢ [w]ܠܚܠܠ ܡܠܬܐ [z]ܗܕܐ ܕܐܡܪܬ
4 ܠܟܘܢ : ܒܬܪܘ ܟܕ ܘܐܢܐ ܟܕܘܢ : ܗܘܝܢ
ܡܢ [a] [b]ܕܟܕܡܬܪܬܐ ܠܐ [c]ܢܝܠܐ [d]ܡܬܬܐ ܦܢܝܢ
ܡܢ ܠܟܘܢ [e]ܐܠܐ ܐ[e] ܡܬܬܐ ܒܨܦܪܐ :
[f]ܗܕܝܢ ܐܡܪ ܐܬܘܢ ܐ ܠܐ ܬܬܬܪܘܢ
5 ܟܕ : ܐܢܐ ܗܘ ܒܨܦܪܐ ܘܐܬܘܢ [g]ܒܡܟܪܬܐ
[f. 99a] ܡܢ ܕܡܬܬܪ ܟܕ ܘܐܢܐ ܟܗ [h]ܗܕܝܢ [i]ܡܬܬܐ
ܦܢܝܢ ܥܡܗ : ܠܟܪ ܡܫܝܚ ܠܝܬ ܐܬܘܢ ܡܢܟܘܢ
6 ܕܬܬܕܟܪܘܢ [j]ܟܘܠܗܝܢ : ܐܠܐ ܗܘܐ [l]ܐܚܪܢ
[m]ܠܐ ܗܘܬܪ ܟܕ [n]ܬܬܕܟܪ ܠܟܪ : ܗܘܝܢ [‡] ܡܢܐ
[o]ܐܢ [p]ܕܟܕܡܬܪܬܐ [q]ܘܟܕܝ : [r]ܘܗܘܢ ܡܫܝܚܝܢ
7 [s]ܬܬܗܘܢ [t]ܘܐܢܫ ܒܘܪܐ [u]ܘܡܢܕܝܢ : [w]ܐ [x]ܕܝ
ܬܬܬܪܘܢ ܟܕ [y]ܘܡܬܠܛܝ ܒܨܦܪܐ [z]ܒܬܬܪܘܢ :
ܡܢ [a]ܕܐܬܘܢ ܢܩܘܡ ܥܠܘܗ [b]ܘܬܬܕܟܪܘܢ ܠܟܘܢ :
8 ܒܗܕܐ ܫܬܬܘܢ ܐܟܕܐ ܕܦܢܝܢ ܥܡܗ ܬܬܬܘܢ
9 ܘܗܬܘܢ ܠܝ ܬܠܡܝܕܝ : ܗܘܝܢ ܡܢܐ ܕܐܫܝܚ

Codex A.

[n]ܐܙܠ
[f]ܡܣܒܪܝܢ
[g]ܠܘܬܟܐ
‡ f. 120a.
[j]ܟܠܗܘܢ
[k]ܟܘܠܗܘܢ [l]ܕܝܕܥܝ
[n]ܗܕܝܢ ܠܝ [p]*add*
[r]ܒܡܟܪܐ
[s]ܗܕܐ [t]ܕܡܬܢܝܬܐ
ܕܝ [u]*omit*
ܗܕܐ [z]*omit*
ܐܢ [a]*add*
[b]ܕܟܕܡܬܪܬܐ
[c]ܢܝܠܐ [d]ܡܬܬܐ
[f]ܗܕܝܢ
[g]ܒܡܟܪܬܐ
[i]ܡܬܬܐ
[j]ܟܘܠܗܝܢ ܠܐ [m]*omit*
[n]ܬܬܕܟܪ ܐܢ [o]*omit*
‡ f. 120b.
[p]ܕܟܕܡܬܪܬܐ [q]ܘܟܕܝ
[r]ܘܗܘܢ [s]ܬܬܗܘܢ
[t]ܘܐܢܫ [u]ܘܡܢܕܝܢ
[y]ܘܡܬܠܛܝ [z]ܒܬܬܪܘܢ
[b]ܘܬܬܕܟܪܘܢ

Codex C.

[f]ܡܣܒܪ
[h]ܡܛܠܠ [i]ܐܬܐ ܗܘ
[l]ܕܝܕܥܝ
[m]ܡܫܝܚ
[o]ܫܘܠ [q]ܡܫܬܠܛܐ
† f. 97a.
[r]ܒܡܟܪܐ
ܕܝ [u]*omit* [w]ܠܚܠܠ
ܗܕܐ [z]*omit*
ܐܢ [a]*add*
[b]ܕܟܕܡܬܪܬܐ [c]ܢܝܠܐ
[d]ܡܬܬܐ
[e]ܐܢ ܐܠܐ[e]
[g]ܒܡܟܪܬܐ
[h]ܗܕܐ
[j]ܟܘܠܗ [l]ܐܚܪܢ
ܠܐ [m]*omit* [n]ܬܬܕܟܪ
ܐܢ [o]*omit*
[p]ܕܟܕܡܬܪܬܐ
[q]ܘܟܕܝ [s]ܬܬܗܘܢ
[t]ܘܐܢܫ [u]ܘܡܢܕܝܢ
[w]ܐܢ [x]ܕܐܢܝ
[y]ܘܡܬܠܛܝ [a]ܐܬܘܢ
[b]ܘܬܬܕܟܪܘܢ

Codex A.	Codex B.	Codex C.
	ܝܬܝ ܐܟܢܐ ܐܘܦ ܐܢܐ ܐܚܒܬ ܝܬܟܘܢ :	
	10 ܟܬܪܘ ܒܚܒܬܝ ܕܝܠܝ : [k]ܐܢ ܬܛܪܘܢ	[k]ܐܝܢ
[l]ܦܩܘܕܝܐ	[l]ܦܩܘܕܝ : [o]ܡܟܬܪܝܢ ܐܢܬܘܢ [p]ܕܝ ܒܚܒܬܝ	[o] *omit* . . . ܡܟܬܪܝܢ
[p] *omit* ܕܝ [r]ܦܩܘܕܘ	ܕܝܠܝ : ܗܝܟ ܡܐ ܕܐܘܦ ܐܢܐ [r]ܦܩܘܕܝ[o] ܕܐܒܐ	. . . ܦܩܘܕܝ
	11 ܢܛܪܬ : ܘܐܢܐ ܡܟܬܪ ܒܚܒܬܗ : ܗܠܝܢ ܡܠܠܬ	
	ܠܟܘܢ † ܕܚܕܘܬܝ ܕܝܠܝ ܬܗܘܐ ܒܓܘܟܘܢ :	† f. 98*a*.
	12 ܘܚܕܘܬܟܘܢ ܬܬܡܠܐ : ܗܕܝܢ ܗܘ ܦܩܘܕܝ	
[s]ܠܚܠܝܦ	ܕܝܠܝ ܕܬܗܘܢ ܡܚܒܝܢ [r]ܦܠܚܒܘܢ [s]ܠܚܠܝܦ :	[r]ܦܠܚܒܘܢ (*sic*)
[t]ܪܒܐ [u] *add* ܡܢ	13 ܗܝܟ ܡܐ ܕܐܚܒܬ ܝܬܟܘܢ : [t]ܪܒܐ [u]ܗܕܐ	[t]ܪܒܐ [u] *add* ܡܢ
[v]ܐܢܫ [w]ܕܝܫܝܡ	ܚܒܬܐ ܠܝܬ [v]ܠܐܢܫ ܐܠܐ [w]ܕܝܫܝܡ ܢܦܫܗ	[w]ܕܝܫܝܡ
[y]ܪܚܡܝܐ	14 ܚܠ ܦܠܓ [x]ܪܚܡܘܝ : ܐܢܬܘܢ [y]ܪܚܡܘܝ ܐܢܬܘܢ	[x]ܪܚܡܝ [y]ܪܚܡܝ
[z]ܡܦܩܕ [a]ܠܟܘܢ	ܐܢ ܬܗܘܢ ܥܒܕܝܢ ܡܐ ܕܐܢܐ [z]ܡܦܩܕ	[z]ܡܦܩܕ
‡ f. 121*a*.	15 ܠܟܘܢ : ܥܘܕ ‡ ܠܝܬ ܐܢܐ ܐܡܪ [a]ܕܐܢܬܘܢ	[a]ܠܟܘܢ
[b]ܠܚܠܠ	ܥܒܕܝܢ : [b]ܠܚܠܠ ܕܥܒܕܐ ܠܐ ܝܕܥ ܡܐ ܥܒܕ ܡܪܗ	
	ܥܒܕ : ܠܟܘܢ ܕܝ ܐܡܪܬ [c]ܕܐܢܬܘܢ [y]ܪܚܡܘܝ :	[c]ܐܢܬܘܢ
	ܕܟܠ ܡܐ ܕܫܡܥܬ ܡܢ ܐܒܐ ܐܘܕܥܬ ܠܟܘܢ :	
	[f. 99*b*] 16 ܠܐ ܐܢܬܘܢ ܒܚܪܬܘܢ ܝܬܝ ܐܠܐ ܐܢܐ	
[d]ܘܐܩܝܡܬ	ܒܚܪܬ ܝܬܟܘܢ : [d]ܘܐܩܝܡܬ ܝܬܟܘܢ ܕܐܢܬܘܢ	[e] *omit* ܕܝ
[e] *omit* ܕܝ	ܬܐܙܠܘܢ [e]ܕܝ ܘܬܝܬܘܢ ܦܐܪܝܢ [f]ܘܦܐܪܝܟܘܢ	[f]ܘܦܐܪܝܟܘܢ
[f]ܘܦܐܪܝܟܘܢ	ܝܗܘܢ ܡܟܬܪܝܢ [g]ܠܥܠܡ : ܘܟܠ ܡܐ [h]ܕܬܫܐܠܘܢ	[g]ܠܥܠܡ
	ܡܢ ܐܒܐ ܒܫܡܝ ܝܬܠ ܠܟܘܢ : [b]ܠܚܠܠ	[h]ܕܬܫܐܠܘܢ
[j]ܡܦܩܕ	17 ܕܡܫܬܒܚ ܐܒܐ [i]ܒܒܪܐ : ܗܠܝܢ ܐܢܐ [j]ܡܦܩܕ	[i]ܒܒܪܗ [j]ܡܦܩܕ
[l]ܠܚܠܝܦ	ܠܟܘܢ [k]ܕܬܗܘܢ ܡܚܒܝܢ ܦܠܚܒܘܢ [l]ܠܚܠܝܦ :	[k]ܕܬܗܘܢ
[n]ܥܠܡܐ	18 [m]ܐܢ ܐܢܬ [n]ܥܠܡܐ ܣܢܐ ܝܬܟܘܢ ܝܕܥܝܢ	[m]ܐܝܢ
[o]ܩܕܡܝ	19 ܐܢܬܘܢ ܕܠܝ [o]ܩܕܡ ܡܢܟܘܢ ܣܢܐ : ܐܠܘ	
	ܗܘܝܬܘܢ ܡܢ ܕܝܢ [n]ܥܠܡܐ : [n]ܥܠܡܐ ܠܕܝܠܗ	
[q]ܪܚܡ	[p]ܗܘܐ [q]ܪܚܡ : [b]ܠܚܠܠ ܕܝ ܕܠܝܬ ܐܢܬܘܢ ܡܢ	[p]ܗܘ
	ܗܕܝܢ [n]ܥܠܡܐ : ܐܠܐ ܐܢܐ ܒܚܪܬ ܝܬܟܘܢ	
[r]ܗܟܢ	† ܡܢ [n]ܥܠܡܐ : [b]ܠܚܠܠ [r]ܗܕܝܢ [n]ܥܠܡܐ ܣܢܐ	† f. 98*b*.
[s]ܚܟܝܪܝܢ	20 ܝܬܟܘܢ : ܗܘܘ [s]ܕܟܝܪܝܢ ܡܠܬܐ ܗܕܐ ܕܡܠܠܬ	
[t]ܥܒܕܐ	ܠܟܘܢ : ܕܠܝܬ [t]ܥܒܕ ܪܒ ܡܢ [u]ܡܪܗ : [x]ܐܢ	[u]ܡܪܘܗ [x]ܐܝܢ

Codex B.

ܠܝ ܪܕܦܘ ܐܘܦ ܠܟܘܢ ܗܢܘܢ ܪܕܦܝܢ܆ ܐܠܘ
ܢܛܪܘ ܡܠܬܝ ܐܘܦ [u]ܠܟܘܢ ܗܘܘ ܡܢܛܪܝܢ܆
21 ܐܠܐ ‡ ܟܘܠ ܗܠܝܢ ܡܥܒܕܘܢ ܠܟܘܢ [v]ܠܓܠܠ
ܫܡܝ: ܕܠܐ ܡܚܟܡܝܢ ܠܕܝ [w]ܕܫܠܚ ܝܬܝ:
22 ܐܠܘ ܠܐ [x]ܐܬܝܬ ܘܡܠܠܬ ܠܗܘܢ ܚܛܝܐ ܠܐ
ܗܘܐ ܠܗܘܢ: ܟܕܘ ܕܝ ܥܠܐ ܠܝܬ ܠܗܘܢ
23 ܥܠ ܦܠܓ [y]ܚܛܝܬܗܘܢ: ܡܢ ܕܣܢܐ ܠܝ ܐܘܦ
24 ܠܐܒܐ ܗܘ ܣܢܐ: ܐܠܘ ܠܐ ܕܥܒܕܬ ܥܘܒܕܐ
ܒܗܘܢ ܡܢܐ ܕܐܢܫ ܚܘܪܝܢ ܠܐ ܥܒܕ:
ܚܛܝܐ ܠܐ ܗܘܬ ܠܗܘܢ: ܟܕܘ ܕܝ ܚܡܘ
25 ܘܣܢܘ ܐܘܦ ܠܝ ܘܠܐܒܐ: ܐܠܐ [z]ܕܬܫܠܡ
ܡܠܬܐ ܗܕܐ [a]ܕܟܬܝܒܐ [c]ܒܢܡܘܣܗܘܢ
[f. 100a]
26 ܕܣܢܘ ܝܬܝ [d]ܠܡܓܢ: ܟܕ ܝܐܬܐ ܡܢܚܡܢܐ ܕܐܢ
ܕܐܢܐ ܡܫܠܚ ܠܟܘܢ ܡܢ ܠܘܬ ܐܒܐ [e]ܪܘܚܐ
ܕܩܘܫܛܐ: ܕܗܝ ܕܡܢ ܠܘܬ ܐܒܐ [e]ܢܦܩ: ܗܘ
27 [f]ܡܣܗܕ ܥܠ ܕܝܠܝ: ܘܐܘܦ ܐܢܬܘܢ ܡܣܗܕܝܢ
XVI. 1 ܕܡܢ ܪܝܫ ܐܬܘܢ ܥܡܝ: ܗܠܝܢ ܡܠܠܬ ܠܟܘܢ
2 ܠܟܕܝܠ ܕܠܐ ܬܬܟܫܠܘܢ: ܡܢ [i]ܟܢܝܫܬܐ
[k]ܝܦܩܘܢ ܝܬܟܘܢ: ܐܠܐ ܐܬܝܐ ܫܥܐ ܕܟܘܠ
ܡܢ ܕܩܛܠ ܝܬܟܘܢ ܣܒܪ [l]ܕܩܘܪܒܢ ܗܘ
3 ܡܩܪܒ ܠܐܠܗܐ: † ܘܗܠܝܢ ܗܢܘܢ ܥܒܕܝܢ
4 ܠܟܘܢ ܕܠܐ ܐܚܟܡܘ ܠܐܒܐ ܘܠܐ ܠܝ: ܐܠܐ
ܗܠܝܢ ܡܠܠܬ ܠܟܘܢ [o]ܟܕ [p]ܬܐܬܐ [q]ܫܥܬܐ: ܬܗܘܘܢ
‡ [r]ܕܟܪܝܢ [s]ܠܗܘܢ ܕܐܢܐ ܐܡܪܬ ܠܟܘܢ: ܗܠܝܢ
5 ܡܢ ܪܝܫ ܠܐ ܐܡܪܬ ܕܥܡܟܘܢ [t]ܗܘܝܬ: ܟܕܘ
[u]ܕܝ ܐܢܐ[u] [v]ܐܙܠ ܠܘܬ ܗܕܝܢ [w]ܕܫܠܚ ܝܬܝ:
ܘܐܢܫ ܡܢܟܘܢ ܠܐ ܫܐܠ ܝܬܝ [x]ܠܗܢ ܐܬ
6 [y]ܐܙܠ: [z]ܐܠܐ ܕܗܠܝܢ [a]ܡܠܠܬ ܠܟܘܢ [b]ܥܩܘܬܐ
7 ܡܠܬ ܠܒܟܘܢ: ܐܠܐ ܐܢܐ ܘܩܘܫܛܐ ܐܢܐ
ܐܡܪ ܠܟܘܢ ܦܠܓ ܠܟܘܢ ܗܝ ܕܐܢܐ [c]ܐܙܠ:
[d]ܐܢ ܠܝܬ ܐܢܐ ܗܝ [y]ܐܙܠ ܡܢܚܡܢܐ ܠܐ

Codex A.

[u]ܕܠܟܘܢ
‡ f. 121b.
[v]ܠܓܠܠ [w]ܕܫܠܚܢ
[x]ܐܬܝܬܝ
[y]ܚܛܝܬܗܘܢ
[z]ܕܬܫܠܡ
[c]ܒܢܡܘܣܗܘܢ
[f]ܡܣܗܕ
[k]ܝܦܩܘܢ
[l]ܣܒܪ
[o]ܟܕ [p]ܬܐܬܐ
‡ f. 122a.
[r]ܕܟܪܝܢ [s]ܠܗܘܢ
[u]ܕܐܢܐ [w]ܕܫܠܚ
[y]ܐܙܠ [b]ܥܩܘܬܐ
[c]ܐܙܠ

Codex C.

[u]ܕܠܟܘܢ
[w]ܕܫܠܚ
[z]ܕܬܫܠܡ
[a]ܕܟܬܝܒܐ
[d]ܠܡܓܢ
[e] ܪܘܚܐ . . . *omit* . . . ܐܒܐ
ܟܢܝܫܬܐ
[k]ܝܦܩܘܢ
† f. 99a.
[o]ܟܕ [q]ܫܥܐ
[t]ܗܘܝܬ
[v]ܐܙܠ [w]ܕܫܠܚ
[x]ܠܗܢ
[z]ܐܠܐ ܕ *omit*
[a]ܡܠܠܬ [b]ܥܩܘܬܐ
[d]ܐܢܝ

Codex A.

^x ܐܫܬܐܠ
ܠܬܘܠܕܬܗܘܢ ^y *omit*
ܗܘ ^z *omit* ^b ܒܠܫܢܐ
^c ܫܘܠܡܬܐ
ܕܝ ^f *add* ^u ܐܙܠ
^g ܕܐܪܒܥܝܢ
^h ܠܝ ^j ܬܬܩܠܡ
^k ܕܬܠܡܝܕܘܗܝ
^l *add* ܗܘܐ
‡ f. 122*b*.
^p ܡܛܠ
^q ܘܡܚܘܐ
^r ܙܥܘܪ
^s ܐܙܠ
^u ܠܦܠܓܐ
ܗܘ ^v *add* ^w ܗܕܝܢ
^x ܗܘ ^y ܕܐܡܪ
^z *omit* ܘܬܘܒ ... ܠܝ
^d ܠܦܠܓܐ

Codex B.

ܐܬܪܐ ܠܬܘܠܕܬܗܘܢ ^w ܐܘ ܕܝ ^x ܐܫܬܐܠ ܐܢܐ
8 ܡܫܠܡܝܢ ܗܘܬ ^y ܠܬܘܠܕܬܗܘܢ : ܘܒܬܪ ^z ܗܘ ܠܐܬܪܐ
ܗܘ ܡܢܟܘܢ ^b ܒܠܫܢܐ ܟܠ ܛܒ ^c ܫܘܠܡܬܐ ܘܟܠ
9 ܛܒ ܝܕܘܥܐ ܘܟܠ ^d ܛܒ ܕܢܣܒܐ : ^e ܟܠ ^d ܛܒ
10 ^c ܫܘܠܡܬܐ ܕܠܐ ^v ܡܬܡܫܚܝܢ ܒܗ : ܟܠ ܛܒ
ܝܕܘܥܐ ^f ܕܐܢܐ ܠܘܬ ܐܒܐ ^u ܐܙܠ : ܘܒܬܪ
11 ܠܘܬ ܐܒܘܗܝ ܣܠܩ ܗܘܐ ܟܠ ܛܒ ܕܢܣܒܐ ܕܝ
12 ^g ܐܪܒܥܝܢ ܕܝܘܡܝܢ ^b ܒܠܫܢܐ ܡܬܚܙܐ : ܒܬܪ
ܫܠܡ ^h ܕܝ ^i ܕܐܬܡܠܝ ܠܗܘܢ : ܐܙܠ ܠܘܬ ܐܒܘܗܝ
[f. 100*b*]
13 ^j ܡܠܘܗܝ ^k ܕܬܠܡܝܕܘܗܝ ܒܬܪ : ܒܬܪ ܐܬܪܐ ^l ܪܘܚܐ
ܕܦܪܩܠܝܛܐ ܗܘ ܡܫܒܪ ܠܒܗܘܢ ܒܦܪܩܠܝܛܐ
ܒܟܠܗ : ܠܐ ܓܪ ^m ܡܡܠܠ ܡܢ ^n ܨܒܝܢܗ : ܐܠܐ
ܟܠ ܡܐ ܕܗܘ ܫܡܥ ܗܘ ^m ܡܡܠܠ ܘܡܐ
14 ^† ܕܐܬܝܐ ܗܘ ^o ܡܚܘܐ ܠܟܘܢ : ܗܘ ܡܫܒܚ
15 ܠܝ : ܕܡܢ ܕܝܠܝ ܗܘ ܢܣܒ ^‡ ܘܡܚܘܐ ܠܟܘܢ :
ܟܠ ܡܐ ܕܐܝܬ ܠܐܒܐ ܕܝܠܝ ܗܘ : ^p ܡܛܠ ܗܢܐ
ܐܡܪܬ ܠܟܘܢ ܕܡܢ ܕܝܠܝ ܗܘ ܢܣܒ ^q ܘܡܚܘܐ
16 ܠܟܘܢ : ^r ܙܥܘܪ ܘܒܬܪ ܠܘܬ ܐܒܘܗܝ ܣܠܩ
ܠܝ : ܘܬܘܒ ^r ܙܥܘܪ ܘܐܒܘܗܝ ܣܠܩ ܠܝ :
17 ܘܐܡܪܘ ^s ܐܙܠ ܠܘܬ ܐܒܐ : ܐܡܪܘ ܕܝ ܐܢܫܝܢ
ܡܢ ^t ܬܠܡܝܕܘܗܝ ܦܠܓܗܘܢ ^u ܠܦܠܓܐ : ܡܢܐ
ܗܘ ^v ^w ܗܕܝܢ ^x ܕܗܘ ^y ܐܡܪ ܠܢ ^r ܙܥܘܪ ܘܒܬܪ
ܠܘܬ ܐܒܘܗܝ ܣܠܩ ܠܝ : ^z ܘܬܘܒ ܙܥܘܪ
ܘܐܒܘܗܝ ܣܠܩ ܠܝ ^z ܘܐܢܐ ^s ܐܙܠ ܠܘܬ
18 ܐܒܐ : ܗܘܘ ܕܝ ܐܡܪܝܢ ܡܢܐ ܗܘ ܗܕܝܢ
^r ܙܥܘܪ ^a ܠܘܬ ܐܢܫ ܡܕܒܪܝܢ ܡܢܐ ܗܘ
19 ^b ܡܡܠܠ : ܘܝܕܥ ܝܫܘܥ ܕܨܒܝܢ ܗܘܘ ܒܡܢ
ܕܢܫܐܠܘܢ ܐܢܘܢ : ܘܐܡܪ ܠܗܘܢ ܟܠ ^c ܛܒ
ܗܕܐ ܐܢܬܘܢ ܡܬܒܥܝܢ ܦܠܓܗܘܢ ^d ܠܦܠܓܐ :
ܕܐܡܪܬ ^r ܙܥܘܪ ܘܠܘܬ ܐܒܘܗܝ ܣܠܩ ܠܝ :
20 ܘܬܘܒ ^r ܙܥܘܪ ܘܐܒܘܗܝ ܣܠܩ ܠܝ : ܐܡܝܢ

Codex C.

^w ܐܘ ^x ܐܙܠ
^z *omit* ܗܘ
^c ܫܘܠܡܗܘܢ
^d ܛܒ ^e ܘܟܠ
^v ܡܬܡܫܚܝܢ
^f *add* ܕܝ
^g ܕܐܪܒܥܝܢ
^h ܠܝ ^i ܕܐܬܡܠܝ
^l *add* ܗܘ
^m ܡܡܠܠ ^n ܨܒܝܢܗ
^o ܡܚܘܐ
† f. 99*b*.
^q ܘܡܚܘܐ
^t ܬܠܡܝܕܘܗܝ
^v *add* ܗܘ
^a *omit* ܠܘܬ
^b ܡܡܠܠ
^c *omit* ܛܒ
^d ܥܡ ܦܠܓܐ ^d

Codex A.	Codex B.	Codex C.
ᵍܐܡܪܢܐ	ܐܡܝܢ ᵍܐܡܪ ܐܢܐᵍ ܠܟܘܢ : ܕܐܢܬܘܢ ܬܒܟܘܢ	
ʰܘܬܐܠܝܢܘܢ	ʰܘܬܐܠܠܘܢ ⁱܥܠܡܐ ܕܝܢ ܚܕܐ : ܐܢܬܘܢ	ʰܘܬܐܠܠܘܢ
ⁱܥܠܡܐ	ʲܬܬܥܝܩܘܢ ܐܠܐ ܥܝܩܬܟܘܢ ܠܚܕܘܐ ܗܝ	
ʲܬܬܥܝܩܘܢ ᵏܝܠܕܐ	[f. 101a] 21 ܡܬܗܦܟܐ : ܐܢܬܬܐ ܟܕ ܗܝ ᵏܝܠܕܐ ܥܝܩܐ	
ᵐܬܘܠܕ	ܗܘܝܐ ܠܗ ܕܐܬܬ ܫܥܬܗ : ܟܕ ܕܝܢ ᵐܬܘܠܕ	ᵐܬܘܠܕ
‡ f. 123a.	ܛܠܝܐ ܒܬܪ ܠܐ ‡ܡܕܟܪܐ ܠܥܘܩܐ : ⁿܒܓܠܠ	ⁿܒܓܠܠ
ᵒܕܐܬܝܠܝܕ	22 ܚܕܘܬܐ ᵒܕܐܬܝܠܝܕ ܒܪܢܫ ᵖܒܥܠܡܐ : ܘܐܦ	ᵖܠܥܠܡܐ
ᵖܠܥܠܡܐ ᵠadd ܕܝܢ	ܐܢܬܘܢ ᵠܟܕܘ ܥܩܐ ܐܝܬ ܠܟܘܢ : †ܬܘܒ	† f. 100a.
ʳܚܙܐ	ܕܝܢ ܐܢܐ ʳܚܙܐ ܠܟܘܢ ܘܠܒܟܘܢ ܚܕܐˢ :	ʳܚܙܐ ᵠadd ܕܝܢ
	ܘܚܕܘܬܟܘܢ ܐܢܫ ܠܐ ܢܣܒ ܡܢܟܘܢ :	ˢadd ܚܕܐ
ᵗܫܐܠܝܢ	23 ܘܒܝܢܬܗ ܝܘܡܐ ܠܝ ܠܝܬ ܐܢܬܘܢ ᵗܫܐܠܝܢ	
ᵘܟܘܠܗܘܡ	ᵘܟܘܠܡ : ܐܡܝܢ ᵍܐܡܪ ܐܢܐᵍ ܠܟܘܢ :	ᵘܟܘܠܡ
	ܕܟܘܠ ܡܐ ʷܕܬܫܐܠܘܢ ܡܢ ܐܒܐ ܒܫܡܝ	ʷܕܬܫܐܠܘܢ
ˣܫܐܠܬܘܢ	24 ܗܘ ܢܗܒ ܠܟܘܢ : ܥܕ ܟܕܘ ܠܐ ˣܫܐܠܬܘܢ	ˣܫܐܠܬܘܢ
ʸܟܘܠܗܘܡ ᵃܒܓܠܠ	ʸܟܘܠܡ ܫܐܠܘ ܘܐܬܘܢ ܢܣܒܝܢ : ᵃܒܓܠܠ	ᵇܕܚܕܘܬܟܘܢ
ᶜܡܫܡܠܝܐ ᵈomit ܕܝܢ	25 ᵇܕܚܕܘܬܟܘܢ ܬܗܘܐ ᶜܡܫܡܠܝܐ : ܗܠܝܢ ᵈܕܝܢ	ᶜܡܫܡܠܝܐ ᵈomit ܕܝܢ
ᶠܫܥܬܐ	ܒܡܬܠܝܢ ܡܠܠܬ ܠܟܘܢ : ܐܬܝܐ ᶠܫܥܬܐ	
	ܕܟܘܕ ᵈܕܝܢ ܒܡܬܠܝܢ ܠܐ ܡܠܠ ܠܟܘܢ : ܐܠܐ	
	ܒܦܪܗܣܝܐ ܥܠ ܐܒܘܗ ܕܐܒܐ ܐܢܐ ܡܬܢܝܐ	
ʲadd ܕܝܢ	26 ܠܟܘܢ : ⁱܒܗܘ ʲܝܘܡܐ ܐܢܬܘܢ ᵏܫܐܠܝܢ	ⁱܒܗܘܢ ʲadd ܕܝܢ
	ܒܫܡܝ ܘܠܝܬ ˡܐܢܐ ܐܡܪ ܠܟܘܢ : ܕܐܢܐ	ᵏܫܐܠܝܢ ˡomit ܐܢܐ
	27 ܒܥܐ ܡܢ ܐܒܐ ܥܠ ܕܝܠܟܘܢ : ܗܘ ܓܪ	
ᵐܪܚܡ	ܐܒܐ ᵐܪܚܡ ܠܟܘܢ ܕܐܢܬܘܢ ܪܚܡܬܘܢ	ᵐܪܚܡ
	ܝܬܝ : ܘܗܝܡܢܬܘܢ ⁿܕܐܢܐ ܡܢ ܠܘܬ ܐܠܗܐ	ⁿomit ܕܐܢܐ
	28 ܢܦܩܬ : ܢܦܩܬ ܓܪ ܡܢ ܠܘܬ ܐܒܐ ܘܐܬܝܬ	
ᵒܠܥܠܡܐ ᵖܥܠܡܐ	ᵒܠܥܠܡܐ : ܬܘܒ ܫܒܩ ܐܢܐ ᵖܥܠܡܐ	ᵒܠܥܠܡܐ
ᵠܘܐܙܠ ʳadd ܠܝ	29 ᵠܘܐܙܠ ʳܠܘܬ ܐܒܐ : ܐܡܪܝܢ ܠܗ ˢܬܠܡܝܕܘܗܝ	ʳadd ܠܝ
‡ f. 123b.	ܗܐ ‡ܟܕܘ ܒܦܪܗܣܝܐ ܐܬ ᵗܡܡܠܠ : ܘܡܬܠ	ᵗܡܡܠܠ
ˢܬܠܡܝܕܘܗܝ	30 ܐܘܦ ܠܐ ܚܕ ᵘܠܝܬ ܐܬ ܐܡܪ : ܟܕܘ ᵛܐܢܚܢ	ᵘomit ܠܝܬ ᵛܐܢܚܢ
ᵛܐܢܚܢ ʷܘܠܝܬ	ܝܕܥܝܢ ܕܐܬ ܝܕܥ ܟܘܠܐ ʷܘܠܝܬ ܐܬ ܨܪܝܟ	
	ܕܢܫܐܠ ˣܡܢܟ ܐܢܫ : ܒܗܕܐ ᵛܐܢܚܢ ܡܗܝܡܢܝܢ	ˣomit ܡܢܟ

Codex A.	Codex B.	Codex C.
	[f. 101b] 31 ܕܡܢ ܐܠܗܐ ܢܦܩܬ : ܐܝܬܝܒ ܡܪܢܐ ܝܫܘܥ	
	ܘܐܡܪ ܠܗܘܢ : ܟܕܘ ܐܢܬܘܢ ܡܗܝܡܢܝܢ :	
[l]ܘܐܬܬ	32 ܗܐ ܐܬܝܐ ܫܥܬܐ [l]ܘܐܬܘܢ [m]ܬܬܒܕܪܘܢ ܟܠ	[m]ܕܬܬܒܕܪܘܢ
[m]ܕܬܬܒܕܪܘܢ	ܚܕ ܘܚܕ ܡܢܟܘܢ ܠܐܬܪܗ : [†] ܘܠܝ ܠܒܠܚܘܕܝ	† f. 100b.
[n]ܕܐܒܐ	ܐܬܘܢ ܫܒܩܝܢ : ܘܠܝܬ ܐܢܐ ܠܒܠܚܘܕܝ [n]ܐܒܐ	[n]ܕܐܒܐ
	33 ܥܡܝ ܐܝܬ ܗܘ : ܗܠܝܢ ܡܠܠܬ ܠܟܘܢ [p]ܠܒܠܠ	[p]ܠܒܠܠ
	ܕܒܝ ܫܠܡ ܝܗܐ ܠܟܘܢ : ܐܠܐ ܐܬܚܝܠܘ	
[o]ܠܥܠܡܐ [a]ܡܠܠ	XVII. 1 ܕܐܢܐ ܢܨܚܬ ܝܬܗ [o]ܠܥܠܡܐ : ܗܠܝܢ [a]ܡܠܠ	[o]ܠܥܠܡܐ
[b]ܥܝܢܘܗܝ	ܡܪܢܐ ܝܫܘܥ ܘܬܠܐ [b]ܥܝܢܘܗ ܠܫܡܝܐ ܘܐܡܪ :	[b]ܥܝܢܘ
[d]ܫܒܚ	ܐܒܐ ܐܬܬ ܫܥܬܐ : [d]ܫܒܚ ܝܬܗ ܠܒܪܟ :	[d]ܫܒܚ
[f]ܠܗ	2 ܕܒܪܟ ܢܫܒܚ ܝܬܟ : ܗܝܟ ܡܐ ܕܝܗܒܬ [f]ܠܗ	[f]ܠܗ
[h] omit ܕܝ	[g]ܫܘܠܛܢܗ ܥܠ ܟܠܗ [h]ܕܝ ܒܣܪܐ : ܕܟܘܠ ܡܐ	[g]ܫܘܠܛܢܗ [h] omit ܕܝ
[j]ܚܝܝܢ [k]ܕܠܥܠܡ	ܕܝܗܒܬ [f]ܠܗ [i]ܢܬܠ ܠܗܘܢ [j]ܚܝܝܢ [k]ܕܠܥܠܡ :	[i]ܢܬܠ [j]ܚܝܝܢ
[l] omit ܗܠܝܢ...ܕܠܥܠܡ	3 [l]ܗܠܝܢ ܕܝ ܗܢܘܢ ܚܝܝܐ ܕܠܥܠܡ[l] : ܕܝܕܥܘܢ	
[m]ܒܠܚܘܕܝܟ	ܡܕܥܝܢ ܠܟ ܕܐܢܬ ܗܘ ܐܠܗܐ ܩܫܝܛܐ [m]ܒܠܚܘܕܝܟ .	
[n]ܘܕܝ [p]ܒܥܒܕܐ	4 [n]ܘܕܝܢ ܕܫܠܚܬ [o]ܝܫܘܥ ܡܫܝܚܐ : ܐܢܐ ܫܒܚܬ	[o] add ܝܬܗ
[q]ܗܕܝܢ [r]ܫܒܚ	ܝܬܟ ܥܠ ܐܪܥܐ : ܕܫܠܡܬ [p]ܒܥܒܕܐ [q]ܗܠܝܢ	[q]ܗܕܝܢ
‡ f. 124a.	5 ܕܝܗܒܬ [‡] ܠܝ ܕܐܥܒܕ : ܐܘܦ ܟܕܘ [r]ܫܒܚ ܝܬܝ	[r]ܫܒܚ
[s]ܒܬܫܒܘܚܬܐ	ܐܒܐ ܠܘܬܟ [s]ܒܬܫܒܘܚܬܐ ܕܗܘܬ ܒܝܢܝ	
[t]ܥܠܡܐ	6 ܠܘܬܟ : ܥܕ ܠܐ ܝܗܐ [t]ܥܠܡܐ : [u]ܐܢܐ	[u] omit ܐܢܐ
[u] omit ܐܢܐ	ܐܘܕܥܬ ܫܡܟ ܠܒܢܝܢܫܐ ܗܠܝܢ ܕܝܗܒܬ ܠܝ ܡܢ	
	[t]ܥܠܡܐ : ܕܝܠܟ ܗܘܘ ܘܠܝ ܝܗܒܬ ܐܢܘܢ :	
[w] add ܡܢ [v] add ܟܠ	7 ܘܡܠܬܟ ܢܛܪܘ : ܟܕܘ ܝܕܥܘ ܕܟܘܠ[v] ܕܝܗܒܬ ܠܝ[w]	[v] add ܟܠ
[x] omit ܕܡܠܐ . . .	8 ܠܘܬܟ ܗܘܝܢ : [x][y]ܕܡܠܐ ܕܝܗܒܬ ܠܝ ܝܗܒܬ	[y]ܕܡܠܐ
. . . ܠܗܘܢ	ܠܗܘܢ[x] : ܘܗܢܘܢ ܩܒܠܘ ܘܐܕܥܘ ܕܡܢ [z]ܘܩܫܛ	[z]ܘܩܫܛ
	[f. 102a] ܡܢ ܠܘܬܟ ܢܦܩܬ : ܘܗܝܡܢܘ ܕܐܢܬ ܫܠܚܬ ܝܬܝ	
[a] add ܥܠ	9 ܐܢܐ ܥܠ ܕܛܠܗܘܢ ܒܥܐ : ܠܐ[a] [b]ܕܛܠܗ	[b] omit ܕ [a] add ܥܠ
[c]ܕܥܠܡܐ [e]ܕܕܝܠܟ	[c]ܕܥܠܡܐ : ܐܢܐ [d]ܒܥܐ : ܐܠܐ ܥܠ ܛܠ ܗܠܝܢ	[d]ܒܥܐ
[f]ܕܝܠܝ	10 ܕܝܗܒܬ ܠܝ[†] [e]ܕܕܝܠܟ ܗܘܢ : ܘܟܘܠ ܡܐ [f]ܕܝܠܝ	† f. 101a.
[g]ܕܝܠ	ܕܝܠܟ ܗܘܢ ܘܕܝܠܟ [g]ܕܝܠܝ : ܘܐܢܐ ܡܫܒܚ	[e]ܕܕܝܠܟ
[h]ܠܝܬܢܐ [i]ܒܥܠܡܐ	11 ܒܗܘܢ : ܘܟܘܕ [h]ܠܝܬ ܐܢܐ[h] [i]ܒܥܠܡܐ ܘܗܠܝܢ	

Codex A.

ܕܝܢ ᵍ *omit* ʰ ܒܡܠܟܐ
ⁱ ܢܦܠܢ ʲ ܒܥܝܢܝܟ
ᵏ ܗܕܝܢ ˡ ܕܐܢܘܢ
ᵐ ܚܙܐ *omit* ⁿ ܗܘܝܬ
ᵒ ܡܬܢܦܢ ᵃ ܗܕܝܢ
ᵖ ܘܚܙܝܬ ᵠ ܐܬܪ

‡ f. 124*b*.

ˢ ܠܟܠܠ
ᵘ ܡܫܟܠܠ
ᵛ ܚܕܘܬܐ

ʷ ܘܒܡܠܟܐ
ˣ ܒܡܠܟܐ ᶻ ܠܬܝܐ
ᵃ ܒܒܢ ᵇ ܕܢܬܪܡ
ᶜ ܕܬܦܠܢ

ᵈ ܡܕܝܢ

ᶠ ܠܡܠܟܐ
ᵍ ܥܠܝܬ

ʰ *add* ܒܢ

ⁱ *add* ܐܢܐ

‡ f. 125*a*.

Codex B.

ᵍ ܕܝܢ ʰ ܒܡܠܟܘܬܐ ܗܘܝܢ: ܘܐܢܐ ܠܘܬܟ ܐܬܝܬ:
ܐܝܟ ܡܕܡܥܐ ⁱ ܢܦܠܢ ܢܬܗܘܢ ʲ ܒܥܝܢܝܟ ᵏ ܗܕܝܢ
ܕܢܗܘܐ ܠܝ: ܕܢܗܘܘܢ ܚܙܐ ܗܢܝܢ ܡܢܐ ˡ ܕܐܢܝܢ
12 ᵐ ܚܙܐ: ܟܕ ⁿ ܗܘܝܬ ᵍ ܕܝܢ ܒܚܙܘܗܘܢ ʰ ܒܡܠܟܘܬܐ
ܐܢܐ ⁿ ܗܘܝܬ ᵒ ܡܬܢܦܢ ܠܗܘܢ ܒܥܝܢܝܟ ᵃ ܗܕܝܢ
ܕܢܗܘܐ ܠܝ: ᵖ ܘܚܙܝܬ ܘܐܬܪ ܡܢܗܘܢ ܠܐ
ᵠ ܐܬܪ ܐܠܐ ‡ ʳ ܐܢ ܒܗ ܕܐܬܪܐ: ˢ ܠܟܠܠ
13 ᵗ ܕܒܬܪܟܐ ܢܬܟܠܐ: ܒܪܘ ܕܝܢ ܠܘܬܟ ܐܢܐ
ܐܬܐ: ܘܗܠܝܢ ܐܢܐ ᵘ ܡܫܟܠܠ ʰ ܒܡܠܟܘܬܐ:
ܕܬܗܘܐ ܒܡܫܘܗܘܢ ᵛ ܚܕܘܬܝ ܕܟܠܝ ܡܫܠܡܐ
14 ܒܫܘܗܘܢ: ܐܢܐ ܡܗܝܢ ܠܗܘܢ ܡܟܠܬܝܟ
ʷ ܘܒܡܠܟܘܬܐ ܗܢܐ ܢܬܗܘܢ ܕܠܬܝ ܗܘܝܢ ܡܢ
ˣ ܒܡܠܟܘܬܐ: ܗܘܝܢ ܡܢܐ ʸ ܕܐܢܐ ᶻ ܠܬܝ ܐܢܐ ᶻ ܡܢ
15 ˣ ܒܡܠܟܘܬܐ: ܠܬܝ ܐܢܐ ᵃ ܒܒܢ ܡܢܝܟ ᵇ ܕܢܬܪܡ
ܢܬܗܘܢ ܡܢ ˣ ܒܡܠܟܘܬܐ: ܐܠܐ ᶜ ܢܦܠܢ ܢܬܗܘܢ
16 ܡܢ ܒܢܫܐ: ܡܢ ˣ ܒܡܠܟܘܬܐ ܠܬܝ ܗܘܝܢ: ܗܘܝܢ
17 ܡܢܐ ܕܐܢܐ ܠܬܝ ܐܢܐ ܡܢ ˣ ܒܡܠܟܘܬܐ ᵈ ܡܕܝܢ
ܢܬܗܘܢ ܒܡܫܬܦܐ: ܡܠܬܝܟ ܕܠܝܟ ᵉ ܗܘ
18 ܘܡܫܬܦܐ: ܗܘܝܢ ܡܢܐ ܕܥܠܝܬ ܢܬܝ ᶠ ܠܡܠܟܘܬܐ
19 ܐܢܐ ᵍ ܥܠܝܬ ܢܬܗܘܢ ᶠ ܠܡܠܟܘܬܐ: ܘܟܠ
[f. 103*b*]
ܕܦܩܘܕܗܘܢ ܐܢܐ ܡܘܕܝܢ ܠܚܝܝܢ: ܕܢܗܘܢ
20 ܐܘܦ ܗܘܝܢ † ܡܘܕܝܢܝܢ ܒܡܫܬܦܐ: ܠܐ
ܟܠ ܕܦܩܘܕܗܘܢ ܕܗܠܝܢ ܐܢܐ ܒܟܐ ܒܠܫܘܢ:
ܐܠܐ ܐܘܦ ܟܠ ܕܦܩܘܕܗܘܢ ܕܗܠܝܢ ܕܡܗܝܡܢܝܢ ʰ
ܒܬܪܟܗ ܕܡܠܬܗܘܢ ܕܒܠܒܗܘܢ ܚܙܐ ܡܢܗܘܢ:
21 ܗܘܝܢ ܡܢܐ ܕܐܬܐ ܐܟܐ ܒܦܘܡܝ ܘܐܢܐ ܐܘܦ ⁱ
ܒܦܘܡܝܟ: ܕܐܘܦ ܗܘܝܢ ܒܦܘܡܝ ܚܙܐ
ܡܢܗܘܢ: ܕܡܗܝܡܢܝܢ ˣ ܒܡܠܟܘܬܐ ܕܐܬܐ ‡ ܥܠܝܬ
22 ܢܬܝ: ܘܐܢܐ ܬܫܒܘܚܬܐ ܗܕܐ ܕܡܗܝܡܢܬ
ܠܝ ܡܗܝܡܢ ܠܗܘܢ: ܕܢܗܘܢ ܚܙܐ ܗܘܝܢ
23 ܡܢܐ ᵏ ܕܐܢܘܢ ܚܙܐ: ܐܢܐ ܒܦܘܡܗܘܢ ܘܐܬܐ

Codex C.

ᵍ *omit* ܕܝܢ
ˡ ܕܐܢܘܢ
ⁿ ܗܘܝܬ
ʳ ܐܢܐ
ᵗ ܕܒܬܪܟܐ
ʸ ܕܐܢܘܢ
ᵃ ܒܒܢ ᵇ ܕܢܬܪܡ
ᶜ ܕܬܦܠܢ
ᵉ ܗܝ
ᶠ ܠܡܠܟܘܬܐ

† f. 1 b.

ʰ *add* ܒܢ

ⁱ *add* ܐܢܐ

ᵏ ܕܐܢܐ

Codex A.	Codex B.	Codex C.
[c]ܠܓܠܠ	ܟܠܗܘܢ ܀ [c]ܠܓܠܠ ܕܝܗܘܢ ܡܫܠܡܝܢ ܠܚܕܐ ܀	
[d]ܘܕܗܘܐ [e]ܥܠܡܐ	[d]ܘܗܘܐ [e]ܥܠܡܐ [f]ܕܒܝ ܕܐܬ ܫܠܚܬ ܝܬܝ ܀	[d]ܘܕܗܘܐ [f]ܕܒܝ
[g]ܘܐܚܒܬ	[g]ܘܐܚܒܬ ܐܢܘܢ ܀ ܗܟܢ ܡܐ ܕܐܚܒܬ	
	24 ܝܬܝ ܀ ܐܒܐ ܗܠܐ ܕܝܗܒܬ ܠܝ ܨܒܐ ܐܢܐ	
	ܕܗܢ ܕܐܢܐ ܗܘܐ ܐܘܦ ܗܢܘܢ ܗܘܘܢ	
[h]ܬܫܒܘܚܬܝ	ܥܡܝ ܀ ܕܝܗܘܢ ܚܡܝܢ [h]ܬܫܒܘܚܬܝ ܗܕܐ	
[j]ܫܘܪܝܗ	ܕܝܗܒܬ ܠܝ ܀ ܕܐܚܒܬ ܝܬܝ ܡܢ ܩܕܡ [j]ܫܘܪܝܗ	[j]ܫܘܪܗ
[k]ܕܥܠܡܐ [l]ܘܥܠܡܐ	25 [k]ܕܥܠܡܐ ܀ ܐܒܐ ܙܕܝܩܐ [l]ܘܥܠܡܐ ܠܐ	[m]ܐܟܪ
	[m]ܐܟܪ ܝܬܟ ܀ ܐܢܐ ܕܝܢ ܐܟܪܬ ܝܬܟ ܀ ܘܐܘܦ	[n] *omit* ܬܗܘܐ
	26 ܗܠܝܢ ܐܟܪܘ ܕܐܬ ܫܠܚܬ ܝܬܝ ܀ ܘܐܘܕܥܬ	[o] *add* ܬܗܘܐ
[n] *omit* ܬܗܘܐ	ܕܐܚܒܬ ܝܬܝ [n]ܬܗܘܐ ܒܗܘܢ [o]܀ ܘܐܢܐ	[p]ܒܗܘܢ
[o] *add* ܬܗܘܐ	XVIII. 1 [p]ܒܗܘܢ ܀ ܒܟܢܐ ܕܝܢ ܕܐܡܪ ܗܠܝܢ ܡܪܢ	[r]ܬܠܡܝܕܘܗܝ [s]ܠܥܒܪ
[t]ܕܩܕܪܘܢܐ	ܝܫܘܥ ܢܦܩ ܥܡ [r]ܬܠܡܝܕܘܗܝ † [s]ܠܥܒܪܗ ܕܢܚܠܐ	† f. 102*a*.
‡ f. 125*b*.	[t]ܕܩܕܪܘܢܐ ܗܢ ܕܗܘܬ ‡ ܓܢܬܐ ܀ ܠܗܢ ܕܥܠ	[t]ܕܩܕܪܘܢܐ
[u]ܘܬܠܡܝܕܘܗܝ	ܗܘ [u]ܘܬܠܡܝܕܘܗܝ ܀	[a]ܐܬܐܚܢ ܠܠܠܬ
[b]ܐܬܐܚܢ ܠܗ	[b a]ܐܬܐܚܢ ܠܠܠܬ ܐܠܟܡܗܘܢ ܣܓܝ [b]ܡܢ ܢܘܣܩܐ[a]	ܐܠܟܡܗܘܢ ܡܢ ܢܘܣܩܐ[a]
ܐܠܟܡܗܘܢ[b]	[f. 103*a*] ܘܒܝܬܗ ܡܢܘܪܐ ܀ [a]ܘܢܦܩ ܥܡ [b]ܬܠܡܝܕܘܗܝ	[a]ܒܟܝܢ ܢܦܩ[a]
[a] *omit* ܘ	ܠܥܒܪܗ ܕܢܚܠܐ [c]ܕܩܕܪܘܢܐ ܗܢ ܕܗܘܬ	[b]ܬܠܡܝܕܘܗܝ
	2 ܓܢܬܐ ܀ ܠܗܢ ܕܥܠ ܗܘ [d]ܘܬܠܡܝܕܘܗܝ ܀ ܗܘܐ	[c]ܕܩܕܪܘܢܐ
[e]ܕܢ [h]ܘܗܐ	ܕܝܢ ܡܟܪ ܐܘܦ [e]ܝܗܘܕܐ [f]ܕܡܢ ܕܡܫܠܡ [g]ܝܬܗ	[d]ܘܬܠܡܝܕܘܗܝ
[v]ܬܠܡܝܕܘܗܝ	[h]ܗܘ ܐܬܪܐ ܕܣܓܝ ܙܒܢܝܢ ܐܬܟܢܫ ܡܪܢ	[f] *omit* ܕܡܫܠܡ
[i]ܝܗܘܕܗ [j]ܠܓܘܕܐ	3 ܝܫܘܥ ܬܡܢ ܥܡ [v]ܬܠܡܝܕܘܗܝ ܀ [i]ܝܗܘܕܐ ܕܝܢ	[g] *add* ܕܡܬܡܪ
[k]ܘܡܢ [l]ܘܦܪܝܫܝܐ	ܢܣܒ [j]ܠܓܘܕܐ [k]ܡܢ ܪܒܝ ܟܗܢܝܐ [l]ܘܦܪܝܫܝܐ	ܘܦܪܝܫܝܐ
[n]ܒܦܢܣܝܢ	[m]ܡܫܡܫܝܢ ܀ ܘܐܬܐ ܠܬܡܢ [n]ܒܦܢܣܝܢ [o]ܘܠܡܦܐܕܝܢ	[k]ܘܡܢ [m]ܡܫܡܫܝܢ
[o]ܘܠܡܦܐܕܝܢ	4 ܘܡܐܢܝܢ ܀ [p]ܘܡܪܢܐ ܝܫܘܥ ܕܝܢ[p] ܚܟܡ ܗܘܐ ܟܠ	[o]ܘܠܡܦܐܕܝܢ
	ܡܐ [q]ܕܐܬܐ ܥܠܘܗܝ ܀ ܢܦܩ [r]ܐܡܪ ܠܗܘܢ	[p] *omit* ܘܡܪܢܐ ܝܫܘܥ ܕܝܢ
[s] *add* ܕܝܢ [t]ܘܐܡܪܝܢ	5 ܠܡܢ ܐܬܘܢ ܒܥܝܢ ܀ [s]ܐܓܝܒܘ [t]ܐܡܪܝܢ ܠܗ	[q]ܕܐܬܐܡܪ
[u]ܢܨܪܝܐ	ܠܝܫܘܥ [u]ܢܨܪܝܐ ܀ ܐܡܪ ܠܗܘܢ [w]ܡܪܢܐ ܝܫܘܥ[w]	[r]ܐܢܐ [s] *add* ܕܝܢ
[x]ܩܐܡ [y]ܝܗܘܕܗ	ܐܢܐ ܗܘ ܀ ܗܘܐ ܕܝܢ [x]ܩܐܡ ܐܘܦ [y]ܝܗܘܕܐ	[w] *omit* ܡܪܢܐ ܝܫܘܥ
[z]ܗܕܢ	6 [z]ܗܕܡܢ ܕܡܫܠܡ ܝܬܗ ܠܗܘܢ ܀ ܟܕ ܕܝܢ ܐܡܪ	[y]ܝܗܘܕܗ
	ܠܗܘܢ ܐܢܐ ܗܘ ܐܙܠܘ [a]ܠܒܣܬܪܗܘܢ ܘܢܦܠܘ	[a]ܠܒܣܬܪܗܘܢ

Codex A.

[t] add ܕܝܢ
[u] ܢܨܘܪܝܐ
[y] ܫܒܘ̈ܩܘ
[z] omit ܕܝܢ [a] add ܗ̈ܠܝܢ
[b] ܕܢܐܙܠܘܢ
[c] ܡܠܬܐ [e] ܕܗ̈ܠܝܢ
‡ f. 126a.
[f] ܚܕ [i] ܫܠܦ
[j] add ܕܝܢ [l] ܕܝ
[m] ܠܐ ܐܫܬܝܬܗ [m]
[n] ܦܘܠܚܢܝ [o] ܘܪ̈ܒܝܢ
[q] ܕܝܗܘܕܝܐ
[r] ܘܐܝܬܝܘ
[s] ܠܘܬ ܚܢܐܢ [s]
[t] ܩܕܡܐܝ [v] ܫܢܬܐ
[w] add ܘܫܕܪܗ ܐܣܝܪ ܠܡܪܢ ܝܫܘܥ ܠܘܬ ܩܝܦܐ
[x] ܘܩܝܦܐ [y] ܕܡܠܟ
[z] ܠܝܗܘܕܝܐ [a] ܕܚܕ
[b] omit ܕ [c] ܘܚܪܢ
[d] omit ܕܝܢ [h] ܝܕܝܥ
[i] ܠܕܪܬܐ [j] ܩܐܡ
[l] ܚܒܪܐ [m] ܘܗܘ
[n] ܕܗܘܐ [o] ܠܬܪܥܝܬܐ
‡ f. 126b.
[r] ܬܪܥܝܬܐ
[t] ܘܩܐܡܝܢ
[v] ܓܘܡܪܝܢ

Codex B.

7 ܚܠ ܐܘܪܚܐ: ܘܬܘܒ ܫܐܠ ܐܢܘܢ ܘܐܡܪ
ܠܗܘܢ ܠܡܢ ܐܢܬܘܢ ܒܥܝܢ: ܗܢܘܢ [t] ܐܡܪܝܢ
8 ܐܡܪܘ ܠܝܫܘܥ [u]ܢܨܪܝܐ: [v]ܐܓܝܒ ܡܪܢ
ܘܐܡܪ ܠܗܘܢ: [w]ܐܡܪܬ ܠܟܘܢ ܕܐܢܐ
ܗܘ: [x]ܐܢ ܠܝ ܐܢܬܘܢ ܒܥܝܢ [y]ܫܒܘܩܘ [z]ܕܝܢ [a]
9 [b]ܐܙܠܝܢ: ܕܬܫܠܡ [c]ܡܠܬܗ ܗܕܐ † [d]ܕܐܡܪ:
[e]ܗܕܝܢ ܕܝܗܒܬ ܠܝ ܠܐ ܐܘܒܕܬ ܡܢܗܘܢ:
10 ܐܘܦ ܠܐ [f]ܚܕܐ: ‡ ܫܡܥܘܢ [g]ܦ̈ܛܪܘܣ [h]ܕܝܢ
ܗܘܐ ܒܝܕܗ ܣܝܦܗ [i]ܫܠܦ ܝܬܗ ܘܡܚܝܐ
ܠܥܒܕܗ ܕܪܒ ܟܗܢܐ: ܘܩܛܥ ܐܕܢܗ ܕܝܡܝܢܐ:
[f. 103b]
11 ܗܘܐ ܕܝܢ ܫܡܗ ܕܥܒܕܐ ܡܠܟܘܣ: ܐܡܪ [j]
ܡܪܢ ܫܡܥܘܢ [k]ܠܦ̈ܛܪܘܣ ܐܦܢܝ ܣܝܦܐ ܠܬܪܬܗ:
ܟܣܐ [l]ܕܝܗܒ ܠܝ ܐܒܐ [m]ܠܫܬܝܬܐ ܠܗ:
12 [n]ܦܘܠܚܢܝ ܕܝܢ [o]ܘܪܒܝ ܐܠܦܐ [p]ܘܣܛܪ̈ܛܝܘܛܐ
[q]ܕܝܗܘܕܝܐ ܐܚܕܘ ܠܡܪܢ ܝܫܘܥ ܘܟܦܬܘ ܝܬܗ:
13 [r]ܘܐܝܬܝܘ ܝܬܗ [s]ܠܚܢܐܢ [t]ܡܩܕܡܝܢ ܗܕܝܢ [u]ܕܗܘܐ
14 ܪܒ ܚܡܘܗܝ ܕܗܘܐ [v]ܫܢܬܐ [w]: ܗܘܐ ܕܝܢ [x]ܘܩܝܦܐ
[y]ܕܡܠܟ [z]ܕܝܗܘܕܝܐ ܕܝܦܩ ܗܘ [a]ܚܕ ܓܒܪܐ
15 [b]ܕܝܡܘܬ ܚܠܦ ܥܡܐ: ܗܘܐ ܕܝܢ [o]ܕܒܬܪܗ
ܠܡܪܢ ܝܫܘܥ ܫܡܥܘܢ [g]ܦ̈ܛܪܘܣ: [c]ܘܚܪܢ
[d]ܕܝܢ [e]ܬܠܡܝܕܝܢ: ܗܘ ܬܠܡܝܕܐ [f]ܕܝܢ ܗܘܐ
[h]ܝܕܝܥ ܠܪܒ ܟܗܢܐ: ܘܥܠ ܥܡ ܡܪܢ ܝܫܘܥ
16 [i]ܠܕܪܬܗ ܕܪܒ ܟܗܢܐ: [g]ܦ̈ܛܪܘܣ ܕܝܢ ܗܘܐ
[j]ܩܐܡ ܥܠ ܬܪܥܐ: ܠܒܪ ܢܦܩ ܕܝܢ [k]ܬܠܡܝܕܐ
[l]ܚܒܪܐ [m]ܗܘ [n]ܕܗܘܐ [h]ܝܕܝܥ ܠܪܒ ܟܗܢܐ
ܘܐܡܪ [o]ܠܬܪܥܝܬܐ ܘܐܥܠܬ [p]ܠܦ̈ܛܪܘܣ
17 [q]ܘܐܡܪܬ ܗܝ ܛܠܝܬܐ [r]ܬܪܥܝܬܐ ܠܦ̈ܛܪܘܣ: [q]
ܕܠܡܐ ܐܘܦ ܐܢܬ ܡܢ [s]ܬܠܡܝܕܘܝ ‡ ܕܗܢܐ ܓܒܪܐ
18 ܐܢܬ: ܘܐܡܪ ܠܗ ܠܝܬ ܐܢܐ: ܗܘܘ ܕܝܢ
[t] † ܩܐܝܡܝܢ ܥܒܕܝܐ [u]ܘܣܛܪ̈ܛܝܘܛܐ ܕܥܒܕܘ
[v]ܓܘܡܪܝܢ ܕܗܘܐ ܩܪܝܪ ܘܗܘܘ ܫܚܢܝܢ: ܗܘܐ

Codex C.

[t] add ܕܝܢ [v] ܐܓܝܒ
[w] omit ܐܡܪܬ
[x] ܐܢ [z] omit ܕܝܢ
[a] add ܗܠܝܢ
† f. 102b.
[b] ܕܢܐܙܠܘܢ [c] ܡܠܬܐ
[d] ܕܐܡܪܬ [e] ܕܗܠܝܢ
[f] ܚܕ [g] ܦܛܪܘܣ
[h] ܕܐܝܢ [i] ܫܠܦ
[j] add ܕܝܢ [k] ܠܦܛܪܘܣ
[m] ܠܐ ܫܬܝܬܐ [m]
[p] ܘܗܣܛܪ̈ܛܝܘܛܐ
[r] ܘܐܝܬܝܘ
[s] ܠܘܬ ܚܢܐܢ
[t] ܡܩܕܡܐܝ
[u] omit ܕܗܘܐ
[v] ܫܢܬܐ [x] ܘܩܝܦܐ
[y] ܕܡܠܟ [z] ܠܝܗܘܕܝܐ
[b] omit ܕ [o] ܒܬܪܗ
[c] ܘܚܪܢܝܢ [d] omit ܕܝܢ
[e] ܬܠܡܝܕܝܢ [f] omit ܕܝܢ
[i] ܠܕܪܬܐ [j] ܘܩܐܡ
[k] ܬܠܡܝܕܐ
[l] ܚܒܪܐ [n] ܕܗܘܐ
[o] ܠܬܪܥܝܬܐ [p] ܠܦܛܪܘܣ
[q] omit ܘܐܡܪܬ . . . ܠܦܛܪܘܣ . . .
[s] ܬܠܡܝܕܘܝ
† f. 103a.
[u] ܘܗܣܛܪ̈ܛܝܘܛܐ

Codex A.	Codex B.	Codex C.
ᵗܦܐܝܩ ᵘܘܥܝܢ	ܕܝ ܐܘܦ ᵍܦ̈ܝܠܛܘܣ ᵗܘܐܝܩ ܒܥܡܗܘܢ ᵘܘܥܝܢ:	ᵍܦܝܠܛܘܣ ᵗܘܐ (sic)
	19 ܝܬܒ ܕܝ ܒܒܝܡܐ ܗܘܐ ܫܠܚ ܠܘܬܗ ܐܢܬܬܗ	
	ܠܐ ܠܟ ܬܬܠܚܡܘܢ ܘܟܠ ܠܟ ܐܬܠܚܡܘܢ:	
	20 ܐܠܝܢ ܕܝ ܪܒܢܐ ܘܐܡܪܘ ܠܗ ܐܢܫܐ ᵛܕܝ	ᵛomit ܕܝ
ᵛomit ܕܝ ʷܠܚܡܠܟܐ	[f. 104a] ܕܩ̈ܫܝܫܐ ܡܠܠܬ ᵛܕܝ ʷܠܚܡܠܟܐ: ܐܢܫܐ ܒܟܘܠ	ʷܠܚܡܠܟܐ
ˣomit ܪܒ ʸܡܠܟܘ	ˣܪܒ ܗܘܬ ʸܡܠܟܘ ᶻܒܟܢܫܬܐ ܘܒܟܘܫܐ ܗܘ	ᶻܒܟܢܫܬܐ
ᵃܫܗܕܝܢ	ܕܟܠܗܘܢ ᵃܫܗܕܝܢ ᵇܡܬܒܥܝܢ ܘܟܦܪܘܢ ܠܐ	ᵇܡܬܒܥܝܢ
ᵇܡܬܒܥܝܢ	21 ᶜܡܠܠܬ ܒܟܘܠܡ: ᵈܡܢܐ ܐܢܬ ᵉܫܐܠ ܠܝ ܥܠ	ᶜܡܠܠܬ ᵈܕܡܢܐ
	ᶠܠܗܠܝܢ ܕܫܡܥܘ ܡܢܐ ܡܠܠܬ ܠܗܘܢ: ܗܐ	ᵉܫܐܠ ᶠܠܗܘܢ
ᵇomit ܕܝ	22 ܗܢܘܢ ܕܚܝܡ ܡܢܐ ܐܡܪܬ ܐܢܐ: ܘܡܕ ᵇܕܝ	ᵇomit ܕܝ
ⁱܕܗܘܐ ʲܦܐܝܩ	ܐܡܪ ܗܠܝܢ ܚܕ ⁱܗܘܐ ʲܘܐܝܩ ܡܢ ܗܦܪ̈ܫܝܢܐ	ⁱܕܗܘܐ ʲܘܐܝܩ
	ܫܡܥ ܠܡܪܐ ܗܢܘܢ ܒܡܫܦܪ: ܘܐܡܪ ܠܗ:	
ˡܒܕ	23 ˡܒܕܝܢ ܐܬ ܡܠܝܢ ܠܦܬ ܒܡܫܝܚܐ: ܘܐܡܪ ܠܗ	
ᵒܐܡܫܪ	ܡܪܐ ܗܘܢ ᵐܐܢ ⁿܒܫܐܝܬ ܐܡܪܬ ᵒܐܡܫܪ	ᵐܐܝܢ ⁿܒܫܝܬ
	ᵖܥܠ ܒܫܬܐ: ᵐܐܢ ܕܝ ܐܘܬ ܠܡܢܐ ܐܬ	ᵒܐܡܫܪ ᵖܥܠ
ᵠܫܢܘ	24 ܡܫܐܠܐ ܠܝ: ܘܥܠܝܫ ܢܬܗ ᵠܫܢܐܘܢ ʳܒܦܫܬ ܠܘܬ	ᵠܫܢܐܘܢ ʳܒܦܫܬ
ˢܦܐܝܩܘܢ ᵗܘܥܝܢ	25 ˢܘܐܝܩܘܢ ܝܬܒ ܒܡܫܝܚܐ: ܗܘܐ ܕܝ ܫܡܥܘܢ	ˢܘܐܝܩܘܢ
‡ f. 127a.	ᵍܦ̈ܝܠܛܘܣ ‡ ʲܘܐܝܩ ᵗܘܥܝܢ: ᵘܘܐܡܪܝܢ ܠܗ	ᵘܘܐܡܪܝܢ
	ܕܡܢܐ ܐܘܦ ܐܬ ܫܕ ܡܢ ᵛܬܠܡܝܕܘܝ ܐܬ:	ᵛܬܠܡܝܕܘܝ
	26 ܘܟܦܪ ܗܘ ܘܐܡܪ ܠܝܬ ܐܢܐ: ܘܐܡܪ ܫܕ ܡܢ	
ʷܒܟܪܕܘ ʸܕܗܕܐ	ʷܒܟܪܕܝ ܕܝܫ ܒܡܫܝܚܐ: ܕܗܘܐ ˣܦܪܒܗ ʸܕܗܕܝܢ	ˣܦܪܒܝ ʸܠܗܕܝܢ
	ܕܦܠܓ ᵍܦ̈ܝܠܛܘܣ † ܐܕܝܢܗ: ܠܐ ܐܢܐ ܫܡܥܬ	† f. 103b.
	27 ܢܬܦ ܒܥܡܗ ܟܠܢܫܬܐ: ܘܬܘܒܡ ܒܥܪ ᵍܦ̈ܝܠܛܘܣ:	
ᶻܘܐܘܒܠ	28 ܘܫܥܐ ܡܪܐ ܬܫܒܘܚܬܐ: ᶻܘܐܘܒ̈ܠܘ ᵃܢܬܗ	ᶻܘܐܘܒܠܘ ᵃomit ܢܬܗ
	ܠܡܪܐ ܫܡܥܘܢ ܡܢ ܠܘܬ ˢܘܐܝܩܘܢ ܠܗܦ̈ܠܝܛܘܪܝܢ:	
ᵇܒܦ̈ܬܐܟܘܢ	ܗܘܐ ܕܝ ܟܦܪܐ: ܘܠܐ ܒܠܘ ܗܢܘܢ ܠܗܦ̈ܠܝܛܘܪܝܢ	ᵇܫܬܐܟܘܢ
ᶜܒܐܟ̈ܠܘܢ	ܕܠܐ ᵇܫܬܗܟܘܢ: ܐܠܐ ᶜܐܟ̈ܠܘܢ ᵈܒܫܝܐ:	ᶜܟ̈ܠܘܢ ᵈܒܫܝܐ

Matt. XXVI. 57—75.

Codex A.	Codex B.	Codex C.
ᵃܐܬܟܢܫ ܐܬܬܠܬ ܡܢ ᵃܬܠܡܝܕܘܝ	ᵃܐܬܟܢܫ ܐܬܬܠܬ ܠܬܠܬ ܐܠܟܣܢܕܪܘܣ ܡܢ	ᵃܐܬܟܢܫ ܐܬܬܠܬ ܠܬܠܬ ᵃܐܠܟܣܢܕܪܘܣ ܡܢ ܡܠܬܐ
ᵃܘܪ̈ܗܒܢܝ ܕܝ ᵇadd	57 ܡܠܐܟܘܢ: ᵃܘܒܢܝܗ ܦܪܘܣܐ: ᵃܘܪ̈ܗܒܢܝ ܗܠܝܢ ᵇ	ᵃܘܪ̈ܗܒܢܐ

Codex B.

[f. 104b]
ܕܐܚܕܘ ܠܡܪܢܐ ܝܣܘܣ ܐܘܒ̈ܠܘ[c] ܝܬܗ ܠܘܬ
ܩܝܦܐ ܪܒ ܟܗܢܐ: ܠܗܢ ܕܐܬܟܢܫܘ [d]ܪܒܢ
58 ܟܗܢܝܐ ܘܣܦܪܝܐ ܘܩܫܝܫܝܐ: ܦ̈ܛܪܘܣ ܕܝܢ
ܗܘܐ ܐܬܐ ܒܬܪܗ ܡܢ ܪܚܘܩ: ܥܕ ܕܪܬܐ
ܠܕܪܬܗ ܕܪܒ ܟܗܢܐ: ܘܥܕ ܥܠ ܠܓܘ ܘܗܘܐ
[g]ܝܬܒ ܥܡ [h]ܗܘ̈ܦܪܝܛܐ ܕܢܚܙܐ [i]ܫܘܠܡܐ:
59 ܪܒܢ ܟܗܢܐ[j] ܘܩܫܝܫܝܐ [k]ܘܟܢܫܬܐ ܟܠܗ: ܗܘܘ
ܒܥܝܢ ܣܗܕܘ [l]ܕܫܩܪ ܥܠ ‡ ܡܪܢܐ ܝܣܘܣ ܗܝܟ
60 [m]ܕܝܡܝܬܘܢ ܝܬܗ: ܘܠܐ ܗܘܘ ܡܫܟܚܝܢ:
ܘܗܕܐ ܕܣܓܝ ܣܗܕܝܢ ܕܫܩܪ ܩܪܒܘ: [o]ܒܚܪܬܐ
61 ܕܝܢ ܩܪܒܘ ܬܪܝܢ: ܘܐܡܪܘ ܗܕܝܢ ܐܡܪ [p]ܐܝܟܠ
ܐܢܐ ܕܐܫܪܐ ܢܘܣܗ ܕܐܠܗܐ ܘܠܬܠܬܐ [r]ܝܘܡܝܢ
62 ܒܢܝܐ ܝܬܗ: ܘܩܡ ܪܒ ܟܗܢܐ ܘܐܡܪ ܠܗ
ܐܘܦ ܠܐ ܬܦܢܐ ܠܢܬ ܐܢܬ ܦܬܓܡܝܢ ܡܢ ܡܐ
63 ܕܗܠܝܢ [t]ܕܝܢ ܡܣܗܕܝܢ ܥܠܝܟ: ܗܘ ܕܝܢ ܡܪܢܐ
ܝܣܘܣ [u]ܗܘܐ [v]ܫܬܩ: ܘܥܢܐ ܪܒ ܟܗܢܐ ܐܡܪ
ܠܗ: ܡܘܡܐ ܐܢܐ [w]ܥܠܝܟ ܒܐܠܗܐ ܚܝܐ
[x]ܕܬܐܡܪ ܠܢ ܐܢ ܐܢܬ ܗܘ ܡܫܝܚܐ [y]ܒܪܗ
64 ܕܐܠܗܐ: †ܐܡܪ ܠܗ ܡܪܢܐ ܝܣܘܣ ܐܢܬ ܐܡܪܬ:
[z]ܒܪܡ ܕܝܢ ܐܡܪ ܐܢܐ ܠܟܘܢ: ܕܡܢ ܟܕܘ
ܬܚܙܘܢ ܠܒܪܗ ܕܓܒܪܐ [b]ܝܬܒ ܡܢ [c]ܝܡܝܢܗ
[d]ܕܚܝܠܐ: ܘܐܬܐ ܥܠ [e]ܥܢܢܝܐ ܕܫܡܝܐ:
65 [f]ܒܟܝܢ ܪܒ ܟܗܢܐ ܒܙܥ [g]ܡܐܢܘܗܝ ܘܐܡܪ
[f. 105a]
[h]ܓܕܦ ܡܢܐ ܥܘܕ [i]ܐܢܚܢ ܨܪܝܟܝܢ ܣܗܕܝܢ ܗܐ
66 ܟܕܘ ܫܡܥܬܘܢ [j]ܓܕܘܦܝܗ ܡܢܐ ܗܘܝܐ ܠܟܘܢ:
ܗܢܘܢ [k]ܐܓܝܒܘ ܐܡܪܝܢ ܚܝܒ ܗܘ [l]ܒܡܘܬܐ:
67 [m]ܒܟܝܢ [n]ܪܩܘ [o]ܒܐܦ̈ܘܝ ܘܡܚܘ ܝܬܗ [p]ܡܠܦܛܝܢ:
68 [q]ܘܐܚܪܢܝܢ ܡܚܘ ‡ ܝܬܗ ܡܣܛܪܘܢ ܘܐܡܪܝܢ:
ܐܬܢܒܐ ܠܢ ܡܫܝܚܐ ܡܢ ܗܘ [r]ܕܡܚܐ ܝܬܟ:
69 [s]ܦ̈ܛܪܘܣ ܕܝܢ ܗܘܐ [t]ܝܬܒ ܠܒܪ ܒܕܪܬܐ ܘܩܪܒܬ
[u]ܚܕܐ [w]ܛܠܝܬܐ [x]ܐܡܪܐ ܠܗ: [y]ܐܦ ܐܢܬ ܗܘܝܬ[z]

Codex A.

[c] ܐܘܒ̈ܠܘ
[d] ܪܒ̈ܢܐ
[h] ܗܘ̈ܦܪܝܛܝܐ
[i] ܫܘܠܡܐ — [j] add ܕܝܢ
[k] ܘܟܢܫܬܐ — [l] ܕܫܩܪ
‡ f. 127b.
[m] ܕܝܡܝܬܘܢ
[o] ܒܚܪ̈ܬܐ
[p] ܝܟܠ
[r] ܝܘ̈ܡܝܢ
[t] omit ܕܝܢ
[v] ܫܬܝܩ
[w] ܠܟ
[x] ܕܬܐܡܪ
[z] ܒܪܡ
[b] ܝܬܒ — [c] ܝܡܝܢܐ
[e] ܥܢܢܝܐ
[f] ܒܟܝܢ — [i] ܐܢܚܢ
[k] add ܕܝܢ — [m] ܒܟܝܢ
[n] ܪܩܩܘ — [o] ܒܐܦ̈ܘܝ
[p] ܡܠܦܛܝܢ
[q] ܘܐܚܪ̈ܢܝܢ
‡ f. 128a.
[r] add ܕܗܘ — [t] ܝܬܒ
[u] ܚܕܐ — [w] ܛܠܝܬܐ
[y] add ܐܘܦ — [z] ܗܘܝܬ

Codex C.

[c] ܐܘܒ̈ܠܘ
[d] ܪܒ̈ܢܐ
[g] ܝܬܒ — [i] ܫܘܠܡܐ
[j] add ܕܝܢ
[l] ܕܫܩܪ
[m] ܕܝܡܝܬܘܢ
[p] ܝܟܠ
[r] ܝܘܡܝܢ
[t] omit ܕܝܢ
[u] omit ܗܘܐ
[w] ܠܟ — [x] ܕܬܐܡܪ
[y] ܒܪܗ
† f. 104a.
[c] ܝܡܝܢܐ — [d] ܕܚܝܠܬܐ
[e] ܥܢܢܝܗ
[g] ܡܐܢܘܝ
[h] ܓܕܦ — [i] ܐܢܚܢ
[j] ܓܕܘܦܝ
[k] add ܕܝܢ — [l] ܒܡܘܬܐ
[o] ܒܐܦ̈ܘܝ
[p] ܡܠܦܛܝܢ
[q] ܘܐܚܪܢܝܢ — [r] add ܕܗܘ
[s] ܦܛܪܘܣ — [u] ܚܕܐ
[x] ܐܡܪܐ — [y] add ܐܘܦ

Codex A.

[x] *add* ܕܝܢ

[y] ܡܚܒܪ

[d] ܕܝܢ

[g] ܕܠܝܬ

[i] ܠܗ [j] ܠܓܒܪܐ

[k] ܙܥܝܪ

[l] ܕܩܐܡܝܢ

[o] ܢܕܥ [p] ܒܟܝܢ

[r] ܘܐܡܪ [s] ܡܟܪ

[v] ܗܕܝܢ

[w] ܬܪܢܓܘܠܐ

[z] *add* ܫܠܡ

[b] ܐܘܢܓܠܝܢ ܐܘܪܒܐ ‡ ܠܠܝܠܝܐ ܐܘܢܓܠܣܛܣ
‡ f. 128*b*. [b] ܐܘܢܓܠܝܣ

[z] *add* ܘܟܬܒܬ ܡܢ ܬܘܡܐ

[c] ܢܬܛܡܐܘܢ

[d] ܢܐܟܠܘܢ

[g] ܩܛܪܓܘܪܝܢ

[h] ܡܩܒܠܝܢ [i] ܗܕܝܢ

[k] ܒܝܫ

[l] ܢܡܘܣܟܘܢ

[o] ܝܗܘܕܝܐ [n] *add* ܕܝܢ

Codex B.

70 ܥܡ ܝܫܘܥ ܓܠܝܠܝܐ[w]: ܗܘ[x] ܟܦܪ ܩܘܕܡ
ܟܠܗܘܢ ܐܡܪ ܠܝܬ ܐܢܐ ܝܕܥ ܡܐ ܐܬܝ
71 ܐܡܪܐ: ܘܠܐ [y]ܡܚܒܪ: ܟܕ ܕܝܢ ܢܦܩ
[a]ܠܬ̈ܪܥܐ [b]ܚܙܬ ܝܬܗ ܚܪܢܝ ܘܐܡܪܐ
[c]ܠܗܠܝܢ ܕܗܘܘ ܬܡܢ ܐܘܦ [d]ܕܝܢ [e]ܗܘܐ ܥܡ
72 ܝܫܘܥ [f]ܢܨܪܝܐ: ܘܬܘܒ ܟܦܪ ܒܡܘܡܬܐ
73 [g]ܠܝܬ ܐܢܐ [h]ܡܟܪ [i]ܠܗܕܝܢ [j]ܓܒܪܐ: ܘܒܬܪ
[k]ܙܥܝܪ ܩܪܒܘ ܗܠܝܢ [l]ܕܩܝܡܝܢ ܘܐܡܪܘ [m]ܠܦ̈ܛܪܘܣ:
[n]ܡܫܪܝܪܬ ܐܘܦ ܐܢܬ ܡܢܗܘܢ ܐܢܬ: ܐܘܦ
74 ܡܡܠܠܟ ܓܪ ܡܒܕܩ ܠܟ [o]ܢܕܥ: [p]ܒܟܝܢ ܫܪܝ
[q]ܡܚܪܡ [r]ܘܡܝܡܐ [†]ܕܠܝܬ ܐܢܐ [s]ܡܟܪ[t]
[u]ܠܓܒܪܐ [v]ܗܕܝܢ: ܘܡܝܕ ܩܪܐ [w]ܬܪܢܓܘܠܐ:
75 [x]ܘܐܬܕܟܪ [y]ܦ̈ܛܪܘܣ ܡܠܬܗ ܕܡܪܢ ܝܫܘܥ
ܕܐܡܪ ܠܗ: ܕܥܕ ܠܐ ܢܩܪܐ ܬܪܢܓܘܠܐ ܬܠܬܐ
ܙܒܢܝܢ ܬܟܦܘܪ ܒܝ: ܘܢܦܩ ܠܗ ܠܒܪ ܘܒܟܐ
ܡܪܝܪܐܝܬ:[z]

John XVIII. 28—XIX. 16.

[ba]ܐܘܢܓܠܝܢ ܐܘܪܒܐ ܠܠܝܠܝܐ ܐܘܢܓܠܣܛܣ[b] ܡܢ
28 ܝܘܚܢܢ[a]:[z] ܘܐܘܒܠܘ ܝܬܗ ܠܡܪܢ ܝܫܘܥ ܡܢ
[f. 105*b*]
ܠܘܬ [a]ܩܝܦܐ [v]ܠܦ̈ܪܛܘܪܝܢ ܗܘܐ ܕܝܢ ܨܦܪܐ:
ܘܠܐ ܥܠܘ ܗܢܘܢ [b]ܠܦ̈ܪܛܘܪܝܢ ܕܠܐ
[c]ܢܬܛܡܐܘܢ: ܐܠܐ [d]ܢܐܟܠܘܢ [e]ܦܨܚܐ
29 ܘܢܦܩ [f]ܦܝܠܛܘܣ ܠܘܬܗܘܢ ܠܒܪ: ܘܐܡܪ
ܠܗܘܢ ܡܢܐ [g]ܩܛܪܓܘܪܝܢ ܐܝܬܘܢ [h]ܡܩܒܠܝܢ
30 ܥܠ [i]ܗܕܝܢ ܓܒܪܐ: ܐܬܝܒܘ ܘܐܡܪܝܢ ܠܗ
ܐܠܘ ܠܐ ܗܘܐ [i]ܗܕܝܢ [j]ܥܒܕ [k]ܒܝܫ: ܠܐ
31 ܗܘܝܢܢ ܡܫܠܡܝܢ ܠܗ ܠܟ: ܐܡܪ ܠܗܘܢ
ܦܝܠܛܘܣ: ܣܒܘ ܝܬܗ ܐܢܬܘܢ ܘܕܘܢܘ
[l]ܟܢܡܘܣܟܘܢ [m]ܕܝܢܘ ܝܬܗ: ܐܡܪܝܢ ܠܗ[n]
[o]ܝܗܘܕܝ ܠܐ [p]ܫܠܝܛ ܠܢ ܕܢܩܛܘܠ ܠܐܢܫ

Codex C.

[w] ܢܨܪܝܐ [x] *add* ܕܝܢ

[a] ܠܬܪܥܐ

[b] ܚܙܬ [c] ܠܗܠܝܢ

[d] ܕܝܢ [e] *omit* ܗܘܐ

[f] ܢܨܪܝܐ

[g] ܕܠܝܬ [h] ܡܟܪ

[l] ܕܩܐܡܝܢ

[m] ܠܦܛܪܘܣ

[n] ܡܫܪܝܪܬ [q] ܡܚܪܡ

† f. 104*b*.

[t] *add* ܠܗܕܝܢ [u] ܓܒܪܐ

[x] ܘܐܬܕܟܪ [y] ܦܛܪܘܣ

[a] ܐܘܢܓܠܝܢ ܐܘܪܒܐ ܕܠܝܠܝܐ ܐܘܢܓܠܣܛܣ ܡܢ ܝܘܚܢܢ[a]

[z] *add* ܘܟܬܒܬܗ.

[a] ܩܝܦܐ

[v] ܠܗܓܡܘܢܝܘܬܐ

[b] ܠܗܓܡܘܢܝܘܬܐ

[c] ܢܬܛܡܐܘܢ

[d] ܢܐܟܠܘܢ [e] ܦܨܚܐ

[f] ܦܝܠܛܘܣ

[g] ܩܛܪܓܘܪܝܢ

[j] *omit* ܥܒܕ

[m] ܕܝܢܘ [n] *add* ܕܝܢ

[p] ܫܠܝܛ

Codex B.

32 ᵃܕܬܫܬܠܡ ܡܠܬܗ ܕܡܪܢܐ ܝܫܘܥ : ᵇܗܕܐ
ܕܐܡܪ ᶜܡܘܕܥ ܒܗܕܝܢ ᵈܡܘܬܗ ܗܘ ܥܬܝܕ
33 ܕܝܡܘܬ : ܥܠ ܕܝܢ ܦ̈ܝܠܛܘܣ ܬܘܒܢ ʰܠܦܪ̈ܛܘܪܝܢ
34 ܘܩܪܐ ܠܡܪܢܐ ܝܫܘܥ ܘܐܡܪ ܠܗ : ᵉܐܢܬ ܗܘ
ܒܪܥܝܢܟ ܐܡܪܬ ܗܕܐ : ܐܐ ܚܘܪܢܝܢ ܐܡܪܘ
35 ܠܟ ܥܠ ܕܦܢܝ : ܐܡܝܢ ᶠܕܝܢ ᵍܦ̈ܝܠܛܘܣ
ܘܐܡܪ ܠܗ : ܕܠܡܐ ܐܢܐ ܝܗܘܕܝ ܐܢܐ ʰܡܫܟ
ⁱܡܠܝܟ : ᵏܘܪܒܢܝ ܟܗܢܐ ܡܫܠܡܘ ܝܬܟ ܠܝ
36 ܡܢܐ ܥܒܕܬ : ܐܡܝܢ ܡܪܢܐ ˡܝܫܘܥ ܘܐܡܪ
ܠܗ ܡܠܟܘܬܝ ܕܝܠܝ ܡܢ ܕܝܢ ᵐܥܠܡܐ :ᵃ
ܐܠܘ ܗܘܬ ܡܠܟܘܬܝ ܡܢ ܗܕܝܢ ᵐܥܠܡܐ :
ܫܡܫܝ ܕܝܠܝ ܐܝܬ ⁿܗܘܘ ᵒܡܬܟܬܫܝܢ ܥܠ
ܕܦܢܝ : ܕܠܐ ܐܫܬܠܡ ᵖܠܝܗܘܕܝܐ : ܟܕܘ ܕܝܢ
37 ᑫܡܠܟܘܬܝ ܠܝܬ ܗܝ ܡܢ ʳܟܐ : ܐܡܪ ܠܗ
ܐܘܦ ܦ̈ܝܠܛܘܣ : ܗܘܝ ܐܘܦ ˢܡܠܝܟ ܐܢܬ :
ᵗܐܡܝܢ ܡܪܢܐ ܝܫܘܥ ܘܐܡܪ ܠܗ ܐܢܬ
ᵘܐܡܪܬ ܕܐܢܐ ᵛܡܠܝܟ : ʷܐܢܐ ˣܠܗܕܝܢ
ʸܐܬܝܠܕܬ ᶻܘܠܗܝܢ ܐܬܝܬ ᵃܠܥܠܡܐ ᵇܕܐܣܗܕ
ܥܠ ܩܘܫܛܐ : ܟܠ ܡܢ ᶜܕܗܘ ܩܘܫܛܐ :
38 ܫܡܥ ܗܘ ܠܩܠܝ : ܐܡܪ ܠܗ ܦ̈ܝܠܛܘܣ ܡܢܐ
ܗܘ ܩܘܫܛܐ : ܘܟܕ ܐܡܪ ܗܕܐ : ܬܘܒܢ ܢܦܩ
ܠܘܬ ᵈܝܗܘܕܝܐ ܘܐܡܪ ܠܗܘܢ : ܐܢܐ ܐܘܦ
ܠܐ ܫܟܚ ܥܠܐ ܠܝܬ ܐܢܐ ܡܫܟܚ ᵉܒܗ :
39 ܐܝܬ ܠܟܘܢ ᶠܐܘܠܦ ᵍܕܐܝܕܐ ܚܕ ܠܟܘܢ
ܫܪܐ ʰܒܦܣܚܐ ܨܒܝܢ ܐܬܘܢ ܐܢܘܢ ⁱܕܐܫܪܐ
40 ܠܟܘܢ ܠܡܠܟܗܘܢ ʲܕܝܗܘܕܝܐ : ᵏܘܨܘܚܘ ܟܘܠܗܘܢ
ܘܐܡܪܝܢ ܠܐ ܗܕܝܢ ܐܠܐ ܠܒܪܐܒܐ : ˡܗܘܐ
XIX. 1 ᵐܒܪܐܒܐ ⁿܠܣܛܝܐ : ܒܟܝܢ ܐܘܦ ܦ̈ܝܠܛܘܣ ܢܣܒ
2 ܠܡܪܢܐ ܝܫܘܥ ܘܢܓܕܗ ᵒܒܦ̈ܪܓܠܐ : ᵖܘܪܘܡܝܢ
ܓܕܠܘ ܟܠܝܠ ᑫܡܢ ܟܘܒܝܢ ʳܘܐܣܝܡܘܗ ܥܠ
ܪܝܫܗ : ˢܘܡܠܒܫܝܢ ܕܐܪܓܘܢ ᵗܟܣܘ ܝܬܗ :

Codex A.

ᵃܕܬܫܬܠܡܬ
ʰܠܦܪܛܘܪܝܢ
ᵉ *add* ܐܢܬ ܗܘ ܡܠܟܗܘܢ ܕܝܗܘܕܝܐ . ܐܡܪ ܠܗ ܡܪܢܐ ܝܫܘܥ :
ᶠ *omit* ܕܝܢ
ʰܡܒܝܢܟ ⁱܕܡܠܝܟ
ᵏܘܪܒܢܝ
ˡ *omit* ܝܫܘܥ
ᵐܥܠܡܐ
ᵃ *add* ܠܝܬ ܗܝ
ⁿܗܘ ᵖܠܝܗܘܕܝܐ
ˢܡܠܝܟ ᵗܐܡܝܢ
ᵛܡܠܝܟ
ˣܠܗܢ ᶻܘܠܗܢ
ᵃܠܥܠܡܐ ᵇܕܐܣܗܕ
ᶜܗܘ
ᵈܝܗܘܕܝܐ
ᶠ *add* ܕܝܢ ᵍܕܐܝܕܐ
ʰܒܦܣܚܐ
ⁱܕܐܫܪܐ
ʲܕܝܗܘܕܝܐ
ᵏܘܨܘܚܘ
ᵐܒܪܐܒܐ
ⁿܠܣܛܝܐ
ᵖܘܪܘܡܝܢ
ᑫ *omit* ܡܢ
ʳܘܐܣܝܡܘܗ ˢܘܡܢ

Codex C.

ᵃܕܬܫܬܠܡ
ᵇܗܕܝܢ
ᶜܡܘܕܥ ᵈܡܘܬܗ
ʰܠܦܪܛܘܪܝܢ
ᶠ *omit* ܕܝܢ
ᵍܦܝܠܛܘܣ
ʰܡܫܟ
ⁱܡܠܝܟ
ᵒܡܬܟܬܫܝܢ
ᵖܠܝܗܘܕܝܐ : ܗܘ
ᑫܡܠܟܘܬܐ
ܟܐ ʳ *omit* ˢܡܠܝܟ
ᵗܐܡܝܢ
ܐܡܪ ܐܢܐ ᵘ ʷ *omit*
ʸܐܬܝܠܕ
ᵃܠܥܠܡܐ
ᵇܕܐܣܗܕ ᶜܕܗܘܐ
ᵉ *omit* ܒܗ
ᶠ *add* ܕܝܢ
ᵍܕܝܗܘܕܝܐ ʰܒܦܣܚܐ
ⁱܕܐܫܪܐ
ʲܕܝܗܘܕܝܐ ᵏܘܨܘܚܘ
ˡ *add* ܕܝܢ
ᵐܒܪܐܒܐ ⁿܠܣܛܝܐ
ᵒܒܦܪܓܠܐ ˢܘܡܢ
ᵗܟܣܘ

Codex B.

3 ܘܗܘܘ ܐܬܝܢ ܠܘܬܗ ܘܐܡܪܝܢ ܫܠܡ ܠܟ
ܡܠܟܗܘܢ [p]ܕܝܗܘܕܝܝܢ ܘܗܘܘ ܡܚܝܢ ܠܗ
4 [q]ܒܣܦܛܘܪܝܢ: ܘܢܦܩ ܐܘܦ ܬܘܒ [r]ܦ̈ܝܠܛܘܣ
ܠܒܪ ܘܐܡܪ ܠܗܘܢ: ܗܐ ܐܢܐ [s]ܡܦܩܐ ܠܗ
ܠܟܘܢ ܠܒܪ ⁝ [t]ܕܐܬܘܢ ܕܬܝܕܥܘܢ [u]ܕܠܐ
5 ܠܝܬ ܐܢܐ [v]ܡܫܟܚ ܒܗ ⁝ ܘܢܦܩ ܐܘܦ ܡܪܢܐ
ܝܫܘܥ ܠܒܪ ܡܟܠܠ ܟܠܝܠܐ ܕܟܘܒܝܐ [w]ܘܡܐܢܐ
ܕܐܪܓܘܢܐ ܘܐܡܪ ܠܗܘܢ ܗܐ ܓܒܪܐ ⁝
6 ܘܟܕ ܚܙܘ ܝܬܗ ܪܒܢܝ ܟܗܢܐ ܘܗܘ̈ܦܪܛܝܐ ⁝
ܒܥܝܢ [x]ܓܥܘ [y]ܘܐܡܪܝܢ [z]ܨܠܘܒ [a z]ܨܠܘܒ [b]ܝܬܗ:
ܘܐܡܪ ܠܗܘܢ [s]ܦ̈ܝܠܛܘܣ [a]ܣܒܘ ܝܬܗ ܐܬܘܢ
[c]ܘܨܠܘܒܘ ܝܬܗ: ܐܢܐ ܓܪ ܠܝܬ ܐܢܐ [d]ܡܫܟܚ
7 ܒܗ ܥܠܐ ⁝ ܘܐܓܝܒܘ [e]ܝܗܘܕܝܝܢ [f]ܘܐܡܪܘ
ܠܗ: ܐܝܬ ܢܡܘܣܐ ܐܝܬ ܠܢ ܘܗܝܟ ܢܡܘܣܐ
ܚܝܒ ܗܘ ܕܝܡܘܬ: ܕܥܒܕ ܢܦܫܗ ܒܪܗ
8 ܕܐܠܗܐ: ܘܟܕ ܐܘܦ ܫܡܥ ܦ̈ܝܠܛܘܣ ܗܕܐ
9 ܡܠܬܐ [g]ܕܚܠ ܠܚܕܐ: ܘܥܠ [h]ܠܦ̈ܠܛܘܪܝܢ ܬܘܒ
ܘܐܡܪ ܠܡܪܢܐ ܝܫܘܥ ܡܢ ܗܘ ܐܢܬ ⁝ ܘܡܪܢܐ
10 ܝܫܘܥ ܕܝܢ ܐܦܢܝ ܘܠܐ [i]ܝܗܒ ܠܗ ⁝ ܘܐܡܪ
ܠܗ [j]ܦ̈ܝܠܛܘܣ [k]ܠܝ [l]ܠܝܬ ܐܢܬ [m]ܡܡܠܠ: ܠܝܬ ܐܢܬ
[n]ܝܕܥ ܕܐܢܐ ܫܠܝܛ ܕܐܨܠܒܟ ܐܢܬ: [o]ܘܫܠܝܛ
11 [p]ܐܢܐ [q]ܕܐܫܪܝܟ ܐܢܬ ⁝ [r]ܘܐܓܝܒ [s]ܡܪܢܐ ܝܫܘܥ
ܘܐܡܪ ܠܗ: ܠܝܬ ܠܟ [t]ܟܠ [u]ܫܘܠܛܢ [v]ܐܘܦ ܠܐ
ܚܕܐ ⁝ ܐܠܘ ܠܐ [i]ܝܗܒ ܠܟ ܡܢ ܠܥܠ:
[w]ܠܟܠܠ [x]ܒܕܝܢ [y]ܕܝܢ ܕܡܫܠܡ ܝܬܝ ܠܟ ܚܛܝܐ
12 ܡܢ ܗܕܐ ܐܝܬܝ ܠܗ ⁝ [z]ܘܒܥܐ ܗܘܐ [a]ܦ̈ܝܠܛܘܣ
[b]ܒܥܝܢ [p]ܕܢܫܪܝܘܢ ܝܬܗ ⁝ [d]ܘܗܘܘ [e]ܝܗܘܕܝܝܢ [f]
[g]ܓܥܘ [h]ܘܐܡܪܝܢ [i]ܐܢ ܫܪܐ ܐܢܬ ܠܗܕܝܢ
[j]ܠܝܬ ܐܢܬ [j] [l]ܪܚܡܗ ܕܩܝܣܪ: ܕܟܠ ܡܢ [m]ܕܥܒܕ
13 ܢܦܫܗ [n]ܡܠܟ ܡܩܒܠ ܠܡܠܟܐ ܩܝܣܪ ⁝ [a]ܦ̈ܝܠܛܘܣ
ܐܘܦ ܟܕ ܫܡܥ ܗܠܝܢ ܡܠܝܐ: [o]ܐܦܩ ܝܬܗ

Codex A.

[p] ܕܝܗܘܕܝ
[q] ܡܒܣܦܛܘܪ̈ܝܢ
[s] ܡܦܩܬܐ
[t] omit ܕܐܬܘܢ
[u] ܕܓܠܐ
[w] ܘܡܐܢܐ
[x] ܓܥ̈ܥܘ [z] ܨܠܘܒ
[a] ܣ̈ܒܘ
[c] ܘܨ̈ܠܘܒܘ
[e] ܝܗܘܕܝ
[g] ܕܚܠ
[j] add ܕܝܢ [l] ܠܝܬܬ
[m] ܡܡܠܠ [n] ܝܕܥܬ
[q] ܕܐܫܪܝܟ [t] omit ܟܠ
[u] ܫܘܠܛܢ [w] ܠܟܠܠ
[x] ܒܕ [y] ܕܝܢ
[d] omit ܘܗܘܘ
[e] ܘܝܗܘ̈ܕܝܝܢ
[f] add ܐܘܦ
[g] ܓܥ̈ܘܥܘ
[h] ܘܐܡܪܝܢ
[i] add ܦܢܝ [j] ܠܝܬܬ
[l] ܪܚܡܗ [m] ܕܒܕ
[n] ܡܠܟ [o] ܐܦܩܬ

Codex C.

[p] ܕܝܘܕܝ
[r] ܦܝܠܛܘܣ
[t] omit ܕܐܬܘܢ
[u] ܕܟܠܐ
[v] ܡܫܟܚ
[w] ܘܡܐܢܐ
[y] ܐܡܪܝܢ [z] ܨܠܘܒ
[a] ܨܠܘܒ
[b] omit ܝܬܗ [d] ܡܫܟܚ
[e] ܘܝܘܕܝ [f] ܘܐܡܪܝܢ
[h] ܠܦܠܛܘܪܝܢ
[i] ܡܗܒ [j] add ܕܝܢ
[k] omit ܠܝ
[l] ܠܝܬܬ [m] ܡܠܠ
[o] ܘܫܠܝܛ
[p] omit ܐܢܐ
[r] ܐܓܝܒ
[s] add ܕܝܢ [t] omit ܟܠ
[u] ܫܘܠܛܢ [z] ܘܠܚܡ
[a] ܦܝܠܛܘܣ [b] ܒܥܐ
[p] ܕܢܫܪܝܘܗܝ [d] omit ܘܗܘܘ
[e] ܘܝܘܕܝܝܢ
[f] add ܐܘܦ [i] ܐܡ
[j] ܠܝܬܬ
[l] ܪܚܡܗ [m] ܕܒܕ

Codex A.	Codex B.	Codex C.
ܕܝ [q] omit	ܠܚܪܢܐ ܫܡܥܘ ܠܒܪ : ܘܐܬܚܢ ܟܠ [o]ܒܝܬܐ [q]ܕܝ	[o]ܒܝܬܐ
[r]ܥܘܒܕܐ	ܕܐܬܬܐ ܗܢ ܕܥܒܕܬܗ [r]ܥܘܒܕܐ [s]ܕܒܝܫܬܐ :	ܕܝ [q] omit [r]ܥܘܒܕܐ
[t]ܣܟܪܝܘܛܐ	14 [t]ܣܟܪܝܘܛܐ ܕܝ [u]ܚܕܬܐ : ܘܗܘܐ ܒܟܢܫܬܗ	[s]ܕܒܝܫܬܐ
	[v]ܕܡܫܝܚܐ : ܗܘܐ ܕܝ ܗܢܘܢ ܫܒܥ ܥܣܪ :	[t]ܣܟܪܝܘܛܐ
[w]ܠܝܗܘܕܝܢ	ܘܗܘܐ ܐܡܪ [w]ܠܝܗܘܕܝܢ ܗܐ [x]ܡܠܟܟܘܢ :	[u]ܚܕܬܐ
	15 ܘܗܢܘܢ ܕܝ ܗܘܘ ܐܡܪܝܢ [y]ܐܪܝܡ [y]ܐܪܝܡ	[v]ܕܦܪܘܩܐ [w]ܠܝܗܘܕܝܢ
	ܙܩܘܦܝ ܠܗ : ܘܐܡܪ ܠܗܘܢ ܦܝܠܛܘܣ	[x]ܡܠܟܟܘܢ
[z] add ܐܚܪܢܐ	ܠܡܠܟܟܘܢ ܙܩܘܦ : [z]ܐܚܪܢܐ [a]ܪܒܝ ܟܗܢܝܐ	[y]ܐܪܝܡ
[a]ܪ̈ܒܝ [b]ܡܠܟܝ	16 ܐܡܪܝܢ ܠܝܬ ܠܢ [b]ܡܠܟܝ ܐܠܐ [c]ܩܣܪ : ܘܟܕܝܢ	[c] add ܐܢ
[d] omit ܫܠܡ	ܟܦܪ ܝܬܗ ܠܗܘܢ ܕܝܙܩܦܘܢ :::: [d]ܫܠܡ .	[d] omit ܫܠܡ

Matt. XXVII. 1.

Codex A.	Codex B.	Codex C.
	ܐܫܠܡܘܢ ܐܢܘܢܗ ܠܦܝܠܛܘܣ ܐܓܡܘܢܐ ܗܝ	
	3 ܗܝܕܝܢ : ܘܟܕ ܚܙܐ ܝܗܘܕܐ : ܕܐܬܚܝܒ ܗܘ	
[a] omit ܐܘܦ	ܥܡܗ [a]ܐܘܦ ܝܗܘܕܗ [b]ܗܘ ܕܡܫܠܡ ܝܬܗ	[a] omit ܐܘܦ
[b] omit ܗܘ	ܕܐܬܚܝܒ ܬܗܘܐ : [c]ܘܐܬܬܘܒ ܬܠܬܝܢ ܕܟܣܦܐ	
[c]ܘܐܬܬܘܒ	4 [e]ܠܪ̈ܒܝ ܟܗܢܝܐ [d]ܘܣܒ̈ܝܐ ܘܐܡܪ : [f]ܐܣܚܠܬ	[f] omit ܐܣܚܠܬ
[d]ܘܣܒ̈ܝܐ	ܕܐܫܠܡܬ ܐܕܡ ܙܟܝ : ܗܢܘܢ ܕܝ ܐܡܪܘ[g]	[g] add ܠܗ
	5 ܡܐ ܠܢ ܐܢܬ ܚܙܝ : [h]ܘܐܫܕܝ [i]ܟܣܦܐ ܒܗܝܟܠܐ	[h]ܡܐ [i]ܘܟܕ
[l]ܪ̈ܒܝ [m] add ܕܝ	6 ܒܗܝܟܠܐ [k]ܘܐܙܠ ܚܢܩ ܢܦܫܗ : [l]ܪܒܝ ܟܗܢܝܐ [m]	[k]ܘܐܙܠ [l]ܪ̈ܒܝ
	ܢܣܒܘ ܟܣܦܐ ܘܐܡܪܘ ܠܐ ܫܠܝܛ ܕܢܪܡܘܢ	[m] add ܕܝ
[n]ܒܩܘܪܒܢܐ	ܝܬܗ [n]ܒܩܘܪܒܢܐ : [o]ܡܛܠ ܕܛܝܡ [p]ܕܕܡܐ	[n]ܒܩܘܪܒܢܐ
[o]ܡܛܠ [q]ܡܠܟܐ	7 ܕܐܕܡ : ܢܣܒܘ ܕܝ [q]ܡܠܟܐ ܘܙܒܢܘ [r]ܒܝܢܗܘܢ	[p]ܕܕܡ [r]ܒܗܘܢ
[r]ܒܗܘܢ	8 ܚܩܠܗ ܕܦܚܪܐ ܠܩܒܘܪܬܐ [s]ܠܐܟܣܢܝܐ : ܠܗܢ	[s]ܠܐܟܣܢܝܐ
[s]ܠܐܟܣܢܝܐ	ܐܬܩܪܝ [t]ܚܩܠܗ [u]ܗܘ ܚܩܠ ܐܕܡܐ ܥܕ ܝܘܡܢܐ	[t]ܚܩܠܐ
[t]ܚܩܠܐ [u]ܗܘ	9 ܠܝܘܡܢܐ : [n]ܟܕܝܢ ܐܫܬܠܡ ܡܐ ܕܐܬܐܡܪ	
[n]ܟܕܝܢ	ܒܐܪܡܝܐ ܢܒܝܐ ܕܐܡܪ : ܢܣܒܘ ܬܠܬܝܢ	[v]ܕܣܦܩ
[v]ܕܣܦܩ	[v]ܕܣܦܩ ܕܡܘܗܝ ܕܡܝܩܪܐ ܡܐ [w]ܕܝܩܪܘ ܡܢ	[w]ܕܝܩܪܘ
[z]ܘܝܗܒܘ	10 [x]ܒܢܝܐ [y]ܕܐܝܣܪܐܝܠ : [z]ܘܝܗܒܘ ܝܬܗܘܢ ܒܚܩܠܗ	[x]ܒܢܝ [y]ܕܐܝܣܪܐܝܠ
[a]ܕܐܬܦܩܕ [b]ܡܪܝܐ	ܕܦܚܪܐ ܗܝܟ ܡܐ [a]ܕܐܬܦܩܕ ܠܝ [b]ܡܪܝܐ[c] :	[c] add ܝܫܘܥ

Codex A.

[d] ܗܠܚܡܘܢܝܐ
[e] ܘܫܐܠ
[i] ܕܝܗܘܕܝܐ
[k] ܐܡܪܬ
[m] ܪ̈ܒܝ
[o] ܟܕܝܢ
[q] ܠܡܕܡ
[r] ܠܡܠܘ
[s] ܐܬܕܡܪ [t] *omit* ܕܝܢ
[u] ܠܐܟܠܘܣܐ
[w] ܚܕ [x] ܝܕܝܥܐ
[y] ܝܫܘܥ
[z] ܠܡܢ [a] ܠܝܫܘܥ
[b] ܕܡܬܩܪܐ
[c] ܕܠܚܣܡܐ
[d] ܝܬܒ
[f] ܠܗܢܐ [g] ܝܘܡܢ
[h] ܠܠܝܐ [i] ܘܪ̈ܒܝ
[k] ܐܦܝܣܘ
[l] ܠܐܟܠܘܣܐ
[o] *omit* ܕܝܢ
[q] ܗܢܐ [r] ܕܡܬܩܪܐ
[t] ܢܙܕܩܦ
[u] *omit* ܢܙܕܩܦ
[s] ܒܝܫ [v] ܡܙܥܩܝܢ
[w] *omit* ܕܝܢ

Codex B.

11 ܗܘ ܕܝܢ ܡܪܢ ܝܫܘܥ ܡܢ ܡܕܝܢܬ [d]ܗܠܚܡܘܢܝܐ:
[e]ܘܫܐܠ ܠܗ [d]ܗܠܚܡܘܢܝܐ [g]ܐܡܪ ܐܢܬ [h]ܗܘ
ܡܠܟܐ [i]ܕܝܗܘܕܝܐ: ܗܘ ܕܝܢ ܡܪܢ ܝܫܘܥ ܐܡܪ
12 ܐܢܬ [k]ܐܡܪܬ: ܘܒܡܐ [l]ܕܗܘܐ ܡܬܩܛܪܓ ܡܢ
[m]ܪ̈ܒܝ ܟܗܢܐ ܘܡܢ ܩܫܝܫܐ: ܘܡܕܡ ܠܐ
13 ܗܘܐ [n]ܡܦܢܐ: [o]ܟܕܝܢ ܐܡܪ ܠܗ [p]ܦܝܠܛܘܣ:
ܠܝܬ ܐܢܬ ܫܡܥ ܟܡܐ ܗܠܝܢ ܡܣܗܕܝܢ ܥܠܝܟ:
14 ܘܠܐ ܐܦܢܝ ܠܗ ܐܘܦ ܠܐ [q]ܠܡܕܡ ܚܕܐ
ܡܠܬܐ: ܗܝܕܝܢ [r]ܠܡܠܘ ܕܝܢ ܕܗܘܐ ܗܠܚܡܘܢܝܐ
15 [s]ܐܬܕܡܪ [t]ܕܝܢ ܠܚܕܐ: ܒܟܠ ܡܥܕܐ ܕܝܢ ܗܘܐ
ܐܠܘܦ ܗܠܚܡܘܢܝܐ ܦܢܐ [u]ܠܐܟܠܘܣܐ ܚܕ
16 ܐܣܝܪ ܡܢ ܕܗܘܘ ܨܒܝܢ: ܗܘܐ ܕܝܢ [v]ܠܗܘܢ
[o]ܟܕܝܢ [w]ܚܕ ܐܣܝܪ [x]ܝܕܝܥܐ ܕܡܬܩܪܐ [y]ܝܫܘܥ ܒܪ
17 ܐܒܐ: ܘܗܝܕܝܢ ܕܗܘܘ ܟܢܝܫܝܢ ܐܡܪ ܠܗܘܢ
[p]ܦܝܠܛܘܣ: [z]ܠܡܢܐ ܐܢܬܘܢ ܒܥܝܢ ܡܢ ܬܪܝܢ
ܕܐܫܪܐ ܠܟܘܢ [a]ܠܝܫܘܥ ܒܪ ܐܒܐ: ܐܘ ܠܝܫܘܥ
18 [b]ܕܡܬܩܪܐ ܡܫܝܚܐ: ܗܘܐ ܓܝܪ ܝܕܥ [c]ܕܠܚܣܡܐ
19 ܦܢܐ ܒܨܦܪܐ ܗܘܐ: ܘܗܝܕܝܢ ܕܗܘ [d]ܝܬܒ ܥܠ
[e]ܒܝܡܐ ܫܠܚܬ ܠܘܬܗ ܐܢܬܬܗ ܐܡܪܐ: ܠܐ
ܠܟ ܘܠܐ [f]ܠܗܢܐ ܙܕܝܩܐ: ܣܓܝ ܓܝܪ ܚܫܬ
20 [g]ܝܘܡܢܐ ܒܚܠܡܐ ܡܢ [h]ܠܠܝܐ: [i]ܘܪ̈ܒܝ
ܟܗܢܐ ܘܩܫܝܫܐ [k]ܐܦܝܣܘ [l]ܠܐܟܠܘܣܐ
ܕܢܫܐܠܘܢ ܠܒܪ ܐܒܐ: ܠܝܫܘܥ ܕܝܢ
21 ܢܘܒܕܘܢ: ܐܡܪ [m]ܕܝܢ [n]ܗܠܚܡܘܢܝܐ ܘܐܡܪ
ܠܗܘܢ: ܠܡܢ [o]ܕܝܢ ܐܢܬܘܢ ܨܒܝܢ ܕܐܫܪܐ
ܠܟܘܢ ܡܢ ܬܪܝܢ: ܗܢܘܢ ܕܝܢ ܐܡܪܘ ܠܒܪ
22 ܐܒܐ: ܐܡܪ ܠܗܘܢ [p]ܦܝܠܛܘܣ ܡܢܐ ܐܥܒܕ
ܠܝܫܘܥ [q]ܗܢܐ [r]ܕܡܬܩܪܐ ܡܫܝܚܐ:
23 ܘܐܡܪܘ ܟܠܗܘܢ [s t]ܢܙܕܩܦ [u t]ܢܙܕܩܦ: ܗܘ
ܕܝܢ ܐܡܪ ܠܗܘܢ ܡܢܐ ܓܝܪ [s]ܒܝܫ ܥܒܕ: ܗܢܘܢ [w]ܕܝܢ
ܝܬܝܪܐܝܬ ܗܘܘ [v]ܡܙܥܩܝܢ [w]ܕܝܢ ܘܐܡܪܝܢ

Codex C.

[g] ܘܐܡܪ
[k] *omit* ܗܘ
[l] *omit* ܕܗܘܐ
[m] ܪ̈ܒܝ [n] ܡܦܢܐ
[p] ܦܝܠܛܘܣ
[s] ܬܕܡܪ [t] *omit* ܕܝܢ
[u] ܠܗܘܢ
[v] *omit* ܠܗܘܢ
[y] ܝܫܘܥ
[z] ܠܡܢ
[a] ܠܝܫܘܥ
[b] ܕܡܬܩܪܐ
[c] *omit* ܕ
[e] ܒܝܡܐ
[i] ܘܪ̈ܒܝ
[k] ܐܦܝܣܘ
[m] ܕܐܢ
[o] *omit* ܕܝܢ
[p] ܦܝܠܛܘܣ
[r] ܕܡܬܩܪܐ
[s] ܢܙܕܩܦ [w] *omit* ܕܝܢ
[u] *omit* ܢܙܕܩܦ
[s] ܒܝܫ [v] ܡܙܥܩܝܢ

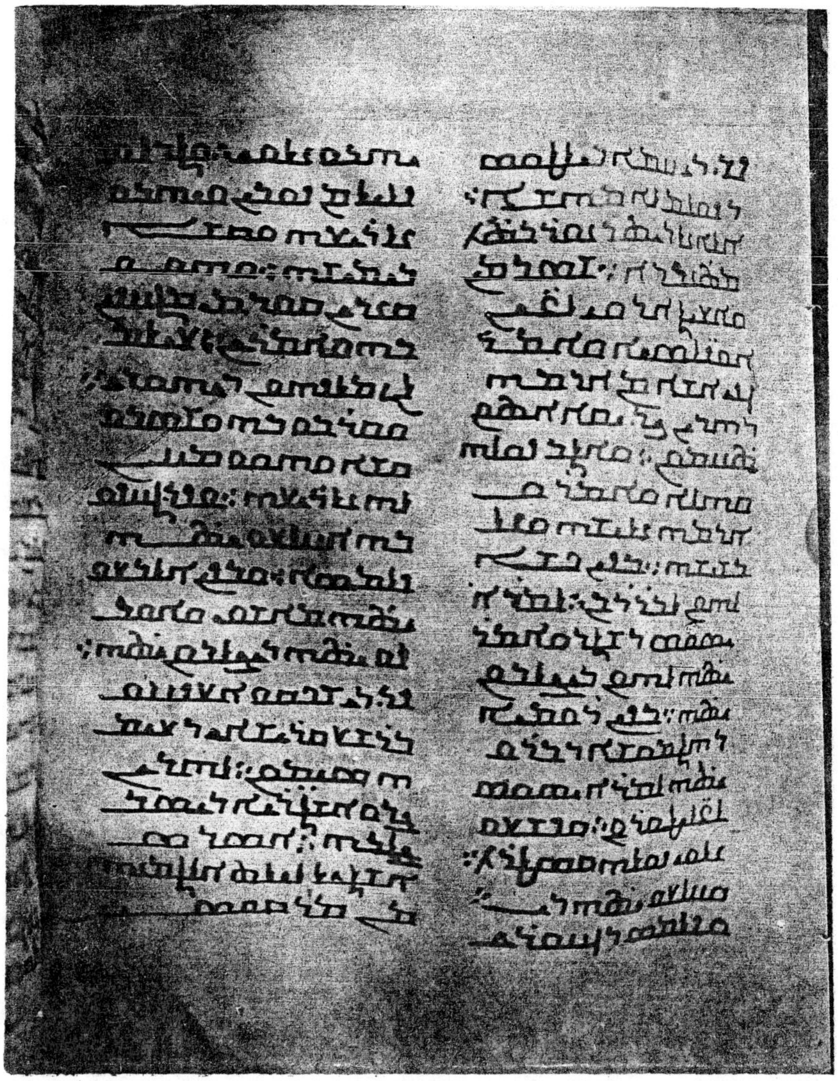

Fol. 107*b*. *Page* 201.

CODEX C.

(MATT. XXVII. 24—32.)

Codex A.

[u] ܕܝܨܠܒ [w] add ܕܝ
[x] ܕܒܬܠܬ
[y] ܕܦܬܪ [z] ܐܕܘܢ
[b] ܠܒܢܝ [c] ܐܘ̈ܩܠܛܣܝܐ
[d] ܐܒܝ [e] ܕܗܕܡ
[g] ܘܐܙܩܦ
[f] ܡܢܝ [h] ܕܝ ܕܢܛܪ
[j] ܕܝܣܠܒܘܢ
[k] ܘܡܢܝܢ [l] ܝܘܡܢܝ
[m] ܕܗܝܡܢܘܬܐ
[n] ܠܐܣܛܝܦܘܪܝܢ
[o] add ܕܝ
[p] ܡܘܕܥܘܢ
[q] ܕܝܗܘܕܝ
[s] ܒܗ [u] ܗܘܐ
[v] ܠܒܘܫܐ
[x] ܐܠܒܫ
[y] ܡܐܢܘܗܝ
[z] ܕܝܨܠܒܘܢ
[b] add ܗܘܐ
[c] ܢܦܩ [d] ܩܘܪܝܢܝܐ
[g] ܨܠܝܒܗ
[h] omit ܥܠܝܗ

[h] ܘܝܘܡܢܝ
[i] add ܕܝ [j] ܕܗܘܝ
[l] ܘܡܢܝܢ [m] ܒܠܒܘܫ
[n] ܕܐܪܓܘܢܐ
[p] omit ܘܗܘܢ
[q] ܘܢܣܒܘ [r] ܥܠܘܝ
[s] omit ܪܫܗ
[t] ܘܫܪܝܘ [u] ܐܫܠܡ

Codex B.

24 [u] ܨܠܒܘܢ : ܒܗ [w] ܫܥܬܐ [p] ܩ̈ܠܝܛܘܣ [x] ܕܒܬܠܬ
ܠܗ ܡܫܝܚܐ : ܐܠܐ ܥܠ [y] ܕܦܬܪ [z] ܥܘܪܒܒܬܐ
ܡܬܟܬܒܐ : ܢܣܒ ܡܢܝ ܘܐܫܟܚܘ [z] ܐܕܘܢ
[b] ܡܘܕܥ [c] ܐܘ̈ܩܠܛܣܝܐ ܘܐܡܪܝܢ : [d] ܐܒܝ ܐܢܐ ܐܢܐ ܡܢ
ܐܕܡܘܗ [e] ܕܗܕܡ ܝܕܥܝܢ ܣܘܟܐ : ܐܬܘ ܬܚܘܙܘܢ :
25 [g] ܘܐܙܩܦܘ ܒܘܠܗ ܩܘܠܐ ܘܐܡܪܘ ܐܕܡܘܗ
26 ܒܠܝܠܗ ܘܥܠ ܒܢܝܢܗ : [f] ܡܢܝ ܒܢܐ ܠܗܘܢ
ܠܒܪ ܪܡ ܠܡܪܐ ܫܘܒܚ [h] ܕܢܛܪ [i] ܘܡܫܡܪ ܗܘܐ
27 ܠܗܘܢ [j] ܕܝܣܠܒܘܢ : ܗܘܐ : [k] ܘܡܢܝܢ [l] ܝܘܡܢܝܐ
[m] ܕܗܝܡܢܘܬܐ ܕܒܪܘ ܗܘܐ ܠܡܪܐ ܫܘܒܚ
[n] ܠܩ̈ܠܝܛܘܪܝܢ : ܘܒܢܫܘ ܒܠܘܢ ܒܘܠܗ ܡܫܦܪܐ :
28 ܘܫܠܡܘ ܗܘܐ [o] : ܘܒܠܒܘܫ ܕܝܣܘܪܝܢ ܢܣܒܘ
29 ܒܠܘܢ : ܘܥܕܠܘ ܒܠܝܠ ܡܢ ܒܘܡܢ ܘܢܣܒܘ ܥܠ
ܪܫܗ ܘܦܠܓܘ ܒܝܡܢܗ : ܘܗܘܘ ܡܕܢܝܢ [p] ܡܘܕܥܗ
ܡܚܫܒܝܢ ܒܗ ܀ ܘܐܡܪܝܢ ܫܠܡ ܠܟ ܡܠܟܗܘܢ
30 [q] ܕܝܗܘܕܝ : [r] ܘܪܘܩܘ [s] ܒܐܦ̈ܘܗܝ ܘܢܩܫܘ ܦܢܝܐ
31 ܘܗܘܘ ܡܚܝܢ ܠܗ ܥܠ ܪܫܗ : ܘܒܬܪ ܕܚܝܟܘ ܒܗ
ܐܫܠܚܘ [u] ܠܗ [v] ܠܒܘܫܐ ܘܡܢܝܢ [x] ܐܫܠܚܘ ܗܘܐ
32 [y] ܡܐܢܝ : ܘܐܘܒܠܘ ܗܘܐ [z] ܕܝܨܠܒܘܢ [b] : ܒܪ
ܕܝ [c] ܢܦܩ ܐܫܟܚܘ ܓܒܪܐ [d] ܩܘܪܝܢܝ ܕܫܡܗ
ܫܡܥܘܢ : [e] ܠܗܕܝܢ [f] ܝܕܥܘ ܐܠܨܘܗܝ ܕܢܣܒ
[g] ܨܠܝܒܗ : [h] ܥܠܝܗ :

Mark XV. 16.

ܐܠܝܢܛܝܠ ܐܫܬܕܘ ܠܠܝܠܝܬ ܐܠܢܛܡܘܢܗ ܡܢ
16 ܕܪܘܣܘ ܘܒܝܬܗ ܦܪܘܣܐ : [i] ܘܩܡܝܢ ܐܘܒܠܘ
ܗܘܐ ܠܒܪ ܕܘܪܬܐ ܡܢܐ [j] ܕܝ [k] ܐܣܛܝܦܘܪܝܢ :
17 ܘܗܘܢ ܩܪܝ ܒܘܠܗ ܡܫܦܪܐ : [l] ܘܡܢܝܢ ܐܠܒܫܘ
ܗܘܐ [m] ܒܠܒܘܫܐ [n] ܕܐܪܓܘܢ ܀ ܘܐܪܢܒܘܢ :
ܘܥܕܠܘ ܒܠܝܠ ܕܒܘܡܢ ܘܗܘܢ [q] ܢܣܒܘ [r] ܥܠ
18 [s] ܪܫܗ : [t] ܘܫܪܘ [u] ܫܠܡ [w] ܒܫܠܡܗ ܘܐܡܪܝܢ ܀ :

Codex C.

[u] ܨܠܒܘܢ [w] add ܕܝ
[p] ܩܠܝܛܘܣ
[z] ܥܘܪܒܒܬܐ
[b] ܠܒܢܝ
[c] ܐܘܩܠܛܣܝܐ
[g] ܘܐܙܩܦ
[h] ܕܢܛܪ [i] ܘܡܫܡܪ
[k] ܡܢܝ [l] ܝܘܡܢܝܐ
[n] ܠܐܣܛܝܦܘܪܝܢ
[v] add ܕܝ
[p] ܡܘܕܥܝܢ
[r] ܘܪܘܩܘ
[s] ܒܗ [u] ܗܘܐ
[v] ܠܒܘܫܐ
[x] ܐܠܒܫܘ [y] ܡܐܢܝ
[b] add ܗܘܐ
[c] ܢܦܩ [d] ܩܘܪܝܢܝ
[f] ܕܝܢ
[h] omit ܥܠܝܗ

[i] add ܕܝ
[j] ܕܗܘܝ [k] ܐܣܛܝܦܘܪܝܢ
[m] ܒܠܒܘܫ [n] ܕܐܪܓܘܢ
[p] omit ܘܗܘܢ [r] ܥܠܘܝ
[s] omit ܪܫܗ [t] ܘܫܪܝ
[u] ܐܫܠܡ [w] ܒܫܠܡܗ

Codex A.	Codex B.	Codex C.
[x] ܕܢܨܪܝܐ	19 ܫܐܠ ܠܗ ܡܠܟܘܬܗܘܢ [x] ܕܢܨܪܝܐ : ܘܗܘܘ ܡܚܝܢ	
[y] ܒܡܠܐ [z] ܡܪܘܡܝܢ	ܠܗ [y] ܒܡܠܐ ܒܠ ܩܕܡܗ : ܘܗܘܘ [z] ܡܪܘܡܝܢ	[z] ܡܪܘܡܝܢ
ܒܠ [b] omit	ܒܠܗ : ܘܗܘܘ [a] ܡܕܒܪܝܢ [b] ܒܠ ܐܪܒܥܬܗܘܢ	[a] ܡܕܒܪܝܢ
	20 ܘܐܡܪܝܢ ܠܗ : ܘܡܢ ܟܝܢܘ ܒܗ ܐܝܠܝܢ ܢܛܘܪܝ ܗܘܬ	
[d] ܡܐܢܘܢ	[c] ܒܠܚܘܕܝܗ ܘܐܪܒܥܐ : ܘܐܠܒܥܘ ܢܛܘܪܝ ܗܘܬ [d] ܡܐܢܘܢ	[c] ܒܠܚܘܕܝܗ
[e] ܩܦܠܝܢ	ܕܠܗܘܢ : ܘܗܘܢ [e] ܡܩܦܠܝܢ ܢܛܘܪܝ ܗܘܬ [f] ܕܝܒܠܘܢ	[d] ܡܐܢܘܢ
[f] ܕܝܒܠܘܢ	21 ܢܛܪܝ : ܘܝܘܡ ܐܪܒܥܐ ܠܟܢܫ ܡܢ ܒܬܪ ܕܫܡܥܘ	[e] ܡܩܦܠܝܢ
[g] ܡܝܬܢܐ	ܫܡܥܘܢ [g] ܡܝܬܢܐ ܕܗܘܐ ܐܬܬܐ ܡܢ ܦܛܪܐ :	[g] ܡܝܬܢܐ
[h] ܐܦܩܘܢ	[h] ܐܦܩܘܢ ܕܐܠܒܫܘܢܐ ܘܕܪܘܦܣ [i] ܕܫܡܥ	[h] ܐܦܩܘܢ [i] ܕܫܡܥ
[i] ܕܫܡܥ	22 ܝܠܒܘܢ : ܘܗܘܢ [j] ܡܢܬܢ ܢܛܘܪܝ ܒܠ ܐܬܪܐ	[j] ܡܢܬܢ
	[k] ܕܝܠܦܠܬܐ ܡܐ ܕܗܘ ܡܬܢܝܢ ܐܬܪܐ	[k] ܕܝܠܦܠܬܐ
	23 ܕܪܘܡܬܐ : ܘܗܘܘ ܡܗܝܢ ܠܗ ܕܫܒܬܐ ܫܡܪ	
	24 [l] ܡܕܢܒ [m] ܒܡܢܪܐ : ܗܘ ܕܝ ܠܐ ܢܫܒ : ܘܒܕ	[l] ܡܕܢܒ [m] ܒܡܢܪܐ
[n] ܡܐܢܘܢ	ܝܠܒܘ ܢܛܘܪܝ ܦܠܛܘ [n] ܡܐܢܘܢ [o] [p] ܘܗܘܘ ܪܡܝܢ	
	[q] ܒܠܫܘܢ ܢܒܝܢ : ܒܘܠ ܚܕ ܘܚܕ ܡܢܗܘܢ	[o] add ܒܠ ܠܒܫܡܗ ܘܒܠ
[r] ܢܫܒ	25 ܡܐ [r] ܢܫܒܒ : ܘܗܘܝ ܕܝ ܗܘܢ ܬܠܬܐ ܫܒܝܢ	ܘܗܘܘ [p]
	26 ܘܝܠܒܘ ܢܛܘܪܝ : ܘܗܘܐ [s] ܒܬܒܐ ܕܒܠܬܗ [s]	[q] omit ܒܠܫܘܢ
[t] ܕܢܨܪܝܐ	27 ܒܬܝܒ ܒܠܘܝ ܡܠܒܐ [t] ܕܢܨܪܝܐ : ܘܝܠܒܘ	[r] ܢܫܒ
[u] ܠܦܪܩܝܢ	ܒܡܒܗ ܬܪܝܢ [u] ܠܦܪܩܝܢ : ܚܕ ܡܢ [v] ܡܢܝܢܐ ܘܚܕ	[s] omit ܒܬܒܐ ܕܒܠܬܗ
[w] ܦܬܠܐ	28 ܡܢ [w] ܦܬܐܠܐ : ܘܐܬܡܠܝ [x] ܒܬܒܐ ܕܐܡܪ :	[v] ܡܢܝܢܐ [w] ܦܬܠܗ
[y] ܕܐܘܦ [z] ܒܕܪܝ	29 [y] ܐܘܦ ܒܡ [z] ܒܕܪ ܢܒܘܫܐ ܐܬܫܒܝ : ܘܗܠܝܢ	[x] ܒܬܒܐ [y] ܕܐܘܦ
[c] ܪܫܘܢ	ܕܗܘܘ ܒܕܪܝܢ ܗܘܘ ܡܕܒܪܝܢ [a] ܒܠܘܝ [b] ܘܡܢܕܝܢ	[a] ܒܠܝ [b] ܘܡܢܕܝܢ
[d] ܐܘ [e] ܗܕܝ	[c] ܪܫܘܢ ܘܐܡܪܝܢ : [d] ܐܘܦ [e] ܗܕܝܢ ܕܫܪܐ	[c] ܪܫܘܢ [d] ܐܘ
[f] ܢܘܗܐ	[f] ܢܘܗܐ [g] ܕܝ ܘܠܬܬܐ [h] ܢܘܡܝܢ ܒܢܐ [i] ܠܗ :	[f] ܢܘܗܐ [g] omit ܕܝ
ܕܝ [g] omit [h] ܢܘܡܝܢ	30 31 ܐܝܟ ܕܐܙܠܝܢ ܘܗܘܬ ܡܢ ܝܠܒܐ : [j] ܘܡܢ ܘܒܘܬ	[h] ܢܘܡܝܢ [i] ܢܛܘܪܝ
[j] ܘܦܢ	ܐܘܦ ܪܫܐ ܒܡܫܐ ܗܘܘ [k] ܡܕܫܡܢ ܦܠܛܘܢ	[k] ܡܕܫܡܢ
[l] ܠܡ ܦܠܝܛ	[l] ܠܦܠܝܛ ܘܒܡ ܫܦܪܐ . [m] ܘܐܡܕܪܝܢ ܠܫܘܪܝܢ	[l] ܠܡ ܦܠܝܛ
[o] ܢܕܠ	32 ܐܝܟ [n] ܘܠܕܪܡܗ ܠܐ [o] ܢܕܠ ܕܫܡܐ : ܡܫܡܫܐ	[m] ܐܡܕܪܝܢ [n] ܘܠܕܪܝܫ
[p] ܕܐܫܦܪܐܠ	ܡܠܒܐ [p] ܕܐܫܦܪܐܠ ܐܬܐ ܗܘ ܫܘܬܐ ܒܕܘ ܡܢ	[p] ܕܫܦܪܠ
	ܝܠܒܐ ܕܫܡܐ ܘܫܡܝܢ : [q] ܫܠܡ .	[q] omit ܫܠܡ

Codex B.

MATT. XXVII. 33.

ܐܠܝܓܝܠ ܐܣܟܒ ܠܠܝܠܬ ܐܠܓܘܡܟܒܗ ܡܢ
33 ܡܬܐܬܘܢ[i] : ܘܟܕ ܐܬܘ [k]ܪܗܛܝܢ ܠܐܬܪܐ [l]ܕܡܬܩܪܐ
[m]ܓܘܠܓܘܠܬܐ : ܗܢܐ ܕܗܘ [n]ܡܬܩܪܐ [r]ܕܝܢ ܐܬܪܐ
34 ܕܩܪܩܦܬܐ : ܘܝܗܒܘ ܠܗ ܕܝܫܬܐ ܚܡܪ [o]ܕܡܒܪܝܒ
[p]ܒܡܪܝܪܐ : ܘܟܕ [q]ܛܥܡ ܠܐ ܗܘܐ ܨܒܐ
35 ܕܝܫܬܐ : ܟܕ ܕܝܢ ܨܠܒܘ ܝܬܗ ܦܠܓܘ [s]ܡܐܢܘܝ :
ܘܪܡܘ ܥܕܒܝܢ : ܕܝܬܡܠܐ ܡܐ ܕܐܬܡܪ ܒܢܒܝܐ
ܕܐܡܪ ܦܠܓܘ [t]ܡܐܢܘܝ ܒܝܢܬܗܘܢ ܘܥܠ
36 ܠܒܘܫܝ ܪܡܘ [u]ܥܕܒ : ܘܗܘܘ [v]ܝܬܒܝܢ ܢܛܪܝܢ ܠܗ
37 ܬܡܢ : ܘܝܗܒܘ [o]ܠܥܠ ܡܢ ܪܝܫܗ : [w]ܥܠܬܗ
[x]ܟܬܒܐ [y]ܕܗܕܝܢ ܐܝܬ ܗܘ ܝܫܘܥ ܡܠܟܗܘܢ
38 [z]ܕܝܗܘܕܝ ܀ [a]ܟܕܝܢ [b]ܕܝܢ [c]ܐܨܛܠܒܘ ܥܡܗ
ܬܪܝܢ [d]ܠܣܛܝܢ ܚܕ ܡܢ [e]ܝܡܝܢܗ ܘܚܕ ܡܢ
39 [f]ܣܡܠܐ : ܗܠܝܢ ܕܝܢ ܕܗܘܘ ܥܒܪܝܢ ܗܘܘ
40 ܡܓܕܦܝܢ [g]ܥܠܘܗܝ ܘܡܢܝܕܝܢ [h]ܪܫܝܗܘܢ ܘܐܡܪܝܢ
ܐܘ [i]ܗܕܝܢ ܕܫܪܐ ܢܘܣܗ ܕܐܠܗܐ ܘܠܬܠܬܐ
[j]ܝܘܡܝܢ ܒܢܐ ܝܬܗ : ܐܚܝ ܢܦܫܟ ܘܚܘܬ
ܡܢ ܨܠܝܒܐ : ܐܢ [k]ܐܝܬ ܐܢܬ [k]ܒܪܗ ܕܐܠܗܐ :
41 [l]ܘܟܢ ܘܟܘܬ [m] [n]ܪܒܢܝ ܟܗܢܝܐ ܗܘܘ ܡܓܚܟܝܢ
ܥܡ ܣܦܪܝܐ ܘܩܫܝܫܝܐ ܘܗܘܘ ܐܡܪܝܢ :
42 [o]ܠܐܘܚܪܢܝܢ ܐܚܝ [p]ܘܠܓܪܡܗ ܠܐ [q]ܝܟܠ ܕܝܚܐ :
ܐܢ [b]ܕܝܢ ܡܠܟܐ [r]ܕܐܝܣܪܝܠ ܐܝܬ ܗܘ [s]ܝܚܘܬ
ܟܕܘ ܡܢ ܨܠܝܒܐ ܘܐܢܢ ܡܗܝܡܢܝܢ ܒܗ : ܐܢ
43 ܣܒܪ ܥܠ ܐܠܗܐ ܝܦܪܘܩ ܝܬܗ : ܟܕܘ ܐܢ
ܐܝܬ ܗܘ ܨܒܐ ܒܗ : ܐܡܪ ܓܪ ܕܐܢܐ ܒܪܗ
44 ܕܐܠܗܐ : [l]ܘܟܢ ܐܘܦ [t]ܠܣܛܝܐ [u]ܕܐܨܛܠܒܘ
45 ܥܡܗ ܗܘܘ ܡܚܣܕܝܢ ܠܗ : ܡܢ ܫܬ ܫܥܝܢ
ܕܝܢ ܗܘܐ ܚܫܘܟܐ ܥܠ ܟܘܠܗ ܐܪܥܐ [v]ܥܕ
46 ܬܫܥܐ [v] [w]ܠܬܫܥ ܫܥܝܢ : ܠܦܢܐ ܕܝܢ ܬܫܥ ܫܥܝܢ
ܐܓܥܝ ܡܪܢ ܝܫܘܥ ܒܩܠܐ [x]ܪܒܐ ܘܐܡܪ

Codex A.

[i] *add* ܘܒܢܬܗܘܢ
ܡܒܪܘܣܐ
[k] ܕܘܡܒܝܢ
[l] ܕܡܬܐܡܪ
[m] ܓܘܠܓܘܠܬܐ
[n] ܡܬܐܡܪ
[o] ܡܒܪܝܒ [q] ܛܥܡ
[s] ܡܐܢܘܗ
[t] ܡܐܢܘܝ
[v] ܝܬܒܝܢ
[o] ܠܥܠ [w] ܥܠܬܗ
[x] ܟܬܒܐ [y] ܕܗܕܝܢ
[z] ܕܝܗܘܕܝܐ
[a] ܟܕܝܢ [b] *omit* ܕܝܢ
[d] ܠܣܛܝܢ [g] ܥܠܘܗܝ
[h] ܪܫܝܗܘܢ
[i] ܗܕܝܢ [j] ܝܘܡܝܢ
[l] ܘܟܢ [m] *add* ܐܘܦ
[n] ܪܒܢܐ
[o] ܠܐܚܪܢܝܢ [q] ܝܟܠ
[r] ܕܐܝܣܪܝܠ
[t] ܠܣܛܝܐ
[v] ܥܕܡܐ
[x] ܪܒܐ

Codex C.

[i] *add* ܘܒܢܬܗܘܢ
[l] ܕܡܬܩܪܐ
[m] ܓܘܠܓܘܠܬܐ
[n] ܡܬܩܪܐ
[r] ܕܐܢ [o] ܡܒܪܝܒ
[p] ܒܡܪܝܪܐ [q] ܛܥܡ
[u] ܥܕܒܝܢ [v] ܝܬܒܝܢ
[o] ܠܥܠ [w] ܥܠܬܗ
[b] *omit* ܕܝܢ [c] ܐܨܛܠܒܘ
[e] ܝܡܝܢܗ
[f] ܣܡܠܗ
[g] ܥܠܘܗܝ [h] ܪܫܝܗܘܢ
[j] ܝܘܡܝܢ
[k] ܐܢܬ ܗܘ
[o] ܠܐܚܪܢܝܢ
[p] ܘܠܓܪܡܟ
[s] ܝܚܘܬ
[t] ܠܣܛܝܐ
[u] ܕܐܨܛܠܒܘ
[v] ܥܕܡܐ
[w] ܠܬܫܥ
[x] ܪܒܐ

Codex A.

[t]ܐܬܠܝ [u]ܦܐܡܪܝܢ
[w]ܠܐܠܝܨܘܗ [x]ܗܕܝ
[y]ܐܣܦܘܠܓܐ [z]ܚܝܠܐ
[b] *add* ܥܠ ܡܢܐ
ܘܡܬܩܪܐ ܗܘܐ ܠܗ
[c]ܘܥܢܝܢܝܬܐ
[d] *add* ܕܝ
[e]ܥܒܘܕ [g]ܐܠܝܨܘܗ
[h]ܚܘܪܝܢ [i] *add* ܕܝ
[j]ܠܟܠܗܘܢ [k]ܡܢ
[l]ܪܒܐ [m]ܠܒܠ
[n]ܠܐܪܥ [o]ܘܥܢܝܢܝܬܐ
[p]ܐܬܦܠܓܬ
[q]ܕܕܡܟܘ
[r]ܠܩܕܝܫܬܐ
[s]ܡܕܝܢܬܐ
[t]ܘܐܬܚܙܝܘ
[u]ܠܣܓܝ
[w]ܘܙܒܘܢܐ [y]ܘܐܡܪܘ
[a]ܗܘ [b] *add* ܥܠܡ

[a]ܒܪ ܡܪܐ
[d]ܒܒܝܫܝ
[f]ܗܕܝ [g]ܕܡܬܩܪܐ
[h]ܓܘܠܓܠܬܐ
[i]ܘܗܠܝܢ
[n]ܘܡܦܠܓܝܢ
[o]ܡܢܝܢ

Codex B.

47 [t]ܐܬܠܝ [t]ܐܬܠܝ ܠܟܢܫܐ ܥܒܘܬ ܝܬܗ : ܐܢܫܝܢ
ܕܝ ܡܢ ܬܠܝܢ ܕܗܘܘ [u]ܡܬܩܪܐ ܝܗܘܕܐ ܚܕ ܥܣܪܬܥ
48 ܐܡܪܘ [w]ܠܐܠܝܨܘ [x]ܗܕܝܢ ܩܪܐ : ܘܥܡܪܐ ܪܗܛ
ܚܕ ܡܢܗܘܢ ܘܢܫܩ [y]ܐܣܦܘܠܓܐ ܘܡܠܐ
49 ܝܬܗ [z]ܚܝܠܐ [a]ܘܐܣܝܪ ܝܬܗ : [b] [c]ܘܫܪܝܬܐ
[d]ܗܘܘ ܐܡܪܝܢ : [e]ܥܒܘܕ [f]ܚܝܠܐ ܐܢ ܐܬܐ
[g]ܐܠܝܨܘ ܕܚܝܠܐ ܝܬܗ : [h]ܚܘܪܝܢ [i]ܢܫܩܝ ܠܘܬܝ
ܘܢܣܥ ܝܬܗ [j]ܠܟܠܗܘܢ : ܘܢܦܩ [k]ܡܢ ܘܐܕܡ
50 ܗܘ ܕܝ ܡܪܐ ܣܦܘܣ ܝܬܗܘܢ ܐܢܚܝܢ ܒܦܠܐ
51 [l]ܪܒܐ ܘܥܒܕ ܪܘܚܐ : ܘܥܡܪܐ ܦܪܣܗ ܕܢܘܣܐ
ܐܬܦܬܚ ܠܬܪܝܢ ܡܢ [m]ܠܒܠ ܚܕ ܡܦܠܐ [n]ܠܐܪܥ :
ܘܐܪܒܐ ܘܚܬ : [o]ܘܥܢܝܢܝܬܐ [p]ܐܬܦܠܓܬ :
52 ܘܡܥܡܘܪܬܐ ܐܬܦܬܚܘ ܘܦܓܪܝ ܒܦܓܪܝܢ ܡܢ
53 ܕܡܕܡܟܐ [q]ܕܡܟܘ ܩܡܘ ܐܬܘ : ܘܥܕ ܢܦܩܘ ܡܢ
ܡܥܡܘܪܬܐ ܐܬܘ [r]ܠܩܕܝܫܬܐ [s]ܡܕܝܢܬܐ [t]ܘܐܬܚܙܝܘ
54 [u]ܠܣܓܝ : ܡܦܪܘܩܢܐ ܕܝ ܘܗܠܝܢ ܕܥܡܗ [v]ܢܦܪܩ
ܠܡܪܐ ܣܦܘܣ : ܚܕ ܚܙܘ [w]ܙܒܘܢܐ ܘܡܢܐ
[x]ܕܐܬܥܒܕ ܕܗܠܘ ܠܡܪܐ [y]ܘܐܡܪܘ [z]ܡܥܦܠܬ
ܒܪܗ ܕܐܠܗܐ [a]ܗܘ ܗܕܝܢ [b].

Luke XXIII. 32.

ܐܠܝܦܠ ܐܬܐܡܪ ܠܠܐܠܬ ܐܠܦܘܡܥܒܗ ܡܢ ܠܘܩܣ :
32 ܘܡܝܬܝܗ [y]ܡܪܘܩܐ : ܘܗܘܘ ܕܝ [z]ܡܬܕܒܪܝܢ ܐܘܦ
[a]ܠܡܪܐ ܣܦܘܣ ܬܪܝܢ ܚܘܪܝܢ [c]ܒܒܪܐ [d]ܒܝܫܝܢ
33 [e]ܕܝܠܝܦܛܘܢ : ܘܟܕ ܐܬܘ ܥܠ ܐܬܪܐ [f]ܗܕܝܢ
[g]ܕܡܬܩܪܐ [h]ܓܘܠܓܠܬܐ ܬܡܢ ܨܠܒܘ ܝܬܗ :
[i]ܘܗܠܝܢ ܒܒܪܝ [j]ܒܝܫܬܐ ܚܕ ܡܢ [k]ܝܡܝܢܐ
34 ܘܚܕ ܡܢ [l]ܣܡܠܐ : ܡܪܐ ܣܦܘܣ ܕܝ ܗܘܐ
ܐܡܪ [m]ܐܒܐ ܫܒܘܩ ܠܗܘܢ : ܠܐ ܓܝܪ ܝܕܥܝܢ
ܡܐ ܗܢܘܢ ܥܒܕܝܢ : [n]ܡܢ ܡܦܠܓܝܢ[n] ܕܝ
35 [o]ܡܐܢܝ ܗܘܘ ܪܡܝܢ ܢܒܝܢ : ܘܗܘܐ ܥܡܐ

Codex C.

[u]ܦܐܡܪܝܢ
[y]ܐܣܦܘܠܓ
[z]ܚܝܠ [a]ܘܐܣܪ
[b] *add* ܥܠ ܡܢܐ
ܘܡܬܩܪܐ ܠܗ
[d] *add* ܕܐܝ
[f]ܕܚܝܠܐ
[i] *add* ܕܝ
[h]ܚܘܪܝܢ [k]ܡܢܐ

[p]ܐܬܦܠܓܬ
[q]ܕܕܡܟܘ
[u]ܠܣܓܝ [v]ܢܦܪܩ
[x]ܕܐܬܥܒܕ
[y]ܘܐܡܪܝܢ
[z]ܡܥܦܠܬ

[y] *omit* ܡܪܘܩܐ
[z]ܡܬܕܒܪܝܢ
[d]ܒܝܫܝܢ [e]ܕܝܠܝܦܛܘܢ
[g]ܕܡܬܩܪܐ
[h]ܓܘܠܓܠܬܐ
[j]ܒܝܫܐ [k]ܝܡܝܢܗ
[l]ܣܡܠܗ
[m] *omit* ܐܒܐ

Codex A.

[p] ܡܩܠܣ̈ܝܢ
[q] ܠܚܘܪ̈ܢܝܢ
[s] *add* ܗܕܝܢ
[t] ܐܝܬܝ [v] ܪ̈ܘܡܝܝܢ
[w] ܩܪܒܝܢ [x] ܚܠܐ
[y] ܕܝܗ̈ܘܕܝܝ
[a] ܥܠܘ
[b] ܗܠܝܢܣܛܝ
[c] ܘܪܗܘܡܐܣܛܝ
[o] ܘܥܒܪܐܣܛܝ
[e] ܕܗܕܢ [f] ܐܝܬܝ
[i] ܥܠܘܝ [k] ܠܐ
[l] ܕܝܢ ܚܘܪܢܐ [m] ܕܚܝܠ
[o] ܩܘܫܛ [p] ܫܘ̈ܝܢ
[q] ܐܝܢܗ [r] ܡܬܦܪܥܝܢ
[s] ܕܢ [t] ܟܠܘܡ
[u] ܐܕܟܪ [y] *add* ܕܝܢ
[z] ܕܝܘܡܕܝܢ
[a] ܘܗܘܐܝ
[b] ܘܚܫܘܟܐ
[c] *omit* ܗܘ [d] ܐܬܟܠ
[e] *add* ܘܫܡܫܐ ܚܫܟ
ܦܪܣܗ ܘܒ̈ܢܘܣܐ
ܢܩܠܗ : ܘܫܒܩܐ
ܒܩܒܗ ܘܡܢܬܪܐ
ܐܬܦܬܚܘ : ܘܦܓܪ̈ܐ
ܕܩܕܝܫܐ ܩܝܡܝܢ
ܡܢܗ : ܘܐܬܚܘܝܘ
ܠܣܓܝܐܐ :
[f] ܪܒ [g] ܐܕ̈ܝܟ
[h] ܐܬܥܒܕ [i] *omit* ܕܝܢ
[k] ܩܘܫܛ [l] ܕܗܕܢ
[m] ܓܒܪܐ [o] ܗܘܐ
[p] ܘܟܠܗܘܢ [q] ܐܘܟܠܘܣܝܐ
[r] ܗܕܢ

Codex B.

ܘܩܐܡ ܥܡܐ : ܗܘܘ ܕܝܢ ܐܘܦ ܐܪܟܘܢܛܐ
[p]ܡܩܠܣܝܢ ܒܗ ܐܡܪܝܢ [q]ܠܚܘܪܢܝܢ ܐܚܝ ܝܚܝ
ܠܢܦܫܗ : [r]ܐܢ [s] [t]ܐܬ ܗܘ ܡܫܝܚܐ [u]ܒܪܗ
36 ܕܐܠܗܐ ܒܚܝܪܗ : ܘܓܚܟܘ ܒܗ ܐܘܦ
[v]ܪܘܡܝܝܢ [w]ܩܪܒܝܢ ܘܡܩܪܒܝܢ ܠܗ [x]ܚܠ
37 ܘܐܡܪܝܢ [r]ܐܢ ܐܬ ܗܘ ܡܠܟܐ [y]ܕܝܗܘܕܝ
38 ܐܚܝ ܢܦܫܟ : ܗܘܐ ܕܝܢ [z]ܟܬܝܒ [a]ܥܠܘܝ
ܒܟܬܒܝܢ [b]ܗܠܝܢܣܛܝ [c]ܘܪܗܘܡܐܣܛܝ
[o]ܘܥܒܪܐܣܛܝ [e]ܕܗܕܝܢ [f]ܐܬ ܗܘ ܡܠܟܗܘܢ
39 [y]ܕܝܗܘܕܝ : ܚܕ ܕܝܢ ܡܢ ܗܠܝܢ ܥܒܕܝ
ܒܝܫܬܐ ܕܐܨܛܠܒܘ ܥܡܗ [h]ܗܘܐ [h]ܡܓܕܦ
[i]ܥܠܘܝ [j]ܘܐܡܪ : [k]ܐܢ ܐܬ ܗܘ ܡܫܝܚܐ
40 ܐܚܝ ܢܦܫܟ ܘܐܚܝܢ ܠܢ : ܐܬܝܒ
[l]ܐܚܪܢܐ ܘܗܘܐ ܙܥܦ ܒܗ ܘܐܡܪ : ܐܘܦ
ܠܐ ܡܢ ܐܠܗܐ ܠܝܬ ܐܬ [m]ܕܚܝܠ [n]ܕܒܗ
41 ܒܕܝܢܐ ܐܝܬܝܟ ܐܘܦ ܐܢ̈ܢ : ܘܐܝܬܝܢ ܡܢ [o]ܩܘܫܛ
[p]ܫܘܝܢ ܒܡܐ ܕܥܒܕܢܢ [q]ܐܝܢ [r]ܡܬܦܪܥܝܢ : [s]ܕܝܢ
42 ܕܝܢ [t]ܟܠܘܡ ܒܝܫ ܠܐ ܥܒܕ : ܘܗܘܐ ܐܡܪ
ܠܡܪܢܐ ܝܫܘܥ [u]ܐܕܟܪܝܢܝ [w]ܡܬܝ ܟܕ [x]ܬܐܬܐ
43 ܒܡܠܟܘܬܟ : [y]ܐܬܝܒ ܡܪܢܐ ܝܫܘܥ ܘܐܡܪ
ܠܗ : ܐܡܝܢ ܐܡܪ ܐܢܐ ܠܟ [z]ܕܝܘܡܕܝܢ ܐܬ
44 ܗܘܐ ܥܡܝ ܒܦܪܕܝܣܐ : [a]ܘܗܘܝ ܗܝܟ
45 ܫܬ ܫܥܝܢ : [b]ܘܚܫܘܟܐ [c]ܗܘ [d]ܐܫܬܠܡ [e]:
ܘܐܬܒܙܥ ܦܪܣܗ ܕܢܘܣܐ ܡܢ ܡܨܥܬܗ :
46 ܘܐܓܥܫ ܡܪܢܐ ܝܫܘܥ ܒܩܠ [f]ܪܒ ܘܐܡܪ :
ܐܒܐ ܒܝܢ [g]ܐܝܕܝܟ ܐܢܐ ܡܦܩܕ ܪܘܚܝ : ܗܕܐ
47 ܕܝܢ ܐܡܪ ܘܥܠܡ : ܘܟܕ ܚܡܐ ܩܢܛܘܪܝܢܐ
ܡܐ [h]ܕܐܬܥܒܕ : ܫܒܚ [i]ܕܝܢ ܠܐܠܗܐ
ܘܐܡܪ : ܡܢ [k]ܩܘܫܛ [l]ܗܕܝܢ [m]ܓܒܪܐ [n]ܙܕܝܩ
48 ܗܘ[o] : [p]ܘܟܠܗܘܢ [q]ܐܘܟܠܘܣܝܢܐ ܕܐܬܘ ܥܠ
[r]ܗܕܝܢ [s]ܡܚܙܝܬܐ : ܘܟܕ ܚܡܘ ܟܠ ܡܐ

Codex C.

[p] ܡܩܠܣܝܢ
[q] ܠܚܘܪܢܝܢ [r] ܐܝܢ
[s] *add* ܗܕܝܢ
[u] ܒܪܗ [w] ܩܪܒܝܢ
[x] ܚܠ [z] ܟܬܝܒ
[a] ܥܠܘ
[b] ܗܠܝܢܣܛܝ
[c] ܘܪܗܘܡܐܣܛܝ
[o] ܘܥܒܪܐܣܛܝ
[f] ܐܝܬܝ
[h] ܗܘܘ ܡܓܕܦܝܢ
[i] ܥܠܘܝ [j] ܘܐܡܪܝܢ
[k] ܠܐ
[l] ܕܝܢ ܚܘܪܢܐ
[n] ܕܒܗ
[p] ܫܘܝܢ [q] ܐܝܢܗ
[r] ܡܬܦܪܥܝܢ
[t] ܟܠܘܡ
[w] *add* ܡܪܐ
[x] ܐܬܬܐ
[y] *add* ܕܝܢ
[a] ܘܗܘܐ
[c] *omit* ܗܘ
[d] ܐܘܟܠ
[f] ܪܒ [h] ܕܐܬܥܒܕ
[i] *omit* ܕܝܢ [k] ܩܘܫܛ
[l] ܕܗܕܝܢ [m] ܓܒܪܐ
[n] *add* ܒܪܗ ܕܐܠܗܐ
[o] ܗܘܐ [p] ܘܟܠܗܘܢ
[q] ܐܘܟܠܘܣܝܐ
[s] ܡܚܙܝܬܐ

E E

Codex A.	Codex B.	Codex C.
ᵗ ܡܣܝܢ	ܕܐܬܒܒܕ : ܗܘܘ ᵗܡܣܝܢ ܥܠ ᵘܚܕܘܬܗܘܢ	ᵗ ܡܣܝܢ
ᵘ ܚܕܘܬܗܘܢ	49 ᵂܘܬܐܡܗܝܢ ∴ ܗܘܘ ˣ ʸܡܐܡܢܝܢ ܟܘܠ ܗܠܝܢ	ᵂ ܘܬܡܗܝܢ
ᵂ ܘܬܐܡܗܝܢ ܕܝ ˣadd	ܕܫܡܥܝܢ ܠܗ ܡܢ ᶻܪܘܚܡܐ : ᵃܢܫܝܐ ˣ ܗܠܝܢ ܕܐܬܝ	ˣ add ܕܝ
ʸ ܦܐܡܢܝܢ	ܒܬܪܗ ܡܢ ܚܠܠܐ ᵇܣܓܝܢ ܗܠܝܢ : ᶜ	ᶻ ܪܘܚܡܐ
ᶻ ܪܘܚܡܐ ᵃ ܢܫܝܐ		ᵇ ܣܓܝܢܐ
ᵇ ܣܓܝܢܐ		
ᶜ add ܥܠܡ		
	JOHN XIX. 25.	
	ܐܠܢܓܝܠ ܐܬܩܪܐ ܠܠܝܠܬ ܐܠܓܡܥܗ ܡܢ	
ᵘ ܡܐܡܝܢ	25 ܝܘܚܢܢ ∴ ܘܩܝܡܢ ܗܘܝ ܩܪܘܒܐ ܗܘܝ ܕܝ ᵘܡܐܡܝܢ	ᵈ ܕܡܠܓܕܠܝܬܐ
ᵐ ܡܪܝܐܡ	ܗܘܢ ܕܝܫܘܥ ܕܡܪܝܐ ܫܡܥܘܢ ܐܡܗ ܘܐܚܬܗ	ᵉ omit ܕܝ
ᵉ omit ܕܝ ᵍ ܕܚܒܝܒ	ܕܐܡܗ ᵐܡܪܝܡ ᵈܕܡܓܕܠܝܬܐ ܘܡܪܝܡ ܡܓܕܠܝܬܐ :	ᶠ ܘܠܬܠܡܝܕܐ
ʰ ܦܐܡܪ	26 ܡܪܝܐ ܝܫܘܥ ܟܕ ᵉܕܝ ܚܡܐ ܠܐܡܗ :	ʰ ܦܐܡܪ
ⁱ ܘܚܙܝܬܝܢ	ᶠܘܠܬܠܡܝܕܐ ܐܘܗܝ ᵍܕܡܚܒܝܒ ᵖ ʰܩܡܪ : ܐܡܪ	ᵏ ܬܠܡܝܕܬܐ
ᵏ ܬܠܡܝܕܬܐ	27 ܠܐܡܗ ܐܢܬܬܐ ܗܐ ܒܪܟܝ : ⁱܘܒܬܪܝܢ ܐܡܪ	ˡ ܕܒܬܪ ᵐ ܬܠܡܝܕܐ
ˡ ܕܒܬܪ ⁿ ܠܒܝܬܗ	ᵏܬܠܡܝܕܐ ܗܐ ܐܡܟܝ : ܘܡܢ ܗܝܕܝܢ ܫܥܬܐ	ᵖ add ܠܗ ᵒ ܥܠܡܐ
ᵃ ܟܘܠ ᵒ ܫܠܡܢ	28 ˡܕܒܬܪ ܗܕܝܢ ᵐܬܠܡܝܕܐ ⁿܠܒܝܬܗ : ܘܒܬܪܝܢ ܚܡܐ	ᑫ ܚܠ ʳ ܡܫܡܫܝܢ
ᵖ add ܠܗ ᑫ ܚܠ	ܡܪܝܐ ܝܫܘܥ ܕܗܐ ᵃܟܘܠܐ ᵒܡܫܠܡܢ ܕܝܬܡܠܐ	ᵃ omit ܡܢܐ
ˢ ܕܚܠ	ܟܬܒܐ ܘܐܡܪ ᵖ ܒܨܗܘܢܝ ᑫܚܠ : ܐܡܪ ܗܐ	ˢ ܕܚܠ ᵘ ܫܫܦܓܐ
ᵗ omit ܡܠܝ : ܘܡܠܘ	29 ܐܢܐ ܨܗܝ : ܗܘܐ ܕܝ ܬܡܢ ʳܡܫܡܫ ᵃܡܢܐ	ˣ ܡܪܝܪܬܐ
ܫܦܓܐ ܚܠ	ˢܕܚܠ ᵗܡܠܝ : ܘܡܠܘ ᵘܫܦܓܐ ᑫܚܠ ᵂܡܡܪܐ	ʸ ܒܩܢܝܐ
ᵂ ܡܡܪܐ	30 ܘܩܪܒܘ ܠܦܘܡܗ : ܟܕ ܐܘܢ ܢܣܒ ܝܫܘܥ	ᶻ omit ܡܕܡ
ˣ ܡܪܝܪܬܐ	ܚܠܐ ܡܢ ˣܡܪܝܪܬܐ ܐܡܪ ܐܘܦ ܫܠܡ	ᵃ omit ܕܝ ᶜ ܦܪܘܩܗ
ᵃ omit ܕܝ	ʸܟܘܠ ᶻܡܕܡ ܘܐܪܟܝܢ ᵃܕܝ ܪܫܗ ܘܡܣܪ	ᵈ add ܕܩܘܫܬܐ
ᵇ omit . . . ܕܝ ܟܕ	ܪܘܚܗ : ᵇ ܟܕ ܕܝ ܡܣܪ ܪܘܚܐ : ᵇ ܐܬܦܠܓ	ᵉ omit ܡܢ ܡܢܓܕܗ
. . . ܠܐܪܥܐ :	ᶜܦܪܘܩܗ ᵈܕܩܘܫܬܐ ᵉܡܢ ܡܢܓܕܗ ᶠܡܢ ܠܥܠ ᵍܥܕ	ᶠ ܕܗܒܐ
ᴶ ܠܓܠܓܠ ⁱ add ܐܘܢ	31 ܠܐܪܥܐ : ʰܘܝܗܘܕܝܐ ⁱܡܢ ᴶܠܓܠܓܠ ܕܗܘܬ	ᵍ omit ܠܐܪܥܐ ܟܕ
ᵏ ܦܓܪܐ	ܥܪܘܒܬܐ ܕܠܐ ܢܬܪܘܢ ᵏܦܓܪܐ ܥܠ ܨܠܝܒܐ	ʰ ܘܝܗܘܕܝܐ
	ܒܫܒܬܐ : ܗܘܐ ˡܓܝܪ ܝܘܡܐ ܕܗܝܕܝܢ ܫܒܬܐ	ⁱ add ܐܘܢ
ᵐ ܪܓܠܝܗܘܢ	ܝܘܡ ܪܒܐ : ܒܥܘ ܡܢ ܦܝܠܛܘܣ ܕܢܬܒܪܘܢ	ᴶ ܠܓܠܓܠ
ⁿ ܘܐܬܘ ⁿ ܪܘܡܝܢ	32 ᵐܪܓܠܝܗܘܢ ܘܢܬܪܡܘܢ : ܘܐܬܘ ⁿܪܘܡܝܢ	ⁿ ܪܘܡܝܢ ˡ omit ܓܝܪ
ᵒ ܘܕܪܩܘܢܐ	ⁿܘܬܒܪܘ ܪܓܠܘܗܝ ܕܩܕܡܝܐ ᵒܘܕܪܩܘܢܐ ܕܐܨܛܠܝܒ	ᵒ ܘܕܪܩܘܢܐ
ᵖ add ܕܝ	33 ܕܐܨܛܠܒܘ ܥܡܗ : ܟܕ ᵖܐܬܘ ܥܠ ܝܫܘܥ	ᵖ add ܕܝ

Codex A.	*Codex* B.	*Codex* C.
ܒܪܐ [q] ܐܬܒܪܝ [s]	ܘܗܘܐ ܝܫܘܥ [q] ܒܒܪ ܕܡܨܠܒ ܠܐ [s] ܐܬܒܪܝ	ܐܬܒܪ [s] ܓ̈ܒܠܢ [t]
ܓ̈ܒܠܢ [t]	34 [t] ܓ̈ܒܠܢ : ܐܠܐ ܚܕ ܡܢ [u] [v] ܒܠܣܛܝܐ ܢܛܪ	[u] *add* ܝܡܝܢܗ
[u] *add* ܝܡܝܢܗ	ܝܬܗ ܒܠܒܗ : [w] ܘܒܥܐ ܝܫܘܥ ܐܝܕܗ [x] ܘܐܡܪ :	ܒܠܣܛܝܐ [v]
ܒܠܣܛܝܐ [v]	35 ܘܗܕܡ ܕܫܡܥܐ [y] ܐܫܒܩ [z] ܕܝܢ [a] ܘܫܘܒܩܢܐ ܐܝܬ	[z] *omit* ܕܝܢ ܐܫܒܩ [y]
[z] *omit* ܕܝܢ ܘܐܡܪ [x]	ܗܘ ܫܒܩܘܬܗ : ܘܗܘ [b] ܢܕܒ [c] ܕܫܘܒܩܢܐ ܗܘ	ܘܫܘܒܩܢܐ [a]
ܘܫܘܒܩܢܐ [a] ܢܕܒ [b]	[z] ܕܝܢ ܐܡܪ : ܕܐܘܦ ܐܢܬܘܢ ܬܫܒܩܘܢ :	ܕܫܘܒܩܢܐ [c]
ܫܒܩ [f]	36 ܐܬܟܒܫܘ ܒܪ ܕܒܬܪܐ ܢܛܠܒ [d] ܕܓ̈ܒܪܝܢ ܒܗܘܢ	ܕܓ̈ܒܪܝܢ [d]
ܕܢܫܒܩ [g]	37 ܠܐ [z] ܕܝܢ ܐܫܬܒܩ : [e] ܘܬܒܥܘܢ ܒܬܪܗ [f] ܫܒܩܘܢ	ܘܬܒܥܘܢ [e]
[i] *omit* ܥܠܡ	ܐܡܪ ܫܡܥܘܢ ܠܗܘ [g] ܕܢܫܟܚ ::: [i] ܥܠܡ :	ܕܐܫܬܟܚ [g]

Mark XV. 43.

Codex A.	*Codex* B.	*Codex* C.
(*deest.*)	ܐܘܢܓܠܝܘܢ ܕܐܠܡܪܩܘܣ ܠܠܝܠܝܐ ܕܐܓܢܐܫܬܐ ܡܢ	ܝܗܘܕܝܢ [z]
	43 ܒܫܪܘܪ ܘܐܬܐ ܝܘܣܦ ܕܡܢ [z] ܝܗܘܕܝܢ [a]	[a] *add* ܘܐܬܐ
	[b] ܠܗ̈ܠܝܢܘܢ ܒܪܬܐ ܕܐܘܦ ܗܘ ܗܘܐ ܡܣܟܐ	ܠܗ̈ܠܝܢܘܢ [b]
	ܠܡܠܟܘܬܗ ܕܐܠܗܐ : ܘܗܘ [c] ܥܠ ܠܘܬ ܦ̈ܝܠܛܘܣ	ܥܠ [c] ܒܝܠܛܘܣ [d]
	44 ܘܫܐܠ ܠܦܓܪܗ ܕܡܪܢ ܝܫܘܥ : [d] ܦ̈ܝܠܛܘܣ ܕܝܢ	ܐܡ [e] ܘܫܐܠ [f]
	ܬܡܗ [e] ܐܢ ܒܒܪ ܡܝܬ ܘܩܪܐ ܠܩܢܛܪܘܢܐ	ܩܢܛܪ [g]
	45 [f] ܘܫܐܠ ܝܬܗ ܐܢ ܒܒܪ ܡܝܬ : ܘܒܕ ܝܕܥ	[h] *omit* ܘܝܘܣܦ
	ܡܢ ܩܢܛܪܘܢܐ ܝܗܒ ܦܓܪܐ [g] ܠܩܢܛܪܘܢܐ	ܕܡܢ [i] ܙܒܢ [k]
	46 ܠܝܘܣܦ : [h] ܘܝܘܣܦ ܕܝܢ [i] ܡܢ [k] ܙܒܢ : [l] ܐܘܦ	[l] *omit* ܐܘܦ
	ܘܐܚܬ ܝܬܗ ܘܥܛܦܗ [m] ܒܟܬܢܐ : ܘܣܡܗ ܐܝܟ	ܒܟܬܢܐ [m]
	ܝܬܗ ܒܩܒܘܪܬܐ ܕܗܘܬ [n] ܢܩܝܪܐ [o] ܒܟܐܦܐ :	ܢܩܝܪܐ [n] ܒܟܐܦܐ [o]
	ܘܓܠܓܠ [p] ܟܐܦ ܥܠ ܬܪܥܐ ܕܩܒܘܪܬܐ :	[p] *omit* ܟܐܦ ܥܠ
	47 ܡܪܝܡ ܕܝܢ ܡܓܕܠܝܬܐ ܘܡܪܝܡ [q] ܒܪܬ ܝܥܩܘܒ	ܒܪ [q] ܗܘ [r]
	ܘܝܘܣܦܐ ܚܙܝܐ ܗܘܝ [r] ܕܐܗܢ [s] ::: [t] ܥܠܡ	[s] *add* ܐܬܬܣܡ
		[t] *omit* ܥܠܡ

John XIX. 38.

Codex A.	*Codex* B.	*Codex* C.
	ܐܘܢܓܠܝܘܢ ܕܐܠܝܘܚܢܢ ܠܠܝܠܝܐ ܕܐܓܢܐܫܬܐ ܡܢ	
	38 ܘܒܬܪܗܝܢ : ܘܒܬܪ ܐܦܢܬܗ ܕܡܪܢ : ܘܡܢ ܒܬܪ ܗܠܝܢ	ܒܠܛܘܣ [z]
ܘܝܘܣܦ [a] ܡܢ [b]	ܫܐܠ ܡܢ [z] ܦ̈ܝܠܛܘܣ : [a] ܝܘܣܦ ܗܕܝܢ [b] ܕܡܢ	ܕܗܘܐ [c]
ܬܠܡܝܕܗ [d]	ܪܡܬܐ [c] ܕܗܘܐ [d] ܬܠܡܝܕܗ ܕܡܪܢ ܝܫܘܥ :	ܬܠܡܝܕܗ [d]

Codex A.	Codex B.	Codex C.

Codex B.

[illegible]
[illegible]
[illegible]
39 [illegible]
[illegible]
[illegible]
40 [illegible]
[illegible]
[illegible]
41 [illegible]
[illegible]
[illegible]
42 [illegible]
[illegible]
[illegible]

Codex A. (variants e–c: [illegible]; i omit [illegible]; p add [illegible])

Codex C. (variants e–d: [illegible]; i omit [illegible]; p add [illegible]; v [illegible] (sic); e omit [illegible])

Matt. XXVII. 1.

Codex B.

[illegible]
[illegible]
[illegible]
[illegible]
3 [illegible]
[illegible]
[illegible]
4 [illegible]
[illegible]
5 [illegible]
[illegible]
6 [illegible]
[illegible]
7 [illegible]

Codex A. (variants a–v: a add [illegible]; o omit [illegible]; n omit [illegible]; u add [illegible])

Codex C. (variants a–v: a add [illegible]; o omit [illegible]; g omit [illegible]; n omit [illegible]; p omit [illegible]; u add [illegible])

Codex B.

ܒܗܘܢ [r]ܢܗܘܪܗ ܕܣܒܪܐ [s]ܠܗܝܡܢܘܬܐ
8 [t]ܠܐܗܝܡܢܝܢ : ܠܟܢ [l]ܕܝܢ ܐܬܘܪܝ [u]ܢܗܘܪܗ [v]ܗܘ
9 [m]ܫܘܠ ܐܕܡܐ [w]ܕܗܕܡܐ ܠܝܘܡܕܝܢ : ܟܕܢ ܐܬܡܠܠ
ܡܐ [x]ܕܐܡܪ ܒܐܘܪܝܬܐ ܢܒܝܐ ܕܐܡܪ ܢܫܒܘ
[y]ܬܠܬܢ [z]ܕܡܫܝܚܐ ܕܡܗܘ [a]ܕܡܝܬܪ ܡܐ
10 [b]ܕܐܡܪܘ ܡܢ ܒܝܢܐ [c]ܕܐܣܪܐܝܠ : ܘܝܗܒ
ܬܗܘܢ ܒܦܘܪܗ ܕܫܒܪܐ : ܗܝܟ ܡܐ [e]ܕܐܬܘܡ
11 ܠܝ [f]ܡܪܐ : ܗܘ ܕܝܢ ܡܪܐ ܫܡܥܘ [g]ܡܢ ܡܘܕܡ
[h]ܗܝܡܢܘܬܐ : [d]*ܘܐܢܐ ܗܘܬ [i]ܗܝܡܢܘܬܐ [j]ܐܡܪ
ܐܬ ܗܘ ܡܠܟܐ [k]ܕܝܗܘܕܝ : ܗܘ ܕܝܢ ܡܪܐ
12 ܫܡܥܘ ܐܡܪ ܐܬ [l]ܐܡܪܬ : ܘܟܡܐ ܕܗܘܐ
ܡܬܦܠܓ ܡܢ [n]ܪܝܫ ܒܗܝܢܐ ܘܡܢ ܡܫܝܚܝܐ :
13 ܘܟܠܡ ܠܐ [o]ܗܘܐ [p]ܡܠܝܟ : [q]ܒܟܢ ܐܡܪ
ܠܗ [r]ܓܠܝܦܘܫ ܠܝܬ ܐܬ ܥܒܕ ܒܡܐ ܗܘܢ
14 ܡܫܝܕܢ ܒܠܝܟ : ܘܠܐ ܐܝܠܝܒ ܢܬܗ ܐܘܦ
ܠܐ [s]ܠܡܒܠ ܚܕܐ ܡܠܐ : ܗܝܟ ܠܡܠܘ ܕܝܢ
15 ܕܝܗܐ [i]ܗܝܡܢܘܬܐ [t]ܬܡܢܗ ܠܚܕܐ : ܒܒܘܠ
[u]ܡܘܒܕ ܕܝܢ ܗܘܐ ܐܠܘܦ ܗܝܡܢܘܬܐ ܒܝܐ
[v]ܠܐܦܠܘܫܝܐ ܚܕ [w]ܐܫܪ ܡܢ ܕܗܘܘ ܓܒܝܢ
16 ܗܘܐ [x]ܕܝܢ ܠܗܘܢ [y]ܒܟܢ ܚܕ [w]ܐܫܪ [a]ܕܝܒ
17 [l]ܕܡܬܘܪܐ [b]ܫܡܥܘ ܒܪ ܪܒܢ : ܘܗܝܟ ܕܗܘܢ
ܡܒܝܢܝܢ ܐܡܪ ܠܗܘܢ [r]ܓܠܝܦܘܫ ܠܟܢ ܐܬܘܢ
ܒܟܢ ܡܢ ܬܘܪܐ ܕܝܒܢܐ ܠܒܘܢ [c]ܐܘܦ
[d]*ܠܫܡܘܫ ܒܪ ܪܒܢ ܐܐ [m]*ܠܫܡܘܫ ܕܡܬܘܪܐ
18 ܡܫܝܚܝܐ : ܗܘܐ ܓܪ ܚܕܒ [n]ܕܠܓܠܝܠ ܡܢܐ
19 ܡܫܪܘ ܢܬܗ : ܘܗܝܟ ܕܗܘ [e]ܢܬܒ ܒܠ
[f]ܒܢܡܐ ܥܠܝܫܬ ܠܪܗ ܐܬܬܗ ܐܡܪܐ[g] : ܠܐ
ܠܝ ܘܠܐ [h]ܠܗܘ [s]ܠܗܘ ܝܕܥܘܐ : ܦܠܢ ܓܪ
ܫܥܬ [i]ܢܡܕܝܢ ܒܫܠܡܢ ܡܢ [j]ܠܓܠܝܠܗ :
20 ܘܪܝܫܐ ܒܗܝܢܐ ܘܡܫܝܚܝܐ [a]ܐܓ̈ܫܘ [k]ܕܝܢ
[l]ܠܐܦܠܘܫܝܐ ܕܫܡܠܝܢ ܠܒܪܝܢ : ܠܡܪܐ [m]ܫܡܥܘ

Codex A.

[t]ܠܐܒܟ̈ܝܢ
[l] omit ܕܝܢ
[u]ܦܘܪܐ — [v]ܗܘ̇ܘ
[w]ܒܕ ܡܠܟܐ
[x]ܕܐܬ̣ܡܪ — [y]ܬܠܬ̣ܝܢ
[z]ܕܡܫ̈ܝܚܐ
[a]ܕܡܝܬܪܐ — [b]ܕܢܘܪܘ
[c]ܕܐܝܣܪܐܝܠ
[e]ܕܐܬܘܡ — [f]ܡܪܐ
[h]ܗܝܡܢ̇ܘܬܐ
[d]ܘܐܢܐ
[i] omit ܗܝܡܢܘܬܐ
[k]ܕܝܗ̈ܘܕܝܢ
[l]ܐܡ̇ܪ
[n]ܪ̈ܝܫܐ — [q]ܒܟܢ
[s]ܠܡܒܠ
[u]ܡܘܒܕ
[v]ܠܐܦ̇ܠܘܫ̈ܝܐ
[y]ܒܟܢ — [w]ܐܫ̇ܪ
[l] omit ܕ — [b]ܫܡܥ̇
[c] omit ܐܘܦ
[d]ܠܫܡܥ̇
[m]ܫܡ̇ܥܘ — [n]ܕܠܓܠܝܠ
[e]ܢܬܒ
[h] omit ܠܗܘ
[i]ܢܡܕܝܢ — [j]ܠܓܠܝܠܗ
[a]ܐܓ̈ܫܘ — [k] omit ܕܝܢ
[l]ܠܐܦ̈ܠܘܫܝܐ
[m] add ܕܝܢ

Codex C.

[r]ܦܘܪܐ
[s]ܠܗܝܡܢܘܬܐ
[t]ܕܐܗܝܡܢܝܢ
[l] omit ܕܝܢ
[u]ܦܘܪܐ — [v]ܗܘܐ
[m]ܫܘܠܐ
[w]ܒܕ ܡܠܟܐ
[x]ܕܐܬܡܪ
[y]ܬܠܬܝܢ — [a]ܕܡܝܬܪܐ
[b]ܕܢܘܪܘ
[c]ܕܐܣܪܐܝܠ — [g]ܘܡܘܕܡ
[d]ܘܐܢܐ
[* *Sic* in Cod. B.]
[j]ܘܐܡܪ
[n]ܪܝܫܐ
[o] omit ܗܘܐ
[r]ܓܠܝܦܘܫ
[t]ܬܡܢܗ
[u]ܡܘܒܕ — [x]ܕܐܝܢ
[a]ܕܝܒ — [b]ܫܡܥ
[c] omit ܐܘܦ
[d]ܠܫܡܥ
[* *Sic* in Cod. B.]
[m]ܠܫܡܘܫ
[f]ܒܢܡܐ
[g] add ܠܗ :
[h]ܠܗܕܝܢ
[s] omit ܠܗܘ
[k] omit ܕܝܢ
[l]ܠܐܦܠܘܫܝܐ
[m] add ܕܝܢ

Codex B.

21 ܘܫܒܩܘܗܝ : [m]ܐܟܒܪ [n]ܕܝܢ [o]ܗܘܠܡܦܝܐ ܘܐܡܪܬ
ܠܗܘܢ : ܠܡܢ ܐܬܝܬܘܢ ܝܕܥܝܢ ܕܡܠܟܐ ܠܟܘܢ
ܡܢ ܬܪܥܐ : ܗܢܘܢ [p]ܕܝܢ ܐܡܪܘ ܠܒܢ̈ܝܢ :
22 ܐܡܪ ܠܗܘܢ [q]ܢܩܛܢܒܘܣ ܡܢܐ ܐܘ ܥܒܕܐ
[r]ܠܢܩܛܢܒܘܣ [s]ܕܝܢ [t]ܕܡܬܕܡܪ ܡܬܒܝܢܐ : ܘܐܡܪ
23 ܒܠܒܗܘܢ [w]ܚܝܠܘܒ : ܗܘ ܕܝܢ ܐܡܪ ܡܢܐ
ܠܟ ܒܢܝܐ ܥܒܕܐ : ܗܢܘܢ [p]ܕܝܢ [v]ܐܬܝܪܐܬ
24 ܗܘܘ ܡܬܕܡܪܝܢ ܘܐܡܪܝܢ [w]ܚܝܠܘܒ : ܟܕ ܕܝܢ
ܫܡܥܐ [q]ܢܩܛܢܒܘܣ [x]ܕܒܠܘܟ ܠܐ ܡܗܝܢܐ : ܐܠܐ
ܥܠ [y]ܕܝܬܝܪ [z]ܒܥܘܬܪܐ ܡܬܒܥܒܕܐ : ܢܦܩ ܡܢ
[a]ܘܐܬܢܚ [b]ܐܕܘܝ ܠܗܝ [c]ܐܠܟܣܢܕܪܘܣ ܘܐܡܪ :
[d]ܐܝܟܢܐ ܐܢܐ ܡܢ ܐܒܘܗܝ [e]ܕܗܕܝܢ *ܝܕܝܥܐ :
25 ܐܬܘܢ ܬܫܡܥܘܢ : [f]ܘܐܟܬܒܘ ܒܟܠܗ ܡܘܠܗܐ
ܘܐܡܪܘ ܐܕܡܗ [g]ܕܝܢ ܟܠܢܗ ܘܟܠ ܒܢܝܢܗ :
26 [h]ܟܡܢ ܦܢܐ ܠܗܘܢ ܠܒܢ̈ܝܢ : ܠܡܪܐ ܢܩܛܢܒܘܣ
ܕܝܢ ܝܗܒ ܘܡܫܩܠ ܢܬܗ ܠܗܘܢ [i]ܕܚܝܠܘܒܘܢ
27 ܢܬܗ : [k]ܘܟܡܢ [l]ܙܘܢܝܐ [j]ܕܗܘܠܡܦܝܐ ܕܒܢܘ
ܢܬܗ ܠܡܪܐ ܢܩܛܢܒܘܣ [m]ܠܦܝܠܝܦܘܣ : ܘܒܥܝܢ
28 [n]ܒܠܝ ܒܟܠܗ ܡܦܩܪܐ : ܘܫܠܒܘ ܢܬܗ ܕܝܢ :
29 [o]ܘܒܠܡܘܣ [a]ܕܙܘܦܪܝ ܝܗܒܘ ܒܠܒܝ : ܘܟܠܒ
ܒܠܒܠ ܡܢ ܒܘܟܝܢ ܘܝܗܒܘ ܒܠ ܙܢܥܗ [b]ܘܦܢܐ
ܒܡܥܝܢܗ : ܘܗܘܘ [c]ܡܕܝܢ [d]ܡܘܕܥܗ ܡܚܝܣܝܢ
ܒܗ : ܘܐܡܪܝܢ ܫܒܠܐ ܠܟ [e]ܡܠܟܡܘܢ
30 [f]ܕܝܗܘܕܝ : [g]ܘܦܘܣ [h]ܒܐܒܘܗ ܘܢܫܩܘ [z]ܦܢܝܐ
31 ܘܗܘܘ [i]ܡܚܝܢ ܠܗ ܒܠ ܙܢܥܗ : ܘܟܕ ܚܙܝܘ
ܒܗ ܐܣܠܥܘ ܢܬܗ [j]ܒܠܡܘܣܐ : [k]ܘܟܡܢ [l]ܐܣܠܥܘ
ܢܬܗ ܡܐܢܝ [n]ܘܐܦܩܘܠ ܢܬܗ [o]ܕܚܝܠܒܘܢ
32 ܢܬܗ : ܟܕ ܕܝܢ [p]ܢܦܩ ܐܣܚܝܘ ܒܪܢܫ [q]ܡܢܝܐܢܝ
ܕܝܡܗܘܢ ܫܝܟܘܢ [r]ܠܗܕܝܢ [s]ܝܕܘ [t]ܐܟܪܙܐ
33 ܕܝܫܒܥ [u]ܚܝܠܒܗ : ܘܒܪ ܐܬܘ [w]ܠܐܬܪܐ
[x]ܗܕܐ [y]ܕܡܬܩܪܐ [z]ܒܘܠܛܠܬܐ : ܡܢܐ ܕܗܘ

Codex A.

[m]ܐܟܒܪ
[o]ܗܘܠܡܦܝܐ
[s]ܗܕܝܢ [t]ܡܬܕܡܪ
[w]ܚܝܠܘܒ
[x]ܕܒܠܘܟ [y]ܕܝܬܝܪ
[z]ܒܥܘܬܪܬܐ
[b]ܐܒܘܗܝ
[c]ܐܘܠܘܡܦܝܐ
[e]ܗܕܝܢ [f]ܘܐܟܬܒ
[g]ܕܝܢ omit [h]ܟܡܢ
[i]ܕܚܝܠܘܒܘܢ
[k]ܘܟܡܢ [l]ܙܘܢܝܐ
[j]ܕܗܘܠܡܦܝܐ
[m]ܠܦܝܠܝܦܘܣ
[o]ܘܒܠܡܘܣ
[a]ܕܙܘܦܪܘ [b]ܘܦܢܝܐ
[d]ܡܘܕܥܗܝ
[f]ܕܝܗܘܕܝܢ [h]ܒܗ
[j]ܒܠܡܘܣܐ
[k]ܘܟܡܢ [l]ܐܠܟܣܢܕ
[n]ܘܐܘܟܠܝܢ
[o]ܕܚܝܠܒܘܢ
[p]ܢܩܘܒ [r]ܠܗܕܝܢ
[s]ܙܐܘ [t]ܐܟܪܙܐ
[u]ܚܝܠܒܗ [w]ܐܬܪܐ
[x]ܗܕܐ omit
[y]ܕܡܬܩܪܐ
[z]ܒܘܠܛܠܬܐ

Codex C.

[m]ܐܟܒܪ [n]ܕܐܝ
[p]ܕܝܢ omit
[q]ܢܩܛܢܒܘܣ
[r]ܠܡܪܐ ܢܩܛܢܒܘܣ
[s]ܗܕܝܢ
[v]ܐܬܪܐܬ
[w]ܚܝܠܘܒ
[x]ܕܒܠܘܟ
[a]ܘܐܬܢܚ [b]ܐܕܘܗ
[* Cod. B. ܝܕܝܥܐ]
[d]ܐܝܟ [f]ܘܐܟܬܒ
[g]ܕܝܢ omit
[m]ܠܦܝܠܝܦܘܣ
[n]ܒܠܝ [c]ܡܕܝܢ
[d]ܡܘܕܥܗ
[e]ܡܠܟܡܘܢ omit
[f]ܕܝܗܘܕܝܢ [g]ܘܦܘܣ
[h]ܒܗ [z]ܦܢܝܐ
[i]ܡܚܝܢ [j]ܒܠܡܘܣܐ
[k]ܘܟܡܢ [l]ܐܣܠܥܘ
[n]ܘܐܦܩܘܠ
[p]ܢܦܩ
[q]ܡܢܝܐܢܝ [t]ܐܟܪܙܐ
[w]ܐܬܪܐ
[x]ܗܕܐ omit
[z]ܒܘܠܛܠܬܐ

Codex A.

ܡܬܦܠܓܝܢ ˣ
ʸ *add* ܕܝ ܐܬܝܢܐ
ܕܦܘܦܣܬܐ ᶻ
ᵐ ܫܠ ᵃ ܕܡܚܝܟܝܢ
ᵉ ܡܐܢܘܗܝ
ᵍ ܡܐܢܘܗܝ ʰ ܢܒܝ :
ᵗ ܢܩܒܝܢ
ⁱ *omit* ܠܗ
ʲ ܠܟܠ ᵏ ܕܠܐܬܗ
ˡ ܕܠܐܬܟܐ
ⁿ ܡܠܟܘܬܗ
ᵒ ܕܝܗܘܕܝܐ
ᵖ ܒܗܡ ᑫ *omit* ܕܝܢ
ˢ ܠܒܗܠܝܢ
ᵐ ܚܕܕܝܢ
ᵒ ܠܐ
ˡ ܫܦܝܪܐ
ᑫ ܕܫܠ ʳ *add* ܕܒܗ
ᵗ ܘܒܢܦܫ ᵘ ܥܒܕܝܢ
ʷ ܐܝܢܗ
ᵇ *omit* ܕܝܢ
ᵈ ܒܡܠܟܟ ᵍ ܬܬܬܐ
ʰ *add* ܐܡܝܢ
ⁱ ܕܡܬܡܟܪ
ᵏ *add* ܒܗܕܐ

ᵐ ܕܗܘ ⁿ *omit* ܕܝܢ

Codex B.

34 *ˣ ܐܬܦܠܓܘ ʸ ᶻܦܘܪܣܬܐ : ܘܩܝܡܘ ܠܗ ܕܚܙܝܬܐ :
ᵐܫܡܪܝ ᵃܡܚܝܟܝܢ ᵇܒܡܚܝܪܐ : ᶜܘܐܡܪ ܠܓܒܪ ܠܐ
35 ܘܗܘܐ ܥܡܐ ܕܚܙܝܬܐ : ᵈܟܕ ܕܝܢ ܥܠܒܘ ܗܘܬ
ܦܠܓܘ ᵉܡܐܢܝܗ ܘܪܡܘ ᶠܢܒܝܢ ᵠܕܝܢ ܕܬܬܡܠܐ
ܡܐ ܕܐܬܐܡܪ ܒܢܒܝܐ ܕܐܡܪ : ܦܠܓܘ ᵍܡܐܢܝ
36 ܒܝܢܬܗܘܢ ܘܥܠ ܠܒܘܫܝ ܪܡܘ ʰܢܒܝܢ : ܘܗܘܘ
37 ᵗܢܬܒܝܢ ܢܛܪܝܢ ܠܗ ܬܡܢ : ܘܣܡܘ ⁱܠܗ ʲܠܟܠ
ܡܢ ܪܝܫܗ ᵏܟܠܝܬܗ ˡܒܬܒܐ ܕܗܕܝܢ ܐܝܬ
38 ܗܘ ܝܫܘܥ ⁿܡܠܟܐ ᵒܕܝܗܘܕܝܐ : ᵖܒܗܝܢ ᑫܕܝܢ
ʳܐܙܕܩܦܘ ܥܡܗ ܬܪܝܢ ˢܠܣܛܝܢ ܚܕ ܡܢ ܝܡܝܢܐ
ܘܚܕ ܡܢ ܣܡܠܐ :

Luke XXIII. 39.

39 ܚܕ ܕܝܢ ܡܢ ˣܗܠܝܢ ᵐܒܝܫܐ ܕܐܙܕܩܦܘ
ܥܡܗ ܗܘܐ ⁿܡܓܕܦ ܥܠܘܝ ܘܐܡܪ : ᵒܐܢ
ܐܢܬ ܗܘ ܡܫܝܚܐ : ܐܚܝ ܢܦܫܟ ܘܐܚܝܢ
40 ܥܢܐ : ܐܚܪܢܐ ܕܝܢ ˡܫܝܐܘܪܐ ᵖܘܗܘܐ ܟܐܒ
ܒܗ ܘܐܡܪ : ܐܘܦ ܠܐ ܡܢ ܐܠܗܐ ܕܚܠ ܐܢܬ
41 ᑫܕܫܠ : ʳܕܒܕܝܢܐ ܐܢܬ ˢܐܘܦ ܐܢܬ ˢ: ܘܐܢܢ
ܡܢ ᵗܘܒܩܘܫܛ ᵘܥܒܕܝܢ ᵛܒܡܐ ܕܥܒܕܢ ʷܐܝܢܢ
ܡܩܒܠܝܢ ᵇܕܝܢ ᶜܕܝܢ ᵈܒܗܠܝܢ ܒܝܫ ܠܐ ܥܒܕ
42 ܘܗܘܐ ܐܡܪ ܠܡܪܐ ܝܫܘܥ ᵉܐܬܕܟܪ ᶠܠܝ ܟܕ
43 ᵍܐܬ ᵍܐܬܐ ܒܡܠܟܘܬܟ : ܐܡܪ ܕܝܢ ܡܪܐ
ܝܫܘܥ ܘܐܡܪ ܠܗ : ʰܐܡܝܢ ܐܡܪ ܐܢܐ ܠܟ
ⁱܕܝܘܡܢ ܐܢܬ ܗܘܐ ᵏܒܦܪܕܝܣܐ :

Matt. XXVII. 39.

39 ܗܠܝܢ ܕܝܢ ܗܘܘ ܡܥܒܪܝܢ ˡܥܠܘܝ ܘܡܢܝܕܝܢ
40 ܪܝܫܗܘܢ : ܘܐܡܪܝܢ ܐܘ ᵐܗܕܝܢ ܕܫܪܐ ᵒܢܟܣܗ
ⁿܕܝܢ ܕܐܠܗܐ ܘܬܠܬܐ ܝܘܡܝܢ ܒܢܐ ܠܗ :
ܐܚܝ ܢܦܫܟ ܘܚܘܬ ܡܢ ܨܠܝܒܐ : ᵖܐܢ ᑫܐܢܬ

Codex C.

[* Cod. B. ܐܬܦܠܓܘ]
ܡܬܦܠܓܝܢ ˣ
ʸ *add* ܕܝ ܐܬܝܢܐ
ܕܦܘܦܣܬܐ ᶻ
ܒܡܚܝܪܐ ᵇ
ᶜ *omit* ܘܐܡܪ ... ܕܚܙܝܬܐ
ᵈ ܘܟܕ ᵉ ܡܐܢܘܗܝ
ᶠ *add* ܥܠܘܗܝ
ᵍ ܡܐܢܘܗܝ ʰ ܢܒܝ
ܢܩܒܝܢ
ⁱ *omit* ܠܗ ᵏ ܕܠܐܬܗ
ⁿ ܡܠܟܘܬܗ
ʳ ܐܙܕܩܦܘ ᑫ *omit* ܕܝܢ
ˣ ܗܠܝܢ ᵐ ܒܝܫܝܢ
ⁿ ܡܓܕܦܝܢ ᵒ ܠܐ
ܫܦܝܪܐ ˡ
ᵖ *add* ܘܐܡܪ
ʳ *add* ܕܒܗ
ˢ ܐܢܬܝܗ
ᵗ ܘܒܩܘܫܛܐ ᵘ ܥܒܕܝܢ
ᵛ ܕܥܒܕܐ
ʷ ܐܝܢܗ ᶜ *omit* ܕܝܢ
ᵈ ܒܡܠܟܘܬܟ ᵉ ܐܬܕܟܪ
ᶠ *add* ܡܪܝ
ܐܬܐܬܐ ᵍ
ᵏ *add* ܒܗܕܐ

ˡ *omit* ܥܠܘܝ
ⁿ *omit* ܕܝܢ
ܢܟܣܐ ᵒ
ᵖ ܐܝܢ ᑫ *omit* ܐܢܬ

Codex A.

[q]ܘܟܝܢ [s]ܪ̈ܫܝܐ
[t]ܗܦܪ̈ܝܐ ܐܢ [u]*omit*
[v]ܠܡܫܝܚܝܢ [x]ܢܚܠ
[z]ܕܐܝܣܪܝܠ
[a]ܐܢܬ [c]ܝܠܒܟܐ
[s]ܘܐܢܢ
[f]ܘܟܝܢ [h]ܠܓܢܝܣܪܐ
[i] *omit* ܗܠܝܢ
[k] *add* ܕܝ [l]ܒܕܡܟܐ
[p]ܪ̈ܚܡܐ [a]ܐܢܠ
[q]ܠܚܟܐ
[b]ܐܠܗܝ
[t]ܦܐܩ̈ܝܢ
[c]ܠܝܠܝܢܐ [u]ܗܕܝܢ
[w]ܫܠ [l]ܡܢܟܐ
[v] *omit* ܕܝ [s] *add* ܕܝ
[m]ܘܫܒܪܬܐ
[y] *omit* ܕܝ
[z] *omit* ܕܝ
[n]ܫܡܥܘ [o]ܐܠܝܦܗ
[p]ܕܚܝܟܐ
[c]ܠܟܠ [d]ܠܙܝܚ
[e]ܘܫܝܢܝܬܐ
[f]ܐܬܩܠܒܠ
[g]ܐܬܦܬܚܝ :
[i]ܕܕܟܟܘ
[l] *omit* ܕܝ
[a]ܠܒܕܝܢܬܐ
[m]ܘܫܢܝܬܐ

Codex B.

41 ܐܢܬ [p]ܒܪܗ ܕܐܠܗܐ : [q]ܘܟܝܢ ܘܟܐܬ [r]ܐܘܦ
[s]ܪܫܝܐ ܒܗܝܢܐ ܗܘܘ ܡܡܠܠܝܢ ܒܢ [t]ܗܦܪܐ
42 ܘܡܫܡܫܢܐ ܗܘܘ ܐܡܪܝܢ : [u]ܐܢ [v]ܠܡܫܝܚܝܢ
ܐܝܟ [w]ܘܠܝܢܬܗ ܠܐ [x]ܡܢܠ ܕܢܝܟܐ : [y]ܐܢ
ܡܠܟܐ [z]ܕܐܝܣܪܝܠ [a]ܐܢܬ ܗܘ [b]ܡܫܝܚܐ ܒܕܘ ܡܢ
43 [c]ܝܠܒܟܐ [s]ܘܐܢܢ [d]ܡܗܡܢܝܢ ܒܗ : [e]ܐܢ ܡܢܪ
ܒܠ ܐܠܗܐ ܡܦܪܘܩ ܝܬܗ : ܒܕܘ ܐܢ ܐܢܬ ܗܘ
ܝܒܟܐ ܒܗ :[e]· ܐܡܪ ܠܝ ܕܐܢܐ ܒܪܗ ܕܐܠܗܐ :
44 [f]ܒܝܢ [g]ܐܘܦ [h]ܠܓܢܝܣܪܐ [i]ܗܠܝܢ ܕܐܝܣܛܠܒܘ
45 ܒܒܢܗ ܗܘܘ ܡܚܣܕܝܢ ܠܗ ܡܢ ܫܢܬ ܫܒܝܢ[k]
ܗܘܐ ܡܬܠܐ ܒܠ ܒܗܠܗ ܐܪܒܐ [l]ܒܕ ܡܬܟܐ[l]
46 [m]ܠܬܫܥܐ ܫܒܝܢ : ܠܦܐ ܕܝ [n]ܬܫܥܐ ܫܒܝܢ ܐܝܟܢ
[o]ܡܪܚܐ ܫܒܩ ܒܡܠܟܐ [p]ܪܒܐ ܘܐܡܪ [a]ܐܠܝܐ
47 [a]ܐܠܝ [q]ܠܝܡܟܐ ܫܒܩܬ ܝܬܝ : [r]ܡܟܐ ܕܐܝܬ
ܗܘ [b]ܐܠܗܝ [b]ܐܠܗܝ [q]ܠܝܡܟܐ ܫܒܩܬ ܝܬܝ[r] :
ܐܢܫܝܢ [s]ܡܢ ܗܠܝܢ ܕܗܘܘ [t]ܩܐܡܝܢ ܬܡܢ : ܒܕ
48 ܫܡܥܘ ܐܡܪܘ [c]ܠܐܠܝܐ [u]ܗܘ ܡܪܐ ܘܫܐܠ
ܪܗܛ ܚܕ [v]ܕܝ ܡܢܗܘܢ ܘܢܣܒ ܐܣܦܘܓ
ܘܡܠܝܗ ܚܠܐ [w]ܘܐܣܩܗ [x]ܒܩܢܝܐ ܘܗܘܐ [l]ܡܫܩܐ ܠܗ
49 ܘܗܘܐ ܡܫܩܐ ܠܗ :· [m]ܘܫܪܬܐ [y]ܕܝ ܗܘܘ
[z]ܕܝ ܐܡܪܝܢ [n]ܫܒܘܩ ܢܚܙܐ ܐܢ [a]ܐܬܐ
50 [o]ܐܠܝܦܗ [p]ܢܚܬ ܠܗ : ܗܘ ܕܝ ܡܪܝܐ ܝܫܘܥ
ܬܘܒ [b]ܐܝܟܢ ܒܩܠܐ ܪܒܐ ܘܫܒܩ ܪܘܚܗ :
51 ܘܗܐ ܦܪܣܗ ܕܗܝܟܠܐ ܐܬܦܠܓ ܠܬܪܝܢ ܡܢ
[c]ܠܥܠ ܥܕ ܡܬܟܐ [d]ܠܐܪܥܐ : ܘܐܪ̈ܥܐ ܙܥܘ ܘܢܬ :·
52 [e]ܘܫܢܝܢܬܐ [f]ܐܬܩܠܒܠܬ : ܘܩܒܘܪܬܐ
[g]ܐܬܦܬܚܬ : ܘܣܓܝ [h]ܦܓܪܝܢ ܡܢ ܕܡܫܝܚܐ
53 [i]ܕܕܟܟܘ [k]ܡܚܝܘ : ܘܒܕ [l]ܕܝ ܢܦܩܘ ܡܢ
ܩܒܘܪܬܐ ܐܬܘ [a]ܠܒܕܝܢܬܐ [m]ܘܫܢܝܬܐ
54 ܘܐܬܚܙܝܘ ܠܣܓܝ : ܡܦܠܛܢܐ ܕܝ ܘܗܠܝܢ
ܕܒܗܡܢ ܢܛܪܝܢ ܠܡܪܐ ܝܫܘܥ : ܒܕ ܚܙܘ

Codex C.

[p] *add* ܗܘ
[r] *omit* ܐܘܦ
[u] *omit* ܐܢ [s]ܪ̈ܫܝܐ
[v]ܠܡܫܝܚܝܢ
[w]ܘܠܝܢܬܗ
[y]ܐܝܟ [z]ܕܐܝܣܪܝܠ
[a]ܐܢܬ [b]ܡܫܝܚ
[d]ܡܗܡܢܝܢ
[e] *omit* ܒܗ ... ܐܢ
[f]ܘܒܝܢ [g] *omit* ܐܘܦ
[i] *omit* ܗܠܝܢ
[k] *add* ܕܝ [l]ܒܕܡܟܐ
[m]ܠܬܫܥܐ [n]ܬܫܥܐ
[o] *omit* ܪܚܐ [p]ܪܒܐ
[q]ܠܝܡܟܐ
[r] *omit* ܝܬܝ ... ܡܟܐ
[s] *add* ܕܝ [t]ܩܐܡܝܢ
[u]ܗܕܝܢ
[v] *omit* ܕܝ
[w]ܫܠ [x]ܘܐܣܩܗ
[y]ܕܐܝܟ [z] *omit* ܕܝ
[a] *omit* ܐܬܐ
[p]ܕܢܚܬ
[b] *omit* ܐܝܟܢ
[d] *add* ܕܝ
[f]ܐܬܩܠܒܠ
[g]ܐܬܦܬܚܢ
[h]ܦܓܪܝܢ
[i]ܕܕܟܟܘ
[l] *omit* ܕܝ [k]ܘܐܡܚܘ
[m]ܘܫܢܝܬܐ

Codex A.	Codex B.	Codex C.
[m]ܘܒܥܘܬܐ [r]ܗܘܐ [s]ܗܕܝܢ	[m]ܘܒܥܘܬܐ ܘܩܠܐ [n]ܕܐܬܒܥܒܥ [o]ܕܫܠܘ ܠܫܕܐ [p]ܘܐܡܪܝܢ : [q]ܡܫܪܪܬ ܒܪܗ ܕܐܠܗܐ [r]ܗܘ [s]ܗܕܝܢ	[n]ܕܐܬܒܥܒܥ [p]ܐܡܪܝܢ [o]omit ܕܫܠܘ [r]ܗܘܐ [q]ܡܫܪܪܬ

John XIX. 31.

Codex A.	Codex B.	Codex C.
[q]ܠܚܠܠ [r] *add* ܕܗܘܬ [s]ܦܓܪܝܐ [t] *add* ܗܘܐ ܓܝܪ ܝܘܡܗ ܕܗܘܬ ܥܪܘܒܬܐ ܝܘܡ ܪܒܐ: [v]ܪܓܠܝܗܘܢ [w] *omit* ܗܘܐ . . . ܪܒܐ [c]ܪܘܡܚܝܢ ܘܬܒܪܘ [g]ܘܕܬܢܝܢܐ [i] *add* ܕܝܢ [k]ܝܫܘܥ [a] *omit* ܕܡܝܬ ܗܘܐ [b]ܟܒܪ [l]ܕܬܒܪܬ [m]ܪܓܠܘܗܝ [n]ܪܘܡܚܝܢ [o]ܒܠܘܟܝܬܐ [q]ܘܢܦܩܘ [s]ܐܣܗܕ [b]ܘܫܪܝܪܐ [p] *omit* ܕܝܢ [d]ܝܕܥ [w]ܕܩܘܫܛ [p] *omit* ܕܝܢ [z]ܘܬܘܒ [a]ܚܙܘܢ [b]ܠܗܘ	31 ܘܝܗܘܕܝܐ ܐܘܦ ܡܢ [q]ܠܚܠܠ [r]ܒܡܘܪܒܬܐ ܕܠܐ ܢܬܪܘܢ [s]ܦܓܪܝܐ ܥܠ ܨܠܝܒܐ ܒܫܘܒܬܐ:[t] ܒܗ ܡܢ [u]ܫܐܠܘܢ ܕܢܬܒܪܘܢ [v]ܪܓܠܝܗܘܢ ܘܢܫܬܩܠܘܢ: [w]ܗܘܐ [x]ܓܝܪ [y]ܝܘܡܗ [z]ܪܒܐ 32 [a]ܕܫܒܬܐ ܝܘܡ [b]ܥܪܘܒܬܐ: ܘܐܬܘ [c]ܘܬܒܪܘ [d]ܥܡܗ [e]ܪܓܠܘܗܝ [f]ܕܩܕܡܝܐ [g]ܘܕܬܢܝܢܐ ܕܨܠܝܒ 33 [h]ܕܐܫܬܠܒܘ ܥܡܗ: ܘܟܕ [i]ܐܬܘ ܥܠ ܡܪܝܐ ܘܚܙܘ [k]ܝܫܘܥ [a]ܕܡܝܬ ܗܘܐ [b]ܟܒܪ [l]ܬܒܪܬ: 34 ܠܐ ܬܒܪܘ [m]ܪܓܠܘܗܝ: ܐܠܐ ܚܕ ܡܢ [n]ܪܘܡܚܝܢ [o]ܒܠܘܟܝܬܐ ܢܩܫ ܝܬܗ ܠܓܒܗ [p]ܕܝܢ [q]ܘܢܦܩܘ 35 ܡܝܐ ܐܕܡ [r]ܘܡܝܢ: ܘܗܕܝܢ ܕܚܙܐ [s]ܐܣܗܕ [b]ܘܫܪܝܪܐ [t]ܐܝܬ ܗܝ ܣܗܕܘܬܗ [p]ܕܝܢ [c]ܘܗܘ [d]ܝܕܥ [w]ܕܩܘܫܛ ܗܘ ܐܡܪ: ܕܐܘܦ ܐܢܬܘܢ 36 ܬܗܝܡܢܘܢ: ܐܬܥܒܕ ܓܝܪ ܕܟܬܒܐ ܬܬܡܠܐ [x]ܕܓܪܡ ܡܢܗ [p]ܕܝܢ ܠܐ ܐܬܬܒܪ: [z]ܘܬܘܒ ܟܬܒ [a]ܚܙܘܢ ܐܡܪ ܢܚܙܘܢ [b]ܠܠܗܘ [c]ܕܢܩܫܘ.	[r] *add* ܗܘܬ [u]ܫܐܠܘ [x] *add* ܪܒܐ [y]ܕܝܘܡܗ [z] *omit* ܪܒܐ [a]ܫܒܬܐ [d] *omit* ܪܘܡܚܝܢ [e]ܪܓܠܝܗ [f]ܕܩܕܡ [g]ܘܕܬܢܝܢܐ [h]ܕܐܫܬܠܒܘ [i] *add* ܕܝܢ [m]ܪܓܠܘܗܝ [l]ܕܬܒܪܬ [o]ܒܠܘܟܝܬܐ [p] *omit* ܕܝܢ [d]ܝܕܥ [c]ܘܗܘܘ [q]ܘܢܦܩ [t] *omit* ܐܝܬ [r]ܘܡܝܢ [p] *omit* ܕܝܢ [w]ܕܩܘܫܛܐ [b]ܠܗܘ [x]ܕܓܪܡ

Matt. XXVII. 55.

Codex A.	Codex B.	Codex C.
[r]ܢܫܝܢ [s]ܚܙܝܢܐ [t]ܕܐܬܝܢ [v]ܡܫܡܫܢ [w]ܠܗ [z]ܐܡܗ [o]ܕܝܥܩܘܒ [r]ܘܐܡܗܘܢ	55 ܗܘܝ ܕܝܢ ܬܡܢ ܐܘܦ [r]ܢܫܝܢ ܣܓܝ ܡܢ ܪܘܚܩܐ [s]ܚܙܝܢ ܗܠܝܢ [t]ܕܐܬܝܢ ܒܬܪ ܡܪܢ ܝܫܘܥ 56 ܡܢ ܓܠܝܠܐ [v]ܡܫܡܫܢ [w]ܝܬܗ: [x]ܕܒܗܝܢ ܗܘܬ [y]ܡܪܝܐܡ ܡܓܕܠܝܬܐ ܘܡܪܝܡ [z]ܐܡܗ [o]ܕܝܥܩܘܒ ܘ[z]ܐܡܗ [a]ܕܝܘܣܦ [r]ܘܐܡܗܘܢ [b]ܕܒܢܝ [c]ܙܒܕܝ	[r]ܢܫܝܢ [s]ܚܙܝܢ [t]ܕܐܬܝܢ [w]ܠܗ [x]ܕܒܗܘܢ [y]ܡܪܝܡ [o]ܕܝܥܩܘܒ [a]ܕܝܘܣܦ [b]ܕܒܢܝ [c]ܙܒܕܝ

Codex A.

[d] omit ܘ   [f]ܪܡܬܝܣ
[g]ܕܫܡܗ
[h]ܬܠܡܝܕ   [k]ܗܝܕܝܢ
[l]ܩܪܒ   [n]ܘܫܐܝܠ
[p] omit ܥܠ   [q]ܒܟܝܢ
[s]ܦܩܕ   [u]ܝܘܣܦ
[w]ܘܟܪܟ   [x]ܘܐܘܣܡܗ
[y] omit ܝܬܗ   [z]ܕܢܩܪ
[a]ܒܟܐܦܐ   [b]ܘܓܠܓܠ
[c]ܘܐܙܠܗ ܠܗ   [d] omit ܠܗ
[e]ܡܪܝܡ
[f]ܘܚܪܬܝܬܐ
[g]ܠܩܘܒܠ

Codex B.

57 [d]ܘܟܕ ܕܝ ܗܘܐ [e]ܪܡܫܐ ܐܬܐ ܓܒܪ ܥܬܝܪ
ܡܢ [f]ܪܡܬܝܣ : [g]ܫܡܗ ܝܘܣܦ : [i]ܕܐܘܦ ܗܘ
58 [h]ܐܬܠܡܕ ܠܝܫܘܥ ܗܢܐ ܝܘܣܦ : [k]ܗܕܝܢ [l]ܩܪܒ
[m]ܠܦܝܠܛܘܣ [n]ܘܫܐܠ [p]ܥܠ ܦܓܪܗ ܕܡܪܐ
ܝܫܘܥ : [q]ܗܝܕܝܢ [r]ܦܝܠܛܘܣ [s]ܦܩܕ [r] [t]ܕܝܬܝܗܒ
59 ܠܗ : ܘܢܣܒ [u]ܝܘܣܦ ܦܓܪܐ [w]ܘܟܪܟ ܝܬܗ
60 ܒܣܕܝܢ ܢܩܝ : [x]ܘܐܣܡܗ [y]ܝܬܗ ܒܡܥܡܘܪܬܐ
ܚܕܬܐ ܗܕܐ [z]ܕܢܩܪ [a]ܒܟܐܦܐ [b]ܘܓܠܓܠ ܟܐܦ
ܪܒܐ ܥܠ ܬܪܥܗ ܕܡܥܡܘܪܬܐ [c]ܘܐܙܠ [d]ܠܗ :
61 ܗܘܬ ܕܝ ܬܡܢ [e]ܡܪܝܡ ܡܓܕܠܝܬܐ [f]ܘܚܪܬܐ
[e]ܡܪܝܡ ܝܬܒܢ [g]ܠܩܒܠ ܡܥܡܘܪܬܐ ⁖ [h]

Codex C.

[d] omit ܘ
[e]ܪܡܫܐ   [g]ܕܫܡܗ
[i] omit ܕܐܘܦ....ܝܫܘܥ
[l]ܩܪܒ   [m]ܠܦܝܠܛܘܣ
[n]ܘܫܐܠ   [p] omit ܥܠ
[r]ܦܩܕ ܦܝܠܛܘܣ
[t] add ܕܝ   [y] omit ܝܬܗ
[x]ܘܐܣܡܗ
[z]ܕܢܩܪܗ
[a]ܒܟܐܦܐ   [b]ܘܓܠܓܠ
[f]ܘܚܪܬܝܬܐ
[h] add ܫܠܡ

CLI.

Matt. XXVII. 62.

Codex A.

[a] omit ܘ
[c] omit ܕܝ
[f]ܐܬܕܟܪܢ
[g]ܡܛܥܝܢܐ
[i] omit ܘ
[j]ܝܘܡܝܢ   [k]ܩܐܡ
[m] omit ܕܝ
[n] omit ܐܡܬܝ
[o]ܬܠܡܝܕܘܗܝ
[q]ܢܓܢܒܘܢ   [s]ܕܩܡ
[r]ܘܢܐܡܪܘܢ
[u]ܒܬܪܝܬܐ

Codex B.

ܠܝܘܡ ܐܫܒܬܐ ܐܠܟܒܝܪ ܒܨܦܪܗ ܡܢ ܡܬܐܘܣ :
62 ܘܒܬܪܗ ܡܩܪܘܒܬܐ : [a]ܘܠܝܘܡܐ ܕܝ ܕܒܬܪ [b]ܗܘܐ
ܕܗܘ ܒܬܪ [c]ܕܝ ܥܪܘܒܬܐ : ܐܬܟܢܫܘ ܪܒܢܐ
63 ܕܟܗܢܐ ܘܦܪܝܫܐ ⁖ ܠܘܬ [d]ܦܝܠܛܘܣ : [e]ܘܐܡܪܝܢ
ܠܗ : ܡܪܢ [f]ܐܬܕܟܪܢ ܕܗܘ [g]ܡܛܥܝܢܐ ܐܡܪ ܟܕ
ܗܘ [h]ܚܝ : [i]ܘܒܬܪ ܬܠܬܐ [j]ܝܘܡܝܢ ܐܢܐ [k]ܩܐܡ :
64 ܦܩܕ ܐܘܢ [l]ܕܬܬܢܛܪ [m]ܕܝ ܡܥܡܘܪܬܐ ܒܕܡܐ
ܠܝܘܡܐ ܬܠܝܬܝܐ : ܕܠܐ [n]ܐܡܬܝ ܢܐܬܘܢ
[o]ܬܠܡܝܕܘܗܝ [p] [q]ܢܓܢܒܘܢ ܝܬܗ [r]ܘܢܐܡܪܘܢ
ܠܥܡܐ [s]ܕܩܐܡ ܡܢ ܒܝܬ ܡܝܬܝܐ : ܘܬܗܘܐ
[m]ܕܝ ܛܥܘܬܐ [u]ܒܬܪܝܬܐ ܒܝܫܐ ܡܢ ܩܕܡܝܬܐ :
65 ܐܡܪ ܠܗܘܢ [w]ܦܝܠܛܘܣ ܗܐ ܠܟܘܢ ܩܘܣܛܘܕܝܐ
66 ܐܙܠܘ ܢܛܪܘ ܗܝܟ [x]ܕܐܬܘܢ ܝܕܥܝܢ : ܗܢܘܢ
ܕܝ ܐܙܠܘ ܢܛܪܘ ܡܥܡܘܪܬܐ ܘܚܬܡܘ ܟܐܦܐ
ܥܡ ܩܘܣܛܘܕܝܐ ⁖

Codex C.

[b] omit ܗܘܐ
[d]ܦܝܠܛܘܣ   [c] omit ܕܝ
[e]ܘܐܡܪܝܢ
[f]ܐܬܕܟܪܢ
[g]ܡܛܥܝܢܐ
[i] omit ܘ   [h]ܚܝ
[k]ܩܐܡ   [j]ܝܘܡܝܢ
[l]ܕܬܬܢܛܪ
[o]ܬܠܡܝܕܘܗܝ   [m] omit ܕܝ
[p] add ܘܗܘܘ
[q]ܢܓܢܒܘܢ
[r]ܘܢܐܡܪܘܢ
[m] omit ܕܝ   [s]ܕܩܡ
[w]ܦܝܠܛܘܣ
[x]ܐܬܘܢ

Codex A.

[z] *add* ܘܒܪܡܫܐ
ܘܒܪܡܫܐ
[a]ܘܒܪܡܫܐ
[e]ܡܪܝܡ ܐܚܪܬܐ
[f]ܕܝܚܡܝܢ
[g]ܘܗܘܐ [h]ܙܘܥܢ
[i]ܕܝܢ [k] *omit* ܘ
[l] *add* ܓܝܪ [m]ܕܡܪܝܐ
[n]ܘܩܪܒ [o]ܓܠܓܠ
[w]ܠܢܫܝܐ
[x]ܬܕܚܠܘܢ
[a]ܠܝܫܘܥ [b]ܕܗܘ
[q]ܐܬܘܢ
[c]ܩܡ [d]ܐܬܝܢ
[e]ܚܡܝܢ [f]ܕܡܟ
[g]ܘܒܥܓܠ
[h]ܐܡܪܝܢ
[i]ܠܬܠܡܝܕܘܝ
[o]ܠܟܘܢ [q]ܒܥܓܠ
[r]ܘܒܚܕܘܐ
[s]ܗܘܝ [m]ܪܗܛܢ
[t]ܕܝܡܪܢ
[x] *add* ܠܗܝܢ [z]ܗܢܝܢ
[b]ܐܚܕܘ
[d]ܒܟܝܢ [e]ܠܗܝܢ
[f]ܬܕܚܠܘܢ
[g]ܬܢܝܢ
[i]ܒܡܝܙܠ [l]ܐܢܫܝܢ
[m]ܠܡܕܝܢܬܐ
[n]ܠܪܒܢܝ

Codex B.

MATT. XXVIII. 1.

ܠܝܘܡ ܐܣܒܬ ܐܠܟܒܝܪ ܦܝ ܐܠܩܕܐܣ ܡܢ
1 ܡܬܐܝ : [z] [a]ܘܒܪܡܫܐ ܕܝܢ[b] [c]ܕܫܒܬܐ [d]ܕܢܓܗ
ܠܚܕ ܒܫܒܐ : ܐܬܬ ܡܪܝܡ ܡܓܕܠܝܬܐ
ܘܐܚܪܬܐ [e]ܡܪܝܡ [f]ܕܝܚܡܝܢ ܡܩܒܪܬܐ :
2 [g]ܘܗܘܐ [h]ܙܘܥܢ [i]ܪܒ ܐܬܥܒܕ [k]ܘܡܠܐܟܗ[l]
[m]ܕܡܪܝܐ ܢܚܬ ܡܢ ܫܡܝܐ [n]ܘܩܪܒ
[o]ܓܠܓܠ ܟܐܦܐ ܡܢ [p]ܬܪܥܐ ܕܡܩܒܪܬܐ ܘܗܘܐ
3 [q]ܝܬܒ [r]ܠܥܠ ܡܢܗ : ܗܘܐ [s]ܕܝܢ ܚܙܘܗ
ܗܝܟ ܡܐ ܕܒܪܩܐ : ܘܠܒܘܫܗ[t] [u]ܚܘܪ ܗܝܟ
4 ܡܐ ܕܬܠܓܐ : ܘܡܢ ܕܚܠܬܗ ܙܥܘ ܗܠܝܢ
5 ܕܢܛܪܝܢ ܘܐܬܥܒܕܘ ܗܝܟ ܡܝܬܝܢ : ܐܓܝܒ ܕܝܢ
ܡܠܐܟܐ [v]ܘܐܡܪ [w]ܠܢܫܝܐ ܠܐ [x]ܬܕܚܠܘܢ
[y]ܐܢܬܝܢ : ܝܕܥ [z]ܐܢܐ [z]ܕܝ [a]ܠܝܫܘܥ [b]ܕܗܘ
6 [r]ܕܐܙܕܩܦ [q]ܐܬܘܢ ܒܥܝܢ : ܠܝܬ ܗܘ ܗܟܐ :
[c]ܩܡ ܓܝܪ ܗܝܟ ܡܐ ܕܐܡܪ : [d]ܐܬܝܢ [e]ܚܡܝܢ
7 ܐܬܪܐ ܗܢ ܕܗܘܐ [f]ܕܡܟ ܡܪܢܐ : [g]ܘܒܥܓܠ
ܐܙܠܝܢ [h]ܐܡܪܝܢ [i]ܠܬܠܡܝܕܘܝ ܕܩܡ ܡܢ ܒܝܢ
ܡܝܬܐ : [k]ܘܗܐ ܗܘ [l]ܡܩܕܡ ܠܟܘܢ ܠܓܠܝܠܐ :
[n]ܬܡܢ ܬܚܡܘܢܗ ܗܐ ܐܡܪܬ [o]ܠܟܘܢ :
8 [p]ܘܐܙܠܝ [q]ܒܥܓܠ ܡܢ ܡܩܒܪܬܐ : ܒܕܚܠܐ
[r]ܘܒܚܕܘܐ ܪܒܐ : [s]ܗܘܝ [m]ܪܗܛܢ [t]ܐܡܪܝܢ
9 [u]ܠܬܠܡܝܕܘܝ : ܘܗܐ ܡܪܢ ܝܫܘܥ [w]ܐܡܪ
[l]ܐܬܝܢ ܘܐܡܪ [x]ܫܠܡ [y]ܠܟܝܢ : [z]ܘܗܢܝܢ ܕܝܢ
10 [a]ܩܪܒܢ [b]ܐܚܕܘ [c]ܪܓܠܘܗܝ ܘܣܓܕܘ ܠܗ : [d]ܒܟܝܢ
ܐܡܪ [e]ܠܗܝܢ ܡܪܢ ܝܫܘܥ : ܠܐ [f]ܬܕܚܠܘܢ :
ܐܠܐ ܐܙܠܝܢ [g]ܬܢܝܢ ܠܐܚܝ ܕܢܐܙܠܘܢ ܠܓܠܝܠܐ
11 ܘܬܡܢ [h]ܢܚܡܘܢܢܝ : [i]ܟܕ ܐܙܠܝ ܕܝܢ : [k]ܗܘܘ
[l]ܐܢܫܝܢ ܡܢ ܐܢܫܝܢ ܡܢ ܩܘܣܛܘܕܝܐ ܐܬܘ
[m]ܠܡܕܝܢܬܐ : ܘܐܘܕܥܘ [n]ܠܪܒܢܝ ܟܗܢܐ ܟܠ ܡܐ
12 [o]ܕܐܬܥܒܕ : ܘܐܬܟܢܫܘ ܥܡ ܩܫܝܫܝܐ ܘܢܣܒܘ ܡܠܟܐ

Codex C.

[z] *add* ܘܒܪܡܫܐ
[c]ܕܫܒܬܐ
[b] *add* ܕܝܢ [d]ܕܢܓܗ
[g]ܘܗܘܐ [h]ܙܘܥܢ
[i]ܕܝܢ [k] *omit* ܘ
[l] *add* ܓܝܪ
[p]ܬܪܥܗ
[q]ܝܬܒ [r]ܠܥܠ
[s] *omit* ܕܝܢ
[t] *add* ܗܝܟ
[u]ܚܘܪ [v]ܘܐܡܪ
[y]ܐܢܬܝܢ
[z]ܓܝܪ ܐܢܐ
[a]ܠܝܫܘܥ
[b]ܕܗܘ [r]ܕܐܙܕܩܦ
[f]ܕܡܟ [g]ܘܒܥܓܠ
[k]ܘܗܐ
[l]ܡܩܕܡ [n]ܬܡܢ
[p]ܐܙܠܝ
[t] *omit* ܐܡܪܝܢ
[u]ܠܬܠܡܝܕܘܝ
[w]ܐܡܪ
[l]ܬܠܬܝܢ
[x] *add* ܠܗܝܢ
[y]ܠܟܝܢ [a]ܩܪܒܢ
[g]ܬܢܝܢ [c]ܪܓܠܘܗܝ
[h] *add* ܡܚܡܘܢ
[k]ܗܘ [n]ܠܪܒܢܝ
[o]ܕܐܬܥܒܕ

Codex A.

[p] ܒܥܩܒ
[q] ܠܪܘܡܐܝܢ
[r] ܐܡܪܘ
[s] ܬܠܡܝܕܘܗܝ
[t] ܕܐܬܘ [u] ܬܫܬܡܥ
[v] ܐܢܘܢ [w] ܡܫܒܩܝܢ
[x] ܘܠܗܘܢ [y] ܩܘܡ
[a] *add* ܕܝܢ [z] ܝܗܒ
[b] ܕܐܬܐܡܪܬ
[c] ܠܘܬ [d] ܝܗܘܕܝܐ
[e] *add* ܠܓܠܝܠܐ
[f] ܗܕ ܢ [g] *add* ܬܡܢ
[h] *add* ܠܗ
[i] ܘܡܪܝܢ [k] ܟܠ
[m] *add* ܠܝ [o] *omit* ܕܝܢ
[p] ܘܕܒܪܐ ܘܕܪܘܚܐ
[q] *omit* ܗܘܐ
[r] ܠܥܠܡܗ
[s] ܕܥܠܡܐ
[t] *add* ܐܡܝܢ

Codex B.

13 ܕܢܐܡܪܘܢ [p] ܬܠܡܝܕܘܗܝ ܐܬܘ [q] ܒܠܠܝܐ ܓܢܒܘܗܝ ܟܕ ܕܡܟܝܢ ܚܢܢ :
[r] ܐܡܪܘ [s] ܬܠܡܝܕܘܗܝ ܐܬܘ ܒܠܠܝܐ [a] ܓܢܒܘ ܝܬܗ
14 ܘܐܢ [t] ܐܬܫܡܥ ܕܐ ܩܕܡ ܡܠܟܐ : ܚܢܢ [u] ܡܦܝܣܝܢ ܚܢܢ ܠܗ
ܠܘܬܗ ܡܦܝܣܝܢ ܚܢܢ [v] ܐܢܘܢ [w] ܡܫܒܩܝܢ [x] ܘܠܟܘܢ ܐܢܘܢ
15 ܘܗܢܘܢ [y] ܢܣܒܘ [z] ܟܣܦܐ : ܥܒܕܘ [a] ܗܟܢܐ ܕܐܬܐܡܪ [b] ܠܗܘܢ :
ܘܢܦܩܬ ܡܠܬܐ ܗܕܐ [c] ܠܘܬ [d] ܝܗܘܕܝܐ ܥܕܡܐ ܠܝܘܡܢܐ
16 ܕܝܘܡܢܐ : ܚܕ ܥܣܪ ܕܝܢ ܬܠܡܝܕܝܢ ܐܙܠܘ
[e] ܠܓܠܝܠܐ [f] ܠܛܘܪܐ ܗܘ ܕܐܡܪ ܠܗܘܢ ܝܫܘܥ :
17 ܘܟܕ ܚܙܘܗܝ [g] ܣܓܕܘ [h] ܠܗ ܡܢܗܘܢ ܕܝܢ ܐܬܦܠܓܘ :
18 [i] ܘܩܪܒ ܝܫܘܥ [k] ܡܠܠ ܥܡܗܘܢ ܘܐܡܪ :
[l] ܐܬܝܗܒ ܠܝ ܟܠ ܫܘܠܛܢ ܒܫܡܝܐ ܘܒܐܪܥܐ
19 ܐܙܠܘ ܗܟܝܠ ܬܠܡܕܘ [m] ܟܠܗܘܢ ܥܡܡܐ
ܘܥܡܕܘ ܐܢܘܢ [o] ܕܝܢ ܒܫܡ ܐܒܐ [p] ܘܒܪܐ ܘܪܘܚܐ [p] ܕܩܘܕܫܐ :
20 ܘܐܠܦܘ ܐܢܘܢ ܕܢܛܪܘܢ ܟܠ ܡܐ ܕܦܩܕܬ
ܐܢܘܢ : ܘܗܐ ܐܢܐ [q] ܥܡܟܘܢ ܐܢܐ
ܟܠܗܘܢ ܝܘܡܬܐ ܥܕܡܐ [r] ܠܚܘܠܩܗ
[s] ܕܥܠܡܐ : [t]

Codex C.

[s] ܬܠܡܝܕܘܗܝ
[a] ܓܢܒܘ
[t] ܕܐܬܘ
[u] ܬܫܬܡܥ [v] ܐܢܘܢ
[w] ܡܫܒܩܝܢ [x] ܘܠܟܘܢ
[y] ܢܣܒܘ
[z] ܟܣܦܐ [a] *add* ܕܝܢ
[c] ܠܘܬ [d] ܝܗܘܕ
[e] *add* ܠܓܠܝܠܐ
[g] *add* ܬܡܢ
[h] *add* ܠܗ
[i] ܘܩܪܒ
[l] ܐܬܝܗܒ
[m] *add* ܠܝ
[o] *omit* ܕܝܢ
[p] ܘܕܒܪܐ ܘܕܪܘܚܐ
[q] *omit* ܗܘܐ

Codex B.

(*deest*)

Codex A.

CLII.

Matt. XXVIII. 16.

16 ܘܬܠܡܝܕܘܗܝ ܚܕܥܣܪ ܕܝܢ ܬܠܡܝܕܝܐ : ܐܙܠܘ ܠܓܠܝܠܐ :
ܐܙܠܘ ܠܓܠܝܠܐ ܠܛܘܪܐ ܗܘ ܕܐܡܪ ܠܗܘܢ
17 ܡܪܢ ܝܫܘܥ : ܘܟܕ ܚܙܘܗܝ ܣܓܕܘ ܠܗ
18 ܠܗ ܡܢܗܘܢ ܕܝܢ ܐܬܦܠܓܘ : ܘܩܪܒ ܡܪܢ
ܝܫܘܥ ܡܠܠ ܥܡܗܘܢ ܘܐܡܪ : ܐܬܝܗܒ ܠܝ
19 ܟܠ ܫܘܠܛܢ ܒܫܡܝܐ ܘܒܐܪܥܐ : ܐܙܠܘ
ܗܟܝܠ ܬܠܡܕܘ ܠܝ ܟܠܗܘܢ ܥܡܡܐ :

Codex C.

(*deest*)

Codex B.	Codex A.	Codex C.
(*deest*)	ܘܐܬܝܬܒ ܗ̇ܢܘܢ ܒܫܒܚܗ ܕܐܒܐ ܘܕܒܪܐ 20 ܘܕܪܘܚܐ ܕܩܘܕܫܐ : ܘܐܠܦܘ ܗ̇ܢܘܢ ܕܫܠܝܚܘܢ ܟܘܠ ܡܐ ܕܦܩܕܬ ܝܬܟܘܢ : ܘܗܐ ܐܢܐ ܥ̇ܡܟܘܢ ܒܟܠܗܘܢ ܝܘܡܝܐ ܘܥܕ ܫܘܠܡܐ ܠܥܠܡܗܘܢ ܕܥܠܡܐ	(*deest*)

Codex A.	Codex B.	Codex C.
	MARK XVI. 2—8.	
	ܒܗܘ ܐܢܓܠ ܐܘܢܓܠܝܘܢ ܐܘܠܬܐ ܫܒܥܪܬܐ : ܘܗܝ ܫܒܥܪܬܐ ܦܢܝܐ ܥܪܘܒܐ ܥܕ : ܒܢܝܗܐ ܫܒܥܪܬܐ ܡܢ ܡܬܐܝ : ܘܗܘ ܦܝ ܐܠܘܪܗ ܐܡܒܪܐ ܠܦܝܠ ܐܠܒܝ ܠܫܡܬ ܐܬܐܝܢ ܒܝܦܪܐ	
[a] omit ܘܒܝܠܬܗ ܡܝܪܘܣܐ :	2 ܡܢ ܡܚܝܡܣ : [a]ܘܒܝܠܬܗ ܡܝܪܘܣܐ : ܘܒܝܦܪܐ [b]ܠܚܕܐ [o]ܒܫܒܐ ܒܨܘܒܚܐ [c]ܗܘܝܢ [d]ܐܬܝܢ ܥܠ	[b] ܠܚܕ
[c] ܗ̇ܘܝܢ [d] ܐܬܝܢ [e] ܕܢܚ [f] ܫܡܫܐ	3 ܩܒܘܪܬܐ : ܒܕ [e]ܕܢܚ [f]ܫܡܫܐ : [g]ܘܗܘܝ	[o] omit ܒܫܒܐ
[g] ܘܗ̇ܘܝܢ [h] ܐܡܪܢ [i] ܠܢܦܫܗܝܢ [j] ܓܪܘܣܗܘܢ	[h]ܐܡܪܝܢ [i]ܠܢܦܫܗܝܢ [j]ܓܪܘܣܗܘܢ ܡܢ [k]ܡܓܠܓܠ	[j] ܓܪܘܣܗܘܢ [k] ܡܓܠܓܠ
[k] ܡܓܠܓܠ [a] omit ܠܗ	4 [a]ܠܗ ܟܐܦܐ ܡܢ [l]ܬܪܥܐ ܕܩܒܘܪܬܐ : ܘܚܙܝܢ ܕܗ ܪܒܐ ܠܚܕܐ : ܘܐܬܝܢ ܘܐܫܟܚܝܢ ܟܐܦܐ	[l] ܬܪܥܐ
[l] ܬܪܥܐ [n] ܒܓܠܝܢ	5 ܡܓܠܠܐ : ܘܥܠ ܟܕ ܠܡܩܒܘܪܬܐ [m]ܚܙܝܢ [n]ܒܓܠܝܢ [o]ܝܬܒ [p]ܠܒܝܫ [q]ܐܣܛܠܝܬ ܚܘܪܐ	[m] ܚܙܝܢ [o] ܝܬܒ [p] ܠܒܝܫ
[s] ܠܗܘܢ [t] ܬܕܚܠܘܢ	6 [r]ܘܕܚܠܝ : ܘܗܘ ܕܝ ܐܡܪ [s]ܠܗܘܢ ܠܐ [t]ܬܕܚܠܘܢ :	[q] ܐܣܛܠܝܬ
[u] ܢܨܪܝܐ [w] ܐܬܝܢ	ܠܝܫܘܥ [u]ܢܨܪܝܐ [w]ܐܬܘܢ [x]ܒܥܝܢ : [y]ܗܐ ܕܝܢ	[r] ܘܕܚܠܘ ܡܢܗ
[x] ܒܥܝܢ [y] ܗ̇ܐ	[f]ܕܐܙܕܩܦ : [z]ܩܡ ܠܝܬ ܗܘ ܗܟܐ : ܗܐ ܐܬܪܐ	[u] ܢܨܪܝܐ [f] ܕܐܙܕܩܦ
[z] ܩܡ [a] ܐܙܝܠܝܢ	7 ܗ̇ܢ [a]ܕܐܣܡܘܢܗ ܬܡܢ : ܐܠܐ ܐܙܠܝܢ [b]ܐܡܪܝܢ	[c] ܠܬܠܡܝܕܘܗܝ
[b] ܐܡܪܝܢ	[c]ܠܬܠܡܝܕܘܗܝ [d]ܘܠܦܛܪܘܣ ܕܗܐ [e]ܐܢܐ ܡܩܕܡ	[d] ܘܠܦܛܪܘܣ
[d] ܘܠܦܛܪܘܣ	ܠܟܘܢ ܠܓܠܝܠܐ : ܬܡܢ ܬܚܙܘܢܗ [f]ܗܘܝܢ	[e] omit ܐܢܐ
[e] omit ܐܢܐ	8 ܟܡܐ ܕܐܡܪ ܠܟܘܢ : ܘܟܕ ܢܦܩܘ ܡܢ ܡܩܒܘܪܬܐ	[f] ܗܘܝܢ [g] ܥܪܩܝܢ
[h] ܐܚܕ [i] ܠܗܘܢ	[g]ܥܪܩܝܢ : ܗܘܐ ܓܝܪ ܪܬܬܐ [h]ܐܚܕ [i]ܠܗܘܢ :	ܘܬܗܝܪܐ
[l] ܡܕܡ	[j]ܘܬܗܝܪܐ : [k]ܘܠܐܢܫ [l]ܡܕܡ ܠܐ ܐܡܪܝܢ	[k] ܘܠܐܢܫ
[m] ܕܕܚܠܝܢ [n] ܗܘܝܢ	[m]ܕܕܚܠܝܢ [n]ܗܘܝܢ ܓܝܪ [o] :·	[o] add ܥܠܡ

Codex A. | *Codex B.* | *Codex C.*

MARK XVI. 9.

Codex A.

[a] *add* ܪܒܢ ܘܒܢܬܗ
ܦܪܘܩܐ
[b] ܡܡ [c] *omit* ܩܕܡܐܝ
[d] ܠܡܪܝܡ [e] ܐܦܩ
[f] ܡܬܐܒܠܝܢ
[g] ܚܐܝ [h] *add* ܕܝ
[k] *omit* ܘܐܙܠܝܢ
[l] ܘܬܢܘ [m] ܠܫܪܟܐ
[n] ܠܗܠܝܢ
[o] ܒܚܪܬܐ
[p] ܗܢܘܢ
[q] ܩܫܝܘܬ
ܗܝܡܢܘܬܗܘܢ
[f] ܕܠܒܗܘܢ
[r] ܕܠܗܠܝܢ
[s] *add* ܠܗܘܢ
[t] *add* ܠܥܠܡܐ
[u] ܟܘܠܗ
[w] *add* ܘܐܟܪܙܘ
ܣܒܪܬܝ ܒܟܠܗ :
[y] ܕܝ [z] *omit* ܐܘܦ
[p] *omit* ܕܝ
[v] *add* ܕܝ [a] ܕܝܢ
[b] ܕܒܢܝܢ [m] ܢܦܩܘܢ
[o] ܘܒܠܫܢܝܢ
[c] ܘܚܘܝܐ
[d] ܢܛܥܢܘܢ
[n] ܕܡܘܬ [e] ܒܐܢܫܝܢ
[g] ܐܝܕܝܗܘܢ
[h] ܘܢܬܐܣܘܢ
[i] *add* ܕܝ [l] ܘܝܬܒ
[p] ܗܘܐ ܡܥܕܪ
[q] *add* ܠܗܘܢ
[s] ܡܠܝܗܘܢ
[t] *add* ܗܠܝܢ
[w] *add* ܥܠܡ

Codex B.

9 ܐܬܐܠܬ ܡܨܦܪܐ ܡܢ ܬܪܘܡܘܗܝ[a] [b]ܘܐܡܪ ܕܝ
ܡܨܦܪܐ ܒܚܕ *ܒܫܒܐ : ܘܐܬܚܙܝ [c]ܩܕܡܐܝ
[d]ܠܡܪܝܡ ܡܓܕܠܝܬܐ : [d]ܕܡܢܗ [e]ܐܦܩ [d]ܫܒܥܐ
10 ܫܐܕܝܢ : ܘܗܝ ܐܙܠܬ ܬܢܝܬ ܠܗܠܝܢ ܕܗܘܘ
11 [f]ܡܬܐܒܠܝܢ ܘܒܟܝܢ ܥܡܗ : ܘܗܠܝܢ ܟܕ ܫܡܥܘ
12 ܕܗܘ [g]ܚܝ ܘܕܐܬܚܙܝ ܠܗ ܠܐ ܗܝܡܢܘ : ܘܡܢ
ܒܬܪ ܗܠܝܢ [h]ܠܬܪܝܢ [i]ܡܢܗܘܢ ܐܬܚܙܝ ܒܚܘܪܝ
[j]ܕܡܘ :· ܗܢܘܢ ܕܗܘܘ ܡܗܠܟܝܢ [k]ܘܐܙܠܝܢ
13 ܠܩܪܝܐ : ܐܘܦ ܗܠܝܢ ܐܙܠܘ [l]ܘܬܢܘ [m]ܠܫܪܟܬܐ
14 ܘܐܘܦ ܠܐ [n]ܠܗܠܝܢ ܗܝܡܢܘ :· [o]ܒܚܪܬܐ
ܕܝ ܗܢܝܢ [p]ܕܗܘܘ ܪܒܝܥܝܢ ܚܕܥܣܪܬܐ ܐܬܓܠܝ
ܠܗܘܢ :· ܘܚܣܕ ܢܬܗܘܢ ܥܠ [q]ܚܣܪܬ
ܗܝܡܢܘܬܗܘܢ [q]: ܘܥܠ ܩܫܝܘܬ [f]ܕܠܒܗܘܢ :·
[r]ܠܟܠܠ ܕܗܠܝܢ ܕܚܙܘ ܝܬܗ ܕܩܡ ܠܐ ܗܝܡܢܘ :·
15 ܘܐܡܪ[s] ܐܙܠܘ[t] [u]ܠܟܘܠܗ [w]ܒܪܝܬܐ : [y]ܕܝܢ
[z]ܐܘܦ [p]ܕܝ ܕܡܗܝܡܢ ܘܡܬܥܡܕ ܡܫܬܘܙܒ :
16 17 [y]ܘܕܝܢ[v] ܕܠܐ ܡܗܝܡܢ ܡܬܚܝܒ : ܗܠܝܢ [a]ܕܝ
ܐܬܘܬܐ [b]ܕܒܢܝܢ ܠܗܠܝܢ ܕܡܗܝܡܢܝܢ ܒܫܡܝ
ܫܐܕܝܢ [m]ܢܦܩܘܢ [o]ܘܒܠܫܢܝܢ ܚܕܬܝܢ ܡܡܠܠܘܢ :
18 [c]ܘܚܘܝܐ [d]ܢܛܥܢܘܢ ܐܘܦ ܐܢ ܡܡܘܬܐ
[n]ܕܡܘܬܐ ܢܫܬܘܢ ܠܐ ܬܒܐܫ ܢܬܗܘܢ ܥܠ
[e]ܒܐܢܫܝܢ [f]ܢܣܝܡܘܢ [g]ܐܝܕܝܗܘܢ [h]ܘܢܬܐܣܘܢ :
19 ܡܪܢ ܝܫܘܥ[i] ܡܢ ܒܬܪ [k]ܕܡܠܠ ܠܗܘܢ ܗܠܝܢ
ܐܬܢܣܒ ܠܥܠ ܠܫܡܝܐ [l]ܘܝܬܒ ܡܢ ܝܡܝܢܗ
20 [m]ܕܐܠܗܐ :· ܗܢܘܢ[i] ܢܦܩܘ ܘܗܘܘ ܡܟܪܙܝܢ
ܒܟܘܠ ܐܬܪ ܕܡܪܢܐ[o] [p]ܡܥܕܪ[q] [r]ܘܡܫܪܪ
[s]ܡܠܬܐ ܒܬܪܝܗ ܐܬܘܬܐ [t]ܕܗܘܘ [u]ܕܒܢܝܢ[w] :·

Codex C.

[a] *add* ܘܒܝܬܗ
[* Cod. B. ܒܫܒܐ]
[b] ܡܡ [c] ܩܕܡܝ
[d] ܗܕܐ ܕܐܦܩܬ ܡܢܗ
[f] ܡܬܐܒܠܝܢ
[g] ܚܐܝ
[h] *add* ܕܝ [i] ܡܢܗܘܢ
[j] ܕܡܘܐ [l] ܘܬܢܘ
[n] ܠܗܠܝܢ
[o] ܒܚܪܬܐ
[r] ܕܠܗܠܝܢ
[z] *omit* ܐܘܦ
[v] *add* ܕܝ [b] ܕܒܢܝܢ
[m] ܢܦܩܘܢ
[o] ܘܒܠܫܢܝܢ
[c] ܘܚܘܝܢ [d] ܢܛܥܢܘܢ
[n] ܕܡܘܬ
[e] ܒܫܡܝ [f] ܢܣܝܡܘܢ
[h] ܘܢܬܐܣܘܢ
[i] *add* ܕܝ [k] ܕܡܠܠ
[l] ܘܝܬܒ [m] ܕܐܠܗܐ
[i] *add* ܕܝ [o] *add* ܗܘܐ
[q] *add* ܠܗܘܢ
[r] ܘܡܫܪܪ
[t] *add* ܗܠܝܢ [u] ܕܒܢܝܢ
[w] *add* ܠܗܘܢ

Codex A.

[z] add ܕܝܢ
[b]ܐܬܘܢ
[c]ܘܐܬܝܢ܀
[d] *omit* ܘܐܝܬܝܝܢ
[e] *add* ܘܐܬܝ ܗܘܐ
[g]ܬܪܥܐ [y] *add* ....
[h]ܦܓܪܐ [j]ܡܬܘܣܟܒܢ
[m]ܒܠܒܫܝܢ
[o]ܗܘܝܢ [n] *omit* ܕܝ
[q]ܡܪܟܢܢ
[x]ܐܦܝܗܝܢ
[u]ܐܬܕܟܪܝܢ
[v]ܡܠܠ [w]ܠܟܘܢ
[x]ܐܡܪ [y]ܕܒܬܪ
[z]ܐܕܝܗܘܢ
[b]ܘܒܟܝܢ [c]ܐܬܕܟܪܝ
[d]ܡܠܝܗ
[e]ܬܐܟܒ [f]ܒܟܝܢ
[g]ܬܐܢܝ
[m]ܒܟܠܗܘܢ
[h]ܘܠܫܪܟܬܐ
[i]ܗܘܝܢ [j]ܡܪܝܡ
[k]ܒܪܬ
[a]ܝܥܩܘܒ
[l]ܘܫܪܟܬܐ
[m]ܕܥܡܗܘܢ
[p]ܡܬܚܙܝܢ
[u]ܩܡ [t] *add* ܕܝ
[v] *omit* ܐܘܦ
[x]ܡܐܢܝ [y]ܒܬܝܢܐ
[b]ܬܡܝܗ [a] *omit* ܕܝܢ

Codex B.

LUKE XXIV. 1.

1 ܐܪܐܟܒ ܕܝܦܪܐ ܡܢ ܠܩܘܫ : [z]ܘܒܚܕ ܒܫܘܒܐ
ܡܢ [a]ܩܪܝܨܐ ܠܚܕܐ : [b]ܐܬܘ ܥܠ ܡܩܒܘܪܬܐ
[c]ܘܐܬܘ ܡܟܐ ܕܟܬܒܘ ܒܣܡܣܢ [d]ܘܐܝܬܝܝܢ[e]
2 ܒܣܡܣܢ [y] [f]ܐܫܟܚܘ ܕܝ ܟܐܦܐ ܡܓܠܓܠܐ ܡܢ
3 [g]ܬܪܥܝ ܕܩܒܘܪܬܐ ܀ ܘܥܠܝ ܕܝ ܘܠܐ
4 ܐܫܟܚܘ [h]ܦܓܪܗ ܕܡܪܢܐ ܝܫܘܥ ܀ ܐܬܟܒܕܝ
ܕܝ ܒܡܟܐ [i]ܕܗܘܐܝ [j]ܡܬܘܣܟܒܢ ܥܠ ܗܕܐ
[k]ܗܕܐ : ܘܗܐ [n]ܕܝ ܬܪܝܢ ܓܒܪܝܢ ܩܡܘ
5 [l]ܠܘܬܗܝܢ [m]ܒܠܒܫܝܢ [n]ܕܝ ܡܒܗܪܢ [o]ܗܘܢ ܕܝ
[p]ܐܬܟܒܕܝ ܒܕܚܠܐ ܙܒܢܐ : ܘܗܘܝ [q]ܡܪܟܢܢ
[x]ܐܦܝܗܝܢ ܠܐܪܥܐ ܀ ܘܐܡܪܘ [r]ܠܗܝܢ [s]ܬܗܘܢ
ܠܒܪܐ ܡܟܐ [t]*ܐܬܝܢ ܒܥܝܢ ܚܝܐ ܥܡ ܡܝܬܐ ܀
6 ܠܝܬ ܗܘ ܗܟܐ : ܐܠܐ ܩܡ ܀ [u]ܐܬܕܟܪܝܢ ܗܝܟ
7 [v]ܡܠܠ [w]ܠܟܘܢ ܟܕ ܗܘ ܒܓܠܝܠܐ [n] [x]ܕܐܡܪ :
[y]ܕܒܬܪ ܗܘ ܒܪܗ ܕܓܒܪܐ ܕܝܬܡܣܪ ܠܐܝܕܝܢ
[z]ܐܕܝܗܘܢ ܕܒܢܝܢܫܐ ܚܛܝܐܝܢ [a]ܘܢܨܛܠܒ
8 ܘܠܝܘܡܐ ܬܠܝܬܝܐ ܝܩܘܡ : [b]ܘܒܟܝܢ [c]ܐܬܕܟܪܝ
9 [d]ܡܠܝ ܘܒܕ [e]ܬܐܟܒ ܡܢ ܡܩܒܘܪܬܐ : [f]ܒܟܝܢ
[g]ܬܐܢܝ ܗܠܝܢ [m]ܒܟܠܗܘܢ ܠܚܕܥܣܪܬܐ [h]ܘܠܫܪܟܬܐ
10 ܒܟܠܗܘܢ : [i]ܗܘܝ ܕܝ [j]ܡܪܝܡ ܡܓܕܠܝܬܐ
ܘܝܘܚܢܐ : [j]ܘܡܪܝܡ [k]ܒܪܬ [a]ܝܥܩܘܒ [l]ܘܫܪܟܬܐ
[m]ܕܥܡܗܘܢ : ܗܘܝ ܐܡܪܢ ܗܠܝܢ [o]ܠܫܠܝܚܝܐ :
11 ܘܗܘܝ [p]ܡܬܚܙܝܢ ܩܕܡܝܗܘܢ ܗܝܟ [q]ܫܛܘ
ܗܠܝܢ ܡܠܝܐ ܘܠܐ ܗܘܘ ܡܗܝܡܢܝܢ [r]ܠܗܝܢ :
12 [s]ܫܡܥܘܢ [t] [u]ܘܩܡ ܪܗܛ [v]ܐܘܦ [w]ܠܡܩܒܘܪܬܐ ܀
ܘܐܕܝܩ ܘܚܙܐ [x]ܡܐܢܝ [y]ܒܬܝܢܐ ܒܠܚܘܕ :
[z]ܘܐܙܠ ܠܒܝܬܗ [a]ܕܝܢ ܘܗܘܐ [b]ܬܡܝܗ ܥܠ
ܡܟܐ [c]ܕܐܬܟܒܕ ܀

Codex C.

[a] *add* ܒܗ
[c]ܘܐܬܘ
[f]ܘܐܫܟܚܘ
[g]ܬܪܥܗ
[h]ܦܓܪܐ
[i]ܕܗܘܐ
[k]ܗܕܐ [l]ܠܘܬܗܘܢ
[m]ܒܠܒܫܝܢ
[n] *omit* ܕܝ
[p]ܐܬܟܒܕܘ
[* Cod. B. ܐܬܝܢ]
[q]ܡܪܟܢܢ [r]ܠܗܘܢ
[s]ܬܗܘܢ [t]ܐܬܝܢ
[u]ܐܬܕܟܪܝܢ
[x]ܐܡܪ [y]ܕܒܬܪ
[a]ܘܢܨܛܠܒ
[c]ܐܬܕܟܪܘ
[d]ܡܠܝ [g]ܬܐܢܝ
[h]ܘܫܪܟܬܐ
[k]ܒܪܬ
[o]ܠܫܠܝܚܐ
[q]ܫܛܘ [r]ܠܗܘܢ
[s]ܫܡܥܘܢ [t] *add* ܕܝ
[v] *omit* ܐܘܦ
[w] *add* ܥܠ
[x]ܡܐܢܝ [z]ܘܐܙܠ
[c]ܕܐܬܟܒܕ [a] *omit* ܕܝܢ

Codex A.	Codex B.	Codex C.

Codex B.

LUKE XXIV. 36.

ܐܠ ܝܫܘܥ ܐܠܬܡܝܕܘܗܝ ܡܢ ܠܗܘܢ ܐܬܚܙܝ
ܗܘ ܐܬܐܬܐ ܒܬܪ ܐܠܩܝܡܬܗ ܘܗܘ ܐܝܟܢ
ܒܩܨܝܐ ܘܗܘܐ ܬܪܝܢ ܡܢܗܘܢ ܐܙܠܘ
ܠܥܡܘܣ ܕܡܫܬܡܥܐ ܦܝ ܐܠܡܘܕܥܬܐ ܘܗܘܐ
ܐܬܚܙܝ ܦܝ ܒܕܕܐ ܨܝܕܝܗܘܢ ܡܢ ܠܗܘܢ :
36 [a]ܘܗܢܘܢ ܕܗܘܘ ܡܡܠܠܝܢ ܐܠܝܢ ܡܠܝܐ ܝܫܘܥ :
ܘܩܡ ܒܡܨܥܬܗܘܢ ܘܐܡܪ ܠܗܘܢ ܫܠܡ
37 ܠܟܘܢ : ܐܢܐ ܗܘ ܠܐ [c]ܬܕܚܠܘܢ : ܗܢܘܢ
ܕܝܢ ܐܬܪܗܒܘ ܘܗܘܘ ܒܕܚܠܐ : ܕܗܘܘ [d]ܕܝܢ
38 ܣܒܪܝܢ ܕܪܘܚ ܗܢܘܢ ܚܡܝܢ : ܘܐܡܪ ܠܗܘܢ
ܡܐ ܐܬܘܢ ܡܬܬܪܦܝܢ : ܘܠܡܐ [e]ܣܠܩܝܢ
39 [f]ܒܠܒܝܢ [g]ܚܫܒܝܢ [h]ܒܠܒܒܟܘܢ : ܚܙܘ [i]ܐܝܕܝ
[j]ܘܪܓܠܝ [k]ܕܐܢܐ ܗܘ : ܓܫܘܫܘ [d]ܕܝܢ ܘܚܙܘ
ܕܪܘܚܐ ܒܣܪ [l]ܘܓܪܡܝܢ ܠܝܬ ܠܗ ܐܝܟ[m]
40 ܐܝܬܝ ܚܙܝܢ [a]ܠܝ [n]: ܘܗܕܐ ܟܕ ܐܡܪ ܐܚܘܝ
41 ܠܗܘܢ [o]ܐܝܕܘܗܝ [p]ܘܪܓܠܘܗܝ : ܘܟܕ ܥܕܟܝܠ ܠܐ
ܗܘܘ ܡܗܝܡܢܝܢ : ܡܢ ܚܕܘܬܐ ܘܗܘܘ [q]ܬܡܝܗܝܢ :
ܘܐܡܪ ܠܗܘܢ ܐܝܬ ܠܟܘܢ ܗܪܟܐ [r]ܡܐܟܘܠܬܐ
42 ܕܢܐܟܘܠ : ܘܗܢܘܢ ܕܝܢ ܝܗܒܘ ܠܗ [s]ܡܢܬܐ
ܡܢ [t]ܢܘܢܐ ܛܘܝܐ ܘܡܢ [d]ܟܘܪܐ [u]ܕܕܒܫܐ [v]:
43 [w]ܘܢܣܒ ܘܐܟܠ ܩܕܡܝܗܘܢ : [x]ܘܢܣܒ ܫܪܟܐ
44 ܘܝܗܒ ܠܗܘܢ : ܘܐܡܪ ܠܗܘܢ ܗܠܝܢ ܐܢܘܢ
ܡܠܝ ܕܡܠܠܬ ܠܟܘܢ ܟܕ ܐܢܐ ܥܡܟܘܢ :
[y]ܕܘܠܐ [z]ܠܡܫܠܡܘ [a]ܟܠ ܗܠܝܢ [b]ܕܟܬܝܒܢ
[c]ܕܟܬܝܒܢ [d]ܒܢܡܘܣܗ [e]ܕܡܘܫܐ [f]ܘܒܢܒܝܐ
45 [f]ܘܒܡܙܡܘܪܐ ܥܠ ܕܝܠܝ : [g]ܒܗܝܕܝܢ ܦܬܚ ܠܗܘܢ
46 [h]ܕܢܣܬܟܠܘܢ ܒܟܬܒܐ : ܘܐܡܪ ܠܗܘܢ
[i]ܕܗܟܢ ܟܬܝܒ ܕܢܚܫ ܡܫܝܚܐ ܘܢܩܘܡ ܡܢ
47 ܒܝܬ [k]ܡܝܬܐ ܠܝܘܡܐ ܬܠܝܬܝܐ : ܘܢܬܟܪܙ ܒܫܡܗ
ܬܝܒܘܬܐ [l]ܘܫܘܒܩܢ [m]ܚܛܗܐ [n]ܒܟܠܗܘܢ ܥܡܡܐ :

Codex A.

[c] ܬܕܚܠܘܢ
[d] omit ܕܝܢ
[e] ܣܠܩܝܢ ܒܠܒܝܢ [f] omit
[g] ܚܫܒܝܢ
[h] ܒܠܒܒܟܘܢ
[i] ܐܝܕܝ
[j] ܘܪܓܠܝ
[k] add ܕܝܢ ܗܘ
[l] ܘܓܪܡܝܢ
[n] ܠܝ [o] ܐܝܕܘܗܝ
[p] ܘܪܓܠܘܗܝ
[r] ܡܐܟܘܠܬܐ [s] ܡܢܬܐ
[v] add ܡܢ [w] ܐܟܠ
[x] ܢܣܒ
[y] ܕܘܠܐ
[a] ܕܡܫܠܡܢ
[c] ܕܟܬܝܒܢ
[f] ܘܒܢܒܝܐ
ܘܒܡܙܡܘܪܐ
[g] ܒܗܝܕܝܢ [i] ܕܗܟܢ
[k] ܡܝܬܐ
[l] ܘܫܘܒܩܢ [m] ܕܚܛܗܐ

Codex C.

[a] add ܒܬܠܡܝܕܘܗܝ
ܒܡܨܥܬܗܘܢ
[d] omit ܕܝܢ
[e] ܚܫܒܝܢ
[i] ܐܝܕܝ [j] ܘܪܓܠܝ
[k] add ܕܝܢ ܗܘ
[l] ܘܓܪܡܝܢ
[a] add ܠܝ [m] add ܐܝܟ
[o] ܐܝܕܘܗܝ [p] ܘܪܓܠܘܗܝ
[q] ܬܡܝܗܝܢ
[r] ܡܐܟܘܠܬܐ
[t] ܢܘܢܐ [d] ܕܝܢ
[u] ܕܕܒܫܐ [w] ܐܟܠ
[z] ܠܗܘܢ
[a] ܕܡܫܠܡܢ
[b] omit ܟܠ
[c] ܕܟܬܝܒܢ
[d] ܒܢܡܘܣܗ
[e] ܕܡܘܫܐ
[f] ܘܒܢܒܝܐ
ܘܒܡܙܡܘܪܐ
[h] ܕܢܣܬܟܠܘܢ
[k] ܡܝܬܐ
[l] ܘܫܘܒܩܢܗܘܢ
[n] ܒܟܠܗܘܢ

Codex A.	Codex B.	Codex C.
[illegible] [v] [illegible] [o] [illegible]	48 [illegible] [v] [illegible] [o] [illegible] [p] [illegible] [q] [illegible] :	[illegible] [v] [illegible] [o] [illegible]
[q] [illegible]	49 [illegible] [r] [illegible] :	[p] add [illegible]
[r] [illegible]	[illegible] [s] [illegible] [t] [illegible] [u] [illegible] [o] [illegible] :	[s] add [illegible] [q] [illegible]
[s] add [illegible] [t] [illegible]	50 [illegible] [v] [illegible] : [illegible] [w]	[w] [illegible] [t] [illegible]
[u] [illegible]	[illegible] † [illegible] [x] [illegible]	† f. 119a.
[o] [illegible]	51 [y] [illegible] : [z] [illegible]	[y] [illegible] [x] [illegible]
[v] [illegible]	[illegible] [a] [illegible]	[a] [illegible] [z] [illegible]
[w] [illegible]	52 [b] [illegible] : [b] [illegible] [c] [illegible] [d] [illegible] : [f. 119a]	[c] [illegible]
[a] [illegible] [x] [illegible]	[illegible] :	[d] omit [illegible]
[b] [illegible]	53 [illegible]	
	[illegible] .	

JOHN XX. 1—10.

Codex A.	Codex B.	Codex C.
[a] [illegible] السابع [a] [illegible]	[a] [b] [illegible] [a] [illegible] [b] : [b] [illegible]	[b] [illegible] [b] [illegible]
[b] omit [illegible]	1 [illegible] : [illegible]	
	[illegible]	
[c] [illegible]	[illegible] : [illegible] [c] [illegible]	[c] [illegible]
[d] [illegible]	2 [illegible] : [illegible] [d] [illegible]	[d] [illegible]
‡ f. 144b.	[illegible] [e] [illegible] [f] [illegible] [g] [illegible]	[f] omit [illegible] [e] [illegible] [g] [illegible]
[h] [illegible] [f] omit [illegible]	[illegible] ‡ [h] [illegible]	
[k] [illegible] [i] omit [illegible]	[i] [illegible] : [illegible] : [illegible] [k] [illegible]	[k] [illegible]
[l] [illegible]	[illegible] [l] [illegible] [l] [m] [illegible]	[n] [illegible]
[m] [illegible]	3 [illegible] : [illegible] [e] [illegible] [q] [illegible] [n] [illegible]	[o] omit [illegible]
[o] omit [illegible]	4 [illegible] [o] [illegible] : [illegible]	[q] [illegible]
[p] [illegible]	[p] [illegible] : [q] [illegible]	[r] [illegible]
[r] [illegible]	[r] [illegible] [s] [illegible] [o] [illegible] [t] [illegible]	[s] [illegible] [t] [illegible]
[v] [illegible]	5 [illegible] : [u] [illegible]	[w] omit [illegible] [u] [illegible]
[y] [illegible] [w] omit [illegible]	6 [v] [illegible] [w] [illegible] : [illegible]	[x] omit [illegible]
[a] [illegible]	[o] [illegible] [x] [illegible] [e] [illegible] [y] [illegible] [z] [illegible] : [illegible]	[z] [illegible]
[b] [illegible]	[illegible] [a] [illegible] [o] [illegible]	
	7 [r] [illegible] : [illegible] [b] [illegible]	

G G

Codex B.

ܐܢܫ ܠܐ ܗܘܐ ܡܬܚܙܐ ܥܡ[a] ܒܠܚܘܕܘܗܝ[†] : ܐܠܐ

8 ܗܝܕܝܢ[b] ܥܠ ܚܘܐ ܐܚܪܢܐ[c] : ܕܐܬܐ ܩܕܡ ܐܦ

ܗܘ ܠܡܥܪܬܐ ܘܚܙܐ ܘܗܝܡܢ[d] ܠܐ ܓܝܪ ܗܘܘ

ܝܕܥܝܢ : ܠܡܩܒܪܬܐ[e] ܘܗܘܐ[f] ܟܬܒܐ ܕܠ

9 ܕܐܡܪ ܕܘܠܐ ܗܘܐ[h] ܠܗ ܡܢ ܒܝܬ ܡܝܬܐ[i] :

10 ܘܐܙܠܘ[j] ܬܠܡܝܕܐ ܠܘܬ ܢܦܫܗܘܢ : ܡܪܝܡ

[f. 119b] ܩܡܬ ܠܡܥܪܬܐ[k] ܠܒܪ ܟܕ ܒܟܝܐ[lk]

John XX. 11—18.

ܐܘܢܓܠܝܘܢ[a b] ܕ[c] ܩܝܡܬܐ[d] : ܕܝܘܚܢܢ ܫܠܝܚܐ :

11 ܡܪܝܡ[i] ܕܝܢ[j] ܩܝܡܐ[k] ܗܘܬ ܠܘܬ ܩܒܪܐ ܠܒܪ

ܟܕ ܒܟܝܐ[l] ܘܟܕ ܒܟܝܐ[m] ܐܬܪܟܢܬ ܚܙܬ

12 ܒܩܒܪܐ : ܘܚܙܬ ܬܪܝܢ ܡܠܐܟܐ[n] ܕܝܬܒܝܢ[o]

ܒܚܘܪܐ[p] ܚܕ[‡] ܡܢ ܪܝܫܗ ܘܚܕ[q] ܡܢ

ܪܓܠܘܗܝ[r] : ܐܝܟܐ[s] ܕܣܝܡ ܗܘܐ[t] ܦܓܪܗ ܕܝܫܘܥ

13 ܘܐܡܪܝܢ[u] ܠܗ : ܐܢܬܬܐ ܡܢܐ ܒܟܝܐ ܐܢܬܝ

ܐܡܪܐ ܠܗܘܢ[v] : ܕܫܩܠܘܗܝ[w] ܠܡܪܝ

[x] ܘܠܐ ܝܕܥܐ ܐܢܐ ܐܝܟܐ[y] ܣܡܘܗܝ

14 ܗܕܐ ܟܕ ܐܡܪܐ : ܐܬܗܦܟܬ ܠܒܤܬܪܗ ܘܚܙܬ

ܠܝܫܘܥ ܕܩܐܡ ܘܠܐ ܝܕܥܐ ܗܘܬ ܕܝܫܘܥ ܗܘ

15 ܐܡܪ ܠܗ[b] ܝܫܘܥ : ܐܢܬܬܐ ܡܢܐ ܒܟܝܐ

ܐܢܬܝ ܠܡܢ ܒܥܝܐ ܐܢܬܝ : ܗܝ ܕܝܢ

ܣܒܪܐ[c] ܗܘܬ ܕܓܢܢܐ[d] : ܐܡܪܐ ܠܗ

ܡܪܝ[e] : ܐܢ ܐܢܬ[f] ܫܩܠܬܝܗܝ : ܐܡܪ ܠܝ

ܐܝܟܐ[g] ܣܡܬܝܗܝ ܘܐܢܐ[†] ܐܙܠ ܐܫܩܠܝܘܗܝ :

16 ܐܡܪ ܠܗ ܝܫܘܥ ܡܪܝܡ[h] : ܘܐܬܦܢܝܬ

ܗܝ ܘܐܡܪܐ ܠܗ[i] ܒܥܒܪܐܝܬ ܪܒܘܠܝ

ܕܡܬܐܡܪ ܡܠܦܢܐ : ܘܐܬܬ[k] ...

17 ܕܬܬܩܪܒ[l] ܠܗ : ܐܡܪ[m] ܠܗ ܝܫܘܥ ܠܐ

Codex A.

ܒܠܚܘܕܘܗܝ[a] ܗܘ[d]

ܠܡܩܒܪܬܐ[e]

ܘܚܙܐ[f] ܘܗܝܡܢ[g]

ܗܘܐ[h] ܡܝܬܐ[i]

ܘܐܙܠܘ[j]

ܠܡܥܪܬܐ[k]

[l] *add* ܥܠܝ

ܐܘܢܓܠܝܘܢ الثامن[a]

ܐܘܢܓܠܝܘܢ[a]

ܩܝܡܐ[i]

ܚܙܬ[k] [j] *add* ܘܚܙܬ

‡ f. 145a.

ܡܠܐܟܐ[n] ܕܝܬܒܝܢ[m]

ܕܝܬܒܝܢ[o] ܒܚܘܪܐ[p]

[s] *omit* ܕܝܢ ܪܓܠܘܗܝ[r]

[t] *add* ܦܓܪܗ

[u] *omit* ܐܡܪܝܢ

ܐܡܪܐ[v] ܕܫܩܠܘܗܝ[w]

ܡܪܝ[x] ܣܡܘܗܝ[y]

ܐܬܗܦܟܬ[z]

ܠܒܤܬܪܗ[a]

[b] *omit* ܝܫܘܥ

ܣܒܪܐ[c]

ܓܢܢܐ[d] ܫܩܠܬܝܗܝ[f]

ܣܡܬܝܗܝ[g]

ܡܪܝܡ[h]

ܒܥܒܪܐܝܬ[i]

ܕܬܬܩܪܒ[l]

Codex C.

† f. 119b.

ܘܗܝܡܢ[b] ܐܚܪܢܐ[c]

ܗܘܐ[h]

ܘܐܙܠܘ[j]

ܐܘܢܓܠܝܘܢ[b]

[c] *add* ܩܝܡܬܐ

ܩܝܡܬܐ[d]

[j] *add* ܘܚܙܬ

ܗܘ[l]

[q] *omit* ܗܘ ܪܓܠܘܗܝ[o]

[s] *omit* ܕܝܢ

[t] *add* ܦܓܪܗ

[u] *omit* ܐܡܪܝܢ

ܐܡܪܐ[v]

ܐܬܗܦܟܬ[z]

ܠܒܤܬܪܗ[a]

ܡܪܝ[e]

† f. 120a.

ܒܥܒܪܐܝܬ[i]

ܘܐܬܬ[k]

ܐܡܪ[m]

Codex A.

ܬܬܩܪܒܝܢ[k]
[l] *add* ܕܝܢ
ܣܠܩ[m] ܘܐܒܘܟܘܢ[n]
ܘܐܠܗܝ[o]
ܘܐܠܗܟܘܢ[p]
ܡܪܝܡ[q]

(*sic*) ܥܪܘܒܬܐ[a]
‡ f. 145*b*.
[b] ܕܫܒܬܐ ܒܚܕ ܒܫܒܐ[b]
ܘܬܪܥܝܐ[c]
[d] *add* التاسع
ܘܬܪܥܐ[h] ܐܚܝܕܝܢ[g]
ܠܚܠܠ[r] ܕܝܗܘܕܝ[s]
ܒܡܨܥܬܐ[u]
ܐܡܪ[w] ܐܘܕܝܥ[v]
ܘܐܠܗܟܘܢ[x] ܚܕܘ[y]
ܢܦܫ[d] [z] *omit* ܝܫܘܥ
ܕܬܫܒܩܘܢ[e]
ܚܛܗܝܗܘܢ[g]
ܬܐܚܕܘܢ[h]
[j] *add* ܚܕ [i] *add* ܥܠܝܗ
ܬܠܡܝܕܝܬܐ[k]
ܬܐܘܡܐ[p] [l] *add* ܗܘ
ܚܙܝܢܢ[q]
ܐܡܪ[r] ܠܬܠܡܝܕܐ[s]
[v] *omit* ܕܝܢ ܐܢܐ[u]
[x] *omit* ܐܝܟܢܐ
ܒܐܨܒܥܬܐ ܕܐܝܕܘܗܝ
ܘܐܚܙܐ

Codex B.

ܬܬܩܪܒܝܢ[k] ܠܝ : ܥܕ ܟܥܢ ܓܝܪ ܠܐ ܣܠܩܬ ܠܘܬ
ܐܒܐ : ܐܙܠܝ[l] ܠܘܬ ܐܚܝ ܘܐܡܪܝ ܠܗܘܢ :
ܗܐ ܐܢܐ ܣܠܩ[m] ܠܘܬ ܐܒܐ ܘܐܒܘܟܘܢ[n]
18 ܘܐܠܗܝ[o] ܘܐܠܗܟܘܢ[p] : ܘܐܬܬ ܡܪܝܡ[q]
[f. 120*a*] ܡܓܕܠܝܬܐ ܡܣܒܪܐ ܠܬܠܡܝܕܝܐ : ܕܚܙܬ
ܠܡܪܢ ܘܗܠܝܢ ܐܡܪ ܠܗ

John XX. 19—25.

ܟܕ ܐܬܐܡܫ[e] ܥܪܘܒܬܐ[a] ܗܘܐ[fb] ܘܝܘܡܐ ܕܚܕ ܒܫܒܐ ܗܘܐ
19 ܗܘܐ ܠܚܫܘܟ[b] ܡܢ[c] ܚܕ ܒܫܒܐ[pf] : ‡ ܘܬܪܥܐ ܐܚܝܕܝܢ ܗܘܘ
ܕܟܢܝܫܝܢ ܗܘܘ ܬܠܡܝܕܘܗܝ ܡܢ ܕܚܠܬܐ[h]
[q] ܕܝܗܘܕܝܐ : ܐܬܐ ܝܫܘܥ ܘܩܡ ܒܡܨܥܬܐ
[r] ܠܚܠܠ ܕܬܠܡܝܕܘܗܝ : ܕܝܗܘܕܝ[s] : ܐܬܐ ܡܪܢ
ܝܫܘܥ[t] ܘܩܡ[u] ܒܡܨܥܬܗܘܢ ܘܐܡܪ ܫܠܡ
20 ܠܟܘܢ : ܘܟܕ ܐܡܪ ܗܕܐ ܐܘܕܥ[v] ܠܗܘܢ
ܐܝܕܘܗܝ[w] ܘܐܠܗܟܘܢ[x] : ܚܕܘ[y] ܕܝܢ ܬܠܡܝܕܐ ܕܚܙܘ
21 ܠܡܪܢ : ܝܫܘܥ[z] ܐܡܪ ܠܗܘܢ ܬܘܒ : ܫܠܡ
ܥܡܟܘܢ : ܐܝܟܢܐ ܕܫܠܚܢܝ ܐܒܐ : ܐܦ ܐܢܐ
ܡܫܕܪ[b] ܐܢܐ ܠܟܘܢ[a] : ܘܟܕ ܐܡܪ ܗܕܐ
22 ܢܦܚ[c] ܒܗܘܢ : ܘܐܡܪ ܠܗܘܢ ܢܦܫ[d] ܩܒܠܘ ܪܘܚܐ
23 ܠܗܘܢ : ܕܩܘܕܫܐ : ܠܡܢ ܕܬܫܒܩܘܢ[e] ܢܫܬܒܩܘܢ ܠܗܘܢ : ܚܛܗܝܗܘܢ[g] [f]
24 ܘܠܡܢ ܕܬܐܚܕܘܢ[y] ܐܚܝܕܝܢ[h] :[i] ܬܐܘܡܐ †
ܕܝܢ ܚܕ[j] ܡܢ ܬܪܥܣܪܬܐ[k] ܕܡܬܐܡܪ[l] ܬܐܘܡܐ[m]
ܠܐ ܗܘܐ[n] ܬܡܢ ܥܡܗܘܢ ܟܕ ܐܬܐ ܝܫܘܥ :
25 ܗܘܘ[o] ܐܡܪܝܢ ܠܗ ܬܠܡܝܕܐ ܐܚܪܢܐ[p]
ܚܙܝܢܢ[q] ܠܡܪܢ : ܗܘ ܕܝܢ ܐܡܪ ܠܗܘܢ : ܐܢ[r]
ܠܐ[s] ܚܙܝܬ ܒܐܝܕܘܗܝ[t] ܐܬܪܐ[u]
ܕܡܣܡܪܐ[v] : ܘܐܪܡܐ ܐܨܒܥܬܐ[x] ܒܐܬܪܐ
ܕܡܣܡܪܐ ܘܐܪܡܐ ܐܝܕܝ[x] ܒܓܢܒܗ[o] ܠܐ[s] ܐܗܝܡܢ[s]
ܠܐ ܡܗܝܡܢ :

Codex C.

ܬܩܪܒܝܢ[k]
[l] *add* ܕܝܢ
(*sic*) ܘܐܒܘܟܘܢ[n]
(*sic*) ܘܐܠܗܟܘܢ[p]

ܐܬܐܡܫ ܥܪܘܒܬܐ[e]
ܡܢ[f] ܚܕ ܒܫܒܐ ܗܘܐ
ܘܬܪܥܐ ܐܚܝܕܝܢ ܗܘܘ
ܚܕ ܡܢ ܕܚܠܬܐ[l]
[p] *add* ܠܗܘܢ
ܝܗܘܕܝܐ
ܬܠܡܝܕܐ[h]
ܘܩܡ[t] ܐܘܕܥ[v]
ܐܝܕܘܗܝ[w] ܘܐܠܗܟܘܢ[x]
ܕܥܠܝ[a] ܡܫܕܪ[b]
ܠܗܘܢ[c] ܢܦܫ[d]
[f] *add* ܠܗܘܢ
ܕܬܐܚܕܘܢ[y]
[j] *add* ܚܕ
† f. 120*b*.
ܬܐܘܡܐ[m]
[n] *omit* ܗܘܐ
ܗܘܘ[o] ܚܙܝܢܢ[q]
ܐܢ[r] ܒܐܝܕܘܗܝ[t]
[x] *omit* ܠܐܨܒܥܬܐ
ܕܐܝܕܘܗܝ ܘܐܚܙܐ
ܐܬܪܐ
ܒܓܢܒܗ[o]

Codex A. | *Codex* B. | *Codex* C.

John XX. 26—31.

Codex B.

26 [a]ܘܒܬܪ ܚܕ ܐܠܦܝܢ[a]: ܘܡܢ ܒܬܪ[x] [y]ܬܠܡܝܕܝܐ
ܘܗܘܢ[y]: ܬܘܡܐ ܗܘܐ ܬܠܡܝܕܝܐ ܠܟܘ ܗܘܢ ܚܕܐ.
ܘ[z]ܬܘܡܐ ܒܥܡܗܘܢ ؛ ܘܐܬܐ ‡ ܡܪܢܐ ܝܫܘܥ
[v]ܘܬܪܥܐ [a]ܐܚܝܕܝܢ: [b]ܘܩܐܡ [c]ܒܡܨܥܬܗܘܢ [f. 120b]
27 ܘܐܡܪ ܫܠܡ ܠܟܘܢ ؛ [w]ܘܡܢ ܒܬܪܟܢ[w] ܐܡܪ
ܠܬܘܡܐ: [d]ܐܝܬܝ [e]ܐܨܒܥܟ ܠܗܪܐ ܘܚܡܝ
[f]ܐܝܕܝ [g]ܘܐܝܬܝ [h]ܐܝܕܟ ܘܪܡܝ [i]ܒܐܠܒܝ:
ܘܠܐ [j]ܬܗܘܝ ܕܠܐ ܡܗܝܡܢ ܐܠܐ [k]ܡܗܝܡܢ:
28 ܘ[l]ܐܬܦܢܝ ܬܘܡܐ ܘܐܡܪ ܠܗ ܡܪܝ [m]ܘܐܠܗܝ:
29 ܐܡܪ [n]ܠܗ ܡܪܢܐ ܝܫܘܥ ܕܚܡܝܬ ܝܬܝ
ܗܝܡܢܬ: ܛܘܒܝܗܘܢ ܗܠܝܢ ܕܠܐ ܚܡܘ
30 ܘܗܝܡܢܘ: ܣܓܝ ܡܢ ܐܘܦ [o]ܐܬܝܢ [p]ܐܘܚܪܢܝܢ
ܥܒܕ ܡܪܢܐ ܝܫܘܥ ܩܕܡ [q]ܬܠܡܝܕܘܝ: ܡܐ
31 ܕܠܝܬ[r] [s]ܟܬܝܒܢ ܒܗܕܝܢ ܣܦܪܐ [t]ܗܠܝܢ[u] [b]ܟܬܝܒܢ:
[c]ܠܡܠܠ [d]ܕܝ [e]ܕܬܗܝܡܢܘܢ ܕܡܪܢܐ ܝܫܘܥ
ܡܫܝܚܐ [f]ܗܘ ܒܪܗ ܕܐܠܗܐ: ܘܟܕܐ ܕܐܬܘܢ
[g]†ܡܗܝܡܢܝܢ ܗܘܝ ܠܟܘܢ [h]ܚܝܝܢ [i]ܒܫܡܗ:

Codex A.

[z]*add* ܐܘܦ [x]*add* ܕܝ
[v]ܘܬܪܥܝܐ
‡ f. 146*a*.
[a]ܐܚܝܕܝܢ [b]ܘܩܡ
[c]ܒܡܨܥܬܗܘܢ
[w]ܘܒܬܪܟܢ
[d]ܐܝܬܝ [e]ܐܨܒܥܟ
[f]ܐܝܕܝ [g]ܘܐܝܬܝ
[h]ܐܝܕܟ [j]ܬܗܘܐ
[k]ܡܗܝܡܢ [m]ܘܐܠܗܝ
[n] *omit* ܠܗ
[o]ܐܬܘܬܐ [p]ܐܘܚܪܢܝܢ
[r] *add* ܗܢܘܢ
[s]ܟܬܝܒܢ [u] *add* ܕܝ
[c]ܠܡܠܠ [d] *omit* ܕܝ
[e]ܕܬܗܝܡܢܘܢ
[g]ܡܗܝܡܢܝܢ
[h]ܚܝܝܢ [i]ܒܫܡܗ

Codex C.

[a]ܠܒܬܪ ܚܕ ܐܠܦܝܢ
ܡܢ ܫܒܬܐ[a]
[x] *add* ܕܝ
[y]ܬܠܡܝܕܝܐ ܘܗܘܢ[y]
[z] *add* ܐܘܦ
[v]ܘܬܪܥܝܐ
[c]ܒܡܨܥܬܐ
[w]ܘܒܬܪܟܢ
[f]ܐܝܕܝ [h]ܐܝܕܟ
[i]ܒܐܠܒܝ [j]ܬܗܘܐ
[l] *omit* ܘ
[p]ܐܘܚܪܢܝܢ
[q]ܬܠܡܝܕܘܝ
[r] *add* ܗܢܘܢ
[t]ܗܕܝܢ [u] *add* ܕܝ
[b]ܟܬܝܒ [d] *omit* ܕܝ
[f] *omit* ܗܘ [h]ܚܝܐܢ
† f. 121*a*.

John XXI. 1—14.

Codex B.

1 [a]ܐܠܒܫܪ ܒܦܪܝܐ[a] ܡܢ [b]ܘܚܙܝܬ[k]: ܘܡܢ ܒܬܪ
ܕܝܢ ܓܠܐ ܡܪܢܐ ܝܫܘܥ ܓܪܡܗ [l]ܠܬܠܡܝܕܘܝ
ܥܠ ܝܡܐ [m]ܕܛܒܪܝܐ: ܓܠܐ [n]ܕܝ ܓܪܡܗ
2 [o]ܟܕܝܢ: ܗܘܘ ܗܡܢ ܚܕܐ [p]ܘܫܡܥܘܢ [q]ܟܐܦܐ:
ܘܬܘܡܐ ܕܡܬܐܡܪ ܬܐܘܡܐ؛ [r]ܘܢܬܢܐܝܠ [s]ܗܕܝܢ
ܕܡܢ [t]ܩܛܢܐ ܕܓܠܝܠܐ [u]ܘܒܢܝ [v]ܙܒܕܝ ܘܬܪܝܢ
3 ܐܚܪܢܝܢ ܡܢ [w]ܬܠܡܝܕܘܝ: ܐܡܪ ‡ [x]ܠܗܘܢ
[q]ܫܡܥܘܢ [y]ܟܐܦܐ ܐܙܠ [z]ܕܗܘܝ ܐܢܐ [a]ܨܝܕ[b]:
ܐܡܪܝܢ ܠܗ [c]ܐܬܝܢ ܐܢܢ ܐܘܦ ܐܢܢ[c] ܥܡܟ:
ܘܢܦܩܘ ܘܣܠܩܘ ܥܠܐ ܠܐܠܦܐ [d]ܘܒܗܘ ܠܠܝܐ
4 [e]ܠܐ ܨܕܘ: ܗܘܐ ܕܝ ܒܬܪ ܨܦܪܐ:

Codex A.

ܩܪܝܢܐ ܕ ... (vertical marginal rubric)
[a]ܐܠܒܫܪ العاشر (sic)
ܐܠܝܫܥܗ[a]
[m]ܕܛܒܪܝܐ
[o]ܟܕ [p] *omit* ܘ
[r]ܘܢܬܢܐܝܠ [s]ܗܕ
[t]ܩܛܢܐ [u]ܘܒܢܝ
[v]ܕܙܒܕܝ [w]ܬܠܡܝܕܘܝ
‡ f. 146*b*.
[x] *add* ܗܘܐ [y]ܟܐܦܐ
[z] *omit* ܕܗܘܝ [a]ܕܐܨܝܕ
[b] *add* ܢܘܢ
[c]ܐܘܦ ܐܢܢ ܐܬܝܢ[c]
[e]ܒܠܘܡ

Codex C.

[b]ܘܚܙܝܬ
[k] *add* ܒܗܢܐ ܦܪܝܣܐ
[l]ܠܬܠܡܝܕܘܝ
[m]ܕܛܒܪܝܐ
[p] *omit* ܘ [n] *omit* ܕܝ
[q]ܟܐܦܐ
[r]ܘܢܬܢܐܝܠ
[x] *add* ܡܪܢܐ
[a]ܕܐܨܝܕ [z]ܕܗܘܝ
[d]ܘܒܗܘ

Codex A.

[g] ܥܠ ܣܦܪ ܝܡܐ [g]
[h] ܝܕܥܝܢ
[k] *add* ܝܫܘܥ
[l] ܠܛܠܝܐ [m] ܒܐܝܕܝܟܘܢ
[n] ܡܢ ܕܡܐ [o] ܕܢܐܟܘܠ
[p] *omit* ܠܗ
[q] ܘܪܡܝܘ [r] ܓܪܕܘ
[t] *omit* ܠܓܠܠ
[w] *add* ܗܘܐ
[z] ܪܚܡ [a] ܗܘ
[b] *add* ܗܘ
[c] *add* ܐܘܢ
[f] ܘܩܘܠܒܗ
[h] *add* ܕܝ [k] ܪܚܝܩܝܢ
[l] *add* ܐܠܐ
[m] ܡܬܬܢܝܢ [n] *add* ܚܘܪ
[o] ܘܚܙܘ [p] ܓܘܡܪܝܢ
[r] *omit* ܕܝ
‡ f. 147*a*.
[t] *omit* ܘܢܘܢ ܡܣܡܟܝܢ
[u] ܡܣܡܟ [v] ܡܒܫܠܝܢ
[x] ܠܚܡ [y] *add* ܘܢܘܢ
[z] *add* ܐܘܢ
[a] ܐܝܬܘ [d] ܪܒܪܒܝܢ
[e] ܡܐܐ [f] ܘܚܡܫܝܢ
[i] ܠܡܫܪܝ [k] *add* ܕܝ
[l] ܬܠܡܝܕܝܐ
[n] ܝܕܥܝܢ [p] ܢܣܒ
[q] ܙܒܢ [r] ܬܠܝܬܝܐ
[s] ܠܬܠܡܝܕܘܗܝ
[t] *omit* ܥܠܡ

Codex B.

[f] ܘܩܡ ܡܪܢ ܝܫܘܥ [g] ܒܚܝܠܐ : ܘܠܐ ܗܘܘ
[h] ܝܕܥܝܢ [i] ܬܠܡܝܕܘܗܝ [f. 121a] ܕܗܘ ܡܪܢ ܝܫܘܥ :
5 [j] ܐܡܪ ܠܗܘܢ ܡܪܢ [k] ܛܠܝܐ : [l] ܕܡܐܟܠ ܐܝܬ
[m] ܒܐܝܕܝܟܘܢ [n] ܡܐܢ [o] ܕܢܛܥܘܡ : ܐܡܪܘ ܘܐܡܪܝܢ
6 [p] ܠܗ ܠܐ : ܐܡܪ ܠܗܘܢ ܪܡܘ ܠܡܨܝܕܬܐ
ܕܐܠܦܐ ܡܢ ܝܡܝܢܐ ܘܐܬܘܢ ܡܫܟܚܝܢ : [q] ܘܪܡܘ
ܪܡܘ ܘܠܐ ܗܘܘ ܡܫܟܚܝܢ [r] ܠܡܓܕ [s] ܝܬܗ ܡܢ
7 [t] ܠܓܠܠ ܣܘܓܝܐ ܕܢܘܢܝܐ : [u] ܐܡܪ [v] ܗܘ [w]
[x] ܬܠܡܝܕܐ ܗܘ ܕܗܘܐ ܡܪܢ [y] ܝܫܘܥ [z] ܪܚܡ.
ܠܗ [o] ܠܦ̈ܛܪܘܣ [a] ܗܘ ܡܪܢ [b] : ܫܡܥܘܢ [c]
[d] ܦ̈ܛܪܘܣ ܟܕ ܫܡܥ ܕܗܘ ܡܪܢ [e] : † [f] ܘܩܘܠܒܗ
[g] ܐܣܪ ܗܘܐ ܟܪ ܚܨܘܗܝ : ܘܪܡܐ ܢܦܫܗ
8 ܠܝܡܐ : ܬܠܡܝܕܝܐ [h] [i] ܫܘܪܝܢܐ ܒܐܠܦܐ ܐܬܘ :
ܠܐ [j] ܓܪ [k] ܪܚܝܩ ܡܢ ܐܪܥܐ [l] ܗܘܘ [m] ܡܬܬܢܝܢ
9 ܐܡܝܢ : ܓܪܝܢ ܡܨܝܕܬܐ [n] ܕܢܘܢܝܐ : ܟܕ ܐܬܘ
ܠܐܪܥܐ [o] ܗܢܘܢ ܚܙܘ [p] ܓܘܡܪܝܢ [q] ܕܢܘܪ
[r] ܕܝ [s] ܡܣܡܟܝܢ [t] ܘܢܘܢ [u] ܡܣܡܟ ܠܓܒܠ [v] ܡܩܘܡܝܢ [w]
10 [x] ܘܠܚܡ [y] : ܐܡܪ ܠܗܘܢ [z] ܡܪܢ ܝܫܘܥ
11 [a] ܐܝܬܘ ܡܢ ܢܘܢܝܐ ‡ ܗܠܝܢ ܕܨܕܬܘܢ : ܟܕܘ
ܣܠܩ ܐܘܢ ܫܡܥܘܢ [b] ܦ̈ܛܪܘܣ ܘܓܕ ܡܨܝܕܬܐ
ܠܐܪܥܐ ܡܠܝܐ [c] ܢܘܢܝܢ [d] ܪܒܪܒܝܢ [e] ܡܐܐ
[f] ܘܚܡܫܝܢ [g] ܘܬܠܬܐ : ܘܒܟܘܠ ܗܠܝܢ ܠܐ
12 [h] ܐܬܦܠܓܬ ܡܨܝܕܬܐ : ܐܡܪ ܠܗܘܢ ܡܪܢ
ܝܫܘܥ ܐܬܘ [i] ܐܫܬܪܘ : ܐܢܫ [k] ܡܢ [l] ܬܠܡܝܕܘܗܝ
ܠܐ ܗܘܐ [m] ܡܬܠܒܒ ܕܢܫܐܠ ܠܗ ܐܢܬ ܡܢ
13 ܐܢܬ : ܕܗܘܘ [n] ܝܕܥܝܢ ܕܗܘ ܡܪܢ [o] : ܘܐܬܐ
ܡܪܢ ܝܫܘܥ ܘܢܣܒ ܠܚܡܐ : ܘܐܬܝܗܒܗ
ܘܗܘܐ [p] ܝܗܒ ܠܗܘܢ : ܘܢܘܢܝܐ ܟܢ ܘܟܘܬ :
14 ܗܕܐ ܕܝ ܟܕܘ [q] ܙܒܢ [r] ܬܠܝܬܝܐ ܐܬܚܙܝ [f. 121b]
ܡܪܢ ܝܫܘܥ [s] ܠܬܠܡܝܕܘܗܝ : ܡܢ ܕܩܡ ܡܢ
ܒܝܬ ܡܝܬܝܐ : [t] ܥܠܡ .

Codex C.

[f] ܥܡ [i] ܬܠܡܝܕܘܗܝ
[j] *add* ܟܕܘ
[k] *add* ܝܫܘܥ
[m] ܒܐܝܕܝܟܘܢ
[n] ܒܡܐܢ [q] *omit* ܠܗ
[s] ܢܓܕܝܢ
[t] *omit* ܠܓܠܠ
[u] ܐܡܪܝܢ
[v] *omit* ܐܘܢ
[w] *add* ܗܘܘ
[x] ܬܠܡܝܕܐ
† f. 121*b*.
[y] *omit* ܝܫܘܥ
[o] ܠܦܛܪܘܣ
[c] *add* ܐܘܢ
[d] ܦܛܪܘܣ
[e] *add* ܝܫܘܥ
[f] ܘܩܘܠܒܗ [g] ܐܣܝܪ
[h] *add* ܕܝ [i] ܐܣܘܪܝܢܐ
[j] *add* ܗܘܘ [k] ܪܚܝܩ
[l] *add* ܐܠܐ
[q] *omit* ܕܢܘܪ
[r] *omit* ܕܝ [s] ܡܣܡܟܝܢ
[t] *omit* ܘܢܘܢ ܡܣܡܟ
[w] *add* ܢܘܢܝܢ [x] ܘܠܚܡ
[z] *add* ܐܘܢ
[b] ܦܛܪܘܣ [c] ܢܘܢܝܢ
[g] *omit* ܘܬܠܬܐ
[h] ܐܬܦܠܓܬ [k] *add* ܕܝܢ
[l] ܬܠܡܝܕܘܗܝ [m] ܡܬܠܒܒ
[o] *add* ܝܫܘܥ [r] ܬܠܝܬܝܐ
[s] ܠܬܠܡܝܕܘܗܝ
[t] *omit* ܥܠܡ

Codex A.	Codex B.	Codex C.
	John XXI. 15—25.	
ᵃالحادى عشر ܡܢܦܢܝܐ	ᵃܐܠܝܢ ܒܬܪ ᵇܡܢ ܕܩܡ ܗܘܐ ܠܝܫܘܥᵇ ܡܢ ܒܝܬ	ᵇܡܢܦܢܝܐ ܡܢ ܒܝܬ
ܐܠܝܩܝܡܘܢ (sic)	15 ܐܠܝܩܝܡܘܢ :ᵃ :ᶻ ܟܕ ܐܫܪܝܘ ܐܡܪ ܡܪܢ ܝܫܘܥ	ᵇܗܘܐ ܝܫܘܥ ܠܬܠܡܝܕܘܗܝ
ܘܠܬܠܡܝܕܘܗܝ ܐܠܝܩܝܡܘܢ	ܠܫܡܥܘܢ ᵒܦܛܪܘܣ : ܫܡܥܘܢ ܒܪ ܝܘܢܐ	ᶻ add ܘܐܫܪܝܘ ܬܠܡܝܕܘܗܝ
ܡܢ ܒܝܬ ܡܝܬܐᵃ	ᵃܪܚܡ ܐܢܬ ܠܝ ܝܬܝܪ ܡܢ ܗܠܝܢ : ܐܡܪ ܠܗ	ᵒܠܦܛܪܘܣ
ᵃܪܚܡ ᶜܪܚܡ	ᵇܐܝܢ ܡܪܝ † ܐܢܬ ܝܕܥ ܕܐܢܐ ᶜܪܚܡ ܠܟ :	† f. 122a.
ᵉܘܬܢܝܢ	16 ܐܡܪ ܠܗ ᵈܪܥܝ ܐܡܪܝ : ᵉܬܢܝܢ ܐܡܪ ܠܗ	ᵇܐܝܢ ᶜܪܚܡ
ᶠܬܢܝܢܘܬ	ᶠܬܢܝܢܘܬ ܫܡܥܘܢ ܒܪ ܝܘܢܐ ᵍܪܚܡ ܐܢܬ	ᵈܪܥܝ ᵉܘܬܢܝܢ
ᵍܪܚܡ ʰܝܕܥ	ܠܝ : ܐܡܪ ܠܗ ܐܝܢ ܡܪܝ ܐܢܬ ʰܝܕܥ ⁱ	ᵍܪܚܡ
ⁱܡܪܝ ʲܪܚܡ	ܕܐܢܐ ʲܪܚܡ ܠܟ : ܐܡܪ ⁿܠܗ ܪܥܝ ܐܡܪܝ :	ⁿ omit ܠܗ ˡܬܠܝܬܝܬܐ
ᵏܐܦ ˡܬܠܝܬܝܬܐ	17 ܐܡܪ ܠܗ ᵏܐܦ ˡܬܠܝܬܝܬܐ ᵐܫܡܥܘܢ ܒܪ	ᵐ omit ܫܡܥܘܢ ܒܪ
‡ f. 147b.	ܝܘܢܐ ʲܪܚܡ ܐܢܬ ܠܝ : ᵖᵒܐܬܟܪܝ ‡ ܦܛܪܘܣ	ܝܘܢܐ
ܘܐܬܟܪܝ	ܕܐܡܪ ܠܗ ᵠܐܦ ʳܬܠܝܬܝܬܐ ܪܚܡ ܐܢܬ ܠܝ :	ᵖ omit . . . ܘܐܬܟܪܝ
ᵠܐܦ ʳܬܠܝܬܝܬܐ	ˢܘܐܡܪ ܠܗ ᵗܡܪܝ ⁿܐܢܬ ܝܕܥ ܒܟܠܐ :	. . . ܐܢܬ ܠܝ
ᵗܡܪܝܐ ᵘܝܕܥ	ܘܐܢܬ ᵛܝܕܥ ܕܐܢܐ ʲܪܚܡ ܠܟ : ܐܡܪ ܠܗ	ˢܐܡܪ ᵗܡܪܝܐ
ᵛܝܕܥ ʷܐܡܪܢܐ	18 ܪܥܝ ܐܡܪܝ : ܐܡܝܢ ܐܡܝܢ ʷܐܡܪ ܐܢܐ ʷ	ˣܗܘܝܬ ʸܛܠܝܐ
ᶻܐܣܪ ᵐܘܗܘܝܬ	ܠܟ ܕܟܕ ˣܗܘܝܬ ʸܛܠܝܐ ˣܗܘܝܬ ᶻܐܣܪ	ᶻ omit ܐܣܪ
ᵇܕܗܘܝܬ	ܠܚܨܝܟ : ᵐܘܗܘܝܬ ᵃܡܗܠܟ ܠܗܢ ᵇܕܗܘܝܬ	ᵃܡܗܠܟ ᵈܬܦܫܛ
ᶜܬܣܒ	ܨܒܐ : ܟܕ ܕܝ ᶜܬܣܒ ܐܢܬ ᵈܬܦܫܛ ᵉܐܝܕܝܟ	ᶠܘܐܚܪܝܢ
ᵈܬܦܫܛ	ᶠܘܐܚܪܝܢ ᵍܝܐܣܪܘܢ ʰܠܟ ܘܡܘܒܠܝܢ ܠܟ	ʰ omit ܠܟ
ᵉܐܝܕܝܟ ᶠܘܐܚܪܝܢ	19 ܠܗܢ ܕܠܝܬ ܐܢܬ ܨܒܐ : ܗܕܐ ܕܝ ܐܡܪ	ⁱ add ܠܗܘܢ
ᵍܢܐܣܪܘܢ	ܡܚܘܝ ⁱܒܗܝܢ ʲܡܘܬܐ ܗܘ ܡܫܒܚ ܠܐܠܗܐ :	ʲܒܡܘܬܐ
ʰ omit ܠܟ	ܘܟܕ ܐܡܪ ܗܕܐ : ܐܡܪ ᵏܠܗ ܗܘܝ ܒܬܪܝ :	ᵏ omit ܠܗ
ʲܒܡܘܬܐ	20 ˡܘܐܬܦܢܝ ᵐܕܝ ⁿܦܛܪܘܣ ܘܚܙܐ : ᵒܬܠܡܝܕܐ	ᵐ omit ܕܝ ˡܘܐܬܦܢܝ
ᵐ omit ܕܝ	ܗܘܝ ܕܗܘܐ ܪܚܡ ᵖܝܫܘܥ ᵠ ʳܕܗܘ	ⁿܠܦܛܪܘܣ
ܕܬܠܡܝܕܐ	ܠܗ : ܗܘܝ ܕܐܬܪܡܝ ܒܚܫܡܝܬܐ ܥܠ	ᵒܬܠܡܝܕܐ
ʳܕܗܘܐ	ܚܕܝܗ ܘܐܡܪ ܠܗ : ܡܪܝ ˢܡܢ ܗܘ ܕܡܫܠܡ ܠܟ :	ᵠ add ܠܗ ᵖܝܫܘܥ
	[f. 122a] 21 ܠܗܕܝܢ ᵗ ܟܕ ܚܙܐ ⁿܦܛܪܘܣ ܐܡܪ ܠܡܪܝܐ	ˢܡܢ ܗܘ
	22 ܫܡܥܘܢ ᵘܡܪܝܐ ᵛܗܢܝܢ ܕܝ ܡܢܐ : ܐܡܪ ܠܗ	ᵗ add ܕܝ ᵘܡܪܝܐ
ʷ omit ܕܝ	ܡܪܝܐ ܫܡܥܘܢ : ܐܢ ܨܒܐ ʷܕܝ ܐܢܐ ܕܢܬܩܘܪ	ʷ omit ܕܝ ᵛܗܢܐ
ˣܕܐܬܐ	ܗܘ ܥܕ ܕܐܬܐ ˣܕܐܬܐ ܡܢܐ ܠܟ : ܐܢܬ	ˣܕܐܬܐ

Codex B.

23 ܕܠܡܐ ܠܐ ܝܗܒܬ ܟܣܦܐ ܕܝܠܝ ܠܛܪܦܝܙܐ† ܘܐܢܐ
ܟܕ ܐܬܝܬ[x] ܐܬܒܥܢܗ[y] ܥܡ ܪܒܝܬܗ[z] : ܠܡ
ܐܡܪ ܠܗܘܢ[a] ܠܗܠܝܢ ܕܩܝܡܝܢ ܩܕܡܘܗܝ : ܣܒܘ
ܡܢܗ[b] ܡܢܐ ܘܗܒܘ ܠܗܘ ܕܐܝܬ ܠܗ‡ ܥܣܪ
24 ܡܢܝܢ[c] ܘܐܡܪܘ[d] : ܡܪܢ ܐܝܬ ܠܗ[e] ܥܣܪ[f] ܡܢܝܢ : ܐܡܪ
ܠܗܘܢ ܐܡܪ ܐܢܐ ܠܟܘܢ ܕܟܠ ܕܐܝܬ ܠܗ[g] ܢܬܝܗܒ
25 ܠܗ ܘܢܬܝܬܪ ܠܗ : ܘܡܢ[h] ܕܠܝܬ ܠܗ ܐܦ ܗܘ
ܕܐܝܬ ܠܗ : ܢܫܬܩܠ ܡܢܗ[i] : ܒܪܡ ܒܥܠܕܒܒܝ
ܗܠܝܢ[k] ܕܠܐ[l] ܨܒܘ[m] ܕܐܡܠܘܟ[n] ܥܠܝܗܘܢ[o]
ܐܝܬܘ[p] ܠܗܘܢ[q] ܠܗܪܟܐ[r] ܘܩܛܘܠܘ[s] ܩܕܡܝ[t] ܘܡܚܢܘܢ[u]
ܩܕܡܝ[w] . ܘܐܡܚܘ[x] ܒܪܫܗܘܢ[y] ܕܒܥܠܕܒܒܝ

CLIII.

Luke XIX. 29—48.

ܘܗܘܐ[a] ܟܕ ܩܪܒ ܠܐܘܪܫܠܡ ܠܒܝܬ ܦܓܐ ܘܠܒܝܬ
29 ܥܢܝܐ[a] : ܠܛܘܪܐ ܕܡܬܩܪܐ ܕܙܝܬܐ : ܫܕܪ ܬܪܝܢ
ܡܢ[b] ܬܠܡܝܕܘܗܝ[c] ܘܐܡܪ ܠܗܘܢ : ܙܠܘ[d] ܠܩܘܪܝܬܐ
30 ܕܠܘܩܒܠܢ : ܘܟܕ ܥܐܠܝܢ ܐܢܬܘܢ[e] ܒܗ ܡܫܟܚܝܢ[f]
ܐܢܬܘܢ ܥܝܠܐ ܕܐܣܝܪ ܕܐܢܫ ܠܐ ܪܟܒ ܥܠܘܗܝ :
ܫܪܘ[g] ܐܝܬܝܘܗܝ[h] : ܘܐܢ[i] ܐܢܫ[k] ܫܐܠ ܠܟܘܢ[l]
ܠܡܢܐ ܫܪܝܢ ܐܢܬܘܢ ܠܗ : ܗܟܢܐ ܐܡܪܘ ܠܗ :
31 ܕܡܪܗ ܨܒܐ ܠܗ : ܘܐܙܠܘ ܗܢܘܢ ܕܐܫܬܕܪܘ ܘܐܫܟܚܘ
ܐܝܟ ܡܐ ܕܐܡܪ ܠܗܘܢ : ܘܟܕ ܫܪܝܢ ܗܘܘ ܠܥܝܠܐ
32 ܐܡܪܘ ܠܗܘܢ ܡܪܘܗܝ : ܠܡܢܐ ܫܪܝܢ ܐܢܬܘܢ
[f. 122b]
ܠܥܝܠܐ : ܗܢܘܢ ܕܝܢ ܐܡܪܘ : ܕܡܪܗ ܨܒܐ ܠܗ
33 ܘܐܝܬܝܘܗܝ ܠܘܬ ܝܫܘܥ : ܘܐܪܡܝܘ[a] ܢܚܬܝܗܘܢ
34 ܥܠ ܥܝܠܐ : ܘܐܪܟܒܘܗܝ ܥܠܘܗܝ : ܘܟܕ ܐܙܠ[b] ܗܘܐ
35 ܡܫܘܚܝܢ ܗܘܘ ܠܒܘܫܝܗܘܢ ܒܐܘܪܚܐ :

Codex A.

[x] add ܕ
[y] ܐܬܒܥܢܗ, [z] ܪܒܝܬܗ
[d] add ܐܬ ܡܢܐ ܚܕܐ
‡ f. 148a.
[g] ܕܢܬܝܗܒ
[h] ܕܝܢ ܐܦ
[i] ܕܐܢܐ, [k] ܫܢܐܐ
[m] ܡܚܝܬܘܢ, [n] ܡܕܝܢ
[r] ܒܥܠܕܒܒܝ, [s] add ܠܐ
[t] ܩܛܘܠܘܢ, [u] ܩܕܡܝ
[x] ܘܡܚܘܢ

(deest)

Codex C.

† f. 122b.
[y] ܐܬܒܥܘ, [a] omit ܠܗܘܢ ܕܝܢ
[b] ܐܡܪ, [c] ܕܐܡܪܬܘܢ
[e] ܠܥܣܪ, [f] ܡܢܝܢ
[g] ܕܢܬܝܗܒ
[h] ܕܝܢ ܐܦ
[i] omit ܕܝܢ
[l] ܘܫܕܪ, [o] ܐܝܟ
[p] ܐܦ, [q] omit ܠܐ
[r] ܒܥܠܕܒܒܝ, [s] add ܠܐ
[u] ܘܐܡܠܘܟ, [w] ܥܠܝܗܘܢ
[y] add ܘܟܠܗܘܢ

ܘܗܘܐ[a] ܟܕ ܐܬܩܪܒ
ܠܐܘܪܫܠܡ ܠܒܝܬ ܦܓܐ
ܕܒܛܘܪ ܠܐ ܡܢ
ܙܝܬܐ[a].

ܘܫܕܪ omit
[b] ܬܠܡܝܕܘܗܝ, [c] ܘܐܡܪ
[d] ܠܩܘܪܝܬܐ
[e] ܕܠܘܩܒܠܢ, [f] ܘܐܫܟܚܘ
[g] ܫܪܝܢ
[h] ܐܢܫ, [i] ܫܐܠ
[k] ܘܢܐܡܪ, [l] ܘܐܢ
[m] add ܐܡܪܘ
† f. 123a.
[a] ܪܡܘ
[b] omit ܠܗܘܢ

Codex A.

(*deest*)

Codex B.

ܘܪܡܘ [b]ܡܐܢܝܗܘܢ ܥܠ ܥܝܠܐ [c]ܘܐܪܟܒܘ
36 ܠܡܪܢ ܝܫܘܥ : ܟܕ ܕܝܢ ܗܘܐ ܐܙܠ ܗܘܘ
37 ܡܫܘܢ [b]ܡܐܢܝܗܘܢ ܒܐܘܪܚܐ : ܟܕ[d] [e]ܗܘܐ
ܩܪܝܒ ܟܒܪ [f]ܠܗܢ ܕܡܚܬܝܬܐ ܕܛܘܪܐ
ܕܙܝܬܐ ܫܪܝ ܟܠ ܣܘܓܐܐ ܕܬܠܡܝܕܘܗܝ ܚܕܝܢ
ܘܡܫܒܚܝܢ ܠܐܠܗܐ : ܒܩܠܐ ܪܒܐ ܥܠ ܟܠ
38 [g]ܚܝܠܝܐ ܕܚܙܘ : [h]ܐܡܪܝܢ ܡܒܪܟ ܗܘ ܡܠܟܐ
ܕܐܬܐ ܒܫܡܗ ܕܡܪܝܐ : [i]ܒܫܘܡܝܐ ܫܠܡܐ
39 [j]ܘܬܫܒܘܚܬܐ [k]ܒܡܪܘܡܝܐ : [l]ܘܐܢܫܝܢ ܡܢ
ܦܪܝܫܐ ܡܢ [v]ܐܟ̈ܠܘܣܐ ܐܡܪܘ ܠܗ ܡܠܦܢܐ
40 ܟܐܐ [m]ܒܬܠܡܝܕܝܟ ܘܐܓܝܒ ܘܐܡܪ ܠܗܘܢ
ܐܡܪ ܐܢܐ ܠܟܘܢ [n]ܕܐܢ ܗܠܝܢ ܢܫܬܩܘܢ
41 ܟܐܦܐ ܢܩܥܘܢ : ܘܟܕ [p]ܩܪܒ ܘܚܡܐ
42 ܡܕܝܢܬܐ ܒܟܐ ܥܠܝܗ : ܘܐܡܪ ܕܐܠܘ ܐܚܟܡܬܝ
ܒܝܘܡܐ ܗܕܝܢ ܐܘܦ ܐܢܬܝ ܡܐ ܕܠܛܒ
[q]ܫܠܡܟܝ : ܗܫܐ ܕܝܢ ܐܬܛܫܝ ܡܢ [r]ܥܝܢܝܟܝ :
43 ܕܢܐܬܘܢ ܥܠܝܟܝ [s]ܝܘܡܝܢ ܘܢܚܕܪܘܢ ܢܬܟܝ
[t]ܒܥܠܕܒ̈ܒܝܟܝ ܫܘܪ [u]ܥܠܝܟܝ : ܘܢܚܕܪܘܢ
ܢܬܟܝ ܘܠܚܘܢ ܢܬܟܝ ܡܢ ܟܘܠ [v]ܐܬܪ :
44 ܘܢܪܡܘܢ [w]ܢܬܟܝ ܠܐܪܥܐ ܘܒܢܝܟܝ ܒܓܘܟܝ :
ܘܠܐ ܢܫܒܩܘܢ ܟܐܦ ܥܠ † ܟܐܦ ܒܓܘܟܝ :
[f. 123*a*]
[x]ܚܘܠܝܦ ܕܠܐ ܐܚܟܡܬܝ ܙܒܢܐ [y]ܕܣܘܥܪܢܝܟܝ :
45 ܘܟܕ ܥܠ ܠܗܝܟܠܐ ܫܪܝ [z]ܡܦܩܢ ܠܗܠܝܢ ܕܡܙܒܢܝܢ
46 ܘܐܡܪ ܠܗܘܢ ܟܬܝܒ ܕܒܝܬܝ ܝܗܐ ܒܝܬ ܨܠܘ :
ܘܐܢܬܘܢ ܥܒܕܬܘܢ ܝܬܗ [a]ܡܥܪܐ [b]ܕܠܝܣܛܝܢ :
47 ܘܗܘܐ [c]ܡܠܝܦ ܟܘܠ ܝܘܡ ܒܗܝܟܠܐ : ܪܒܝ
ܟܗܢܐ ܕܝܢ ܘܣܦܪܐ ܘܟܘܠ [d]ܪܘܪܒܢܝܗ ܕܥܡܐ :
48 ܗܘܘ ܒܥܝܢ ܕܢܘܒܕܘܢ ܝܬܗ : ܘܠܐ ܗܘܘ
ܡܫܟܚܝܢ ܕܡܐ [e]ܢܥܒܕܘܢ ܠܗ : ܥܡܐ ܟܘܠܗ
ܬܠ ܗܘܐ ܠܬܐ [f]ܟܕ [g]ܘܫܡܥ ܡܢܗ : : : :
ܫܠܡ

Codex C.

[b] ܡܢܝܗܘܢ
[c] ܘܪܟܒܘ
[d] *add* ܕܝܢ
[e] *omit* ܗܘܐ
[f] ܠܗܘܢ
[g] ܚܝܠܐ
[h] ܘܐܡܪܝܢ
[i] ܒܫܡܝܐ
[j] ܘܬܫܒܚܬܐ
[k] ܒܡܪܘܡܐ
[l] ܘܐܢܫ
[v] ܐܟ̈ܠܘܣܝܐ
[m] ܒܬܠܡܝܕܟ
[n] ܕܐܢ
[p] ܩܪܒ
[q] ܫܠܡܟܝ [r] ܥܝܢܝܢ
[s] ܝܘܡܐ
[t] ܒܥܠܕܒܒܝܢ
[u] ܥܠܝܢ [v] ܐܬܪܐ
[w] ܢܬܝܢ
† f. 123*b*.
[x] ܚܘܠܦ
[y] ܕܣܘܥܪܢܟܝ
[z] ܡܦܩ
[a] ܡܥܪܝܢ [b] ܕܠܣܛܝܢ
[c] ܡܠܦ
[d] ܪܘܪܒܢܝܗܘܢ
[e] ܢܥܒܕܘܢ
[f] ܒܗ [g] ܫܡܥ

Codex A.	Codex B.	Codex C.

[CLXI.]

CLIV.

Luke IV. 16.

ܐܘܠܦܠ ܬ̈ܠܬܝܢ ܘܚܕܐ ܒܡܕܗ ܐܬܒܥܝܪ ܫܒܗ
ܘܠܝܠܗ ܘܡܗܪܐܗ ܐܫܢܗ ܐܘܠ ܝܘܡ ܚܕ ܐܘܠܦܠ
ܬܕܒܐܪ ܐܠܩܕܝܣ ܡܪܝ ܫܡܥܘܢ ܐܠܚܠܒܝ : ܡܢ
16 ܠܘܩܣ : [a] ܘܐܬܐ ܡܪܢ ܝܫܘܥ [b] ܠܢܨܪܬ ܠܗܢ
ܕܗܘܐ ܡܪܒܝܐ : ܘܥܠ ܗܝܟ ܕܗܘܐ ܐܠܝܦ
17 ܒܝܘܡ ܫܒܬܐ [c] ܠܟܢܫܬܐ : ܘܐܬܝܗܒ [d] ܗܘܢ
[f] ܣܦܪܗ [g] ܕܐܫܥܝܐ ܢܒܝܐ [h] ܘܦܬܚ ܕܣܦܪܐ :
[i] ܘܗܘ ܦܬܚ [k] ܣܦܪܐ [l] ܘܐܫܟܚ ܐܬܪܐ ܗܢ
18 [m] ܕܟܬܝܒ ܪܘܚܗ [n] ܕܡܪܝܐ [o] ܥܠܝ : ܠܒܕܠ
ܕܡܢ [p] ܡܫܚ ܝܬܝ ܕܐܒܣܪ ܠܡܣܟܢܝܐ ܫܠܚ ܝܬܝ
19 ܕܐܣܐ ܠܬܒܝܪܝ [q] ܕܠܒܐ ܒܠܒܐ : ܕܐܟܪܙ
[r] ܠܫܒܝܐ [s] ܫܘܒܩܢ ܘܠܥܘܪܝܐ [t] ܕܢܚܙܘܢ :
ܕܐܫܠܚ ܠܬܒܝܪܝܐ ܒܫܘܒܩܢܐ : [u] ܕܐܟܪܙ ܫܢܬܗ
20 [w] ܕܡܪܝܐ ܡܩܒܠܬܐ : [x] ܘܟܪܟ [y] ܣܦܪܐ
[z] ܘܐܫܠܡܗ ܠܗ [a] ܠܫܡܫܐ ܘܝܬܒ ܠܗ :
ܘܥܝܢܝܗܘܢ ܕܟܠ ܗܠܝܢ [b] ܕܒܟܢܫܬܐ [c] ܗܘܝ
21 [d] ܡܕܡܟܝܐ ܠܗ : ܘܗܘ ܫܪܝ ܐܡܪ ܠܗܘܢ
ܝܘܡܢ ܐܬܡܠܝ [e] ܗܕܝܢ ܟܬܒܐ ܒܐܕܢܝܟܘܢ :
22 ܘܟܠܗܘܢ ܗܘܘ [f] ܕܝ ܡܣܗܕܝܢ ܒܠܗ : ܘܗܘܘ
[g] ܡܬܡ̈ܗܝܢ ܒܠ ܟܘܠ ܡܠܝܐ [h] ܕܛܝܒܘܬܐ ܕܗܘܝ
[i] ܢܦܩܝܢ ܡܢ ܦܘܡܗ .

Codex A (variants): [a] *add* ܘܒܬܪܗ ܡܝܪܘܬܐ — [b] ܠܢܨܪܬ — [d] ܠܗ — [f] ܣܦܪܗ — [g] ܕܐܫܥܝܐ — [i] *omit* ܗܘ — [k] ܣܦܪܐ — [l] ܘܐܫܟܚ — [n] ܕܡܪܝܐ — [o] ܥܠܝ — [p] ܡܫܚ — [q] ܕܬܒܝܪܝ — [r] ܠܫܒܝܐ — [s] ܫܘܒܩܢ — [u] ܕܐܟܪܙ — [w] ܕܡܪܝܐ — [x] ܘܟܪܟ — [c] ܗܘܘ — [e] ܗܕܝܢ — [f] *omit* ܕܝ — [h] ܕܛܝܒܘܬܐ — [i] ܢܦܩܝܢ

Codex C (variants): [c] ܠܟܢܫܬܐ — [d] ܘܐܬܝܗܒܠܗ — [g] ܕܐܫܥܝܐ — [h] ܘܦܬܚ — [i] *omit* ܗܘ — [k] ܣܦܪܐ — [l] ܘܐܫܟܚ — [m] ܕܟܬܝܒ — [p] ܡܫܚ — [q] ܕܬܒܝܪܝ — [r] ܠܫܒܝܐ — [t] ܕܢܚܙܘܢ — [y] ܣܦܪܐ — [z] ܘܐܫܠܡܗ — [a] ܠܫܡܫܐ — [b] ܕܒܟܢܫܬܐ — [d] ܡܕܡܟܝܢ — [f] *omit* ܕܝ — [g] ܡܬܡ̈ܗܝܢ

Codex B.	Codex A.	

[CLXIV.]

Luke X. 1.

Codex B: (deest)

ܪܐܒܥ ܬܕܒܐܪ ܐܠܩܕܝܣ ܒܫܢܘܕܐ ܘܠܐܦܓܐܠ
ܘܐܠܩܕܝܣܝܢ ܐܠܬܝ ܡܟܗ ܡܢ ܠܘܩܣ : ܘܒܬܪ

Codex C: (deest)

Codex B.	*Codex* A.	*Codex* C.
(*deest*)	1 ܡܒܝܪܘܬܐ ܐܘܕܝܬ ܡܪܝܐ ܕܫܡܥܬ ܗܘ ܐܦܣ ܬܠܡܝܕܘܗܝ ܫܘܒܚܐ: ܘܫܠܝܚ ܡܬܩܦ ܬܪܝܢ ܬܪܝܢ ܡܢܗܘܢ ܐܝܟ ܠܟܠ ܠܟܠ ܡܕܝܢܬܐ ܘܠܟܠ 2 ܐܬܪ ܕܗܘܐ ܥܬܝܕ ܕܢܐܙܠ: ܘܗܘܐ ܐܡܪ ܠܗܘܢ ܚܨܕܐ ܡܢ ܦܠܚܐ: ܘܚܨܘܕܐ ܙܥܘܪܐ: ܒܥܘ ܡܢ ܡܪܗ ܕܚܨܕܐ ܕܢܦܩ ܦܥܠܐ ܠܚܨܕܗ: 3 ܐܙܠܘ ܗܐ ܫܠܚ ܐܢܐ ܠܟܘܢ ܗܝܟ ܐܡܪܐ 4 ܒܝܬ ܕܐܒܐ: ܠܐ ܬܫܩܠܘܢ ܟܝܣܐ ܒܫܡܐ. ܘܠܐ ܦܪܐ: ܘܠܐ ܡܣܐܢܐ: ܘܒܫܠܡܐ ܕܐܢܫ 5 ܕܠܡܫܐܠ ܐܘܪܚܐ ܠܐ ܬܫܐܠܘܢ: ܘܠܟܠ ܒܝܬ ܕܬܥܠܘܢ ܠܗ ܡܩܕܡ ܗܘܘ ܐܡܪܝܢ ܫܠܡܐ 6 ܠܒܝܬܐ ܗܢܐ: ܘܐܢ ܬܡܢ ܐܝܬ ܒܪ ܫܠܡܐ ܬܬܢܝܚ ܥܠܘܗܝ ܫܠܡܟܘܢ: ܘܐܢ ܕܝܢ ܠܐ. 7 ܫܠܡܟܘܢ ܠܘܬܟܘܢ ܢܗܦܘܟ: ܘܒܗ ܒܒܝܬܐ ܗܘ ܗܘܘ ܐܟܠܝܢ ܘܫܬܝܢ ܡܢ ܕܠܘܬܟܘܢ: ܫܘܝܐ ܗܘ ܓܝܪ ܦܥܠܐ ܠܐܓܪܗ: ܠܐ ܬܫܢܘܢ 8 ܡܢ ܒܝܬ ܠܒܝܬ:: ܘܠܟܠ ܡܕܝܢܬܐ ܕܬܥܠܘܢ ܠܗ ܘܢܩܒܠܘܢ ܟܘܢ: ܗܘܘ 9 ܐܟܠܝܢ ܡܕܡ ܕܡܣܬܝܡ ܩܕܡܝܟܘܢ: ܘܗܘܘ ܡܐܣܝܢ ܠܟܪܝܗܐ ܕܒܗ: ܘܗܘܘ ܐܡܪܝܢ ܠܗܘܢ ܩܪܒܬ ܥܠܝܟܘܢ ܡܠܟܘܬܗ ܕܐܠܗܐ: 10 ܘܡܕܝܢܬܐ ܕܬܥܠܘܢ ܠܗ ܘܠܐ ܢܩܒܠܘܢ ܟܘܢ. ܟܕ ܬܦܩܘܢ ܠܫܘܩܝܗ ܐܡܪܘ 11 ܕܐܦ ܥܦܪܐ ܕܕܒܩ ܒܪ̈ܓܠܝܢ ܡܢ ܡܕܝܢܬܟܘܢ. ܐܢܚܢ ܡܦܨܝܢ ܚܢܢ ܠܟܘܢ: ܒܪܡ ܕܝܢ ܗܕܐ ܗܘܘ ܝܕܥܝܢ. ܕܩܪܒܬ ܥܠܝܟܘܢ ܡܠܟܘܬܗ ܕܐܠܗܐ: 12 ܐܡܪ ܐܢܐ ܠܟܘܢ ܕܝܢ ܕܠܣܕܘܡ ܒܝܘܡܐ ܗܘ ܢܗܘܐ ܢܝܚ ܐܘ ܡܢ ܠܗܝ ܡܕܝܢܬܐ	(*deest*)

Codex A.	Codex B.	Codex C.

Codex B.

CLV.

Matt. XXIII. 29.

ܬܐܡܢ. ܗܘܐ ܟܕ ܐܡܠܠ ܬܘܕܝܪ ܐܠܗܝܕܝܐ ܡܛܝܪ
ܐܡܪܐ: ܐܬܠܡܒ. ܗܘܐ ܐܬܝܢ ܡܒܠ ܐܣܛܪܝܗ
ܘܗܘ ܢܦܩ ܐܬܝܬܠ ܐܝܟܐ ܗܘ ܠܒܘܟܐ ܡܣܬܠܐ
ܘܗܘ ܡܢ ܡܣܝܣܐ ܬܠܬ ܗܘܐ ܬܘܕܝܪ ܐܬܢܡܬܘܣ
ܐܬܠܒ* ܫܡܥܘܢ ܦܢ ܐܡܠܠ ܬܘܕܝܪ ܐܠܗܝܐ
ܡܝܢ ܘܡܪܝܐ ܡܢ ܡܬܐܘܣ ܗܘ ܗܕܝܢ: ܐܡܪ
29 ܡܪܝܐ [w]ܫܡܥܘܢ: ܘܝ ܠܟܘܢ ܣܦܪܝܐ [x]ܘܦܪܝܫܝ
ܫܒܪܝܐ: ܕܐܬܘܢ ܒܢܝܢ ܡܩܒܪܝܬܗܘܢ
[y]ܕܢܒܝܐ: ܘܡܬܩܢܝܢ [z]ܡܒܪܝܗܘܢ ܕܨܕܝܩܝܐ:
30 ܘܐܬܘܢ ܐܡܪܝܢ ܕܐܠܘ [a]ܗܘܝܢ ܒܝܘܡܝܗܘܢ
[b]ܕܐܒܗܬܢ ܠܐ [c]ܗܘܝܢ ܫܘܬܦܝܢ ܒܡܕܡܗܘܢ
31 ܒܐܕܡܐ [y]ܕܢܒܝܐ :* ܗܘܐ ܐܘܢ ܐܬܘܢ
ܡܣܗܕܝܢ ܥܠ ܢܦܫܟܘܢ ܕܐܬܘܢ [e]ܒܢܝܗܘܢ
32 ܕܩܛܠܝܢ ܕܩܛܠܘ [e]ܢܒܝܐ: ܐܦ ܐܬܘܢ ܡܠܘ
33 [f]ܡܟܝܠܬܗܘܢ ܕܐܒܗܬܟܘܢ: [g]ܚܘܘܬܐ [h]ܘܠܝܕܗܘܢ
[i]ܕܥܩܪܒܐ ܗܝܟ [k]ܬܥܪܩܘܢ ܡܢ ܕܝܢܐ ܕܓܗܢܐ:
34 [l]ܠܟܠܠ [m]ܟܕܝܢ ܗܐ ܐܢܐ [n]ܡܫܠܚ ܠܘܬܟܘܢ
[o]ܢܒܝܢ ܘܚܟܝܡܝܢ ܘܣܦܪܝܢ: [p]ܘܡܢܗܘܢ [q]
[r]ܬܩܛܠܘܢ [s]ܘܬܙܩܦܘܢ: ܘܡܢܗܘܢ ܬܢܓܕܘܢ
[t]ܒܟܢܫܬܟܘܢ [u]ܘܬܪܕܦܘܢ ܡܢ ܡܕܝܢܐ ܠܡܕܝܢܐ:
35 [v]ܠܡܟܠ ܕܝܐܬܐ ܥܠܝܟܘܢ ܟܠ ܐܕܡ ܙܟܝ
[w]ܕܡܢ [x]ܕܐܫܬܦܟ ܥܠ ܐܪܥܐ ܡܢ ܐܕܡܗ
ܕܗܒܝܠ ܙܟܝܐ ܥܕܡܐ ܠܐܕܡܗ ܕܙܟܪܝܐ
ܒܪ [y]ܒܪܟܝܐ ܗܕܝܢ ܕܩܛܠܬܘܢ ܒܝܢ ܢܘܣܐ
36 [z]ܠܡܕܒܚܐ: ܐܡܝܢ [o]ܐܡܪ ܐܢܐ[o] ܠܟܘܢ
ܕܝܐܬܝܢ ܟܠܗܝܢ [a]ܟܘܠܗܘܢ ܥܠ ܗܕܝܢ ܕܪܐ:
37 [b]ܝܪܘܫܠܡ [c]ܝܪܘܫܠܡ ܗܕܐ [d]ܕܩܛܠܐ [e]ܢܒܝܐ
ܘܪܓܡܐ ܠܗܠܝܢ [f]ܕܡܫܬܠܚܝܢ ܠܘܬܗ: ܟܡܐ

Codex A.

[CLXV.]

[w] *omit* ܫܡܥܘܢ
[x] ܘܦܪܝܫܝܐ
[y] ܕܢܒܝܐ
[b] ܕܐܒܗܬܢ
[c] ܗܘܝܢ [e] ܢܒܝܐ
[f] ܡܟܝܠܬܗܘܢ
[g] ܚܘܘܬܐ
[h] ܘܝܠܕܝܗܘܢ
[i] ܕܥܩܪܒܐ
[k] ܬܥܪܩܘܢ
[l] ܠܟܠܠ [m] ܟܕ
[n] ܡܫܠܚ [o] ܢܒܝܝܢ
[r] ܬܩܛܠܘܢ
[s] ܘܬܙܩܦܘܢ
[u] ܘܬܪܕܦܘܢ
[v] ܠܡܟܠܐ [w] *omit* ܕܡܢ
[x] ܕܐܫܬܦܟ
[y] ܒܪܟܝܐ [o] ܐܡܪ ܐܢܐ
[a] ܟܘܠܗܝܢ
[c] ܝܪܘܫܠܡ
[d] ܕܩܛܠܐ
[e] ܢܒܝܐ
[f] ܕܡܫܬܠܚܝܢ

Codex C.

[* Cod. B. in margine ܬܠܬ ܥܣܪ ܗܘܐ ܡܢ ܬܫܪܝܢ ܐܚܪܝܐ]

[w] *omit* ܫܡܥܘܢ
[z] ܡܒܪܝܗܘܢ
[a] ܗܘܝܢ
[e] ܒܢܝ ܗܘ
[h] ܘܠܝܕܝܗܘܢ
[i] ܕܥܩܪܒܐ
[n] ܡܫܠܚ
[p] ܡܢܗܘܢ
[q] *add* ܕܝ
[t] ܒܟܢܫܬܗܘܢ
[w] *omit* ܕܡܢ
[y] ܒܪܟܝܐ
[z] ܡܕܒܚܐ
[b] ܝܪܘܫܠܡ
[d] ܕܩܛܠܐ
[f] ܕܡܫܬܠܚܝܢ

Codex A.

ܕܒܚܕܘ [f]

[g] *omit* ܒܚܕܘܗ

[h] *add* ܟܘܠ

ܕܬܬܢܛܪܘܢ ܠܟܘܢ [i]

ܦܪܘܫܝܗ [j] ܒܝܕܝܗ [k]

ܥܒܝܕ [l] ܢܛܪܝܢ [m]

ܕܬܒܝܥܘܢ [n]

ܗܕܝܢ [o] ܕܟܝܪܐ [p]

Codex B.

(deest)

Codex B.

ܘܟܠܝܢ ܝܫܡܥܘܢ ܕܡܫܝܚܐ[f] ܒܝܫܘܥ ܒܚܕܘܗ[g] ܗܘܝܢ[h]

ܗܘܐ ܕܬܬܢܛܪܘܢ ܠܟܘܢ[i] ܡܬܝܐܢܐ ܦܪܘܫܝܗ[j] ܠܬܘܠܕܬ

38 ܒܝܕܝܗ[k] ܘܠܐ ܝܫܘܥܘܢ ܗܘܐ ܥܒܝܕ[l] ܠܗܘܢ

39 ܒܝܬܗܘܢ ܢܛܪܝܢ[m] : ܐܡܪ ܐܢܐ ܠܗܘܢ ܠܝ

ܕܠܐ ܬܫܡܥܘܢ ܡܢ ܡܢ ܒܗܘ ܒܕܡܝܐ ܕܬܒܝܥܘܢ[n]

ܡܢܗܘܢ ܗܘ ܗܕܝܢ[o] ܕܐܬܐ ܒܫܡܝܗ ܕܟܝܪܐ[p] :

Codex A.

[CLXVI.]

Mark XII. 28—37.

28 ܘܒܬܪܗ ܩܪܝܒܐ ܐܢܫ ܘܡܢܗ ܚܕ ܡܢ ܣܦܪܝܐ.

ܕܫܡܥ ܠܗܘܢ ܕܡܬܕܪܫܝܢ : ܘܚܙܐ ܕܝܐܝܘܬ

ܐܝܒܗ ܠܗܘܢ : ܫܐܠ ܠܗ ܗܘ ܚܕ ܦܘܩܕ

29 ܩܕܡܝ ܡܢ ܟܠܗܘܢ : ܐܡܪ ܝܫܘܥ ܐܝܒܗ

ܠܗ : ܩܕܡܝ ܗܘ ܦܘܩܕܐ ܩܕܡܝܐ : ܫܡܥ

ܐܝܣܪܐܝܠ ܡܪܝܐ ܐܠܗܢ ܡܪܝܐ ܚܕ ܗܘ :

30 ܘܬܪܚܡ ܠܡܪܝܐ ܐܠܗܟ ܡܢ ܟܘܠܗ ܠܒܟ :

ܘܡܢ ܟܘܠܗ ܢܦܫܟ : ܘܡܢ ܟܘܠܗ ܚܝܠܟ : ܗܕܝܢ

31 ܗܘ ܦܘܩܕܐ ܩܕܡܝܐ : ܘܬܢܝܢܐ ܕܕܡܝ ܠܗ.

ܕܬܪܚܡ ܩܪܝܒܟ ܗܝܟ ܕܠܢܦܫܟ : ܪܒ ܡܢ

32 ܗܠܝܢ ܣܓܝ ܦܘܩܕ ܠܝܬ : ܘܐܡܪ ܠܗ ܗܘ

ܣܦܪܐ ܝܐܝܘܬ ܡܠܦܢܐ ܒܩܘܫܛ ܐܡܪܬ

ܕܚܕ ܗܘ ܐܠܗܐ ܘܠܝܬ ܣܓܝ ܠܒܪ ܡܢܗ :

33 ܘܕܬܪܚܡ ܝܬܗ ܡܢ ܟܘܠܗ ܠܒܐ ܘܡܢ ܟܘܠܗ

ܟܘܢܝܬܐ : ܘܡܢ ܟܘܠܗ ܢܦܫܐ : ܘܡܢ ܟܘܠܗ

ܚܝܠܐ : ܘܕܬܪܚܡ ܐܢܫ ܩܪܝܒܗ ܗܝܟ ܕܠܢܦܫܗ

ܝܬܝܪ ܗܝ ܡܢ ܟܘܠ ܩܘܪܒܢܐ : ܘܡܢ

34 ܕܒܚܝܬܐ : ܘܚܙܐ ܝܫܘܥ ܕܒ ܝܐܝܘܬ ܥܢܐ ܗܘܐ

ܕܒܟܘܢܝ ܐܝܒܗ ܘܐܡܪ ܠܗ ܕܠܝܬ ܐܢܬ ܪܚܝܩ

ܡܢ ܡܠܟܘܬܗ ܕܐܠܗܐ : ܘܐܢܫ ܟܘܪ ܠܐ

Codex C.

ܕܫܡܥܝܢ [f] ܒܝܫܘܥ [h] ܟܘܠܗܘܢ

ܕܬܬܢܛܪܘܢ ܠܟܘܢ [i]

ܢܛܪܝܢ [m]

(deest)

Codex B. (*deest*)

Codex A.

35 ܗܘܐ ܥܢܐ ܕܝܫܘܥ ܠܗܘܢ: ܘܐܠܦܝܢ ܡܪܢ
ܒܗܝܟܠܐ ܗܘܐ ܐܡܪ ܟܠܗ ܒܢܗܘܐ: ܗܝܟ
ܐܡܪܝܢ ܣܦܪܝܐ ܕܡܫܝܚܐ ܗܘ ܒܪܗ ܕܕܘܝܕ ܀
36 ܗܘ ܓܝܪ ܕܘܝܕ ܐܡܪ ܒܪܘܚܐ ܕܩܘܕܫܐ:
ܐܡܪ ܡܪܝܐ ܠܡܪܝ ܬܒ ܡܢ ܝܡܝܢܝ ܥܕܡܐ
ܕܐܫܘܐ ܒܥܠܕܒܒܝܟ ܟܘܒܫܐ ܬܚܘܬ ܪ̈ܓܠܝܟ ܀
37 ܐܝ ܗܘ ܕܘܝܕ ܩܪܐ ܠܗ ܡܪܝ ܗܝܟ ܗܘ
ܒܪܗ: ܘܣܓܝ ܕܝܢ ܕܐܘܟܠܘܣܝܢ ܗܘܐ ܫܡܥ
ܡܢܗ ܒܚܕܘܬܐ ܀ ܫܠܡ

Codex C. (*deest*)

Codex A. [CCVII.]

Codex B.

CLVI.

Luke X. 16—21.

ܫܪܘܐ ܣܡܟ ܦܝ ܐܠܘܠ ܬܕܒܐܪ ܡܫܝܚܐ ܪܒܘܫ
ܐܠܡܠܐܟܐ ܡܢ ܠܗܘܬ : ܐܡܪ ܡܪܢ
16 ܠܬܠܡܝܕܘܗܝ[y]: ܡܢ ܕܫܡܥ[z] ܠܟܘܢ ܠܝ ܗܘ
ܫܡܥ[a]: ܘܡܢ ܕܛܠܡ ܠܟܘܢ ܠܝ ܗܘ ܛܠܡ:
ܘܡܢ[b] ܕܛܠܡ ܠܝ ܛܠܡ ܠܕܡ[c] ܕܫܠܚܢܝ[d] ܗܘ:
ܘܡܢ ܕܫܡܥ ܠܝ ܫܡܥ ܠܕܡ[c] ܕܫܠܚܢܝ[d] ܗܘ:
17 ܘܬܒܘ ܗܢܘܢ ܫܒܥܝܢܬܐ[j] ܒܚܕܘܐ ܐܡܪܝܢ
ܡܪܢ ܐܘܦ ܫܐܕܐ ܡܫܬܥܒܕܝܢ ܠܢ[e] ܒܫܡܟ:
18 ܘܐܡܪ ܠܗܘܢ ܚܙܝܐ ܗܘܝܬ ܠܣܛܢܐ[f] ܕܢܦܠ
19 ܗܝܟ ܒܪܩܐ ܕܡܢ ܫܡܝܐ: ܗܐ ܝܗܒܬ[g]
ܠܟܘܢ ܫܠܝܛܘ ܘܥܩܪܒܐ[h] ܕܬܕܘܫܘܢ[i] ܠܥܠ[k] ܡܢ
ܫܘܠܛܢܐ[l] ܘܥܩܪ̈ܒܐ: ܘܥܠ ܚܝܠܗ ܕܒܥܠܕܒܒܐ[n]:
20 ܘܡܕܡ ܠܐ ܡܟܐ ܢܬܟܘܢ: ܒܪ[o] ܕܝܢ
ܒܗܕܐ ܠܐ ܬܚܕܘܢ: ܕܪܘܚܬܐ ܡܫܬܥܒܕܝܢ[p]
ܠܟܘܢ: ܚܕܘ ܕܝܢ ܕܫܡܗܬܟܘܢ[q] ܟܬܝܒܝܢ[r]
21 ܒܗ ܒܫܥܬܐ: ܘܗܘ ܒܚܕܘܬܐ ܐܬܚܕܝ ܡܪܢ

Codex A. variants:

[z] ܕܫܡܥ [a] ܫܡܥ
[b] ܘܡܢ [c] ܠܕ
[d] ܕܫܠܚܢܝ
[j] ܫܒܥܝܢܬܐ
[e] ܠܢ [f] ܠܣܛܢܐ
[g] ܝܗܒܬ
[h] ܘܥܩܪܒܐ [k] ܠܥܠ
[l] ܫܘܠܛܢܐ
[n] ܕܒܥܠܕܒܒܐ
[o] ܒܪ
[p] ܡܫܬܥܒܕܝܢ
[q] ܫܡܗܬܟܘܢ
[r] ܟܬܝܒܝܢ

Codex C. variants:

[y] ܠܬܠܡܝܕܘܗܝ
[b] ܘܡܢ [c] ܠܕ
[d] ܕܫܠܚܢܝ
[e] ܠܢ
[f] ܠܣܛܢܐ
[h] ܘܥܩܪܒܐ
[i] ܕܬܕܘܫܘܢ [k] ܠܥܠ
[n] ܕܒܥܠܕܒܒܐ
[r] ܟܬܝܒܝܢ

Codex A.	*Codex* B.	*Codex* C.
	ܫܘܗ ܒܪܘܚܐ [s] ܕܩܘܕܫܐ ܘܐܡܪ : ܡܫܬܘܕܐ	[s] *omit* ܕܩܘܕܫܐ
[t] ܕܫܡܝܐ	ܐܢܐ ܠܟ ܐܒܐ ܡܪܐ [t] ܕܫܡܝܐ ܘܕܐܪܥܐ :	
[u] ܚܟܝܡܝܢ	ܕܛܡܪܬ ܗܠܝܢ ܡܢ [u] ܚܟܝܡܝܢ ܘܡܢ ܡܣܬܟܠܝܢ :	[u] ܚܟܝܡܝܢ
[w] *add* ܐܢܝܢ ܠܝܠܘܕܝܢ :	ܘܓܠܝܬ [w] : ܐܝ ܐܒܐ [x] ܕܟܢ ܐܬܪܥܝܬ ܨܒܝܢܐ	
[x] ܕܟܢ [z] ܩܘܕܡܝܟ	[z] ܩܘܕܡܝܟ : :	[z] ܩܘܕܡܝܟ

[CLXVIII.]	CLVII.	
	LUKE I. 39.	
	ܬܫܒܘܚܬܗ ܒܗ ܐܡܠܠ ܡܠܐܟ ܓܒܪܐܝܠ ܠܡܪܝܡ	
	ܡܪܝܡ ܗܘܐ ܒܣܦܪܐ ܡܢ ܠܘܩܣ : ܘܒܫܬܗ	
[a] ܘܒܗܠܝܢ	39 ܡܫܝܪܘܬܐ : [a] ܘܒܗܠܝܢ ܝܘܡܝܐ ܩܡܬ ܕܝ	
[b] ܡܪܝܡ	[b] ܡܪܝܡ ܘܐܙܠܬ [c] ܠܛܘܪܐ ܒܥܝܓܠܘ [d] ܕܝ	[c] ܠܛܘܪܬܐ
[c] ܠܛܘܪܬܐ	40 [e] ܠܡܕܝܢܬܐ [f] ܕܝܗܘܕܐ : ܘܥܠܬ ܠܒܝܬܗ [g] ܕܙܟܪܝܐ :	[d] *omit* ܕܝ
[d] *omit* ܕܝ	41 [h] ܘܫܐܠܬ [i] ܒܫܠܡܗ [j] ܕܐܠܝܫܒܥ : [k] ܘܗܘܐ [l] ܟܕ	[e] ܠܡܕܝܢܬܗ
[e] ܠܡܕܝܢܬܐ	ܕܫܡܥܬ ܐܠܝܫܒܥ [m] ܫܠܡܗ ܕܡܪܝܡ ܩܦܨ	[h] ܘܫܐܠܬ [i] ܒܫܠܡܗ
[f] ܕܝܗܘܕܐ	ܛܠܝܐ ܒܟܪܣܗ : [n] ܘܐܬܡܠܝܬ ܐܠܝܫܒܥ ܡܢ ܪܘܚܐ	[j] ܕܐܠܝܫܒܥ
[g] ܕܙܟܪܝܐ [k] ܘܗܘܐ	42 ܕܩܘܕܫܐ : ܘܐܓܥܬ ܒܩܠܐ ܪܒܐ ܘܐܡܪܐ :	[m] ܫܠܡܗ
[l] *omit* ܕ ܟܕ	ܡܒܪܟܐ [o] ܐܬܝ [p] ܒܢܫܝܐ : ܘܡܒܪܟ ܗܘ	[n] ܘܐܬܡܠܝܬ
[p] ܒܢܫܝܐ	43 ܦܐܪܗ ܕܒܪܥܣܝܟܝ : ܘܡܢ [q] ܗܝ ܠܝ ܗܕܐ	[o] ܐܬܝ [q] ܗܠܝܢ
[t] ܕܬܐܬܐ	44 [t] ܕܬܐܬܐ [u] ܐܡܗ ܕܡܪܝ ܠܘܬܝ : ܗܐ ܓܝܪ	[t] ܕܬܐܬܐ
[u] ܐܡܗ	ܟܕ [v] ܕܐܫܬܡܥ ܩܠ [w] ܫܠܡܝܟܝ ܒܐܕܢܝ :	[w] ܫܠܡܟܝ
[v] ܕܐܫܬܡܥܬ	45 ܩܦܨ ܛܠܝܐ ܒܚܕܘܐ [x] ܒܟܪܣܝ : ܘܛܘܒܝܗ	[x] ܒܟܪܣܝ
[y] ܫܠܡ	ܠܗܕܐ ܕܗܝܡܢܬ ܕܗܘܐ [y] ܫܠܡ [z] ܠܗܠܝܢ	[y] ܫܠܡ
[b] ܡܪܐ [c] *omit* ܕܝ	46 ܕܐܬܡܠܠ ܠܗ [a] ܡܢ ܠܘܬ [b] ܡܪܐ : ܘܐܡܪܬ	[a] *omit* ܡܢ [z] ܠܗܠܝܢ
[d] ܡܪܝܡ [e] ܠܡܪܐ	[c] ܕܝ [d] ܡܪܝܡ : ܡܪܒܝܐ ܗܝ ܢܦܫܝ [e] ܠܡܪܐ	[b] ܡܪܐ
	47 [f] ܘܐܬܚܕܝܬ ܪܘܚܝ ܥܠ ܐܠܗܐ ܡܚܝܝܢܝ :	[f] ܘܐܬܚܕܬ
[g] ܝܗܒܝܢ [h] ܠܝ	48 ܕܐܣܬܟܠ ܥܠ ܡܟܝܟܘܬܗ ܕܐܡܬܗ : ܗܐ ܓܝܪ	
[i] *add* ܗܘ	ܡܢ ܟܕܘ [g] ܝܗܒܝܢ [h] ܠܝܒܝ ܛܘܒܐ ܟܠܗܘܢ	[g] ܝܗܒܝܢ [h] ܠܝ
[j] ܕܫܠܝܛܐ	49 ܕܪܝܐ : ܕܥܒܕ ܠܝ ܪܒܪܒܢ [i] [j] ܫܠܝܛܐ ܘܩܕܝܫ	

Codex A.	Codex B.	Codex C.
[k] add ...ܠܗܠܝܢ ܕܫܡܥܝܢ ܡܠܬܗ .... ܘܢܛܪ ...ܡܢ...[53]ܠܥܡܘܕܐ ܐܫܒܥܐ ⌐ܡܢ⌐ ܠܦܬܐ ܘܠܟܬܪܐ ܥܠܝ ... [54]ܘܒܠ ܠܡܫܪܠ ܦܠܝܗ ܘܫܒܪ ܐܫܒܝܢܐ [55]ܗܟܢ ܒܥܠܡܐ ܕܒܠܠ ܠܗܬ ܐܒ ܗ ܐ ܠܐܒܘܗܝ ܘܠ[ܐ]ܡ[ܗ] ܕܒܗܘ ܠܒܠܗ : [l] ܡܪܝܡ [m] omit ܠܗ [n] omit ܥܠܡ [CLXVIII.] [a] add ܝܫܘܥ ܡܪܢ [b] ܐܙܠ [c] ܘܐܬܬܐ [d] add ܠܗ [e] ܡܪܝܡ [f] ܝܬܒܐ [g] ܕܬܒܠܝܢ [i] add ܕܝܢ [j] ܬܫܡܫܝ [l] ܒܥܠ [m] ܕܐܚܬܝ [n] ܒܠܚܘܕܝ [o] ܐܘ [p] ܝܨܦܐ [q] ܘܝܨܒܕ [r] ܡܪܝܡ [s] ܡܢܬܐ [t] ܐܬܬܐ [w] ܐܟܠܘܣܐ [x] ܘܐܡܪܬ [y] add ܠܗ [a] ܠܟܪܣܐ [c] ܘܬܕܝܐ [d] ܕܐܝܢܩܘ [CLXXV.]	50 ܗܘ ܢܝܫܗ :[k] ܟܠܬܗ ܕܝܢ [l]ܡܪܝܡ ܠܬܘܠܗ ܗܟܢ ܬܠܬܐ ܢܛܪܐ ܘܬܒܬ [m]ܠܗ ܠܒܠܒܗ :: [n]ܥܠܡ . **CLVIII.** LUKE X. 38. ܘܗܘܐ ܠܡܗܕܐ ܘܗܘ ܢܩܘܪܐ ܢܡܩ ܐܠܝܩܒܐ ܐܫܢܗ ܒܥܠܡܐ ܡܢ ܠܥܘܡ : ܘܒܝܬܗ ܡܢܘܪܫܐ : 38 ܘܗܘܐ ܗܟܢ ܕܗܘܐ[a] [b]ܐܙܠ : ܘܗܘ ܒܠ ܠܢܝܫܐ ܩܪܝܐ : [c]ܘܐܬܬܐ ܚܕܐ ܕܫܡܗ ܡܪܬܐ 39 ܩܒܠܬ ܢܬܗ ܒܒܝܬܗ : ܘܠܗܕܐ ܗܘܬ [d]ܐܚܐ ܡܬܩܪܝܐ [e]ܡܪܝܡ : ܗܕܐ ܕܝܢ [f]ܝܬܒܬ ܠܗ ܗܘ [g]ܕܬܒܠܝܢ ܕܡܪܐ ܢܫܡܥ ܘ[h]ܗܘܬ ܥܒܕܐ 40 ܡܠܝܗ : ܡܪܬܐ [i]ܗܘܬ ܡܫܬܦܩܐ ܠܦܒ ܫܡܫ [j]ܬܫܡܫܝ : ܘܩܡܬ [k]ܕܝܢ ܡܪܬܐ ܘܐܡܪܬ ܡܪܝ ܠܐ [l]ܒܥܠ ܠܟ [m]ܕܐܚܬܝ ܫܒܩܬ ܢܬܝ [n]ܒܠܚܘܕܝ ܡܫܡܫܫܐ : ܐܡܪ ܠܗ [o]ܐܘ 41 ܕܬܫܡܫ ܢܬܝ : ܐܦܢܝ ܕܝܢ ܡܪܐ ܝܫܘܥ ܘܐܡܪ ܠܗ ܡܪܬܐ ܡܪܬܐ : ܫܦܝܠ ܐܬܝ [p]ܝܨܦܐ ܘܡܫܬܦܩܐ [q]ܘܝܨܒܕ ܗܘ ܙܘܪܐ : 42 [r]ܡܪܝܡ ܕܝܢ [s]ܡܢܝܬܐ ܛܒܬܐ ܒܚܪܬ ܠܗ : XI. 27 ܗܕܐ ܕܠܐ ܡܬܢܫܒܐ ܡܢܗ : ܘܗܘܐ ܗܟܢ ܕܗܘ ܐܡܪ ܗܠܝܢ : ܩܠܬ ܚܕܐ [t]ܐܬܬܐ [u]ܠܗ ܡܢ ܟܘ [w]ܐܟܠܘܣܐ [x]ܘܐܡܪܬ[y] [z]ܠܡܪܐ ܝܫܘܥ : [a]ܠܟܪܣܐ ܒܪܣܐ ܕܛܥܢܬ [b]ܝܬܟ : [c]ܘܬܕܝܐ 28 [d]ܕܐܝܢܩܘ ܝܬܟ : ܘܗܘ ܐܡܪ ܠܟܘܒܢܘܗܝ ܠܗܠܝܢ ܕܫܡܥܝܢ ܡܠܬܗ ܕܐܠܗܐ ܘܢܛܪܝܢ[e] . **CLIX.** ܘܟܕ ܬܫܒܚ ܡܢ ܗܘܠܐ ܬܪܬܐ ܝܘܡܝܢ ܘܝܘܝ : ܐܦܠܘܢ ܐܫܒܬ ܐܗܘܝ ܡܢ ܠܥܘܡܐ :	[c] ܘܐܬܬܐ [d] add ܠܗ [h] add ܗܘ [i] add ܕܝܢ [j] ܬܫܡܫܝ [k] ܕܝܢ [s] ܡܢܬܐ [t] ܐܬܬܐ [u] ܠܗ [w] ܐܟܠܘܣܐ [x] ܘܐܡܪ [y] add ܠܗ [z] ܡܪܐ [a] ܠܟܪܣܐ [b] ܝܬܟ (sic) [e] add ܠܗ

Codex A.	Codex B.	Codex C.
	ܘܦܢ ܒܒܪܗ : ܠܡܫܡܫܐ ܐܡܝܢ ܐܠܗܘܬܗ :	
	ܐܦܠܘܢ ܐܘܩܡܬ ܐܘܪܝܐ ܡܢ ܡܬܠܘܬܗ ܚܕܝ	
	ܒܪ ܠܡܫܡܫ ܐܡܝܢ : ܐܦܠܘܢ ܗܘܐ ܐܬܬܐܬ	
	ܦܢ ܫܒܗ ܒܒܪ ܐܠܗܘܬ : ܐܬܒܪܒܪ ܠܡܫܡܫ	
	ܐܡܝܢ : ܐܦܠܘܢ ܗܘܐ ܐܬܬܝܢ ܫܒܘ ܫܒܗ	
	ܒܒܪ ܐܠܗܝܢ : ܬܬܬܒܪ ܠܡܫܡܫ ܐܡܝܢ	
	ܐܦܠܘܢ ܗܘܐ ܐܬܬܬܐ ܫܒܘ ܫܒܗ ܒܒܪ	
	ܐܠܗܘܬ ܐܘܩܡܬ ܐܠܗܝ ܡܢܠ ܢܦܩ ܐܡܝܢ	° add ܘܒܢܝܗܘܢ
	ܐܦܠܘܢ ܐܘܩܡܬ ܐܘܐܒܝܢ ܡܢ ܡܬܠܘܬܗ ܚܕ	ܩܕܝܫܐ
	ܡܢܠ ܢܦܩܢ ܐܡܝܢ ܡܢ ܗܘܫܥ ܘܗܘ ܗܒܝ°	

JOHN III. 13.

Codex A.	Codex B.	Codex C.
a omit ܝܫܘܥ	13 ※ ܐܡܪ ܡܪܢ a ܝܫܘܥ : b ܘܐܝܬ ܠܐ ܣܠܩ	a omit ܝܫܘܥ
c add ܕܝ e ܚܘܝܐ	ܠܫܡܝܐ ܐܠܐ ܐ c ܕܢܚܬ ܡܢ ܫܡܝܐ	b ܘܠܐܝܬ
f ܟܕܒܟܘܪܐ	ܒܪܗ ܕܓܒܪܐ ܗܘܝܢ ܕܗܘܐ ܒܫܡܝܐ :	c add ܕܗܝ
g ܗܟܕܝ	14 ܘܗܝܟ ܡܫܐ ܕܐܪܝܡ ܒܡܕܒܪܐ e ܠܚܘܝܐ	e ܚܘܝܐ
h ܩܒܠܗܘ i ܠܟܠ	f ܟܕܒܟܢܐ g ܗܟܢܝܢ ܠܗ h ܩܒܠܗܘ ܕܢܬܪܘܡ	h ܟܒܠܗܘ
l ܚܝܝܢ m ܕܠܥܠܡ :	15 ܒܪܗ ܕܓܒܪܐ : i ܠܟܠ ܕܗܝܡܢ ܒܗ ܕܡܗܝܡܢ	
n ܠܥܠܡܐ	16 ܟܢ ܗܟܐ k ܠܗ l ܚܝܝ m ܕܠܥܠܡ : g ܗܟܢܝܢ ܓܝܪ	k omit ܠܗ l ܚܝܐܝܢ
o ܝܗܒ q ܝܗܒܗ	ܪܚܡ ܐܠܗܐ n ܠܥܠܡܐ ܕܠܒܪܗ ܝܚܝܕܝܗ	
r ܚܝܝܢ s ܕܠܥܠܡ	o ܝܗܒ : ܕܟܠ ܡܢ ܕܡܗܝܡܢ ܒܗ p ܠܐ q ܝܐܒܕ :	o ܝܗܒ p omit ܠܐ
t ܥܠܡ u ܠܥܠܡܐ	17 ܐܠܐ ܢܗܐ ܠܗ r ܚܝܝ s ܕܠܥܠܡ : ܠܐ ܓܝܪ	q ܝܐܒܕ r ܚܝܐܝܢ
w ܥܠܡܐ	t ܫܠܚ ܐܠܗܐ ܠܒܪܗ u ܠܥܠܡܐ : ܐܠܐ ܕܢܚܝܐ	s ܕܠܥܠܡ u ܠܥܠܡܐ
x omit ܥܠܡ	w ܥܠܡܐ ܒܐܝܕܗ : : : : x ܥܠܡ	x omit ܥܠܡ

CLX.

JOHN XIX. 6—35.

ܐܘܪܟܣܝܣ ܗܘܐ ܦܢ ܐܝܟܠ ܐܬܐܒܝ ܐܡܝܢ
ܒܘܟܪܗ ܐܦܠܘܢ ܗܘܝܐ ܬܬܬܐ ܫܒܘ ܫܒܗ

Codex B.

ܒܪ̈ ܐܠܦܝܣܢ ܗܘܐ ܡܢ ܝܘܡ. ܐܠܝܦܝܢ ܐܘܠܗ
ܐܝܟܐ ܕܟܬܝܒ ܘܗܕܐ ܠܝܘܡ ܐܪܒܥ ܒܫ ܐܠܦܘܕܐܘܣ Mat. XXVII.
1 ܡܢ ܨܦܪ ܡܬܟܢܫܝܢ : [x]ܘܒܬܪܗ ܦܫܘܪܝܐ : ܐܬܚܫܒܘ
ܪܝܫ ܟܗܢܝܐ ܘܦܪ̈ܝܫܝܐ ܠܟܠ ܥܡܐ[y]
ܕܝܗܘܕܝܐ ܥܠܘܗܝ[x] : ܘܐܬܝܗ ܠܡܬܠ [c]ܕܝܢ [z]ܦܝܠܛܘܣ : Jno. XIX.
6 [a]ܟܕ [b]ܚܙܐ [c]ܕܝܢ ܘܐܡܪܝܢ [d]ܨܠܘܒ [d]ܨܠܘܒ.
ܥܠܘܗܝ : ܘܐܡܪ ܠܗܘܢ [z]ܦܝܠܛܘܣ [f]ܣܒܘ
ܥܠܘܗܝ ܐܢܬܘܢ [g]ܘܨܠܘܒܘ ܥܠܘܗܝ ܐܢܐ ܠܐ ܐܫܟܚ ܠܗ
7 ܐܢܐ [h]ܡܫܟܚ ܒܗ [i]ܥܠܠܐ : ܘܐܡܪܘ [k]ܕܝܢ
9 [l]ܝܗܘܕܝܐ ܘܐܡܪܘ ܠܗ : ܢܡܘܣ [m]ܘܐܡܪܘ
ܠܝܫܘܥ ܡܢ ܗܢ ܐܢܬ : [n]ܘܐܡܪܘ ܝܫܘܥ
10 [o]ܕܝܢ [p]ܐܓܝܒܗ ܠܐ [q]ܝܗܒ ܠܗ : [r]ܘܐܡܪ ܠܗ
ܕܝܢ [z]ܦܝܠܛܘܣ ܠܝ [s]ܠܝܬ [t]ܐܢܬ [s]ܡܡܠܠ[u] : ܠܝܬ
ܐܢܬ [w]ܝܕܥ ܕܐܝܬ ܫܘܠܛܢ ܕܨܠܘܒܟ ܘܫܪܝܟ :
11 [x]ܘܫܘܠܛܢ ܐܝܬ ܕܡܫܒܩܟ ܘܫܪܝܟ : [y]ܘܐܓܝܒ[v]
ܝܫܘܥ ܘܐܡܪ ܠܗ : ܠܝܬ ܠܟ [a]ܫܘܠܛܢܐ
[b]ܥܠܝ ܐܘܦ ܠܐ ܚܕܐ : ܐܠܐ ܠܐ [c]ܝܗܒ
13 ܠܟ ܡܢ ܠܥܠ : ܐܘ [z]ܦܝܠܛܘܣ ܟܕ ܫܡܥ
ܡܠܝܢ ܗܠܝܢ : [d]ܐܦܩܗ ܠܝܫܘܥ ܠܒܪܐ ܘܝܬܒ
ܠܒܪ : ܘܝܬܒ ܥܠ [e]ܒܝܡܐ ܕܐܬܪܐ [f]ܕܡܬ
ܕܡܬܩܪܐ [g]ܫܘܥܐ [h]ܕܟܐܦܐ : [i]ܒܥܒܪܐܝܬ [j]ܕܝܢ
14 [k]ܓܒܬܐ : ܘܗܘܬ [l] [m]ܥܪܘܒܬܐ [n]ܕܦܨܚܐ : [o]ܗܘ
ܕܝܢ ܗܟܢ ܫܬ ܫܥܝܢ : [p]ܘܗܘ ܐܡܪ [q]ܠܝܗܘܕܝܐ
15 ܗܐ ܡܠܟܟܘܢ : [r]ܘܗܢܘܢ ܕܝܢ ܗܘܘ ܐܡܪܝܢ
ܐܪܝܡ ܐܪܝܡ ܨܠܘܒ ܠܗ : ܘܐܡܪ ܠܗܘܢ
[s]ܕܝܢ [z]ܦܝܠܛܘܣ ܠܡܠܟܟܘܢ [t]ܐܨܠܘܒ ܐܝܟܢܐ[u]
[s]ܕܝܢ [w]ܪܝܫ ܟܗܢܝܐ ܐܡܪܝܢ ܠܝܬ ܠܢ [x]ܡܠܟܐ
16 ܐܠܐ ܩܣܪ : [y]ܘܟܕܝܢ ܐܘ ܫܠܡ ܠܗ
ܠܗܘܢ [a]ܕܢܨܛܠܒ : ܒܪ ܐܘ ܕܒܪܘ ܠܗ
ܠܝܫܘܥ [b] [c]ܕܝܢ ܐܦܩܘܗܝ ܟܕ ܛܥܝܢ ܨܠܝܒܗ :
17 ܘܢܦܩ ܠܗ ܢܦܩ ܠܗܘܢ[d] ܐܬܪܐ ܕܡܬܩܪܐ

Codex A.

[x] *omit* . . . ܘܒܬܪܗ
. . . ܐܬܝܗ :

[c] *omit* ܕܝܢ

[a] ܟܕ [b] ܚܙܘ

[c] *omit* ܕܝܢ [d] ܨܠܘܒ.

[f] ܣܒܘ

[h] ܡܫܟܚ

[i] ܥܠܠܐ [k] *omit* ܕܝܢ

[l] ܝܗܘܕܝܐ

[m] ܘܐܡܪܘ [n] ܘܐܡܪܘ

[q] ܝܗܒ

[s] ܠܝܬܟ [t] *omit* ܐܢܬ

[u] ܡܡܠܠ

[b] ܥܠܝ [c] ܝܗܒ

[d] ܐܦܩܗ

[f] ܕܝܢ [g] ܫܘܥܐ

[h] ܕܟܐܦܐ

[i] ܒܥܒܪܐܝܬ

[k] ܓܒܬܐ

[m] ܥܪܘܒܬܗ

[o] ܗܘ [p] ܘܗܘܐ

[q] ܠܝܗܘܕܝܐ

[r] ܘܗܢܘܢ [s] *omit* ܕܝܢ

[u] *add* ܐܢܬܘܢ

[w] ܪܝܫ

[x] ܡܠܟ [y] ܘܟܕ

[b] *add* ܠܐܣܛܪܛܝܘܛܐ

[c] *omit* ܕܝܢ

Codex C.

[y] *add* ܕܝܗܘܕܝܐ

[c] *omit* ܕܝܢ

[z] ܦܝܠܛܘܣ :

[b] ܚܙܘ [d] ܨܠܘܒ

[f] ܣܒܘ [g] ܘܨܠܘܒܘ

[i] ܥܠܠܐ [k] *omit* ܕܝܢ

[l] ܝܗܘܕܝܐ [m] ܘܐܡܪ

[n] ܘܐܡܪ [o] *omit* ܕܝܢ

[p] ܐܓܝܒܗ [q] ܝܗܒ

[r] ܐܡܪ [z] ܦܝܠܛܘܣ

[s] ܠܝܬܟ [t] *omit* ܐܢܬ

[w] ܝܕܥ [x] ܘܫܘܠܛܢ

[y] *omit* ܘ [v] *add* ܕܝܢ

[a] ܫܘܠܛܢ [b] ܥܠܝ

[e] ܒܝܡܐ

[i] ܒܥܒܪܐܝܬ

[j] ܕܐܝܬ [l] *add* ܕܝܢ

[m] ܥܪܘܒܬܐ

[n] ܕܦܨܚܐ [p] ܘܗܘܐ

[s] *omit* ܕܝܢ [t] ܨܠܘܒ

[x] ܡܠܟ

[y] ܟܕܝܢ

[a] ܕܢܨܛܠܒ

[c] *omit* ܕܝܢ

[d] ܠܗܘܢ

Codex A.

[f] *omit* ܕܝ
[g] ܒܒܪ̇ܐܣܛܐ
[h] ܒܡܢܓܒ̇ܝܬܐ
[i] ܠܗܘ ܩ̈ܠܝܠܩܘܣ
[k] ܘܐܪ̈ܝܡܘ [l] ܒܬܪ̈ܝܗ
[m] ܕܝܘ̈ܕܝܢ [o] ܠܗܕ̄
[p] ܠܡܕܝܢܬܐ
[q] ܕܐܝܬܠܝܒ
[s] ܒܒܪ̇ܐܣܛܐ
[t] ܘܪܘܡܐ̇ܣܛܐ
[u] ܘܗ̇ܠܝܢܣܛܐ
[w] ܡܐܡ̈ܢܝܢ
[x] ܕܐܒܡܢܗ [y] ܡ̇ܪܝܒ̇ܣ
[z] ܕܩܘܠܝܩ̈ܘܣ
[a] ܘܠܬܠܡܝܕܝܐ
[b] *omit* ܐܐ [c] ܐܗܘ
[d] ܕܡܣܒܒ̇ [j] ܘܒܬܪ̇ܝܢ
[f] ܬܠܡܝܕܝܐ
[g] ܐܡ̇ܝܢ [h] ܕܒ̇ܪ
[i] ܠܕܝܠܗ
[k] *add* ܕܗ̇ܘܐ [l] ܒܠܘ
[m] ܡ̇ܫܠܛ [n] *omit* ܗܘ
[o] ܘܐܪ̇ܝܢ [p] *omit* ܕܝ
[a] *omit* ܘ [b] ܒܪܘܒ̇ܬܐ
[q] ܦܓ̇ܪ̈ܐ
[s] ܪ̈ܓܠܘܗ̄
[t] ܪܘܡܝܢ
[u] ܘܕܫ̇ܪܝܐ [v] *add* ܕܝ
[w] ܥܠ ܡܪܐ
[x] ܪ̈ܓܠܘܗܝ
[y] ܒܠܘܢܟ̇ܝܬܐ [z] ܘܡܢ

Codex B.

ܦܪܘܣܬܐ : ܐܝܟ ܕܗܘ [e]ܡܬܬܡܪ [f]ܕܝ [g]ܒܒܪܝܣܛܐ
18 ܒܓܠܓܠܛܝܐ : ܗ̄ܘ ܕܝܠܗ ܗܘܬ : ܘܒܢܝܗ
ܣܘܪܝܢ ܬܪܝܢ ܚܕ ܡܢ ܒܐ ܘܚܕ ܡܢ ܒܐ :
19 [h]ܒܡܢܓܒܐ ܕܝ ܠܡܕܝܢܬܐ ܫܡܗ ܀ ܘܡܬܒ ܐܘܦ
[i]ܩ̈ܠܝܩܘܣ ܠܗܘ[i] [k]ܘܐܣܩܘܢܗ ܝܬܗ ܥܠ ܝܠܕܐ :
ܗܘܐ ܕܝ [l]ܒܬܪܗ ܒܗ ܫܡܗ ܢܘܪܐ ܡܠܟܘܬܗ̄
20 [m]ܕܝܘܕܝܢ : ܠܗ [n]ܕܝ [o]ܠܗܕܝܢ ܠܗܢܐ ܦܪܘ
ܣܛܝܢ ܡܢ ܢܘܕܝܐ ܕܗܘܐ ܦܪܝܒ ܐܬܪܐ
[p]ܠܡܕܝܢܬܐ : ܗ̄ܘ [q]ܕܐܝܬܠܝܒ ܡܪܐ ܫܡܗ :
ܘܗܘܐ [r]ܒܬܪܒ [s]ܒܒܪܐܣܛܐ [t]ܘܪܘܡܐܣܛܐ
25 [u]ܘܗܠܝܣܛܐ : ܗܘܝ [v]ܕܝ [w]ܡܐܝܡܢܝܢ ܗ̄ܘ
ܕܝܠܗܘܢ ܕܡܪܐ ܫܡܗ ܀ ܐܝܟ ܗܢܐ ܘܐܝܬܘܗܝ
[x]ܕܐܝܡܢܗ : [y]ܘܡܪܝܢܘܣ [z]ܕܩܘܠܘܢ̈ܝܐ ܘܡܪܝܢܘܣ
26 ܡܓܕܠܝܬܐ : ܡܪܐ ܫܡܗ ܒܗ ܚܒܝܒܐ ܠܐܝܠܗ :
[a]ܘܠܬܠܡܝܕܐ [b]ܐܐ [c]ܗܘ [d]ܕܡܣܒܒ [e]ܡܐܝܟ :
27 ܐܡܪ ܠܐܝܠܗ ܐܬܬܐ ܗܐ ܒܪܝܟ : [j]ܘܒܬܪܝܢ
ܐܡܪ ܠܝܬܗ [f]ܬܠܡܝܕܐ ܗܐ [g]ܐܡܝܢ ܘܡܢ
ܝܬܗ ܫܡܥܐ [h]ܕܒܝܪ ܝܬܗ ܬܠܡܝܕܐ [i]ܠܕܝܠܗ :
28 ܘܒܬܪܝܢ ܫܡܥܐ ܡܪܐ ܫܡܗ [k] [l]ܒܠܘܐ
30 [m]ܡܫܠܝܛ : [n]ܗܘ [o]ܐܘܪܝܢ ܪܫܗ [p]ܕܝ ܘܡܫܡܪ
31 ܪܘܫܗ : ܒܗ ܕܝ ܡܫܡܪ ܪܘܚܐ : [a]ܘܡܕܝܢܐ ܐܘ̄
ܡܢ ܠܚܠܠ ܕܗܘܬ [b]ܒܪܘܒܬܐ ܕܠܐ ܡܬܪܘ̄
[q]ܦܓܪܐ ܥܠ ܝܠܕܐ ܒܥܘܒܬܐ . ܒܗܘ ܡܢ
[r]ܩ̈ܠܝܩܘܣ ܕܬܪܝܢܘ̄ [s]ܪ̈ܓܠܘܗ̄ ܘܬܪܥܘ̄ :
ܗܘܐ ܠܐ ܘܗܒܐ ܕܬܗ ܥܘܒܬܐ ܗܝ ܪܒܐ :
32 ܘܐܬܐ ܘܬܒܪܘ [t]ܪܘܡܝܢ ܪ̈ܓܠܘܗܝ ܕܡܫܝܚܐ
33 [u]ܘܕܫܪܝܐ ܕܗܠܝܢ ܕܐܝܬܠܝܗܘ ܒܗܘܢ : ܘܒܗ[v]
ܐܬܘ [w]ܠܡܕܝܢܬܐ ܫܡܗ : ܥܡܝ ܕܫܡܗ ܗܘܬ
34 ܒܒܪ ܕܡܢܬ : ܠܐ ܬܒܪܘ [x]ܪ̈ܓܠܘܗܝ ܐܠܐ
ܚܕ ܡܢ [t]ܪܘܡܝܢ [y]ܒܠܘܢܟܝܬܐ ܢܩܫ ܥܒܕ ܝܬܗ
35 ܠܒܠܒܗ ܘܢܦܩ ܥܒܐ ܐܡܪ [z]ܘܡܢ : ܘܗܕܝܢ

Codex C.

[e] *omit* ܡܬܬܡܪ
[f] *omit* ܕܝ
[g] ܒܒܪܐܣܛܐ
[h] ܒܡܢܓܒܝܬܐ
[i] ܠܗܘ ܒܠܝܩܘܣ
[k] ܘܐܣܩܘܗ
[m] ܕܝܘܕܝܢ
[n] *omit* ܕܝ
[r] ܒܬܪܒ
[s] ܒܒܪܐܣܛܐ
[t] ܘܪܘܡܐܣܛܐ
[u] ܘܗܠܝܣܛܐ
[v] *omit* ܕܝ
[w] ܕܐܡܢܝܢ
[y] ܡܪܝܢܘܣ [z] ܕܩܘܠܝܩܘܣ
[a] ܘܠܬܠܡܝܕܝܐ
[b] *omit* ܐܐ [c] ܐܗܘ
[e] *add* ܠܗ
[f] ܬܠܡܝܕܝܐ
[g] ܐܡܝܢ [h] ܕܒܪ
[k] *add* ܕܗܘܐ
[m] ܡܫܠܛ [n] *omit* ܗܘ
[o] ܘܐܪܝܢ
[p] *omit* ܕܝ
[b] ܒܪܘܒܬܐ
[r] ܒܠܝܩܘܣ
[v] *add* ܕܝ
[w] ܥܠ ܡܪܐ
[z] ܘܡܢ

Codex A.

[a]ܘܡܬܒܥܝܐ
[d] *add* ܫܠܡ

Codex B.

ܕܢܒܝܐ ܐܘܣܝܕ [a]ܘܡܬܒܥܝܐ ܐܝܬ [b]ܗܘܝ
[c]ܡܫܬܘܕܥܬܗ [d] : : : : :

In totis tribus codicibus desunt vv. 8, 12, deest pars v. 7, pars v. 9 quoque.

Desunt vv. 21, 22, 23, 24.

Deest v. 29, deest pars vv. 28, 30 quoque.

Codex C.

[a]ܘܡܬܒܥܝܐ [b]ܗܘ
[c]ܡܫܘܕܥܘ

CLXI.

ܩܒܠܬ ܒܒܪ ܚܒܪ ܐܝܠܝܢ ܐܬܠܗܘܢ ܗܘܝ
ܐܬܦܪܣܘ ܦܝ ܐܘܩܒܗ ܐܪܒܥܗ ܒܒܪ
ܐܠܗܘܬ: ܚܕ ܒܒܪ ܚܕ ܐܝܠܝܢ ܐܬܠܗܘܢ ܬܠܬ
ܚܕ ܦܝ ܐܝܩܘܢ ܒܪܘܬ ܢܘܚܐ ܐܠܗܝܬܐ
ܦܝ ܬܠܬ ܗܘ ܒܪܫܝܬ ܡܢ ܐܝܠܘܠ ܐܬܠܗܘܢ
ܡܢ ܢܦܩ ܐܠܠܝܢ ܦܝ ܡܠܘܬܐ ܠܦܪܘܣ ܦܝ
ܫܬܝܢ ܐܪܒܥܗ ܘܒܪܫܝܬ ܬܕܒܪ ܐܠܗܝܬܗܘܢ
ܡܪܬܝ ܬܘܠܗ: ܐܬܠܗܘܢ ܩܒܠܬܪ ܩܒܠܬ ܡܢ
ܒܪܢܬ ܡܬܐܘܩ ܬܡܢܝܗ ܘܒܪܫܝܬ ܗܘܐ ܬܕܒܪ
ܐܠܒܪܝܬܐ ܡܢ ܡܬܐܝ:

MATT. XI. 27—30.

Codex A.

[CCCCXI.]

[d] *omit* ܘܒܝܬܗ ܦܪܘܣܐ
[e]ܠܬܠܡܝܕܘܗܝ
[f]ܐܬܡܣܪܬ [g]ܚܟܡ
[a] *add* ܠܐ
[d]ܘܦܟܝܢܝܢ
[e]ܡܘܩܠܝܢ
[f]ܢܝܪ [g]ܘܠܦܘ
[i]ܢܝܚܐ
[k]ܒܣܝܡ
[l] *omit* ܫܠܡ

Codex B.

[d]ܘܒܝܬܗ ܦܪܘܣܐ: ܐܡܪ ܡܪܢܐ [e]ܠܬܠܡܝܕܘܗܝ:
27 ܟܘܠܐ [f]ܐܬܡܣܪ ܠܝ ܡܢ ܠܘܬ ܐܒܐ: ܘܐܢܫ
ܠܐ [g]ܡܚܟܡ ܠܒܪܐ ܐܠܐ ܐܢ ܐܒܐ: ܘܐܘܦ
[a]ܠܐܒܐ [b]ܐܢܫ ܠܐ [g]ܡܚܟܡ [c] ܐܠܐ ܐܢ
ܒܪܐ: ܘܠܡܢ ܕܨܒܐ ܒܪܐ ܕܝܓܠܐ ܗܘ ܠܗ:
28 ܐܬܘ ܠܘܬܝ ܟܘܠ ܗܠܝܢ ܕܠܐܝܢ [d]ܘܦܟܝܢܝܢ
29 [e]ܡܘܩܠܝܢ ܘܐܢܐ ܡܢܝܚ ܠܟܘܢ: ܫܒܘ [f]ܢܝܪܝ
ܥܠܝܟܘܢ [g]ܘܠܦܘ ܡܢܝ ܕܐܢܐ ܢܝܚ ܘܡܟܝܟ
ܒܠܒܝ: [h]ܘܐܬܘܢ ܡܫܟܚܝܢ [i]ܢܝܚ ܠܢܦܫܬܟܘܢ:
30 ܢܝܪܝ [h] ܓܝܪ [k]ܡܒܣܡ ܘܡܘܒܠܝ ܩܠܝܠܐ ܐܝܬ
ܗܝ: [l]ܫܠܡ.

Codex C.

[f]ܐܬܡܣܪܬ
[a]ܠܐ ܐܒܐ
[b]ܐܢܫ - [c] *add* ܠܗ
[e]ܡܘܩܠܝܢ
[g]ܘܠܦܘ
[h] *omit* ܘܐܬܘܢ . . . ܢܝܪܝ . . .
[k]ܒܣܝܡ
[l] *omit* ܫܠܡ

Codex A.	Codex B.	Codex C.

Codex B.

CLXII.

Luke XXI. 12.

ܬܫܪܝܢ ܐܠܘܠܐ ܚܕ ܘܬܠܬܝܢ ܝܘܡܐ : ܬܐܝܢ
ܝܘܡ ܦܢܚ ܒܬܪܐ ܠܡܪܝܢ ܡܒܬܪܐ ܐܬܠܘܒ
ܝܘܡ ܐܬܠܝܢ ܐܦܝܣܩܘܦܗ ܘܦܝ ܫܠܝܚܐ ܝܘܡ
ܬܪܝܢ ܐܠܘܠܐ ܡܪܝ ܬܘܒܐ : ܐܬܠܘܒ
ܚܕ ܐܠܬܝܢ ܘܦܝ ܫܒܥܐ ܒܝܪ ܐܠܘܢܣܝܢ
ܫܪܒܐ ܘܪܘܫܐ ܡܢ ܠܘܩܐ : ᵛܘܒܝܬܗ ܡܪܘܫܐ
12 ܐܡܪ ܡܪܢܐ ʷܝܫܘܥ : ˣܩܕܡ ܢܪܡܘܢ ܥܠܝܟܘܢ
ʸܐܝܕܝܗܘܢ ᶻܒܒܝܫܬܐ ᵃܘܪܕܦܘܢ ᵇܝܬܟܘܢ
ᶜܘܡܫܠܡܘܢ ᵈܠܟܘܢ ᵉܕܝܢ ᶠܒܟܢܫܬܐ ᵍܘܒܝܬܐܣܝܪܐ
ʰܘܬܝܬܘܢ ܠܩܕܡ ܡܠܟܝܢ : ⁱܘܠܩܕܡ ʲܗܓܡܘܢܝܢ
13 ᵏܡܛܠ ܫܡܝ : ˡܬܗܘܐ ܕܝܢ ܗܠܝܢ ܠܟܘܢ
14 ܠܣܗܕܘ : ܐܣܝܡܘ ܗܘ ᵐܒܠܒܒܟܘܢ ܕܠܐ ܡܢ
ܩܕܡ ܬܗܘܘܢ ܡܬܪܢܝܢ ᵒܕܬܬܦܠܓܘܢ ᵃܐܦܘܠܘܓܝܐ :
15 ᵖܐܢܐ ᵠܝܬܠ ܠܟܘܢ ˢܦܘܡ ᵗܕܝܢ ܘܚܟܡܬܐ :
ܕܠܐ ᵘܝܟܠܘܢ ᵛܡܩܝܡܝܢ ܐܦ ܐܡܪܝܢ ʳܠܩܘܒܠܗ :
ܗܠܝܢ ʷܕܗܘܝܢ ܡܩܝܡܝܢ ˣܠܩܘܒܠܟܘܢ : ʸܐܬܘܢ
16 ܬܬܡܣܪܘܢ ܕܝܢ ܐܘܦ ᶻܡܢ ܐܒܗܬܟܘܢ ܘܡܢ
ᵃܐܚܝܟܘܢ ܘܡܢ ܩܪܝܒܝܟܘܢ : ܘܡܢ ܪܚܡܝܟܘܢ
17 ᵇܘܝܩܛܠܘܢ ܡܢܟܘܢ : ܘܐܬܘܢ ܗܘܝܢ ܡܣܢܝܢ
18 ܡܢ ܟܘܠܐ ᵏܡܛܠ ܫܡܝ : ᶜܘܣܥܪܐ ܕܝܢ ܡܢ
19 ܪܫܝܟܘܢ ܠܐ ᵈܬܐܒܕ : ᵉܒܣܝܒܪ ᶠܒܡܣܒܪܢܘܬܟܘܢ
ܐܬܘܢ ܩܢܝܢ ᵍܐܘܦ ʰܠܢܦܫܬܟܘܢ :

Codex A.

[CLXXXIV.]

ᵛ *omit* ܘܒܝܬܗ ܡܪܘܫܐ
ʷ *omit* ܝܫܘܥ
ˣ *add* ܡܢ ܐܢܫܝܢ
ʸ ܐܝܕܝܗܘܢ
ᶻ *omit* ܒܒܝܫܬܐ
ᵃ ܘܪܕܦܘܢ
ᵇ *omit* ܝܬܟܘܢ
ᶜ ܘܡܫܠܡܘܢ
ᵈ ܝܬܟܘܢ ᵉ *omit* ܕܝܢ
ᵍ ܘܒܝܬ ܐܣܝܪܐ
ʲ ܗܓܡܘܢܝܢ
ᵏ ܡܛܠ ˡ ܬܗܘܐ
ᵒ ܕܬܬܦܠܓܘܢ
ᵃ ܐܦܘܠܘܓܝܐ
ᵖ *add* ܒܪ ᵠ ܝܬܠ
ˢ ܦܘܡܐ ᵗ *omit* ܕܝܢ
ᵘ ܝܟܠܘܢ
ˣ ܠܩܘܒܠܟܘܢ
ʸ *omit* ܐܬܘܢ
ᵇ ܘܝܩܛܠܘܢ
ᵏ ܡܛܠ ᶜ ܘܣܥܪܐ
ᵈ ܬܐܒܕ ᵉ ܡܣܒܪ
ᶠ ܒܡܣܒܪܢܘܬܟܘܢ
ᵍ *omit* ܐܘܦ
ʰ ܢܦܫܬܟܘܢ

Codex B.

(deest.)

Codex A.

[CLXXXV.]

Luke XI. 29—33.

ܘܐܚܕ ܘܒܟܝܢ ܬܕܟܪ ܐܠܟܝܢ ܗܐܟܝܢ (*sic*)
29 ܡܢ ܠܘܩܐ ܘܒܝܬܗ ܡܪܘܫܐ ܘܟܕ ܗܘܘ

Codex C.

(deest)

Codex B.	Codex A.	Codex C.
(*deest*)		(*deest*)

ܐܦܠܘܩܐ ܬܟܢܫܘܢ ܥܘܪܝ ܡܢܗ ܢܫܦܘܢ ܐܡܪ
ܗܢܘܢ ܕܐܪ ܕܘ ܚܝܥ ܐܝܬܗܘ: ܐܬܘ ܢܟܒܫ
ܘܐܬܘ ܠܐ ܡܬܢܣܒ ܠܗ ܥܠܬܐ ܐܬܘܗ ܕܝܩܪܢ
30 ܗܘܝ ܬܪܝܢ ܠܒܪ ܕܗܘܐ ܢܦܩ ܐܬܐ ܠܒܬܘܟ:
ܗܘܢ ܢܗܒ ܒܪܗ ܕܝܒܪܐ ܐܬ ܠܗܘܢ
31 ܕܐܪ: ܡܠܟܘܬܐ ܕܫܡܝܐ ܬܦܫܛ ܒܕܝܢܐ ܒܗ
ܒܒܪܘܝ ܕܗܘܢ ܕܐܪ ܘܬܫܒ ܠܬܦܩܘܢ:
ܕܒܬܬ ܒܡ ܦܢܩܝܗ ܕܐܪܥܐ ܕܬܒܚܦܠ
ܣܒܚܬܗ ܕܥܦܠܒܚܦܢ: ܘܗܐ ܡܢܬܪ ܒܡ
32 ܥܦܠܒܚܦܢ ܒܐ: ܠܒܪܝܐ ܕܝܒܘܐ ܝܦܘܩܘܢ
ܒܕܝܢܐ ܒܗ ܗܕܡ ܕܐܪ ܘܝܫܬܒܘܢ ܢܬܗ:
ܠܒܕܝܠ ܕܬܗܘ ܒܐܒܪܘܬܗ ܕܝܩܪܢ: ܘܗܐ
33 ܡܢܬܪ ܡܢ ܢܘܝܢ ܒܐ: ܠܝܬ ܐܝܬ ܡܕܠܝܡ
ܒܘܝܡ ܘܢܗܒ ܠܗ ܒܡܠܚܘܪܝ ܘܠܐ ܬܦܣܬ
ܡܘܕܐ: ܐܠܐ ܒܠ ܡܢܪܬܐ ܕܗܠܝܡ ܟܠܝܡ
ܫܡܚܘܢ ܢܦܘܪܗ ܥܠܡ

[CXCVII.]

Matt. XIII. 44—54.

ܬܐܠܬ ܐܠܦܪܝܣ ܕܐܝܘܣܝܘܣ ܐܠܩܕܝܣ ܡܢ
44 ܡܢܬܘܣ: ܐܡܪ ܡܪܢ ܡܕܢ ܒܬܠܬܐ ܕܡܒܝܐ
ܗܝ ܡܠܟܘܬܐ ܕܫܡܝܐ ܠܣܝܡܐ ܠܒܝܬܪܐ
ܒܚܩܠܐ: ܗܘܐ ܕܐܫܟܚܗ ܒܪܢܫ ܘܛܫܝܗ:
ܘܡܢ ܚܕܘܬܗ ܗܘ ܐܙܠ ܘܡܙܒܢ ܒܠ ܡܐ
45 ܕܗܘܐ ܠܗ ܘܙܒܢ ܢܬܗ ܠܒܪܐ: ܬܘܒ ܕܡܝܐ
ܗܝ ܡܠܟܘܬܐ ܕܫܡܝܐ ܠܬܓܪ ܬܒܥ ܕܡܒܐ
46 ܡܪܓܠܝܬܐ ܛܒܢ: ܒܕ ܕܝ ܐܫܟܚ ܚܕܐ ܡܪܓܠܝ
ܦܛܝܬܐ ܕܡܢ ܐܙܠ ܘܙܒܢ ܒܠ ܡܐ ܕܗܘܐ
47 ܠܗ ܘܙܒ ܢܬܗ: ܬܘܒ ܕܡܝܐ ܗܝ ܡܠܟܘܬܐ

Codex B.	Codex A.	Codex C.
(deest)	ܕܢܡܘܣܐ ܠܡܪܕܐ ܕܐܬܡܪܚܡܬ ܠܟܘ ܒܡܟܐ ܀	(deest)
	48 ܘܡܢ ܟܘܠ ܓܒܪ ܒܢܫܐ ܀ ܘܟܕ ܐܬܚܙܝܬ ܐܘܫܦܐ	
	ܗܘܬ ܥܠ ܓܒܪܐ ܀ ܘܩܛܠܘ ܠܟܠܗܘܢ ܓܒܪ̈ܝܐ	
	49 ܠܡܬܝܢܗܘܢ ܘܩܛܠܝܢ ܥܒܕ ܠܒܝ ܀ ܗܟܢ	
	ܗܘܐ ܒܥܒܕܗܘܢ ܕܟܠܡܐ ܢܩܡܘ ܡ̈ܠܐܟܝܐ	
	50 ܘܡܦ̈ܪܫܝܢ ܒܢ̈ܝܐ ܡܢ ܟܢ ܬ̈ܕܡܝܐ ܀ ܘܪ̈ܚܡܝܢ	
	ܠܗܘܢ ܠܡܫܒܚܐ ܕܢܘܪܐ ܀ ܬܡܢ ܗܘܐ ܒܦܒܥܐ	
	51 ܘܣ̈ܘܣܘܬܗܘܢ ܕܒ̈ܢܝܢܐ ܀ ܘܐܡܪ ܠܗܘܢ ܡܪܝܐ	
	ܒܚܫܒ ܢܚܬܘܢ ܘܐܬܟܢܫܘܢ ܟܠܗܘܢ	
	52 ܒܟܠܗܘܢ ܐܡ̈ܪܝܢ ܠܗ ܐܝܢ ܀ ܐܡܪ ܠܗܘܢ	
	ܠܟܠܒ ܟܕ ܟܘܠ ܚܙܪ ܕܐܬܠܡܕ ܠܡܠܟܘܬܐ	
	ܕܫܡܝܐ ܕܡܟܐ ܗܘ ܠܒܝܬ ܡܪܐ ܟܐܝ ܕ	
	53 ܕܢܦܩܝܢ ܡܢ ܐܘܨܪܗ ܚ̈ܕܬܐ ܘܥ̈ܬܝܩܝܢ ܀ ܘܗܘܐ	
	ܟܕ ܫܠܡ ܡܪܐ ܒܫܘܦܗ ܡ̈ܠܝܢ ܡܬܠܝܐ ܢܦܩ ܡܢ	
	54 ܬܡܢ ܘܐܬܐ ܠܡܕܝܢܬܐ ܕܝܠܗ ܀ ܘܗܘܐ ܡܠܦ	
	ܠܗܘܢ ܒܟܢܫܬܗܘܢ	

[CC.]

John VIII. 1—11.

ܬܐܡܢ ܐܠܦܪܝܫܝܐ ܦܠܓܢܝܐ ܡܢ ܘܐܝܢܝܢܐ

1 ܘܐܙܠ ܝܫܘܥ ܠܛܘܪܐ ܕܙܝܬܐ

3 ܘܐܝܬܝܘ ܣܦܪ̈ܐ ܘܦܪ̈ܝܫܐ ܠܐܢܬܬܐ ܕܐܬܬܦܝܣܬ

ܠܡܘܕܡ ܡܪܝܐ ܒܫܦܘ ܐܬܬܐ ܕܐܬܬܦܝܣܬ

ܡܫܡܠܐ ܀ ܘܩܝܡܘ ܐܢܘܢܗ ܒܡܨܥܬܐ

4 ܘܐܡܪܝܢ ܠܗ ܡܠܦܢܐ ܗܕܐ ܐܬܬܐ ܟܕܘ

5 ܐܬܬܦܝܣܬ ܡܫܡܠܐ ܀ ܒܢܝܡܘܣܐ ܕܝܢ ܡܘܫܐ

ܦܩܕ ܘܒܘܐ ܪ̈ܓܡܝܢ ܠܟܠܗܝܢ ܕܟܠܝܢ ܀ ܐܬ

6 ܕܝܢ ܡܢܐ ܐܬ ܐܡܪ ܀ ܗܕܐ ܕܝܢ ܐܡܪ̈ܘ

ܡܢܣܝܢ ܠܗ ܕܢܗܘܐ ܠܗܘܢ ܡܢܐ ܕܢܐܟܠܘܢ

Codex B.	*Codex* A.	*Codex* C.
(*deest*)	ܢܬܗ: ܘܗܘܐ ܫܡܥܘܢ ܐܦܝܢ ܐܦܩܘܢ ܠܐܪܒܥܐ	(*deest*)
	7 ܘܗܘܐ ܒܬܪ ܒܐܝܓܒܗ ܒܐܪܒܥܐ :: ܒܡܚܐ	
	ܕܝ ܕܫܡܒܪܘ ܬܐܠܝܢ ܠܗ: ܒܡ ܬܠܬܐ ܐܦܩܘܢ	
	ܘܐܡܪ ܠܗܘܢ: ܗܢܘܢ ܡܒܗܘܢ ܕܠܐ ܐܫܡܥ:	
	8 ܗܘ ܡܒܐܢ ܝܕܥܐ ܒܠܝܠܗ ܒܝܒܫܐ: ܘܬܗܘܡ	
	ܐܒܝܢ ܐܦܩܘܢ ܘܗܘܐ ܒܬܪ ܒܐܪܒܥܐ ::	
	9 ܘܗܘܢܘܢ ܒܕ ܥܒܘ ܐܢܠܝܢ ܠܗܘܢ ܚܕ ܚܕ	
	ܠܒܝܬܗ: ܡܢ ܦܒܝܢܐ ܒܝܡܢܐ ܠܓܠܝܠܐ: ܘܐܝܬܥܒܕ	
	ܗܘ ܒܠܚܘܕܘܗܝ: ܘܐܬܬܐ ܗܘܬ ܡܐܡܢܐ	
	10 ܒܡܢ ܒܬܗ: ܘܬܠܐ ܒܪܡܗ ܡܢܪܐ ܝܫܘܥ	
	ܘܐܡܪ ܠܗ̇ ܐܬܬܐ ܗܘ ܗܘܢܘܢ: ܐܝܟ ܠܐ	
	11 ܫܒܩ ܢܬܒܝ: ܗܘ ܕܝ ܐܡܪܬ ܘܠܐ ܐܝܟ	
	ܡܪܝ: ܘܐܡܪ ܠܗ̇ ܡܪܢܐ ܝܫܘܥ: ܐܦܘ ܠܐ	
	ܐܝܢܐ ܠܝܬ ܐܝܢܐ ܡܚܝܒ ܠܝܒܕܝ: ܐܙܠܝ ܘܡܢ	
	ܟܕܘ ܠܐ ܬܗܘܝܢ ܡܚܛܝܐ	

Codex A.	*Codex* B.	
[CCXIII.]	CLXIII.	
	ܬܐܫܥܝ ܝܘܡ ܬܪܝܢ ܐܠܦܪܘܣ ܕܫܒܘܥܐ ܡܢ	
	ܫܠܝܚܐ ܐܓܦܠܘܣ ܐܘܠ ܚܕ ܡܢ ܠܗܘܢ ܬܠܡܝܕܘܗܝ	
	ܝܘܡ ܦܢ ܬܪܝܢ ܐܠܦܠ ܬܪܝܢ ܐܠܦܪܘܣ	
	ܠܗܘܢ: ܐܓܦܠܘܣ ܫܬܗ ܦܢ ܐܠܦܠ: ܬܠܬܗ	
	ܘܒܪܝܢ ܒܝܕ ܐܠܦܪܘܣ ܡܪܢ ܒܫܘܥ ܐܫܘ	
	ܐܪܒ: ܐܓܦܠܘܣ ܬܡܢܫܗ ܘܒܪܝܢ ܦܢ ܒܐܫܘܢ	
	ܐܠܦܠ ܫܡܫܗ ܘܒܪܝܢ ܝܘܡ ܬܪܝܢ ܐܠܦܪܘܣ	
	ܐܠܦܬܒܗ ܡܢ ܠܗܘܢ: ܘܗܘ ܝܘܡܪܐ ܠܒܘܠ	
	ܐܠܦܪܘܣ ܘܒܢܬܗ ܡܢܘܫܐ:	
	LUKE XII. 2—12.	
[b] *omit* ܕܝ	2 ܐܡܪ ܡܪܢܐ [a]ܠܬܠܡܝܕܘܗܝ: ܠܝܬ [b]ܕܝ ܟܣܝ	[a] ܠܬܠܡܝܕܘܗܝ

Codex A.

[e]ܣܘܠܩܗ
[f]ܐܬܐܡܪܘܢ
[g]ܕܐܠܗܘܬܐ [i]ܐܬܦܢܝܘ
[l]ܠܡܦܪܫܘܢ
[m]ܬܬܕܚܠܘܢ
[n]ܘܒܬܪܟܝܢ [p]ܕܚܠܘ
[q]ܗܘ ܡܢ [r] *omit*
[s]ܫܘܠܛܢܐ [u]ܐܝܟ
[v]ܐܡܪ ܐܢܐ
[w]ܫܒܥܐ [y]ܡܙܕܒܢܝܢ
[z]ܐܣܪܝܢ
[a]ܘܚܕܐ [b]ܡܢܗܘܢ
[d]ܕܪܫܟܘܢ
[l]ܟܠܗܘܢ [f]ܡܢܝܢ
[g]ܬܕܚܠܘܢ
ܕܝ ܕܟܠ [j] *add*
[l]ܡܠܐܟܘܗܝ
ܕܝ [m] *omit* [n]ܕܢܟܦܘܪ
[o]ܐܦ ܐܢܐ
[p]ܡܠܐܟܘܗܝ
[q]ܘܟܠ ܕܝ [t] *add*
[u]ܕܢܓܕܦ
[v]ܠܟܢܘܫܬܐ
[w]ܪܫܘܬܐ
[x]ܘܫܘܠܛܢܘܬܐ
[y]ܬܬܦܢܘܢ
[a]ܐܦܠܘܓܝܐ
[b]ܬܬܦܢܘܢ [c]ܬܠܦ
[d]ܕܬܬܦܢܘܢ

Codex B.

ܒܫܡܐ ܕܠܐ [c]ܡܬܓܠܝܐ : ܘܠܐ [d]ܦܬܓܡܢ ܕܠܐ
3 ܡܬܝܕܥܝܢ : [e]ܣܘܠܩܗ ܗܢܐ ܕܒܫܡܠܝܐ [f]ܐܡܪܘ
ܐܬܘܢ [f] ܒܢܝܡܘܗܝ ܗܘ ܡܫܬܡܥܝܢ : ܘܗܢܐ
[g]ܕܐܠܗܘܬܐ ܡܫܬܠܛܘܢ ܒܬܘܕܝܬܐ : [h]ܘܥܠ
4 ܐܦܢܝܐ [i]ܐܬܦܢܝ ܘܒܥܝܘ ܫܘܐܠܐ : ܐܡܪ
ܐܢܐ ܠܟܘܢ [k]ܕܝ [l]ܠܡܦܪܫܘ ܠܟ ܠܐ [m]ܬܬܕܚܠܘܢ
ܡܢ ܗܠܝܢ ܕܬܠܝܢ ܒܦܓܪܐ : [n]ܘܒܬܪܟܝܢ ܠܝܬ
5 ܠܗܘܢ ܒܘܠܡ ܡܕܡ ܕܢܒܥܘܢ : [o]ܡܕܡ ܐܢܐ
ܠܟܘܢ ܕܝ ܡܢ ܡܢ [m]ܬܕܚܠܘܢ : [p]ܕܚܠܘ ܡܢ
[q]ܗܘܝܘ ܕ[r]ܡܢ ܒܬܪ ܕܗܘ ܩܛܠ ܐܝܬ ܠܗ [s]ܫܘܠܛܢܐ
ܕܢܪܡܐ [t]ܒܓܗܢܐ : [u]ܐܝ [v]ܐܡܪܢܐ[v] ܠܟܘܢ
6 ܡܢ ܗܘܝܘ [p]ܕܚܠܘ : ܠܐ [w]ܫܒܥܐ [x]ܦܪܬܝܢ [y]ܡܙܕܒܢܝܢ
ܒܬܪܝܢ [z]ܐܣܪܝܢ [a]ܘܚܕ [b]ܡܢܗܘܢ ܠܐ [c]ܦܓܥܐ
7 ܩܕܡ ܐܠܗܐ : ܐܠܐ ܐܦ ܣܥܪܐ [d]ܕܪܫܟܘܢ
[l]ܟܠܗܝܢ [e]ܡܢܝܢܢ [f]ܗܝܢ : ܠܐ [g]ܬܕܚܠܘܢ
8 ܡܢ ܣܓܝܐ [h]ܦܪܬܝܢ [i]ܐܢܬܘܢ ܡܝܬܪܝܢ[i] : ܐܡܪ
ܐܢܐ ܠܟܘܢ [j]ܡܢ ܕܢܘܕܐ ܒܝ ܩܕܡ ܒܢܝܢܫܐ
ܐܦ ܒܪܗ ܕܐܢܫܐ ܢܘܕܐ [k]ܒܗ ܩܕܡ [l]ܡܠܐܟܘܗܝ
9 [m]ܕܝ ܕܐܠܗܐ : ܘܡܢ [n]ܢܟܦܘܪ ܒܝ ܩܕܡ
ܒܢܝܢܫܐ ܢܟܦܘܪ ܒܗ [o]ܐܢܐ ܐܦ[o] ܩܕܡ
10 [p]ܡܠܐܟܘܗܝ ܕܐܠܗܐ : [q]ܘܟܠ ܡܢ [r]ܕܢܐܡܪ
ܡܠܬܐ ܥܠ [s]ܒܪܗ ܕܐܢܫܐ ܢܫܬܒܩ ܠܗ : [t]ܘܡܢ
[u]ܕܢܓܕܦ ܥܠ ܪܘܚܐ ܕܩܘܕܫܐ ܠܐ ܢܫܬܒܩ
11 ܠܗ : ܟܕ ܕܝ ܡܩܪܒܝܢ ܠܟܘܢ [v]ܠܟܢܘܫܬܐ
ܘܠܩܕܡ [w]ܪܫܘܬܐ [x]ܘܫܘܠܛܢܘܬܐ : ܠܐ
[y]ܬܬܦܢܘܢ ܗܝܟ ܐܝܟ ܡܢܐ [z]ܬܬܠܘܢ [a]ܐܦܠܘܓܝܐ
12 ܐܘ ܡܢܐ [b]ܬܐܡܪܘܢ : ܪܘܚܐ ܕܩܘܕܫܐ ܓܝܪ
[c]ܬܠܦܟܘܢ ܢܬܠܦ ܒܫܥܬܗ ܗܝ ܡܢܐ ܕܘܠܐ
[d]ܕܬܐܡܪܘܢ

Codex C.

[c]ܡܬܓܠܝܐ
[d]ܦܬܓܡܢ [e]ܣܘܠܩܗ
[f]ܐܡܪܘܢ
[g]ܕܐܠܗܘܬܐ [h]ܥܠ
[i]ܐܬܦܢܝ
[k]ܕܝ
[o]ܡܕܡ
[r] *omit* ܡܢ
[s]ܫܘܠܛܢܐ
[t]ܠܓܗܢܐ [u]ܐܝܟ
[v]ܐܡܪ [w]ܫܒܥܐ
[x]ܦܪܬܝܢ [z]ܐܣܪܝܢ
[c]ܦܓܥܐ [l]ܟܠܗܘܢ
[e]ܡܢܝܢ [h]ܦܪܬܝܢ
[i]ܡܝܬܪܝܢ ܐܢܬܘܢ
[j] *add* ܕܝ ܕܟܠ
[k] *omit* ܒܗ
[l]ܡܠܐܟܘܗܝ
[m] *omit* ܕܝ
[n]ܕܢܟܦܘܪ
[o]ܐܦ ܐܢܐ
[p]ܡܠܐܟܘܗܝ
[r]ܕܢܐܡܪ [s]ܒܪܗ
[v]ܠܟܢܘܫܬܐ
[w]ܪܫܘܬܐ
[x]ܘܫܘܠܛܢܘܬܐ
[y]ܬܬܦܢܘܢ
[z]ܬܬܠܘܢ [c]ܬܠܦ

Codex B.	Codex A.	Codex C.

[CCXIV.]

Matt. VIII. 23—27.

Codex B: (deest)

Codex C: (deest)

ܦܐܕܘ ܘܒܥܪܘܒ ܐܠܡܫܝܚ ܕܡܬܩܪܝܢܘ ܘܒܪܒ
ܐܠܠܠܗ ܡܢ ܡܣܬܐ : ܘܡܣܬܘܢ ܡܢܘܪܝܐ
23 ܘܟܕ ܣܠܩ ܠܐܠܦܐ ܐܬܘ ܒܬܪܗ ܬܠܡܝܕܘܝ
24 : ܘܗܐ ܙܘܥ ܪܒ ܐܬܥܒܕ ܒܝܡܐ .: ܗܟܢ
ܕܬܬܟܣܝ ܐܠܦܐ ܡܢ ܓܠܠܝܐ : ܗܘܐ ܓܪ
ܪܘܚܐ ܠܩܘܒܠܗܘܢ : ܗܘ ܕܝܢ ܗܘܐ ܕܡܟ .:
25 ܘܩܪܒܘ ܬܠܡܝܕܘܝ ܐܩܝܡܘܢ ܝܬܗ ܐܡܪܝܢ :
26 ܡܪܢܐ ܐܚܝ ܝܬܢ ܕܗܐ ܐܒܕܝܢ : ܘܐܡܪ
ܠܗܘܢ ܡܢܐ ܐܬܘܢ ܕܚܠܬܢܝܢ ܙܥܘܪܝ
ܗܝܡܢܘܬܐ : ܒܟܢ ܩܡ ܘܐܟܐ ܒܪܘܚܐ ܘܒܝܡܐ
27 ܘܐܬܥܒܕ ܫܠܝܢ ܪܒ : ܒܢܝ ܐܢܫܐ ܕܝܢ ܬܡܗܘܢ
ܘܐܡܪܝܢ . ܕܐܝܟ ܡܢ ܗܘ ܗܢܐ ܕܐܦ
ܪܘܚܐ ܘܝܡܐ ܠܗ ܡܫܬܡܥܝܢ .

Codex A.	Codex B.	

CLXIV.

Matt. X. 1, 5—8.

Codex A: [CCXVIII.] [CCCLX.]

ܦܬܓܡ ܘܒܬܪܝܢ ܝܘܡ ܒܗ ܬܫܪܝܢ ܐܠܘܠ ܬܫܪܝ
ܐܠܡܫܝܚ ܕܡܬܩܪܝܢܘ ܐܦܘܠܘܢ ܬܠܬ ܫܒܬ ܒܒܪ
ܐܠܫܡܫ . ܬܫܪܝܢ ܐܬܐܝܚ ܬܠܬܝܢ ܒܫܪܗ ܒܫܪ
ܦܐܒܬ ܘܠܘܠܗ ܐܪܒܥܬܥܫܪܬ ܝܘܡ ܘܡܒܐ ܐܘܠ ܝܘܡ
ܬܫܪܝ ܐܦܘܠܒܐ ܡܘܢܒܐ ܘܕܡܬܝܢܘ ܡܢ ܡܬܝܐ
1 ܘܡܣܬܘܗ ܡܢܘܪܝܐ : ܘܡܢܘܪܐ ܡܢܪܐ ܝܫܘܥ
ܠܬܪܝܣܪܬܐ [a] ܕܝܢ [b] ܬܠܡܝܕܘܝ ܘܝܗܒ ܠܗܘܢ
[c] ܫܘܠܛܢ ܥܠ [d] ܪܘܚܬܐ [e] ܡܣܐܒܬܐ ܕܝܦܩܘܢ
[f] ܡܣܐܝܢ ܝܬܗܘܢ : ܘܕܝܐܣܘܢ [g] ܡܣܐܒܝܢ ܟܘܠ
5 [h] ܟܐܒܝܢ ܘܟܘܠ ܡܪܥܝܢ : [k] ܠܗܠܝܢ [i] ܬܪܝܣܪ

Codex A (variants):
[a] *omit* ܕܝܢ
[c] ܫܘܠܛܢ
[d] ܪܘܚܬܐ
[e] ܡܣܐܒܬܐ
[g] ܡܣܐܒܝܢ [h] ܟܐܒܝܢ
[k] *omit* ܠܗܠܝܢ ܬܪܝܣܪ ܬܗܘܢ

Codex C (variants):
[a] *omit* ܕܝܢ
[b] ܬܠܡܝܕܝܐ
[c] ܫܘܠܛܢ
[e] ܡܣܐܒܬܐ
[f] ܡܣܐܝܢ [g] ܡܣܐܒܝܢ
[i] ܬܪܝܣ

Codex A.	Codex B.	Codex C.
ˡ add ܗܘ ܠܝ	ܢܛܪܘܢ ˡ ܕܢܟܪܝܐ ܫܡܥܘܢ ᵐ ܘܡܫܡܥܝܢ ܢܛܪܘܢ	ᵐ ܘܡܫܡܥܝܢ ⁿ ܠܐܘܚܪܢ
ܕܡܫܝܚܘܬܗܘܢ	ܘܐܡܪ ⁿ ܠܐܘܚܪܢ ° ܕܡܫܝܚ ܠܐ ܬܫܠܘܢ :	° ܕܡܫܝܚ
ᵐ ܘܡܫܡܥܝܢ ⁿ ܠܐܘܚܪܢܝܐ	6 ܘܠܡܕܝܢܬܐ ܕܡܫܝܚ ܠܐ ᵖ ܬܫܡܥܘܢ : ܐܠܐ	ᵖ ܬܫܡܥܘܢ
° ܕܡܫܝܚ	ܐܙܠܘ ܠܘܬ ᑫ ܐܡܪܬܐ ʳ ܗܠܝܢ ˢ ܕܐܡܬܝܢܐ ܡܢ	ʳ omit ܗܠܝܢ
ᵖ ܬܫܡܥܘܢ	7 ᵗ ܒܬܪܐ ᵘ ܕܐܡܪܝܢ : ܘܒܕ ܬܗܘܢ ܐܙܠܝܢ ܗܘܘ	ᵗ ܒܬܪܗ ᵘ ܕܡܪܝܢ
ᑫ ܐܡܪܬܐ	ܡܢܕܝܢ ܘܐܡܪܝܢ : ܕܩܪܒܬ ᵛ ܡܠܟܘܬܗܘܢ	ᵛ ܡܠܟܘܬܗܘܢ
ʳ omit ܗܠܝܢ	8 ܕܫܡܝܐ :· ʷ ܒܝܫܝܢ ܗܘܘ ˣ ܡܣܩܝܢ ܘܡܬܦܢܝܢ	ʷ ܟܐܝܫܝܢ
ˢ ܕܐܡܬܝܢ	ܗܘܘ ܡܕܒܪܝܢ : ܘܫܕܝܐ ܗܘܘ ʸ ܡܦܩܝܢ :· ᶻ ܡܓܢ	ʸ ܡܦܩܝܢ ᶻ ܡܓܢ
ᵘ ܕܐܡܪܝܢ	ܢܣܒܬܘܢ ᵃ ܡܓܢ ܗܒܘ :	ᵃ ܡܓܢܐ
ᵛ ܡܠܟܘܬܗܘܢ		
ʷ ܟܐܝܫܝܢ ˣ ܡܣܩܝܢ		

[CLXIII.]

CLXV.

John X. 9—16.

ܗܘ ܒܝ ܬܠܬܗ ܝܘܡ ܒܝܗ ܬܕܒܪ ܐܠܗܝܢ ܡܪܝ
ܠܘܩܒܠ ܐܝܫܘܥ ܐܢܓܠܝܘܢ ܐܡܟܬ ܐܠܝܚܢ
ܒܒܕ ܐܠܗܝܢ ܬܠܡܝܕܗ ܒܝܗ ܬܕܒܐܪ ܐܠܡܠܟ
ܡܫܝܚ ܐܢܓܠܝܘܢ ܗܬ ܐܝܟ ܒܝ ܐܠܬܠ ܚܕܝ
ܒܪ ܝܘܡ ܬܕܒܪ ܡܪܝ ܡܫܝܚܐ ܘܪܒܘܬܗ ܐܢܓܠܝܘܢ
7 ܬܠܬ ܗܒܬ ܒܒܕ ܐܠܗܝܢ : ܘܒܝ ܐܬܒܒܪ ܒܝܗ
ܐܠܗܝܢ ܡܪܝ ܝܫܘܥ ܐܪܫܘܥ: ܐܢܓܠܝܘܢ ܝܘܡ
ܐܬܠܬܐ ܒܒܕ ܐܩܕܝܗ : ܬܠܬܒܒܪ ܬܕܒܪ
ܝܫܘܥ ܒܝܘܡ ܐܕܗܒ ܗܘܘ ܕܝܢ ܡܢ ܝܫܘܥ :
9 ܐܡܪ ܡܪܝܐ :° ܐܢܐ ᵖ ܬܪܥܐ : ᑫ ܟܠ ᵃ ܕܟܠ
ܡܢ ᵇ ܕܟܠ ܚܝܐ : ܘܟܠܠ ܘܢܦܩ ܘܡܫܟܚ
10 ܡܪܥܝܐ : ܓܢܒܐ ܠܐ ܐܬܐ ܐܠܐ ܕܝܓܢܘܒ
ܘܢܩܛܘܠ ܘܢܘܒܕ : ܐܢܐ ܐܬܝܬ ᵈ ܕܚܝܝܢ ܝܗܐ
11 ܠܗܘܢ : ܘܡܘܬܪ ܝܗܐ ܠܗܘܢ : ܐܢܐ ܗܘ
ܪܥܝܐ ܛܒܐ : ܘܪܥܝܐ ᵉ ܛܒܐ ܢܦܫܗ ܗܘ
12 ᶠ ܝܗܒ ܥܠ ܥܢ ܐܡܪܘܬܗ : ᵍ ܕܝܢ ʰ ܕܐܓܝܪ ܘܠܝܬ

Codex A.	Codex C.
⁷ ܕܐܡܪܝܢ ܗܘ ° add	
ܬܪܥܐ ܕܐܡܪܬܐ:	
⁸ ܟܘܠ ܗܠܝܢ ܕܐܬܘ	
ܠܩܕܡܝ ܗܘܘ	
ܘܠܓܢܒܐ ܐܠܐ	
ܠܐ ܫܡܥܘ ܠܗܘܢ	
ܐܡܪܬܐ:	
ᵖ add ܗܘ	ᵖ add ܗܘ ᑫ ܟܠ
ᵃ ܕܥܠܝܠ ᵇ ܕܥܠܠ	ᵃ ܕܥܠܝܠ ᵇ ܕܥܠܠ
ᵈ ܕܢܚܝܢ	ᵈ ܕܢܚܝܢ
ᵉ ܛܒܐ ᶠ ܝܗܒ	ᵉ ܛܒܐ ᶠ ܝܗܒ
ᵍ ܕ ʰ add ܕܝ	ʰ add ܕܝ

Codex A.	*Codex* B.	*Codex* C.
[e]ܪܥܝܐ	ܗܘ [e]ܪܥܝܐ : [f]ܗܘܝܢ ܕܠܝܬ [g]ܐܡܪܬܐ ܕܝܠܗ	
[f]ܗܘܝܢ	ܚܡܐ ܗܘ ܕܐܒܐ ܐܬܐ ܘܫܒܩ [g]ܐܡܪܬܐ	
[g]ܐܡܪܬܐ	13 ܘܥܪܩ : ܘܕܐܒܐ ܚܛܦ ܝܬܗܘܢ ܘܡܒܕܪ ܕܗܘ	
[h]ܚܫܠ	ܐܓܝܪ : ܘܠܐ [h]ܚܫܠ ܠܗ ܥܠ ܥܒܪ [i]ܐܡܪܬܐ :	[i]ܐܡܪܬܐ
[i]ܐܡܪܬܐ	14 ܐܢܐ ܗܘ ܪܥܝܐ ܛܒܐ : ܘܐܢܐ [j]ܡܚܟܡ ܕܝܠܝ	
[j]ܡܚܟܡ	15 ܘܕܝܠܝ [k]ܡܚܟܡܝܢ ܠܝ : ܗܝܟ ܡܐ ܕܐܒܐ [l]ܡܚܟܡ	[k]ܡܚܟܡܝܢ
	ܠܝ : ܘܐܢܐ [l]ܡܚܟܡ ܠܐܒܐ : ܘܢܦܫܝ ܐܢܐ	[l]ܡܚܟܡ
[m]ܘܐܡܪܝܢ	16 ܡܣܝܡ ܥܠ ܕܓܒܪ ܐܡܪܬܝ : [m]ܘܐܡܪܝܢ	
[n]ܗܘܝܢ	ܐܚܪܢܝܢ ܐܝܬ ܠܝ ܗܠܝܢ ܕܠܝܬ [n]ܗܘܝܢ	
[* Cod. B. ܘܠܝܩܘܢ]	ܡܢ ܗܕܐ ܕܪܬܐ : ܐܦ ܠܗܠܝܢ *ܘܠܝܩܘܢ ܠܝ	[o] *add* ܗܘܝܢ
[p]ܢܫܡܥܘܢ	ܕܐܝܬܐ : ܘܠܩܠܝ [o] [p]ܢܫܡܥܘܢ : [q]ܘܢܗܘܘܢ	[p]ܫܡܥܝܢ
[q]ܘܬܗܘܘܢ [s]ܘܚܕ	[r]ܚܕܐ ܡܪܥܝܬܐ [s]ܘܚܕ ܪܥܝܐ :	[r]ܚܕ [s]ܘܚܕ

CLXVI.

ܐܘܢܓܠܝܘܢ ܬܕܝܪ ܦܠܩܘܣ ܐܥܠܝܢ ܘܡܐܦܩܝܢ
ܝܘܡ ܐܣܦܪܗ ܐܦܠܘܢ ܐܠܦܝܠ ܐܠܝܢ ܦܝ
ܐܠܝܓܠ ܝܘܡ ܐܠܐܪܒܥܐ ܒܥܕ ܐܠܦܨܚ ܫܡܥ
ܒܥܪ ܬܕܒܪ ܐܬܠܬ ܡܕܝܢ ܐܠܡܣܬܪܦܝܢ :
ܐܦܠܘܢ ܫܡܥܘܢ ܘܒܥܪܝܢ ܦܝ ܬܕܝܢ ܐܠܠܝ :
ܘܦܝ ܡܦܬܥܪ ܬܕܒܪ ܐܠܡܥܪ ܡܬܐܝ ܐܦܠܘܢ
ܐܡܥܒܬ ܐܠܫܐܡܥ ܡܢ ܡܬܐܝ : ܡܥܬܦܪ
ܬܕܒܪ ܐܠܡܪܩܘܣ ܦܪܦܪܘܣ ܐܠܦܝܫܒܐ ܐܦܠܘܢ
ܐܘܠ ܐܥܫܪ ܬܡܥܬܦܪܪ ܝܘܡ ܦܝ ܬܥܪܝܢ
ܐܬܐܝܫ ܒܥܕ ܐܠܩܪܘܡܝܐ ܠܐܦܝܘܣ ܘܐܪܡܥܘܣ
ܐܦܠܘܢ ܬܠܬ ܥܒܬ ܒܥܕ ܐܠܥܡܫ : ܬܥܬܦܪ
ܬܕܒܪ ܐܒܥܝ ܒܘܒܕܢܐ :: ܐܦܠܘܢ ܫܡܥܘܢ ܦܝ
ܐܠܠܘܠ ::: ܘܫܕ ܘܒܥܪܝܢ ܕܫܘܠ ܐܥܫܪܗ
ܐܠܡܥܠ ܐܦܠܘܢ ܬܡܚܝܢ ܦܝ ܐܠܠܘܠ ܥܒܥܗ
ܘܒܥܪܝܢ ܝܘܡ ܬܕܒܪ ܐܠܡܪܩܘܣ ܡܪܝ ܒܘܡܘܒ
ܐܠܦܪܫܝ ܐܦܠܘܢ ܝܘܡ ܐܬܢܝܢ ܐܥܫܪܗ ܬܠܬܝܢ

Codex A.	Codex B.	Codex C.
	ܬܕܒܪ ܐܚܝܢ ܐܝܬܘܗܝ ܐܠܦܠܢ ܗܘܐ ܐܬܟܪܗ ܐܠܦܝܢ ܐܢܐ ܢܦܩ ܐܠܦܠܢ	
	ܒܟܝܢ ܐܠܗܐ ܚܕ ܘܬܠܬܝܢ ܗܘܐ: ܐܡܠ ܗܘܐ ܐܢ ܦܢܗ ܚܕ ܐܒܢܐ ܠܐܝܢܗܘܢ ܬܐܢ ܗܘܐ ܚܕ ܐܒܢܐ ܫܬܡܘ ܬܠܬ ܗܘܐ ܚܕ ܐܒܢܐ ܢܦܫܢ ܐܠܦܠܢ ܫܬܡܗ ܦܢ ܐܡܠܠ ܠܡܘ ܡܢ ܬܠܬ ܬܡܘܡܐ ܙܒܢܐ ܗܘܐ ܚܕ ܐܠܦܝܫܘ ܒܢܝܗ: ܡܢ ܡܪܝܡ ܘܒܢܬܗ ܡܪܝܡܐ	
[CCXLIV.]	MARK V. 24.	
ܘܐܙܠ[y] ܐܟܠܘܣ[z]	24 ܘܐܙܠ[y] ܥܡܗ ܐܟܠܘܣ[z] ܣܓܝ ܒܬܪܗ[a]: ܘܗܘܘ	ܐܟܠܘܣ[z]
ܕܚܩܘ[b] ܐܙܠ[c]	ܕܚܩܘ[b] ܐܙܠ[c] ܥܡܗ: ܘܗܘܐ[d] ܐܟܠܘܣ[e] ܣܓܝ	ܒܬܪܗ[a] ܕܚܩܘ[b]
ܐܟܠܘܣ[e] ܘܐܢܬܬܐ[f]	25 ܘܗܘܐ ܕܚܩܝܢ ܠܗ: ܘܐܢܬܬܐ[f] ܕܗܘܬ ܒܕܘܒܗ	[d] *omit* ܘܗܘܐ
ܬܬܝܒܘܣܬܪ[g] ܥܫܝܢ[h]	26 ܕܐܕܡܐ[g] ܬܬܝܒܘܣܬܪ[h] ܥܫܝܢ: ܘܣܓܝ ܚܫܬ ܡܢ	ܐܟܠܘܣ[e] ܘܐܢܬܬܐ[f]
ܠܗ[i] ܐܬܒܗܠܬ[j]	ܣܓܝ ܐܣܘܢ: ܘܗܘܐ[x] ܐܦܩܬ ܟܘܠ ܡܐ ܕܗܘܐ	ܬܬܝܒܘܣܬܪ[g] ܐܦܩܬ[x]
ܬܬܝܒܢܬ[k]	ܠܗ[i]: ܘܟܘܠ ܠܐ ܐܬܒܗܠܬ[j] ܐܠܐ ܬܬܝܒܢܬ[k]	ܠܗ[i] ܐܬܒܗܠܬ[j]
ܟܕ[l] ܘܟܕ[m]	27 ܠܡܣܒ ܡܢ[l] ܚܝܢ: ܐܬܬ[m] ܟܕ ܫܡܥܬ ܠܝܫܘܥ	ܬܬܝܢܬ[k] ܘܟܕ[m]
ܒܐܟܠܘܣܐ[n]	ܕܐܬܐ ܡܢ ܒܐܟܠܘܣܐ[n]: ܐܬܬ ܡܢ	ܠܒܣܬܪ[o] ܕܡ [p] *omit*
ܕܡ [p] *omit* ܡܢܡܢܐ[t]	28 ܠܒܣܬܪ[o]: ܘܩܪܒܬ ܕܡ[p] ܠܡܐܢܘܗܝ: ܗܘܬ ܕܡ[p]	ܐܢ[q] ܠܡܐܢܘܗܝ[r]
ܕܐܕܡܗܐ[u] ܘܐܬܚܬ[v]	ܐܢ ܐܡܪܐ: [q]ܐܢ ܩܪܒܬ ܠܒܘܫܗ[r] ܠܡܐܢܘܗܝ	ܡܢܡܢܐ[t]
ܕܐܬܚܠܡܬ[w]	29 ܚܝܢ ܐܢܐ: ܘܡܚܕܐ ܝܒܫ ܕܡ[p] ܡܢܡܢܐ[t]	ܕܐܕܡܗܐ[u]
ܒܝܕܥܬܗ[x] ܝܕܥ[y]	ܕܐܕܡܗܐ[u] ܘܐܬܚܬ ܒܦܓܪܗ[v] ܕܐܬܚܠܡܬ[w] ܡܢ	ܕܐܬܚܠܡܬ[w] ܘܐܬܚܬ[v]
ܒܐܟܠܘܣܐ[z]	30 ܒܝܕܥܬܗ[x]: ܘܡܚܕܐ ܝܕܥ ܝܫܘܥ[y] ܒܢܦܫܗ	ܒܝܕܥܬܗ[x] ܝܕܥ[y]
ܘܗܘܐ[s] ܡܐܪ[a]	ܕܚܝܠܐ ܢܦܩ ܡܢܗ: ܘܐܬܦܢܝ ܒܐܟܠܘܣܐ[z]	ܘܗܘܐ[s]
ܬܠܡܝܕܘܗܝ[b]	31 ܘܗܘܐ[s] ܐܡܪ ܡܢ[a] ܡܐܪ ܠܡܐܢܘܗܝ: ܘܗܘܘ ܕܡ[p]	ܡܐܪ[a] ܬܠܡܝܕܘܗܝ[b]
ܐܟܠܘܣܐ[c] ܚܙܝܢ[d]	ܐܡܪܝܢ ܠܗ ܬܠܡܝܕܘܗܝ[b] ܚܙܝ ܐܢܬ ܐܟܠܘܣܐ[c]	ܘܐܟܠܘܣܐ[c]
ܘܐܢܬ ܐܡܪ[gf]	[d]ܚܙܝܢ ܠܟ ܘܐܢܬ[f] ܐܡܪܬ[g] ܡܢ[h] ܡܐܪ	[f] *omit* ܘܐܢܬ ܚܙܝܢ[d]
[j] *add* ܗܕܐ ܡܐܪ[h]	32 ܠܝ: ܘܗܘܐ ܡܚܙܐ[i] ܕܢܚܙܐ ܡܢ ܗܝ[j]	ܡܚܙܐ[i] ܕܥܒܕܬ[g]
ܕܗ[k] ܕܥܒܕܬ[l]	33 ܕܥܒܕܬ ܕܗ[k]: ܘܐܢܬܬܐ ܕܥܒܕܬ[l] ܘܕܚܠܬ ܘܪܬܝܬ	ܕܥܒܕܬ[l] [j] *add* ܗܕܐ
ܝܕܥܬ[n] ܘܐܬܬ[o]	ܝܕܥܬ ܡܐ[m] ܕܗܘܐ[n] ܠܗ: ܐܬܬ ܘܢܦܠܬ[o]	[m] *omit* ܡܐ ܕܗܘܐ

Codex A.	*Codex* B.	*Codex* C.
[o] ܘܩܕܡܘܗܝ	34 ܘܩܕܡܘܗܝ[o] ܘܐܡܪܬ ܠܗ ܒܩܠܐ ܒܥܘܫܦ: ܡܪܐ	[p] *add* ܕܝ
[p] *add* ܕܝ [q] ܝܬܓܒܝ	ܫܡܥܘܢ[p] ܐܡܪ ܠܗ ܒܪܬܐ ܗܝܡܢܘܬܟܝ ܐܚܝܬ	[q] ܝܬܡܒܝ
[r] ܐܙܠܝ [s] ܒܫܠܡܐ	[q]ܝܬܒܝ [r]ܐܙܠܝ [s]ܒܫܠܡ[r] :	[r] *omit* ܐܙܠܝ ܒܫܠܡ

CLXVII.

	ܫܡܥܘܗ ܬܕܒܪ ܐܠܗܝܢ ܡܪܝ ܗܐܟܢܐ : ܐܬܠܘܒ	
	ܫܘܝ ܒܪܢ ܡܢ ܟܠܗܘܢ ܐܬܐܝܢ ܗܐܬܘܗ ܒܪܝ	
	ܐܠܗܝܢ ܡܪܝ ܢܦܩܠܐ : ܐܬܠܘܒ ܝܘܡ	
	ܐܬܠܬܐ ܒܒܪ ܐܗܠܝܗ : ܬܗܦܟܗ ܫܪ ܠܫܝܗ	
	ܐܠܗܝܢܗ ܐܬܠܘܒ ܐܗܒܬ ܐܗܐܪܗ ܡܢ	
	ܠܗܦܐ ܦܝ ܫܘܝ ܒܪܢ ܒܪ [a]ܐܠܒܐܪ ܕܝܫܐܠ	[a] ܐܒܐ
	ܐܠܗܝܢ : ܐܬܠܘܒ ܬܦܫܝܗ ܘܒܪܢܡ ܡܢ	
	ܐܬܠܘܠ : : ܬܠܬܐ ܒܪܢ ܬܕܒܪ ܐܠܗܝܢܗܝܢ	
	[b]ܐܗܪܬܘܗ ܘܐܨܝܚܗ : ܐܬܠܘܒ ܦܝ ܐܫܝܪ	[b] ܐܗܪܝܬܘܗ
	ܐܠܝܟܠ : ܗܡܟܬܪ ܬܕܒܪ ܐܢܒܝ ܕܝܫܐܠ	
	ܘܐܠܗܝܢܗܝܢ ܐܬܠܬܐ ܦܬܝܗ : ܐܬܠܘܒ ܫܡܥܘܗ	
	ܡܢ ܐܬܠܘܠ : ܒܒܪܢ ܒܪ ܐܠܗܝܢ ܐܨܝܚܘܗ	
	ܡܢ ܡܪܝܘܗ : ܘܒܝܬܗ ܦܢܘܪܐ :	

[CCLI.]	MARK : IX. 32—40.	
	32 ✠ ܘܐܬܐ ܡܪܝܐ ܫܡܥܘܢ [z]ܘܬܠܡܝܕܘܗܝ ܠܒܬܪ ܝܫܘܥ :	[z] ܘܬܠܡܝܕܘܗܝ
[b] ܐܡܪ	ܘܟܕ ܗܘܐ ܒܟܘ ܒܝܬܐ [a]ܫܐܠ ܐܢܘܢ [b]ܘܐܡܪ	[a] ܫܐܠ [b] ܐܡܪ
	ܡܢܐ ܗܘܝܬܘܢ ܡܬܚܫܒܝܢ ܒܐܘܪܚܐ ܦܠܓܘܢ	[d] ܡܬܕܒܪܝܢ
[c] ܦܠܓ	33 ܠܘܬ [c]ܦܠܓ : ܘܗܢܘܢ ܗܘܘ [e]ܫܬܝܩܝܢ : ܦܠܓܘܢ	[e] ܫܬܝܩܝܢ [f] ܪܒ
	ܓܝܪ ܥܡ [c]ܦܠܓ ܗܘܘ [d]ܡܬܕܒܪܝܢ ܒܐܘܪܚܐ ܡܢ	[g] ܘܝܬܒ [h] ܩܕܡܝܐ
[f] ܪܒ [g] ܘܝܬܒ	34 ܡܢܗ [f]ܪܒ : [g]ܘܝܬܒ ܘܩܪܐ ܠܬܪܥܣܪܬܐ	[i] *omit* ܘܫܡܫܐ ܕܟܘܠܐ
[h] ܩܕܡܝܐ	ܘܐܡܪ ܠܗܘܢ : ܡܢ ܕܨܒܐ ܕܝܗܘܐ [h]ܩܕܡܝܐ	
[l] *omit* ܕܝ	ܗܘ ܝܗܘܐ ܒܬܪܐ ܕܟܘܠܐ [i]ܘܫܡܫܐ ܕܟܘܠܐ :	[j] ܛܠܝܐ [k] ܘܐܩܝܡ
[m] ܒܝܢܝܗܘܢ	35 ܘܢܣܒ [j]ܛܠܝܐ [k]ܘܐܩܝܡܗ ܒܝܢܬܗ [l]ܕܝ [m]ܒܝܢܝܗܘܢ :	[l] *omit* ܕܝ
[n] ܘܓܦܦ [o] ܕܪܥܗ	[n]ܘܓܦܦܗ ܘܗܘ ܥܠ [o]ܕܪܥܘܗܝ ܘܐܡܪ ܠܗܘܢ :	[m] ܒܝܢܝܗܘܢ [o] ܕܪܥܗ

Codex B.

36 ܡܢ ⁿܕܡܦܩܕܢ ᵒܪܒܐ ܗܘ ܡܢ ܗܠܝܢ ܬܠܝܐ ܟܠ
ܢܡܘܣܐ: ܠܝ ܗܘ ᵖܡܦܩܕܢ ܘܡܢ ᵠܕܡܦܩܕܢ
ܐܡܪ ܠܗ ܠܐ ᵖܡܦܩܕܢ: ܐܠܐ ʳܠܡܪܝ ܕܐܠܗܟ
37 ܐܡܪ: ܘܐܡܪ ˢܘܣܝܡܘ ܘܐܡܪ ܠܗ ܡܠܦܢܐ
ܡܢ ܟܠ ܠܒܟ ᵗܕܝ ᵘܡܢܗܘܢ ܥܡܝܗ ܒܢܦܫܟ:
38 ᵛܘܡܠܝܢܗ ܐܡܪ ܕܠܐ ܝܬܪܐ ˣܒܬܪܢ: ܘܡܪܐ
ܣܡܘܣ ܐܡܪ ܠܗ ܬܚܘܡ ܐܡܪ: ܠܒܪ ܡܢ
ܐܚܪ ʸܕܟܬܒ ܟܠ ܥܠܡܐ ܚܝܠ ᶻܘܡܠܝܢ ܒܟܘܠܗ
39 ܕܐܡܪܘܢ ᵃܟܠܗܝ ܒܢܝܐ: ܡܢ ܒܪ ܕܠܒܬ ܗܘ
40 ᵇܠܡܦܩܢ ܟܠ ܕܠܒܢ ܗܘ: ܡܢ ܒܪ ܕܫܡܥܐ
ܐܡܪܘܗܝ ܒܗ ᶜܕܡܢ ܟܠ ܥܡܐ ܕܐܬܐܘܗܝ ᵈ
ܕܡܫܝܚܐ: ܐܡܪܝܢ ܐܡܪ ܐܢܐ ܠܟܘܢ ܕܠܐ
ܝܕܥ ܐܢܬܘܢ :·

CLXVIII.

Mark XII. 38—44.

ܘܚܕ ܘܐܡܪܝܢ ܚܕ ܐܠܡܝܕܘܗܝ ܐܝܬܘܗܝ
ܐܬܠܡܕ ܐܘܠܦܢܗ ܡܢ ܒܢܝ ܐܢܫ: ܐܬܝܗ
ܘܐܡܪܝܢ ܚܕ ܐܠܡܝܕܘܗܝ ܢܦܩܘܗܝ ܡܢ ܡܪܢܐ.
38 ܘܒܬܪܗ ܢܦܩܘܢܐ: ܐܡܪ ܡܪܢܐ ᵃܠܬܠܡܝܕܘܗܝ
ܐܬܠܡܝܕܘܗܝ ᵇܗܐܟܘ ܒܠܒܘܢ ܡܢ ܣܦܪܝܐ:
ܗܠܝܢ ܕܨܒܝܢ ܕܝܗܠܟܘܢ ᶜܒܐܣܛܠܝܬܐ ᵈܘܫܐܠܢ
39 ܫܠܡܐ ܒܫܘܩܝܐ: ܘܪܫܝܐ ᵉܡܬܥܒܕܢܘܬܐ
ᶠܒܟܢܫܬܐ: ܘܪܫܝܐ ܡܪܟܒܝܐ ᵍܒܡܟܣܘܬܐ:·
40 ܗܠܝܢ ܕܐܟܠܝܢ ʰܒܬܝܗܘܢ ⁱܕܐܪܡܠܬܐ ܘܕܝܬܡܐ:
ܘܒܥܠܬܐ ᵏܡܨܠܝܢ ˡܐܪܝܟܝܢ: ܗܠܝܢ ܝܣܒܘܢ ᵐܕܝ
41 ܡܬܚܪ: ܘܗܘܐ ⁿܩܐܡ ܡܪܢܐ ܝܫܘܥ ᵒܠܡܫܩܠ
ܒܬܪ ᵖܩܘܪܒܢܐ ᵠܘܗܘ ʳܣܓܝܐܐ ܗܘܝ ˢܐܦܩܠܘܣܐ
ᵗܙܒܢܐ ܠܝܫܐ ܒܒܝܬ ᵘܩܘܪܒܢܐ: ܘܣܓܝ
42 ܒܬܪܝܢ ܗܘܘ ܙܒܢܝܢ ܣܓܝ: ܘܐܬܬ ܚܕܐ ᵛ

Codex A.

ᵖ ܡܦܩܕܢ
ᵠ ܕܡܦܩܕܢ
ʳ ܠܡܪܢ
ˢ ܘܣܝܡܘ
ᵗ omit ܕܝ
ᵘ ܬܚܘܡ
ˣ ܒܬܪܢ
ʸ ܕܟܬܒ
ᶻ ܘܡܠܝܢ
ᵃ ܟܠܗܝ
ᵇ ܠܡܦܩܢ

[CCLIII.]

ᵇ ܗܘܢ
ᶜ ܒܐܣܛܠܝܬܐ
ᵈ ܘܫܐܠܢ
ᵉ ܡܬܥܒܕܢܘܬܐ
ᵍ ܒܡܟܣܘܬܐ
ʰ ܒܬܝܗܘܢ
ᵏ add ܗܘܢ
ˡ ܐܪܝܟܝܢ ᵐ ܕܝܢ
ⁿ ܩܐܡ ᵒ ܠܡܫܩܠ
ᵖ ܩܘܪܒܢܐ ᵠ ܗܘܐ
ˢ ܐܦܩܠܘܣܐ
ᵗ ܙܒܢܐ ᵘ ܩܘܪܒܢܐ
ᵛ add ܕܝ

Codex C.

ⁿ ܕܡܦܩܕܢ
ᵒ ܪܒܐ ܗܘ ᵖ ܡܦܩܕܢ
ᵠ ܕܡܦܩܕܢ
ʳ ܠܡܪܢ
ᵗ omit ܕܝ
ᵘ ܡܢܗܘܢ ᵛ ܘܡܠܝܢܗ
ʸ ܕܟܬܒ ᶻ ܟܠܗܝ
ᵇ ܠܡܦܩܢ ܠܝ
ᶜ ܡܢ
ᵈ add ܬܠܡܝܕܘܗܝ

ᵃ ܬܠܡܝܕܘܗܝ ᵇ ܗܘܢ
ᵉ ܡܬܥܒܕܢܘܬܐ
ᶠ ܒܟܢܫܬܐ
ᵍ ܕܡܟܣܘܬܐ
ʰ ܒܬܝܗܘܢ
ⁱ ܕܐܪܡܠܬܐ
ᵏ add ܗܘܢ ᵐ ܕܝܢ
ᵖ ܩܘܪܒܢܐ ᵠ ܗܘܐ
ʳ omit ܣܓܝ
ᵗ ܙܒܢܐ
ᵛ add ܕܐܦ

Codex A.	*Codex* B.	*Codex* C.
	ܐܪܟܠܐ [v]ܡܫܒܚܐ ܕܢܫܬ ܦܐܪܝܟ ܐܡܪܝܟ ܡܢܐ	[v] ܡܫܒܚܐ
	43 ܕܗܘ ܡܕܪܝܩܝܢ: ܘܡܢܐ [w]ܠܝܬܡܘܢ ܘܐܡܪ	[w] ܠܝܬܡܘܢ
[x] ܐܡܪܢܐ	ܠܗܘܢ : ܐܡܪܢ [x]ܐܡܪ ܐܢܐ[x] ܠܟܘܢ ܕܗܘܐ	
[y] ܡܫܒܚܬܬܐ	ܐܪܟܠܬܐ [y]ܡܫܒܚܬܐ ܕܢܫܬ ܡܠܟ ܡܢ ܟܠ	
[z] ܡܪܒܢܝܐ	44 ܗܠܝܢ ܕܝܕܥ ܒܒܢܝܬ [z]ܡܪܒܢܝܐ ∶ ܒܗܠܘܢ	
[b] ܕܝܬܪ [c] ܠܗ	[a]ܟܪ ܡܢ ܡܢܐ [b]ܕܝܬܪ ܠܗܘܢ[a] ܪܒܘ : ܗܕܐ ܕܝ	[a] omit ܟܪ ... ܠܗܘܢ
[d] *omit* ܕܝ	ܡܢ ܫܦܪܘܢܗ ܒܟܠ ܡܢܐ ܕܗܘܐ [c]ܠܗ [d]ܕܝ ܪܒܬ	[d] *omit* ܕܝ
[e] *add* ܥܠܡ ܥܠܡ	ܒܟܠ ܡܢܝܢܗ ∶[e]	

ܐܠ ܚܕ ܐܠܦܝ ܒܒܪ ܐܠܦܫ ܒܡܢܝܢܗ ܐܦܠܘܢ
ܡܢ ܡܬܐܝ ܐܠܦܝ ܠܠܡܝܡܗ ܐܠܦܠ :: ܚܕܐ
ܫܢܝܢ :: ܐܦܠܘܢ ܡܢ ܡܢܝܢܗ ܘܗܘܐ ܬܠܬ
ܐܠܦܝ ܐܠܦܝ ܠܠܡܟܠܠ : ܐܦܠܘܢ ܡܢ ܠܘܩܐ
ܘܗܘ ܐܪܐܒܒ :: ܐܠܦܝ ܐܠܦܝ ܠܫܡܪܝܢܗ
ܐܦܠܘܢ ܡܢ ܢܘܚܐ ܘܗܘ ܐܫܐܒܒ : ܚܕ
ܐܠܦܝܢ ܐܦܠܘܢ ܡܢ ܢܘܚܐ ܘܗܘ ܐܬܐ
ܡܢ : ܫܡܝܫ ܐܦܠܘܢ ܐܦܠܘܢ ܡܢ ܡܢܝܢܗ
ܘܗܘ ܐܬܐܬܐ : ܚܕ ܐܠܦܝ ܠܠܐܒܐ : ܐܦܠܘܢ
ܡܢ ܢܘܚܐ ܘܗܘ ܐܠܐܒܪ : ܐܠܦܝ ܐܠܦܝ
ܠܠܚܝܢܗ ܐܦܠܘܢ ܡܢ ܢܘܚܐ ܘܗܘ ܐܬܐܫܒ
ܫܒܬ ܡܟܠ ܚܕ ܐܠܐܒܐ ܐܦܠܘܢ ܚܕܒܪ
ܫܒܬ ܡܢ ܠܘܩܐ ; ܚܕ ܡܟܠ ܚܕ ܐܠܐܒܐ ::
ܐܦܠܘܢ ܚܕܒܪ ܚܕ ܡܢ ܠܘܩܐ : ܐܫܒܬ
ܐܠܦܝ ܡܟܠ ܐܠܡܠܐܕ ܐܦܠܘܢ ܐܬܒܪ
ܫܒܬ ܡܢ ܠܘܩܐ : ܚܕ ܡܟܠ ܐܠܡܠܐ ܠܠܐܒܐ
ܐܠܡܕܫܝܢ ܘܗܘ ܐܢܫܘܪܗ ܡܢ ܡܬܐܝ ܘܒܢܬܗ
ܡܪܘܫܐ

[CCLVII.]

CLXIX.

Matt. I. 1.

Codex A.	*Codex* B.	*Codex* C.
[a] ܟܬܒܐ	1 ✠ ܟܬܒܐ[a] ܕܬܘܠܕܬܗ[b] ܕܝܫܘܥ ܡܫܝܚܐ : ܒܪܗ	
[b] ܕܬܘܠܕܬܗ		
[c] ܕܕܘܝܕ [d] ܐܘܠܕ	2 ܕܕܘܝܕ[c] ܒܪܗ ܕܐܒܪܗܡ : ܐܒܪܗܡ ܐܘܠܕ[d]	[d] ܐܘܠܕ

Codex A.

[c]ܠܐܝܣܚܩ
[e]ܐܝܣܚܩ ܕܝ [d]*add*
[f]ܘܠܐܚܘܗܝ
ܕܝ [j]*omit* ܕܝ [d]*add*
[l]ܐܘܠܕ
[m]ܠܥܡܝܢܕܒ
[q]ܥܡܝܢܕܒ [n]ܐܘܠܕ
[o]ܐܘܠܕ ܕܝ [x]*add*
[p]ܠܥܘܒܕ [r]ܪܥܘܬ
[s]ܥܘܒܕ [t]ܠܝܫܝ
[u]ܐܝܫܝ [v]ܠܕܘܕ
[y]ܠܫܠܝܡܘܢ
[z]ܕܐܘܪܝܐܣ
[a]ܫܠܝܡܘܢ
[c]ܠܐܒܝܘܕ [e]ܐܒܝܘܕ
[f]ܠܐܣܐ [g]ܠܝܗܘܫܦܛ
[h]ܝܗܘܫܦܛ
[l]ܠܝܘܐܩܝܡ
[m]ܝܘܐܩܝܡ
[t]*omit* ܕܝ
[o]ܘܠܐܚܘܗܝ
[p]ܒܓܠܘܬܐ
[r]ܓܠܘܬܐ [d]*add* ܕܝ
[s]*omit* ܕܝ
[n]ܐܘܠܕ [w]ܠܙܪܘܒܒܠ
[x]ܙܪܘܒܒܠ [a]ܠܐܟܝܡ
[c]ܐܘܠܕ [e]ܐܠܝܥܙܪ
[f]ܠܡܬܢ
[g]ܕܡܪܝܡ
[h]ܕܡܢܗ [i]ܕܝ
[k]ܕܬܘܠܕܬܐ

Codex B.

[c]ܠܐܝܣܚܩ [e]ܐܝܣܚܩ ܐܘܠܕ ܠܝܥܩܘܒ : ܝܥܩܘܒ[d]
3 ܐܘܠܕ ܠܝܗܘܕܐ [f]ܘܠܐܚܘܝ : [g]ܝܗܘܕܐ ܕܝ [n]ܐܘܠܕ
[h]ܠܦܪܨ [j]ܕܝ ܘܠܙܪܚ ܡܢ ܬܡܪ : ܦܪܨ ܕܝ
[k]ܐܘܠܕ ܠܚܨܪܘܢ : ܚܨܪܘܢ [d] [o]ܐܘܠܕ ܠܐܪܡ :
4 ܐܪܡ ܕܝ [o]ܐܘܠܕ [m]ܠܥܡܝܢܕܒ : [q]ܥܡܝܢܕܒ ܕܝ
[k]ܐܘܠܕ ܠܢܚܫܘܢ : ܢܚܫܘܢ ܕܝ [k]ܐܘܠܕ
5 ܠܣܠܡܘܢ : ܣܠܡܘܢ ܕܝ [o]ܐܘܠܕ ܠܒܘܥܙ ܡܢ
ܪܚܒ : ܒܘܥܙ[x] [n]ܐܘܠܕ [p]ܠܥܘܒܕ ܡܢ [r]ܪܘܬ :
[s]ܥܘܒܕ[d] [n]ܐܘܠܕ [t]ܠܐܝܫܝ : [u]ܐܝܫܝ ܕܝ [n]ܐܘܠܕ
6 [v]ܠܕܘܕ ܡܠܟܐ[v] : [w]ܕܘܕ[x] ܐܘܠܕ [y]ܠܫܠܝܡܘܢ ܡܢ
7 ܐܢܬܬܗ [z]ܕܐܘܪܝܐܣ : [a]ܫܠܝܡܘܢ ܕܝ ܐܘܠܕ [j]ܕܝ
[b]ܠܪܚܒܥܡ : ܪܚܒܥܡ ܕܝ ܐܘܠܕ [c]ܠܐܒܝܐ :
8 [e]ܐܒܝܐ ܕܝ [n]ܐܘܠܕ [f]ܠܐܣܐ : ܐܣܐ ܕܝ
ܐܘܠܕ [g]ܠܝܗܘܫܦܛ : [h]ܝܗܘܫܦܛ [i]ܕܝ ܐܘܠܕ ܠܝܘܪܡ :
9 ܝܘܪܡ ܕܝ ܐܘܠܕ ܠܥܘܙܝܐ : ܥܘܙܝܐ ܕܝ ܐܘܠܕ
ܠܝܘܬܡ : ܝܘܬܡ ܕܝ ܐܘܠܕ [j]ܠܐܚܙ : [k]ܐܚܙ ܕܝ
10 ܐܘܠܕ ܠܚܙܩܝܐ : ܚܙܩܝܐ ܕܝ ܐܘܠܕ ܠܡܢܫܐ :
ܡܢܫܐ ܕܝ ܐܘܠܕ ܠܐܡܘܢ : ܐܡܘܢ ܕܝ
11 ܐܘܠܕ ܠܝܘܫܝܐ : ܝܘܫܝܐ ܕܝ ܐܘܠܕ [l]ܠܝܘܐܩܝܡ :
[m]ܝܘܐܩܝܡ [t]ܕܝ ܐܘܠܕ [n]ܠܝܘܟܢܝܐ [o]ܘܠܐܚܘܝ
12 [p]ܒܓܠܘܬܗ ܕܒܒܠ : ܡܢ ܒܬܪ [d] [r]ܓܠܘܬܗ
ܕܒܒܠ : ܝܘܟܢܝܐ [s]ܕܝ [n]ܐܘܠܕ [u]ܠܫܠܬܐܝܠ :
13 [v]ܫܠܬܐܝܠ ܕܝ ܐܘܠܕ [w]ܠܙܪܘܒܒܠ : [x]ܙܪܘܒܒܠ
ܕܝ ܐܘܠܕ ܠܐܒܝܘܕ : ܐܒܝܘܕ ܕܝ [n]ܐܘܠܕ
14 ܠܐܠܝܩܝܡ : ܐܠܝܩܝܡ ܕܝ ܐܘܠܕ [y]ܠܥܙܘܪ : [z]ܥܙܘܪ
ܕܝ ܐܘܠܕ ܠܨܕܘܩ : ܨܕܘܩ ܕܝ ܐܘܠܕ [a]ܠܐܟܝܡ :
15 [b]ܐܟܝܡ ܕܝ ܐܘܠܕ ܠܐܠܝܘܕ : ܐܠܝܘܕ ܕܝ
[c]ܐܘܠܕ [d]ܠܐܠܝܥܙܪ : [e]ܐܠܝܥܙܪ ܕܝ ܐܘܠܕ ܠܡܬܢ :
16 ܡܬܢ ܕܝ ܐܘܠܕ ܠܝܥܩܘܒ : ܝܥܩܘܒ ܕܝ
ܐܘܠܕ [f]ܠܝܘܣܦ ܒܥܠܗ [g]ܕܡܪܝܡ [h]ܕܡܢܗ ܐܬܝܠܕ
17 ܣܟܘܡ [i]ܕܝ [k]ܕܬܘܠܕܬܐ ܡܥܢܝܢܐ : ܟܠܗܘܢ

Codex C.

[f]ܘܠܐܚܘܗܝ [g]ܝܗܘܕܐ
[h]ܠܦܪܨ ܕܝ [j]*omit*
[k]ܐܘܠܕ ܕܝ [d]*add*
[m]ܠܥܡܝܢܕܒ
[q]ܥܡܝܢܕܒ
[n]ܐܘܠܕ ܕܝܢ [x]*add*
[p]ܠܥܘܒܕ
[s]ܥܘܒܕ [t]ܠܐܝܫܝ
[u]ܐܝܫܝ
[v]ܡܠܟܐ ܕܘܕ
[w]ܕܘܕ [z]ܐܘܪܝܐ
[a]ܫܠܝܡܘܢ
[b]ܠܪܚܒܥܡ
[c]ܠܐܒܝܐ [e]ܐܒܝܐ
[f]ܠܐܣܐ [g]ܠܝܗܘܫܦܛ
[h]ܝܗܘܫܦܛ
[j]ܠܐܚܙ [k]ܐܚܙ
[l]ܠܝܘܐܩܝܡ
[m]ܝܘܐܩܝܡ [t]ܕܝܢ
[n]ܠܝܘܟܢܝܐ
[p]ܒܓܠܘܬܗ
[r]ܓܠܘܬܐ [d]*add* ܕܝ
[s]*omit* ܕܝ
[n]ܐܘܠܕ [u]ܠܫܠܬܐܝܠ
[v]ܫܠܬܐܝܠ
[w]ܠܙܪܘܒܒܠ
[x]ܙܪܘܒܒܠ
[y]ܠܠܥܙܪ [z]ܠܥܙܘܪ
[a]ܠܐܟܝܡ [b]ܐܟܝܡ
[d]ܠܐܠܝܥܙܪ
[k]ܕܬܘܠܕܬܐ

Codex A. | *Codex B.* | *Codex C.*

Codex B.

ܐܘܦ ܕܪܝܐ [e]ܕܡܢ ܐܒܪܗܡ [f]ܥܕ [g]ܕܘܝܕ
[m]ܕܪܝܢ [h]ܐܪܒܥܣܪ ∴ ܘܡܢ [i]ܕܘܝܕ ܥܕܡܐ [j]ܕܝ
[k]ܠܓܠܘܬܐ ܕܒܒܝܠ [m]ܕܪܝܢ [h]ܐܪܒܥܣܪ : ܘܡܢ
[l]ܓܠܘܬܐ ܕܒܒܝܠ ܥܕܡܐ ܠܡܫܝܚܐ [m]ܕܪܝܢ
[h]ܐܪܒܥܣܪ ∴

CLXX.

Matt. I. 18—25.

18 ܠܝܫܘܥ ܐܠܡܫܝܚܐ ܡܢ [a]ܡܬܐܘܢ [l]ܬܘܠܕܬܗ[z] [a]
ܕܝܫܘܥ ܡܫܝܚܐ : [b]ܡܟܕܝܢ [c]ܗܘܬ ∴ ܒܕ [h]ܐܬܡܟܪܬ
[d]ܡܪܝܡ [d]ܐܡܗ [e]ܠܝܘܣܦ ܥܕ ܠܐ ܢܬܩܪܒܘܢ
ܐܫ ܠܗܘܬ ܒܕ [f]ܐܫܬܟܚܬ [g]ܡܥܒܪܐ [h]ܒܪܘܚ ܡܢ
19 ܪܘܚܐ ܕܩܘܕܫܐ : [i]ܝܘܣܦ ܕܝ ܓܒܪܗ ܗܘܐ
ܙܕܝܩ : ܘܠܐ ܗܘܐ [f. 132a] ܨܒܐ ܕܝܦܪܣ ܢܬܗ : [k]
20 ܘܗܘܝܢ ܕܗܘ ܡܬܚܫܒ ܗܠܝܢ [l]ܘܗܐ ܡܠܐܟܗ
[m]ܕܡܪܝܐ ܐܬܚܡܝ ܠܗ [n]ܒܚܠܡܗ ܘܐܡܪ
ܠܗ : [o]ܝܘܣܦ ܒܪܗ [p]ܕܕܘܝܕ ܠܐ [q]ܕܝ ܬܕܚܠ
ܬܕܒܪ [r]ܠܡܪܝܡ ܐܬܬܟ [s]ܗܕܝܢ ܕܝ [t]ܕܡܬܝܠܕ
21 ܒܗ ܡܢ ܪܘܚܐ ܕܩܘܕܫܐ ܐܝܬ ܗܘ : ܬܝܠܕ [u]
ܒܪ [v]ܘܡܬܩܪܐ [q]ܕܝ ܫܡܗ ܝܫܘܥ : ܗܘ ܓܪ
22 ܝܚܐ ܥܡܗ ܡܢ [w]ܚܛܝܗܘܢ ∴ ܗܕܐ [x] ܒܟܠܗ
[y]ܐܬܥܒܕܬ [z]ܕܝܬܡܠܐ ܡܐ [a]ܕܐܬܐܡܪ ܡܢ [b]ܡܪܝܐ
23 ܒܢܒܝܗ [q]ܕܝ [c]ܕܐܫܥܝܐ ܢܒܝܐ [d]ܕܐܡܪ ∴ ܗܐ
[e]ܒܬܘܠܬܐ [f]ܡܥܒܪܐ [g]ܒܪܗ [h]ܘܝܠܕܬ [i]ܒܪ [j]ܘܩܪܘܢ
ܫܡܗ [i]ܥܡܢܘܐܝܠ : ܡܐ[†] ܕܗܘ ܡܬܦܪܫ
24 ܥܡܢ ܗܘ ܐܠܗܐ : ܟܕ ܕܝ [k]ܩܡ ܝܘܣܦ ܡܢ
[l]ܫܢܬܗ : ܘܥܒܕ ܗܝܟ ܡܐ [m]ܕܦܩܕ ܠܗ
ܡܠܐܟܗ [n]ܕܡܪܝܐ ∴ ܘܕܒܪ ܠܗ ܠܐܬܬܗ :
25 ܘܠܐ ܗܘܐ ܚܟܡ ܠܗ ܥܕ [o]ܠܐ ܕܝܠܕܬ [p]ܒܪ [q]
[r]ܘܩܪܐ ܫܡܗ ܝܫܘܥ [s] :

Codex A.

[e] omit ܕ
[f]ܒܕܘܝܕ [g]ܠܕܘܝܕ
[h]ܐܪܒܥܬܥܣܪܝܢ
[i]ܕܘܝܕ [j] omit ܕܝ
[k]ܠܓܠܘܬܐ
[l]ܓܠܘܬܐ

[CCLVIII.]
[f. 166b]
[a] omit ܡܢ ܡܬܐܘܢ
[l] add ܓܝܪ
[z]ܬܘܠܕܬܗ
[a] add ܕܝ [b]ܡܟܕ
[c]ܗܘܬ [h]ܐܬܡܟܪܬ
[d]ܐܡܗ ܡܪܝܡ
[e]ܠܝܘܣܦ [g]ܡܥܒܪܐ
[h]ܒܪܘܚ [i]ܝܘܣܦ
[k] add ܐܠܐ ܐܬܚܫܒ ܕܒܛܘܫܝܐ ܢܫܒܩ ܠܗ : [m]ܕܡܪܝܐ
[o]ܝܘܣܦ [p]ܕܘܝܕ
[q] omit ܕܝ [r]ܠܡܪܝܡ
[t] omit ܕ [s]ܗܕܐ
[u] add ܕܝ [v]ܘܬܩܪܐ
[w]ܚܛܗܝܗܘܢ
[x] add ܕܝ [y]ܐܬܥܒܕܬ
[z]ܕܬܬܡܠܐ
[a]ܕܐܬܐܡܪ [b]ܡܪܝܐ
[q] omit ܕܝ
[c]ܕܐܝܫܥܝܐ
[f]ܡܥܒܪܐ [h]ܘܝܠܕܐ
[i]ܒܪܐ [j]ܘܩܪܘܢ
[i]ܥܡܢܘܐܝܠ
[k]ܩܡ [l]ܫܢܬܗ
[m]ܕܦܩܕ [n]ܕܡܪܝܐ
[o]ܠܐ [p]ܒܪܗ
[q] add ܒܘܟܪܐ
[r]ܘܩܪܬ [s] add ܥܠܝ

Codex C.

[e] omit ܕ
[f]ܒܕܘܝܕ [g]ܠܕܘܝܕ
[h]ܐܪܒܥܣܪܝܢ
[k]ܠܓܠܘܬܗ [j] omit ܕܝ
[l]ܓܠܘܬܗ [m]ܕܕܪܝܢ

ܠܝܫܘܥ ܐܠܡܫܝܚܐ ܕܝܢ
[l] add ܘܝܠܕܗ ܗܟܢܐ ܗܘܬ :
[c]ܗܘܬ [a] add ܕܝ
[h]ܐܬܡܟܪܬ
[d]ܐܡܗ ܡܪܝܡ
[e]ܠܝܘܣܦ [f]ܐܫܬܟܚܬ
[k] add ܐܠܐ ܐܬܚܫܒ ܕܒܛܘܫܝܐ ܢܫܒܩ ܠܗ :
[l]ܘܗܐ
[n]ܒܚܠܡܗ
[q] omit ܕܝ
[v]ܘܬܩܪܐ
[y]ܐܬܥܒܕ [x] add ܕܝ
[z]ܕܬܬܡܠܐ
[c]ܕܐܫܥܝܐ
† f. 133b.
[d] omit ܕܐܡܪ
[e]ܒܬܘܠܬܐ
[g]ܒܪܘܚ [h]ܘܝܠܕܐ
[i]ܥܡܢܘܐܝܠ
[m]ܕܦܩܕ [o]ܡܐ

Codex A.	Codex B.	Codex C.

CLXXI.

Luke II. 1—20.

Codex B.

ܐܪܒܗ [a]ܘܡܫܪܝܢ [b]ܠܠܝܠܬ [c]ܐܠܝܠܕܐ ܡܢ ܠܘܩܣ[d]: [a]
1 ܘܗܘܐ [b]ܒܗܠܝܢ [c]ܝܘܡܝܐ: ܢܦܩܬ [d]ܕܝܢ [e]ܦܩܘܕ
ܡܢ ܠܘܬ [f]ܐܓܘܣܛܘܣ [g]ܩܣܪ: [h]ܕܬܬܟܬܒ ܟܠܗ
2 [i]ܡܥܡܘܪܬܐ: [k]ܗܕܐ ܗܘܬ ܐܟܬܒܘܬܐ ܩܕܡܝܬܐ:
3 ܟܕ ܗܘܐ [l]ܩܘܪܝܢܘܣ[m]: ܘܗܘܘ ܐܙܠܝܢ ܟܠܗܘܢ
ܕܬܬܟܬܒܘܢ ܟܠ [n]ܐܢܫ ܐܢܫ [o]ܒܡܕܝܢܬܗ:
4 ܘܣܠܩ ܐܦ ܝܘܣܦ ܡܢ ܓܠܝܠܐ ܡܢ [p]ܡܕܝܢܬܐ
[q]ܢܨܪܬ ܠܝܗܘܕܐ [r]ܠܡܕܝܢܬܗ [d]ܕܝܢ [s]ܕܕܘܝܕ: ܗܕܐ
[t]ܕܡܬܩܪܝܐ ܒܝܬ [u]ܠܚܡ: [v]ܡܛܠ ܕܗܘܐ ܡܢ
5 ܒܝܬܗ ܘܡܢ ܫܪܒܬܗ [s]ܕܕܘܝܕ: ܕܬܬܟܬܒ ܥܡ
[f. 132b]
[w]ܡܪܝܡ ܗܕܐ ܕܗܘܬ [x]ܡܐܪܣܐ ܠܗ: [y]ܘܗܝ
6 ܗܘܬ [z]ܒܛܢܐ: ܘܗܘܐ [a]ܕܗܝܟ ܕܗܘܘ ܬܡܢ
7 ܐܬܡܠܝܘ ܝܘܡܝܐ ܕܬܠܕ ܘܝܠܕܬ [b]ܒܪܗ
[c]ܒܘܟܪܗ ܘܟܪܟܬ ܝܬܗ [d]ܒܥܙܪܘܩܝܢ: [e]ܘܐܫܟܒܬ
ܝܬܗ [f]ܒܐܘܪܝܐ: [g]ܡܛܠ ܕܠܐ ܗܘܐ [h]ܠܗܘܢ
8 ܐܬܪ [i]ܒܒܝܬ ܡܫܪܝܐ:[j] [k]ܘܗܘܘ ܬܡܢ ܪܥܘܝܢ
ܒܝܬܗ [l]ܐܪܥܐ ܡܒܝܬܝܢ [m]ܒܚܩܠܐ ܘܢܛܪܝܢ
9 [n]ܡܛܪܬܗ ܕܠܠܝܐ ܥܠ ܡܪܥܝܬܗܘܢ: [o]ܘܗܐ
ܡܠܐܟܗ [p]ܕܡܪܝܐ [q]ܩܡ [r]ܥܠܝܗܘܢ: ܘܬܫܒܘܚܬܗ
[p]ܕܡܪܝܐ ܐܢܗܪܬ ܠܗܘܢ: ܘܕܚܠܘ [†] ܕܚܠܐ ܪܒܐ:
10 ܘܐܡܪ ܠܗܘܢ ܡܠܐܟܐ ܠܐ [s]ܬܕܚܠܘܢ: ܗܐ
ܐܢܐ ܓܪ ܡܣܒܪ ܠܟܘܢ [t]ܚܕܘܐ ܪܒܐ: ܗܕܐ
11 ܕܬܗܘܐ ܠܟܠܗ ܥܡܐ ܕܐܬܝܠܕ ܠܟܘܢ
[u]ܝܘܡܢ ܦܪܘܩܐ: ܡܢ ܕܗܘ ܡܫܝܚܐ [p]ܕܡܪܝܐ
12 [v]ܒܡܕܝܢܬܗ [w]ܕܕܘܝܕ: [x]ܘܗܕܝܢ ܠܟܘܢ [y]ܐܬܐ
ܗܐ ܐܬܘܢ [z]ܐܫܟܚܝܢ ܡܥܛܦܝܢ ܠܛܠܝܐ [a]ܡܟܪܟܝܢ
13 [b]ܘܡܫܬܒܚ [c]ܒܐܘܪܝܐ: ܘܡܢ [d]ܫܠܝܐ ܗܘܐ ܥܡ
[e]ܡܠܐܟܐ [f]ܣܓܝܐܝܢ ܕܚܝܠܘ ܕܫܡܝܐ: [g]ܡܫܒܚܝܢ

Codex A.

[CCLIX.]
[f. 167a]

ܘܡܫܪܝܢ [b]ܐܠܝܠܬ
[c]ܐܠܝܠܕܐ
[d] add ܐܠܘܩܣ
[b]ܒܗܠܝܢ [c]ܝܘܡܝ̈ܐ
[d] omit ܕܝܢ [e]ܦܩܘܕ
[f]ܐܓܘܣܛܘܣ
[g]ܩܝܣܪ [h]ܕܬܬܟܬܒ
[i]ܡܥܡܘܪܬܐ
[k]ܗܕܐ [l]ܩܘܪܝܢܘܣ
[m] add ܡܕܒܪܢܐ
[o]ܒܡܕܝܢܬܗ
[p]ܡܕܝܢܬܐ
[r]ܠܡܕܝܢܬܗ
[s]ܕܕܘܝܕ [u]ܠܚܡ
[v]ܡܛܠ [w]ܡܪܝܡ
[x]ܐܪܘܣܐ [y]ܕܗ ܗܝ
[z]ܒܛܢܐ
[a]ܗܝܟ [c]ܒܘܟܪܗ
[d]ܒܥܙܪܘܩܝܢ
[f]ܒܐܘܪܝܐ [g]ܡܛܠ
[h] omit ܠܗܘܢ [i]ܒܒܝܬ
[l]ܕܐܪܥܐ
[n]ܡܛܪܬܗ
[o] omit ܗܐ
[p]ܕܡܪܝܐ
[q]ܩܡ [r]ܥܠܝܗܘܢ
[s]ܬܕܚܠܘܢ
[t]ܚܕܘܐ [u]ܝܘܡܢ
[v]ܒܡܕܝܢܬܗ
[w]ܕܕܘܝܕ [x]ܘܗܕܐ
[y]ܐܬܐ [z] omit ܐܫܟܚܝܢ
[a]ܡܟܪܟܝܢ [d]ܫܠܝܐ
[g]ܡܫܒܚܝܢ

Codex C.

ܐܪܒܗ ܘܡܫܪܝܢ
ܠܠܝܠܬ ܐܠܝܠܕܐ ܡܢ
ܠܘܩܣ
[a] add ܘܒܟܬܒܗ
ܦܪܘܩܐ
[b]ܒܗܠܝܢ
[d] omit ܕܝܢ [e]ܦܩܘܕ
[f]ܐܓܘܣܛܘܣ
[h]ܕܬܬܟܬܒ
[l]ܩܘܪܝܢܘܣ
[m] add ܥܠ ܣܘܪܝܐ:
[n] omit ܐܢܫ
[o]ܒܡܕܝܢܬܗ [q]ܢܨܪܬ
[t]ܕܡܬܩܪܝܐ
[x]ܐܪܘܣܐ
[a]ܗܝܟ [b]ܒܪ
[e]ܘܐܫܟܒܬ
[f]ܒܐܘܪܝܐ
[h] omit ܠܗܘܢ
[i]ܒܒܝܬ [j] add ܪܥܝܐ
† f. 134a.
[k]ܘܗܘܘ [l]ܕܐܪܥܐ
[m]ܒܚܩܠܐ
[n]ܡܛܪܬܗ
[o] omit ܗܐ
[q]ܩܡ [r]ܥܠܝܗܘܢ
[z] omit ܐܫܟܚܝܢ [y]ܐܬܐ
[b]ܘܡܫܬܒܚ [c]ܒܐܘܪܝܐ
[e]ܡܠܐܟܐ [f]ܣܓܝܐܝܢ

Codex A.

ᶠܬܫܒܘܚܬܐ
ⁱܘܗܘܐ ʲܐܙܠܘ
ᵈܡܠܐܟܝܐ
ᵏomit ܠܓܘ ˡܠܫܡܝܐ
ᵐܠܦܠܓܗ ⁿܢܐܙܠ
ᵒܠܚܡ
ᵖܕܡܪܝܐ
ʳܘܐܫܟܚܘ
ᵗܒܐܘܪܝܐ
ᵛܕܐܬܡܠܠܬ
ʷ add ܡܢ
ˣܕܫܡܥܘ ܘܚܡܘ
ʸܡܠܐܟܐ
ᶻ add ܥܠܡ

[CCLX.]
[f. 168a]
ᵃܘܒܥܐܪܝܢ
ᵇܦܫܝܢ ܡܢ ܡܬܝܘܣ
ܐܘܢܓܠܒ ܡܢ ܝܘܚ. ܫܕ.
ᶻܒܒܝܬ ܠܚܡ
ᵃܒܝܘܡܘܗܝ
ᵇܕܗܪܘܕܣ
ᵈܡܓܘܫܝܐ
ᵉܕܝܗܘܕܝܐ
ᶠܟܘܟܒܗ
ᵍܘܐܬܝܢ
ʰܗܪܘܕܣ

Codex B.

14 ܠܐܠܗܐ ܘܐܡܪܝܢ ⁘ ᶠܬܫܒܘܚܬܗ ܠܐܠܗܐ
ܒܡܪܘܡܐ ⁘ ᵍܘܥܠ ܐܪܥܐ ᵍ ܫܠܡܐ ܒܒܢܝܢܫܐ
15 ʰܨܒܝܢܐ ⁘ ⁱܘܗܘܐ ܟܕ ʲܐܙܠܘ ܠܗܘܢ ܡܢܗܘܢ
ᵈܡܠܐܟܐ ᵏܠܓܘ ˡܫܡܝܐ : ܐܡܪܘ ܪܥܝܐ
ܦܠܓܗܘܢ ᵐܠܦܠܓܗ : ܐܬܘ ⁿܢܐܙܠ ܥܕܡܐ
ܠܒܝܬ ᵒܠܚܡ : ܘܢܚܡܐ ܡܠܬܐ ܗܕܐ
16 ܕܐܬܥܒܕܬ ܗܕܐ ᵖܕܡܪܝܐ ᵠܐܘܕܥ ܠܢ ⁘ ܘܐܬܘ
ܡܬܥܒܝܢ ʳܘܐܬܘ ܫܟܚܘ ʳ ܝܬܗ ܠܡܪܝܡ
[f. 133a]
17 ܘܠܝܘܣܦ ܘܠܛܠܝܐ ˢܡܫܟܒ ᵗܒܘܪܝܐ : ܘܟܕ
ܚܡܘ ܐܘܕܥܘ ܥܠ ܡܠܬܐ ܕܐܬܡܠܠܬ
18 ܠܗܘܢ : ܥܠܘܗܝ ܕܛܠܝܐ ܗܕܝܢ : ܘܟܠ ܗܠܝܢ
ܕܫܡܥܘ ܗܘܘ ᵘܬܡܗܝܢ ܥܠ ܥܠ ܟܠ ܗܠܝܢ
19 ᵛܕܡܡܠܠܘ ܠܗܘܢ ʷ ܪܥܝܐ : ܘܡܪܝܡ ܗܘܬ
ܢܛܪܐ ܟܠ ܗܠܝܢ ܡܠܝܐ ܘܪܥܝܐ ܒܓܘ ܠܒܗ ⁘
20 ܘܬܒܘ ܪܥܝܐ ܡܫܒܚܝܢ ܘܡܫܒܚܝܢ ܠܐܠܗܐ ܥܠ
ܟܠ ܗܠܝܢ ˣܕܫܡܥܘ ܘܚܡܘ ˣ ܗܟܢ ܕܐܬܡܠܠ
ܠܗܘܢ ܡܢ ʸܡܠܐܟܐ ᶻ

CLXXII.

Matt. II. 1—12.

ܫܡܫܗ ᵃܘܒܥܪܝܢ ܝܘܡ ܐܠܡܝܠܕ : ᵇܘܗܕܐ ܗܘ
1 ܠܠܗܕܐܘܣ ܡܢ ܡܬܝܐ ᵇ ܘܟܕ ܐܬܝܠܕ ܡܪܢ
ܝܫܘܥ ᶻܒܒܝܬ ܠܚܡ ᶻ ܕܝܗܘܕܐ ᵃܒܝܘܡܝ
ᵇܗܪܘܕܣ ܡܠܟܐ ᶜܗܘܐ ᵈܡܓܘܫܝܢ ܡܢ
2 ܡܕܢܚܐ ܐܬܘ ܠܐܘܪܫܠܡ ⁘ ܐܡܪܝܢ ܗ̇ ܗܘ
ܗܕܝܡ ܕܐܬܝܠܕ ܡܠܟܗܘܢ ᵉܕܝܗܘܕܝܐ : ܚܡܝܢܢ
ܓܝܪ ᶠܟܘܟܒܗ ܒܡܕܢܚܐ ᵍܘܐܬܝܢܢ ܕܢܣܓܘܕ
3 ܠܗ : ܘܟܕ ܫܡܥ ʰܗܪܘܕܣ ܡܠܟܐ ܐܬܥܪܒܒ
4 ⁱܘܟܠܗ ܐܘܪܫܠܡ ܥܡܗ ⁘ ᵏܘܟܢܫ ܟܠܗܘܢ

Codex C.

ᵍܠܐܪܥܐ
ʰܨܒܝܢܐ ⁱܘܗܘܐ
ʲܐܙܠܘ ᵈܡܠܐܟܐ
ᵏomit ܠܓܘ ˡܠܫܡܝܐ
ⁿܢܐܙܠ ᵒܠܚܡ
ᵠܐܘܕܥ
ʳܘܐܫܟܚܘ ˢܡܫܟܒ
ᵗܒܐܘܪܝܐ
ᵘܬܡܗܝܢ
ᵛܕܐܬܡܠܠ
ˣܕܫܡܥܘ ܘܚܡܘ
ʸܡܠܐܟܐ

ܫܡܫܗ ܘܒܥܪܝܢ
ܝܘܡ ܐܠܡܝܠܕ
ܒܘܪܗ ܡܢ ܡܬܝܐ
ܐܘܢܓܠܒ ܡܢ ܝܘܚ
ܫܕ ܐܠܟܐ
[† f. 134b]
ܘܗܘ ܬܠܕܬܗ
†ܕܝ ܕܡܪܢܐ ܝܫܘܥ
ܡܫܝܚܐ ܘܗܕܐ
ܠܠܗܕܘ ܝܘܡ ܐܠܡܝܠܕ
ܡܢ ܡܬܝܐ ܘܟܝܬܗ
ܦܢܪܘܣܐ
ᶻܒܒܝܬ ܠܚܡ
ᶜܘܗܘܐ
ᵏܘܟܢܫܘ ⁱܘܟܠ

Codex A.

[k] ܘܟܢܫ [l] ܡܫܐܠ

[m] *add* ܗܘ

[o] ܟܕܢ ܠܒܝܬ [r] *add*

[s] ܕܝܗܘܕܐ

[t] *omit* ܒܢܒܝܐ

[u] *add* ܠܝܬ

[j] ܒܡܠܟܘܬܐ

[w] *add* ܓܝܪ

[z] ܢܪܥܝܘܢ [a] ܠܥܡܝ

[b] ܐܝܣܪܐܝܠ

[c] ܟܕܢ [d] ܗܪܘܕܝܣ

[g] ܠܡܓܘܫܝܐ

[i] *add* ܠܗܘܢ

[k] ܠܒܝܬ [o] *omit* ܗܘ

[l] *omit* ܐܙܠܘ

[n] *omit* ܐܢܐ

[o] ܗܕܝܢ [q] ܠܓܠ

[s] ܢܘܗܪܐ

[t] ܚܡܝܘܢ [u] ܦܬܚܘ

[v] ܕܗܒ [w] ܘܠܒܘܢܐ

[y] ܗܪܘܕܝܣ

[z] *omit* ܐܠܐ

[a] ܒܐܘܪܚ

[b] *omit* ܐܬܪܗܘܢ

[c] ܠܐܬܪܗܘܢ

[CCLXI.]
[f. 168*b*]
ܘܟܕ ܐܙܠܘ [b] ܡܓܘܫܐ [c] ܗܐ ܡܠܐܟܐ ܕܡܪܝܐ
ܐܬܚܙܝ

[o] *add* ܗܘ

[a] ܕܗܘ ܬܪܝܠܗ

Codex B.

ܘܟܢܫ[k] ܟܠܗܘܢ ܪܒܝ ܟܗܢܝܐ ܘܣܦܪܝܐ ܕܥܡܐ : ܘܗܘܐ
ܡܫܐܠ[l] ܠܗܘܢ ܗܢܘܢ ܡܫܝܚܐ ܗܝܟܐ ܡܬܝܠܕ :
5 ܘܐܡܪܘ[m] ܠܗ ܒܒܝܬ ܠܚܡ[n] ܕܝܗܘܕܐ
6 ܟܕܢ[o] ܓܪ ܟܬܝܒ[p] ܒܢܒܝܐ : ܐܢܬ[q] ܐܢܬ
ܒܝܬ[r] ܐܪܥܐ[s] ܕܝܗܘܕܐ[t] ܒܢܒܝܐ[u] ܐܢܬ
ܙܥܘܪܐ[j] ܒܡܠܟܘܬܐ[v] ܕܝܗܘܕܐ : ܒܢܒܝܐ[w] ܡܢܟ
ܢܦܩ[x] ܡܕܒܪܢܐ[y] ܕܗܘ[z] ܢܪܥܐ[a] ܠܥܡܝ[b] ܐܝܣܪܐܝܠ :
7 ܟܕܢ[c] ܗܪܘܕܝܣ[d] ܩܪܐ[e] ܒܛܡܝܪܐܝܬ[f] ܠܡܓܘܫܐ[g]
ܘܥܩܒ ܡܢܗܘܢ ܙܒܢܗ ܕܟܘܟܒܐ[h] ܕܐܬܚܙܝ[i]:
8 ܘܫܠܚ[j] ܐܢܘܢ ܠܒܝܬ ܠܚܡ[k] ܘܐܡܪ : ܐܙܠܘ
ܐܬܒܩܘ ܒܚܦܝܛܘ ܥܠ ܛܠܝܐ[o] ܗܘ ܡ[f. 133*b*]ܬܒܩܘ
ܛܠܝܐ : ܘܟܕ[l] ܐܫܟܚܬܘܢ ܐܘܕܥܘܢܢܝ[m] ܕܐܦ ܐܢܐ
ܐܬܐ[n] ܘܐܣܓܘܕ ܠܗ :
9 ܗܢܘܢ ܕܝܢ ܟܕ ܫܡܥܘ ܡܢ ܡܠܟܐ ܐܙܠܘ : ܘܗܐ
ܟܘܟܒܐ ܗܘ[o] ܕܚܙܘ ܒܡܕܢܚܐ ܗܘܐ[t]
ܐܙܠ ܩܕܡܝܗܘܢ ܥܕܡܐ ܕܐܬܐ[p] ܘܩܡ
10 ܠܥܠ[q] ܡܢ[r] ܐܬܪܐ ܕܗܘܐ ܛܠܝܐ : ܟܕ ܕܝܢ ܚܙܘ
11 ܟܘܟܒܐ ܚܕܝܘ[s] ܚܕܘܐ ܪܒܐ ܠܚܕܐ : ܘܥܠܘ
ܠܒܝܬܐ ܚܙܘ ܠܛܠܝܐ ܥܡ ܡܪܝܡ ܐܡܗ[t] :
ܘܢܦܠܘ[u] ܣܓܕܘ ܠܗ : ܘܦܬܚܘ ܣܝܡܬܗܘܢ
ܘܩܪܒܘ ܠܗ ܩܘܪܒܢܐ . ܕܗܒܐ[v] ܘܠܒܘܢܬܐ[w]
12 ܘܡܘܪܐ[x] : ܘܐܬܚܙܝ ܠܗܘܢ ܒܚܠܡܐ ܕܠܐ
ܢܗܦܟܘܢ ܠܘܬ ܗܪܘܕܝܣ[y] : ܐܠܐ[z] ܒܐܘܪܚܐ[a]
ܐܚܪܝܬܐ ܐܙܠܘ ܠܐܬܪܗܘܢ[b] ܠܐܬܪܗܘܢ[c] :

CLXXIII.

MATT. II. 13—23.

ܘܟܕ[a] ܐܙܠܘ[b] ܡܓܘܫܐ ܗܐ ܡܠܐܟܐ[c] ܕܡܪܝܐ ܐܬܚܙܝ
13 ܠܝܘܣܦ ܒܚܠܡܐ[c] : ܘܐܡܪ ܠܗ ܩܘܡ ܕܒܪ[a]

Codex C.

[k] ܘܟܢܫ [m] *add* ܗܘ

[n] ܠܒܝܬ [p] ܟܬܝܒ

[q] *add* ܐܢܬ

[r] *add* ܠܒܝܬ

[t] *omit* ܒܢܒܝܐ

[j] ܒܡܠܟܘܬܐ [u] *add* ܠܝܬ

[v] ܕܝܗܘܕܐ [w] *add* ܓܝܪ

[x] ܡܕܒܪܢܐ [y] *add* ܕܗܘ

[z] ܢܪܥܐ [a] ܠܥܡܝ

[e] ܒܛܡܝܪܐܝܬ

[f] ܩܪܐ [g] ܠܡܓܘܫܐ

[h] ܕܐܬܚܙܝ

[j] ܘܫܠܚ [o] *omit* ܗܘ

[l] *omit* ܐܙܠܘ

† f. 135*a*.

[m] ܐܘܕܥܘ

[p] *omit* ܘܩܡ

[r] *omit* ܡܢ

[u] ܦܬܚܘ [v] ܕܗܒ

[w] ܘܠܒܘܢܐ [x] ܘܡܘܪܐ

[y] ܗܪܘܕܝܣ

[z] *omit* ܐܠܐ

[a] ܒܐܘܪܚ

[b] *omit* ܐܬܪܗܘܢ

[c] ܠܐܬܪܗܘܢ

ܘܟܕ ܐܙܠܘ
ܡܓܘܫܐ ܗܐ ܡܠܐܟܐ
ܕܡܪܝܐ ܐܬܚܙܝ
ܠܝܘܣܦ ܒܚܠܡܐ

[a] *add* ܗܘ

Codex A.

[b] *add* ܡܓܘܫܝܐ

[c]ܕܡܪܝܐ [d]ܕܒܪ

[e]ܘܠܐܡܗ

[f]ܘܥܪܘܩ

[h]ܥܕ ܕ [i] *add* ܒܪ

[k]ܗܪܘܕܣ [l]ܕܒܪ

[m]ܘܠܐܡܗ [n]ܘܐܙܠ

[j]ܗܪܘܕܣ

[o]ܡܪܝܐ [p]ܟܕܝܢ

[q]ܡܓܘܫܝܐ

[r]ܠܚܡ [s]ܘܟܠܗ

[t]ܬܚܘܡܝܗ

[u]ܫܢܝܢ [x]ܡܓܘܫܝܐ

[y]ܗܝܕܝܢ [a]ܩܠܐ

[b]ܒܟܝܐ

[c]ܘܬܘܚܐ [o]ܣܓܝܐ

[d]ܪܐܚܝܠ [e] *add* ܒܟܝܐ

[f]ܒܢܝܗ [h] *add* ܥܠܡ

[i]ܗܪܘܕܣ [k]ܕܡܪܝܐ

[l]ܠܝܘܣܦ

ܕܝܢ [m] *omit* [n]ܕܒܪ

[o]ܘܠܐܡܗ

[p]ܘܐܙܠ ܠܟ [q] *omit*

[r]ܕܐܝܣܪܝܠ

[u]ܕܐܝܣܪܝܠ

[v]ܕܐܪܟܠܘܣ

[w]ܡܠܟ [x]ܒܝܗܘܕܐ

[y]ܐܒܘܗ [z]ܕܚܠ

ܗܘ [a] *omit* [b]ܠܗ

ܕܝܢ [d] *omit*

Codex B.

[a]ܠܗܘܢ [b]܀ ܗܐ ܡܠܐܟܗ [c]ܕܡܪܝܐ ܐܬܚܡܝ
ܒܚܠܡܐ ܠܝܘܣܦ ܘܐܡܪ ܠܗ: ܩܘܡ [d]ܕܒܪ
ܝܬܗ ܠܛܠܝܐ [e]ܘܠܐܡܗ ܀ [f]ܘܥܪܘܩ ܠܡܨܪܝܢ
ܘܗܘܝ ܬܡܢ ܒܡܕܝܢܬܐ [g]ܕܐܡܪܢܐ ܠܟ: [h]ܥܕ ܕ
ܗܘ [i] [k]ܗܪܘܕܣ ܕܡܒܥܐ ܝܬܗ ܠܛܠܝܐ ܕܝܘܒܕ
14 ܝܬܗ: ܘܗܘ ܕܝܢ ܩܡ [l]ܕܒܪ ܝܬܗ ܠܛܠܝܐ
[m]ܘܠܐܡܗ ܒܠܠܝܐ [n]ܘܐܙܠ ܠܗ ܠܡܨܪܝܢ:
15 ܘܗܘܐ ܬܡܢ ܥܕܡܐ ܕܡܝܬ [j]ܗܪܘܕܣ ܕܝܬܡܠܐ
ܡܐ ܕܐܬܐܡܪ ܡܢ [o]ܡܪܝܐ ܒܢܒܝܐ ܕܐܡܪ ܡܢ
16 ܡܨܪܝܢ ܩܪܝܬ ܝܬܗ ܠܒܪܝ: [p]ܟܕܝܢ [j]ܗܪܘܕܣ
ܟܕ ܚܙܐ ܕܐܬܒܙܚ ܡܢ [q]ܡܓܘܫܝܐ ܐܬܚܡܬ
ܠܚܕܐ: ܘܫܠܚ ܩܛܠ ܟܠ ܛܠܝܐ ܕܗܘܘ ܒܒܝܬ
[r]ܠܚܡ: [s]ܘܟܠܗ [t]ܬܚܘܡܝܗ ܡܢ ܒܪ ܬܪܬܝܢ
[f. 134a]
[u] † ܫܢܝܢ [w]ܘܠܬܚܬ: ܗܝܟ ܐܟܘܬܐ ܕܐܬܥܩܒ ܡܢ
17 [x]ܡܓܘܫܝܐ: [y]ܗܝܕܝܢ ܐܬܡܠܝ ܡܐ [z]ܕܐܬܐܡܪ
18 ܒܐܪܡܝܐ ܢܒܝܐ ܕܐܡܪ: [a]ܩܠ ܒܪܡܐ
ܐܫܬܡܥ [b]ܒܟܝ [c]ܘܬܘܚܐ [o]ܣܓܝ: [d]ܪܐܚܝܠ
[e]ܥܠ [f]ܒܢܝܗ ܘܠܐ [g]ܒܥܝܐ ܕܬܬܢܚܡ ܕܠܝܬ
19 ܗܢܘܢ: [h] ܘܟܕ ܡܝܬ [i]ܗܪܘܕܣ ܗܐ ܡܠܐܟܗ
[k]ܕܡܪܝܐ ܐܬܚܡܝ [l]ܠܝܘܣܦ [m]ܕܝܢ ܒܡܨܪܝܢ
20 ܘܐܡܪ ܠܗ: ܩܘܡ [n]ܕܒܪ ܠܛܠܝܐ [o]ܘܠܐܡܗ
[p]ܘܐܙܠ [q]ܠܟ: ܠܐܪܥܐ [r]ܕܐܝܣܪܝܠ: [s]ܡܝܬܘ
21 ܓܝܪ ܗܠܝܢ ܕܗܘܘ ܒܥܝܢ ܢܦܫܗ ܕܛܠܝܐ: ܘܩܡ
[t]ܕܒܪ ܝܬܗ ܠܛܠܝܐ [o]ܘܠܐܡܗ ܘܐܬܐ ܠܐܪܥܐ
22 [u]ܕܐܝܣܪܝܠ: ܟܕ ܕܝܢ ܫܡܥ [v]ܕܐܪܟܠܘܣ [w]ܡܠܟ
[x]ܒܝܗܘܕܐ ܚܠܦ [i]ܗܪܘܕܣ [y]ܐܒܘܗ [z]ܕܚܠ
ܕܝܐܙܠ ܠܬܡܢ: ܘ[a]ܗܘ ܐܬܚܡܝ [b]ܕܝܢ ܒܚܠܡܐ
23 [c]ܕܝܐܙܠ ܠܗ ܠܐܪܥܐ ܕܓܠܝܠܐ ܘ[a]ܗܘ ܐܬܐ
ܘܥܡܪ [d]ܕܝܢ ܒܡܕܝܢܬܐ ܗܕܐ [e]ܕܡܬܩܪܝܐ
ܢܨܪܬ: ܕܢܬܡܠܐ ܡܐ ܕܐܬܐܡܪ ܒܢܒܝܐ ܕܢܨܪܝ
ܢܬܩܪܐ ܀ [f]ܫܠܡ ܀

Codex C.

[a] *omit* ܠܗܘܢ

[b] *add* ܡܓܘܫܝܐ

[d]ܕܒܪ

[g]ܕܐܡܪܢܐ [h]ܥܕ ܕ

[i] *add* ܒܪ

[l]ܕܒܪ

[m]ܘܠܐܡܗ (*sic*)

[j]ܗܪܘܕܣ

[s]ܘܟܠܗ

[t]ܬܚܘܡܝܗܘܢ

[w]ܘܠܬܚܬ

† f. 135*b*.

[x]ܡܓܘܫܝܐ

[z]ܕܐܬܐܡܪ

ܘܠܐ [b]ܒܟܝ

[d]ܪܐܚܝܠ

[e] *add* ܒܟܝܐ

[f]ܒܢܝܗ [g]ܒܥܝܐ

[h] *add* ܥܠܡ ܐܢܫ

[i]ܗܪܘܕܣ

ܕܝܢ [m] *omit* [n]ܕܒܪ

[r]ܕܐܝܣܪܝܠ [s]ܡܝܬܘ

[t] *omit* ܝܬܗ

[v]ܕܐܪܟܠܘܣ

[x]ܒܝܗܘܕܐ [y]ܐܒܘܗܝ

ܗܘ [a] *omit* [b]ܠܗ

[c]ܕܐܙܠ ܕܝܢ [d] *omit*

[e]ܕܡܬܩܪܝܐ

[f] *omit* ܫܠܡ

Codex A.	Codex B.	Codex C.
[CCLXIII.] [f. 169b]	CLXXIV. MARK VI. 1—5.	
[Syriac text]	[Syriac text]	[Syriac text]
[Syriac text]	[Syriac text]	[Syriac text] g add
[Syriac text]	[Syriac text]	[Syriac text]
[Syriac text]	1 [Syriac text]	i omit [Syriac text]
(sic) [Syriac text]	2 [Syriac text]	[Syriac text]
g add [Syriac text]	[Syriac text]	[Syriac text]
i omit [Syriac text]	[Syriac text]	f omit [Syriac text]
[Syriac text]	[Syriac text] †	† f. 136a.
[Syriac text]	[Syriac text]	[Syriac text]
f omit [Syriac text]	3 [Syriac text]	[Syriac text]
[Syriac text]	[Syriac text] [f. 134b]	[Syriac text]
[Syriac text]	[Syriac text]	[Syriac text]
[Syriac text]	[Syriac text]	[Syriac text]
[Syriac text]	4 [Syriac text]	[Syriac text]
[Syriac text]	[Syriac text]	[Syriac text]
[Syriac text]	5 [Syriac text]	t omit [Syriac text]
[Syriac text]	[Syriac text]	v omit [Syriac text]
[Syriac text]	[Syriac text]	[Syriac text]
[Syriac text]	[Syriac text]	
v add [Syriac text]	[Syriac text]	[Syriac text]
z add [Syriac text]	[Syriac text]	[Syriac text]
	[Syriac text]	b add [Syriac text]

Codex A.	Codex B.	Codex C.
[CCLXVIII.] [f. 170a]	CLXXV. LUKE II. 20, 21, 40—52.	[Syriac text]
(sic) كانون الثاني [a]		[Syriac text]
[Syriac text] (sic)	[Syriac text]	[Syriac text]
[Syriac text] (sic)	[Syriac text]	[Syriac text]
[Syriac text]	[Syriac text]	[Syriac text]
[Syriac text]	[Syriac text]	[Syriac text]

Codex A.	Codex B.	Codex C.
[a]ܘܐܬܦܢܘ	20 ܘܒܬܪܗ ܦܢܘ ܪܥܘܬܐ [a]ܘܐܬܦܢܘ ܪܥܝܐ ܡܫܒܚܝܢ	
	ܘܡܫܒܚܝܢ ܠܐܠܗܐ ܥܠ ܟܘܠ ܗܠܝܢ ܕܫܡܥܘ	
	ܘܚܙܘ : ܗܝܟ ܕܐܬܡܠܠ ܠܗܘܢ ܡܢ [b]ܡܠܐܟܐ :	[b]ܡܠܐܟܐ
[c]add ܕܝܢ	21 ܘܟܕ ܫܠܡܘ[c] [d]ܬܡܢܝܐ [e]ܝܘܡܝܢ ܠܛܠܝܐ	[c]add ܕܝܢ
[d]ܬܡܢܝܐ [e]ܝܘܡܝܢ	[f]ܕܝܓܙܪܘܢ ܝܬܗ : ܐܬܩܪܝ ܫܡܗ ܝܫܘܥ	[d]ܬܡܢܝܐ [e]ܝܘܡܝܢ
[f]ܕܝܓܙܪܘܢ	[g]ܗܕܝܢ ܕܐܬܩܪܝ ܡܢ [h]ܡܠܐܟܐ ܥܕ ܠܐ ܝܬܒܛܢ	[h]ܡܠܐܟܐ
[g]ܗܕܝܢ	40 ܒܟܪܣܐ : ܘܛܠܝܐ ܕܝܢ ܗܘܐ ܪܒܐ ܘܡܫܬܪܪ	[i]add ܒܟܪܣܐ
[k]ܘܚܣܕܗ	ܒܪܘܚܐ [i]ܘܡܬܡܠܐ ܡܢ ܚܟܡܬܐ : [k]ܘܚܣܕܗ	[l]ܗܘܐ
[l]ܗܘܐ [m]ܥܠܘ	41 ܕܐܠܗܐ †[l]ܗܘܬ [m]ܥܠܘܝ : ܘܗܘܘ ܐܒܗܘܬܗ	† f. 136b.
[n]omit ܕܝܢ	ܐܙܠܝܢ ܠܝܪܘܫܠܡ [n]ܕܝܢ ܒܟܘܠ ܫܢܐ [o]ܒܥܐܕܐ	[n]omit ܕܝܢ
[o]ܒܥܐܕܐ	42 [p]ܕܦܨܚܐ : ܘܟܕ ܗܘܐ ܒܪ [q]ܬܪܬܝܢ ܥܣܪ[q]	[p]ܕܦܨܚܐ
[q]ܬܪܬܝܢܥܣܪܝ [j]ܫܢܝܢ	[j]ܫܢܝܢ : ܣܠܩܘ ܠܝܪܘܫܠܡ ܗܝܟ ܐܬܥܝܕܘܬܗ	[q]ܬܠܬܥܣܪܝ
[r]ܕܥܐܕܐ	43 [r]ܕܥܐܕܐ : ܘܟܕ ܫܠܡܘ ܝܘܡܝܐ ܒܗܦܟܐ	[r]ܕܥܐܕܐ :
[s]ܐܬܦܢܝܢ [t]ܡܪܢ	ܕܗܘܘ [s]ܐܬܦܢܝܢ : ܦܫܪ ܕܝܢ ܛܠܝܐ [t]ܡܪܢܐ [f. 135a]	[t]ܡܪܢ
	ܝܫܘܥ ܒܝܪܘܫܠܡ : ܘܠܐ ܝܕܥܘ ܐܒܗܘܬܗ	
	44 ܘܗܘܘ ܣܒܪܝܢ ܕܗܟܐ ܥܡ ܒܢܝ [a]ܠܘܬܗܘܢ	[a]ܠܘܬܗܘܢ
[u]ܕܗܠܝܟ	ܗܘ : ܘܐܬܘ [u]ܕܗܠܝܟ ܚܕ ܝܘܡ ܒܐܘܪܚܐ :	[u]ܕܗܠܝܟ
	ܘܗܘܘ ܒܥܝܢ ܠܗ ܒܝܢ ܩܪܝܒܝܗܘܢ ܘܒܗܠܝܢ	
	45 ܕܝܕܥܝܢ ܠܗܘܢ : ܘܟܕ ܠܐ ܐܫܟܚܘ ܝܬܗ	
	46 [v]ܬܒܘ ܠܗܘܢ ܠܝܪܘܫܠܡ : ܒܥܝܢ ܠܗ : ܘܗܘܐ	[v]ܬܒܘ
[w]ܝܘܡܝܢ	ܡܢ ܒܬܪ ܬܠܬܐ [w]ܝܘܡܝܢ ܐܫܟܚܘ ܝܬܗ ܒܗܝܟܠܐ	[w]ܝܘܡܝܢ
[x]ܝܬܒ [y]ܘܫܐܠ	[x]ܝܬܒ ܒܡܨܥܬ ܡܠܦܢܐ : ܫܡܥ ܡܢܗܘܢ [y]ܘܫܐܠ	[y]ܘܫܐܠ
	47 ܠܗܘܢ ܘܗܘܘ [o]ܡܬܡܗܝܢ ܟܘܠ ܗܠܝܢ ܕܗܘܘ	[o]ܡܬܡܗܝܢ
[a]ܦܬܓܡܬܗ	ܫܡܥܝܢ ܡܢܗ : ܥܠ *ܒܣܘܟܠܬܗ ܘܥܠ [a]ܦܬܓܡܬܗ :	[*Cod. B. ܒܣܘܟܠܬܗ]
[c]ܐܬܡܗܘ	48 ܘܟܕ ܕܝܢ [b]ܚܙܘ ܝܬܗ [c]ܐܬܡܗܘ : ܘܐܡܪܬ ܠܗ	[b]omit ܚܙܘ ܝܬܗ
[d]add ܠܢ [e]ܥܒܕ	ܐܡܗ ܒܪܝ ܠܡܐ [d]ܥܒܕܬ [e]ܠܢ : [f]ܗܐ ܐܢܐ	[d]add ܠܢ [f]ܕܗܐ
[f]ܗܐ [g]ܘܐܒܘܟ	49 [g]ܘܐܒܘܟ ܗܘܝܢ ܡܒܥܝܢ ܒܥܝܢ ܠܟ : ܘܐܡܪ	[g]ܘܐܒܘܟ
[h]ܡܢܐ [i]ܠܐ	ܠܗܘܢ [h]ܡܐ ܗܘܝܬܘܢ ܒܥܝܢ ܠܝ : [i]ܠܐ	[i]ܠܐ [k]ܕܒܝܬ
[k]ܕܒܝܬ [l]ܕܝܗܘܝ	ܗܘܝܬܘܢ ܝܕܥܝܢ [k]ܕܒܝܬ ܐܒܐ ܢܦܠ ܠܝ [l]ܕܝܗܘܝ	[l]ܕܝܗܘܝ
[m]omit ܐܢܐ	50 [m]ܐܢܐ : ܘܗܢܘܢ [n]ܕܝܢ ܠܐ ܐܬܒܝܢܘ [o]ܡܠܬܐ	[m]omit ܐܢܐ
[n]omit ܕܝܢ [o]ܠܡܠܬܐ	51 [p]ܕܡܠܠ ܠܗܘܢ : ܘܢܚܬ ܥܡܗܘܢ ܘܐܬܐ ܠܢܨܪܬ	[p]ܕܡܠܠ [n]omit ܕܝܢ

Codex A.	Codex B.	Codex C.
ܘܐܡܗ[q]	ܘܗܘܐ ܡܫܬܥܒܕ ܠܗܘܢ ܀ ܘܐܡܗ[q] ܗܘܬ ܢܛܪܐ	ܡܬܪܒܐ[n]
	52 ܟܠܗܝܢ ܡ̈ܠܝܐ ܐܠܝܢ ܒܠܒܗ ܀ †ܘܡܪܢ ܝܫܘܥ ܗܘܐ	† f. 137a.
ܡܬܪܒܐ[n]	ܡܬܪܒܐ[n] ܒܚܟܡܬܐ ܘܒܩܘܡܬܐ ܘܒܛܝܒܘܬܐ	ܘܒܚܘܒܐ[o]
ܘܒܚܘܒܐ[o]	ܘܒܚܘܒܗ[o] ܠܘܬ ܐܠܗܐ ܘܠܘܬ ܒܢܝ ܐܢܫܐ ܀ ܥܠܡ[p] ܀	[p] omit ܥܠܡ

Codex A.	Codex B.	Codex C.
[CCLXIX.] [f. 170b]	**CLXXVI.**	
	JOHN III. 1, 12; MATT. III. 1, 5—11.	ܐܬܐ ܐܢܫ ܐܠܘܠܐ ܚܕ ܡܢ ܦܪܝܫܐ ܫܡܗ ܢܝܩܕܡܘܣ
ܐܬܐ ܐܢܫ[a]	ܐܬܐ[a] ܐܢܫ[b] ܐܠܘܠܐ ܫܡܗ[c] ܚܕ[d] ܢܝܩܕܡܘܣ	
[b] omit ܐܢܫ	ܡܢ[d] [e]ܐܘܚܕܢܐ ܡܠܟܘܬܗ[f] ܗܘܐ ܗܘ ܗܘ ܡܢ[g]	ܘܗܘܐ[f]
ܫܡܗ ܢܝܩܕܡܘܣ[c] (sic)	[h]ܦܪܝܫܐ [g]ܘܫܡܗ [i]ܢܝܩܕܡܘܣ ܘܐܬܐ ܠܘܬܗ	[g] omit ܦܪܝܫܐ ܡܢ
[d] omit ܡܢ . . . ܚܕ	ܕܝܫܘܥ ܬܘܒ ܐܡܪ ܗܘܐ ܀ [m]ܡܢ ܐܢܫ[k] [l]ܡܬܝܠܕ	ܢܝܩܕܡܘܣ[i]
ܐܘܚܕܢܐ[e] ܦܪܝܫܐ[h]	1 ✠ ܘܐܬܐ[a] [b]ܝܘܚܢܢ ܡܥܡܕܢܐ [c]ܡܟܪܙ ܒܡܕܒܪܐ	ܡܬܝܠܕ ܡܢ[m]
ܢܝܩܕܡܘܣ[i]	5 ܕܝܗܘܕܐ[d] ܗܝܕܝܢ ܢܦܩܘ ܠܘܬܗ[e]	ܡܬܠܕ ܘܡܠܟܘܬܗ
ܡܬܝܠܕ[l] [k]omit ܐܢܫ	[f. 135b] ܐܘܪܫܠܡ ܘܟܠܗ ܝܗܘܕ[f] ܘܟܠܗ	ܐܬܐ[a]
[CCLXX.]		
ܐܬܐ[a] ܕܝܗܘܕܐ[d]	6 ܐܬܪܐ [g]ܕܝܪܕܢܐ [h]ܘܡܬܥܡܕܝܢ ܗܘܘ ܡܢܗܘܢ	ܝܘܚܢܢ[b] ܡܟܪܙ[c]
ܕܝܪܕܢܐ[g]	ܡܢܗ ܒܝܪܕܢܐ[i] ܢܗܪܐ ܘܡܘܕܝܢ [k]ܚܛܗܝܗܘܢ ܀	ܕܝܗܘܕܐ[d] ܠܘܬܗ[e]
ܒܝܪܕܢܐ[h] ܒܝܪܕܢܐ[i]	7 ܟܕ ܚܙܐ ܣܓܝܐܐ ܡܢ [l]ܦܪܝܫܐ ܘܡܢ [m]ܨܕܘܩܝܐ	ܕܝܗܘܕܐ[f]
ܚܛܗܝܗܘܢ[k]	ܐܬܝܢ [v]ܠܡܥܡܕܘܬܗ ܐܡܪ ܠܗܘܢ ܀ [n]ܝܠܕܝ ܐܟܕܢܐ	ܒܝܪܕܢܐ[i]
ܦܪܝܫܐ[l] ܨܕܘܩܝܐ[m]	[o]ܕܚܝܘܬܐ ܡܢ [p]ܐܚܘܝܟܘܢ ܠܡܥܪܩ [q]ܡܢ ܪܘܓܙܐ	ܕܥܡܕܘܬܗ[v]
ܕܡܥܡܕܘܬܗ[v]	8 ܕܥܬܝܕ[r] ܥܒܕܘ ܗܟܝܠ ܦܐܪܐ ܕܫܘܝܢ	ܝܠܕܝ[n] ܐܟܕܢܐ
ܝܠܕܝ ܐܟܕܢܐ[n]	9 ܠܬܝܒܘܬܐ[s] ܘܠܐ [t]ܬܗܘܘܢ ܐܡܪܝܢ [u]ܐܒܘܢ	ܕܚܝܘܬܐ[o]
ܕܚܝܘܬܐ[o] ܐܚܘܝ[p]	ܐܒܪܗܡ ܐܝܬ ܠܢ ܐܡܪ ܐܢܐ ܠܟܘܢ : ܐܡܪ	ܠܬܝܒܘܬܐ[s]
ܕܪܘܓܙܐ[q]	ܐܢܐ ܠܟܘܢ ܕܝܟܘܠ[w] ܗܘ ܐܠܗܐ ܕܡܢ ܟܐܦܐ	[t] omit ܬܗܘܘܢ
ܕܥܬܝܕ[r]	10 ܗܠܝܢ ܢܩܝܡ[x] ܒܢܝܐ ܠܐܒܪܗܡ : ܗܐ ܕܝܢ[z]	ܕܝܟܘܠ[w]
ܠܬܝܒܘܬܐ[s]	ܢܪܓܐ[y] ܣܝܡ ܥܠ[b] ܥܩܪܐ[c] ܕܐܝܠܢܐ ܀	ܢܩܝܡ[x]
[t] omit ܬܗܘܘܢ	ܟܠ ܐܝܠܢ ܕܠܐ ܥܒܕ[d] ܦܐܪܐ[e] ܛܒܐ ܡܬܦܣܩ	ܕܝܢ[z] ܢܪܓܐ[a]
ܐܒܘܢ[u]	11 ܘܒܢܘܪܐ ܢܦܠ : ܐܢܐ[f] ܡܢ ܩܕܡ	ܥܩܪܐ[c]
ܢܪܓܐ[y] ܕܝܢ[z]	ܠܟܘܢ ܡܥܡܕ ܒܡܝܐ : [g]† ܗܘ ܕܝܢ[h] ܕܒܬܪܝ	ܐܝܠܢ[o]
[b] omit ܥܠ ܢܪܓܐ[a]	ܗܘ ܚܝܠܬܢ ܡܢܝ ܕܠܐ ܫܘܐ ܐܢܐ ܠܡܫܪܐ ܡܣܢܘܗܝ	† f. 137b.
ܥܩܪܐ[c]	ܗܘ ܢܥܡܕܟܘܢ ܒܪܘܚܐ ܕܩܘܕܫܐ ܘܒܢܘܪܐ[i] ܀	ܥܒܕ[d]
ܥܒܕ[d] ܦܐܪܐ[e]		ܢܥܡܕ[i]
[f] omit ܡܢ ܗܘ[g]		
ܕܝܢ[h] ܢܥܡܕܟܘܢ[i]		

Codex A.

[CCLXXI.]

[f. 171*a*]

ܐܪܟܝܢ ܐܬܓܠܝ[b]

ܡܬܝܘܗܝ[d]

[e] *add* ܥܡ ܕܝܘܡ M. ܕܢܘܪܐ

[y] *add* ܡܒܝܬܐ ܡܪܢܐ :

ܡܫܝܚܐ[z] ܡܟܪܙ[c]

ܕܥܡܘܕܐ[d] [e]*add* ܠܗ

ܕܡܠܟܘܬܐ[f] ܗܘ[g]

ܕܐܬܐܡܪ[h] ܒܝܕ[j]

ܕܐܫܥܝܐ[i] ܢܒܝܐ[k]

ܡܥܡܕܝܢ ܗܘܘ[m]

ܗܘ[o] *add* ܕܡܠܐܟܐ[v]

ܕܡܫܝܚܐ[q] ܐܬܐܡܪ[r]

ܡܫܝܚܐ[u] ܚܒܝ[w]

ܝܘܪܕܢܢ[y] ܕܡܠܟܘܬܐ[b]

ܝܘܕܢܐ[c] ܒܢܗܪܐ[e]

ܚܛܗܝܗܘܢ[f]

Codex B.

CLXXVII.

MATT. III. 1—6.

ܐܘܪܝܢܗ[a] ܐܬܦܠܓܬ ܗܘܐ ܐܬܓܠܝ[b] ܐܠܗܐ : :
ܗܝܟ ܡܐ ܕܡܪܐ[c] ܐܠܗܐ ܥܡ ܡܬܐ[d] ܕܝܠܗ :[e] [y]
ܒܗܝܢ ܝܘܡܬܐ[z] ܡܫܝܚܐ[a] ܥܡܕܢܐ[b] ܟܕ ܐܬܐ[c] ܡܟܪܙ 1
ܒܡܕܒܪܐ[d] ܕܝܗܘܕ ܘܐܡܪ[e] ܬܘܒܘ ܡܠܟܘܬܐ 2
ܕܡܠܟܘܬܐ[f] : ܗܘܐ[g] ܗܘ ܕܐܬܐܡܪ[h] ܒܝܕ ܐܫܥܝܐ[i] ܢܒܝܐ 3
ܕܐܡܪ[k] ܒܡܕܒܪܐ ܡܠܐ : ܛܝܒܘ ܐܘܪܚܗ ܕܡܪܝܐ 4
ܘܗܘ[j] ܕܢܒܝܐ ܠܒܘܫܗ[l] ܡܢ ܣܥܪܐ[m] ܕܓܡܠܐ : ܗܘ[n] ܗܘ
ܡܫܝܚܐ[z] ܠܒܘܫܗ ܕܡܫܟܐ[o] ܡܢ ܚܨܗ[p] ܕܡܠܐ[v]
ܘܐܬܐ[q] ܕܡܫܝܚܐ ܐܡܪ[r] ܒܡܕܒܪܐ : ܘܡܠܟܘܬܗ[s]
5 ܗܘܬ ܡܫܝܚܐ[t] ܘܡܬܐ[u] ܕܝܘܕܢܐ : ܟܠܗ[w] ܗܘܬ[x]
ܢܦܩܐ ܠܘܬܗ ܝܪܘܫܠܡ[y] ܘܟܠܗ ܝܗܘܕܐ ܐܪܥܐ
[f. 136*a*]
ܕܡܫܝܚܐ[z] ܘܟܠܗ[a] ܐܬܪܐ ܕܣܚܪ[b] ܝܘܪܕܢܢ[c] :
6 ܘܗܘܘ ܡܬܥܡܕܝܢ[d] ܡܢܗ ܒܝܘܪܕܢܢ[e] ܢܗܪܐ
ܘܡܘܕܝܢ ܚܛܗܝܗܘܢ[f]

Codex C.

ܐܪܟܝܢ[a] ܐܬܓܠܝ[b]

ܗܘܘ[c] ܡܬܐ[d]

[y] *add* ܡܒܝܬܐ ܡܪܢܐ

ܡܥܡܕܢܐ[a]

[b] *add* ܘܐܡܪ : ܐܢܐ

ܕܡܠܟܘܬܐ[d]

[e] *add* ܠܗ

ܕܐܬܐܡܪ[h]

ܒܡܕܒܪܐ[i] ܐܫܥܝܐ[l]

ܡܥܡܕܝܢ ܗܘܘ[m]

ܕܐܢܐ[n] ܗܘܐ[p]

ܕܡܫܝܚܐ[q] ܐܬܐܡܪ[r]

ܘܡܠܟܘܬܗ[s]

ܘܡܫܝܚܐ[t] ܗܘܐ[x]

ܝܘܪܕܢܢ[y]

ܕܡܫܝܚܐ[z] ܘܟܠܗ[a]

ܡܬܥܡܕܝܢ[d]

CLXXVIII.

LUKE III. 23—38.

Codex A deest.]

Codex B.

ܘܐܝܬܐ ܗܘ ܡܢ ܟܠ ܥܡܐ ܐܠܗܐ ܘܗܘܐ
23 ܘܗܘܐ ܝܫܘܥ ܐܝܬ ܗܘܐ ܡܢ ܫܢܝܢ ܬܠܬܝܢ ܕܐܬܝܠܕ
ܒܪܐ ܐܝܟ ܕܡܬܚܫܒ ܗܘܐ ܒܪ ܝܘܣܦ ܬܠܬܝܢ ܫܢܝܢ : ܘܗܘܐ
ܕܐܬܝܠܕ ܗܘ ܒܪ ܝܘܣܦ : ܒܪ ܗܠܝ :
24 ܒܪ ܡܛܬ : ܒܪ ܠܘܝ : ܒܪ ܡܠܟܝ : ܒܪ ܝܢܐ
25 ܒܪ ܝܘܣܦ : ܒܪ ܡܬܬܝܐ : ܒܪ ܐܡܘܨ : ܒܪ ܢܚܘܡ :
26 ܒܪ ܚܣܠܝ : ܒܪ ܢܓܝ : ܒܪ ܡܐܬ : ܒܪ ܡܬܬܝܐ : ܒܪ
ܒܪ ܫܡܥܝ : ܒܪ ܝܘܣܦ : ܒܪ ܝܗܘܕܐ : ܒܪ
27 ܒܪ ܝܘܚܢܢ : ܒܪ ܪܝܣܐ : ܒܪ ܙܘܪܒܒܠ : ܒܪ
ܒܪ ܫܠܬܐܝܠ : ܒܪ ܢܪܝ : ܒܪ ܡܠܟܝ : ܒܪ

Codex C.

[f. 154*a*]

ܗܘܐ ܝܫܘܥ ܡܢ ܟܠ ܥܡܐ ܐܠܗܐ
23 ܘܗܘܐ ܝܫܘܥ ܐܝܬ ܗܘܐ ܡܢ ܫܢܝܢ ܬܠܬܝܢ 23
ܒܪܐ ܐܝܟ ܕܡܬܚܫܒ ܗܘܐ ܒܪ ܝܘܣܦ
ܬܠܬܝܢ ܫܢܝܢ : ܕܗܘܐ ܒܪ ܝܘܣܦ ܒܪ
ܗܠܝ ܒܪ ܡܛܬ ܒܪ ܠܘܝ ܒܪ ܡܠܟܝ :
24 ܒܪ ܝܢܐ : ܒܪ ܝܘܣܦ : ܒܪ ܡܬܬܝܐ ܒܪ 24 25
26 ܐܡܘܨ : ܒܪ ܢܚܘܡ ܒܪ ܚܣܠܝ : ܒܪ 26
27 ܢܓܝ ܒܪ ܡܐܬ : ܒܪ ܡܬܬܝܐ ܒܪ 27
28 ܘܙܘܪܒܒܠ : ܒܪ ܫܠܬܐܝܠ ܒܪ ܢܪܝ : ܒܪ 28
29 ܡܠܟܝ ܒܪ ܐܕܝ : ܒܪ ܩܘܣܡ ܒܪ ܐܠܡܘܕܕ : 29

Codex B.

28 ܢܝܪܐ ܒܪ ܡܠܟܝ : ܒܪ ܐܕܝ ܒܪ ܩܘܣܡ : ܒܪ
29 ܐܠܡܕܡ : ܒܪ ܥܝܪ : ܒܪ ܝܫܘܥ : ܒܪ
ܐܠܝܥܙܪ : ܒܪ ܝܘܪܡ ܒܪ ܡܛܬܐ : ܒܪ ܠܘܝ
30 ܒܪ ܫܡܥܘܢ : ܒܪ ܝܗܘܕܐ ܒܪ ܝܘܣܦ :
31 ܒܪ ܝܘܢܡ ܒܪ ܐܠܝܩܝܡ : ܒܪ ܡܠܝܐ ܒܪ
ܡܝܢܐ : ܒܪ ܡܛܬܐ ܒܪ ܢܬܢ : ܒܪ
32 ܕܘܝܕ ܒܪ ܐܝܫܝ : ܒܪ ܝܘܒܝܕ ܒܪ ܒܘܥܙ :
33 ܒܪ ܫܠܡܐ ܒܪ ܢܚܫܘܢ : ܒܪ ܐܪܡ ܒܪ
ܐܡܝܢܕܒ : ܒܪ ܐܪܡܝ ܒܪ ܐܪܢܝ ܒܪ ܚܨܪܘܢ
34 ܒܪ ܦܪܨ : ܒܪ ܝܗܘܕܐ ܒܪ ܝܥܩܘܒ : ܒܪ
ܐܝܣܚܩ ܒܪ ܐܒܪܗܡ : ܒܪ ܬܪܚ ܒܪ ܢܚܘܪ :
35 ܒܪ ܣܪܘܓ ܒܪ ܐܪܥܘ : ܒܪ ܦܠܓ ܒܪ ܥܒܪ
36 ܒܪ ܫܠܚ ܒܪ ܩܝܢܢ ܒܪ ܐܪܦܟܫܪ ܒܪ ܫܡ
37 ܒܪ ܢܘܚ ܒܪ ܠܡܟ ܒܪ ܡܬܘܫܠܚ ܒܪ
[f. 136b]
ܚܢܘܟ ܒܪ ܝܪܕ ܒܪ ܡܗܠܠܐܝܠ ܒܪ ܩܝܢܢ
38 ܒܪ ܐܢܘܫ : ܒܪ ܫܝܬ ܒܪ ܐܕܡ : ܒܪܗ
ܕܐܠܗܐ

Codex C.

25 ܒܪ ܠܘܝ ܒܪ ܝܐܢܝ : ܒܪ ܡܛܬܝܐܘ ܒܪ
ܢܚܘܡ : ܒܪ ܢܓܝ ܒܪ ܡܛܬܝ : ܒܪ ܫܡܥܝ
ܒܪ ܝܘܕܐ ܒܪ ܪܝܫܐ : ܒܪ ܫܠܬܐܝܠ ܒܪ
ܡܠܟܝ : ܒܪ ܩܘܣܡ ܒܪ ܗܪ : ܒܪ ܐܠܥܙܪ
30 ܒܪ ܡܛܬܝ : ܒܪ ܠܘܝ ܒܪ ܫܡܥܘܢ : ܒܪ
ܝܗܘܕܐ ܒܪ ܝܘܣܦ : ܒܪ ܝܢܡ ܒܪ ܐܠܝܩܝܡ :
31 ܒܪ ܡܠܝܐ ܒܪ ܡܢܝܢܐ : ܒܪ ܡܛܬܐ ܒܪ
32 ܢܬܢ : ܒܪ ܕܘܝܕ ܒܪ ܐܝܫܝ : ܒܪ ܐܘܒܝܕ
ܒܪ ܒܘܥܙ : ܒܪ ܫܠܐ ܒܪ ܢܚܫܘܢ : ܒܪ
33 ܐܪܡ ܒܪ ܐܡܝܢܕܒ : ܒܪ ܐܪܡܝܢ ܒܪ ܐܪܢܝ :
34 ܒܪ ܚܨܪܘܢ ܒܪ ܦܪܨ : ܒܪ ܝܗܘܕܐ ܒܪ
ܝܥܩܘܒ : ܒܪ ܐܝܣܚܩ ܒܪ ܐܒܪܗܡ : ܒܪ
35 ܬܪܚ ܒܪ ܢܚܘܪ : ܒܪ ܣܪܘܓ ܒܪ ܥܘ : ܒܪ
36 ܦܠܓ ܒܪ ܥܒܪ : ܒܪ ܫܠܚ ܒܪ ܩܝܢܢ : ܒܪ
[f. 154b]
ܐܪܦܟܫܪ : ܒܪ ܫܡ : ܒܪ ܢܘܚ ܒܪ ܠܡܟ :
37 ܒܪ ܡܬܘܫܠܚ ܒܪ ܚܢܘܟ : ܒܪ ܝܐܪܕ ܒܪ
38 ܡܗܠܠܐܝܠ : ܒܪ ܩܝܢܢ ܒܪ ܐܢܘܫ ܒܪ
ܫܝܬ ܒܪ ܐܕܡ ܒܪ ܐܠܗܐ

Codex A.

[CCLXXI.]

[f. 171b]

ܚܕ ܩܒܠ ܩܘܕܘ
ܐܠܡܚܐ ܡܢ ܡܪܩܘܣ
ܚܕ ܒܫܒܐ M.

[b] ܒܐܫܥܝܐ

[c] ܡܫܠܚ   [f] ܕܡܪܝܐ

[h] ܫܒܝܠܘܗܝ

[j] ܡܥܡܕ   [k] ܕܝ *omit*

[l] ܒܡܕܒܪܐ

[m] ܘܡܟܪܙ   [n] ܕܬܝܒܘܬܐ

[o] ܠܫܒܘܩܢ   [p] ܕܚܛܗܝܢ

Codex B.

CLXXIX.

Mark I. 1—8.

ܘܗܕܐ ܝܘܩܪܐ ܡܒܟܐ ܐܘܢܓܠܝܗ ܡܢ ܡܪܩܘܣ :
1 ܒܫܘܪܝܗ ܕܣܒܪܐ ܝܫܘܥ ܡܫܝܚܐ : ܗܝܟ
2 [a] ܕܟܬܝܒ [b] ܒܐܫܥܝܐ ܢܒܝܐ : ܕܗܐ ܐܢܐ [c] ܡܫܠܚ
ܡܠܐܟܝ ܩܕܡ [d] ܐܦܝܟ : ܕܗܘ [e] ܢܫܠܠ
3 ܐܘܪܚܟ : ܩܠ ܡܟܪܝܙ ܒܡܕܒܪܐ ܬܩܢܘ ܐܘܪܚܗ
4 [f] ܕܡܪܝܐ [g] ܫܘܝܢ ܒܒܕܘ [h] ܫܒܝܠܘܗ : ܗܘܐ
ܕܝ [i] ܝܘܚܢܢ [j] ܡܥܡܕ [k] ܕܝ [l] ܒܡܕܒܪܐ :
[m] ܘܡܟܪܙ † ܡܥܡܘܕ [n] ܕܬܘܒܘ [o] ܠܫܒܘܩܢ [p] ܕܚܛܠܢ :

Codex C.

ܚܕ ܩܒܠ ܩܕܐܘ
ܐܠܡܚܐ ܡܢ ܡܪܩܘܣ
ܘܒܢܬܗ

1
2 [a] ܕܟܬܝܒ   [b] ܒܐܫܥܝܐ

[c] ܡܫܠܚ   [d] ܐܦܝܟ

[e] ܢܫܠܠ   [g] ܫܘܝܢ

3 [h] ܫܒܝܠܘܗܝ   [i] ܝܘܚܢܢ

4 [j] ܡܥܡܕ   [k] ܕܝ *omit*

[o] ܠܫܒܘܩܢ

† f. 138a.

Codex A.

ܒܟܠܗ [p]
ܒܝܕܝܗܐ [q]
ܡܫܠܡܬܗܘܢ [r]
ܢܦܫܬܟܘܢ [s]
ܕܝܡܠܐ [t]
ܘܐܡܪ [w]
ܕܡܚܝܢ [y] ܗܘܐ [z]
ܕ [a] ܕܗܘܝܠܝܗ [b]
ܕܚܫܘܒܝܗ [d]
ܐܬܒܟܝܬ [e] ܒܝܕܝܗ [f]

[CCLXXII.]
[f. 171*b*]

ܗܘܐ ܕܝܢ [a] ܒ*omit* [b]
ܠܫܠܝܛܘܬ [c] ܕܛܒܪܝܘܣ [d]
ܡܢ ܠܩܝܣܪ *omit* [e]
ܕܗܓܡܘܢ [b]
ܕܦܝܠܛܘܣ [d]
ܦܘܢܛܝܘܣ [e]
ܦܝܠܝܦܘܣ [f] ܒܝܗܘܕܐ [g]
ܗܪܘܕܝܣ [h]
ܘܠܝܣܢܝܘܣ [i]
ܦܝܠܝܦܘܣ [k]
ܕܐܒܝܠܝܢܐ [n]
ܕܚܢܢ [o] ܕܩܝܦܐ [p]
ܘܩܝܦܐ [q]
ܢܦܫܬܟܘܢ [h] ܕܝܘܪܕܢܐ [i]
ܠܥܡܡܝܐ [j] ܕܝܘܚܢܢ [k]
ܝܘܪܕܢܐ [l] ܡܟܪܙ [m]
ܠܫܘܒܩܢ [o] ܕܚܛܝܢ [p]
ܒܡܕܒܪܐ [r]
ܕܐܫܥܝܐ ܢܒܝܐ [s]
ܕܡܪܝܐ [t] ܫܒܝܠܘ [w]
ܫܒܝܠܘܗܝ [x]
ܟܠ [y] ܢܚܬ [a]
ܘܪܡܬܐ [c] ܘܟܠ [b] *add*

Codex B.

5 ܘܬܬܓܠܐ ܐܝܩܪܗ ܕܡܪܝܐ ܘܢܚܙܘܢ ܟܠ ܒܣܪ [p] ܐܟܚܕܐ ܦܘܪܩܢܗ ܕܐܠܗܐ :
ܘܟܠ ܚܕ ܢܫܡܥ : ܘܗܘܐ ܡܬܐܡܪ ܡܢܗ
ܒܝܕ ܢܒܝܐ [q] : ܡܫܡܠܝܐ ܡܫܠܡܬܗܘܢ [r] :
6 ܘܗܘܐ ܢܦܫܗ [s] ܠܒܝܫ ܡܢ [t] ܕܝܡܠܐ ܘܐܘܪܚܐ
ܕܡܫܝܚܐ [u] ܐܬܐ ܟܠܗܘܢ [v] : ܘܐܡܪ [w] ܡܢܗܘܢ
7 ܘܡܢ [x] ܐܠܗܐ ܕܢܛܪ ܘܗܘܐ [y] ܡܚܝܢ ܘܐܡܪ ܐܢܬ
ܗܘ [z] ܗܘ ܕܗܘܐ ܒܟܠܗ ܒܝܘܡܬܐ : [a] ܕܝ
ܕܒܥܝܬ ܐܢܬ [b] ܕܗܘܝܠܝܗ [c] ܕܡܫܝܚܐ ܢܦܪ
8 ܒܪܘܚܐ [d] ܕܚܫܘܒܝܗ : ܐܢܬ [e] ܐܬܒܟܝܬ ܒܝܕܝܗ
ܒܗܘܢ : ܗܘ ܕܝ [f] ܐܬܒܟܝܬ ܒܝܕܝܗ ܒܪܘܚܐ
ܕܡܫܝܚܐ :

CLXXX.

Luke III. 1—18.

ܐܡܪ [a] ܗܘܐ ܕܝܢ [b] ܠܫܠܝܛܘܬ [c] ܕܛܒܪܝܘܣ [d] ܩܝܣܪ [e] ܡܢ [f] ܠܩܝܣܪ :
1 ܘܒܫܢܬܐ ܕܝ [b] ܚܡܫܬܥܣܪܐ [c] ܕܫܘܠܛܢܗ
ܕܦܝܠܛܘܣ [d] ܦܘܢܛܝܘܣ : ܕܗ ܗܘܐ [e] ܗܓܡܘܢ [f] ܒܝܗܘܕܐ
ܒܝܗܘܕܐ [g] ܕܝܗܘܕܐ : [h] ܘܗܪܘܕܝܣ ܛܛܪܪܟܐ
ܕܓܠܝܠܐ : [i] ܘܦܝܠܝܦܘܣ [j] ܐܚܘܗܝ [k] ܛܛܪܪܟܐ
ܕܐܝܛܘܪܝܐ [l] ܘܐܪܥܐ ܕܛܪܟܘܢܝܛܐ :
[f. 137*a*]
2 ܘܠܘܣܢܝܘܣ [m] ܛܛܪܪܟܐ [k] ܕܐܒܝܠܝܢܐ [n] : ܥܠ
ܝܕ [o] ܚܢܢ ܘܩܝܦܐ [q] ܕܗܘܘ [p] ܪܒܝ ܟܗܢܐ : ܗܘܬ
ܡܠܬܐ ܕܐܠܗܐ ܥܠ [h] ܝܘܚܢܢ ܒܪ [i] ܙܟܪܝܐ
3 ܒܡܕܒܪܐ : ܘܐܬܐ [j] ܠܟܠܗ ܐܬܪܐ [k] ܕܚܕܪܝܗ
[l] ܝܘܪܕܢܐ : [m] ܡܟܪܙ [n] ܡܥܡܘܕܝܬܐ ܕܬܝܒܘܬܐ [o] ܠܫܘܒܩܢ
4 [p] ܕܚܛܗܝܢ : ܐܝܟ [q] ܕܟܬܝܒ [r] ܒܣܦܪܐ ܕܡܠܘܗܝ
[s] ܕܐܫܥܝܐ ܢܒܝܐ ܕܐܡܪ : ܩܠ ܕܩܪܐ ܒܡܕܒܪܐ
ܕܡܪܝܐ [t] ܐܘܪܚܗ [u] ܛܝܒܘ [w] ܫܒܝܠܘܗܝ
5 [x] ܫܒܝܠܘܗܝ : ܟܠ [y] ܢܚܠ ܢܬܡܠܐ : [z] ܘܟܠ ܛܘܪ
[a] ܘܪܡܬܐ ܢܬܡܟܟ : ܘܢܗܘܐ [b] ܥܩܡܬܐ [c] ܠܦܫܝܛܬܐ
6 ܘܟܠ ܥܒܪܬܐ [d] ܠܡܫܘܚܬܐ ܘܬܗܘܐ ܠܦܩܥܬܐ

Codex C.

ܒܟܠܗ [p]

ܒܝܕܝܗܐ [q]
ܕܡܫܝܚܐ [u] ܟܠܗܘܢ [v]
ܘܐܡܪ [w]
ܘܡܢ [x]
ܕܗܘܝܠܝܗ [b]
ܕܡܫܝܚܐ [c]
ܕܚܫܘܒܝܗ [d]
ܐܬܒܟܝܬ [e] ܐܬܒܟܝܬ [f]

ܗܘܐ ܕܝܢ [a] ܒ*omit* [b]
ܠܫܠܝܛ [c] ܕܛܒܪ [d]
ܠܩܝܣܪ [f]
ܘܒܫܢܬܗ *add* [a]
ܕܚܡܫܬܥܣܪܐ [b]
ܫܢܝܢ *add* [c]
ܕܦܝܠܛܘܣ [d]
ܦܘܢܛܝܘܣ [e]
ܦܝܠܝܦܘܣ [f]
ܗܪܘܕܝܣ [h]
ܘܠܝܣܢܝܘܣ [i]
ܛܛܪܪܟܐ [k] ܐܚܘܗܝ [j]
ܘܐܬܪܐ [l]
ܘܠܘܣܢܝܘܣ [m]
ܕܐܒܝܠܢܐ [n]
ܘܩܝܦܐ [q] ܕܚܢܢ [p]
ܕܝܘܪܕܢܐ [i] ܘܡܟܪܙ [m]
ܡܥܡܘܕܝܬܐ [n]
ܕܟܬܝܒ [q] ܒܣܦܪܐ [r]
† f. 138*b*.
ܕܐܫܥܝܐ [s] ܐܘܪܚܗ [u]
ܫܒܝܠܘܗܝ [x] ܢܚܠ [y] (*sic*)
ܘܟܠ *omit* [z] ܢܬܡܟܟ [a]
ܥܩܡܬܐ [c] ܠܡܫܘܚܬܐ [d]

<table>
<tr><th>Codex A.</th><th>Codex B.</th><th>Codex C.</th></tr>
<tr><td></td><td>7 ܒܟܠ ܙܒܢ ܡܫܝܚܗ ܕܐܠܗܐ: ܗܘܐ ܐܘܢ</td><td></td></tr>
<tr><td>[d]ܠܐܦܩܠܘܣܝܐ</td><td>ܐܡܪ [d]ܠܐܦܩܠܘܣܐ [e]ܕܢܦܫܢ ܡܬܠܒܒܝܢ ܡܢܗ:</td><td>[e]ܕܢܦܫ</td></tr>
<tr><td>[f]ܘܠ̈ܕܝܫܝܢ</td><td>[f]ܘܠܕܝܫܘܗܝ ܕܚܝܝܐ ܡܢ ܐܘܒܕܢ ܠܟܘܢ</td><td></td></tr>
<tr><td>[g]ܕܬܒܪ̈ܘܢܘܢ</td><td>8 [g]ܕܬܒܪܘܢܘܢ ܡܢ ܪܘܓܙܐ ܕܥܬܝܕ: ܒܒܕܘ</td><td></td></tr>
<tr><td></td><td>ܐܘܢ ܦܪܘܩ [h]ܥܡܡ ܒܬܫܒܘܚܬܐ: ܘܠܐ ܬܬܒܪܘܢ</td><td>[h]ܥܡܡܝ</td></tr>
<tr><td>[i]ܐܡܪܝܢ</td><td>[i]ܐܡܪܝܢ [j]ܒܢܦܫܟܘܢ ܐܝܟ ܐܢܬ ܠܝ ܐܒܪܗܡ:</td><td>[j]ܒܢ ܢܦܫܟܘܢ</td></tr>
<tr><td>[k]ܐܡܪܢܐ</td><td>[k]ܐܡܪ ܐܢܐ [k]ܠܟܘܢ ܕܢ [l]ܕܝܟܠ ܗܘ ܐܠܗܐ ܕܡܢ</td><td>[k]ܐܢܐ ܐܡܪ</td></tr>
<tr><td>[m]ܢܩܝܡ [o]ܡܩ̈ܝܡ</td><td>9 ܗܠܝܢ ܟܐܦܐ [m]ܕܢܩܝܡ ܒܢܝܢ ܠܐܒܪܗܡ: ܟܕ</td><td>[l]ܕܝܟܠ [m]ܢܩܝܡ</td></tr>
<tr><td>[p]ܫܪ̈ܫܝܗܘܢ</td><td>ܕܝܢ [n]ܒܥܠܡܐ [o]ܡܩܝܡ ܟܠ [p]ܫܘܪܝܫܘܢ</td><td>[n]ܒܥܠܡܐ</td></tr>
<tr><td></td><td>[q]ܕܐܝܠܢܐ: ܒܟܠ [z]ܐܝܟ ܐܘܢ ܕܠܐ ܥܒܕ ܦܐܪܝܢ</td><td>[q]ܕܐܝܠܢܐ [z]ܐܝܟ</td></tr>
<tr><td>[r]ܡܬܦܣܩ ܗܘ</td><td>ܛܒܝܢ [r]ܗܘ ܡܬܦܣܩ [r] [s]ܘܠܢܘܪܐ ܡܬܪܡܐ:</td><td>[r]ܡܬܦܣܩ ܗܘ</td></tr>
<tr><td>[s]ܘܠܢܘܪܐ</td><td>10 ܘܗܘܘ [t]ܫܐܠܝܢ ܠܗ [u]ܐܘܟܠܘܣܐ ܘܐܡܪܝܢ:</td><td>[t]ܫܐܠܝܢ</td></tr>
<tr><td>[t]ܫ̈ܐܠܝܢ [u]ܐܘ̈ܟܠܘܣܐ</td><td>11 ܡܢܐ ܐܘܢ ܢܥܒܕ: [v]ܐܦܢܝ ܕܝܢ ܘܐܡܪ</td><td>[u]ܐܘܟܠܘܣܐ</td></tr>
<tr><td>ܕܝܢ [v]*omit* [w]ܣܠܘ̈ܩܝܢ</td><td>ܠܗܘܢ: ܡܢ ܕܠܗ ܬܪܝܢ [w]ܣܘܠܩܝܢ ܢܬܠ [x]ܠܗܘ</td><td>[w]ܣܘܠܩܝܢ</td></tr>
<tr><td>[z]ܡܢ [a]ܡ̈ܟܣܝܢ</td><td>ܕܠܝܬ ܠܗ: ܘܡܢ ܕܠܗ [y]ܡܝܟܘܠ [z]ܟܢ ܘܗܟܘܬ</td><td>[x]ܠܗܘ [y]ܡܐܟܘܠܝܢ</td></tr>
<tr><td>ܕܝܢ [b]*omit*</td><td>12 ܢܥܒܕ: ܐܬܘ ܕܝܢ ܐܘܦ [a]ܡܟܣܝܢ [b]ܕܝܢ [c]ܕܝܬܥܡܕܘܢ
[f. 137*b*]</td><td>ܕܝܢ [b]*omit*</td></tr>
<tr><td></td><td>13 ܡܢܗ: ܘܐܡܪܘ ܠܗ ܡܠܦܢܐ ܡܐ ܢܥܒܕ: ܗܘ</td><td>[c]ܕܡܬܥܡܕܘܢ</td></tr>
<tr><td></td><td>ܕܝܢ ܐܡܪ ܠܗܘܢ: ܒܘܠܡ ܡܘܬܪ ܡܢ ܡܐ</td><td></td></tr>
<tr><td>[b]ܕܡܬܦܩܕ</td><td>[b]ܕܡܬܦܩܕ ܠܟܘܢ ܠܐ ܬܥܒܕܘܢ ܘܠܐ [c]ܬܬܒܥܘܢ:</td><td>[c]ܬܬܒܥܘܢ</td></tr>
<tr><td>[e]ܪ̈ܘܡܚܝܢ</td><td>14 [d]ܫܐܠܘ ܝܬܗ ܕܝܢ ܐܘܦ [e]ܪܘܡܚܝܢ ܐܡܪܝܢ:</td><td>[d]ܫܐܠܘ</td></tr>
<tr><td>[g]ܬܛ̈ܠܡܘܢ</td><td>ܐܘܦ ܐܢܚܢ ܡܐ ܢܥܒܕ: ܘܐܡܪ ܠܗܘܢ:</td><td>[f]ܠܐܢܫ</td></tr>
<tr><td>[h]ܬܥܒ̈ܘܢ</td><td>[f]ܠܐܢܫ ܠܐ †[g]ܬܛܠܡܘܢ ܘܠܐ [h]ܬܥܒܘܢ:</td><td>† f. 139*a*.</td></tr>
<tr><td>[i]ܘܝ̈ܗܘܢ [k]ܣܦ̈ܩܝܢ</td><td>[i]ܘܝܗܘܢ [b]ܕܝܢ [k]ܣܦܩܝܢ ܠܟܘܢ ܐܦܣܘܢ ܕܠܟܘܢ:</td><td>[i]ܘܝܗܘܢ [k]ܣܦܩܝܢ</td></tr>
<tr><td>[m]ܒܠܒ̈ܝܗܘܢ</td><td>15 ܟܕ ܕܝܢ ܗܘܐ ܡܣܟܐ ܥܡܐ [l]ܘܡܬܚܫܒܝܢ</td><td>ܕܝܢ [b]*omit*</td></tr>
<tr><td>[n]ܕܝܘܚ̈ܢܢ [o]ܝܘܚܢܢ</td><td>ܟܘܠܗܘܢ [m]ܒܠܒܒܝܗܘܢ ܠܝܘܚܢܢ [n]ܕܝܘܚܢܢ ܕܠܡܐ</td><td>[l]ܘܡܬܚܫܒܝܢ</td></tr>
<tr><td>[p]ܠܗܘܢܗܘܢ</td><td>16 ܗܘ ܡܫܝܚܐ: ܐܦܢܝ [o]ܝܘܚܢܢ ܘܐܡܪ [p]ܠܗܘܢ:</td><td></td></tr>
<tr><td>ܡܢ [q]*omit*</td><td>ܐܢܐ [q]ܡܢ [r]ܡܥܡܕ [s]ܠܟܘܢ ܒܡܝܢ: ܐܬܐ ܕܝܢ</td><td>[s]ܠܟܘܢ</td></tr>
<tr><td>[r]ܡܥܡܕ [s]ܠܟܘܢ</td><td>[t]ܕܢ ܕܠܝܬ ܐܢܐ [u]ܕܡܫܠܐ ܕܫܪܐ ܥܪܩܬܐ</td><td>[u]ܕܡܫܠܐ</td></tr>
<tr><td>[t]ܕܢ [u]ܕܡܫܠܐ</td><td>[w]ܕܡܣܢܘܗܝ: ܗܘ [x]ܡܥܡܕ ܠܟܘܢ ܒܪܘܚܐ</td><td>[w]ܕܡܣܢܘܗܝ</td></tr>
<tr><td>[w]ܕܡܣܢ̈ܘܗܝ [y]ܗ̈ܕܢ</td><td>17 ܕܩܘܕܫܐ ܘܒܢܘܪܐ: [y]ܗܕܝܢ ܕܪܦܫܗ ܒܐܝܕܗ:</td><td>[x]ܡܥܡܕ</td></tr>
<tr><td>[z]ܘܡܟܢܫ [a]ܚܛ̈ܐ</td><td>ܘܗܘ ܡܕܟܐ ܐܕܪܗ [z]ܘܡܟܢܫ [a]ܚܛܝܐ</td><td>[z]ܘܡܟܢܫ</td></tr>
</table>

Codex A.	Codex B.	Codex C.
ᵇܘܐܬܕܒܚܐ ᶜ *add* ܕܝܢ	ᵃܠܐܚܪܢܝܗ ᵇܘܐܬܕܒܚܐ ᶜ ᵈܗܘܐ ܒܡܘܥܕܐ : ܕܠܐ	ᵃܠܐܚܪܢܝܗ
ᵈܢܚܬ ᶠܝܫܘܥܢ	18 ᵉܦܠܚܐ : ܥܠܝ ܡܢ ܐܢܘܢ ܐܬܐ ᶠܝܫܘܥ ܗܘܐ	ᵈܢܚܬ ᶜ *add* ܕܝܢ
	ܟܕ ܐܢܘܢ ܒܥܡܐ ᵍܘܡܥܡܕ ܠܗܘܢ ᵍ	ᵉܦܠܚܐ ᶠܝܫܘܥ
		ᵍ *omit* ܘܡܥܡܕ ܠܗܘܢ

[CCLXXIII.]
[f. 173*a*]

CLXXXI.

Mark I. 9—11.

Codex A.	Codex B.	Codex C.
ᵇܘܐܬܐ ᶜܘܗܘܐ	ᵇᵃܘܐܬܐ ܗܘܐ ᶜܝܫܘܥ ᵃܐܠܗܐ ᵈܒܢܨܪܬ ܡܢ	ᵃܘܐܬܐ ܗܘ ܝܫܘܥ
ᵈܢܨܪܬ	9 ܓܠܝܠܐ :ʸ ܘܗܘܐ ᶻܐܬܥܡܕ ܒܝܘܪܕܢܢ ᵃܕܐܬܐ	ܐܬܐ ܗܘܐ
ʸ *add* ܘܒܝܘܡܬܐ ܗܢܘܢ :	ܡܢ ܝܘܚܢܢ ᵇܒܝܘܪܕܢܢ ܕܓܠܝܠܐ : ܘܐܬܥܡܕ	ʸ *add* ܘܒܝܘܡܬܐ
ᵃ *omit* ܕ	10 ᶜܘܟܕ ܣܠܩ ܡܢ ᵈܡܝܐ : ܘܚܙܐ ܕܦܬܝܚܝܢ	ᶻܐܬܥܡܕ
ᵇܢܚܬܬ ᶜܒܕܡܘܬܐ	ܫܡܝܐ : ܘܪܘܚܐ ᵉܕܩܘܕܫܐ ܕܢܚܬܐ ܡܢ	
ᵈܫܡܝܐ ᵉܦܬܝܚܝܢ	11 ܥܠܘܗܝ ܒܕܡܘܬ ܝܘܢܐ : ܘܩܠܐ ᶠܡܢ ܫܡܝܐ	ᶠ *add* ܗܘܐ
ᶠ *add* ܗܘܐ ᵍܨܒܝܬ	ܐܡܪ : ܐܢܬ ܗܘ ܒܪܝ ܚܒܝܒܐ ᵍܕܒܟ ܨܒܝܬ :	ᵍܨܒܝܬ

[CCLXXIII.]
[f. 173*a*]

CLXXXII.

Matt. III. 13—17.

Codex A.	Codex B.	Codex C.
ᵃܠܐܠܝܘܡܐ ܡܢ ܒܬܪ ᵃܕܢܚܐ	ᵃܒܝܘܡܐ ܕܢܚܐ ܕܒܗ ᵃܐܬܓܠܝ ܡܪܢ ܡܢ ܫܡܝܐ :	ᵃܠܐܠܝܘܡܐ ܡܢ ܒܬܪ ᵃܕܢܚܐ
	13 ʸܒܗܝܢ ܥܕܢܐ ܐܬܐ ܝܫܘܥ ܡܢ ܓܠܝܠܐ	ܘܒܝܘܡܬܐ ܗܢܘܢ
ʸܒܗܝܢ	ᶻܠܝܘܪܕܢܢ ܠܘܬ ᵃܝܘܚܢܢ ᵇܕܢܬܥܡܕ ܡܢܗ :	ᶻܠܝܘܪܕܢܢ
ᶻܠܝܘܪܕܢܢ ᵃܝܘܚܢܢ	14 ᵃᶜܘܝܘܚܢܢ ܗܘܐ ᵈܡܟܠܐ ܠܗ ܘܐܡܪ ᵉܕܝ	ᶜ*add* ܗܘ ᵇܕܢܬܥܡܕ
ᶜ *add* ܗܘ	ܐܢܐ ܣܢܝܩ ܕܐܬܥܡܕ ܡܢܟ † ܘܐܢܬ ܐܬܝܬ	† f. 139*b*.
ᵉ *omit* ܕܝ ᵈܟܠܝ	15 ܠܘܬܝ : ܘܐܬܥܡܕ [f. 138*a*] ܥܢܐ ܝܫܘܥ ܘܐܡܪ ܠܗ	ᵉ *omit* ܕܝ ᵈܟܠܐ
ᶠܗܫܐ	ܫܒܘܩ ܗܫܐ ᶠܗܟܢܐ ܓܝܪ ܝܐܐ ܠܢ ܕܢܡܠܐ ܟܠ	ᶦܐܬܥܡܕ
ᵍܟܝܢ ʰܒܗܝܢ	16 ᵍܟܐܢܘ : ʰܘܒܗܝܢ ܫܒܩ ܠܗ : ܘܟܕ ܕܝ ᵉ ᶦܐܬܥܡܕ	ᵏ *add* ܘܣܠܩ ܡܢ ܡܝܐ
ᶦܐܬܥܡܕ	ܝܫܘܥ ᵏܣܠܩ ʲܫܡܝܐ ܐܬܦܬܚܘ ܠܗ :	ʲܫܡܝܐ ˡܠܗ
ᵏ *add* ܘܣܠܩ ܡܢ ܡܝܐ	ܘܚܙܐ ܪܘܚܗ ܕܐܠܗܐ ܕܢܚܬܐ ˡܥܠܘܗܝ ᵒܐܝܟ	ᵒ *add* ܥܠܘܗܝ
ⁿܩܠܐ ᵖܨܒܝܬ	17 ܘܡܬܝܐ ᵐܥܠܘܗܝ : ܘܗܐ ⁿܩܠܐ ܡܢ ܫܡܝܐ	ⁿܩܠܐ ᵐ *omit* ܥܠܘܗܝ
ᑫ *add* ܥܠܡ	ܐܡܪ ܐܢܬ ܗܘ ᵒܒܪܝ ܚܒܝܒܐ ܕܒܟ ᵖܨܒܝܬ :ᑫ	ᵖܨܒܝܬ ᵒ *omit* ܒܪܝ

Codex A. | Codex B. | Codex C.

[CCLXXIV.]
[f. 173b]

CLXXXIII.

John I. 29—34.

[illegible]
[illegible]
29 [illegible]
[illegible]
30 [illegible]
[illegible]
[illegible]
31 [illegible]
[illegible]
[illegible]
32 [illegible]
[illegible]
33 [illegible]
[illegible]
[illegible]
[illegible]
34 [illegible]
[illegible]

Codex A: [a] [illegible]; [b] [illegible] *omit* . . . [illegible]; [c] [illegible]; [d] *add* [illegible]; [f] [illegible]; [z] [illegible]; [a] [illegible] [b] [illegible]; [c] [illegible] [e] [illegible]; [d] [illegible]; [f] [illegible] [g] [illegible]; [h] [illegible] [i] [illegible]; [j] [illegible] [l] [illegible]; [m] [illegible] [n] [illegible]; [r] [illegible] [s] [illegible]; [t] [illegible] [u] [illegible]; [v] [illegible]; [w] [illegible]; [x] *add* [illegible]

Codex C: [b] [illegible] *omit* . . . [illegible]; [c] [illegible]; [e] [illegible]; [f] [illegible]; [b] [illegible]; [e] *omit* [illegible]; [f] [illegible] [j] [illegible]; [k] [illegible]; [n] [illegible]; [o] [illegible]; [p] [illegible]; [q] [illegible]; [r] [illegible] [s] [illegible]; [u] [illegible]; [v] [illegible] (*sic*)

[CCLXXIV.]
[f. 173b]

CLXXXIV.

Matt. IV. 1—11.

[illegible]
1 [illegible]
[illegible]
2 [illegible]
3 [illegible]
[f. 138b]
[illegible]

Codex A: [c] [illegible]; [d] *add* [illegible] M.; [a] [illegible] [b] [illegible]; [d] [illegible] [e] [illegible]; [f] [illegible] [g] [illegible]; [i] [illegible]; [k] *omit* [illegible]

Codex C: † f. 140a. [a] [illegible] [b] [illegible]; [c] [illegible]; [e] *omit* [illegible]; [c] [illegible] [d] [illegible]; [e] [illegible] [h] [illegible]; [i] [illegible] [j] *omit* [illegible]

Codex A.

[j] ܕܗܠܝܢ
[k] ܒܟܐܦܐ [l] ܢܬܥܒܕܢ
[m] ܠܚܡܐ ܕܝܢ [n] omit
[p] ܟܬܝܒ
[r] ܘܒܟܝܢ
[t] ܠܡܕܝܢܬܐ
[u] ܩܕܝܫܬܐ [y] ܠܬܚܬ
[z] ܕܡܠܐܟܘܗܝ [o] ܘܥܠ
[b] ܬܬܩܠ [c] ܪܓܠܝܟ
[d] omit ܓܪ
[e] ܬܢܣܐ [f] ܠܡܪܝܐ
[g] ܐܠܗܟ [h] ܘܬܘܒ
[j] ܕܥܠܡܐ
[k] ܘܟܠ ܕܝܢ [l] omit
[m] ܬܫܒܘܚܬܗܘܢ
[n] ܬܦܠ [o] ܒܟܝܢ
[p] ܐܙܠ [q] ܟܬܝܒ
[r] ܠܡܪܝܐ [t] ܐܠܗܟ
[w] ܘܒܟܝܢ
[x] ܡܠܐܟܝܐ
[y] add ܥܠܡ

[CCLXXIV.]
[f. 174*b*]
[a] ܫܕܪ [c] ܡܛܠܬܗ
[d] add ܫܕ ܟܕ
ܕܡܬܩܪܐ M.
[a] add ܝܫܘ
[b] ܕܐܬܡܣܪ
[c] ܝܘܚܢܢ
[d] ܐܙܠ [f] ܓܝܦ
[g] ܒܬܚܘܡܝܗܘܢ
[h] ܕܙܒܘܠܘܢ
[i] ܒܐܫܥܝܐ

Codex B.

ܐܡܪ [j] ܠܗܕܝܢ [k] ܟܐܦܝܐ [l] ܬܬܥܒܕܘܢ [m] ܠܚܡ:
4 ܘܗܘ ܐܓܝܒ [n] ܕܝܢ ܘܐܡܪ [o] ܠܗ [p] ܟܬܝܒ ܕܠܐ
ܥܠ ܠܚܡܐ ܒܠܚܘܕ [q] ܝܚܐ [v] ܒܪܢܫܐ: ܐܠܐ ܥܠ
5 ܟܠ ܡܠܬܗ ܕܐܠܗܐ: [r] ܘܒܟܝܢ ܕܒܪ ܝܬܗ
[s] ܣܛܢܐ [t] ܠܡܕܝܢܬܐ [u] ܩܕܝܫܬܐ [w] ܘܐܩܝܡ ܝܬܗ
6 ܥܠ ܟܢܦܗ ܕܗܝܟܠܐ ܘܐܡܪ ܠܗ: ܐܢ [x] ܐܢܬ
[v] ܒܪܗ ܕܐܠܗܐ ܪܡܝ ܓܪܡܟ ܡܢ ܟܐ
[y] ܠܬܚܬ: ܟܬܝܒ ܓܪ [z] ܕܡܠܐܟܘܗܝ ܗܘ ܡܦܩܕ
ܥܠ ܕܝܠܟ: [o] ܘܥܠ ܐܝܕܝܗܘܢ ܢܣܒܘܢ ܝܬܟ
7 ܕܠܐ [a] [b] ܬܬܩܠ ܒܟܐܦܐ [c] ܪܓܠܟ: ܘܐܡܪ ܠܗ
ܡܪܢܐ ܝܫܘܥ: ܟܬܝܒ [d] ܓܪ ܕܠܐ [e] ܬܢܣܐ
8 [f] ܠܡܪܝܐ [g] ܐܠܗܟ: [h] ܘܬܘܒ ܕܒܪ ܝܬܗ [s] ܣܛܢܐ
ܠܛܘܪ ܪܡ [i] ܠܚܕܐ: ܘܐܚܙܝ ܠܗ ܟܠܗܘܢ
ܡܠܟܘܬܗ [j] ܕܥܠܡܐ [k] ܘܫܘܒܚܗܘܢ [l] ܕܝܢ
9 [m] ܬܫܒܘܚܬܗܘܢ ܘܐܡܪ ܠܗ ܟܠ ܗܠܝܢ
ܐܢܐ ܝܗܒ ܠܟ: ܐܢ [n] ܬܦܠ ܘܬܣܓܘܕ
10 ܠܝ: [o] ܒܟܝܢ ܐܡܪ ܠܗ ܡܪܢܐ ܝܫܘܥ [p] ܐܙܠ
ܠܟ [s] ܣܛܢܐ: [q] ܟܬܝܒ ܓܪ [r] ܠܡܪܝܐ [t] ܐܠܗܟ
11 ܬܣܓܘܕ ܘܠܗ ܒܠܚܘܕ [u] ܬܫܡܫ: [w] ܘܒܟܝܢ
ܫܒܩ ܝܬܗ [s] ܣܛܢܐ: ܘܗܐ [x] ܡܠܐܟܐ ܩܪܒܘ
ܘܗܘܘ ܡܫܡܫܝܢ ܠܗ: [y]

CLXXXV.

Matt. IV. 12—17.

12 [a] ܫܕ ܟܕ [b] ܘܫܕܪܗ ܐܠܗܐ † ܡܢ [c] ܡܛܠܬܐ [d]: [a] ܘܟܕ
ܫܡܥ ܡܪܢܐ ܝܫܘܥ [b] ܕܐܬܡܣܪ [c] ܝܘܚܢܢ
13 [d] ܐܙܠ ܠܗ ܠܐܪܥܐ ܕܓܠܝܠܐ: [e] ܘܫܒܩ ܝܬܗ
ܠܢܨܪܬ: ܘܐܬܐ ܘܥܡܪ ܒܟܦܪܢܚܘܡ ܥܠ
[f] ܓܝܦ ܝܡܐ: [g] ܒܬܚܘܡܝܢ [h] ܕܙܒܘܠܘܢ ܘܢܦܬܠܝ:
14 ܕܬܬܡܠܐ ܡܐ ܕܐܬܐܡܪ [i] ܒܐܫܥܝܐ ܢܒܝܐ ܕܐܡܪ:

Codex C.

[j] ܠܗܠܝܢ [m] ܠܚܡ
[n] omit ܕܝܢ
[o] ܠܗܘܢ [p] ܟܬܝܒ
[q] ܕܝܚܐ [v] ܒܢܝܢܫܐ
[s] ܣܛܢܐ [w] ܘܐܩܝܡ
[x] omit ܐܢܬ
[v] add ܗܘ
[z] ܕܡܠܐܟܘܗܝ
[o] ܕܥܠ
[a] add ܐܡܬܝ
[d] omit ܓܪ
[e] ܬܢܣܐ [f] ܠܡܪܝܐ
[h] ܬܘܒ [i] omit ܠܚܕܐ
[k] ܘܟܠ ܕܝܢ [l] omit
[m] ܬܫܒܘܚܬܗܘܢ
[q] ܟܬܝܒ
[u] ܬܫܡܫ [w] ܘܒܟܝܢ
[x] ܡܠܐܟܘܗܝ

† f. 140*b*.
[b] ܘܫܕܪܗ
[c] ܡܛܠܬܐ
[a] add ܘܒܬܪܗ
[e] ܘܫܒܩ
[h] ܕܙܒܘܠܘܢ

Codex A.

[h] ܕܐܒܢܬܐ
[i] ܕܐܘܪܕܢܐ
[j] ܣܗܕܐ ܕܝܢ [l] omit
[m] ܕܢܬܒܝܢ
[o] ܒܟܡ [p] ܡܟܪܙ
[q] add ܒܪ
[r] ܡܠܟܘܬܐ
[s] ܕܫܡܝܐ

[CCLXXVI.]
[f. 174b]

[a] ܬܘܒ ܐܢܝܚܘ
[b] omit ܗܘܐ [c] ܥܒܕܬ
[d] omit ܗܘ ܕܝܢ
[z] add ܘܒܬܪܗ ܡܪܕܘܬܐ :
[a] ܗܪܘܕܣ
[b] ܛܛܪܪܟܐ
[c] ܡܢܗ [d] ܕܐܚܘܗܝ
[e] ܒܟܠ [f] ܗܪܘܕܣ
[h] ܠܝܘܚܢܢ
[i] ܒܒܝܬܐ
[e] omit ܕܝܢ
[o] ܕܝܗ [r] ܨܒܝܬ

[CCLXXVII.]
[f. 175a]
[a] ܒܥܘ [b] ܝܫܘܥ
[a] add: ܘܒܬܪܗ ܡܪܕܘܬܐ
[b] omit ܬܘܒ
[c] ܕܢܬܦܣܘܢܗ
[d] ܐܬܦܪܩ ܡܢܗܘܢ
[e] ܘܐܙܠ [f] ܠܥܒܪ
[g] ܕܐܘܪܕܢܐ
[h] ܝܘܚܢܢ [i] ܡܥܡܕ

Codex B.

15 ܐܪܟܐ [h] ܕܐ̈ܬܠܘܢ ܐܪܟܐ ܕܡܬܩܠܬ ܐܡܪܘܣܗ
ܕܡܢܐ ܒܒܪܗ [i] ܕܝܘܪܕܢܢܐ ܚܠܠܐ ܕܡܫܝܚܐ :
[f. 139a]
16 ܡܗܠܐ ܕܐܬܐ ܟܡܟܠܐ ܢܗܘܪ [k] ܙܝ [j] ܣܗܕܐ [k] :
ܘܗܠܝܢ [l] ܕܝܢ [m] ܕܢܬܒܝܢ ܒܫܘܥܒܕܐ ܘܟܠܠܗܘܢ
17 ܕܒܡܘܬܐ ܢܗܘܪ ܕܝܚ [n] ܠܗܘܢ : [o] ܒܟܡ ܡܢ ܬܘܒ
ܘܒܟܐ ܥܝܢ ܡܟܪܐ ܫܡܥܘܢ [p] ܡܟܪܙ ܘܐܡܪ :
ܬܘܒ ܩܪܒܬ [q] [r] ܡܠܟܘܬܗ [s] ܕܫܡܝܐ

CLXXXVI.

Luke III. 19—22.

[a] ܬܘܒ [b] ܗܘܐ ܐܬܠܘܒ [c] ܐܥܒܕܬ ܐܠܟܣܕ ܬܗܡܘܢ
19 [d] ܗܘ ܕܝܢ [d] ܡܢ ܠܗܘܐ : [z] [a] ܗܪܘܕܣ ܕܝܢ [b] ܛܛܪܪܟܐ
ܕܗܘܐ ܡܬܒܟܣ [c] ܡܢܗ ܥܠ ܐܦ ܗܪܘܕܝܐ
ܐܢܬܬܗ [d] ܕܐܚܘܗܝ : ܘܥܠ ܟܠ [e] ܕܝܢ ܒܝܫܬܐ
20 ܕܥܒܕ [f] ܗܪܘܕܣ : ܘܐܘܣܦ ܐܦ ܗܕܐ ܥܠ
[g] ܟܘܠܗܝܢ : ܘܚܒܫ [h] ܠܝܘܚܢܢ [i] ܒܒܝܬܐ :
21 ܐܬܥܒܕ ܕܝܢ ܟܕ ܐܬܥܡܕ ܟܘܠܗ [e] ܕܝܢ ܥܡܐ :
ܘܐܦ ܝܫܘܥ ܥܡܕ ܟܕ [l] ܐܬܥܡܕ ܘܨܠܝ :
22 ܐܬܦܬܚܘ [e] ܕܝܢ ܫܡܝܐ [n] ܘܢܚܬܬ ܪܘܚܐ
ܕܩܘܕܫܐ ܒܕܡܘ ܕܓܘܫܡ ܗܝܟ [o] ܝܘܢܐ [p] ܥܠܘܗܝ :
ܘܩܠܐ ܡܢ ܫܡܝܐ ܐܬܥܒܕ [†] [q] ܐܡܪ
ܐܢܬ ܗܘ ܒܪܝ ܚܒܝܒܐ ܕܒܟ [r] ܨܒܝܬ :

CLXXXVII.

John X. 39—42.

39 [a] ܒܥܘ ܗܘ ܡܢ [b] ܝܫܘܥ : [a] ܗܘܘ ܒܥܝܢ [b] ܬܘܒ
[c] ܕܢܬܦܣܘܢܗ : ܘܢܦܩ ܡܢ [d] ܐܝܕܝܗܘܢ
40 [e] ܘܐܙܠ ܠܗ ܬܘܒ [f] ܠܥܒܪܗ [g] ܕܝܘܪܕܢܢܐ ܠܐܬܪܐ
ܗܘ ܕܗܘܐ [h] ܝܘܚܢܢ [i] ܡܥܡܕ ܡܢ ܩܕܡ :

Codex C.

[h] ܕܒܢܬܐ
[i] ܕܝܘܪܕܢܐ
[k] ܐܪܟ ܣܗܕܐ
[l] omit ܕܝܢ
[n] ܠܗܘܢ
[q] add ܒܪ

[a] ܬܘܒ ܐܢܝܚܘ [b] omit ܗܘܐ
[c] ܥܒܕܬ ܗܘ ܕܝܢ [d] omit
[z] add ܘܒܬܪܗ ܡܪܕܘܬܐ
[c] ܡܢܗ
[d] ܕܐܚܘܗܝ
[e] omit ܕܝܢ
[g] ܟܘܠܗܘܢ
[l] ܐܬܥܡܕ
[n] ܘܢܚܬܬ
[o] ܕܝܘܢܐ [p] ܥܠܘܗܝ
† f. 141a.
[q] ܘܐܡܪ [r] ܨܒܝܬ

[b] ܝܫܘܥ
[a] add ܘܒܬܪܗ
[i] ܡܥܡܕ

Codex A.

[i] ܕܡܫܢܝܡܣ
[k] *add* ܕܝ
[f] ܡܫܢܝܡܣ
[l] ܕܗܕ̈ܝ [m] ܡܘܣܦ
[o] *omit* ܥܠܡ

[CCLXXVIII.]
[f. 175*a*]
[a] ܚܕ ܐܝܕ̈ܢ [b] ܠܝܘܡܐ
[c] *omit* ܕܝܢ
[z] *add* ܘܟܢܫܬܗ
ܡܢ ܦܠܘܛܐ :
[b] ܡܠܟܘܬܐ
[c] ܘܩܡܘ [d] ܘܟܗܢ̈ܝ
[e] ܒܡܕܝܢܬܐ [f] ܕ݁ܝ
[g] ܒܫܠܝܛܘܬܝ
[h] ܘܐܡܪܘ
[a] ܡܢܝܢܝܟܘܬܐ
[k] ܕܡܫܢܝܡܣ
[l] *omit* ܫܡܥܘܢ
[m] ܡܬܚܫܒܝܢ
[n] ܠܡܡܠܠ
[o] ܢܐܡܪ [p] ܐܡܪ
[r] ܡܘܠܝܐ ܒܡܠܬ
‡ f. 175*b*.
[s] ܪܓܡ
[t] ܡܩܒܠ [u] ܡܫܢܝܡܣ
[w] ܠܝܬܝ ܐܢܐ [x] *omit* ܐܢܐ
[y] ܐܡܪ [z] ܒܡܕܝܢܬܐ
[a] *add* ܥܠܡ

CCLXXVIII.
[CCIX.] [f. 160*a*]
[a] ܬܕܒܪܬܐ
[b] ܬܠܡܝܕܝܐ ܕܝܫܘܥ [c] ܠܝܘܡܐ
[a] *omit* ܐܡܪ
[[a] *omit* ܡܪܝ ܝܫܘܥ]

Codex B.

41 [h] ܘܗܘܐ ܟܕ ܩܪܒ ܚܡܐ ܘܒܟܐ ܐܬܐ ܠܘܬܗ :
ܘܗܘܘ ܐܡܪܝܢ [i] ܕܡܫܝܚܐ ܠܐ ܚܕܐ ܐܬܝ ܐܘܦ
42 ܠܐ ܚܕ : ܟܘܠ ܡܟܐ [k] ܕܐܡܪ [f] ܡܫܝܚܐ ܟܠ
ܠܟܘܢ [l] ܕܗܕܝܢ [m] ܡܘܣܦܝܢ ܗܘܐ : ܘܡܠܟ
ܗܘܬܘܢ ܟܗ [n] ܬܡܢ [o] ܥܠܡ [n] ⁖

CLXXXVIII.

Luke XX. 1—8.

1 [a] ܚܕ ܒܝܘ̈ܡܐ [a] ܡܢ [b] ܠܝܘܡܐ [c] ܐܝܬ [z] ܘܗܘܐ ܟܕ
ܡܢ [b] ܡܠܟܐ ܗܘܢ ܕܗܘܐ ܡܠܦ ܠܥܡܐ ܒܗܝܟܠܐ
ܘܡܣܒܪ [c] ܗܘ ܐܝܬ ܒܗܝܟܠܐ ܘܡܦܪܫܐ ܟܡ
2 [d] ܡܠܝܟܝܢ ܘܐܡܪܘ ܠܝܬܗ : ܐܡܪ ܠܢ [e] ܒܡܕܝܢܬܐ
ܫܠܝܛܘ ܐܢܬ ܚܕܐ ܗܠܝܢ ⁖ ܐܘ ܡܢ ܗܘ [f] ܕܝܢ
[f. 139*b*]
3 ܕܝܗܒ ܠܟ ܗܕܐ ܫܠܝܛܘܬܐ : ܘܐܬܦܢܝ
ܘܐܡܪ ܠܗܘܢ [g] ܫܘܐܠ [i] ܠܟܘܢ [g] ܐܘܦ ܐܢܐ
4 ܚܕܐ ܡܠܐ : [h] ܐܡܪܘ ܠܝ : [a] ܡܥܡܘܕܝܬܐ
[k] ܕܡܫܝܚܐ ܡܢ ܗܘܢ ܡܢ ܫܡܝܐ ܐܘ
5 ܡܢ ܒܢܝܢܫܐ : ܘܗܘܢ ܗܘܘ [l] ܫܡܥܘܢ [m] ܘܡܬܚܫܒܝܢ
[n] ܠܡܡܠܠ ܠܒܢܝܗܘܢ ܐܡܪܝܢ : ܐܢ [o] ܢܐܡܪ ܡܢ
ܫܡܝܐ [p] ܐܡܪ ܗܘ ܠܢ ܠܡܐ ܠܐ ܗܝܡܢܬܘܢ
6 [q] ܠܗ ⁖ ܘܐܢ [o] ܢܐܡܪ ܡܢ ܒܢܝܢܫܐ [r] ܟܠܗ
[r] ܥܡܐ [s] ܪܓܡܝܢ ܠܢ ⁖ [‡] [t] ܡܩܒܠ ܗܘ ܓܪ
7 [u] ܕܡܫܝܚܐ ܢܒܝܐ ܐܝܬ ܗܘ : ܘܐܬܦܢܝܘ ܕܠܐ
8 ܝܕܥܝܢ ܡܢ ܗܘܢ ܗܘ ⁖ ܘܐܡܪ ܝܫܘܥ ܐܡܪ
ܠܗܘܢ : ܐܘܦ [v] ܠܐ ܐܢܐ [w] ܠܝܬ [x] ܐܢܐ [y] ܐܡܪ
ܠܟܘܢ [z] ܒܗܕܐ ܫܠܝܛܘ ܐܢܐ ܚܕܐ ܗܠܝܢ [a] ⁖

CLXXXIX.

Luke VI. 17—23.

ܘܢܦܩ ܗܘܐ ܐܠܗܢ [a] ܚܕ ܐܝܕܢ [b†] ܬܠܡܝܕܝܐ ܕܝܫܘܥ
17 ܡܢ [c] ܠܝܘܡܐ : ܘܟܢܫܬܗ ܡܢ ܦܠܘܛܐ : ܘܩܡ [a a] ܡܪܝܐ

Codex C.

[h] ܘܗܘܐ

[k] *add* ܕܝ
[m] ܡܘܣܦ
ܬܡܢ : ܥܠܡ : [n] *omit*

[b] ܠܝܘܡܐ [c] *omit* ܐܝܬ
[z] *add* ܘܟܢܫܬܗ ܡܢ
[b] ܡܠܟܘܬܐ

[f] ܗܕܝܢ

[i] *add* ܐܢܐ
[h] ܘܐܡܪܘ
[a] ܡܢܝܢܝܟܘܬܗ
[l] *omit* ܫܡܥܘܢ
[m] ܡܬܚܫܒܝܢ
[p] ܐܡܪ [q] ܟܗ
[r] ܡܘܠܝܐ ܒܡܠܬ
[s] ܪܓܡ
[t] ܡܩܒܠ

[w] ܠܝܬ [v] *omit* ܠܐ
[y] ܐܡܪ

† f. 141*b*.
[a] ܬܕܒܪ
[b] ܬܠܡܝܕܝܐ ܕܝܫܘܥ [c] ܠܝܘܡܐ

Codex A.

[b]ܐܘܦܠܣܗ
ܡܢ . . . [γ] *omit*
(v. 19) ܠܚܠܠܘܢ . . .
[e]ܚܠܠܗ [f]ܚܒܪܘܗܝ
[g]ܩܦܪܗ [i]ܢܛܪܝܢ
[j]ܕܡܬܚܡܝܢ
[k]ܘܡܬܐܡܪܝܢ
[l]ܡܬܐܡܪܝܢ
[m]ܐܩܠܝܣܐ
[n]ܕܡܩܕܡܝܢ
[ܡܟܗܢܝܐ[β]]
[δs]ܠܡܒܟܝܢ
[εt]ܒܪܘܚܐ
[ζu]ܕܕܠܚܝܢ
[η]ܕܡܟܣܐ
[v]ܕܐܟܣܐ
[θx]ܕܐܬܐ
[ιy]ܡܬܚܝܒܝܢ
ܒܪ [zγ] *omit*
[κb]ܢܚܒܝܢ [λc]ܠܠܠܠ
[ܘܐܫܡܥ[μ]] [dδ] *omit* ܕܝ
[νg]ܐܟܪܝܢ
‡ f. 176*a*
[i] *omit* ܫܠܡ

[CCXCI.]

[z]ܠܡܫܚܐ[z]
[x] *add* ܡܢ ܡܬܝܘܣ
(*sic*) [b]ܐܚܕܘ
[c] *omit* . . . ܐܬܦܠܩ
. . . ܐܘܠܦܢܗ
[d]ܘܐܫܕܘܗ ܚܕܪ
[e]ܘܠܘܠܗ

Codex B.

ܗܘܘܢ ܥܠ ܐܘܪܚܐ : ܘܩܡܘ [a]ܟܡܝܪܝܢ : [βb]ܐܩ̈ܠܝܣܗ [γ]ܡܢ
[c]ܬܠܡܝܕܘܝ [d]ܘܩܡܘ ܩܡ ܡܢ ܩܕܡܝܗ :· ܘܡܢ
[e]ܚܠܠ ܫܡܥܘܢ ܘܡܢ [f]ܚܒܪܘܗܝ : ܘܡܢ [g]ܩܦܪܗ
[h]ܕܡܟܐ : ܘܡܢ ܢܛܪ ܘܡܢ [i]ܢܛܪܝܢ : ܗܠܝܢ
ܕܐܬܐܘ [j]ܕܡܬܚܡܝܢ ܡܢܗ [k]ܘܡܬܐܡܪܝܢ ܡܢ
18 ܚܡܫܝܢܘܢ : ܘܗܠܝܢ ܕܗܘܘ ܡܬܠܡܝܕܝܢ ܡܢ
19 ܪܘܚܬܐ ܠܦܫܩܬܐ ܗܘܘ [l]ܡܬܐܡܪܝܢ : ܘܒܠܠ
[m]ܐܩ̈ܠܝܣܐ ܗܘܘ ܒܥܝܢ [n]ܕܡܩ̈ܕܡܝܢ ܠܗ ܕܡܠܟܐ
[o]ܗܘܐ ܢܦܩ ܡܢܗ : ܘܗܘܐ [p]ܡܟܐܫ ܐܘܬܗܘܢ
20 ܠܚܠܠܘܢ[γ] : ܘܗܘ ܐܬܠܐ [q]ܚܝܠܘܝ ܥܠ [r]ܬܠܡܝܕܘܝ :·
ܘܗܘܐ ܐܡܪ [δs]ܠܡܒܟܝܢܘܢ [β]ܡܟܗܢܝܐ [εt]ܕܪܘܚܐ
21 [ζu]ܕܠܠܘܢ ܗܝ ܡܠܒܘܫܬܐ [ηv]ܕܡܟܣܐ : [δs]ܠܡܒܟܝܢܘܢ
ܗܠܝܢ [w]ܕܟܡܝܢ ܒܪܘ [θx]ܐܬܐܘ [ιy]ܬܬܚܝܒܘܢ :
ܠܡܒܟܝܢ ܗܠܝܢ ܕܟܡܝܢ ܒܪܘ ܕܐܬܐܘ
22 ܬܫܒܚܘܢ : ܠܡܒܟܝܢ [z]ܒܪ ܫܡܥܘܢ ܢܚܒܘܢ
ܒܢܝܢܐ ܘܒܪ ܡܦܪܝܢ ܢܚܒܘܢ ܘܢܫܡܥܘܢ
[f. 140*a*]
ܢܚܒܘܢ [a]ܘܢܩ̈ܡܘܢ [κb]ܢܚܒܝܢܘܢ ܡܢܝ ܒܢܝܢ
23 [λc]ܠܠܠܠ ܒܪܗ [δd]ܕܝ ܕܐܬܚܪܐ : [e]ܢܛܪܘ ܕܝ [μf]ܒܡܗܘ
ܡܟܐܡ ܘܡܪܦܝܢ : ܗܐ ܠܪ [νg ‡]ܐܟܪܝܢܘܢ
[h]ܡܥܠ ܒܝܗ ܡܢܚܡܐ ܫܠܡ : : : [i]ܫܠܡ

CXC.

[z]ܡܬܚܦܠܪܢ ܕܬܘܕܐ ܐܘܠܦܢܗ ܕܝܫܘܥ ܡܫܝܚܐ[xz] [a]ܝܫܘܥ
[b]ܐܘܠܦܢܗ ܐܬܦܠܩ [c]ܕܢܘܠܐ ܡܢ ܐܬܐܡܪ ܒܪܒ
[d]ܐܘܫܕܗ [d]ܘܦܠܪܢ [e]ܠܘܠܘܗܝ [f]ܐܬܦܪܘܝܗ [g]ܐܬܠܝ
[h]ܠܟܪܝ [i]ܩܦܪܘܗ :· [e]ܐܬܦܠܩ : [k]ܘܗܒܬ [l]ܐܘܫܕܗ :·
[m]ܘܡܚܦܠܪܢ [n]ܬܘܕܐ [o]ܐܠܗܐ [p]ܐܬܦܢܘܗ : ܐܬܦܠܩ

Codex C.

[a]ܟܡܝܪܝܢ [b]ܐܘܦܠܣܗ
[c]ܬܠܡܝܕܘܝ
[d]ܘܩܡܘ
[e]ܚܠܠܗ
[h]ܕܡܬܐܡܪܐ
[m]ܐܩ̈ܠܝܣܐ
[o]ܗܘ [p]ܡܟܐܫ
[q]ܚܝܠܗ [r]ܬܠܡܝܕܘܝ
[s]ܠܡܒܟܝܢ
[t]ܒܪܘܚܐ
[u]ܕܕܠܚܝܢ
[w]ܕܟܡܝܢ
[x]ܕܐܬܐ
[a]ܘܢܚܒܝܢ
[b]ܢܚܒܝܢ
[d] *omit* ܕܝ
[e]ܢܛܪܘ [f]ܒܐܘܗ
[h] *omit* ܡܥܠ
[i] *omit* ܫܠܡ

[y]ܡܬܚܦܠܪܢ
[a]ܝܫܘܥ [d]ܬܘܡܚܦܠܪܢ
[f]ܐܬܦܪܘܝܗ [g]ܐܬܠܝ
[h]ܒܪ ܐܘܠܦܢܗ ܒܪ
[i]ܩܦܪܘܗ
[k]ܘܐܬܘܗ
[m]ܘܡܚܦܠܪܢ
[o]ܐܬܠܝ

[*Codex* A.—cont.

[m]ܘܐܡܪ ܚܕܪ [n] *omit* ܬܘܕܐ ܐܠܗܐ [f] *omit* ܠܟܪܝ . . . ܐܬܦܪܘܝܗ [i]ܩܦܪܘܗ [l]ܐܬܠܝܡܬܦܠܩܬܝܢ [p]ܐܬܦܢܘܗ

Codex A.	Codex B.	Codex C.
[q]ܐܝܠܝܢ ܬܠܡܝܕܘܗܝ ܡܢ ܐܚܘܗܝ[q]	[q]ܚܙܐ ܒܬܪ ܚܕ ܗܕܐ ܐܫܟܚ[q] : [sr]ܬܠܡܝܕܝܢ ܬܪܝܢ	[s]ܬܠܡܝܕܝܢ ܬܪܝܢ
[r]ܬܐܡܘܡ ܒܬܪ ܐܠܗܝܗܘܢ ܒܡܐܪܘܗܘܢ[r]	[t]ܐܒܐ ܡܢܗ [u]ܒܢܘܗܝ[r] : [†] ܐܦܠܘܣ[u] ܚܙܐ ܒܬܪ	† f. 142a.
[u]ܫܒܩܘ ܣܦܝܢܬܗ ܒܬܪ ܡܢ ܡܚܘܬܗܘܢ[u]	ܫܒܩܘ ܡܢ ܠܗܘܢ[u] :: ܒܬܪܝܢ [w]ܗܘܢ ܦܝ ܒܐܝܘܢ	[t]ܐܒܘܗܝ [u]ܒܢܘܗܝ
[w]omit ܗܘܢ...ܐܬܐܡܘܢ	ܐܬܐܡܘܢ[w] [g]ܬܪܝܢ [ih]ܐܦܝܩܝܢܘܢ : ܐܦܠܘܣ	[w]omit ܗܘܢ...ܐܬܐܡܘܢ
[h]add ܐܠܗܐ ܬܪܝܢ[g]	[k]ܬܡܢ ܘܒܬܪܝܢ [l]ܦܝ ܐܠܗܠ[k] :[m]ܫܡܥܘܢ[n] ܘܒܬܪܝܢ	[g]ܬܪܝܢ
[k]ܦܝ ܐܚܘܗܝ ܐܠܝܐܠ ܬܠܡܝܕܗ[k]	[o]ܒܬܪ ܬܪܝܢ ܐܠܗܝܗܘܢ [p]ܠܡܠܝܢܘܢ ܐܦܠܘܣ[sq] [rv]ܬܠܬ	[i]ܐܦܝܩܝܢܘܢ
[m]add ܬܐܡܘܢ ܒܬܪܝܢ	ܒܬܪ ܗܘܢ ܦܝ ܬܪܝܢ ܐܬܐܡܘܢ[rv] [t]ܫܡܥܘܢ	[l]ܡܢ ܒܬܪ omit[o]
ܐܠܗܝܗܘܢ ܒܡܫܡܫܘܢ	ܘܒܬܪܝܢ [u]ܢܦܠ ܥܒܕ ܐܠܗܝܗܘܢ[wu] ܗܘܢܐ ܦܢ	[p]ܠܡܠܝܢܘܢ
[n]ܫܡܥܘܢ	[x]ܐܒܘܗܘܢ [y]ܐܦܠܘܣ[z] [a]ܬܠܡܝܕܝܢ[z] [b]ܡܢ ܬܪܝܢ	[q]add ܡܢ ܗܘܢ ܐܚܘܗܝ ܐܠܝܫܡܥ ܒܪ ܐܠܗܝܢ
	[c]ܐܬܐܡܘܢ[y] [d]ܬܡܢܝܗ ܘܒܬܪܝܢ [e]ܬܪܝܢ [f]ܐܠܗܐ	[v]omit ܐܬܐܡܘܢ...ܬܠܬ
	ܐܒܘܢܐ [g]ܐܦܩܘ ܡܢ [h]ܒܬܪܐ [i]ܘܒܬܪܗ [j]ܡܪܘܢܐ :	[z]add ܦܝ [w]add ܒܢܝܐ
		[a]ܬܠܡܝܕܝܢ [b]ܦܝ
		[c]ܐܬܐܡܘܢ
		[g]ܐܦܩܘ [j]ܡܪܘܢ

[Codex A.—cont.

ܐܠܗܝܗܘܢ ܐܦܠܘܣ ܫܡܥܘܢ ܘܒܬܪܝܢ ܡܢ ܬܪܝܢ ܐܠܗܠ [m] ܫܡܥܘܢ[n]
ܒܬܪ ܬܪܝܢ omit[o] [p]ܠܡܠܝܢܘܢ ܗܘܢ ܘܒܬܪܝܢ ܐܦܩܘܡܝܢ [s]add
ܘܐܠܗܗ ܐܦܠܘܣ ܐܝܠܝܢ ܬܠܡܝܕܘܗܝ ܡܢ ܐܚܘܗܝ[s] [r]ܬܐܡܘܡ ܡܢ ܐܠܗܠ[r]
[t]ܫܡܥܘܢ ܢܦܠ ... ܐܠܗܝܗܘܢ omit[u] [x]ܐܒܘܗܘܢ [y]ܐܦܠܘܣ ܬܠܬ
ܡܢ ܐܠܗܠ[y] [d]ܬܐܚܘܗܝ [e]ܬܪܝܢ [f]ܐܠܗܐ [g]ܐܦܩܘ
[h]ܒܬܪܘܗܝ ܘܒܬܪܗ ܡܪܘܢܐ omit[j]

Matt. V. 14—19.

Codex A.	Codex B.	Codex C.
[a]ܠܥܠܡܝܢ	14 ܐܢܬܘܢ ܢܗܘܪܐ [a]ܠܥܠܡܝܢ : ܐܢܬܘܢ ܗܘܝܢ	
[b]ܕܥܠܡܐ [c]ܝܟܠܐ	ܢܗܘܪܗ [b]ܕܥܠܡܐ : ܠܐ [c]ܝܟܠ ܡܕܝܢܐ	[c]ܝܟܠܐ
[e]ܡܬܛܫܝܐ	ܕܬܬܛܫܐ ܗܝܐ [d]ܕܠܥܠ ܡܢ ܛܘܪ [e]ܡܬܛܫܝܐ :	[d]ܕܠܥܠ
	15 ܘܠܐ ܡܕܠܩܝܢ ܒܘܨܝܢܐ ܘܡܣܝܡܝܢ ܠܗ ܬܚܘܬ	[f]ܡܕܘ
[h]ܗܟܕ	[f]ܡܕܘܕܐ : ܐܠܐ ܥܠ ܡܢܪܬܐ ܘܗܘ ܡܢܗܪ ܠܟܘܠ	[i]ܢܗܘܪܟܘܢ
[j]ܠܟܘܠ	16 ܗܠܝܢ ܕܒܒܝܬܐ : [h]ܗܟܕܝܢ ܢܢܗܪ [i]ܢܗܘܪܟܘܢ	[j]ܠܟܘܠ
‡ f. 177a.	ܩܕܡ ܒܢܝܢܫܐ : [j]ܠܡܚܙܝ ‡ ܕܝܚܙܘܢ [k]ܥܒܕܝܟܘܢ	[k]ܥܒܕܝܟܘܢ
[l]omit ܕܝ	ܛܒܝܐ : ܘܝܫܒܚܘܢ ܠܐܒܘܟܘܢ ܕܒܫܡܝܐ :	[l]omit ܕܝ
[m]ܬܣܒܪܘܢ	17 ܠܐ [l]ܕܝ [m]ܬܣܒܪܘܢ ܕܐܬܝܬ [l]ܕܝ ܕܐܫܪܐ [n]ܢܡܘܣܐ	[m]ܬܣܒܪܘܢ
[o]add ܓܝܪ	ܐܘ ܢܒܝܐ : ܠܐ ܐܬܝܬ ܕܐܫܪܐ ܐܠܐ ܕܐܫܠܡܐ :	[o]add ܓܝܪ [n]ܢܡܘܣܐ
[v]omit ܐܡܝܢ	18 ܐܡܝܢ[o] ܐܡܝܢ[v] ܐܡܪ ܐܢܐ ܠܟܘܢ : ܕܥܕܡܐ	[v]omit ܐܡܝܢ

Codex A.	*Codex* B.	*Codex* C.
ᵖ ܕܡܕܒܪܝܢ	ᵖ ܕܡܕܒܪܝܢ ܥܡܡܐ ܘܐܪܟܢܐ ᵠ ܘܡܠܟܐ ܚܕ : ܐܢܐ	ᵠ ܡܠܟܐ
ʳ ܬܬܒܥܘܢ	ܚܙܐ ܡܠܟܐ ܠܐ ʳ ܬܬܒܥܘܢ ܡܢ ܢܒܝܘܬܐ : ܐܢܐ [f. 140*b*]	
ˢ ܢܒܝܐ	19 ܡܢ ˢ ܢܒܝܐ : ܒܪܢܫܐ ܕܡܠܟܐ ᵗ ܐܬܒܥܘ : ܟܠ	ᵗ ܐܬܒܥܘ
ᵗ ܐܬܒܥܘ	ܡܢ ܐܢܘܢ ܕܥܒܪܐ ܚܕ ܡܢ ܗܠܝܢ ܦܘܩܕܢܐ :	
ᵘ ܒܗ ʷ ܥܒܕܘ	ܘܢܘܦܐ ܗܠܝܢ ᵘ ܒܗ ܠܒܢܝܢܫܐ ʷ ܥܒܕܘ ˡ ܕܝ ܢܬܩܪܐ	ʷ ܥܒܕܘ
	ܒܡܠܟܘܬܐ ܕܫܡܝܐ : ܡܢ ˣ ܕܝ ܕܥܒܕ ܘܠܗ :	ˣ *omit* ܕܝ
ʸ ܗܢ ᶻ ܕܫܡܝܐ	ʸ ܗܢܘܢ ܕܝ ܢܬܩܪܐ ܒܡܠܟܘܬܐ ᶻ ܕܫܡܝܐ	ᵃ *omit* ܘܥܒܕܝܢ
	ܬܗܘܐ ᵃ ܘܥܒܕܝܢ ܬܒܥ ܐܠܗܐ ᵇ ܐܬܒܥܘܗ	ᵇ ܐܬܒܥܘܗ
	ܐܬܠܒܫ ܥܒܕܝܢ ܗܘ ᶜ ܒܗܘܢ ܐܠܗܐ † ܡܢ	† f. 142*b*.
	ܠܗܘܢ :	ᶜ ܒܗܘܢ

[CCXCV.]
[f. 177*a*]

CXCI.

Luke II. 22—40.

Codex A.	Codex B.	Codex C.
ᵇ*omit* ܐܡܪ ... ܢܗܘܐ	ᵃ ᵇ ܐܡܪ ܐܘܢܓܠܝܣܛܐ ܗܘ ܒܥܕܢ ܢܗܘܐ :	ᵃ ܐܡܪ ܥܠ ᶜ ܐܬܐ
ᵈ ܢܗܘ ᵉ *add* ܐܢ	ᶜ ܐܬܐ ᵈ ܢܗܘܐ ᵉ ܕܡܟܠ ܫܒܐ ᶠ ᵍ ܡܘܫܐ ܢܒܝܐ ᶠ	ᵈ ܢܗܘ
ᵍ ܐܡܪ ʰ ܐܠܗܘܬ	22 ܐܠܡܫܝܚܐ ʰ ܠܡܘܬ ܡܢ ܠܗܘܢ : ⁱ ܘܒܪ ᵠ ܐܬܬܡܠܝܘ	ᶠ *omit* ܡܘܫܐ ܢܒܝܐ
ʳ *omit* . . . ܘܒܪ	ܢܗܘܐ ܕܕܒܝܚܝܢ ܗܝܟ ܢܬܒܫܢ ܕܡܢܘܚܬܐ :ʳˢ	ⁱ *add* ܘܒܢܘܬܗ
. . . ܕܡܢܘܚܬܐ	ᵗ ܐܣܩܘܗ ᵘ ܠܗ ܠܐܘܪܫܠܡ ʷ ܕܢܩܝܡܘܢ ܠܗ	ᵠ ܐܣܩܘܗ ʷ ܕܢܩܝܡܘܢ
ˢ *add* ܘܒܢܘܬܗ	23 ܩܕܡ ܡܪܝܐ : ܗܝܟ ˣ ܕܟܬܝܒ ܒܢܡܘܣܗ	ˣ ܕܟܬܝܒ
ܦܪܘܩܢܐ	ܕܡܪܝܐ ܕܟܠ ܕܟܪ ‡ ܕܦܬܚ ᶻ ܡܚܙܐ ܩܕܝܫ	ᶻ ܒܟܪ ܩܠܘܕܝܬ
ᵗ ܐܣܩܘܗ	24 ܢܬܩܪܐ ܠܡܪܝܐ ܘܕܢܬܠ ܢܟܣܐ ܗܝܟ ᵃ ܕܐܡܝܪ	ᵇ ܒܢܡܘܣܗ
‡ f. 177*b*.	ᵇ ܒܢܡܘܣܗ ܕܡܪܝܐ : ܐܘ ᶜ ܦܪܘܓܝܢ : ܐܢܐ ܬܪܝܢ	ᶜ ܕܝܘܢܝܢ
ᵘ *add* ܐܡܪ ܡܠܟܐ ܠܗܘܢ	25 ܓܘܙܠܝܢ ᵈ ܕܝܘܢܐ : ˣˣˣˣˣ ᵉ ܬܪܝܢ : ᶠ ܘܗܘܐ ܚܕ	ᵈ ܕܝܘܢܐ
ʷ ܕܢܩܝܡܘܢ	ܓܒܪ ᵍ ܡܢ ܐܘܪܫܠܡ ʰ ܕܫܡ ܗܘܐ ܫܡܥܘܢ	ᵉ *omit* ܬܪܝܢ
ᶻ ܡܚܙܐ	26 ܫܡܥܘܢ : ܘܗܘܐ ܙܕܝܩ ⁱ ܘܕܚܝܠ ܡܢ	ᶠ ܘܗܘܐ ᵍ ܒܐܘܪܫܠܡ
ᵃ ܕܐܡܝܪ	ܐܠܗܐ ʲ ܘܗܘ ܡܣܟܐ ᵏ ܠܒܘܝܐܗ	ʲ *add* ܗܘܐ
ᵇ ܒܢܡܘܣܗ	ˡ ܕܐܝܣܪܝܠ : ܘܪܘܚܐ ܕܩܘܕܫܐ ܗܘܬ ܥܠܘܗܝ :	ᵏ ܠܒܘܝܐܗ
ᶜ ܕܝܘܢܝܢ	ܘܗܘܐ ᵐ ܕܐܬܒܪܬ ܠܗ ܡܢ ܪܘܚܐ ܕܩܘܕܫܐ :	ˡ ܕܐܝܣܪܝܠ ᵐ ܕܐܬܒܪܬ
ᶠ ܘܗܘܐ ᵍ ܒܐܘܪܫܠܡ	ܕܠܐ ܢܚܙܐ ܡܘܬܐ ⁿ ܥܕܡܐ ܕܢܚܙܐ	ⁿ ܕܥܕܡܐ
ʰ ܕܝ	27 ܠܡܫܝܚܗ ܕܡܪܝܐ : ᵒ ܘܐܬܐ ܒܪܘܚܐ ܠܗܝܟܠܐ	ᵒ *omit* ܘ
ⁱ ܘܕܚܝܠ ʲ *add* ܗܘܐ		
ᵏ ܠܒܘܝܐܗ		
ˡ ܕܐܝܣܪܝܠ		

Codex A.

[p]ܡܫܐܠܝܢ ܡܢܐ [q] *omit*
[r]ܕܐܠܦܝܢ
[s]ܘܡܫܠܗ [t]ܒܦܠܓܗ
[u]ܘܒܪܟܢ [w]ܚܝܠܐܝ
[y]ܕܒܬܕܬ
[a]ܢܗܘܪ [b]ܠܦܠܓܐܝ
[c]ܐܫܬܪܝ [d]ܘܐܝܟܢܗ
[e]ܬܬܡܗܝܢ [g]ܡܬܡܠܠܝܢ
[h]ܠܡܬܪܐܡ [i]ܐܝܟܢܗ
[b]ܗܕܝܢ [d]ܠܡܦܩܠܐ
[e]ܒܐܫܬܪܝ

‡ f. 178a.

[f]ܘܐܠܦܬ [h]ܬܫܒܚܬܐ
[i]ܫܡܥܝܢ [k]ܢܒܝܬܐ
[l]ܕܦܢܘܐܝܠ
[m]ܫܘܒܚܗ [n]ܕܐܫܬܪ
[o]ܒܠܘܠܬ [p]ܘܡܢܝܢ
[q]ܕܢܫܐܬ [t]ܫܢܝܢ
[u]ܒܬܘܠܘܬܗ
[v]ܬܬܗܡܝܢ
[w]ܪܘܚܐ [y]ܒܡܘܡܝܢ
[z]ܘܒܪܘܠܐ
[a]ܠܝܠܐ [b]ܘܐܝܡܡܐ
[c]ܠܒܘܠ [d]ܠܦܪܘܢܐ
[i]ܠܡܕܝܢܬܗܘܢ
[l]ܫܒܥܐ ܕܝ [m] *omit*
[n]ܒܡܘܡܬܐ
[o]ܒܡܠܬܐ [p]ܘܚܫܕܗ
[q]ܗܘܐ [r]ܥܠܘܝ

Codex B.

ܘܒܡܒܐ ܕܗܘܘ ܐܢܫܘܬܗ ܕܒܪܐ ܢܫܘܦ:
[p]ܡܫܐܠܝܢ ܠܗ ܕܡܫܒܒܘܢ ܠܗ ܗܝܢ [q]ܡܢܐ
28 [r]ܕܐܠܦܝܢ ܡܢ ܢܫܡܘܬܗ ܠܦܠܓܗ [s]ܘܡܫܝܠ
ܥܡܗܘܢ [t]ܒܦܠܓܗ [u]ܘܒܪܟܢ ܠܐܠܗܐ ܘܐܡܪܝܢ:
[f. 141a]
29 ܒܪܘ ܐܢܬ [v]ܦܢܐ ܒܒܪܝܢ ܡܪܐ ܗܝܢ ܡܠܬܢ
30 31 ܒܥܠܡ ܕܫܡܝܐ [w]ܚܝܠܝ [x]ܡܫܝܚܢ: ܡܢܐ [y]ܕܒܬܕܬ
32 ܘܡܕܡ [z]ܐܦܝܗܘܢ ܕܒܗܠ ܘܡܠܝܐ [a]ܢܗܘܪ [b]ܠܦܠܓܝ
33 ܕܚܝܢܝܢ: [v]ܘܠܬܫܒܘܚܬܗ ܕܫܡܟܝ [c]ܐܫܬܪܝ:
34 †ܘܗܘܐ ܢܫܩܐ [d]ܘܐܝܡ [e]ܬܬܡܗܝܢ ܒܠ ܗܠܝܢ
ܕܗܘܝ [g]ܡܬܡܠܠܝܢ ܒܠ ܕܦܠܓܗ: [f]ܘܒܪܟܢ
ܬܗܘܢ ܥܡܗܘܢ ܘܐܡܪܝܢ [h]ܠܡܬܪܐܡ [i]ܐܝܟܢܗ:
ܐܝܟ [b]ܗܕܝܢ [c]ܡܫܡܫ [d]ܠܡܒܘ̈ܠܐ ܘܠܡܦܩܢܐ ‡ܕܫܡܝܐ
35 [e]ܒܐܫܬܪܝ [f]ܘܠܝܬ ܕܡܫܬܘܕܥܝܢ ܠܗ: ܘܐܬܝܢ
ܒܬܫܒܚܬ ܬܒܥܘܪ ܣܓܝܐ: ܠܡܠܟܐ ܕܝ [h]ܬܬܒܠܝܢ
36 [i]ܫܡܥܝܢ ܡܢ ܠܒܒܝܢ ܦܠܓܐ: ܘܗܘܬ ܫܢܝܐ [k]ܡܬܢܒܝܐ (*sic*)
ܒܪܬܗ [l]ܕܦܢܘܐܝܠ ܡܢ [m]ܫܘܒܚܗ [n]ܕܐܫܬܪ: ܘܗܕܐ
ܗܘܬ [o]ܒܠܘܠܬ [p]ܘܡܢܝܢ ܦܠܓܐ [q]ܕܐܫܬ ܒܡ
37 ܒܪܬܗ [r]ܫܘܒܚ [t]ܫܢܝܢ ܡܢ [u]ܒܬܘܠܘܬܗ: ܘܗܝ
ܗܘܬ ܐܪܡܠܬܐ ܗܝܢ [s]ܒܪܬ [v]ܬܬܗܡܝܢ ܘܐܪܒܥ
[t]ܫܢܝܢ ܗܕܐ ܕܠܐ ܗܘܬ [w]ܪܘܚܐ ܡܢ ܢܘܗܪܐ [x]
[y]ܒܡܘܡܝܢ [z]ܘܒܪܘܠܐ ܡܫܡܫܐ [a]ܠܝܠܐ [b]ܘܐܝܡܡܐ:
38 ܘܗܝ ܒܗ ܒܫܥܬܐ ܡܛܬ ܘܗܘܬ ܡܫܬܘܕܝܐ
ܠܡܪܝܐ: ܘܗܘܬ ܡܡܠܠܐ ܠܦܠܓܗ [c]ܕܒܠ ܗܠܝܢ
39 ܕܗܘܘ ܡܣܟܝܢ [d]ܠܦܪܘܩܐ [e]ܒܐܘܪܫܠܡ: ܘܒܪ
[f]ܫܠܡ ܒܘܠܐ ܗܝܢ [g] [h]ܕܢܫܡܬܗ ܕܡܪܝܐ: ܬܒܘ
40 ܠܗܘܢ ܠܟܠܠܐ [i]ܠܡܕܝܢܬܗܘܢ ܢܦܩܬ: [k]ܘܦܠܐ
ܕܝ ܗܘܐ [l]ܫܒܥܐ ܘܡܫܬܪܪ [m]ܕܝ [n]ܒܡܘܡܬܗ
[o]ܘܡܬܩܒܠܐ ܡܢ ܚܡܬܐ [p]ܘܚܫܕܗ ܕܐܠܗܐ
[q]ܗܘܬ [r]ܥܠܘܗܝ:

Codex C.

[p]ܡܫܐܠܝܢ
[s]ܘܡܫܠܗ [t]ܒܦܠܓܗ
[u]ܘܒܪܟܢ [v]ܦܢܝ
[x]ܠܡܫܝܚܢ [y]ܕܒܬܕܫ
[z]ܐܦ̈ܝܗܘܢ
[a]ܢܗܘܪ
[v]ܘܬܫܒܘܚܬܗ
[d]ܘܐܡܗ

† f. 143a.

[e]ܬܬܡܗܝܢ [f]ܘܒܪܟܢ
[c]ܕܡܫܡܫ
[d]ܠܡܒܘܠܐ [e]ܒܫܪܝܠ
[f]ܘܐܠܦܬ [k]ܢܒܝܐ
[l]ܕܦܢܘܐܝܠ [m]ܫܘܒܚܗ
[n]ܕܐܫܬܪ [o]ܒܠܘܠܬ
[q]ܕܢܫܐܬ [r]ܫܘܒܚ
[s]ܒܪܬ [v]ܬܬܗܡܝܢ
ܕܡܪܝܐ [x] *add* [a]ܠܝܠܐ
[c]ܠܒܘܠ [d]ܠܦܪܘܢܐ
[e]ܒܪܘܫܠܡ [f]ܫܠܡ
[g] *add* ܕܒܬܒܒ
[h]ܒܢܫܡܬܗ
[i]ܠܡܕܝܢܬܗܘܢ
[k]ܘܦܠܐ [l]ܫܒܥܐ
[m] *omit* ܕܝ
[n]ܒܡܘܡܬܐ
[o]ܘܡܠܬܡܠܐ
[q]ܗܘܐ [r]ܥܠܘܝ

Codex A.	Codex B.	Codex C.
[CCCIX.] [f. 178b]	CXCII.	

CXCII.

Luke VII. 19—29.

Codex B.

ܬܠܬܗܘܢ[z] ܕܗܘܐ ܐܝܕܘܡ ܥܡܗܘܢ [a]ܐܬܠܡܝܕܘܗܝ

ܐܠܝܫ ܐܠܝܫܥ ܡܢ ܠܘܬܐ[a] ܕܡܕܝܢܬܗ ܕܗܘܐ [b]ܬܪܝܢ

ܐܝܬܝ[b] ܐܬܠܡܝܕܘܗܝ [c]ܘܫܕܪܗܘܢ [d]ܘܐܡܪ ܠܗ ܐܬܠܡܝܕ[z] ܀

[e]ܐܝܟܢܢܗ ܘܟܢܝܫܝܢ ܒܟܘܠ ܐܬܪ [f]ܗܘܐ [g]ܘܝܫܘܥ

19 [h]ܐܬܠܡܝܕܝܗܝ [ij]ܘܫܕܪܐ [k]ܠܘܬܗ ܕܝܫܘܥ [j]ܡܢ ܠܘܬܐ:[a]

ܘܐܡܪܐ [b]ܘܝܫܘܥ ܐܬܝܢ ܐܢܬ ܡܢ [c]ܐܬܠܡܝܕܘܗܝ ܘܥܠܝܢ

[f. 141b]

ܠܘܬܗ [d]ܡܪܢ ܝܫܘܥ [e]ܐܡܪ: ܐܢܬ [f]ܗܘ [g]ܗܘ ܕܐܬܐ

20 ܕܐܬܝܬ ܐܢܬ [h]ܠܝܫܘܥ ܐܢܗ ܡܫܝܚܐ: ܒܪ ܕܒ

ܐܬܘ [†]ܘܫܠܚܢ ܠܟܢܫܐ ܠܘܬܗ ܡܪܝܐ ܝܫܘܥ

ܐܡܪܘ ܠܗ: [i]ܘܝܫܘܥ [‡]ܡܢ ܟܢܫܐ ܥܠܝܟ ܐܬܝ

ܠܘܬܟ: ܐܡܪ ܐܢܬ [g]ܗܘ ܕܐܬܐ ܕܐܬܐ ܐܢܐ

21 [h]ܠܝܫܘܥ [i]ܐܝܬܝ ܡܫܝܚܐ: [l]ܘܒܗ [m]ܒܥܕܢܐ

ܐܝܟ ܡܪܐ ܝܫܘܥ ܠܟܠ [n]ܡܢ ܟܘܪܗܢܐ ܘܡܢ

[o]ܡܚܘܬܐ ܘܡܢ [p]ܪܘܚܐ ܒܝܫܬܐ: [q]ܘܠܥܘܝܪܐ

22 ܣܓܝ ܝܗܒ [r]ܕܢܚܙܘܢ: [s]ܘܐܦܢܝ ܡܪܢܐ

ܝܫܘܥ ܘܐܡܪ ܠܗܘܢ: ܐܙܠܘ [t]ܕܒ ܐܡܪܘ

ܠܝܘܚܢܢ ܡܐ ܕܚܙܝܬܘܢ ܘܫܡܥܬܘܢ: ܕܥܘܝܪܐ

[u]ܚܙܝܢ: [w]ܘܚܓܝܪܐ ܡܗܠܟܝܢ: ܘܓܪܒܐ [y]ܡܬܕܟܝܢ:

ܘܚܪܫܐ ܫܡܥܝܢ ܘܡܝܬܐ [z]ܩܝܡܝܢ: ܘܡܣܟܢܐ

23 [a]ܡܬܒܣܪܝܢ: [b]ܘܛܘܒܘܗܝ ܡܢ ܕܠܐ ܢܬܬܟܫܠ ܒܝ:

24 ܘܡܢ ܕܐܙܠܘ ܠܗܘܢ [c]ܫܠܝܚܘܗܝ [d]ܕܝܘܚܢܢ ܫܪܝ

ܡܪܢܐ ܝܫܘܥ ܐܡܪ [e]ܠܟܢܫܐ ܥܠ ܝܘܚܢܢ

[f]ܝܘܚܢܢ ܡܢܐ ܢܦܩܬܘܢ [g]ܠܡܕܒܪܐ ܠܡܚܙܐ

25 ܩܢܝܐ [h]ܡܢ ܪܘܚܐ [i]ܡܬܬܙܝܥ: [j]ܐܠܐ ܡܢܐ

ܢܦܩܬܘܢ ܠܡܚܙܐ ܓܒܪܐ ܕܢܚܬܐ [k]ܪܟܝܟܐ

[l]ܠܒܝܫ: ܗܐ ܗܠܝܢ ܕܢܚܬܐ ܪܟܝܟܐ ܠܒܫܝܢ

ܒܒܬܝ [m]ܡܠܟܐ ܐܝܬܝܗܘܢ: [n]ܡܠܟܘܬܐ ܀

26 ܐܠܐ ܡܢܐ ܢܦܩܬܘܢ ܠܡܚܙܐ ܢܒܝܐ [o]ܐܝ

Codex A.

[z] omit . . . ܬܠܬܗܘܢ . . . ܐܬܠܡܝܕ

[e] ܐܝܟܢܢܗ

[h] ܠܡܚܕܐ

[j] [illegible]

[a] add ܘܡܢ ܠܘܬܗ ܕܝܫܘܥ

[b] ܘܝܫܘܥ

[c] ܐܬܠܡܝܕܘܗܝ

[d] ܡܪܢ [g] ܗܘ

‡ f. 179a.

[g] ܕܒ [h] ܠܝܫܘܥ

[i] ܐܝܬܝ [l] ܘܒܗ

[m] ܒܥܕܢܐ [o] ܡܚܘܬܐ

[p] ܪܘܚܐ [q] ܘܠܥܘܝܪܐ

[s] ܘܐܦܢܝ [t] omit ܕܒ

[u] ܚܙܝܢ [w] ܘܚܓܝܪܐ

[y] ܡܬܕܟܝܢ [z] ܘܩܝܡܝܢ

[a] ܡܬܒܣܪܝܢ

[b] ܘܛܘܒܘܗܝ

[c] ܫܠܝܚܘܗܝ

[d] ܕܝܘܚܢܢ

[e] ܠܟܢܫܐ

[f] ܝܘܚܢܢ

[g] ܠܡܕܒܪܐ

[i] ܡܬܬܙܝܥ [j] ܐܠܐ

[k] ܪܟܝܟܐ

[m] ܡܠܟܘܬܗܘܢ

[n] ܡܠܟܘܬܐ [o] ܐܝ

Codex C.

[a] omit . . . ܐܬܠܡܝܕ . . . ܠܘܬܐ

[b] ܐܝܬܝ ܬܪܝܢ

[c] ܘܫܕܪܗܘܢ [d] ܐܡܪ

[f] add ܠܘܬܗ ܐܬܠܡܝܕܘܗܝ [g] ܝܫܘܥ

[h] omit ܐܬܠܡܝܕܝܗܝ

[i] ܘܫܕܪܐ ܠܘܬܗ [k] omit

[a] add ܘܡܢ ܠܘܬܗ ܕܝܫܘܥ

† f. 143b.

[b] ܘܝܫܘܥ

[d] ܡܪܢ [e] ܘܐܡܪ

[f] omit ܗܘ

[h] ܠܝܫܘܥ [i] ܘܝܫܘܥ

[g] ܕܒ [i] ܐܝܬܝ

[l] ܘܒܗ [m] ܒܥܕܢܐ

[n] omit ܡܢ [o] ܡܚܘܬܐ

[q] ܘܠܥܘܝܪܐ

[r] ܕܢܚܙܘܢ

[s] ܘܐܦܢܝ

[t] omit ܕܒ [u] ܚܙܝܢ

[w] ܘܚܓܝܪܐ

[x] ܡܗܠܟܝܢ

[z] ܘܩܝܡܝܢ

[d] ܕܝܘܚܢܢ

[h] ܡܢ [i] ܡܬܬܙܝܥ

[j] ܐܠܐ [k] ܪܟܝܟܐ

[l] ܠܒܝܫ

[m] ܒܒܬܝ ܡܠܟܐ

[n] ܡܠܟܘܬܐ [o] ܐܝ

Codex B.

ܐܡܪ ܐܢܐ ܠܟܘܢ ܕܐܘܦ ܝܬܝܪ ܡܢ ܢܒܝܐ
27 ܗܘ : [p]ܗܕܝܢ ܗܘ ܗܘ ܕܥܠܘܗܝ [q]ܟܬܒ ܗܐ
ܐܢܐ ܡܫܠܚ ܡܠܐܟܝ ܩܕܡ [r]ܐܦܝܟ : ܕܗܘ
28 ܡܫܠܠ [s]ܠܟ ܐܘܪܚܐ [t]ܘܡܬܩܢ : ܐܡܝܢ ܐܡܪ
ܐܢܐ ܠܟܘܢ ܕܠܝܬ [u]ܒܝܠܘܕܝܗܘܢ ܕܢܫܝܐ [‡] ܪܒ ܡܢ
[w]ܝܘܚܢܢ : [x]ܘܙܥܘܪܐ ܕܝ ܒܡܠܟܘܬܗ ܕܐܠܗܐ
29 ܪܒ ܗܘ ܡܢܗ : ܘܟܠܗ ܕܝ ܥܡܐ [y]ܕܫܡܥܘ
[z]ܘܡܟܣܐ [†]ܙܕܩܘ ܠܐܠܗܐ ܕܐܨܛܒܥܘ [a]ܒܝܘܚܢܢ :

Codex A.

[p]ܗܕܝܢ ܟܬܒ [q]omit
[r]ܐܦܝܟ ܠܟ [s]omit
[t]ܘܡܬܩܢ
[u]ܒܝܠܘܕܝܗܘܢ
[w]ܝܘܚܢܢ
‡ f. 179b.
[x]ܘܙܥܘܪܐ
[y]ܕܫܡܥܘ
[z]ܘܡܟܣܐ
[a]ܒܝܘܚܢܢ

Codex C.

[r]ܐܦܝܟ ܠܟ [s]omit
[u]ܒܝܠܘܕܝܗܘܢ
[x]ܘܙܥܘܪܐ
[y]ܕܫܡܥܘ
[z]ܘܡܟܣܐ
[a]ܡܢ ܝܘܚܢܢ
† f. 144a.

CXCIII.

Matt. XI. 2—15.

Codex B.

[a]ܘܗܕܐ ܗܘ[a] [b]ܠܬܠܡܝܕܘܗܝ : ܘܗܘܐ[c] [d]ܠܬܠܬܐ
[f. 142a]
ܐܦܢܗ ܒܥܠܡܐ ܡܢ [e]ܡܬܐܬܝ[f] :[g] ܫܡܥ
2 [y]ܝܘܚܢܢ ܕܝ ܟܕ [z]ܒܒܝܬ [a]ܐܣܝܪܐ [b]ܐܘܦ
[c]ܒܥܒܕܘܝ ܕܡܫܝܚܐ : [d]ܫܠܚ ܬܪܝܢ ܡܢ
3 [e]ܬܠܡܝܕܘܗܝ ܘܐܡܪ ܠܗ : ܐܬ ܗܘ[f] ܕܝܢ
ܕܐܬܐ ܐܘ [g]ܠܐܚܪܢ ܐܢܚܢ ܡܣܟܝܢ :
4 ܘܐܓܝܒ ܡܪܢ ܝܫܘܥ ܘܐܡܪ ܠܗܘܢ : ܐܙܠܘ
[h]ܐܡܪܘ [i]ܠܝܘܚܢܢ ܡܐ [j]ܕܐܬܚܙܝܬܘܢ [k]ܚܙܝܢ
5 [l]ܘܫܡܥܝܢ : ܣܡܝܐ ܚܙܝܢ [m]ܘܚܓܝܪܐ ܡܗܠܟܝܢ :
ܘܓܪܒܢܐ [n]ܡܕܟܝܢ ܘܚܪܫܢܐ ܫܡܥܝܢ : [o]ܘܡܝܬܐ
6 [p]ܩܐܡܝܢ ܘܡܣܟܢܝܐ [q]ܡܬܒܣܪܝܢ : [r]ܘܛܘܒܝ
7 ܡܢ ܕܠܐ ܡܬܟܫܠ ܒܝ : ܘܟܕ ܐܙܠܘ ܠܗܘܢ
ܫܪܝ ܡܪܢ ܝܫܘܥ ܐܡܪ [t]ܠܐܟܠܘܣܝܐ
ܥܠ [u]ܝܘܚܢܢ ܡܐ ܢܦܩܬܘܢ [v]ܠܡܕܒܪܐ
8 ܕܬܚܙܘܢ [w]ܩܢܝܐ [x]ܡܢ ܪܘܚܐ [y]ܡܙܕܥܙܥ : [z]ܐܠܐ
ܡܐ ܢܦܩܬܘܢ ܕܬܚܙܘܢ[w] ܒܪܢܫ [a]ܒܡܐܢܝܢ

Codex A.

[CCCIX.]
[f. 179b]

[a]ܘܗܕܐ ܗܘ omit
[b]ܠܬܠܡܝܕܘܗܝ [c]add ܝܗܒ
[d]ܐܬܠܬܐ [e]ܡܢܐܬܗܘܢ
[g]add ܘܒܥܠܡܗ ܡܢܗܘܢ ܐܦܢܗ
[y]ܝܘܚܢܢ [z]ܒܒܝܬ
[a]ܐܣܝܪܐ
[b]omit ܐܘܦ
[c]ܒܥܒܕܘܝ
[e]ܬܠܡܝܕܘܗܝ
ܕܝܢ [f]omit [g]ܠܐܚܪܢ
[h]ܘܐܡܪܘ
[i]ܠܝܘܚܢܢ [j]ܕܐܬܚܙܝ
[m]ܘܚܓܝܪܐ
[n]ܡܗܠܟܝܢ
[o]ܘܡܝܬܐ [p]ܩܐܡܝܢ
[q]ܡܬܒܣܪܝܢ
[r]ܘܛܘܒܝ
[t]ܠܐܟܠܘܣܝܐ
[u]ܝܘܚܢܢ
[v]ܠܡܕܒܪܐ [x]ܕܬܚܙܘܢ
[y]ܡܙܕܥܙܥ
[z]ܐܠܐ [a]ܒܡܐܢܝܢ

Codex C.

[a]omit ܘܗܕܐ ܗܘ
[b]ܠܬܠܡܝܕܘܗܝ
[c]add ܝܗܒ
[d]ܐܬܠܬܐ
[e]ܡܢܐܬܗ
[f]add ܒܥܠܡܗ
[z]ܒܒܝܬ
[b]omit ܐܘܦ
[d]ܫܠܚ
[e]ܬܠܡܝܕܘܗܝ
ܕܝܢ [f]omit [g]ܠܐܚܪܢ
[k]ܚܙܝܢ
[l]ܘܫܡܥܝܢ
[m]ܘܚܓܝܪܐ
[o]ܘܡܝܬܐ
[p]ܩܐܡܝܢ
[q]ܡܬܒܣܪܝܢ
[v]omit ܠܡܕܒܪܐ
[w]omit ܡܐ . . .
. . . ܕܬܚܙܘܢ
[a]ܒܡܐܢܝܢ

Codex A.

[d]ܡܐܢܝܐ
[e]ܡܦܩܢܝܐ
[f]ܒܒܬܝܗܘܢ [h]ܐܝܢ
‡ f. 180*a*.
[l]ܗܕ [o]ܐܦܝܟ
[p]ܕ [r]ܩܘܕܡܝܟ
[t]ܒܝܠܝܕܝܗܘܢ
[u]ܕܢܫܝܐ [v]ܝܘܚܢܢ
[w] *omit* ܐܘܦ
[y]ܝܘܡܝ
[z]ܕܝܘܚܢܢ
[b]ܢܒܝܐ
[c]ܐܬܢܒܝܘ
[e]ܐܠܝܐ [f]ܗܘ
[h]ܝܫܡܥ

Codex B.

[b]ܡܐܢܝܢ [c]ܡܦܩܢܝܢ : ܗܐ ܗܠܝܢ ܕܡܦܩܢܝܢ [d]ܡܢܝܐ[c]
[e]ܡܦܩܢܝܐ [f]ܒܒܬܝܗܘܢ ܕܡܠܟܝܐ ܗܢܘܢ :
9 ܐܠܐ ܡܢܐ ܢܦܩܬܘܢ ܕܬܚܙܘܢ [g]ܢܒܝܐ : [h]ܐܝܢ
[i]ܐܡܪ ܐܢܐ [i]‡[k]ܠܟܘܢ ܕܐܘܦ ܝܬܝܪ ܡܢ [g]ܢܒܝܐ :
[l]ܗܕܝܢ ܗܘ ܥܠ ܕܠܘܬܗ [m]ܟܬܝܒ ∴ ܕܗܐ ܐܢܐ
ܡܫܠܚ [n]ܡܠܐܟܝ ܩܕܡ [o]ܐܦܝܟ [p]ܕܝܢ [q]ܕܝܫܘܐ
11 ܐܘܪܚܐ [r]ܩܘܕܡܝܟ ∴ ܐܡܝܢ ܐܡܪ ܐܢܐ ܠܟܘܢ
ܒܪ ܕܠܐ [s]ܩܡ [t]ܒܝܠܝܕܝܗܘܢ [u]ܕܢܫܝܐ ܪܒ ܡܢ
[v]ܝܘܚܢܢ ܡܥܡܕܢܐ : [p]ܕܝܢ ܕܝ [w]ܐܘܦ ܕܙܥܘܪ
12 [x]ܒܡܠܟܘܬܐ ܕܫܡܝܐ ܪܒ ܗܘ ܡܢܗ ܡܢ
[y]ܝܘܡܝ ܕܝ [z]ܕܝܘܚܢܢ ܡܥܡܕܢܐ [a]ܡܠܟܘܬܗܘܢ
ܕܫܡܝܐ ܡܬܐܢܣܐ ܘܒܢܝ ܚܛܦܝܢ ܠܗ
13 [†]ܟܠܗܘܢ ܓܝܪ [b]ܢܒܝܐ ܘܢܡܘܣܐ ܥܕ ܡܠܦܐ
14 [v]ܝܘܚܢܢ [c]ܐܬܢܒܝܘ ∴ [d]ܘܐܢ ܨܒܝܢ ܐܢܬܘܢ
ܕܬܩܒܠܘܢ ܗܘ ܐܝܬ ܗܘ [e]ܐܠܝܐ [f]ܗܘܕܝܢ
[f. 142*b*]
15 [g]ܕܥܬܝܕ ܕܝܐܬܐ : ܡܢ ܕܐܝܬ ܠܗ ܐܕܢܝܢ ܕܝܫܡܥ
[h]ܝܫܡܥ

Codex C.

[b]ܡܐܢܝܐ
[c] *omit* ܡܦܩܢܝܢ . . . ܡܢܝܐ . . .
[g]ܢܒܝܐ
[i]ܐܢܐ ܐܡܪ
[m]ܟܬܝܒ
[n]ܡܠܐܟܝ
[s] *add* ܕܝ [q]ܕܝܫܘܐ
[w] *omit* ܐܘܦ
[x]ܒܡܠܟܘܬܗ
[y] *add* ܕܝ
[a]ܡܠܟܘܬܗ
† f. 144*b*.
[c]ܐܬܢܒܝܘ
[d]ܘܐܝܢ [e]ܐܠܝܐ
[g]ܕܥܬܝܕ
[h]ܝܫܡܥ

[CCCXVIII.]
[f. 180*b*]

CXCIV.

Matt. XX. 1—16.

Codex A.

[z] *omit* ܫܒܪ . . . ܘܩܝ
[d] *omit* ܝܘܡ ܡܢܝܗ
[f]ܚܕܐܪܗ
[g]ܐܪܒܥܝܢ
[h] *add* ܒܡܣܟܢܝܬܗ
[i]ܬܠܡܝܕܘܗܝ
[k] *omit* ܘܟܢܫܬܗ
[z]ܗܕܡܐ [b] *add* ܓܒܪ
[c]ܒܝܬܐ [f]ܫܠܝܚ
[h]ܘܐܚܪܢܝܢ
[i] *add* ܒܫܘܩܐ

Codex B.

[z]ܫܒܪ ܐܕܐܪ ܐܚܕ [a]ܘܬܠܬܐ [b]ܝܘܡܐ : [c]ܘܩܝ[z]
ܬܐܡܪ [d]ܝܘܡ [e]ܡܢܝܗ[d] [f]ܚܝܪ [g]ܐܪܒܥܝܢ [g]ܫܐܗܕ[h] ܡܢ
[i]ܬܠܡܝܕܘܗܝ [k]ܘܟܢܫܬܗ ∴ ܐܡܪ ܡܪܢ [y]ܠܬܠܡܝܕܘܗܝ
1 [z]ܗܕܝܢ ܡܬܠܬܐ [a]ܕܫܡܝܐ [b]ܗܝ ܡܠܟܘܬܐ
ܕܫܡܝܐ ܠܓܒܪ [x]ܡܪܐ [c]ܒܝ : ܕܢܦܩ ܒܨܦܪܐ
2 ܕܝܓܘܪ ܦܥܠܝܢ ܠܟܪܡܗ : [d]ܟܕ [e]ܕܝ ܦܣܩ ܥܡ
ܦܥܠܝܐ ܡܢ ܙܘܙ ܒܝܘܡܐ ∴ [f]ܫܠܚ ܐܢܘܢ
3 ܠܟܪܡܗ ∴ ܘܢܦܩ ܠܘܬ ܬܠܬ ܫܥܝܢ ܘܚܙܐ
4 [g]ܚܪܢܝܢ [h]ܩܝܡܝܢ [i]ܒܛܠܝܢ : ܘܐܡܪ ܠܗܘܢ
ܐܡܪ ܐܙܠܘ [j]ܐܘܦ ܐܢܬܘܢ ܠܟܪܡܐ : ܘܡܐ

Codex C.

[z] *omit* ܫܒܪ
[a]ܘܬܠܬܐ [b]ܝܘܡ
[c] *omit* ܘܩܝ [e]ܡܢܝܗ
[f]ܬܐܪܒܥܝܢ [g]ܫܗܕ
[i]ܬܠܡܝܕܝ
[k] *omit* ܘܟܢܫܬܗ
[y]ܠܬܠܡܝܕܘܗܝ [z]ܗܕܐ
[a]ܬܕܡܐ [b] *add* ܓܒܪ
[x]ܡܪܐ [c]ܒܝܬܐ
[d]ܟܕ [e]ܕܐܝܢ
[g]ܚܪܢܝܢ
[i] *add* ܒܫܘܩܐ
[j] *omit* ܐܘܦ

Codex B.

5 ܕܝܗܘܐ [k]ܟܕܝܢ ܐܢܐ ܗܘ ܡܢ ܠܒܪ ܡܢܝ : ܗܘܝܢ
ܕܝ ܐܠܗܐ : ܚܝܠܬܟ ܕܝ [l]ܢܚܡ [m]ܠܟܝ ܝܕܥܬ [n]ܥܡܝ
6 [o]ܘܬܝܕܥܘܢ ܥܡܝܢ ܕܡܕ [p]ܢܚ ܘܡܥܪܒ : [q]ܘܠܡܥܪܒܐ ܕܝ
ܠܝܬ [r]ܒܪ ܡܢܝ ܐܠܗܐ ܥܡܝ ܒܪ ܢܚܡ [s]ܐܢܫܝܢ ܣܘܓܝܢ
[t]ܡܬܩܢ [u]ܢܗܘܪܐ ܘܒܪܐ ܚܫܘܟܐ ܘܥܒܕ ܫܠܡܐ ܡܢ
ܗܘܘܬܐ [v]ܡܬܩܢ ܡܢ [w]ܒܝܫܬܐ ܕܢܚܡ ܢܗܘܪܐ ܒܝܫܬܐ
7 ܐܡܪ ܠܗ : [x]ܕܐܢܐ ܠܐ [y]ܐܡܪܬ ܠܟܘܢ :
ܐܡܪ ܠܟܘܢ ܐܠܗܐ ܐܘܦ ܐܢܬܘܢ ܠܚܝܘܬܐ :[z]
8 ܘܒܪ ܗܘܐ [a]ܪܘܚܡܢܐ ܐܡܪ ܡܪܝܐ ܕܒܪܝܬܐ
[b]ܠܡܢܚܡܗ ܢܦܪܐ ܦܠܥܝܐ ܘܝܬܒܐ ܠܟܘܢ
[c]ܐܬܚܪܘܟܘܢ : ܘܝܗܒ ܡܢ [d]ܒܡܢܝܢܐ ܒܕܡܐ
9 [e]ܠܡܚܢܝ : [†]ܐܬܐ ܕܝ [f]ܗܠܝܢ [g]ܕܠܟܝ ܚܕ
10 [h]ܒܚܪܐ [i]ܥܡܝ : ܘܢܥܡܘ ܡܢ ܗܘ : ܘܒܪ ܐܬܐ
[k]ܕܝ [l]ܡܬܩܢ [m]ܡܒܝܪܝܢ ܕܡܘܬܪ ܢܦܫܗܘܢ :
11 ܘܢܦܫܗ ܐܘܦ ܗܘܝܢ ܡܢ ܗܘ : [n]ܘܒܪ ܢܦܫܗ
ܐܘܦ ܗܘܝܢ ܡܢ [o]ܗܘ[n] ܗܘܘ ܡܒܝܢܝܢ ܒܠ
12 ܡܪܗ [p]ܕܒܝܬܐ ܐܡܪܝܢ : [q]ܗܠܝܢ ܒܡܢܝܢܐ ܚܕܐ
ܥܒܕܐ ܒܒܕܘ : ܘܥܡܝܢ [r]ܒܒܕܬ ܢܦܫܗܘܢ :
[f. 143a]
13 ܐܢܗ ܕܐܠܒܝܗ [h]ܘܢܦܪܗ ܕܝܗܒܐ [i]ܘܥܪܒܗ : ܗܘ
ܕܝ ܐܠܒܝܢ ܘܐܡܪ ܠܚܕ ܡܢܗܘܢ : [l]ܣܒܝܒܝ
ܠܝܬ ܐܢܐ [m]ܐܠܝܨ ܠܝ : ܠܐ [n]ܡܢ ܗܘ ܒܫܠܡܬ
14 ܒܡܢܝ : ܗܒ. ܕܠܝ [o]ܘܐܙܠ : ܟܝܢܐ ܕܝ ܐܢܐ
[p]ܠܗܕܝܢ [q]ܒܡܢܝܢܐ ܡܬܠ ܗܘܝ [r]ܕܠܝ : [s]ܐܢܐ [t]ܠܝܬ
15 ܐܢܐ ܥܠܝܟ ܕܝܒܕ ܡܢܐ [s]ܕܐܢܐ ܟܝܢܐ ܒܕܝܠܝ :
16 ܐܢܐ ܕܡܢܐ ܒܢܝܢ ܒܫܡܐ ܕܐܢܐ ܐܠܒ : [u]ܗܒܕܝܢ
ܢܦܩܘܢ [v]ܡܬܩܢܝܢ [w]ܒܡܢܝܢ : [x]ܘܒܡܢܝܢ [v]ܡܢܝܢ :
[y]ܗܠܝܢ ܗܘܝܢ ܡܢܐ [z]ܘܟܝܢܝܕ ܗܘܝܢ
ܒܢܝܐ :

Codex A.

[k]ܟܕܝܢ
[n] *omit* ܥܡܝ
[p]ܡܢ
[s]ܐܢܫܝܢ
[t]ܦܐܬܩܢ [v]ܦܐܬܩܢ
[w]ܒܦܠܝܗ [y]ܐܠܢ
[z] *add* ܘܦܠܐ ܕܝܗܘܐ ܟܕܝܢ ܐܢܐ ܢܚܡ ܠܟܘܢ
[a]ܪܘܚܡܢܐ
[b]ܠܡܢܚܡܝܢܗ
[c]ܐܬܚܪܘܟܘܢ
[e]ܠܡܚܢܝܢ
[k] *omit* ܕܝ
[l]ܡܬܩܢܝܢ [m]ܡܒܝܪܝܢ
[o]ܘܗܘܐ
[q]ܗܠܝܢ
[r] *add* ܠܝ
[i]ܘܥܪܒܗ
[m]ܐܠܝܨ
[o]ܘܐܙܠ
[p]ܠܗܕܝܢ [q]ܒܡܢܝܢܐ
[s]ܐܢܐ ... ܡܢܐ ܕ *omit*
[u]ܗܒܕܝ [v]ܦܩܬܢܝܢ
[w]ܒܦܩܬܢܝܢ
[x]ܘܒܡܢܝܢ
[y] *add* ܐܠ
[z]ܘܟܝܢܝܕ

o o

Codex C.

[l] *add* ܕܝ [m]ܠܟܝ
[n] *omit* ܥܡܝ
[o]ܘܬܝܕܥܘܢ [q]ܘܠܡܥܪܒܐ
[r]ܒܚܪ [u]ܢܗܘܪܐ.
[v]ܡܬܩܢ [w]ܒܦܠܗ
[x]ܐܢܐ [y]ܐܠܢ
[b]ܠܡܢܚܡܝܢܗ
[d]ܒܡܢܝܢܐ
† f. 145a.
[f]ܗܠܝܢ [g]ܕܠܟܝ
[h]ܒܚܪ [i]ܥܡܝ (sic)
[k] *omit* ܕܝ [l]ܡܬܩܢ
ܘܒܪ . . . ܗܘ [n] *omit*
[p]ܕܒܝܬܐ [q]ܗܠܝܢ
[r] *add* ܠܝ [s]ܒܒܕ
[h]ܘܢܦܪܐ
[i]ܘܥܪܒܗ
[l]ܣܒܝܒ
[m]ܐܠܝܨ ܡܢ [n] *omit*
[p]ܕܠܗܝܢ
[r]ܕܠܝ [t]ܠܝܬ
[v]ܡܢܝܢ
[y] *add* ܐܠ

(ܪܥܚ)

Codex A. | Codex B. | Codex C.

CXCV.

LUKE I. 24—38.

Codex B.

[a]ܘܦܢ ܫܡܥܗ ܘܒܟܪܝܢ[b] [c]ܗܘܐ [d]ܒܥܪܬ [e i]ܐܠܝܫܒܥ
[f]ܡܪܬܗ ܡܪܝܡ [f]ܒܡܪܝܗ[i] : ܐܬܠܒܫܬ[j] [g]ܠܒܝܬܗ
[h]ܦܢ ܐܠܝܫܒܥ ⁘ [k]ܘܗܕܐ [l]ܗܘ[k] ܠܫܠܡܐ ܕܝܠܗ ܡܢ
24 [n]ܠܝܘܡܘܗܝ ⁖[z] [a]ܘܡܢ [b]ܒܬܪ [c]ܗܠܝܢ [d]ܕܝܢ ܝܘܡܝܐ
ܒܛܢܬ [e]ܐܠܝܫܒܥ ܐܢܬܬܗ [f]ܕܙܟܪܝܐ [d]ܕܝܢ ܘܗܘܬ
[d]ܕܝܢ ܡܛܫܝܐ ܢܦܫܗ [g]ܚܡܫܐ ܝܪܚܝܢ : ܐܡܪܐ
25 [h]ܕܗܟܢ ܥܒܕ ܠܝ ܡܪܝܐ : [i]ܒܝܘܡܝܐ ܕܚܙܐ :
26 [j]ܕܢܣܒ [k]ܚܣܕܝ ܡܢ [v]ܒܢܝܢܫܐ : ܘܒܝܪܚܐ
ܫܬܝܬܝܐ ܐܫܬܠܚ ܡܠܐܟܐ [l]ܓܒܪܝܠ ܡܢ
ܠܘܬ ܐܠܗܐ : [m]ܠܡܕܝܢܬܐ ܡܢ ܓܠܝܠܐ ܕܫܡܗ
27 [n]ܢܨܪܬ : ܠܘܬ ܒܬܘܠܬܐ [o]ܐܪܘܣܐ ܠܓܒܪ ܕܫܡܗ
[p]ܝܘܣܦ ܡܢ ܒܝܬܗ [q]ܕܕܘܕ : [†]ܘܫܡܗ ܕܝܢ
28 [r]ܕܒܬܘܠܬܐ [s]ܡܪܝܡ ⁖ ܘܥܠ ܠܘܬܗ ܡܠܐܟܐ
ܘܐܡܪ ܠܗ : ܫܠܡ ܠܝܟܝ [t]ܚܕܝܬܐ [u]ܡܪܝܐ
29 ܥܡܟܝ ⁖ ܗܝ ܕܝܢ ܐܬܒܪܒܪܬ ܥܠ ܡܠܬܗ
ܘܗܘܬ ܡܬܚܫܒܐ ⁖ [w]ܕܐܝܟܢ ܗܝܟ ܗܘ [x]ܗܕܝܢ
30 [y]ܐܝܟܠ [z]ܫܠܡܐ : ܘܐܡܪ [a]ܠܗ ܡܠܐܟܐ ܠܐ
[b]ܬܕܚܠܝܢ [c]ܡܪܝܡ : [d]ܐܫܟܚܬܝ ܓܪ [e]ܚܣܕ ܠܘܬ
31 ܐܠܗܐ : ܘܗܐ ܐܬܝ ܢܣܒܐ [f]ܒܪܫ [g]ܘܝܠܕܐ
32 ܒܪ [h]ܘܬܩܪܝܢ ܫܡܗ ܝܫܘܥ : [i]ܗܕܝܢ ܝܗܐ
[f. 143b]
ܪܒ ܘܒܪܗ ܕܡܪܘܡܐ ܝܬܩܪܐ ⁖ ܘܝܬܢ ܠܗ
[k]ܡܪܝܐ ܐܠܗܐ ܟܘܪܣܝܗ [l]ܕܕܘܕ [m]ܐܒܘܗܝ ⁖
33 ܘܝܡܠܘܟ ܥܠ ܒܝܬܗ ܕܝܥܩܘܒ [n]ܠܥܠܡ [o]ܘܡܠܟܘܬܗ
34 ܠܐ ܝܗܐ [p]ܠܗ [q]ܫܘܠܡܗ : [r]ܐܡܪܬ [c]ܡܪܝܡ ܠܘܬ
ܡܠܐܟܐ ܗܝܟ [t]ܕܝܢ ܝܗܘܐ ܠܝ ܗܕܐ ܥܠ
35 [u]ܓܒܪ ܠܝܬ ܐܢܐ [w]ܡܚܒܪܐ* [x]ܘܐܓܒ ܡܠܐܟܐ
ܘܐܡܪ ܠܗ ܪܘܚܐ ܕܩܘܕܫܐ [y]ܬܐܬܐ ܥܠܝܟܝ ⁖
ܘܚܝܠܗ [z]ܕܡܪܘܡܐ [a]ܝܛܠܠ ܥܠܝܟܝ : [b]ܠܓܠܠ

Codex A.

[CCCXXIV.]
[f. 181b]

[a] omit ܘܦܢ
[c] omit ܗܘܐ [d]ܒܥܐܪܗ
[i]ܘܐܬܠܗ ܐܠܗ ܐܬܢܒܠ
ܫܡܥܪ (sic) ܡܢ ܠܘܩܐ[i]
[j] add ܦܢ
[g]ܬܒܝܬܗ [h]ܡܢ
ܘܗܕܐ ܗܘ omit [k]
[n]ܠܘܩܐ
[a]ܡܢ [b] add ܕܝܢ
ܕܝܢ omit [d] [e]ܐܠܝܫܒܥ
[g]ܚܡܫܐ [h]ܕܒܗ
[i]ܒܝܘܡܝܐ [j]ܕܢܣܒ
[k]ܚܣܕܐ ܝ
[v]ܒܢܝܢܫܐ
[l]ܓܒܪܝܠ
[m]ܠܡܕܝܢܬܐ [n]ܢܨܪܬ
[o]ܐܪܘܣܐ [p]ܝܘܣܦ
[q]ܕܕܘܕ [s]ܡܪܝܡ
[t]ܚܕܝܬܐ
[x]ܗܕܝ [y]ܐܝܟܠ
[a]ܠܗ [b]ܬܕܚܠܝܢ
[c]ܡܪܝܡ [e]ܚܣܕ
[f]ܒܪܫ [g]ܘܝܠܕܐ
[h]ܘܬܩܪܝܢ [i]ܗܕܝ
[k]ܡܪܝܐ [l]ܕܕܘܕ
[m]ܐܒܘܗܝ [n]ܠܥܠܡܐ
[o]ܘܡܠܟܘܬܗ
[p] omit ܠܗ [q]ܫܘܠܡܐ
[r] add ܕܝܢ [t] omit ܕܝܢ
[u]ܓܒܪ [w]ܡܚܒܪܐ
[x]ܘܐܓܒ [v]ܬܐܬܐ

[* Sic in Cod. B.]

[z]ܕܡܪܘܡܐ
[a]ܝܛܠܠ [b]ܠܓܠܠ

Codex C.

[a] omit ܘܦܢ [b] add ܦܢ
[c]ܐܕܐܪ [d]ܠܒܥܪܗ
[e] omit ܐܠܝܫܒܥ
[f]ܐܬܢܣܒܗ [g]ܬܒܝܬܗ
[h]ܡܢ [j] add ܦܢ
[l] omit ܗܘ
[m]ܠܫܠܡܗ [n]ܠܘܩܐ
[z] add ܘܒܬܪܗ ܦܪܘܩܐ
[a]ܡܢ [b] add ܕܝܢ
[c]ܗܠܝܢ [d] omit ܕܝܢ

† f. 145b.

[e]ܐܠܝܫܒܥ [f]ܙܟܪܝܐ
[j]ܕܢܣܒ [k]ܚܣܕܐ ܝ
[o]ܐܪܘܣܐ [r]ܒܬܘܠܬܐ
[t]ܚܕܝܬܐ [u]ܘܡܪܝܐ
[w]ܕܐܝܟܢ [y]ܥܠ
[z]ܫܠܡܐ [b]ܬܕܚܠܝܢ
[d]ܐܫܟܚܬ [e]ܚܣܕ
[h]ܘܬܩܪܐ
[m]ܐܒܘܗܝ [n]ܠܥܠܡܐ
[o]ܘܡܠܟܘܬܗ
[p] omit ܠܗ
[q]ܫܘܠܡܗ [r] add ܕܐܝ
[t] omit ܕܝܢ
[u]ܕܓܒܪ [w]ܡܚܒܪܐ
[x]ܘܐܓܒ [y]ܬܐܬܐ
[z]ܕܡܪܘܡܐ

Codex A.

ܗܘܐ[t] ܢܚܬ ܬܘܠܡܝ̈ܕܘܗܝ[u]

[y] *add* ܐܘܦ

ܗܘܘ[z] ܐܬܬܠܝܘ[b]

[d] *add* ܕܝ

ܡܬܪܓܡ[x]

ܕܡܬܪܓܡܐ[e]

ܘܐܡܪ[g] ܠܘܬܗ[h]

[i] *add* ܥܠܡ

CCCXXXI. [f. 182*b*]

[CLXXX.] [f. 155*a*]

[z] *add* ܢܝܣܢܐ نيسان ܢܚܘܡ

[b] *omit* ܥܢܐ . . . ܗܢܘܢ

ܡܬܪܓܡ[g]

[η] *add* ܐܢܬ ܐܘ ܗܘܝܬ ܐܢ ܗܘ ܢܚܘܡܐ

[θ] *omit* ܒܥܘܬܗ

ܠܡܐܟܠ[ι]

[[χ] *add* ܥܢܝ]

[a β] *add* ܘܥܠܬܗ ܦܪܘܫܐ

[i κ] *omit* ܕܝ

[b γ] *omit* ܘܐܡܪ . . . ܫܡܥܘܢ . . .

ܕܐܫܬܟܚ[δ c] ܦܪܝܫܐ[ε d]

ܐܢܬܬܐ[a d] ܡܚܝܒܬܐ[λ e]

ܝܕܥܬ[β f] ܦܪܝܫܐ[d]

ܘܐܬܬ[γ] ܕܒܣܡ[δ g]

ܠܦܘܪܝܐ[ε h]

ܕܪܓܠܘܗܝ[ζ i]

ܘܒܕܡܥܝܗ[η j]

ܡܬܢܐ[θ l] ܡܥܦܪܐ[ς n]

ܪܓܠܘܗܝ[ι o m]

ܒܒܣܡܐ[κ p]

ܗܘ[λ q] ܗܕܝܢ[μ r]

[ܗܘܐ[ν]] ܡܒܣܪ[ξ t]

Codex B.

ܕܐܘܦ ܗܘܝܢ[t] ܕܬܠܡܝܕܘܗܝ[s] ܡܢܗ ܬܪܝܢ[u] ܟܢܘܢ

36 ܕܐܠܗܐ[v] : ܘܗܘܐ[y] ܐܠܝܢ ܐܬܪܟܒܘܢ ܟܠܗܘܢ

ܟܕ ܫܡܥܘܢܗ :· ܘܗܕܝܢ[z] ܠܗ ܬܪܝܢ[a] ܐܬܬܠܝܘ[b] :

37 ܠܗܕܐ[c] ܕܡܬܪܓܡܐ ܒܥܒܪܐ : ܕܠܐ ܡܢܢܐ ܥܡܠ

38 ܡܠܐܟ ܠܘܬܗ ܐܠܗܐ : ܐܡܪܬ[d] ܡܬܪܓܡ[x] ܗܘܐ

ܐܢܐ ܐܡܪܬܗ[e] ܕܡܪܐ ܗܘܐ ܠܝ[f] ܗܘܝܢ ܡܠܬܟ :

ܘܐܡܪ[g] ܠܗ ܡܠܐܟܐ ܡܢ[h] ܚܙܝܢ[i] ܬܫܟܚܗ[k]

ܘܡܪܝܡ ܬܫܟܚܪ[l †] ܚܙܝܬ ܐܠܗܝܟ[l] :· ܐܬܠܡܒ

ܫܬܗ ܦܝ[m] ܐܠܗܐ[n] ܘܦܝ ܬܬܠܝܢ[o] ܘܗܡ[p] ܬܬܕܟܪ

ܐܠܝܢ[q] ܢܘܚܝܐ[r] ܐܠܗܝܢܘܢ ܐܬܠܡܒ

ܬܫܟܚܘܢܗ[s] ܘܡܪܝܡ ܦܝ ܐܠܗܐ

CXCVI.

Luke VII. 36—50.

ܥܢܐ[baz] ܝܫܘܥ ܢܫܐ ܬܬܠܝܢ[c] ܘܗܘ ܐܡܪ ܗܘ ܐܢ[d]

ܗܢܘܢ[b] ܕܐܬܡܪ[e] ܐܠܟܘܢܗ[f] ܡܬܪܓܡ[g] ܐܠܦܪܝܣܗ[η]:

36 ܡܢ ܒܥܘܬܗ[θh] ܕܠܡܐܟܘܠ[ιj] ܘܗܘܐ[aβχ] ܒܟܠܐ ܕܝ[κi] ܥܡܗ

ܫܡ ܦܪܝܫܐ : ܘܐܡܪ[γb] ܠܡܪܐ ܫܡܥܘܢ[bγ] ܕܐܫܬܟܚ[δc]

ܒܒܝܬܗ ܘܥܠ ܠܒܝܬܗ ܕܗܘܐ ܦܪܝܫܐ[εd] :· ܘܐܟܠ :

37 ܘܗܐ ܐܢܬܬܐ[ad] ܚܕܐ ܕܗܘܬ ܒܗܝ ܡܚܝܒܬܐ[λe]

ܒܥܠܡܐ ܝܕܥܬ ܕܗܘ ܝܕܥܬ[βf] ܒܒܝܬܗ ܕܗܘ

38 ܦܪܝܫܐ[d] : ܘܐܬܬ[γ] ܠܘܬܗ ܕܒܣܡ[δg] ܘܩܡܬ

ܠܦܘܪܝܐ[εh] ܗܘ ܕܪܓܠܘܗܝ[ζi] :· ܒܒܟܝܐ ܘܒܕܡܥܝܗ[ηj]

ܫܪܝܬ[k] ܡܬܢܐ[θl] ܪܓܠܘܗܝ[ιm] ܘܒܣܥܪܗ ܕܪܫܗ ܗܘܬ

ܡܥܦܪܐ[ςn] : ܘܗܘܬ ܡܢܫܩܐ ܪܓܠܘܗܝ[ιo] ܘܡܫܝܚܐ

[f. 144*a*]

39 ܒܒܣܡܐ[κp] : ܘܟܕ ܚܙܐ ܗܘܐ[λq] ܦܪܝܫܐ

ܐܡܪ ܒܠܒܗ : ܗܕܝܢ[μr] ܐܠܘ ܗܘܐ ܢܒܝܐ :

ܐܬܝ ܗܘ[νs] ܡܒܪ[ξt] ܡܢ ܗܝ : ܘܐܝܟܐ ܗܝ ܗܕܐ

Codex C.

[s] *add* ܡܢܟܘܢ

ܬܘܠܡܝܕܐ[u]

ܕܡܬܩܪܝܐ[v]

ܬܪܝܢ[a] ܐܬܬܠܝܘ[b]

ܕܡܬܪܓܡܐ[c]

[f] *omit* ܠܝ [d] *add* ܕܝ

ܚܙܝܢ[h] ܬܫܟܚܗ[k]

ܬܫܟܚܪ[l] ܐܠܗܝܟ

ܚܙܝܬ[l]

† f. 146*a*.

ܐܠܗܐ[m] ܘܦܝ *omit*[n]

ܘܗܡ *omit*[o] ܬܬܕܟܪ[p]

ܐܠܝܢܘܚܝܐ[q]

ܐܠܗܝܢܘܢ[r]

ܬܫܟܚܘܢܗ[s]

ܥܢܐ *omit*[a] ܘܗܢܐ[c]

[d] *omit* ܐܢ

ܬܬܕܟܪ[e] ܐܠܟܘܢܗ[f]

[g] *omit* ܡܬܪܓܡ

[h] *omit* ܒܥܘܬܗ

ܡܢ ܠܡܐܟܠ[j] ܕܝ *omit*[i]

[a] *add* ܘܥܠܬܗ ܦܪܘܫܐ

[b] *omit* ܘܐܡܪ . . . ܫܡܥܘܢ . . .

ܕܐܫܬܟܚ[c] ܦܪܝܫܐ[d]

ܐܢܬܬܐ[d] ܠܦܘܪܝܐ[h]

ܫܪܝܬ[k] ܡܬܢܐ[l]

ܪܓܠܘܗܝ[m] ܡܥܦܪܐ[n]

ܗܘ[q] ܗܘܐ[s]

Codex A.

ܘܐܦܠܝܢ [ou]
ܕܐܡܐܡܪܬ [πw] ܕܝܢ omit [xρ]
ܫܘܒܚܐ [σa]
ܕܐܘܦܠܝܢܘܣ [τc]
ܡܢܐܐ [ςe]
ܫܒܝܥܝܢ [υx] ܕܗܕܐ [y]
ܚܠܝܬ [φb] ܘܗܟܢ [χc]
ܠܬܪܥܝܐ [ψd]
ܒܕܡܟܝܢ [ωe]
[[α] add ܕܢܦܬܗ]
ܬܪܬܝܢ ܬܢ [fβ]
ܬܪܥܝܐ [g] [[γ] ܬܪܥܝܐ]
ܘܒܫܒܪܝܗ [h]
ܕܝܢ omit [iδ]
ܒܦܪܬ [εm] ܥܘܠܡ [ζn]
ܬܪܥܝܐ [o]
[[η] ܬܪܥܠ]
ܒܡܥܢܝܢ [θp] ܬܪܥܢ [ιq]
ܒܒܫܡܐ [κr] ܬܪܥܝܐ [λs]
ܒܕ [μt] ܕܥܒܝܕܝܢ [νu]
ܫܠܝܬܗ [ξw]
ܘܕ [ox] ܕܡܢܫܐ [πy]
ܡܢܫܐ [ρz] ܥܒܝܕܝܢ [σb]
ܫܠܝܬܢ [τc]
ܕ [αw] ܥܒܕ [βy]
ܕܝܢ omit [aγ]
ܒܥܠܡܐ [δb]
ܬܠܬܐ [a]
ܘܒܥܣܪ [b]
ܬܕܐܒܪ [c]
[d] add ܐܠܦܝܣ
ܡܢܝ [e] ܠܦܪܓܣ [f]
[i] omit ܦܝ ... ܐܠܦܣܟܗ
[k] ܫܒܫܗ ܘܒܥܪܝܢ [k]
[m] add ܐܠܘ ܬܕܐܒܪ [l]
[n] add ܐ
ܐܬܬܝܢ [o]

Codex B.

40 ܐܬܬܐ ܕܡܟܝܪܬ ܠܗ ܕܗܘܐ ܣܗܕܐ : [ou]ܘܐܦܠܝܢ
ܡܪܬܐ ܫܡܘܢܐ ܘܐܡܪܬ ܠܗ : ܫܡܘܢܐ [v]ܐܝܬ ܠܝ
ܡܢܐ [πw]ܕܣܒܪܬ ܠܟܝ : ܘܗܘ [ρx]ܕܝܢ ܐܡܪ ܡܠܦܢܐ
41 [y]ܐܡܪܬ ·: ܐܡܪ ܠܗ [z]ܬܪܝܢ ܣܗܕܐ [σa]ܫܘܕܐ [b]ܘܗܘ
ܠܫܕ [τc]ܕܐܘܦܠܝܢܘܣ : ܫܕ ܗܘܐ ܫܒܥ ܠܗ [d]ܫܒܝܢ
42 [ςe]ܡܢܐ [w]ܕܫܢܝܢ : ܘܫܘܪܢܐ [υx]ܫܒܝܥܝܢ [w]ܕܫܢܝܢ : ܘܗܟܢ
ܕܠܐ ܗܘܐ ܠܗܘܢ ܕܢܦܩܘܢ ܠܬܪܥܗܘܢ ܥܡܗ :
ܡܢ ܐܢܘܢ ܡܢܗܘܢ ܫܒܥܬܗ ܗܦܟܬ ܐܡܪܬ ܠܗ :
43 ܐܦܠܝܢ ܕܝܢ ܫܡܘܢܐ ܐܡܪ : ܫܡܥ ܐܢܐ
[y]ܕܗܕܝܢ ܕܥܒܕ [z]ܠܗ ܗܦܟܝ : ܘܐܡܪ ܠܗ [†]ܬܐܥܘܬ
44 ܕܢܬ : ܘܬܒ ܠܘܬ ܐܬܬܐ ܘܐܡܪ ܠܫܡܘܢܐ
[a]ܫܒܝܬ [b]ܗܕܐ ܐܬܬܐ : ܐܢܐ [φb]ܚܠܝܬ ܠܒܢܝܟܝ
[χc]ܘܗܟܢ ܠܐ ܫܒܩܬ ܠܝ [ψd]ܠܬܪܥܝܐ ·: ܘܗܕܐ
[ωe]ܒܕܡܟܝܢ [α] [βf]ܬܪܬܝܢ [γg]ܬܪܥܝܐ : [h]ܘܒܫܒܪܝܗ [δi]ܕܝܢ
45 [εm]ܒܦܪܬ : [ζn]ܥܘܠܡ ܠܐ ܫܒܩܬ ܠܝ : ܘܗܕܐ ܡܢ
46 ܕܚܠܬ ܠܐ ܫܠܝܬ ܡܥܠܝܐ [ηo]ܬܪܥܝܐ ·: [θp]ܒܡܥܢܝܢ
ܠܐ ܡܫܒܩ [ιq]ܬܪܥܝܐ : ܘܗܕܐ [κr]ܒܒܫܡܐ ܡܥܢܝܬ
47 [λs]ܬܪܥܝܐ : ܠܒܕܠ [μt]ܒܕܡ ܐܡܪ ܐܢܐ ܠܟܝ :
[νu]ܕܥܒܝܕܝܢ ܠܗ [ξw]ܫܠܝܬܗ ܕܗܦܟܝ ܕܐܫܟܚ ܗܦܟܝ ·:
[ox]ܘܕܡ [πy]ܕܡܢܫܐ ܡܫܬܟܚ ܠܗ [ρz]ܡܢܫܐ [a]ܡܫܒܩ :
48 49 ܘܐܡܪ ܠܗ [σb]ܥܒܝܕܝܢ ܠܝܟܝ [τc]ܫܠܝܬܢ ܘܥܪܘ
ܗܠܝܢ [d]ܕܪܒܝܢ ܒܒܗ ܐܡܪܝܢ ܒܬܪܗܘܢ ܡܢ
50 ܗܘ [αw]ܕܝܢ ܕܐܘܦ [x]ܫܒܠ ܗܘ [βy]ܥܒܕܘ : ܘܐܡܪ
ܠܐܬܬܐ ܗܝܡܢܘܬܝܢ ܐܫܬ ܢܬܝܒܝܢ [z]ܐܙܠܝܢ
[γa]ܕܝܢ [δb]ܒܥܠܡܐ : :
[a]ܬܠܬܗ [b]ܘܒܥܣܪܝܢ [c]ܬܕܒܪ [d] [e]ܡܢܝܢ [f]ܠܦܪܓܘܣ :
ܐܦܠܘܢ ܬܠܬ ܫܢܝܢ ܒܝܕ [g]ܐܠܦܣܘܣ [h]ܦܝ [i]
ܐܠܕܪܐ ܡܕܝܢܬܗ ܐܦܠܘܢ ܢܘܡ ܐܠܟܣܢܕܪܘܣ
[i]ܐܠܦܣܟܗ [k]ܐܠܫܒܫܗ ܦܝ [h] [c]ܩܦܠܟܪ [k]
[f. 144b]
[l]ܬܕܒܪ ܐܠܥܪܝܢ ܡܪܘܢܘܣ : ܐܦܠܘܢ [m]ܢܘܡ [n]
ܦܝ ܬܥܪܝܢ [o]ܐܬܬܝܢ ܬܠܬܝܢ [l]ܬܕܒܪ ܐܠܥܒܝܢ

Codex C.

ܘܐܦܠܝܢ [u]
ܐܝܬܝܢ [v] ܕܝܢ omit [x]
ܐܡܪܬ [y]
ܡܪܬܐ ܫܡܘܢܐ add [z]
ܫܘܪܐ [a] ܘܗܘ omit [b]
ܫܒܝܢ [d] ܕܫܢܝܢ [w]
ܠܗ omit [z]
ܫܒܝܬ [a] ܗܕܐ [b]
ܚܠܝܬ [b] ܘܗܟܢ [c]
† f. 146b.
ܠܬܪܥܝܐ [d]
ܒܕܡܟܝܢ [e]
ܬܪܬܝܢ [f]
ܬܪܥܝܐ [g] ܕܝܢ omit [i]
ܬܪܥܝܐ [o]
ܒܡܥܢܝܢ [p]
ܬܪܥܝܐ [q]
ܡܫܒܩ omit [a]
ܕܪܒܝܢ [d]
ܫܒܠ [x] ܥܒܕܘ [y]
ܕܝܢ omit [a]
[d] add ܐܠܦܝܣ
ܐܠܦܣܘ [g]
[h] omit ܦܝ . . . ܦܝ
[k] ܫܒܫܗ ܘܒܥܪܝܢ [k]
[m] add ܐܘܠ
ܐܬܬܝܢ [o]

Codex A.

[p]ܐܡܢ [q]ܘܟܕܐܡܪ

[r] *add* ايار

[s] *omit* ܐܣܪ ܘܬܠܬܝܢ ܗܘܢ

[u] *add* ܐܘ [w]ܬܕܟܪܐܢܪ

[x] *omit* ܐܢܒܢ

[y]ܫܐܡܥܘܬܐܡܪ (*sic*)

[z] *omit* ܥܕܪܐ [a]ܘܩܬܗ

[b] *add* ܐܝܢ [c]ܬܕܟܪܐܢܪ

[d]ܗܘܒܐ [e]ܣܕܝ ܟܬܪܐܢܪ

[f]ܬܕܟܪܐܢܪ [g]ܐܥܠܝܢܪ

[h]ܐܡܢ [i]ܘܟܕܐܡܪ

[CCCXXXVII.]

[f. 183b]

[y] *add* ܘܟܝܢܬܗ ܡܪܝܐ

[z]ܩܐܝܡܝܢ [c]ܡܪܝܡ

[e]ܘܬܠܡܝܕܐ

[f]ܕܪܚܡ

[g] *add* ܗܐ [h]ܘܒܬܪܟܢ

[j]ܬܠܡܝܕܐ [k]ܕܒܪ

[n]ܘܟܬܒ [o]ܕܫܪܝܪܐ

[t] *omit* ܕܝ [v]ܫܒܪ

[w]ܥܠܡܐ [x]ܡܣܝܒܪ

[z] *add* ܐܡܝܢ

[z] *omit* ܘܟܕ...ܐܬܐܢܝ

[c]ܬܫܒܗ

[d] *omit* ܬܕܟܪ

[e]ܘܐܬܦܠܓܘܢܗܘ
ܐܣܪ ܗܘܒ ܬܠܬܐ
ܟܕܪ ܐܠܦܝܐ
ܟܐܢܪ ܐܥܠܝܢ
ܗܘܢܟܘ ܐܬܦܠܓܘ
ܐܬܦܠܓܘܬ ܐܬܠܬܐ ܡܢ
ܠܥܠܐ[e]

Codex B.

ܡܡܘܒ [p]ܐܡܢ [q]ܘܟܕܐܡܪ : ܐܬܦܠܓܘܒ ܦܐܟܒ
ܫܒܬ ܡܢ ܠܥܠܐ :
ܐܟܐܪ[r] [s]ܐܣܪ ܘܬܠܬܝܢ ܗܘܢ[s] ܐܘܠ ܗܘܢ[u] ܦܝܗ
[w]ܟܣܪ ܐܪܥܐ [x]ܐܢܒܢ : ܐܬܦܠܓܘܒ [y]ܫܐܡܥܘ ܗܘܢ[y]
ܦܝ [z]ܥܕܪܐ ܐܠܠܐ : [a]ܘܩܬܗ[b] [c]ܟܝܢܕܐ [d]ܗܘܒ
ܐܢܕܝܗ † ܐܬܦܠܓܘܒ [e]ܣܕܝ ܟܬܪ[e] ܫܒܬ ܡܢ ܠܥܠܐ :
ܬܡܢܝܗ [f]ܬܕܟܪ [g]ܐܥܠܝܢ ܗܣܝܐ [h]ܐܡܢ [i]ܘܟܕܐܡܪ :
ܡܢ [k]ܗܘܝܘܒ :

CXCVII.

John XIX. 25—27; XXI. 24, 25.

25 [y]ܗܘܘܝ [a]ܕܝ [z]ܩܝܡܝܢ[a] ܠܗ ܕܙܩܝܦܗ ܕܡܪܢܐ
ܝܫܘܥ : ܐܡܗ ܘܐܚܬܗ [b]ܕܐܡܗ : [c]ܡܪܝܡ
26 [d]ܕܩܠܝܘܦܐ ܘ[c]ܡܪܝܡ ܡܓܕܠܝܬܐ : ܡܪܢܐ ܝܫܘܥ
ܟܕ ܚܡܐ ܠܐܡܗ : [e]ܘܬܠܡܝܕܐ ܐܝܟܘ [f]ܕܪܚܡ
ܩܐܝܡ : ܐܡܪ ܠܐܡܗ ܐܢܬܬܐ[g] ܒܪܟܝ :
27 [h]ܘܒܬܪܟܢ ܐܡܪ [i]ܠܬܠܡܝܕܐ [j]ܗܐ ܐܡܟ :
ܘܡܢ ܗܝ ܫܥܬܐ [k]ܕܒܪ ܗܝ ܬܠܡܝܕܐ[j]
XXI. 24 ܠܕܝܠܗ : ܗܢܘ [l]ܬܠܡܝܕܐ [m]ܕܡܣܗܕ ܥܠ ܗܠܝܢ
[n]ܘܟܬܒ ܗܠܝܢ ܘܐܝܬ ܝܕܥܝܢ [o]ܕܫܪܝܪܐ ܗܝ
25 ܣܗܕܘܬܗ ܐܝܬ ܕܝ ܐܘܦ ܣܓܝܐܢ ܐܚܪܢ [p]ܕܥܒܕ
ܡܪܢ ܝܫܘܥ : ܗܠܝܢ [q]ܕܐܢ ܡܬܟܬܒܢ ܟܠ
[r]ܚܕ [s]ܘܚܕ [t]ܕܝ [u]ܡܣܬܒܪ : [v]ܫܒܪ ܐܢܐ
ܕܐܦ ܠܐ ܥܠܡܐ [w]ܠܐ [x]ܡܣܝܒܪ [y]ܣܦܪܐ
ܕܡܬܟܬܒܝܢ :[z]
[z]ܘܟܕ ܗܕܐ ܐܠܝܦ [a]ܘܗܘ ܬܕܒܪ ܐܠܒܪ
ܐܪܝܣܘܣ : ܐܬܦܠܓܘܒ ܣܕܝ ܟܬܪ ܡܢ ܟܘ
[b]ܐܬܐܢܝ :[z] [c]ܬܫܒܗ [d]ܬܕܟܪ ܐܢܒܢ ܥܒܝܐ : :
[e]ܐܬܦܠܓܘܢ ܗܘܢ ܐܠܪܒܥܐ [f]ܦܝ [g]ܫܒܬ ܐܫܕܫܗ

Codex C.

[q]ܘܟܕܐ

[s] *omit* ܐܣܪ ܘܬܠܬܝܢ ܗܘܢ

[x] *omit* ܐܢܒܢ [w]ܬܕܟܪܐ

[y]ܫܐܡܥܘ ܐܡܪ[y]

[z] *omit* ܥܕܪܐ

† f. 147a.

[a] *omit* ܘ [c]ܬܕܟܪ

[d]ܗܘܒܐ [g]ܐܥܠܝܢܪ

[i]ܘܟܕܐ [k]ܗܣܝܐ

[y] *add* ܘܟܝܢܬܗ ܡܪܝܐ

[a]ܕܩܐܝܡܝܢ

[b]ܕܐܡܗ

[d]ܕܩܠܝܘܦܐ

[e]ܘܬܠܡܝܕܐ

[g] *add* ܗܐ

[i]ܠܗ [j]ܬܠܡܝܕܐ

[k]ܕܒܪ [l]ܬܠܡܝܕܐ

[m]ܕܡܣܗܕ

[n]ܘܟܬܒ [o]ܕܫܪܝܪܐ

[p]ܕܥܒܕ [q]ܕܐܢ

[r]ܚܕ [s]ܘܚܕ

[t] *omit* ܕܝ [v]ܡܣܬܒܪ

[y]ܣܦܪܐ

[a] *omit* ܘܗܘ

[b]ܐܬܐܢܝ

[f] *omit* ܦܝ [g]ܐܫܕܫܗ

Codex A.

[i]ܐܬܢܝܚ ܒܫܢ̇
ܐܦܝܦܢܝܘܣ
ܘܦܛܪܝܪܟܐ ܘܐܚܕ
ܘܒܫܢ̇ ܡܢ ܬܫܪܝܢ
ܐܠܦ ܬܠܬ ܒܫܢ̇
ܐܠܟܣ̇ ܐܠܟܣܢܕܪܘܣ
ܐܠܦܐ ܫܒܬ
ܬܠܬ (*sic*) ܒܫܢ̇
ܐܠܦܝܢ ܫܬܝܢ
ܒܫܢ̇ ܐܠܟܐܪ
ܒܫܘܡܘܣ ܐܠܦܐ
ܫܬܗ ܡܢ ܒܐܝܘ
ܐܠܦܪ (*sic*) ܫܐܕܘ
ܒܫܢ̇ ܐܠܟܣ̇[i]

ܐܝܒܐ [v] *omit* [x]ܡܢ

[y]ܫܐܕܘ (*sic*) ܒܫܢ̇
ܐܠܦܝܢ ܗܘܕܐ
ܐܠܦܐ ܬܡܢܝܢܬܪ
ܡܢ ܬܫܪܝܢ ܐܠܦܪ
ܫܐܒܒܗ ܘܒܫܢ̇
ܬܐܘܕܐܪܘܣ ܘܕܘܡܐ
ܐܠܦܐ ܒܫܢܝܢ ܡܢ
ܐܠܘܬܬܐ ܡܢ ܘܒܫܢܝܢ
ܐܦܪܣܝܢܩܘܣ
ܘܐܝܫܟܗ ܐܠܦܐ
ܐܠܝܕ ܐܠܘܠ ܡܢ
ܡܢܬܐ ܘܚܕ
ܘܬܠܬܝܢ ܐܠܟܣ̇
ܐܪܡܝܐ

احزيران ܚܙܝܪܐܢ
ܐܘܠ ܚܪܝܛܝܡ
ܘܐܚܟܗ ܐܠܦܐ
ܫܒܬ ܒܫܢ̇ ܐܠܦܝܢ
ܐܬܢܝܚ ܢܦܘܪܕܝܪܐ
ܐܠܦܝܢܝܢܗ (*sic*)
ܐܠܦܐ ܬܠܬ (*sic*)
ܡܢ ܐܝܠܘܠ ܬܠܬ

Codex B.

ܒܫܢ̇ [h]ܐܠܦܝܢ[e]: [i]ܐܬܢܝܚ [k]ܗܘ ܡܪܝ ܐܠܘܣܝܘܣ
[l]ܐܦܝܦܢܝܘܣ ܦܛܪܝܪܟܐ: ܐܠܦܐ ܬܡܢܝܢ ܘܒܫܢܝܢ
[m]ܦܢ ܒܢܘ [n]ܐܬܢܝܚ: [o]ܦܢ [p]ܫܬܝܢܬܪ ܬܡܢܝܢ [f. 145*a*]
ܐܠܦܪ [q]ܡܪܘܫܘ: ܐܠܦܐ ܚܕ ܒܫܢ̇ [r]ܦܢ
[s]ܒܐܝܘ [t]ܐܬܢܝܚ: [u]ܫܬܝܢܬܪ ܬܡܢܝܢ [i] [w]ܐܢܐܪܐ
[v]ܐܝܒܐ[w] ܐܠܦܐ ܚܡܫܝܢ [x]ܦܢ ܐܝܠܘܠ [†] [a y]ܐܚܕ
ܘܒܫܢܝܢ [b]ܬܡܢܝܢ ܐܠܟܠܝܢ [d]ܘܫܬܝܢܬܝܢ ܘܚܕܝܢ:
ܐܠܦܐ ܗܘ ܐܠܫܡܗܘܢ [e]ܦܢ [f]ܐܡܫܬܐ ܐܠܟܣܢܕܪܘܣ
ܒܫܢ̇ [g]ܐܠܦܝܢ ܡܢ ܢܝܦ ܐܠܝܛܠ ܐܪܒܥܝܢ
ܘܒܫܢܝܢ [h]ܬܡܢܝܢ [j]ܫܒܥܐ [k]ܐܠܟܣܢܕܪܘܣ:
ܐܠܦܐ ܬܫܥܝܢ ܘܒܫܢܝܢ [l]ܡܢ [m]ܒܐܝܘ
[n]ܐܬܢܝܚ: ܚܡܫܝܢ ܘܒܫܢܝܢ ܘܬܠܬ [o]ܪܐܫ
[p]ܢܣܒܐ [q]ܐܠܟܣܢܕܪܘܣ ܐܠܦܐ ܐܪܒܥܝܢ ܘܒܫܢܝܢ
ܦܢ [r]ܪܗܛ [s]ܐܬܟܣܝܦ:

[t]ܚܙܝܪܐ [u][v]ܬܠܬܝܢ ܘܬܫܥܐ [w]ܢܝܣܢ ܫܬܝܢܬܪ
ܫܢܬ ܘܠܝܠܗ ܬܫܥܐ ܫܐܟܡܐܬ [w y]ܬܫܥܝܢ [x]ܦܢܗ
ܬܡܢܝܢ[z] [v]ܬܡܢܝܢܫ[a] [b]ܐܠܦܢܘܬܝ: [c]ܐܠܦܐ ܚܡܫܝܢ
[d]ܘܒܫܢܝܢ ܦܢ ܬܫܪܝܢ ܐܝܠܘܠ: [e f]ܘܚܕ ܒܫܢ̇
ܬܡܢܝܢ[f] ܐܫܠܝܚܝܢ [g]ܪܬܠܐܘܒܝܢ [h]ܦܐܪܝܪܐ
ܐܠܦܐ ܐܘܠ ܗܘ ܦܢ ܬܫܪܝܢ [i]ܐܬܢܝܚ:
ܐܬܢܝܚܝܢ [k]ܬܡܢܝܢ [l]ܐܠܦܪ ܐܢܦܪܘܫ [m]ܐܫܚܝܢ
ܐܠܦܐ ܬܫܥܝܢ [n]ܘܒܫܢܝܢ ܦܢ ܐܝܠܘܠ:
ܐܪܒܥܝܢ [k]ܬܡܢܝܢ ܐܝܒܐ ܐܠܝܟܒ: ܡܢ [o]ܒܫܘܪܗ
[p]ܕܠܘܫ:

[*Codex* A.—cont.

ܐܠܟܣܢܕ ܠܒܝܢܝܘܫ ܐܠܦܐ ܚܡܫܝܢ ܐܒܫܪ ܡܢ ܐܝܠܘܠ[y]
ܦܢܗ [x]*omit* ܬܡܢܝܢܐܪ[z] ܐܠܦܢܘܬܝ [v]*add* [a]ܬܪܘܪܐܘ (*sic*)
ܐܠܦܐ [c]*omit* [d]ܘܒܫܢܝܢ [f]ܚܕ ܒܫܢܐܪ ܬܡܢܝܢܐܪ[f] [g]ܪܬܠܐܘܒ
[h]ܦܐܪܝܪܐ [i]ܐܬܢܝܚ [k]ܬܡܢܝܢܐܪ [l]ܐܠܦܪܐܢܪ (*sic*) [m]ܐܫܚܝܢ
[n]ܘܒܫܢܝܢ ܒܫܘܪܗ [o]*omit* [p]ܠܘܫܐ

Codex C.

[h]ܐܠܦܝܢ
ܗܘ [k]*omit*
[l]ܐܦ̈ܝܦܢܝܘ
[m]ܡܢ [n]ܐܬܢܝܚ
ܦܢ [o]*omit*
[p]ܫܬܝܢܬܪ
† f. 147*b*.
[q]ܪܫܒܘܫ [r]ܡܢ
[s]ܒܐܝܘ [t]ܐܬܢܝܚ
[u]ܫܬܝܢܬܪ
[w]ܐܝܒܐ ܐܢܐܪܐ[w]
[a]ܘܐܚܕ [b]ܬܡܢܝܢܐܪ
[d]ܘܫܬܝܢܬܝܢ
ܦܢ [e]*omit* [f]ܐܡܫܬܗ
[g]ܐܠܦܝܢ [h]ܬܡܢܝܢܐܪ
ܐܠܦܪ [j]*add*
[k]ܐܠܟܣܢܕܪܘܣ
[l]ܦܢ [m]ܒܐܝܘ
[n]ܐܬܢܝܚ [o]ܪܫ
[p]ܢܣܒܐ
ܐܠܟܣܢܕܪܘܣ [q]*omit*
ܪܗܛ [r]*omit*
[s]ܐܬܟܣܝܦ [t]ܚܙܝܪܐ
ܘܚܕ [u]*add*
[v]ܘܬܠܬܝܢ
ܢܝܣܢ . . . [w]*omit*
. . . ܫܐܟܡܐܬ
ܐܠܦܢܘܬܝ [v]*add*
[b]ܐܠܦܢܘܬܝ [e]ܚܕ
[g]ܪܬܠܐܘܒܝܢ
[h]ܦܐܪܝܪܐ
[i]ܐܬܢܝܚ
ܒܫܘܪܗ [o]*omit*
[p]ܠܘܫܐ

Codex A. | Codex B. | Codex C.

CXCVIII.

Luke IV. 22—30.

22 [z] ܘܗܘܘ [a] ܡܬܡ̈ܗܝܢ ܥܠ ܟܘܠ [b] ܡܠܝܐ [c] ܕܚܣܕܐ
ܕܗܘܘ [d] ܢܦܩܝܢ ܡܢ ܦܘܡܗ ܡܪܢܐ ܝܫܘܥ :
ܘܗܘܘ [f] ܐܡܪܝܢ [g] ܠܐ [h] ܗܕܝܢ ܗܘ [i] ܒܪܗ [j] ܕܝܘܣܦ :
23 ܘܐܡܪ ܠܗܘܢ ܩ̈ܬܠܘܗ [k] ܬܐܡܪܘܢ ܠܝ [l] ܗܕܝܢ
[m] ܡܬܠܐ : ܐܣܝܐ ܐܣܝ ܢܦܫܟ : ܘܟܘܠܡܐ
ܕܫܡܥܢܗ ܕܥܒܕܬ ܒܟܦܪܢܚܘܡ ܥܒܕ ܐܘܦ ܗܟܐ
24 [n] ܒܡܕܝܢܬܟ : ܘܐܡܪ ܠܗܘܢ ܐܡܝܢ [o] ܐܡܪ
ܐܢܐ [o] ܠܟܘܢ : ܕܠܝܬ ܢܒܝ ܡܩܒܠ [p] ܒܡܕܝܢܬܗ :
[f. 145b]
25 ܡܢ [p] ܩܘܫܛ ܕܝ ܐܢܐ ܐܡܪ ܠܟܘܢ : ܕܣܓܝܢ
[q] ܐܪܡܠܝܢ ܗܘܝ [r] ܒܝܘܡܝ [e] ܕܐܠܝܐ ܢܒܝܐ
[s] ܒܐܝܣܪܐܝܠ : [t] ܟܕ [u] ܐܬܚܒܫܘ [v] ܫܡܝܐ ܬܠܬ
[w] ܫܢܝܢ [x] ܘܫܬܐ ܝܪ̈ܚܝܢ : ܟܕ ܗܘܐ ܟܦܢܐ ܪܒܐ
26 ܥܠ ܐܪܥܐ : ܘܠܘܬ ܚܕܐ [y] ܡܢܗܘܢ ܠܐ
ܐܫܬܠܚ ܐܠܝܐ ܐܠܐ [z] ܐܢ † ܠܨܪܦܬ [a] ܕܨܝܕܢ :
27 ܘܠܘܬ [b] ܐܬܬܐ ܐܪܡܠܬܐ : ܘܣܓܝܢ ܓܪ̈ܒܝܢ ܗܘܘ
[s] ܒܐܝܣܪܐܝܠ ܥܠ [c] ܝܘܡܝ ܕܐܠܝܫܥ ܢܒܝܐ :
ܘܚܕ ܡܢܗܘܢ ܠܐ [d] ܐܬܕܟܝ ܐܠܐ [z] ܐܢ ܢܥܡܢ
28 [e] ܣܘܪܝܐ : [f] ܘܐܬܡܠܝܘ ܟܘܠܗܘܢ ܚܡܬܐ ܟܕܘ
29 [g] ܒܫܡܥܬܐ ܫܡܥܝܢ ܗܠܝܢ : [h] ܘܩܡܘ [i] ܐܦܩ̈ܘ ܝܬܗ
ܠܒܪ ܡܢ [k] ܡܕܝܢܬܐ : [l] ܘܐܝܬܝܘ ܝܬܗ ܥܕܡܐ
[m] ܠܟܢܦܗ ܕܛܘܪܐ [n] ܕܝܢ ܕܗܘܬ ܡܕܝܢܬܗܘܢ
30 ܒܢܝܐ ܥܠܘܝ ܗܘܝ [o] ܕܢܩܦܘܢ ܝܬܗ : ܗܘ ܕܝ
ܥܒܪ [p] ܘܐܙܠ ܠܗ [q] ܒܡܨܥܬܗܘܢ : [r] ܥܠܡ
[a] ܫܡܥܦܛܪ [b] ܬܕܟܪ ܐܢܝ [c] ܒܟܡܝ : ܐܬܦܠܓܒ
ܫܡܥܘܢ ܦܝ ܐܝܠܘܠ : ܬܫܡܥܦܛܪ [b] ܬܕܟܪ
ܐܠܦܝܫ [d] ܠܬܠܡܝܕܘܗܝ : [e] ܐܬܦܠܓܒ. ܬܠܬ [f] ܫܒܬ ܒܟܕ
[g] ܐܠܦܫܝ : ܐܪܒܥܗ [h] ܘܒܥܬܝܡ [i] ܡܠܝܐ [k] [l] ܕܝܫܘܥ
ܐܠܬܒܕܝܐ [m] : [v] ܐܬܦܠܓܒ ܐܪܒܥܗ ܘܒܥܬܝܡ ܒܝ
[n] ܐܫܟܚܦ :: ܘܗܕܐ [o] ܗܘ [p] ܠܠܡܘܕܐܝܫ [q] ܡܢ [r] ܠܘܐܝܫ :

Codex A.

[CCCLIV.]
[z] *add* ܘܒܝܘܡܗ ܦܪܘܩܢܐ
[c] ܕܚܣܕܐ
[d] ܢܦܩܝܢ [f] ܐܡܪܝܢ
[g] *add* ܠܗ
[h] ܗܕܝܢ [i] ܒܪܗ
[j] ܕܝܘܣܦ
[k] ܬܐܡܪܘܢ
[l] ܗܕܐ [m] ܡܬܠܬܐ
[o] ܐܡܪܢܐ
[p] ܒܡܕܝܢܬܗ
[p] ܩܘܫܛ [q] ܐܪܡܠܝܢ
[r] ܒܝܘܡܝ
[e] ܕܐܠܝܐ
[s] ܒܐܝܣܪܐܝܠ
[v] ܫܡܝܐ [w] ܫܢܝܢ
[x] ܘܫܬܐ [y] ܡܢܗܘܢ
[a] ܕܨܝܕܢ [b] ܐܬܬܐ
[c] ܘܣܓܝܢ [d] ܐܬܕܟܝ
[e] ܣܘܪܝܐ [f] ܘܐܬܡܠܝܘ
[g] ܒܫܡܥܬܐ
[i] ܐܦܩܘ [k] ܡܕܝܢܬܐ
[l] ܘܐܝܬܝܘ
[m] ܠܟܢܦܗ
[n] ܕܝ [o] ܕܢܩܦܘܢ
[r] *omit* ܥܠܡ [p] ܘܐܙܠ
[a] ܫܡܥܦܛܪ
[b] ܬܕܟܪ [c] ܒܟܡܝ
[d] ܠܬܠܡܝܕܘܗܝ
[f] ܫܒܬ [g] ܐܬܦܠܓܘ
[h] ܘܒܥܬܝܡ [i] ܡܠܝܐ
[k] *add* ܐܠܦܝܫ
[l] ܡܢ ܢܘܫܐ [l]
[m] *add* ܫܡܥ (sic)
[n] ܘܐܫܟܚܦ
[o] *omit* ܗܘ
[p] ܠܠܡܘܕܐܝܫ [r] ܠܘܐܝܫ

Codex C.

[z] *add* ܘܒܝܘܡܗ ܦܪܘܩܢܐ
[a] ܡܬܡ̈ܗܝܢ
[b] ܡܠܝܐ [c] ܕܚܣܕܐ
[i] ܒܪܗ
[m] ܡܬܠܬܐ
[n] ܒܡܕܝܢܬܟ
[p] ܒܡܕܝܢܬܗ
[q] ܐܪܡܠܝܢ
[s] ܕܐܝܣܪܐܝܠ [t] ܘܟܕ
[u] ܐܬܚܒܫܘ
[z] ܐܢ [b] ܐܬܬܐ
† f. 148*a*.
[d] ܐܬܕܟܝ [h] ܘܩܡܘ
[i] ܐܦܩܘ [l] ܘܐܝܬܝܘ
[m] ܠܟܢܦܗ
[q] ܒܡܨܥܬܗܘܢ
[r] *omit* ܥܠܡ
[a] ܫܡܥܦܛܪ
[d] ܠܬܠܡܝܕܘܗܝ
[e] ܐܬܦܠܓܒ [g] ܐܬܦܠܓܘ
[i] ܡܠܝܐ
[k] *add* ܐܠܦܝܫ
[l] ܢܘܫܐ
[m] *add* ܒܪܗ
[v] ܐܬܦܠܓܒ [n] ܐܫܟܚܦ
[p] ܠܠܡܘܕܐܝܫ [o] *omit* ܗܘ
[q] *omit* ܡܢ ܠܘܐܝܫ

Codex A.

[CCCLVII.]
[f. 185a]

[a]ܠܡܛܠ [c]ܕܟܡ
[d] *omit* ܕܝ
[g]ܫܡܫܝܢܝܗ
[h]ܘܫܡܫܝܢܝܗ
[i]ܕܡܠܬܗ
[j]ܬܫܥܝܬܐ
[l]ܕܐܬܬܠܡܢܬ
[m]ܠܟܘܢ [n] *omit* ܐܢܐ
[o]ܗܘܐ [p]ܒܝܘܡܝ
[q]ܕܗܪܘܕܝܣ
[r]ܕܝܗܘܕܐ
[s]ܘܫܡܗ [v]ܕܐܗܪܘܢ
[w]ܕܐܢܬܬܗ
[y] *add* ܕܝ [z]ܦܘܩܕܢܘܗܝ
[a]ܘܕܝܢܘܗܝ
[b]ܘܠܐ [c]ܠܟܠܗܝ
[g]ܐܬܦܢܝ [h]ܡܫܡܫ
[i] *omit* ܐܝܟ
[k]ܕܡܫܡܫܘܬܐ
[l]ܕܐܠܗܐ [n]ܕܢܥܘܠ
[q]ܠܗܝܟܠܗ [s] *omit* ܕܝ
[t]ܟܡܪܐ
[u]ܕܡܠܐܟܐ [v]ܘܩܡ
[w] *add* ܕܡܕܒܚܐ
[x]ܠܡܘܬܗ [y]ܘܐܬܥܬܝ
[z]ܠܟܠܗܝ [b]ܡܠܬܝ
[c]ܒܪܐ [d]ܘܒܬܘܪܐ
[e]ܐܢܫܝܗ
[f]ܘܚܕܘ

Codex B.

CXCIX.

Luke I. 1—25, 57—68, 76, 80.

1 [az]ܘܠܡܛܠ ܕܣܓܝܢ ܐܬܟܠܟܠܘ ܠܡܕܟܪܐ : ܬܫܥܝܬܐ[b]
2 ܠܟܠ ܡܣܬܒܪܐ ܗܠܝܢ [c]ܕܟܡ ܐܫܠܡܘ : ܗܝܟ
ܕܡܫܠܡܘ ܠܢ [f]ܗܠܝܢ ܕܡܢ ܫܪܝ. ܗܘܘ [g]ܫܡܫܝܢܝܗ
3 [h]ܘܫܡܫܝܢܗ [d]ܕܝ ܕܡܠܬܐ : ܝܐܝ ܠܝ ܐܦ
ܠܝ [d]ܕܝ ܕܡܩܒܠ ܠܟܘܠܗܘܢ : ܡܢ ܫܪܝ ܒܥܘܡܩ
ܥܠ ܠܟܬܒܐ [i]ܕܡܠܬܐ ܠܟ : ܐܘܢ ܚܝܠܬܐ
4 [j]ܬܘܩܝܠܐ : ܠܡܛܠ [k]ܕܬܫܡܥ ܫܪܝܪܐ ܕܡܠܝܐ
5 ܗܠܝܢ [l]ܕܐܬܠܡܕܬ [m]ܠܟܘܢ + [n]ܐܢܐ [o]ܘܗܘܐ
[p]ܒܝܘܡܝ [q]ܕܗܪܘܕܣ ܡܠܟܐ [r]ܕܝܗܘܕܐ : ܟܗ ܢ
[f. 146a]
ܫܡ [s]ܙܟܪܝܐ [t]ܐܦܪܝܡ ܡܢ [u]ܡܫܡܫܬܗ [v]ܐܒܝܐ :
ܘܐܢܬܬܗ ܗܘܬ ܡܢ ܒܢܬܗ [w]ܕܐܗܪܘܢ [x]ܘܫܡܗ[y]
6 ܐܠܝܫܒܥ : ܗܘܘ[y] ܬܪܝܗܘܢ[x] ܙܕܝܩܝܢ ܩܕܡ
ܐܠܗܐ : ܡܗܠܟܝܢ ܒܟܠܗ [z]ܦܘܩܕܢܘܗܝ [a]ܘܕܝܢܘܗܝ
7 [†]ܕܡܪܝܐ ܕܠܐ [b]ܥܠܠܐ : ܘܒܪ ܠܐ ܗܘܐ ܠܗܘܢ :
[c]ܠܟܠܠ ܕܗܘܬ ܐܠܝܫܒܥ ܥܩܪܐ ܘܬܪܝܗܘܢ
8 ܗܘܘ [e]ܥܠܝܠܝܢ [f]ܒܝܘܡܝܗܘܢ : [g]ܘܐܬܚܕܬ ܕܝ
ܗܝܟ ܕܗܘܐ [h]ܡܫܡܫ [i]ܐܝܟ [k]ܒܐܬܦܠܓܘܬܗ
9 [l]ܕܝܘܡܐ ܕܡܫܡܫܢܘܬܐ ܩܕܡ ܐܠܗܐ : ܗܝܟ
ܐܝܟ ܥܝܕܐ [m]ܕܡܫܡܫܢܘܬܐ : ܡܛܠܐ ܠܗ [n]ܕܢܥܘܠ
10 [o]ܒܗܝܟܠܐ : ܕܡܪܝܐ ܘܠܒܣܡܐ : [p]ܘܟܠܗ
[q]ܥܡܐ ܕܡܠܝܐ [p][r]ܗܘܐ ܡܨܠܐ ܠܒܪ [s]ܕܝ
11 [t]ܒܫܥܬܐ ܕܒܣܡܐ : ܘܐܬܚܙܝ ܠܗ [u]ܡܠܐܟܗ
ܕܡܪܝܐ [v]ܘܩܡ ܡܢ ܝܡܝܢܗ ܕܡܕܒܚܐ :[w]
12 ܘܐܬܕܠܚ ܙܟܪܝܐ ܟܕ ܚܙܐ ܘܕܚܠܬܐ ܢܦܠܬ
13 [x]ܥܠܘܗܝ : ܘܐܡܪ ܠܗ ܡܠܐܟܐ ܠܐ [s]ܕܝ ܬܕܚܠ
[y]ܙܟܪܝܐ [z]ܠܟܠܠ [a]ܕܐܫܬܡܥܬ ܒܥܘܬܟ ܘܗܐ
ܐܢܬܬܟ ܐܠܝܫܒܥ [b]ܬܠܕ ܠܟ [c]ܒܪ [d]ܘܬܩܪܐ
14 [e]ܫܡܗ [f]ܝܘܚܢܢ : ܘܬܗܘܐ ܠܟ ܚܕܘܐ ܘܪܘܙܐ :
15 ܘܣܓܝܐܐ ܒܡܘܠܕܗ ܢܚܕܘܢ ܡܛܠ ܕܢܗܘܐ ܪܒ ܩܕ

Codex C.

[z] *add* ܘܒܥܘܬܗ
ܫܪܝܪܐ
[a]ܠܡܛܠ [b]ܬܫܥܝܬ
[d] *omit* ܕܝ [f]ܗܠܝܢ
[i]ܕܡܠܬܐ
[j]ܬܘܩܝܠܘܬܗ [k]ܕܐܬܠܡܕ
[l]ܕܐܬܠܡܕܬ
[m]ܠܟܘܢ [p]ܒܝܘܡܝ
[q]ܕܗܪܘܕܣ
[r]ܕܝܗܘܕܐ [t]ܐܒܝܐ
[u]ܡܫܡܫܬܗ [v]ܕܐܒܝܐ
[x] *omit* . . . ܘܫܡܗ
. . . ܬܪܝܗܘܢ

† f. 148b.

[a]ܘܕܝܢܘܗܝ [b]ܥܠܠܐ
[e]ܥܠܝܠܝܢ [f]ܒܝܘܡܝܗܘܢ
[g]ܐܬܚܕܬ
[i] *omit* ܐܝܟ
[k]ܕܐܬܦܠܓܘܬܐ
[l]ܕܝܘܡܐ
[m]ܕܡܫܡܫܢܘܬܐ
[n]ܕܢܥܘܠ [o]ܒܗܝܟܠܐ
[p] *omit* . . . ܘܟܠܗ
. . . ܕܡܠܝܐ
[s] *omit* ܕܝ [r] *add* ܕܝ
[t]ܒܫܥܬܐ
[w] *add* ܕܡܕܒܚܐ
[x]ܥܠܘܗܝ [y]ܙܟܪܝܐ
[a]ܕܐܫܬܡܥܬ

Codex A.

ܘܡܫܒܚ[t]
[u] *add* ܕܝ
ܐܠܝܫܒܥ[w]
[a]ܘܢܦܩܬ [c]ܕܐܠܗܘܢ
ܠܒܪܝܐ[e]
ܡܬܒܥܝܢ[f]
[h]ܡܫܡܠܝܢ [i]ܕܪܒܝܗ
ܠܡܠܐܟܐ[j]
[k] *add* ܓܝܪ [x]ܣܒ
[l]ܒܥܠܠܐ [m]ܒܝܘܡܝܗ
ܘܐܓܒ[n]
ܓܒܪܐܝܠ[o]
[p]ܕܩܐܡ [q]ܠܟ
[r]ܫܬܝܩ [t]ܡܫܟܚ
ܕܢܗܘܝܢ[v]
ܢܫܠܡܢ[x]
ܒܙܒܢܗܘܢ[y]
[z]ܠܙܟܪܝܐ [a] *add* ܕܝ
[b] *add* ܗܘܐ
ܚܙܘܢܐ[c]
ܕܬܫܡܫܬܗ[e]
[f]ܐܙܠ [g] *add* ܕܝܢ
ܚܡܫܐ[h]
ܕܗܟܢܐ[i]
[k]ܒܝܘܡܬܐ [l]ܕܢܣܒ
ܚܣܕܝ[m]
[n]ܒܢܝܢܫܐ [o]ܙܒܢܗ
[p] ܕܝ *omit* [r] *add* ܕܝ
ܘܩܪܝܒܘܗ[t]
ܕܢܓܙܪܘܢ[u]

P P

Codex B.

ܘܡܘܕܐ ܡܪܝܐ : ܘܫܡܥ [t]ܘܡܫܒܚ ܠܗ ܠܐ ܫܬܩܐ :
ܘܡܢ ܪܘܚܐ[u] ܕܩܘܕܫܐ ܡܬܡܠܝܐ. ܟܕ ܗܘ
16 ܒܟܪܣܗ ܕܐܡܗ ܀ ܘܫܠܡ ܡܢ ܟܢܝ [w]ܐܠܝܫܒܥ
17 [x]ܢܦܩܬ ܠܘܬ ܡܪܝܐ [y]ܐܠܗܘܢ : ܘܗܘ [z]ܢܩܕܡ
[a]ܘܐܬܬܐ [b]ܡܘܕܝܢ ܒܪܘܚܐ ܘܒܚܝܠܗ [c]ܕܐܠܗܐ :
[d]ܕܝܠܕܬ [e]ܠܒܪܝܐ ܐܚܝܢ ܀ ܟܠ ܟܢܝܢ : ܘܗܠܝܢ
[f. 146*b*]
ܕܠܐ [f]ܡܬܒܥܝܢ [g]ܒܒܝܘܬܗܘܢ ܕܝܕܘܥܐ :
18 ܕܝܠܬܗ ܠܡܪܝܐ ܘܩܠ [h]ܡܫܡܠܝܢ : ܘܐܡܪ
†[i]ܕܪܒܝܗ [j]ܠܡܠܐܟܐ : ܒܡܢܐ ܐܢܐ ܝܕܥ ܗܕܐ :
ܐܢܐ [k]ܓܝܪ [x]ܣܒܐ ܘܐܬܬܝ [l]ܒܥܠܠܐ [m]ܒܝܘܡܝܗ ܀
19 [n]ܘܐܓܒ ܡܠܐܟܐ ܘܐܡܪ ܠܗ ܐܢܐ ܗܘ
[o]ܓܒܪܐܝܠ [p]ܕܩܐܡ ܩܕܡ ܐܠܗܐ : ܘܐܫܬܠܚܬ
20 ܕܐܡܠܠ ܠܟ ܘܐܣܒܪ [q]ܠܟ ܗܠܝܢ : ܘܗܐ ܐܢܬ
ܗܘܐ [r]ܫܬܝܩ [s]ܘܠܐ [t]ܡܫܟܚ [u]ܕܬܡܠܠ ܒܝܘܡܐ
ܠܝܘܡܐ [v]ܕܢܗܘܝܢ ܗܠܝܢ : ܚܠܦ ܕܠܐ ܗܝܡܢܬ
ܠܡܠܝ ܗܠܝܢ ܀ [w]ܕܗܢܝܢ [x]ܢܫܠܡܢ [y]ܒܙܒܢܗܘܢ :
21 ܘܗܘܐ ܥܡܐ ܡܣܟܐ [z]ܠܙܟܪܝܐ : ܘܗܘܘ
22 ܡܬܡܗܝܢ ܒܗܕܐ ܕܐܘܚܪ ܒܗܝܟܠܐ : ܟܕ[a]
ܢܦܩ ܠܐ[b] [t]ܡܫܟܚ ܕܢܡܠܠ ܥܡܗܘܢ ܀ ܘܝܕܥܘ
[c]ܕܚܙܘܢܐ ܚܙܐ ܒܗܝܟܠܐ : ܘܗܘ ܗܘܐ ܪܡܙ
23 ܠܗܘܢ : ܘܫܬܩ ܕܠܐ [d]ܡܡܠܠ : ܘܗܘܐ ܟܕ
ܫܠܡܘ ܝܘܡܬܐ [e]ܕܬܫܡܫܬܗ [f]ܐܙܠ ܠܗ ܠܒܝܬܗ :[g]
24 ܡܢ ܒܬܪ ܕܝܢ ܗܠܝܢ ܝܘܡܬܐ ܒܛܢܬ ܐܠܝܫܒܥ
ܐܢܬܬܗ ܘܗܘܬ ܡܛܫܝܐ ܢܦܫܗ [h]ܚܡܫܐ
25 ܝܪܚܝܢ : ܐܡܪܐ : [i]ܕܗܟܢܐ ܥܒܕ ܠܝ ܡܪܝܐ
[k]ܒܝܘܡܬܐ ܕܚܙܐ : [l]ܕܢܣܒ [m]ܚܣܕܝ ܡܢ
57 [n]ܒܢܝܢܫܐ :: ܘܐܬܡܠܝ [o]ܙܒܢܗ ܕܐܠܝܫܒܥ
58 [p]ܕܝ [q]ܕܬܠܕ : ܘܝܠܕܬ ܒܪ ܘܫܡܥܘ [r] [s]ܫܒܒܘܬܗ
[p]ܕܝ [t]ܘܩܪܝܒܘܗ ܕܐܪܒܝ ܡܪܝܐ ܚܢܢܗ ܥܡܗ :
59 ܘܗܘܘ ܚܕܝܢ ܠܗ ܘܗܘܐ ܒܝܘܡܐ ܬܡܝܢܝܐ
†ܐܬܘ [u]ܕܢܓܙܪܘܢ ܠܛܠܝܐ ܗܘ ܀ ܘܗܘܘ ܩܪܝܢ

Codex C.

ܘܡܫܒܚ[t]
[u] *add* ܕܝ
[x]ܢܦܩܬ [y]ܐܠܗܘܢ
[z]ܢܩܕܡ [b]ܡܘܕܝܢ
[d]ܕܝܠܕܬ [e]ܠܒܪܝܐ
ܡܬܒܥܝܢ[f]
ܒܒܝܘܬܗܘܢ[g]
† f. 149*a*.
[k] *add* ܓܝܪ [x]ܣܒ
ܒܥܠܠܐ[l]
ܘܐܓܒ[n]
[o]ܓܒܪܐܝܠ [p]ܕܩܐܡ
[q]ܠܟ [r]ܫܬܝܩ
[s]ܠܐ [u]ܕܬܡܠܠ
ܕܢܗܘܝܢ[v]
ܕܗܢܝܢ[w]
ܒܙܒܢܗܘܢ[y]
ܠܙܟܪܝܐ[z]
[a] *add* ܕܝ
[b] *add* ܗܘܐ
ܡܡܠܠ[d]
ܕܬܫܡܫܬܗ[e]
ܚܣܕܝ[m]
[o]ܙܒܢܗ [p] *omit* ܕܝ
[q]ܕܬܠܕ [r] *add* ܕܝ
ܫܒܒܘܬܗ[s]
† f. 149*b*.

Codex A.

[m] ܕܐܒ̈ܘܗܝ [o] ܐܡܗ
[p] ܠܐ [q] ܐܬܩܪܝ
[r] ܝܘܚܢܢ
[s] ܫܪܒܬܟ
[u] ܒܗܕܝܢ [v] ܠܐܒ̈ܘܗܝ
[w] ܕܬܬܩܪܐ [y] ܦܢ̈ܩܝܬܐ
[z] ܘܟܬܒ [a] ܕܝܘܚܢܢ
[c] ܒܪ ܫܥܬܗ
[d] ܘܠܫܢܗ
[f] ܘܟܘܠܗ
[g] ܕܝܗܘܕܐ
[i] ܡܬܡܠܠܝܢ
[o] ܐܝܕܗ [p] ܐܒܘܗܝ
[q] ܐܠܗܗ [s] *omit* ܕܝܢ
[t] ܛܠܝܐ [w] ܘܬܗܠܟ
[x] *add* ܓܝܪ [z] ܐܦܘܗܝ
[a] ܘܬܬܒܪ [b] *omit* ܕܝܢ
[c] ܒܡܕܒܪܐ
[d] ܕܐܘܚܕܢܘܬܗ
[e] ܐܝܣܪܐܝܠ

[CCCLIX.]
[f. 187*a*]

[z] ܬܕܒܪ [a] ܐܠܟܣܢܕܪܝܣ
[b] ܒܪܘܡܢܘܣ
[d] ܐܣܩܒܐ
[e] ܐܫܠܝܚܝܢ (*sic*)
[f] *add* ܒܪ
[h] *omit* ܘܦܘ̈ܠܘܣ
[b] ܕܩܣܪܝܐ
[c] ܕܦܝܠܝܦܘܣ
[d] ܫܐܠ [e] ܚܒܪ
[f] ܠܬܠܡܝܕܘܗܝ [h] *add* ܕܝܢ

Codex B.

60 ܠܗ ܥܠ ܫܡܗ ܕܐܒ̈ܘܗܝ[m] ܙܟܪ̈ܝܐ[n]: ܘܐܬܦܢܝܬ
ܐܡܗ[o] ܘܐܡܪܬ ܐܠܐ[p] ܬܬܩܪܐ[q] ܫܡܗ
61 ܝܘܚܢܢ[r]: ܘܐܡܪܘ ܠܗ ܕܠܝܬ ܐܢܫ ܡܢ
[f. 147*a*]
62 ܫܪܒܬܟ[s] ܕܡܬܩܪܐ[t] ܒܗܕܝܢ[u] ܫܡܐ: ܘܗܘܘ
ܪܡܙܝܢ ܠܐܒ̈ܘܗܝ[v] ܗܝܟ ܗܘ ܨܒܐ ܕܝܬܩܪܐ[w]:
63 ܘܫܐܠ[x] ܦܢ̈ܩܝܬܐ[y] ܘܟܬܒ[z] ܐܡܪ ܕܝܘܚܢܢ[a] ܗܘ
64 ܫܡܗ ܘܬܡܗܘ[b] ܟܘܠܗܘܢ: ܘܐܬܦܬܚ ܦܘܡܗ
ܒܫܥܬܗ[c] ܘܠܫܢܗ[d] ܘܗܘܐ ܡܡܠܠ[e] ܘܡܒܪܟ
65 ܠܐܠܗܐ: ܘܗܘܬ ܕܚܠܬܐ ܥܠ ܟܘܠ ܡܩܪ̈ܒܝܗܘܢ
ܘܟܘܠ[f] ܛܘܪܝܬܐ ܕܝܗܘܕܐ[g]: ܗܘܝܢ[h] ܡܬܡܠܠܝܢ[i]
66 ܟܘܠ ܗܠܝܢ ܡܠܝܐ[k]: ܘܐܣܝܡܘ ܟܘܠ ܗܠܝܢ[k]
ܕܫܡܥܘ ܒܠܒܗܘܢ[l]: ܐܡܪܝܢ ܐܪܐ ܡܐ ܗܘ[m]
ܗܕܝܢ ܛܠܝܐ[n] ܝܗܘܐ ܐܝܕܗ[o] ܕܡܪܝܐ ܗܘܬ ܥܡܗ:
67 ܘܙܟܪ̈ܝܐ ܐܒ̈ܘܗܝ[p] ܐܬܡܠܝ ܡܢ ܪܘܚܐ ܕܩܘܕܫܐ:
68 ܘܐܬܢܒܝ ܘܐܡܪ: ܡܒܪܟ ܗܘ ܡܪܝܐ ܐܠܗܗ[q]
76 ܕܐܝܣܪܐܝܠ[r]: ܘܐܢܬ ܕܝܢ[s] ܛܠܝܐ[t] ܢܒܝܗ[u] ܕܡܪܘܡܐ
ܬܬܩܪܐ: ܘܬܗܠܟ[w] [x]ܩܕܡܘܗܝ ܘܬܐܙܠ[y] ܩܕܡ ܐܦ̈ܘܗܝ[z]
80 ܕܡܪܝܐ ܘܬܬܒܪ[a] ܐܘܪܚܬܗ: ܘܛܠܝܐ ܗܘܐ ܪܒܐ[b] ܕܝܢ
ܫܟܝܚ ܘܡܬܚܝܠ ܒܪܘܚܐ: ܘܗܘܐ ܒܡܕܒܪܐ[c]
ܥܕܡܐ ܠܝܘܡܐ ܕܐܘܚܕܢܘܬܗ[d] ܠܘܬ ܐܝܣܪܐܝܠ[e]:

CC.

Matt. XVI. 13—19.

ܬܫܡܫܬܗ ܘܫܪܝܢ ܬܕܒܪ[z] ܐܠܟܣܢܕܪܝܣ[a] ܒܪܘܡܢܘܣ[b] †
ܐܦܝܠܘܒ[c] ܐܣܩܒܐ ܐܣܩܒܐ[d] ܡܢ ܠܘܩܐ: ܬܫܡܫܬܗ
ܘܫܪܝܢ ܬܕܒܪ[z] ܐܫܠܝܚܝܢ[e] [f]ܦܛ̈ܪܘܣ[g] ܘܦܘ̈ܠܘܣ[h] ::
13 ܡܢ ܬܚܘܡܝ[i] ܐܬܐ: [k] ܘܟܕ ܐܬܐ ܡܪܢ ܝܫܘܥ
ܠܐܬܪܐ[a] ܕܩܣܪܝܐ[b] ܕܦܝܠܝܦܘܣ[c]: [d]ܫܐܠ.
ܗܘܐ [e]ܥܡ [f]ܬܠܡܝܕܘܗܝ ܘܐܡܪ: ܡܢ ܐܡܪܝܢ
14 ܒܢܝܢܫܐ ܕܗܘ ܒܪܗ ܕܓܒܪܐ: ܗܢܘܢ[g] [h]ܐܡܪܘ

Codex C.

[m] ܕܐܒ̈ܘܗܝ [n] ܙܟܪ̈ܝܐ
[p] ܠܐ [s] ܫܪܒܬܟ
[t] ܕܡܬܩܪܐ [v] ܠܐܒܘܗܝ
[w] ܕܬܬܩܪܐ [x] ܘܫܐܠ
[y] ܦܢ̈ܩܝܬܐ [z] ܘܟܬܒ
[b] ܘܬܡܗܘ
[c] ܒܪ ܫܥܬܗ
[e] ܡܡܠܠ
[f] ܘܟܘܠܗ
[g] ܕܝܗܘܕܐ [h] ܗܘܘ
[k] ܡܠܝܐ : *omit*
ܘܐܣܝܡܘ ܟܘܠ
ܗܠܝܢ
[l] ܒܠܒܗܘܢ
[m] ܗܘܝܢ [n] ܛܠܝܐ *omit*
[p] ܐܒܘܗܝ [q] ܐܠܗܗ
[r] ܕܐܝܣܪܐܝܠ [t] ܛܠܝܐ
[u] ܢܒܝܐ [w] ܘܬܬܩܕܡ
[y] ܘܬܙܠ
[a] ܘܬܬܒܪ [b] *omit* ܕܝܢ

[a] *omit* ܐܠܟܣܢܕܪܝܣ
[b] ܒܪܘܡܢܘܣ
[c] ܐܦܝܠܘ
[d] ܐܣܩܒܐ [e] ܐܫܠܝܚܝܢ
† f. 150*a*.
[g] ܦܛܪܘܣ
[h] *omit* ܘܦܘ̈ܠܘܣ
[i] ܬܚܘܡܝ
[k] *add* ܘܟܕ ܡܛܐ
[a] ܠܐܬܪܐ
[b] *omit* ܕܩܣܪܝܐ
[c] ܕܦܝܠܝܦܘܣ [e] ܥܡ
[g] ܐܢܘܢ [h] *add* ܕܝܢ

Codex A.

[e] ܕܐܡܪܝܢ
[f] ܝܘܚܢܢ
[g] ܡܥܡܕܢܐ
[h] *add* ܕܝ [i] ܐܠܝܗܘ
[k] ܢܒܝܝܐ
[l] *add* ܗܘܘܢ
[n] ܛܘܒܝܟ
[o] ܕܐܢܬ
[r] ܒܥܕܬܝ
[s] ܘܬܪܥܝܗ
[t] ܕܫܝܘܠ
[x] ܕܬܐܣܘܪ
[y] ܢܗܘܐ [z] ܫܪܐ

[CCCLX.] [f. 187*b*]
[a] *omit* ܗܘܐ [b] ܬܕܒܪܐ
[c] ܐܠܝܫܥ
[d] ܐܬܠܬܝܢ
[e] *add* ܗܘܐ ܢܦܩ ܐܠܝܫܥ ܢܒܝܐ ܕܐܠܗܐ
[f] ܡܬܝ
[a] *add* ܘܒܬܪ
ܗܕܐ
[b] ܐܟܠܘܣܝܐ
[d] ܐܝܟ [e] ܠܗܘܢ
[f] ܠܬܠܡܝܕܘܗܝ
[h] *add* ܕܝ
[i] ܙܥܘܪܝܢ [k] *omit* ܕܝ
[m] ܕܝܦܩ [n] ܬܠܡܝܕܘܗܝ
[p] ܪܘܚܬܐ
[q] ܡܣܐܒܬܐ
[r] ܡܦܩܝܢ

Codex B.

ܠܗ ܐܝܬ ܡܢܗܘܢ [e]ܐܡܪܝܢ [f]ܝܘܚܢܢ [g]ܡܥܡܕܢܐ :
ܐܚܪܢܝܢ[h] [i]ܐܠܝܐ [j]ܘܐܚܪܢܝܢ ܕܝ ܐܪܡܝܐ ܐܘ
15 ܚܕ ܡܢ [k]ܢܒܝܐ : ܐܡܪ ܠܗܘܢ [l]ܐܢܬܘܢ ܕܝ
[f. 147*b*]
16 ܡܢ ܐܢܬܘܢ ܐܡܪܝܢ [m]ܥܠܝ ܕܐܝܢܐ : ܐܓܝܒ
ܫܡܥܘܢ [t]ܦܛܪܘܣ ܘܐܡܪ : ܐܢܬ ܗܘ ܡܫܝܚܐ
17 ܒܪܗ ܕܐܠܗܐ ܚܝܐ : ܐܓܝܒ [h]ܡܪܐ ܝܫܘܥ
ܘܐܡܪ ܠܗ [n]ܛܘܒܝܟ ܫܡܥܘܢ ܒܪ ܝܘܢܐ
ܕܒܣܪ ܘܐܕܡ ܠܐ ܓܠܐ ܠܟ ܐܠܐ ܐܒܐ
18 ܕܒܫܡܝܐ : ܘܐܦ ܐܢܐ ܐܡܪ ܠܟ :
[o]ܐܢܬ ܗܘ [p]ܦܛܪܘܣ : ܘܥܠ ܗܕܐ ܟܐܦܐ ܐܒܢܐ
[q]ܒܢܝ [r]ܒܥܕܬܝ : [s]ܘܬܪܥܝܗ [t]ܕܫܝܘܠ ܠܐ
19 ܢܬܚܝܠܘܢ [u]ܥܠܝܗ : ܘܐܬܠ [w]ܠܟ [h]ܡܦܬܚܝܐ
ܕܡܠܟܘܬܐ ܕܫܡܝܐ : ܘܡܐ [x]ܕܬܐܣܘܪ ܥܠ
ܐܪܥܐ ܢܗܘܐ ܐܣܝܪ ܒܫܡܝܐ : ܘܡܐ
ܕܬܫܪܐ ܥܠ ܐܪܥܐ [y]ܢܗܘܐ [z]ܫܪܝ ܒܫܡܝܐ :

CCI.

Matt. IX. 36—X. 8.

ܬܠܬܝܢ [a]ܗܘܐ [b]ܕܒܪܬ [c]ܐܠܝܫܥ [d]ܐܬܠܬܝܢ ܒܥܪ[d] [e]ܡܢ
36 [f]ܡܬܝ : [a]ܘܟܕ ܚܙܐ ܡܪܢ ܝܫܘܥ [b]ܐܟܠܘܣܝܐ
ܐܬܪܚܡ ܥܠܝܗܘܢ : ܕܗܘܘ ܡܫܪܦܝܢ [c]ܘܪܡܝܢ
37 ܐܝܟ [d]ܐܡܪܝܢ ܕܠܝܬ [e]ܠܗܘܢ ܪܥܝܐ : † ܗܝܕܝܢ
ܐܡܪ [f]ܠܬܠܡܝܕܘܗܝ [g]ܚܨܕܐ ܡܢ ܣܓܝ ܘܦܥܠܝܐ[h]
38 [i]ܙܥܘܪܝܢ : ܒܥܘ ܐܘܢ ܡܢ ܡܪܗ [k]ܕܝ [l]ܕܚܨܕܐ
X. 1 [m]ܕܝܦܩ ܦܥܠܝܢ ܠܚܨܕܗ : ܘܩܪܐ ܠܬܪܥܣܪܬܐ
[k]ܕܝ [n]ܬܠܡܝܕܘܗܝ (*sic*) ܘܝܗܒ ܠܗܘܢ [o]ܫܘܠܛܢܐ ܥܠ
[p]ܪܘܚܬܐ [q]ܡܣܐܒܬܐ ܕܝܗܘܢ [r]ܡܦܩܝܢ

Codex C.

[e] ܕܐܡܪܝܢ
[g] ܡܥܡܕܢܐ
[h] *add* ܕܝ [i] ܐܠܝܐ
[j] ܘܐܚܪܢܝܢ [m] ܥܠܝ
[t] ܦܛܪܘܣ
[o] ܕܐܢܬ [p] ܟܐܦܐ
[q] ܒܢܝ [r] ܒܥܕܬܝ
[u] ܥܠܝ [w] ܕܝ
[x] ܕܬܐܣܘܪ
[y] ܢܗܘܐ [z] ܫܪܐ

[a] *omit* ܗܘܐ
[c] ܘܪܡܝܢ
[d] ܐܬܠܬܝܢ [f] ܡܬܝ
[a] *add* ܘܒܬܪ
ܗܕܐ
[c] ܘܪܡܝܢ [d] ܐܝܟ
† f. 150*b*.
[f] ܠܬܠܡܝܕܘܗܝ
[h] *add* ܕܝ [g] ܚܨܕܐ
[k] *omit* ܕܝ [l] ܕܚܨܕܐ
[m] ܕܝܦܩ [n] ܬܠܡܝܕܘܗܝ
[o] ܫܘܠܛܢܐ
[q] ܡܣܐܒܬܐ
[r] ܡܦܩܝܢ

Codex A.

ˢܬܐܣܘ̇ܢ
ᵗ *omit* ܟܡܘܠܐ
ᵘܫܡܗܬܗܘܢ
ʷ *add* ܕܝ
ˢܫ̈ܠܝܚܐ ᵗܩܕܡܝ
ᵘܗ̇ܕܝ ʷܕܡܬܩܪܐ
ˣ *omit* ܕܝ
ᶻܘܐܢܕܪܐܘܣ
ᵛܐܚܘܗܝ
ᵃܘܝܥܩܘ̇ܒ
ᶜܘܝܘܚܢܢ ᵈܦܝܠܝ̈ܦܘܣ
ᵉܒܪ ܬܘ̇ܠܡܝ
ᶠܬܐܘ̇ܡܐ
ᵍ *add* ܡܟܣܐ
ⁱܘܝܥܩܘ̇ܒ ʲܚܠܦܝ
ᵖ *omit* ܕܐܘܦ
ᑫܕܐܫܠܡܗ ʳܥܠܝ
ˢܘܠܡܕܝܢܬܐ
ᵗܬܥܘܠܘ̇ܢ
ᵛܐܡܪܬܐ ᵘ*add* ܬܘܒ
ʷ *omit* ܗܠܝܢ
ˣܕܐܒܕܝܢ ᶻܕܐܝܣܪܠ
ᵃܡܐܣܝܢ ᵇܡܕܟܝܢ
ᵇ *add* تموز ᵃ *omit* ܫܒܪ
ᶜ *omit* ܐܡܪ . . . ܘܢܣܒ
ᶠ *add* ܐܢ ܗܘ
ᵍܬܘܕܪܐ ʰܡܘܕܝܐ
ⁱܘܕܡܝܢܗܘܢ
ᵏ *add* ܐܢ ˡܐܬܝܚ
ᵐܐܬܝܚܢ
ⁿ *omit* ܡܘܕܝܐ
ʰ *add* ܡܢ ܕܝܢܗ
ᵒ *omit* ܐܠܗܐ
ᵖܫܡܥܐ
ᑫܐܬܝܢ ܡܢ ᑫ
ʳܒܐܢ
ˢ *add* ܫܡܥܘܢ ܕܝܢ ܐܠܗܐ . . . ܐܠܡܝܢ
ᵗܫܘܐܫܘܢ
ʷܫܕܪ ܒܪ

Codex B.

ˢܠܗܘ̇ܢ ܘܕܝܣܘܢ ܡܟܐܒܝܢ ܟܘܠ ܟܐܒܝܢ ܘܟܘܠ
2 ܡܪܥܘ ᵗܟܡܘܠܐ : ᵘܫܡܗܬܗ ʷܕܬܪܥܣܪܬܐ
ˢܫܠܝܚܝܐ ܗܢܘܢ ܗܠܝܢ ᵗܩܕܡܝ ܫܡܥܘܢ
ᵘܗܕܝܢ ʷܕܡܬܩܪܐ ˣܕܝ ʸܦ̈ܛܪܘܣ ᶻܘܐܢܕܪܐܘܣ
3 ᵛܐܚܘܝ : ᵃܘܝܥܩܘܒ ܒܪܗ ᵇܕܙܒܕܝ ᶜܘܝܘܚܢܢ
ܐܚܘܝ : ᵈܘܦܝܠܝ̈ܦܘܣ ᵉܘܒܪܬܘܠܡܝ ᶠܘܬܐܘܡܐ ᵍ
ʰܘܡܬܬܝ ܡܟܣܐ ⁱܘܝܥܩܘܒ ܒܪ ʲܚܠܦܝ :
[f. 148*a*]
4 ᵏܘܠܒܝܘܣ ܗܕܝܢ ˡܕܐܬܦܪܝ ᵐܬܕܐܝ ⁿܫܡܥܘܢ
ܩܢܢܝܐ ᵒܘܝܗܘܕܗ ܐܣܟܪܝܘܛܐ ܗܘ ᵖܕܐܘܦ
5 ᑫܡܫܠܡ ܠܗ : ܠܗܠܝܢ ˣܕܝ ܬܪܥܣܪܬܐ ʳܫܠܚ
ܡܪܢ ܝܫܘܥ : ܘܦܩܕ ܠܗܘܢ ܘܐܡܪ ܠܐܘܪܚ
ܕܥܡܡܝܢ ܠܐ ܬܐܙܠܘܢ ˢܘܠܐ ܠܡܕܝܢܬܐ ˢܕܫܡܪܝܢ
6 ܠܐ ᵗܬܥܠܘܢ : ܐܠܐ ܐܙܠܘ ᵘ ᵛܠܐܡܪܬܐ
ʷܗܠܝܢ ˣܕܐܒܕܝܢ ܡܢ ʸܒܝܬܐ ᶻܕܐܝܣܪܝܠ :
7 ܘܟܕ ܬܗܘܘܢ ܐܙܠܝܢ ܗܘܘ ܡܟܪܙܝܢ ܘܐܡܪܝܢ
8 ܕܩܪܒܬ ܡܠܟܘܬܐ ܕܫܡܝܐ : ܒܝܫܝܐ ܗܘܘ
ᵃܡܐܣܝܢ : ܘܡܝܬܝܐ ܗܘܘ ܡܩܝܡܝܢ : ܘܓܪܒܝܐ
ܗܘܘ ᵇܡܕܟܝܢ : ᶜܡܓܢ ܢܣܒܬܘܢ ᶜܡܓܢ
ܗܒܘ :

ᵃܫܒܪ ᵇܬܡܢܝ ᶜܐܡܪ ܘܬܠܬܝܢ ܡܫܝܚܐ ܘܐܒܐ ᵈܐܚܘܗ ᵈ
ᵉܕܬܠܡܝܕܝ ܫܐܠܘܗ ܘܝܚܢ ܘܐܡܠܝܠ ܒܥܝܢܗ
ܘܝܚܢ ᶜ : ܐܘܠ ܝܗܒ ᵉᶠ ܬܘܕܪܐ ᵍ ܐܠܗܐ ʰܡܘܕܝܐ
ⁱܘܕܡܝܢ ܐܠܗܐ ܐܘܠ ܝܗܒ ᵏ ܡܢ ܬܫܪܝܢ
ˡܐܬܝܚܗ : † ᵐܐܬܝܚܢ ⁿܡܘܕܝܐ ᵍܬܘܕܪܐ ܐܫܡܥܗ ʰ
. . . . ᵒܐܠܗܐ ܬܫܒܚܬܗ ܡܢ ܐܠܗܐ ܫܡܥܗ ᵍܬܘܕܪ
ܐܠܗܐ ܡܬܒܪܟ ܐܢ ܐܠܗܝܢ ᵖܫܡܥܢ ܐܠܗܐ
ᑫܫܡܥܢ ܡܢ ᑫ ʳܒܐܢ ܐܠܗܐ ˢܫܡܥܗ ᵍܬܘܕܪ ܐܠܗܐ
ᵗܫܘܐܫܘܢ ᵘܐܠܗܐ ʷܫܕܪ ܒܪ ʷ ܡܢ ˣܒܐܢ

Codex C.

ˢܬܐܣܘ̇ܢ
ᵗ *omit* ܟܡܘܠܐ
ᵘܫܡܗܬܗܘܢ
ʷ *add* ܕܝ
ˣ *omit* ܕܝ ᵗܩܕܡܝ
ʸܟܐܦܐ ᵇܕܙܒܕܝ
ᶜܘܝܘܚܢܢ
ᶠܬܐܘ̇ܡܐ ᵈܦܝܠܝ̈ܦܘܣ
ʰܡܬܬܝ
ⁱܡܟܣܐ
ᵏܘܠܒܝܘܣ ˡܕܐܬܦܪܝ
ᵐ *omit* ܬܕܐܝ
ⁿܩܢܢܝܐ ᵒܘܝܗܘܕܗ
ʳܥܠܝ ˢܘܠܡܕܝܢܬܐ
ᵘ *add* ܬܘܒ
ᵛܐܡܪܬܐ
ʷ *omit* ܗܠܝܢ
ʸܒܝܬܗ ᶻܐܝܣܪܝܠ
ᵇܡܕܟܝܢ ᶜܡܓܢ
ᵃ *omit* ܫܒܪ
ᵈܐܘܠ ܝܗܒ ܐܢ
ᵈܕܝܢ
ᵉ *omit* . . . ܕܬܠܡܝܕܝ
. . . ܝܗܒ
ʰܡܘܕܝܐ ⁱܘܕܡܝܢܗ
ˡܐܬܝܚ ᵐܐܬܝܚܢ
† f. 151*a*.
ⁿ *omit* ܡܘܕܝܐ
ᑫܐܬܝܢ ܒܗ ᑫ
ᵗܫܘܐܫܘܢ
ᵘܐܠܗܐ ˣܒܐܢ

Codex A.

ܐܬܐܠܝܢ[y] ܬܪܝܢ[k]ܬܠܡܝܕܝܢ
ܟܪܘܣܘܬܗ[z]
ܫܡܥܝܢ[a]
ܬܠܡܝܕܝܢ[b] ܟܪܝܠ[c]
[e] *add* ܘܟܕ ܠܛܘܪܐ
ܐܠܝܢ[f] ܚܙܘܢܗ[h]
ܟܪܝܢ[j]
ܐܠܝܢ[l]
[m] *omit* ܚܝܐ
[o] *add* ܟܕ ܠܡܪܢ
ܘܐܡܪ ܐܠܝܢ
ܐܝܢ ܠܝ
ܐܝܟܢ[o]

Codex B.

ܐܬܐܠܝܢ[y] ... ܬܪܝܢ[k] ... ܟܪܘܣܘܬܗ[z] ::
ܬܠܡܝܕܝܢ[u] ... ܫܡܥ[a] ... ܬܠܡܝܕܝܢ[b]
ܬܪܝܢ[k] ... ܟܪܝܠ[c] :: ܬܠܡܝܕܝܢ[u] ...
...
ܟܪܘܣܘܬܗ[d] [e] ... ܐܠܝܢ[f] ...
ܚܙܘܢܗ[h] :: ܟܪܝܢ[j i] ... [k] ... ܐܠܝܢ[l]
... [m] ... [i] ::[o]

Codex C.

ܐܬܐܠܝܢ[y]
ܟܪܘܣܘܬܗ[z]
[a] ܫܡ ܥܝܢ[a]
ܟܪܝܠ[c]
ܟܪܘܣܘܬܗ[d] ܚܙܘܢܗ[h]
[i] *omit* ܟܪܝܢ ... ܐܝܟ

Codex A.

[CCCLXVIII.]

Matt. XVII. 10—13.

[f. 188*b*]

[Syriac text]
[Syriac text]
[Syriac text]
[Syriac text]
[Syriac text]
[Syriac text]
[Syriac text]
[Syriac text]
[Syriac text]
[Syriac text]

[vv. 14—23 in Lesson LXXII.]

Codex A. (*deest*)

Codex C. (*deest*)

Codex A.

[CCCLXIX.] [f. 188*b*]

ܐܬܐܠܝܢ[p]
[q] *add* ܐܠܡܝܢ
[z] *add* ܘܬܠܡܝܕܘܗܝ
ܬܪܝܢ
ܟܠ[a] ܘܟܠ[b]
ܩܪܝܐ[c] ܟܪܙ[d]

Codex B.

CCII.

Luke VIII. 1—3.

[Syriac text][p] ... [k] ... [q] ...
1 [Syriac text][z] ... [f. 148*b*] ... [a] ...
[Syriac text][b] ... [c] ... [d] ...

Codex C.

[q] *add* ܐܠܡܝܢ
[z] *add* ܘܬܠܡܝܕܘܗܝ
ܟܠ[a]

Codex A.	Codex B.	Codex C.
[e]ܘܒܢܝܢ	2 ܕܐܠܗܐ : ܘܡܕܡ ܬܘܪܓܡܢܘܬܐ [e]ܘܢܒܝܐ ܗܠܝܢ	[e]ܘܢܒܝܐ
[f]ܕܐܬܬܗܒ [g]ܪܘܚܐ	[f]ܕܐܬܬܗܒ ܡܢ [g]ܪܘܚܐ [h]ܒܢܒܝܐ: ܘܡܢ ܒܬܪܝܢ	[g]ܪܘܚܐ
[h]ܒܢܝܢ [i]ܡܢܐܡܪ	[i]ܡܢܝܢ ܡܫܡܠܝܘܬܐ ܗܘ [l]ܕܒܡܘܒܠܐ [m]ܚܕܐ	[l]ܕܒܡܘܒܠܬܐ
[m]ܚܕܐ	3 ܢܗܘܐ ܡܢܗ : ܘܗܘܐ ܐܬܬܗ ܕܒܪܐ	[n]ܡܬܩܪܝܢܘܬܗ
[n]ܡܬܩܪܝܢܘܬܗ	[n]ܡܬܩܪܝܢܘܬܗ [o]ܕܡܬܪܒܝܐ [p]ܘܐܬܚܝܝܢ [q]ܘܡܬܪܝܡ	[o]ܕܡܬܪܒܝܐ
[o]ܕܡܬܪܒܝܐ	ܗܢܐ: ܗܠܝܢ [r]ܕܗܘܘ [s]ܡܬܡܠܝܢ [t]ܠܗܘܢ ܡܢ	[p]ܘܐܬܚܝܝܢ
[p]ܘܐܬܚܝܝܢ	[u]ܡܢܐܠܗܘܢ :	[q]ܘܡܬܪܝܡ
[q]ܘܡܬܪܝܡܐ	[a]ܬܠܬ [b]ܘܥܣܪܝܢ [c]ܬܪܬܝܢ [d][e]ܚܘܝܐ ܐܠܗܐ :[d]	[u]ܡܢܐܠܗܘܢ
[r]ܕܗܘܘ [s]ܡܬܡܠܝܢ	ܐܝܟ ܗܢܐ ܐܡܪ ܗܘ [f]ܬܪܬܝܢ [g]ܐܬܐܝܢ	[a]ܬܠܬܗ
[t]ܠܗܘܢ [u]ܡܢܐܠܗܘܢ	ܐܝܟܢܐ ܘܥܣܪܝܢ [c]ܬܪܬܝܢ ܐܠܦܘܣܗ [h]ܩܪܝܢܘܬܗ :	[e]omit ܚܘܝܐ
[a]ܬܠܬܗ [b]ܘܥܣܪܝܢ	ܐܝܟ ܗܢܐ [i]ܡܬܩܪܝܢ [i]ܗܢܐ ܡܢ [j]ܡܬܐܡܪ:	[j]ܡܬܐ
[c]ܬܪܬܝܢ	ܫܡܥܢܐ [k]ܘܥܣܪܝܢ [c]ܬܪܬܝܢ ܚܕܐ [l]ܐܝܟ ܐܡܪܗ : :	
[d]ܐܝܟ ܚܘܝܐ [d]	ܐܝܟ ܗܢܐ ܐܡܪܬ ܡܢ ܠܗܘܢ ܐܡܪܗ : ܡܡܠܠ	
[f]ܬܪܬܝܢ [g]ܐܬܐܝܢ (sic)	[b]ܘܥܣܪܝܢ [c]ܬܪܬܝܢ ܐܠܦܘܣܗ ܒܬܠܝܬܝܗܘܢ :	[m]ܬܠܬܐ ܡܫܬ [m]
[h]ܩܪܝܢܘܬܗ	ܐܝܟ ܗܢܐ [m]ܐܡܪܬ [n]ܐܬܬܠܬ ܒܗ [o]ܐܠܦܘܣ [p]: :	[o]ܐܠܦܘܣ
[i]ܗܢܐ ܐܡܪ ܐܠܝܥܙܪ[i]		
[j]ܡܬܐܡܪ [k]ܘܥܣܪܝܢ		
[l]ܐܝܟ [n]ܐܬܬܠܬ		
[p]add ܐܒ ܐܒ		
CCCLXXIV. [f. 189*a*]		
[CLXXIX.]		

CCIII.

Matt. X. 16—22.

Codex A.	Codex B.	Codex C.
[b]omit ܝܫܘܥ ... ܡܫܝܚܐ	[a]ܝܫܘܥ[b] ܐܡܪ ܐܒ ܐܒܘܢ ܬܠܡܝܕܘܗܝ ܡܫܝܚܐ[b] : ܐܠܗ[c]	[a]omit ܝܫܘܥ
[c]ܐܠܗ [d]ܬܠܡܝܕܘܗܝ	ܗܐ ܐܢܐ ܫܠܚ [d]ܬܠܡܝܕܘܗܝ [e]ܐܠܫܠܝܚܝܗ [f]ܐܡܫܕܪܬ	[c]ܐܠܫܠܝܚܝܗ
[e]ܐܡܫܕܪܬܐ	[g]ܘܫܠܝܚܐ : ܡܢ [h]ܒܥܘܬܗ [i]ܕܡܫܬܘܬܗ : [a † z]ܐܡܪ	† f. 151*b*.
[f]ܐܡܫܕܪܬ	16 ܡܢܐ [βd]ܠܬܠܡܝܕܘܗܝ ܗܐ ܐܢܐ [γe]ܡܫܕܪ ܠܟܘܢ	[z]add ܐܡܪ ܘܫܠܚ ܬܠܡܝܕܘܗܝ
[g]ܘܫܠܝܚܐ	ܐܝܟ [δf]ܐܡܪܝܢ [eg]ܡܢ [sh]ܕܒܝܢ ܗܘܘ ܐܢܬܘܢ [ζi]ܚܟܝܡܝܢ	[g]ܘܫܠܝܚܐ
[h]omit ܒܥܘܬܗ	ܐܝܟ [ηj]ܚܘܝܬܐ : [θk]ܘܬܡܝܡܝܢ ܐܝܟ [l]ܝܘܢܐ :	[h]omit ܒܥܘܬܗ
[i]ܕܡܫܬܘܬܗ [α][ܡܫܒܚܬܐ]	17 ܘܗܘ ܠܟܘܢ[ιm] ܡܢ ܒܢܝܢܫܐ : [κn]ܡܫܠܡܝܢ ܠܟܘܢ	[e]ܡܫܕܪ [i]ܚܘܝܬܐ
[d]ܠܬܠܡܝܕܘܗܝ	ܠܒܬܝ ܕܝܢܐ [λo]ܠܟܢܘܫܬܐ ܘܒܟܢܘܫܬܗܘܢ ܢܢܓܕܘܢܟܘܢ	[g]ܡܢ [h]ܕܒܝܢ
[β]ܠܬܠܡܝܕܘܗܝ	18 ܘܩܕܡ ܗܓܡܘܢܐ ܘܡܠܟܐ ܬܩܪܒܘܢ ܡܛܠܬܝ	[k]ܘܬܡܝܡܝܢ
[γe]ܡܫܕܪ [δf]ܐܡܪܝܢ	[μp]ܠܣܗܕܘܬܐ ܠܗܘܢ : [νq]ܠܥܡܡܐ [ξr]ܕܗܢܘܢ	[r]ܠܣܗܕܘܬܐ [m]add ܕܗܢ
[eg]ܡܢ [sh]ܕܒܝܢ		
[ζi]ܚܟܝܡܝܢ [ηj]ܚܘܝܬܐ		
[θk]ܘܬܡܝܡܝܢ [l]ܝܘܢܐ		
[m ι]add ܕܗܢ		
[κn]ܡܫܠܡܝܢ		
[λo]ܠܟܢܘܫܬܐ		
[μp]ܠܣܗܕܘܬܐ		
[νq]ܠܥܡܡܐ [ξr]ܕܗܢܘܢ		

Codex A.	Codex B.	Codex C.

Codex A.

[m ι] *add* ܕܝܢ
[π s] ܡܥܡܕܢܘܢ
[ρ t] ܐܬܢܒܝܘܢ
[σ u] ܗܝܟ ܐܐ ܡܐ
[τ v] ܬܡܠܠܘܢ
[υ] ܡܬܚܫܒ
[y χ] *omit* ܕܝܢ [φ x] ܒܗܐܘ
[a] ܗܘ [s b] ܕܡܡܠܠܝܢ
[c] ܗܕܐ [ψ e] ܠܐܢܫܝܢ
[h] ܟܘܠ [i] ܠܐܠܠ
[α k] ܗܕܐ [l ω] *add* ܕܝܢ
[n] ܚܝܐ [β] ܚܝܐ
[o] *omit* ܫܠܡ

Codex B.

19 ܠܗܘܢ ܘܠܚܝܫܐ: ܒܕ[ι m] ܡܥܡܕܢܐ[π s] ܘܐܚܪܢܝܢ ܐܠܝܐ
[f. 149a] ܠܐ ܐܬܢܒܝܘܢ[ρ t] ܠܒܐ[σ u] ܕܬܡܠܠܝܢ[τ v] ܡܬܚܫܒ[υ w]
ܗܘ ܠܟܘܢ ܐܢ ܒܗܘ[φ x] ܗܘܝܢܐ ܡܢ ܕܝ[χ y]
20 ܬܡܠܠܘܢ[z] : ܠܐ ܐܢ ܐܬܘܢ ܗܘܝܢ[a] ܕܡܠܠܝܢ[s b] :
ܐܠܐ ܪܘܚܗ ܕܐܒܘܟܘܢ ܗܘ ܗܕܝܢ[c] ܕܡܡܠܠ[d]
21 ܒܟܘܢ : ܡܫܝܚܐ[ι m] ܐܝܟ ܠܐܢܫܝܗ[ψ e] ܠܡܘܬܐ
ܘܐܒܕ ܠܒܪܗ : ܘܝܡܘܬܘܢ[f] ܒܢܝܢ ܥܠ
22 ܐܒܗܬܗܘܢ ܘܢܡܝܬܘܢ[g] ܝܬܗܘܢ : ܘܐܬܘܢ
ܗܘܝܢ ܡܣܬܢܝܢ ܡܢ ܟܘܠܐ[h] ܠܐܠܠ[i] ܫܡܝ :
::: ܗܕܝܢ[α k] ܕܡܣܝܒܪ[ω l] ܠܥܠܡܝܢ[m] ܗܘ ܚܝܐ[β n] :::
ܫܠܡ[o] :

Codex C.

[m] *add* ܕܝܢ
[t] ܐܬܢܒܝܘܢ
[u] ܗܝܟ ܐܐ ܡܐ
[v] ܬܡܠܠܘܢ
[y] *omit* ܕܝܢ [x] ܒܗܐܘ
[z] ܬܡܠܠܘܢ
[a] ܗܘ [b] ܕܡܡܠܠܝܢ
[d] ܕܡܡܠܠܐ
[e] ܠܐܢܫܝܢ [f] ܘܝܡܘܬܘܢ
[g] ܘܢܡܝܬܘܢ
[l] *add* ܕܝܢ [m] ܠܥܠܡܝܢ
[n] ܚܝܐ [o] *omit* ܫܠܡ

CCIV.

Luke IX. 28—36.

Codex A.

[CCCLXXV.] [f. 189b]
[a] ܐܬܐܒܝܢ
[b] *omit* ܗܘܐ [c] ܬܕܒܪ
[d] ܐܦܐܠܐܣܘܢ
[e] *add* ܐܘܠ
ܐܫܒܐܦܐܣܗ
[f] ܬܠܦܠܚܢܪ
[g] ܡܬܝܘܣ
[CCCLXXIX.] [f. 189b]
[j] ܗܐܕܣ ܬܠܬܝܢ
ܪܒܝܐ ܫܘܒܥܐ
ܐܠܡܣܝܚ ܒܝ ܦܛܪ
ܬܐܒܘܪ ܫܒܬ[j]
[a] ܦܪܫܐ [b] ܠܦܛܪܘܣ
[c] ܘܠܝܘܚܢܢ
[d] *omit* ܐܘܦ
[e] ܘܠܝܥܩܘܒܘܣ
[f] ܕܐܦܘܗܝ
[h] ܡܒܗܩ [i] ܘܗܐ
[j] ܕܗܢܘܢ [k] ܘܐܠܝܐ
[l] ܒܬܫܒܘܚܬܐ
[m] *add* ܟܠ
[n] ܡܦܩܢܘܬܗ [p] *add* ܕܝܢ
[q] ܝܩܝܪܝܢ [r] ܒܫܢܬܐ
[s] *add* ܕܝܢ
[t] *add* ܬܫܒܘܚܬܗ
ܘܠܬܪܝܢ
[u] *omit* ܕܝܢ [w] ܓܒܪܐ
[x] ܕܩܐܡܝܢ

Codex B.

ܬܐܒܝܢ[a] ܗܘܐ[b] ܬܕܒܪ[c] ܐܠܗܝܢ ܐܦܐܠܐܣܘܢ[d]
ܐܦܠܠܒ[e] ܬܠܦܠܚܢܪ[f] ܚܕ[g] ܡܢ ܬܠܡܝܕܝ[h] : ܘܒܝ[j i]
ܫܬܗ ܚܝܕ ܦܛܪ[k] ܬܐܒܘܪ[l] ܡܢ ܒܘܒܪܗ[j] : ܡܢ
28 ܠܘܩܐ ܘܒܝܘܬܗ ܦܪܩܐ[a] : ܘܒܬܪ ܡܠܝܐ ܗܠܝܢ
ܠܦܛܪܘܣ[b] ܘܠܝܘܚܢܢ[c] ܐܘܦ[d] ܘܠܝܥܩܘܒ[e] ܘܣܠܩ
29 ܠܛܘܪܐ ܕܝܨܠܐ : ܘܗܘܐ ܟܕ ܗܘܐ ܡܨܠܐ :
ܐܘܦ[d] ܡܫܬܚܠܦܐ ܕܐܦܘܗܝ[f] ܐܬܚܠܦ ܘܠܒܘܫܗ
30 ܐܬܚܘܪ ܣܓܝ[g] ܡܒܗܩ[h] : ܘܗܐ[i] ܬܪܝܢ ܓܒܪܝܢ
ܗܘܘ ܡܡܠܠܝܢ ܥܡܗ : ܗܢܘܢ[j] ܗܘܘ ܡܘܫܐ[†]
31 ܘܐܠܝܐ[k] ܕܐܬܚܙܝܘ ܒܬܫܒܘܚܬܐ[l] : ܘܗܘܘ ܐܡܪܝܢ[m]
ܡܦܩܢܘܬܗ[n] ܗܕܐ ܕܗܘܐ ܥܬܝܕ ܕܢܡܠܐ
32 ܒܐܘܪܫܠܡ[o] : ܦܛܪܘܣ[o] ܘܗܠܝܢ[p] ܕܗܘܘ ܥܡܗ
ܗܘܘ ܝܩܝܪܝܢ[q] ܒܫܢܬܐ[r] : ܟܕ[s] ܐܬܥܝܪܘ[p] ܚܙܘ[t]
33 ܕܝܢ[u][t] ܓܒܪܐ[w] ܕܩܐܡܝܢ[x] ܥܡܗ : ܘܗܘܐ

Codex C.

[b] *omit* ܗܘܐ
[d] ܐܦܐܠܐܣܘܢ
[g] *omit* ܚܕ [h] ܬܠܡܝܕܐ
[i] *omit* ܘܒܝ [k] ܐܦܛܪ
[l] *omit* ܡܢ ܬܐܒܘܪ
[b] ܠܦܛܪܘܣ
[d] *omit* ܐܘܦ
[e] ܘܠܝܥܩܘܒ
[f] ܕܐܦܘܗܝ [g] ܣܓܝ
[h] ܡܒܗܩ [j] ܕܗܢܘܢ
[n] ܡܦܩܢܘܬܗ

† f. 152a.

[o] ܒܐܘܪܫܠܡ
[o] ܦܛܪܘܣ
[s] *add* ܕܝܢ [p] ܐܬܥܝܪܘ
[t] *add* ܬܫܒܘܚܬܗ
ܘܠܬܪܝܢ
[u] *omit* ܕܝܢ [x] ܕܩܐܡܝܢ

Codex B.

ܒܡܐ ܕܦܪܫܘ[t] ܡܢܗ ܐܡܪ[u] ܦ̈ܛܪܘܣ[w] ܠܡܪܢܐ
ܝܫܘܥ : ܪܒܝ[x] ܛܒ ܠܢ ܕܢܗܘܐ[y] ܗܟܐ[z] ܕܝ ܢܥܒܕ
ܬܠܬ ܡܛܠܝܢ : ܠܟ[a] ܚܕ ܘܠܡܘܫܐ ܚܕܐ
[b]ܘܠܐܠܝܐ ܚܕܐ : ܕܠܐ ܝܕܥ ܡܐ ܗܘ
[f. 149b]
34 [c]ܐܡܪ :[d] [e]ܘܗܘܐ ܥܢܢܐ ܐܬܥܒܕ[f] ܘܐܛܠܠ
ܥܠܝܗܘܢ : ܕܚܠܘ ܕܝ ܟܕ ܥܠܘ[g] ܗܢܘܢ ܠܥܢܢܐ :
35 ܘܩܠܐ ܡܢ ܥܢܢܐ ܗܘܐ ܐܡܪ[h] ܗܕܝܢ[i] ܗܘ ܒܪܝ
36 ܚܒܝܒܝ ܠܗ[j] ܫܡܥܘ : ܘܒܡܐ ܕܗܘܐ[h] ܗܕܝܢ
ܩܠܐ :[k] ܐܫܬܟܚ ܡܪܢܐ ܝܫܘܥ[l] ܒܠܚܘܕܘܝ :·
ܘܗܢܘܢ ܫܬܩܘ ܘܠܐܢܫ ܠܐ ܬܢܝܘ ܒܗܘܢ ܝܘܡܝܢ ܒܗܠܝܢ
ܘܡܕܡ ܡܢ ܗܟܐ[m] ܕܚܙܘ :·

CCV.

Matt. XVII. 1—9.

[z]ܘܗܕܐ[a] ܠܠܘܩܕܐܝܣ[b] [c]ܠܛܘܪ ܬܐܒܘܪ[c] [d]ܡܢ
1 [e]ܡܬܐܘܣ[a][d] :· ܘܒܬܪ[b] ܝܘܡܝܢ ܫܬܐ[c] ܠܦ̈ܛܪܘܣ
[d]ܘܠܝܥܩܘܒ[e] ܘܠܝܘܚܢܢ[f] ܐܚܘܗܝ[g] ܘܐܣܩ ܐܢܘܢ
2 ܠܛܘܪ ܪܡ ܠܒܠܚܘܕܝܗܘܢ :[h] ܘܐܫܬܚܠܦ ܗܘ ܡܪܢܐ
ܝܫܘܥ ܩܕܡܝܗܘܢ :·[i] ܘܐܢܗܪܘ[k] ܐܦ̈ܘܗܝ ܗܝܟ
[l]ܕܫܡܫܐ[m] ܡܐܢܝ ܕܝ ܐܬܥܒܕܘ[n] ܚܘܪܝܢ ܗܝܟ
3 ܕܢܗܘܪܐ :[o] ܘܐܬܚܙܝܘ ܠܗܘܢ ܡܘܫܐ[p] ܘܐܠܝܐ
4 ܡܡܠܠܝܢ ܥܡܗ : ܐܥܢܐ ܕܝ[j] ܦ̈ܛܪܘܣ ܘܐܡܪ
ܠܡܪܢܐ ܝܫܘܥ ܡܪܝ[†] [q]ܛܒ ܠܢ ܕܢܗܘܐ[r] ܗܟܐ
ܐܢܬ ܨܒܐ ܕܢܥܒܕ[s] ܗܟܐ ܬܠܬ ܡܛܠܝܢ : ܠܟ ܚܕܐ
5 [t]ܘܠܡܘܫܐ ܚܕܐ[u] ܘܠܐܠܝܐ ܚܕܐ : ܘܥܕ ܗܘ
[v]ܡܡܠܠ ܗܐ[w] :[x] [y]ܢܗܪ[z] ܐܛܠܠ[a] ܥܠܝܗܘܢ :
ܘܗܐ ܩܠܐ ܡܢ ܓܘ[b] ܥܢܢܐ ܐܡܪ :[c] ܗܕܝܢ
ܗܘ ܒܪܝ ܚܒܝܒܝ ܕܒܗ[d] ܨܒܝܬ ܠܗ[e] ܗܘܘ
6 [f]ܫܡܥܝܢ ܬܠܡܝܕܘܝ ܢܦܠܘ ܥܠ[g] ܐܦ̈ܝܗܘܢ
7 ܘܕܚܠܘ ܠܣܓܝ: ܘܩܪܒ ܡܪܢܐ ܝܫܘܥ:[i] ܘܐܬܦܫ

Codex A.

[w] ܠܡܪܢ
[z] *omit* ܕܝ
[a] ܚܕܐ
[b] ܘܠܐܠܝܐ
[d] *add* ܗܠܝܢ ܕܝ ܟܕ ܗܘܐ ܐܡܪ
[e] ܘܗܘܐ [f] ܘܐܛܠܠ
[h] ܗܕܝܢ
[j] ܫܡ̈ܥܘܢ
[l] ܒܠܚܘܕܘܝ

[CCCLXXIX.]
[f. 192a]

[a] *omit* ܘܗܕܐ
[b] *add* ܡܢ ܡܬܐܘܣ
[d] *omit* ܡܢ ܡܬܐܘܣ
[a] *add* ܘܒܬܪܗ ܦܪܘܣܐ
[b] ܡܪܢ
[d] ܘܠܝܥܩܘܒ
[e] ܘܠܝܘܚܢܢ
[f] ܐܚܘܗ [i] ܘܢܗܪܘ
[k] ܐܦ̈ܘܗ [l] ܕܫܡܫܐ
[m] ܡܐܢܘܗ [n] ܚܘܪܝܢ
[p] ܘܐܠܝܐ [q] *add* ܗܘ
[r] *add* ܗܐ
[t] ܘܠܐܠܝܐ
[u] ܘܠܡܘܫܐ
[w] *add* ܗܐ [x] *add* ܥܢܢ
[z] ܐܛܠܠ [a] ܥܠܝܗܘܢ
[b] ܥܢܢܐ [c] ܗܕܝܢ
[f] ܫܡܥܘ [i] ܘܐܬܦܫ

Codex C.

[t] ܕܦܪܫܘ [u] ܦܛܪܘܣ
[x] *omit* ܛܒ [y] ܗܟܐ
[z] *omit* ܕܝ
[a] ܚܕܐ [c] ܡܛܠܠ
[d] *add* ܗܠܝܢ ܕܝ ܟܕ ܗܘܐ ܐܡܪ
[f] ܘܐܛܠܠ [g] ܗܘܢ
[i] *omit* ܗܘ
[k] ܐܫܬܟܚ
[l] ܒܠܚܘܕܘܝ
[m] *omit* ܕܚܙܘ

[z] *omit* ܘܗܕܐ
[a] ܠܠܘܩܕܝܣ
[c] *omit* ܠܛܘܪ ܬܐܒܘܪ
[e] ܡܬܐܘܣ
[a] *add* ܘܒܬܪܗ ܦܪܘܣܐ
[c] ܠܦܛܪܘܣ
[f] ܐܚܘܗ [g] ܘܣܠܩ
[h] ܘܐܫܬܚܠܦ [i] ܘܢܗܪܘ
[k] ܐܦ̈ܘܗ [m] ܘܡܐܢܘܗ
[o] ܘܐܬܚܙܝܘ
† f. 152b.
[j] ܦܛܪܘܣ
[s] *omit* ܗܟܐ [q] *add* ܗܘ
[v] ܡܡܠܠ
[w] *add* ܗܐ
[y] ܢܗܘܪ [a] ܥܠܝܗܘܢ
[b] ܥܢܢܐ [d] ܨܒܝܬ
[f] ܫܡܥܘ [e] *omit* ܗܘܘ
[g] ܐܦ̈ܝܗܘܢ [i] ܘܐܬܦܫ

Codex A.

[h] *omit* ܕܝ
[i] ܬܛܥܢܘܢ
[n] ܒܠܘܫܗ [o] ܐܡܪ
[p] ܬܬܡܪܘܢ
[q] ܒܬܫܡܫܬܐ
[r] *add* ܗܢܐ
[a] ܬܬܕܝܪ [b] ܡܪܝ
[c] ܕܘܡܝܟ [d] ܐܚܕ
[e] ܐܬܝܘܡ (*sic*)
[f] ܣܡܦܠܩܝܢ ܒܥܪ [f]
[g] *add* ܘܐܬܠܗ ܐܠܗ
[h] *omit* ܡܪܬܝ ܡܪܝܡ
[j] ܬܡܥܝܢܗ [k] ܡܢ
[l] *omit* ܗܘܡ ܦܝ ܐܚܝ
[m] *omit* ܬܕܒܪ
[n] ܐܠܢܒܝ [o] ܝܚܘܠ
[p] ܡܢ [q] *omit* ܦܝ ܐܚܝ
[r] ܣܐܕܝ [t] ܐܬܐܝܢ

Codex B.

8 [h] ܕܝ ܒܗܘܢ ܘܐܡܪ ܠܐ [i] ܬܛܥܢܘܢ : ܘܬܠܘ
ܚܫܘܟܘܢ ܘܠܐ ܣܡܗ ܠܚܘܕ ܐܠܐ [k] ܐܢ
[f. 150b]
9 [h] ܕܝ [m] ܠܡܪܐ ܣܘܡܟ [n] ܒܠܘܫܝܗܘܢ ܘܒܕ ܢܣܬܘ
ܡܢ ܦܬܘܪܐ ܦܘܡ ܢܬܘܢ ܡܪܐ ܣܘܡܟ [o] ܘܐܡܪ :
ܠܟܝܢ ܠܐ [p] ܬܬܡܪܘܢ [h] ܕܝ [q] ܒܬܫܡܫܬܐ [r] ܒܕܡܟܐ
ܕܬܥܘܠ ܒܝܬܗ [h] ܕܝ ܕܬܒܥܐ ܡܢ ܒܝܢ ܡܬܢܬܐ :
ܗܒܒܡ [a] ܬܬܕܝܪ ܐܠܗܝܗܘܢ [b] ܡܪܝ [c] ܕܘܡܝܟ : ܐܝܠܠܘܢ
ܬܬܠܬ [d] ܚܕ ܡܢ [e] ܐܬܝܘܡ [f] ܣܡܦܠܩܝܢ ܬܐܚ ܐܥܝܢܗ
[g] ܡܪܬܝ ܡܪܝܡ [h] [i] ܐܝܠܠܘܢ [j] ܬܡܥܝܢܗ [k] ܦܝ ܐܬܠܘܢ :
ܒܪܝܡ [l] ܗܘܡ ܦܝ ܐܚܝ [l] [m] ܬܕܒܪ [n] ܐܢܒܝ [o] ܝܚܘܠ :
[i] ܐܝܠܠܘܢ ܣܡܥܗ [p] ܦܝ ܐܬܠܘܢ ܬܡܥܝܢܗ ܘܒܥܪܝܡ
[q] ܦܝ ܐܚܝ [q] [a] ܬܬܕܝܪ ܡܦܩܐ ܐܠܣܒܝ : [i] ܐܝܠܠܘܢ
[r] ܣܕܝ ܒܥܪ ܡܢ [s] ܒܐܢܘܢ [t] ܐܬܐܝܢ

Codex C.

[h] *omit* ܕܝ
[k] ܐܝܢ
[m] ܡܪܐ [n] ܒܠܘܫ
[q] ܒܬܫܡܫܬܐ
[g] *omit* ܡܪܬܝ ܡܪܝܡ
[i] ܐܝܠܠ
[j] ܬܡܥܝܢܗ [k] ܡܢ
[l] *omit* ܗܘܡ ܦܝ ܐܚܝ
[o] ܒܚܘܠ
[q] *omit* ܦܝ ܐܚܝ
[s] ܒܢܘܢ [t] ܐܬܐܝܢ

[CCCXCVI.]

Codex A.

[f. 193a]
[u] ܡܐܠܟܐ [v] ܪܐܫ
[w] *add* ܐܠܗܝܗܘܢ
[x] ܐܠܗܕܒܪܐ
[y] ܫܢܝܐܪ [a] ܫܒܐܝܟ
[b] *omit* ܗܘ [c] ܠܠܡܕܐܫ
[e] *add* ܘܒܢܬܗ ܡܪܫܐ
[d] ܗܪܘܕܝܫ [e] ܕܕܒܝ
[f] ܕܝܘܚܢܢ
[g] *add* ܗܘ ܕܐܢܐ ܦܣܩܬ ܪܝܫܗ ܘܗܘ
[h] ܩܡ [i] ܘܠܓܠܠ
[j] ܡܬܥܒܕܝܢ [k] ܘܐܚܪܢܝܢ
[m] ܢܒܝܐ [n] *omit* ܕܝ
[o] ܗܪܘܕܝܣ [p] ܗܘܐ
[q] ܗܕܝܢ [r] *add* ܗܕܝܢ
[v] ܐܦܣܩܬ

CCVI.

Mark VI. 14—30.

Codex B.

ܬܫܡܥ ܘܒܥܪܝܡ [u] ܡܠܟܐ [v] ܪܘܫ [w] ܘܫܢܝ ܐܢܫܐ [x] ܐܠܗܕܒܪܐ
[y] ܒܗܒܪܗ [z] ܐܝܠܠܘܢ ܐܪܒܥܗ ܘܒܥܪܝܡ ܡܢ
[a] ܐܥܒܐܝܟ : ܘܗܕܐ [b] ܗܘ [c] ܠܠܡܕܐܝܫ ܡܢ
14 [d] ܡܪܘܡܫ [e] [d] ܗܘܪܕܝܫ ܘܥܒܕ ܡܠܟܐ : [e] ܝܪ ܠܟ
ܐܬܒܒܕ ܥܢܡܗ ܕܡܪܐ ܣܘܡܟ : ܘܗܘܐ ܐܡܪ
[f] ܕܝܘܚܢܢ ܡܥܡܕܢܐ [g] [h] ܩܡ ܡܢ ܒܝܢ ܡܝܬܝܐ :
[i] ܘܠܓܠܠ ܟܕܡ ܚܝܠܐ [j] ܡܬܥܒܕܝܢ ܒܗ : [k] ܘܐܚܪܢܝܢ ܗܘܘ
15 [l] ܐܡܪܝܢ [l] ܕܗܘ ܐܠܝܐ : ܘܐܚܪܢܝܢ ܗܘܘ ܐܡܪܝܢ
16 ܕܢܒܝܐ ܗܘ : [†] ܐܝܟ ܚܕ ܡܢ [m] ܢܒܝܐ : ܘܟܕ
ܫܡܥ [n] ܕܝ [o] ܗܪܘܕܝܣ [p] ܗܘ ܐܡܪ : [q] ܗܕܝܢ [r] [t] ܗܘ
[u] ܝܘܚܢܢ ܕܐܢܐ [v] ܐܦܣܩܬ ܪܝܫܗ [g] ܗܘ ܩܡ :

Codex C.

[v] ܪܐܫ
[x] ܐܠܗܕܒܪܝܢ
[z] ܐܝܠܠ [b] *omit* ܗܘ
[c] ܠܠܡܕܐܫ [d] ܡܪܘܡܫ
[e] *add* ܘܒܢܬܗ
[d] ܗܪܘܕܝܫ [e] ܕܕܒܝ
[h] ܩܡ [j] ܡܬܥܒܕܝܢ
[k] ܘܐܚܪܢܝܢ
[l] *omit* ܕܗܘ . . . ܐܡܪܝܢ . . .
† f. 153a.
[n] *omit* ܕܝ
[o] ܗܪܘܕܝܣ [p] ܗܘܐ
[t] *omit* ܗܘ [u] ܝܘܚܢܢ

Codex A.

[x] ܕܝܢ *omit*
[o] ܗܪܘܕܝܣ [y] ܫܠܚ
[z] ܠܝܘܚܢܢ [a] ܘܚܒܫܗ
[b] ܒܟܠܝܒܐ [c] ܒܓܠܠ
[d] ܕܦܝܠܝܦܘܣ
[g] ܘܝܘܚܢܢ [i] ܠܗܪܘܕܝܣ
[k] ܫܠܝܛ [l] ܕܝܢ *omit*
[n] ܡܫܟܚܐ [p] ܗܪܘܕܝܣ
[q] ܕܚܝܠ [s] ܗܘ
[t] ܘܗܘܐ
[u] ܘܒܥܕܢܬܐ
[w] ܝܕܥ [x] ܓܢܣܝܐ
[y] ܒܫܡܘܬ [z] ܥܡ *omit*
[a] ܪܒܪܒܢܘܗܝ
[b] ܘܠܪܫܝܐ [d] ܘܠܪܫܝܗ
[e] ܕܝܢ *omit* [f] ܘܫܦܪܬ
[g] ܠܗܪܘܕܝܣ
[s] ܠܐܡܗ
[t] ܕܝܘܚܢܢ
[w] ܕܣܩܘܣܐ
[x] ܕܝܘܚܢܢ
[y] ܘܐܬܥܩ [z] ܒܓܠܠ
[a] *add* ܕܝܢ
[b] ܡܘܡܬܐ
[c] ܕܝܢ *omit* [d] ܫܠܚ
[e] ܠܣܦܩܘܠܛܘܪܐ
[f] ܕܝܝܬܐ [g] ܐܙܠ
[h] ܒܟܠܝܒܐ
[i] ܘܐܝܬܝ
[k] ܕܣܩܘܣܐ
[n] ܕܝܢ *omit* [o] *add* ܕܝܢ

Codex B.

17 ܘܗܘ[w] ܕܝܢ[x] ܓܝܪ[w] ܗܪܘܕܣ[o] ܫܠܚ[y] ܐܚܕ ܠܝܘܚܢܢ[z]
ܘܐܣܪܗ[a] ܝܬܗ ܒܟܠܘܒܐ[b] : ܒܓܠܠ[c] ܗܪܘܕܝܐ
ܐܢܬܬܗ ܕܦܝܠܝܦܘܣ[d] ܐܚܘܝ[e] ܕܐܬܢܣܒܬ[f] ܠܗ :
18 ܗܘܐ ܓܝܪ[g] ܝܘܚܢܢ ܐܡܪ[h] ܠܗܪܘܕܣ[i] ܠܐ
ܫܠܝܛ[k] ܠܟ ܕܬܗܘܐ ܠܟ ܐܢܬܬܗ ܕܐܚܘܟ : [f. 151a]
19 ܘܗܝ[l] ܕܝܢ ܗܪܘܕܝܐ ܗܘܬ[l] ܕܝܢ[m] ܐܟܪܝܐ ܠܗ :
ܘܒܥܝܐ ܕܬܩܛܠ ܝܬܗ ܘܠܐ ܗܘܬ[n] ܡܫܟܚܐ :
20 ܗܘܐ ܓܝܪ[p] ܗܪܘܕܣ[q] ܕܚܝܠ ܡܢ[r] ܝܘܚܢܢ ܕܗܘܐ
ܝܕܥ[s] ܕܗܘ ܓܒܪ ܙܕܝܩ[l] ܕܝܢ ܘܩܕܝܫ : [t] ܘܗܘ
ܢܛܪ ܠܗ ܘܫܡܥ ܡܢܗ ܣܓܝ ܘܥܒܕ :
21 [u] ܘܒܥܕܢܬܐ[v] ܗܘܐ ܥܒܕ ܡܢܗ : ܘܗܘܐ ܝܘܡ
[w] ܝܕܥ ܟܕ ܥܒܕ[o] ܗܪܘܕܣ[x] ܓܢܣܝܐ ܕܝܠܗ
[y] ܒܫܡܘܬ[z] ܥܡ[a] ܪܒܪܒܢܘܗܝ[b] ܘܠܪܫܝ[c] ܐܠܦܘܗܝ
22 [d] ܘܠܪܫܝܗ ܕܓܠܝܠܐ : ܘܥܠܬ[e] ܕܝܢ ܒܪܬܗ ܕܗܪܘܕܝܐ
ܘܪܩܕܬ[f] ܘܫܦܪܬ[g] ܠܗܪܘܕܣ : ܘܠܟܠܗܘܢ ܕܗܘܘ
ܪܒܝܥܝܢ ܥܡܗ : ܘܐܡܪ ܡܠܟܐ ܠܛܠܝܬܐ ܫܐܠܝ
ܡܢܝ ܡܐ ܕܐܢܬܝ ܨܒܝܐ : ܘܐܢܐ ܝܗܒ ܠܝܟܝ :
23
24 ܒܕܡܐ[r] ܠܦܠܓܘܬ ܡܠܟܘܬܝ : ܗܝ ܕܝܢ ܢܦܩܬ
ܐܡܪܬ[s] ܠܐܡܗ ܡܐ ܐܫܐܠ : ܘܗܝ ܐܡܪܬ
25 ܪܫܗ[t] ܕܝܘܚܢܢ ܡܥܡܕܢܐ : ܘܥܠܬ ܥܘܝ
ܒܣܘܚ ܠܘܬ ܡܠܟܐ : ܘܫܐܠܬ ܐܡܪܐ[u] ܨܒܝܐ
ܐܢܐ ܒܥܝ[v] ܕܬܬܠ ܠܝ ܥܠ[w] ܕܣܩܘܣܐ ܪܫܗ
26 [x] ܕܝܘܚܢܢ ܡܥܡܕܢܐ : [y] ܘܐܬܥܩ ܡܠܟܐ[z] ܒܓܠܠ[a]
ܡܘܡܬܐ[b] : [t] ܘܗܠܝܢ[e] ܕܝܢ[p] ܕܪܒܝܥܝܢ ܥܡܗ ܠܐ
27 ܨܒܐ ܕܢܥܓܠ ܗܝܕܐ ܘܫܠܚ[d] ܗܝܕܐ[c] ܕܝܢ
28 [e] ܠܣܦܩܘܠܛܘܪܐ ܘܦܩܕ[f] ܕܝܝܬܐ ܪܫܗ : ܘܗܘ
ܕܝܢ[g] ܐܙܠ ܦܣܩ ܪܫܗ[h] ܒܟܠܘܒܐ : [i] ܘܐܝܬܐ
ܪܫܗ[j] ܥܠ[k] ܕܣܩܘܣܐ : ܘܝܗܒ ܗܝܕܐ ܠܛܠܝܬܐ
29 ܘܛܠܝܬܐ ܝܗܒܬ ܗܝܕܐ[l] ܠܐܡܗ : ܘܫܡܥܘ
[m] ܬܠܡܝܕܘܗܝ ܘܐܬܘ ܐܪܝܡܘ[c] ܕܝܢ ܦܓܪܗ ܘܩܒܪܘ [f. 151b]
30 ܗܝܕܐ[n] ܕܝܢ ܒܩܒܘܪܬܐ : ܘܐܬܟܢܫܘ[o] ܫܠܝܚܐ

Codex C.

[w] ܗܘܐ ܓܝܪ
[o] ܗܪܘܕܣ
[y] ܫܠܚ [a] ܘܚܒܫܬ
[e] ܐܚܘܝ [f] ܕܐܬܢܣܒܬ
[h] *add* ܠܗ
[i] ܗܪܘܕܣ
[l] ܕܝܢ *omit* [m] ܐܟܪܝܐ
[n] ܡܫܟܚܐ [p] ܗܪܘܕܣ
[r] ܝܘܚܢܢ [t] ܘܗܘܐ
[u] ܘܒܥܕܢܬܐ
[v] ܘܗܘܐ
[y] ܒܫܡܘܬ [z] ܥܡ *omit*
[a] ܪܒܪܒܢܘܗܝ
[b] ܘܠܪܫܝܐ [c] ܐܠܦܘܗܝ
[e] ܕܝܢ *omit* [f] ܘܫܦܪܬ
[g] ܠܗܪܘܕܣ
[r] ܠܦܠܓܘܬ
[t] ܕܝܘܚܢܢ
[u] ܨܒܝܐ [v] ܕܬܬܠ
[y] ܘܐܬܥܩ
[b] ܡܘܡܬܐ
[c] ܕܝܢ *omit*
[p] ܕܪܒܝܥܝܢ [d] ܫܠܚ
† f. 153*b*.
[f] ܕܝܝܬܐ [h] ܒܟܠܘܒܐ
[i] ܘܐܝܬܝ [j] ܥܠ *omit*
[k] ܕܣܩܘܣܐ
[l] ܠܐܡܗ
[m] ܬܠܡܝܕܘܗܝ
[n] ܕܝܢ *omit*
[o] *add* ܕܐܝܢ

Codex A.

ܚܠܦ. ᵒ*add* ᵖܘܬܠܡܝܕܘܗܝ
ᵃ*omit* ܗܘܐ ܡܢ ܐܒܐ ܬܪܒܪ
ᵇܠܒܝܬ ᶜܐܠܦܝܗ
ᵈ*add* ܘܐܠܦܝܗ ܐܠܗ
ᵉܬܠܡܝܕܗ ܡܢ ܐܕܝ.

Codex B.

(deest)

‡ f. 194*b*.

Codex B.

ܠܘܬ ܡܪܐ ⁿܫܡܥܘܢ ܘܬܘܒ ܠܗ ܒܡܠܬܐ: ܒܗܠ
ܡܢܐ ܕܒܥܒܕܘ ܘܐܠܗܐ:ᵒ ܘܫܪ ᵖܘܬܠܡܝܕܐ ᵃܗܘܐ ܡܢ
ܐܒܐ ᵃܬܪܒܪ ᵃ ᵇܘܫܢܐ ᶜܕܐܘܪܚܗ ᵈܐܬܠܡܕ ᵉܐܘܟܬ
ܐܘܪܗ ܡܢ ܠܘܩܐ:ᵉ

Codex A.

ܬܐܠܬܝܢ ܐܠܦܝܢ ܬܪܝܢ ܐܬܠܡܕ ܫܡܥܘܢ ܘܒܢܝܢ
ܡܢ ܢܫܐ
ܘܫܪ ܘܬܠܬܝܢ ܠܒܝܬ ܐܠܦܝܗ ܘܐܠܦܝܗ ܐܠܗ
ܐܬܠܡܕ ܬܠܡܝܕܗ ܡܢ ܐܕܝ
ܐܝܟܢ ܗܘܪܐ ܠܒܝܬܢܝܐ ܒܝ ܬܠܡܝܕܐ ܐܠܦܝܗ
ܐܬܠܡܕ ܡܢ ܘܗܦ ܐܝܟܢ ܗܘܐ ܐܠܦܝܗ
ܐܠܦܝܗ ܐܠܦܝܗܘܢ ܒܒܪ ܐܠܦܝܗ ܐܘܠܗ
ܒܝ ܐܬܬܠܡܕ ܒܐܘܪܫܠܡ (John x. 22.)
ܐܝܟܢ ܠܠܘܠܝܗ ܐܬܠܡܕ ܒܝ ܫܬܗ ܘܒܬܪܝܢ
ܡܢ ܬܪܬܝܢ ܐܘܠ
‡ܐܝܟܢ ܠܠܒܢܐ ܐܬܠܡܕ ܒܝ ܐܬܝܗ ܡܢ ܐܠܦܝܗ
ܐܠܬܠܬܗ (sic) ܒܒܪ ܐܠܦܝܗ
ܐܝܟܢ ܠܡܘܬܐ ܐܬܠܡܕ ܗܘܐ ܐܠܬܒܒܐ ܐܠܦܝܗ
ܐܠܬܝܗ ܒܒܪ ܐܠܦܝܗ
ܐܝܟܢ ܠܦܠܝܢ (sic) ܐܬܠܡܕ ܐܘܠ ܗܘܐ ܡܢ ܬܡܘܢ
ܐܝܟܢ ܠܠܡܘܐܬ ܐܬܠܡܕ ܘܫܪ ܘܒܬܪܝܢ ܡܢ
ܬܪܬܝܢ ܐܘܠ
ܐܝܟܢ ܠܠܒܪܐܪ ܐܬܠܡܕ ܒܬܪܝܢ ܡܢ ܒܐܝܘ ܐܠܝܪ
ܐܝܟܢ ܠܠܝܫܘܥ ܐܬܠܡܕ ܫܬܗ ܐܒܬܪ ܡܢ
ܐܘܠ
ܐܝܟܢ ܠܠܝܒܢܐ ܐܬܠܡܕ ܒܝ ܫܡܥܘܢ ܡܢ
ܐܘܠ
ܐܝܟܢ ܠܠܥܡܕܐ ܐܬܠܡܕ ܒܝ ܒܬܪܝܢ ܡܢ ܐܘܠ
ܐܝܟܢ ܠܠܕܝܢ ܒܠܐ ܐܦܣܩܘܦ ܐܬܠܡܕ ܒܝ
ܬܡܢܝܒܬܪ ܡܢ ܬܪܬܝܢ ܐܘܠ

Codex C.

ⁿ*omit* ܫܡܥܘܢ
ᵖܘܬܠܡܝܕܘܗܝ
ᵃ*omit* ܗܘܐ ܡܢ ܐܒܐ
ᵇܘܫܢܐ ᶜܐܘܪܚܗ

(deest)

Codex B. (*deest*)

Codex A.

ܬܐܡܪܐܬ ܒܬܘܒܬ ܗܕܐ ܐܠܝܨܒܬ ܐܠܟܡܘܢܘܣ
ܢܘܡ ܐܠܐܪܒܥܐ ܐܬܦܩܗ ܦܝ ܦܐܟܒܗܐܬ
ܐܝܢܡ ܡܚܪܬ ܘܗܘ ܐܒ ܦܝܗ ܘܒܬܒ ܐܠܢܣܟ
ܐܠܕܝܦ ܐܠܝܐ ܐܠܝܘܡ ܐܠ ܒܒܘܕܝ ܒܢܣܟܗ
ܐܢܕܗ ܢܗܒ ܠܐܬܘܬܗ ܦܝ ܕܝܪ ܐܢܒܐ ܡܘܫܐ
ܒܡܐܕܝܢܗ ܐܠܦܠܣܛܝܢ ܢܐܚܝܬ ܐܪܕܘܢ ܘܗܘ
[f. 195 r]
ܢܚܠ ܒܘܠ ܡܢ ܡܪܐ ܦܝܗ ܐ ܢܝܫ ܕܠܢܗ
ܢܝܡ ܐܠܗ ܡܢ ܡܐܪܐ ܘܡܢ ܒܬܒ ܐܡܝܢ
ܘܕܠܟ ܦܝܗ ܐܠܦ ܘܬܠܬܡܐܝܗ ܘܐܚܕ
ܘܐܪܒܥܝܢ ܐܠܡܣܝܚܝܗ ܐܠܝܘܢܐܢܝܗ ܘܒܐܠܗ
ܐܬܬܘܦܝܩ

Codex C. (*deest*)

Lesson CCCCX.—Matt. xxv. 1—13, vide pp. 96, 97.
CCCCXI.—Matt. xi. 27—30, vide p. 239.

[CCCCXII.]

Matt. XV. 21—28.

21 ܣܒ. ܒܥ. ܝܐ ܡܢ ܡܟܐܬܐܘܣ : ܒܬܚܘ ܕܝ ܘܨܝܕܢܐ
22 ܐܬܬܐ ܟܢܥܢܝܬܐ ܠܬܚܘܡܐ ܕܨܘܪ ܘܨܝܕܢ. ܘܗܘܐ
ܐܬܬܐ ܟܢܥܢܝܬܐ ܡܢ ܬܚܘܡܝܐ ܗܢܘܢ ܢܦܩܬ
ܒܪ ܡܩܥܐ ܘܐܡܪܐ. ܐܬܪܚܡ ܥܠܝ ܡܪܝ
ܒܪܗ ܕܕܘܝܕ ܒܪܬܝ ܒܝܫܐܝܬ ܡܬܕܒܪܐ ܡܢ
23 ܫܐܕܐ. ܗܘ ܕܝ ܠܐ ܦܢܝ ܠܗ ܦܬܓܡܐ.
ܘܩܪܒܘ ܬܠܡܝܕܘܗܝ ܒܥܘ ܡܢܗ ܘܐܡܪܝܢ ܫܪܝ
24 ܠܗ ܕܩܥܝܐ ܒܬܪܢ. ܗܘ ܕܝ ܥܢܐ ܘܐܡܪ
ܠܗܘܢ : ܠܐ ܐܫܬܕܪܬ ܐܠܐ ܠܘܬ ܥܪܒܐ
25 ܕܐܒܕܘ ܡܢ ܒܝܬ ܐܝܣܪܐܝܠ ܗܝ ܕܝܢ ܐܬܬܐ
26 ܐܬܬ ܣܓܕܬ ܠܗ ܘܐܡܪܐ .... ܠܝܫܘܥ
27 ܕܬܝܒܐ ܠܡܪܚܡܘ ܠܡܪܚܡܐ (*sic*). ܗܝ ܕܝ ܐܡܪܬ.
ܐܝܢ ܡܪܝ ܐܦ ܟܠܒܐ ܐܟܠܝܢ ܡܢ ܦܪܬܘܬܐ

Codex B.	*Codex* A.	*Codex* C.
(*deest*)	28 ܕܬܫܠܡ ܡܢ ܦܘܫܩܐ ܕܡܪܩܘܣ ܘܣܐܝܡ. ܗܢܐ ܟܬܒܐ ܠܗ ܒܥܘܕ. ܐܘ ܟܬܒܬܐ ܪܒܬܐ ܗܝ ܘܡܫܒܚܬܐ. ܢܗܘܐ ܠܟܠ ܟܬܝܒ ܕܢܩܪܐ ܐܢܫ. ܘܢܬܟܬܒ ܒܣܦܪܐ ܕܚܝܐ ܒܓܘ ܟܬܒܐ :::	(*deest*)

Codex B.

ܬܡ ܗܕܐ ܐܠܐܢܓܝܠ ܒܥܘܢ ܐܠܠܗ
ܐܠܒܪ ܐܠܡܥܝܢ ܥܠܐ ܟܠ ܐܠܟܬܒܐ ܦܝ
ܫܗܪ ܫܒܐܛ ܣܢܗ ܐܠܦܘܬܡܢܝܗ ܦܝ ܫܗܪ
ܘܥܫܪܝܢ ܡܢ ܐܝܒܐܬ ܘܡܢ ܫܢܝܢ ܐܕܡ
ܫܬ ܐܠܐܦ ܘܬܡܢ ܡܐܝܗ ܘܐܪܒܥܝܢ ܣܢܗ :
ܘܗܘ ܒܝܕ ܐܠܥܒܕ ܐܠܚܩܝܪ ܐܠܡܣܟܝܢ
ܐܠܡܣܟܝܢ ܐܠܡܫܬܗܝ ܓܦܪܐܢ ܐܒܢ ܐܒܪܐܗܝܡ
ܐܒܘ ܐܠܚܪ ܐܠܟܬܒܝ ܢܝܚ ܐܠܠܗ ܢܦܣܗ ܘܓܦܪ
ܠܗ ܘܪܚܡܗ ܐܡܝܢ : ܘܠܘܠܕܗ ܐܠܡܬ
[ܡܣܝܚܝ] ܒܥܦܪܬ ܐܠܡܣܝܚ ܡܢܬ ܡܪܝܡ
ܘܩܘܣܬܐ ܐܠܡܩܕܣܐ ܘܓܡܝܥ ܐܠܩܝܣܐ
ܘܐܠܩܕܝܣܝܢ ܘܐܠܩܕܝܣܐܬ ܘܐܪܘܐܚ ܐܠܒܫܪ:
ܪܚܡ ܐܠܗ ܡܢ ܩܪܐ ܘܥܬܒ ܘܩܐܠ ܐܡܝܢ
ܐܡܝܢ ܐܡܝܢ
ܘܗܕܐ ܐܠܐܢܓܝܠ ܠܠܩܣܝܣ ܐܒܘ ܥܠܝ ܐܒܢ ܠܣܝܕ

انتقل هذا الانجيل الى القس
ابى العلى ابن لسيد رحمة الله

Codex C.

ܬܡ ܒܥܘܢ ܐܠܡܣܝܚ ܘܬܘܦܝܩܗ ܐܡ ܐܠܢܘܪ
ܘܓܡܝܥ ܐܠܩܕܝܣܝܢ ܐܡܝܢ ܐܡܝܢ ܐܡܝܢ ܘܟܐܢ
ܐܠܦܪܘܓ ܦܝ ܬܠܬ ܫܗܪ ܡܢ ܐܝܐܪ ܣܢܗ
ܐܫܦܬ ܦܝ ܝܘܡ ܐܚܕ ܡܢ ܐܒ ܫܗܪ ܫܬ
ܐܠܐܦ ܘܫܬ ܡܝܗ ܘܬܣܥܝܢ ܫܢܗ ܡܢ
ܫܢܝ ܐܕܡ ܐܪܚܡܗ ܒܟܬܒܗ ܐܠܠܗ ܒܓܪܘܒ
ܐܚܪܝ ܐܠܫܝܟ ܐܓܢܒܝ ܘܗܘ ܢܩܠ ܒܟܠ
ܡܢ ܩܪܐ ܦܝܗ ܢܒܝ ܠܗ ܒܓܦܪܐܢ
ܐܠܫܝܟܗ ܪܚܡ ܐܠܠܗ ܡܢ ܟܬܒ ܘܩܪܐ
ܐܡܝܢ ܐܡܝܢ ܐܡܝܢ
ܪܒ ܐܠܥܠܡܝܢ ܢܩܘܠ ܐܡܝܢ

Codex A.

ܒܫܡ ܐܠܠܗ ܢܒܬܕܝ ܐܠܥܡܠ
ܢܩܘܠ ܐܢܐ ܐܠܡܣܟܝܢ ܐܝ ܥܠܝܐ ܐܠܡܬܘܟܠ. ܒܬܪܬܝܒ ܐܠܡܣܝܚ ܡܢܗ ܐܠܝܐ ܐܠܡܚܒܗ.
ܒܟܬܐܪ ܒܘܒܥ ܐܠܬܝ ܘܡܢ ܥܠܝܐ ܢܨܪ ܬܪܝܐܝ ܘܐܠܫܝܪܝܢ ܘ....ܪ ܡܢ ܐܢܩܠ
ܒܒܬܪ ܦܠܡܣܝܚ ܡܬܪܒܘܡ ܘܓܦܪ ܠܗܡ ܡܬܡ ܬܒܪܪ ܠܗ ܫܓܐܝܗ ܘܡܝܫ ܢܦܣ ܐܒܡܘܬ

Codex A.

ܒܡܥܘܢܬ ܐܠܩܕܝܣܗ ܡܪܬ ܡܪܝܐܡ ܘܒܪܟܬ ܐܠܐܒܐ ܡܪܝ ܐܠܝܐ ܘܒܪܟܬ ܠܟܡܝܠ
ܐܠܩܕܝܣܝܢ ܐܡܝܢ ܦܝܗ̈ ܗܕܐ ܐܠܟܬܒ ܡܣܝܚܝ ܥܠܐ ܕܝܪ ܟܘܟܒ ܘܠܟܠ ܦܝܗ ܝܩܪܐ
ܐܘ ܝܬܠܘܗ ܡܟܝ ܠܝܣ ܘܡܢ ܟܬܒ ܒܕܐܠܗ ܢܟܝ ܡܣܝܚܝ ÷ ܡܢ ܟܬܒ ܐܠܩܕܝܣ ܘܡܢ
ܦܐܟܬܒ ܐܢܐ ܐܠܚܛܝ ܐܠܬܐ ܐܠܩܣܝܣ ܐܠܦܩܝܪ ܒܫܠܛܗ ܪܚܡ ܐܠܠܗ... ܕܡ ܘܚܢܢ ܢܥܡ
ܐܡܝܢܐܬܗ ܐܡܝܢ [ܡܢ ܒ]ܬܒ ܘܡܢ ܩܪܐ ܐܡܝܢ ܐܡܝܢ ܐܡܝܢ

The following inscription was read by St. E. and J. S. Assemanus in A.D. 1758, but it had disappeared when Miniscalchi Erizzo saw it in 1848 :—

ܐܩܘܠ ܐܢܐ ܐ̄ ܐܠܝܐ ܐܠܩܣ ܬܠܡܝܕ ܐ̄ ܡܘܣܐ ܐܢܝ ܟܬܒܬ ܗܕܐ ܐܠܐܢܓܝܠ
ܘܟܬܒ ܐܠܐܥܝܐܕ ܘܐܠܩܝܐܡܗ ܘܣܬ̈ ܡܝܢܐܘܢ ܚܕܡܗ ܐܠܟܢܝܣܗ ܐܠܡܩܕܣܗ ܘܣܐܝܪ
ܐܠܟܬܒ ܐܠܕܝ ܓܬ ܡܥܝ ܡܢ ܐܢܛܐܟܝܗ ܐܠܥܪܒ ܘܩܦܗ ܠܠܩܕܝܣ ܡܪܝ ܐܠܝܐ
ܐܠܡܥܪܘܦ ܒܕܝܪ ܟܘܟܒ ܐܠܕܝ ܓܪܬ ܥܡܐܪܬܗ ܥܠܝ ܝܕܝ ܬܟܘܢ ܗܕܐ ܐܠܐܢܓܝܠ ܘܐܠܟܬܒ
ܠܡܢ ܣܟܢ ܐܠܕܝܪ ܝܩܪܐ ܦܝܗܐ ܘܝܬܪܚܡ ܥܠܝ ܐܢܐ ܐܠܚܛܝ ܘܠܐ ܝܟܘܢ ܠܐܚܕ ܣܠܛܐܢ
ܠܐ ܝܒܝܥ ܘܠܐ ܝܫܬܪܝ ܘܟܠ ܡܢ ܚܐܠܦ ܝܟܘܢ ܡܚܪܘܡ ܡܦܪܘܙ ܡܢ ܐܠܠܗ : ܪܚܡ
ܐܠܠܗ ܡܢ ܩܪܐ ܘܡܢ ܟܬܒ. ܐܡܝܢ ܐܡܝܢ

It was translated by the Assemanii into Arabic thus :—

اقول انا انبا اليا القس تلميذ انبا موسى انى كتبت هذا الانجيل وكتب الاعياد والقيامة وستة ميناون خدمة الكنيسة المقدسة وسائر الكتب الذى جاءت معى من انطاكيه العرب وقف القديس مار اليا المعروف بدير كوكب الذى جرت عمارته على يدى تكون هذا الانجيل والكتب لمن سكن الدير يقرا فيها ويترحم على انا الخاطى ÷ ولا يكون لاحد سلطان لا يبيع ولا يشترى : وكل من خالف يكون محروم مفروز من الله ÷ رحم الله من قرء ومن كتب امين امين ÷

LIST OF RUBRICS NOT PRINTED WITH THE TEXT.

CODEX A.

(*Copied from De Lagarde's Evangeliarium Hierosolymitanum.*)

			PAGE
40	ܩܪܝܢ ܦܬܓܡܗ ܠܫܠܝܚ ܦܘܠܘܣ ܡܢ ܡܟܪܘܙܘܬ ܡܬܟܬܒ ܗܘܐ ܠܛܝܡܬܐ ܡܢ ܐܢܛܝܘܟܝܐ ܠܩܘܪܢܬܝܐ ܘܗܘ ܠܛܝܡܬܐ ܩܪܝܢ ܠܩܘܪܢܬܝܐ ܠܗܘܠܘܢ ܡܢ ܠܘܩܐ ܡܬܟܬܒ ܗܘܐ ܠܛܝܡܬܐ ܠܣܝܪܘܣ ܡܢ ܐܢܛܝܘܟܝܐ ܠܩܘܪܢܬܝܐ السادس ܘܐܣܪ ܘܥܒܕܝ ܩܪܝܢ	30[1]	50
85	M ܩܪܝܢ ܗܘܝ ܒ ܕܒܬܪ ܥܐܕܐ ܕܨܠܝܒܐ قراة انجيل لوقا من بعد عيد الصليب بسبين وحدين		+ 99
150[5] Matth. xxvii. 3-32.	ܠܨܦܪܐ ܕܥܪܘܒܬܐ ܠܛܘܒܢܗ ܠܡܫܝܚܗ ܡܢ ܡܬܝܐܘܣ M ܗ	130[2]	199
	M[4], ubi ܡ vocis ܠܡܫܝܚ possit ܘܡ esse vel aliud nescio quid. ܠܡܫܝܚ ܕܡܫܝܚܐ ܡܫܝܚ		
Marc. xv. 16-32. πιστεύσωμεν	ܐܦܪܘܣ ܕܥܪܘܒܬܗ ܠܛܘܒܢܗ ܡܢ ܡܪܩܘܣ M ܘ ܕܬܠܬ ܫܥܝܢ	132[1]	201
Matth. xxvii. 33-54.	ܫܬ ܫܥܝܢ ܠܛܘܒܢܗ | ܠܡܫܝܚܗ ܡܢ ܡܬܝܐܘܣ M ܐ	133[1]	203
Luc. xxiii. 32-49.	ܠܬܫܥ ܫܥܝܢ ܠܛܘܒܢܗ ܡܢ ܠܘܩܐ M ܬܫܥ ܫܥܝܢ	134[1]	204
Ioh. xix. 25-37.	ܠܪܡܫ ܕܥܪܘܒܬܗ ܠܛܘܒܢܗ ܠܡܫܝܚܗ ܡܢ ܝܘܚܢܢ M ܠܐ	135[1]	206
Ioh. xix. 38-42.	ܠܨܦܪ ܕܫܒܬܐ ܐܘܢܓܠܝܘܢ ܠܡܫܝܚܗ ܡܢ ܝܘܚܢܢ M ܒ	135[4]	207
Matth. xxvii. 1 συμβούλιον—38.	ܩܪܝܢ ܐܘܢܓܠܝܘܢ ܕܠܠܝܐ ܡܢ ܡܬܝܐܘܣ M ܠܝܠܝܐ ܕܥܪܘܒܬܐ	136[2]	208
Luc. xxiii. 39-43, Matth. xxvii. 39-54, Ioh. xix. 31-37.			211-13

---

40. Vocabula ܡܬܟܬܒ ܗܘܐ ܠܛܝܡܬܐ ܡܢ ܐܢܛܝܘܟܝܐ delere radendo conatus est nescio quis. ܠܛܝܡܬܐ sero in ܠܛܝܡܬܐܘܣ mutatum.

150[6]. ܠܛܘܒܢܗ A: ܢ minio ab eo quo librarius ipse utitur diverso supra versum scripta.

150[10]. ܡܘܫܐ ab ipso librario supra alio nomine nescio quo scriptum.

150[11]. Crediderim ܕܠܠܝܐ scriptum, non ܕܠܠܝܡ, quod edidit Miniscalchius.

				PAGE
	Matth. xxvii. 55-61.	ܡܐ ܕܫܠܡܐ M	139[4]	213
151	Matth. xxvii. 62-66.	ܠܝܘܡ ܥܪܘܒܬܐ ܕܒܬܪ ܕܢܚܐ (*sic*) ܡܢ ܡܬܝ M ܡܢ ܕܫܠܡܐ	140[1]	214
	Matth. xxviii. 1-20.	ܠܝܘܡ ܥܪܘܒܬܐ ܕܒܬܪ ܕܢܚܐ ܡܢ ܡܬܝ	140[2]	215
152		ܟܬܒܐ ܕܐܘܢܓܠܝܘܢ ... ܐܘܢܓܠܝܘܢ ܕܩܝܡܬܐ ... ܐܘܢܓܠܝܘܢ ܕܩܝܡܬܐ	141[3]	
	Matth. xxviii. 16-20.	... ܡܢ ܡܬܝ M الاول M ا ܡܢ ܡܐ	141[3]	216
	Marc. xvi. 2-8.	... الثانى ܡܢ ܡܪܩܘܣ M ܒ ܡܢ ܡܐ	141[4]	217
	Marc. xvi. 9-20 σημείων.	... الثالث ܡܢ ܡܪܩܘܣ M ܓ ܡܢ ܡܐ	142[2]	218
	Luc. xxiv. 1-12.	... الرابع ܡܢ ܠܘܩܐ M ܕ ܡܢ ܡܐ	142[4]	219
		... الخامس ܡܢ ܠܘܩܐ	143[3]	
	Luc. xxiv. 36-53.	... السادس ܕܩܝܡܬܐ ܡܢ ܠܘܩܐ M ܘ ܡܢ ܡܐ	143[3]	220
	Ioh. xx. 1-10.	... السابع ܕܩܝܡܬܐ ܡܢ ܝܘܚܢܢ M ܙ ܡܢ ܡܐ	144[2]	221
	Ioh. xx. 11-18.	... الثامن ܕܩܝܡܬܐ ܡܢ ܝܘܚܢܢ M ... ܡܢ ܡܐ	144[4]	222
	Ioh. xx. 19-25.	... (*sic*) ... التاسع M ... ܡܢ ܡܐ	145[3]	223
	Ioh. xx. 26-31.	...	145[4]	224
	Ioh. xxi. 1-14.	... العاشر (*sic*) ܕܩܝܡܬܐ ܡܢ ܝܘܚܢܢ M ... ܡܢ ܡܐ	146[2]	224
	Ioh. xxi. 15-25.	الحادى عشر ... (*sic*) ... ܡܢ ܝܘܚܢܢ M ... ܡܐ ܡܢ ܡܐ	147[2]	226
		...	148[1]	
153		... ܡܢ ܡܐ	148[1]	
154		... (*sic*)	148[1]	227
155		...	148[2]	
156		...	148[2]	
157		...	148[2]	
158		...	148[2]	
159		...	148[2]	

151[1]. ܕܢܚܐ A: ... minio ab eo quo librarius ipse utitur diverso supra versum scripta. M minio eodem usus est quo corrector. ... lego, non ... = ...

151[2]. ... A.: minio de quo saepius et dixi et dicam, ... supra versum addita.

152. Titulus capitibus praemissus ita scriptus ut a titulo capiti primo praefixo non separatus sit. ... codex. ... serius intra versus additum.

153. ... ante ... supra versum scriptum manu primâ. Mox ܡܢ ܡܐ minio alio quam quo librarius ipse utitur scriptum.

	Lection	Rubric		Fol.	PAGE
160		[Syriac] (*sic*) [Syriac]		148^2	
		[Syriac]		148^2	
161		[Syriac]		148^2	
	Luc. iv. 16-22 στόματος αὐτοῦ.	[Syriac]			229
162		[Syriac] (*sic*) [Syriac]	[Syriac]	148^4	
	Ioh. xv. 1.	[Syriac]			
163	Ioh. x. 7-16.	[Syriac]	[Syriac]	148^4	246
164		[Syriac]	[Syriac]	149^3	
	Luc. x. 1-12.	[Syriac]			229
165	Matth. xxiii. 29-39.	[Syriac]	[Syriac]	150^2	231
166		[Syriac] (*sic*) [Syriac]	[Syriac]	150^4	
	Marc. xii. 28-37.	[Syriac]		151^1	232
167		[Syriac]	[Syriac]	151^4	
168	Luc. . 39-56.	[Syriac]	[Syriac]	151^4	234
	Luc. x. 38-42, xi. 27-28.	[Syriac]		152^2	235
169		[Syriac]	[Syriac]	152^4	
170		[Syriac]	[Syriac]	152^4	
171		[Syriac]	[Syriac]	152^4	
172		[Syriac]	[Syriac]	153^1	
173		[Syriac]	[Syriac]	153^1	
174	[Syriac] M	[Syriac] (*sic*) [Syriac] (*sic*) [Syriac]		153^1	
175	Ioh. iii. 13-17. [Syriac] M	[Syriac]		153^1	236

161. [Syriac] A[1].

162. [Syriac] manu non primâ in righturâ scriptum. mox [Syriac] codex. numeri dierum quos in hac mensium recensione editurus sum, a librario omnes in margine positi sunt.

164. [Syriac] altera nominis [Syriac] pr m supra versum scripta: antea [Syriac] cum [Syriac] sequenti conexa erat: quae conexio radendo nunc deleta est.

166. [Syriac] codex: deleta est [Syriac]. [Syriac] altera vocis [Syriac] minio non primi librarii scripta, quo et puncta nomini Michaelis subdita picta sunt.

167. numerus [Syriac] a primâ manu bis scriptus.

168^1. [Syriac] manu primâ serius scriptum. Mittheilungen 4 10.

168^2. [Syriac] codex, quem Miniscalchius tacitus emendaverat.

169. [Syriac] A: pr m correctum.

No.	Lesson	Rubric		Fol.	PAGE
176		[Syriac]	[Syriac]	153²	
	Ioh. xii. 28.	[Syriac]			
	Ioh. xi. 53, xix. 6 ἐκραύγασαν—35 μαρτυρία.	[Syriac] (sic) [Syriac] (sic) [Syriac]		153³	236
177		[Syriac]		154⁴	
		M [Syriac]			
178		[Syriac] M [Syriac]		154⁴	
179	Matth. x. 16-22.	[Syriac]	[Syriac]	155¹	290
180	Luc. vii. 36-50.	[Syriac]	[Syriac]	155²	280
181		[Syriac]	[Syriac]	156²	
		[Syriac] . . .			
182		[Syriac]	[Syriac]	156²	
183		[Syriac]	[Syriac]	156²	
184	Luc. xxi. 12-19.	[Syriac]	[Syriac]	156²	240
185	Luc. xi. 29-33.	[Syriac] (sic) [Syriac]	[Syriac]	156⁴	240
186		[Syriac]	[Syriac]	157²	
187		[Syriac]	[Syriac]	157²	
		[Syriac]			
188		[Syriac]	[Syriac]	157²	
189		[Syriac]	[Syriac]	157²	
190		[Syriac]	[Syriac]	157³	
191		[Syriac]	[Syriac]	157³	
192		[Syriac]	[Syriac]	157³	

176. [Syriac] edidi : [Syriac] codex, quod recenti manu in [Syriac] [sic] correctum. [Syriac] habet [Syriac] pr m supra versum scriptam.

177. [Syriac] A[1] : punctum litterae [Syriac] subditum utrum ab A[1] an ab A[2] sit, nescio.

178. [Syriac] punctum et supra et infra litteram primam scriptum, in fine [Syriac] habet.

181. quod nomen in fine tituli voluerit auctor, non expedio. [Syriac] ex [Syriac] vel ex [Syriac] pr m (ni fallor) factum. Aut vice versâ.

182. vocis [Syriac] punctum dexterum solum servatum voluit C.

187. [Syriac] et [Syriac] habent [Syriac] et [Syriac] pr m supra versum scriptas.

188. [Syriac] vocis [Syriac] pr m, [Syriac] manu vetustâ supra versum scriptum.

189. [Syriac] A, minio lucidiore correctum. puncta duo supra [Syriac] scripta recentia.

190. [Syriac] minio alio quam quo librarius ipse utitur, lucidiore illo, de quo dixi, serius additum. [Syriac] prior vocis τοῦ θεολόγου eodem minio serius addita. scribitur ipsa [Syriac] littera.

192. nomen sancti habet [Syriac] minio alio quam quo librarius utitur, supra versum scriptam.

					PAGE
193		ܬܫܡܫܬܐ ܘܬܫܡܫܬܐ ܕܦܘܠܚܢܐ ܘܚܕ ܘܬܫܡܫܬܐ ܕܥܠ ܬܫܥܝܐ ܐ	ܕܠܗ	157[3]	
194	Matth. xxiv. 42-51.	ܬܫܠܡܬܐ ܐܠܝܣܝܣܘܪܘܣ ܕܐܡܪ ܐܢܐ ܕܥܠ ܡܢܚܢܐ	ܠ	157[3]	162
		ܬܫܥܝܐ ܠܗܘܢ		158[1]	
195		ܐܘ ܠܗ ܠܩܕܝܫܐ ܣܡܝܐ ܘܠܩܘܝܘ ܐܪܒܥܝܢ ܐܠܗܐ ܐܬܐ ܐܡܝܢ	ܐ	158[1]	
196		ܐܬܐ ܕܒܪܝܬܐ ܐܠܗܐ ܬܠܬܐ ܥܠ ܐܡܝܢ	ܐܬܐ	ܒ	158[2]	
197	Matth. xiii. 44-54 αὐτῶν.	ܬܠܬܐ ܠܩܘܝܘ ܕܦܘܠܚܢܐ ܠܗܘܢ ܥܠ ܡܢܚܢܐ	ܓ	158[2]	241
198		ܗܦܝܟ ܠܩܕܝܫܐ ܘܐܬܐ ܐܠܗܐ ܡܢ ܠܩܘܝܘ	ܘ	158[4]	
199		ܗܒܐ ܗܝܡܢ ܘܒܫܡܐ	ܐܠܗܐ ܕܥܠ ܐܡܝܢ	ܐ	159[1]	
200	Ioh. viii. 1-11.	ܬܫܒܘܚܬܐ ܠܩܘܝܘ ܦܠܓܝܐ ܥܠ ܡܘܣܝܩܐ	ܡ	159[1]	242
201		ܬܫܡܫܬܐ ܕܒܬܪ ܠܩܕܝܫܐ ܡܚܕܐ ܐܬܝܬܐ ܬܫܡܫܬܐ ܕܥܠ ܬܫܥܝܐ ܠܗܘܢ ܘܐܡܪ ܠܩܘܝܘ ܗܠܘܢ ܘܐܬܝܢ ܐܠܗܐ ܗܢܐ ܗܒܐ ܕܥܠ ܡܢܚܢܐ	ܠ	159[3]	
202		ܕܐܦ ܐܬܠܝܘܬ ܐܠܗܐ ܗܢܐ ܗܒܐ ܕܥܠ ܠܘܩܐ	ܡ	159[3]	
203		ܐܬܐܠܝܦ (*sic*) ܠܗܘܢ ܐܬܐܪܝܬ ܘܐܢܛܘܢܝܘܣ	ܘܐܬܝܢ ܐܠܗܐ ܕܥܠ ܐܡܝܢ	ܡܓ	159[4]	
204		ܕܐܬܒܪܟ ܠܩܘܝܘ ܠܐܒܘܗܝ ܐܠܗܐ ܗܢܐ ܐܬܠܬܐ ܥܠ ܠܥܠܡ	ܡܕ	159[4]	
205		ܗܐܠܝܦ ܕܒܝܬ ܥܠܡ ܥܠܡ ܐܠܗܐ ܕܐܬܐܠܝܦ ܥܠ ܐܡܝܢ	ܡܗ	159[4]	
206		ܗܒܐ ܕܥܠ ܠܩܘܝܘ ܕܒܝܬ ܘܬܫܡܫܬܐ ܐܠܗܐ ܕܥܠ ܐܡܝܢ	ܡܘ	159[4]	
207	Luc. x. 16-21.	ܬܫܒܘܚܬܐ ܕܥܠ ܠܩܕܝܫܐ ܠܐܦܝܣܩܘܦܐ ܠܟܠ ܥܠ ܠܘܩܐ	ܡܙ	159[4]	233
208		ܕܥܠ ܠܩܘܝܘ ܠܒܢܝ ܐܪܡܝܐ ܐܠܗܐ ܗܢܐ ܐܬܠܬܐ ܕܥܠ ܠܥܠܡ	ܡܚ	160[2]	
209	Luc. vi. 17-23 οὐρανῷ.	ܘܐܦ ܬܫܡܫܬܐ ܠܟܠ ܠܐܪܥܐ ܕܗܠܝܢ ܘܡܢ ܗܘ ܕܠܐ ܠܡܫܝܚܐ ܥܠ ܠܘܩܐ	ܕܐ	160[2]	
210		ܐܬܐ ܬܫܡܫܬܐ ܠܟܠ ܐܬܠܝܘܬ ܐܠܗܐ ܕܥܠ ܕܐܒܘܗܝ ܐܬܐ	ܐܬܐ	ܕܒ	160[4]	
211		ܬܠܬܐ ܬܫܡܫܬܐ ܡܚܕܐ ܐܦ ܠܟܠ ܗܢܐ ܗܦܝܟ ܥܠ ܠܘܩܐ	ܕܓ	160[4]	
212		ܐܬܒܪܝ ܬܫܡܫܬܐ ܠܟܠ ܐܬܐ ܘܐܬܝܢ ܐܠܗܐ ܠܟܠ ܠܗܘܢ ܥܠ ܡܢܚܢܐ	ܕܕ	160[4]	

193. fin serius manu non primâ addita.

194. ܐܠܝܣܝܣܘܪܘܣ edidi e sententiâ librarii eius qui minio lucidiore utitur: ܐܠܝܣܘܣܘܪܘܣ A. subter ܐ punctum adest.

200. super ܡ nominis Pelagiae litura. ܦܠܓܝܐ codex.

201. ܐܬܝܬܐ clare legitur; vide Uebersicht 75[r]. voces ܐܠܗܐ ܗܢܐ ܗܒܐ ܕܥܠ ܡܢܚܢܐ manu, si non primâ, vetustâ tamen, serius additae. post ܬܫܡܫܬܐ punctum supernum recens.

203. ܘ prior vocis ܘܐܢܛܘܢܝܘܣ minio non primo addita. ante ܐܡܝܢ radendo deletum ܐܡ

205. ܝ numeri xv pr m inter scribendum addita.

206. ܬܫܡܫܬܐ minio non primo inter versus additum.

208. ܐܪ nominis ܐܪܡܝܐ pr m ex ܐ efficta.

209. in nomine Hilarionis ܠ prior serius, sed primâ manu, scripta.

210. ܐܠܗܐ ex ܐܠܗܘܢ facta credi possit. ܕܐܒܘܗܝ fuerat: ܢ altera si non spongiâ deleta, certe instaurata a C non est.

212. punctum prius non sub ܐ, sed sub ܠ habet codex.

					PAGE
213	Luc. xii. 2-12. [Syriac] (*sic*) [Syriac]	[Syriac]	160^4	243
214	Matth. viii. 23-27. [Syriac] ※	[Syriac]	161^3	245
215	[Syriac]	[Syriac]	161^4	
216	[Syriac]	[Syriac]	161^4	
217	[Syriac] M [Syriac] تشرين الاخر	[Syriac]	162^1	
	[Syriac] (*sic*)		162^1	
218	Matth. x. 1, 5-8. [Syriac]	[Syriac]	162^1	245
219	[Syriac]	[Syriac]	162^2	
220	[Syriac]	[Syriac]	162^2	
221	[Syriac] (*sic*) [Syriac]	[Syriac]	162^3	
222	[Syriac]	[Syriac]	162^3	
223	[Syriac]	[Syriac]	162^3	
224	[Syriac]	[Syriac]	162^3	
225	[Syriac]	[Syriac]	162^3	
226	[Syriac]	[Syriac]	162^4	
227	[Syriac] (*sic*) [Syriac]	[Syriac]	162^4	
228	[Syriac]	[Syriac]	162^4	
229	[Syriac]	[Syriac]	162^4	
230	[Syriac]	[Syriac]	162^4	
231	[Syriac]	[Syriac]	162^4	
232	[Syriac]	[Syriac]	163^1	

213. [Syriac] serius addidit C.

214. ※ scripsit C.

217. [Syriac] habetur: quod utrum ab A an a C sit, nescio. [Syriac] serius, تشرين الاخر non in margine, sed in versus ipsius fine, qui vacuus remanserat, scriptum.

220. [Syriac] A: non pr m correctum.

221. [Syriac] vocis [Syriac] a C esse videatur.

222. cave credas [Syriac] vocis [Syriac] non .. sed [Syriac] habere. librarius .. scripserat: quum punctum dexterum signi nimis prope ad [Syriac] accessisse videret, repetivit paulo altius.

223. [Syriac], sed [Syriac] manu vetustâ super versum addita.

226. [Syriac] sub versu serius scriptum.

229. [Syriac] habet [Syriac] primâ manu inter scribendum additam.

230. [Syriac] pr m ante versum suppletum. [Syriac] vocis [Syriac] manu recentissimo atramento utenti addita.

232. [Syriac] A, [Syriac] C, licet fuerit cum ab A^2 correctum crederem. [Syriac] A, [Syriac] serius additum.

No.	Reference	Rubric		Page	Page
233		[Syriac text]	[Syriac text]	163^1	
234		[Syriac text]	[Syriac text]	163^1	
235		[Syriac text] (*sic*) [Syriac text]	[Syriac text]	163^1	
236		[Syriac text] (*sic*) [Syriac text]	[Syriac text]	163^1	
237		[Syriac text]	[Syriac text]	163^1	
238		[Syriac text]	[Syriac text]	163^2	
239		[Syriac text]	[Syriac text]	163^2	
240		[Syriac text]	[Syriac text]	163^2	
		كانون الاول [Syriac text]		163^2	
241		[Syriac text]	[Syriac text]	163^2	
242		[Syriac text]	[Syriac text]	163^2	
243		[Syriac text]	[Syriac text]	163^2	
244	Marc. v. 24-34 εἰρήνην.	[Syriac text]	[Syriac text]	163^3	248
245		[Syriac text] (*sic*) [Syriac text]	[Syriac text]	164	
246		[Syriac text]	[Syriac text]	164^1	
247		[Syriac text]	[Syriac text]	164^1	
248		[Syriac text] (*sic*) [Syriac text]	[Syriac text]	164^2	
249		[Syriac text] (*sic*) [Syriac text]	[Syriac text]	164^2	
250		[Syriac text]	[Syriac text]	164^2	
251	Marc. ix. 32-40 Vulg.	[Syriac text]	[Syriac text]	164^2	249
252		[Syriac text]	[Syriac text]	164^4	
253	Marc. xii. 38-44.	[Syriac text]	[Syriac text]	165^1	250
254		[Syriac text]		165^2	
255		[Syriac text]		165^3	
256		[Syriac text] (*sic*) [Syriac text]		165^3	

235. [Syriac text] A: sero correctum: [Syriac text] nominis [Syriac text] minio alio quam quo librarius utitur, supra versum addita.

237. fortasse [Syriac text] prior vocis [Syriac text] puncto caret in codice.

240. [Syriac text] A: antiquâ manu correctum.

242. [Syriac text] manu recenti in liturâ scr.

245. inter [Syriac text] et [Syriac text] vocis [Syriac text] sero: [sic] supra versum additum. [Syriac text] C.

248. [Syriac text] codex: Miniscalchius tacitus correxit.

250. [Syriac text] altera vocis [Syriac text] manu non primâ supra versum scripta.

251. [Syriac text] (fortasse pr m) in margine scriptum.

252. [Syriac text] C: [Syriac text] + C?

					PAGE
257	[Syriac] M² [Syriac]			165^3	251
	Matth. i. 1-17. [Syriac]				
258	Matth. i. 18-25.	[Syriac]		166^3	253
259	Luc. ii. 1-20.	[Syriac] (*sic*) [Syriac]	[Syriac]	167^1	254
260		[Syriac]	[Syriac]	168^1	
	Matth. i. 18.	[Syriac]			
	Matth. ii. 1-12.	[Syriac]		168^1	255
261	Matth. ii. 13-23.	[Syriac]	[Syriac]	168^4	256
262		[Syriac]	[Syriac]	169^3	
263	Marc. vi. 1-5.	[Syriac] (*sic*) [Syriac]	[Syriac]	169^3	258
264		[Syriac]		170^1	
265		[Syriac]		170^1	
266		[Syriac] (*sic*)		170^1	
267		[Syriac] (*sic*) [Syriac]		170^1	
		كانون الثانى (*sic*) [Syriac] (*sic*) [Syriac]		170^1	
268	Luc. ii. 20-21, 40-52.	[Syriac] (*sic*) [Syriac] (*sic*) [Syriac]	[Syriac]	170^1	258
269	Ioh. iii. 1.	[Syriac] (*sic*) [Syriac]	[Syriac]	170^4	260
	Ioh. iii. 12.	[Syriac]			
270	Matth. iii. 15-11 ἁγίῳ	[Syriac]	[Syriac]	170^4	
279	Luc. vi. 17-23 οὐρανῷ.	[Syriac]		176^1	269

257. [Syriac] altera vocis [Syriac] minio alio quam quo librarius utitur, scripta.

260. [Syriac] A : pr m [Syriac] supra versum addita.

263. [Syriac] vocis [Syriac] minio alio quam quo librarius utitur, supra versum scripta.

264-266. numeri dierum in margine non adsunt. similia videant deinceps ex editione meâ qui eâ utentur vel non moniti.

264. [Syriac] scripsi : codex [Syriac], additâ [Syriac] super [Syriac] pr m.

265, 266. manu vetustâ in intercolumnio scripta.

266. fortasse [Syriac] voluit librarius.

267. in titulo legeret كانعان vel كانعاز qui librarii morem non nosset.

269. [Syriac] edidi : puncta [Syriac] scripta sunt.

279. [Syriac] fuerat : punctum superius prius deletum, punctum inferius non additum.

PAGE

280 [illegible] 176[1]

281 [illegible] (*sic*) [illegible] 176[1]

292 Matth. v. 14-19. [illegible] 177[2] 271

293 [illegible] 177[2]

294 [illegible] (*sic*) [illegible] (*sic*) [illegible] 177[2]

[illegible] السابعاط اول 177[2]

296 Luc. ii. 25. [illegible] 178[2] 273

297 [illegible] 178[2]

298 [illegible] 178[3]

299 [illegible] 178[3]

300 [illegible] 178[3]

301 [illegible] (*sic*) [illegible] 178[3]

302 [illegible] 178[3]

303 [illegible] 178[3]

304 [illegible] 178[3]

305 [illegible] 178[3]

306 [illegible] 178[4]

307 [illegible] 178[4]

308 [illegible] 178[4] 273

Matth. xi. 2-15.

310 [illegible] 180[2] 275

311 [illegible] 180[2]

---

292. [illegible] tacitus edidit Miniscalchius, quem secutus sum: in codice non adest.

293. [illegible] A: radendo emendatum. supra [illegible] nominis [illegible] liturulâ.

294. [illegible] puncto in codice carere memineris.

296. [illegible] codex, omissâ litterâ ultimâ.

298. supra [illegible] nominis sancti signum : primâ manu scriptum.

300. in voce [illegible] videatur [illegible] puncto superno, [illegible] signo .. notatum esse.

305. [illegible] nominis [illegible] non certus lego. [illegible] A, pr m inter scribendum correctum.

PAGE

312 ܗܟܢܘ ܘܟܡܢ ܡܢ ܕܡܐܡܘܣ ܐܡܝܢ ܕܐܡܘ ܐܘܢܓܠܝܘܢ ܕܠܘܩܐ ܡܢ ܡܬܝ 180[2]

313 ܬܫܥܝܢ ܘܟܡܢ ܠܩܕܝܫܐ ܕܐܘܢܓܠܝܘܢ ܠܫܒܬܐ ܕܫܒܥܬ ܡܢ ܡܬܝ 180[2]

ܨܦܪ 180[2]

314 ܐܘ ܠܒܝܬܗ ܘܝܗܒ ܐܘܢܓܠܝܘܢ ܫܡܥܘ ܐܡܪ (sic) ܡܢ ܡܬܝ 180[2]

315 ܬܠܝܬ ܠܩܕܝܫ ܬܘܪܝܬܐ (sic) ܐܡܝܢ ܕܘܢܗ | ܐܘܢܓܠܝܘܢ ܕܠܘܩܐ ܡܢ ܡܬܝ 180[3]

316 ܝܚ ܬܠܬܐ ܠܩܕܝܫܐ ܕܫܡܫܐ ܘܪܚܡܗ ܐܘܢܓܠܝܘܢ ܗܟܢܘ ܐܡܪ ܡܢ ܡܬܝ 180[3]

317 ܝ ܨܦܪܐ ܕܚܘܠܡ ܘܬܢܝܢ ܡܟܬܒܝܢ ܐܘܢܓܠܝܘܢ ܕܟܢܝܢ ܡܢ ܡܬܝ 180[3]

Matth. xx. 1-16.

319 ܝܛ ܕܡܢ ܠܚܡܐ ܡܢܘܢܝܗ ܐܘܢܓܠܝܘܢ ܫܒܐ ܣܦܪ ܕܟܢܝܢ ܡܢ ܠܘܩܐ 181[2] 276

320 ܝܗ ܩܕܡܝܬܐ ܠܚܡܐ ܠܩܕܝܫܐ ܐܟܢܝ ܐܘܢܓܠܝܘܢ ܠܬܠܬܐ ܡܢ ܡܬܝ 181[2]

321 ܝܘ ܫܒܥܐ ܕܡܢ ܠܚܡܐ ܠܩܕܝܫܐ ܬܐܡܐ ܐܘܢܓܠܝܘܢ ܕܟܢܝܢ ܡܢ ܡܬܝ 181[2]

322 ܝܙ ܫܒܬܐ ܕܝܘܡ ܠܟܘܢ ܐܬܡܘ ܐܘܢܓܠܝܘܢ ܚܕ ܬܠܬܐ ܡܢ ܡܪܩܘܣ 181[2]

323 ܝܚ ܕܟܢܝܢ ܠܥܪܘܒܬܐ ܠܠܝܐ ܩܕܡܝ ܕܝܢ ܗܘ ܫܒܬܐ ܕܟܢܝܢ ܡܢ ܕܝܘܡ ܠܟܠ 181[2]

Luc. i. 24-38. 278

325 ܟܗ ܫܒܬܗ ܘܟܢܝܢ ܬܪܬܝܢ ܥܣܪܐ ܠܥܒܕܐ ܐܘܢܓܠܝܘܢ ܫܒܬܗ ܕܝ ܡܢ ܡܬܝ 182[2] 279

326 ܟܘ ܫܒܥܐ ܕܟܢܝܢ ܠܩܕܝܫܐ ܡܬܬܪܥܐ ܐܘܢܓܠܝܘܢ ܫܒܬ ܫܒܥܐ ܕܡܢ ܡܢ ܡܬܬܝܐ 182[2]

327 ܟܙ ܬܪܝܢ ܘܟܢܝܢ ܠܩܕܝܫܐ ܕܐܠܝܫܒܥ ܫܒܬܗ ܘܟܢܝܢ ܡܢ ܫܘܒܬܐ 182[2]

328 ܟܚ ܬܫܥܐ ܘܟܢܝܢ ܠܡܘܬܐ ܕܬܪܝܢ ܠܩܘܡܐ ܡܢܕܡܢ ܡܢ ܠܘܩܐ 182[2]

329 ܟܛ ܬܠܬܝܢ (sic) ܠܠܒܝܬ ܡܘܬܐ ܘܠܡܬܡܘܡ ܐܘܢܓܠܝܘܢ ܕܟܢܝܢ ܡܢ ܕܝܘܡ ܠܟܠ 182[2]

330 ܠ ܘܚܕ ܘܬܠܬܝܢ (sic) ܫܒܝܥܐ ܘܬܪܝܢܬܗ ܐܘܢܓܠܝܘܢ ܕܟܢܝܢ ܡܢ ܡܬܝ 182[2]

Matth. x. 16-22. 290

376 ܝܚ ܬܠܬܐ ܠܩܕܝܫܐ ܕܫܒܬܐ ܐܘܢܓܠܝܘܢ ܕܟܢܝܢ ܡܢ ܕܝܘܡ ܠܟܠ 189[3] 291

377 ܝ ܨܦܪܐ ܠܩܕܝܫܐ ܘܝܗܒ ܐܘܢܓܠܝܘܢ ܬܫܥܝܢ ܐܡܪ ܡܢ ܡܬܝ 189[3]

---

315. quartum nominis sancti elementum puncto in codice caret.

321. ܝ vocis ܕܟܢܝ pr m serius scripta esse videatur.

322. ܠܟܘܢ sero in ܠܟܘܢ mutatum.

323. ܝ vocis ܕܟܢܝ pr m serius scripta videatur.

326. ܝ in ܕܟܢܝ serior, etsi vetusta.

327. ܬ vocis ܬܪܝܢ inter scribendum ex ܫ effecta. ܘܟܢܝܢ habet ܘ in liturâ scriptam, ܝ fortasse serius additam.

328. ܘ vocis ܘܟܢܝܢ supra ܬ radendo deletâ.

377. sub ultimis litteris nominis ܘܝܗܒ punctum deletum.

				PAGE
378	ܩ̈ܪܝܢܐ ܠܥܐܕܐ ܕܐܘܣܩܠܝܛܘ ܐܘܢܓܠܝܘܢ ܕܨܦܪܐ ܡܢ ܠܠܘܩܐ	ܗ	189[3]	
	Matth. xvii. 1 καὶ παραλαμβάνει—9.			292
381	ܬܪ̈ܝܢ ܠܣܗ̈ܕܐ ܫܡܘܢܐ ܘܒ̈ܢܝܗ̇ ܠܥܙܪܐ ܐܘܢܓܠܝܘܢ ܬܫܥܐ ܡܢ ܕܐܢܘܢ ܠܡܬܝ	ܣ	192[4]	293
382	ܬܪܘܢ ܠܩܕܝܫܐ ܡܪܐ ܐܘܢܓܠܝܘܢ ܕܪ̈ܡܫܐ ܐܚܪ ܡܢ ܕܐܬܐ	ܠ	192[4]	
383	ܕܐܦ ܠܣܗ̈ܕܐ ܕܒܪܬܗ ܐܘܢܓܠܝܘܢ ܕܨܦܪ ܡܢ ܬܫܥܐ ܠܡܬܝ	ܢ	192[4]	
384	ܚܕܝܡ ܕܨܦܪ ܠܥܐܕܐ ܘܒܬܪܗ ܫܒܬ ܬܠܬܐ ܡܢ ܒܬܪ ܠܡܪܩܘܣ	ܚ	192[4]	
385	ܬܠܬܐ ܕܨܦܪ ܠܣܗ̈ܕܐ ܠܒܪ ܡܕܒܪܢܐ ܐܘܢܓܠܝܘܢ ܫܒ ܠܡܬܝ	ܝ	192[4]	
386	ܕܐܒܐ ܕܨܦܪ ܠܩܕܝܫܐ ܡܬܩܕܫܐ ܐܘܢܓܠܝܘܢ ܐܘܦ ܡܢ ܕܐܢܘܢ ܠܡܬܝ	ܡ	192[4]	
387	ܩ̈ܪܝܢܐ ܕܨܦܪ ܢܒܝܐ ܐܠܝܫܥ ܘܠܐܒܘܗ ܠܗ | ܐܘܢܓܠܝܘܢ ܬܫܥܐ ܡܢ ܠܠܘܩܐ	ܡܗ	193[1]	
388	ܗܘܝܐ ܕܨܦܪ ܠܣܗ̈ܕܐ ܕܐܒܪܗܡ ܫܒܬ ܬܠܬܐ ܒܬܪ ܠܡܪܩܘܣ	ܡܘ	193[1]	
389	ܗܘܠܐ ܕܨܦܪ ܠܣܗ̈ܕܐ ܡܪܩܘܣ ܘܐܪܣܛܘܒܘܠܘܣ ܩ̈ܪܝܢܐ ܘܕܨܦܪ ܡܢ ܬܫܥܐ ܠܡܬܝ	ܡܙ	193[1]	
390	ܬܪܝܢ ܕܨܦܪ ܠܣܗ̈ܕܐ ܐܦܪܝ ܘܐܪܣܛܘܒܘܠܘܣ ܐܘܢܓܠܝܘܢ ܩ̈ܪܝܢܐܦܪܝ ܡܢ ܠܠܘܩܐ	ܡܣ	193[1]	
391	ܬܪܘܢ ܕܨܦܪ ܠܣܗ̈ܕܐ ܐܒܪܡ ܠܣܝܒܪܝ ܐܘܢܓܠܝܘܢ ܕܨܦܪܐ ܡܢ ܠܠܘܩܐ	ܡܛ	193[1]	
392	ܕܨܦܪ ܠܩܕܝܫܐ ܕܐܦܪܝܡ ܐܘܢܓܠܝܘܢ ܩ̈ܪܝܢܐ ܡܢ ܠܠܘܩܐ	ܢ	193[1]	
393	ܘܫܒ ܘܕܨܦܪ ܠܣܗ̈ܕܐ ܓܪܓܝܣ ܘܐܠܝܫܥ ܐܘܢܓܠܝܘܢ ܕܨܦܪ ܡܢ ܠܠܘܩܐ	ܢܐ	193[1]	
394	ܬܠܬܐ ܘܕܨܦܪ ܠܩܕܝܫܐ ܕܬܪܬܥܣܪ ܐܘܢܓܠܝܘܢ ܐܘܦ ܡܢ ܝܘܚܢܢ (sic)	ܢܒ	193[1]	

CODEX C.

			FOL.	PAGE
150	Matt. xxvii. 3-22.	ܐܠܫܘܡܐ ܐܚܪܢܐ ܠܠܝܐ ܐܘܢܓܠܝܘܢ ܡܢ ܡܬܝ	106*a*	199
	Mark xv. 16-32.	ܐܦܐܪܘ ܐܚܪܢܐ ܠܠܝܐ ܐܘܢܓܠܝܘܢ ܡܢ ܡܪܩܘܣ	107*b*	201
	Matt. xxvii. 33-54.	ܐܦܐܟܒ ܠܠܝܐ ܐܘܢܓܠܝܘܢ ܡܢ ܡܬܝ	108*b*	203
	Luke xxiii. 32-49.	ܐܬܪܬܐ ܠܠܝܐ ܐܘܢܓܠܝܘܢ ܡܢ ܠܘܩܐ	109*b*	204

381. supra versum ad ܣ nominis ܫܡܘܢܐ adiecta est ܐ manu recentiori eâdem ܥܙ vocis ܠܥܙܪܐ supra versum scr.

383. dubitare possis utrum ܕܨܦܪ voluerit librarius an ܕܨܦܪ inter scribendum emendaverit.

387. ܐܠܝܫܥ esse videatur, sed ܢ punctum litterae ܝ est.

390. ܩ̈ܪܝܢܐܦܪܝ codex, quem tacitus Miniscalchius correxerat.

392. ܕܐ nominis ܕܐܦܪܝܡ supra versum scripta serius.

393. ܓܪܓܝܣ habet : subter ܓ scriptum.

			FOL.	PAGE
	John xix. 25-37.	ܐܬܐܡܢ ܠܝܠܬ ܐܠܓܡܥܗ ܡܢ ܝܘܚܢܐ	110*b*	206
	Mark xv. 43-47.	ܘܗܘ ܠܝܠܬ ܐܠܓܡܥܗ ܡܢ ܡܪܩܘܣ	111*a*	207
	John xix. 38-42.	ܬܐܣܥ ܒܥܕ ܠܝܠܬ ܐܠܓܡܥܗ ܡܢ ܝܘܚܢܐ	111*b*	207
	Matt. xxvii. 1*b*-38.	ܠܝܘܡ ܐܠܓܡܥܗ ܒܠܒܟܪ ܡܢ ܡܬܝܐ	112*a*	208
151	Matt. xxvii. 62-66.	ܠܝܘܡ ܣܒܬ ܐܠܟܒܝܪ ܒܟܪܗ ܡܢ ܡܬܝܐ	115*b*	214
152	Matt. xxviii. 1-20.	ܠܝܘܡ ܐܚܕ ܐܠܟܒܝܪ ܒܥܕ ܠܠܩܕܐܣ ܘܒܩܝܬܗ	115*b*	215
		ܒܫܡܗ ܕܐܒܐ ܘܒܪܐ ܘܪܘܚܐ ܕܩܘܕܫܐ ܠܥܠܡ ܐܡܝܢ		
		ܐܠܐܘܠ ܒܟܪܐ ܠܠܩܕܐܣ ܘܗܘ ܡܢ ܡܬܝܐ ܘܒܩܝܬܗ ܡܪܩܘܣܐ	116*b*	216
	Mark xvi. 2-8.	ܐܬܐܢܝ ܒܟܪܐ ܡܢ ܡܪܩܘܣ	116*b*	217
	Mark xvi. 9-20.	ܐܬܐܠܬ ܒܟܪܐ ܡܢ ܡܪܩܘܣ	117*a*	218
	Luke xxiv. 1-12.	ܐܪܐܒܥ ܒܟܪܐ ܡܢ ܠܘܩܐ ܘܒܩܝܬܗ	117*b*	219
	Luke xxiv. 36-53.	ܐܠܚܐܡܣ ܒܟܪܐ ܡܢ ܠܘܩܐ ܐܢܓܝܠ ܐܬܐܠܬ		
		ܒܥܕ ܐܠܥܝܕ ܐܣܕܣ ܒܟܪܐ ܡܢ ܠܘܩܐ ܘܒܩܝܬܗ ܡܪܩܘܣܐ	118*a*	220
154	Luke iv. 16-22.	ܐܠܐܚܕ ܬܠܬܝܢ ܦܨܚܐ ܐܘܠ ܝܘܡ ܦܝܗ ܪܐܣܝܗ ܘܬܕܒܐܪ ܐܠܡܕܝܣ		
		ܡܪܝ ܫܡܥܢ ܐܠܫܠܝܚ ܡܢ ܠܘܩܐ ܘܒܩܝܬܗ	123*b*	229
155	Matt. xxiii. 29-39.	ܐܬܢܝܢ ܦܝ ܐܝܠܘܠ ܬܫܪܝ ܐܠܡܕܝܣ ܡܪܝ ܡܐܟܡܐ ܐܠܫܝܟ ܝܘܡ ܐܬܢܝܢ		
		ܐܣܩܦܗ ܡܢ ܢܝܚ ܐܠܫܝܟ ܡܢ ܚܠܒ ܐܝܢܐ ܗܘܬܦܢܐ		
		ܣܒܥܬܗ ܦܝ ܐܝܠܘܠ ܬܫܪܝ ܐܠܡܕܝܣ ܡܪܝ ܝܥܩܘܒ ܡܢ ܡܬܝܐ ܘܒܩܝܬܗ	124*a*	231
156	Luke x. 16-21.	ܬܣܥܬܗ ܦܝ ܐܝܠܘܠ ܬܫܪܝ ܡܪܩܐ ܐܠܡܥܠܡ ܡܢ ܠܘܩܐ ܘܒܩܝܬܗ	124*b*	233
157	Luke i. 39-49.	ܬܡܢܝܗ ܦܝ ܐܝܠܘܠ ܡܘܠܕ ܐܠܣܝܕܗ ܐܡ ܐܢܘܪ ܘܗܘ ܠܒܟܪܗ ܡܢ ܠܘܩܐ	125*a*	234
158	Luke x 38—xi. 27, 28.	ܘܗܕܐ ܠܠܩܕܐܣ ܡܢ ܠܘܩܐ ܘܗܘ ܝܩܪܐ ܠܝܘܡ ܐܠܬܪܟܝܐ		
		ܐܣܝܡܗ ܒܥܠܡܐ ܡܢ ܠܘܩܐ	125*b*	235
159	John iii. 13-17.	ܬܣܥܗ ܬܕܒܐܪܗ ܝܐܣܝܡ ܘܢܝܚ ܐܠܟܢ ܐܣܒܬ ܐܣܕܣ ܡܢ ܠܘܩܐ : ܒܥܕܗ ܠܨܠܝܒ ܐܠܟܪܝܡ ܐܠܡܒܪܟ ܐܠܟܢ ܐܣܒܬ ܐܣܒܬ ܡܢ ܡܬܝܐ : ܫܕܝ ܒܥܕ ܠܨܠܝܒ ܐܠܟܪܝܡ ܐܠܡܒܪܟ ܐܠܟܢ ܝܘܡ ܐܬܢܝܢ ܬܐܢܝ ܗܒܗ ܐܠܥܝܕ ܬܐܢܝ ܒܥܕ ܠܨܠܝܒ ܐܠܟܪܝܡ ܐܠܡܒܪܟ ܐܠܟܢ ܝܘܡ ܐܬܠܬܝܢ ܗܐܕܗ ܐܝܐܡܗ ܒܥܕ ܐܠܥܝܕ ܬܬܬܒܪ ܠܨܠܝܒ ܐܠܟܪܝܡ ܐܠܟܢ ܝܘܡ ܐܬܐܠܬܐ ܗܐܕܗ ܐܝܐܡܗ		

FOL. PAGE

ܒܬܪ ܐܠܗܝܢ ܫܒܬܐ ܕܟܠ ܢܘܗܪ ܐܢܓܝܢ. ܐܘܢܓܠܝܘܢ ܐܫܒܬܐ
ܐܫܒܒܐ ܡܢ ܥܣܬܐ ܚܕ ܕܟܠ ܢܘܗܪ ܐܢܓܝܢ 126a 235-6
160 John xix. 6-35. ܐܪܒܥܣܪ ܠܝܘܡ ܐܝܠܘܠ ܐܢܓܝܢ ܐܠܦܪܝܘܢ ܒܡܪܝܢ
ܐܘܢܓܠܝܢ ܝܘܡ ܐܝܬܐܝܬ ܫܐܪܘ ܫܒܥ ܒܬܪ ܐܠܗܝܢ
ܫܒܥܐ ܠܠܡܐܕܘ ܢܟܢ ܐܚܪܢ ܡܢ ܢܫܢܐ. 126b 236
161 Matt. xi. 27-30. ܫܒܬ ܒܬܪ ܚܒܪ ܐܢܓܝܢ ܐܘܢܓܠܝܢ ܝܘܡ ܐܠܦܪܝܘܢ ܦܢ
ܐܫܐܒܘ ܐܪܒܥ ܒܬܪ ܐܠܗܝܢ ܚܕ ܒܬܪ ܚܒܪ ܐܢܓܝܢ ܐܘܢܓܠܝܢ
ܬܠܬ ܚܕ ܡܢ ܐܝܘܡ ܐܪܒܥ ܘܒܪܝܢ ܬܪܬܝܢ ܐܠܦܪܝܘܢ ܬܠܬܐ
ܐܘܢܓܠܝܢ ܫܪܒܥܣܪ. ܫܒܬ ܡܢ ܥܣܬܐ ܬܫܥܢ ܘܒܪܝܢ
ܬܪܬܝܢ ܐܪܒܥܣܪܝܢ ܡܢ ܥܣܬܐ ܘܫܒܥܘܬ 127-8 239
162 Luke xxi. 12-19. ܬܪܝܢ ܐܬܠܬ ܬܢܝ ܝܘܡ ܦܢܘ ܬܪܬܝܢ ܐܠܦܪܝܘܢ
ܡܢܬܐ ܐܘܢܓܠܝܢ ܝܘܡ ܐܬܢܝ ܐܫܢܬܐ = ܫܬܐ ܬܪܬܝܢ ܐܠܦܪܝܘܢ
ܡܢܝ ܬܫܥܐ ܐܘܢܓܠܝܢ (*sic*) ܚܕ ܐܠܦܪܝܢ ܫܒܥܐ ܦܢܘ ܐܠܦܪܝܘܢ ܫܢܝܢ
ܘܬܫܥܐ ܬܫܥܐ ܬܪܬܝܢ ܐܠܦܪܝܘܢ ܢܫܒܥܢ ܐܡ ܚܠܦ ܐܘܢܓܠܝܢ
ܐܬܠ ܚܕ ܡܢ ܠܝܘܡܐ ܫܒܥܐ ܐܠܝܬܠ ܠܠܡܐܕܘ ܫܢܝܢ ܘܬܫܥܐ
ܡܢ ܠܝܘܡܐ 128a 240
163 Luke xii. 2-12. ܬܪܝܢܣܪ ܦܢ ܬܪܝܢ ܐܬܠܬ ܬܪܬܝܢ ܐܠܦܪܝܢ ܠܝܘܡܐ ܐܘܢܓܠܝܢ
ܫܬܐ ܦܢ ܐܬܠܬ ܬܠܬܝܢ ܘܒܪܝܢ ܬܪܬܝܢ ܐܠܦܪܝܘܢ ܡܢܝ ܢܫܒܥܢ
ܐܚܕ ܐܪܝ ܐܘܢܓܠܝܢ ܬܫܥܢ ܘܒܪܝܢ ܦܢ ܚܕܐ ܐܬܠܬ ܚܫܥܢ ܘܒܪܝܢ
ܬܪܬܝܢ ܐܠܦܪܝܘܢ ܐܠܦܬܢ ܫܘܘ ܢܝܪܐ ܠܚܬܠ ܐܠܦܪܝܢ ܡܢ ܠܝܘܡܐ
ܘܒܫܘܬ ܡܢܝܘܡܐ 128b 243
164 Matt. x. 1, 5-8. ܬܪܝܢ ܐܬܬܐܝܢ ܬܠܬܝܢ ܢܫܒܥܐ ܫܬܐ ܘܒܪܝܢ ܬܪܬܝܢ
ܐܠܦܪܝܘܢ ܕܬܪܬܝܢܘ ܐܘܢܓܠܝܢ. ܬܠܬ ܫܒܬ ܒܬܪ
ܐܠܗܝܢ ܘܐܬܠ ܝܘܡ ܐܡ ܦܢܘ ܬܪܬܝܢ ܐܠܦܪܝܢ
ܡܢܫܐ ܘܬܫܥܐ ܡܢ ܥܣܬܐ 129a 245
165 John x. 9-16. ܬܠܬܐ ܦܢܘ ܬܪܬܝܢ ܐܠܦܪܝܘܢ ܡܢܝ ܠܬܪܝܢ ܐܢܝܢܝܐ
ܐܘܢܓܠܝܢ ܐܫܒܬ ܐܠܫܒܥ ܒܬܪ ܐܠܗܝܢ ܬܫܥܢ ܦܢܘ ܬܬܫܐܝܢ
ܐܠܦܠܝܢ ܡܫܝܚ ܐܘܢܓܠܝܢ ܫܬܐ ܐܫܐ ܦܢ ܐܬܠܬ ܚܕܝ ܚܪܝ
ܬܪܬܝܢ ܐܠܦܪܝܘܢ ܡܢܝ ܡܫܝܚܐ ܢܪܒܥܘܘ ܐܘܢܓܠܝܢ ܬܠܬ ܫܒܬ
ܒܬܪ ܐܠܗܝܢ ܐܬܪܬܝܢ ܬܪܬܝܢ ܐܠܦܪܝܘܢ ܡܢܝ ܢܫܝܚܐ ܐܪܒܥ ܐܘܢܓܠܝܢ
ܝܘܡ ܐܬܬܠܬ ܒܬܪ ܐܫܒܥܐ ܬܠܬܝܢ ܬܪܬܝܢ ܐܫܪܝܘ ܢܫܝܚܐ
ܦܢܘ ܐܪܒܥ ܡܢ ܢܫܝܚܐ ܘܒܫܘܬ 129b 246

FOL. PAGE

166 Mark v. 24-34. ܐܘܢܓܠܝܘܢ ܕܡܪܢ ܐܡܠܝܟ ܦܠܚܘܗ ܐܬܠܘܢ. ܐܠܦܝܠ ܐܠܕܝ.
ܦܝ ܐܠܝܘܡ ܗܘܕ ܐܘܪܫܠܝܡ ܟܕܐ ܐܠܦܬܝ ܘܡܬܠܓܝܢ ܕܡܟܐܢ ܐܬܠܬ
ܘܡܫܐܝ ܐܠܡܬܠܡܝܕܝܢ ܐܬܠܘܢ. ܘܡܫܝܗ ܘܟܢܝܣܐ ܦܝ ܕܝܢܐ ܐܠܟܠ
ܫܟܢܝ ܕܡܟܐܢ ܐܠܟܢܝܢ ܡܬܐ ܐܬܠܘܢ. ܐܫܥܬ ܐܠܡܣܝܚ ܡܢ
ܡܬܐ ܫܡܬܠܓܝܢ ܕܡܟܢ ܐܠܡܥܝܗ ܠܠܡܝܘܗ ܐܠܝܘܟܢ ܐܬܠܘܢ. ܐܘܠ
ܐܫܡܢ ܕܡܬܬܟܢܝܢ ܕܡܟܢ ܐܠܡܥܝܗ ܠܝܬܘܗ ܘܐܢܡܘܘܗ ܐܬܠܘܢ.
ܬܐܠܬ ܫܟܬ ܟܕܐ ܐܠܦܬܝ ܠܫܡܬܠܢ ܕܡܟܢ ܐܢܟܝ ܟܘܟܒܐ ܐܬܠܘܢ.
ܫܐܡܢܗ ܗܘܕ ܦܝ ܐܠܘܠ ܘܐܫܝ ܘܟܢܝܣܐ ܕܟܘܠ ܐܫܘܪܗ ܐܠܡܫܟܠ
ܐܬܠܘܢ. ܬܡܢܝܗ ܦܝ ܐܠܘܠ ܫܟܢܗ ܘܟܢܝܣܐ ܕܡܟܢ ܐܠܡܥܝܗ
ܟܪܝ ܝܡܘܢ.
ܐܠܦܪܘܝ ܐܬܠܘܢ. ܗܘܕ ܐܬܢܝܢ ܐܫܟܪܗ ܬܠܬܐ ܬܡܟܢ ܐܫܠܝܚ
ܐܝܪܘܗ ܗܘܕ ܐܠܪܟܢܐ ܐܬܟܪܝ ܐܠܐ ܝܝܦ ܐܠܝܘܡ ܟܐܝܘܢ ܐܠܟܠ
ܐܝܫ ܘܬܠܬܝܢ ܝܘܟܢܐ ܐܘܠ ܗܘܕ ܦܝܗ ܕܡܟܢܐ ܐܢܟܝ ܝܘܡܗ ܬܐܝܢ
ܐܢܟܝ ܫܟܘܘܡ ܬܠܬ ܐܢܟܝ ܝܘܟܢܐ ܐܬܠܘܢ. ܫܟܫܡܗ ܦܝ ܐܠܘܠ
ܐܘܪܟܢܐ ܕܡܟܢܐ ܐܡܘܢܫܡܗ ܟܪܟܝܗ ܡܢ ܡܪܩܘܣ 130*a* 248

167 Mark ix. 32-40. ܫܟܫܡܗ ܕܡܟܢ ܫܟܢܐ ܐܬܠܘܢ. ܫܢܝ ܟܫܢܐ ܦܝ ܟܝܘܡ ܐܬܝܢ
ܫܬܗ ܕܡܟܢ ܐܠܡܥܝܗ ܡܟܪܝ ܢܡܘܠܐ ܐܬܠܘܢ ܢܘܕ ܐܬܬܠܬܐ
ܟܕܐ ܐܫܟܪܗ ܬܫܟܗ ܫܟܠ ܐܠܡܥܝܫܗ ܫܝܗ ܐܬܠܘܢ.
ܐܫܘܪܗ ܡܢ ܠܘܡܐ ܫܟܢܝ ܕܡܟܢܐ ܐܟܢܐ ܕܫܐܠ ܐܠܡܣܝܚ
ܐܬܠܘܢ. ܬܡܟܢܗ ܘܟܢܝܣܐ ܡܢ ܐܠܘܠ ܬܠܓܟܢ ܕܡܟܢ
ܐܠܡܥܝܫܝܢ ܐܘܫܢܝܗ ܘܐܝܫܟܬܗ ܐܬܠܘܢ. ܦܝ ܐܫܢܝ ܐܠܝܘܡ
ܫܟܠܓܟܢ ܕܡܟܢ ܐܢܟܝ ܕܫܠܠ ܘܐܠܡܥܝܫܝܢ ܬܠܬ
ܦܬܗ ܐܬܠܘܢ. ܫܟܫܡܗ ܡܢ ܐܠܘܠ ܟܫܢܐ ܕܡܟܢ ܐܠܡܥܝܗ ܐܝܬܝܘܗ
ܡܢ ܡܪܩܘܣ ܘܠܘܩܐ 130*b*-1*a* 249

168 Mark xii. 38-44. ܘܐܫ ܘܟܢܝܣܐ ܕܡܟܢܐ ܐܠܡܥܝܫܗ ܐܘܠܝܗ ܐܬܠܘܢ.
ܐܘܟܢܗ ܡܢ ܟܝܘܡ ܐܠܘܠ ܐܬܢܝܢ ܘܟܢܝܣܐ ܕܡܟܢ ܐܠܡܥܝܫܗ ܫܠܓܫܝܗ
ܡܢ ܡܪܩܘܣ 131*b* 250

169 Matt. i. 1-17. ܐܠܫܐ ܟܕܐ ܐܦܬܝ ܟܘܟܪܗ ܐܠܐ ܠܠܡܣܝܚܗ ܐܬܠܘܢܗ ܡܢ
ܡܬܠܐ ܘܗܘ
ܐܠܘܠ ܫܐ ܐܫܡܘ ܐܬܠܘܢܗ ܡܢ ܡܪܩܘܣ ܘܗܘ ܐܬܠܬ ܫܟܐ ܐܠܡܫܠܟ
ܐܬܠܘܢܗ ܡܢ ܠܘܡܐ ܘܗܘ ܐܪܐܟܢ ܫܟܐ ܐܫܟܪܘܗ ܐܬܠܘܢܗ ܡܢ
ܫܢܟܐ

FOL. PAGE

ܘܗܘ ܐܬܐܡܪ ܫܪܝܘ ܐܦܠܘܣ ܐܦܠܛܘܢ ܡܢ ܡܕܝܢܬܐ ܘܗܘ ܐܬܬܬܐ
ܫܐܪ: ܐܠܟܣܢܕܪܐ ܐܦܠܛܘܢ ܡܢ ܚܟܝܡܐ ܫܐܪ: ܐܠܟܣܢܕܪܘܣ ܐܦܠܛܘܢ ܐܠܟܣܢܕܪ
ܚܟܝܡܐ ܗܘܐ

ܐܠܟܣ ܐܠܗܐ ܡܠܟ ܚܕ ܐܪܣܛܘ ܡܘܪܐ ܒܡܠܟܘܬܐ ܚܟܝܡܐ
ܚܕ ܐܪܣܛܘ ܐܢܬܠ ܐܠܦܠܛܘܢ ܐܠܗܐ ܕܠܟܬ ܡܢ ܐܪܥ ܦܘܠܘܣ
ܡܟܐܪܒ

ܦܟܬ ܡܠܟ ܐܠܟܐ ܐܦܠܛ ܚܕܟܪ ܦܟܬ ܡܢ ܠܘܩܐ ܫܐܪ: ܡܠܟ
ܐܠܡܫܠܐ

ܐܦܠܛ ܚܕ ܟܪ ܡܢ ܠܘܩܐ ܦܟܬ ܡܠܟ ܐܡܫܠ ܐܦܠܘܛ ܬܘܢ ܟܪ
ܦܟܬ ܡܢ ܠܘܩܐ ܚܕ ܡܠܟ ܐܠܡܫܠ ܠܠܐܟܐ ܐܠܡܕܝܢ ܡܢ ܟܣܪܘܗ
ܕܟܬܐܘܣ 132a 251

From the Remains of another Lectionary now bound up with Codex B.

(Collated on the Text of Codex B.)

Fol. 1*a*.

John xi. 21. ܐܚܘܝ] ܐܚܝ || ܡܪܝܐ] ܡܪܝ || ܐܡܪܬ] + ܕܝܢ

22. ܗܫܒ] ܗܫܒ || ܕܬܫܐܠ] ܕܬܝܫܐܠ || ܝܗܒ] ܝܗܒܐ

23. omit ܠܗ

24. ܐܚܪܝܬܐ] ܐܚܪܝܐ || ܝܘܡܐ] ܝܘܡܐ || ܐܡܪܐ] + ܠܗ

25. ܚܝܐ] ܚܝܝܐ || ܕܡܗܝܡܢ] ܕܡܗܝܡܢܝܢ

26. ܕܚܝ] ܕܚܝܐ || ܘܡܗܝܡܢ] ܘܡܗܝܡܢܝܢ || ܝܡܘܬ] ܝܡܘܬ

27. ܡܗܝܡܢܐ ܐܢܐ] ܐܢܐ ܡܗܝܡܢܬ

29. ܒܦܪܝܥ] ܒܐܦܪܝܥ

30. ܐܬܐ] ܕܐܬܐ || omit ܗܘܐ

31. ܐܠܗܐ] || omit ܕܝܢ || ܩܡܬ] ܘܐܩܡܬ || ܕܒܦܪܝܥ] ܒܐܦܪܘܥ || ܘܕܐܝܢ] ܘܕܐܢ
ܕܬܒܟܐ] ܕܬܒܟܝ || ܐܠܗܐ

32. || ܕܢܦܠܬ] ܢܦܠܬ || ܪܓܠܘܗܝ] ܕܪܓܠܘܗܝ || ܡܪܝ] ܡܪܝܐ || omit ܐܘ
ܐܚܘܝ] ܐܚܝ || ܘܐܡܪܐ] ܘܐܡܪܬܐ

33. ܘܒܟܝܢ] ܘܒܟܝܢ || ܕܐܬܘ] ܐܬܘ || omit ܥܡܗ || ܘܝܗܘܕܝܐ] ܘܝܗܘܕܝܐ || omit ܕܝܢ

36. ܝܗܘܕܝܐ] ܝܗܘܕܝܐ || ܕܝܢ] ܐܘ

37. ܕܡܢܗܘܢ] ܕܡܢܗܘܢ || ܕܥܡܝܐ] ܕܥܡܝܐ || ܐܡܪܝܢ ܗܘܘ] ܐܡܪܘ

38. ܒܥܩܐ] ܒܥܩܬ || omit ܗܘܐ || ܕܝܢ + [ܥܠ

39. ܕܐܠܢ] ܐܠܢ

Fol. 1*b*.

Rubric. .... ܠܝܫ ܐܘܢܓܠܝܘܢ ܕܝܘܡ ܐܠܘܕܐܘ ܕܫܒ ܐ ....

John xi. 39. ܠܗ] + ܠܗ || ܝܘܡܝܢ] + ܕܝܘܡܬܐ

John xi. 40. ܬܚܙܘܢ] ܬܚܙܝܢ

41. ܡܫܒܚܬܐ] ܡܫܒܚܬܢ

42. ܫܡܥ] ܫܡܥܬ ‖ ܩܝܡ] ܩܝܡܝܢ

43. ܐܬܐ] ܐܬܝܐ ‖ ܐܠܥܙܪ] ܠܥܙܪ

44. ܟܘܪܝܢ] ܟܘܪܝܐ ‖ ܘܐܩܝܡܘܢ] ܘܐܩܝܡܘ ‖ ܘܐܙܠܘܢ] ܘܐܙܠܘ ‖ ܪܓܠܘܗܝ] ܪܓܠܘܗܝ

44, 45. omit ܫܪܘ ܗܘܝܗ ܘܫܒܘܩܘ : ܡܢ ܝܗܘܕܝܐ

45. ܠܘܬ + [ܗܘ ‖ ܘܚܙܘ] ܘܚܙܝܘ ‖ ܕܥܒܕ ܝܫܘܥ ܗܘܝܢ + [ܕܥܒܕ ‖ ܗܝܡܢܘ] ܘܗܝܡܢܘ

Rubric. ܩܪܝܢ ܚܕ ܡܢ ܐܘܢܓܠܝܘܢ ܕܝܘܚܢܢ ܕܥ ܡܢ ܥܢܝܢܐ ܕܥܢܝܢܐ

John xii. 1. omit ܝܫܘܥ ‖ ܕܐܩܝܡ] ܕܐܩܝܡܗ ‖ ܐܠܥܙܪ] ܠܥܙܪ

2. ܥܒܕܘ ܚܫܡܝܬܐ] ܚܫܡܝܬܐ

3. ‖ ܟܠܗ omit ‖ ܪܓܠܘܗܝ] ܪܓܠܘܗܝ ‖ ܒܣܥܪܗ] ܒܣܥܪܗ ‖ ܕܢܪܕܝܢ] ܢܪܕܝܢ
ܕܒܣܡܐ] ܒܣܡܐ

4. ܬܠܡܝܕܘܗܝ] ܬܠܡܝܕܘܗܝ ‖ ܕܐܫܠܡܗ] ܕܐܫܠܡܗ

5. ܠܡܣܟܢܐ] ܠܡܣܟܢܐ ‖ ܒܡܐܬܐ] ܒܡܐܬܐ

6. ‖ ܟܐܢܫ] ܟܐܢܫ ‖ ܗܘܐ] ܕܗܘܐ ‖ ܗܘ] ܗܘ ‖ ܡܚܫܒ] ܡܚܫܒ ‖ ܐܠܐ ܕܓܢܒ] ܓܢܒ
ܠܗ + [ܕܝܗܒܝܢ ‖ (sic) ܕܗܘܐ] ܗܘܐ

7. ܫܒܘܩܘ] ܫܒܘܩܘܗ ‖ ܕܩܒܘܪܬܝ] ܕܩܒܘܪܬܝ

9. ‖ ܕܝܫܘܥ] ܝܫܘܥ ‖ ܐܠܥܙܪ (sic)] ܠܥܙܪ ‖ ܕܐܩܝܡ omit ‖ ܘܚܙܘܢ] ܘܚܙܘܢ
ܕܐܩܝܡ] ܕܩܡ

10. ܘܐܬܡܠܟܘ] ܘܐܬܡܠܟܘ ‖ ܕܢܩܛܠܘܢ + [ܠܗ ‖ ܕܢܩܛܠ] ܢܩܛܠ

Fol. 2a.

(On Lesson XXXVIII.)

John xii. 25. ܕܠܚܝܘܗܝ] ܕܠܚܝܘܗܝ ‖ ܠܢܦܫܗ] ܠܢܦܫܗ

26. ‖ ܐܢ ܐܢܫ ܗܘܐ] ܐܢ ܗܘܐ ܐܢܫ ‖ ܗܘܐ] ܗܘܐ ‖ ܡܫܡܫܢܐ] ܡܫܡܫܢܝ
ܢܝܩܪܗ] ܢܝܩܪܗ

27. omit ܐܢܐ ‖ ܠܗܕܐ] ܠܗܕܐ ‖ ܗܕܐ] ܗܕܐ

28. ܐܬܐ] ܐܬܐ

29. omit ܕܝܢ ‖ ܫܡܥܘ] ܫܡܥܘ ‖ ܡܠܐܟܐ] ܡܠܐܟ ‖ ܐܬܡܠܠ] ܐܬܡܠܠ

30. ܠܡܠܘܗܝ] ܠܡܠܘܗܝ ‖ ܩܠܐ ܗܢܐ] ܩܠܐ ‖ ܐܬܐ] ܐܬܐ

31. omit ܗܢܐ

32. ܐܬܪܝܡܬ (sic)] ܐܬܪܝܡܬ ‖ ܐܬܪܝܡܬ] ܐܬܪܝܡܬ

John xii. 33. ܥܬܝܕ]ܡܥܬܝܕ || (*homœoteleuton*) ܐܡܪ ܡܗܘܕܥ ܒܗܕܝܢ ܡܘܬ ܗܘܐ *omit*

34.]ܐܬ ܐܡܪ || ܫܡܥܢܢ]ܫܡܥܢܗ || ܐܝܟܢ]ܐܝܟܢܗ || ܐܟ̈ܠܘܣܐ]ܐܟ̈ܠܘܣܣܐ

ܟܕܢ ܐܡܪܝܢ]ܐܡܪܝܢ ܠܗ || ܥ̈ܠܡܘܗ]ܕܥ̈ܠܡܘܗ || ܐܬ ܐܡܪ ܐܬ

35. ܡܗܠܟ]ܡܗܠܟ

36. ܕܒܢܘܝ]ܕܒܢܝ

Rubric. ܬܫܡܫܬܗ ܘܬܠܬܝܢ ܝܘܡ ܐܠܐܪܒܥܐ ܡܢ ܝܘܚܢܢ ܩܕܝܫܐ ☼ ܐܡܪ ܡܪܢܐ ܠܝܗܘܕܝܐ

(On Lesson XXXIX.)

John xii. 36. *omit* ܡܠܠ

38.]ܠܡܫܡܥܘܢ || ܕܐܫܥܝܐ]ܕܐܫܥܝܝܐ || ܡܠܬܗ]ܕܡܠܬܗ || ܠܓܠܠ]ܠܓܠܝܠ

ܕܡܪܐ +]ܘܐܕܪܥܗ || ܠܡܫܡܫܘܢ (*sic*)

39. ܐܫܥܝܐ]ܐܫܥܝܝܐ || ܠܓܠܠ]ܠܓܠܝܠ

40. ܘܐܥܝܪ]ܘܐܥܪܐ || ܠܒܗܘܢ]ܠܒܒܗܘܢ || ܘܝܬܘܪܘܢ]ܘܝܬܘܒܘܢ

41. ܕܚܙܗ]ܕܚܙܝܗ || ܐܫܥܝܐ]ܐܫܥܝܝܐ

42. ܒܥܫܬܐ]ܒܥܫܝܬܐ || ܠܓܠܠ]ܠܓܠܝܠ

43. *omit* ܓܪ

Fol. 2b.

44. ܐܠܐ +]ܒܝ || ܕܫܠܚܢ]ܕܫܠܚܢܝ || ܒܗܕܝܢ]ܒܕܝܢ || ܒܠܚܘܕܝ +]ܒܝ

45. ܕܫܠܚܢ]ܕܫܠܚܢܝ

46. ܢܗܘܪ]ܡܢܗܘܪ || ܕܡܗܝܡܢܝܢ]ܕܡܗܝܡܢ

47. || ܝܐܫܡ (*sic*)]ܕܐܫܡ || ܘܡܛܪ ܠܗܘܢ]ܘܡܛܪܘ ܠܗܘܢ || ܡܬܠܐܝ]ܡܬܐܠܝ

ܓܪ +]ܠܐ

Rubric. ܐܪܒܥܝܢ ܝܘܡ ܐܠܚܡܝܣ ܠܩܠܘܬܗ ܕܡܫܝܚܐ ܡܢ ܐܬܐܟܠ ܐܠܦܨܚܐ ܡܢ ܠܘܩܐ

ܘܗܝܢ ܕܗܘܝܢ ܡܬܠܠܝܢ ܐܬܐܡܪܬܐ

ܘܫܢ ܘܐܪܒܥܝܢ ܝܘܡ ܐܠܓܡܥܗ ܐܟܣܪܝܘܣܗ ܡܢ ܝܘܚܢܢ ☼

(On Lesson XL.)

John xiv. 2. ܐܡܪ]ܐܡܪܬ || ܡܢܝܚܢ]ܡܢܝܚ

3. ܘܕܒܪ]ܘܐܕܒܪ || ܘܬܗܘܢ]ܬܗܘܢ

5. ܐܝܟܢ (*bis*)]ܐܝܟܢܗ

6. ܕܟܐܠܗܝ]ܕܟܠܗܝ || ܕܟܠ]ܟܠ || ܠܘܬܝ (*sic*)]ܠܘܬ

8. ܐܘܕܝܥ]ܐܘܕܥ || ܦܠ̈ܩܘܣ]ܦܠܩ̈ܘܣ

9. ܦܠ̈ܩܘܣ]ܦܠܩܣܐ || ܐܒܪܝܬ]ܐܒܪܬ

John xiv. 10. ܐܢܬܗܘ + [ܒܝ

Rubric. ܐܬܝܢ ܘܐܡܪܝܢ ܗܘܐ ܐܠܗܬ ܐܠܦܘܡܒܗ ܐܦܘܣܕܘܪܗ ܡܢ ܗܘܫܢܐ ✡

(On Lesson XLI.)

John xiv. 10. ܡܡܠܠ [ܡܡܠܠ || ܡܠܠ [ܡܡܠܠ || ܗܠܝܢ *omit* || ܠܬܠܡܝܕܐܝ [ܠܬܠܡܝܕܘܗܝ
ܗܕܝܢ ܕܐܢܐ ܥܒܕ + [ܒܥܒܕܐ

11. ܠܓܠܠ [ܠܓܠܠ

12. ܘܪܒܪܒܢ ܡܢ ܗܠܝܢ ܥܒܕܢܐ + [ܥܒܕܐ (*homœoteleuton*)

13. ܠܓܠܠ [ܠܓܠܠ || ܠܗܘܢ + ܥܒܕܢܐ [ܥܒܕܐ || ܐܒܐ [ܕܐܒܐ || ܕܬܫܬܒܚ [ܕܬܫܬܒܚܘܢ
ܒܝ + [ܐܒܐ

14. (*omitted*)

15. ܢܛܪܘ ܦܘܩܕܢܝ [ܦܘܩܕܢܝ ܢܛܪܘ || ܐܢ [ܐܢ

16. ܠܥܠܡ [ܠܥܠܡ || ܚܘܪܢ [ܚܘܪܢܝ || ܢܗܒ [ܢܗܒ

Fol. 3a.

Rubric. ܗܘܝܢ ܐܠܠܫܕ (*sic*) ܐܘܐܢܒܝ ܒܒܕ ܐܠܦܝܫ

John xiv. 17. ܘܒܓܘܒܘܢ [ܕܒܓܘܒܘܢ || ܫܡܥܐ [ܡܫܡܥ || ܡܚܝܠ [ܡܚܠ

18. ܐܬܝܢ [ܐܬܐ || ܢܬܡܢ [ܢܬܡܢ || ܢܬܒܘܢ (*sic*) + [ܢܬܒܘܢ || ܘܠܝܬ [ܠܝܬ

19. ܚܝܝܢ [ܚܐܝܢ || ܚܝܝܢ [ܚܐܝ

20. ܬܕܥܘܢ [ܬܕܥܘܢ

21. ܥܠܡ *omit* || ܗܘܝ [ܗܘ || ܠܝ [ܠܝ || ܘܢܛܪ [ܘܢܛܪ || ܦܘܩܕܢܝ [ܦܘܩܕܢܝ

Rubric. ܬܠܬܗ ܘܐܡܪܝܢ ܗܘܐ ܐܠܝܫ ܐܠܬܝ ܒܐܠܩܕܝܣܐ ܘܗܘ ܐܠܝܫ ܐܘܐܢܒܝ ܒܒܕ
ܐܠܦܨܚ ܡܢ ܗܘܫܢܐ ✡

(On Lesson XLII.)

John xvii. 1. ܥܒܕ [ܥܒܕ || ܐܬܬ [ܐܬܬ || ܒܪܗ [ܒܪܘܢ || ܡܠܠ [ܡܠܠ

2. ܕܠܥܠܡ [ܕܠܥܠܡ || ܚܝܝ [ܚܝܝ || ܠܝ [ܠܗ || ܒܣܪܐ [ܒܣܪ || ܒܘܠܗ [ܒܘܠ

3. ܚܝܝܢ [ܚܝܝܐ

4. ܒܬܫܒܘܚܬܐ [ܒܬܫܒܘܚܐ || ܕܥܒܕܢ [ܕܥܒܕܢ || ܗܕܝܢ [ܗܠܝܢ || ܕܫܠܡܬ [ܕܫܠܡܬ

6. ܘܠܬܠܡܝܕܝܟ [ܘܠܬܠܡܝܕܝܟ || ܘܐܘܕܥܬ [ܐܘܕܥܬ

7. ܝܗܒܘ [ܝܗܒܬ

8. ܫܠܚܬ [ܫܠܚܬ

9. ܕܦܠܚܘܢ [ܕܦܠܚܘܢ || *omit* ܠܐ ܥܠ ܕܦܠܚܘ ܕܥܠܡܐ ܐܠܐ ܥܠ ܗܠܝܢ (*homœoteleuton*) ||
ܡܢ *omit* || ܕܝܠܟ [ܕܕܝܠܟ || ܕܝܠܟ [ܕܝܠܟ

John xvii. 10. ܕܝܠܝ] + ܗܘ

11. *omit* ܐܢܐ ܘܐܬܐ ‖ ܗܟܢ] + ܗܘܐ ‖ ܕܐܒܘܗܝ] ܕܐܝܬ

12. ܒܥܠܡܐ ܥܡܗܘܢ] ܥܡܗܘܢ ܒܥܠܡܐ ‖ ܗܘܝܬ] (*bis*) ܗܘܝܬ ‖ ܐܒܕܘ] ܐܒܕ ‖
ܐܠܐ] ܐܝܢ

13. ܡܡܠܠܐ] ܡܡܠܠ ‖ ܚܕܘܬܐ] ܚܕܘܬܝ

Fol. 3b.

Rubric. ܐܘܢܓܠܝܘܢܗ ܕܝܘܚܢܢ ܩܘܡ .... ܩܪܝܢܐ ܗܘܐ ....

(On Lesson XLIII.)

John xiv. 28. ܐܬܚܕܝܬܘܢ] ܚܕܝܬܘܢ ܐܢܬܘܢ

29. ܬܗܝܡܢܘܢ] ܬܗܝܡܢܘܢ

30. ܡܡܠܠ] ܡܡܠܠܐ ‖ *omit* ܗܪܟܐ ‖ ܠܗ] ܗܘ

31. ܕܢܕܥ] ܢܕܥ ‖ ܕܢܕܥܘܢ] ܢܕܥܘܢ

xv. 1. *omit* ܗܘ ‖ ܫܪܝܪܬܐ] ܫܪܝܪܬܐ

2. ܦܐܪܐ] ܦܐܪܐ ‖ ܫܒܝܫܬܐ] ܫܒܝܫܬܐ ‖ ܡܕܡ] ܡܕܡ ‖ ܡܕܟܐ] ܡܕܟܐ ‖
ܝܬܝܪܬܐ] ܝܬܝܪܬܐ ‖ ܡܛܠ] ܡܛܠ

3. ܡܛܠ] ܡܛܠ ‖ ܕܟܝܢ] ܕܟܝܢ

4. ܫܒܝܫܬܐ] ܫܒܝܫܬܐ ‖ ܕܒܓܦܬܐ] ܕܒܓܦܬܐ

5. ܫܒܝܫܬܐ] ܫܒܝܫܬܐ ‖ ܡܢ] ܡܢ ‖ ܦܐܪܐ] ܦܐܪܐ ‖ ܡܕܡ] ܡܕܡ ‖ ܟܠܗܝܢ] ܟܠܗܝܢ

6. ܗܘܐ] ܗܘܐ ‖ *omit* ܠܗ ‖ ܫܒܝܫܬܐ] ܫܒܝܫܬܐ ‖ ܘܝܒܫܐ] ܘܝܒܫܐ ‖
ܢܘܪܐ] ܢܘܪܐ ‖ + ܠܗܘܢ ‖ ܘܡܘܩܕܝܢ] ܘܡܘܩܕܝܢ + ܠܗܘܢ

7. ܐܢ] ܐܢ ‖ *omit* ܠܗ ‖ ܘܡܠܝ] ܘܡܠܝ ‖ ܬܫܐܠܘܢ] ܬܫܐܠܘܢ

Rubric. ܫܠܡܬ ܘܫܘܪܝ ܕܝܘܚܢܢ .... ܐܘܢܓܠܝܘܢܗ ܐܠܐ ܟܕ ܬܠܬܐ ܩܘܡ ܐܡܪ .... ܡܢ ܩܝܡܬܐ

(On Lesson XLIV.)

John xvi. 2. ܫܥܬܐ] ܫܥܬܐ ‖ ܢܦܩܘܢ] ܢܦܩܘܢ ‖ ܡܩܪܒ] ܡܩܪܒ

4. ܥܕܢܐ] ܥܕܢܐ ‖ ܠܗܘܢ] ܠܗܘܢ ‖ ܠܟܘܢ] *omit* ܕܝ ‖ ܗܘܝܬ] ܗܘܝܬ

7. ܐܠܐ] *omit* ܐܢܐ ‖ ܐܢ] ܐܢ ‖ ܐܙܠ ܐܢܐ] ܐܙܠ ܐܢܐ ‖ ܡܢܚܡܢܐ] ܡܢܚܡܢܐ

Fol. 4a.

John xvi. 8-11. ܥܠܡܐ] ܥܠܡܐ

10. ܟܐܢܘܬܐ] + ܕܝ

John xvi. 13. ܐܬܝܐ] ܐܬܝܐ || ܗܘ] ܗܘܐ || ܡܕܒܪ] ܡܕܒܪ || ܠܟܘܢ] ܠܟܘܢ || ܩܘܫܛܐ] ܩܘܫܛ

Rubric. ܫܠܡܬ ܘܩܪ⌜ܝܢ⌝ ܝܘܡ ܐܠܦܬܚܐ ܕܡ ܢܘܚܐ ✡

(On Lesson XLV.)

John xvi. 14. ܘܡܚܘܐ] ܘܡܚܘܐ || ܠܟ] ܠܟܘܢ || ܠܟܠܡܕܐܢ] ܠܟܠܡܕܝܢ

15. ܘܡܚܘܐ] ܘܡܚܘܐ || ܟܠ] ܟܠܠ

16. ܘܐܢܐ] ܐܢܐ || ܙܥܘܪ (bis)] ܙܥܘܪ

17. omit ܙܥܘܪ || ܙܥܘܪ (bis)] ܙܥܘܪ

18. ܡܠܠ] ܡܡܠܠ || ܐܝܟ] ܐܝܬܐ || ܘܐܡܪܝܢ + || ܙܥܘܪ] + ܗܕܐ || ܗܘܘ] ܗܘܘ

19. ܙܥܘܪ] ܙܥܘܪ (bis) || ܠܩܒܠܟ] ܡܢ ܩܒܠܟ || ܠܟܐ] ܠܟܐ || ܘܐܡܪ] ܐܡܪ
ܘܬܘܒ ܙܥܘܪ ܘܐܡܪܝܢ + [ܕܚܡ ܠܟܘܢ

20. ܘܬܥܘܢ] ܘܬܥܘܢܝܢ || ܘܬܥܘܢ] ܘܬܬܥܒܕܝܢ || ܘܬܒܟܘܢ] ܘܬܒܟܘܢ

21. ܟܠ] ܟܠܠ || ܠܚܘܒܐ] ܠܠܚܘܒܐ || ܡܕܒܪܐ] ܡܕܒܪܐ || ܝܘܡ] ܝܘܡܐ
ܠܥܠܡܐ] ܠܥܠܡܐ || ܕܐܬܝܠܕ] ܕܐܬܝܠܕܬ

22. ܘܬܚܕܘܢ] ܘܬܚܕܘܢ || omit ܫܠܡ || ܚܕܐ] ܚܕܘܐ || ܚܕܐ] ܚܕܘܐ || ܝܘܡ] ܝܘܡܐ

23. ܢܬܠ] ܢܬܠ

Rubric. ܫܠܡܬ ܘܩܪܝܢ ܝܘܡ ....

ܠܟܠܡܕܝܢ] ܠܟܠܡܕܘܗܝ

(vv. 8-13 very indistinct.)

Fol. 4*b*.

Defective, and stained by leather binding against which the page was folded.

(On Lesson XLVI.)

John xvi. 25. ܐܬܐ + [ܥܡ] || ܡܚܘܐ] ܡܚܘܐ

27. ܪܚܡ] ܪܚܡ

29. ܐܡܪ] ܡܡܠܠ

30. omit ܐܬ || ܐܝܟ] ܐܝܬܘܗܝ

31. ܐܝܟ] ܐܝܟܢ

32. omit ܠܒܝܬܗ ܐܢܐ ܘܠܝ : ܥܡܝ ܐܒܘܢ (*homœoteleuton*)

33. ܥܠܡ + [ܠܟܘܢ || ܟܠ] ܟܠܠ

Rubric. ܬܫܡܫܬ ܘܩܪܝܢ ܝܘܡ ܐܠܝܚܢܢܘܗܝ ܐ ....

(On Lesson XLVII.)

John xvii. 20. ܕܡܗܝܡܢܝܢ] ܕܡܗܝܡܢܝܢ || ܕܡܠܝܗܘܢ] ܕܡܠܝܗܘܢ (bis)

21. ܕܢܗܘܘܢ] ܕܢܗܘܘܢ || ܘܐܝܟ ⌜ܐܢܐ⌝] ܘܐܢܐ ܐܝܟ

John xvii. 22. omit ܗܕܐ || ܕܐܢܗ] ܕܐܢܐ

24. ܓܒܐ] ܓܒܐܝ || ܕܝܗܘܢ] ܕܗܢ

Defective, being partly covered with the leather binding.

(On Lesson XXV.)

John vii. 18. ܕܕܡ] ܕܡ || ܥܠܝܗ] ܕܥܠܝܗ || ܘܢܥܦ] ܡܢܥܦ || ܘܦܘܠܘܡ] ܘ⌜ܦܘ⌝ܠܡ

19. ܝܗܒ] ܡܗܒ || ܠܗܘܢ] ܠܟܘܢ || ܥܒܕ] ܥܒܕܐ

20. ܐܓܝܒ] ܐܓܝܒܘ || ܒܟܐ] ܒܟ

21. ܥܒܕ] ܥܘܒܕ || ܬܡܗܝܢ] (sic) ܬܡܗܝܢ

22. ܠܒܕܠ] ܠܟܠܠ || ܘܒܫܒܘܬܐ] ܘܫܒܘܬܐ || ܐܬܘܢ] ܐܬܘ || ܒܪܝܡ] ܒܪܝܡ

23. ܚܠܦ] ܚܠܘܦ || ܡܬܚܣܬܡ] ܡܬܚܣܬܢ || ܒܫܒܘܬܐ] ܕܫܒܘܬܐ

24. ܐܩ̈ܝܡ] ܐܩܝܡ

25. ܪܘܫܠܡ] ܪܘܫܘܠܡ

26. ܡܡܠܠ] ܡܡܠܝܠ || ܘܟܘܠܡ] ܘܟܠܡ

In Binding. (Partly covered up.)

(On Lesson XLVIII.)

John vii. 38*b*—viii. 3 :

39. ܡܫܝܚܐ] ܡܫܝܚܐ || ܠܟܠܝܠ] ܠܟܠܠ

40. ܐܘܟ̈ܠܣܐ] ܐܘܟܠܣܐ

42. ܕܕܘܕ] ܕܕܘܝܕ || ܠܚܡ] ܠܚܡ || ܩܪܝܬܐ] ܩܪܬܐ

43. ܒܐܠ . . . .] ܒܝܢ ܐܘܟ̈ܠܣܐ

44. ܐܕܘܐ] ܐܕܐ || ܕܢܣܒܘܢ] ܕܢܣܒܘܢ

45. ܐܬܘ] + ܕܝ || ܗܒ̈ܪܦܝܐ] ܗܒܪܦܝܐ || ܘܦܪܝܫܝܐ] ܘܦܪܝܫܝܢ

46. ܡܫܡܥܝܢ] ܡܫܡܥ

48. ܡܫܡܥܝܢ] ܡܫܡܥ || ܦܪܝܫܝܐ] ܦܪܝܫܝܐ

49. ܡܐܟܝܢ] ܡܐܟܝܢ

51. ܢܡܘܣܐ] ܢܡܘܣܘܢ || ܕܐܡ] ܕܡ || ܡܫܡܥ] ܡܫܡܥ

52. ܕܐܒ] + ܐܘܦ || ܢܒܝܐ] ܢܒܝ

viii. 2. ܗܝܟܠܐ] omit ܗܘܐ

At the end of John viii. 2 is ܫܠܡ. Then follows:—

John xi. 1. ܫܠܡܗܝܢ] ܫܠܡܗ